HANDBOOK OF
SEXUALITY-RELATED MEASURES
THIRD EDITION

This classic and invaluable reference Handbook of use to sex researchers and their students worldwide has now been completely revised in a new edition complete with its own companion website. It remains the only easy and efficient way for researchers to learn about, evaluate, and compare instruments that have previously been used in sex research. In this third edition of the *Handbook*, 218 scales, complete with full descriptions and psychometric data, are made available, with additional information provided at the companion website for this volume.

Terri D. Fisher has been on the psychology faculty of The Ohio State University since 1982. She has conducted research on various aspects of sexual behavior and is Past-President of the Midcontinent Region of the Society for the Scientific Study of Sexuality, and Consulting Editor for *The Journal of Sex Research*.

Clive M. Davis taught at Syracuse University. Davis' research was focused on sexuality and communications. He was Editor of *The Journal of Sex Research* and President of the Society for the Scientific Study of Sexuality. He was the founding president of the Foundation for the Scientific Study of Sexuality.

William L. Yarber is professor of applied health science and professor of gender studies at Indiana University, Bloomington. He is also a senior research fellow at The Kinsey Institute for Research in Sex, Gender, and Reproduction and the senior director of the Rural Center for AIDS/STD Prevention at Indiana University. He is a Past-President of the Society for the Scientific Study of Sexuality.

Sandra L. Davis was an Executive Assistant in the New York State Assembly for 15 years. From 1983-1988, she was Managing Editor of *The Journal of Sex Research* and then served as Assistant Editor for the *Annual Review of Sex Research* for 10 years. She currently edits the online series "What Sexual Scientists Know About..." published by the Society for the Scientific Study of Sexuality.

Summaries of all scales, additional information regarding some of the scales, and complete versions of several others may be found at the companion website to the *Handbook*: http://www.routledge.com/textbooks/9780415801751

Routledge Titles of Related Interest

Sex For Sale, *Second Edition*
Ronald Weitzer

Global Gender Research
Bose and Kim

Regression Analysis for the Social Sciences
Rachel Gordon

GIS and Spatial Analysis for the Social Sciences
Robert Parker and Emily Asencio

State of Sex: Tourism, Sex, and Sin in the New American Heartland
Barbara Brents, Crystal Jackson, and Kathryn Hausbeck

Gender Circuits: Bodies and Identities in a Technological Age
Eve Shapiro

HANDBOOK OF SEXUALITY-RELATED MEASURES
THIRD EDITION

Edited by

Terri D. Fisher

Clive M. Davis

William L. Yarber

Sandra L. Davis

Routledge
Taylor & Francis Group

NEW YORK AND LONDON

First edition published 1988
by Clive M. Davis, William L. Yarber, and Sandra L. Davis

Second edition published 1998
by Sage Publications, Inc.

This edition published 2011
by Routledge
711 Third Avenue, New York, NY 10017

Simultaneously published in the UK
by Routledge
2 Park Square, Milton Park, Abingdon, Oxon OX14 4RN

Routledge is an imprint of the Taylor & Francis Group, an informa business

© 1988 Clive M. Davis, William L. Yarber, and Sandra L. Davis
© 1998 Sage Publications, Inc.
© 2011 Taylor & Francis

Typeset in Times New Roman by Swales & Willis Ltd, Exeter, Devon

Library of Congress Cataloging in Publication Data
Handbook of Sexuality related measures / edited by Terri D. Fisher ... [et al.]. — 3rd ed.
p. cm.
Includes bibliographical references and index.
1. Sexology—Research—Handbooks, manuals, etc. 2. Birth control—Research—Handbooks, manuals, etc.
3. Hygiene, Sexual—Research—Handbooks, manuals, etc. 4. Sexual behavior surveys—Handbooks, manuals, etc.
5. Questionnaires. I. Fisher, Terri D.
HQ60.H36 2010
3067072—dc22
2009048685

ISBN13: 978–0–415–80174–4 (hbk)
ISBN13: 978–0–415–80175–1(pbk)

Contents

Communication

Compatibility

Compulsion

Condoms

Homophobia

Homosexualities (also see Attraction)

Love

Male Sexuality

Masculinity (see Male Sexuality)

Masturbation (also see Attitudes, Behavior, Female Sexuality, and Self-Stimulation)

Molestation (see Abuse)

Motivation (see Sexual Motivation)

Myths (see Attitudes, Beliefs and Cognitions, and Knowledge)

Narcissism

Orgasm (also see Female Sexuality)

Paraphilia (also see Compulsion, and Transvestism)

Pedophilia (see Abuse)

Permissiveness (also see Attitudes)

Preface

Research is fundamental to increasing the understanding of individual and societal sexual expression. Reliable and valid measurement is fundamental to sound research. Although there have been many questionnaires, scales, inventories, interview schedules, etc. developed to measure a myriad of sexuality-related states and traits, attitudes and behaviors, variations and deviations, in the past, relatively few of these were used sufficiently for their reliability and validity to have been firmly established. Instead, there was a tendency for researchers to reinvent the wheel when they had need of a sexuality-related measure.

For an instrument to be used, it must be available to the community of professionals in the field. In order to solve the problem of accessibility of scales, Clive M. Davis, William L. Yarber, and Sandra L. Davis edited and published *Sexuality-Related Measures: A Compendium* in 1988. Prior to the publication of this compendium, there was no easy or efficient way for researchers to learn about, evaluate, and compare instruments that had been previously used in sex research. Although this task has become easier with the advent of the Internet, tracking down available sexuality-related measures has remained a challenge.

The first edition, which consisted of 110 scales, was revised in 1998 by Davis, Yarber, and Davis, with the assistance of Robert Bauserman and George Schreer. The second edition, published by Sage, contained 225 scales. Since the previous edition, sex research has progressed, expanded, and transformed, but despite the increase in physiologically based measures there is still a great need for sound psychometric instruments.

In this third edition of the *Handbook*, we have included 218 scales, with some additional ones at the companion website for this volume, which may be found at http://www.routledge.com/textbooks/9780415801751. However, because of the large expansion of the field, we have made the decision that this edition will focus more directly on solid sexuality-related measures. Therefore, we have eliminated a few categories of measures that were included in the previous two editions; for example, we have not included measures of abortion attitudes or of sex-role behavior. We have also eliminated a number of obsolete measures. This edition consists of 87 new scales, 43 revised entries from the previous edition, and 88 entries from the previous edition for which we did not receive a revision but which we chose to retain nonetheless.

Notable entries in this edition of the *Handbook* include revisions and updates of some well-established measures, scales that reflect expansions into sexual medicine, scales that have resulted from new theoretical constructs, and scales that reflect societal changes in attitudes toward women and toward homosexuality. As with the previous editions, there are a few instruments that are described only briefly, primarily because the author of the instrument was not able to provide us with a more complete paper. In some instances, we have been able to include only a sampling of items from the instrument. In most cases, this is because the instrument is sold commercially and restricted by copyright regulations. In these instances, details about how to obtain the instrument are included. Also, there are some instruments that will be known to many readers that are not mentioned at all. These are not included, unfortunately, because we were unable to obtain a response from the author(s) to our request for a paper or the necessary information. We welcome suggestions from readers about other instruments to include in future editions, and we invite authors to submit material without invitation. As this project has grown, it has become increasingly difficult to identify all of the available instruments and to track down the authors, so assistance from the community of sexual scientists and practitioners is most welcome.

Acknowledgments

We wish to thank all of those who have contributed to the third edition of this handbook. Without the authors of the more than 200 separate chapters contained herein, this edition could not have been produced. We also want to thank the many people who reported to us that they had found the first two editions very useful and encouraged us to undertake a revision. Without that support, it is unlikely we would have taken on the task again. We need to single out for special thanks Paul J. Loeber, who served as an editorial assistant and copyeditor on this project for an extended period of time, with little compensation other than his pride in a job well done. We also wish to acknowledge the support of The Ohio State University at Mansfield in providing workspace and supplies. Finally, we want to thank all of those at Routledge who have provided support and assistance in completing this project, most notably Steve Rutter and Leah Babb-Rosenfeld.

Terri D. Fisher
Mansfield, Ohio

Clive M. Davis
Syracuse, New York

William L. Yarber
Bloomington, Indiana

Sandra L. Davis
Syracuse, New York

Childhood Sexual Abuse Scale

MATTHEW C. AALSMA[1] AND J. DENNIS FORTENBERRY, *Indiana University School of Medicine, Indianapolis*

The Child Sexual Abuse Scale (CSAS; Aalsma, Zimet, Fortenberry, Blythe, & Orr, 2002) is a self-report instrument that was developed to measure the occurrence of childhood sexual abuse in adolescent and adult populations. The measurement of childhood sexual abuse varies widely from brief, single-item measures to lengthy clinical interviews. The scale was developed with two issues in mind. First, a benefit of the current measure is it is very brief (four items) and can therefore be utilized in a wide variety of studies. For instance, many measures of childhood sexual abuse are interviews or are lengthy self-report inventories, which are difficult to incorporate into studies assessing many areas of sexual functioning and behavior. Second, because the CSAS is a multiple-item rather than single-item measure, internal reliability can be assessed.

Description

The CSAS consists of four items. Participants are instructed that the items refer to events that may have occurred prior to age 12. The use of this particular age cutoff was based, in part, on focus groups with adolescents in which the participants reached a consensus that the term childhood sexual abuse involved events occurring up to 12 years of age. We also wanted the CSAS to address an age range during which consensual sexual experiences were less likely. In order to maintain brevity, the CSAS did not include items regarding the specific nature of the abuse (e.g., whether penetration was involved) or the participant's relationship with the perpetrator. Given that the age range for childhood sexual abuse is set at below 12, as well as the reading level of this scale, it is most appropriate for adolescent and adult populations.

Response Mode and Timing

The participants are asked to circle *Yes* or *No* to each statement.

Scoring

The total score for this scale is calculated by summing across items and can range from zero to four.

Reliability

The CSAS was originally utilized in a study of female adolescent and young adult subjects (14 to 24 years of age) recruited from urban health clinics and a sexually transmitted disease clinic in a large midwestern city. The scale, measuring a single construct, demonstrated excellent internal reliability at baseline (alpha = .81) and 7-month follow-up (alpha = .84; Aalsma et al., 2002).

Validity

The content validity of this scale was established by exploring other childhood sexual abuse scales. When compared to other scales, the current CSAS demonstrates strong face validity. Support for the construct validity of the CSAS is demonstrated by its relationship with other variables. In the original study assessing the role of consistent reporting of childhood sexual abuse, consistent nonreporters of childhood sexual abuse were compared to inconsistent (endorsed at least one item at one time point and not at another time point) and consistent reporters of childhood sexual abuse. We found that reporters (either inconsistent or consistent) endorsed marked increases in measures of pathology (i.e., depression) and health-compromising behavior (i.e., sexual coercion and lifetime sexual partners). Moreover, a linear trend was evident with lifetime number of sexual partners and depression. Consistent reports of childhood sexual abuse reported the highest number of sexual partners and increased depression. Lastly, we conducted a logistic regression in order to predict membership in the consistent or inconsistent reporting group. The results indicated that adolescents who endorsed at least two items on the CSAS were over five times more likely to be consistent childhood sexual abuse reporters. The results of this analysis demonstrate the utility and importance of using a scale to measure childhood sexual abuse rather than a single-item measure. The above findings were extended in an additional analysis with the same sample (Fortenberry & Aalsma, 2003).

[1]Address correspondence to Matthew C. Aalsma, Section of Adolescent Medicine, Indiana University School of Medicine, 575 N. West Dr., Rm. 070, Indianapolis, IN 46202; e-mail: maalsma@iupui.edu

The CSAS was also employed in a study of homeless youth (Rew, Whittaker, Taylor-Seehafer, & Smith, 2005). Significant differences among homeless youth by sexual orientation categories on the CSAS were found. Specifically, gay and lesbian youth were more likely to have left home due to sexual abuse than heterosexual and bisexual youth. The authors of the study utilized the full scale as well as individual items in the analysis.

References

Aalsma, M. C., Zimet, G. D., Fortenberry, J. D., Blythe, M. J., & Orr, D. P. (2002). Report of childhood sexual abuse by adolescents and young adults: Stability over time. *The Journal of Sex Research, 39,* 259–263.

Fortenberry, J. D. & Aalsma, M. C. (2003). Abusive sexual experiences before age 12 and adolescent sexual behaviors. In J. Bancroft (Ed.), *Sexual Development in Childhood* (pp. 359–369). Bloomington, IN: Indiana University Press.

Rew, L., Whittaker, T. A., Taylor-Seehafer, M. A., & Smith, L. R. (2005). Sexual health risks and protective resources and gay, lesbian, bisexual, and heterosexual homeless youth. *Journal for Specialists in Pediatric Nursing, 10,* 11–19.

Exhibit

Childhood Sexual Abuse Scale

Instructions: These next questions are about activity before you were 12 years old.

1. Someone tried to touch me in a sexual way against my will.
2. Someone tried to make me touch them in a sexual way against my will.
3. I believe that I have been sexually abused by someone.
4. Someone threatened to tell lies about me or hurt me unless I did something sexual with them.

Early Sexual Experiences Checklist

ROWLAND S. MILLER[1] AND JAMES A. JOHNSON, *Sam Houston State University*

Self-report biases and definitional problems have plagued studies of sexual abuse of children. Various investigators have forced respondents to label themselves as "sexually abused" (e.g., Kercher & McShane, 1984) or to make subtle distinctions among vague categories (e.g., "kissing or hugging in a sexual way"; Kilpatrick, 1986) in order to be counted as victims of deleterious, unwanted childhood sexual experiences. Miller, Johnson, and Johnson (1991) created the Early Sexual Experiences Checklist (ESEC) to provide an efficient, accessible procedure for detecting such experiences that avoids these methodological and conceptual problems. The ESEC merely asks respondents to check any specific, overt sexual behaviors that occurred when the respondents did not want them to. Coupled with reports of (a) the respondent's age during the events, (b) the age of the person who initiated the events, or (c) any coercion, the ESEC allows diverse operationalizations of unwanted sexual experience that span the existing literature on sexual abuse (Kendall-Tackett, Williams, & Finkelhor,

1993). The straightforward, mechanical checklist method eschews evaluative, pejorative terminology and is thus relatively noninvasive. It is also simple and direct and very inexpensive, making it practical for use with large heterogenous populations.

Description

The ESEC contains nine items listing explicit sexual behaviors and two additional items that allow respondents either to describe a further sexual event or to pick *none of the above.* The checklist ordinarily includes additional questions—which may vary according to investigators' needs—that obtain (a) the respondent's sex, (b) the respondent's age at the time of the most bothersome event, (c) the age of the other person involved, (d) the identity (e.g., "stranger") of the other person, (e) the frequency and duration of the most bothersome experience, and (f) the presence and type of any coercion. Items using a 1 (*not at*

---

[1]Address correspondence to Rowland Miller, Division of Psychology and Philosophy, Sam Houston State University, Huntsville, TX 77341–2447; e-mail: psy_rsm@shsu.edu

all) to 7 (*extremely*) Likert-type format also obtain various ratings of the most bothersome event (e.g., "How much did it bother you then?" "How much does it bother you now?").

Response Mode and Timing

Respondents are ordinarily instructed to indicate with a check any sexual behaviors that were unwanted and that occurred before they were 16 years old. (This age limit may be changed for different applications of the checklist.) Thereafter, because many respondents will have encountered more than one type of sexual experience, respondents are typically asked to circle the experience that bothered them the most and to answer any further questions with regard to that specific event. The checklist and any additional questions usually fit on two sheets that take only 4 or 5 minutes to complete.

Scoring

Respondents who report unwanted sexual experiences can readily be distinguished from those who do not, and the percentage of the sample reporting each type of unwanted experience is easily calculated. A useful distinction can also be made, however, between those who have encountered relatively severe events, such as oral-genital contact or anal or vaginal intercourse, and those who have encountered less severe events, such as the exhibition of, or fondling of, sexual organs. Miller et al. (1991) showed that such distinctions are made by lay judges, and Anderson, Miller, and Miller (1995) demonstrated that the two different types of experiences are linked to different adult outcomes.

The results obtained by the ESEC resemble those obtained by the laborious, much costlier face-to-face interviews often advocated by methodologists (Wyatt & Peters, 1986). Anderson et al. (1995) found that 9% of the women and 3% of the men in a heterogenous college sample reported a youthful history of severe victimization by another person 5 or more years older than themselves. An additional 15% of the women and 6% of the men reported less severe experiences that were initiated by substantially older partners. Remarkably, if all such experiences are counted—regardless of the age of the partner—nearly half of the sample (48%) had some unwanted sexual experience during childhood or young adolescence.

Reliability

Using Cohen's kappa, a conservative statistic that corrects for chance agreement among diverse categories, the average 1-month test-retest reliability of the ESEC is .92 (Miller & Johnson, 1997).

Validity

Importantly, the ESEC captures reports of childhood sexual abuse that escape other paper-and-pencil techniques. Using the ESEC, Miller and Johnson (1997) found that 56% of a college sample who reported abuse in the form of unwanted, bothersome childhood experiences with partners 5 or more years older than themselves nevertheless specifically reported that they had *not* been "sexually abused." Thus, fewer than half of those who had encountered sexual abuse actually labeled themselves as "abused." Nonetheless, their experiences were detected by the ESEC. Anderson et al. (1995) have also found that adult respondents reporting any unwanted experiences on the ESEC evidenced more depression and neuroticism, and lower self-esteem, than did those who had encountered no such experiences. Furthermore, those reporting relatively severe experiences (i.e., unwanted oral-genital contact or anal or vaginal intercourse) were more impulsive, used more alcohol and other drugs, and were less secure and more anxious and avoidant in their interpersonal relations than were those who had not had such severe experiences. The ESEC methodology thus replicated the findings of other techniques for assessing abuse, but also extended those findings by allowing comparison of the sequelae of different types of abuse experiences.

References

Anderson, J. H., Miller, R. S., & Miller, G. A. (1995, August). *Adult sequelae of unwanted childhood sexual experiences*. Paper presented at the meeting of the American Psychological Association, New York.

Kendall-Tackett, K. A., Williams, L. M., & Finkelhor, D. (1993). Impact of sexual abuse on children: A review and synthesis of recent empirical studies. *Psychological Bulletin, 113*, 164–180.

Kercher, G., & McShane, M. (1984). Prevalence of child sexual abuse victimization in an adult sample of Texas residents. *Child Abuse and Neglect, 8*, 495–501.

Kilpatrick, A. (1986). Some correlates of women's childhood sexual experiences: A retrospective study. *The Journal of Sex Research, 22*, 221–242.

Miller, R. S., & Johnson, J. A. (1997). *Abuse victims don't always feel "abused": Using checklists to detect childhood sexual abuse.* Unpublished manuscript.

Miller, R. S., Johnson, J. A., & Johnson J. K. (1991). Assessing the prevalence of unwanted childhood sexual experiences. *Journal of Psychology & Human Sexuality, 4*, 43–54.

Wyatt, G. E., & Peters, S. D. (1986). Methodological considerations in research on the prevalence of child sexual abuse. *Child Abuse and Neglect, 10*, 241–251.

Exhibit

Early Sexual Experiences Checklist

Your sex: _____ Male _____ Female

Early Sexual Experiences

When you were under the age of sixteen (16), did any of these incidents ever happen to you *when you did not want them to?*

Please check those that occurred:

_____ Another person showed his or her sex organs to you.
_____ You showed your sex organs to another person at his or her request.
_____ Someone touched or fondled your sexual organs.
_____ You touched or fondled another person's sex organs at his or her request.
_____ Another person had sexual intercourse with you.
_____ Another person performed oral sex on you.
_____ You performed oral sex on another person.
_____ Someone told you to engage in sexual activity so that he or she could watch.
_____ You engaged in anal sex with another person.
_____ Other (please specify): _____
_____ None of these events ever occurred.

If any of these incidents ever happened to you, please answer the following questions by *thinking about the one behavior that bothered you the most.*

In addition, please *circle* the behavior above that bothered you the most.

1. How old were you when it happened? _____
2. Approximately how old was the other person involved? _____
3. Who was the other person involved?

    _____ relative   _____ friend or acquaintance   _____ stranger

4. If the other person was a relative, how were they related to you? (i.e., cousin, father, sister, etc.) _____
5. How many times did this behavior occur?

    _____ just once   _____ twice   _____ 3 or 4 times   _____ 5 times or more

6. Over how long a period did this behavior occur?

    _____ just once   _____ a month or less   _____ several months   _____ a year or more

7. How much did the experience *bother* you at the time?

1	2	3	4	5	6	7
not at all			moderately			extremely

8. How much does the experience *bother* you now?

1	2	3	4	5	6	7
not at all			moderately			extremely

9. What kind of psychological pressure or physical force did the person use, if any? *Please check all that apply:*

    _____ They tried to talk you into it.
    _____ They scared you because they were bigger or stronger.
    _____ They said they would hurt you.
    _____ They bribed you.
    _____ They pushed, hit, or physically restrained you.
    _____ You were afraid they wouldn't like or love you.
    _____ They physically harmed or injured you.
    _____ They threatened you with a weapon.

_____ They drugged you or got you drunk.
_____ Other (please specify): _____
_____ None of these occurred.

What-If-Situations-Test

ALAN G. NEMEROFSKY,[1] *Community College of Baltimore County*
DEBORAH T. CARRAN, *Johns Hopkins University*

The What-If-Situations-Test (WIST; Nemerofsky, 1986) was developed to measure performance of preschool-age children in sexual abuse prevention programs. The WIST is constructed from the learning objectives of the Children's Primary Prevention Training Program (Nemerofsky, Sanford, Baer, Cage, & Wood, 1986) and is composed of situations that require the child to determine how he or she would respond. The test items measure the skills and concepts taught in the prevention program and address skills and concepts thought to be essential in reducing the risk of sexual victimization (Conte, Rosen, & Saperstein, 1986; Wurtele, 1987). The WIST can be used as a pretest measure, as well as a measure of performance in sexual abuse prevention programs.

Description

The WIST consists of 29 items addressing (a) the names and location of the child's "private parts," (b) appropriate requests to touch or to examine the child's genitals by physicians, (c) requests for touching of the child's genitals by others, (d) requests for the child to touch another individual's genitals, (e) the child's right to refuse to be touched, (f) appropriate requests to touch (hug/kiss) the child by others, (g) requests to keep secrets, (h) requests to keep secrets about genital touching, (i) attempts to provide gifts/bribes/presents/incentives to touch child's genitals or have the child touch the genitals of another person, (j) actions to be taken if the child was afraid and/or uncomfortable, and (k) the child's role in potential abuse situations.

Eleven items require the child to make a determination about the appropriateness of an action or situation (e.g., If someone touches a child's private parts, should the child tell?). Seventeen items deal with actions that a child should take in abuse situations (e.g., What would you do if someone touched your private parts?). One item addresses the names and locations of the child's private parts.

Response Mode and Timing

The WIST is administered, on an individual basis, by the child's teacher. The child's responses are written down verbatim and scored by comparison to a key. The test requires approximately 15 minutes to complete.

Scoring

Scores can range from 0 to 64, with higher scores indicating greater understanding of child sexual abuse prevention skills and concepts. WIST items are differently keyed according to the nature of the item. The 11 WIST items requiring the child to make a determination about the appropriateness of an action or situation are scored 0 points for a wrong answer and 1 point for a correct response. The 17 items addressing actions a child could take in abuse situations receive 1 point for an assertive or motoric response, 2 points for disclosure, and 3 points for both an assertive and a disclosure response. The WIST item that requires the child to name and locate his or her private parts receives 0 points for a wrong answer, 1 point for a partial answer (e.g., child names only one private part), and 2 points for a complete correct answer (e.g., a girl's private parts are her vagina, buttocks, and breasts).

Reliability

In a sample of 1,044 3- to 6-year-old children (Nemerofsky, 1991), the Cronbach's alpha for the WIST was .83, indicating good reliability.

Validity

In a study using the WIST pretest mean score as the covariate, WIST posttest mean scores of children who had completed a sexual abuse prevention training program were compared to the control group of children who had not received the training. A significant difference was found between groups, with the experimental group of children scoring significantly higher on the WIST posttest following participation in the sexual abuse prevention training program than the control group of children who had not received the training (Nemerofsky, Carran, & Rosenberg, 1994).

[1]Address correspondence to Alan G. Nemerofsky, CCBC Essex, 7201 Rossville Blvd., Baltimore, MD 21237; e-mail: ANemerofsky@ccbcmd.edu

References

Conte, J. R., Rosen, C., & Saperstein, L. (1986). An analysis of programs to prevent the sexual victimization of children. *Journal of Primary Prevention, 6,* 141–155.

Nemerofsky, A. G. (1986). *The What-If-Situations-Test.* Baltimore, MD: Author.

Nemerofsky, A. G. (1991). *Child sexual abuse prevention: Teacher and child variables affecting the learning of skills and concepts in a sexual abuse prevention program.* Unpublished doctoral dissertation, The Johns Hopkins University, Baltimore, MD.

Nemerofsky, A. G., Carran, D. T., & Rosenberg, L. A. (1994). Age variation in performance among preschool age children in a sexual abuse prevention program. *Journal of Child Sexual Abuse, 3,* 85–102.

Nemerofsky, A. G., Sanford, H. J., Baer, B., Cage, M., & Wood, D. (1986). *The children's primary prevention training program.* Baltimore, MD: Author.

Wurtele, S. K. (1987). School-based sexual abuse prevention programs: A review. *Child Abuse and Neglect, 11,* 483–495.

Exhibit

What-If-Situations-Test

Child Code Number:

Circle: Pretest   Posttest

1. Tell me the names of your private parts.
2. What would you do if someone touched you in a way you did not like?
3. What would you do if someone touched you in a way that you liked?
4. What would you do if someone asked you to keep a secret?
5. What would you do if someone tried to touch your private parts?
6. What would you do if someone touched you in a way that made you feel uncomfortable?
7. Is it OK for a mom or dad to give you a hug if you want one? (Circle) Yes   No
8. Do you have to let anyone touch you on your private parts? (Circle) Yes   No
9. What would you do if someone touched your private parts?
10. What would you do if someone said they would give you a present if you would keep a secret?
11. If someone makes a child touch their private parts:

    a. Did the child do anything wrong? Yes   No
    b. Is it the child's fault? Yes   No
    c. Should the child tell? Yes   No
    d. Should the child ask for help? Yes   No

12. What would you do if someone asked you to touch their private parts?
13. What would you do if someone asked you to keep a secret about touching private parts?
14. What would you do if someone said they would give you a present if you would touch their private parts?
15. What would you do if someone made you touch their private parts?
16. If someone touches a child's private parts:

    a. Did the child do anything wrong? Yes   No
    b. Is it the child's fault? Yes   No
    c. Should the child tell? Yes   No
    d. Should the child ask for help? Yes   No

17. Would it be OK for your doctor to look at your private parts if you were hurt there? Yes   No
18. What would you do if you were scared or confused or felt uncomfortable?
19. What would you say if someone asked you to touch their private parts?
20. What should a child do if someone touched his/her private parts and promised not to do it again?
21. If someone touched your private parts:

    a. What would you say?
    b. What would you do?
    c. Who would you tell?

Empathy for Children Scale

Gerard A. Schaefer,[1] *Institute of Sexology and Sexual Medicine, Charité— Universitätsmedizin Berlin, Freie und Humboldt-Universität zu Berlin, Germany* **Steven Feelgood,** *Clinical Psychology and Psychotherapy, Technical University, Dresden, Germany*

Empathy can be defined as one individual's reactions to the observed experiences of another (Davis, 1983). A four-stage model of empathy by Marshall, Hudson, Jones, and Fernandez (1995) includes emotion recognition, perspective taking, emotional response, and appropriate action. Several measures have been developed to assess general empathy, such as the Interpersonal Reactivity Index (IRI; Davis, 1983), Hogan's Empathy Scale (Hogan, 1969), or the Emotional Empathy Scale (Mehrabian & Epstein, 1972).

Sexual offenders typically display a lack of empathy for their victims (Marshall, 1997). Child sexual abuse offenders' empathy deficits are greatest for their own victims compared to nonsexual offenders (Marshall, Hamilton, & Fernandez, 2001). Contact sexual offenders score lower than child pornography offenders in victim empathy (Bates & Metcalf, 2007; Elliott, Beech, Mandeville-Norden, & Hayes, 2009).

The Empathy for Children Scale (ECS) was developed to measure an individual's cognitive and emotional empathy for child victims. Three scenarios are used, assessing empathy with respect to an "accident victim," a "stranger child sexual abuse victim," and "(fantasized) own child sexual abuse victim." The ECS can be used as a research tool in examining respective empathy deficits of various subsamples. It can also serve as a clinical tool for therapists in treatment planning and treatment outcome assessment.

Description

The ECS is based on the Child Molester Empathy Measure (CMEM; Fernandez & Marshall, 2003; Fernandez, Marshall, Lightbody, & O'Sullivan, 1999), in that it uses the same three scenarios to assess empathy for child victims using two subscales (cognitive and emotional empathy) for each scenario. However, as the ECS was specifically developed for administration with pedophilic nonoffenders, the original "own child sexual abuse victim" scenario was modified to offer a fantasized own victim. Changes to the scenarios also improved the comparability of the scenarios. Furthermore, the ECS assesses data regarding age and gender of (fantasized) own victim and imagined general sexual abuse victim. With 75 items rated on 5-point Likert-type scales, the ECS is less complex to rate for the respondents, as well as more economic to administer (the CMEM has 150 items and uses 11-point Likert-type scales). Higher scores indicate more empathy. Owing to its design, it may be used in both forensic and nonforensic settings. Therefore, its use is not limited to individuals with known victims, such as convicted sexual offenders. The instrument is available in English, French, and German (Feelgood & Schaefer, 2005).

Response Mode and Timing

For each item, respondents are to circle the number (0–4; 0 = *Not at all*; 4 = *Very Much*) that best describes how, in their opinion, the child might feel (cognitive empathy) and how they feel when imagining what the child experienced (emotional empathy). It typically takes 20 to 30 minutes to complete the instrument.

Scoring

The items for each subscale are added to form total scores. Items 4 and 7 are reverse scored for cognitive empathy, and Items 1, 8, and 9 are reverse scored for emotional empathy. It is possible to have an overall empathy score for each scenario by simply adding the total scores for cognitive and emotional empathy for the respective scenarios.

Reliability

One hundred and fifty men (83 reporting sexual contacts with children, 67 "potential" perpetrators) who volunteered for a treatment program for individuals with a sexual interest in minors, the Berlin Prevention Project Dunkelfeld (PPD), completed the ECS as part of an assessment battery (Beier, Ahlers et al., 2009; Beier, Neutze et al., 2009). Cognitive distortion and social desirability were controlled using the Bumby MOLEST Scale (BMS; Bumby, 1996) and the Balanced Inventory of Desirable Responding (BIDR-20; Paulhus, 1991; German version: Musch, Brockhaus,

[1]Address correspondence to Gerard A. Schaefer, Institute of Sexology and Sexual Medicine, University Clinic Charité Campus Mitte, Freie und Humboldt-Universität zu Berlin, Luisenstraße 57, D-10117 Berlin-Mitte, Germany; e-mail: gerard.schaefer@charite.de

& Bröder, 2002). Significant correlations with the BMS-cognitive distortion scale were found (−.42 to −.50) and only one small correlation with social desirability (−.19 for accident victim). Internal consistency (Cronbach's alpha = .96) supports the structure of the scale (Schaefer & Feelgood, 2006).

Validity

Comparing child sexual abuse offenders diagnosed with pedophilia, no differences were found between undetected and detected offenders concerning emotional empathy regarding their own victims (Schaefer, Neutze, Mundt, & Beier, 2008). Similar profiles to those found in samples of detected offenders (Marshall et al., 2001) were identified in a sample of PPD offenders (i.e., undetected child sexual abuse offenders). They displayed less empathy for their own victim than for other victims of child sexual abuse and the greatest empathy for a child car accident victim (Schaefer & Feelgood, 2006). Differences between these groups support discriminant validity. The lack of social desirability responding relative to the ECS supports divergent validity.

Other Information

When using the instrument to assess empathy deficits within a population of known (e.g., convicted) offenders, the text passages in italicized uppercase letters must be deleted.

Steven Feelgood is also affiliated with the Social Therapy Unit, Brandenburg an der Havel Prison, Brandenburg, Germany.

Copies of the instrument and information regarding revisions of any part of the instrument may be requested by e-mail to the first author.

References

Bates, A., & Metcalf, C. (2007). A psychometric comparison of Internet and non-Internet sex offenders from a community treatment sample. *Journal of Sexual Aggression, 13,* 11–20.

Beier, K. M., Ahlers, C. J., Goecker, D., Neutze, J., Mundt, I. A., Hupp, E., et al. (2009). Can pedophiles be reached for primary prevention of child sexual abuse? First results of the Berlin Prevention Project Dunkelfeld (PPD). *Journal of Forensic Psychiatry and Forensic Psychology, 20,* 851–867.

Beier, K. M., Neutze, J., Mundt, I. A., Ahlers, C. J., Goecker, D., Konrad, A., et al. (2009). Encouraging self-identified pedophiles and hebephiles to seek professional help: First results of the Berlin Prevention Project Dunkelfeld (PPD). *Child Abuse and Neglect, 33,* 545–549.

Bumby, K. M. (1996). Assessing the cognitive distortions of child molesters and rapists: Development and validation of the MOLEST and RAPE scales. *Sexual Abuse: Journal of Research and Treatment, 8,* 37–54.

Davis, M. H. (1983). Measuring individual differences in empathy: Evidence for a multidimensional approach. *Journal of Personality and Social Psychology, 44,* 113–126.

Elliott, I. A., Beech, A. R., Mandeville-Norden, R., & Hayes, E. (2009). Psychological profiles of Internet sexual offenders: Comparisons with contact sexual offenders. *Sexual Abuse: A Journal of Research and Treatment, 21,* 76–92.

Feelgood, S., & Schaefer, G. A. (2005). *German version of the Empathy for Children Scale (ECS).* Unpublished manuscript.

Fernandez, Y. M., & Marshall, W. L. (2003). Victim empathy, social self-esteem and psychopathy in rapists. *Sexual Abuse: A Journal of Research and Treatment, 15,* 11–26.

Fernandez, Y. M., Marshall, W. L., Lightbody, S., & O'Sullivan, C. (1999). The Child Molester Empathy Measure. *Sexual Abuse: A Journal of Research and Treatment, 11,* 17–31.

Hogan, R. (1969). Development of an empathy scale. *Journal of Consulting and Clinical Psychology, 33,* 307–316.

Marshall, W. L. (1997). The relationship between self-esteem and deviant sexual arousal in non-familial child molesters. *Behavior Modification, 21,* 86–96.

Marshall, W. L., Hamilton, K., & Fernandez, Y. (2001). Empathy deficits and cognitive distortions in child molesters. *Sexual Abuse: A Journal of Research and Treatment, 13,* 123–130.

Marshall, W. L., Hudson, S. M., Jones, R., & Fernandez, Y. M. (1995). Empathy in sex offenders. *Clinical Psychological Review, 15,* 99–113.

Mehrabian, A., & Epstein, N. (1972). A measure of emotional empathy. *Journal of Personality, 40,* 525–543.

Musch, J., Brockhaus, R., & Bröder, A. (2002). Ein Inventar zur Erfassung von zwei Faktoren sozialer Erwünschtheit [An inventory for the assessment of two factors of social desirability]. *Diagnostica, 48*(3), 121–129.

Paulhus, D. L. (1991). Measurement and control of response bias. In J. P. Robinson, P. R. Shaver, & L. S. Wrightsman (Eds.), *Measures of personality and social psychological attitudes* (pp. 17–41). San Diego, CA: Academic Press.

Schaefer, G. A., & Feelgood, S. (2006, September). *Validation of a new scale for measuring victim empathy in pedophiles: The Empathy for Children Scale (ECS).* Paper presented at the 9th International Conference of the International Association for the Treatment of Sexual Offenders (IATSO), Hamburg, Germany.

Schaefer, G. A., Neutze, J., Mundt, I. A., & Beier, K. M. (2008, October). *Pedophiles and hebephiles in the community: Findings from the Berlin Prevention Project Dunkelfeld (PPD).* Paper presented at the 27th Annual Meeting of the Association for the Treatment of Sexual Abusers, Atlanta, GA.

Exhibit

Empathy for Children Scale

Instructions: In the following you will find three short stories. You will be asked to indicate at first how you believe the *child* in the story feels, and afterwards how *you* feel when thinking about the child.

Story 1:

Imagine a child that was badly injured in road traffic and had to spend some time in hospital. The child is now out of hospital and will live with a permanent disability.

In your opinion, how may the child feel or have felt, what may it experience or have experienced while in hospital and afterwards? For each of the following descriptions, please circle the number that best indicates **the child's experience**.

The child	Not at all				Very Much
1. feels guilty.	0	1	2	3	4
2. feels sad.	0	1	2	3	4
3. feels angry.	0	1	2	3	4
4. is self-confident.	0	1	2	3	4
5. has nightmares.	0	1	2	3	4
6. has suicidal thoughts.	0	1	2	3	4
7. is successful in school.	0	1	2	3	4
8. has sleep disturbances.	0	1	2	3	4
9. feels lonely.	0	1	2	3	4
10. is withdrawn from others.	0	1	2	3	4
11. has psychological problems.	0	1	2	3	4
12. feels helpless.	0	1	2	3	4
13. is suffering.	0	1	2	3	4
14. is tense.	0	1	2	3	4
15. feels ashamed.	0	1	2	3	4

Now please circle the number that best indicates **how you feel** when imagining what the child experienced.

I feel . . . / I am . . .	Not at all				Very Much
1. cheerful.	0	1	2	3	4
2. furious.	0	1	2	3	4
3. disturbed.	0	1	2	3	4
4. distraught.	0	1	2	3	4
5. devastated.	0	1	2	3	4
6. helpless.	0	1	2	3	4
7. upset.	0	1	2	3	4
8. good.	0	1	2	3	4
9. stimulated.	0	1	2	3	4
10. shocked.	0	1	2	3	4

How old was the child you imagined?   Ca. _____ years

Of what gender was the child you imagined?

O female
O male

Story 2:

Now imagine a child that had sex with an adult male. *(THE RELATIONSHIP WITH THE CHILD AS WELL AS THE NATURE AND FREQUENCY OF SEXUAL CONTACT MATCH YOUR OWN SEXUAL EXPERIENCE WITH CHILDREN. IF YOU HAVE NOT HAD ANY SEXUAL EXPERIENCE WITH CHILDREN, THEN IMAGINE THE STORY MATCHED YOUR USUAL SEXUAL FANTASIES OF CHILDREN.)* *In your opinion*, how may the child feel or have felt, what may it experience or have experienced while this sexual contact was occurring and afterwards?

For each of the following descriptions, please circle the number that best indicates **the child's experience**.

The child . . .	Not at all				Very Much
1. feels guilty.	0	1	2	3	4
2. feels sad.	0	1	2	3	4
3. feels angry.	0	1	2	3	4
4. is self-confident.	0	1	2	3	4
5. has nightmares.	0	1	2	3	4
6. has suicidal thoughts.	0	1	2	3	4
7. is successful in school.	0	1	2	3	4
8. has sleep disturbances.	0	1	2	3	4
9. feels lonely.	0	1	2	3	4
10. is withdrawn from others.	0	1	2	3	4
11. has psychological problems.	0	1	2	3	4
12. feels helpless.	0	1	2	3	4
13. is suffering.	0	1	2	3	4
14. is tense.	0	1	2	3	4
15. feels ashamed.	0	1	2	3	4

Now please circle the number that best indicates **how you feel** when imagining what the child experienced.

I feel . . . / I am . . .	Not at all				Very Much
1. cheerful.	0	1	2	3	4
2. furious.	0	1	2	3	4
3. disturbed.	0	1	2	3	4
4. distraught.	0	1	2	3	4
5. devastated.	0	1	2	3	4
6. helpless.	0	1	2	3	4
7. upset.	0	1	2	3	4
8. good.	0	1	2	3	4
9. stimulated.	0	1	2	3	4
10. shocked.	0	1	2	3	4

How old was the child you imagined?   Ca. _____ years

Of what gender was the child you imagined?

O female

O male

Story 3:

Now think of a child with whom *you* have had sexual contact. *(IF YOU HAVE NOT HAD ANY SEXUAL CONTACT WITH CHILDREN, PLEASE IMAGINE A CHILD YOU HAD OR HAVE SEX WITH IN YOUR FANTASIES.)* **In your opinion**, how may the child feel or have felt, what may it experience or have experienced while this sexual contact was occurring and afterwards?

For each of the following descriptions, please circle the number that best indicates **the child's experience**.

IF YOU HAVE NOT HAD ANY SEXUAL CONTACT WITH CHILDREN PLEASE TICK THE BOX TO THE RIGHT. ☐

The child . . .	Not at all				Very Much
1. feels guilty.	0	1	2	3	4
2. feels sad.	0	1	2	3	4
3. feels angry.	0	1	2	3	4
4. is self-confident.	0	1	2	3	4
5. has nightmares.	0	1	2	3	4
6. has suicidal thoughts.	0	1	2	3	4
7. is successful in school.	0	1	2	3	4
8. has sleep disturbances.	0	1	2	3	4
9. feels lonely.	0	1	2	3	4
10. is withdrawn from others.	0	1	2	3	4
11. has psychological problems.	0	1	2	3	4
12. feels helpless.	0	1	2	3	4
13. is suffering.	0	1	2	3	4
14. is tense.	0	1	2	3	4
15. feels ashamed.	0	1	2	3	4

Now please circle the number that best indicates **how you feel** when imagining what the child experienced.

IF YOU HAVE NOT HAD ANY SEXUAL CONTACT WITH CHILDREN PLEASE TICK THE BOX TO THE RIGHT. ☐

I feel . . . / I am . . .	Not at all				Very Much
1. cheerful.	0	1	2	3	4
2. furious.	0	1	2	3	4
3. disturbed.	0	1	2	3	4
4. distraught.	0	1	2	3	4
5. devastated.	0	1	2	3	4
6. helpless.	0	1	2	3	4
7. upset.	0	1	2	3	4
8. good.	0	1	2	3	4
9. stimulated.	0	1	2	3	4
10. shocked.	0	1	2	3	4

How old was the child you imagined?   Ca. _____ years

Of what gender was the child you imagined?

○ female

○ male

Unwanted Childhood Sexual Experiences Questionnaire

MICHAEL R. STEVENSON,[1] *Ball State University*

The Unwanted Childhood Sexual Experience Questionnaire can be used to document the age and extent of respondents' unwanted childhood sexual experiences with adults. Instructions intentionally refer to *unwanted* childhood sexual experiences rather than abusive sexual experiences or experiences of sexual *victimization* in an attempt to avoid unintended bias in reporting. It defines an adult as someone who is at least 5 years older than the respondent.

Description

Each of the 13 items refers to a different set of behaviors that can be categorized as minimal contact (Items 1–3), moderate contact (Items 4–8), or maximal contact (Items 9–13). Items were drawn from a larger questionnaire designed by Finkelhor (1979) and have been used in other studies (e.g., Fromuth, 1986; Stevenson & Gajarsky, 1992).

Response Mode and Timing

Respondents simply indicate in the space provided the age or ages at which any of the unwanted sexual behaviors occurred. The scale can be completed in less than 5 minutes.

Scoring

The questionnaire allows for the reporting of the frequency with which each of the behaviors occur in the sample, and the ages at which the behaviors occurred.

Reliability

The intention of this questionnaire is to document whether specific unwanted behaviors have occurred, and the items are not intended to constitute a scale. Reliability has not been assessed directly.

Validity

Using this measure, Stevenson and Gajarsky's (1992) sample of college students reported frequencies of unwanted sexual experiences that were consistent with earlier reports (e.g., Finkelhor, 1979, 1984; Groth, 1979). Although the percentage of men reporting unwanted sexual experiences was somewhat higher than some previous estimates, it was quite consistent with others (e.g., Popen & Segal, 1988).

References

Finkelhor, D. (1979). *Sexually victimized children*. New York: Free Press.

Finkelhor, D. (1984). *Child sexual abuse: New theory and research*. New York: Free Press.

Fromuth, M. E. (1986). The relationship of childhood sexual abuse with later psychological and sexual adjustment in a sample of college women. *Child Abuse and Neglect, 10*, 5–15.

Groth, N. A. (1979). Sexual trauma in the life histories of rapists and child molesters. *Victimology: An International Journal, 4*(1), 10–16.

Popen, P. J., & Segal, H. J. (1988). The influence of sex and sex-role orientation on sexual coercion. *Sex Roles, 19*, 689–701.

Stevenson, M. R., & Gajarsky, W. M. (1992). Unwanted childhood sexual experiences relate to later revictimization and male perpetration. *Journal of Psychology & Human Sexuality, 4*, 57–70.

Exhibit

Unwanted Childhood Sexual Experiences Questionnaire

It is now generally realized that most people have sexual experiences as children and while growing up. By "sexual" it is meant any behavior or event that might seem "sexual" to you. Please try to remember the unwanted, that is, sexual experiences that were forced on you or done against your will by an adult (someone at least five or more years older than you), while growing up. Indicate if you had any of the following experiences *before* the age of 16.

1. An invitation or request to do something sexual.   Age(s)_____
2. Kissing and hugging in a sexual way.   Age(s)_____
3. An adult showing his/her sex organs to you.   Age(s)_____
4. You showing your sex organs to an adult.   Age(s)_____
5. An adult fondling you in a sexual way.   Age(s)_____

[1]Address correspondence to Michael R. Stevenson, P O Box 15700, Northern Arizona University, Flagstaff, AZ 86011; e-mail: Michael.Stevenson@nau.edu

6. You fondling an adult in a sexual way.   Age(s)_____
7. An adult touching your sex organs.   Age(s)_____
8. You touching an adult person's sex organs.   Age(s)_____
9. An adult orally touching your sex organs.   Age(s)_____
10. You orally touching an adult person's sex organs.   Age(s)_____
11. Intercourse, but without attempting penetration of the vagina.   Age(s)_____
12. Intercourse (penile-vaginal penetration).   Age(s)_____
13. Anal intercourse (penile-anal penetration).   Age(s)_____

Sexual History and Adjustment Questionnaire

ROBIN J. LEWIS[1] AND LOUIS H. JANDA, *Old Dominion University*

This measure was developed to assess participants' retrospective reports of (a) frequency of sleeping in the bed with parents between the ages of 0–5 and 6–11 years; (b) frequency of seeing parents, as well as others, naked between 0–5 years and 6–11 years; (c) parental attitudes toward sexuality; (d) participants' level of comfort in discussing sexuality with parents; and (e) perceptions of parental discomfort regarding sexuality. Information on current adjustment and sexual behavior was also obtained.

Description

This instrument would be appropriate for populations of older adolescents and adults. Items 1–10 assess retrospective reports of childhood experiences with nudity and sleeping in the parental bed. Items 11–19 assess the participant's perceptions of parental attitudes toward sex and discussion of sexuality, as well as how often there was demonstration of physical affection in the family. Items 20–29 assess the participant's current sexual behavior and attitudes toward himself or herself. Item 30 addresses feelings of discomfort about the physical contact and affection displayed in one's family.

Response Mode, Timing, and Scoring

Respondents are asked to indicate their response to each item by circling the number that best reflects their answer to a question using a 5-point Likert-type scale. The anchors of the scale vary by section. Investigators may be interested in individual responses, such as frequency of seeing one particular parent naked, and may wish to sum responses across ages (e.g., index for maternal nudity would be sum

of response for nudity at ages 0–5 plus nudity at ages 6–11). Or investigators may wish to sum for a total parental nudity index (cf. Lewis & Janda, 1988) by summing all responses for mother and father across ages.

A similar approach is used with the items about parental attitudes. Investigators may combine items for maternal attitudes (e.g., comfort discussing sexual matters; positive vs. negative attitude), as well as similar items for paternal attitudes. Alternatively, a global measure of attitudes may be generated. In our previous research (Lewis & Janda, 1988), however, we found some differences in maternal and paternal attitudes. Thus, investigators are urged to be cautious in this regard.

In our previous research (Lewis & Janda, 1988), we examined the sexual adjustment items separately. Interested investigators might wish to combine items to generate a more global measure of adjustment.

Reliability

A number of subscales for this measure can be constructed, depending on researchers' interests. Internal consistency was demonstrated for the following subscales using coefficient alpha:

1. Parental Nudity Subscale (Sum Items 1, 2, 3, 4): .74
2. Overall Nudity Subscale (Sum Items 1–8): .77
3. Parental Bed Subscale (Sum Items 9–10): .80
4. Maternal Attitudes Subscale (Sum Items 11, 13, 15): .77
5. Paternal Attitudes Subscale (Sum Items 12, 14, 16): .78
6. Overall Attitudes Subscale (Sum Items 11–16): .78

[1]Address correspondence to Robin J. Lewis, Department of Psychology, Old Dominion University, Norfolk, VA 23529–0267; e-mail: rlewis@odu.edu

No test-retest reliability has been obtained for this measure.

Validity

No formal validation of this measure has been reported. It would be appropriate to demonstrate validity by correlating subscales of this measure with established measures of sexual adjustment and perhaps global attitudes about one's family. The items on this measure clearly demonstrate face validity. It would also be helpful to examine the degree to which a socially desirable response set might influence responses. To that end, examination of the correlation between these items and a measure of social desirability (e.g., Reynolds, 1982) would provide useful information.

References

Lewis, R. J., & Janda, L. H. (1988). The relationship between adult sexual adjustment and childhood experiences regarding exposure to nudity, sleeping in the parental bed, and parental attitudes toward sexuality. *Archives of Sexual Behavior, 17*, 349–362.

Reynolds, W. M. (1982). Development of reliable and valid short forms of the Marlowe-Crowne Social Desirability Scale. *Journal of Clinical Psychology, 38*, 119–125.

Exhibit

Sexual History and Adjustment Questionnaire

Retrospective Reports of Childhood Experiences with Nudity and Sleeping in the Parental Bed

Please use the following scale for questions 1–10:

1	2	3	4	5
almost never	rarely	sometimes	often	very often

1. When you were between the ages of 0–5, how often do you remember seeing your mother naked?
2. When you were between the ages of 6–11, how often do you remember seeing your mother naked?
3. When you were between the ages of 0–5, how often do you remember seeing your father naked?
4. When you were between the ages of 6–11, how often do you remember seeing your father naked?
5. When you were between the ages of 0–5, how often do you remember seeing your same-sex siblings or friends naked?
6. When you were between the ages of 6–11, how often do you remember seeing your same-sex siblings or friends naked?
7. When you were between the ages of 0–5, how often do you remember seeing your opposite-sex siblings or friends naked?
8. When you were between the ages of 6–11, how often do you remember seeing your opposite-sex siblings or friends naked?
9. When you were between the ages of 0–5, how often do you remember sleeping in the same bed as your parents?
10. When you were between the ages of 6–11, how often do you remember sleeping in the same bed as your parents?

Parental Attitudes Items

Please use the following scale for questions 11–14:

1	2	3	4	5
extreme discomfort	moderate discomfort	neither comfort nor discomfort	moderate comfort	extreme comfort

11. In general, over the course of your childhood, please rate the degree of comfort you felt in talking about sexual matters with your mother:
12. In general, over the course of your childhood, please rate the degree of comfort you felt in talking about sexual matters with your father:
13. While you were growing up, please rate the degree of comfort you think your mother felt when talking about sexuality:
14. While you were growing up, please rate the degree of comfort you think your father felt when talking about sexuality:
15. How would you characterize your mother's attitude toward sexuality when you were growing up?

1	2	3	4	5
extremely negative	moderately negative	neither positive nor negative	moderately positive	extremely positive

16. How would you characterize your father's attitude toward sexuality when you were growing up?

1	2	3	4	5
extremely negative	moderately negative	neither positive nor negative	moderately positive	extremely positive

17. Overall, how well do you feel that your upbringing prepared you to deal with issues of sexuality and sexual relationships?

1	2	3	4	5
not at all	poorly	adequately	pretty well	very well

18. How often do you remember issues of sexuality being discussed in your home when you were growing up?

1	2	3	4	5
almost never	rarely	sometimes	often	very often

19. In general, how often was there physical contact/affection displayed in your family?

1	2	3	4	5
almost never	rarely	sometimes	often	very often

Sexual Adjustment Items

Please use the following scale for questions 20–29:

1	2	3	4	5
strongly disagree	somewhat disagree	neither agree nor disagree	somewhat agree	strongly agree

20. I feel good about myself.
21. I experience guilt or anxiety when it comes to my sex life.
22. I am happy with my sex life.
23. I am heterosexual.
24. I have sex more often than most people of my age and situation (e.g., married versus single).
25. I tend to engage in casual sexual relationships.
26. I have experienced sexual problems.
27. I would like my sex life to be more active than it is.
28. I am very consistent in making certain that birth control is a part of my sexual encounters.
29. I am knowledgeable about sex.
30. Regarding physical contact and affection in your family how often do you remember having feelings of discomfort about this contact?

1	2	3	4	5
almost never	rarely	sometimes	often	very often

Sexual Knowledge and Attitude Test for Adolescents

William Fullard, *Temple University*
Lawrence M. Scheier,[1] *LARS Research Institute, Inc.*

The Sexual Knowledge and Attitude Test for Adolescents (SKAT-A) is a developmentally appropriate, paper-and-pencil self-report questionnaire for assessing subjective evaluations and knowledge proficiency regarding sexual behavior and sexual experience for adolescents (Fullard, Scheier & Lief, 2005).

Description

The current version of the SKAT-A (2005) represents a considerable revision from the previous two versions (e.g., Fullard, Johnston, & Lief, 1998; Lief, Fullard, & Devlin, 1990). The original Sexual Knowledge and Attitude Scale (Lief & Reed, 1972) was developed for use with adult health professionals and is described in detail by Lief (1988). Previous versions of the adolescent-focused test were constructed to be appropriate for youth ages 12–18 and utilized the original SKAT as a basis for developing and constructing scales. Sections collecting demographic information and sexual behavior were added to equip the SKAT-A for broad-based use in a variety of settings including program evaluations, and educational courses in human sexuality, and as a means to collect relevant information about adolescent sexuality not otherwise available. The SKAT-A is also suitable for use with young adults.

The SKAT-A contains 40 attitudinal items with a 5-point Likert-type response format ranging from 1 = *Strongly Agree* to 5 = *Strongly Disagree*. Eleven of the attitudinal items are reverse scored. Preliminary exploratory factor analysis resulted in five content scales (Masturbation, Homosexuality, Pornography, Premarital sex, and Abortion).

A confirmatory factor analysis model was configured with simple structure. Based on prior factor analytic work with a young adult sample (Fullard et al., 1998), six factors were specified tapping Premarital Sexuality, Rape/Coercion, Masturbation, Abortion, Homosexuality, and Pornography. This base six-factor model fit adequately, $\chi^2 (465) = 3861.98$, $p < .001$, Comparative Fit Index (CFI: .831), Root Mean Square Error of Approximation (RMSEA = .051), and Standardized Root Mean Residual

(SRMR = .065).[2] The six factors were all psychometrically reliable with significant factor loadings (all $ps < .001$). Average loadings within factors ranged from $\lambda = .61$ for Masturbation to $\lambda = .40$ for Abortion.

Table 1 contains the factor intercorrelations (estimates of internal consistency are on the diagonal). A model positing a higher-order factor structure did not improve appreciably on the primary first-order model, $\Delta\chi^2(37) = 2767.46$, $p < .001$.

The SKAT-A also includes 40 trichotomously scored knowledge items (*True, False,* and *Not Sure*). Scale scores are derived by assigning a 1 to correct responses and 0 to incorrect answers. The response *Not Sure* is not penalized in the computation of knowledge proficiency scale scores (number correct—number incorrect). Six proficiency scales assess knowledge of pregnancy/contraception, abstinence/sexual awareness, orgasm, masturbation, negative consequences of sex, and homosexuality.

The Sexual Behavior Inventory obtains information about a wide variety of sexual and experiential behaviors including dating experience, onset of sexual activity, contraceptive practices, number of sexual partners, sexually transmitted diseases and other experiences relevant to adolescent sexuality and education.

TABLE 1
Correlations Among Latent Factor Constructs From Six-Factor Model

	F1	F2	F3	F4	F5	F6
Premarital Sexuality (F1)	71	.10	.29**	.49***	−.15*	.65***
Rape/Coercion (F2)		.71	.46***	.48**	−.40***	.36***
Masturbation (F3)			.78	.55***	−.58***	.67***
Abortion (F4)				.50	−.60***	.46***
Homosexuality (F5)					.74	−.29**
Pornography (F6)						.54

Note: Numbers on diagonals are error-free estimates of internal consistency computed using Werts, Linn, & Jöreskog's (1974) formula (reliability presented as unstandardized alpha).
*p < .05; **p < .01; ***p < .001

[1]Address correspondence to Lawrence Scheier, LARS Research Institute, Inc., 11735 Glowing Sunset Lane, Las Vegas NV 89135; e-mail: Scheier@cox.net
[2]The model fit indices could be improved considerably with the addition of correlated residuals and cross-factor loadings. This would likely improve the CFI, which should hover above .95 (Hu & Bentler, 1998), and reduce the magnitude of both the RMSEA and SRMR (both of which should be below .05 indicating the amount of off-diagonal residual variances unaccounted for by the hypothetical model). However, for the purpose of deriving *pure* factor loadings and providing a basis for cross-validation with a moderately small sample, we chose to model simple structure and not to include any model refinements based on post-hoc specification searches. In addition, the robust nature of correlated residuals has been brought into question with Monte Carlo simulations with *N*s less than 500, a number that approximates our sample size (MacCallum, 1986).

Response Mode and Timing

With standard survey administration procedures, the SKAT-A can be completed in 20–30 minutes. The Attitude and Knowledge sections include forced-choice question formats. The Demographics and Behavior sections require a combination of checked items (e.g., grade in school) and open-ended questions (e.g., age of first menstrual period, father's occupation).

Reliability

The psychometric information presented here is based on a sample ($N = 516$) of urban high school students (59% female; 9th through 12th grades) from a northeastern city. The mean age of the sample was 16.7 (range 15 to 20 years). Racial self-identification indicated 19.5% White, 20% African American, 19.% African Caribbean, 18% Hispanic, 10% Asian, and 13.5% Other. Some comparative information is included from a sample of college students at an urban university in the northeast ($N = 240$; 74% female; mean age = 23.0; racial self-identification: 58% White, 31% African American, 5% Hispanic, 4% Asian, 2% Other; Fullard et al. 1998; Johnston, 1998).

Reliability analyses of the five derived attitudinal subscales indicated adequate reliability (see Fullard et al., 1998), with adequate internal consistency coefficients (.84 for high school students, .88 for college students). Test-retest coefficients over a 2-week period were .88 (high school sample, $N = 45$) and .89 (college sample, $N = 52$; Fullard et al., 1998; Johnston, 1998).

Total scale reliabilities for the knowledge items are as follows: internal consistency (high school sample = .79, college sample = .75); test-retest stability over a 2-week period was .78 (high school sample) and .85 (college sample; Fullard et al., 1998; Johnston, 1998).

Validity

We examined the associations between the six latent factors and various sexual behavior measures. Space limitations do not permit presenting of all of these relations; however, the most pronounced were between a 7-item scale assessing frequency of sexual experiences (e.g., dating, kissing, petting, oral sex; $\alpha = .80$) and Premarital Sexuality attitudes ($r = .42$, $p < .001$) followed by Pornography attitudes ($r = .35$, $p < .001$). Other notable associations included intercourse with Premarital Sexuality attitudes ($r = .31, p < .001$) and with Pornography attitudes ($r = .18$, $p < .05$). Reports of homosexual experiences were inversely related to Rape/ Coercion attitudes ($r = -.14, p < .05$) and abortion attitudes were related to the use of contraception ($r = .28, p < .01$).

Associations between knowledge and behavior. Mean levels of proficiency for the six knowledge scales were 33% (pregnancy), 25% (virginity), 27% (orgasm), 28% (masturbation), 33% (negative consequences), and 32%

(homosexuality). It should be noted that knowledge scores were substantially higher with the college sample, as would be expected. The low proportion of youth scoring correct and moderate skew for all six scales indicated the knowledge items are difficult for this age group. Knowledge of orgasm issues had the largest association with a composite tapping frequency of sexual behavior ($r = .15, p < .01$), followed by knowledge of masturbation issues ($r = .11, p < .05$). Relations between the six knowledge scales and behavior indicated that more knowledge of abstinence/ sexual awareness was related to frequency of contraceptive use ($r = .24, p < .01$), knowledge of homosexuality issues was related to contraception ($r = .24, p < .01$) and inversely with frequency of contraceptive use ($r = -.15, p < .05$). A similar comparison with the college sample may be found in Fullard et al. (1998).

Associations between attitudes and knowledge. Correlations between the six attitudinal latent factors and the six knowledge scale scores indicated relatively low overlap between knowledge and Premarital Sexuality attitudes ($r_{avg} = .07$ for the six associations), and likewise relatively low associations with Rape ($r_{avg} = .10$), Masturbation ($r_{avg} = .13$), Abortion ($r_{avg} = .12$), Homosexuality ($r_{avg} = .12$), and Pornography attitudes ($r_{avg} = .12$). Overall, these patterns indicate a clear divergence between attitudinal and knowledge proficiency scales. See Fullard et al. (1998) for attitude/knowledge relationships in the college sample.

Other Information

The SKAT-A is registered with the U.S. Copyright Office (Fullard, Scheier, & Lief, 2005) and available from LARS Research Institute, Inc. (www.larsri.org). A nominal handling fee is charged.

Lawrence M. Scheier is also affiliated with Washington University, St. Louis, Cornell University, and the Department of Public Health, Division of Prevention and Health Behavior, Institute for Prevention Research. Howard I. Lief is deceased.

References

Fullard, W., Johnston, D. A., & Lief, H. I. (1998). The Sexual Knowledge and Attitude Test for Adolescents. In C. M. Davis, W. L. Yarber, R. Bauserman, G. Schreer, & S. L. Davis (Eds.), *Handbook of sexuality-related measures* (pp. 33–35). Thousand Oaks, CA: Sage.

Fullard, W., Scheier, L., & Lief, H. L. (2005). *The Sexual Knowledge and Attitude Scale for Adolescents (SKAT-A)*. Available from LARS Research Institute, Inc. (www. larsri.org).

Hu, L., & Bentler, P. M. (1998). Fit indices in covariance structural equation modeling: Sensitivity to underparameterized model misspecification. *Psychological Methods, 3,* 424–453.

Johnston, D. A. (1998). *A psychometric evaluation of the Sexual Knowledge and Attitude Test for Adolescents*. Unpublished doctoral dissertation, Temple University, Philadelphia, PA.

Lief, H. I. (1988). The Sex Knowledge and Attitude Test (SKAT). In C. M. Davis, W. L. Yarber, & S. L. Davis (Eds.), *Sexuality-related measures: A compendium* (pp. 213–216). Lake Mills, IA: Graphic Publishing Company.

Lief, H. I., Fullard, W., & Devlin, S. J. (1990). A new measure of adolescent sexuality: SKAT-A. *Journal of Sex Education and Therapy, 16,* 79–91.

Lief, H. I., & Reed, D. M. (1972). *Sex Knowledge and Attitude Test.* Philadelphia: University of Pennsylvania, Center for the Study of Sex Education in Medicine.

MacCallum, R. (1986). Specification searches in covariance structure modeling. *Psychological Bulletin, 100,* 107–120.

Werts, C. E., Linn, R. L., & Jöreskog, K. J. (1974). Interclass reliability estimates: Testing structural assumptions. *Educational and Psychological Measurement, 34,* 25–33.

Mathtech Questionnaires: Sexuality Questionnaires for Adolescents

DOUGLAS KIRBY,[1] *ETR Associates*

The questionnaires have two purposes: first, to measure the most important knowledge areas, attitudes, values, skills, and behaviors that either facilitate a positive and fulfilling sexuality or reduce unintended pregnancy among adolescents; and second, to measure important possible outcomes of sexuality education programs.

The Center for Disease Control funded Mathtech, a private research firm, to develop methods of evaluating sexuality education programs. Mathtech reviewed existing questionnaires for adolescents and determined that it was necessary to develop new questionnaires. With the help of about 20 professionals in the field of adolescent sexuality and pregnancy, Mathtech identified more than 100 possible outcomes of sexuality education programs and then had 100 professionals rate (anonymously) each of those outcomes according to its importance in reducing unintended pregnancy and facilitating a positive and fulfilling sexuality. Mathtech then calculated the mean ratings of those outcomes and developed questionnaires to measure many of the most important outcomes. The questionnaires, which measure these important outcomes, include the Knowledge Test, the Attitude and Value Inventory, and the Behavior Inventory.

KNOWLEDGE TEST

Description

The Knowledge Test is a 34-item multiple-choice test. It includes questions in the following areas: adolescent physical development, adolescent relationships, adolescent sexual activity, adolescent pregnancy, adolescent marriage, the probability of pregnancy, birth control, and sexually transmitted disease. It has been used successfully with both junior and senior high school students.

To develop the questionnaires, we completed the following steps: (a) generated between 5 and 20 items in each of the content areas that the 100 professionals indicated as important; (b) pretested the questionnaire with small groups of adolescents and adults, and clarified many items; (c) administered the questionnaire to 729 adolescents, analyzed their answers, removed items that were too easy or too difficult, and also removed items not positively related to the overall test score; (d) removed questions from content domains that had too many questions; and (e) made numerous refinements following subsequent administrations of the questionnaires and reviews by other professionals.

Response Mode and Timing

Respondents circle the single best answer to each question. Bright students commonly take about 15 to 20 minutes; slower students may take as long as 45 minutes to complete the questionnaire.

Scoring

The answers to the test are included at the end of the test (see the Exhibit). To obtain the percentage correct, count the number of correct answers and divide by 34. No special provisions are made for students who do not answer questions.

Reliability

The test was administered to 58 adolescents on one occasion, and then again 2 weeks later. The test-retest reliability coefficient was .89.

Validity

Older students obtained higher scores than younger students; and students with overall higher grade point

[1]Address correspondence to Douglas Kirby, ETR Associates, P. O. Box 1830, Santa Cruz, CA 95061–1830; e-mail: dougk@etr.org

averages had higher scores than students with lower grade point averages. Content validity was determined by experts who selected both the domains and the items for the domains.

ATTITUDE AND VALUE INVENTORY

Description

The Attitude and Value Inventory includes 14 different scales, each consisting of five 5-point Likert-type items. The responses include *strongly disagree, disagree, neutral, agree, strongly agree*. The scales are identified in Table 1.

To develop the questionnaires, we completed the following steps: (a) generated 5 to 10 items for each of the psychological outcomes rated important by the 100 experts; (b) had the items reviewed by small groups of both adults and adolescents who made suggestions for changes; (c) had two psychologists trained in questionnaire design and scale construction examine each item for unidimensionality and clarity; and (d) had more than 200 adolescents complete the questionnaire, removing those items that had a correlation coefficient greater than .30 with the Crowne-Marlowe (1964) Social Desirability Scale, that had the lowest scale loadings on each scale, and that had mean scores near the minimum or maximum possible score.

Response Mode and Timing

Respondents should circle the number indicating their agreement/disagreement with each item. Bright adolescents complete the questionnaire in about 10 minutes; slower students may take a half hour.

Scoring

Following the Attitude and Value Inventory are all the scales, with the items grouped by scale. In front of each item is a plus sign or minus sign indicating whether the item

should be positively scored or reverse scored. The mean score for each scale should be determined by adding the responses and dividing by 5. Higher scores represent more favorable attitudes.

Reliability

Reliability was determined by administering the questionnaire to 990 students and calculating Cronbach's alpha. These are included in Table 1.

BEHAVIOR INVENTORY

Description

Many behaviors have at least three important components or aspects to them: the skill with which the behavior is completed, the comfort experienced during that behavior, and the frequency of that behavior. The Behavior Inventory measures these three aspects of several kinds of behavior. The actual measures are identified in Tables 2 and 3.

The questions measuring skills use 5-point scales with answers ranging from *almost always* to *almost never*; those measuring comfort use 4-point scales ranging from *comfortable* to *very uncomfortable*; those measuring sexual activity, use of birth control, and frequency of communication ask how many times during the previous month the respondent engaged in the specified activity.

TABLE 1
Reliability Coefficients for the Scales in the Attitude and Value Inventory

Cronbach's alpha	Scale
.89	Clarity of long term goals
.73	Clarity of personal sexual values
.81	Understanding of emotional needs
.78	Understanding of personal social behavior
.80	Understanding of personal sexual response
.66	Attitude toward gender roles
.75	Attitude toward sexuality in life
.72	Attitude toward the importance of birth control
.94	Attitude toward premarital sex
.58	Attitude toward the use of force and pressure in sexual activity
.70	Recognition of the importance of the family
.73	Self esteem
.85	Satisfaction with personal sexuality
.81	Satisfaction with social relationships

TABLE 2
Reliability Coefficients for the Scales in the Behavior Inventory

Test Retest r^a	n	Alpha^b	n	Scale
.84	39	.58	541	Social decision making skills
.65	36	.61	464	Sexual decision making skills
.57	41	.75	529	Communication skills
.68	32	.62	409	Assertiveness skills
.88	17	.58	243	Birth control assertiveness skills
.69	40	.81	517	Comfort engaging in social activities
.66	36	.66	461	Comfort talking with friends, girl/boyfriend, and parents about sex
.40	33	.63	133	Comfort talking with friends, girl/boyfriend, and parents about birth control
.62	39	.73	156	Comfort talking with parents about sex and birth control
.44	41	NA^c	NA	Comfort expressing concern and caring
.68	35	.68	455	Comfort being sexually assertive (saying no)
.70	37	NA	NA	Comfort having current sex life, what ever it may be
.38	14	.86	449	Comfort getting and using birth control

^{a}The test retest coefficient is the correlation coefficient based upon two administrations of the same questionnaire 2 weeks apart.
^{b}Alpha is Cronbach's alpha based upon all the intercorrelations within each scale.
^{c}NA means not applicable because alpha requires two or more items, and these scales had only one item.

TABLE 3
Test retest Reliability Coefficients for the Behavior Questions in the Behavior Inventory

r^a	Question
1.00	Q43: Ever had sexual intercourse
.78	Q44: Had intercourse last month
.88	Q45: Frequency of intercourse last month
.97	Q46: Frequency of intercourse last month with no birth control
.89	Q47: Frequency of intercourse last month using diaphragm, withdawal, rhythm, or foam (without condoms)
.97	Q48: Frequency of intercourse last month using pill, condoms, or IUD
.80	Q49: Frequency of conversations with parents about sex last month
.81	Q50: Frequency of conversations with friends about sex last month
.83	Q51: Frequency of conversations with boy/girlfriend about sex last month
.71	Q52: Frequency of conversations with parents about birth control last month
.69	Q53: Frequency of conversations with friends about birth control last month
.75	Q54: Frequency of conversations with boy/girlfriend about birth control last month

Note: $N = 41$.
[a] The measure of reliability is the correlation coefficient between the two administrations of the questionnaire given 2 weeks apart.

It is important to realize that the questions measuring skill do not try to assess skill in the classroom but, instead, measure the frequency with which respondents actually use important skills in everyday life.

The panel of 100 experts rated *most highly* most of the skills, areas of comfort, and behaviors for which we developed measures. We tried many different ways of measuring skills and after a variety of attempts and pretests with small groups of adolescents, we settled on the current approach in which we identified key behaviors in various skills and simply asked what proportion of the time respondents engage in those behaviors.

The scales measuring comfort and behaviors flowed directly from the outcomes specified by the experts. We conducted minitests with both adults and adolescents to determine for how many months they could accurately measure their communication and sexual behavior. Nearly all adolescents could remember their behavior for the previous month.

The entire inventory was reviewed by psychologists who examined each item for clarity, unidimensionality, and comprehensibility. More than 100 adolescents completed the questionnaire; their responses indicated that most data were reliable.

Because of the great sensitivity of these questions, the researcher should (a) get appropriate approval to administer the questionnaire, (b) emphasize to the students that completing the questionnaire is voluntary, and (c) take every reasonable measure to assure that the answers remain absolutely anonymous. Remember, if students learn that some

particular girl (or boy) has experienced (or not experienced) sex, that person's reputation can be greatly damaged.

Response Mode and Timing

Respondents should circle the number indicating their agreement/disagreement with each item. The questionnaire takes adolescents between 20 and 45 minutes to complete. Adolescents who are brighter or not sexually active complete it more quickly.

Scoring

Most of the questions measuring skills or comfort should be combined into scales. Following the inventory are the items grouped into scales. In front of each item measuring a skill or area of comfort is a plus sign or minus sign, indicating whether the item should be positively scored or reverse scored. The mean score for these scales should be determined by adding the responses and dividing by the number of items. Higher scores represent more favorable attitudes.

The questions measuring the existence and frequency of sexual behavior should not be combined into scales. Moreover, higher scores do not commonly represent more favorable behaviors.

Reliability

For all items test-retest reliability was determined by administering the questionnaire twice, 2 weeks apart. However, because some students were not sexually active, the sample sizes are unreasonably low for some items. Moreover, the test-retest reliability coefficients are artificially low for some items because the sexual activities of teenagers change from one 2-week period to the next. Consequently, Cronbach's alpha is also given for those scales having two or more items. All of these coefficients are presented in Tables 2 and 3.

Validity

The most sensitive of the behavior questions had other questions that should have been consistent. For example, 10 different questions provide information about whether or not the respondent had had sex. Specifically written computer programs indicated that more than 95% of the questionnaires had answers that were consistent.

Other Information

These questionnaires are in the public domain and can be used without permission. However, appropriate citation is requested. They are included in Kirby (1984).

References

Crowne, D. P., & Marlowe, D. (1964). *The approval motive: Studies in evaluative dependence*. New York: Wiley.

Kirby, D. (1984). *Sexuality education: An evaluation of programs and their effects*. Santa Cruz, CA: Network Publications.

Exhibit

Knowledge Test

We are trying to find out is this program is successful. You can help us by completing this questionnaire.

To keep your answers confidential and private, do *not* put your name anywhere on this questionnaire. Please use a regular pen or pencil so that all questionnaires will look about the same and no one will know which is yours.

Because this study is important, your answers are also important. Please answer each question carefully. Thank you for your help.

Name of school or organization where course was taken:_____

Teacher's name: _____

Your birth date: Month Day _____

Your sex (Check one): Male Female _____

Your grade level in school (Check one): 9_10_11_12_

Please circle the one best answer to each of the questions below.

1. By the time teenagers graduate from high schools in the United States:
    a. only a few have had sex (sexual intercourse).
    b. about half have had sex.
    c. about 80% have had sex.
2. During their menstrual periods, girls:
    a. are too weak to participate in sports or exercise.
    b. have a normal, monthly release of blood from the uterus.
    c. cannot possibly become pregnant.
    d. should not shower or bathe.
    e. all of the above.
3. It is harmful for a woman to have sex (sexual intercourse) when she:
    a. is pregnant.
    b. is menstruating.
    c. has a cold.
    d. has a sexual partner with syphilis.
    e. none of the above.
4. Some contraceptives:
    a. can be obtained only with a doctor's prescription.
    b. are available at family planning clinics.
    c. can be bought over the counter at drug stores.
    d. can be obtained by people under 18 without their parents' permission.
    e. all of the above.
5. If 10 couples have sexual intercourse regularly without using any kind of birth control, the number of couples who become pregnant by the end of 1 year is about:
    a. one.
    b. three.
    c. six
    d. nine.
    e. none of the above.
6. When unmarried teenage girls learn they are pregnant, the largest group of them decide:
    a. to have an abortion.
    b. to put the child up for adoption.
    c. to raise the child at home.
    d. to marry and raise the child with the husband.
    e. none of the above.
7. People having sexual intercourse can best prevent getting a sexually transmitted disease (VD or STD) by using:
    a. condoms (rubbers).
    b. contraceptive foam.
    c. the pill.
    d. withdrawal (pulling out).

8. When boys go through puberty:
   a. they lose their "baby fat" and become slimmer.
   b. their penises become larger.
   c. they produce sperm.
   d. their voices become lower.
   e. all of the above.

9. Married teenagers:
   a. have the same social lives as their unmarried friends.
   b. avoid pressure from friends and family.
   c. still fit in easily with their old friends.
   d. usually support themselves without help from their parents.
   e. none of the above.

10. If a couple has sexual intercourse and uses no birth control, the woman might get pregnant:
    a. anytime during the month.
    b. only 1 week before menstruation begins.
    c. only during menstruation.
    d. only 1 week after menstruation begins.
    e. only 2 weeks after menstruation begins.

11. The method of birth control which is *least* effective is:
    a. a condom with foam.
    b. the diaphragm with spermicidal jelly.
    c. withdrawal (pulling out).
    d. the pill.
    e. abstinence (not having intercourse).

12. It is possible for a woman to become pregnant:
    a. the first time she has sex (sexual intercourse).
    b. if she has sexual intercourse during her menstrual period.
    c. if she has sexual intercourse standing up.
    d. if sperm get near the opening of the vagina, even though the man's penis does not enter her body.
    e. all of the above.

13. Physically:
    a. girls usually mature earlier than boys.
    b. most boys mature earlier than most girls.
    c. all boys and girls are fully mature by age 16.
    d. all boys and girls are fully mature by age 18.

14. It is impossible now to cure:
    a. syphilis.
    b. gonorrhea.
    c. herpes virus # 2.
    d. vaginitis.
    e. all of the above.

15. When men and women are physically mature:
    a. each female ovary releases two eggs each month.
    b. each female ovary releases millions of eggs each month.
    c. male testes produce one sperm for each ejaculation (climax).
    d. male testes produce millions of sperm for each ejaculation (climax).
    e. none of the above.

16. Teenagers who choose to have sexual intercourse may possibly:
    a. have to deal with a pregnancy.
    b. feel guilty.
    c. become more close to their sexual partners.
    d. become less close to their sexual partners.
    e. all of the above.

17. As they enter puberty, teenagers become more interested in sexual activities because:
    a. their sex hormones are changing.
    b. the media (TV, movies, magazines, records) push sex for teenagers.
    c. some of their friends have sex and expect them to have sex also.

    d. all of the above.

18. To use a condom the correct way, a person must:

    a. leave some space at the tip for the guy's fluid.

    b. use a new one every time sexual intercourse occurs.

    c. hold it on the penis while pulling out of the vagina.

    d. all of the above.

19. The proportion of American girls who become pregnant before turning 20 is:

    a. 1 out of 3.

    b. 1 out of 11.

    c. 1 out of 43.

    d. 1 out of 90.

20. In general, children born to young teenage parents:

    a. have few problems because their parents are emotionally mature.

    b. have a greater chance of being abused by their parents.

    c. have normal birth weight.

    d. have a greater chance of being healthy.

    e. none of the above.

21. Treatment for venereal disease is best if:

    a. both partners are treated at the same time.

    b. only the partner with the symptoms sees a doctor.

    c. the person takes the medicine only until the symptoms disappear.

    d. the partners continue having sex (sexual intercourse).

    e. all of the above.

22. Most teenagers:

    a. have crushes or infatuations that last a short time.

    b. feel shy or awkward when first dating.

    c. feel jealous sometimes.

    d. worry a lot about their looks.

    e. all of the above.

23. Most unmarried girls who have children while still in high school:

    a. depend upon their parents for support.

    b. finish high school and graduate with their class.

    c. never have to be on public welfare.

    d. have the same social lives as their peers.

    e. all of the above.

24. Syphilis:

    a. is one of the most dangerous of the venereal diseases.

    b. is known to cause blindness, insanity, and death if untreated.

    c. is first detected as a chancre sore on the genitals.

    d. all of the above.

25. For a boy, nocturnal emissions (wet dreams) means he:

    a. has a sexual illness.

    b. is fully mature physically.

    c. is experiencing a normal part of growing up.

    d. is different from most other boys.

26. If people have sexual intercourse, the advantage of using condoms is that they:

    a. help prevent getting or giving VD.

    b. can be bought in drug stores by either sex.

    c. do not have dangerous side effects.

    d. do not require a prescription.

    e. all of the above.

27. If two people want to have a close relationship, it is important that they:

    a. trust each other and are honest and open with each other.

    b. date other people.

    c. always think of the other person first.

    d. always think of their own needs first.

    e. all of the above.

28. The physical changes of puberty:
    a. happen in a week or two.
    b. happen to different teenagers at different ages.
    c. happen quickly for girls and slowly for boys.
    d. happen quickly for boys and slowly for girls.
29. For most teenagers, their emotions (feelings):
    a. are pretty stable.
    b. seem to change frequently.
    c. don't concern them very much.
    d. are easy to put into words.
    e. are ruled by their thinking.
30. Teenagers who marry, compared to those who do not:
    a. are equally likely to finish high school.
    b. are equally likely to have children.
    c. are equally likely to get divorced.
    d. are equally likely to have successful work careers.
    e. none of the above.
31. The rhythm method (natural family planning):
    a. means couples *cannot* have intercourse during certain days of the woman's menstrual cycle.
    b. requires the woman to keep a record of when she has her period.
    c. is effective less than 80% of the time.
    d. is recommended by the Catholic church.
    e. all of the above.
32. The pill:
    a. can be used by any woman.
    b. is a good birth control method for women who smoke.
    c. usually makes menstrual cramping worse.
    d. must be taken for 21 or 28 days in order to be effective.
    e. all of the above.
33. Gonorrhea:
    a. is 10 times more common than syphilis.
    b. is a disease that can be passed from mothers to their children during birth.
    c. makes many men and women sterile (unable to have babies).
    d. is often difficult to detect in women.
    e. all of the above.
34. People choosing a birth control method:
    a. should think only about the cost of the method.
    b. should choose whatever method their friends are using.
    c. should learn about all the methods before choosing the one that's best for them.
    d. should get the method that's easiest to get.
    e. all of the above.

Answers to the Knowledge Test

Question	Answer	Question	Answer	Question	Answer
1	b	12	e	23	a
2	b	13	a	24	d
3	d	14	c	25	c
4	e	15	d	26	e
5	d	16	e	27	a
6	a	17	d	28	b
7	a	18	d	29	b
8	e	19	a	30	e
9	e	20	b	31	e
10	a	21	a	32	d
11	c	22	e	33	e
				34	c

Attitude and Value Inventory

The questions below are not a test of how much you know. We are interested in what you believe about some important issues. Please rate each statement according to how much you agree or disagree with it. Everyone will have different answers. Your answer is correct if it describes you very well.

Circle: 1 = if you Strongly Disagree with the statement.[a]
               2 = if you Somewhat Disagree with the statement.
               3 = if you feel Neutral about the statement.
               4 = if you Somewhat Agree with the statement.
               5 = if you Strongly Agree with the statement.

1. I am very happy with my friendships.
2. Unmarried people should not have sex (sexual intercourse).
3. Overall, I am satisfied with myself.
4. Two people having sex should use some form of birth control if they aren't ready for a child.
5. I'm confused about my personal sexual values and beliefs.
6. I often find myself acting in ways I don't understand.
7. I am not happy with my sex life.
8. Men should not hold jobs traditionally held by women.
9. People should never take "no" for an answer when they want to have sex.
10. I don't know what I want out of life.
11. Families do very little for their children.
12. Sexual relationships create more problems than they're worth.
13. I'm confused about what I should and should not do sexually.
14. I know what I want and need emotionally.
15. No one should pressure another person into sexual activity.
16. Birth control is not very important.
17. I know what I need to be happy.
18. I am not satisfied with my sexual behavior (sex life).
19. I usually understand the way I act.
20. People should not have sex before marriage.
21. I do not know much about my own physical and emotional sexual responses.
22. It is all right for two people to have sex before marriage if they are in love.
23. I have a good idea of where I'm headed in the future.
24. Family relationships are not important.
25. I have trouble knowing what my beliefs and values are about my personal sexual behavior.
26. I feel I do not have much to be proud of.
27. I understand how I behave around others.
28. Women should behave differently from men most of the time.
29. People should have sex only if they are married.
30. I know what I want out of life.
31. I have a good understanding of my own personal feelings and reactions.
32. I don't have enough friends.
33. I'm happy with my sexual behavior now.
34. I don't understand why I behave with my friends as I do.
35. At times I think I'm no good at all.
36. I know how I react in different sexual situations.
34. I have a clear picture of what I'd like to be doing in the future.
38. My friendships are not as good as I would like them to be.
39. Sexually, I feel like a failure.
40. More people should be aware of the importance of birth control.
41. At work and at home, women should not have to behave differently from men, when they are equally capable.
42. Sexual relationships make life too difficult.
43. I wish my friendships were better.
44. I feel that I have many good personal qualities.
45. I am confused about my reactions in sexual situations.

46. It is all right to pressure someone into sexual activity.
47. People should not pressure others to have sex with them.
48. Most of the time my emotional feelings are clear to me.
49. I have my own set of rules to guide my sexual behavior (sex life).
50. Women and men should be able to have the same jobs, when they are equally capable.
51. I don't know what my long-range goals are.
52. When I'm in a sexual situation, I get confused about my feelings.
53. Families are very important.
54. It is all right to demand sex from a girlfriend or boyfriend.
55. A sexual relationship is one of the best things a person can have.
56. Most of the time I have a clear understanding of my feelings and emotions.
57. I am very satisfied with my sexual activities just the way they are.
58. Sexual relationships only bring trouble to people.
59. Birth control is not as important as some people say.
60. Family relationships cause more trouble than they're worth.
61. If two people have sex and aren't ready to have a child, it is very important they use birth control.
62. I'm confused about what I need emotionally.
63. It is all right for two people to have sex before marriage.
64. Sexual relationships provide an important and fulfilling part of life.
65. People should be expected to behave in certain ways just because they are male or female.
66. Most of the time I know why I behave the way I do.
67. I feel good having as many friends as I have.
68. I wish I had more respect for myself.
69. Family relationships can be very valuable.
70. I know for sure what is right and wrong sexually for me.

ªThe five response options are repeated following each item.

Scales in the Attitude and Value Inventory

Clarity of Long-Term Goals:	−Q10, +Q23, +Q30, +Q37, +Q51.
Clarity of Personal Sexual Values:	−Q5, −Q13, −Q25, +Q49, +70.
Understanding of Emotional Needs:	+Q14, +Q17, +Q48, +Q56, −Q62.
Understanding of Personal Social Behavior:	−Q6, +Q19, +Q27, −Q34, +Q66.
Understanding of Personal Sexual Responses:	−Q21, +Q31, +Q36, −Q45, −Q52.
Attitude Toward Various Gender Role Behaviors:	−Q8, −Q28, +Q41, +Q50, +Q65.
Attitude Toward Sexuality in Life:	−Q12, −Q42, +Q55, −Q58, +64.
Attitude Toward the Importance of Birth Control:	+Q4, −Q16, +Q40, −Q59, +Q61.
Attitude Toward Premarital Intercourse:	+Q2, +Q20, −Q22, +Q29, −Q63.
Attitude Toward the Use of Pressure and Force in Sexual Activity:	−Q9, +Q15, −Q46, +Q47, +Q54.
Recognition of the Importance of the Family:	−Q11, −Q24, +Q53, −Q60, +Q69.
Self-Esteem:	+Q3, −Q26, −Q35, +Q44, −Q68.
Satisfaction with Personal Sexuality:	−Q7, −Q18, +Q33, −Q39, +Q57.
Satisfaction with Social Relationships:	+Q1, −Q32, −Q38, −Q43, +Q67.

Note. + means that the item is positive; − means the item is negative and should be reverse scored. On some scales, people will have different views about whether larger scores represent socially desirable or undesirable scores.

Behavior Inventory

Part 1

The questions below ask how often you have done some things. Some of the questions are personal and ask about your social life and sex life. Some questions will not apply to you. Please do not conclude from the questions that you should have had all of the experiences the questions ask about. Instead, just mark whatever answer describes you best.

Circle: 1 = if you do it *almost never*, which means about 5% of the time or less.

2 = if you do it *sometimes*, which means about 25% of the time.

3 = if you do if *half the time*, which means about 50% of the time.

4 = if you do it *usually*, which means about 75% of the time.

5 = if you do it *almost always*, which means about 95% of the time or more.

DNA = if the question *does not apply* to you.

1. When things you've done turn out poorly, how often do you take responsibility for your behavior and its consequences?[a]
2. When things you've done turn out poorly, how often do you blame others?
3. When you are faced with a decision, how often do you take responsibility for making a decision about it?
4. When you have to make a decision, how often do you think hard about the consequences of each possible choice?
5. When you have to make a decision, how often do you get as much information as you can before making the decision?
6. When you have to make a decision, how often do you first discuss it with others?
7. When you have to make a decision about your sexual behavior (for example, going out on a date, holding hands, kissing, petting, or having sex), how often do you take responsibility for the consequences?
8. When you have to make a decision about your sexual behavior, how often do you think hard about the consequences of each possible choice?
9. When you have to make a decision about your sexual behavior, how often do you first get as much information as you can?
10. When you have to make a decision about your sexual behavior, how often do you first discuss it with others?
11. When you have to make a decision about your sexual behavior, how often do you make it on the spot without worrying about the consequences?
12. When a friend wants to talk with you, how often are you able to clear your mind and really listen to what your friend has to say?
13. When a friend is talking with you, how often do you ask questions if you don't understand what your friend in saying?
14. When a friend is talking with you, how often do you nod your head and say "yes" or something else to show that you are interested?
15. When you want to talk with a friend, how often are you able to get your friend to really listen to you?
16. When you talk with a friend, how often do you ask for your friend's reaction to what you've said?
17. When you talk with a friend, how often do you let your feelings show?
18. When you are with a friend you care about, how often do you let that friend know you care?
19. When you talk with a friend, how often do you include statements like "my feelings are . . .," "the way I think is . . .," or "it seems to me"?
20. When you are alone with a date or boy/girlfriend, how often can you tell him/her your feelings about what you want to do and do not want to do sexually? (If you are a boy, boy/girlfriend means girlfriend; if you are a girl, it means boyfriend.)
21. If a boy/girl puts pressure on you to be involved sexually and you don't want to be involved, how often do you say "no"? (If you are a boy, boy/girl means girl; if you are a girl, it means boy.)
22. If a boy/girl puts pressure on you to be involved sexually and you don't want to be involved, how often do you succeed in stopping it?
23. If you have sexual intercourse with your boy/girlfriend, how often can you talk with him/her about birth control?
24. If you have sexual intercourse and want to use birth control, how often do you insist on using birth control?

Part 2

In this section, we want to know how uncomfortable you are doing different things. Being "uncomfortable" means that it is difficult for you and it makes you nervous and uptight. For each item, circle the number that describes you best, but if the item doesn't apply to you, circle DNA.

Circle: 1 = if you are *comfortable*.

2 = if you are a *little uncomfortable*.

3 = If you are *somewhat uncomfortable*.

4 = If you are *very uncomfortable*.

DNA = if the question *does not apply* to you.

25. Getting together with a group of friends of the opposite sex.[b]
26. Going to a party.
27. Talking with teenagers of the opposite sex.
28. Going out on a date.
29. Talking with friends about sex.
30. Talking with a date or boy/girlfriend about sex. (If you are a boy, boy/girlfriend means girlfriend; if you are a girl, it means boyfriend.)

31. Talking with parents about sex.
32. Talking with friends about birth control.
33. Talking with a date or boy/girlfriend about birth control. (If you are a boy, boy/girlfriend means girlfriend; if you are a girl, it means boyfriend.)
34. Talking with parents about birth control.
35. Expressing concern and caring for others.
36. Telling a date or boy/girlfriend what you want to do and do not want to do sexually.
37. Saying "no" to a sexual come-on.
38. Having your current sex life, whatever it may be (it may be doing nothing, kissing, petting, or having intercourse).

If you are not having sexual intercourse, circle DNA in the four questions below.

39. Insisting on using some form of birth control, if you are having sex.
40. Buying contraceptives at a drug store, if you are having sex.
41. Going to a doctor or clinic for contraception, if you are having sex.
42. Using some form of birth control, if you are having sex.

Part 3

Circle the correct answer to the following two questions.

43. Have you ever had sex (sexual intercourse)?	yes	no
44. Have you had sex (sexual intercourse) during the last month?	yes	no

Part 4

The following questions ask how many times you did some things during the last month. Put a number in the right hand space to show the number of times you engaged in that activity. If you did not do that during the last month, put a "0" in the space.

Think *carefully* about the times that you have had sex during the last month. Think also about the number of times you did not use birth control and the number of times you used different types of birth control.

45. Last month, how many times did you have sex (sexual intercourse)   _____ times in the last month
46. Last month, how many times did you have sex when you or your partner did not use any form of birth control?   _____ times in the last month
47. Last month, how many times did you have sex when you or your partner used a diaphragm, withdrawal (pulling out before releasing fluid), rhythm (not having sex on fertile days), or foam without condoms?   _____ times in the last month
48. Last month, how many times did you have sex when you or your partner used the pill, condoms (rubbers), or an IUD?   _____ times in the last month

If you add your answer to questions #46, #47, and #48, the total number should equal your answer to #45. (If it does not, please correct your answers.)

49. During the last month, how many times have you had a conversation or discussion about sex with your parents?   _____ times in the last month
50. During the last month, how many times have you had a conversation or discussion about sex with your friends?   _____ times in the last month
51. During the last month, how many times have you had a conversation or discussion about sex with a date or boy/girlfriend? (If you are a boy, boy/girlfriend means girlfriend; if you are a girl, it means boyfriend.)   _____ times in the last month
52. During the last month, how many times have you had a conversation or discussion about birth control with your parents?   _____ times in the last month
53. During the last month, how many times have you had a conversation or discussion about birth control with your friends?   _____ times in the last month
54. During the last month, how many times have you had a conversation or discussion about birth control with a date or boy/girlfriend?   _____ times in the last month

Thank you for completing this questionnaire.

[a]The six response options are repeated following Items 1–24.
[b]The five response options are repeated following Items 25–42.

Scales in the Behavior Inventory

Social decision-making skills

+Q1
−Q2
+Q3
+Q4
+Q5
+Q6

Sexual decision-making skills

+Q7
−Q8
+Q9
+Q10
−Q11

Communication skills

+Q12
+Q13
+Q14
+Q15
+Q16
+Q17
+Q18
+Q19

Assertiveness skills

+Q20
+Q21
+Q22

Birth control assertiveness skills

+Q23
+Q24

Comfort engaging in social activities

−Q25
−Q26
−Q27
−Q28

Comfort talking with friends, girl/boy-
friend, and parents about sex

Q29
Q30
Q31

Comfort talking with friends, girl/boyfriend, and parents about birth control

−Q32
−Q33
−Q34

Comfort talking with parents about sex and birth control

−Q31
−Q34

Comfort expressing concern and caring

−Q35

Comfort being sexually assertive (saying "No")

−Q36
−Q37

Comfort having current sex life, whatever it may be

−Q38

Comfort getting and using birth control

−Q39
−Q40
−Q41
−Q42

Note. + means the item is positive; − means the item is negative and should be reverse scored.

Worry About Sexual Outcomes Scale

JESSICA MCDERMOTT SALES,[1] *Emory University*
ROBIN R. MILHAUSEN, *University of Guelph*
JOSH SPITALNICK, *Emory University*
RALPH J. DICLEMENTE, *Emory University*

The Worry About Sexual Outcomes (WASO) Scale was developed to assess adolescents' worry regarding outcomes of risky sexual behavior (i.e., STIs/HIV infection and unintended pregnancy; Sales et al., 2008).

Description

The WASO was developed as part of an NIMH-funded intervention grant (Sales et al., 2008). Domains pertinent to worry about the outcomes of risky sexual behavior were selected based on a review of the empirical literature. Three topics were frequently noted in the literature with regard to worry pertaining to the sexual outcomes of risky sexual behavior: (a) pregnancy, (b) STI, and (c) HIV. Focus groups of African American adolescent females were conducted to verify that these topics were relevant in their sexual relationships. Eighteen items were created to assess worry in these domains. Health educators assessed face validity of the items. The measure was pilot-tested on 15 African American adolescent females 14 to 18 years of age. Based on their suggestions, items were revised to enhance reading comprehension. Items that were highly correlated and thought to assess the same construct, as well as items that decreased the Cronbach's alpha below .90, were deleted, leaving a 10-item scale consisting of two subscales: STI/HIV Worry (8 items) and Pregnancy Worry (2 items). Data from a longitudinal evaluation study were used to validate the measure (Sales et al., 2008).

Though the WASO was designed for adolescent females and validated with an African American female sample, the items are likely more broadly applicable to individuals of other racial or ethnic backgrounds and other age groups, and to males.

Response Mode and Timing

A single stem is used for all items, "In the past 6 months, how often did you worry that . . ." Each item requires a response based on a 4-point Likert-type scale: 1 (*Never*), 2 (*Sometimes*), 3 (*Often*), and 4 (*Always*). The scale typically takes less than 5 minutes to complete.

Scoring

All items are coded so that higher values indicate more frequent worrying about these health outcomes. Scores can be calculated in two ways: (a) items are summed to create a total scale score for the full 10 items, or (b) items are summed to create two subscale scores: STI/HIV Worry (8 items) and Pregnancy Worry (2 items). Scores on the total scale range from 10 to 40. Scores on the STI/HIV Worry subscale range from 8 to 32. Scores on the Pregnancy Worry subscale range from 2 to 8.

The mean score for participants in our validation sample for the total scale was 16.81 ($SD = 6.43$). Participants in the validation sample had a mean score of 15.52 ($SD = 5.96$) for the STI/HIV Worry subscale and a mean score of 4.43 ($SD = 2.03$) for the Pregnancy Worry subscale (Sales et al., 2008).

Reliability

Stability of the measure was assessed by Pearson correlation. Because it has been suggested that the length of time between reliability assessments mirrors the length of time in intervention studies (Gliner, Morgan, & Harmon, 2001), measurement stability was assessed with 6 months between administrations. Baseline scores on the full WASO (all 10 items) were significantly correlated with scores at 6-month follow-up ($r = .38$, $p < .01$) and with scores at 12-month follow-up ($r = .27$, $p < .01$). Further, scores at 6-month follow-up were significantly correlated with scores at 12-month follow-up ($r = .44$, $p < .01$; Sales et al., 2008).

Validity

The WASO was correlated with other related constructs in the predicted directions (Sales et al., 2008). Specifically, frequency of worry about sexual outcomes was negatively associated with sexual communication self-efficacy (with new partner and steady partner), frequency of sexual communication with partner (Milhausen et al., 2007), attitudes about condom use (St. Lawrence et al., 1994), and

[1]Address correspondence to Jessica McDermott Sales, Emory University, Rollins School of Public Health, Department of Behavioral Sciences and Health Education, 1520 Clifton Rd., NE, Room 266, Atlanta, GA 30322; e-mail: jmcderm@emory.edu

social support (Zimet, Dahlem, Zimet, & Farley, 1988). Additionally, it was positively associated with barriers to condom use (St. Lawrence et al., 1999), condom negotiation, external locus of control, and depression (Melchior, Huba, Brown, & Reback, 1993). The STI/HIV Worry subscale correlations mirror the findings for the overall scale score. The Pregnancy Worry subscale was negatively associated with frequency of sexual communication with partner (Milhausen et al., 2007) and positively associated with barriers to condom use (St. Lawrence et al., 1999), external locus of control, and depression (Melchior et al., 1993).

The WASO was negatively correlated with condom use at last vaginal sex with steady partners, condom use during the previous 30 days with steady partners, and condom use with steady partner over the previous 6 months. Again, the STI/HIV Worry subscale mirrored the findings for the overall scale score. The Pregnancy Worry subscale was also negatively correlated with aforementioned condom use variables. Additionally, Pregnancy Worry scores were positively correlated with frequency of vaginal intercourse with steady and nonsteady partners in the previous 30 days. The correlations were all significant and effect sizes were small to moderate (Cohen, 1988).

Other Information

The WASO is a brief, self-administered behavioral scale measuring adolescents' worry regarding outcomes of risky sexual behavior (i.e., STIs/HIV infection and unintended pregnancy), suitable for low-literate samples (requiring a fourth grade reading level). Researchers may find the

WASO particularly useful in sexual health education interventions for assessing worry of STI/HIV and pregnancy pre- and postintervention to evaluate intervention efficacy. The authors would appreciate receiving information about the results obtained with this measure.

References

Cohen, J. (1988). *Statistical power analysis for the behavioral sciences* (2nd ed.). Hillsdale, NJ: Lawrence Erlbaum Associates.

Gliner, J. A., Morgan, G. A., & Harmon, J. J. (2001). Measurement reliability. *Journal of the American Academy of Child and Adolescent Psychiatry, 4,* 486–488.

Melchior, L., Huba, G., Brown, V., & Reback, C. (1993). A short depression index for women. *Educational and Psychological Measurement, 53,* 1117–1125.

Milhausen, R. R., Sales, J. M., Wingood, G. M., DiClemente, R. J., Salazar, L. F., & Crosby, R. A. (2007). Validation of a partner communication scale for use in HIV/AIDS prevention interventions. *Journal of HIV/AIDS Prevention in Children and Youth, 8,* 11–33.

Sales, J. M., Spitalnick, J., Milhausen, R. R., Wingood, G. M., DiClemente, R. J., Salazar, L. F., et al. (2008). Validation of the worry about sexual outcomes scale for use in STI/HIV prevention interventions for adolescent females. *Health Education Research, 24,* 140–152.

St. Lawrence, J., Chapdelaine, A., Devieux, J., O'Bannon, R., Brasfield, T., & Eldridge, G. (1999). Measuring perceived barriers to condom use: Psychometric evaluation of the Condom Barriers Scale. *Assessment, 6,* 391–404.

St. Lawrence, J., Reitman, D., Jefferson, K., Alleyne, E., Bradsfield, T. L., & Shirley, A. (1994). Factor structure and validation of an adolescent version of the condom attitude scale: An instrument for measuring adolescents' attitudes toward condoms. *Psychological Assessment, 6,* 352–359.

Zimet, G., Dahlem, N. V., Zimet, S. G., & Farley, G. K. (1988). The multidimensional scale of perceived social support. *Journal of Personality Assessment, 52,* 30–41.

Exhibit

Worry About Sexual Outcomes Scale

In the past 6 months, how often did you worry that . . .	Never	Sometimes	Often	Always
. . . you might get the HIV virus[a]	1	2	3	4
. . . you might already have the HIV virus[a]	1	2	3	4
. . . your sex partner may be infected with the HIV virus[a]	1	2	3	4
. . . your partner may become infected with the HIV virus[a]	1	2	3	4
. . . you might get an STI[a]	1	2	3	4
. . . you might already have an STI[a]	1	2	3	4
. . . your partner may be infected with an STI[a]	1	2	3	4
. . . your partner may become infected with an STI[a]	1	2	3	4
. . . you might get pregnant[b]	1	2	3	4
. . . you might already be pregnant[b]	1	2	3	4

[a]STI/HIV Worry subscale item; [b]Pregnancy Worry subscale item.

Adolescent Perceived Costs and Benefits Scale for Sexual Intercourse

STEPHEN A. SMALL,[1] *University of Wisconsin-Madison*

The Adolescent Perceived Costs and Benefits Scale for Sexual Intercourse (Small, Silverberg, & Kerns, 1993) was developed to measure the costs and benefits that adolescents perceive for engaging in nonmarital sexual intercourse. Adolescent sexual activity is often viewed as problematic because of its potential risk to the adolescent's health and life prospects, as well as the possible negative consequences for the broader society. The present measure considers the adolescent as a decision maker and is based on the assumption that if we wish to understand why adolescents become sexually active, it is important to understand the positive and negative consequences adolescents associate with engaging in the behavior.

Description

The Adolescent Perceived Costs and Benefits Scale for Sexual Intercourse consists of two independent subscales of 10 items each. The Perceived Costs subscale assesses the perceived costs associated with engaging in sexual intercourse; the Perceived Benefits subscale assesses the perceived benefits of sexual activity. Each item is responded to using a 4-point Likert-type format. Responses range from 0 (*strongly disagree*) to 3 (*strongly agree*). The scale is based on current research and theory on adolescent development, which views the adolescent as a decision maker and recognizes the importance of understanding the meanings that adolescents ascribe to behavior.

The scale was developed over a multiyear period and involved extensive interviews with a diverse sample of adolescents. It underwent a number of refinements as a result of pilot testing. A parallel measure for assessing adolescents' perceptions of the costs and benefit of using alcohol is also available (see Philipp, 1993; Small et al., 1993).

Response Mode and Timing

Respondents are asked to indicate the number corresponding to their degree of agreement or disagreement with each of the items. This can be done by circling the appropriate response or filling it in on a machine-scorable answer sheet. Each subscale takes approximately 3 to 5 minutes to complete.

Scoring

For each subscale a total perceived costs or benefits score is obtained by summing the 10 individual items. Scores can range from 0 to 30 with a higher score reflecting higher perceived costs or benefits. Individual items can also be examined to gain insight into the primary or modal reasons particular groups of adolescents perceive for engaging or not engaging in sexual intercourse.

Reliability

Internal reliability, as determined by Cronbach's alpha, was .86 for both the perceived costs and the perceived benefits subscales based on a sample of 2,444 male and female adolescents. Based on a sample of 124 male and female adolescents, the subscales had a test-retest reliability over a 2-week period of .70 and .65 for the cost and benefits scales respectively.

Validity

As expected, Small et al. (1993) found that adolescents who were not sexually active perceived significantly more costs for engaging in sexual intercourse than their sexually active peers. The correlation between sexual intercourse status and perceived costs was $r = .32$. Females perceived more costs ($M = 17.30$) for engaging in sexual intercourse than their male counterparts ($M = 14.80$).

Small et al. (1993) reported that adolescent females perceived fewer significant benefits ($M = 17.68$) for engaging in sexual intercourse than their male peers ($M = 18.22$). The correlation between sexual activity status and the perceived benefits subscale was small but significant ($r = .11$). Overall, sexually active teens perceived more benefits than adolescents who were not sexually active. However, although the perceived benefits scores for the nonsexually active teens remained stable across grade levels, after the 9th grade there was a decrease in the perceived benefits scores of teens who were sexually active. Small et al. suggested two possible explanations for this finding. First, with experience sexually active teens may come to realize that many of their beliefs regarding the benefits of sexual intercourse do not hold true. Second, at younger ages, when sexual intercourse is generally less acceptable, teens must first believe there are many benefits for sexual intercourse before becoming sexually active. At older ages, when sexual activity is more acceptable, there is less of a need to be convinced of the value of the behavior before engaging in it.

[1]Address correspondence to Stephen Small, Department of Human Development-Related and Family Studies, University of Wisconsin-Madison, 1430 Linden Drive, 201 HDFS Building, Madison, WI 53706; e-mail: sasmall@wisc.edu

In unpublished data, Small (1996) found that the regularity of birth control use among sexually active teens was positively correlated ($r = .24$) with the perceived costs subscale but was not correlated with the perceived benefits subscale. In addition, adolescents who reported more supportive and positive relations with their parents perceived more costs for engaging in sexual intercourse than adolescents who had a poorer relationship with their parents.

Small (1991) found that adolescents who intended to go on to college were more likely than their non-college-bound peers to report that fear of pregnancy was a primary reason for not having sexual intercourse. Consistent with the literature on adolescent peer influence, as the age of the adolescent increased, fewer agreed that peer pressure was a major reason why a teen would engage in sexual intercourse. Similarly, older teens were much more likely than younger teens to report that curiosity (i.e., "Teens have sex to see what it's like") was a reason for having sexual intercourse.

References

Philipp, M. (1993). *From the adolescent's perspective: Understanding the costs and benefits of using alcohol.* Unpublished doctoral dissertation, University of Wisconsin-Madison.

Small, S. A. (1991, October). *Understanding the reasons underlying adolescent sexual activity.* Paper presented at the symposium, Teen Sexuality Challenge . . . Bridging the Gap between Research and Action, University of Wisconsin-Green Bay.

Small, S. A. (1996). [Teen Assessment Project findings]. Unpublished data. Department of Child and Family Studies, University of Wisconsin-Madison.

Small, S. A., Silverberg, S. B., & Kerns, D. (1993). Adolescents' perceptions of the costs and benefits of engaging in health-compromising behaviors. *Journal of Youth and Adolescence, 22*, 73–87.

Exhibit

Adolescent Perceived Costs and Benefits Scale for Sexual Intercourse

Perceived Costs Subscale

Why Teenagers Don't Have Sexual Intercourse

Instructions: Below are some of the reasons that teens give for *NOT* having sexual intercourse. Please indicate how much you agree or disagree with each reason. If you're not sure, give your best guess.

1. Teenagers don't have sex because they think it is morally wrong or against their religion.
2. Teenagers don't have sex because they don't want to get a sexually transmitted disease (STD) or a disease like AIDS.
3. Teenagers don't have sex because their parent(s) don't approve.
4. Teenagers don't have sex because they don't feel old enough to handle it.
5. Teenagers don't have sex because their friends won't approve.
6. Teenagers don't have sex because they or their partner might get pregnant.
7. Teenagers don't have sex because they aren't in love with anyone yet.
8. Teenagers don't have sex because they don't need it to make them happy.
9. Teenagers don't have sex because they would feel guilty.
10. Teenagers don't have sex because they or their partner might get pregnant which might mess up their future plans for college, school or a career.

Responses: 0 = Strongly Agree 1 = Agree 2 = Disagree 3 = Strongly Disagree

Perceived Benefits Subscale

Why Teenagers Have Sexual Intercourse

Instructions: Below are some of the reasons that teens give for having sexual intercourse. Please indicate how much you agree or disagree with each reason. If you're not sure, give your best guess.

1. Teenagers have sex because it helps them forget their problems.
2. Teenagers have sex because it makes them feel grown up.
3. Teenagers have sex because they *want* to get pregnant or become a parent.
4. Teenagers have sex as a way to get or keep a boyfriend or girlfriend.
5. Teenagers have sex because it makes them feel good.
6. Teenagers have sex because it makes them feel loved.
7. Teenagers have sex because they want to fit in with their friends.
8. Teenagers have sex because they want to see what it's like.
9. Teenagers have sex because it makes them feel more confident and sure of themselves.
10. Teenagers have sex because people they admire or look up to make it seem like a "cool" thing to do.

Responses: 0 = Strongly Agree 1 = Agree 2 = Disagree 3 = Strongly Disagree

Multidimensional Measure of Comfort With Sexuality

PHILIP TROMOVITCH,[1] *Tokyo Medical and Dental University*

One of the goals of sexuality educators has been to increase student comfort with sexuality, including comfort talking about sexual issues. This chapter reports on a multidimensional measure of comfort with sexuality—the MMCS1—and a nine-item short form, the MMCS1-S, which correlates well with the total score from the MMCS1.

The MMCS1 is a multidimensional measure of comfort with sexuality that can be easily administered in college-level sexuality classrooms. Note that comfort with sexuality is not the same as acceptance of sexuality as a positive thing. For example, a person might be comfortable talking about a sexual behavior they believe people should not do; the MMCS1 measures comfort, not necessarily acceptance.

Although scale development work typically proceeds with a single ordering of items (thereby embedding each item in a specific context), in the "real" world, scales are often misused; researchers often extract and administer only those items that constitute a particular subscale. This practice pulls the items out of the context in which they were validated, raising questions about the validity of the subscale using the new format. The MMCS1 was developed using data from three semirandom orderings of the items—only items that were relatively position/context independent were retained—allowing more confidence to be placed in the use of a single subscale.

The MMCS1 was developed using a convenience sample of 463 college students, most of whom were recruited from sexuality education classrooms. The MMCS1 was developed as part of my doctoral work. See my doctoral dissertation for full details on the development of the instrument (Tromovitch, 2000; available as a PDF).

Description

The MMCS1 contains 32 items, each of which is written as a statement. Respondents indicate the extent to which they agree or disagree with each statement by checking one of six non-numbered boxes. Data from the MMCS1 produces four subscales:

- *Comfort discussing sexuality.* This subscale is designated as the TS subscale (Talking, Sexuality). The TS subscale contains 11 items. Most were designed to tap comfort talking about sexuality of a personal nature, and a few were designed to tap comfort talking about

sexuality of a nonpersonal nature (contrary to my expectations, statistical analyses did not support a psychometrically meaningful distinction between personal and nonpersonal discussions of sexual topics).
- *Comfort with one's own sexual life.* This subscale is designated as the AP subscale (Activities, Personal). The AP subscale contains 8 items, all of which were designed to tap comfort with one's own sexual activities.
- *Comfort with the sexual activities of others.* This subscale is designated as the AO subscale (Activities, Others). This subscale contains nine items, all of which were designed to tap comfort interacting with people who engage in various sexual activities.
- *Comfort with the taboo sexual activities of others.* This subscale is designated as the AT subscale (Activities, Taboo). This subscale contains four items, all of which were designed to tap comfort interacting with people who engage in a variety of sexual activities. They are distinguished from those constituting the AO subscale in that they all deal with taboo sexual activities (e.g., sibling incest, youth-adult sex, bestiality).

A 9-item short form, the MMCS1-S, was also created so as to have a high correlation with the total score from the MMCS1 ($r = .93$) and good internal consistency ($\alpha = .80$).

The instruments were derived for use in college-level sexuality education classrooms, but may have applicability with other populations.

Response Mode and Timing

The full, 32-item MMCS1 takes approximately 10 minutes to complete. Respondents indicate the degree to which they agree or disagree with the 32 statements by checking one of six non-numbered boxes with the anchors *Strongly Disagree* and *Strongly Agree*.

Scoring

Subscale scores are calculated as the arithmetic mean of the individual responses for the appropriate items, after adjusting for reverse valence items. This approach keeps all subscales on the same measurement scale (1 to 6) and allows for an easy way to deal with missing data (i.e., if an item is left blank, it does not enter into the calculation). A

[1]Address correspondence to Philip Tromovitch, College of Liberal Arts and Sciences, Tokyo Medical and Dental University, 2-8-30 Konodai, Ichikawa, Chiba, 272-0827, Japan; e-mail: tromovitch.las@tmd.ac.jp

single blank item is not expected to meaningfully reduce the validity of the scores; however, if multiple items are left blank, scores should be interpreted with caution.

By summing the TS, AP, and AO subscales, a comfort with sexuality total score is formed (thus having a range of 3 to 18). It must be remembered that this total score is not necessarily related to comfort with the taboo sexual activities of others (statistical analyses indicated that a total score is warranted, yet is relatively independent of the construct measured by the AT subscale).

For normal valence items, *Strongly Disagree* is scored as 1, with scores increasing to *Strongly Agree*, which is scored as 6—higher scores indicating greater comfort. See Table 1 for item numbers and the subscale to which they belong; items with an asterisk are reverse scored.

The MMCS1-S is scored by averaging the responses to its 9 items; it does not contain reverse valence items.

Reliability

Cronbach's alpha indicated excellent reliability for the TS, AP, and AO subscales and low but acceptable reliability for the AT subscale (see Table 1).

Item-total correlation analyses were also performed. All 32 MMCS1 items were found to have item-total correlations in the commonly recommended ranges (.2 or .3 through .8).

Validity

To ensure face and content validity, an initial pool of items was reviewed by an expert panel including expertise in both sexuality education and psychometric scale development. The panel included one MD, one psychology PhD, and two sexuality educators. Only 60 of the items passing the first expert panel were considered for use.

To ensure construct validity, over 400 factor analyses were calculated. Factor analytic methods included principal components analysis, common factor analysis, and image analysis. Types of rotation employed included varimax, equamax, and promax (with $k = 2$ and $k = 3$). In addition to analyzing the entire derivation dataset as a whole, various subgroups were separately examined including, but not limited to, males, females, respondents aged 18–20, respondents aged 21–23, White/Caucasian respondents, and data from each of the three different semirandom ordered forms of the derivation instrument. The 32 items retained in the MMCS1 possess a clear factor structure evidencing great reproducibility across factor analytic method, type of rotation, and subsample.

As a further check on face and content validity, a second expert panel reviewed the 34 best items (based on numerous statistical analyses, at both the factor level and the individual item level (e.g., kurtosis, means, and standard deviations of responses to each item). The second expert panel consisted of this author and two others, both of whom have PhDs in sexuality.

TABLE 1
Information on the MMCS1 Subscales

Subscale	Subscale Intercorrelations			Cronbach's α	Items Constituting Subscales
	AP	*AO*	*AT*		
TS (Talking, Sexuality)	.38	.46	.08	.89	2, 4, 5*, 7, 8, 13, 15, 19, 24, 27, 31
AP (Activities, Personal)		.23	−.01	.84	3, 9, 10, 12*, 14, 16*, 21, 29
AO (Activities, Others)			.19	.83	1, 11*, 17, 23, 25, 26, 28*, 30, 32
AT (Activities, Taboo)				.62	6, 18, 20*, 22*

Note. Items marked with an asterisk (*) are reverse scored. An α greater than .9 may indicate the presence of bloated specifics, which raise α without improving a scale's usefulness; an α less than .6 indicates low reliability.

The four factors that were used to define the subscales accounted for over 40% of the variance in the 32 items. This large value suggests the four subscales significantly explain response variance in items dealing with comfort with sexuality, further supporting construct validity.

As a final test of construct validity, a confirmatory analysis was conducted (oblique principal components cluster analysis), which also indicated high construct validity.

Image analysis indicated that the TS, AO, and AP subscales shared common variance, supporting their use (and excluding the AT subscale) in calculating a comfort with sexuality total score.

Other Information

In the derivation sample, males and females did not significantly differ in most of their comfort levels; people who masturbate more than one time per month were more comfortable discussing sexuality and with the sexuality of others than people who rarely masturbate or who declined to indicate their masturbation frequency; people who described themselves as liberal were more comfortable with sexuality; people whose family of origin was open about sexual issues and nudity were more comfortable discussing sexuality and with their own sexual lives; and people reporting higher frequencies of religious attendance or importance showed significantly less comfort with the sexuality of others.

Because of the small number of items on the AT subscale, its lower reliability, and the fact that what constitutes taboo activity varies greatly from one population to another, the AT subscale should be interpreted carefully; further, owing to widely varying and constantly changing definitions of *taboo*, when feasible the AT subscale should be tested for internal consistency.

Note that, as with most measures containing subscales, the scoring of the MMCS1 produces raw scores, not standardized scores. Consequently scores cannot be precisely compared across subscales (e.g., if a respondent has an AP subscale score of 3.2 and a TS subscale score of 3.4, one cannot conclude that the respondent is more comfortable talking about sexuality than the respondent is with his or her own sexual life).

The intercorrelations among the subscales are provided in Table 1.

Reference

Tromovitch, P. (2000). The Multidimensional Measure of Comfort With Sexuality (MMCS1): The development of a multidimensional objective measure of comfort with sexuality for use in sexuality education and research (Doctoral dissertation, University of Pennsylvania). *Dissertation Abstracts International, 61*, 2277.

Exhibit

The MMCS1: The Multidimensional Measure of Comfort With Sexuality

For each item please check (✓) the box that best represents your answer.

1. I am completely comfortable knowing and interacting with people whose sexual activities significantly differ from my own. — Strongly Disagree ☐ ☐ ☐ ☐ ☐ ☐ Strongly Agree

2. I would be completely comfortable talking to a friend about sexual problems I was having with my lover. — Strongly Disagree ☐ ☐ ☐ ☐ ☐ ☐ Strongly Agree

3. I have lived my sex life in a way that is consistent with my moral beliefs. — Strongly Disagree ☐ ☐ ☐ ☐ ☐ ☐ Strongly Agree

4. I would be comfortable telling a good friend about sexual experiences I have had which I consider to be out of the norm. — Strongly Disagree ☐ ☐ ☐ ☐ ☐ ☐ Strongly Agree

5. Talking about the details of my own sexual experiences would be embarrassing, even with friends. — Strongly Disagree ☐ ☐ ☐ ☐ ☐ ☐ Strongly Agree

6. I could be comfortable interacting with a person who I thought might be having a sexual relationship with their sibling. — Strongly Disagree ☐ ☐ ☐ ☐ ☐ ☐ Strongly Agree

7. Talking about my personal sexual views is as natural as talking about current events. — Strongly Disagree ☐ ☐ ☐ ☐ ☐ ☐ Strongly Agree

8. I enjoy the opportunity to share my personal views about sexuality. — Strongly Disagree ☐ ☐ ☐ ☐ ☐ ☐ Strongly Agree

9. My sexual experiences and explorations are a positive, on-going part of who I am. — Strongly Disagree ☐ ☐ ☐ ☐ ☐ ☐ Strongly Agree

10. I am comfortable with my sexual activities, both past and present. — Strongly Disagree ☐ ☐ ☐ ☐ ☐ ☐ Strongly Agree

11. Having a lot of sexually active bisexual friends would make me feel uncomfortable. — Strongly Disagree ☐ ☐ ☐ ☐ ☐ ☐ Strongly Agree

12. I am ashamed of my past sexual conduct. — Strongly Disagree ☐ ☐ ☐ ☐ ☐ ☐ Strongly Agree

13. I am comfortable talking about my sexual views, my sexual fantasies, and sexual experiences that I have had. — Strongly Disagree ☐ ☐ ☐ ☐ ☐ ☐ Strongly Agree

14. My past sexual experiences and explorations have been very worthwhile. — Strongly Disagree ☐ ☐ ☐ ☐ ☐ ☐ Strongly Agree

15. I would be comfortable talking about my sexual fantasies in a small group. — Strongly Disagree ☐ ☐ ☐ ☐ ☐ ☐ Strongly Agree

16. It is disturbing for me to think about my past sexual experiences. — Strongly Disagree ☐ ☐ ☐ ☐ ☐ ☐ Strongly Agree

17. I would be comfortable having a close friend who was engaging in homosexual activities. — Strongly Disagree ☐ ☐ ☐ ☐ ☐ ☐ Strongly Agree

18. I could comfortably interact with an adult who I thought might have had a sexual encounter with a pubescent 12-year-old. — Strongly Disagree ☐ ☐ ☐ ☐ ☐ ☐ Strongly Agree

19. I am comfortable talking about my sexual views with people I do not know well. — Strongly Disagree ☐ ☐ ☐ ☐ ☐ ☐ Strongly Agree

20. I would never maintain a friendship with someone who engaged in sexual activity with animals.　Strongly Disagree ☐ ☐ ☐ ☐ ☐ ☐ Strongly Agree

21. The sexual activities I have engaged in are completely and perfectly natural.　Strongly Disagree ☐ ☐ ☐ ☐ ☐ ☐ Strongly Agree

22. I would be repulsed and appalled if a 21-year-old friend told me they recently had oral sex with a 13-year-old.　Strongly Disagree ☐ ☐ ☐ ☐ ☐ ☐ Strongly Agree

23. It would not bother me if I knew that a good friend enjoys anal stimulation during masturbation.　Strongly Disagree ☐ ☐ ☐ ☐ ☐ ☐ Strongly Agree

24. I am comfortable discussing my sexual fantasies with close friends.　Strongly Disagree ☐ ☐ ☐ ☐ ☐ ☐ Strongly Agree

25. I would be perfectly comfortable working with a person who I knew enjoys spanking during sexual activity with their sex partner.　Strongly Disagree ☐ ☐ ☐ ☐ ☐ ☐ Strongly Agree

26. A person can be a good friend of mine, even if they enjoy sadomasochism with their sex partners.　Strongly Disagree ☐ ☐ ☐ ☐ ☐ ☐ Strongly Agree

27. I can freely discuss sexual topics in a small group of peers.　Strongly Disagree ☐ ☐ ☐ ☐ ☐ ☐ Strongly Agree

28. I would find it awkward knowing that a friend's favorite sexual activity was anal sex.　Strongly Disagree ☐ ☐ ☐ ☐ ☐ ☐ Strongly Agree

29. If I had my life to live over, I would relive most of my past sexual experiences.　Strongly Disagree ☐ ☐ ☐ ☐ ☐ ☐ Strongly Agree

30. I think it is good for people to experiment with a wide range of sexual practices.　Strongly Disagree ☐ ☐ ☐ ☐ ☐ ☐ Strongly Agree

31. Talking to a sexuality researcher about my sexual history would be easy for me.　Strongly Disagree ☐ ☐ ☐ ☐ ☐ ☐ Strongly Agree

32. I would continue to accept a 21-year-old friend who I discovered was sexually involved with an elderly person.　Strongly Disagree ☐ ☐ ☐ ☐ ☐ ☐ Strongly Agree

The MMCSI-S: The Multidimensional Measure of Comfort With Sexuality Short Form

For each item please check (✓) the box that best represents your answer.

1. I am completely comfortable knowing and interacting with people whose sexual activities significantly differ from my own.　Strongly Disagree ☐ ☐ ☐ ☐ ☐ ☐ Strongly Agree

2. I enjoy the opportunity to share my personal views about sexuality　Strongly Disagree ☐ ☐ ☐ ☐ ☐ ☐ Strongly Agree

3. My sexual experiences and explorations are a positive, on-going part of who I am.　Strongly Disagree ☐ ☐ ☐ ☐ ☐ ☐ Strongly Agree

4. I am comfortable with my sexual activities, both past and present　Strongly Disagree ☐ ☐ ☐ ☐ ☐ ☐ Strongly Agree

5. I am comfortable talking about my sexual views, my sexual fantasies, and sexual experiences that I have had.　Strongly Disagree ☐ ☐ ☐ ☐ ☐ ☐ Strongly Agree

6. My past sexual experiences and explorations have been very worthwhile.　Strongly Disagree ☐ ☐ ☐ ☐ ☐ ☐ Strongly Agree

7. It would not bother me if I knew that a good friend enjoys anal stimulation during masturbation.　Strongly Disagree ☐ ☐ ☐ ☐ ☐ ☐ Strongly Agree

8. I can freely discuss sexual topics in a small group of peers.　Strongly Disagree ☐ ☐ ☐ ☐ ☐ ☐ Strongly Agree

9. I think it is good for people to experiment with a wide range of sexual practices.　Strongly Disagree ☐ ☐ ☐ ☐ ☐ ☐ Strongly Agree

Possible cover page for use with the MMCSI

Thank you for filling out the attached questionnaire. Your responses to this questionnaire are anonymous. Do not put your name on these sheets.

Instructions: This is not a test. It is a survey about attitudes and sexuality. You will not have to reveal any details about sexual experiences you may have had. There are no correct or incorrect answers. Please answer all of the questions and answer each question truthfully. Your honest answer to each question is the best answer.

Thank you for your participation!

Sincerely,

[fill in name of researcher]
Principal Investigator

If you have any questions about this research and would like to contact me, I can most easily be reached by [fill in: e-mail, phone, postal mail] at:

[fill in contact information]

Possible demographics page for use with the MMCSI

What is your age?   _____

What is your sex?   _____

What is your race/ethnicity (if you are mixed race, please check all that apply):

☐ White/Caucasian   ☐ Black/African American   ☐ Other (please specify:

☐ Asian/Pacific Islander   ☐ Hispanic/Latino   _____

How open about sexual issues were your parents while you were growing up?

Not Open   ☐   ☐   ☐   ☐   ☐   ☐   Very Open

How open was your family about nudity while you were growing up?

Not Open   ☐   ☐   ☐   ☐   ☐   ☐   Very Open

How would you describe your social views?

Conservative ☐   ☐   ☐   ☐   ☐   ☐   Liberal

To what extent are you sexually aroused by people of the *other* sex?

Not At All   ☐   ☐   ☐   ☐   ☐   ☐   Very Much

To what extent are you sexually aroused by people of the *same* sex?

Not At All   ☐   ☐   ☐   ☐   ☐   ☐   Very Much

How do you rate your sex drive (libido)?

Very Mild   ☐   ☐   ☐   ☐   ☐   ☐   Very Strong

With *how many people* of the *other* sex have you had sexual experiences
(e.g., masturbating with them, oral sex, anal sex, penis-vagina intercourse)?   _____

With *how many people* of the *same* sex have you had sexual experiences
(e.g., masturbating with them, oral sex, anal sex)?   _____

How many sexual *experiences* have you had with people of the *other* sex?

☐ None   ☐ 1 or 2   ☐ 3 to 5   ☐ 6 to 10   ☐ 11 to 20   ☐ 21+

Of those, approximately how many times have you engaged in coitus (i.e., penis-vagina intercourse)?

☐ None ☐ 1 or 2 ☐ 3 to 5 ☐ 6 to 10 ☐ 11 to 20 ☐ 21+

How many sexual *experiences* have you had with people of the *same* sex?

☐ None ☐ 1 or 2 ☐ 3 to 5 ☐ 6 to 10 ☐ 11 to 20 ☐ 21+

In a typical month, how many times do you masturbate? _____

How frequently do you attend religious services?

☐ Never ☐ 1–4 times/year ☐ 5–12 times/year
☐ 2–3 times/month ☐ Once a week ☐ More than once a week

Attraction to Sexual Aggression Scale

N. M. Malamuth, *University of California, Los Angeles*

This instrument was developed by Malamuth (1989a, 1989b) to measure attraction to sexual aggression. It is reprinted by permission of the author.

References

Malamuth, N. M. (1989a). The Attraction to Sexual Aggression Scale: Part one. *The Journal of Sex Research, 26*, 26–49.
Malamuth, N. M. (1989b). The Attraction to Sexual Aggression Scale: Part two. *The Journal of Sex Research, 26*, 324–354.

Exhibit

Attraction to Sexual Aggression Scale

Social Relationships Research

Instructions: On the following pages there are a variety of different questions. Please answer all the questions to the best of your ability. If you are unsure of the answer to a question, please give your best guess. It is important that all of the questions be answered. There are no right or wrong answers, and no trick questions. Please answer the question by placing a tick in the box you choose, like this: Y. Please work quickly and be AS HONEST as possible. Your responses will be kept completely confidential. Thank you for your cooperation.

1. People frequently think about different activities even if they never do them. For each kind of activity listed, please indicate how often you have thought of trying it:

	Never	Sometimes	Often

   a. Necking (deep kissing)[a]
   b. Petting
   c. Oral sex
   d. Heterosexual intercourse
   e. Anal intercourse
   f. Homosexual acts
   g. Group sex
   h. Bondage sex
   i. Whipping, spanking sex
   j. Robbing a bank
   k. Raping a woman
   l. Forcing a female to do something sexual she didn't want to
   m. Being forced to do something sexual you didn't want to

n. Transvestism (wearing women's clothes)
o. Sex with children
p. Killing someone
q. Selling illegal drugs

2. Whether or not you have ever thought of it, do you find the idea of:

Very unattractive	Somewhat unattractive	Somewhat attractive	Very attractive

a. Necking (deep kissing)[b]

3. What percentage of *males* do you think would find the following activities sexually arousing?

a. Anal intercourse[c]
b. Group sex
c. Homosexual acts
d. Armed robbery
e. Bondage sex
f. Whipping, spanking sex
g. Rape
h. Robbing a bank
i. Forcing a female to do something sexual she really didn't want to
j. Killing someone
k. Transvestism
l. Sex with a child
m. Being forced to do something sexual they didn't want to

4. What percentage of *females* do you think would find the following activities sexually arousing?

a. Anal intercourse[d]

5. How sexually arousing do you think you would find the following activities if you engaged in them (even if you have never actually engaged in them and never would)?

Not arousing at all	Very arousing

a. Oral sex[e]
b. Heterosexual intercourse
c. Anal intercourse
d. Homosexual acts
e. Group sex
f. Bondage sex
g. Whipping, spanking sex
h. Robbing a bank
i. Raping a female
j. Forcing a female to do something sexual she didn't want to do
k. Transvestism (wearing women's sex)
l. Being forced to do something sexual you didn't want to do
m. Sex with children
n. Killing someone

6. If you were sure that no one would ever find out and that you'd never be punished for it, how likely would you be to do the following?

Very unlikely	Very likely

a. Oral sex[f]
b. Heterosexual intercourse
c. Anal intercourse
d. Homosexual acts

e. Group sex
f. Bondage sex
g. Whipping, spanking sex
h. Robbing a bank
i. Raping a female
j. Forcing a female to do something sexual she didn't want to
k. Transvestism (wearing women's clothes)
l. Sex with children
m. Killing someone
n. Selling illegal drugs

7. If your best male friend were assured that no one would find out and that he'd never be punished for it, how likely do you think he would be to do the following:

| Very | Very |
| unlikely | likely |

a. Oral sex[g]

8. Approximately what percentage of your male friends, would you estimate, have done the following:

a. Anal intercourse[h]
b. Group sex
c. Homosexual acts
d. Armed robbery
e. Bondage sex
f. Whipping, spanking sex
g. Rape
h. Robbing a bank
i. Forcing a female to do something sexual she didn't want to
j. Killing someone
k. Transvestism
l. Sex with a child
m. Being forced to do something sexual they didn't want to
n. Selling illegal drugs

9. How likely do you think it is that at some point in the future you might try to following activities?

| Very | Very |
| unlikely | likely |

a. Oral sex[i]

End of questionnaire

Thanks for your responses.

---

[a]These items are followed by boxes under each of the response options, providing a place for the respondent to ✓ option chosen.
[b]The same items as shown for Question 1 are repeated, with boxes under each of the four response options.
[c]The response options are indicated by 11 boxes identified from 0% to 100%.
[d]The same items and response options as shown for #3 repeated.
[e]Seven boxes between the two anchors are provided for responses.
[f]Seven boxes between the two anchors are provided for responses.
[g]The same items and response options as shown for Question 6 are repeated.
[h]The response options are indicated by 11 boxes identified from 0% to 100%.
[i]The same items and response options as shown for Question 6 are repeated.

Aggressive Sexual Behavior Inventory

DONALD L. MOSHER,[1] *University of Connecticut*

The Aggressive Sexual Behavior Inventory (ASBI; Mosher & Anderson, 1986) was developed to measure sexual aggression by men against women that occurs in dating or other heterosocial-heterosexual situations. College men, but particularly college men with a macho personality constellation that includes callous sexual attitudes toward women, frequently use these tactics (Mosher & Anderson, 1986). In studies of sexual aggression, answers to a single question about the occurrence of date rape or to a hypothetical question asking about the likelihood of rape if one were not going to be caught suffer from problems of unreliability and false reporting. Although men might also under- or overreport on these 20 items, the summed score, when anonymous, is a better estimate of each man's history of aggressive sexual behavior. The ASBI can be treated as an individual-differences measure of sexual aggression or as a dependent variable when studying predictive correlates of aggressive sexual behavior.

Description

The ASBI consists of 20 items (or a 10-item short form) arranged in a 7-point Likert-type format to rate frequency of occurrence from 1 (*never*) to 7 (*extremely frequently*). From the responses of a sample of 125 college men to 33 items, a varimax factor analysis with an orthogonal rotation extracted six factors that were named Sexual Force, Drugs and Alcohol, Verbal Manipulation, Angry Rejection, Anger Expression, and Threat.

Response Mode and Timing

Respondents can circle the number from 1 to 7 corresponding to their frequency of using the tactic, but the more common scoring is to mark the answers on machine-scoreable answer sheets. The inventory requires approximately 5 minutes to complete.

Scoring

All 20 items are keyed in the same direction with a higher score indicating a greater frequency of aggressive sexual behavior. Scores can range from 20 to 140 or from 10 to 70 on the short form. For each specific factor, the percentage of 125 University of Connecticut college men who endorsed one or more items in the factor and the numbers of the items loading most highly on specific factors follows: Sexual Force, 28% (3, 9, 11, 14, 17, 19); Drugs and Alcohol, 75% (2, 6, 15); Verbal Manipulation, 64% (1, 4, 7, 20); Angry Rejection, 43% (10, 13); Anger Expression, 46% (8, 16, 18); and Threat, 13% (5, 12). The 10-item short form includes Items 1, 4, 5, 6, 11, 12, 13, 15, 18, and 19.

Reliability

In a sample of 125 college men (Mosher & Anderson, 1986), the Cronbach alpha for the summed scores from the 20 items was .94. It is recommended that the summed score of the 20 items be regarded as a homogeneous measure of aggressive sexual behavior. The short form of 10 items had a Cronbach alpha of .87 in a sample of 55 male rock musicians (Zaitchik, 1986).

Validity

As expected, Mosher and Anderson (1986) found that the summed score of the ASBI was significantly correlated with Macho Personality, $r = .33$, Callous Sexual Attitudes, $r = .53$, Violence as Manly, $r = .23$, and Danger as Exciting, $r = .26$, as measured by the Hypermasculinity Inventory (Mosher & Sirkin, 1984). As expected, aggressive sexual behavior (Anderson, 1983) was significantly negatively correlated with Sex-Guilt, $r = -.53$, and Hostility-Guilt, $r = -.49$, as measured by the Mosher Forced-Choice Guilt Inventory (Mosher, 1966). When 125 college men imagined themselves in the role of rapist during guided imagery of a realistic-violent and nonerotic-rape, men scoring higher on aggressive sexual behavior, in comparison to men scoring lower, reported significantly more subjective sexual arousal, as hypothesized, but contrary to expectations they also experienced more affective anger, distress, fear, shame, and guilt (Mosher & Anderson, 1986). These results were interpreted as consistent with the revivification by the guided imagery of rape of the sexually aggressive men's mood-congruent, state-memories (Bower, 1981) of their own previous acts of sexual aggression. In a sample of rock musicians, Zaitchik (1986) found that the ASBI was correlated .75 with macho personality, .72 with cocaine use, .70 with amphetamine use, .50 with marijuana use, and −.35 with life satisfaction.

[1]Address correspondence to Donald L. Mosher, 648 Ternberry Forest Drive, The Villages, FL 32162; e-mail: dlmosher@aol.com

References

Anderson, R. D. (1983). *Hyper-masculine attitudes, aggressive sexual behaviors, and the reactions of college men to a guided imagery presentation of realistic rape*. Unpublished master's thesis, University of Connecticut, Storrs.

Bower, G. H. (1981). Mood and mercy. *American Psychologist, 36*, 129–148.

Mosher, D. L. (1966). The development and multitrait-multimethod matrix analysis of three measures of guilt. *Journal of Consulting Psychology, 30*, 25–29.

Mosher, D. L., & Anderson, R. D. (1986). Macho personality, sexual aggression, and reactions to guided imagery of realistic rape. *Journal of Research in Personality, 20(2)*, 77–94.

Mosher, D. L., & Sirkin, M. (1984). Measuring a macho personality constellation. *Journal of Research in Personality, 18*, 150–163.

Zaitchik, M. (1986). *Macho personality and life satisfaction in rock musicians*. Unpublished master's thesis, University of Connecticut, Storrs.

Exhibit

Aggressive Sexual Behavior Inventory

Instructions: The following 20 items sample behavior that sometimes occurs in dating or man-woman sociosexual interactions. The items describe various techniques, which may or may not be successful, for gaining increased sexual access to women. Some of the behaviors are acceptable to some men and others are not. Because you are an anonymous subject in a psychological study, you are asked to be as truthful as you can be. Each item is to be rated on a 7-point scale of the frequency of past use of the tactic in which 1 means *never* and 7 means *extremely frequent*. If, for example, an item said, "I shave with an electric razor," you would mark the item with a 1, if you never shave with an electric razor, with a 7, if you shaved extremely frequently with an electric razor, and with a number between 2–6 to represent the relative frequency with which you shaved with an electric razor. Record your answers on the separate answer sheet.

1. I have threatened to leave or to end a relationship if a woman wouldn't have sex with me.
2. I have gotten a woman drunk in order to have sex with her.
3. I have waited my turn in line with some other guys who were sharing a "party girl."
4. I have told a woman that I wanted to come into her apartment so I could get her where I wanted.
5. I have warned a woman that she could get hurt if she resisted me, so she should relax and enjoy it.
6. I have gotten a woman high on marijuana or pills so she would be less able to resist my advances.
7. I have told a woman I was petting with that she couldn't stop and leave me with "blue balls."
8. I have blown my top and sworn or broken something to show a woman that she shouldn't get me angry.
9. I have brought a woman to my place after a date and forced her to have sex with me.
10. I have told a woman I was going out with that I could find someone else to give me sex if she wouldn't.
11. I have calmed a woman down with a good slap or two when she got hysterical over my advances.
12. I have promised a woman that I wouldn't harm her if she did everything that I told her to do.
13. I have called a woman an angry name and pushed her away when she would not surrender to my need for sex.
14. I have forced a woman to have sex with me and some of my pals.
15. I have turned a woman on to some expensive drugs so that she would feel obligated to do me a sexual favor.
16. I have roughed a woman up a little so that she would understand that I meant business.
17. I have pushed a woman down and made her undress or torn her clothes off if she wouldn't cooperate.
18. I have gripped a woman tightly and given her an angry look when she was not giving me the sexual response I wanted.
19. I have gotten a little drunk and forced a woman that I'm with to have sex with me.
20. I have told a woman that her refusal to have sex with me was changing the way I felt about her.

Senior Adult Sexuality Scales

ESTELLE WEINSTEIN,[1] *Hofstra University*

The SASS (Senior Adult Sexuality Scales) is a multidimensional measurement instrument suitable for assessing senior adult (60+) sexual attitudes and sexual interests, and a specific set of sexual activities.

Description

The SASS consists of five parts. Part I, the first Biographical Information section, includes 14 questions that gather general descriptive information (see the Exhibit).

Part II, the Sexual Attitude Scale, consists of 16 items that address approval or disapproval of various sexually related activities or concepts (e.g., premarital and extramarital sexual activity, abortion, contraception, and masturbation). It is intended to measure the extent to which the sexual orientation of an individual is liberal or conservative.

Part III, the Sexual Interest Scale, refers to a concept of "interest," encompassing a feeling of concern for, desire for, or preference for a particular set of sexual activities, whether or not one is a participant. The interest subscales (Experimental and Traditional) were developed as a quantitative measure of the degree of interest in a fairly comprehensive set of sexual activities. The items were selected from a taxonomy of items that represent the range of sexual activities commonly practiced or of interest to middle-aged to older adults.

The Experimental subscale consists of 10 items covering sexual behaviors involving partner choices (e.g., group sex, sex with considerably younger partners, nonmarital sex). The Traditional subscale consists of seven items covering intimate sexual behaviors such as kissing, petting, intercourse, orgasm, and so forth. Interest levels are based on desire for a specific activity if it was readily available whenever one wanted it.

Part IV, the Sexual Activities Scale, was designed to assess the construct *sexual activity*. Sexual activity refers to the wide range of activities or behaviors involved in sexual expression and interaction. This scale was developed to measure a limited range of specific sexual activities such as sexual intercourse, cuddling, petting, sexual initiation, orgasm, and so on.

Part V, Biographical Information II, asks the respondents the degree to which their participation in athletic, social, and sexual activities has changed from their 30s or 40s as compared to now. Also included here are questions that will allow for an identification of the sexual orientation of the sample and/or individual, as well as space for the respondents to comment on the total instrument.

The 68-item preliminary questionnaire was developed from an initial pool of 100 items selected from extant measures applicable to other subpopulations and from colleagues' suggestions. Face validity, clarity, and applicability to the desired constructs were determined by five professionals and five senior adults, who assigned the items to three hypothesized underlying factors (attitudes, interests, activities).

To substantiate that the scales representing the hypothesized factors were psychometrically sound, data from 314 respondents were subjected to a principal axis factor analysis with squared multiple correlation coefficients as initial estimates of communality. The criteria used to determine the number of factors included an examination of the proportion of variance (POV) accounted for, the number of factors with eigenvalues greater than 1, and an assessment of the substantive interpretability of the factors. Solutions were explored with one to six factors. The best solution found was a four-factor solution, accounting for 51% of the common factor variance.

The result of factor analyses performed on the three preliminary scales separately—to determine if any interpretable pattern was being masked by an overall solution—further substantiated acceptance of the combined solution. The existence of the hypothesized constructs was strongly substantiated in that each factor emerged separately. The only modification to the initial expectation is that two factors explaining sexual interest emerged rather than one, hence the Traditional and Experimental subscales.

The retained solution was rotated orthogonally and obliquely. The oblique solution revealed no meaningful correlations among the factors; thus, the orthogonal solution was used to interpret the factors and to select the final items to be included in the scales and subscales.

Because a minimum criterion of .4 on the factor loadings was considered meaningful or substantial, the items included in the final scales had factor loadings of .4 or more on one factor and less than .4 on all other factors. If two items were redundant, then other theoretical criteria were applied. Each final scale consisted of a homogeneous set of items influenced by one major factor (Allen & Yen, 1979).

Response Mode and Timing

Respondents are instructed to answer the questions by circling an appropriate number or placing a check in a space provided. On the average, 30 to 40 minutes are required to complete the entire questionnaire.

---

[1]Address correspondence to Estelle Weinstein, Department of Health Professions and Family Studies, Hofstra University, Hempstead, Long Island, NY 11549; e-mail: estelle.weinstein@hofstra.edu

Scoring

Each item on the Sexual Attitude Scale (Part II) is scored on a 7-point scale where 1 = *Strongly Agree* and 7 = *Strongly Disagree.* When the entire scale is summed, low scores will represent a more conservative sexual attitude orientation and high scores a more liberal sexual attitude orientation. A liberal or conservative attitude of the group toward a particular item can also be assessed.

Each item on the Sexual Interest Scale (Part III, both Experimental and Traditional subscales) is scored on a 7-point scale where 7 = *Very Interested* and 1 = *Not Interested.* All items are worded so that a high score represents a high degree of interest, and a low score represents a low degree of interest. To check for consistency of responses, some items were worded differently, although addressing the same concerns. The items on each subscale can be added and comparisons made between groups. The subscales should be administered as one scale but scored separately because collapsing them into one scale may result in invalid and inappropriate conclusions.

The items on the Sexual Activities Scale (Part IV) are rated in a somewhat new format successfully tested in a major study of teen behavior by the Centers for Disease Control (Kirby, Alter, & Scales, 1979). The question format is "How often do you . . . ?" The respondent is instructed to fill in the correct number on the line provided, next to *times per day, times per week, times per month, times per year,* or *never.*

Applying statistical procedures to the raw data to arrive at the common denominator of weekly, monthly, or yearly participation is necessary for comparisons. When this is completed, the scores can be added. A high number reflects more frequent sexual activity. Individual items can be examined separately, describing frequency for a particular activity. The total frequency for any one individual or one item is best discussed as a relative comparison to some group or individual. The Sexual Activities Scale should be used by researchers interested only in the quantity of activity.

Reliability

Cronbach's alpha reliability coefficients were calculated for each of the scales of the SASS (Nunnally, 1978). The Sexual Attitude Scale and the Sexual Interest Scale, Part A and Part B, have respectable reliabilities of .87, .90, and

.84, respectively. The Sexual Activities Scale has a somewhat lower reliability coefficient of .66.

Validity

Face validity and content validity were substantiated by a professional and senior adult review. Construct validity is strongly confirmed by the results of the factor analysis, as the items in each scale and subscale intercorrelated and loaded separately on the respective factor, with no overlap. The orthogonal solution, as the most appropriate solution to explain the data, showed the distinctness of the factors, which acts as further confirmation of construct validity.

The SASS was used in a study of age-segregated and age-integrated living arrangements of senior adults as they relate to their sexual attitudes, interest, and activities. The data across scales were collected on the SASS and subjected to a discriminant function analysis where significant differences were detected between the groups (Weinstein, 1984). Research of this nature serves to support the construct validity of the scales.

Other Information

The scales have been discussed in journal articles, including Weinstein and Rosen (1988, 1989). The full SASS (preliminary and final versions) is available from Estelle Weinstein.

References

Allen, M. J., & Yen, W. M. (1979). *Introduction to measurement theory.* Monterey, CA: Brooks/Cole.

Kirby, D., Alter, J., & Scales, P. (1979). *An analysis of U.S. sex education programs and evaluation methods.* Springfield, VA: National Technical Information Service.

Nunnally, J. (1978). *Psychometric theory.* New York: McGraw-Hill.

Weinstein, E. (1984). Senior adult sexuality-community living styles. *Dissertation Abstracts International.* (University Microfilms No. 1015, 3)

Weinstein, E., & Rosen, E. (1988). Senior adult sexuality in age-segregated and age-integrated living styles. *International Journal of Aging and Human Development, 27,* 261–270.

Weinstein, E., & Rosen, E. (1989). A new senior adult sexuality scale for assessing sexual attitudes, interests and activities. In R. Harris & S. Harris (Eds.), *Physical activity, aging, and sports, Volume I: Scientific and medical aspects.* Albany, NY: Center for the Study of Aging.

Exhibit

Senior Adult Sexuality Scales

Biographical Information I (Part I)

Instructions: Please answer all questions by placing a check or a statement in the appropriate space provided.

1. Relationship Status:

    Married _____   Committed Partners _____   Remarried _____

    Single _____   Divorced _____   Widowed _____

    Separated _____   Other (specify) _____

2. If remarried or in a committed partnership:

    More than 10 years _____   Less than 10 years _____

3. How many children do your have?

    None _____   One _____   Two _____   Three _____   Four or More _____

4. Education:

    Completed Elementary School _____   Some High School _____

    College Graduate _____   Some College _____

    Other (specify) _____   Graduate School _____

5. Religious Affiliation:

    Catholic _____   Protestant _____   Jewish _____   Other (specify) _____

6. How religious do you consider yourself?

    Very Religious _____   Moderately Religious _____

    Somewhat Religious _____   Not Religious _____

7. State of Retirement:

    Fully Retired _____   Partially Retired _____   Full-Time Employed _____

8. How would you rate your present state of health?

    Excellent _____   Good _____   Fair _____   Poor _____

9. Lifetime Occupation (i.e., homemaker, salesperson, executive, lawyer, etc.):

    _____

10. Current income from all sources:

    Under $15,000 _____   Between $15–25,000 _____   Between $25–35,000 _____

    Between $35–50,000 _____   Above $50,000 _____

11. Type of community in which you are living more than half of each year:

    Small Town _____   Small City _____   Large City _____

    Retirement Community _____   Suburban Community _____

12. If you checked retirement type community in question 11, where was the original residence in which you spent the major portion of your working life?

Small Town_____   Small City_____   Large City_____

Suburban Community_____   Other (specify)_____

13. What is your age? _____years

14. What is your sex? _____Female   _____Male

Senior Adult Sexuality Scales (SASS) (Part II)

Attitudes—Scale I

1. I think there is too much sexual freedom today.[a]
2. Abortion is a greater evil than bringing an unwanted child into the world.
3. Sexual activity amongst older single senior citizens is not acceptable behavior.
4. Premarital sexual intercourse is morally wrong.
5. Women should not initiate sexual activity as often as men.
6. Stronger laws should be passed to curb homosexuality.
7. Frequent desire for oral-genital sex is an indicator of an excessive sex drive.
8. Sexual intercourse should only occur between married partners.
9. Masturbation is generally an unhealthy practice.
10. Sexual activity between young adults simply for enjoyment is unacceptable behavior.
11. Men who lose their spouses generally need sexual activity more frequently than women who lose their spouses.
12. Women should not experience sexual intercourse with their mate prior to marriage.
13. I think people are too sexually active today.
14. Laws should be passed to ban pornography.
15. Too much information about sex and contraception is available to young people today.
16. Modern attitudes and morals about sex are responsible for the breakdown in the American family.

Senior Adult Sexuality Scales (SASS) (Part III)

Interest—Scale II

Part A

1. Having sex with someone I have recently met[b]
2. Stimulating my own genitals until climax (ejaculation, orgasm)
3. Having sex with someone other than my spouse or regular mate
4. Having sex with more than one partner at a time (group sex)
5. Having sex with partners considerably younger than myself
6. Watching sex movies
7. Reading sex books or magazines
8. Receiving oral sex to climax (ejaculation, orgasm)
9. Receiving oral sex until partner reaches climax
10. Extramarital/extra committed partner sex activity

Part B

1. Kissing, cuddling, touching, petting
2. Having my breasts stroked or kissed
3. Body massage as sex play
4. Having sex in the shower
5. Extended foreplay that leads to intercourse

6. Sex only with someone of the opposite sex
7. Talking about sex with my partner

Senior Adult Sexuality Scales (SASS) (Part IV)

Activities—Scale III

1. How often do you engage in sexual intercourse?

___times per day   ___times per week   ___times per month
___times per year   ___never[c]

2. How often do you engage in touching, cuddling, petting as foreplay to sexual intercourse?
3. How often do you engage in oral sex as foreplay to sexual intercourse?
4. How often do you reach orgasm (climax)?
5. How often do you use a vibrator or other objects for sexual stimulation with a partner?
6. How often do you initiate (start) sexual activity with your partner?

Senior Adult Sexuality Scales (SASS) (Part V)

Biographical Information II

1. How would you rate your current participation in athletic activities?[d]
2. How would you rate your participation in athletic activities when you were 35–45 years old?
3. How would you rate your current participation in social functions?
4. How would you rate your participation in social functions when you were 35–45 years old?
5. How would you rate your current participation in sexual activities?
6. How would you rate your participation in sexual activities when you were 35–45 years old?
7. How would you rate your current interest in sexual activities, if it were available whenever you wanted it?[e]
8. How would you rate your interest in sexual activity when you were 35–45 years old?
9. How would you rate your current sexual attitudes?[f]
10. How would you rate your sexual attitudes when you were 35–45 years old?
11. (Circle the appropriate statement)
    Do you consider yourself a:

    Heterosexual person (preference for sexual partner of opposite sex)
    Homosexual person (preference for sexual partner of same sex)
    Bisexual person (can prefer sexual partner of either sex)

[a]Each item in this section is followed by 7-point *Strongly Agree-Strongly Disagree* scales.
[b]Each item in this section is followed by 7-point *Very Interested-Not Interested* scales.
[c]The remaining items in this section are followed by the same response options.
[d]Items 1–6 are followed by 7-point *Inactive-Very Active* scales.
[e]Items 7 and 8 are followed by 7-point *Not Interested-Very Interested* scales.
[f]Items 9 and 10 are followed by 7-point *Very Conservative-Very Liberal* scales.

Aging Sexual Knowledge and Attitudes Scale

CHARLES B. WHITE,[1] *Trinity University*

The Aging Sexual Knowledge and Attitudes Scale (ASKAS) is designed to measure two realms of sexuality: (a) knowledge about changes (and nonchanges) in sexual response to advanced age in males and females and (b) general attitudes about sexual activity in the aged. The items are largely specific to the elderly rather than a general sexual knowledge-attitudes scale. The ASKAS was developed for use in assessing the impact of group or individual interventions on behalf of sexual functioning in the aged utilizing, for example, a pretest-posttest procedure. Further, the measure may form the basis for group and individual discussion about sexual attitudes and/or sexual knowledge. The scale is also appropriate for use in educational programs for those working with the aged.

The actual numerical scores may be conveniently used for research purposes, but the individual items are also useful to assess the extent of an individual's knowledge upon which to base clinical interventions, as well as identifying attitudinal obstacles to sexual intimacy in old age.

Description, Response Mode, and Timing

The ASKAS consists of 61 items, 35 true/false/don't know in format and 26 items responded to on a 7-point Likert-type scale as to degree of agreement or disagreement with the particular item. The 35 true/false questions assess knowledge about sexual changes and nonchanges which are or are not age related. The 26 agree/disagree items assess attitudes toward sexual behavior in the aged. The items are counterbalanced. The instrument takes 20–40 minutes to complete.

Scoring

The ASKAS may be given in an interview of paper-and-pencil format and may be group administered or individually administered. The nature of the scoring and items are readily adaptable to computer scoring systems.

Scoring is such that a low knowledge score indicates high knowledge and a low attitude score indicates a more permissive attitude. The rationale for the low knowledge score reflecting high knowledge is that *don't know* was given a value of 3, indicating low knowledge. In the Knowledge section, Questions 1 through 35, the following scoring applies: *true* = 1, *false* = 2, and *don't know* = 3. Items 1, 10, 14, 17, 20, 30, and 31 are reversed scored. In the Exhibit, the correct answers are in parentheses for Items 1 through 35. The attitude questions, 36 through 61, are each scored according to the value selected by the respondent with the

exception of Items 44, 47, 48, 50–56, and 59 in which the scoring is reversed.

Reliability

The reliability of the ASKAS has been examined in several different studies, and in varying ways, summarized in Table 1. As can be seen, reliabilities are very positive and at acceptable levels.

Validity

Presented in Table 2 are the means and standard deviations of ASKAS scores from several studies. These means are not meant to be viewed as normative, but rather illustrative of group variation in ASKAS performance.

The validity of the ASKAS has been examined in a sexual education program for older persons, by individuals working with older persons, and by adult family members of aged persons in which each group received the psychological-educational intervention separately (White & Catania, 1981). Each experimental group had a comparable

TABLE 1
Aging Sexual Knowledge and Attitudes Scale (ASKAS) Reliabilities

Type of reliability	Reliability coefficient	Sample size	Type of sample
		Knowledge	
Split-half[a]	.91	163	Nursing home staff
Split-half[a]	.90	279	Nursing home residents
Alpha	.93	163	Nursing home staff
Alpha	.91	279	Nursing home residents
Alpha	.92	30	Community older adults
Alpha	.90	30	Nursing home staff
Alpha	.90	30	Families of older adults
Test-retest	.97	15	Community older adults
Test-retest	.90	30	Staff of nursing home and families of the older adults
		Attitudes	
Split-half[a]	.86	163	Nursing home staff
Split-half[a]	.83	279	Nursing home residents
Alpha	.85	163	Nursing home staff
Alpha	.76	279	Nursing home residents
Alpha	.87	30	Community older adults
Alpha	.87	30	Nursing home staff
Alpha	.86	30	Families of older adults
Test-retest	.96	15	Community older adults
Test-retest	.72	30	Staff of nursing home and families of the aged

[a]These correlations have been corrected for test length.

[1]Address correspondence to Charles B. White, Trinity University, 1 Stadium Drive, San Antonio, TX 78212; e-mail: cwhite@Trinity.Edu

TABLE 2
Aging Sexual Knowledge and Attitudes Scale (ASKAS)
Score Means and Standard Deviations Score by Group

Group	n	Mean	SD
Nursing home residents[a]	273		
Attitudes		84.56	23.32
Knowledge		65.62	15.09
Community older adults[b]	30		
Attitudes		86.40	17.28
Knowledge		73.73	12.52
Families of older adults[b]	30		
Attitudes		75.00	22.66
Knowledge		78.00	13.61
Persons who work with older adults[b]	30		
Attitudes		76.00	17.60
Knowledge		62.46	12.50
Nursing home staff[b]	163		
Attitudes		61.08	25.79
Knowledge		64.19	17.25

Note. The possible range of ASKAS scores are as follows: Knowledge = 35–105; Attitudes = 26–182. All scores reported here are the pretest scores in cases where both pretests and posttests were administered.
[a]White, 1981.
[b]White and Catania, 1981.

nonintervention control group. In all cases, the educational intervention resulted in significant increases in knowledge and significant changes in the direction of a more permissive attitude, both relative to their own pretest scores and relative to the appropriate control group, whereas the control group posttest scores were not significantly changed relative to their pretest scores. There was a 4–6 week period between pre- and posttests.

Hammond (1979) utilized the ASKAS in a sexual education program for professionals working with the aged. She reported significant changes from pre- to posttest toward increased knowledge and more permissive attitudes in the interception group, as in the White and Catania (1981) research, whereas the control group scores were unchanged from pre- to posttest.

White (1982a), in a study of nursing home residents in 15 nursing homes, reported that both ASKAS attitude and knowledge scores were associated with whether an individual was sexually active or not such that more activity was associated with greater knowledge and with more permissive attitudes.

A factor analysis of the ASKAS results (White, 1982b) from the studies in Table 2 resulted in a two-factor solution, with each item loading most heavily on its hypothesized membership in either the attitude or knowledge section of the measure.

Other Information

The ASKAS may be utilized without permission. It is only requested that all findings be shared with the test author.

References

Hammond, D. (1979). *An exploratory study of a workshop on sex and aging.* Unpublished doctoral dissertation, University of Georgia, Athens, GA.

White, C. B. (1982a). Interest, attitudes, knowledge, and sexual history in relation to sexual behavior in the institutionalized aged. *Archives of Sexual Behavior, 11,* 11–21.

White, C. B. (1982b). A scale for the assessment of attitudes and knowledge regarding sexuality in the aged. *Archives of Sexual Behavior, 11,* 491–502.

White, C. B., & Catania, J. (1981). Sexual education for aged people, people who work with the aged, and families of aged people. *International Journal of Aging and Human Development, 15,* 121–138.

Exhibit

Aging Sexual Knowledge and Attitudes Scale

Knowledge Questions (Correct answer shown in parentheses.)

*1. Sexual activity in aged persons is often dangerous to their health. (F)

        True   False   Don't know[a]

2. Males over the age of 65 typically take longer to attain an erection of their penis than do younger males. (T)

3. Males over the age of 65 usually experience a reduction in intensity of orgasm relative to younger males. (T)

4. The firmness of erection in aged males is often less than that of younger persons. (T)

5. The older female (65+ years of age) has reduced vaginal lubrication secretion relative to younger females. (T)

6. The aged female takes longer to achieve adequate vaginal lubrication relative to younger females. (T)

7. The older female may experience painful intercourse due to reduced elasticity of the vagina and reduced vaginal lubrication. (T)

8. Sexuality is typically a life-long need. (T)

9. Sexual behavior in older people (65+) increases the risk of heart attack. (F)

*10. Most males over the age of 65 are unable to engage in sexual intercourse. (F)

11. The relatively most sexually active younger people tend to become the relatively most sexually active older people. (T)

12. There is evidence that sexual activity in older persons has beneficial physical effects on the participants. (T)

13. Sexual activity may be psychologically beneficial to older person participants. (T)

*14. Most older females are sexually unresponsive. (F)

15. The sex urge typically increases with age in males over 65. (F)
16. Prescription drugs may alter a person's sex drive. (T)
*17. Females, after menopause, have a physiologically induced need for sexual activity. (F)
18. Basically, changes with advanced age (65+) in sexuality involve a slowing of response time rather than a reduction of interest in sex. (T)
19. Older males typically experience a reduced need to ejaculate and hence may maintain an erection of the penis for a longer time than younger males. (T)
*20. Older males and females cannot act as sex partners as both need younger partners for stimulation. (F)
21. The most common determinant of the frequency of sexual activity in older couples is the interest or lack of interest of the husband in a sexual relationship with his wife. (T)
22. Barbiturates, tranquilizers, and alcohol may lower the sexual arousal levels of aged persons and interfere with sexual responsiveness. (T)
23. Sexual disinterest in aged persons may be a reflection of a psychological state of depression. (T)
24. There is a decrease in frequency of sexual activity with older age in males. (T)
25. There is a greater decrease in male sexuality with age than there is in female sexuality. (T)
26. Heavy consumption of cigarettes may diminish sexual desire. (T)
27. An important factor in the maintenance of sexual responsiveness in the aging male is the consistency of sexual activity throughout his life. (T)
28. Fear of the inability to perform sexually may bring about an inability to perform sexually in older males. (T)
29. The ending of sexual activity in old age is most likely and primarily due to social and psychological causes rather than biological and physical causes. (T)
*30. Excessive masturbation may bring about an early onset of mental confusion and dementia in the aged. (F)
*31. There is an inevitable loss of sexual satisfaction in post-menopausal women. (F)
32. Secondary impotence (or non-physiologically caused) increases in males over the age of 60 relative to young males. (T)
33. Impotence in aged males may literally be effectively treated and cured in many instances. (T)
34. In the absence of severe physical disability, males and females may maintain sexual interest and activity well into their 80s and 90s. (T)
35. Masturbation in older males and females has beneficial effects on the maintenance of sexual responsiveness. (T)

Attitude Questions (7-point Likert-type scale, where *disagree* = 1, *agree* = 7)
36. Aged people have little interest in sexuality. (Aged = 65+ years of age.)
37. An aged person who shows sexual interest brings disgrace to himself/herself.
38. Institutions, such as nursing homes, ought not to encourage or support sexual activity of any sort in its residents.
39. Male and female residents of nursing homes ought to live on separate floors or separate wings of the nursing home.
40. Nursing homes have no obligation to provide adequate privacy for residents who desire to be alone, either by themselves or as a couple.
41. As one becomes older (say past 65) interest in sexuality inevitably disappears.

For Items 42, 43, and 44:
If a relative of mine, living in a nursing home, was to have a sexual relationship with another resident I would:
42. Complain to the management.
43. Move my relative from this institution.
+44. Stay out of it as it is not my concern.
45. If I knew that a particular nursing home permitted and supported sexual activity in residents who desired such, I would not place a relative in that nursing home.
46. It is immoral for older persons to engage in recreational sex.
+47. I would like to know more about the changes in sexual functioning in older years.
+48. I feel I know all I need to know about sexuality in the aged.
49. I would complain to the management if I knew of sexual activity between any residents of a nursing home.
+50. I would support sex education courses for aged residents of nursing homes.
+51. I would support sex education courses for the staff of nursing homes.
+52. Masturbation is an acceptable sexual activity for older males.
+53. Masturbation is an acceptable sexual activity for older females.
+54. Institutions, such as the nursing home, ought to provide large enough beds for couples who desire such to sleep together.
+55. Staff of nursing homes ought to be trained or educated with regard to sexuality in the aged and/or disabled.
56. Residents of nursing homes ought not to engage in sexual activity of any sort.
57. Institutions, such as nursing homes, should provide opportunities for the social interaction of men and women.

58. Masturbation is harmful and ought to be avoided.

+59. Institutions, such as nursing homes, should provide privacy such as to allow residents to engage in sexual behavior without fear of intrusion of observation.

60. If family members object to a widowed relative engaging in sexual relations with another resident of a nursing home, it is the obligation of the management and staff to make certain that such sexual activity is prevented.

61. Sexual relations outside the context of marriage are always wrong.

---

^aThese options are repeated for Items 2–35.

*Indicates that the scoring should be reversed such that 2 = 1, and 1 = 2 (i.e., a low score indicates high knowledge).

+Reverse scoring on these items. A low score indicates a permissive attitude.

Sex Anxiety Inventory

LOUIS H. JANDA,[1] *Old Dominion University*

The Sex Anxiety Inventory (SAI) measures anxiety regarding sexual matters, defined as a generalized expectancy for nonspecific external punishment for the violation of, or the anticipation of violating, perceived normative standards of acceptable sexual behavior. A major goal was to be able to distinguish sexual anxiety from sexual guilt, which Mosher (1965) defined as "a generalized expectancy for self-mediated punishment for violating, anticipating the violation of, or failure to attain internalized standards of proper behavior" (p. 162).

Description

The 25 items on the scale are in a forced-choice format, with one alternative representing an anxiety response and the other a nonanxiety response. The form of the scale used by its developers includes 15 filler items. Items were included on the final version of the scale if they met the following criteria: (a) The correlation between the item and the total score of the SAI was significant at the .05 level (two-tailed), (b) the item-total correlation exceeded the correlation between that item and the score on the Sex Guilt subscale of the Mosher Forced-Choice Guilt Inventory, (c) the item-total correlation exceeded the correlation between that item and the score on the Crowne and Marlowe (1964) Social Desirability Scale, and (d) there was no significant difference between the item-total correlations for males and females. Of the 25 items that appear on the scale, only 4 were significantly correlated with social desirability, 2 in the positive direction and 2 in the negative direction. The scale was developed with a college student population.

Response Mode and Timing

The respondents circle the letter of the alternative that comes closest to describing their feelings. The scale rarely requires more than 15 minutes for completion.

Scoring

For Items 2, 3, 5, 6, 8, 11, 12, 13, 14, 15, 17, 22, 24, and 25, alternative "a" is the anxiety response. For the remaining items, alternative "b" is the anxiety response. Each anxiety response is scored as 1 point, resulting in a possible range of scores from 0 to 25.

Reliability

Janda and O'Grady (1980) reported that the internal consistency of the scale (using the Kuder-Richardson formula) was .86. Test-retest reliability, with a time interval of 10 to 14 days, was .85 for males and .84 for females.

Validity

Concurrent validity of the scale has been demonstrated by using it to predict self-reported sexual experiences of both men and women (Janda & O'Grady, 1980). Vanwesenbeeck (2001) reported that women high in sex anxiety were less likely to watch Dutch sexually explicit television for leisure than low-anxious women.

Other Information

A copy of the scale, complete with filler items, can be obtained at no cost from the author.

---

[1]Address correspondence to Louis H. Janda, Department of Psychology, Old Dominion University, Norfolk, VA 23508; e-mail: ljanda@odu.edu

References

Crowne, D. P., & Marlowe, D. (1964). *The approval motive: Studies in evaluative dependence*. New York: Wiley.

Janda, L. H., & O'Grady, K. E. (1980). Development of a sex anxiety inventory. *Journal of Consulting and Clinical Psychology, 48*, 169–175.

Mosher, D. L. (1965). Interaction of fear and guilt in inhibiting unacceptable behavior. *Journal of Consulting Psychology, 29*, 161–167.

Vanwesenbeeck, I. (2001). Psychosexual correlates of viewing sexually explicit sex on television among women in the Netherlands. *The Journal of Sex Research, 38*, 361–368.

Exhibit

Sex Anxiety Inventory

1. Extramarital sex . . .

   a. is OK if everyone agrees.
   b. can break up families.

2. Sex . . .

   a. can cause as much anxiety as pleasure.
   b. on the whole is good and enjoyable.

3. Masturbation . . .

   a. causes me to worry.
   b. can be a useful substitute.

4. After having sexual thoughts . . .

   a. I feel aroused.
   b. I feel jittery.

5. When I engage in petting . . .

   a. I feel scared at first.
   b. I thoroughly enjoy it.

6. Initiating sexual relationships . . .

   a. is a very stressful experience.
   b. causes me no problem at all.

7. Oral sex . . .

   a. would arouse me.
   b. would terrify me.

8. I feel nervous . . .

   a. about initiating sexual relations.
   b. about nothing when it comes to members of the opposite sex.

9. When I meet someone I'm attracted to . . .

   a. I get to know him or her.
   b. I feel nervous.

10. When I was younger . . .

    a. I was looking forward to having sex.
    b. I felt nervous about the prospect of having sex.

11. When others flirt with me . . .

    a. I don't know what to do.
    b. I flirt back.

12. Group sex . . .

    a. would scare me to death.
    b. might be interesting.

13. If in the future I committed adultery . . .

    a. I would probably get caught.
    b. I wouldn't feel bad about it.

14. I would . . .

    a. feel too nervous to tell a dirty joke in mixed company.
    b. tell a dirty joke if it were funny.

15. Dirty jokes . . .

    a. make me feel uncomfortable.
    b. often make me laugh.

16. When I awake from sexual dreams . . .

    a. I feel pleasant and relaxed.
    b. I feel tense.

17. When I have sexual desires . . .

    a. I worry about what I should do.
    b. I do something to satisfy them.

18. If in the future I committed adultery . . .

    a. it would be nobody's business but my own.
    b. I would worry about my spouse finding out.

19. Buying a pornographic book . . .

    a. wouldn't bother me.
    b. would make me nervous.

20. Casual sex . . .

    a. is better than no sex at all.
    b. can hurt many people.

21. Extramarital sex . . .

    a. is sometimes necessary.
    b. can damage one's career.

22. Sexual advances . . .

    a. leave me feeling tense.
    b. are welcomed.

23. When I have sexual relations . . .

    a. I feel satisfied.
    b. I worry about being discovered.

24. When talking about sex in mixed company . . .

    a. I feel nervous.
    b. I sometimes get excited.

25. If I were to flirt with someone . . .

    a. I would worry about his or her reaction.
    b. I would enjoy it.

Sexual Arousability Inventory and Sexual Arousability Inventory—Expanded

EMILY FRANCK HOON,[1] *Gainesville, Florida*
DIANNE CHAMBLESS, *University of Pennsylvania*

The Sexual Arousability Inventory (SAI) and the Sexuality Arousability Inventory—Expanded (SAI-E) measure sexual arousability and anxiety. The SAI has clinical utility, as it is capable of discriminating between a normal population and individuals seeking therapy for sexual dysfunction (Hoon, Hoon, & Wincze, 1976). The SAI-E can help determine if a client has an arousal dysfunction problem and/or sexual anxiety, which may be inhibiting normal functioning. Furthermore, it can help pinpoint which erotic experiences may be problematic. The SAI is sensitive to therapeutic changes (e.g., Murphy, Coleman, Hoon, & Scott, 1980) and can, therefore, help to determine the efficacy of various therapy programs (or components thereof) for a given individual or group(s) of individuals.

The SAI-E is also a valuable research tool for determining the relationship of sexual arousability and anxiety to the characteristics, attitudes, and experiences of subjects (e.g., Burgess & Krop, 1978; Coleman, Hoon, & Hoon, 1983; Hoon & Hoon, 1982) and for investigating underlying dimensions of arousability (Chambless & Lifshitz, 1984; Hoon & Hoon, 1978).

Description

The SAI is a 28-item self-report inventory measuring perceived arousability to a variety of sexual experiences. The SAI-E is the same inventory rated both on arousability and anxiety dimensions. The two dimensions are uncorrelated, providing independent information.

The SAI is suitable for either heterosexual or lesbian women. The SAI-E is suitable for administration to men or women regardless of sexual orientation or marital status. The items are descriptions of sexual experiences and situations which are rated along a 7-point Likert-type scale on the basis of (a) how sexually aroused and (b) how anxious the respondent feels (or would feel) when engaged in the described activity. Response options on the arousability dimension range from –1, *adversely affects arousal; unthinkable, repulsive, distracting* to 5, *always causes sexual arousal; extremely arousing.* Extremes of the anxiety scale are –1, *relaxing, calming* to 5, *always causes anxiety; extremely anxiety producing.*

When frequent evaluations are desired, alternate forms of the arousability scale are available. Comprised of 14 items, each from the original scale, the shortened versions of the SAI may be used interchangeably to assess sexual arousability throughout therapy for sexual dysfunction.

Response Mode and Timing

Using a paper/pencil format, respondents circle the number indicating their degree of arousal during each of the described activities. They then independently circle the numbers indicating their perceived anxiety during each of the same activities. A card sort format may also be used for individual assessment. The inventory takes an average of 10 minutes to complete by either method. It takes less than 5 minutes to complete the 14-item version.

Scoring

Arousability score is the sum of the arousability ratings (subtracting any –1s). Anxiety score is a sum of anxiety ratings (subtracting –1s). For ease of interpretation, available normative data are presented in Table 1.

Reliability

Arousability, female samples. Reliability information from the original research (Hoon et al., 1976) follows with additional information, as noted. Cronbach alpha coefficients for the original validation ($N = 151$) and cross-validation ($N = 134$) samples were .91 and .92,

TABLE 1
Mean Arousability and Anxiety Score on the Sexual Arousability Inventory—Expanded (SAI-E)

Group	N	MSAI-E score	SD	M age
Arousability				
Heterosexual females				
Validation group	370	82.00	23.30	25.80
Undergraduates	252	78.93	24.84	18.91
Community women	90	99.14	14.27	26.26
Lesbians	371	92.34	14.37	28.20
Heterosexual males	205	90.60	14.70	25.80
Anxiety				
Heterosexual females				
Undergraduates	252	34.34	33.14	18.91
Community women	90	6.36	16.11	26.26

[1]Address correspondence to Emily Franck Hoon, 2531-C NW 41st Street, Gainesville, FL 32606; e-mail: efhoon@remconsults

respectively. Spearman-Brown corrected split-half coefficients were .92 for each sample, indicating high internal consistency. A test-retest coefficient on a subsample (n = 48) with an 8-week interval was .69. Split-half reliability was later confirmed by Chambless and Lifshitz (1984), who obtained a Spearman-Brown corrected coefficient of .92 utilizing a sample (N = 252) from another geographic location.

Cumulative percentile norms have remained remarkably consistent. The addition of a sample of women over the age of 25 to the original sample, and subsequent reanalysis of the data, did not appreciably alter the cumulative percentile distribution (M age = 28.4, revised N = 370). Similarly, the distributions obtained from independent samples (Chambless & Lifschitz, 1984) were remarkably similar with two minor differences. A slightly lower average arousability score was obtained from the younger sample (M age = 18.91, N = 252) and a slightly higher average score was obtained from the older sample (M age = 26.26, N = 90; see Table 1).

Flax (1980) has provided reliability information on the 14-item shortened versions of the arousability scale for women. In a sample of 158 White married women, half with ileostomies, she obtained Cronbach alpha coefficients of .88 and .86 for Forms A and B, respectively. Test-retest coefficients after a 3-week interval were .97 and .98 (N = 39) respectively.

Anxiety, female samples. Split-half reliability was calculated on responses of 252 female undergraduates yielding an excellent corrected reliability coefficient of .94 (Chambless & Lifshitz, 1984). Test-retest data are unavailable.

Arousability and anxiety, male samples. Reliability information on the SAI-E and SAI for men is not available.

Validity

Arousability, female samples. Construct validity has been demonstrated by consistently high correlations with four criterion variables: awareness of physiological changes during sexual arousal, satisfaction with sexual responsiveness, frequency of intercourse, and total episodes of intercourse before marriage (Hoon et al., 1976). Separate factor analyses of the original SAI data and a subsequent independent heterosexual female sample both resulted in five highly interpretable solutions with similar factor loadings on the respective factors (Chambless & Lifshitz, 1984). Factor analysis of SAI data obtained on a sample of lesbian women (N = 407) resulted in six underlying dimensions, three of which were analogous to factors found on the heterosexual samples. The other three factors were consistent with lesbian sexual practices, one differing in genitally oriented items, another representing oral sex, and the last representing nudity (Coleman et al., 1983).

Burgess and Krop (1978) found a significant correlation between SAI scores and satisfaction with intercourse frequency in heterosexual women (N = 74). They also found a significant positive relationship between sexual arousability and heterosexual attitude and significant negative relationships with sexual anxiety and trait anxiety. Trait anxiety was not significantly related to sexual anxiety, which implies that these two forms of anxiety are independent entities.

Discriminant validity has been demonstrated between normal and sexually dysfunctional women, with the mean score of the latter falling at the 5th percentile of the former (Hoon et al., 1976). Significant and theoretically interpretable response differences to specific items have been found according to sex (Hoon & Hoon, 1977), experience with cohabitation (Hoon & Hoon, 1982), orientation (Coleman et al., 1983), and distinct styles of sexual expression (Hoon & Hoon, 1978).

Anxiety, female samples. The initial stages of validation of the anxiety scale yielded encouraging results. Validity data were collected on two samples of women by Chambless and Lifshitz (1984), who predicted the anxiety scale should be negatively correlated with frequency of orgasm and with greater sexual experience. In the undergraduate sample (N = 252), the more sexually experienced were found to be significantly less anxious (tau = −.14), and in a sample of community women (N = 90), higher frequency of coital orgasm was significantly associated with lower anxiety (tau = −.25).

A principal components analysis with oblique rotation was conducted on the undergraduate responses. Three interpretable factors, accounting for 61% of the variance, were extracted. Factor 1 (45%) and Factor 3 (5%) were similar in being general factors defined more by their exclusion of pornography and masturbation than by items they included. Factor 1, however, seemed more related to intercourse and foreplay, whereas Factor 3 was weighted more heavily with items concerning noncoital genital stimulation. Factor 2 (12%) concerned pornography and masturbation. These factors are similar in content to three of those on the arousability scale, indicating these may be consistent dimensions of sexual stimuli. The two factors pertaining to partner sex were modestly negatively correlated with the masturbation factor.

Arousability and anxiety, male samples. Validity information on the SAI-E and SAI is unavailable for men.

Other Information

Samples of the measure, factor analytic information, item means and standard deviation are available from the first author.

References

Burgess, D., & Krop, H. (1978, October). *The relationship between sexual arousability, heterosexual attitudes, sexual anxiety, and general anxiety in women.* Paper presented at the South East Regional American Association of Sex Educators, Counselors and Therapists, Asheville, NC.

Chambless, D. L., & Lifshitz, J. L. (1984). Self-reported sexual anxiety and arousal: The Expanded Sexual Arousability Inventory. *The Journal of Sex Research, 20,* 241–254.

Coleman, E., Hoon, P. W., & Hoon, E. F. (1983). Arousability and sexual satisfaction in lesbian and heterosexual women. *The Journal of Sex Research, 19,* 58–73.

Flax, C. C. (1980). *Comparison between married women with ileostomies and married women without ileostomies on sexual anxiety, control, arousability and fantasy.* Unpublished doctoral dissertation, New York University, New York.

Hoon, E. F., & Hoon, P. W. (1977, September). *Sexual differences between males and females on a self-report measure.* Paper presented at the Fifth Annual Canadian Sex Research Forum, Banff, Alberta.

Hoon, E. F., & Hoon, P. W. (1978). Styles of sexual expression in women: Clinical implications of multivariate analyses. *Archives of Sexual Behavior, 7,* 106–116.

Hoon, E. F., Hoon, P. W., & Wincze, J. P. (1976). The SAI: An inventory for the measurement of female sexual arousability. *Archives of Sexual Behavior, 5,* 291–300.

Hoon, P. W., & Hoon, E. F. (1982). Effects of experience in cohabitation on erotic arousability. *Psychological Reports, 50,* 255–258.

Murphy, W., Coleman, E., Hoon, E. F., & Scott, C. (1980). Sexual dysfunction and treatment in alcoholic women. *Sexuality and Disability, 3,* 240–255.

Exhibit

Sexual Arousability Inventory

Instructions: The experiences in this inventory may or may not be sexually arousing to you. There are no right or wrong answers. Read each item carefully, and then circle the number which indicates how sexually aroused you feel when you have the described experience, or how sexually aroused you think you would feel if you actually experienced it. *Be sure to answer every item.* If you aren't certain about an item, circle the number than seems about right. Rate feelings of arousal according to the scale below.

-1 adversely affects arousal; unthinkable, repulsive, distracting
 0 doesn't affect sexual arousal
 1 possibly causes sexual arousal
 2 sometimes causes sexual arousal; slightly arousing
 3 usually causes sexual arousal; moderately arousing
 4 almost always sexually arousing; very arousing
 5 always causes sexual arousal; extremely arousing

* 1. When a loved one stimulates your genitals with mouth and tongue[a]
* 2. When a loved one fondles your breasts with his/her hands
  3. When you see a loved one nude
  4. When a loved one caresses you with his/her eyes
* 5. When a loved one stimulates your genitals with his/her finger
* 6. When you are touched or kissed on the inner thighs by a loved one
  7. When you caress a loved one's genitals with your fingers
  8. When you read a pornographic or "dirty" story
* 9. When a loved one undresses you
*10. When you dance with a loved one
*11. When you have intercourse with a loved one
*12. When a loved one touches or kisses your nipples
 13. When you caress a loved one (other than genitals)
*14. When you see pornographic pictures or slides
*15. When you lie in bed with a loved one
*16. When a loved one kisses you passionately
 17. When you hear sounds of pleasure during sex
*18. When a loved one kisses you with an exploring tongue
*19. When you read suggestive or pornographic poetry
 20. When you see a strip show
 21. When you stimulate your partner's genitals with your mouth and tongue
 22. When a loved one caresses you (other than genitals)
 23. When you see a pornographic movie (stag film)
 24. When you undress a loved one
 25. When a loved one fondles your breasts with mouth and tongue
*26. When you make love in a new or unusual place
 27. When you masturbate
 28. When your partner has an orgasm

Note. Asterisks indicate those items comprising shortened form A. Form B consists of items without asterisks.
[a]The seven response options are repeated following each item.

Sexual Anxiety Inventory

Now rate each of the items according to how anxious you feel when you have the described experience. The meaning of anxiety is extreme uneasiness, distress. Rate feelings of anxiety according to the scale below:

  −1 relaxing, calming
   0 no anxiety
   1 possibly causes some anxiety
   2 sometimes causes anxiety; slightly anxiety producing
   3 usually causes anxiety; moderately anxiety producing
   4 almost always causes anxiety; very anxiety producing
   5 always causes anxiety; extremely anxiety producing

 1. When a loved one stimulates your genitals with mouth and tongue[a]
 2. When a loved one fondles your breasts with his/her hands
 3. When you see a loved one nude
 4. When a loved one caresses you with his/her eyes
 5. When a loved one stimulates your genitals with his/her finger
 6. When you are touched or kissed on the inner thighs by a loved one
 7. When you caress a loved one's genitals with your fingers
 8. When you read a pornographic or "dirty" story
 9. When a loved one undresses you
10. When you dance with a loved one
11. When you have intercourse with a loved one
12. When a loved one touches or kisses your nipples
13. When you caress a loved one (other than genitals)
14. When you see pornographic pictures or slides
15. When you lie in bed with a loved one
16. When a loved one kisses you passionately
17. When you hear sounds of pleasure during sex
18. When a loved one kisses you with an exploring tongue
19. When you read suggestive or pornographic poetry
20. When you see a strip show
21. When you stimulate your partner's genitals with your mouth and tongue
22. When a loved one caresses you (other than genitals)
23. When you see a pornographic movie (stag film)
24. When you undress a loved one
25. When a loved one fondles your breasts with mouth and tongue
26. When you make love in a new or unusual place
27. When you masturbate
28. When your partner has an orgasm

[a]The seven response options are repeated following each item.

Multiple Indicators of Subjective Sexual Arousal

DONALD L. MOSHER,[1] *University of Connecticut*

Three self-report measures of subjective sexual arousal were developed to serve as standard measures. Construction of the measures was designed to permit comparison of male and female subjective sexual arousal. To secure more uniform measurement across laboratories, item selection and analysis were guided by past research and theory, and careful attention was paid to the psychometric properties of the measures. From the perspective of involvement theory (Mosher, 1980), *subjective sexual arousal* is defined as a specific *affect-cognition* blend, in consciousness, of physiological sexual arousal with its accompanying sexual affects. The multiple indicators of self-reported sexual arousal were derived from past research that had variously used Likert-type rating scales (Jakobovits, 1965; Mosher & Abramson, 1977; Schmidt & Sigusch, 1970), adjective checklists (Mosher & Abramson, 1977; Mosher & Greenberg, 1969), and a checklist of genital sensations (Mosher & Abramson, 1977; Schmidt & Sigusch, 1970). Mosher, Barton-Henry, and Green (1988) developed the three measures of subjective sexual arousal presented here.

Descriptions and Scoring

Ratings of Sexual Arousal consists of the five items, selected from a pool of 11 items, yielding the highest alpha coefficients across self-reports to four types of erotic fantasies. The five items selected were sexual arousal, genital sensations, sexual warmth, nongenital physical sensations, and sexual absorption. Each item is further defined: for example, "Sexual Warmth—a subjective estimate of the amount of sexual warmth experienced in the genitals, breasts, and body as a function of increasing vasocongestion (i.e., engorgement with blood)." If a sixth item is desired, the next best item is "Sexual Tension—subjective estimate of the sexual tension that presses toward release." A 7-point Likert-type format is used to rate the items with anchors of, for example, 1, *no sexual arousal at all* to 7, *extremely sexually aroused*. This measure is appropriate for educated populations of men and women. The definitions of the concepts include technical vocabulary.

Respondents respond to these instructions: "For each item, place a circle around the number that best describes how you felt during the experience." Average completion time is 2 minutes. Scores are summed and a mean item score can be calculated. Higher scores indicate more subjective sexual arousal.

Affective Sexual Arousal consists of five adjective prompts selected from a pool of 10 items embedded in a 70-item adjective checklist patterned after the Differential Emotions Scale (Izard, Doughty, Bloxom, & Kotsch, 1974; Mosher & White, 1981). The adjective prompts that were included, following the item analysis across the four erotic fantasies, were sexually aroused, sensuous, turned-on, sexually hot, and sexually excited. If a sixth item is needed, it should be "sexy." Each adjective prompt was rated on a 5-point Likert-type scale as follows: 1, *very slightly or not at all*; 2, *slightly*; 3, *moderately*; 4, *considerably*; or 5, *very strongly*. This measure of subjective sexual arousal contains standard and slang vocabulary understandable by both men and women, but it probably should be embedded within an affect adjective checklist.

Respondents respond by circling the number which best describes "how they felt during the experience." Completion time can be estimated at 10 items per minute if embedded in a larger affect checklist. Scores are summed across the five items, and a mean item score can be computed. Higher scores indicate more subjective sexual arousal.

Genital Sensations is an 11-item checklist modified from earlier versions of self-reports of genital sensations (Mosher & Abramson, 1977; Schmidt & Sigusch, 1970) by placing the items in an ordinal order and by writing brief descriptions of the genital sensations and bodily responses. The 11 items are as follows: no genital sensations, onset of genital sensations, mild genital sensations, moderate genital sensations, prolonged moderate genital sensations, intense genital sensations, prolonged intense genital sensations, mild orgasm, moderate orgasm, intense orgasm, and multiple orgasm. An example of the definitions given is "(4) Moderate genital sensations—vasocongestion sufficient to erect penis fully or to lubricate vagina fully." The vocabulary is appropriate for educated populations, but the arrangement into an ordered scale educates and helps a less educated group to respond.

Respondents check the peak or highest level of genital sensations felt during the experience, and, thus, achieve a score of 1 to 11. The measure requires 2 to 3 minutes to complete.

Reliability

Cronbach alpha coefficients for the two 5-item measures—Ratings of Sexual Arousal and Affective Sexual Arousal—in a sample of 120 male and 121 female college students, as measured across four fantasy conditions, ranged from .92 to .97 and were robust across erotic conditions (Mosher et al., 1988). Median Cronbach alpha coefficients for Ratings of Sexual Arousal were .97 and for Affective Sexual Arousal were .96.

---

[1]Address correspondence to Donald L. Mosher, 648 Ternberry Forest Drive, The Villages, FL 32162; e-mail: dlmosher@aol.com

Validity

Evidence of convergent validity between the measures when cast into an intercorrelation matrix was strong, with a median validity coefficient—same scale across erotic conditions—of .52. Intercorrelations of the three measures of subjective sexual arousal within an erotic condition revealed median intercorrelations of approximately .81 for Ratings of Sexual Arousal with Affective Sexual Arousal, .74 for Ratings of Sexual Arousal with Sensations, and .69 of Affective Sexual Arousal with Genital Sensations (Mosher et al., 1988). Further evidence of construct validity is available in the body of literature cited above which used similar measures.

References

Izard, C. E., Dougherty, F. E., Bloxom, B. M., & Kotsch, W. E. (1974). *The Differential Emotions Scale: A method of measuring the subjective experience of discrete emotions.* Unpublished manuscript, Department of Psychology, Vanderbilt University.

Jakobovits, L. (1965). Evaluational reactions to erotic literature. *Psychological Reports, 16,* 985–994.

Mosher, D. L. (1980). Three dimensions of depth of involvement in human sexual response. *The Journal of Sex Research, 16,* 1–42.

Mosher, D. L. (1984). *Sexual desire in involvement theory: Sexual motivators.* Unpublished manuscript.

Mosher, D. L., & Abramson, P. R. (1977). Subjective sexual arousal to films of masturbation. *Journal of Consulting and Clinical Psychology, 35,* 796–807.

Mosher, D. L., Barton-Henry, M., & Green, S. E. (1988). Subjective sexual arousal and involvement theory: Development of multiple indicators. *The Journal of Sex Research, 25,* 412–425.

Mosher, D. L., & Greenberg, I. (1969). Females' affective responses to reading erotic literature. *Journal of Consulting and Clinical Psychology, 33,* 472–477.

Mosher, D. L., & White, B. B. (1981). On differentiating shame from shyness. *Motivation and Emotions, 5,* 61–74.

Schmidt, G., & Sigusch, V. (1970). Sex differences in responses to psychosexual stimulation by films and slides. *The Journal of Sex Research, 6,* 268–283.

Exhibit

Multiple Indicators of Subjective Sexual Arousal

Ratings of Sexual Arousal

Instructions: For each item, place a circle around one number that best described how you felt during the experience.

1. Sexual Arousal—a subjective estimate of your overall level of sexual arousal.

   1   2   3   4   5   6   7
  No sexual   Extremely
  arousal at all   sexually aroused

2. Genital Sensations—a subjective estimate of the amount and quality of sensation experienced in your genitals.

   1   2   3   4   5   6   7
  No   Extreme
  sensation at all   genital sensation

3. Sexual Warmth—a subjective estimate of the amount of sexual warmth experienced in the genitals, breasts and body as a function of increasing vasocongestion, i.e., engorgement with blood.

   1   2   3   4   5   6   7
  No sexual   Extreme
  warmth at all   sexual warmth

4. Non-Genital Physical Sensations—a subjective estimate of the physical sensations such as tickling, floating, or fullness that accompany your experience of sexual arousal.

   1   2   3   4   5   6   7
  No   Extreme
  sensation at all   non-genital
                                                      physical sensation

5. Sexual Absorption—a subjective estimate of your level of absorption in the sensory components of the experience.

   1   2   3   4   5   6   7
  No   Extreme
  absorption at all   absorption

Ratings of Affective Sexual Arousal

Instructions:[a] This scale consists of a number of words that describe different emotions or feelings. Please indicate the extent to which each word describes the way you felt during the preceding experiences. Record your answers by indicating the appropriate number on the five-point scale on the attached answer sheet. Presented below is the scale for indicating the degree to which each word describes the way you feel.

1	2	3	4	5
Very slightly	Slightly	Moderately	Considerably	Very strongly

In deciding on your answer to a given item or word, consider the feeling connoted or defined by that word. Then, if during the experience you felt that way *very slightly* or *not at all*, you would darken the blank under the number 1 on the scale; if you felt that way to a *moderate* degree, you would darken the blank under 3; if you felt that way *very strongly*, you would darken the circle under 5, and so forth.

Remember, you are requested to make your responses on the basis of the way you felt during the experience. Work at a good pace. It is not necessary to ponder; the first answer you decide on for a given word is probably the most valid. It should not take more than a few minutes to complete the scale.

Items:
1. Sexually aroused
2. Sensuous
3. Turned-on
4. Sexually hot
5. Sexually excited

Ratings of Genital Sensations

Instructions: Genital sensations refer to sensory sensations in the genital region that accompany any source of somatogenic or psychogenic sexual stimulation and that are a function of increasing vasocongestion in the genital area. Males experience these sensations as accompaniments of penile erections and females experience these sensations as a function of the engorgement of the labia and the orgasmic platform in the vagina with accompanying vaginal lubrication. Below, indicate the peak level of genital sensation that you felt during the experience. The items are:

_____ 1. No genital sensations.
_____ 2. Onset of genital sensations—onset of swelling of penis or vulva or nipple erection.
_____ 3. Mild genital sensations—vascongestion sufficient to begin penile erection or to begin vaginal lubrication.
_____ 4. Moderate genital sensations—vasocongestion sufficient to erect penis fully or to lubricate vagina fully.
_____ 5. Prolonged moderate genital sensations—maintain erection for several minutes or considerable vaginal lubrication for several minutes.
_____ 6. Intense genital sensations—hard or pulsing erection and elevation of testicles in the scrotum; or receptive, engorged vagina or sex flush, or breast swelling or retraction of clitoris or ballooning of vagina.
_____ 7. Prolonged intense genital sensations—near orgasmic levels of genital sensations; swelling of head of penis or high levels of muscular tension or heavy breathing or high heart rate; lasting several minutes and will produce orgasm if continued.
_____ 8. Mild orgasm—mild orgasmic release, slow reduction of vasocongestion, 3–5 contractions.
_____ 9. Moderate orgasm—moderate orgasmic release, average time to resolution of vascongestion, 5–8 contractions.
_____ 10. Intense orgasm—intense orgasmic release with rapid resolution of vasocongestion, 8–12 contractions.
_____ 11. Multiple orgasm—repeated orgasmic release in a single sexual episode.

[a]These instructions assume the five sexual prompts are embedded within a longer affect adjective checklist.

Hurlbert Index of Sexual Assertiveness

David F. Hurlbert,[1] *U.S. Department of Health and Human Services*

The Hurlbert Index of Sexual Assertiveness (HISA) is described by Hurlbert (1991).

Reference

Hurlbert, D. F. (1991). The role of assertiveness in female sexuality: A comparative study between sexually assertive and sexually nonassertive women. *Journal of Sex & Marital Therapy, 17,* 183–190.

Exhibit

Hulbert Index of Sexual Assertiveness

This inventory is designed to measure the degree of sexual assertiveness you have in the sexual relationship with your partner. This is not a test, so there are no right or wrong answers. Please answer each item as accurately as you can by placing a number by each question as follows:

0 = All of the time
1 = Most of the time
2 = Some of the time
3 = Rarely
4 = Never

1. I feel uncomfortable talking during sex.
2. I feel that I am shy when it comes to sex.
3. I approach my partner for sex when I desire it.
4. I think I am open with my partner about my sexual needs.
5. I enjoy sharing my sexual fantasies with my partner.
6. I feel uncomfortable talking to my friends about sex.
7. I communicate my sexual desires to my partner.
8. It is difficult for me to touch myself during sex.
9. It is hard for me to say no even when I do not want sex.
10. I am reluctant to describe myself as a sexual person.
11. I feel uncomfortable telling my partner what feels good.
12. I speak up for my sexual feelings.
13. I am reluctant to insist that my partner satisfy me.
14. I find myself having sex when I do not really want it.
15. When a technique does not feel good, I tell my partner.
16. I feel comfortable giving sexual praise to my partner.
17. It is easy for me to discuss sex with my partner.
18. I feel comfortable in initiating sex with my partner.
19. I find myself doing sexual things that I do not like.
20. Pleasing my partner is more important than my pleasure.
21. I feel comfortable telling my partner how to touch me.
22. I enjoy masturbating myself to orgasm.
23. If something feels good, I insist on doing it again.
24. It is hard for me to be honest about my sexual feelings.
25. I try to avoid discussing the subject of sex.

Note. Reverse-score item numbers: 3, 4, 5, 7, 12, 15, 16, 17, 18, 21, 22, and 23.

[1]Address correspondence to David F. Hurlbert, 140 Farnworth Lane Roswell, Georgia 30075; e-mail: david.hurlbert@acf.hhs.gov

Intimate Relationships Questionnaire

GEORGIA YESMONT,[1] *Hofstra University*

The Intimate Relationships Questionnaire (IRQ) was created to measure assertive, nonassertive, and aggressive tendencies specific to safer-sex behaviors in unmarried adolescents and young adults (Yesmont, 1992b). The AIDS epidemic has highlighted the serious health problems created by less fatal, yet more prevalent, sexually transmitted diseases (STDs). The rates of STDs are highest in the young adult population. The IRQ is a convenient and promising measure that is easily incorporated into assertiveness training to increase safer-sex behaviors and reduce the incidence of STDs. The IRQ offers a structured format that can be used in an individual or group setting, or with couples. It may be used in conjunction with role-play and rehearsal of precautionary behaviors and to identify those aspects of safer sex behaviors that are especially difficult for respondents.

Description

The IRQ consists of 10 items, each with three response alternatives that measure assertive, nonassertive, and aggressive tendencies. The items describe intimate situations involving the precautionary behaviors of condom use, asking a date about his (her) STD history, about prior AIDS testing, and wanting to know a date better before engaging in sexual intercourse. The assertive, nonassertive, and aggressive responses are randomly sequenced throughout the items. There are an additional four items (1, 3, 5, and 8), pertaining to nonsexual intimate situations that are included as detractors. The IRQ items present the three types of responses in a 5-point Likert scale, from (1) *not at all like me* to (5) *just like me*. Respondents are asked to rate each alternative according to their own probable cognitive or behavioral response in each scenario.

The precautionary sex situations were inspired by research in AIDS-prevention programs (Kelly, St. Lawrence, Hood, & Bransfield, 1989; Rotheram-Borus & Koopman, 1989). The assertive, nonassertive, and aggressive response alternatives were formulated from the most universally accepted definitions of these terms (Alberti & Emmons, 1986).

In a content validation procedure, a panel of clinicians rated the three response alternatives according to the given definitions of the three assertiveness dimensions. Further revisions resulted in the present content that had been unanimously rated by a second group of clinicians, according to the intended conceptualizations of assertiveness.

Although the IRQ was normed on predominantly heterosexual college students, its gender-nonspecific format renders it useful for individuals with other sexual orientations.

Response Mode and Timing

Respondents circle the number from 1 to 5 on each of the three alternatives to every test item, according to their self-perceived similarity to the proposed response. The IRQ requires approximately 10 minutes to complete.

Scoring

The numerical values of the Likert-type choices (1 to 5) are summed for each assertiveness dimension (assertiveness, nonassertiveness and aggression) according to the response key. The answers to the detractor items (1, 3, 5 and 8) are not added into the score. The score range is from 10 to 50, with larger sums representing a stronger response tendency. Correlational analysis of the IRQ assertiveness dimensions revealed a significantly positive relationship between assertive and aggressive scores, $r = .15$ and a significantly negative relationship between assertiveness and nonassertiveness, $r = -.21$ (Yesmont, 1992a). Nonassertive and aggressive scores were unrelated.

Reliability

In a sample of 253 unmarried, predominantly white undergraduates (159 females; 94 males), the Cronbach alphas for the three assertiveness categories on the safer sex questions were as follows: assertiveness, .77; aggressiveness, .67, and nonassertiveness, .71 (Yesmont, 1992b). Using a Spanish version of the IRQ, Batista (1995) reported similar alpha coefficients in a sample of 103 older high school students in Puerto Rico (assertiveness, .76; aggressiveness, .76, and nonassertiveness, .76).

Validity

In the Yesmont study (1992b), the college students' IRQ assertiveness scores were significantly correlated with their degree of using Caution in a new, intimate relationship ($r = .35$) and Asking (inquiry about drug use, STD history, prior contact with high-risk partners and AIDS testing;) $r = .36$. Their aggressiveness scores also were significantly related to Caution, $r = .22$ and Asking, $r = .19$. As predicted, the students' nonassertiveness scores correlated negatively and significantly with their degree of Caution ($r = -.41$) and Asking ($r = -.34$).

IRQ assertiveness was significantly correlated to the percentage of time that condoms were used for coitus, $r = .24$. IRQ nonassertiveness had a significantly negative relationship to condom use, as expected, $r = -.25$.

[1]Address correspondence to Georgia Yesmont, Life Span Services, 14 Ketewomoke Drive, Huntington, NY 11743; e-mail: DoctorGeorgia@optonline.net

The students who reported 100% condom use, as compared to nonusers, had higher assertiveness scores ($M = 35.01$ vs. $M = 33.74$), $t(87) = -2.17$, $p < .05$ and significantly lower nonassertiveness scores ($M = 14.65$ vs. $M = 19.53$), $t(85) = 4.95$, $p < .001$. The females were significantly more assertive and aggressive on the IRQ than the males. Conversely, the males endorsed nonassertive responses to a significantly greater extent than the females.

References

Alberti, R. E., & Emmons, M. L. (1986). *Your perfect right: A guide to assertive living*. San Luis Obispo, CA: Impact Publishers.

Batista, N. (1995). *The design and evaluation of a counseling intervention program in sexual assertiveness in adolescents*. Unpublished doctoral dissertation. University of Puerto Rico, Rio Piedras.

Kelly, J. A., St. Lawrence, J. S., Hood, H. V., & Brasfield, T. L. (1989). Behavioral intervention to reduce AIDS risk activities. *Journal of Counseling and Clinical Psychology, 57*, 60–67.

Rotheram-Borus, M. J., & Koopman, C. (1989, January). *Research on AIDS prevention among runaways: The state of the art and recommendations for the future*. Paper presented at the National Institute of Child Health and Human Development Technical Review and Research Planning Meeting on Adolescents and HIV Infection. Bethesda, MD.

Yesmont, G. (1992a, April). *The development of the Intimate Relationships Questionnaire*. Paper presented at the 63rd Annual Meeting of the Eastern Psychological Association. Boston, MA.

Yesmont, G. (1992b). The relationship of assertiveness to college students' safer sex behaviors. *Adolescence, 27*, 253–272.

Exhibit

Intimate Relationships Questionnaire

Each item below describes a situation and three responses that are thoughts or behaviors. These intimate situations involve a dating couple. Try to imagine a situation in your life that is as close to the one described as possible.

After reading each item, circle a number to the right of each response, indicating how similar it might be to the thought you might have or the behavior you might show, in the actual situation.

Please rate every response to each situation. Use the following scale for your ratings:

1	2	3	4	5
Not at all like me	Slightly like me	Somewhat like me	Mostly like me	Just like me

1. During the past few weeks your boyfriend (girlfriend) seems less enthusiastic and caring about your relationship.
    (AG)[a]   a. You'll decide to confront him (her) on your next date and let out your angry feelings.   1 2 3 4 5
    (NON)   b. You'll wait for him (her) to call you and you'll complain to your friends.   1 2 3 4 5
    (AS)   c. You'll decide to speak to him (her) frankly and suggest you try to work things out.   1 2 3 4 5

2. When your date says he (she) won't have sex with you if you insist on using a condom, you say. . .
    (AS)   a. O.K. Then how about trying some other things besides intercourse?   1 2 3 4 5
    (AG)   b. Your attitude doesn't make any sense! That's it for us. Let's go home.   1 2 3 4 5
    (NON)   c. O.K. You're more important to me, we don't need to use it.   1 2 3 4 5

3. You're at a party with your boyfriend (girlfriend) and notice that he (she) is very attentive to someone of the opposite sex that you've never seen before. You think. . .
    (NON)   a. I'll make the best of it—after all, he's (she's) going home with me tonight.   1 2 3 4 5
    (AS)   b. I really would like more of his (her) attention tonight and I'm going to tell him (her).   1 2 3 4 5
    (AG)   c. How could he (she) ignore me like this—I'll find someone on my own I can talk to and make him (her) jealous.   1 2 3 4 5

4. You want to tell your date that you'd like to use a condom when making love tonight and you think. . .
    (AS)   a. If I can't convince him (her) to use a condom tonight, we can find other safe ways of enjoying ourselves for now.   1 2 3 4 5
    (NON)   b. Using a condom is a good idea but I don't think I have the nerve to ask him (her) to use one.   1 2 3 4 5
    (AG)   c. He (she) should do what I ask without any hesitation if he (she) loves me.   1 2 3 4 5

5. Your boyfriend (girlfriend) gets silent instead of saying what's on his (her) mind. You think. . .
    (AG)   a. Here it comes. The big silent treatment. I'm going to get mad and force him (her) to talk to me.   1 2 3 4 5

(NON) b. If I make a joke and distract him (her), maybe he'll (she'll) forget what's bothering him (her).   1 2 3 4 5

(AS) c. I'll tell him (her) it bothers me when he (she) gets silent because it leaves me confused about what he's (she's) thinking.   1 2 3 4 5

6. When you're asked by your date if you have any disease that you could give him (her) if you make love that night, you think. . .

(AG) a. Who does he (she) think I am—some degenerate who runs around infecting people?   1 2 3 4 5

(AS) b. I'm glad he (she) asked because it gives me a chance to ask the same question.   1 2 3 4 5

(NON) c. I'd better answer or he (she) may get annoyed with me.   1 2 3 4 5

7. When your date asks you if you agree to using a condom when you both make love tonight, you think. . .

(AG) a. This is a turn-off. I don't want anybody telling me what we should do when we make love.   1 2 3 4 5

(NON) b. I'd better do what he (she) says or he'll (she'll) be frustrated tonight.   1 2 3 4 5

(AS) c. I'm glad he (she) brought this up, now we're both protected.   1 2 3 4 5

8. Your boyfriend (girlfriend) has criticized your appearance in front of your friends. You say. . .

(AS) a. It hurt my feelings when you criticized me. If you have something to say, please bring it up before we go out.   1 2 3 4 5

(AG) b. How could you do such a rotten thing to me? If you do that again—we're through!   1 2 3 4 5

(NON) c. I guess I don't look so great tonight since you criticized me in front of my friends.   1 2 3 4 5

9. When you suggest to your date that a condom be used for mutual protection when you make love tonight, your date teases you about being such a worrier. . .

(NON) a. You then become silent for a while, until he (she) comes around to agreeing with you.   1 2 3 4 5

(AS) b. You then tell your date you'd love to make love with him (her), but you always use condoms.   1 2 3 4 5

(AG) c. You then tell your date he's (she's) being really immature.   1 2 3 4 5

10. You want to ask if your date's been tested for AIDS and you say. . .

(NON) a. I was wondering about. . . well this is embarrassing to talk about. . . but. . . have you ever been tested for AIDS? You don't have to answer that if you don't want to.   1 2 3 4 5

(AG) b. I want you to tell me right now if you've been tested for AIDS.   1 2 3 4 5

(AS) c. I really like you a lot, but with all this talk about AIDS, I'd like to be a little careful. I've been tested for AIDS, have you?   1 2 3 4 5

11. If your date refuses to use a condom you think. . .

(AS) a. I can find out what he (she) has against them and we can talk about it.   1 2 3 4 5

(NON) b. I'm afraid he (she) won't want to see me again if I insist.   1 2 3 4 5

(AG) c. If he (she) won't do what I say—that's it for us.   1 2 3 4 5

12. When neither you nor your date has any condoms one evening, you say. . .

(NON) a. Oh. . . that's O.K. I suppose we can do it just once without one.   1 2 3 4 5

(AG) b. That's irresponsible. If you like me you'd always have them when we're together.   1 2 3 4 5

(AS) c. I don't have any either, but we can satisfy each other without intercourse tonight.   1 2 3 4 5

13. You tell your date that you'd like to wait until know each other a little you better before having sex. When he (she) gets annoyed you would. . .

(AG) a. Tell your date that you couldn't go out with someone who argues with you about this.   1 2 3 4 5

(AS) b. Re-state your feeling that you'd like to wait.   1 2 3 4 5

(NON) c. Change your mind and have sex with him (her) sooner than you'd planned.   1 2 3 4 5

14. When you suggest to your date that you a condom be used when you make love tonight, he (she) says, "You don't trust me. I told you I've never been exposed to AIDS or herpes, or any other disease."

(AS) a. You say, "I'm sorry, but we have no way of knowing that. I'd feel so much better if we used condoms."   1 2 3 4 5

(AG) b. You say, "It's not a question of trust. You don't understand what I'm saying."   1 2 3 4 5

(NON) c. You say, "I'm sorry. I do trust you. Let's drop the whole subject. I don't want to argue."   1 2 3 4 5

---

[a]Response classification: AG = Aggressive; AS = Assertive; NON = Nonassertive

Attitudes Toward Sexuality Scale

TERRI D. FISHER,[1] *The Ohio State University at Mansfield*

The Attitudes Toward Sexuality Scale (ATSS) was developed to allow the comparison of the sexual attitudes of adolescents between the ages of 12 and 20 and their parents. An instrument was needed that was brief, simplistic, and nonoffensive in order to facilitate its use with younger adolescents and yet still be valid for adults. To this end, items from Calderwood's Checklist of Attitudes Toward Human Sexuality (1971) were modified and an objective scoring system was added. The result was a brief, general sexual attitudes measure that is equally appropriate for adolescents and adults (Fisher & Hall, 1988).

Description

The ATSS consists of 13 statements related to topics such as nudity, abortion, contraception, premarital sex, pornography, prostitution, homosexuality, and sexually transmitted diseases. The 5-point Likert response format ranges from *Strongly Disagree* to *Strongly Agree*. The original scale contained 14 items, but one of the items contributed so little to the total score variance that it was dropped from the scale. Several of the terms used in the scale have dropped out of usage since its development. The exhibit indicates the newer terminology that researchers would likely wish to use, with the original terms indicated in brackets.

Response Mode and Timing

Respondents indicate the degree of their agreement/disagreement with the statement by circling the number on the response scale that most closely reflects their reaction. The ATSS requires no more than 5 minutes to complete.

Scoring

Items 1, 4, 5, 7, 8, 11, and 13 are reverse scored by assigning a score of 1 if 5 was marked, a score of 2 if 4 was marked, etc. Then the number of points is totaled. Scores can range from 13 to 65, with lower scores indicating greater conservatism about sexual matters and higher scores indicating greater permissiveness about sexual matters.

Reliability

For a sample of 35 early adolescents (ages 12–14), the Cronbach alpha coefficient was .76. Among 47 middle adolescents (ages 15–17), the alpha was .65, and for a group of 59 late adolescents (18–20 years old) the alpha was .80. The alpha for the total group of adolescents was .75. Among 141 parents (ages 31–66), the alpha was .84. The test-retest reliability coefficient, using an independent sample of 22 college students between the ages of 18 and 28 over a 1-month time period, was .90.

Validity

In a sample of college students between the ages of 18 and 28 (Fisher & Hall, 1988), the ATSS correlated highly with the Heterosexual Relations (Liberalism) scale of the Sexual Knowledge and Attitudes Test (SKAT; Lief & Reed, 1972), $r(42) = .83$. The ATSS was also correlated with the Abortion scale, $r(42) = .70$, the Autoeroticism scale $r(42) = .54$, and the Sexual Myths scale, $r(42) = .59$.

In studies of adolescents and their parents (Fisher, 1986; Fisher & Hall, 1988), age was negatively correlated with the ATSS score, $r(280) = -.18$, although, for the young and middle adolescents combined, age was positively related to the ATSS score, $r(82) = .37$. Amount of education was found to be significantly correlated with the total scale score for the adult subjects, $r(139) = .20$. Religiosity, as measured by church attendance, was significantly correlated to ATSS scores for the middle adolescents, $r(45) = -.32$; the older adolescents, $r(57) = -.44$; and the adults, $r(139) = -.41$, such that people who regularly attended church tended to be more conservative in their sexual attitudes. Chia (2006) reported that adolescents with more permissive scores on a slightly modified version of the ATSS were significantly more likely to report having experienced sexual intercourse, having experienced it at an earlier age, and having experienced it in more casual situations.

As has been found on other measures of sexual attitudes, males generally indicate more permissive sexual attitudes on the ATSS than females. In more recent research with this measure, sex difference was mixed, with Fisher (2007) reporting a significant sex difference, but no sex differences found in other studies with similar samples (Alexander & Fisher, 2003; Fisher, 2009).

Other Information

Richard G. Hall assisted with the initial development of this scale.

[1]Address correspondence to Terri D. Fisher, The Ohio State University at Mansfield, 1760 University Drive, Mansfield, OH 44906; e-mail: fisher.16@osu.edu

References

Alexander, M. G., & Fisher, T. D. (2003). Truth and consequences: Using the bogus pipeline to examine sex differences in self-reported sexuality. *The Journal of Sex Research, 40,* 27–35.

Calderwood, D. (1971). *About your sexuality.* Boston: Beacon.

Chia, S. C. (2006). How peers mediate media influence on adolescents' sexual attitudes and sexual behavior. *Journal of Communication, 56,* 585–606.

Fisher, T. D. (1986). An exploratory study of parent-child communication about sex and the sexual attitudes of early, middle, and late adolescents. *The Journal of Genetic Psychology, 147,* 543–557.

Fisher, T. D. (2007). Sex of experimenter and social norm effects on reports of sexual behavior in young men and women. *Archives of Sexual Behavior, 36,* 89–100.

Fisher, T. D. (2009). The impact of socially conveyed norms on the reporting of sexual behavior and attitudes by men and women. *Journal of Experimental Social Psychology, 45,* 567–572.

Fisher, T. D., & Hall, R. G. (1988). A scale for the comparison of the sexual attitudes of adolescents and their parents. *The Journal of Sex Research, 24,* 90–100.

Lief, H. I., & Reed, D. M. (1972). *Sex Knowledge and Attitude Test.* Philadelphia: Center for the Study of Sex Education in Medicine, University of Pennsylvania.

Exhibit

Attitudes Toward Sexuality Scale

For each of the following statements, please circle the response which best reflects your reaction to that statement.

1	2	3	4	5
Strongly Disagree	Somewhat Disagree	Neutral	Somewhat Agree	Strongly Agree

1. Nudist camps should be made completely illegal.

1	2	3	4	5

2. Abortion should be made available whenever a woman feels it would be the best decision.[a]
3. Information and advice about contraception (birth control) should be given to any individual who intends to have intercourse.
4. Parents should be informed if their children under the age of eighteen have visited a clinic to obtain a contraceptive device.
5. Our government should try harder to prevent the distribution of pornography.
6. Prostitution should be legalized.
7. Petting (a stimulating caress of any or all parts of the body) is immoral behavior unless the couple is married.
8. Premarital sexual intercourse for young people is unacceptable to me.
9. Sexual intercourse for unmarried young people is acceptable without affection existing if both partners agree.
10. Homosexual behavior is an acceptable variation in sexual orientation [original term: preference].
11. A person who catches a sexually transmitted [original term: venereal] disease is probably getting exactly what he/she deserves.
12. A person's sexual behavior is his/her own business, and nobody should make value judgments about it.
13. Sexual intercourse should only occur between two people who are married to each other.

[a]The 5-point scale is repeated after each item.

Trueblood Sexual Attitudes Questionnaire

ROSEANN HANNON, DAVID HALL,[1] VIANEY GONZALEZ, AND HOLLY CACCIAPAGLIA,
University of the Pacific, Stockton

The original Trueblood Sexual Attitudes Questionnaire (TSAQ) (Trueblood, Hannon, & Hall, 1998) was developed to reliably measure attitude change regarding the most common topics relating to sexual behavior covered in human sexuality courses. The authors were also interested in comparing attitudes by gender, ethnicity, sexual experience, etc. Based on Story's (1979) approach, the TSAQ was divided into sexual attitudes acceptable for oneself versus acceptable for others. TSAQ items were developed based on an analysis of the content of college sexuality course textbooks, with a final scale containing 90 items divided into five subscales: Autoeroticism, Heterosexuality, Homosexuality, Sexual Variations, and Commercial Sex. Topics less directly related to sexual behavior per se (e.g., abortion, marital relationships) were not included. Internal consistency (reliability) was assessed using coefficient alpha, which was .93 for the Self scale and .96 for the Other scale. Subscale coefficients (e.g., Autoeroticism-Self) ranged from .67 to .97, with the lowest coefficients for Heterosexuality and Commercial Sex. The revision (Hannon, Hall, Gonzalez, & Cacciapaglia, 1999) was designed to shorten the scale, replace poor items, and to assess test/retest reliability.

Description

The current questionnaire contains 80 items reflecting Self (40 items) versus Other (40 items) across the five subscales. Each item is rated on a 9-point Likert-type scale, ranging from 1, *I completely disagree* to 9, *I completely agree*. Some questions are reverse scored. For total and subscale scores, higher numbers indicate a more liberal attitude. Questions from the five subscales are randomly ordered within the Self scale. The same 40 questions were reworded to reflect attitudes toward others and then randomly ordered within the Other scale. The following list shows sample items.

The division of the items into Self versus Other, with five major areas of content coverage in each, allows for more refined measurement of attitudes following a sexuality course. Changes in attitudes toward Self versus Others can be compared. One can note differential change in the five content areas, as they may vary in amenability to change. The questionnaire can also be used to study subgroups of particular interest (e.g., ethnic, age, Greek (fraternity/sorority) versus non-Greek. Information from responses to the questionnaire may be used to guide the development of future courses, depending on course goals. Although the scale has been used primarily with college students, there is no reason it cannot be used on other populations. It has been used by Duyan and Duyan (2005), by Petroski, Spears, Dempsey, and Kapalka (2007), and is listed in the GASP Measures Database, an American Psychological Association division site.

Response Mode and Timing

This questionnaire can be implemented as a paper instrument or by using online survey software. It typically takes 15–20 minutes to complete.

Scoring

The mean rating for the 8 questions in each subscale is normally reported, as well as the overall mean rating for Self and Other. The attached questionnaire has the subscale indicated for each question, as well as an R for reverse scoring.

Reliability and Validity

The questionnaire was tested in 1999 on 143 female and 51 male college students (median age = 20) in Northern California. Coefficient alpha was .97 for the entire mea-

TABLE 1
Mean and Standard Deviation for the Basic Scales

	Self	Other
Single test ($N = 194$)	3.47 (1.33)	5.21 (1.92)
Retest ($N = 104$)	3.55 (1.48)	5.24 (2.04)

sure, .93 for the Self scale, and .96 for the Other scale. Test-retest reliability after 3 weeks was .94 ($p < .01$). Caucasians were significantly more liberal on both the Self and Other scales than Asians and Hispanics, who did not differ from each other, $F(2, 157) = 10.86, p < .001$. Gender differences were not significant.

Mean scores for the Self and Other scales for the single test and retesting are shown in Table 1. Test-retest reliability is excellent. Self versus Other comparisons were significantly different on both testings ($p < .001$). As expected, the participants were more liberal about others' behavior than their own.

Coefficient alpha for each subscale is shown in Table 2, along with the mean rating for each of the 10 subscales. Ratings were acceptable for all subscales except

[1]Please address correspondence to David S. Hall, 2111 Lido Circle, Stockton, CA 95207; e-mail: airsafe1@comcast.net

TABLE 2
Mean (SD) and Reliability (Coefficient Alpha) for the Five Subscales

	Self	Other	F	p <
Autoeroticism	4.33 (2.13) .88	6.13 (2.29) .91	260.06	.001
Heterosexuality	4.79 (1.52) .68	4.98 (1.37) .56	5.96	.015
Homosexuality	1.91 (1.57) .91	4.93 (3.15) .98	217.26	.001
Variations	2.90 (1.52) .78	7.96 (2.22) .88	306.05	.001
Commercial Sex	3.43 (1.48) .76	5.07 (1.86) .81	328.06	.001

Heterosexuality. The mean ratings for Self were significantly more conservative than for Other in each of the five areas. The largest mean difference between Self and Other occurred for Homosexuality.

The revised questionnaire had acceptable internal consistency for the total score, the Self and Other scores, and 8 of the 10 subscale scores. The Heterosexuality subscale scores were weaker.

References

Duyan, V., & Duyan, G. (2005). Turkish social work students' attitudes toward sexuality. *Sex Roles, 52,* 697–706. GASP Measures Database. Retrieved October 4, 2008, from apps.psych.utah.edu/psych/gasp/newbindes.jsp

Hannon, R., Hall, D., Gonzalez, V., & Cacciapaglia, H. (1999). Revision and reliability of a measure of sexual attitudes. *Electronic Journal of Human Sexuality, 2.* Retrieved October 4, 2008, from ejhs.org/volume2/hannon/attitudes.htm

Petroski, J., Spears, J., Dempsey, A., & Kapalka, G. M. (2007). Relationship between attachment style and risky sexual behavior. In G.M. Kapalka (Ed.), *Proceedings of the Annual Conference of the New Jersey Counseling Association* (pp. 111–124). Retrieved on April 30, 2009 from www.njcounseling.org/index.php?option=com_docman&task=cat_view&gid=38&Itemid=129

Story, M. D. (1979). A longitudinal study of the effects of a university human sexuality course on attitudes toward human sexuality. *The Journal of Sex Research, 15,* 184–204.

Trueblood, K., Hannon, R., & Hall, D. S. (1998, June). *Development and validation of a measure of sexual attitudes.* Paper presented at the meeting of the Society for the Scientific Study of Sexuality Western Region Annual Conference, Honolulu, HI.

Exhibit

Trueblood Sexual Attitudes Questionnaire

Subscales

1 Masturbation/Erotic

2 Heterosexual

3 Homosexual

4 Variations

5 Commercial

Please answer the following questions about your attitudes toward your personal sexual behavior by writing the number between 1 and 9 that best represents how you feel in response to each question.

1......................2......................3......................4......................5......................6......................7......................8......................9

I Completely
Disagree

I Completely
Agree

_1_ 1. I find that masturbating is an acceptable sexual outlet when I am not currently involved with a partner.

_2_ 2. I would engage in sexual intercourse with my fiancée before marriage.

_3_ 3. I would engage in oral genital sexual stimulation with a partner of the same sex.

_5_ 4. I would watch pornography with my partner to learn new sexual techniques.

_4_ 5. I could be involved in more than one sexual relationship at a time.

_4_ 6. I would find it acceptable to dress in the clothing of the opposite gender if I found it sexually arousing.

_3_ 7. It is acceptable for me to engage in bisexuality.

_1_ 8. Videotaping myself and my partner during sexual activity is acceptable to me if it is arousing.

_5_ 9. I do not believe there should be censorship of sexual materials because I want the freedom to enjoy sexual materials.

_3_ 10. It is acceptable for me to be attracted to members of the same sex as well as members of the opposite sex.

_4_ 11. I would find it acceptable to inflict pain on a consenting individual if I found it sexually arousing.

_4_ 12. I find it acceptable to watch other people engage in sexual activity.

_1_ 13. I personally believe it is acceptable for me to think or daydream about sexual activity.

_5_ 14. I believe I would engage in sex more often if I watched pornography.

_2R_ 15. I would use my sexual activity only for reproduction, not for pleasure.

_1_ 16. When I am engaged in sexual activity with my partner, it is acceptable to fantasize about someone else.

_5_ 17. I would sell my sexual services for money.

_4_ 18. I would enjoy being dominated in a sexual relationship.

_2___ 19. I would use sexual activity for my own personal sexual pleasure.
_4___ 20. I would enjoy being the dominator in a sexual relationship.
_1___ 21. Even if I were married, I would engage in masturbation as an acceptable means of sexual outlet.
_3___ 22. It would be acceptable to me if a member of my own sex made an advance toward me.
_5___ 23. I would watch pornography to enhance my sexual relationships.
_5___ 24. I would appear in sexually explicit entertainment for money.
_3___ 25. I would engage in sexual intercourse with a partner of the same sex.
_1___ 26. I would use erotica (magazines, videos, books) as a means to stimulate sexual arousal for myself.
_2R___ 27. I would engage in sexual intercourse only with my spouse.
_4___ 28. I would find it acceptable to receive a sexually obscene phone call if I found it sexually arousing.
_3___ 29. I would engage in mutual touching with a partner of the same sex.
_3___ 30. It is acceptable for me to engage in homosexuality.
_4___ 31. I would engage in group sex (3 or more people consenting).
_2___ 32. I would engage in sexual intercourse with a person of the opposite sex the first time we met.
_1___ 33. If I were single, I would engage in masturbation as a means of sexual outlet.
_2R___ 34. I would engage in sexual intercourse only if I loved my partner.
_5___ 35. It is acceptable for me to engage in prostitution.
_3___ 36. I consider it acceptable for me to be attracted to members of the same sex.
_2___ 37. I would engage in oral genital sexual stimulation with a partner of the opposite sex.
_5R___ 38. I would not watch pornography because it is harmful.
_2___ 39. I would engage in anal sexual stimulation with a partner of the opposite sex.
_1___ 40. When I am in a sexual relationship, I think it is still acceptable to fantasize about someone else.

The following questions refer to your beliefs about others.

_4___ 41. It is acceptable if other people are involved in more than one sexual relationship at a time.
_1___ 42. While other people are engaged in sexual activity with their partner, it is acceptable for them to fantasize about someone else.
_1___ 43. It is acceptable if other people use erotica (magazines, videos, books) as a means to stimulate sexual arousal for themselves.
_3___ 44. It is acceptable for another person to engage in oral genital sexual stimulation with a partner of the same sex.
_4___ 45. It is acceptable for other people to receive sexually obscene phone calls if they find this sexually arousing.
_1___ 46. It is acceptable for other people to think or daydream about sexual activity.
_5___ 47. It is acceptable for other people to engage in prostitution.
_5___ 48. It is acceptable if other people appear in sexually explicit entertainment for money.
_1___ 49. It is acceptable for other people to engage in masturbation as a means of sexual outlet if they are single.
_5___ 50. It is acceptable for other people to watch pornography to enhance their sexual relationships.
_5R___ 51. Other people should not watch pornography because it is harmful.
_1___ 52. It is acceptable for other people to videotape themselves and their partner during sexual activity if it is arousing to them.
_4___ 53. It is acceptable for other people to engage in group sex (3 or more people consenting).
_3___ 54. It is acceptable for another person to be attracted to members of the same sex as well as the opposite sex.
_3___ 55. It is acceptable if other people find it acceptable when someone of their same sex makes an advance toward them.
_4___ 56. It is acceptable for another person to enjoy being dominated in a sexual relationship.
_2___ 57. It is acceptable for another person to engage in anal sexual stimulation with a partner of the opposite sex.
_5___ 58. It is acceptable if other people watch pornography with their partner to learn new sexual techniques.
_2___ 59. It is acceptable for other people to engage in sexual intercourse with a person of the opposite sex the first time they meet.
_5___ 60. I believe other people would engage in sex more often if they watched pornography.
_3___ 61. It is acceptable for another person to engage in sexual intercourse with a partner of the same sex.
_3___ 62. It is acceptable for other people to engage in homosexual activity.
_1___ 63. Even if they are married, it is acceptable for other people to engage in masturbation as a means of sexual outlet.
_4___ 64. It is acceptable for other people to dress in the clothing of the opposite gender if they find it sexually arousing.
_3___ 65. It is acceptable if other people are attracted to members of the same sex.
_2___ 66. It is acceptable if other people use sexual activity for their personal sexual pleasure.
_2___ 67. It is acceptable if other people engage in sexual intercourse with their fiancée before marriage.
_1___ 68. When they are in a sexual relationship, it is still acceptable for other people to fantasize about someone else.
_2___ 69. It is acceptable for another person to engage in oral genital sexual stimulation with a partner of the opposite sex.

_2R__ 70. It is acceptable if other people engage in sexual intercourse only with a partner they love.

_1__ 71. It is acceptable for other people to use masturbation as a sexual outlet when they are not currently involved with a partner.

_2R__ 72. It is acceptable for other people to use sexual activity only for reproduction, not pleasure.

_4__ 73. It is acceptable for other people to inflict pain on another consenting individual if they find it sexually arousing.

_3__ 74. It is acceptable for another person to engage in mutual touching with a partner of the same sex.

_3__ 75. It is acceptable for other people to engage in bisexuality.

_4__ 76. It is acceptable for another person to enjoy being the dominator in a sexual relationship.

_2R__ 77. It is acceptable if other people only engage in sexual intercourse with their own spouse.

_4__ 78. It is acceptable if another person watches others engage in sexual activity.

_5__ 79. It is acceptable for other people to believe there should not be censorship of sexual materials because they want the freedom to enjoy sexual materials.

_5__ 80. It is acceptable for other people to sell their sexual services for money.

Note. Numbers in the answer space indicate the subscale the question is associated with, and the R is reversed scored. Contact David Hall at airsafe1@comcast.net for a printable copy without scoring information. There is no copyright on this questionnaire.

Sexual Attitudes Scale and Brief Sexual Attitudes Scale

SUSAN S. HENDRICK[1] AND CLYDE HENDRICK, *Texas Tech University*

SEXUAL ATTITUDES SCALE

The Sexual Attitudes Scale (SAS; Hendrick & Hendrick, 1987) was developed to broaden the assessment of sexual attitudes from a heavy reliance on sexual permissiveness to a more comprehensive and multidimensional approach. Although we viewed sexual attitudes as more than just permissiveness, we realized that permissiveness is extremely important and included it as a major aspect of our measurement of sexual attitudes. The SAS was also designed to assess attitudes generically, including maritally, premaritally, and for nonmarital couples. Finally, the scale was intended to be psychometrically sound and to complement rather than duplicate existing measures.

Description

Initial work on the SAS (Hendrick, Hendrick, Slapion-Foote, & Foote, 1985) involved item generation and reduction via principal components analysis (PCA) to a 58-item scale measuring Sexual Permissiveness, Sexual Responsibility, Sexual Communion, Sexual Instrumentality, and Sexual Conventionality. After additional sampling of nearly 1,400 university students from both Florida and Texas and extensive analyses employing PCA with Varimax rotation, 43 items across four factors were retained in a final scale (Hendrick & Hendrick, 1987). Given the nature of PCA, the factors were orthogonal, and the subscales were only modestly related. The subscales and number of items are as follows (the full scale is reproduced in the Exhibit). Permissiveness (21 items) measures a casual, open attitude toward sex. Sexual Practices (7 items) measures responsible (e.g., birth control) and tolerant (e.g., masturbation) sexual attitudes. Communion (9 items) presents sex as an ideal or "peak experience." Finally, Sexual Instrumentality (6 items) reflects sex as a natural, biological, self-oriented aspect of life. The items are all written as statements and are in a Likert format with which the respondent rates his/her degree of agreement. As noted, the scale is appropriate for partnered couples of all types whose relationships have a sexual component.

Response Mode and Timing

Instructions for the SAS are included in the Exhibit. The items are rated on a 5-point basis in a Likert format, with 1 = *strongly agree*, 2 = *moderately agree*, 3 = *neither agree nor disagree*, 4 = *moderately disagree*, and 5 = *strongly disagree*.

Scoring

The lower the score, the greater the endorsement of a subscale, although direction of scoring can be reversed. Two

[1]Address correspondence to Susan S. Hendrick, Department of Psychology, Texas Tech University, Lubbock, TX 79409–2051; e-mail: s.hendrick@ttu.edu

items on the Permissiveness subscale are reverse-scored. The SAS can be completed typically in 10 minutes or less. Scores for a given subscale are represented by subscale mean scores (i.e., total the item scores and divide by the number of items). We have not found it useful to obtain a total score on the SAS, given that the subscales are relatively independent, representing different orientations toward sex (see following section).

Reliability

Reliability indices for the SAS are taken from Hendrick and Hendrick (1987); however, the scale has been used fairly widely for over 20 years and has been translated from English into a variety of languages. Reliability herein refers to internal consistency (Cronbach's alpha), test-retest reliability, and intersubscale (i.e., intra SAS) correlations. Values were quite similar across two studies, with standardized alphas ranging from .71 for Sexual Practices to .94 for Permissiveness (Study I). Test-retest correlations (Study I only) ranged from .66 for Instrumentality to .88 for Permissiveness. Finally, intrascale correlations ranged from $r = .00$ between Permissiveness and Sexual Practices to $r = .44$ between Permissiveness and Instrumentality (Study II).

Validity

Initial criterion validity was demonstrated (Hendrick & Hendrick, 1987) by appropriate correlations between the SAS and measures such as the Reiss Male and Female Sexual Permissiveness Scales (Reiss, 1967) and the Revised Mosher Guilt Inventory (Green & Mosher, 1985). In other research (Hendrick & Hendrick, 1995), men reported themselves to be more permissive and instrumental in their sexual attitudes than women reported themselves to be. Relating these sexual attitudes to love attitudes for both women and men separately (see Hendrick & Hendrick, 1986, for a description of the Love Attitudes Scale), Permissiveness was positively related to game-playing love and negatively related to friendship love, practical love, and altruistic love. Sexual Practices was related inconsistently to love attitudes. Communion was positively related to passionate love, possessive love, and altruistic love. Instrumentality was positively related to game-playing love and negatively related to altruistic love.

The SAS has been used in variety of studies: along with personality measures in a study of women with eating problems (Evans & Wertheim, 1998); to explore relationship infidelity and distress (Cann, Mangum, & Wells, 2001); using the internet for casual dating (Peter & Valkenburg, 2007); predicting sexual experiences and attitudes from religious variables (Murray, Ciarrocchi, & Murray-Swank, 2007); comparing men who commit different types of sexual assault (Abbey, Parkhill, Clinton-Sherrod, & Zawacki, 2007); using sexual terms and personality terms to predict sex and relationships (Shafer, 2001); and examining

religious and sexual attitudes of Irish youth (Grey & Swain, 1996). The SAS was also used in a study of French adults (Le Gall, Mullet, & Riviere Shafighi, 2002), wherein the scale performed well but was found to have a scale structure differing slightly from the original four-factor structure. Thus, the SAS is a solid and widely used scale, but some questions were raised about its factor structure. The Le Gall et al. findings and changes in language use and cohort influences over 2 decades prompted us to conduct a series of studies that resulted in the revision of the Sexual Attitudes Scale to the Brief Sexual Attitudes Scale, described below.

Other Information

The Sexual Attitudes Scale and the Brief Sexual Attitudes Scale are shown in the Exhibit, along with scoring instructions. The scales are in the public domain and free for research and clinical use. In the Exhibit, all 43 items in the SAS are shown; however, only the items in the BSAS are numbered.

BRIEF SEXUAL ATTITUDES SCALE

Description

The Brief Sexual Attitudes Scale (BSAS; Hendrick, Hendrick, & Reich, 2006) was developed because our recent research and that of others (e.g., Le Gall et al., 2002) indicated that the factor structure had shifted slightly. In addition, attitudes and language usage change rapidly in our technology-oriented society. Finally, all indices being equal, the briefer the measure, the greater its practicality for both research and clinical use. Based on data from three studies (two existing data sets and one prospective study), and analyses that included principal components analyses, confirmatory factor analyses (CFA), alphas, subscale intercorrelations, test-retest correlations, correlations with relevant measures, and assessment of gender differences, the 43-item SAS was refined into the 23-item BSAS. The final four scales include Permissiveness (10 items), Birth Control (3 items), Communion (5 items), and Instrumentality (5 items).

Response Mode, Timing, and Scoring

The response format for the BSAS is similar to that for the SAS, and completion time ranges from 5–10 minutes. Scoring is handled similarly to the SAS, using mean scores for the subscales and no overall scale score.

Reliability and Validity

In Studies 1 and 2, using existing data sets (Hendrick et al., 2006), the BSAS and SAS performed similarly, though CFA fit indices were significantly better for the BSAS. Gender differences and correlations with other measures (e.g., love attitudes, relationship satisfaction) were very similar. In

Study 3, the prospective study (Hendrick et al. 2006), the analytic strategy was similar to that for the previous two studies. CFA indices for the BSAS showed a Goodness of Fit Index (*GFI*) of .98, *AGFI* of .95, *RMSEA* of .05, *CFI* of .99, and χ^2 (21, 518) = 52.3 (Hendrick et al., 2006). The alphas were .95 for Permissiveness, .88 for Birth Control, .73 for Communion, and .77 for Instrumentality. Inter-sub-scale correlations were .20 or less except for one that was .40 (Permissiveness with Instrumentality). Test-retest correlations were .92 for Permissiveness, .57 for Birth Control, .86 for Communion, and .75 for Instrumentality. The BSAS subscales correlated as expected for the most part with love attitudes and with other relationship-oriented measures. Finally, gender differences were consistent with Studies I and II. Women "were less endorsing of Permissiveness and Instrumentality than were men, and the genders did not differ on Birth Control or Communion" (Hendrick et al., p. 84, 2006). The BSAS has been used in other published research (Hendrick & Hendrick, 2006), and the article has been cited by Rathus and colleagues (Rathus, Nevid, & Fichner-Rathus, 2008).

Other Information

As noted above, the Brief Sexual Attitudes Scale is readily available.

References

Abbey, A., Parkhill, M. R., Clinton-Sherrod, A. M., & Zawacki, T. (2007). A comparison of men who committed different types of sexual assault in a community sample. *Journal of Interpersonal Violence, 22,* 1567–1580.

Cann, A., Mangum, J. L., & Wells, M. (2001). Distress in response to relationship infidelity: The roles of gender and attitudes about relationships. *The Journal of Sex Research, 38,* 185–190.

Evans, L., & Wertheim, E. H. (1998). Intimacy patterns and relationship satisfaction of women with eating problems and the mediating effects of depression, trait anxiety, and social anxiety. *Journal of Psychosomatic Research, 44,* 355–365.

Green, S. E., & Mosher, D. L. (1985). A causal model of sexual arousal to erotic fantasies. *The Journal of Sex Research, 21,* 1–23.

Grey, I. M., & Swain, R. B. (1996). Sexual and religious attitudes of Irish students. *The Irish Journal of Psychology, 17,* 213–227.

Hendrick, C., & Hendrick, S. S. (1986). A theory and method of love. *Journal of Personality and Social Psychology, 50,* 392–402.

Hendrick, C., Hendrick, S. S., & Reich, D. A. (2006). The Brief Sexual Attitudes Scale. *The Journal of Sex Research, 43,* 76–86.

Hendrick, S. S., & Hendrick, C. (1987). Multidimensionality of sexual attitudes. *The Journal of Sex Research, 23,* 502–526.

Hendrick, S. S., & Hendrick, C. (1995). Gender differences and similarities in sex and love. *Personal Relationships, 2,* 55–65.

Hendrick, S. S., & Hendrick, C. (2006). Measuring respect in close relationships. *Journal of Social and Personal Relationships, 23,* 881–899.

Hendrick, S. S., Hendrick, C., Slapion-Foote, M. J., & Foote, F. H. (1985). Gender differences in sexual attitudes. *Journal of Personality and Social Psychology, 48,* 1630–1642.

Le Gall, A, Mullet, E., & Shafighi, S. R. (2002). Age, religious beliefs, and sexual attitudes. *The Journal of Sex Research, 39,* 207–216.

Murray, K. M., Ciarrocchi, J. W., & Murray-Swank, N. A. (2007). Spirituality, religiosity, shame and guilt as predictors of sexual attitudes and experiences. *Journal of Psychology and Theology, 35,* 222–234.

Peter, J., & Valkenburg, P. M. (2007). Who looks for casual dates on the internet? A test of the compensation and the recreation hypotheses. *New Media & Society, 9,* 455–474.

Rathus, S. A., Nevid, J. S., & Fichner-Rathus, L. (2007). *Human sexuality in a world of diversity* (7th ed.). Boston, MA: Allyn & Bacon.

Reiss, I. L. (1967). *The social context of premarital sexual permissiveness.* New York: Holt, Rinehart & Winston.

Shafer, A. B. (2001). The Big Five and sexuality trait terms as predictors of relationships and sex. *Journal of Research in Personality, 35,* 313–338.

Exhibit

Sexual Attitudes Scale and Brief Sexual Attitudes Scale

Listed below are several statements that reflect different attitudes about sex. For each statement fill in the response on the answer sheet that indicates how much you agree or disagree with that statement. Some of the items refer to a specific sexual relationship, while others refer to general attitudes and beliefs about sex. Whenever possible, answer the questions with your current partner in mind. If you are not currently dating anyone, answer the questions with your most recent partner in mind. If you have never had a sexual relationship, answer in terms of what you think your responses would most likely be.

For each statement:

A = Strongly Agree with the Statement
B = Moderately Agree with the Statement
C = Neutral—Neither Agree nor Disagree
D = Moderately Disagree with the Statement
E = Strongly Disagree with the Statement

1. I do not need to be committed to a person to have sex with him/her.
2. Casual sex is acceptable.
3. I would like to have sex with many partners.
4. One-night stands are sometimes very enjoyable.

5.   It is okay to have ongoing sexual relationships with more than one person at a time.

P   It is okay to manipulate someone into having sex as long as no future promises are made.

6.   Sex as a simple exchange of favors is okay if both people agree to it.
7.   The best sex is with no strings attached.
8.   Life would have fewer problems if people could have sex more freely.
9.   It is possible to enjoy sex with a person and not like that person very much.

P   Sex is more fun with someone you don't love.
P   It is all right to pressure someone into having sex.
P   Extensive premarital sexual experience is fine.
P   Premarital affairs are all right as long as one's partner doesn't know about them.
P   Sex for its own sake is perfectly all right.
P   I would feel comfortable having intercourse with my partner in the presence of other people.
P   Prostitution is acceptable.

10. It is okay for sex to be just good physical release.

P   Sex without love is meaningless.
P   People should at least be friends before they have sex together.
P   In order for sex to be good, it must also be meaningful.

11. Birth control is part of responsible sexuality.
12. A woman should share responsibility for birth control.
13. A man should share responsibility for birth control.

SP   Sex education is important for young people.
SP   Using "sex toys" during lovemaking is acceptable.
SP   Masturbation is all right.
SP   Masturbating one's partner during intercourse can increase the pleasure of sex.

C   Sex gets better as a relationship progresses.

14. Sex is the closest form of communication between two people.
15. A sexual encounter between two people deeply in love is the ultimate human interaction.

C   Orgasm is the greatest experience in the world.

16. At its best, sex seems to be the merging of two souls.
17. Sex is a very important part of life.
18. Sex is usually an intensive, almost overwhelming experience.

C   During sexual intercourse, intense awareness of the partner is the best frame of mind.
C   Sex is fundamentally good.

19. Sex is best when you let yourself go and focus on your own pleasure.
20. Sex is primarily the taking of pleasure from another person.
21. The main purpose of sex is to enjoy oneself.
22. Sex is primarily physical.
23. Sex is primarily a bodily function, like eating.

I   Sex is mostly a game between males and females.

Note. Items included in the original SAS have a letter denoting their subscale and are not numbered. The BSAS includes the instructions shown at the top, which are the same as for the SAS. The items are administered in the order shown. For purposes of analyses, we have A = 1 and E = 5. (The scoring may be reversed, so that A = strongly disagree, etc.) P = Permissiveness; SP = Sexual Practices; C = Communion; I = Instrumentality. Items 1–10 = Permissiveness; 11–13 = Birth Control; 14–18 = Communion; 19–23 = Instrumentality.

Sexual Attitude Scale

WALTER W. HUDSON,[1,2] *WALMYR Publishing Co.*
GERALD J. MURPHY, *New Orleans, Louisiana*

The Sexual Attitude Scale (SAS) is a short-form scale designed to measure liberal versus conservative attitudes toward human sexual expression.

Description

The SAS contains 25 category partition (Likert type) items, two of which are worded negatively to partially offset the potential for response set bias. Each item is scored on a relative frequency scale as shown in the scoring key of the instrument. Obtained scores range from 0 to 100, where higher scores indicate greater degrees of conservatism and lower scores indicate more liberal attitudes. The SAS has a cutting score of 50, such that scores above that value indicate the presence of an increasingly conservative attitude toward human sexual expression, whereas scores below that value indicate the presence of an increasingly liberal orientation. A score of 0 represents the most liberal position and a score of 100 represents the most conservative position. The SAS can be used with all English speaking populations aged 12 or older.

Readability statistics are as follows: Flesch Reading Ease: 63; Gunning's Fog Index: 10; and Flesch-Kincaid Grade Level: 7.

Response Mode and Timing

The SAS is a self-report scale that is normally completed in 5–7 minutes.

Scoring

Items 21 and 22 must first be reverse-scored by subtracting the item response from $K + 1$, where K is the number of response categories in the scoring key. After making all appropriate item reversals, compute the total score as $S = (\sum SX_i - N)(100) / [(K-1)N]$, where X is an item response, 1st small i is italic K is the number of response categories, and N is the number of properly completed items. Total scores remain valid in the face of missing values (omitted items) provided the respondent completes at least 80% of the items. The effect of the scoring formula is to replace missing values with the mean item response value so that scores range from 0 to 100 regardless of the value of N.

Reliability

Cronbach's alpha = .94 and the SEM = 4.20. Test-retest reliability is not available.

Validity

The known-groups validity coefficient is .73 as determined by the point-biserial correlation between group status (liberal vs. conservative criterion groups) and the SAS scores. Detailed information about content, factorial, and construct validity are reported in the *WALMYR Assessment Scale Scoring Manual* which is available from the publisher.

Other Information

The proper use of the WALMYR assessment scales is easily mastered, and the scales can be readily understood by qualified professional practitioners. These measurement tools are not intended for use by untrained individuals. The scales are simple, powerful devices that, when used by trained professionals, are capable of revealing both minor and serious problems that individuals might have in many areas of personal and social functioning. They are not intended for use by persons who are not trained to deal with such problems and should be used only by competent professionals, researchers, scholars and those who are engaged in supervised study and training.

The SAS is a copyrighted commercial assessment scale and may not be copied, reproduced, altered, or translated into other languages. The scale may not be administered online nor placed on a website for others to use. It may be purchased in tear-off pads of 50 copies each for $22.50 at www.walmyr.com.

References

Hudson, W. W., Murphy, G. J., & Nurius, P. S. (1983). A short-form scale to measure liberal vs. conservative orientations toward human sexual expression. *The Journal of Sex Research, 19*, 258–272.

Nurius, P. S., & Hudson, W. W. (1993). *Human services practice, evaluation & computers.* Pacific Grove, CA: Brooks/Cole.

[1]Walter W. Hudson, 1934–1999.
[2]Address correspondence to WALMYR Publishing Co., P.O. Box 12217, Tallahassee, FL 32317–2217; e-mail: walmyr@walmyr.com

Exhibit

Sexual Attitude Scale (SAS)

Name:_____   Today's Date:_____

This questionnaire is designed to measure the way you feel about sexual behaviour. It is not a test, so there are no right or wrong answers. Answer each item as carefully and as accurately as you can by placing a number beside each one as follows.

    I = Strongly disagree
    2 = Disagree
    3 = Neither agree nor disagree
    4 = Agree
    5 = Strongly agree

1._____ I think there is too much sexual freedom given to adults these days.
2._____ I think that increased sexual freedom undermines the American family.
3._____ I think that young people have been given too much information about sex.
4._____ Sex education should be restricted to the home.
5._____ Older people do not need to have sex.
6._____ Sex education should be given only when people are ready for marriage.
7._____ Pre-marital sex may be a sign of a decaying social order.
8._____ Extra-marital sex is never excusable.
9._____ I think there is too much sexual freedom given to teenagers these days.
10._____ I think there is not enough sexual restraint among young people.
11._____ I think people indulge in sex too much.
12._____ I think the only proper way to have sex is through intercourse.
13._____ I think sex should be reserved for marriage.
14._____ Sex should be only for the young.
15._____ Too much social approval has been given to homosexuals.
16._____ Sex should be devoted to the business of procreation.
17._____ People should not masturbate.
18._____ Heavy sexual petting should be discouraged.
19._____ People should not discuss their sexual affairs or business with others.
20._____ Severely handicapped (physically and mentally) people should not have sex.
21._____ There should be no laws prohibiting sexual acts between consenting adults.
22._____ What two consenting adults do together sexually is their own business.
23._____ There is too much sex on television.
24._____ Movies today are too sexually explicit.
25._____ Pornography should be totally banned from our bookstores.

Note. Item 21 and 22 are reverse scored.

Revised Attitudes Toward Sexuality Inventory

WENDY PATTON[1] AND MARY MANNISON, *Queensland University of Technology*

In an attempt to develop a scale providing a focus for sexuality issues of the 1990s, we undertook the construction of this attitude scale, with a particular focus on sexual coercion.

Description

The 1980s and 1990s had seen a focus on attitudes toward sexual coercion, both in terms of their implications for female and male psychological development and their relationship to unintended pregnancy and Sexually transmitted diseases (STDs). As such, a broad array of items focusing on attitudes toward sexual relationships, in addition to more specific issues, such as abortion, masturbation, homosexuality, contraception, sexuality in childhood and the aged, and sexuality education, were seen as important for inclusion in the inventory.

The initial Attitudes Toward Sexuality Inventory (Patton & Mannison, 1993) was a 72-item questionnaire representing 10 attitudinal categories designed to evaluate a university course in human sexuality. There were 5 to 11 items in each category. The categories were selected to represent the main content areas of the course and included (a) contraception, (b) masturbation, (c) sexuality across the lifespan, (d) gender roles, (e) gay and lesbian relationships, (f) abortion, (g) STDs, (h) child sexual abuse, (i) rape, and (j) sexuality education.

Items in the initial inventory were derived from a number of different sources. These questionnaires included a number of the Burt (1980) scales, such as Sexual Conservatism, Rape Myth Acceptance, Interpersonal Violence, and Sex Role Stereotyping. Other measures used included those focusing on attitudes toward homosexuality (Herek, 1988), AIDS (Greiger & Ponterotto, 1988), rape (Deitz, Blackwell, Daley, & Bentley, 1982; Dull & Giacopassi, 1987; Feild, 1978), dating relationships (Giarusso, Johnson, Goodchild, & Zellman, 1979), and women (Spence, Helmreich, & Stapp, 1973).

As a result of preliminary research (Patton & Mannison, 1993, 1994), evaluations from independent experts in university sexuality education, and a review of item content and wording by a group of secondary school sexuality educators, changes were made. Several items were deleted, the focus of a number of items was changed, and other items were reworded to reflect subtle language shifts in the young adult population (Hall, Howard, & Boezio, 1986). Also, new items were added to capture various topical questions. In all, 35 items reflecting diverse issues in sexuality, including masturbation, sexuality in children and the aged,

sexual coercion and assault in childhood and adulthood, homosexuality, abortion, and contraception were included in the revised inventory. Five items focusing on attitudes toward women (adapted from Spence et al., 1973) were also included, making a total of 40 items in the Revised Attitudes Toward Sexuality Inventory.

Three reliable and clear factors were found in a factor analysis, and two other factors were less clear (Patton & Mannison, 1995). The three factors were Attitudes Toward Sexual Coercion and Assault (Items 2, 5, 6, 13, 17, 18, 25, 27, 29, 33, 37, 38), Attitudes Toward Sexuality Issues (Items 4, 7, 8, 15, 19, 20, 23, 35), and Attitudes Toward Gender Roles (Items 9, 28, 31, 32, 35).

Response Mode and Timing

The response format is a 6-point scale to which respondents reply from *Strongly Agree* through *Strongly Disagree*. The 6-point format was chosen in order to avoid a midpoint and invite a choice for one side or the other. The inventory typically requires 5–10 minutes to complete.

Scoring

Items were worded to counter any tendency to simply agree (or disagree) with all of them. This resulted in the reverse scoring of the following items: 4, 7, 13, 15, 19, 20, 23. On the Attitudes Toward Sexual Coercion and Assault factor, higher scores reflect greater acceptance of rape myths and sexual coercion. Higher scores on the Attitudes Toward Sexuality factor reflect less traditional attitudes toward sexuality. Higher scores on the Attitudes Toward Gender Roles factor reflect more traditional attitudes toward gender roles.

Reliability

The Cronbach alpha for the overall revised inventory was .85, and for the three clear factors, the alphas were .85, .79, and .68, respectively (Patton & Mannison, 1995).

Validity

The initial version of the Attitudes Toward Sexuality Inventory has been used to evaluate attitude change following a university course. Pre- and posttest data were received from 115 students (Patton & Mannison, 1993). Patton and Mannison (1994) also used the initial version of the inventory in a study designed to measure attitude and behaviour

[1]Address correspondence to Wendy Patton, School of Learning and Development, Queensland University of Technology, Kelvin Grove Campus 4059, Brisbane, Australia; e-mail: w.patton@qut.edu.au

change (measured by responses to problem situations) following a university human sexuality course. Patton and Mannison (1995) found significant differences. For Factor 1, there was a significant difference between men and women on all 12 items, with 10 of these at the $p < .001$ level. In every instance, men reported less disagreement with the item, indicating that women have a more negative response to sexual coercion. A similar pattern emerged with regard to the attitudes toward rape myths, as well as those items which reflected sexual coercion between people who knew each other. It must be noted that the difference was one of degree; all means were between 1.00 and 3.00 (i.e., between *Strongly Disagree* and *Mildly Disagree*).

On Factor 2 there were fewer items (four of eight) with a significant gender difference. The significant items showed women more accepting of the expression of sexuality in children and in the elderly, and more rejecting of the notion that male and female homosexuality is a threat to society. Again, the difference was one of degree on most items.

In Factor 3, all five items showed significant differences between women and men. These differences reflected greater acceptance of traditional gender role attitudes by men—that women being whistled at in public is a compliment, intoxication in women is worse than in men, and homosexuality is a threat to societal institutions.

Analyses of variance were also performed on the summed factor scores for the reliable factors, Factors 1, 2, and 3. As expected, the consistent gender differences found on individual items generally remained for the total factor score, with Factors 1 and 3 showing significant gender differences. Overall means for Factor 2, the general attitudes toward sexuality factor, showed no significant difference between women and men. Although the items reflected specific area differences, the summed score results reflected a representative look at gender differences, illustrating differences on some dimensions of sexuality attitudes only.

Patton and Mannison (1995) indicated that additional redefinition of the measure is necessary. Although the first two factors may be used as independent measures, accepting the multidimensional complexity of attitudes toward sexuality suggests further refinement while continuing to include a wide range of content.

References

Burt, M. (1980). Cultural myths and supports for rape. *Journal of Personality and Social Psychology, 38*, 217–230.

Deitz, S. R., Blackwell, K. T., Daley, P. C., & Bentley, B. J. (1982). Measurement of empathy toward rape victims and rapists. *Journal of Personality and Social Psychology, 43*, 372–384.

Dull, R. T., & Giacopassi, D. (1987). Demographic correlates of sexual and dating attitudes: A study of date rape. *Criminal Justice and Behaviour, 14*, 175–193.

Feild, H. S. (1978). Attitudes toward rape: A comparative analysis of police, rapists, crisis counselors, and citizens. *Journal of Personality and Social Psychology, 37*, 176–179.

Giarusso, R., Johnson, P., Goodchild, J., & Zellman, G. (1979, April). *Adolescent cues and signals: Sexual assault.* Paper presented at the annual meeting of the   Western Psychological Association, San Diego, CA.

Greiger, I., & Ponterotto, J. G. (1988). Students' knowledge of AIDS and their attitudes toward gay men and lesbian women. *Journal of College Student Development, 29*, 415–422.

Hall, E., Howard, J., & Boezio, S. (1986). Tolerance of rape: A sexist or antisocial attitude? *Psychology of Women Quarterly, 10*, 101–118.

Herek, G. M. (1988). Heterosexuals' attitudes toward lesbians and gay men. *The Journal of Sex Research, 25*, 451–477.

Patton, W., & Mannison, M. (1993). Effects of a university subject on attitudes towards human sexuality. *Journal of Sex Education and Therapy, 19*, 93–107.

Patton, W., & Mannison, M. (1994). Investigating attitudes towards sexuality: Two methodologies. *Journal of Sex Education and Therapy, 20*, 185–197.

Patton, W., & Mannison, M. (1995). Sexuality attitudes: A review of the literature and refinement of a new measure. *Journal of Sex Education and Therapy, 21*, 268–295.

Spence, J. T., Helmreich, R., & Stapp, J. (1973). A short version of the Attitudes Toward Women Scale. *Bulletin of the Psychonomic Society, 2*, 219–220.

Exhibit

Revised Attitudes Toward Sexuality Inventory

Your Attitudes

This page and the next asks you about your attitudes toward a number of sexual issues. Please offer your frank opinion by ticking one of the following options:

SA   Strongly Agree
A   Agree
MA   Mildly Agree
MD   Mildly Disagree
D   Disagree
SD   Strongly Disagree

	SA	A	MA	MD	D	SD
1. Some girls will only respond sexually if a little force is used.	☐	☐	☐	☐	☐	☐
2. Women falsely report rape in order to call attention to themselves.	☐	☐	☐	☐	☐	☐

3. Engaging in sex, e.g., for athletes, does not affect their energy and concentration. ☐ ☐ ☐ ☐ ☐ ☐

4. A woman's decision to have an abortion is a good enough reason to have one. ☐ ☐ ☐ ☐ ☐ ☐

5. A girl will often pretend she doesn't want intercourse because she doesn't want to seem loose, but she's really hoping the guy will force her. ☐ ☐ ☐ ☐ ☐ ☐

6. In the majority of rapes, the woman already has a bad reputation. ☐ ☐ ☐ ☐ ☐ ☐

7. Children should be encouraged to accept the practice of masturbation. ☐ ☐ ☐ ☐ ☐ ☐

8. Easily accessible abortion will probably cause people to become unconcerned and careless. ☐ ☐ ☐ ☐ ☐ ☐

9. There's nothing wrong with a little sweet talk to get what you want. ☐ ☐ ☐ ☐ ☐ ☐

10. A woman cannot be forced to have intercourse against her will. ☐ ☐ ☐ ☐ ☐ ☐

11. The primary goal of sexual intercourse should be to have children. ☐ ☐ ☐ ☐ ☐ ☐

12. Sexual inaccessibility of a man's partner is a common cause of child sexual abuse in the home. ☐ ☐ ☐ ☐ ☐ ☐

13. It's not okay for a guy to pressure for more sex even if he thinks the girl has led him on. ☐ ☐ ☐ ☐ ☐ ☐

14. Normal males can commit rape. ☐ ☐ ☐ ☐ ☐ ☐

15. Children should be ignored if found playing "doctors and nurses" or other games of sexual exploration. ☐ ☐ ☐ ☐ ☐ ☐

16. It doesn't hurt children to have a little bit of sex play with their older relatives. ☐ ☐ ☐ ☐ ☐ ☐

17. If the couple have dated a long time, it's only natural for the guy to pressure her for sex. ☐ ☐ ☐ ☐ ☐ ☐

18. Women who are raped are usually a little to blame for the crime. ☐ ☐ ☐ ☐ ☐ ☐

19. The elderly in nursing homes should have as much sexual access to each other as they want. ☐ ☐ ☐ ☐ ☐ ☐

20. Contraceptives should be readily available to teenagers. ☐ ☐ ☐ ☐ ☐ ☐

21. Even if the guy gets sexually excited, it's not okay for him to use force. ☐ ☐ ☐ ☐ ☐ ☐

22. Rape is usually planned and premeditated. ☐ ☐ ☐ ☐ ☐ ☐

23. Masturbation is a normal sexual activity throughout life. ☐ ☐ ☐ ☐ ☐ ☐

24. Women should receive preferential treatment right now to make up for past discrimination. ☐ ☐ ☐ ☐ ☐ ☐

25. If a guy spends a lot of money on a girl, he's got a right to expect a few sexual favours. ☐ ☐ ☐ ☐ ☐ ☐

26. Forcing a woman to have sex when she doesn't want to is rape. ☐ ☐ ☐ ☐ ☐ ☐

27. A woman who initiates a sexual encounter will probably have sex with anybody. ☐ ☐ ☐ ☐ ☐ ☐

28. Being whistled at in public is like getting a compliment. ☐ ☐ ☐ ☐ ☐ ☐

29. You can't blame a guy for not listening when the girl changes her mind at the last minute. ☐ ☐ ☐ ☐ ☐ ☐

30. No woman harbours a secret desire to be raped. ☐ ☐ ☐ ☐ ☐ ☐

31. Sexuality education probably leads to experimentation and increased sexual activity. ☐ ☐ ☐ ☐ ☐ ☐

32. Intoxication among women is worse than among men. ☐ ☐ ☐ ☐ ☐ ☐

33. A girl should give in to a guy's advances so as not to hurt his feelings. ☐ ☐ ☐ ☐ ☐ ☐

34. Rape has nothing to do with an uncontrollable desire for sex. ☐ ☐ ☐ ☐ ☐ ☐

35. Male and female homosexuality is a threat to many of society's institutions. ☐ ☐ ☐ ☐ ☐ ☐

36. If there are rules about corporal punishment in schools, they should apply equally to boys and girls. ☐ ☐ ☐ ☐ ☐ ☐

37. If a girl engages in necking or petting and she lets things get out of hand, it is her own fault if her partner forces sex on her. ☐ ☐ ☐ ☐ ☐ ☐

38. A woman who claims she was raped by a man she knows can be described as a "woman who changed her mind afterward." ☐ ☐ ☐ ☐ ☐ ☐

39. Most adults who contract AIDS get pretty much what they deserve. ☐ ☐ ☐ ☐ ☐ ☐

40. No clubs should be allowed to refuse membership, terms, or conditions of membership on the basis of gender. ☐ ☐ ☐ ☐ ☐ ☐

Attitudes Toward Unconventional Sex Scale

CAROLYN A. WENNER,[1] V. MICHELLE RUSSELL, AND JAMES K. MCNULTY,
University of Tennessee, Knoxville

The Attitudes Toward Unconventional Sex Scale (ATUSS) was developed to assess a general disposition to engage in unconventional sexual practices. In contrast to the two existing measures of conventional sex (Hendrick & Hendrick, 1987; Purnine, Carey, & Jorgensen, 1996), which confound general tendencies toward unconventional sex with specific unconventional behaviors, the ATUSS contains only global items assessing individuals' general preferences for unconventional sex. Accordingly, the ATUSS can be used to determine the extent to which a general tendency toward unconventional sex predicts specific behaviors that may or may not be unconventional, without concern that item overlap may lead to spurious associations (see Fincham & Bradbury, 1987).

Description

The 5-item ATUSS assesses the extent to which individuals perceive that they enjoy sexual behaviors that deviate from traditional, conventional sexual practices. Items are rated on a 7-point Likert-type scale ranging from 1 (*Strongly Disagree*) to 7 (*Strongly Agree*).

Response Mode and Timing

The ATUSS can be administered in either paper-pencil or computerized response formats. Respondents should be instructed to choose the Likert rating that best describes their current attitudes or beliefs and assured that there are no "right or wrong" sexual attitudes. The ATUSS takes less than 2 minutes to complete.

Scoring

Items are coded such that higher scores indicate more unconventional sexual preferences. A total ATUSS score is computed by summing all scores (possible range = 5–35, see Exhibit).

Reliability

The ATUSS demonstrated high internal consistency in both a sample of 204 undergraduate college students ($\alpha = .80$ for males; $\alpha = .76$ for females) and a sample of 36 recently married couples ($\alpha = .86$ for husbands; $\alpha = .70$ for wives).

Validity

The ATUSS also demonstrated predictive validity in both samples. Specifically, in the sample of 204 undergraduate college students, scores on the ATUSS were strongly associated with enjoyment of various unconventional sexual behaviors, such as anal sex ($r = .39$), dominant/submissive sex ($r = .58$), and sex in unique places ($r = .59$). Likewise, in the sample of 36 recently married couples, scores on the ATUSS were strongly associated with enjoyment of anal sex ($r = .61$ for husbands; $r = .42$ for wives), dominant/submissive sex ($r = .76$ for husbands; $r = .60$ for wives), and sex in unique places ($r = .62$ for husbands; $r = .39$ for wives). Notably, husbands ($M = 19.39, SD = 6.79$) reported more unconventional preferences than wives ($M = 15.39, SD = 4.74$), $t(35) = 3.94, p < .001$, though husbands' and wives' unconventional sexual preferences were highly correlated ($r = .48$). In contrast, although male undergraduates ($M = 20.18, SD = 6.50$) reported slightly more unconventional preferences than female undergraduates ($M = 19.13, SD = 5.65$), that difference was not statistically significant, $t(202) = 1.23, p = .22$.

Other Information

The ATUSS may be useful in determining whether a general disposition toward unconventional sex is a risk factor for negative sexual outcomes (e.g., sexually transmitted infections, unwanted pregnancy). The ATUSS may also be useful in determining the distal sources of unconventional sexual preferences (e.g., personality, previous sexual experiences). Finally, the ATUSS may be useful in determining whether particular levels or combinations of unconventional sexual preferences are beneficial or harmful for relationships. For example, partners may be more satisfied to the extent that both prefer unconventional sex, or to the extent that they both prefer conventional sex, or to the extent that the male is more conventional than the female, or to the extent that the female is more conventional than the male.

References

Fincham, F. D., & Bradbury, T. N. (1987). The assessment of marital quality: A reevaluation. *Journal of Marriage and the Family, 49,* 797–809.

Hendrick, S., & Hendrick, C. (1987). Multidimensionality of sexual attitudes. *The Journal of Sex Research, 23,* 502–526.

Purnine, D., Carey, M., & Jorgensen, R. (1996). The inventory of dyadic heterosexual preferences: Development and psychometric evaluation. *Behaviour Research and Therapy, 34,* 375–387.

[1]Address correspondence to Carolyn Wenner, Department of Psychology, University of Tennessee, Knoxville, TN 37996; e-mail: cwenner@utk.edu

Exhibit

Attitudes Toward Unconventional Sex Scale

I would describe my sexual preferences as "non-traditional."

I like sex most when it is out-of-the-ordinary.

I like sex with my partner to be unpredictable.

I like to experiment with different sexual practices.

Some people might think my sexual preferences are unusual.

Assessing Multiple Facets of Attraction to Women and Men

LISA M. DIAMOND,[1] *University of Utah*

This measure is designed to provide an assessment of both the frequency and the intensity of an individual's attractions to women and men. The measure is written so that it can be administered to either women or men, thereby yielding estimates of same-sex and other-sex attractions (depending on the gender of the respondent). All of the items are phrased with respect to "woman" and "man," instead of "same-sex" and "other-sex." The items are not designed to be aggregated into a single scale. Rather, the intent is to provide a more detailed, nuanced assessment of an individual's pattern of sexual and emotional feelings than that which is provided by global measures such as the Kinsey scale. Depending on the specific research questions being asked, and the population being studied, different items (and combinations of items) may prove meaningful. Modifications of this scale have been administered in Diamond (1998, 2000, 2003, 2005, 2008a, 2008b).

Description

Items 1–3 assess the *relative* frequency of same-sex and opposite-sex attractions and fantasies (similar to the Kinsey scale), but they use a different response format than the Kinsey scale. Specifically, respondents are prompted to provide a number between 0 and 100 to represent the degree to which they are more frequently attracted to women versus men. The 0%-to-100% response format has been found to be more intuitive and easier to understand than the Kinsey scale items. For example, whereas respondents need to be given a specific operational definition for each different number on the Kinsey scale, most individuals intuitively

understand the distinctions between, for example, "75%" and "95%." Note that physical and emotional attractions are assessed separately, and operational definitions are provided for each type.

In contrast to the items assessing relative frequency, Items 4, 7, and 10 (for women) and 14, 17, and 20 (for men) provide information on the *overall* frequency of attractions and fantasies. This is useful for differentiating between (for example) a woman who experiences 90% of her physical attractions for men, but experiences such attractions less than once a month, versus a woman who experiences 90% of her attractions for men, and experiences such attractions every single day.

Depending on the research question at hand, researchers might consider averaging together the responses assessing frequency of attractions and fantasy, but are advised to carefully examine the correlations between attraction-fantasy items (and in particular, to examine scatterplots) before doing so. In my own research on women, I have found tremendous interindividual variation in the degree to which women's attractions correspond to their sexual fantasies, perhaps because some women feel self-conscious about engaging in sexual fantasy. When such discrepancies are observed, it is advisable to analyze attraction and fantasy as separate constructs.

Items 5, 6, 8 and 9 (for women) and 15, 16, 18, and 19 (for men) are designed to assess the *breadth* of an individual's attractions. In other words, are respondents only capable of experiencing same-sex attractions for one specific individual (and, perhaps, someone that they are currently involved with) or do respondents experience them

[1]Address correspondence to Lisa M. Diamond, University of Utah, 380 South 1530 East, Room 502, Salt Lake City, UT 84112-0251; e-mail: diamond@psych.utah.edu

for many different individuals? Previous research indicates that some individuals experience their attractions as "based on the person rather than the gender," or report that they have only *ever* experienced same-sex (or other-sex) attractions for one particular person. These items are designed to identify such individuals so that they can be meaningfully contrasted with individuals who experience more general, stable patterns of same-sex or other-sex attraction.

Items 11–13 (for women) and 21–23 (for men) focus on the intensity of attractions experienced in the previous 6 months, and the degree to which these attractions are experienced as an urge for sexual activity. Researchers may wish to average these measures (within target gender, of course), but should carefully inspect correlations and scatterplots before doing so, as (again) there may be considerable inter-individual variation in the degree of correspondence among these items.

Response Mode and Timing

The measure is designed so that it can be administered on paper, online, or verbally during an interview. Administration takes about 10 minutes.

Scoring

As indicated during the description, the scale is not designed to provide an aggregated index. Rather, different items may be of interest to researchers investigating different components of sexual attraction. Not all of the items have comparable scales. Hence, if researchers

decide to aggregate certain items after inspecting correlations and scatterplots, they should standardize the relevant variables before doing so.

Reliability and Validity

No formal information is available on reliability and validity. However, I have used different subsets of these items during my own long-standing research on female sexual identity development. Relevant publications appear in the references. I have not collected comparable data on men, and hence the degree to which the items capture the same types of variation in female versus male sexual attraction is not yet known.

References

Diamond, L. M. (1998). Development of sexual orientation among adolescent and young adult women. *Developmental Psychology, 34,* 1085–1095.

Diamond, L. M. (2000). Sexual identity, attractions, and behavior among young sexual-minority women over a two-year period. *Developmental Psychology, 36,* 241–250.

Diamond, L. M. (2003). Was it a phase? Young women's relinquishment of lesbian/bisexual identities over a 5-year period. *Journal of Personality and Social Psychology, 84,* 352–364.

Diamond, L. M. (2005). A new view of lesbian subtypes: Stable vs. fluid identity trajectories over an 8-year period. *Psychology of Women Quarterly, 29,* 119–128.

Diamond, L. M. (2008a). Female bisexuality from adolescence to adulthood: Results from a 10-year longitudinal study. *Developmental Psychology, 44,* 5–14.

Diamond, L. M. (2008b). *Sexual fluidity: Understanding women's love and desire.* Cambridge, MA: Harvard University Press.

Exhibit

Assessing Multiple Facets of Attraction to Women and Men

The first few questions below ask about how OFTEN you are attracted to women versus men. It does not matter if the attractions are strong or weak; we are just trying to get a sense of how often they occur. The first question focuses on physical attractions and the second question focuses on emotional attractions. By "physical," we mean the type of attraction that you would associate with a desire for sexual activity. By "emotional," we mean the type of attraction that is usually associated with romantic love, including strong desires for emotional closeness and intimacy. Physical and emotional attractions often occur together, but not always. This is why we are asking about them separately.

1. Please provide a number between 0 and 100 to represent the percentage of your day-to-day PHYSICAL attractions which have been directed toward women versus men over the past 6 months. For example, 0% would mean that you have NEVER experienced attractions for women during the past 6 months, 100% would mean that you have ONLY experienced attractions for women during the past 6 months, and 50% would mean that you have been physically attracted to women about as often as you have been physically attracted to men during the past 6 months. You can provide any number between 0 and 100 (for example 20%, 83%, 99%).
   Percentage of physical attractions directed toward women: _____

2. Now provide a number from 0% to 100% for the percentage of your EMOTIONAL attractions which are directed to women versus men. Percentage of emotional attractions directed toward women: _____

3. In general, what percentage of your sexual fantasies have been about women versus men over the past 6 months?
   Percentage of sexual fantasies about women: _____

4. How often have you experienced a physical attraction for a woman during the past 6 months?

_____ Almost never
_____ Less than once a month
_____ Once or twice a month
_____ About once a week
_____ More than once a week
_____ About every day

5. About how many *different* women have you been physically attracted to in the past 6 months? _____

6. If you answered "1" on the last question, is this someone that you are currently sexually or romantically involved with?
_____ yes _____ no

7. How often have you experienced an emotional attraction for a woman during the past 6 months?
_____ Almost never
_____ Less than once a month
_____ Once or twice a month
_____ About once a week
_____ More than once a week
_____ About every day

8. About how many *different* women have you been emotionally attracted to in the past 6 months? _____

9. If you answered "1" on the last question, is this someone that you are currently sexually or romantically involved with?
_____ yes _____ no

10. How often have you had sexual fantasies about a woman, or women in general, in the past MONTH?
_____ Almost never
_____ Less than once a month
_____ Once or twice a month
_____ About once a week
_____ More than once a week
_____ About every day

11. The next question concerns the intensity of your physical attractions for women. This is on a 1 to 5 scale, so that 1 is "no attraction," 3 is a moderate attraction (right in the middle of the scale), and 5 is the most intense attraction you can experience. Thinking about ALL of the attractions to women you have experienced in the past 6 months, how would you rate the AVERAGE intensity of those attractions? _____

12. How would you rate the intensity of the STRONGEST attraction to a woman that you've experienced in the past 6 months? _____

13. When you have sexual thoughts about a woman, or women in general, how strong is your desire to engage in sexual activity? Use the same 1 to 5 scale, so 1 is basically "no desire for sexual activity," 3 is in the middle, and 5 is maximum desire for sexual activity. _____

The next set of questions focus on men.

14. How often have you experienced a physical attraction for a man during the past 6 months?
_____ Almost never
_____ Less than once a month
_____ Once or twice a month
_____ About once a week
_____ More than once a week
_____ About every day

15. About how many *different* men have you been physically attracted to in the past 6 months? _____

16. If you answered "1" on the last question, is this someone that you are currently sexually or romantically involved with?
_____yes _____no

17. How often have you experienced an emotional attraction for a man during the past 6 months?
_____ Almost never
_____ Less than once a month
_____ Once or twice a month

_____ About once a week

_____ More than once a week

_____ About every day

18. About how many *different* men have you been emotionally attracted to in the past 6 months? _____

19. If you answered "I" on the last question, is this someone that you are currently sexually or romantically involved with?

    _____ yes   _____ no

20. How often have you had sexual fantasies about a man, or men in general, in the past MONTH?

_____ Almost never

_____ Less than once a month

_____ Once or twice a month

_____ About once a week

_____ More than once a week

_____ About every day

21. Thinking about all of the attractions to MEN that you have experienced in the past 6 months, how would you rate the AVERAGE intensity of those attractions? As before, this is on a I to 5 scale, so that I is "no attraction," 3 is a moderate attraction (right in the middle of the scale), and 5 is the most intense attraction you can experience. _____

22. How would you rate the intensity of the STRONGEST attraction to a man that you've experienced in the past 6 months? _____

23. When you have sexual thoughts about a man, or men in general, how strong is your desire to engage in sexual activity? Use the same I to 5 scale, so I is basically "no desire for sexual activity," 3 is in the middle, and 5 is maximum desire for sexual activity.

_____

Sexual Awareness Questionnaire

WILLIAM E. SNELL, JR.,[1] *Southeast Missouri State University*
TERRI D. FISHER, *The Ohio State University at Mansfield*
ROWLAND S. MILLER, *Sam Houston State University*

The Sexual Awareness Questionnaire (SAQ; Snell, Fisher, & Miller, 1991) is an objective, self-report instrument designed to measure four personality tendencies associated with sexual awareness and sexual assertiveness: (a) *sexual consciousness*, defined as the tendency to think and reflect about the nature of one's sexuality; (b) *sexual preoccupation*, defined as the tendency to think about sex to an excessive degree; (c) *sexual monitoring*, defined as the tendency to be aware of the public impression which one's sexuality makes on others; and (d) *sexual assertiveness*, defined as the tendency to be assertive about the sexual aspects of one's life.

Description

The SAQ consists of 36 items arranged in a format whereby respondents indicate how characteristic of them each

statement is. A 5-point Likert scale is used, with each item being scored from 0 to 4: *Not at all characteristic of me* (0), *Slightly characteristic of me* (1), *Somewhat characteristic of me* (2), *Moderately characteristic of me* (3), *Very characteristic of me* (4). In order to create subscale scores (discussed below), the items on each subscale are summed. Higher scores thus correspond to greater amounts of the relevant tendency.

To confirm the conceptual dimensions assumed to underlie the SAQ, the questionnaire items were subjected to a principal axis factor analysis with varimax rotation. Four factors accounting for 42% of the variance were interpreted. The first factor contained items that pertained to sexual consciousness (Items 1, 4, 10, 13, 22, and 25). The items on the second factor (Items 2, 5, 14, 17, 23, 26, 28, 31, and 32) referred to sexual monitoring tendencies. The third factor was composed of items assessing sexual assertive-

[1]Address all correspondence to William E. Snell, Jr., Department of Psychology, Southeast Missouri State University, One University Plaza, Cape Girardeau, MO 63701; e-mail wesnell@semo.edu

ness (Items 3, 6, 9, 12, 15, 18, and 24), and the fourth factor was concerned with sex-appeal consciousness (Items 8, 11, and 29). A second cross-validation factor analysis reported by Snell et al. (1991) also showed that the SAQ subscales were factorially consistent with the anticipated factor structure. The results of these statistical analyses provided strong preliminary evidence supporting the factor structure of the SAQ.

Response Mode and Timing

In most instances, people respond to the 36 items on the SAQ by marking their answers on separate machine-score-able answer sheets. The scale usually requires about 15–30 minutes to complete.

Scoring

All of the SAQ items are coded so that A = 4; B = 3; C = 2; D = 1; and E = 0, except for six specific items which are reverse coded (Items 23, 31, 32, 30, 6, and 9); these items are designated with an "R" on the copy of the SAQ shown in the Exhibit. The relevant items on each subscale are first coded so that A = 0; B = 1; C = 2; D = 3; and E = 4. Next, the items on each subscale are summed, so that higher scores correspond to greater amounts of each respective psychological tendency. Scores on the sexual-consciousness subscale can range from 0 to 24; sexual-monitoring scores can range from 0 to 32; sexual-assertiveness scores can range from 0 to 36; and scores on the sex-appeal consciousness subscale can range from 0 to 12.

Reliability

The internal consistency of the four subscales on the SAQ was determined by calculating Cronbach alpha coefficients, using participants from two separate samples (Sample I consisted of 265 females, 117 males, and 4 gender unspecified; Sample II consisted of 265 females, 117 males, and 4 gender unspecified) drawn from lower division psychology courses at a small midwestern university (Snell et al., 1991). The average age of Sample I was 24.1, with a range of 17 to 60; the average age of Sample II was also 24.1, $SD = 6.87$. Results indicated that all four subscales had clearly acceptable levels of reliability (Snell et al., 1991). In Sample I the alphas were: for sexual consciousness, alpha = .83 for males and .86 for females; for sexual monitoring, alpha = .80 for males and .82 for females; for sex-appeal consciousness, alpha = .89 for males and .92 for females; and for sexual assertiveness, alpha = .83 for males and .81 for females. For Sample II, the internal consistency of the sexual-consciousness subscale was .85 for males and .88 for females; for sexual monitoring, .81 for males and .82 for females; for sex-appeal consciousness, .92 for males and .92 for females; and for sexual assertiveness, .80 for males and .85 for females.

Validity

Evidence for the validity of the SAQ comes from a variety of findings. Snell et al. (1991) provided evidence supporting the convergent and discriminant validity of the SAQ. All four SAQ subscales tended to be negatively related to measures of sex-anxiety and sex-guilt for both males and females, and sexual-consciousness was directly related to erotophilic feelings. Other findings indicated that women's and men's responses to the four SAQ subscales were related in a predictable fashion to their sexual attitudes, dispositions, and behaviors. Other findings indicated that men reported greater sexual assertiveness than did women, with no gender differences found for sexual consciousness, sexual monitoring, or sex-appeal consciousness. Snell (1994) revealed that sexual assertiveness in both males and females was predictive of greater contraceptive use, but only among males was sexual consciousness and sexual monitoring found to predict more favorable attitudes toward condom use. In addition, for both females and males, sexual consciousness, sexual monitoring, and sexual assertiveness were positively associated with a greater variety and a more extensive history of sexual experiences.

References

Snell, W. E., Jr., Fisher, T. D., & Miller, R. S. (1991). Development of the Sexual Awareness Questionnaire: Components, reliability, and validity. *Annals of Sex Research, 4*, 65–92.

Snell, W. E., Jr. (1994, April). *Sexual awareness: Contraception, sexual behaviors and sexual attitudes*. Paper presented at the 63rd annual meeting of the Southwestern Psychological Association, Tulsa, OK.

Exhibit

Sexual Awareness Questionnaire

Instructions: The items listed below refer to the sexual aspects of people's lives. Please read each item carefully and decide to what extent it is characteristic of you. Give each item a rating of how much it applies to you by using the following scale:

A = *Not at all* characteristic of me.
B = *Slightly* characteristic of me.
C = *Somewhat* characteristic of me.

D = *Moderately* characteristic of me.

E = *Very* characteristic of me.

1.   I am very aware of my sexual feelings.
2.   I wonder whether others think I'm sexy.
3.   I'm assertive about the sexual aspects of my life.
4.   I'm very aware of my sexual motivations.
5.   I'm concerned about the sexual appearance of my body.
6.   I'm not very direct about voicing my sexual desires. (R)
7.   I'm always trying to understand my sexual feelings.
8.   I know immediately when others consider me sexy.
9.   I am somewhat passive about expressing my sexual desires. (R)
10. I'm very alert to changes in my sexual desires.
11. I am quick to sense whether others think I'm sexy.
12. I do not hesitate to ask for what I want in a sexual relationship.
13. I am very aware of my sexual tendencies.
14. I usually worry about making a good sexual impression on others.
15. I'm the type of person who insists on having my sexual needs met.
16. I think about my sexual motivations more than most people do.
17. I'm concerned about what other people think of my sex appeal.
18. When it comes to sex, I usually ask for what I want.
19. I reflect about my sexual desires a lot.
20. I never seem to know when I'm turning others on.
21. If I were sexually interested in someone, I'd let that person know.
22. I'm very aware of the way my mind works when I'm sexually aroused.
23. I rarely think about my sex appeal. (R)
24. If I were to have sex with someone, I'd tell my partner what I like.
25. I know what turns me on sexually.
26. I don't care what others think of my sexuality.
27. I don't let others tell me how to run my sex life.
28. I rarely think about the sexual aspects of my life.
29. I know when others think I'm sexy.
30. If I were to have sex with someone, I'd let my partner take the initiative. (R)
31. I don't think about my sexuality very much. (R)
32. Other people's opinions of my sexuality don't matter very much to me. (R)
33. I would ask about sexually-transmitted diseases before having sex with someone.
34. I don't consider myself a very sexual person.
35. When I'm with others, I want to look sexy.
36. If I wanted to practice "safe sex" with someone, I would insist on doing so.

Sexual Activity Questionnaire

E. SANDRA BYERS,[1] *University of New Brunswick*

Sexual activity occurs on a particular occasion as a result of individual and dyadic processes (see Byers & Heinlein, 1989, Figure 1). The Sexual Activity Questionnaire (SAQ) assesses the frequency of each step of the sequence of behaviors leading up to and during sexual interactions, as well as the specific behaviors used to initiate sexual activity and to respond to a sexual initiation. The SAQ has been used with married and cohabiting partners (Byers & Heinlein, 1989) and with dating partners (O'Sullivan & Byers, 1992). The term *sexual activity* includes all activities that the subjects experience as sexual, from holding hands to kissing to sexual intercourse. The SAQ could be easily adapted for use by same-sex couples.

Description

The SAQ is administered as a self-monitoring measure. At the end of each day, or as soon after a sexual interaction as possible, participants indicate (a) whether sexual activity had been initiated on that day, and, if so, by the man or by the woman; (b) if sexual activity was initiated, whether the noninitiator's first response was interest or disinterest in engaging in sexual activity at that time; and (c) if sexual activity was not initiated by either partner, whether the respondent had considered initiating sexual activity. When used with dating, rather than cohabiting, partners, respondents first indicate on each day whether they had been on a "date" (defined as any social situation in which the person was with a member of the other sex).

Participants then provide detailed information about one or more of the sexual initiations that occurred that week. For example, participants can be asked to describe the first sexual initiation by the man and/or by the woman (O'Sullivan & Byers, 1992), the first sexual initiation to which the partner responded positively (if any), and/or the first sexual initiation to which the partner responded negatively (if any; Byers & Heinlein, 1989). For the specified situation(s), respondents indicate the verbal and nonverbal behaviors used to initiate the sexual activity and to respond to the sexual initiation, as well as where the couple was and what they were doing when the initiation occurred. Respondents also indicate, from a list of 22 behaviors, those used by the initiator to demonstrate a desire for sexual activities. For the situation in which the partner initially was not interested in engaging in sexual activity, respondents indicate the reason(s) for the disinterest, how long the disagreement continued, how the disagreement was resolved, and they rate how satisfied they were with their own and their partner's parts in resolving the disagreement.

They also indicate whether they engaged in sexual activity at that time and, if so, why the initially disinterested person decided to engage in the activity. For the situation in which the partner was initially interested in engaging in the sexual activity, respondents indicate how satisfied they were with the way sex was initiated.

For those situations in which sexual activity resulted from the initiation, respondents indicate the types of sexual activities that resulted and their duration. They also rate how enjoyable the sexual interaction was for themselves and for their partner. Using an open-ended format, respondents are given the opportunity to provide additional information about the interaction they had described. Finally, they rate their confidence in the accuracy of their responses.

Dating partners are asked to provide information about their dating partner that is not included on the marital/cohabiting form. Questions assess their relationship with their dating partner (type of relationship, number of previous dates), their romantic interest in their date, and their perception of their date's romantic interest in them before they went on the date, and their own and their date's romantic interest at the end of the evening.

Response Mode and Timing

The SAQ takes approximately 10 minutes to complete. Most of the questions are objective. However, participants describe their activities and location at the time of the sexual initiation. Activities are coded for whether the partners are actively interacting. Location is coded as to whether the initiation occurred in a bedroom, other room in the house, or elsewhere. In addition, respondents describe the words and behaviors used to initiate sexual activity and to respond to a partner's initiation. The categories used to code descriptions of verbal initiations are no verbal initiation, indirect (ambiguous) statement, statement of feelings, and direct statement. Nonverbal initiations are coded as no nonverbal initiation, nonsexual touching or suggestive look, kissing, and sexual fondling. The checklist of 22 initiation behaviors is collapsed into five categories: direct verbal initiation, ambiguous verbal cues, physical contact, sexual cues, and suggestive movements and actions.

Different categories are used to code descriptions of negative and positive responses to initiations. For negative responses to initiations, the verbal responses are coded as no verbal response, verbal refusal without reason, refusal with physical reason, refusal indicating that there was not time, and refusal with a mood-related reason. The nonver-

[1]Address correspondence to E. Sandra Byers, Department of Psychology, University of New Brunswick, Fredericton, NB, Canada E3B 6E4; e-mail: byers@unb.ca

bal responses are coded as no physical response, positive response to a lower level of sexual activity only, stopping or not responding to the partner's sexual advances, and moving away. For positive responses to initiations, the verbal responses are coded as no verbal response, agreement or invitation, and request for clarification. The nonverbal responses are coded as follows: no nonverbal response, initiated sexual activity, and continued sexual interaction. Alternately, ratings of positive and negative responses to initiations can be combined.

Reliability

The SAQ has good reliability. Byers and Heinlein (1989) found a mean interrater agreement for the open-ended questions of .86. In general, respondents were moderately or very sure that their responses were accurate ($M = 5.5$ on a 6-point scale). Eno (1994) found the average agreement between spouses from 36 couples to be .75 for initiations and .90 for responses to initiations. O'Sullivan and Byers (1992) found an average interrater agreement of .87 and an average confidence rating of 5.2, demonstrating good reliability with dating couples.

Validity

There is support for the validity of some aspects of the SAQ. Byers and Heinlein (1989) found that younger individuals, individuals newer to their relationships, and those who reported greater marital and sexual satisfaction reported more initiations. When the number of initiations was controlled, more negative responses were associated with men and women who experienced less sexual pleasure, lower sexual satisfaction, and lower dyadic adjustment. Those individuals who had been in the relationship longer, and who reported less sexual pleasure for the woman and less sexual satisfaction, reported considering initiating sex despite not doing so more often. Eno (1994) found significant positive correlations between retrospective measures of the frequency of sexual initiations and positive responses in the week before self-monitoring and self-monitoring measures of these behaviors, ($M = .71$). O'Sullivan and Byers (1992) found that respondents who had dated more frequently in the month before the study or who were in steady dating relationships reported more sexual initiations.

References

Byers, E. S., & Heinlein, L. (1989. Predicting initiations and refusals of sexual activity in married and cohabiting heterosexual couples. *The Journal of Sex Research, 26,* 210–231.

Eno, R. (1994). *Factors related to sexual initiations and responses to initiations within long-term heterosexual relationships.* Unpublished doctoral dissertation, University of New Brunswick, Fredericton.

O'Sullivan, L. F., & Byers, E. S. (1992). College students' incorporation of initiator and restrictor roles in sexual dating interactions. *The Journal of Sex Research, 29,* 435–446.

Exhibit

Sexual Activity Questionnaire (Married/Cohabiting Version)[a]

Instructions: We are interested in learning more about how couples initiate sexual activities, and how their partners respond to these initiations. By initiation of sexual activities, we mean any word and/or action that one person uses to indicate his or her interest in engaging in sexual activities, at a point in time when the couple is not engaging in any sexual activities. Notice that we are interested in initiations, whether or not any sexual activity results from the initiation. For example, one person may initiate sexual interactions by complimenting his or her partner on his or her looks or using a code phrase that the partner knows indicates sexual interest. Other examples of initiations would be if one person moved closer to their partner or if one person loosened or removed some of his or her own or the partner's clothing. We are interested in the initiation of all levels of sexual activity from kissing (if you consider it a sexual activity and not an expression of affection) to intercourse.

Please complete the attached questionnaire on a daily basis for one week. It is divided into 3 parts.

Part I. Part I of the questionnaire asks you to indicate, for each day of that particular week, whether either you or your partner initiated sexual activity. You are also asked to indicate for each "initiation" who initiated the sexual activity, and whether the noninitiator's *first response* was interest or disinterest in sex. By first response we mean the first thing he or she said or did in response to the initiation. In some cases, the noninitiator's first response might not be the same as their response a few seconds or minutes later. If sexual activity was not initiated by either partner on that day, please indicate whether you considered initiating and your reasons for not doing so. Further instructions for filling out this part of the questionnaire are on the questionnaire itself.

Part II. Fill in Part II of the questionnaire (the blue sheets) for the *first* occasion (if any) in that week on which sex was initiated, and the noninitiator's first response was that he or she was *not interested.* If no such initiation occurred in your relationship that week, leave this part of the questionnaire blank.

Part III. Fill in Part III of the questionnaire (the yellow sheets) for the *first* occasion (if any) in that week on which sex was initiated, and the noninitiator's first response was that he or she was *interested* in sex—that is, when both partners were interested from the outset. If no such initiation occurred that week, leave this part of the questionnaire blank.

Since it is easy to forget the specifics of any particular communication or interaction, it is important that you complete Parts II and III of the questionnaire as soon as possible after the initiation occurs. Try to be as accurate as possible in completing the questionnaire.

Definitions:

> *Sexual Activity:* Any activity of a sexual (as opposed to purely affectionate) nature. Thus, this can include anything from kissing and touching to sexual intercourse. "SEX" is not necessarily intercourse.

> *Initiation:* Any communication (verbal or nonverbal) of a "desire" to participate in sexual activity. Sexual activity may or may not follow.

Sexual Initiation Questionnaire

Part I. For each day of the week, please indicate the following (see Instruction Sheet for definitions):

(a) Whether sexual activity was initiated.

(b) If sexual activity was initiated, indicate whether it was initiated by you or by your partner (male or female). Then indicate what the first response was of the noninitiator. That is, if sex was initiated by you, indicate what your partner's first response was; if sex was initiated by your partner, indicate what your first response was.

(c) If neither you nor your partner initiated sex on that day, indicate if you considered initiating sex but did not do so. If you did change your mind, indicate the reasons for doing so.

Date and day of week	Was sex initiated?	By whom?	Noninitiator's first response	Did you consider initiating?	If yes, why didn't you initiate?
			If sex initiated	If sex not initiated	
_____	___ yes	___ woman	___ interested	___ yes	_____
	___ no	___ man	___ uninterested	___ no	_____
_____	___ yes	___ woman	___ interested	___ yes	_____
	___ no	___ man	___ uninterested	___ no	_____
_____	___ yes	___ woman	___ interested	___ yes	_____
	___ no	___ man	___ uninterested	___ no	_____
_____	___ yes	___ woman	___ interested	___ yes	_____
	___ no	___ man	___ uninterested	___ no	_____
_____	___ yes	___ woman	___ interested	___ yes	_____
	___ no	___ man	___ uninterested	___ no	_____
_____	___ yes	___ woman	___ interested	___ yes	_____
	___ no	___ man	___ uninterested	___ no	_____
_____	___ yes	___ woman	___ interested	___ yes	_____
	___ no	___ man	___ uninterested	___ no	_____

The first of these days on which either you or your partner initiated sex and found that the noninitiator was *initially not interested* was _____ (write in day of the week). Please fill in Part II of the questionnaire on the *blue paper* for this occasion.

The first of these days on which either you or your partner initiated sex and found that the noninitiator was *initially interested* _____ (write in day of the week). Please fill in Part III of the questionnaire on the *yellow paper* for this occasion.

Part II. Complete Questions 1–14 (blue paper) if either you or your partner initiated sexual activity and the first response of the non-initiator was that he or she was *not interested*.

1. At the time of the initiation, where were you and your partner (e.g., in the kitchen of our home)?_____
_____

2. Briefly describe the main thing(s) you and your partner were doing prior to the initiation (e.g. reading, talking)._____
_____

3. The noninitiator indicated a desire for sexual activity by

   saying: _____

   doing: _____

4. The noninitiator responded to the initiator's initial advances by:

   saying: _____

   doing: _____

5. The initiator then responded to this reaction by:

   saying: _____

   doing: _____

6. How long did the disagreement continue? _____ minutes

7. How was the disagreement resolved? _____

8. (a) How satisfied are you with how sexual activity was initiated?

   _____ very satisfied

   _____ satisfied

   _____ neutral

   _____ dissatisfied

   _____ very satisfied

   (b) Why? _____

9. (a) Overall, how satisfied are you with how the disagreement was resolved?

   _____ very satisfied

   _____ satisfied

   _____ neutral

   _____ dissatisfied

   _____ very dissatisfied

   b) Why? _____

10. What behaviors did the initiator use to demonstrate a desire for sexual activities? (Check all that apply.)

    _____ asked directly

    _____ used some code words
            with which the man was
            familiar

    _____ used pet names

    _____ used more eye contact

    _____ touched her date

    _____ massaged or stroked

    _____ snuggled or cuddled

    _____ kissed date

    _____ shared a drink

    _____ moved closer

    _____ talked about the
            relationship

    _____ used "suggestive" body
            movements or postures

    _____ others: _____

    _____ removed or loosened clothing

    _____ played with man's hair

    _____ lay down

    _____ changed tone of voice

    _____ made indirect talk of sex

    _____ set mood atmosphere
            (music, lighting, etc.)

    _____ played games or light
            "rough-housing"

    _____ made compliments

    _____ used some force

    _____ allowed hand to wander

    _____ looked at sexual material

11. If you did engage in sexual activities at that time,

    (a) Why did the person who was initially not interested decide to have sex? _____

    _____

    (b) Which behaviors did you and your partner engage in at that time (check all that apply)?

    _____ hugging, cuddling

    _____ kissing

    _____ necking

    _____ fondling or kissing breast

    _____ fondling woman's genitals

    _____ fondling man's genitals

_____ oral-genital stimulation

_____ coitus

_____ other (please specify) _____

(c) About how long did you and your partner spend in sexual activity at that time? _____ minutes

(d) How enjoyable was this occasion of love-making for you?

_____ extremely unpleasant

_____ moderately unpleasant

_____ slightly unpleasant

_____ slightly pleasant

_____ moderately pleasant

_____ extremely pleasant

(e) How enjoyable do you think this occasion of love-making was for your partner?

_____ extremely unpleasant

_____ moderately unpleasant

_____ slightly unpleasant

_____ slightly pleasant

_____ moderately pleasant

_____ extremely pleasant

12. If you did not engage in sexual activity at that time,

(a) was sex initiated again later that day?

____ yes   ____ no

(b) If yes, by whom?   ____ the man   ____ the woman   ____ mutual consent

13. If there is any additional information that would help us to understand the situation that you described above, please provide it.

_____ _____

14. How confident are you that your responses are accurate?

_____ very unsure

_____ moderately unsure

_____ slightly unsure

_____ slightly sure

_____ moderately sure

_____ very sure

Part III. Complete Questions 15–25 (yellow paper) if either you or your partner initiated sexual activity and the first response of the noninitiator was that he or she was _interested._

15. At the time of the initiation, where were you and your partner (e.g., in the kitchen of our home)? _____

_____

16. Briefly describe the main thing(s) you and your partner were doing prior to the initiation (e.g. reading, talking)._____

_____

17. The initiator indicated a desire for sexual activity by:

saying: _____

doing: _____

18. The noninitiator responded to the initiator's initial advances by:

saying: _____

doing: _____

19. (a) How satisfied are you with how sexual activity was initiated?

_____ very satisfied

_____ satisfied

_____ neutral

_____ dissatisfied

_____ very dissatisfied

(b) Why? _____

20. What behaviors did the initiator use to demonstrate a desire for sexual activities? (Check all that apply.)

_____ asked directly
_____ used some code words
　　　 with which the man was
　　　 familiar
_____ used pet names
_____ used more eye contact
_____ touched her date
_____ massaged or stroked
_____ snuggled or cuddled
_____ kissed date
_____ shared a drink
_____ moved closer
_____ talked about the
　　　 relationship
_____ used "suggestive" body
　　　 movements or postures
_____ others: _____

_____ removed or loosened clothing
_____ played with man's hair
_____ lay down
_____ changed tone of voice
_____ made indirect talk of sex
_____ set mood atmosphere
　　　 (music, lighting, etc.)
_____ played games or light
　　　 "rough-housing"
_____ made compliments
_____ used some force
_____ allowed hand to wander
_____ looked at sexual material

21 Did you and your partner engage in sexual activity at that time?
___ yes   ___ no

22. If you did have sex at that time,

(a) which sexual behaviors did you and your partner engage in (check all that apply)?
_____ hugging, cuddling
_____ kissing
_____ necking
_____ fondling or kissing breast
_____ fondling woman's genitals
_____ fondling man's genitals
_____ oral-genital stimulation
_____ coitus
_____ others (please specify) _____

(b) About how long did you and your partner spend in sexual activity at that time?
_____ minutes

(c) How enjoyable was this occasion of love-making for you?
_____ extremely unpleasant
_____ moderately unpleasant
_____ slightly unpleasant
_____ slightly pleasant
_____ moderately pleasant
_____ extremely pleasant

(d) How enjoyable do you think this occasion of love-making was for your partner?
_____ extremely unpleasant
_____ moderately unpleasant
_____ slightly unpleasant
_____ slightly pleasant
_____ moderately pleasant
_____ extremely pleasant

23. If you did not engage in sexual activity at that time,
(a) was sex initiated again later that day?
___ yes   ___ no

(b) If yes, by whom?   ___ the man   ___ the woman   ___ mutual consent

24. If there is any additional information that would help us to understand the situation that you described above, please provide
it. _____

25. How confident are you that your responses are accurate?

_____   very unsure

_____   moderately unsure

_____   slightly unsure

_____   slightly sure

_____   moderately sure

_____   very sure

[a]This version of the questionnaire is designed to be completed by cohabiting partners. The questionnaire can be modified for use by dating couples.

Cowart–Pollack Scale of Sexual Experience

DEBRA COWART-STECKLER,[1] *University of Mary Washington*
ROBERT H. POLLACK, *University of Georgia*

The Cowart–Pollack Scale of Sexual Experience consists of two checklists of heterosexual activities: one for men and another for women. It was developed to assess the sexual experience of an individual or group of individuals in research, therapy, or the classroom.

Description

The checklists comprise a wide range of sexual activities for men and women, including oral contacts, masturbation, various intercourse positions, anal intercourse, and bondage. The female scale consists of 30 sexual activities. They range from "your nude breast felt by male" to "anal intercourse." The male scale consists of 31 sexual activities, ranging from "feeling female's nude breast" to "bondage."

Initially, the sexual experience scales consisted of 47 items drawn from previous studies (Bentler, 1968a, 1968b; Zuckerman, 1973). These 47-item scales were distributed to 153 men and 226 women during a group-testing session. After completion, the items were ordered from most to least frequent according to the percentages of subjects who reported that they had engaged in such behavior. In accordance with the Cornell technique of Guttman scaling with two response categories, the top and bottom 10% of the items were discarded. This procedure yielded the present scales.

Investigations of the range of heterosexual experiences have shown a predictable sequence of experiences for men and women (Cowart & Pollack, 1979; Cowart-Steckler, 1984). These experiences can be described using the Cornell technique of Guttman scaling in which the behaviors are ordered from most frequent to least frequent (Guttman, 1947). Guttman scaling assumes that an individual who experiences a less frequent behavior previously has experienced the more common behavior (Edwards, 1957). Applying the

Guttman scaling technique to sexual experiences suggests that heterosexual relationships progress through similar sequences of experiences. An individual who responds to this scale, then, can be compared to the normative sample and the level of sexual experience can be ascertained.

The Cowart–Pollack scale has been standardized using a college-aged sample (aged 18 to 21) and, therefore, is appropriate for people in that age group. Distributing the questionnaire to people of different ages may yield a different ordering in the sequence of behaviors.

Response Mode and Timing

When the scale is used in research, therapy, or to assess one's level of sexual experience, the items are ordered randomly. Respondents indicate that they have or have not experienced each behavior by circling *yes* or *no* in answer to the question "Have you experienced the following?" The scale usually requires an average of 10 minutes for completion.

Scoring

No scoring per se is required. A comparison between the ordering of the respondent's experiences and the norms established by the Cowart–Pollack scale will give an accurate indication of the respondent's level of sexual experience.

Reliability and Validity

The Cowart–Pollack scale has been distributed twice to large groups of college-aged individuals. In 1979 (Cowart & Pollack, 1979), the 31-item scale for men and the 30-item scale for women were administered in a group-testing situation to 199 men and 213 women. The coefficient of

[1]Address correspondence to Debra Cowart-Steckler, Department of Psychology, University of Mary Washington, Fredericksburg, VA 22401; e-mail: dsteckle@umw.edu

reproducibility for the male and female scales was .85 and .88, respectively. A coefficient of at least .85 indicates reliability in the ordering of behaviors (Edwards, 1957).

In 1983 the Cowart–Pollack scale was distributed to 197 men and 212 women (Cowart-Steckler, 1984). These subjects were demographically similar to the subjects in 1979. The coefficient of reproducibility was .88 for the male scale and .87 for the female scale.

The major difference in the results of the 1979 and 1983 distribution was not in the ordering of sexual experiences but in the numbers of men and women engaging in most types of sexual experiences. There were significantly more men and women from the 1983 sample engaging in sexual activities. This finding suggests that, at least for individuals aged 18 to 21, there has been an increase in sexual activity from 1979. As the coefficients of reproducibility indicate,

the results of the 1983 distribution represent a reliable and stable sequence of events.

References

Bentler, P. M. (1968a). Heterosexual behavior assessment-I. Males. *Behavior Research and Therapy, 6*, 21–25.

Bentler, P. M. (1968b). Heterosexual behavior assessment-II. Females. *Behavior Research and Therapy, 6*, 27–29.

Cowart, D. A., & Pollack, R. H. (1979). A Guttman scale of sexual experience. *Journal of Sex Education & Therapy, 1*, 3–6.

Cowart-Steckler, D. (1984). A Guttman scale of sexual experience: An update. *Journal of Sex Education & Therapy, 10*, 49–52.

Edwards, A. L. (1957). *Techniques of attitude scale construction.* New York: Appleton-Century-Crofts.

Guttman, L. (1947). The Cornell technique of scale and intensity analysis. *Educational and Psychological Measurement, 7*, 247–280.

Zuckerman, M. (1973). Scales for sexual experience for males and females. *Journal of Consulting & Clinical Psychology, 11*, 27–29.

Exhibit

Cowart–Pollack Scale of Sexual Experience

Men (N = 197)		Women (N = 212)	
Activity	% Yes[a]	Activity	% Yes
Feeling female's nude breast	98	Your nude breast felt by male	91
Male mouth contact with female's nude breast	94	Male mouth contact with your breast	91
Exposure to erotic materials sold openly in newsstands	93	Penetration of vagina by male's finger	83
Male finger penetration of vagina	92	Male lying prone on female without penetration	83
Your observation of nude partner	91	Partner's observation of your nude body	80
Partner's observation of your nude body	91	Clitoral manipulation by male	79
Clitoral manipulation by male	90	Your observation of nude partner	78
Manipulation of penis by female	90	Male manipulation of vulva	77
Male lying prone on female without penetration	87	Manipulation of penis by female	76
Female mouth contact with penis	86	Sexual intercourse, male superior	67
Male manipulation of vulva	84	Female mouth contact with penis	67
Sexual intercourse, male superior	83	Male mouth contact with vulva	66
Masturbation	81	Male tongue manipulation of clitoris	66
Clitoral manipulation to orgasm by male	78	Male tongue penetration of vagina	66
Male mouth contact with vulva	77	Sexual intercourse, face to face, side	60
Sexual intercourse, partially clothed	77	Showering or bathing with partner	58
Male tongue penetration of vagina	76	Exposure to erotic materials sold openly in newsstand	58
Male tongue manipulation of clitoris	75	Sexual intercourse, partially clothed	56
Mutual oral stimulation of genitals to orgasm	74	Clitoral manipulation to orgasm by male	55
Sexual intercourse, face to face, side	73	Sexual intercourse, female superior	55
Exposure to hardcore erotic materials	72	Masturbation	54
Sexual intercourse, female superior	71	Sexual intercourse, vagina entered from rear	46
Showering or bathing with partner	68	Mutual oral stimulation of genitals to orgasm	45
Male tongue manipulation of female genitals to orgasm	66	Male tongue manipulation of your genitals to orgasm	45
Sexual intercourse, vagina entered from rear	63	Hand contact with partner's anal area	40
Hand contact with partner's anal area	61	Sexual intercourse, sitting position	37
Sexual intercourse, standing	48	Sexual intercourse, standing	28
Sexual intercourse, sitting	48	Exposure to hardcore erotic materials	24
Finger penetration of partner's anus	39	Finger penetration of partner's anus	19
Use of mild pain	16	Anal intercourse	13

[a]From Cowart-Steckler (1984).

Human Sexuality Questionnaire

MARVIN ZUCKERMAN,[1] *University of Delaware*

The experience scales are designed to measure cumulative *heterosexual experience* and *homosexual experience* in terms of the variety of sexual activities of each type and the frequency. Separate 1-item scales assess the *number of heterosexual partners* and the *number of homosexual partners*. An *orgasmic experience* scale measures the variety of sexual activities leading to orgasm and their cumulative frequency. A 1-item *masturbation* scale measures cumulative masturbatory experience.

Attitude scales are designed to measure (a) *parental attitudes* toward manifestations of sexual curiosity and behavior in children, (b) *attitudes toward heterosexual activities* as a function of the *social relationship* to the other person, (c) *attitudes toward heterosexual activities* as a function of the *emotional relationship* to the other person, and (d) *attitudes toward homosexuality* in general.

EXPERIENCE SCALES

Description and Scoring of Subscales

1. The Heterosexual Experience scale is an extension of prior Guttman-type scales. It consists of 14 items ranging from kissing to manual petting, oral stimulation of the breast, genital manipulation, oral-genital contact, and coitus in various positions. For each of the 14 items, the subject rates his or her experience on a 5-point scale from 1 (*never*) to 5 (*10 times or more*). The score is the sum of the weighted item responses.

Reliability. Coefficients of reproducibility were .97 for males and females on a 12-item earlier version of the scale (Zuckerman, 1973) and .93 and .94 on the current 14-item version (Zuckerman, Tushup, & Finner, 1976). Coefficients of scalability in the latter study were .77 and .81 in males and females, respectively. Retest reliabilities after a 15-week interval were .80, .92, .94, and .95 in four groups (Zuckerman et al., 1976).

Validity. Subjects electing to take a course in human sexuality scored significantly higher than subjects in a personality course (Zuckerman et al., 1976). There were no initial sex differences. The males, but not the females, taking the sexuality course showed a greater increase than the control group. Heterosexual experience was positively correlated with all Sensation Seeking subscales in both males and females. Heterosexual college males scored higher

than male members of a gay university group (Zuckerman & Myers, 1983). The scale correlated positively with levels of plasma testosterone and estradiol in college males (Daitzman & Zuckerman, 1980).

2. The Homosexual Experience scale consists of four items describing experiences of genital manipulation (active and passive) and oral-genital stimulation (active and passive) with members of one's own sex. The subject responds on a 5-point scale for each item that ranges from 1 (*never*) to 5 (*10 times or more*). The score is the sum of the weighted item responses.

Reliability. Coefficients of reproducibility were .98 and 1.00 and coefficients of scalability were .76 and 1.00 for males and females, respectively (Zuckerman et al., 1976). Retest reliabilities after a 15-week interval were .84 and .49 for two groups of males (the lower one after taking a sexuality course), and .67 and .80 for two groups of females.

Validity. Males scored higher than females. Males, but not females, taking a course in human sexuality showed more increase than a control group (Zuckerman et al., 1976). Males in two gay groups scored higher than males in two heterosexual groups with practically no overlap in the two distributions (Zuckerman & Myers, 1983). The scales correlated positively with plasma estradiol levels in males, but not with testosterone (Daitzman & Zuckerman, 1980).

3. The Number of Heterosexual Partners scale consists of one item:. "With how many different persons of the opposite sex have you had sexual relationships in your lifetime?". The subject responds on a 5-point scale ranging from 1 (*none*) to 5 (*four or more*). The score is the weight (1 to 5) of the response choice.

Reliability. Retest reliabilities after a 15-week interval were .91 and .76 for two groups of males and .85 and .94 for two groups of females (Zuckerman et al., 1976).

Validity. Subjects taking a course in human sexuality scored higher than those taking a course in personality, and males scored higher than females (Zuckerman et al., 1976). The scale was unaffected by the course in human sexuality. It correlated positively with the Sensation Seeking subscales in both sexes. A heterosexual college male group scored higher than two gay male groups and a college church group (Zuckerman & Myers, 1983). The scale correlated positively with both plasma testosterone

[1]Address correspondence to Marvin Zuckerman, Department of Psychology, 220 Wolf Hall, University of Delaware, Newark, DE 19711; e-mail: zuckerma@udel.edu

and estradiol in college males (Daitzman & Zuckerman, 1980).

4. The Number of Homosexual Partners scale consists of one item: "With how many different persons of your own sex have you had sexual relations in your lifetime?". The subject responds on a 5-point scale from 1 (*none*) to 5 (*four or more*).

Reliability. Retest reliabilities were very low on this scale after a 15-week interval: .56 and .37 for males and .26 and .27 for females (Zuckerman et al., 1976). Instability may be due to changing interpretations of the term *sexual relations* in a homosexual context or more willingness to admit such relations on one occasion relative to another. Another reason is the highly restricted range; most persons respond *none*, so the stability depends on the responses on the few individuals who respond *one or more*.

Validity. A group taking a sexuality course scored higher than a group taking a personality course. There were no sex differences (Zuckerman et al., 1976). Males taking the sexuality course increased on the scale relative to control males. Two groups of gay males scored higher than two groups of heterosexual males (Zuckerman & Myers, 1983). The scale did not correlate with either testosterone or estradiol in males (Daitzman & Zuckerman, 1980).

5. The Orgasmic Experience scale consists of eight items describing various ways in which orgasm can be achieved: masturbation, petting, genital manipulation, heterosexual and homosexual intercourse, oral stimulation from another, dreams, and fantasy alone. The scale is similar to Kinsey's (Kinsey, Pomeroy, & Martin, 1948) "total outlet" measure which also includes all types of sexual activity. Subjects rate how many times they have reached orgasm by each of the specified methods on the scale ranging from 1 (*never*) to 5 (*10 times or more*). The score is the sum of weighted item responses.

Reliability. Retest reliabilities after a 15-week interval are .75 and .80 for males and .84 and .80 for females (Zuckerman et al., 1976).

Validity. Males scored significantly higher than females, but there was no difference between those taking sexuality and personality courses (Zuckerman et al., 1976). All Sensation Seeking subscales correlated with the scale in males, but only the Experience Seeking subscale correlated with Orgasmic Experience in females. Both gay groups (college and church-affiliated) and the heterosexual college male group scored higher than the church-affiliated college male group on this scale (Zuckerman & Myers, 1983). Orgasmic experience correlated with plasma testosterone but not with estradiol in college males (Daitzman & Zuckerman, 1980).

6. The Masturbation scale is a one-item scale referring to "Manipulation of your own genitals." The subject responds on a 5-point scale ranging from 1 (*once or twice*) to 5 (*10 times or more*). The score is the weighted item response.

Reliability. Retest reliabilities for a 15-week interval were .76 and .63 for males and .90 and .77 for females.

Validity. Males scored higher than females, but there were no differences between those taking sexuality and personality courses (Zuckerman et al., 1976). Males, but not females, increased more than a control group after taking a sexuality course. Gay groups had higher scores than the college church group but did not differ from the college heterosexual group (Zuckerman & Myers, 1983).

ATTITUDE SCALES

Description and Scoring of Subscales

1. The Parental Attitudes scale consisted of the five items in the Suppression of Sex scale from the Parental Attitude Research Instrument (PARI; Schaefer & Bell, 1958); the five corresponding reversed items from the reversed PARI (Zuckerman, 1959), constructed to control acquiescence set in the PARI; and two additional items dealing with attitudes toward exposing children to pornography. The 12 items are in a 4-response Likert format *strongly disagree* to *strongly agree*. The score consists of the weighted sum of responses scored in the direction of permissiveness.

Reliability. Retest reliabilities after a 15-week interval were .63 and .64 for males and .44 and .56 for females (Zuckerman et al., 1976).

Validity. Students taking a sexuality course scored higher (more permissive) than those taking a personality course. There were no sex differences (Zuckerman et al., 1976). Females, but not males, taking a sexuality course showed significantly greater increases than a control group.

2. The Attitudes Toward Heterosexual Activities scales are modifications of the Reiss (1967) scale, which separates social relationships and emotional relationships as criteria for permissiveness.

a. The Social Relationship attitude scale consists of the 14 activities described in the Heterosexual Experience scale. For each item the subjects are asked to indicate the relationship of partners for which they would consider the particular activity *all right* or *not all right* for someone of their own sex. The response scale options are 1 = *never all right*; 2 = *all right with someone you are married to*; 3 = *all right with someone you are engaged to*; 4 = *all right with someone you know well*; and 5 = *all right with anyone, no matter how long you have known them*. The total score, in the direction of permissiveness, is the sum of the weighted responses to each of the items.

b. The Emotional Relationship attitude scale uses the same 14 sexual activities, but here the subjects indicate whether the activity is all right under the following conditions: 1 = *never all right regardless of how much you love the person*; 2 = *all right if you are deeply in love with the person*; 3 = *all right if you feel strong affection toward the person*; 4 = *all right if you really like the person*; 5 = *all right, regardless of how you generally feel about the person*.

Reliabilities. For the Social Relationship scale, coefficients of reproducibility were .96 and 1.00, and coefficients of scalability were .89 and .96 for males and females, respectively. For the Emotional Relationship scale, coefficients of reproducibility were .96 and .98 and coefficients of scalability were .91 for both males and females. Retest reliabilities after a 15-week interval for the Social Relationship scale were .83 and .64 for males and .86 and .85 for females. For the Emotional Relationship scale retest reliabilities were .48 and .72 for males and .75 and .72 for females (Zuckerman et al., 1976).

Validity. Persons taking a sexuality course scored higher (more permissive) than those taking a personality course, and males scored higher than females on both attitude scales. The highly significant sex differences on the attitude scales were a marked contrast to the absence of difference on the Heterosexual Experience scale, which used the same activities in the items (Zuckerman et al., 1976). Attitude scales were more highly correlated with Experience scales for females than for males. Both males and females taking the sexuality course showed more change in the permissive attitude direction than did those in the control group. Permissive attitudes correlated positively with estradiol, but not testosterone, in males (Daitzman & Zuckerman, 1980).

3. The Attitudes Toward Homosexuality scale consists of four Likert-type items (*strongly disagree* to *strongly agree*) regarding the rights of homosexuals to marry or adopt children and whether homosexuals are regarded as normal or disturbed. The score is weighted based on the sum of the responses (1 to 4) for the items.

Reliability. No reliability data are available.

Validity. Unpublished data show no sex differences but do show a significant influence of a course in human sexuality in increasing permissiveness of attitudes toward homosexuality. Two gay groups had more permissive attitudes than two college heterosexual groups, and the heterosexual college group had more permissive attitudes than the heterosexual college church group (Zuckerman & Myers, 1983). Permissive attitudes correlated positively with estradiol, but not testosterone, in males (Daitzman & Zuckerman, 1980).

Other Information

This test is not copyrighted and may be used with the permission of the author for research purposes only.

References

Daitzman, D., & Zuckerman, M. (1980). Disinhibitory sensation seeking and gonadal hormones. *Personality and Individual Differences, 1,* 103–110.

Kinsey, A. C., Pomeroy, W. B., & Martin, C. E. (1948). *Sexual behavior in the human male.* Philadelphia: Saunders.

Reiss, I. L. (1967). *The social context of premarital sexual permissiveness.* New York: Holt, Rinehart & Winston.

Schaefer, E. S., & Bell, R. Q. (1958). Development of the Parental Attitude Research Instrument. *Child Development, 29,* 339–361.

Zuckerman, M. (1959). Reversed scales to control acquiescence response set in the Parental Attitude Research Instrument. *Child Development, 30,* 523–532.

Zuckerman, M. (1973). Scales for sex experience for males and females. *Journal of Consulting and Clinical Psychology, 41,* 27–29.

Zuckerman, M., & Myers, P. L. (1983). Sensation seeking in homosexual and heterosexual males. *Archives of Sexual Behavior, 12,* 347–356.

Zuckerman, M., Tushup, R., & Finner, S. (1976). Sexual attitudes and experience: Attitude and personality correlates and changes produced by a course in sexuality. *Journal of Consulting and Clinical Psychology, 44,* 7–19.

Exhibit

Human Sexuality Questionnaire

Ordering of Scales: Generally, the Attitude Scales are given before the Experience Scales, beginning with the Parental Attitudes Scale.

Parental Attitudes Scale

Response options for all items are:

    A) Strongly agree
    B) Mildly agree
    C) Mildly disagree
    D) Strongly disagree

1. A young child should be protected from hearing about sex.
2. Children should be taught about sex as soon as possible.

3. Children are normally curious about sex.
4. Young children should be prevented from contact with pornographic pictures.
5. There is usually something wrong with a child who asks a lot of questions about sex.
6. Sex play is a normal thing in children.
7. Sex is one of the greatest problems to be contended with in children.
8. Pornography is not harmful to young children and there is no need to be concerned about their coming into contact with it.
9. There is nothing wrong with bathing boys and girls in the same bathtub.
10. Sex is no great problem for child if the parent does not make it one.
11. It is very important that young boys and girls not be allowed to see each other completely undressed.
12. Children who take part in sex play become sex criminals when they grow up.

Scoring: Items 2, 3, 6, 8, 9, and 10 are weighted: A = 1; B = 2; C = 3; D = 4
          Items 1, 4, 5, 7, 11, and 12 are reverse weighted: A = 4; B = 3; C = 2; D = 1
          Score is sum of weighted responses: range = 12–48.

Attitudes Toward Heterosexual Activities: I. Social Relationship

Instructions: Answer these based on what you feel is right for *most persons* of your own sex and age.

Response options for all items are:

   A) Never
   B) All right with someone you are married to
   C) All right with someone you are engaged to, or intend to marry
   D) All right with someone you have been going with for some time
   E) All right with anyone, no matter how long you have known them

1. Kissing without tongue contact.
2. Kissing with tongue contact.
3. Male feeling covered female breasts.
4. Male feeling nude female breasts.
5. Male lying prone on the female, petting without penetration of her vagina.
6. Male mouth contact with female breast.
7. Female manipulation of male penis.
8. Male manipulation of female genitalia (vaginal and clitoral area).
9. Sexual intercourse in face to face position with the male on top.
10. Female mouth contact with male's penis.
11. Male mouth contact with female genitalia.
12. Sexual intercourse, face to face with female on top.
13. Sexual intercourse, face to face, in side position.
14. Sexual intercourse, entering from the rear.

Scoring: Response options are weighted as follows for all items:
         A = 1; B = 2; C = 3; D = 4; E = 5
         Score is sum of weighted response: range = 14–70.

Attitudes Toward Heterosexual Activities: II. Emotional Relationship

Instructions: Answer these based on what you feel is right for *most persons* of your own sex and age.

Response options for all items are:

   A) Never all right regardless of how much you love the person
   B) All right if you are deeply in love with the person
   C) All right if you feel strong affection for the person
   D) All right if you really like the person
   E) All right regardless of how you generally feel about the person

1. Kissing without tongue contact.
2. Kissing with tongue contact.
3. Male feeling covered female breasts.
4. Male feeling nude female breasts.
5. Male lying prone on the female, petting without penetration of her vagina.
6. Male mouth contact with female breast.

7.   Female manipulation of male penis.
8.   Male manipulation of female genitalia (vaginal and clitoral area).
9.   Sexual intercourse in face to face position with the male on top.
10. Female mouth contact with male's penis.
11. Male mouth contact with female genitalia.
12. Sexual intercourse, face to face, with female on top.
13. Sexual intercourse, face to face, in side position.
14. Sexual intercourse, entering vagina from the rear.

Scoring: Response options are weighted as follows for all items:
    A = 1; B = 2; C = 3; D = 4; E = 5
    Score is sum of weighted responses: range = 14–70.

Attitudes Toward Homosexuality

1.   Do you think homosexuals (male or female) should have the right to legally marry?
    A) Definitely not
    B) No, I don't think so
    C) Yes, maybe
    D) Yes, definitely
2.   Do you think homosexual couples (male or female) should have the right to adopt children?
    A) Definitely not
    B) No, I don't think so
    C) Yes, maybe
    D) Yes, definitely
3.   Nearly all homosexuals are psychiatrically disturbed:
    A) Strongly agree
    B) Mildly agree
    C) Mildly disagree
    D) Strongly disagree
4.   Except for differences in sexual preference, homosexuals are as normal as heterosexuals:
    A) Strongly agree
    B) Mildly agree
    C) Mildly disagree
    D) Strongly disagree

Scoring: Items 1, 2, and 4 are weighted: A = 1; B = 2; C = 3; D = 4
    Item 3 is reverse weighted: A = 4; B = 3; C = 2; D = 1
    Score is sum of weighted responses: range = 4–16.

Heterosexual Experience

Instructions: Heterosexual experience (with persons of the opposite sex). If you are male, substitute yourself for "male" in the item; if you are female, substitute yourself for "female" in the item (e.g., for a female, Item 4 is "having your nude breast felt by a male.")

Response options for all items are:

    A) Never
    B) Once or Twice
    C) Several times
    D) More than several times, less than ten times
    E) Ten times or more

How many times have you done the following?

1.   Kissing without tongue contact.
2.   Kissing with tongue contact.
3.   Male feeling covered female breasts.
4.   Male feeling nude female breasts.
5.   Male lying prone on the female, petting without penetration of her vagina.

6. Male mouth contact with female breast.
7. Female manipulation of male's penis.
8. Male manipulation of female genitalia (vaginal and clitoral areas).
9. Sexual intercourse in face to face position with the male on top.
10. Female mouth contact with male's penis.
11. Male mouth contact with female genitalia.
12. Sexual intercourse, face to face, with female on top.
13. Sexual intercourse, face to face, in side position.
14. Sexual intercourse, entering vagina from the rear.

Scoring: Response options are weighted as follows:
       For all items A = 1; B = 2; C = 3; D = 4; E = 5
       Score is sum of weighted responses: range = 14–70.

Homosexual Experience

Instructions: Homosexual experience (with a person of your own sex).

Response options for all items are:

    A) Never
    B) Once or twice
    C) Several times
    D) More than several, less than ten times
    E) Ten times or more

How many times have you done the following?

1. Manipulating the genitals of a person of your own sex.
2. Having your genitals manipulated by a person of your own sex.
3. Performing mouth-genital contact on a person of your own sex.
4. Having mouth-genital contact performed on you by a person of your own sex.

Scoring: Response options are weighted as follows:
       A = 1; B = 2; C = 3; D = 4; E = 5
       Score is sum of weighted responses: range = 4–20.

One-Item Scales

Masturbation Experience

How many times have you engaged in manipulation of your own genitals:
    A) Never
    B) Once or twice
    C) Several times
    D) More than several, less than ten times
    E) Ten times or more

Score is weighted response: A = 1; B = 2; C = 3; D = 4; E = 5: range = 1–5

Number of Heterosexual Partners[a]

With how many different persons *of the opposite sex* have you had sexual intercourse in your lifetime?
    A) None
    B) One
    C) Two
    D) Three
    E) Four or more

Score is weighted response: A = 1; B = 2; C = 3; D = 4; E = 5: range = 1–5

Number of Homosexual Partners

With how many different persons *of your own sex* have you had sexual relations in your lifetime?

    A) None
    B) One
    C) Two
    D) Three
    E) Four or more

Score is weighted response: A = 1; B = 2; C = 3; D = 4; E = 5: range = 1–5

Orgasmic Experience[b]

Instructions: Orgasmic Experience (orgasm = sudden spasmodic discharge of sexual tension usually accompanied by ejaculation in the male).

Response options for all items are:

    A) Never
    B) Once or twice
    C) Several times
    D) More than several, less than ten times
    E) Ten times or more

How many times have you experienced orgasm through:

1. Masturbation
2. Petting, or body contact without manipulation of genitals
3. Manipulation of your genitals by someone else
4. Heterosexual intercourse
5. Homosexual relations
6. Oral stimulation by another
7. Dreams (nocturnal emissions)
8. Fantasy alone

Scoring: Response options are weighted as follows for all items:
    A = 1; B = 2; C = 3; D = 4; E = 5
    Score is sum of weighted responses: range = 8–40

---

[a]Note that the Number of Partners scales may be used as a consistency check on the heterosexual sexual intercourse item and any of the homosexual experience items in regard to the report or denial of this type of experience.

[b]Note that the Orgasmic Experience scale may be used for a consistency check on heterosexual and homosexual activities and partners scales.

Sexual Dysfunctional Beliefs Questionnaire

PEDRO J. NOBRE,[1] *Universidade de Trás-os-Montes e Alto Douro, Portugal*
JOSÉ PINTO-GOUVEIA, *Universidade de Coimbra, Portugal*

The Sexual Dysfunctional Beliefs Questionnaire (SDBQ; Nobre, Pinto-Gouveia, & Gomes, 2003) is an instrument designed to assess sexual dysfunctional beliefs as an indicator of vulnerability factors to sexual disorders in both men and women. The SDBQ may be useful in both clinical practice and educational programs.

Description

The SDBQ is a self-report measure with a male and a female version that can be used in both clinical and nonclinical samples. The SDBQ is a 40-item questionnaire assessing an assortment of specific stereotypes and beliefs presented in the clinical literature as predisposing factors to the development and maintenance of the different male and female sexual dysfunctions.

Response Mode and Timing

Participants may respond to the SDBQ using paper and pencil or computer. The response scales are Likert type. Respondents are asked to identify the degree of concordance with 40 statements regarding diverse sexual issues, from 1 (*Completely Disagree*) to 5 (*Completely Agree*). Respondents take an average of 10 minutes to complete the SDBQ.

Scoring

Both male and female versions of the SDBQ were submitted to factor analysis (Nobre, Pinto-Gouveia, & Gomes, 2003). A principal component analysis with varimax rotation of the female version identified six factors accounting for 43% of the total variance: (a) Sexual Conservatism, (b) Sexual Desire and Pleasure as a Sin, (c) Age-Related Beliefs, (d) Body-Image Beliefs, (e) Denying Affection Primacy, (f) Motherhood Primacy (see Table 1).

The principal component analysis with varimax rotation of the SDBQ male version identified six factors that accounted for 49% of the total variance (Nobre, Pinto-Gouveia, & Gomes, 2003): (a) Sexual Conservatism, (b) Female Sexual Power, (c) "Macho" Belief, (d) Beliefs About Women's Sexual Satisfaction, (e) Restricted Attitude Toward Sexual Activity, (f) Sex as an Abuse of Men's Power (see Table 2).

TABLE 1
Domain and Total Scores of the SDBQ (Female Version)

	Domains	Item numbers	Min	Max
F1	Sexual Conservatism	2, 4, 7, 13, 14, 17, 27, 28, 32	9	45
F2	Sexual Desire and Pleasure as a Sin	15, 34, 35, 36, 37, 39	6	30
F3	Age-Related Beliefs	5, 6, 8, 11, 20	5	25
F4	Body-Image Beliefs	10, 12, 38, 40	4	20
F5	Denying Affection Primacy	1, 3, 18, 22, 23, 24	6	30
F6	Motherhood Primacy	26, 30, 31, 33	4	20
Total			34	170

Note. Items 1, 3, 22, 23, and 24 are scored in reverse order.

TABLE 2
Domain and Total Scores of the SDBQ (Male Version)

	Domains	Item numbers	Min	Max
F1	Sexual Conservatism	2, 5, 9, 18, 21, 24, 25, 26, 32, 33	10	50
F2	Female Sexual Power	11, 15, 19, 27, 29, 38, 39, 40	8	40
F3	"Macho" Belief	1, 4, 6, 17, 28, 31, 37	7	35
F4	Beliefs About Women's Satisfaction	3, 7, 16, 35, 36	5	25
F5	Restrictive Attitude Toward Sex	8, 12, 13, 30	4	20
F6	Sex as an Abuse of Men's Power	10, 22, 34	3	15
Total			37	185

Note. Item 37 is scored in reverse order.

An index of dysfunctional sexual beliefs might be calculated by summing all SDBQ items (after reversing the scores of the inverted items).

Reliability

Internal Consistency

Internal consistency of the instrument was assessed by calculating Cronbach's alpha statistic for the total scale and also for each dimension of both male and female versions. Results for the total scale (Cronbach's $\alpha = .93$ for the male and .81 for the female version) supported the high

[1]Address correspondence to Pedro Nobre, Universidade de Trás-os-Montes e Alto Douro, Apartado 1013, 5001–801 Vila Real, Portugal; e-mail: pnobre5@gmail.com

internal consistency of the SDBQ. The Cronbach's α for each dimension of the SDBQ ranged from .50 to .89 for the female version and from .54 to .89 for the male version (Nobre, Pinto-Gouveia, & Gomes, 2003).

Test-Retest Reliability

Test-retest reliability for both male and female versions was assessed by computing Pearson product-moment correlations between two consecutive administrations of the questionnaires with a 4-week interval. Both male and female versions presented statistically significant results ($p < .05$) for the total scale ($r = .73$ and $r = .80$ respectively), demonstrating that the instrument presented good stability over time (Nobre, Pinto-Gouveia, & Gomes, 2003).

Validity

Convergent Validity

Our analysis of convergent validity indicated that the SDBQ is associated with validated measures of sexual and more general beliefs, as well as with measures of sexual functioning (Nobre, Pinto-Gouveia, & Gomes, 2003). Our findings showed statistically significant correlations between the SDBQ and the Sexual Beliefs and Information Questionnaire (SBIQ; Adams et al., 1996). The SDBQ also correlated significantly with the Female Sexual Function Index (FSFI; Rosen et al., 2000) and the International Index of Erectile Function (IIEF; Rosen et al., 1997).

Discriminant Validity

We conducted a discriminant validity analysis, using a clinical sample (49 men and 47 women with sexual dysfunction) and a matched control group (49 men and 46 women without sexual dysfunction). Findings for both men and women, although not reaching statistical significance, showed that participants from the clinical group presented higher scores on several domains of the SDBQ compared to individuals in the control group. Women in the clinical group presented higher scores in Sexual Conservatism (F1), Sex as a Sin (F2), and Body-Image Beliefs (F4), whereas men with sexual dysfunction showed higher scores on "Macho" Belief (F3; Nobre, Pinto-Gouveia, & Gomes, 2003; Nobre & Pinto-Gouveia, 2006).

Other Information

For more information regarding the SDBQ and permission for its use, please contact Pedro J. Nobre.

References

Adams, S. G., Dubbert, P. M., Chupurdia, K. M., Jones, A., Lofland, K. R., & Leermakers, E. (1996). Assessment of sexual beliefs and information in aging couples with sexual dysfunction. *Archives of Sexual Behavior, 25,* 249–260.

Nobre, P. J., & Pinto-Gouveia, J. (2006). Dysfunctional sexual beliefs as vulnerability factors to sexual dysfunction. *The Journal of Sex Research, 43,* 68–75.

Nobre, P. J., Pinto-Gouveia, J., & Gomes, F. A. (2003). Sexual Dysfunctional Beliefs Questionnaire: An instrument to assess sexual dysfunctional beliefs as vulnerability factors to sexual problems. *Sexual and Relationship Therapy, 18,* 171–204.

Rosen, R. C., Brown, C., Heiman, J., Leiblum, S., Meston, C., Shabsig, R., et al. (2000). The Female Sexual Function Index (FSFI): A multidimensional self-report instrument for the assessment of female sexual function. *Journal of Sex & Marital Therapy, 26,* 191–208.

Rosen, R. C., Riley, A., Wagner, G., Osterloh, I. H., Kirkpatrick, J., & Mishra, A. (1997). The International Index of Erectile Function (IIEF): A multidimensional scale for assessment of erectile dysfunction. *Urology, 49,* 822–830.

Exhibit

Sexual Dysfunctional Beliefs Questionnaire

Male Version

The list presented below contains statements related to sexuality. Please read each statement carefully and circle the number in the right-hand column which corresponds to the extent to which you agree or disagree with each statement (circle only one option per statement), from 1 (completely disagree) to 5 (completely agree). There are no wrong or right answers, but it is very important that you be honest and that you answer all items.

Sexual Beliefs

	Completely Disagree	Disagree	Don't Disagree or Agree	Agree	Completely Agree
1. A real man has sexual intercourse very often	1	2	3	4	5
2. Orgasm is possible only by vaginal intercourse	1	2	3	4	5
3. Penile erection is essential for a woman's sexual satisfaction	1	2	3	4	5
4. Homosexuality is a sickness	1	2	3	4	5
5. A woman has no other choice but to be sexually subjugated by a man's power	1	2	3	4	5
6. A real man must wait the necessary amount of time to sexually satisfy a woman during intercourse	1	2	3	4	5
7. A woman may have doubts about a man's virility when he fails to get an erection during sexual activity	1	2	3	4	5
8. Repeated engagement in oral or anal sex can cause serious health problems	1	2	3	4	5
9. A shorter duration of intercourse is a sign of a man's power	1	2	3	4	5
10. Sex is an abuse of a male's power	1	2	3	4	5
11. The consequences of a sexual failure are catastrophic	1	2	3	4	5
12. Women only pay attention to attractive younger men	1	2	3	4	5
13. It is not appropriate to have sexual fantasies during sexual intercourse	1	2	3	4	5
14. There are certain universal rules about what is normal during sexual activity	1	2	3	4	5
15. In bed the woman is the boss	1	2	3	4	5
16. Men who are not capable of penetrating women can't satisfy them sexually	1	2	3	4	5
17. In sex, getting to the climax is most important	1	2	3	4	5
18. In sex, anything but vaginal intercourse is unacceptable	1	2	3	4	5
19. A woman's body is her best weapon	1	2	3	4	5
20. A woman may stop loving a man if he is not capable of satisfying her sexually	1	2	3	4	5
21. Vaginal intercourse is the only legitimate type of sex	1	2	3	4	5
22. The quality of the erection is what most satisfies women	1	2	3	4	5
23. A successful career implies the control of sexual urges	1	2	3	4	5
24. Foreplay is a waste of time	1	2	3	4	5
25. Sex is meant only for procreation	1	2	3	4	5
26. In sex, the quicker/faster the better	1	2	3	4	5
27. People who don't control their sexual urges are more easily controlled by others	1	2	3	4	5
28. A real man is always ready for sex and must be capable of satisfying any woman	1	2	3	4	5
29. If a man lets himself go sexually he is under a woman's control	1	2	3	4	5
30. Anal sex is a perverted activity	1	2	3	4	5
31. A man must be capable of maintaining an erection until the end of any sexual activity	1	2	3	4	5
32. There is only one acceptable way of having sex (missionary position)	1	2	3	4	5
33. Sexual intercourse before marriage is a sin	1	2	3	4	5
34. Sex is a violation of a woman's body	1	2	3	4	5
35. A man who doesn't sexually satisfy a woman is a failure	1	2	3	4	5
36. Whenever the situation arises, a real man must be capable of penetration	1	2	3	4	5
37. Sex can be good even without orgasm	1	2	3	4	5
38. A real man doesn't need much stimulation to reach orgasm	1	2	3	4	5
39. A woman at her sexual peak can get whatever she wants from a man	1	2	3	4	5
40. The greater the sexual intimacy, the greater the potential for getting hurt	1	2	3	4	5

Female Version

The list presented below contains statements related to sexuality. Please read each statement carefully and circle the number in the right-hand column which corresponds to the extent to which you agree or disagree with each statement (circle only one option per statement), from 1 (completely disagree) to 5 (completely agree). There are no wrong or right answers, but it is very important that you be honest and that you answer all items.

Sexual Beliefs

		Completely Disagree	Disagree	Don't Disagree or Agree	Agree	Completely Agree
1.	Love and affection from a partner are necessary for good sex	1	2	3	4	5
2.	Masturbation is wrong and sinful	1	2	3	4	5
3.	The most important component of sex is mutual affection	1	2	3	4	5
4.	The best gift a woman could bring to marriage is her virginity	1	2	3	4	5
5.	After menopause women lose their sexual desire	1	2	3	4	5
6.	Women who have sexual fantasies are perverted	1	2	3	4	5
7.	Masturbation is not a proper activity for respectable women	1	2	3	4	5
8.	After menopause women can't reach orgasm	1	2	3	4	5
9.	There are a variety of ways of getting pleasure and reaching orgasm	1	2	3	4	5
10.	Women who are not physically attractive can't be sexually satisfied	1	2	3	4	5
11.	In the bedroom the man is the boss	1	2	3	4	5
12.	A good mother can't be sexually active	1	2	3	4	5
13.	Reaching climax/orgasm is acceptable for men but not for women	1	2	3	4	5
14.	Sexual activity must be initiated by the man	1	2	3	4	5
15.	Sex is dirty and sinful	1	2	3	4	5
16.	Simultaneous orgasm for two partners is essential for a satisfying sexual encounter	1	2	3	4	5
17.	Orgasm is possible only by vaginal intercourse	1	2	3	4	5
18.	The goal of sex is for men to be satisfied	1	2	3	4	5
19.	A successful professional career implies control of sexual behavior	1	2	3	4	5
20.	As women age the pleasure they get from sex decreases	1	2	3	4	5
21.	Men only pay attention to young, attractive women	1	2	3	4	5
22.	Sex is a beautiful and pure activity	1	2	3	4	5
23.	Sex without love is like food without flavor	1	2	3	4	5
24.	As long as both partners consent, anything goes	1	2	3	4	5
25.	Any woman who initiates sexual activity is immoral	1	2	3	4	5
26.	Sex is meant only for procreation	1	2	3	4	5
27.	Sexual intercourse during menstruation can cause health problems	1	2	3	4	5
28.	Oral sex is one of the biggest perversions	1	2	3	4	5
29.	If women let themselves go sexually they are totally under men's control	1	2	3	4	5
30.	Being nice and smiling at men can be dangerous	1	2	3	4	5
31.	The most wonderful emotions that a woman can experience are maternal feelings	1	2	3	4	5
32.	Anal sex is a perverted activity	1	2	3	4	5
33.	In the bedroom the woman is the boss	1	2	3	4	5
34.	Sex should happen only if a man initiates	1	2	3	4	5
35.	There is just one acceptable way of having sex (missionary position)	1	2	3	4	5
36.	Experiencing pleasure during sexual intercourse is not acceptable in a virtuous woman	1	2	3	4	5
37.	A good mother must control her sexual urges	1	2	3	4	5
38.	An ugly woman is not capable of sexually satisfying her partner	1	2	3	4	5
39.	A woman who only derives sexual pleasure through clitoral stimulation is sick or perverted	1	2	3	4	5
40.	Pure girls don't engage in sexual activity	1	2	3	4	5

Sexual Modes Questionnaire

PEDRO J. NOBRE,[1] *Universidade de Trás-os-Montes e Alto Douro, Portugal*
JOSÉ PINTO-GOUVEIA, *Universidade de Coimbra, Portugal*

The Sexual Modes Questionnaire (SMQ; Nobre & Pinto-Gouveia, 2003) is a measure designed to assess the interaction among cognitions, emotions, and sexual responses.

Description

The SMQ is a self-report measure, with a male and a female version that can be used in both clinical and nonclinical samples. It is composed of three interdependent subscales: the Automatic Thought (AT) subscale, the Emotional Response (ER) subscale, and the Sexual Response (SR) subscale.

Automatic Thought Subscale

The AT subscale is composed of 30 items (male) or 33 items (female) developed to evaluate automatic thoughts and images experienced by the participants during sexual activity. Thoughts included in the scale were selected based on their theoretical and clinical relevance. For the male version we generated items pertaining to sexual performance thoughts (especially the erectile response), thoughts of potential failure, sexually negative or conservative thoughts toward sexuality, and thoughts about the negative impact of age on sexual functioning. We generated items for the female version to assess failure and disengagement thoughts, low body-image thoughts, sexual abuse thoughts, thoughts about a partner's lack of affection, and sexual passivity and control thoughts (Nobre & Pinto-Gouveia, 2003).

Emotional Response Subscale

The ER subscale is composed of 30 items (male) or 33 items (female) that assess emotions that the respondents experience during sexual activity. Respondents are given a list of 10 emotions (worry, sadness, disillusion, fear, guilt, shame, anger, hurt, pleasure, satisfaction) to select from in evaluating their responses to the AT items.

Sexual Response Subscale

The SR subscale is composed of 30 items (male) or 33 items (female) that assess subjective sexual responses pertaining to the items of the AT subscale.

Response Mode and Timing

Using Likert-type scales, the participants may respond to the SMQ using paper and pencil or computer. Respondents begin with the AT subscale by rating how frequently they experience each of the automatic thoughts during sexual activity (from 1 = *Never* to 5 = *Always*). Respondents then check from the list of 10 emotions (worry, sadness, disillusion, fear, guilt, shame, anger, hurt, pleasure, satisfaction) those that they usually experience whenever they engage in each automatic thought. Finally respondents rate the intensity of their subjective sexual arousal (from 1 = *Very Low* to 5 = *Very High*) when related to their previous thoughts and emotions.

Scoring

Both versions (male and female) of the AT subscale were submitted to factor analysis (Nobre & Pinto-Gouveia, 2003). We conducted a principal component analysis with varimax rotation of the female version, identifying six factors accounting for 53.1% of the total variance: (a) Sexual Abuse Thoughts, (b) Failure and Disengagement Thoughts, (c) Partner's Lack of Affection, (d) Sexual Passivity and Control, (e) Lack of Erotic Thoughts, and (f) Low Self Body-Image Thoughts (see Table 1).

TABLE 1
Items, Minimums, and Maximums of Female AT Factors and Totals

Factors	Item Number	Minimum	Maximum
Sexual Abuse Thoughts	1, 2, 3, 4, 6, 15, 32, 33	8	40
Failure/Disengagement Thoughts	19, 22, 26, 30	4	20
Partner's Lack of Affection	7, 12, 24, 27, 28	5	25
Sexual Passivity and Control	10, 14, 17, 21, 23, 29	6	30
Lack of Erotic Thoughts	5, 8, 11, 25, 31	5	25
Low Self Body-Image Thoughts	9, 16, 20	3	15
Total		31	155

Note. Items 5, 8, 11, 25, and 31 are scored in reverse order.

[1]Address correspondence to Pedro Nobre, Universidade de Trás-os-Montes e Alto Douro, Apartado 1013, 5001–801 Vila Real, Portugal; e-mail: pnobre5@gmail.com

In the male version, we conducted a principal component analysis that identified five factors accounting for 54.7% of the total variance: (a) Failure Anticipation Thoughts, (b) Erection Concern Thoughts, (c) Age and Body Function-Related Thoughts, (d) Negative Thoughts Toward Sex, and (e) Lack of Erotic Thoughts (see Table 2).

TABLE 2
Items, Minimums, and Maximums of the Male AT Factors and Totals

Factors	Item Numbers	Minimum	Maximum
Failure Anticipation Thoughts	1, 2, 3, 4, 6, 7, 16	7	35
Erection Concern Thoughts	5, 8, 9, 10, 11, 12, 29	7	35
Age and Body-Related Thoughts	19, 21, 22, 28	4	20
Negative Thoughts Toward Sex	20, 23, 24, 25, 30	5	25
Lack of Erotic Thoughts	14, 17, 18, 26	4	20
Total		27	135

Note. Items 14, 17, 18, and 26 are scored in reverse order.

An index of negative automatic thoughts may be calculated by summing all automatic thought items (thoughts related to erotic cues were scored in reverse order).

An index for each emotional response may be calculated based on the following formula: total number of each emotion endorsed / total number of emotions endorsed. The emotional response index ranges from 0.0 to 1.0.

An index of sexual response may be calculated based on the following formula: sum of the sexual response for each item / total number of sexual response items endorsed. The sexual response index ranges from 1 to 5.

Reliability

Internal consistency of both male and female AT subscales was assessed using Cronbach's α for the total scales and for each factor separately. Results were high for male and female total scales ($α = .88$ and .87, respectively), showing the general consistency of the measures (Nobre & Pinto-Gouveia, 2003). The internal consistency of the specific dimensions within each factor indicated Cronbach's α statistics ranging from .71 to .80 for the female version and from .69 to .83 for the male version (Nobre & Pinto-Gouveia, 2003).

We assessed test-retest reliability of both male and female AT subscales by computing Pearson product-moment correlation between two consecutive administrations with a 4-week interval. Results from the female version show the stability of the measure across time, with a high correlation for the total scale ($r = .95$, $p < .01$) and correlations from the specific dimensions ranging from $r = .52$, $p < .05$ to $r = .90$, $p < .01$. Results from the male version show a more moderate Pearson product-moment correlation between the two consecutive administrations ($r = .65$, $p = .08$), with

correlations for the several specific dimensions ranging from $r = .20$, $p < .05$ to $r = .95$, $p < .01$ (Nobre & Pinto-Gouveia, 2003).

Validity

Convergent Validity

Convergent validity of the SMQ was assessed through the relationship with validated measures of sexual functioning in men (International Index of Erectile Function [IIEF]; Rosen et al., 1997) and women (Female Sexual Function Index [FSFI]; Rosen et al., 2000). Several statistically significant correlations were found between both versions of the SMQ and the FSFI and IIEF, indicating that thoughts and emotions during sexual activity are closely linked to sexual response. The FSFI presented high negative correlations with the AT subscale, particularly with Sexual Abuse Thoughts (F1), Failure and Disengagement Thoughts (F2), and Lack of Erotic Thoughts (F5). The IIEF showed significant negative correlations with the AT subscale, particularly with Failure Anticipation Thoughts (F1), Erection Concern Thoughts (F2), and Lack of Erotic Thoughts (F5; Nobre & Pinto-Gouveia, 2003).

Correlations between the ER subscale and the male and female sexual function indices were also statistically significant. The FSFI was strongly negatively correlated with the emotions of sadness, guilt, and anger, and positively correlated with pleasure. For males, there were higher correlations between the IIEF and sadness, disillusionment, pleasure, and satisfaction (Nobre & Pinto-Gouveia, 2003, 2006).

Discriminant Validity

We conducted a discriminant validity analysis, using a clinical group (men and women with sexual dysfunction) and a control group (matched men and women without sexual dysfunction). Our results indicated significant differences in the automatic thoughts, emotions, and sexual responses of clinical and control group participants of both sexes. The women in the clinical group presented significantly higher scores on Failure and Disengagement Thoughts (F2), Lack of Erotic Thoughts (F5), and the total scale. The men in the clinical group presented significantly higher scores (compared to the control group) on Failure Anticipation (F1), Erection Concern (F2), and Lack of Erotic Thoughts (F5; Nobre & Pinto-Gouveia, 2003, 2008).

Other Information

For more information regarding the SMQ and permission for its use, please contact Pedro J. Nobre.

References

Nobre, P. J., & Pinto-Gouveia, J. (2003). Sexual Modes Questionnaire: Measure to assess the interaction between cognitions, emotions and sexual response. *The Journal of Sex Research, 40,* 368–382.

Nobre, P. J., & Pinto-Gouveia, J. (2006). Emotions during sexual activity: Differences between sexually functional and dysfunctional men and women. *Archives of Sexual Behavior, 35,* 8–15.

Nobre, P. J., & Pinto-Gouveia, J. (2008). Differences in automatic thoughts presented during sexual activity between sexually functional and dysfunctional males and females. *Journal of Cognitive Therapy and Research, 32,* 37–49.

Rosen, R. C., Brown, C., Heiman, J., Leiblum, S., Meston, C., Shabsigh,

R., et al. (2000). The Female Sexual Function Index (FSFI): A multidimensional self-report instrument for the assessment of female sexual function. *Journal of Sex & Marital Therapy, 26,* 191–208.

Rosen, R. C., Riley, A., Wagner, G., Osterloh, I. H., Kirkpatrick, J., & Mishra, A. (1997). The International Index of Erectile Function (IIEF): A multidimensional scale for assessment of erectile dysfunction. *Urology, 49,* 822–830.

Exhibit

Sexual Modes Questionnaire

Male Version

The items presented below are a list of thoughts one can have during sexual activity. In the first column, please indicate the frequency with which you experience these **thoughts** by circling a number (1—Never to 5—Always). Next, indicate the **types of emotions** you typically experience when having these thoughts by marking an X in the columns for the appropriate emotions. Finally, in the last column, for each thought experienced indicate the intensity of your typical **sexual response** (arousal) while you are having that thought by circling a number (1—Very Low to 5—Very High).

NOTE: For thoughts that you indicate as never experiencing, you do not need to fill out the emotion or sexual response column.

Example: Imagine that the thought "Making love is wonderful" comes to your mind very often whenever you are engaged in a sexual activity, that this idea is accompanied by pleasurable emotions, and that your sexual arousal becomes very high. In this case your answer should be:

Thoughts / Type of Thoughts	Frequency (Never, Seldom, Sometimes, Often, Always)	Types of Emotions (Worry, Sadness, Disillusioned, Fear, Guilt, Shame, Anger, Hurt, Pleasure, Satisfaction)	Sexual Response Intensity (Very Low, Low, Moderate, High, Very High)
Example: Making love is wonderful	1 2 3 **X** 5	X (Pleasure)	1 2 3 4 **X**

Thoughts / Type of Thoughts	Frequency	Types of Emotions	Sexual Response Intensity
	Never Seldom Sometimes Often Always	Worry Sadness Disillusioned Fear Guilt Shame Anger Hurt Pleasure Satisfaction	Very Low Low Moderate High Very High
1. These movements and positions are fabulous	1 2 3 4 5		1 2 3 4 5
2. This time I cannot disappoint my partner	1 2 3 4 5		1 2 3 4 5
3. She will replace me with another guy	1 2 3 4 5		1 2 3 4 5
4. I'm condemned to failure	1 2 3 4 5		1 2 3 4 5
5. I must be able to have intercourse	1 2 3 4 5		1 2 3 4 5
6. This is not going anywhere	1 2 3 4 5		1 2 3 4 5
7. I'm not satisfying her	1 2 3 4 5		1 2 3 4 5
8. I must achieve an erection	1 2 3 4 5		1 2 3 4 5
9. I'm not penetrating my partner	1 2 3 4 5		1 2 3 4 5
10. My penis is not responding	1 2 3 4 5		1 2 3 4 5
11. Why isn't this working?	1 2 3 4 5		1 2 3 4 5
12. I wish this could last longer	1 2 3 4 5		1 2 3 4 5
13. What is she thinking about me?	1 2 3 4 5		1 2 3 4 5
14. These movements and positions are fabulous	1 2 3 4 5		1 2 3 4 5

		Frequency	Emotions	Sexual response
15.	What if others knew I'm not capable . . . ?	1 2 3 4 5		1 2 3 4 5
16.	If I fail again I am a lost cause	1 2 3 4 5		1 2 3 4 5
17.	I'm the happiest man on earth	1 2 3 4 5		1 2 3 4 5
18.	This is turning me on	1 2 3 4 5		1 2 3 4 5
19.	If I don't climax now, I won't be able to later	1 2 3 4 5		1 2 3 4 5
20.	She is not being as affectionate as she used to	1 2 3 4 5		1 2 3 4 5
21.	She doesn't find my body attractive anymore	1 2 3 4 5		1 2 3 4 5
22.	I'm getting old	1 2 3 4 5		1 2 3 4 5
23.	This is disgusting	1 2 3 4 5		1 2 3 4 5
24.	This way of having sex is immoral	1 2 3 4 5		1 2 3 4 5
25.	Telling her what I want sexually would be unnatural	1 2 3 4 5		1 2 3 4 5
26.	She is really turned on	1 2 3 4 5		1 2 3 4 5
27.	I must show my virility	1 2 3 4 5		1 2 3 4 5
28.	It will never be the same again	1 2 3 4 5		1 2 3 4 5
29.	If I can't get an erection, I will be embarrassed	1 2 3 4 5		1 2 3 4 5
30.	I have other more important matters to deal with	1 2 3 4 5		1 2 3 4 5

Female Version

The items presented below are a list of thoughts one can have during sexual activity. In the first column, please indicate the frequency with which you experience these **thoughts** by circling a number (1—Never to 5—Always). Next, indicate the **types of emotions** you typically experience when having these thoughts by marking an X in the columns for the appropriate emotions. Finally, in the last column, for each thought experienced indicate the intensity of your typical **sexual response** (arousal) while you are having that thought by circling a number (1—Very Low to 5—Very High).

NOTE: For thoughts that you indicate as never experiencing, you do not need to fill out the emotion or sexual response column.

Example: Imagine that the thought "Making love is wonderful" comes to your mind often whenever you are engaged in a sexual activity, that this idea is accompanied by pleasurable emotions, and that your sexual arousal becomes very high. In this case your answer should be:

Thoughts / Type of Thoughts	Frequency (Never Seldom Sometimes Often Always)	Types of Emotions (Worry Sadness Disillusioned Fear Guilt Shame Anger Hurt Pleasure Satisfaction)	Sexual response Intensity (Very Low Low Moderate High Very High)
Making love is wonderful	1 2 3 **X** 5	X (Pleasure)	1 2 3 4 **X**

Thoughts / Type of Thoughts	Frequency (Never Seldom Sometimes Often Always)	Types of Emotions (Worry Sadness Disillusioned Fear Guilt Shame Anger Hurt Pleasure Satisfaction)	Sexual response Intensity (Very Low Low Moderate High Very High)
1. He is abusing me	1 2 3 4 5		1 2 3 4 5
2. How can I get out of this situation?	1 2 3 4 5		1 2 3 4 5
3. He only wants to satisfy himself	1 2 3 4 5		1 2 3 4 5
4. Sex is all he thinks about	1 2 3 4 5		1 2 3 4 5
5. The way he is talking turns me on	1 2 3 4 5		1 2 3 4 5
6. He is violating me	1 2 3 4 5		1 2 3 4 5

		Left scale		Right scale
7.	This way of having sex is immoral	1 2 3 4 5		1 2 3 4 5
8.	These movements and positions are fabulous	1 2 3 4 5		1 2 3 4 5
9.	I'm getting fat/ugly	1 2 3 4 5		1 2 3 4 5
10.	If I let myself go he is going to think I'm promiscuous	1 2 3 4 5		1 2 3 4 5
11.	Making love is wonderful	1 2 3 4 5		1 2 3 4 5
12.	He is not being as affectionate as he used to be	1 2 3 4 5		1 2 3 4 5
13.	I'm not satisfying my partner	1 2 3 4 5		1 2 3 4 5
14.	I must not show that I'm interested	1 2 3 4 5		1 2 3 4 5
15.	This is disgusting	1 2 3 4 5		1 2 3 4 5
16.	I'm not as physically attractive as I used to be	1 2 3 4 5		1 2 3 4 5
17.	I should not take the lead in sexual activity	1 2 3 4 5		1 2 3 4 5
18.	He only cares about me when he wants sex	1 2 3 4 5		1 2 3 4 5
19.	I'm not getting turned on	1 2 3 4 5		1 2 3 4 5
20.	I'm not feeling physically attractive	1 2 3 4 5		1 2 3 4 5
21.	These activities shouldn't be planned ahead of time	1 2 3 4 5		1 2 3 4 5
22.	I can't feel anything	1 2 3 4 5		1 2 3 4 5
23.	I don't want to get hurt emotionally	1 2 3 4 5		1 2 3 4 5
24.	Why doesn't he kiss me?	1 2 3 4 5		1 2 3 4 5
25.	My body turns him on	1 2 3 4 5		1 2 3 4 5
26.	When will this be over?	1 2 3 4 5		1 2 3 4 5
27.	If only he'd whisper something romantic in my ear	1 2 3 4 5		1 2 3 4 5
28.	He only loves me if I'm good in bed	1 2 3 4 5		1 2 3 4 5
29.	I should wait for him to make the first move	1 2 3 4 5		1 2 3 4 5
30.	I am only doing this because he asked me to	1 2 3 4 5		1 2 3 4 5
31.	I'm the happiest woman on earth	1 2 3 4 5		1 2 3 4 5
32.	I have other more important matters to deal with	1 2 3 4 5		1 2 3 4 5
33.	If I refuse to have sex, he will cheat on me	1 2 3 4 5		1 2 3 4 5

Sexual Cognitions Checklist

CHERYL A. RENAUD, *Federal Medical Center Devens*
E. SANDRA BYERS,[1] *University of New Brunswick*

The Sexual Cognitions Checklist (SCC) was developed to assess sexual cognitions that are experienced as positive as well as those that are experienced as negative (Renaud, 1999). Most conceptual definitions and measures of sexual cognitions (often referred to as fantasies) assume that they are pleasant, enjoyable, and deliberate (Leitenberg & Henning, 1995). However, many individuals report having negative sexual thoughts that are experienced as ego-dystonic, unwanted, and personally unacceptable (Byers, Purdon, & Clark, 1998). To fully understand sexual cognitions, it is important to distinguish between those that are experienced as positive and those that are experienced as negative.

Description

The SCC consists of a checklist of 56 sexual cognitions. Forty of the items were taken from the Wilson Sex Fantasy Questionnaire (WSFQ; Wilson, 1988). The WSFQ has been used extensively in sexual fantasy research and has been found to have strong internal consistency ($\alpha = .98$).

[1]Address correspondence to Sandra Byers, University of New Brunswick, Psychology Department, Fredericton, New Brunswick, Canada E3B 6E4; e-mail: byers@unba.ca

The remaining 16 items were taken from the Revised Obsessional Intrusions Inventory—Sex Version (ROII–v2), which also has demonstrated high internal consistency (α = .92; Byers et al., 1998). For the SCC, the wording of some of the items was changed so that they could be experienced as either positive or negative. The SCC is appropriate for men and women of any age and sexual orientation.

Response Mode and Timing

The SCC can be administered individually, or in a group format, and takes approximately 30 minutes to complete. Respondents are first provided with definitions of positive and negative sexual cognitions. Positive sexual cognitions are defined as purposeful or nonpurposeful cognitions that are experienced as acceptable and pleasant, are the types of thoughts one would expect to have, and might or might not result in sexual arousal. Negative sexual cognitions are defined as purposeful or nonpurposeful cognitions that are experienced as highly unacceptable, upsetting, unpleasant, and repugnant, and might or might not result in sexual arousal. Participants then indicate how often they have had each of the listed sexual thoughts when it was a positive thought as well as when it was a negative thought on a scale ranging from *I have never had this thought* (0) to *I have this thought frequently during the day* (6).

The SCC also contains two nonoverlapping subscales, one reflecting themes of sexual dominance and one reflecting themes of sexual submission. To develop these subscales, six doctoral students in human sexuality independently rated each of the 56 sexual cognitions on the SCC as reflecting sexual submission, sexual dominance, both sexual submission and sexual dominance, or neither sexual submission nor sexual dominance. Six items were judged to have dominance but not submission themes and make up the dominance cognitions subscale. Ten items were judged to reflect submission but not dominance themes and make up the sexual submission subscale.

Scoring

The total frequency scores for positive sexual cognitions (POSCOG) and negative sexual cognitions (NEGCOG) are calculated by summing the item ratings for the 56 items. Thus, scores range from 0 to 336, with higher scores indicating more frequent positive or negative cognitions. Scores on the positive sexual dominance (POSDOM) and negative sexual dominance subscales (NEGDOM) are determined by summing frequency ratings on the six dominance items such that scores range from 0 to 36. A similar procedure is used to calculate scores on the 10 positive sexual submission (POSSUB) and negative sexual submission (NEGSUB) subscales, with scores ranging from 0 to 60.

Reliability

In a study of 148 female and 144 male undergraduate students, Renaud and Byers (1999) found high internal consistencies

for the POSCOG and NEGCOG subscales for both men (α = .95 and .96, respectively) and women (α = .95 and .95, respectively). Acceptable internal consistencies have also been found for men and women for POSDOM (α = .76 and .71, respectively), NEGDOM (α = .84 and .66, respectively), POSSUB (α = .81 and .80, respectively), and NEGSUB (α = .85 and .82, respectively; Renaud & Byers, 2005, 2006).

Validity

Renaud and Byers (1999) found that the sexual cognitions most commonly experienced as positive by individuals differed from those most commonly experienced as negative. The most commonly reported POSCOG revolved around themes of romance and intimacy, whereas the most commonly reported NEGCOG reflected themes of anonymous sex and sexual embarrassment. In addition, Renaud and Byers (2001) found that, compared to negative cognitions, positive cognitions were associated with more positive affect, less negative affect, more frequent subjective general physiological and sexual arousal, and less frequent upset stomach. They also found that positive sexual cognitions are more deliberate than are negative sexual cognitions and result in fewer attempts to control them. Further, in line with previous sexual fantasy research findings (Alfonso, Allison, & Dunn, 1992), a greater frequency of positive sexual cognitions is associated with better sexual adjustment, including more masturbation experience, a greater number of sexual partners, and greater sexual satisfaction (Renaud & Byers, 2001). In contrast, when the frequency of positive cognitions was controlled, the frequency of negative sexual cognitions was not associated with sexual adjustment.

Renaud and Byers (2005, 2006) provided evidence for the validity of the dominance and submission subscales. Consistent with previous research (e.g., Gold & Clegg, 1990), self-reported use of sexual coercion was uniquely associated with the frequency of sexual dominance cognitions experienced as positive but not sexual dominance cognitions experienced as negative (Renaud & Byers, 2005). Consistent with prior research that had found that individuals who reported having been sexually abused as children reported fantasizing about being forced to have intercourse more often than did individuals without a history of child sexual abuse (Briere, Smiljanich, & Henschel, 1994), a greater frequency of positive sexual submission cognitions was uniquely associated with a history of child sexual abuse (Renaud & Byers, 2006).

References

Alfonso, V. C., Allison, D. B., & Dunn, G. M. (1992). Sexual fantasy and satisfaction: A multidimensional analysis of gender differences. *Journal of Psychology and Human Sexuality, 5*(3), 19–37.

Briere, J., Smiljanich, K., & Henschel, D. (1994). Sexual fantasies, gender, and molestation history. *Child Abuse and Neglect, 18,* 131–137.

Byers, E. S., Purdon, C., & Clark, D. A. (1998). Sexual intrusive thoughts of college students. *The Journal of Sex Research, 35,* 359–369.

Gold, S. R., & Clegg, C. L. (1990). Sexual fantasies of college students with coercive experiences and coercive attitudes. *Journal of Interpersonal Violence, 5,* 464–473.

Leitenberg, H., & Henning, K. (1995). Sexual fantasy. *Psychological Bulletin, 117,* 469–496.

Renaud, C.A. (1999). *Differentiating between positive and negative sexual cognitions.* Unpublished doctoral dissertation, University of New Brunswick, Fredericton.

Renaud, C. A., & Byers, E. S. (1999). Exploring the frequency, diversity, and content of university students' positive and negative sexual cognitions. *Canadian Journal of Human Sexuality, 8,* 17–30.

Renaud, C. A., & Byers, E. S. (2001). Positive and negative sexual cognitions: Subjective experience and relationships to sexual adjustment. *The Journal of Sex Research, 38,* 252–262.

Renaud, C.A., & Byers, E. S., (2005). Relationship between sexual violence and positive and negative cognitions of sexual dominance. *Sex Roles, 53,* 253–260.

Renaud, C. A., & Byers, E. S. (2006). Positive and negative cognitions of sexual submission: Relationship to sexual violence. *Archives of Sexual Behavior, 35,* 483–490.

Wilson, G. D. (1988). Male-female differences in sexual activity, enjoyment, and fantasies. *Personality and Individual Differences, 8,* 125–127.

Exhibit

Sexual Cognitions Checklist

We all have thoughts about sex from time to time. Sexual thoughts can be divided into different types:

Positive Sexual Thoughts. Sometimes we experience our sexual thoughts as positive. Positive sexual thoughts may include thoughts that we purposely engage in to enhance our sexual feelings or sexual arousal. Positive sexual thoughts may also include thoughts that pop into our heads out of the blue. Whether we purposely engage in positive sexual thoughts, or they pop into our minds out of the blue, positive sexual thoughts are thoughts that we find acceptable and pleasant. They are the types of thoughts that we would expect to have. We can have positive sexual thoughts while we are engaging in masturbation, while we are engaged in sexual activity with a partner, and while we are involved in non-sexual activities.

Negative Sexual Thoughts. Sometimes, we have sexual thoughts that we experience as negative. Negative sexual thoughts are thoughts that we dislike having. They are the types of thoughts that we would not expect to have because they are uncharacteristic of our usual thoughts and habits. That is, negative sexual thoughts are thoughts of things we would never want to do or say. Therefore, negative sexual thoughts are highly unacceptable, upsetting, and unpleasant. We tend to find these thoughts disgusting and we wonder why we are having such repugnant thoughts. However, because they are sexual in content, we may experience sexual arousal to these thoughts even though we find them unacceptable, unpleasant, and upsetting. Like positive sexual thoughts, we can have negative sexual thoughts while we are engaging in masturbation, while we are engaged in sexual activity with a partner, and while we are involved in non-sexual activities.

Sometimes Positive and Sometimes Negative Sexual Thoughts. Although some thoughts are clearly positive or clearly negative for us, there are some sexual thoughts that we experience as positive at times and as negative at other times. For example, you may have had a thought about seeing your neighbor undress. If that thought was about the good-looking neighbor in apartment "B," the thought might be positive. That is, it might be the type of thought you would expect to have and it is acceptable and pleasant. On the other hand, if you thought about the neighbor in apartment "A," who you find disgusting, the thought might be negative. In this case, the thought is unacceptable, unpleasant, and not the type of thought you would expect to have. So, in this case, the same thought, "Seeing your neighbor undress," is sometimes positive and sometimes negative. Other factors, such as your mood or what you are doing when you have a sexual thought, may also make a certain thought sometimes positive and sometimes negative.

INSTRUCTIONS: The questionnaire on the following few pages deals with a variety of very common sexual thoughts. On this questionnaire, we would like you to indicate *how often* you have had each of the listed sexual thoughts *when it was a positive sexual thought,* and *when it was a negative sexual thought* using the following scale:

0   I have *never* had this thought
1   I have had this thought only *once or twice ever*
2   I have had this thought *a few times a year*
3   I have had this thought *once or twice a month*
4   I have had this thought *once or twice a week*
5   I have had this thought *daily*
6   I have had this thought *frequently during the day*

Example:
Watching my neighbor undress.
How often have you had this thought when it was positive?   0   1   ②   3   4   5   6
How often have you had this thought when it was negative?   0   1   2   3   ④   5   6

This example shows that I have had this thought a few times a year (I circled "2") when it was positive (pleasant and acceptable) and that I have had this thought once or twice a week (I circled "4") when it was negative.

Please indicate how often you have had each of the following sexual thoughts.

   0 I have *never* had this thought
   1 I have had this thought only *once or twice ever*
   2 I have had this thought *a few times a year*
   3 I have had this thought *once or twice a month*
   4 I have had this thought *once or twice a week*
   5 I have had this thought *daily*
   6 I have had this thought *frequently during the day*

In the past year, I have had sexual thoughts of:

1. Making love out of doors in a romantic setting (e.g. field of flowers; beach at night).
    How often have you had this thought when it was positive? 0 1 2 3 4 5 6[a]
    How often have you had this thought when it was negative? 0 1 2 3 4 5 6[a]
2. Having intercourse with a loved partner.
3. Having intercourse with someone I know but have not had sex with.
4. Having sex with an anonymous stranger.
5. Engaging in a sexual act with someone who has authority over me.
6. Being pressured into engaging in sex.
7. Engaging in a sexual act with someone who is "taboo" (family member, religious figure).
8. Having sex with two other people at the same time.
9. Participating in an orgy.
10. Being forced to do something sexually.
11. Forcing someone to do something sexually.
12. Engaging in sexual activity contrary to my sexual orientation (e.g. homosexual or heterosexual).
13. Throwing my arms around and kissing an authority figure.
14. Lifting my skirt or dropping my pants, thereby indecently exposing myself in public.
15. Receiving oral sex.
16. Giving oral sex.
17. Watching others have sex.
18. Having sex with an animal or non-human object.
19. Being overwhelmed by a stranger's sexual advances.
20. Being sexually victimized.
21. Receiving or giving genital stimulation.
22. Whipping or spanking someone.
23. Being whipped or spanked.
24. Taking someone's clothes off.
25. Having my clothes taken off.
26. Engaging in a sexual act which I would not want to do because it violates my religious principles.
27. Forcing another adult to engage in a sexual act with me.
28. Making love elsewhere than the bedroom (e.g. kitchen or bathroom).
29. Being excited by material or clothing (e.g. rubber, leather, underwear).
30. Hurting a partner.
31. Being hurt by a partner.
32. Partner-swapping.
33. Being aroused by watching someone urinate.
34. Being tied up.
35. Masturbating in a public place.
36. Authority figures (minister, boss) being naked.
37. People I come in contact with being naked.
38. Having sex in a public place.
39. Tying someone up.
40. Having incestuous sexual relations (sexual relations with a family member).
41. Exposing myself provocatively.
42. Wearing clothes of the opposite sex.

43. Being promiscuous.
44. Having sex with someone much younger than myself.
45. Having sex with someone much older than myself.
46. Being much sought after by the opposite sex.
47. Being seduced as an "innocent."
48. Seducing an "innocent."
49. Being embarrassed by failure of sexual performance.
50. Having sex with someone of a different race.
51. Using objects for stimulation (e.g. vibrator, candles).
52. Being masturbated to orgasm by a partner.
53. Looking at obscene pictures or films.
54. Kissing passionately.
55. While engaging in a sexual act with my partner I have had sexual thoughts of saying something to my partner that I know would upset him/her.
56. While engaging in a sexual act with my partner I have had sexual thoughts of doing something to my partner that I know would upset him/her.
57. Any other sexual thought not listed above. (SPECIFY):

Note. Items 11, 22, 27, 30, 39, and 48 constitute the Sexual Dominance Subscale. Items 5, 6, 10, 19, 20, 23, 26, 31, 34, and 47 constitute the Sexual Submission Subscale.

Attitudes Toward Women's Genitals Scale

DEBRA HERBENICK,[1] *Indiana University*

Women's sexual and sexual health behaviors may be influenced by a range of factors including their perceptions of female genitals, such as whether vaginas are clean or dirty, attractive or unattractive, or whether they smell or taste pleasant. As an example, women who believe that vaginas generally smell bad or are "dirty" may avoid receiving cunnilingus or may avoid annual pelvic exams. The Attitudes Toward Women's Genitals Scale (ATWGS) was designed with the intent to measure individuals' perceptions of women's genitals (Herbenick, 2006) rather than genital self-image, a concept that relates to how one perceives one's own genitals, which is measured by other scales.

Description

The ATWGS is a 10-item measure composed of statements with which respondents are asked to indicate their agreement or disagreement. The scale was developed in multiple stages. In Phase One, nine brief pilot surveys were completed by 370 women and men in order to elicit perceptions of women's genitals using open-ended and closed-ended items. These data, in combination with a review of literature related to women's genitals, were examined for common themes. A total of 14 themes were found: genital appearance, vaginal birth, size in relation to function, menstruation, hygiene, pubic hair, smell, taste, communication, femininity, "looking" (e.g., either looking at oneself or allowing another to look), wetness, touching, and oral sex. Based on these themes, 101 items were written by the author and informed by feedback from a team of experts in the areas of gender studies, medicine, public health, psychology, and women's sexuality. The items were then administered as part of a larger survey to 604 undergraduate and graduate students (362 women, 242 men; mean age = 20.0) and, through an iterative process involving the use of reliability analysis, the scale was reduced to 10 items. Further research is recommended in order to understand the scale properties among other adult populations and clinical samples. The ATWGS may be particularly well suited for use in research that purports to understand how educational curricula or interventions can help to change attitudes toward women's genitals over time. It may also be a useful measure among clinical samples of women who have experienced a change in their genital appearance or function, such as in samples of women with vulvar cancer or lichen sclerosus.

[1]Address correspondence to Debra Herbenick, HPER 116, Indiana University, Bloomington, IN 47405; e-mail: debby@indiana.edu

Response Mode and Timing

Respondents are asked to read a series of 10 statements and to indicate their agreement or disagreement using the response options of *Strongly Disagree, Disagree, Agree*, or *Strongly Agree*. Time to completion is typically less than 5 minutes.

Scoring

ATWGS scores are calculated by summing the scores of Items 1, 2, 4, 7, 9, and 10 (1 = *Strongly Disagree*, 2 = *Disagree*, 3 = *Agree*, 4 = *Strongly Agree*) with the reverse-coded scores from Items 3, 5, 6, and 8. A higher score indicates more positive attitudes toward women's genitals.

Reliability

Cronbach's alpha for the scale was .85 among women, .82 among men, and .86 for the genders combined. Corrected item-to-total correlations exceeded .38 for each item (Herbenick, 2009). The temporal stability of the ATWGS over a 2-week period for a group of 16 women and men was .93 ($p < .001$).

Validity

The ATWGS correlated with the 5-item Sexual Opinion Survey (Fisher, 1998), $r = .43$, $p < .001$, lending support for the convergent validity of the ATWGS (Herbenick,

2009). In addition, the ATWGS exhibited evidence of predictive capacity in that women who had experienced a gynecological exam, who had received cunnilingus three or more times, who had examined their genitals three or more times, or who had used a vibrator scored significantly higher on the ATWGS than women who had not. Men who had performed oral sex on a woman three or more times scored higher on the ATWGS, indicating more positive attitudes toward women's genitals, than men who had not.

Gender Differences

In the initial testing of the scale, men scored significantly higher on the ATWGS, on average, than women (29.77 vs. 26.48, $p < .001$). Further research is recommended to understand the stability and consistency of these gender differences.

References

Fisher, W. A. (1998). The Sexual Opinion Survey. In C. M. Davis, W. L. Yarber, R. Bauserman, G. Schreer, & S. L. Davis (Eds.), *Handbook of Sexuality-Related Measures* (pp. 218–223). Thousand Oaks, CA: Sage Publications.

Herbenick, D. (2006). The development and validation of a scale to measure college students' attitudes toward women's genitals. Unpublished doctoral dissertation, Indiana University.

Herbenick, D. (2009). The development and validation of a scale to measure attitudes toward women's genitals. *International Journal of Sexual Health, 21,* 153–166.

Exhibit

Attitudes Toward Women's Genitals Scale

The following items are about people's feelings and beliefs related to women's genitals (both the vulva and the vagina). The world *vulva* refers to a woman's external genitals (the parts that one can see from the outside such as the clitoris, pubic mound and vaginal lips). The word *vagina* refers to the inside part, also called the birth canal.

Please mark an "X" in the box to indicate how strongly you agree or disagree with each statement.

	Strongly Disagree	Disagree	Agree	Strongly Agree
1. Women's genitals are beautiful.				
2. Women should feel proud of their genitals.				
3. Women's genitals smell bad.				
4. I wish more people could appreciate the beauty of women's genitals.				
5. In general, women's genitals probably taste disgusting.				
6. Women's genitals are ugly.				
7. I wish our society was more open about women's genitals.				
8. Women's genitals are dirty.				
9. I feel positively toward women's genitals.				
10. I can see how some people would think that women's genitals feel good to touch.				

Male Body Image Self-Consciousness Scale

LORRAINE K. McDONAGH, *National University of Ireland, Galway*
TODD G. MORRISON,[1] *University of Saskatchewan, Canada*
BRIAN E. McGUIRE, *National University of Ireland, Galway*

The Male Body Image Self-Consciousness Scale (M-BISC) measures body image self-consciousness during sexual intimacy, which may be defined as the extent to which one feels self-conscious about one's body and physical features when engaged in physically intimate situations, such as sexual intercourse.

Description

Items were generated through a focus group with male participants. Conversations were recorded and transcribed verbatim, and the text was analyzed, resulting in the development of 39 items. All items were written such that men, with and without sexual experience involving a partner (male or female), can respond. To reduce the number of scale items, corrected item-total and inter-item correlations were inspected. Twenty-two items were removed. To gauge the dimensionality of the 17 remaining items, an exploratory factor analysis was conducted, with unweighted least squares serving as the extraction method and parallel analysis in conjunction with the scree plot being used for factor retention. A one-factor solution provided an acceptable representation of the data (eigenvalue = 7.61, accounting for 44% of the variance).

Response Mode and Timing

Respondents indicate their answer by circling the number that best corresponds to their agreement or disagreement with each statement. Responses are coded on a 5-point Likert scale (1 = *Strongly Disagree*; 2 = *Disagree*; 3 = *Don't Know*; 4 = *Agree*; and 5 = *Strongly Agree*). The anchors should be reversed for a random subset of items (i.e., 1 = *Strongly Agree*; 5 = *Strongly Disagree*), so as to prevent acquiescent and response set behaviors. The scale takes no more than 5 minutes to complete.

Scoring

Items are summed to provide a total scale score (possible range is 17 to 85), with higher scores denoting greater levels of body image self-consciousness during physical intimacy.

Reliability

Cronbach's alpha for the 17-item M-BISC was .92 (95% CI = .90 to .94), which suggests good scale score reliability (McDonagh, Morrison, & McGuire, 2008).

Validity

To assess the construct validity of the M-BISC, five hypotheses were tested. Levels of body image self-consciousness were related to levels of body esteem, $r(131) = -.56, p < .001$; sexual esteem, $r(130) = -.56, p < .001$; sexual anxiety, $r(131) = .40, p < .001$; self-rated physical attractiveness, $r(130) = -.50, p < .001$; and the drive for muscularity, $r(131) = .26, p < .005$. A series of point-biserial and Pearson's correlation coefficients also revealed that higher levels of body image self-consciousness during physical intimacy were associated with being less likely to have: (a) engaged in vaginal intercourse, $r_{pb}(129) = -.24, p < .01$, (b) performed oral sex on another person, $r_{pb}(129) = -.28, p < .001$, or (c) received oral sex from another person, $r_{pb}(129) = .27, p < .01$.

Reference

McDonagh, L. K., Morrison, T. G., & McGuire, B. E. (2008). The naked truth: Development of a scale designed to measure male body image self-consciousness during physical intimacy. *Journal of Men's Studies, 16,* 253–265.

[1]Address correspondence to Todd G. Morrison, University of Saskatchewan, Saskatoon, SK, CA S7N 5A5; e-mail: todd.morrison@usask.ca

Exhibit

Male Body Image Self-Consciousness Scale

Instructions: Please read each item carefully and then CIRCLE the most appropriate response UNDER each statement. The term partner refers to someone with whom you are romantically or sexually intimate.

The response format is:

1 = Strongly Disagree
2 = Disagree
3 = Don't Know
4 = Agree
5 = Strongly Agree

1. During sex, I would worry that my partner would think my chest is not muscular enough.[a]
2. During sexual activity, it would be difficult not to think about how unattractive my body is.
3. During sex, I would worry that my partner would think my stomach is not muscular enough.
4. I would feel anxious receiving a full-body massage from a partner.
5. The first time I have sex with a new partner, I would worry that my partner would get turned off by seeing my body without clothes.
6. I would feel nervous if a partner were to explore my body before or after having sex.
7. I would worry about the length of my erect penis during physically intimate situations.
8. During sex, I would prefer to be on the bottom so that my stomach appears flat.
9. The worst part of having sex is being nude in front of another person.
10. I would feel embarrassed about the size of my testicles if a partner were to see them.
11. I would have difficulty taking a shower or a bath with a partner.
12. During sexual activity, I would be concerned about how my body looks to a partner.
13. If a partner were to put a hand on my buttocks I would think, "My partner can feel my fat."
14. During sexually intimate situations, I would be concerned that my partner thinks I am too fat.
15. I could only feel comfortable enough to have sex if it were dark so that my partner could not clearly see my body.
16. If a partner were to see me nude I would be concerned about the overall muscularity of the body.
17. The idea of having sex without any covers over my body causes me anxiety.

[a]The 5-point scale is repeated after each item.

Questionnaire on Young Children's Sexual Learning

PATRICIA BARTHALOW KOCH,[1] *The Pennsylvania State University*
PEGGY BRICK, *Sexuality Education Consultant*

Sexual development and sexual learning are ongoing processes from womb to tomb. One reason that the sexual learning and development of young children is very important is because it is the foundation for becoming a sexually healthy adult (Early Childhood Sexuality Education Task Force, 1995). Frayser (1994) noted "the bulk of evolutionary, developmental, and cross-cultural evidence demonstrating that children are sexual beings, whose exploration of sexual knowledge and play, is an integral part of their development as fully functioning human beings" (p. 210). Unfortunately, there is a dearth of research-based information and understanding regarding typical sexual development and sexual expression of young children. This has led to a great deal of denial, misunderstanding, and discomfort about this topic among adults who personally or professionally interact with

[1]Address correspondence to Patricia Barthalow Koch, Department of Biobehavioral Health, The Pennsylvania State University, University Park, PA 16802; e-mail: p3k@psu.edu

children (Davies, Glaser, & Kossoff, 2000). Adults' attitudes affect how they respond to children's sexual expressions, for example in a punitive or accepting manner (Davies et al., 2000). Without normative data about children's typical sexual expression and behaviors, adults might either overreact and pathologize typical behavior as deviant or underreact and minimize behavior that might indicate an underlying concern or problem (Sandnabba, Santtila, Wannas, & Krook, 2003). Therefore, it is important to collect data regarding knowledge, attitudes, and comfort levels related to young children's sexual development and learning from various adults (e.g., preschool teachers, daycare workers, health professionals, parents) who interact with children.

The Questionnaire on Young Children's Sexual Learning was developed to assess the knowledge, attitudes/beliefs, and degree of comfort of adult caretakers regarding young children's (infants to preschoolers) sexual development and learning. It has served as a useful tool in assessing the effectiveness of the Healthy Foundations professional development workshop. Healthy Foundations is a nationwide initiative that includes a variety of resources designed to teach early childhood educators how to form a positive foundation for young children's growth toward healthy adult sexuality (Brick, Montfort, & Blume, 1993; Montfort, Brick, & Blume, 1993). The initiative includes a one-day workshop designed for adults who deal with young children in settings such as preschools, daycare centers, and community agencies. The goals of the workshop include helping adults to become more knowledgeable about childhood sexual development and learning, to develop more positive attitudes and beliefs in these areas, and to become more comfortable and competent in dealing with these areas with young children and their families. The questionnaire also could be used in other educational, research, or clinical settings to determine the knowledge, attitudes/beliefs, or comfort levels of professionals, parents, students, or other groups of adults regarding young children's sexual development and learning. The terminology referring to the adult caretaker may be changed from "teacher" to "participant," for example to make the items more appropriate for the group. Use with adults of differing backgrounds in various settings would help to further establish the psychometric properties and norms for the scales.

Description

The Questionnaire on Young Children's Sexual Learning is composed of three separate scales. The Knowledge About Young Children's Sexual Learning Scale consists of 21 true-or-false statements designed to assess knowledge about young children's sexual development and learning. The Attitudes/Beliefs About Young Children's Sexual Learning Scale contains 28 statements to which a respondent indicates on a 5-point Likert scale his or her attitudes and beliefs about sexual development and how young

children should learn about various aspects of sexuality. The Comfort With Young Children's Sexual Learning Scale lists 10 topics that adults typically need to discuss or deal with when interacting with young children. Respondents indicate their comfort level with these topics on a 4-point Likert-type scale.

Response Mode and Timing

On the Knowledge About Young Children's Sexual Learning Scale, respondents choose the answer to each statement that best reflects their level of knowledge from 1 = *Definitely True*, 2 = *Probably True*, 3 = *Probably False*, 4 = *Definitely False*, 5 = *Don't Know*. This scale requires no more than 10 minutes to complete.

Respondents choose the response which best reflects their attitudes/beliefs toward each statement on the Attitudes/Beliefs About Young Children's Sexual Learning Scale from 1 = *Strongly Agree*, 2 = *Agree*, 3 = *Uncertain*, 4 = *Disagree*, 5 = *Strongly Disagree*. This scale requires no more than 15 minutes to complete.

On The Comfort With Young Children's Sexual Learning Scale, respondents indicate their comfort level in interacting with young children about each sexual topic from 1 = *Very Comfortable*, 2 = *Somewhat Comfortable*, 3 = *Somewhat Uncomfortable*, 4 = *Very Uncomfortable*. Respondents can complete this scale in less than 5 minutes.

Scoring

One point is given for every correct answer on the Knowledge About Young Children's Sexual Learning Scale. Following are the correct answers for each item: definitely true, Items 1, 2, 3, 6, 8, 13, 16, 18; definitely false, Items 4, 5, 7, 9, 10, 11, 12, 14, 15, 17, 19, 20, 21. All other responses are counted as 0. Thus, the highest knowledge score would be 21. In a study of 183 participants attending eight different Healthy Foundations programs around the country, the average preworkshop knowledge score was 10 (Brick & Koch, 1996).

Scores on the Attitudes/Beliefs about Young Children's Sexual Learning Scale may range from 28, indicating the most negative or nonsupportive attitudes/beliefs, to 140, indicating the most positive and supportive attitudes toward young children's sexual learning. The following items need to be reverse scored: Items 3, 7, 10, 11, 12, 13, 15, 16, 19, 24, 25, 27, 28. The study of Healthy Foundations program participants found their preworkshop attitudes to be slightly negative to ambivalent (*M* = 78; Brick & Koch, 1996).

On the Comfort With Young Children's Sexual Learning Scale, scores may range from 10, indicating the highest level of comfort, to 40, indicating the lowest level of comfort. Preworkshop comfort scores for a sample of Healthy Foundations program participants indicated that overall they felt somewhat comfortable in interacting with young children about various sexual topics (*M* = 17.6; Brick &

Koch, 1996). Respondents indicated most discomfort with masturbation.

Reliability

Internal reliability for each of the three scales, using Cronbach's alpha coefficient, was established with a nationwide sample of 183 Healthy Foundations participants (Brick & Koch, 1996). The alpha coefficients follow: for the Knowledge About Young Children's Sexual Learning Scale, .46; for the Attitudes/Beliefs About Young Children's Sexual Learning Scale, .92; for the Comfort With Young Children's Sexual Learning Scale, .93. Weak questions on the knowledge scale have been revised since that time.

Validity

The content validity for the three scales was determined through an extensive review of the literature on children's sexual development and learning. Initial items were constructed through collaboration of the researchers with the staff at the Family Life Education Center. Items were then reviewed and content validity was established by a panel of experts that included practicing preschool teachers and professionals in the field of sexology. Because some researchers have found knowledge and attitudinal differences among various types of professionals who work with children, including child psychologists, teachers, 4-H leaders, and medical students (Haugaard, 1996; Heiman, Leiblum, Equilin, & Pallitto, 1998), it is recommended that these scales be used with a variety of professionals and the results compared.

Other Information

Information about the Healthy Foundations Program Learning may be obtained from Peggy Brick, Center for Family Life Education, Planned Parenthood of Greater Northern New Jersey, Hackensack, NJ.

References

Brick, P., & Koch, P. B. (1996, November). *Healthy Foundations: An early childhood educators' sexuality program and its effectiveness.* Paper presented at the Annual Meeting of the Society for the Scientific Study of Sexuality, Houston, TX.

Brick, P., Montfort, S., & Blume, N. (1993). *Healthy Foundations: The teacher's book—Responding to young children's questions and behaviors regarding sexuality.* Hackensack, NJ: Planned Parenthood of Greater Northern New Jersey.

Davies, S. L., Glaser, D., & Kossoff, R. (2000). Children's sexual play and behavior in pre-school settings: Staff's perceptions, reports, and responses. *Child Abuse and Neglect, 24,* 1329–1343.

Early Childhood Sexuality Education Task Force. (1995). *Right from the start: Guidelines for sexuality issues (birth to five years).* New York: Sexuality Information and Education Council of the U.S.

Frayser, S. (1994). Defining normal childhood sexuality: An anthropological approach. *Annual Review of Sex Research, 5,* 173–217.

Haugaard, J. J. (1996). Sexual behaviors between children: Professionals' opinions and undergraduates' recollections. *Families in Society: The Journal of Contemporary Human Services, 77*(2), 81–89.

Heiman, M. L., Leiblum, S., Equilin, S. C., & Pallitto, L. M. (1998). A comparative survey of beliefs about "normal" childhood sexual behaviors. *Child Abuse and Neglect, 22,* 289–304.

Montfort, S., Brick, P., & Blume, N. (1993). *Healthy Foundations: Developing positive policies and programs regarding young children's learning about sexuality.* Hackensack, NJ: Planned Parenthood of Greater Northern New Jersey.

Sandnabba, N. K., Santtila, P., Wannas, M., & Krook, K. (2003). Age and gender specific sexual behaviors in children. *Child Abuse and Neglect, 27,* 579–605.

Exhibit

Questionnaire on Young Children's Sexual Learning

I. Knowledge About Young Children's Sexual Learning Scale

Please indicate if the following statements are "Definitely True" (1), "Possibly True" (2), "Possibly False" (3), or "Definitely False" (4). If you are unsure of the correct answer, circle "Don't Know" (5).

Scale[a]
1 = *Definitely True*; 2 = *Possibly True*; 3 = *Possibly False*; 4 = *Definitely False*; 5 = *Don't Know*

1. Young children's sexual learning can affect how they feel about sexuality as adults.
2. Infants have sexual responses like clitoral/penile erections and orgasms.
3. Even if there is no formal program, children are learning about sexuality in their preschool.
4. It is unusual for young children to masturbate.
5. Most preschoolers are fearful of sexual topics.
6. By 3 years of age, most children can tell the difference between males and females.
7. It is of little concern for a child to be preoccupied with sexual behavior over an extended period of time.
8. Healthy and natural sex play usually occurs between friends and playmates of about the same age.
9. Children do not stimulate their own genitals until after they are 3 years old.
10. The vagina of female infants is not capable of lubrication.
11. Most 3- and 4-year-olds are really not curious about the differences in boys' and girls' bodies.

12. A person's body image does *not* begin to form until 4 years of age.
13. Children can be taught that it is O.K. to masturbate in private but not in public.
14. Young children understand human sexuality best when it is taught using plants and other animals as the examples rather than talking about people.
15. Adult responses to a child's sexual behavior have little effect upon how "good" or "bad" children think sex is.
16. Before answering a child's question about sexuality, you should try to find out what the child thinks.
17. When answering a child's questions about sexuality, you should only provide information and not deal with their feelings or attitudes.
18. Before responding to a child's sexuality-related behavior, you should try to find out what meaning this behavior has to the child.
19. The most effective method for dealing with sexuality-related behavior in children is to ignore the behavior.
20. It is too upsetting for preschoolers to tell them how babies are actually born.
21. Young children that have received age-appropriate sexuality education are more likely to be sexually exploited and abused.

II. Attitudes/Beliefs About Young Children's Sexual Learning Scale

Please circle the number which best represents your feelings or ideas toward the following statements.

Scale
1 = *Strongly Agree*; 2 = *Agree*; 3 = *Uncertain*; 4 = *Disagree*; 5 = *Strongly Disagree*

1. Preschool children can be sheltered from sexual messages in our society.
2. Biology is the main influence on a person's sexual attitudes and behaviors.
3. Masturbation is natural and healthy for children.
4. Sexual information is too complex for most preschool children to understand.
5. Adults/teachers must be careful not to allow little boys to act too much like girls.
6. Sexual learning for young children is primarily about where babies come from.
7. It is fine for young children to be curious about sexual topics.
8. Children receive positive messages about sexuality when adults use cute nicknames for genitals.
9. Most preschool children are too young to be able to use the correct names for their genitals (like "penis," "scrotum," "vulva," and "clitoris").
10. It is O.K. for preschool children to realize that their genitals feel good when they touch them.
11. It is better to use nonsexist language (i.e., "firefighter" instead of "fireman") with young children.
12. Children should feel positively about sexuality.
13. It is O.K. to allow children to touch their own genitals when their diapers or pants are being changed.
14. Teachers who have strong religious beliefs about sex should teach these to the children they care for.
15. It is important to begin discussing sexuality openly in early childhood.
16. Traditional gender role stereotypes discourage responsible sexual behaviors for both genders.
17. Anatomically detailed dolls or picture books promote unhealthy sexual curiosity in young children.
18. Talking about sexuality with young children encourages them to experiment.
19. Adults/teachers need to understand their own attitudes about sexual topics since these attitudes may influence their children.
20. Adults/teachers must be careful not to allow little girls to act too much like boys.
21. Seeing children of the other sex without clothes on encourages children to experiment with sexual behaviors.
22. Preschool programs should only deal with sexual information; dealing with sexual attitudes and values should be left up to parents.
23. Preschool teachers should refrain from affectionately touching their children.
24. Children have the right to choose who they want and do not want to touch their bodies.
25. A positive rather than a punitive approach is better when handling children's sexuality-related behaviors (like sex play and masturbation).
26. An early childhood sexuality program is adequate if it only deals with preventing sexual abuse.
27. Children should be encouraged to ask their teachers questions about sexuality.
28. A sexually healthy adult demonstrates tolerance for people with different sexual values, lifestyles, and orientations.

III. Comfort With Young Children's Sexual Learning Scale

Please circle the number which best represents how comfortable you currently feel in interacting with young children about the following sexuality topics.

Scale

1 = *Very Comfortable*; 2 = *Somewhat Comfortable*; 3 = *Somewhat Uncomfortable*; 4 = *Very Uncomfortable*

1. Female and male roles and behavior.
2. Male and female body differences.
3. Names of genital or "sexual" body parts.
4. Being partially clothed (e.g., changing diapers, going topless, nude swimming, etc.).
5. Masturbation.
6. Sex play (e.g., "doctor," "mommies & daddies").
7. How babies are made ("get in").
8. How babies are born ("get out").
9. "Sexual" language use (e.g. "poopy-head," "boobies").
10. The privacy of their bodies (e.g. giving and receiving permission for touching).

[a]The appropriate scale follows each item.

Sexual Coercion Scale

MATTHEW C. AALSMA[1] AND J. DENNIS FORTENBERRY,
Indiana University School of Medicine, Indianapolis

Sexual coercion is a relatively common event in young women's lives. The Sexual Coercion Scale (SCS; Aalsma, Zimet, Fortenberry, Blythe, & Orr, 2002) was developed in order to measure the occurrence of unwanted sexual behavior in adolescent and adult populations. Our definition of sexual coercion includes the use of pressure, threat, or force by one partner to obtain sex that is unwanted by the other partner (Blythe, Fortenberry, Temkit, Tu, & Orr, 2006). The SCS is a brief measure of sexual coercion that still retains multiple items in order to assess internal reliability as well as consistency of reporting. It is particularly important to have brief, multiple-item scales in studies in which a goal is to assess a wide range of sexual functioning and behavior items.

Description

The SCS consists of four items. Because we assessed a wide variety of sexual behaviors, we felt it was important to make a distinction between sexual coercion from other sexual behaviors, including childhood sexual abuse. One distinction between coercion and sexual abuse that was evident in focus groups with adolescents was age. Hence, our instructions for the scale include an age break because focus groups indicated sexual coercion was distinguished from childhood sexual abuse as being a more recent experience, occurring after age 12. This age break is also developmentally appropriate, as children at this age are beginning to engage in romantic and sexual partnerships. In addition, the instructions specifically instruct the participant that sexual coercion can occur within a romantic or sexual partnership. ("Unwanted" means any kind of sex that you didn't agree to, even if it was with someone you knew.) The scale describes a wide variety of unwanted sexual experiences, including undesired sex. We wanted to include a range of power and relational imbalances, including overt physical threats as well as covert relational tactics. Given the age restriction and the reading difficulty, the SCS is most appropriate for adolescent and adult populations.

Response Mode and Timing

A 3-point Likert-type response format is utilized with this scale (1 = *Never*, 2 = *Once*, 3 = *Two Times or More*). The participant is asked to circle the correct descriptor.

[1]Address correspondence to Matthew C. Aalsma, Section of Adolescent Medicine, Indiana University School of Medicine, 575 N. West Dr., Rm. 070, Indianapolis, IN 46202; e-mail: maalsma@iupui.edu

Scoring

The total score for this scale is calculated by summing across items and can range from 0 to 12.

Reliability

The SCS was utilized in a study of female adolescent and young adult subjects (14 to 24 years of age) recruited from urban health clinics and a sexually transmitted disease clinic in a large midwestern city. The scale demonstrated good internal reliability at baseline (alpha = .67; Aalsma et al., 2002).

Validity

Items in the SCS are comparable to other scales assessing sexual coercion, which is an indicator of content validity. Support for the construct validity of the SCS can be achieved by assessing its relationship with other variables. In previous research, we found consistent reporters of childhood sexual abuse were more likely to have elevated levels of sexual coercion based on the SCS (Aalsma et al., 2002).

References

Aalsma, M. C., Zimet, G. D., Fortenberry, J. D., Blythe, M. J., & Orr, D. P. (2002). Report of childhood sexual abuse by adolescents and young adults: Stability over time. *The Journal of Sex Research, 39,* 259–263.

Blythe, M. J., Fortenberry, J. D., Temkit, M., Tu, W., & Orr, D. P. (2006). Incidence and correlates of unwanted sex and relationships of middle and late adolescent women. *Archives of Pediatrics and Adolescent Medicine, 160,* 591–595.

Exhibit

Sexual Coercion Scale

Instructions: These next questions are about unwanted sexual activity after you were 12 years old. "Unwanted" means any kind of sex that you didn't agree to, even if it was with someone you knew.

1. How often has someone used physical force (like punching you or holding you down) to make you have sex?

   Never   Once   Two or More

2. How often has someone used a weapon (like a gun or a knife) to make you have sex?

   Never   Once   Two or More

3. How often have you had sex with someone because you were afraid of them?

   Never   Once   Two or More

4. How often have you had sex when you really didn't want to?

   Never   Once   Two or More

Survey of Unwanted Sexual Attention in University Residences

KATHLEEN V. CAIRNS[1] AND JULIE WRIGHT, *The University of Calgary*

The Survey of Unwanted Sexual Attention in University Residences is an amalgamation of several previous instruments (see below) with the addition of demographic descriptions and site-specific questions. It was used to identify the types of sexual harassment and coercion problems that occurred in undergraduate residence halls on campus and to determine how student attitudes and beliefs about sexual harassment and coercion were related to their occurrence. Specific outcomes of the study can be found in several published articles (Cairns, 1993a, 1993b, 1994a, 1994b). The narrative sections of the survey proved to be particularly valuable; qualitative analysis of the narratives confirmed and further developed the findings from the quantitative analyses.

Description

The final version of the survey contains 10 sections (only Sections D, G, H and I appear in the exhibit), each of which addresses a different set of issues relevant to sexual harassment and coercion. Each of these sections is outlined in this article.

Section A. This section contains a series of general questions intended to provide a demographic picture of the sample population. The specific items selected for this section were chosen to reflect characteristics that the literature on harassment suggests may be useful in understanding variation in individual responses (i.e., age, gender) as well as information about issues unique to the residences, which might also be expected to systematically affect responses (i.e., type of residence, floor activity level, gender composition of the floor, length of time the participant had lived in residence). Additional questions elaborate on participants' backgrounds (i.e., length of time since leaving home, whether they had lived independently before moving into a university residence) and inquire about how content they were with their current living arrangements.

Section B. This section contains two standardized test instruments, the Sexual Harassment Attitude Scale (Lott, Reilly, & Howard, 1982) and the Attitudes Toward Sex, Dating and Rape Scale (Dull & Giacopassi, 1987). The items on these instruments include a range of beliefs about gender interaction and sex roles. Respondents indicate the extent of their agreement with each statement, using a 5- point Likert scale ranging from *strongly agree* to *strongly disagree*.

Section C. This section was a modified version of Muehlenhard and Cook (1988), which provided a series of 16 possible reasons for engaging in unwanted sexual activity. Respondents were asked to indicate whether they had ever engaged in unwanted sexual activity for any of these reasons, and, if so, what type of sexual activity was involved.

Section D. Section D contains items asking specifically about a series of 10 behaviors that the research literature indicates may be widely considered to constitute sexual harassment. The 10 behaviors include the use of sexually obscene language; display of sexually explicit, offensive, or pornographic materials; putting down women as a group; putting down men as a group; discussion or spreading rumors about the sexual activities of other residents; unwanted, sexually suggestive looks or gestures; unwanted sexual teasing, jokes, comments, or questions; unwanted pressure for social contact; unwanted deliberate touching or physical closeness; and unwanted attempts to kiss or fondle (Reilly, Lott, & Gallogly, 1986). An additional question, added by residents' focus groups prior to survey administration, asks about residents being exposed, against their wishes, to members of the opposite sex in states of undress.

For each problem behavior, residents were asked about whether and with what frequency the behavior had been observed, how offensive it was considered to be, and whether the respondent thought of it as sexual harassment. For Items 6 through 11, which were considered to be more problematic forms of harassment, an additional set of questions was asked concerning frequency of occurrence; maximum number of times any one resident behaved in this manner; how upsetting the incidents were; how the person responded to the incidents; how the person thought he or she would have responded were the person precipitating the incident not another resident; whether the responding person had ever engaged in the behavior him-or herself; and how often, why, and how upsetting the respondent thought the behavior was to the other person.

Section E. This section contains the Sexual Experiences Survey (Koss & Oros, 1982). Items on this instrument ask for information about eight types of unwanted sexual activity personally experienced by residents. These activities range from unwanted fondling, kissing, or petting to sexual intercourse. The questions consider possible sexual coercion, the involvement of alcohol and drugs, and the use of physical force. Because the literature indicates that offenders in these more serious types of offense are overwhelmingly likely to be men, and that victims are almost exclusively women, the sections for each gender were written accordingly. Section E

[1]Address correspondence to Kathleen V. Cairns, Department of Educational Psychology, The University of Calgary, 2500 University Drive N.W., Calgary, Alberta, Canada T2N 1N4; e-mail: kcairns@ucalgary.ca

(Female) focuses on unwanted sexual activity as recipient, asking each woman whether she has had a particular experience, and, if so, how often, when and where it occurred, to whom (if anyone) it was reported, and whether she considered it sexual assault. Section E (Male) asks about unwanted sexual activity from the perspective of the offender, using a comparable set of questions.

Section F. Section F requests further details about the most severe incident reported by the respondent in Section E, including the number of offenders involved, the relationship of the victim to the offender, where the offense had occurred, whether drugs or alcohol were involved, and various aspects of victim and offender perceptions of the incident. Again, this section is worded differently for female and male respondents reflecting the predominance of male offenders and female victims.

Qualitative Sections G, H, and I. Section G asks for written descriptions of incidents that the respondent felt had not been addressed in the previous sections. Section H provides descriptions of incidents of physical abuse of a nonsexual nature occurring between men and women in the residence complex. Section I requests narrative descriptions of a particular incident of sexually inappropriate behavior that the respondents felt had affected them most or that they remember best. The specific wording of the qualitative sections is contained in the Exhibit.

Section J. The final section includes questions about the participants' perceptions of the level of their personal knowledge about sexual harassment and sexual assault, their judgements about current levels of education about these issues in the residences, and their impressions of their own personal safety in residence.

References

Cairns, K. V. (1993a). Sexual entitlement and sexual accommodation: Male and female responses to sexual coercion. *The Canadian Journal of Human Sexuality, 2,* 203–214.

Cairns, K. V. (1993b). Sexual harassment in student residences: A response to Dekeseredy and Kelly. *Journal of Human Justice, 4,* 73–84.

Cairns, K. V. (1994a). A narrative study of qualitative data on sexual assault, coercion and harassment. *Canadian Journal of Counselling, 28,* 193–205.

Cairns, K. V. (1994b). Unwanted sexual attention in university residences. *Journal of College and University Student Housing, 24,* 30–36.

Dull, R. T., & Giacopassi, D. J. (1987). Demographic correlates of sexual and dating attitudes. *Criminal Justice and Behavior, 14,* 175–193.

Koss, M. P., & Oros, C.J. (1982). Sexual experiences survey: A research instrument investigating sexual aggression and victimization. *Journal of Consulting and Clinical Psychology, 50,* 455–457.

Lott, B., Reilly, M., & Howard, D. R. (1982). Sexual assault and harassment: A campus community case study. *Signs, 8,* 296–319.

Muehlenhard, C. L., & Cook, S. W. (1988). Men's self-reports of unwanted sexual activity. *The Journal of Sex Research, 24,* 58–72.

Reilly, M. E., Lott, B., & Gallogly, S. M. (1986). Sexual harassment of university students. *Sex Roles, 15,* 333–358.

Exhibit

Survey of Unwanted Sexual Attention in University Residences (Sections D, G, H, and I, Only)

Section D (adapted from Reilly, Lott, & Gallogly, 1986). In this section you will find descriptions of several behaviors. Each brief description is followed by several questions regarding your perceptions of and experience with the behavior.

Section G: Are there any other incidents that have occurred in the residence complex that you would classify as sexual harassment or sexually inappropriate that have not been addressed in the previous two sections? If so, please describe.

Section H: Have you ever experienced or been aware of physical abuse of a non-sexual nature occurring between men and women in the residence complex? If yes, please tell us about the incident or incidents.

Section I: Now we'd like you to think about the questions that have been asked and the types of behavior that have been addressed in this survey. We would like you to describe in your own words a particular incident of sexually inappropriate behavior that you feel has affected you the most or that you remember best. Please describe this incident as fully as possible (e.g., what occurred, why it occurred, how you felt, how you responded, the consequences of your response, how it affected your life and you personally, how it affected your relationships, etc.).

Sexual Coercion in Intimate Relationships Scale

AARON T. GOETZ,[1] *California State University, Fullerton*
TODD K. SHACKELFORD, *Florida Atlantic University*

Sexual coercion sometimes includes violence and physical force, and in an intimate relationship also may include subtle tactics, such as emotional manipulation. Because relationship partners have a vested interest in each other, one might expect that sexual coercion is sometimes achieved by more subtle manipulations. We developed the Sexual Coercion in Intimate Relationships Scale (SCIRS) to assess the prevalence and severity of varied forms of sexual coercion in relationships.

Although other measures of sexual coercion exist, we developed the SCIRS to address limitations of these measures. Previous measures assess the lifetime occurrence of sexually coercive acts but not the frequency and severity of these acts. Also, because some measures of sexual coercion assess lifetime experience with sexual coercion, they cannot differentiate sexual coercion by an intimate partner and, for example, molestation experienced in childhood. Finally, although some measures of sexual coercion include assessments of threats as coercive tactics, they are not able to differentiate types of threats (e.g., threats of physical harm, threats to terminate the relationship).

Description

The 34 SCIRS items assess communicative tactics, such as hinting and subtle manipulations, in addition to tactics such as use of force. The SCIRS assesses use of psychological and behavioral tactics of sexual coercion, such as threats, withholding of resources, and violence. The SCIRS also assesses the use of tactics that range in subtlety.

The SCIRS uses a 6-point scale to assess how often in the past month each of 34 acts has occurred in the participant's relationship. Values are: 0 = *Act did not occur*, 1 = *Act occurred 1 time*, 2 = *Act occurred 2 times*, 3 = *Act occurred 3 to 5 times*, 4 = *Act occurred 6 to 10 times*, 5 = *Act occurred 11 or more times*. A male version of the SCIRS assesses men's self-reports of their own sexually coercive behaviors, whereas a female version assesses women's reports of their partner's sexually coercive behaviors.

Studies using the SCIRS have secured data primarily from heterosexual young adults (mean age 24 years) residing in North America.

Response Mode and Timing

The SCIRS is a self-administered survey but can be adapted for an interview, and standardized instructions make self-administration uncomplicated. When self-administered, the SCIRS takes about 10 minutes to complete. Although the SCIRS assesses men's sexual coercion in the past month, one can adjust this period to assess the success of an intervention program, for example.

Scoring

Full-scale scores are calculated by summing response values (0–5) for each item in the entire scale. The full scale has a range of 0 to 170 (34 acts × 5). Shackelford and Goetz (2004) conducted a component analysis that produced three components: Resource Manipulation/Violence, Commitment Manipulation, and Defection Threat. Resource Manipulation/Violence includes coercive acts in which men withhold or give gifts and benefits and threaten or use violence and physical force. Commitment Manipulation includes coercive acts in which men manipulate their partners by telling them that the couple's relationship status obligates sexual access. Defection Threat includes coercive acts in which men threaten to pursue relationships with other women.

Reliability

In all studies in which the SCIRS has been used, acceptable reliabilities have been observed, using male samples, female samples, and a combination of both. For example, alpha reliabilities for the three components (Resource Manipulation/Violence, Commitment Manipulation, and Defection Threat) and the total scale were .92, .91, .95, and .96, respectively, in the development and initial validation of the SCIRS (Shackelford & Goetz, 2004).

Validity

A valid measure of sexual coercion might be expected to (a) illustrate that women who are sexually coerced are less satisfied with their relationships, (b) reflect personality differences between men who sexually coerce and those who do not, and (c) differentiate men who would be more upset from those who would be less upset by their partners' denials of sexual access. These predictions have received support. Relationships between men's sexual coercion and women's relationship satisfaction are negative (Shackelford & Goetz, 2004); men who are lower

[1]Address correspondence to Aaron T. Goetz, Department of Psychology, California State University, Fullerton, P. O. Box 6846, Fullerton, CA 92834; e-mail: agoetz@fullerton.edu

(relative to men who are higher) on conscientiousness are more likely to sexually coerce their partners (Goetz & Shackelford, 2009); and the more that men report being upset if their partners denied them sexual access, the more sexually coercive these men are (Shackelford & Goetz, 2004).

The SCIRS also has demonstrated convergent and discriminative validity. Correlations between SCIRS scores and scores on a sexual coercion subscale of the Violence Assessment Index are positive and statistically significant, according to men's self-reports and women's partner-reports (Shackelford & Goetz, 2004). Correlations between SCIRS scores and scores on the Controlling Behavior Index (Dobash, Dobash, Cavanagh, & Lewis, 1995), Violence Assessment Index (Dobash et al., 1995), Injury Assessment Index (Dobash et al., 1995), Women's Experience with Battering Scale (Smith, Earp, & DeVellis, 1995), Mate Retention Inventory (Buss, Shackelford, & McKibbin, 2008), and Partner-Directed Insults Scale (Goetz, Shackelford, Schipper, & Stewart-Williams, 2006) are uniformly positive but do not share more than 20% of the response variance, providing evidence of convergent and discriminative validity of the SCIRS (Buss et al., 2008; Goetz & Shackelford, 2006; Shackelford & Goetz, 2004; Starratt, Goetz, Shackelford, McKibbin, & Stewart-Williams, 2008; Starratt, Popp, & Shackelford, 2008; Starratt, Shackelford, Goetz, & McKibbin, 2009). These correlations suggest that the SCIRS measures behaviors that are related to, but distinct from, nonsexual violence and control.

References

Buss, D. M., Shackelford, T. K., & **McKibbin, W. F.** (2008). The Mate Retention Inventory—Short Form (MRI-SF). *Personality and Individual Differences, 44*, 322–334.

Dobash, R. E., Dobash, R. P., Cavanagh, K., & Lewis, R. (1995). Evaluating criminal justice programmes for violent men. In R. E. Dobash, R. P. Dobash, & L. Noaks (Eds.), *Gender and crime* (pp. 358–389). Cardiff: University of Wales Press.

Goetz, A. T., & Shackelford, T. K. (2006). Sexual coercion and forced in-pair copulation as sperm competition tactics in humans. *Human Nature, 17*, 265–282.

Goetz, A. T., & Shackelford, T. K. (2009). Sexual coercion in intimate relationships: A comparative analysis of the effects of women's infidelity and men's dominance and control. *Archives of Sexual Behavior, 38*, 226–234.

Goetz, A. T., Shackelford, T. K., Schipper, L. D., & Stewart-Williams, S. (2006). Adding insult to injury: Development and initial validation of the Partner-Directed Insults Scale. *Violence and Victims, 21*, 691–706.

Shackelford, T. K., & Goetz, A. T. (2004). Men's sexual coercion in intimate relationships: Development and initial validation of the Sexual Coercion in Intimate Relationships Scale. *Violence and Victims, 19*, 541–556.

Smith, P. H., Earp, J., & DeVellis, R. (1995). Measuring battering: Development of the Women's Experience with Battering (WEB) Scale. *Women's Health, 1*, 273–288.

Starratt, V. G., Goetz, A. T., Shackelford, T. K., McKibbin, W. F., & Stewart-Williams, S. (2008). Men's partner-directed insults and sexual coercion in intimate relationships. *Journal of Family Violence, 23*, 315–323.

Starratt, V. G., Popp, D., & Shackelford, T. K. (2008). Not all men are sexually coercive: A preliminary investigation of the moderating effect of mate desirability on the relationship between female infidelity and male sexual coercion. *Personality and Individual Differences, 45*, 10–14.

Starratt, V. G., Shackelford, T. K., Goetz, A. T., & McKibbin, W. F. (2009). *Only if he thinks she's cheating: Perceived risk of female infidelity moderates the relationship between objective risk of female infidelity and sexual coercion.* Manuscript under editorial review.

Exhibit

Sexual Coercion in Intimate Relationships Scale

Instructions: Sexuality is an important part of romantic relationships and can sometimes be a source of conflict. Your honest responses to the following questions will contribute profoundly to what is known about sexuality in romantic relationships and may help couples improve the sexual aspects of their relationships. We appreciate that some of the questions may be uncomfortable for you to answer, but keep in mind that your responses will remain confidential.

Below is a list of acts that can occur in a romantic relationship. Please use the following scale to indicate HOW OFTEN in the *past ONE month* these acts have occurred in *your* current romantic relationship. Write the number that best represents your response in the blank space to the left of each act.

0 = Act *did NOT* occur in the past month

1 = Act occurred *1 time* in the past month

2 = Act occurred *2 times* in the past month

3 = Act occurred *3 to 5 times* in the past month

4 = Act occurred *6 to 10 times* in the past month

5 = Act occurred *11 OR MORE times* in the past month

_____ 1. My partner *hinted* that he would withhold benefits that I depend on if I did not have sex with him.

_____ 2. My partner *threatened* to withhold benefits that I depend on if I did not have sex with him.

_____ 3. My partner withheld benefits that I depend on to get me to have sex with him.

_____ 4. My partner *hinted* that he would give me gifts or other benefits if I had sex with him.

_____ 5. My partner gave me gifts or other benefits so that I would feel obligated to have sex with him.

_____ 6. My partner reminded me of gifts or other benefits he gave me so that I would feel obligated to have sex with him.

_____ 7. My partner persisted in asking me to have sex with him, even though he knew that I did not want to.

_____ 8. My partner pressured me to have sex with him against my will.

_____ 9. My partner initiated sex with me when I was unaware (for example, I was asleep, drunk, or on medication) *and continued against my will.*

_____ 10. My partner *threatened* to physically force me to have sex with him.

_____ 11. My partner physically forced me to have sex with him.

_____ 12. My partner made me feel obligated to have sex with him.

_____ 13. My partner *hinted* that he would have sex with another woman if I did not have sex with him.

_____ 14. My partner *threatened* to have sex with another woman if I did not have sex with him.

_____ 15. My partner told me that other couples have sex more than we do, to make me feel like I should have sex with him.

_____ 16. My partner *hinted* that he might pursue a long-term relationship with another woman if I did not have sex with him.

_____ 17. My partner *threatened* to pursue a long-term relationship with another woman if I did not have sex with him.

_____ 18. My partner *hinted* that if I were truly committed to him I would have sex with him.

_____ 19. My partner *told me* that if I were truly committed to him I would have sex with him.

_____ 20. My partner *hinted* that if I loved him I would have sex with him.

_____ 21. My partner *told me* that if I loved him I would have sex with him.

_____ 22. My partner *threatened* violence against me if I did not have sex with him.

_____ 23. My partner *threatened* violence against someone or something I care about if I did not have sex with him.

_____ 24. My partner *hinted* that other women were interested in a relationship with him, so that I would have sex with him.

_____ 25. My partner *told me* that other women were interested in a relationship with him, so that I would have sex with him.

_____ 26. My partner *hinted* that other women were interested in having sex with him, so that I would have sex with him.

_____ 27. My partner *told me* that other women were interested in having sex with him, so that I would have sex with him.

_____ 28. My partner *hinted* that other women were willing to have sex with him, so that I would have sex with him.

_____ 29. My partner *told me* that other women were willing to have sex with him, so that I would have sex with him.

_____ 30. My partner *hinted* that it was my obligation or duty to have sex with him.

_____ 31. My partner *told me* that it was my obligation or duty to have sex with him.

_____ 32. My partner *hinted* that I was cheating on him, in an effort to get me to have sex with him.

_____ 33. My partner *accused me* of cheating on him, in an effort to get me to have sex with him.

_____ 34. My partner and I had sex, even though I did not want to.

Sexual Beliefs Scale

CHARLENE L. MUEHLENHARD,[1] *University of Kansas*
ALBERT S. FELTS, *San Marcos, Texas*

We developed the Sexual Beliefs Scale (SBS) to measure five beliefs related to rape: the beliefs (a) that women often indicate unwillingness to engage in sex when they are actually willing (the Token Refusal, or TR, subscale); (b) that if a woman "leads a man on," behaving as if she is willing to engage in sex when in fact she is not, then the man is justified in forcing her (the Leading On Justifies Force, or LOJF, subscale); (c) that women enjoy force in sexual situations (the Women Like Force, or WLF, subscale); (d) that men should dominate women in sexual situations (the Men Should Dominate, or MSD, subscale); and (e) that women have a right to refuse sex at any point, at which time men should stop their sexual advances (the No Means Stop, or

NMS, subscale). There were existing measures of rape-related beliefs that yielded one global score (e.g., Burt's Rape Myth Acceptance Scale, 1980) or that measured one belief (e.g., Burt's Adversarial Sexual Beliefs Scale, 1980), but we could find no scales that yielded separate scores for different beliefs.

Description

The short form of the SBS is a 20-item scale consisting of five 4-item subscales; the long form is a 40-item scale consisting of five 8-item subscales. Each item is rated on a 4-point scale, from *Disagree Strongly* (0) to *Agree Strongly*

[1]Address correspondence to Charlene Muehlenhard, Department of Psychology, University of Kansas, 426 Fraser Hall, 1415 Jayhawk Blvd., Lawrence, KS 66045-7556; e-mail: charlene@ku.edu

(3). Many respondents found the long form repetitious, and correlations between the short and long forms were high, ranging from .96 to .98 for the five subscales. Thus, we recommend the short form for most purposes.

Response Mode and Timing

The SBS can be administered using numerous formats (e.g., as a paper-and-pencil questionnaire or online questionnaire). The short form requires less than 5 minutes to complete; the long form requires less than 10 minutes.

Scoring

Items on each subscale are summed, yielding five subscale scores ranging from 0 to 12 (short form) or from 0 to 24 (long form). Higher scores reflect greater agreement with the belief measured by the subscale.

Reliability

For a sample of 337 male and female undergraduates, Cronbach's alphas for the short and long forms, respectively, were as follows: TR, .71 and .84; LOJF, .90 and .92; WLF, .92 and .95; MSD, .85 and .93; NMS, .94 and .96. In other samples, Milhausen, McBride, and Jun (2006) found alphas for the five subscales ranging from .62 to .86, with a median of .80 ($N = 261$). Dill, Brown, and Collins (2008) found alphas ranging from .71 (TR) to .94 (NMS); the alpha for the 20-item composite was .83 ($N = 180$).

Validity

Muehlenhard and Hollabaugh (1988) found that women who had engaged in token refusal of sexual intercourse—indicating no but meaning yes—scored higher than other women on the TR subscale, indicating that they regarded token refusal as a widespread behavior.

Muehlenhard and MacNaughton (1988) compared women whose LOJF scores fell at the lowest, middle, and highest 15% of the distribution. Compared with low-LOJF women, high-LOJF women rated a hypothetical rape victim as more responsible for the rape, rated the rape as more justified, and so forth. Medium- and high-LOJF women were more likely than low-LOJF women to report engaging in unwanted intercourse because a man had become so aroused that they felt it was useless to stop him; perhaps they believed that they had "led him on" and thus were obligated to satisfy him.

Muehlenhard, Andrews, and Beal (1996) compared men with high LOJF scores (LOJF men), men with low LOJF but high TR scores (TR men), and men with low LOJF and TR scores (Low-Myth men). LOJF men scored higher than TR men, and both scored higher than Low-Myth men, on self-rated likelihood of attempting intercourse with a woman after she said no. When asked to assume that she really had meant no, TR men no longer differed significantly from Low-Myth men, suggesting that TR men really had not believed her refusal; in contrast, LOJF men still

scored significantly higher than Low-Myth men. The distinct pattern for each group illustrates the value of measuring these beliefs separately.

Jones and Muehlenhard (1990) investigated the effects of a classroom lecture aimed at decreasing rape-supportive beliefs. Four weeks later, students who had received the lecture scored significantly lower than students in control classes on the TR, LOJF, WLF, and MSD subscales (as well as on Burt's Rape Myth Acceptance, Adversarial Sexual Beliefs, and Acceptance of Interpersonal Violence scales, 1980). The two groups did not differ significantly on the NMS subscale; even the control group had high NMS scores. Assessing another sexual assault prevention program, Milhausen et al. (2006) found significant pre- to posttest decreases on the WLF and TR subscales. Paradoxically, scores on the NMS subscale also decreased slightly but significantly.

Dill et al. (2008) found that SBS composite scores correlated significantly with exposure to violent video games ($r = .24, p < .001$). The correlation was even higher for exposure to *first-person shooter* games ($r = .26, p < .0001$).

Finally, consistent with numerous studies showing that men endorse rape-supportive beliefs more strongly than women do, Milhausen et al. (2006) found that men scored higher than women on all the SBS subscales except the NMS subscale. Similarly, Dill et al. (2008) found that men scored higher than women on the 20-item composite.

In summary, numerous studies support the validity of the SBS. The No Means Stop subscale, however, seems less useful than the others. Some respondents endorsed NMS items, agreeing that women have the right to say no at any point, but also endorsed items agreeing that no often means yes and that women who "lead men on" deserve to be forced. Similar patterns have been found in other studies (e.g., Goodchilds & Zellman, 1984); some respondents state that forced intercourse is *never* justified *and* that forced intercourse *is* justified in some circumstances.

References

Burt, M. R. (1980). Cultural myths and supports for rape. *Journal of Personality and Social Psychology, 38*, 217–230.

Dill, K. E., Brown, B. P., & Collins, M. A. (2008). Effects of exposure to sex-stereotyped video game characters on tolerance of sexual harassment. *Journal of Experimental Social Psychology, 44*, 1402–1408.

Goodchilds, J. D., & Zellman, G. L. (1984). Sexual signaling and sexual aggression in adolescent relationships. In N. M. Malamuth & E. Donnerstein (Eds.), *Pornography and sexual aggression* (pp. 234–243). Orlando, FL: Academic Press.

Jones, J. M., & Muehlenhard, C. L. (1990, November). *Using education to prevent rape on college campuses.* Paper presented at the Annual Meeting of the Society for the Scientific Study of Sex, Minneapolis, MN.

Milhausen, R. R., McBride, K. R., & Jun, M. K. (2006). Evaluating a peer-led, theatrical sexual assault prevention program: How do we measure success? *College Student Journal, 40*, 316–328.

Muehlenhard, C. L., Andrews, S. L., & Beal, G. K. (1996). Beyond "just saying no": Dealing with men's unwanted sexual advances in heterosexual dating contexts. *Journal of Psychology and Human Sexuality, 8*, 141–168.

Muehlenhard, C. L., & Hollabaugh, L. C. (1988). Do women sometimes say no when they mean yes? The prevalence and correlates of women's token resistance to sex. *Journal of Personality and Social Psychology, 54*, 872–879.

Muehlenhard, C. L., & MacNaughton, J. S. (1988). Women's attitudes toward women who "lead men on." *Journal of Social and Clinical Psychology, 7*, 65–79.

Exhibit

Sexual Beliefs Scale

Below is a list of statements regarding sexual attitudes. Using the scale below, indicate how much you agree or disagree with each statement. There are no right or wrong answers, only opinions.

Disagree Strongly	Disagree Mildly	Agree Mildly	Agree Strongly
0	1	2	3

*M	1.	Guys should dominate girls in bed.
N	2.	Even if a man really wants sex, he shouldn't do it if the girl doesn't want to.
L	3.	Girls who are teases deserve what they get.
*W	4.	By being dominated, girls get sexually aroused.
W	5.	A little force really turns a girl on.
N	6.	It's a girl's right to refuse sex at any time.
T	7.	Girls usually say No even when they mean Yes.
L	8.	When a girl gets a guy obviously aroused and then says No, he has the right to force sex on her.
W	9.	Girls really want to be manhandled.
*M	10.	Men should decide what should happen during sex.
*L	11.	A man is justified in forcing a woman to have sex if she leads him on.
M	12.	A man's masculinity should be proven in sexual situations.
*T	13.	Girls generally want to be talked into having sex.
*W	14.	Girls think it is exciting when guys use a little force on them.
*N	15.	A guy should respect a girl's wishes if she says No.
M	16.	The man should be the one who dictates what happens during sex.
T	17.	Girls say No so that guys don't lose respect for them.
W	18.	Feeling dominated gets girls excited.
L	19.	A girl who leads a guy to believe she wants sex when she really doesn't deserves whatever happens.
*T	20.	Women often say No because they don't want men to think they're easy.
*N	21.	When girls say No, guys should stop.
M	22.	During sex, guys should be in control.
*L	23.	When a girl toys with a guy, she deserves whatever happens to her.
T	24.	Girls just say No so as not to look promiscuous.
*N	25.	At any point, a woman always has the right to say No.
*M	26.	Guys should have the power in sexual situations.
*W	27.	Women really get turned on by men who let them know who's boss.
*T	28.	Girls just say No to make it seem like they're nice girls.
*L	29.	Girls who tease guys should be taught a lesson.
*M	30.	The man should be in control of the sexual situation.
L	31.	Girls who act like they want sex deserve it when the guy follows through.
*N	32.	Even if a man is aroused, he doesn't have the right to force himself on a woman.
*L	33.	Girls who lead guys on deserve what they get.
N	34.	If a woman says No, a man has no right to continue.
M	35.	Men should exercise their authority over women in sexual situations.
*T	36.	When girls say No, they often mean Yes.
W	37.	It really arouses girls when guys dominate them in bed.
N	38.	If a girl doesn't want sex, the guy has no right to do it.
T	39.	Girls who act seductively really want sex, even if they don't admit it.
*W	40.	Girls like it when guys are a little rough with them.

Note. T = Token Refusal subscale; L = Leading On Justifies Force subscale; W = Women Like Force subscale; M = Men Should Dominate subscale; N = No Means Stop subscale.

*These items are on the short form.

Dyadic Sexual Communication Scale

JOSEPH A. CATANIA,[1] *San Francisco State University*

The Dyadic Sexual Communication Scale (DSC) is a Likert-type scale assessing respondents' perceptions of the communication process encompassing sexual relationships. The original 13-item scale discriminated people reporting sexual problems from those not reporting sexual problems (Catania, 1986). The shortened and modified versions of the DSC scales, which have been used in nationally sampled sexual-risk studies, discriminated significant differences in disclosure of extramarital sex (Choi, Catania, & Dolcini, 1994) and have also been correlated with incidence of multiple partners (Dolcini, Coates, Catania, Kegeles, & Hauck, 1995).

Description

The DSC scale is a 13-item scale that measures how respondents perceive the discussion of sexual matters with their partners. Items are rated on a 6-point Likert-type scale (1 = *Disagree Strongly*, 6 = *Agree Strongly*). When frequent evaluations are desired, shortened, modified versions of the DSC scale are available to assess respondents' quality of communication.

Response Mode and Timing

For each item respondents are instructed to choose the rating that most adequately describes their feelings. All forms of the DSC scale are interviewer administered. Scales are available in English and Spanish, and all versions of the DSC scale take 1–2 minutes to complete.

Scoring

Sum across items for a total score.

Reliability and Validity

The DSC scale has been administered to college and adolescent populations, as well as national urban probability samples constructed to adequately represent White, Black, and Hispanic ethnic groups, as well as high HIV-risk factor groups (Choi et al. 1994; Dolcini et al., 1995). The DSC scale was assessed in a pilot study (*N* = 144 college students) that examined the internal consistency, test -retest reliability, and factor structure of the scale (Cronbach's alpha = .81 total sample, .83 cohabiting couples; test-retest = .89; a single factor was obtained; Catania, Pollack, McDermott, Qualls, & Cole, 1990). In a larger study (*N* = 500), the scale

was administered to respondents who had been recruited from pleasure parties in the California Bay Area (82%), and at church meetings and college classes in Colorado (18%). A slightly higher Cronbach's alpha was obtained (.87), and a factor analysis revealed that the DSC scale was composed of a single dimension. The communication measure discriminated people reporting sexual problems from those not reporting sexual problems, with the problem group (*M* = 53, *SD* = 13.0) reporting poorer sexual communication than the no problem group (*M* = 63.7, *SD* = 10.2), *t*(416) = 9.32, *p* = .0001.

A shortened, four-item version of the DCS scale was examined in a study of the correlates of extramarital sex (Choi et al., 1994). The analysis was a part of the 1990–1991 National AIDS Behavior Survey (NABS) longitudinal study, which was composed of three interlaced samples designed to oversample African-Americans and Hispanics for adequate representation. (For further details on sample construction and weighting of the NABS cohort study see Catania, Coates, Kegeles, et al., 1992.) The interlaced samples included a national sample, an urban sample of 23 cities with high prevalences of AIDS cases, and a special Hispanic urban sample. To examine the correlates of extramarital sex, we restricted our analysis to married, 18–49 year olds who reported having a primary sex partner. In Choi et al. (1994), the shortened, four-item version of the DSC scale was administered to those respondents (*N* = 5,900) who were married and between the ages of 18–49. Reliability was good (Cronbach's alpha = .62 for the total sample). Means, standard deviations, range, median, and reliabilities are given for White, Black, and Hispanic groups, males and females, and levels of education for both national and urban/high risk city samples in Table 1. In the national sample, significant differences in test scores were found between education levels and gender. In the urban/high-risk city groups, differences were found between ethnic groups as well as levels of education and gender. A regression analysis revealed that Hispanics who scored poorly on the dyadic communication scale were more likely to report extramarital sex. A *t* test revealed gender differences (*t* = 2.02, *p* < .04) with women scoring higher than men.

A six-item version of the DSC scale was developed on 114 adolescent females who participated in a study that examined psychosocial correlates of condom use and multiple partner sex (Catania, Coates, & Kegeles, 1989). Respondents, recruited from a family planning clinic in

[1]Address correspondence to Joseph A. Catania, College of Health and Human Sciences, Oregon State University, 320B Waldo Hall, Corvallis, OR 97331; e-mail: Joseph.Catania@oregonstate.edu

TABLE 1
Normative Data for the Dyadic Sexual Communications Scale

	N	Mean	SD	Range	Mdn	Alpha
NABS[a] Study						
National Sample	1,217	13.35	2.21	11.0	14.0	.65
High Risk Cities	4,683	13.14	2.26	12.0	13.0	.62
Ethnicity						
White						
National Sample	843	13.48	2.14	11.0	14.0	.67
High Risk Cities	1,816	13.20	2.22	12.0	13.0	.68
Black						
National Sample	213	13.25	2.38	9.0	14.0	.64
High Risk Cities	1,797	13.53	2.22	12.0	14.0	.58
Hispanic						
National Sample	128	12.57	2.31	8.0	12.0	.53
High Risk Cities	3,062	12.45	2.39	12.0	12.0	.59
Gender						
Male						
National Sample	499	13.22	2.22	9.0	13.0	.65
High Risk Cities	2,059	12.98	2.25	11.0	13.0	.62
Female						
National Sample	723	13.48	2.17	11.0	14.0	.65
High Risk Cities	2,617	13.32	2.24	12.0	14.0	.62
Education						
< 12 years						
National Sample	125	13.46	2.37	9.0	14.0	.60
High Risk Cities	694	12.39	2.31	11.0	12.0	.54
= 12 years						
National Sample	330	13.09	2.23	11.0	13.0	.62
High Risk Cities	1,163	13.20	2.30	12.0	13.0	.56
> 12 years						
National Sample	765	13.46	2.13	11.0	14.0	.67
High Risk Cities	2,286	13.32	2.18	12.0	14.0	.66
AMEN[b] Study						
Total	558	20.73	2.97	14.0	21.0	.67
Ethnicity						
White	259	20.49	2.94	12.0	21.0	.73
Black	124	21.48	2.60	10.0	22.5	.53
Hispanic	124	20.59	3.35	14.0	21.5	.66
Gender						
Male	250	20.44	2.97	12.0	21.0	.67
Female	308	20.96	2.96	14.0	21.0	.66
Education						
< 12 years	58	20.45	3.44	14.0	21.0	.61
= 12 years	109	20.95	2.95	12.0	21.0	.66
> 12 years	390	20.71	2.91	14.0	15.0	.70

[a]National AIDS Behavior Survey.
[b]AIDS in Multi-Ethnic Neighborhoods.

California, were White (92%), Hispanic (4%), and other (4%). The majority of respondents were heterosexual, unmarried, and sexually active. Reliability was good (Cronbach's alpha = .77).

The six-item DSC scale was also administered to 558 respondents who participated in a study (Dolcini et al., 1995) examining incidence of multiple partners and related psychosocial correlates, as part of the AIDS in Multi-Ethnic Neighborhoods (AMEN) Study (Catania, Coates, Stall, et al., 1992). The AMEN study is a longitudinal study (three waves) examining the distribution of HIV, sexually transmitted diseases (STDs), related risk behaviors, and their correlates across social strata. Respondents for the AMEN study were recruited from 16 census tracts of San Francisco that are characterized by high rates of STDs and drug use. (For further information regarding sampling techniques see Catania, Coates, Stall, et al., 1992; Fullilov-e et al., 1992.) The multiple-partner study sample, which obtained data at Wave 2, was restricted to heterosexuals who reported having a primary sexual partner and being sexually active. Respondents ranged from 20–44 years of age. Reliability was good (Cronbach's alpha = .67). The mean, standard deviation, median, range, and reliabilities of ethnic groups, gender, and levels of education are provided in Table 1. The communication scale was relevant only to those with a primary partner. A multiple regression revealed the DSC scale to be associated with having two or more partners.

References

Catania, J. (1986). *Help-seeking: An avenue for adult sexual development*. Unpublished doctoral dissertation. University of California, San Francisco.

Catania J., Coates, T., Golden, E., Dolicini, M., Peterson, J., Kegeles, S., Siegel, D., & Fullilove, M. (1994) Correlates of condom use among Black, Hispanic, and White heterosexuals in San Francisco: The AMEN Longitudinal Survey. *AIDS Education and Prevention, 6,* 12–26.

Catania, J., Coates, T., & Kegeles, S. (1989) Predictors of condom use and multiple partnered sex among sexually active adolescent women: Implications for AIDS-related health interventions. *The Journal of Sex Research, 26,* 514–524.

Catania, J., Coates, T., Kegeles, S., Thompson-Fullilove, M., Peterson, J., Marin, B., Siegel, D., & Hulley, S. (1992). Condom use in multi-ethnic neighborhoods of San Francisco: The population-based AMEN (AIDS in Multi-Ethnic Neighborhoods Study). *American Journal of Public Health, 82,* 284–287.

Catania, J., Coates, T., Peterson, J., Dolcini, M., Kegeles, S., Siegel, D., Golden, E., & Fullilove, M. (1993). Changes in condom use among Black, Hispanic and White heterosexuals in San Francisco: The AMEN Longitudinal Survey. *The Journal of Sex Research, 30,* 121–128.

Catania, J. A., Coates, T. J., Stall, R., Turner, H., Peterson. J., Hearst, N., Dolcini, M. M., Hudes, E., Gagnon, J., Wiley, J., & Groves, R. (1992). Prevalence of AIDS-related risk factors and condom use in the United States. *Science, 258,* 1101–1106.

Catania, J., Pollack, L., McDermott, L., Qualls, S., & Cole, L. (1990). Help-seeking behaviors of people with sexual problems. *Archives of Sexual Behavior, 19,* 235–250.

Choi, K. H., Catania, J. A., & Dolcini, M. M. (1994). Extramarital sex and HIV risk behavior among US adults: Results from the National AIDS Behavioral Survey. *American Journal of Public Health, 84,* 2003–2007.

Dolcini, M. M., Coates. T. J., Catania, J. A., Kegeles, S. M., & Hauck, W. W. (1995). Multiple sexual partners and their psychosocial correlates: The population-based AIDS in Multi-Ethnic Neighborhoods (AMEN) Study. *Health Psychology, 14,* 1–10.

Fullilove, M., Wiley, J., Fullilove, R., Golden, E., Catania, J., Peterson, J., Garrett, K., Siegel, D., Marin, G., Kegeles, S., Coates, T., & Hulley, S. (1992). Risk for AIDS in multi-ethnic neighborhoods in San Francisco, California: The population-based AMEN study. *Western Journal of Medicine, 157,* 32–40.

Exhibit

Dyadic Sexual Communication Scale

Instructions: Now I am going to read a list of statements different people have made about discussing sex with their primary partner. As I read each one, please tell me how much you agree or disagree with it.

1. My partner rarely responds when I want to talk about our sex life.
2. Some sexual matters are too upsetting to discuss with my sexual partner.
3. There are sexual issues or problems in our sexual relationship that we have never discussed.
4. My partner and I never seem to resolve our disagreements about sexual matters.
5. Whenever my partner and I talk about sex, I feel like she or he is lecturing me.
6. My partner often complains that I am not very clear about what I want sexually.
7. My partner and I have never had a heart to heart talk about our sex life together.
8. My partner has no difficulty in talking to me about his or her sexual feelings and desires.
9. Even when angry with me, my partner is able to appreciate my views on sexuality.
10. Talking about sex is a satisfying experience for both of us.
11. My partner and I can usually talk calmly about our sex life.
12. I have little difficulty in telling my partner what I do or don't do sexually.
13. I seldom feel embarrassed when talking about the details of our sex life with my partner.

Note. The short, four-item questionnaire used in the NABS study includes Items 2, 8, 10, and 12. The six-item version used in the AMEN and adolescent study includes Items 1, 2, 3, 8, 10, and 12. Questions in the original study have been modified for respondents who participated in subsequent studies.

The exact wording of the shortened, four-item versions of the DSC scale are as follows: 1. Do you find some sexual matters too difficult to discuss with your spouse? 2. Does your spouse have difficulty in talking to you about what he/she likes during sex? 3. Is talking about sex with your spouse fun for the both of you? 4. Do you find that it is easy for you to tell your spouse what you do or do not like to do during sex?

The exact wording of the six-item versions of the DSC scale is as follows: 1. I find some sexual matters are too upsetting to talk about with my primary partner. 2. I think it is difficult for my primary partner to tell me what (he/she) likes to do sexually. 3. It is easy for me to tell my primary partner what I do or don't like to do during sex. 4. My primary partner hardly ever talks to me when I want to talk about our sex life. 5. My primary partner really cares about what I think about sex. 6. Talking about sex with my primary partner is usually fun for the both of us.

Weighted Topics Measure of Family Sexual Communication

Terri D. Fisher,[1] *The Ohio State University at Mansfield*

The Weighted Topics Measure of Family Sexual Communication (WTM) was developed to enable researchers to assess quickly and objectively the amount of communication about sexuality that has occurred between parents and their adolescent children. This scale combines a relatively objective measure (number of topics discussed) with a more subjective one (extent of discussion).

Description

This measure asks respondents to indicate the extent to which nine specific sexual topics have been discussed,

using a scale of 0–4, with 0 corresponding to *None* and 4 corresponding to *A Lot*. Possible scores range from 0–36, with higher scores indicating greater amounts of communication. Adolescents may be asked to give separate reports for communication with the mother and the father.

Response Mode and Timing

Respondents indicate the extent of communication about each topic by indicating which of the five possible ratings mentioned above best corresponds to the amount of

[1]Address correspondence to Terri D. Fisher, The Ohio State University at Mansfield, 1760 University Drive, Mansfield, OH 44906; e-mail: fisher.16@osu.edu

communication experienced. This measure takes no more than 2 to 3 minutes to complete.

Scoring

To score the WTM, simply add up the weights for each topic.

Reliability

In a study of 129 male and 234 female unmarried college students between the ages of 18 and 24 (Fisher, 1993), the Cronbach alpha reliability coefficient was .89 for males reporting on communication with mothers, .91 for males reporting on communication with fathers, .90 for females reporting on communication with mothers, and .91 for females reporting on communication with fathers. Among the 336 mothers, the Cronbach alpha coefficient was .87, and for the 233 fathers it was .89. More recently, in a study of college students aged 18–21 (Clawson & Reese-Weber, 2003), the overall reliability coefficient was .91 for communication with fathers and .88 for communication with mothers.

Validity

In a validity study (Fisher, 1993) of nine measures of sexual communication using 129 male and 234 female college students between the ages of 18 and 25, the WTM was significantly correlated with general family communication as measured by the Openness in Family Communication subscale of Olson and Barnes' Parent-Adolescent Communication Scale (Olson et al., 1982). Correlation coefficients ranged from a low of .28 based on fathers' reports of communication to a high of .53 based on sons' reports of communication with their mothers. The WTM was not significantly correlated with a measure of social desirability responding (Strahan & Gerbasi, 1972). The correlation between the various measures of sexual communication and the validity measures were generally non-significant, but this was largely due to the use of Bonferroni corrections to account for the very large number of correlation coefficients that were calculated. In general, for most analyses, the WTM appeared to be the strongest of the measures.

Recently, Zamboni and Silver (2009) compared the WTM with Warren and Neer's Family Sex Communication Quotient (FSCQ; 1986). The WTM for communication with mothers was highly correlated (.64) with the comfort subscale of the FSCQ. For WTM reports of communication with fathers, the correlation with the comfort subscale of the FSCQ was .40 for females and .44 for males. Correlations of the WTM with the Value subscale of the FSCQ ranged from .22 to .46. Zamboni and Silver provided support for the concurrent validity of both the WTM and the FSCQ and concluded that "Because of these conceptual strengths and because the instruments have good psychometric properties, future studies might consider using these instruments to assess family sex communication" (p. 71).

Other Information

Previous studies with the WTM have consistently indicated that, when families are categorized as "high communication" and "low communication" families by means of a median split using this measure, adolescents and parents in the high communication families have sexual attitudes that are much more strongly correlated than those in the low communication families (Fisher, 1986, 1987, 1988). The WTM was also used to determine predictors of parental communication about sexuality (Fisher, 1990).

References

Clawson, C. L., & Reese-Weber, M. (2003). The amount and timing of parent-adolescent sexual communication as predictors of late adolescent sexual risk-taking behaviors. *The Journal of Sex Research, 40,* 256–265.

Fisher, T. D. (1986). An exploratory study of parent-child communication about sex and the sexual attitudes of early, middle, and late adolescents. *Journal of Genetic Psychology, 147,* 543–557.

Fisher, T. D. (1987). Family communication and the sexual behavior and attitudes of college students. *Journal of Youth and Adolescence, 16,* 581–595.

Fisher, T. D. (1988). The relationship between parent-child communication about sexuality and college students' sexual behavior and attitudes as a function of parental proximity. *The Journal of Sex Research, 24,* 305–311.

Fisher, T. D. (1990). Characteristics of mothers and fathers who talk to their adolescent children about sexuality. *Journal of Psychology and Human Sexuality, 3,* 53–70.

Fisher, T. D. (1993). A comparison of various measures of family sexual communication: Psychometric properties, validity, and behavioral correlates. *The Journal of Sex Research, 30,* 229–238.

Olson, D. H., McCubbin, H. I., Barnes, H., Larsen, A., Muxen, M., & Wilson, M. (1982). *Family inventories.* St. Paul: University of Minnesota.

Strahan, R., & Gerbasi, K. C. (1972). Short, homogeneous versions of the Marlowe-Crowne Social Desirability Scale. *Journal of Clinical Psychology, 28,* 191–193.

Warren, C., & Neer, M. (1986). Family sex communication orientation. *Journal of Applied Communication Research, 14,* 86–107.

Zamboni, B. D., & Silver, R. (2009). Family sex communication and the sexual desire, attitudes, and behavior of late adolescents. *American Journal of Sexuality Education, 4,* 58–78.

Exhibit

Weighted Topics Measure of Family Sexual Communication

Using a scale from 1 to 4 with 0 = None and 4 = A Lot, please indicate how much discussion you have had with your child about the following topics.

None   0   1   2   3   4   A Lot

_____ Pregnancy
_____ Fertilization
_____ Intercourse
_____ Menstruation
_____ Sexually Transmitted Disease [originally Venereal Disease]
_____ Birth Control
_____ Abortion
_____ Prostitution
_____ Homosexuality

Female Partner's Communication During Sexual Activity Scale

ALEXANDRA McINTYRE-SMITH[1] AND WILLIAM A. FISHER, *University of Western Ontario*

This scale assesses female respondents' perceptions of how easy it is to communicate with a partner during sexual activity, and how frequently they communicate their sexual preferences and the type of stimulation they desire to their partners.

Description

The scale is composed of three items measuring how easy it is for respondents to communicate with a partner during sexual activity, rated on a 7-point scale from *Very Difficult* to *Very Easy*, and three items measuring the frequency of use of different verbal and nonverbal communication strategies, rated on a 6-point scale ranging from *0% of the time* to *100% of the time*.

Scale development followed an iterative process, whereby items were developed and refined over a series of three studies. An initial pool of 20 items was developed and administered to 198 female undergraduate students. Items were subject to individual item analyses and exploratory factor analyses. Fourteen items were deleted owing to poor empirical performance or poor conceptual overlap with the construct. The six remaining items were provided to 16 graduate students who rated the items for clarity and provided feedback and suggestions for wording changes (see Hinkin, 1998; Streiner & Norman, 2008, for evidence for the use of students as item judges). Recommendations to improve item wording were considered if they were suggested by two or more people. For this scale, no wording changes were made. The six items were then administered to a second sample of 242 female undergraduate participants, and items were subjected to item analyses and exploratory factor analyses. Two items were deleted and two additional items were written. The six remaining items were administered to 211 female undergraduate participants, and responses were subjected to item analyses and test-retest reliability analyses. All six items were retained for the final scale.

Decision-making regarding item deletion was based on the following scale development guidelines (see Netemeyer, Bearden, & Sharma, 2003; Streiner & Norman, 2008): (a) range restriction problems (i.e., more than 50% of the sample endorsed a single response option, low standard deviations), (b) poor inter-item correlations with two or more scale items ($r < .30$), (c) poor corrected item-total

[1]Address correspondence to Alexandra McIntyre-Smith or William Fisher, Department of Psychology, The University of Western Ontario, London, Ontario, Canada N6A 5C2; e-mail: amcsmith@gmail.com or fisher@uwo.ca

correlations ($r < .30$), (d) high cross-loadings on nontarget factors ($> .35$ or more), (e) low percentage of variance accounted for within items (i.e., poor communalities; $< .30$), (f) low clarity ratings by expert raters ($M < 5.5$ on a 7-point scale), (g) poor item wording as judged by expert raters, (h) redundancy with other items, (i) poor conceptual overlap (i.e., item was judged to be too dissimilar from other items and/or to poorly reflect the construct).

Sampling was conducted with three groups of female undergraduate students, aged 17–49 ($M = 18.83$–19.24, $SD = 2.67$–3.38), who were heterosexually active (i.e., they reported having sexual intercourse with a male partner at least twice per month). As this scale was developed based on responses from undergraduate female participants, it is most appropriate for use with this population. Future studies examining the use of this measure with additional populations are needed.

Response Mode and Timing

Respondents are provided with the scale and instructions, and are asked to complete the survey on their own, and with as much privacy as possible. The scale was administered using the Internet for the purpose of scale development research. Paper-and-pencil administration of the scale requires 2 to 5 minutes.

Scoring

1. Score Items 1–3, 5 as follows: *Very Difficult* = 1, *Moderately Difficult* = 2 . . . *Very Easy* = 7.
2. Score Items 4–6 as follows: 0% = 0, 1–25% = 1, 26–50% = 2, 51–75% = 3, 76–99% = 4, 100% = 5.
3. Because Items 4–6 are essentially keyed on a 5-point scale (i.e., there is no conceptual equivalent to the 0% response option on the 7-point scales for Items 1–3), and the rest of the items are coded on a 7–point scale, items should be weighted in the following manner:

    a. Multiply Items 1–3 by 5.
    b. Multiply Items 4–6 by 7.

4. Calculate the average score or the total score for all items. Higher scores indicate a greater self-rated ease and frequency of sexual communication with a partner during sexual activity.
5. Calculate subscale scores if desired as follows:

    a. Ease of Sexual Communication—Items 1–3
    b. Frequency of Sexual Communication—Items 4–6

When calculating subscale scores, items do not need to be weighted within a given subscale because the response options are the same for all items (e.g., Items 1–3 are all answered on a 7-point scale).

Reliability

In Study III, when all six items were available for calculating reliability, internal consistency of the total scale was good ($\alpha = .83$). In Studies I and II, only four of the final six items were available, and internal consistency scores were somewhat lower as a result ($\alpha = .76$–.77). The corrected item-to-total correlations across all three studies were good, $r = .54$–.63, as were the inter-item correlations, $r = .27$–.64. Four-week test-retest reliability was reasonable for the total scale ($r = .72$).

As the two subscales comprised only two or three items each (two items in Studies I and II, and three items in Study III), internal consistency estimates were somewhat lower than for the total scale ($\alpha = .64$–.79). Nonetheless, the intercorrelations between subscale items were in the range $r = .51$–.64, suggesting that the items can be combined to form a subscale. Four-week test-retest reliability was reasonable for both subscales ($r = .65$–.67).

Validity

We hypothesized that correlations between scores on the Female Sexual Function Index (FSFI; Rosen et al., 2000) and scores on the Female Partner's Communication During Sexual Activity Scale would provide evidence of convergent validity because communication with a partner has been shown to facilitate sexual response during sexual activity with a partner (e.g., Hayes et al., 2008). As hypothesized, the Female Partner's Communication During Sexual Activity Scale and subscales scores were associated with the total FSFI score ($r = .30$–.37), as well as scores on the Desire ($r = .19$–.23), Arousal ($r = .19$–.22), and Satisfaction ($r = .26$–.30) subscales.

Other evidence of convergent validity includes the correlation of the total score and subscales with the Sexual Opinion Survey measure of erotophobia-erotophilia, $r = .16$–.27, which is the tendency to respond to sexual stimuli with negative-to-positive affect and avoidant-to-approach behavior (Fisher, Byrne, White, & Kelley, 1988), and with the Dyadic Sexual Regulation Scale, $r = .33$–.47, which measures the degree to which the respondent initiates sexual activity (vs. waiting for a partner to do so), and is an active (vs. more passive) participant during sexual activity (Catania, McDermott, & Wood, 1984). Frequency of intercourse ($r = .25$–.47) and frequency of masturbation ($r = .22$–.26$) were also correlated with the total scale and subscale scores. The Female Partner's Communication During Sexual Activity Scale and subscales were not correlated with the Marlowe-Crowne Social Desirability Scale (Crowne & Marlowe, 1964) or with measures of depression and anxiety (Henry & Crawford, 2005), providing evidence of discriminant validity and freedom from response bias.

References

Catania, J. A., McDermott, L. V., & Wood, J. A. (1984). Assessment of locus of control: Situational specificity in the sexual context. *The Journal of Sex Research, 20,* 310–324.

Crowne, D. P., & Marlowe, D. (1964). *The approval motive: Studies in evaluative dependence.* New York: Wiley.

Fisher, W. A., Byrne, D., White, L. A., & Kelley, K. (1988). Erotophobia-erotophilia as a dimension of personality. *The Journal of Sex Research, 25,* 123–151.

Hayes, R. D., Dennerstein, L., Bennett, C. M., Sidat, M., Gurrin, L. C., & Fairley, C. K. (2008). Risk factors for female sexual dysfunction in the general population: Exploring factors associated with low sexual function and sexual distress. *Journal of Sexual Medicine, 5,* 1681–1693.

Henry, J. D., & Crawford, J. R. (2005). The short-form version of the Depression Anxiety Stress Scales (DASS-21): Construct validity and normative data in a large non-clinical sample. *British Journal of Clinical Psychology, 44,* 227–239.

Hinkin, T. R. (1998). A brief tutorial on the development of measures for use in survey questionnaires. *Organizational Research Methods, 1,*

104–121.

Netemeyer, R. G., Bearden, W. O., & Sharma, S. (2003). *Scaling procedures: Issues and applications.* Thousand Oaks, CA: Sage.

Rosen, R., Brown, C., Heiman, J., Leiblum, S., Meston, C., Shabsigh, R., et al. (2000). The Female Sexual Function Index (FSFI): A multidimensional self-report instrument for the assessment of female sexual function. *Journal of Sex and Marital Therapy, 26,* 191–208.

Streiner, D. L. & Norman, G. R. (2008). *Health measurement scales: A practical guide to their development and use* (4th ed.). New York: Oxford University Press.

Exhibit

Female Partner's Communication During Sexual Activity Scale

Instructions: The following questions ask about your thoughts and feelings concerning sexual activities with a partner and your sexual experiences. You are asked to rate each item on the scale provided. Please check off one box per item to indicate your response.

1. *Telling* my partner what to do to stimulate me during intercourse would be:

☐ Very Difficult ☐ Moderately Difficult ☐ Slightly Difficult ☐ Neither Easy nor Difficult ☐ Slightly Easy ☐ Moderately Easy ☐ Very Easy

2. *Showing* my partner what to do to stimulate me during intercourse would be:

☐ Very Difficult ☐ Moderately Difficult ☐ Slightly Difficult ☐ Neither Easy nor Difficult ☐ Slightly Easy ☐ Moderately Easy ☐ Very Easy

3. *Asking* my partner to stimulate me to orgasm (i.e., by massaging my genitals/clitoris) when I have intercourse with my partner would be:

☐ Very Difficult ☐ Moderately Difficult ☐ Slightly Difficult ☐ Neither Easy nor Difficult ☐ Slightly Easy ☐ Moderately Easy ☐ Very Easy

4. When having sex with a partner, how *often do you tell your partner what feels good?*
☐ 0% of the time
☐ 1–25% of the time
☐ 26–50% of the time
☐ 51–75% of the time
☐ 76–99% of the time
☐ 100% of the time

5. When having sex with a partner, how *often do you show your partner what feels good?*
☐ 0% of the time
☐ 1–25% of the time
☐ 26–50% of the time
☐ 51–75% of the time
☐ 76–99% of the time
☐ 100% of the time

6. When having sex with a partner, how *often do you ask your partner to stimulate your clitoris to orgasm?*
☐ 0% of the time
☐ 1–25% of the time
☐ 26–50% of the time
☐ 51–75% of the time
☐ 76–99% of the time
☐ 100% of the time

Partner Communication Scale

ROBIN R. MILHAUSEN,[1] *University of Guelph*
JESSICA MCDERMOTT SALES, *Emory University*
RALPH J. DICLEMENTE, *Emory University*

The Partner Communication Scale (PCS) was developed to assess frequency of communicating about sexual topics with a male sex partner among African American adolescent females (Milhausen et al., 2007).

Description

The PCS was developed as part of an NIMH-funded intervention grant (Milhausen et al., 2007). Domains pertinent to sexual communication were selected based on a review of the empirical literature. These were (a) pregnancy; (b) STDs; (c) HIV/AIDS; (d) condom use; and (e) partner's sex history. Focus groups of African American adolescent females were conducted to verify that these topics were relevant in their sexual relationships. Thirty-six items were created to assess communication in these domains. Health educators assessed face validity of the items. The measure was pilot-tested on 15 African American adolescent females, 14 to 18 years of age. Based on their suggestions, items were revised to enhance reading comprehension. Items that were highly correlated and thought to assess the same construct, as well as items that decreased the Cronbach's alpha below .90, were deleted, leaving a 5-item scale. Data from three studies were used to validate the measure (Milhausen et al., 2007).

Though the PCS was designed for, and validated with, samples of African American adolescent females, the items are likely more broadly applicable to individuals of other racial or ethnic backgrounds, to other age groups, and, as well, to males.

Response Mode and Timing

A single stem is used for all items, "During the past 6 months, how many times have you and your sex partner discussed . . ." Each item requires a response based on a Likert-type scale: 0 (*Never*); 1 (*Sometimes, 1–3 Times*); 2 (*Often, 4–6 Times*); 3 (*A Lot, 7 or More Times*). The scale typically takes less than 5 minutes to complete.

Scoring

All items are coded so that higher values indicate more frequent sexual communication. Scores on the five items are summed to create a scale score. Scores range from 0 to 15. The mean score for participants in Study 1 was 8.47 (*SD* = 4.31); in Study 2 the mean score was 7.59 (*SD* = 5.04; Milhausen et al., 2007). In Study 3, the mean score was 6.46 (*SD* = 4.32; Milhausen et al., 2007).

Reliability

Stability of the measure was assessed by Pearson correlation. Because it has been suggested that the length of time between reliability assessments should mirror the length of time in intervention studies (Gliner, Morgan, & Harmon, 2001), measurement stability was assessed with 6 months between administrations. In Study 1, baseline and 6-month follow-up responses were correlated at .44. Baseline and 12-month follow-up responses were correlated at .38 (Milhausen et al., 2007). In Study 2, baseline and 6-month follow-up responses were correlated at .37. Correlations may be low because participants were referring to different partners at each completion point. In Study 1, the Cronbach's alpha was .80 at baseline (*N* = 522), .87 at 6-month follow-up, and .87 at 12-month follow-up. In Study 2, the Cronbach's alpha for the PCS was .90 (*N* = 243). In Study 3, the Cronbach's alpha was .84 at baseline (*N* = 715) and .89 at 6-month follow-up (*N* = 313; Milhausen et al., 2007).

Validity

The PCS was correlated with other related constructs in the direction that was predicted in both Study 1 and Study 2 (Milhausen et al., 2007). Specifically, in Study 1, the PCS was correlated with frequency of sexual communication with a parent (Sales et al., 2008) and sexual communication self-efficacy (with new partner and boyfriend), and the effect sizes were moderate (Cohen, 1988). Small but significant positive correlations were found between the PCS and relationship satisfaction and self-esteem. Small but significant negative correlations were found between the PCS and fear of consequences of condom negotiation and partner-related barriers to condom use (St. Lawrence et al., 1999). The PCS was correlated positively with condom use at last vaginal sex with steady and nonsteady partners, condom use during the past 30 days with steady

[1]Address correspondence to Robin R. Milhausen, Department of Family Relations and Applied Nutrition, Room 217 MINS Building, University of Guelph, Guelph, Ontario, N1G 2W1, Canada; e-mail: rmilhaus@uoguelph.ca

and nonsteady partners, and condom use with a steady partner over the previous 6 months. Discriminant validity was assessed by correlating the PCS with measures of watching movies or television. These correlations were not significant. In Study 2, the PCS was correlated with sexual communication with parents (Sales et al., 2008), self-esteem (Rosenberg, 1965, 1989), sexual refusal self-efficacy, and receiving sex education in schools (Milhausen et al., 2007). In Study 2, the PCS did not correlate significantly with partner-related barriers to condom use (St. Lawrence et al., 1999).

Other Information

The PCS is a brief, self-administered behavioral scale measuring frequency of sexual communication with a male partner, suitable for low-literate samples (requiring a fourth grade reading level). Researchers may find the PCS particularly useful in sexual health education interventions, assessing frequency of sexual communication pre- and postintervention to evaluate intervention efficacy. The authors would appreciate receiving information about the results obtained with this measure.

Additional affiliation information: Robin R. Milhausen: The Kinsey Institute; Rural Center for AIDS/STD Prevention, Indiana University, Bloomington.

References

Cohen, J. (1988). *Statistical power analysis for the behavioral sciences* (2nd ed.). Hillsdale, NJ: Lawrence Erlbaum.

Gliner, J. A., Morgan, G. A., & Harmon, J. J. (2001). Measurement reliability. *Journal of the American Academy of Child and Adolescent Psychiatry, 4,* 486–488.

Milhausen, R. R., Sales, J. M., Wingood, G. M., DiClemente, R. J., Salazar, L. F., & Crosby, R. A. (2007). Validation of a partner communication scale for use in HIV/AIDS prevention interventions. *Journal of HIV/ AIDS Prevention in Children and Youth, 8,* 11–33.

Rosenberg, M. (1965). *Society and the adolescent self-image.* Princeton, NJ: Princeton University Press.

Rosenberg, M. (1989). *Society and the adolescent self-image* (Rev. ed.). Middletown, CT: Wesleyan University Press.

Sales, J. M., Milhausen, R. R., Wingood, G. M., DiClemente, R. J., Salazar, L. F., & Crosby, R. A. (2008). Validation of a parent-adolescent communication scale for use in STD/HIV prevention interventions. *Health Education and Behavior, 35,* 332–345.

St. Lawrence, J. S., Chapdelaine, A. P., Devieux, J. G., O'Bannon, R. E., III, Brasfield, T. L., & Eldridge, G. D. (1999). Measuring perceived barriers to condom use: Psychometric evaluation of the Condom Barriers Scale. *Assessment, 6,* 391–404.

Exhibit

Partner Communication Scale

During the past six months, how many times have you and your sex partner discussed . . .	Never	Sometimes (1–3 Times)	Often (4–6 Times)	A Lot (7 or More Times)
. . . how to prevent pregnancy	0	1	2	3
. . . how to use condoms	0	1	2	3
. . . how to prevent the AIDS virus	0	1	2	3
. . . how to prevent STDs	0	1	2	3
. . . your partner's sex history	0	1	2	3

Parent-Adolescent Communication Scale

JESSICA MCDERMOTT SALES,[1] *Emory University*
ROBIN R. MILHAUSEN, *University of Guelph*
RALPH J. DICLEMENTE, *Emory University*

The Parent-Adolescent Communication Scale (PACS) was developed to assess adolescent girls' frequency of sexual communication with their parents (Sales et al., 2008).

Description

The PACS was developed as part of an NIMH-funded intervention grant (Sales et al., 2008). Domains pertinent to sexual communication were selected based on a review of the empirical literature. These included (a) pregnancy, (b) STDs, (c) HIV/AIDS, (d) condom use, and (e) general information about sex. Focus groups of African American adolescent females were conducted to verify that these topics were relevant in their sexual relationships. Thirty-six items were created to assess communication in these domains. Health educators assessed face validity of the items. The measure was pilot-tested on 15 African American adolescent females 14 to 18 years of age. Based on their suggestions, items were revised to enhance reading comprehension. Items that were highly correlated and thought to assess the same construct, as well as items that decreased the Cronbach's alpha below .90, were deleted, leaving a 5-item scale. Data from one longitudinal evaluation study were used to validate the measure (Sales et al., 2008).

Though the PACS was designed for adolescent females, and validated with an African American female sample, the items are likely more broadly applicable to individuals of other racial or ethnic backgrounds, other age groups, and males.

Response Mode and Timing

A single stem is used for all items: "In the past 6 months, how often have you and your parent(s) talked about the following things . . ." Each item requires a response based on a Likert-type scale: 1 (*Never*); 2 (*Rarely*); 3 (*Sometimes*); 4 (*Often*). The scale typically takes less than 5 minutes to complete.

Scoring

All items are coded so that higher values indicate more frequent sexual communication with parents. Scores on the five items are summed to create a scale score. Scores range from 5 to 20. The mean score for participants in our validation sample was 14.20 ($SD = 4.79$; Sales et al., 2008).

Reliability

Stability of the measure was assessed by Pearson correlation. Because it has been suggested that the length of time between reliability assessments mirrors the length of time in intervention studies (Gliner, Morgan, & Harmon, 2001), measurement stability was assessed with 6 months between administrations. The intercorrelation between baseline and 6-month follow-up scores was significant ($r = .58$, $p < .001$), as was the intercorrelation between baseline and 12-month follow-up scores ($r = .53$, $p < .001$; Sales et al., 2008).

Validity

The PACS was correlated with other related constructs in the predicted directions (Sales et al., 2008). Concurrent validity was assessed by correlating frequency of sexual communication with parent(s) as measured by PACS at baseline and other related constructs also assessed at baseline. Specifically, the PACS was positively associated with frequency of sexual communication with partner (Milhausen et al., 2007) and sexual communication self-efficacy (with new partner), family support (Zimet, Dahlem, Zimet, & Farley, 1988), and perceived parental knowledge about their whereabouts. In addition, PACS scores were negatively associated with depressive symptoms. Also, the PACS was positively correlated with recent condom use (last vaginal sex, past 30 days, and past 6 months) with steady partners and was inversely correlated with frequency of vaginal intercourse (past 30 days). The correlations were all significant, and effect sizes were small to moderate (Cohen, 1988). Predictive validity was assessed by correlating baseline PACS scores to related constructs assessed at 6- and 12-month follow-up assessments. At the 6-month follow-up interval, baseline PACS scores were significantly positively associated with frequency of sexual communication with partner (Milhausen et al., 2007) and sexual communication self-efficacy with a new partner. Also, the PACS was significantly positively associated with condom use during the intervening 6 months between the baseline and 6-month follow-up assessment. At the

[1]Address correspondence to Jessica McDermott Sales, Emory University, Rollins School of Public Health, Department of Behavioral Sciences and Health Education, 1520 Clifton Rd., NE, Room 266, Atlanta, GA 30322; e-mail: jmcderm@emory.edu

12-month follow-up interval, baseline PACS scores were significantly positively associated with frequency of sexual communication (Milhausen et al., 2007) and condom use during the intervening 6 months between the 6-month and 12-month follow-up assessments. Discriminant validity was assessed by correlating the PACS with measures of watching movies or television. These correlations were not significant.

Other Information

The PACS is a brief, self-administered behavioral scale measuring frequency of sexual communication with a parent or parents, suitable for low-literate samples (requiring a fourth grade reading level). Researchers may find the PACS particularly useful in sexual health education interventions, particularly family-level interventions, for assessing frequency of sexual communication pre- and postintervention to evaluate

intervention efficacy. The authors would appreciate receiving information about the results obtained with this measure.

References

Cohen, J. (1988). *Statistical power analysis for the behavioral sciences* (2nd ed.). Hillsdale, NJ: Lawrence Erlbaum.

Gliner, J. A., Morgan, G. A., & Harmon, J. J. (2001). Measurement reliability. *Journal of the American Academy of Child and Adolescent Psychiatry, 4,* 486–488.

Milhausen, R. R., Sales, J. M., Wingood, G. M., DiClemente, R. J., Salazar, L. F., & Crosby, R. A. (2007). Validation of a partner communication scale for use in HIV/AIDS prevention interventions. *Journal of HIV/AIDS Prevention in Children and Youth, 8,* 11–33.

Sales, J. M., Milhausen, R. R., Wingood, G. M., DiClemente, R. J., Salazar, L. F., & Crosby, R. A. (2008). Validation of a parent-adolescent communication scale for use in STD/HIV prevention interventions. *Health Education and Behavior, 35,* 332–345.

Zimet, G., Dahlem, N. V., Zimet, S. G., & Farley, G. K. (1988). The multidimensional scale of perceived social support. *Journal of Personality Assessment, 52,* 30–41.

Exhibit

Parent–Adolescent Communication Scale

In the past 6 months, how often have you and your parent(s) talked about the following things . . .	Never	Rarely	Sometimes	Often
. . . sex	1	2	3	4
. . . how to use condoms	1	2	3	4
. . . protecting yourself from STDs	1	2	3	4
. . . protecting yourself from AIDs	1	2	3	4
. . . protecting yourself from becoming pregnant	1	2	3	4

Family Sex Communication Quotient

CLAY WARREN,[1] *The George Washington University*

The Family Sex Communication Quotient (FSCQ) was developed as a diagnostic tool to measure a general family orientation to discussion about sex between parents and children (Warren & Neer, 1982, 1983). This orientation is assessed across three dimensions: comfort, information, and value. The *comfort* dimension was chosen as a main FSCQ measure because people positively experience supportive climates regarded as essential to the exchange of sex-related information between parents and children. The *information* dimension was included because the home

can function as a primary source of sexual learning only through sufficient sharing of information. The *value* dimension was selected because long-range positive values about family sex communication will influence the likelihood of discussing sex with one's own children.

Description

The 18-item FSCQ instrument incorporates six statements for each of three dimensions assessed on a 5-point Likert

[1]Address correspondence to Clay Warren, Department of Organizational Sciences and Communication, The George Washington University, 600 21st Street NW, Washington, DC, 20052; e-mail: claywar@gwu.edu

scale from *Strongly Agree* to *Strongly Disagree*. The *comfort* dimension measures the perceived degree of openness with which sex is discussed in the family (e.g., "I feel free to ask my parents questions about sex"). The *information* dimension measures perception of the amount of information learned and shared during discussions (e.g., "I feel better informed about sex if I talk with my parents"). The *value* dimension measures the perceived overall importance of the family role in sexual learning (e.g., "The home should be a primary place for learning about sex").

Descriptive statistics from inception to the present show respondents demonstrating a modest orientation (between 65 and 36) toward family sex communication (Warren, 2006). Basing a strong orientation on a minimum score of 72 that would result if respondents "agree" with all 18 statements, approximately 1 in 10 respondents represent a strong orientation. Range levels of orientation have been generalized as low (18–39), moderate (40–69), and high (70–90).

The FSCQ is appropriate for American and Canadian populations (Warren, 2000). The extent to which families in other developed countries have effective family sex communication is generally not available (Warren, 1992). When the FSCQ was administered to a Danish sample, however, results were distributed differently from those of the U.S. (Warren, 1987).

Response Mode and Timing

Respondents are informed that the FSCQ represents personal feelings about family discussions of sex. They are asked to circle one of five response categories that best describes their opinion: SA = *Strongly Agree*, A = *Agree*, N = *Neutral* (or *Don't Know*), D = *Disagree*, SD = *Strongly Disagree*. They are advised to answer the questions regardless of whether they have talked about sex with their parents, not to spend much time on any one question, and not to ask others how they are answering their questions. The FSCQ can be completed in 5 minutes or less.

Scoring

Comfort is measured by Items 2, 5, 8, 11, 14, and 17, *Information* by Items 3, 6, 9, 12, 15, and 18, and *Value* by Items 1, 4, 7, 10, 13, and 16. Each SA answer gets a "5," each A a "4," each N a "3," each D a "2," and each SD a "1." Six of the items need to be reverse scored (Items 4, 9, 10, 13, 14, and 16). The numbers are totaled and represent the FSCQ score. Three subscores are available by summing the items in each dimension.

Reliability and Validity

Statements were constructed along definitional lines of face validity for inclusion in the FSCQ dimensions. In the early stages of development, four independent measures on frequency, impact, parental style, and attitudes toward sexual practices were employed to serve as criterion-related validity tests for the FSCQ.

The initial statistical assessments of the FSCQ showed it to be a highly reliable instrument (*a* = .92; Warren & Neer, 1986). Across the years, the *alpha* coefficient has averaged above .90 (Warren, 2006). In a study analyzing parental, in addition to children's, completion of the FSCQ, the *alpha* for mothers was .91 (Warren & Olsen, 2005).

Early development work on analysis of the 18 items demonstrated that two-thirds of the items correlated above .60, one-sixth above .40, and one-sixth above .30. Dimension-to-dimension correlations further supported the internal consistency of the FSCQ. All dimensions correlated above .60, with the comfort and information dimensions correlating above .80. Dimension-to-total correlations provided very strong evidence for the internal consistency of the FSCQ with all dimensions correlating above .80, while the value and information dimensions each correlated above .90 with the FSCQ.

The internal structure of the FSCQ was examined with factor analysis, and only two items from the value dimension failed to contribute to the factor structure. (They were not deleted because they did not reduce the *alpha* estimate of the instrument.) Evidence for the reliability of the orientation levels assigned to the FSCQ summed scores was found in significant univariate F ratios that ranged from 6.85 to 70.80, with one-half of the items producing F ratios above 40.00, while only four items yielded F ratios lower than 20.00. Discriminant analysis resulted in a single discriminant function that correctly classified 87% of respondents within their respective membership category.

A full discussion of reliability and validity measures can be found in Warren (1995) and Warren and Neer (1986). A recent study (Zamboni & Silver, 2009) evaluating properties of the FSCQ as well as Fisher's Weighted Topics Scale (1987) found the two scales to be significantly and positively correlated with one another, and together to encompass all aspects of measurement that Fisher deemed important in the area of family sex communication (i.e., extent, frequency, quality, and content). Because of the conceptual strengths and good psychometric properties of the scales, the researchers proposed their use to assess family sex communication.

Other Information

The FSCQ was initially copyrighted in the *Journal of Applied Communication Research*. The instrument can be reprinted for profit with the permission of the journal and author. It can be used, without obtaining permission of the journal or author, for noncommercial purposes. Michael Neer contributed to designing the instrument.

References

Fisher, T. D. (1987). Family communication and the sexual behavior and attitudes of college students. *Journal of Youth and Adolescence, 16*, 481–495.

Warren, C. (1987, May). *Family sex communication in Denmark*. Paper presented at International Communication Association conference, Montreal.

Warren, C. (1992). Perspectives on international sex practices and American family sex communication relevant to teenage sexual behavior in the United States. *Health Communication, 4,* 121–136.

Warren, C. (1995). Parent-child communication about sex. In T. J. Socha & G. Stamp (Eds.), *Parents, children, and communication: Frontiers of theory and research* (pp. 173–201). Hillsdale, NJ: Lawrence Erlbaum.

Warren, C. (2000). Talking with your children about sex. In C. G. Waugh, W. I. Gorden, & K. M. Golden (Eds.), *Let's talk: A cognitive skills approach to interpersonal communication* (pp. 292–295 & 451). Dubuque, IA: Kendall/Hunt.

Warren, C. (2006). Communicating about sex with parents and partners. In K. M. Galvin & P. J. Cooper (Eds.), *Making connections: Readings in relational communication* (4th ed., pp. 319–326). New York: Oxford University Press.

Warren, C., & Neer, M. (1982, May). *Family sexual communication: A preliminary study of patterns of interaction*. Paper presented at International Communication Association conference, Boston.

Warren, C., & Neer, M. (1983, May). *Determinants and effects of family sexual communication*. Paper presented at International Communication Association conference, Dallas.

Warren, C., & Neer, M. (1986). Family sex communication orientation. *Journal of Applied Communication Research, 14,* 86–107.

Warren, C., & Olsen, N. (2005, November). *A paired analysis of parent-child communication about sex*. Paper presented at National Communication Association conference, Boston.

Zamboni, B. D., & Silver, R. (2009). Family sex communication and the sexual desire, attitudes, and behavior of late adolescents. *American Journal of Sexuality Education, 4,* 58–78.

Exhibit

Family Sex Communication Quotient

Directions: The following statements represent personal feelings about family discussions of sex. Please circle one of the five response categories that best describes your opinion: SA = Strongly Agree, A = Agree, N = Neutral (or Don't Know), D = Disagree, SD = Strongly Disagree. Also, please answer these questions regardless of whether you have ever talked about sex with your parents. Don't spend much time on any one question; make a choice and move to the next. Don't ask others how they are answering their questions, or how they think you should answer yours.

1.	Sex should be one of the most important topics for parents and children to discuss.	SA A N D SD
2.	I can talk to my parents about almost anything related to sex.	SA A N D SD
3.	My parents know what I think about sex.	SA A N D SD
4.	It is not necessary to talk to my parents about sex.	SA A N D SD
5.	I can talk openly and honestly with my parents about sex.	SA A N D SD
6.	I know what my parents think about sex.	SA A N D SD
7.	The home should be a primary place for learning about sex.	SA A N D SD
8.	I feel comfortable discussing sex with my parents.	SA A N D SD
9.	My parents have given me very little information about sex.	SA A N D SD
10.	Sex is too personal a topic to discuss with my parents.	SA A N D SD
11.	My parents feel comfortable discussing sex with me.	SA A N D SD
12.	Much of what I know about sex has come from family discussions.	SA A N D SD
13.	Sex should not be discussed in the family unless there is a problem to resolve.	SA A N D SD
14.	Sex is too hard a topic to discuss with my parents.	SA A N D SD
15.	I feel better informed about sex if I talk to my parents.	SA A N D SD
16.	The least important thing to discuss with my parents is sex.	SA A N D SD
17.	I feel free to ask my parents questions about sex.	SA A N D SD
18.	When I want to know something about sex, I generally ask my parents.	SA A N D SD

Scoring: The FSCQ measures a general orientation toward discussion about sex in the family unit along three dimensions: Comfort (Items 2, 5, 8, 11, 14, and 17), Information (Items 3, 6, 9, 12, 15, and 18), and Value (Items 1, 4, 7, 10, 13, and 16). You can give each SA answer a "5," A answer a "4," N answer a "3," D answer a "2," and SD answer a "1." Six of the questions need to be reverse scored (Items 4, 9, 10, 13, 14, and 16). Reverse scoring means the 5 and 1 weights are interchanged, the 4 and 2 weights are interchanged, and the 3 remains the same. It is used in questionnaire design to detect set-response behavior—a tendency of some folks to not think about the questions and, thus, to use the same answers regardless of the question asked. After pairing a number with the 18 questions, you can total the numbers for your FSCQ score. Range levels of orientation have been generalized as low (18–39), moderate (40–69), and high (70–90).

Hurlbert Index of Sexual Compatibility

DAVID F. HURLBERT,[1] *U.S. Department of Health and Human Services*

The Hurlbert Index of Sexual Compatibility (HISC) is described by Hurlbert, White, Powell, and Apt (1993).

Reference

Hurlbert, D. F., White, L. C., Powell, R. D., & Apt, C. (1993). Orgasm consistency training in the treatment of women reporting hypoactive sexual desire: An outcome comparison of women-only groups and couples-only groups. *Journal of Behaviour Therapy & Experimental Psychiatry, 24*, 3–13.

Exhibit

Hurlbert Index of Sexual Compatibility

1. My sexual beliefs are similar to those of my partner. (R)
2. I think my partner understands me sexually. (R)
3. My partner and I share the same sexual likes and dislikes. (R)
4. I think my partner desires too much sex.
5. My partner is unwilling to do certain sexual things for me that I would like to experience.
6. I feel comfortable during sex with my partner. (R)
7. I am sexually attracted to my partner. (R)
8. My partner sexually pleases me. (R)
9. My partner and I argue about the sexual aspects of our relationship.
10. My partner and I share the same level of interest in sex. (R)
11. I feel uncomfortable engaging in some of the sexual activities that my partner desires.
12. When it comes to sex, my ideas and values are different from those of my partner.
13. I do not think I meet my partner's sexual needs.
14. My partner and I enjoy the same sexual activities. (R)
15. When it comes to sex, my partner and I get along well. (R)
16. I think my partner is sexually attracted to me. (R)
17. My partner enjoys doing certain sexual things that I dislike.
18. It is hard for me to accept my partners' views on sex.
19. In our relationship, my partner places too much importance on sex.
20. My partner and I disagree over the frequency in which we should have sex.
21. I have the same sexual values as my partner. (R)
22. My partner and I share similar sexual fantasies. (R)
23. When it comes to sex, my partner is unwilling to do certain things that I would like to experience.
24. I think I sexually satisfy my partner. (R)
25. My partner and I share about the same level of sexual desire. (R)

Note. This 25-item inventory is scored on the following 5-point Likert-type scale: *all of the time* (0); *most of the time* (+1); *some of the time* (+2); *rarely* (+3); *never* (+4). (R) = reverse-score items.

[1]Address correspondence to David F. Hurlbert, 140 Farnworth Lane, Roswell, Georgia 30075; e-mail: david.hurlbert@acf.hhs.gov

Compulsive Sexual Behavior Inventory

ELI COLEMAN[1] AND REBECCA E. SWINBURNE ROMINE, *University of Minnesota*

The Compulsive Sexual Behavior Inventory (CSBI) is a 22-item self-report measure consisting of multiple-choice items about compulsive sexual behavior. Compulsive sexual behavior (CSB) is defined as a clinical syndrome characterized by intense, distressing, and recurrent sexual urges and fantasies that interfere with a person's daily functioning. Despite a desire to be free of their symptoms, individuals with CSB are unable to control their distressing behaviors and thoughts. There are two basic types of CSB: paraphilic and nonparaphilic. Paraphilic CSB involves both compulsive or impulsive thoughts and behaviors and deviant or nonconventional sexual interests, whereas nonparaphilic CSB describes similar compulsivity and impulsivity but around normative or conventional sexual behaviors. The CSBI is used to assess the severity of both forms of CSB.

Description

The CSBI contains items that assess two factors of compulsive sexual behavior: control and violence. To develop the initial version of the scale, experts including the first author generated 42 items designed to assess components of CSB. These items included items designed to assess control over one's sexual behavior, as well as items assessing behaviors that had been clinically observed to be associated with CSB. The first version of the scale included items that assessed control, violence, and abuse (Coleman, Miner, Ohlerking, & Raymond, 2001). The abuse items were later removed, and the total number of items has been reduced to 22. Each of the items is scored on a 5-point rating scale ranging from *Never* to *Very Frequently*. A Spanish version is also available, and shows comparable structure and reliability to the English version (see Exhibit). Preliminary research on the CSBI has focused on its use with Spanish- and English-speaking adult men. The first validity study compared CSBI scores in three groups of men: those clinically diagnosed with nonparaphilic CSB, those diagnosed with pedophilia, and a community control group. The second validity study focused on Latino men who have sex with men participating in an online survey. Current research is being conducted to evaluate the CSBI for use with adult women, as well as with a larger and more representative group of adult men.

Response Mode and Timing

The individual completing the CSBI responds to 22 items. Each of the items is scored on a 5-point rating scale ranging from *Never* to *Very Frequently*. Completing the measure takes approximately 10 minutes. It has been administered both in a pencil-and-paper form and online.

Scoring

The CSBI is scored by assigning a value of 1 for every *Never* response, 2 for every *Rarely*, 3 for every *Occasionally*, 4 for every *Frequently*, and 5 for every *Very Frequently*, and summing across the 22 items. Higher scores indicate more CSB. The CSBI consists of two factors: Control and Violence. The control scale consists of Items 1 through 13, and the violence scale consists of Items 14 through 22.

Reliability

The CSBI has shown consistent factor structure in both English and Spanish. Test-retest reliability has been assessed in both languages and results have indicated a reliability of $r = .86$ for the English version, and $r = .93$ in Spanish ($p < .001$; Miner, Coleman, Center, Ross, & Rosser, 2007).

Validity

Respondents with CSBI scores above the median report greater numbers of sexual partners and more unprotected anal intercourse, and were more likely to report being intoxicated or feeling depressed, lonely, or driven during intercourse than those who scored below the median both on the full scale and on each of the factors. The exception to that was self-reports of depression, which were linked to the total score and the control score, but not to the violence score (Miner et al., 2007).

References

Coleman, E., Miner, M., Ohlerking, F., & Raymond, N. (2001). Compulsive Sexual Behavior Inventory: A preliminary study of reliability and validity. *Journal of Sex and Marital Therapy, 27*, 325–332.

Miner, M. H., Coleman, E., Center, B. A., Ross, M., & Rosser, B. R. S. (2007). The Compulsive Sexual Behavior Inventory: Psychometric properties. *Archives of Sexual Behavior, 36*, 579–587.

[1]Address correspondence to Eli Coleman, Professor and Director, Program in Human Sexuality, Department of Family Practice and Community Health, Medical School, 1300 South 2nd Street, Suite 180, Minneapolis, MN 55454; e-mail: colem001@umn.edu

Exhibit

Compulsive Sexual Behavior Inventory

CSBI (English Version)

Circle the answer that most accurately describes your response.

	Never	Rarely	Occasionally	Frequently	Very Frequently
1. How often have you had trouble controlling your sexual urges?	1	2	3	4	5
2. Have you felt unable to control your sexual behavior?	1	2	3	4	5
3. How often have you used sex to deal with worries or problems in your life?	1	2	3	4	5
4. How often have you felt guilty or shameful about aspects of your sexual behavior?	1	2	3	4	5
5. How often have you concealed or hidden your sexual behavior from others?	1	2	3	4	5
6. How often have you been unable to control your sexual feelings?	1	2	3	4	5
7. How often have you made pledges or promises to change or alter your sexual behavior?	1	2	3	4	5
8. How often have your sexual thoughts or behaviors interfered with the formation of friendships?	1	2	3	4	5
9. How often have you developed excuses and reasons to justify your sexual behavior?	1	2	3	4	5
10. How often have you missed opportunities for productive and enhancing activities because of your sexual activity?	1	2	3	4	5
11. How often have your sexual activities caused financial problems for you?	1	2	3	4	5
12. How often have you felt emotionally distant when you were engaging in sex with others?	1	2	3	4	5
13. How often have you had sex or masturbated more than you wanted to?	1	2	3	4	5
14. Have you forced anyone against his or her will to have sex?	1	2	3	4	5
15. Have you ever hit, kicked, punched, slapped, thrown, choked, restrained, or beaten any of your sexual partners?	1	2	3	4	5
16. Have you given others physical pain for sexual pleasure?	1	2	3	4	5
17. In fighting, have you been hit, kicked, punched, slapped, thrown, choked, restrained, or beaten by your current or most recent partner?	1	2	3	4	5
18. Have you received physical pain for sexual pleasure?	1	2	3	4	5
19. Have you received money to have sex?	1	2	3	4	5
20. Have you been forced to have sex with your husband, wife, or lover?	1	2	3	4	5
21. Have you been watched masturbating or having sex without giving permission?	1	2	3	4	5

Compulsive Sexual Behavior Inventory (CSBI)
© Eli Coleman, Ph.D.
Program in Human Sexuality

Inventario de Comportamiento Sexual Compulsivo (Spanish Version)

Circule la respuesta que más aplique.

	Nunca	Rara	Ocasional	Frec	Muy Frec
1. ¿Con qué frecuencia ha tenido usted dificultad en controlar sus impulsos sexuales?	1	2	3	4	5
2. ¿Se ha sentido usted incapaz de controlar su comportamiento sexual?	1	2	3	4	5
3. ¿Con qué frecuencia ha usado usted el sexo para tratar sus preocupaciones o problemas?	1	2	3	4	5
4. ¿Con qué frecuencia se ha sentido usted culpable o avergonzado acerca de los aspectos de su comportamiento sexual?	1	2	3	4	5
5. ¿Con qué frecuencia ha ocultado usted su comportamiento sexual a otros?	1	2	3	4	5
6. ¿Con qué frecuencia se ha sentido usted incapaz de controlar sus sentimientos sexuales?	1	2	3	4	5
7. ¿Con qué frecuencia ha hecho usted compromisos o promesas de cambiar o de alterar su comportamiento sexual?	1	2	3	4	5

8. ¿Con qué frecuencia sus pensamientos o comportamientos sexuales han interferido con la formación
    de amistades?   1   2   3   4   5
9. ¿Con qué frecuencia ha inventado usted excusas y razones para justificar su comportamiento sexual?   1   2   3   4   5
10. ¿Con qué frecuencia ha perdido usted la oportunidad para hacer actividades productivas debido a su
    actividad sexual?   1   2   3   4   5
11. ¿Con qué frecuencia su actividad sexual le ha causado a usted problemas financieros?   1   2   3   4   5
12. ¿Con qué frecuencia se ha sentido emocionalmente distante cuando ha tenido sexo con otros?   1   2   3   4   5
13. ¿Con qué frecuencia ha tenido sexo o masturbación más de lo que usted ha querido?   1   2   3   4   5
14. ¿Con qué frecuencia ha sido arrestado o legalmente sancionado por su comportamiento sexual?   1   2   3   4   5
15. ¿Ha obligado usted a algún hombre/mujer hacer algo en contra de su voluntad?   1   2   3   4   5
16. ¿Alguna vez ha golpeado, empujado, cacheteado, lanzado, sofocado, sometido o le ha pegado
    usted a alguna de sus parejas sexuales?   1   2   3   4   5
17. ¿Le ha causado usted a otras personas dolor físico por placer sexual?   1   2   3   4   5
18. En peleas, ¿ha sido usted golpeado, pateado, empujado, cacheteado, ha sido tirado, estrangulado,
    frenado, o le ha pegado su pareja actual o la más reciente?   1   2   3   4   5
19. ¿Ha recibido usted dolor físico por placer sexual?   1   2   3   4   5
20. ¿Ha recibido dinero por tener sexo?   1   2   3   4   5
21. ¿Ha sido obligado a tener sexo con su esposo, esposa u amantes?   1   2   3   4   5
22. ¿Ha sido usted visto masturbándose o teniendo sexo sin dar su permiso?   1   2   3   4   5

Inventario de Comportamiento Sexual Compulsivo (ICSC)
© Eli Coleman, Ph.D.
Program in Human Sexuality

Sexual Compulsivity Scale

SETH C. KALICHMAN,[1] *University of Connecticut*

The Sexual Compulsivity Scale was designed to serve as a brief psychometric instrument to assist in the assessment of insistent, intrusive, and uncontrolled sexual thoughts and behaviors. Sexual compulsivity is conceptually and clinically similar to sexual addiction. Clinically, sexually compulsive individuals may present with an array of social problems that stem from their sexual preoccupation and conduct, including disturbances in their interpersonal relationships, occupation, and other facets of daily living. Sexual compulsivity can lead to sexual assault and other criminal behavior, especially when the compulsivity occurs in the context of a paraphilia. However, the Sexual Compulsivity Scale is not intended to detect paraphilias. Most available research has examined sexual compulsivity as a correlate of risks for sexually transmitted infections, including HIV/AIDS. The scale content concentrates on sexual preoccupations rather than acting as an indicator of overt sexual behaviors.

Description

The Sexual Compulsivity Scale was originally derived from self-descriptive statements contained in a brochure advertising a sexual addiction support group (CompCare, 1987). The brochure stated that a person should contact the group "if your sexual appetite has gotten in the way of your relationships . . . or if your sexual thoughts and behaviors are causing problems in your life . . . or if your desires to have sex have disrupted your daily life. . . ." We, therefore, extracted self-identifying affirmations from the brochure and framed them as items written in the first person. The scale consists of 10 items that were pilot-tested with men and women in community samples (Kalichman et al., 1994). Items were refined following community feedback and were placed on 4-point scales, 1 = *Not at all Like Me*, 2 = *Slightly Like Me*, 3 = *Mainly Like Me*, 4 = *Very Much Like Me*. The scale was developed for use with men and women and has shown utility with adults of all ages.

Response Mode, Timing, and Scoring

The 10-item Sexual Compulsivity Scale requires less than 5 minutes to self-administer or interview-administer. The scale does not have formally developed subscales. However, factor analysis has shown two principal

[1]Address correspondence to Seth C. Kalichman, Department of Psychology, 406 Babbidge Road, University of Connecticut, Storrs, CT 06269; e-mail: seth.k@uconn.edu

components to the scale: (a) uncontrolled thoughts and behaviors and (b) social and interpersonal problems and disruptions. The scale is scored by summing the items or by taking the mean response (sum of items/10). There are no reverse-scored items.

Reliability

The Sexual Compulsivity Scale has demonstrated excellent internal consistency across several diverse populations including male ($\alpha = .77$) and female ($\alpha = .81$) college students (Dodge, Reece, Cole, & Sandfort, 2004), community samples of HIV-positive men and women ($\alpha = .89$; Kalichman & Rompa, 1995), gay and bisexual men (α's are in range .86–.90; Dodge et al., 2008; Kalichman et al., 1994; Parsons & Bimbi, 2007), young adults in Croatia ($\alpha = .87$; Stulhofer, Buško, & Landripet, 2010), and patients seeking help for hypersexuality ($\alpha = .79$; Reid, Carpenter, Spackman, & Willes, 2008). Item-total correlations range from .49 to .73, with no single item substantially reducing or improving the internal consistency when deleted from the total. The scale has also demonstrated acceptable time stability over 2 weeks ($r = .95$; Kalichman & Rompa, 1995) and 3 months ($r = .64$; Kalichman et al., 1994).

Validity

Studies have demonstrated evidence for the construct validity of the Sexual Compulsivity Scale. Kalichman and colleagues (Kalichman et al., 1994; Kalichman and Rompa, 1995) found the scale to correlate with numbers of sexual partners ($r = .21$), lower intentions to reduce sexual risks ($r = -.35$), lower self-esteem ($r = -.35$), and lower sexual control ($r = -.61$). Sexually transmitted infection clinic patients who score higher on the scale report greater numbers of sex partners, greater numbers of one-time sex partners, and greater rates of sexual acts (Kalichman & Cain, 2004). Other researchers have shown that Sexual Compulsivity Scale scores predict Internet use for sexual content. For example, people who score higher on the scale spend more time online pursuing sexual partners than individuals who score lower (Cooper, Sherer, Boies, & Gordon, 1999). Dodge et al. (2008) found that gay and bisexual men who score higher on the scale are more likely to seek sex partners on the Internet as well as in anonymous sexual exchange venues and clubs. Demonstrating discriminant validity, patients who seek help for hypersexuality score more than a standard deviation higher on the Sexual Compulsivity Scale than nonclinical samples (Reid et al.,

2008). Discriminant validity is also supported by researchers who have demonstrated that gay and bisexual men who engage in high-risk sexual behavior fully understanding their risks for HIV/AIDS score higher on the scale (Halkitis et al., 2005; Parsons & Bimbi, 2007). For additional information, see Kalichman & Rompa (2001).

Other Information

The Sexual Compulsivity Scale is in the public domain and available for open use. National Institute of Mental Health (NIMH) grant R01-MH71164 supported preparation of the chapter.

References

CompCare. (1987). Hope and recovery: A twelve-step guide for healing from compulsive sexual behavior [Brochure]. Minneapolis, MN.

Cooper, A., Sherer, C., Boies, S., & Gordon, B. (1999). Sexuality on the Internet: From sexual exploration to pathological expression. *Professional Psychology: Research and Practice, 30,* 154–164.

Dodge, B., Reece, M., Cole, S. L., & Sandfort, T. G. (2004). Sexual compulsivity among heterosexual college students. *The Journal of Sex Research, 41,* 343–350.

Dodge, B., Reece, M., Herbenick, D., Fisher, C., Satinsky, S., & Stupiansky, N. (2008). Relations between sexually transmitted infection diagnosis and sexual compulsivity in a community-based sample of men who have sex with men. *Sexually Transmitted Infections, 84,* 324–327.

Halkitis, P. N., Wilton, L., Wolitski, R. J., Parsons, J. T., Hoff, C. C., & Bimbi, D. S. (2005). Barebacking identity among HIV-positive gay and bisexual men: Demographic, psychological, and behavioral correlates. *AIDS, 19*(Suppl. 1), S27–35.

Kalichman, S. C., Adair, V., Rompa, D., Multhauf, K., Johnson, J., & Kelly, J. (1994). Sexual sensation-seeking: Scale development and predicting AIDS-risk behavior among homosexually active men. *Journal of Personality Assessment, 62,* 385–397.

Kalichman, S. C., & Cain, D. (2004). The relationship between indicators of sexual compulsivity and high risk sexual practices among men and women receiving services from a sexually transmitted infection clinic. *The Journal of Sex Research, 41,* 235–241.

Kalichman, S. C., & Rompa, D. (1995). Sexual sensation seeking and sexual compulsivity scales: Reliability, validity, and predicting HIV risk behaviors. *Journal of Personality Assessment, 65,* 586–602.

Kalichman, S. C., & Rompa, D. (2001). The Sexual Compulsivity Scale: Further development and use with HIV positive persons. *Journal of Personality Assessment, 76,* 379–395.

Parsons, J. T., & Bimbi, D. S. (2007). Intentional unprotected anal intercourse among men who have sex with men: Barebacking—from behavior to identity. *AIDS and Behavior, 11,* 277–287.

Reid, R. C., Carpenter, B. N., Spackman, M., & Willes, D. L. (2008). Alexithymia, emotional instability, and vulnerability to stress proneness in patients seeking help for hypersexual behavior. *Journal of Sex and Marital Therapy, 34,* 133–149.

Stulhofer, A., Buško, V., & Landripet, I. (2010). Pornography, sexual socialization, and satisfaction among young men. *Archives of Sexual Behavior, 39,* 168–178.

Exhibit

Sexual Compulsivity Scale

A number of statements that some people have used to describe themselves are given below. Read each statement and then circle the number to show how well you believe the statement describes you.

	Not at all Like Me	Slightly Like Me	Mainly Like Me	Very Much Like Me
1. My sexual appetite has gotten in the way of my relationships.	1	2	3	4
2. My sexual thoughts and behaviors are causing problems in my life.	1	2	3	4
3. My desires to have sex have disrupted my daily life.	1	2	3	4
4. I sometimes fail to meet my commitments and. responsibilities because of my sexual behaviors	1	2	3	4
5. I sometimes get so horny I could lose control.	1	2	3	4
6. I find myself thinking about sex while at work.	1	2	3	4
7. I feel that my sexual thoughts and feelings are stronger than I am.	1	2	3	4
8. I have to struggle to control my sexual thoughts and behavior.	1	2	3	4
9. I think about sex more than I would like to.	1	2	3	4
10. It has been difficult for me to find sex partners who desire having sex as much as I want to.	1	2	3	4

Cognitive and Behavioral Outcomes of Sexual Behavior Scale

KIMBERLY R. MCBRIDE,[1] MICHAEL REECE, AND STEPHANIE A. SANDERS, *Indiana University*

The term *sexual compulsivity* (SC) is used to describe sexual behaviors that may be beyond an individual's control and that subsequently could lead to impairment in functioning as well as a range of negative outcomes. The Society for the Advancement of Sexual Health (SASH) has offered a list of outcomes that may occur if a person or behaviors are sexually compulsive. This outcomes-based understanding of sexual compulsivity would suggest that individuals and their behaviors (including behaviors that they do alone, such as masturbation, as well as those that they do with other people, such as having intercourse) could lead to negative consequences in various domains, including social, emotional, physical, legal, financial/occupational, and spiritual areas of life (Reece, Dodge, & McBride, 2006). The Cognitive and Behavioral Outcomes of Sexual Behavior Scale (CBOSBS) was developed to

measure the extent to which an individual has experienced negative outcomes in one or more of the six domains identified by SASH.

Description

Items were generated by the researchers based on theoretical understandings of SC and guided by the outcomes suggested by SASH. The scale includes a cognitive outcomes component and a behavioral outcomes component to measure both the extent to which a person is concerned about negative outcomes resulting from their sexual behaviors, and the extent to which such outcomes are actually experienced. For each, items assess six potential types of outcomes (financial/occupational, legal, physical, psychological, spiritual, social). The cognitive outcomes scale

[1]Address correspondence to Kimberly R. McBride, Department of Psychological and Brain Sciences, Indiana University, Bloomington, IN 47405; e-mail: kmcbride@indiana.edu

consists of 20 items based on a 4-point Likert-type scale ranging from *Never* to *Always*. The behavioral outcomes scale includes 16 items that are measured dichotomously, using a *Yes* or *No* option.

Pilot testing was conducted in a nonclinical sample of young adults (Perera, Reece, Monahan, Billingham, & Finn, 2009a, 2009b). Scale validation was performed in a nonclinical sample of young adults ($N = 390$; McBride, Reece, & Sanders, 2007, 2008). Analyses were conducted to assess the psychometric properties of the CBOSBS and the extent to which those in the sample reported experiencing negative outcomes resulting from their sexual behaviors.

Response Mode and Timing

The cognitive items ask participants to rate the extent to which they have worried that the things they have done sexually in the past year have resulted in a specified outcome. The behavioral items ask participants to indicate whether they have experienced a particular outcome within the previous year. The scale is self-administered and typically takes 10 minutes to complete.

Scoring

Cognitive items are scored on a scale of $0 = $ *Never* to $3 = $ *Always*. Total score range for the cognitive outcome items is 0 to 60. The dichotomous behavioral items are scored by assigning a 0 score to items answered "No" and 1 to "Yes" responses. Total score range for the behavioral items is 0 to 16. Total CBOSBS scores range from 0 to 76 and are calculated by adding cognitive and behavioral scores. The threshold for SC is reached when scores meet or exceed the 80th percentile.

Reliability

Reliability of the CBOSBS was assessed using Cronbach's alpha for internal consistency reliability; separate analyses of the cognitive and behavioral items were conducted. Internal consistency for the 20-item cognitive scale was high ($\alpha = .89$), with a slightly lower level of reliability ($\alpha = .75$) for the 16-item behavioral scale. However, given that the response scale for the behavioral items was dichotomous, this level is quite acceptable. Separate reliability estimates were calculated for each of the six factors (or subscales). Cronbach's alpha for internal consistency was found to be high for all of the factors, or subscales, indicating scale reliability in this sample. Although some of the subscales

with high Cronbach's alpha levels and elevated correlations may be worth revising, the overall inter-item correlation matrix, again, does not suggest a unidimensional scale. Testing in large samples with diverse demographic characteristics and perhaps greater numbers of negative outcomes is warranted before making the decision to drop items. Given the low occurrence of negative outcomes associated with sexual behaviors in this young nonclinical sample, the decision was made to use total scale scores for remaining analyses.

Validity

Construct validity for the 20 cognitive outcomes items was tested using a principal component analysis with varimax rotation, specifying six factors because items were constructed to focus on the six outcome categories articulated by SASH. Overall, the six-factor solution explained 74.8% of the total variance. The inter-item correlation matrix did not yield correlations high enough to suggest that the scale is unidimensional. However, a few specific inter-item correlations were high enough that it may be appropriate to eliminate one or more of the items. For example, items assessing worry about financial problems and worry about wasting money were highly correlated, suggesting they were essentially measuring the same thing in this sample.

Additional Information

Kimberly McBride is also affiliated with The Academic Edge, Inc., Bloomington, Indiana.

References

McBride, K. R., Reece, M., & Sanders, S. A. (2007). Predicting negative outcomes of sexuality using the Compulsive Sexual Behavior Inventory. *International Journal of Sexual Health, 19*(4), 51–62.

McBride, K. R., Reece, M., & Sanders, S. A. (2008). Using the Sexual Compulsivity Scale to predict outcomes of sexual behavior in young adults. *Journal of Sexual Addiction and Compulsivity, 15,* 97–115.

Perera, B., Reece, M., Monahan, P., Billingham, R., & Finn, P. (2009a). Childhood characteristics and personal dispositions to sexually compulsive behavior among young adults. *Sexual Addiction and Compulsivity, 16*(2), 131–145.

Perera, B., Reece, M., Monahan, P., Billingham, R. & Finn, P. (2009b). Relations between substance use and personal dispositions towards out-of-control sexual behaviors among young adults, *International Journal of Sexual Health, 21*(2), 87–95.

Reece, M., Dodge, B., & McBride, K. (2006). Sexual compulsivity: Issues and challenges. In R. McAnulty & M. Burnette (Eds.), *Sex and sexuality* (pp. 213–231). London: Praeger Press.

Exhibit

Cognitive and Behavioral Outcomes of Sexual Behavior

Below is a list of things that some people worry about as a result of their sexual activities (including things people do alone and those they do with others). Please indicate the extent to which the following apply to you:

Never = A   Sometimes = B   Often = C   Always = D

I am worried that the things I have done sexually:

1.   might have placed me or one of my sex partners at risk for pregnancy.[a]
2.   might have placed me or one of my sex partners at risk for a sexually transmitted infection (like herpes, gonorrhea, or crabs).
3.   might have placed me or one of my sex partners at risk for HIV.
4.   might have resulted in pain, injury, or other problems for one of my sex partners.
5.   might have resulted in pain, injury, or other problems for myself.
6.   might have presented the potential for serious physical injury or death.
7.   might be leading to problems with my friends.
8.   might be leading to problems with my family members.
9.   might be leading to problems with my boyfriend/girlfriend/spouse.
10. might have placed me at risk of being arrested.
11. might have been against the law.
12. might have led to financial problems.
13. might have caused me to waste my money.
14. were interfering with my ability to complete tasks for work or school.
15. might have presented the potential for me to lose my job.
16. could lead to school-related problems, such as probation, expulsion, or other sanctions.
17. were inconsistent with my spiritual beliefs.
18. were inconsistent with my religious values.
19. were making me feel guilty.
20. were making me ashamed of myself.

Instructions: Below is a list of things that sometimes happen to people as a result of their sexual activities (including those they do alone and those they do with others). Please indicate whether these things have happened to you during the last year as a result of your sexual activities.

In the past year, as a result of the things you have done sexually, did the following happen to you:

21. I or my sexual partner(s) became pregnant.

     A. Yes
     B. No

22. I contracted a sexually transmitted infection.[a]
23. I contracted HIV.
24. I gave someone else a sexually transmitted infection.
25. I gave someone else HIV.
26. I caused pain, injury, or other physical problems for myself.
27. I caused pain, injury, or other physical problems for a sex partner.
28. My relationships with friends and/or family members were damaged.
29. My relationships with a spouse or other relationship partner were damaged.
30. I was arrested.
31. I experienced financial problems.
32. I experienced problems at school.
33. I experienced problems at work.
34. I experienced spiritual distress.
35. I was embarrassed or ashamed of myself.
36. I felt guilty.

[a]The response scale directly above is repeated after each item.

Sexuality Scale

WILLIAM E. SNELL, JR.,[1] *Southeast Missouri State University*

The Sexuality Scale (SS; Snell & Papini, 1989) is an objective, self-report instrument designed to measure of three aspects of human sexuality: *sexual esteem*, defined as positive regard for and confidence in the capacity to experience one's sexuality in a satisfying and enjoyable way; *sexual depression,* defined as the experience of feelings of sadness, unhappiness, and depression regarding one's sex life; and *sexual preoccupation*, defined as the tendency to think about sex to an excessive degree.

Factor analysis confirmed that the items on the SS form three conceptual clusters corresponding to the three concepts (Snell & Papini, 1989). Other results indicated that all three subscales had clearly acceptable levels of reliability. Additional findings indicated that whereas there were no gender differences on the measures of sexual esteem and sexual depression, men reported higher levels of sexual preoccupation than did women. Other evidence showed that among both women and men, sexual esteem was negatively related to sexual depression, with the relationship being quite substantial among male subjects. Also Snell and Papini (1989) found that women's sexual esteem was positively associated with sexual preoccupation, whereas among men sexual depression was directly related to their sexual preoccupation.

Description

The SS consists of 30 items arranged in a format allowing respondents to indicate how much they agree (versus disagree) with that statement. A 5-point Likert scale is used, with responses for each item being scored from +2 to –2: *agree* (+2), *slightly agree* (+1), *neither agree nor disagree* (0), *slightly disagree* (–1), *disagree* (–2). To create subscale scores (discussed below), the items on each subscale are summed. Higher positive scores thus correspond to greater agreement with the statements, and more extreme negative scores indicate greater disagreement with the statements.

To confirm the three conceptual dimensions assumed to underlie the SS, the 30 items were subjected to a principal components factor analysis. A three-factor solution was specified and rotated to orthogonal simple structure with the varimax procedure. The first factor had an eigenvalue of 8.39 and accounted for 56% of the common variance; the first factor was characterized by the items on the sexual-esteem subscale. All 10 sexual-esteem items loaded on this factor with coefficients ranging from .52 to .82 (average coefficient, .69). The second factor had an eigenvalue of

4.75 and accounted for 32% of the common variance. All 10 of the sexual-preoccupation items loaded substantially on this factor (i.e., greater than .41), with an average loading of .65 (range = .41 to .86). The third factor, accounting for 13% of the common variance and having an eigenvalue of 1.88, dealt with the sexual-depression items; 8 of the 10 items on this sexual-depression subscale had loadings ranging from .48 to .84; average coefficient = .67. The other two items had loadings less than .20, and thus it was decided to consider them "filler items."

Response Mode and Timing

In most instances, people respond to the 30 items by marking their answers on separate machine-scoreable answer sheets. The scale usually requires about 15–20 minutes to complete.

Scoring

After several items are reverse coded (designated with an "R"), the relevant items on each subscale are then coded so that A = –2; B = –1; C = 0; D = +1; and E = +2. Next, the items on each subscale are summed, so that higher scores correspond to greater sexual esteem, sexual depression, and sexual preoccupation. Scores on the sexual-esteem and sexual-preoccupation scales can range from –20 to +20; scores on the sexual-depression scale range from –16 to +16. The items on the three SS subscales are: sexual esteem (Items 1, 4, 7, 10R, 13R, 16, 19R, 22, 25R, 28R); sexual depression (Items 2, 5R, 8, 17, 20, 23R, 26, 29R); and sexual preoccupation (Items 3, 6, 9R, 12, 15, 18, 21R, 24R, 27R, 30R).

An abbreviated version of the three subscales was developed by Wiederman and Allgeier (1993). The 15-item SS short-form includes the following items: sexual esteem (Items 1, 4, 16, 19R, 22); sexual depression (Items 2, 5R, 8, 17, 23R); and sexual preoccupation (Items 3, 6, 12, 15, 18).

Reliability

The internal consistency of the three subscales on the SS was determined by calculating Cronbach alpha coefficients, using a sample of 296 participants (209 females and 87 males) drawn from lower division psychology courses at a small midwestern university (Snell & Papini, 1989). The average age of the women in this study was 23.5 years (*SD* = 5.9), with a range of 19 to 53; the males averaged 23.7

[1]Address correspondence to William E. Snell, Jr., Department of Psychology, Southeast Missouri State University, One University Plaza, Cape Girardeau, MO 63701; e-mail: wesnell@semo.edu

years of age (*SD* = 4.4), with a range of 19 to 37. The alpha coefficients were computed for each of the three subscales for women and men separately and together. Each coefficient was based on 10 item scales, except for the measure of sexual depression which consists of eight items. The alphas for the sexual-esteem scale were: .92 for women, .93 for men, and .92 for all subjects. For the sexual-depression subscale, the alpha for women was .88 and the alpha for men was .94 (combined alpha = .90). The alphas for the sexual-preoccupation scale were: .88 for women, .79 for men, and .88 for all subjects.

Snell, Fisher, and Schuh (1992) also provided additional reliability evidence for the SS: sexual esteem (alpha range = .91 to .92), sexual depression (alpha range = .85 to .93), and sexual preoccupation (alpha range = .87 to .91). Test-retest reliability, as reported by Snell et al. (1992), was sexual esteem (range = .69 to .74), sexual depression (range = .67 to .76), and sexual preoccupation (range = .70 to .76). In brief, the three subscales had more than adequate internal consistency and test-retest reliability.

The 15-item short-form SS, 5 items per subscale, had Cronbach alphas for men and women, respectively, of .92 and .94 for sexual esteem, .89 and .89 for sexual depression, and .96 and .92 for sexual preoccupation (Wiederman & Allgeier, 1993).

Validity

Evidence for the validity of the SS comes from a variety of sources. Snell and Papini (1989) found that among university students, women's and men's scores on sexual esteem and sexual depression were negatively correlated. However, for women, sexual preoccupation was positively correlated with sexual esteem. In contrast, for men, sexual preoccupation was positively correlated with sexual depression. Snell et al. (1992) provided evidence that the SS measures of sexual esteem, sexual depression, and sexual preoccupation were related in predictable ways to men's and women's sexual behaviors and attitudes; evidence for the discriminant validity of the SS was also documented by Snell et al. (1992). Wiederman and Allgeier (1993) indicated that men score higher than do women on both the sexual-esteem and sexual-preoccupation scales. Finally, other researchers have used the SS within a therapy treatment context (Hurlbert, White, Powell, & Apt, 1993).

References

Hurlbert, D. F., White, L. C., Powell, R. D., & Apt, C. (1993). Orgasm consistency training in the treatment of women reporting hypoactive sexual desire: An outcome comparison of women-only groups and couples-only groups. *Journal of Behavior Therapy and Experimental Psychiatry, 24*, 3–13.

Snell, W. E., Jr., & Papini, D. R. (1989). The Sexuality Scale: An instrument to measure sexual-esteem, sexual-depression, and sexual-preoccupation. *The Journal of Sex Research, 26*, 256–263.

Snell, W. E., Jr., Fisher, T. D., & Schuh, T. (1992). Reliability and validity of the Sexuality Scale: A measure of sexual-esteem, sexual-depression, and sexual-preoccupation. *The Journal of Sex Research, 29*, 261–273.

Wiederman, M. W., & Allgeier, E. R. (1993). The measurement of sexual-esteem: Investigation of Snell and Papini's (1989) Sexuality Scale. *Journal of Research in Personality, 27*, 88–102.

Exhibit

Sexuality Scale

Instructions: The statements listed below describe certain attitudes toward human sexuality which different people may have. As such, *there are no right or wrong answers*, only personal responses. For each item you will be asked to indicate how much you agree or disagree with the statement listed in that item. Use the following scale to provide your responses:

(A) Agree	(B) Slightly agree	(C) Neither agree nor disagree	(D) Slightly disagree	(E) Disagree

1. I am a good sexual partner.
2. I am depressed about the sexual aspects of my life.
3. I think about sex all the time.
4. I would rate my sexual skill quite highly.
5. I feel good about my sexuality. (R)
6. I think about sex more than anything else.
7. I am better at sex than most other people.
8. I am disappointed about the quality of my sex life.
9. I don't daydream about sexual situations. (R)
10. I sometimes have doubts about my sexual competence. (R)
11. Thinking about sex makes me happy.
12. I tend to be preoccupied with sex.
13. I am not very confident in sexual encounters. (R)

14. I derive pleasure and enjoyment from sex.
15. I'm constantly thinking about having sex.
16. I think of myself as a very good sexual partner.
17. I feel down about my sex life.
18. I think about sex a great deal of the time.
19. I would rate myself low as a sexual partner. (R)
20. I feel unhappy about my sexual relationships.
21. I seldom think about sex. (R)
22. I am confident about myself as a sexual partner.
23. I feel pleased with my sex life. (R)
24. I hardly ever fantasize about having sex. (R)
25. I am not very confident about my sexual skill. (R)
26. I feel sad when I think about my sexual experiences.
27. I probably think about sex less often than most people. (R)
28. I sometimes doubt my sexual competence. (R)
29. I am not discouraged about sex. (R)
30. I don't think about sex very often. (R)

Condom Use Errors/Problems Survey

RICHARD A. CROSBY,[1] *University of Kentucky*
CYNTHIA A. GRAHAM, *University of Oxford*
ROBIN R. MILHAUSEN, *University of Guelph*
STEPHANIE A. SANDERS AND WILLIAM L. YARBER,[2] *Indiana University*

For sexually active persons wanting to prevent sexually transmitted infections (STIs) and pregnancy, condom use for all sexual episodes is necessary. Consistent use of the male, latex condom is an effective method of reducing the risk of transmitting and acquiring many STIs, including HIV infection, and unintended pregnancy (Centers for Disease Control and Prevention [CDC], 2009; Holmes, Levine, & Weaver, 2004). However, consistently using condoms is not sufficient—condoms must also be used correctly (CDC, 2009; Crosby, DiClemente, Holtgrave, & Wingood, 2002; Steiner, Cates, & Warner, 1999). Indeed, evidence suggests that condom failure typically stems from user error rather than product defect (Graham, Crosby, Sanders, & Yarber, 2005). Thus, identifying prevalent user errors and problems can be a valuable starting point toward the goal of promoting improved quality of condom use (Crosby, Yarber, Sanders, Graham, & Arno, 2008).

Description

The Condom Use Errors/Problems Survey (CUES) is a comprehensive assessment of errors and problems that people may experience when using male condoms that may lead to condom failures. Errors such as forms of incorrect use (e.g., putting condom on after starting sex) and problems such as breakage or slippage, erection difficulties, and discomfort are assessed using the CUES. The questionnaire has been refined through use in several studies involving samples of adolescent and adult men and women recruited from STI clinics, college students, rural men from a random telephone sampling, and participants from an online survey (e.g., Crosby, Milhausen, Sanders, Graham, & Yarber, 2008; Crosby, Sanders, Yarber, Graham, & Dodge, 2002; Graham et al., 2006; Sanders et al, 2003; Sanders, Milhausen, Crosby, Graham, & Yarber, 2009; Yarber, Graham, Sanders, & Crosby, 2004; Yarber et al., 2005). We

[1]Authors listed alphabetically.
[2]Address correspondence to William L. Yarber, Department of Applied Health Science, Indiana University, Bloomington, Indiana 47405; e-mail: yarber@indiana.edu

have two versions: (a) Condom Use Errors/Problems—Men (M-CUES), for men who placed the condom on themselves, and (b) Condom Use Errors/Problems—Women (W-CUES), for women who placed condoms on their male partners. Both versions are presented in the Exhibit.

The CUES assesses the last three times a condom was used during the past 3 months as the recall period. The CUES has also been used to assess use errors and problems the last time the condom was used or during all occasions of condom use during a specified time period. We used a limited event and time frame because accuracy of recall is considered vital (Graham et al., 2005). However, researchers are encouraged to adopt a recall period that reflects their study goals and objectives.

The survey can be used to measure condom use errors and problems during either penile-vaginal or penile-anal sexual intercourse. As seen in the CUES versions presented below, a blank space is provided before the word "intercourse" so that researchers can tailor the measure to assess the specific behavior of interest (i.e., penile-vaginal intercourse or penile-anal intercourse).

Response Mode and Timing

Respondents indicate whether or not each condom use error or problem occurred during the last three times they used and applied a male condom and, if so, if it occurred on one, two, or three occasions. The survey takes an average of 10 minutes to complete.

Scoring

Although analysis of individual items provides greater insight, summative scores of error items and problem items can be calculated. Error Items are 1, 2, 3, 4, 6, 7, 9, 10, and 11. Problem Items are 5, 8, 12, 13, 14, 15, and 16. For a recall period based on the last three times a condom was used, the summative error score indicates the total number of times errors were reported (minimum 0, maximum 27 [9 errors × 3 occasions]). Items 1, 3, and 4 are reversed scored such that a *no* response is scored as 3, one occasion scored as 2, two occasions scored as 1, and all three occasions scored as 0 (for an example of this scoring, see Crosby, Milhausen, et al., 2008). Alternatively, an error occurring during any of the last three occasions or that occurred at least once during a specific time period could be scored a 1 and a correct condom use or no problem is scored as 0 (Crosby, Sanders, et al., 2002; Milhausen et al., 2009).

Reliability

Reliability refers to the consistency of a measure within the same subject under the same conditions. It is usually measured in terms of internal consistency and test-retest reliability. Behavioral measures such as the CUES do not easily lend themselves to such evaluations, as they are not measuring a trait or construct assessed with multiple questions. Instead, the items are designed to measure distinct behavioral experiences. Making one type of error is not assumed to correlate with making other errors. Relative to test-retest, the same person may have different behavioral experiences over time; test-retest assessments may not be highly correlated over time unless the person has the same behavioral experiences. Although it is possible that a person who reports a specific error or problem at "test" may also be inclined to the same error/problem in the future "retest" (assuming that taking the CUES does not alter the behavior), this has not been evaluated longitudinally with the CUES.

Validity

The survey items have evidence of content and face validity because they were informed by widely cited condom use guidelines (CDC, 1998; Warner & Hatcher, 1999). Our studies have found, for example, that respondents who reported previous instruction on correct condom use were found to have lower error scores than those who had not had such instruction (Crosby, Sanders, et al., 2002), and correlations have been reported between errors and specific problems, such as incomplete use and erection difficulties (Graham et al., 2006) and using sharp objects to open the package and condom breakage (Yarber et al., 2004).

References

Centers for Disease Control and Prevention. (1998). *Facts about condoms and their use in preventing HIV infection and other STDs*. Atlanta, GA: U.S. Department of Health and Human Services.

Centers for Disease Control and Prevention. (2009). *Condoms and STDs: Fact sheet for public health personnel*. Retrieved May 18, 2009, from http://www.cdc.gov/condomeffectiveness/latex.htm

Crosby, R., Milhausen, R., Sanders, S., Graham, C., & Yarber, W. (2008). Two heads are better than one: The association between condom decision-making and condom use errors and problems. *Sexually Transmitted Infections, 84*, 196–201.

Crosby, R. A., DiClemente, R. J., Holtgrave, D. R., & Wingood, G. M. (2002). Design, measurement, and analytic considerations for testing hypotheses relative to condom effectiveness against nonviral STIs. *Sexually Transmitted Infections, 32*, 513–515.

Crosby, R. A., Sanders, S. A., Yarber, W. L., Graham, C. A., & Dodge, B. (2002). Condom use errors and problems among college men. *Sexually Transmitted Diseases, 29*, 552–557.

Crosby, R. A., Yarber, W. L., Sanders, S. A., Graham, C. A., & Arno, J. N. (2008). Slips, breaks and "falls": Condom errors and problems reported by men attending an STD clinic. *International Journal of STD and AIDS, 19*, 90–93.

Graham, C. A., Crosby, R. A., Sanders, S. A., & Yarber, W. L. (2005). Assessment of condom use in men and women. *Annual Review of Sex Research, 16*, 1–33.

Graham, C. A., Crosby, R. A., Yarber, W. L., Sanders, S. A., McBride, K., Milhausen, R. R., et al. (2006). Erection loss in association with condom use among young men attending a public STI clinic: Potential correlates and implications for risk behavior. *Sexual Health, 3*, 255–260.

Holmes, K. K., Levine, R., & Weaver, M. (2004). Effectiveness of condoms in preventing sexually transmitted infections. *Bulletin of the World Health Organization, 82*, 454–461.

Milhausen, R. R., Wood, J., Sanders, S. A., Crosby, R. A., Yarber, W. L. & Graham, C. A., (2009). *A novel, self-guided home-based* intervention to promote condom use among young men: A pilot study. Manuscript submitted for publication.

Sanders, S. A., Graham, C. A., Yarber, W. L., Crosby, R. A., Dodge, B., & Milhausen, R. R. (2003). Condom use errors and problems among women who put condoms on their male partners. *Journal of the American Medical Women's Association, 58,* 95–98.

Sanders, S. A., Milhausen, R. R., Crosby, R. A., Graham, C. A., & Yarber, W. L. (2009). Do phosphodiesterase type 5 inhibitors protect against condom-associated erection loss and condom slippage? *Journal of Sexual Medicine, 6,* 1451–1456.

Steiner, M., Cates, W., & Warner, L. (1999). The real problem with male condoms in non-use. *Sexually Transmitted Diseases, 26,* 459–462.

Warner, D. L., & Hatcher, R. A. (1999). Male condoms. In R. A. Hatcher, W. Cates, Jr., J. Trussell, F. Stewart, F. Guest, G. K. Stewart, et al. (Eds.), *Contraceptive technology* (17th ed., pp. 325–352). New York: National Academy Press.

Yarber, W. L., Graham, C. A., Sanders, S. A., & Crosby, R. A. (2004). Correlates of condom breakage and slippage among university students. *International Journal of STD and AIDS, 15,* 467–472.

Yarber, W. L., Kennedy, J., Sanders, S. A., Crosby, R. A., Graham, C. A., Heckman, T. G., et al. (2005). Prevalence of condom use errors and problems among Indiana rural men: An exploratory telephone survey. *The Health Education Monograph, 22*(3), 36–38.

Exhibit

Condom Use Errors/Problems Survey

Condom Use Errors/Problems Survey—Men (M-CUES)

Directions: The questionnaire is designed for a man who has used male condoms at least three times in the past three months for _____ [Researchers choose penile-vaginal (penis in vagina) or penile-anal (penis in rectum/butt)] intercourse and who put the condom on his penis all of the three times. Thinking about the last three times you (not your partner) put the condom on your penis, indicate whether or not you engaged in the behavior or if the event happened and, if so, how often it occurred.

1. For the last three times you used a condom for _____ [Researchers choose: penile-vaginal or penile-anal] intercourse, did you *check for visible damage before having* _____ *intercourse?*
   ___ no
   ___ if yes, did you do it on 1 occasion, on 2 occasions, or on all 3 occasions?
   ___ I did it on 1 occasion
   ___ I did it on 2 occasions
   ___ I did it on all 3 occasions

2. For the last three times you used a condom for _____ intercourse, did you *put it on the wrong side up and have to flip it over?*
   ___ no
   ___ if yes, did you do it on 1 occasion, on 2 occasions, or on all 3 occasions?
   ___ I did it on 1 occasion
   ___ I did it on 2 occasions
   ___ I did it on 3 occasions

3. For the last three times you used a condom for _____ intercourse, did you *leave space at the tip of the condom when putting it on?*
   ___ no
   ___ if yes, did you do it on 1 occasion, on 2 occasions, or on all 3 occasions?
   ___ I did it on 1 occasion
   ___ I did it on 2 occasions
   ___ I did it on 3 occasions

4. For the last three times you used a condom for _____ intercourse, did you *squeeze the air out after putting it on?*
   ___ no
   ___ if yes, did you do it on 1 occasion, on 2 occasions, or on all 3 occasions?
   ___ I did it on 1 occasion
   ___ I did it on 2 occasions
   ___ I did it on 3 occasions

5. For the last three times you used a condom for _____ intercourse, did you *lose or start to lose your erection while putting it on?*
   ___ no
   ___ if yes, did you do it on 1 occasion, on 2 occasions, or on all 3 occasions?

___ I did it on 1 occasion

___ I did it on 2 occasions

___ I did it on 3 occasions

6. For the last three times you used a condom for _____ intercourse, did you *use a condom* **without** *a water-based lubricant such as K-Y jelly or spermicidal cream (meaning the condom did not have lubricant on it and you or your partner did not put any on it)?*

    ___ no

    ___ if yes, did you do it on 1 occasion, on 2 occasions, or on all 3 occasions?

    ___ I did it on 1 occasion

    ___ I did it on 2 occasions

    ___ I did it on 3 occasions

7. For the last three times you used a condom for _____ intercourse, did you *also use an oil-based lubricant, such as Vaseline or baby oil, with the condom?*

    ___ no

    ___ if yes, did you do it on 1 occasion, on 2 occasions, or on all 3 occasions?

    ___ I did it on 1 occasion

    ___ I did it on 2 occasions

    ___ I did it on 3 occasions

8. For the last three times you used a condom for _____ intercourse, did *you lose or start to lose your erection after* _____ *intercourse had begun while using the condom?*

    ___ no

    ___ if yes, did you do it on 1 occasion, on 2 occasions, or on all 3 occasions?

    ___ I did it on 1 occasion

    ___ I did it on 2 occasions

    ___ I did it on 3 occasions

9. For the last three times you used a condom for _____ intercourse, did you *let it contact sharp jewelry, fingernails, piercings, or teeth anytime before or during* _____ *intercourse?*

    ___ no

    ___ if yes, did you do it on 1 occasion, on 2 occasions, or on all 3 occasions?

    ___ I did it on 1 occasion

    ___ I did it on 2 occasions

    ___ I did it on 3 occasions

10. For the last 3 times you used a condom for _____ intercourse, did you *start having* _____ *intercourse without the condom and then put it on later and continued* _____ *intercourse?*

    ___ no

    ___ if yes, did you do it on 1 occasion, on 2 occasions, or on all 3 occasions?

    ___ I did it on 1 occasion

    ___ I did it on 2 occasions

    ___ I did it on 3 occasions

11. For the last time you used a condom for _____ intercourse, did you *start having intercourse with it on and then take it off and continue having* _____ *intercourse without it on?*

    ___ no

    ___ if yes, did you do it on 1 occasion, on 2 occasions, or on all 3 occasions?

    ___ I did it on 1 occasion

    ___ I did it on 2 occasions

    ___ I did it on 3 occasions

12. For the last three times you used a condom for _____ intercourse, did *it break during* _____ *intercourse?*

    ___ no

    ___ if yes, did it do it on 1 occasion, on 2 occasions, or on all 3 occasions?

    ___ it did it on 1 occasion

    ___ it did it on 2 occasions

    ___ it did it on 3 occasions

13. For the last three times you used a condom for _____ intercourse, did *it slip off during* _____ *intercourse?*
  ___ no
  ___ if yes, did it do it on 1 occasion, on 2 occasions, or on all 3 occasions?
    ___ it did it on 1 occasion
    ___ it did it on 2 occasions
    ___ it did it on 3 occasions

14. For the last three times you used a condom for _____ intercourse, did *it slip off as you were taking your penis out of the* _____ *[vagina or anus/rectum/butt]?*
  ___ no
  ___ if yes, did it do it on 1 occasion, on 2 occasions, or on all 3 occasions?
    ___ it did it on 1 occasion
    ___ it did it on 2 occasions
    ___ it did it on 3 occasions

15. For the last three times you used a condom for _____ intercourse, did *you have any problems with the way it fit?*
  ___ no
  ___ if yes, did I on 1 occasion, on 2 occasions, or on all 3 occasions?
    ___ I did on 1 occasion
    ___ I did on 2 occasions
    ___ I did on 3 occasions

16. For the last three times you used a condom for _____ intercourse, did *you or your partner have any problems with the way it felt?*
  ___ no
  ___ if yes, did it happen on 1 occasion, on 2 occasions, or on all 3 occasions?
    ___ it happened on 1 occasion
    ___ it happened on 2 occasions
    ___ it happened on 3 occasions

Condom Use Errors/Problems Survey—Women (W-CUES)

Directions: The questionnaire is designed for a woman who has used a male condom at least three times in the past three months for _____ [Researchers choose penile-vaginal (penis in vagina) or penile-anal (penis in rectum/butt)] intercourse and who put the condom on her partner's penis all of the three times. Thinking about the last three times you (not your partner) put the condom on his penis, indicate whether or not you engaged in the behavior or if the event happened and, if so, how often it occurred.

1. For the last three times you used a condom for _____ [Researchers choose: penile-vaginal or penile-anal] intercourse, did *you check for visible damage before having* _____ *intercourse?*
  ___ no
  ___ if yes, did you do it on 1 occasion, on 2 occasions, or on all 3 occasions?
    ___ I did it on 1 occasion
    ___ I did it on 2 occasions
    ___ I did it on all 3 occasions

2. For the last three times you used a condom for _____ intercourse, did you *put it on the wrong side up and have to flip it over?*
  ___ no
  ___ if yes, did you do it on 1 occasion, on 2 occasions, or on all 3 occasions?
    ___ I did it on 1 occasion
    ___ I did it on 2 occasions
    ___ I did it on 3 occasions

3. For the last three times you used a condom for _____ intercourse, did you *leave space at the tip of the condom when putting it on?*
  ___ no
  ___ if yes, did you do it on 1 occasion, on 2 occasions, or on all 3 occasions?
    ___ I did it on 1 occasion

____ I did it on 2 occasions

____ I did it on 3 occasions

4. For the last three times you used a condom for _____ intercourse, did you *squeeze the air out after putting it on?*

    ____ no

    ____ if yes, did you do it on 1 occasion, on 2 occasions, or on all 3 occasions?

    ____ I did it on 1 occasion

    ____ I did it on 2 occasions

    ____ I did it on 3 occasions

5. For the last three times you used a condom for _____ intercourse, did your partner *lose or start to lose his erection while you were putting it on his penis?*

    ____ no

    ____ if yes, did he do it on 1 occasion, on 2 occasions, or on all 3 occasions?

    ____ he did it on 1 occasion

    ____ he did it on 2 occasions

    ____ he did it on 3 occasions

6. For the last three times you used a condom for _____ intercourse, did you *use a condom **without** a water-based lubricant such as K-Y jelly or spermicidal cream (meaning the condom did not have lubricant on it and you or your partner did not put any on it)?*

    ____ no

    ____ if yes, did you do it on 1 occasion, on 2 occasions, or on all 3 occasions?

    ____ I did it on 1 occasion

    ____ I did it on 2 occasions

    ____ I did it on 3 occasions

7. For the last three times you used a condom for _____ intercourse, did you *also use an oil-based lubricant, such as Vaseline or baby oil, with the condom?*

    ____ no

    ____ if yes, did you do it on 1 occasion, on 2 occasions, or on all 3 occasions?

    ____ I did it on 1 occasion

    ____ I did it on 2 occasions

    ____ I did it on 3 occasions

8. For the last three times you used a condom for _____ intercourse, did *your partner lose or start to lose his erection after _____ intercourse had begun while using the condom?*

    ____ no

    ____ if yes, he did on 1 occasion, on 2 occasions, or on all 3 occasions?

    ____ he did it on 1 occasion

    ____ he did it on 2 occasions

    ____ he did it on 3 occasions

    ____ not sure

9. For the last three times you used a condom for _____ intercourse, did you *let it contact sharp jewelry, fingernails, piercings, or teeth anytime before or during _____ intercourse?*

    ____ no

    ____ if yes, did you do it on 1 occasion, on 2 occasions, or on all 3 occasions?

    ____ I did it on 1 occasion

    ____ I did it on 2 occasions

    ____ I did it on 3 occasions

10. For the last three times you used a condom for _____ intercourse, did you *start having _____ intercourse without the condom and then put it on later and continued _____ intercourse?*

    ____ no

    ____ if yes, did you do it on 1 occasion, on 2 occasions, or on all 3 occasions?

    ____ I did it on 1 occasion

    ____ I did it on 2 occasions

    ____ I did it on 3 occasions

11. For the last time you used a condom for _____ intercourse, did you *start having intercourse with it on and then take it off and continue having* _____ *intercourse without it on?*
    ___ no
    ___ if yes, did you do it on 1 occasion, on 2 occasions, or on all 3 occasions?
    ___ I did it on 1 occasion
    ___ I did it on 2 occasions
    ___ I did it on 3 occasions

12. For the last three times you used a condom for _____ intercourse, did *it break during* _____ *intercourse?*
    ___ no
    ___ if yes, did it do it on 1 occasion, on 2 occasions, or on all 3 occasions?
    ___ it did it on 1 occasion
    ___ it did it on 2 occasions
    ___ it did it on 3 occasions
    ___ not sure

13. For the last three times you used a condom for _____ intercourse, did *it slip off during* _____ *intercourse?*
    ___ no
    ___ if yes, did it do it on 1 occasion, on 2 occasions, or on all 3 occasions?
    ___ it did it on 1 occasion
    ___ it did it on 2 occasions
    ___ it did it on 3 occasions
    ___ not sure

14. For the last three times you used a condom for _____ intercourse, did *it slip off while your partner was taking his penis out of your* _____ *[vagina or anus/rectum/butt]?*
    ___ no
    ___ if yes, did it do it on 1 occasion, on 2 occasions, or on all 3 occasions?
    ___ it did it on 1 occasion
    ___ it did it on 2 occasions
    ___ it did it on 3 occasions
    ___ not sure

15. For the last three times you used a condom for _____ intercourse, did *your partner have any problems with the way it fit?*
    ___ no
    ___ if yes, did he on 1 occasion, on 2 occasions, or on all 3 occasions?
    ___ he did on 1 occasion
    ___ he did on 2 occasions
    ___ he did on 3 occasions
    ___ not sure

16. For the last three times you used a condom for _____ intercourse, did *you or your partner have any problems with the way it felt?*
    ___ no
    ___ if yes, did it happen on 1 occasion, on 2 occasions, or on all 3 occasions?
    ___ it happened on 1 occasion
    ___ it happened on 2 occasions
    ___ it happened on 3 occasions

Correct Condom Use Self-Efficacy Scale

RICHARD A. CROSBY,[1] *University of Kentucky*
CYNTHIA A. GRAHAM, *University of Oxford*
ROBIN R. MILHAUSEN, *University of Guelph*
STEPHANIE A. SANDERS AND WILLIAM L. YARBER,[2] *Indiana University*

Consistent and correct male condom use has been noted as one effective method for preventing the transmission of HIV and reducing the risk of other STDs (Centers for Disease Control and Prevention, 2009). Although a number of psychosocial constructs have been associated with condom use, a central construct, from a theoretical and an empirical perspective, has been condom use self-efficacy. Bandura (1994) defined self-efficacy as beliefs about one's capabilities to produce designated levels of performance and suggested that self-efficacy largely determined how individuals feel, think, motivate themselves, and behave. Condom use self-efficacy, therefore, refers to an individual's confidence in the ability to exert control over his or her motivation, behavior, and social environment to use condoms (Forsyth & Carey, 1998).

A number of previous measures of self-efficacy assess knowledge, behavioral intentions, or attitudes, but not an individual's perception about his or her ability to perform specific behaviors (e.g., Goldman & Harlow, 1993; Lux & Petosa, 1994; Schaalma, Kok, & Peters, 1993). Other measures of self-efficacy are limited by their conceptualization of self-efficacy as a stable trait across different contexts (e.g., St. Lawrence, Brasfield, Jefferson, Alleyne, & Shirley, 1994) as opposed to a more domain-specific behavior. Many researchers also have relied on a single-item measure of self-efficacy that may limit the precision of measurement (e.g., Wulfert & Wan, 1993). Therefore, a scale that measures individuals' perceptions of their ability to perform behaviors specific to correct condom use would have utility in public health research.

Description

The Correct Condom Use Self-Efficacy Scale (CCUSS) is a 7-item scale designed to measure an individual's perception of the ease or difficulty with which he or she can apply and use male condoms correctly. This scale emerged from our earlier research on the prevalence and predictors of male condom use errors and problems (e.g., Crosby, Milhausen, Sanders, Graham, & Yarber, 2008; Crosby, Sanders, Yarber, Graham, & Dodge, 2002; Graham et al., 2006; Milhausen et al., 2009; Sanders et al., 2003; Sanders, Milhausen, Crosby, Graham, & Yarber, 2009; Yarber,

Graham, Sanders, & Crosby, 2004; Yarber et al., 2005). CCUSS items reflect the condom use errors and problems that might occur before, during, and after sex.

Response Mode and Timing

Respondents are asked how easy or difficult it would be for them to perform various correct condom use tasks. Responses are provided using a scale ranging from 1 (*Very Difficult*) to 5 (*Very Easy*).

Scoring

Items are summed such that a higher score indicates greater self-efficacy for correct use of male condoms. The mean score among a sample of 278 adult male clients attending a sexually transmitted infections (STI) clinic was 27.61 (*SD* = 4.37, range = 8–35; Crosby, Salazar, et al., 2008).

Reliability

The scale produced a Cronbach's alpha of .70 among the aforementioned STI clinic sample (Crosby, Salazar, et al., 2008).

Validity

Crosby, Salazar, et al. (2008) found that greater self-efficacy for correct use of condoms was associated with fewer condom use errors and problems.

References

Bandura, A. (1994). Social cognitive theory and exercise of control over HIV infection. In R. J. DiClemente & J. Peterson (Eds.), *Preventing AIDS: Theories and methods of behavioral interventions* (pp. 25–59). New York: Plenum.

Centers for Disease Control and Prevention. (2009). Condoms and STDs: Fact sheet for public health personnel. Retrieved May 18, 2009, from http://www.cdc.gov/condomeffectiveness/latex.htm

Crosby, R., Milhausen, R., Sanders, S., Graham, C., & Yarber, W. (2008). Two heads are better than one: The association between condom decision-making and condom use errors and problems. *Sexually Transmitted Infections, 84*, 196–201.

Crosby, R. A., Salazar, L. F., Yarber, W. L., Sanders, S. A., Graham, C. A., Head, S., et al. (2008). A theory-based approach to understanding

[1]Authors listed alphabetically.
[2]Address correspondence to William L. Yarber, Department of Applied Health Science, Indiana University, Bloomington, Indiana 47405; e-mail: yarber@indiana.edu

condom errors and problems reported by men attending an STI clinic. *AIDS and Behavior, 12*, 412–418.

Crosby, R. A., Sanders, S. A., Yarber, W. L., Graham, C. A., & Dodge, B. (2002). Condom use errors and problems among college men. *Sexually Transmitted Disease, 29*, 552–557.

Forsyth, A. D., & Carey, M. P. (1998). Measuring self-efficacy in the context of HIV risk reduction: Research challenges and recommendations. *Health Psychology, 17*, 559–568.

Goldman, J. A., & Harlow, L. L. (1993). Self-perception variables that mediate AIDS-preventive behavior in college students. *Health Psychology, 12*, 489–498.

Graham, C. A., Crosby, R. A., Yarber, W. L., Sanders, S. A., McBride, K., Milhausen, R. R., et al. (2006). Erection loss in association with condom use among young men attending a public STI clinic: Potential correlates and implications for risk behavior. *Sexual Health, 3*, 255–260.

Lux, K. M., & Petosa, R. (1994). Using the health belief model to predict safer sex intentions of incarcerated youth. *Health Education Quarterly, 21*, 487–497.

Milhausen, R. R., Wood, J., Crosby, R. A., Graham, C. A., Sanders, S. A., & Yarber, W. L. (2009). *A novel home-based intervention to promote condom use among young heterosexual males: A pilot study.* Manuscript in preparation.

Sanders, S. A., Graham, C. A., Yarber, W. L., Crosby, R. A., Dodge, B., & Milhausen, R. R. (2003). Condom use errors and problems among women who put condoms on their male partners. *Journal of the American Medical Women's Association, 58*, 95–98.

Sanders, S. A., Milhausen, R. R., Crosby, R. A., Graham, C. A., & Yarber, W. L. (2009). Do phosphodiesterase type 5 inhibitors protect against condom-associated erection loss and condom slippage? *Journal of Sexual Medicine, 6*, 1451–1456.

Schaalma, H., Kok, G., & Peters, L. (1993). Determinants of consistent condom use by adolescents: The impact of experience of sexual intercourse. *Health Education Research, 8*, 255–269.

St. Lawrence, J. S., Brasfield, T. L., Jefferson, K. W., Alleyne, E., & Shirley, A. (1994). Social support as a factor in African American adolescents' sexual risk behavior. *Journal of Adolescent Health, 9*, 292–310.

Wulfert, E., & Wan, C. K. (1993). Condom use: A self-efficacy model. *Health Psychology, 12*, 346–353.

Yarber, W. L., Graham, C. A., Sanders, S. A., & Crosby, R. A. (2004). Correlates of condom breakage and slippage among university students. *International Journal of STD and AIDS, 15*, 467–472.

Yarber, W. L., Kennedy, J., Sanders, S. A., Crosby, R. A., Graham, C. A., Heckman, T. G., et al. (2005). Prevalence of condom use errors and problems among Indiana rural men: An exploratory telephone survey. *The Health Education Monograph, 22*(3), 36–38.

Exhibit

Correct Condom Use Self-Efficacy Scale

Directions: Please circle the number that represents *how easy or difficult* it would be to do what each question asks. For example, if you thought a behavior in the statement would be very easy, you would circle number "5."

1. How easy or difficult would it be for you to find condoms that fit you properly?

Very Difficult   Very Easy

   1   2   3   4   5

2. How easy or difficult would it be for you to apply condoms correctly?

Very Difficult   Very Easy

   1   2   3   4   5

3. How easy or difficult would it be for you to keep a condom from drying out during sex?

Very Difficult   Very Easy

   1   2   3   4   5

4. How easy or difficult would it be for you to keep a condom from breaking during sex?

Very Difficult   Very Easy

   1   2   3   4   5

5. How easy or difficult would it be for you to keep an erection while using a condom?

Very Difficult   Very Easy

   1   2   3   4   5

6. How easy or difficult would it be for you to keep a condom on when withdrawing after sex?

Very Difficult   Very Easy

   1   2   3   4   5

7. How difficult would it be for you to wear a condom from start to finish of sex with your partner?

Very Difficult   Very Easy

   1   2   3   4   5

UCLA Multidimensional Condom Attitudes Scale

MARIE HELWEG-LARSEN,[1] *Dickinson College*

The purpose of the UCLA Multidimensional Condom Attitudes Scale (MCAS) is to measure condom attitudes in five independent areas: (a) the *reliability and effectiveness* of condoms, (b) the sexual *pleasure* associated with condom use, (c) the *stigma* associated with people proposing or using condoms, (d) the *embarrassment about negotiating and using* condoms, and (e) the *embarrassment about purchasing* condoms. The scale can be used with individuals who do and do not have personal experience with condoms.

Description

The 25-item MCAS assesses five independent factors associated with condom use. The MCAS was found to be reliable and valid in three studies using ethnically diverse samples of UCLA undergraduates (Helweg-Larsen & Collins, 1994). As of August 2008 it had been cited 97 times; the scale has been used in 31 of these articles (see companion website at www.routledge.com/text-books/9780415801751 to view the complete list). The scale has been used with a range of populations, such as HIV-positive individuals from urban clinics in California (Milam, Richardson, Espinoza, & Stoyanoff, 2006), Chinese and Filipina American college women (Lam & Barnhart, 2006), sexually active adult cocaine or heroin users (Rosengard, Anderson, & Stein, 2006), cocaine-abusing, opioid-dependent HIV-positive adults entering a methadone program (Avants, Warburton, Hawkins, & Margolin, 2000), individuals in a large public psychiatric hospital diagnosed primarily with schizophrenia and mood disorders (Weinhardt, Carey, & Carey, 1997), American Indian men in New York City who identified as gay/bisexual/two-spirit and heterosexual (Simoni, Walters, Balsam, & Meyers, 2006), and HIV-positive Zambian women (Jones, Ross, Weiss, Bhat, & Chitalu, 2005). Furthermore, the MCAS has been translated to Spanish (DeSouza, Madrigal, & Millan, 1999; Unger & Molina, 1999), Japanese (Kaneko, 2007), and various Zambian languages such as Bemba, Nyanja, and Nsenga (Jones et al., 2005). Overall, the body of research using the MCAS shows that it has been a reliable and valid measure of condom attitudes in a wide range of participants. A complete list of studies which have used the MCAS may be found at the companion website for this book (http://www.routledge.com/textbooks/9780415801751).

Scoring

We found that the five dimensions of the MCAS cannot meaningfully be summed to generate a single global score because the factors are independent. The statistical independence of the five factors was established via factor analyses and confirmatory factor analysis in structural equation modeling which showed that a model with five independent factors was superior in fitting the data compared to a unidimensional model (all 25 questions averaged). Thus, it is important that the five factors are scored separately. If researchers do not have room to use all 25 questions, they may select one or several of the factors that they are particularly interested in and use all 5 questions in that factor. Another option is to select a few questions from each of the five factors; Table 1 in Helweg-Larsen and Collins (1994) shows factor loadings (separately for men and women) that can guide researchers in the selection of questions. Our research indicates that important information is lost if questions are added together across factors.

Our research also demonstrated the importance of examining condom attitudes separately for men and women. First, results indicated gender differences on several of the five factors; compared to women, men were less embarrassed about purchasing condoms but more concerned about stigma. Second, the MCAS factors showed different patterns of correlations with criterion variables for men and women. For example, women's past condom use was not correlated with any of the five MCAS factors, whereas men's past condom use was correlated with positive attitudes toward pleasure and embarrassment about buying condoms.

Some of the MCAS items are worded negatively (i.e., indicate a negative attitude toward condoms), and the score must therefore be reversed before adding or averaging the scores (higher scores will then indicate more positive condom attitudes). The scoring for these items is as follows:

1. Reliability and Effectiveness of Condoms: Reverse score Questions 6 and 14; then add Questions 4, 6, 9, 14, and 20.
2. Pleasure Associated With Condoms: Reverse score Questions 2, 8, and 25; then add Questions 2, 8, 15, 19, and 25.
3. Stigma Associated With Condoms: Reverse score Questions 3, 13, 18, 22, and 24; then add Questions 3, 13, 18, 22, and 24.

[1]Address correspondence to Marie Helweg-Larsen, PhD, Department of Psychology, Dickinson College, Carlisle, PA 17013; e-mail: helwegm@dickinson.edu

4. Embarrassment About Negotiation and Use of Condoms: Reverse score Questions 1, 7, and 16; then add Questions 1, 7, 12, 16, and 21.
5. Embarrassment About Purchasing Condoms: Reverse score Questions 5, 11, 17, and 23; then add Questions 5, 10, 11, 17, and 23.

Reliability

We established internal consistency in three independent samples (separately for men and women) using factor analysis and confirmatory factor analysis in structural equation modeling (Helweg-Larsen & Collins, 1994). Acceptable Cronbach's alpha values for each factor have been found in many subsequent studies (e.g., Maisto et al., 2004; Rosengard et al., 2006).

Validity

We established construct validity for the MCAS by showing that gender and sexual experience were associated with the five factors of the MCAS (Helweg-Larsen & Collins, 1994). Furthermore, past and intended condom use was related to the five factors of the MCAS, again showing different patterns for men and women. The MCAS has also been validated in a sample of low-acculturated Hispanic women (Unger & Molina, 1999) and among Mexican undergraduate students (DeSouza et al., 1999).

References

Avants, S. K., Warburton, L. A., Hawkins, K. A., & Margolin, A. (2000). Continuation of high-risk behavior by HIV-positive drug users: Treatment implications. *Journal of Substance Abuse Treatment, 19,* 15–22.

DeSouza, E., Madrigal, C., & Millan, A. (1999). A cross-cultural validation of the Multidimensional Condom Attitudes Scale. *Interamerican Journal of Psychology, 33,* 191–204.

Helweg-Larsen, M., & Collins, B. E. (1994). The UCLA Multidimensional Condom Attitudes Scale: Documenting the complex determinants of condom use in college students. *Health Psychology, 13,* 224–237.

Jones, D. L., Ross, D., Weiss, S. M., Bhat, G., & Chitalu, N. (2005). Influence of partner participation on sexual risk behavior reduction among HIV-positive Zambian women. *Journal of Urban Health: Bulletin of the New York Academy of Medicine, 82,* iv92–iv100.

Kaneko, N. (2007). Association between condom use and perceived barriers to and self-efficacy of safe sex among young women in Japan. *Nursing and Health Sciences, 9,* 284–289.

Lam, A. G., & Barnhart, J. E. (2006). It takes two: The role of partner ethnicity and age characteristics on condom negotiations of heterosexual Chinese and Filipina American college women. *AIDS Education and Prevention, 18,* 68–80.

Maisto, S. A., Carey, M. P., Carey, K. B., Gordon, C. M., Schum, J. L., & Lynch, K. G. (2004). The relationship between alcohol and individual differences variables on attitudes and behavioral skills relevant to sexual health among heterosexual young adult men. *Archives of Sexual Behavior, 33,* 571–584.

Milam, J., Richardson, J. L., Espinoza, L., & Stoyanoff, S. (2006). Correlates of unprotected sex among adult heterosexual men living with HIV. *Journal of Urban Health—Bulletin of the New York Academy of Medicine, 83,* 669–681.

Rosengard, C., Anderson, B. J., & Stein, M. D. (2006). Correlates of condom use and reasons for condom non-use among drug users. *The American Journal of Drug and Alcohol Abuse, 32,* 637–644.

Simoni, J. M., Walters, K. L., Balsam, K. F., & Meyers, S. B. (2006). Victimization, substance use, and HIV risk behaviors among gay/bisexual/two-spirit and heterosexual American Indian men in New York City. *American Journal of Public Health, 96,* 2240–2245.

Unger, J. B., & Molina, G. B. (1999). The UCLA Multidimensional Condom Attitudes Scale: Validity in a sample of low-acculturated Hispanic women. *Hispanic Journal of Behavioral Sciences, 21,* 199–211.

Weinhardt, L. S., Carey, M. P., & Carey, K. B. (1997). HIV risk reduction for the seriously mentally ill: Pilot investigation and call for research. *Journal of Behavior Therapy and Experimental Psychiatry, 28,* 87–95.

Exhibit

MCAS Multidimensional Condom Attitudes Scale

Please respond to all questions *even if you are not sexually active* or *have never used* (or had a partner who used) condoms. In such cases indicate how you *think you would feel* in such a situation.

Choose a number on the scale below that best represents your feelings about each statement. There are no right or wrong responses to any of these statements. Write the number that best represents your opinion in the blank beside each question.

Strongly Disagree	Disagree	Slightly Disagree		Slightly Agree	Agree	Strongly Agree
1	2	3	4	5	6	7

_____ 1. It is really hard to bring up the issue of using condoms to my partner.

_____ 2. Use of a condom is an interruption of foreplay.

_____ 3. Women think men who use condoms are jerks.

_____ 4. Condoms are an effective method of preventing the spread of AIDS and other sexually transmitted diseases.

_____ 5. I always feel really uncomfortable when I buy condoms.

_____ 6. Condoms are unreliable.

_____ 7. When I suggest using a condom I am almost always embarrassed.

_____ 8. Condoms ruin the sex act.

_____ 9. I think condoms are an excellent means of contraception.

_____ 10. I don't think that buying condoms is awkward.

_____ 11. It is very embarrassing to buy condoms.

_____ 12. It is easy to suggest to my partner that we use a condom.

_____ 13. If a couple is about to have sex and the man suggests using a condom, it is less likely that they will have sex.

_____ 14. Condoms do not offer reliable protection.

_____ 15. Condoms are a lot of fun.

_____ 16. I never know what to say when my partner and I need to talk about condoms or other protection.

_____ 17. It would be embarrassing to be seen buying condoms in a store.

_____ 18. People who suggest condom use are a little bit geeky.

_____ 19. The use of condoms can make sex more stimulating.

_____ 20. Condoms are an effective method of birth control.

_____ 21. I'm comfortable talking about condoms with my partner.

_____ 22. Men who suggest using a condom are really boring.

_____ 23. When I need condoms, I often dread having to get them.

_____ 24. A woman who suggests using a condom does not trust her partner.

_____ 25. Condoms are uncomfortable for both parties.

Condom Fit and Feel Scale

MICHAEL REECE,[1] **DEBBY HERBENICK, AND BRIAN DODGE,** *Indiana University*

Those who promote condoms in their sexual health promotion efforts have been challenged by the assertion from some men that their resistance to condoms is based upon their perceptions that they do not fit properly or feel comfortable during use. The Condom Fit and Feel Scale was developed to provide the field with an empirical measure for assessing men's perceptions of the extent to which condoms fit and feel comfortable along specific points of the penis (e.g., base, shaft, glans). The scale was designed for use by both sexual health researchers and sexual health practitioners (e.g., clinicians, educators, therapists, and community-based organization staff and volunteers). For researchers, the scale is designed to provide a quantitative assessment of men's perceptions of condom fit and feel and can be used for studies that seek to include a construct such as "perceived condom fit and feel" in their work related to condom use, condom attitudes, and other cognitive, affective, and behavioral aspects of using condoms. For practitioners, the scale was designed to be a useful tool that would help condom-resistant men to articulate their specific concerns with the fit and feel of condoms in a way that is sensitive to the challenges that both men and providers may face during discussions related to male sexual anatomy. For practitioners involved in the promotion of correct and consistent condom use, the scale can be quickly scored or individual items can be reviewed in order to assist providers with making recommendations for specific condoms that are designed for men with varying penile dimensions or that have properties (e.g., shape, texture, lubricant type) that men may perceive as better fitting or more comfortable given their particular concerns.

Description

The Condom Fit and Feel Scale is a 14-item Likert-type scale on which men indicate their experiences with the fit and feel of condoms. Items were developed by sexual health researchers in collaboration with sexual health practitioners, condom manufacturers, and condom distributors based upon the specific issues that men have presented during sexual health interventions and upon the specific issues with condom fit and feel that men have expressed to condom companies and condom retailers when seeking condom recommendations. The scale has five subscales, including

[1]Address correspondence to Michael Reece, Center for Sexual Health Promotion, HPER 116, Indiana University, Bloomington, IN 47405; e-mail: mireece@indiana.edu

Condoms Fit Fine, Condoms Feel Too Loose, Condoms Feel Too Tight, Condoms Are Too Long, and Condoms Are Too Short. Each item is assessed using a 4-point response option (1 = *Never Applies to Me*; 2 = *Sometimes Applies to Me*; 3 = *Often Applies to Me*; 4 = *Always Applies to Me*).

Response Mode and Timing

Respondents are asked to read a series of 14 statements and to indicate the extent to which the specific perception of condom fit and feel has applied to them over the course of their past sexual activities during which condoms were used. The scale is preceded by the instruction: "Please rate the extent to which each of the following statements has applied to you as you have used condoms for sexual activities in the past." Completion of the scale takes approximately 5 minutes.

Scoring

A mean score for each subscale is calculated by summing the scores on items within each subscale and dividing the total subscale score by the number of items in each subscale. The subscale mean scores can be used independently to assess men's experiences with specific aspects of condom fit and feel. One can also calculate an overall score of Condom Fit and Feel Problems by reverse scoring the two positive items in the Condoms Fit Fine subscale and creating a summed score.

Reliability

Reliability coefficients of the subscales have ranged from .60 (Condoms Are Too Long subscale) to .89 (Condoms Feel Too Loose subscale) during administration to samples of heterosexual, bisexual, and gay men (Reece, Dodge, Herbenick, Fisher, & Alexander, 2007; Reece, Herbenick, & Dodge, 2009). In addition to the English version of the scale, similar levels of reliability have been demonstrated in multiple languages including Spanish, German, French,

Dutch, and Slovenian (Dodge, Reece, & Herbenick, 2009). Reliability of the scale has also been established among individuals living with HIV (Briggs, Reece, Dodge, Glover, & Herbenick, 2009).

Validity

Factorial validity was established through exploratory and confirmatory factor analyses (Reece et al., 2008) following its initial implementation among a sample of 1,842 men with a history of condom use in the United States. Factor analyses indicated a five-factor solution (the five subscales) that explained 54.3% of the variance. Known-groups validity has been established by exploring the extent to which subscale scores converge with self-reported measures of erect penile circumference and penile length (Reece et al., 2009). Convergent validity of the total scale and individual subscales has been further established through the use of the scale with measures of condom use, condom breakage, and condom slippage (Reece et al., 2007; Reece et al., 2009).

References

Briggs, L., Reece, M., Dodge, B., Glover, R., & Herbenick, D. (2009, November). *Perceptions of condom fit and feel and relations with condom use among men living with HIV*. Paper presented at the Annual Meeting of the American Public Health Association, Philadelphia, PA.

Dodge, B., Reece, M., & Herbenick, D. (2009, November). *Experiences of condom fit and feel among men in five European nations*. Paper presented at the Annual Meeting of the American Public Health Association, Philadelphia, PA.

Reece, M., Dodge, B., Herbenick, D., Fisher, C., & Alexander, A. (2007). Experiences of condom fit and feel among African-American men who have sex with men. *Sexually Transmitted Infections, 83,* 454–457.

Reece, M., Herbenick, D., & Dodge, B. (2009). Penile dimensions and men's perceptions of condom fit and feel. *Sexually Transmitted Infections, 85,* 127–131.

Reece, M., Herbenick, D., Monahan, P., Sanders, S., Temkit, M., & Yarber, W. L. (2008). Breakage, slippage and acceptability outcomes of a condom fitted to penile dimensions. *Sexually Transmitted Infections, 84,* 143–149.

Exhibit

Condom Fit and Feel Scale

Please rate the extent to which each of the following statements has applied to you as you have used condoms for sexual activities in the past.

Response Options:

1. Never Applies to Me
2. Sometimes Applies to Me
3. Often Applies to Me
4. Always Applies to Me

Scale Items by Subscale (subscale titles provided for information, not to be included in the actual scale when administered).

Condoms Fit Fine
Condoms fit my penis just fine.
Condoms feel comfortable once I have them on my penis.

Condoms Are Too Long
Condoms are too long for my penis.
I have some unrolled condom left at the base of my penis after I unroll it.

Condoms Are Too Short
Condoms are too short for my penis.
Condoms will not roll down far enough to cover my penis completely.

Condoms Feel Too Tight
Condoms are too tight on my penis.
Condoms feel too tight along the shaft of my penis.
Condoms feel too tight on the head of my penis.
Condoms feel too tight around the base of my penis.

Condoms Feel Too Loose
Condoms are too loose on my penis.
Condoms feel too loose along the shaft of my penis.
Condoms feel too loose around the head of my penis.
Condoms feel too loose around the base of my penis.

Condom Embarrassment Scale

KAREN VAIL-SMITH[1] AND THOMAS W. DURHAM, *East Carolina University*
H. ANN HOWARD, *University of North Carolina at Chapel Hill*

Embarrassment as a construct inhibiting effective contraceptive use has been supported in the literature (Baffi, Schroeder, Redican, & McCluskey, 1989; Beckman, Harvey, & Tiersky, 1996; Bell, 2009; Dahl, Gorn, & Weinberg, 1998; Herold, 1981; Hingson, Strunin, Berlin, & Heeren, 1990; Hughes & Torre, 1987; Kallen & Stephensen, 1980; Moore, Dahl, Gorn, & Weinberg, 2006; Moore et al., 2008; Valdiserri, Arena, Proctor, & Bonati, 1989). The Condom Embarrassment Scale (CES) was developed to measure the level of embarrassment in college men and women regarding condom use (Vail-Smith, Durham, & Howard, 1992). Condom embarrassment is here defined as the psychological discomfort, self-consciousness, and feeling of being ill at ease associated with condom use. The researchers hypothesized that this psychological discomfort would be experienced when an individual makes an acquisition of condoms, negotiates with a partner to use condoms, and actually uses a condom as a part of a sexual encounter.

Description

The 18-item CES employs a Likert scale (5-point) with response options labeled from *Strongly Disagree* to *Strongly Agree*. From the responses of a sample of 256 college students, a principal factor analysis with varimax rotation revealed three major components of condom embarrassment that accounted for 59.4% of the total variance. Items 1, 2, 3, 4, 5, 6, 7, and 12 loaded heavily on the first factor. This factor accounted for 45.0% of the shared variance explained by the three factors and appears to be character-

[1]Address correspondence to Karen Vail-Smith, Department of Health Education and Promotion, East Carolina University, Greenville, NC 27858; e-mail: vailsmithk@ecu.edu

ized by embarrassment associated with acquiring, purchasing, obtaining or possessing condoms. Items 14, 15, 16, 17, and 18 loaded on the second factor, which accounted for 30.1% of the common variance and appears to be associated with actually using condoms. Items 8, 9, 10, 11, and 13 loaded on the third factor. Factor three appears to be associated with negotiating the use of condoms and accounts for 24.9% of the explainable variance.

Response Mode and Timing

Respondents indicate their level of agreement with each item by circling the letter (A-E) corresponding with their answer choice. The CES requires approximately 10 minutes to complete.

Scoring

Each item on the CES is scored from 1 to 5 with 1 corresponding to *Strongly Disagree* (low embarrassment) and 5 corresponding to *Strongly Agree* (high embarrassment). Point values for all answers were summed to provide the CES score. The possible range of CES scores is from 18 to 90, with 90 indicating the highest embarrassment and 18 indicating the lowest. Among the 256 college students who participated in the original study, the mean score on the CES was 44.88 ($SD = 14.85$). Women ($M = 46.54, SD = 14.65$) scored significantly higher than men ($M = 41.81, SD = 14.74$), $t(254) = 2.48, p = .01$.

Reliability

To assess the stability of the test over time, a Pearson product-moment correlation coefficient was computed using the scores from the 226 college students who completed two administrations of the CES. The obtained reliability coefficient was .78, $p < .001$. The Cronbach's alpha for the summed scores from the 18 items was .92.

Validity

As expected, Vail-Smith, Durham, and Howard (1992) found that the summed score of the CES was significantly correlated with the Sex Anxiety Inventory (Janda & O'Grady, 1980), $r = .39$. It was also predicted that those persons with greater knowledge about condom use and sexually transmitted diseases (STDs) would feel less embarrassed about buying, discussing, and using condoms. When comparing the scores on an STD/condom knowledge test (Solomon & DeJong, 1989) and the CES across both men and women, the Pearson product-moment correlation for these two variables was .34, $p < .01$, also indicating a significant correlation in the predicted direction. The relationship of CES scores with the STD/condom knowledge test scores differs by gender, however. For the 163 women, the correlation between the two variables was −.35, $p < .001$, indicating that women who scored higher on the knowledge test felt

less embarrassment about condom acquisition and use. For the 93 men, this correlation was −.13, $p > .20$, revealing no significant relationship between the variables.

In addition to the attitude measures described above, variation on CES scores as a function of various behaviors was also examined. As expected, those who have actually purchased a condom do feel less condom embarrassment than those who have not made such a purchase and consequently scored significantly lower on the CES. Another factor supporting construct validity is that sexually active respondents have a lower embarrassment score than those who are not sexually active.

Other Information

The use of the CES for educational or research purposes is encouraged. The authors would appreciate receiving information about the results.

References

Baffi, C. R., Schroeder, K. K., Redican, K. J., & McCluskey, L. (1989). Factors influencing selected heterosexual male college students' condom use. *Journal of American College Health, 38*, 137–141.

Beckman, L. J., Harvey, S. M., & Tiersky, L. A. (1996). Attitudes about condoms and condom use among college students. *Journal of American College Health, 44*, 243–249.

Bell, J. (2009). Why embarrassment inhibits the acquisition and use of condoms: A qualitative approach to understanding risky sexual behaviour. *Journal of Adolescence, 32*, 379–391.

Dahl, D. W., Gorn, G. J., & Weinberg C. B. (1998). The impact of embarrassment on condom purchase behaviour. *Canadian Journal of Public Health, 89*, 368–370.

Herold, E. S. (1981). Contraceptive embarrassment and contraceptive behavior among young single women. *Journal of Youth and Adolescence, 10*, 233–242.

Hingson, R. W., Strunin, L., Berlin, M., & Heeren, T. (1990). Beliefs about AIDS, use of alcohol and drugs, and unprotected sex among Massachusetts adolescents. *American Journal of Public Health, 80*, 295–299.

Hughes, C. B., & Torre, C. (1987). Predicting effective contraceptive behavior in college females. *Nurse Practitioner, 12*, 44–54.

Janda, L. H., & O'Grady, K. E. (1980). Development of a sex anxiety inventory. *Journal of Consulting and Clinical Psychology, 48*, 169–175.

Kallen, J. D., & Stephensen, J. (1980). The purchase of contraceptives by college students. *Family Relations, 29*, 358–364.

Moore, S. G., Dahl, D. W., Gorn, G. J., & Weinberg, C. B. (2006). Coping with condom embarrassment. *Psychology, Health and Medicine, 11*, 70–79.

Moore, S. G., Dahl, D. W., Gorn, G. J., Weinberg, C. B., Park, J., & Jiang, Y. (2008). Condom embarrassment: Coping and consequences for condom use in three countries. *AIDS Care, 20*, 553–559.

Solomon, M. Z., & DeJong, W. (1989). Preventing AIDS and other STDs through condom promotion: A patient education intervention. *American Journal of Public Health, 79*, 453–458.

Vail-Smith, K., Durham, T. W., & Howard, H. A. (1992). A scale to measure embarrassment associated with condom use. *Journal of Health Education, 29*, 209–214.

Valdiserri, R. O., Arena, V. C., Proctor, D., & Bonati, F. A. (1989). The relationship between women's attitudes about condoms and their use: Implications for condom promotion programs. *American Journal of Public Health, 79*, 499–501.

Exhibit

Condom Embarrassment Scale

Instructions: The following items assess how embarrassed you do feel (or would feel) about condom use. Using the following scale, please respond to each of the items listed below.

A = Strongly Disagree
B = Disagree
C = Neither Agree nor Disagree
D = Agree
E = Strongly Agree

1. I am embarrassed or would be embarrassed about buying a condom from a drug store near campus.
2. I am embarrassed or would be embarrassed about buying a condom from a drug store close to where my parents live.
3. I am embarrassed or would be embarrassed about buying a condom from a place where I could be certain no one I know would see me.
4. I am embarrassed or would be embarrassed about obtaining condoms from Student Health Services (School Infirmary).
5. I am embarrassed or would be embarrassed about obtaining condoms from a local health department.
6. I am embarrassed or would be embarrassed about asking a pharmacist or drug store clerk where condoms are located in the store.
7. I am embarrassed or would be embarrassed about asking a doctor or other health care professional questions about condom use.
8. I am embarrassed or would be embarrassed about stopping during foreplay and asking my partner to use a condom.
9. I would be embarrassed if a new partner insisted that we use a condom.
10. I am embarrassed or would be embarrassed to tell my partner during foreplay that I am not willing to have sexual intercourse unless we use a condom.
11. I am embarrassed or would be embarrassed about being prepared and providing a condom during lovemaking if my partner didn't have one.
12. I am embarrassed or would be embarrassed about carrying a condom around in my wallet/purse.
13. I am embarrassed or would be embarrassed about talking to my partner about my thoughts and feelings about condom use.
14. I am embarrassed or would be embarrassed if my partner watched me dispose of a condom after we had used it.
15. I am embarrassed or would be embarrassed about *watching my partner* put on a condom OR if my *partner watched me* put on a condom.
16. I am embarrassed or would be embarrassed about *helping my partner* put on a condom OR if my *partner helped me* put on a condom.
17. I am embarrassed or would be embarrassed about *watching my partner* remove a condom OR if my *partner watched me* remove a condom.
18. I am embarrassed or would be embarrassed about *helping my partner* remove a condom OR if my *partner helped me* remove a condom.

Sexual Situation Questionnaire

E. SANDRA BYERS,[1] AND LUCIA F. O'SULLIVAN, *University of New Brunswick*

The Sexual Situation Questionnaire (SSQ) measures behavior during interactions in which heterosexual dating partners disagree about the level of sexual intimacy in which they desire to engage (Byers & Lewis, 1988; O'Sullivan & Byers, 1993; O'Sullivan & Byers, 1996). It also assesses coercive and noncoercive behaviors individuals use to influence a reluctant partner to engage in the disputed sexual activity. Parallel forms measure disagreement situations in which the male or the female is the reluctant partner and differ only in the pronouns used to designate the initiating and the reluctant partner. The term *sexual activity* is defined to include all activities that the subjects experience as sexual, ranging from holding hands and kissing to sexual intercourse. *Dating* is defined broadly as any social situation in which the respondent was with a member of the other sex, even if it was not part of what they would consider to be a true date. The SSQ could easily be adapted to assess same-sex sexual interactions.

Description

The SSQ can be administered retrospectively (O'Sullivan & Byers, 1993, 1996) or as a self-monitoring device (Byers & Lewis, 1988). The self-monitoring version requires participants to keep a daily record of whether they had been on a date, whether the date involved sexual activity, and whether they and their partner differed about the desired level of sexual activity. The retrospective version requires participants to indicate whether they have ever experienced the designated type of disagreement situation (i.e., a disagreement situation in which the woman desired the higher level of sexual activity or a disagreement situation in which the man desired the higher level of sexual activity). There are male and female versions of each questionnaire.

Respondents who report having experienced such an interaction then complete a 19-item questionnaire assessing characteristics of the first (self-monitoring) or most recent (retrospective) incident. Questions assess their relationship with their dating partner (i.e., type of relationship, number of previous dates, romantic interest in their partner), where they were at the time of the disagreement, the disputed level of sexual activity, whether they had engaged in the disputed sexual activity with that partner on a previous occasion, and the consensual sexual activities preceding the disagreement (if any). Respondents also provide the reasons why the reluctant partner did not want to engage in the initiated sexual activity. Respondents provide detailed information regarding the communication about the disputed sexual activity by reporting the verbal and/or nonverbal behaviors

used by (a) the man or woman to indicate his or her desire to engage in the sexual activity (i.e., initiation behaviors), (b) the reluctant partner to indicate unwillingness to engage in the initiated sexual activity (i.e., response behaviors), and, (c) the initiator in response to the noninitiating partner's reluctance (i.e., influence behaviors). Respondents rate how clearly the initiator had indicated a desire for the sexual activity and how clearly the partner had indicated reluctance. Respondents also indicate, from a list of 34 possible influence strategies, those strategies (if any) used to influence the reluctant partner to engage in the unwanted sexual activity. For each strategy endorsed, respondents indicate whether the impact on the reluctant partner was positive (i.e., pleasing), negative (i.e., displeasing), or neutral (i.e., neither pleasing nor displeasing). Respondents indicate whether they had engaged in the disputed level of sexual activity following the disagreement, and they rate the pleasantness associated with the disagreement interaction both at the time of the disagreement and at the time the questionnaire is completed. They also rate the amount of romantic interest felt toward their dating partner both before and after the disagreement.

Using an open-ended format, respondents are given the opportunity to provide additional information about the interaction they had described. Finally they rate their confidence in the accuracy of their responses.

Response Mode and Timing

The SSQ takes approximately 10 minutes to complete. The format is primarily multiple choice. Five items are open-ended: location of incident, reasons for reluctance to engage in the disputed level of sexual activity, and the verbal and nonverbal components of the disagreement. Location was rated as occurring in a bedroom or not in a bedroom. The following categories are used to rate reasons for reluctance to engage in the sexual activity: unknown, timing in relationship, inappropriate relationship, situational (wrong time or location), moral beliefs, physical reasons, and mood. Verbal initiation behavior is categorized as no verbal initiation, indirect verbal initiation, or direct verbal initiation. Nonverbal initiation is categorized as no nonverbal initiation, suggestive look or action, kissing or sexual fondling, or coercion using physical tactics. Responses can be rated categorically (O'Sullivan & Byers, 1993, 1996) or on two definiteness scales (Byers & Lewis, 1988). Categories for verbal responses are no verbal response, refusal without reason, refusal with situation reason, and refusal with personal reason. Categories for nonverbal responses are no nonverbal response, no

---

[1]Address correspondence to E. Sandra Byers, Department of Psychology, University of New Brunswick, Fredericton, NB, Canada, E3B 6E4; e-mail: byers@unb.ca

resistance, passive acceptance, physical counteraction, or nonsexual touch. The verbal definiteness scale consists of the following 4-point scale: no verbal refusal, refusal implying advances might be accepted at some other time or place, unqualified refusal, and refusal with anger or threat that date should leave. Nonverbal definiteness is scored on the following 4-point scale: no physical refusal, blocked or did not perform sexual activity, moved away or pushed partner away, and got up or slapped. Similarly, influence behaviors can be rated categorically (O'Sullivan & Byers, 1993, 1996) or on a compliance scale (Byers & Lewis, 1988). The categories for influence behaviors are compliance using no influence behaviors, compliance using influence behaviors, or noncompliance. Alternately, compliance is scored on a 5-point scale consisting of: stopped without questioning, stopped and asked for clarification, stopped and attempted to persuade partner, stopped and expressed displeasure or anger, and continued unwanted advances.

Reliability and Validity

The SSQ has good reliability. The mean interrater agreement for open-ended questions was .87 (range .83 to 1.0)

(O'Sullivan & Byers, 1993, 1996) and .85 (range .71 to 1.00; Byers & Lewis, 1988).

Respondents' mean confidence ratings of 5.1 (O'Sullivan & Byers, 1993) and 5.2 (O'Sullivan & Byers, 1996; Byers & Lewis, 1988)) on a 6-point scale provide evidence for the validity of the responses. Men have been found to rate themselves as less likely to comply with women's refusal of their sexual advances in response to less definite than to more definite verbal responses, providing evidence for the validity of the definiteness scale. More traditional men have been found to be less compliant in their responses to a woman's refusal of their sexual advances, providing evidence for the validity of the compliance scale.

References

Byers, E. S., & Lewis, K. (1988). Dating couples' disagreements over the desired level of sexual intimacy. *The Journal of Sex Research, 24,* 15–29.

O'Sullivan, L. F., & Byers, E. S. (1993). Eroding stereotypes: College women's attempts to influence reluctant male sexual partners. *The Journal of Sex Research, 30,* 270–282.

O'Sullivan, L. F., & Byers, E. S. (1996). Gender differences in responses to discrepancies in desired level of sexual intimacy. *The Journal of Psychology & Human Sexuality, 8*(1/2), 49–67.

Exhibit

Sexual Situation Questionnaire for Men (Reluctant Woman Version)[a]

Instructions: We are interested in learning more about communication in dating situations in which you, a man, wished to engage in a higher level of sexual activity than your date, a woman, wanted to engage in at that time. For example, you may have wanted to kiss a woman when she did not wish to kiss you. Another example would be if you wanted to have intercourse and your date only wanted to go as far as sexual fondling. Notice that we are interested in communication about *all* levels of sexual activity from holding hands and kissing to intercourse. And, while we use the term "date," we are interested in any sexual situation that you are in with a member of the other sex, even if it is not part of what you may consider to be a true "date." Also, when we use the term "disagreement," we are referring to those situations in which you indicate a desire to engage in a higher level of sexual activity than a woman wanted—even if she later changed her mind and engaged in the sexual activity anyway or she was convinced to engage in the sexual activity some other way. In other words, the term "disagreement" means that you and your date differed in the level of sexual activity desired. It does not imply that you argued or fought about this issue.

1. Have you ever been on a date where you wanted to engage in a higher level of sexual activity than your date, a woman, did? —
   _____ Yes   _____ No
   If No, then you do not need to complete the rest of the questionnaire.
   If Yes, please complete the rest of the questionnaire for the *most recent* time that this occurred.
2. How long ago was the *most recent* time that you wanted to engage in a higher level of sexual activity than your date did?
   _____ (specify number and whether it was days, weeks, or months).
3. Prior to the disagreement, how many previous dates had you and this woman had together? _____
4. What type of relationship did you have with your date prior to the disagreement?
   _____ first date
   _____ casual date
   _____ steady date
5. Where were you and your date at the time of the disagreement?
   _____

6. The sexual activity that you wished to engage in but your date did not wish to engage in was: (check all that apply)
   _____ hugging
   _____ a kiss
   _____ necking
   _____ you fondling or kissing your date's breasts
   _____ you fondling your date's genitals

_____ your date fondling your genitals

_____ oral sex (male to female)

_____ oral sex (female to male)

_____ intercourse

_____ anal sex

_____ other (please specify) _____

7. Why did your date *not* wish to engage in this sexual activity?

_____

8. Had you ever engaged in this sexual activity before with this woman?

_____ Yes   _____ No

9. The sexual activity (or activities) that you and your date were engaging in *immediately prior* to the disagreement was (were): (check as many as apply)

_____ no sexual activity

_____ hugging

_____ a kiss

_____ necking

_____ you fondling or kissing your date's breasts

_____ your date fondling your genitals

_____ you fondling her genitals

_____ oral sex (male to female)

_____ oral sex (female to male)

_____ intercourse

_____ anal sex

_____ other (please specify) _____

10. How clearly did you indicate to your date that you wanted to engage in the higher level of sexual activity that you specified in Question 6?

_____ extremely clearly

_____ moderately clearly

_____ somewhat clearly

_____ somewhat unclearly

_____ moderately unclearly

_____ extremely unclearly

11. What did you say and/or do to indicate that you wanted to engage in the higher level of sexual activity that you specified in Question 6? (Please write the exact words you used [if any] and/or describe the actions that you used [if any] to indicate that you wanted to engage in the sexual activity.)

I said: _____

_____

I did: _____

_____

12. How clearly did your date indicate that she did not want to engage in this sexual activity?

_____ extremely clearly

_____ moderately clearly

_____ somewhat clearly

_____ somewhat unclearly

_____ moderately unclearly

_____ extremely unclearly

13. What did she say and/or do to indicate that she did not want to engage in this sexual activity? (Please write the exact words she used [if any] and/or describe the actions that she used [if any] to indicate that she did not want to engage in the sexual activity.)

She said: _____

_____

She did: _____

_____

14. How did you respond after she had indicated that she did *not* want to engage in this sexual activity? (Please write the exact words you used [if any] and/or describe the actions that you used [if any] after she had indicated that she did not want to engage in the sexual activity.)

I said: _____

_____

I did: _____
_____

15. Did you and your date end up engaging in the sexual activity that you had disagreed upon?

    Yes, then _____
    Yes, later on that date _____
    No, not on that date _____

16. Please indicate which of the following behaviors you used (if any) in attempting to influence your date to engage in the higher level of sexual activity once she had indicated that she did not want to by placing a check mark in the left hand column below.

    Then, for each behaviour you used, indicate the impact of the behaviour on your date *at that time*. Use a "P" if the impact of the behavior was positive or pleasing to your date, a "D" if the impact of the behavior was negative or displeasing, or an "N" if the impact of the behavior was neutral. (Check as many behaviours as occurred.)

Did you use this?	Impact on woman (P, D, or N)	
_____	_____	asked her if she found you sexually attractive
_____	_____	pouted, sulked, or refused to talk
_____	_____	told her that you were too sexually aroused to stop
_____	_____	said things to her that you did not really mean (e.g., told her that you loved her and you do not)
_____	_____	talked about your real feelings toward her (e.g., told her that you loved her and you do)
_____	_____	threats (e.g. to end the date, end the relationship or tell others)
_____	_____	discontinued all sexual activity
_____	_____	complimented her on her body or sexuality
_____	_____	made negative comments (e.g. about her sexuality, her personality, her appearance or the relationship)
_____	_____	pinched, poked her
_____	_____	tickled her
_____	_____	pleaded
_____	_____	tried to reason with her
_____	_____	bargained, negotiated, or suggested a compromise
_____	_____	took off or loosened clothing
_____	_____	flirted
_____	_____	pretended to become disinterested in the sexual activity that you had wanted to engage in previously
_____	_____	cried
_____	_____	grabbed her or used some other form of physical pressure
_____	_____	touched, stroked her
_____	_____	tried to get her drunk, stoned
_____	_____	started an argument
_____	_____	made positive comments about her appearance
_____	_____	made positive comments about her personality
_____	_____	made positive comments about the relationship
_____	_____	told her how enjoyable it would be
_____	_____	made her feel guilty
_____	_____	used humor
_____	_____	moved away from her
_____	_____	made her jealous (e.g., flirted with someone else)
_____	_____	ignored refusal and engaged in the higher level of sexual activity anyway
_____	_____	asked her why she didn't want to do it
_____	_____	put on clothing, music that you hoped she would find arousing
_____	_____	danced, moved seductively
_____	_____	other (please specify) _____

17. *At the time* when you wanted to engage in the higher level of sexual activity than your date did, how pleasurable was it being with your date?

    _____ extremely unpleasant
    _____ moderately unpleasant

_____ slightly unpleasant

_____ slightly pleasant

_____ moderately pleasant

_____ extremely pleasant

18. How do you *now* evaluate this time with your date (when you wanted to engage in a higher level of sexual activity)?

_____ extremely unpleasant

_____ moderately unpleasant

_____ slightly unpleasant

_____ slightly pleasant

_____ moderately pleasant

_____ extremely pleasant

19. Before this incident, how romantically interested did you feel toward your date?

_____ no romantic interest

_____ slightly romantically interested

_____ moderately romantically interested

_____ very romantically interested

_____ extremely romantically interested

20. After this incident, how romantically interested did you feel toward your date?

_____ no romantic interest

_____ slightly romantically interested

_____ moderately romantically interested

_____ very romantically interested

_____ extremely romantically interested

21. If there is any additional information that would help us to understand the incident that you described above, please provide it.

_____

_____

22. How confident are you that your responses are accurate?

_____ very unsure

_____ moderately unsure

_____ slightly unsure

_____ slightly sure

_____ moderately sure

_____ very sure

ªThis version of the questionnaire is designed for men to report on incidents in which they desired a higher level of sexual activity than did their female partner. Men can also be asked to report on situations in which their female partner desired to engage in a higher level of sexual activity than they did, and women can be asked to report on either of these disagreement situations by altering the pronouns and use of the terms *man* and *woman*.

Sexual Consent Scale, Revised

TERRY P. HUMPHREYS,[1] *Trent University*

The purpose of the Sexual Consent Scale, Revised (SCS-R; Humphreys, 2004; Humphreys & Brousseau, 2009; Humphreys & Herold, 2007) is to assess attitudes and behaviors about the negotiation of sexual consent between sexual partners. This scale was normed on heterosexual undergraduate students at three universities.

Description

The SCS was initially developed using semistructured focus group interviews with university students to gain an initial understanding of the key themes regarding sexual consent negotiations. These themes were then translated into Likert-type items for the quantitative survey. Use of focus

[1]Address correspondence to Terry P. Humphreys, Psychology Department, Trent University, 1600 West Bank Drive, Peterborough, Ontario, Canada, K9J 7B8; e-mail: terryhumphreys@trentu.ca

groups prior to developing the survey instrument improved the phrasing and relevance of the items, as well as ensuring adequate coverage of the topic area. The original SCS (Humphreys & Herold, 2007) is a 35-item scale containing both attitude and behavior items, each with two subscales: *Asking for consent first is important, Commitment reduces asking for consent, Consent discussions/awareness,* and *Consent is negotiated once,* respectively.

The Theory of Planned Behavior (TPB; Ajzen, 1985, 2001, 2005) was used to redesign the original sexual consent scale to maximize its use as a predictive tool. Additional items were added to the SCS to ensure adequate coverage of the three predictors of behavioral intent in the TPB (i.e., attitude toward the action, subjective norms, and perceived behavioral control).

The SCS-R is a 40-item, self-report questionnaire that is answered using a 7-point Likert-type scale ranging from 1 (*Strongly Disagree*) to 7 (*Strongly Agree*). Factor analysis with varimax rotation revealed four attitudinal subscales and two behavioral subscales. The four attitudinal subscales are Positive Attitude Towards Establishing Consent (9 items, $M = 4.67$), Lack of Perceived Behavioral Control (9 items, $M = 3.18$), Relationship Length Norms (5 items, $M = 5.02$), and (Pro) Assuming Consent (7 items, $M = 3.08$). The two behavioral subscales are Indirect Consent Behaviors (6 items, $M = 4.97$) and Awareness of Consent (4 items, $M = 3.55$). The final 40-item factor structure accounted for 48.7% of the variance (Humphreys & Brousseau, 2009).

Response Mode and Timing

Two alternate modes are possible. As a paper-and-pencil survey, respondents circle a number from 1 to 7 corresponding to their degree of agreement or disagreement with each item. As an online survey (using an internal or external service), respondents click on the bullet response from 1 to 7 corresponding to their degree of agreement or disagreement with each item. The SCS-R requires approximately 20 minutes to complete.

Scoring

Items are scored 1 for *Strongly Disagree* to 7 for *Strongly Agree,* with the exception of the reversed items. Items 17, 34, 40 are reverse scored. To obtain subscale scores, add together the score on each item and divide by the number of items for each subscale.

Reliability

Based on a dataset of 396 completed surveys, the reliability for the whole SCS-R was .89. Internal consistency for each subscale, using coefficient alpha, was as follows: Positive Attitude Towards Establishing Consent ($\alpha = .83$), Lack of Perceived Behavioral Control ($\alpha = .85$), Relationship Length Norms ($\alpha = .72$), (Pro) Assuming Consent ($\alpha = .68$), Indirect Consent Behaviors ($\alpha = .78$), and Awareness of Consent ($\alpha = .72$; Humphreys & Brousseau, 2009).

Test-retest reliability was conducted on a sample of 45 students over a 5-week interval. Coefficients for the 6 subscales ranged from .63 to .71 (Humphreys & Brousseau, 2009).

Validity

Construct validity was examined by comparing the six subscales of the SCS-R to two previously established scales, the Sexual Sensation Seeking Scale (SSSS; Kalichman & Rompa, 1995) and Hurlbert's Index of Sexual Assertiveness (HISA; Hurlbert, 1991). The SSSS assesses the willingness to take physical and social risks to achieve varied and novel sexual sensations and experiences. Given that establishing sexual consent is a "safe" behavior that guards against miscommunication and, possibly, coercion, there should be a logical connection between the two measures: As the trait of sensation seeking increases, the formal negotiation of sexual consent between sexual partners should decrease. Sensation seeking was negatively correlated with positive attitude towards establishing consent ($r = -.15, p < .05$) and positively correlated with assuming consent ($r = .15, p < .05$), believing that longer relationships reduce the need for establishing consent (relationship length norms; $r = .15, p < .05$) and using more indirect consent behaviors ($r = .18, p < .05$; Humphreys & Brousseau, 2009).

Likewise, sexual assertiveness would be logically connected to sexual consent because both concepts are characterized by a willingness to communicate about sex. Assertive communication about sexuality includes aspects of consenting to sexual activity, such as initiating, talking about contraceptives, past partners, desires and general comfort (Morokoff et al., 1997). Sexual assertiveness was negatively correlated with a lack of perceived behavioral control ($r = -.35, p < .01$) and positively correlated with awareness of consent issues ($r = .24, p < .01$) and using more indirect consent behaviors ($r = .23, p < .01$; Humphreys & Brousseau, 2009).

Extending the Theory of Planned Behavior to sexual consent, the intent to negotiate sexual consent should be based on attitudes in favor of establishing consent first and attitudes in favor of assuming consent, a perceived lack of behavioral control, relationship length norms, and past sexual behavior. Predictive validity was assessed by conducting a standard regression analysis using *intent to verbally ask for sexual consent in the next five sexual encounters* (2 items) with the 6 subscales of the SCS-R. Being male ($B = -.36, \beta = -.15$), perceiving greater behavioral control over negotiating consent ($B = -.22, \beta = -.22$), having positive attitudes towards establishing consent before sexual activity begins ($B = .20, \beta = .17$), using fewer indirect approaches to negotiate consent in the past ($B = -.41, \beta = -.39$), and having more awareness and discussions of consent ($B = .07, \beta = .08$) were all statistically unique predictors of the intent to verbally negotiate sexual consent in the near future, $F(6,380) = 33.31, p < .001, R^2 = .39$ (Humphreys & Brousseau, 2009).

Other Information

Permission to use the SCS or the SCS-R may be obtained from T. Humphreys. I acknowledge the assistance of Ed Herold, University of Guelph and Melanie Brousseau, UQAM in the development of this scale.

References

Ajzen, I. (1985). From intentions to actions: A theory of planned behavior. In J. Kuhi & J. Beckmann (Eds.), *Action-control: From cognition to behavior* (pp. 11–39). Heidelberg, Germany: Springer.

Ajzen, I. (2001). Attitudes. *Annual Review of Psychology, 52,* 27–58.

Ajzen, I. (2005). *Attitudes, personality, and behavior* (2nd ed.). Milton Keynes, UK: Open University Press/McGraw-Hill.

Humphreys, T. P. (2004). Understanding sexual consent: An empirical investigation of the normative script for young heterosexual adults.

In M. Cowling & P. Reynolds (Eds.), *Making sense of sexual consent* (pp. 209–225). Aldershot, UK: Ashgate.

Humphreys, T. P., & Brousseau, M. (2009). The Sexual Consent Scale—Revised: Development, reliability, and preliminary validity. *The Journal of Sex Research, 46,* 1–9.

Humphreys, T. P., & Herold, E. (2007). Sexual consent in heterosexual dating relationships: Attitudes and behaviours of university students. *Sex Roles, 57,* 305–315.

Hurlbert, D. F. (1991). The role of assertiveness in female sexuality: A comparative study between sexually assertive and sexually non-assertive women. *Journal of Sex and Marital Therapy, 17*(3), 183–190.

Kalichman, S. C., & Rompa, D. (1995). Sexual sensation seeking and sexual compulsivity scales: Reliability, validity, and predicting HIV risk behavior. *Journal of Personality Assessment, 65,* 586–601.

Morokoff, P. J., Quina, K., Harlow, L. L., Whitmire, L., Grimley, D. M., Gibson, P. R., et al. (1997). Sexual assertiveness scale (SAS) for women: Development and validation. *Journal of Personality and Social Psychology, 73,* 790–804.

Exhibit

Sexual Consent Scale, Revised

Instructions: Please note that the term *sexual consent* is used extensively throughout this questionnaire. Please use the definition of sexual consent below when answering the questions that follow.

Sexual consent: the freely given verbal or nonverbal communication of a feeling of willingness to engage in sexual activity.

Using the following scale, please circle the number that best describes how strongly you agree or disagree with each statement. Remember, there are no right or wrong answers, just your opinions.

Strongly Disagree	Disagree	Somewhat Disagree Disagree	Neither Agree nor	Somewhat Agree	Agree	Strongly Agree
1	2	3	4	5	6	7

Factor 1: Positive Attitude Towards Establishing Consent

1. I feel that sexual consent should always be obtained before the start of any sexual activity.
2. I think it is equally important to obtain sexual consent in all relationships regardless of whether or not they have had sex before.
3. I believe that asking for sexual consent is in my best interest because it reduces any misinterpretations that might arise.
4. I feel that verbally asking for sexual consent should occur before proceeding with any sexual activity.
5. When initiating sexual activity, I believe that one should always assume they do not have sexual consent.
6. I believe that it is just as necessary to obtain consent for genital fondling as it is for sexual intercourse.
7. I think that consent should be asked before any kind of sexual behavior, including kissing or petting.
8. I feel it is the responsibility of both partners to make sure sexual consent is established before sexual activity begins.
9. Before making sexual advances, I think that one should assume 'no' until there is clear indication to proceed.

Factor 2: (Lack of) Perceived Behavioral Control

10. I would have difficulty asking for consent because it would spoil the mood.
11. I am worried that my partner might think I'm weird or strange if I asked for sexual consent before starting any sexual activity.
12. I think that verbally asking for sexual consent is awkward.
13. I would worry that, if other people knew I asked for sexual consent before starting sexual activity, they would think I was weird or strange.
14. I would have difficulty asking for consent because it doesn't really fit with how I like to engage in sexual activity.
15. I believe that verbally asking for sexual consent reduces the pleasure of the encounter.
16. I would have a hard time verbalizing my consent in a sexual encounter because I am too shy.
17. I feel confident that I could ask for consent from a new sexual partner [R].
18. I would not want to ask a partner for consent because it would remind me that I'm sexually active.

Factor 3: Relationship Length Norms

19. I believe that the need for asking for sexual consent decreases as the length of an intimate relationship increases.
20. I think that obtaining sexual consent is more necessary in a casual sexual encounter than in a committed relationship.
21. I think that obtaining sexual consent is more necessary in a new relationship than in a committed relationship.
22. If a couple has a long history of consenting sexual activity with each other, I do not believe that they need to ask for consent during each sexual encounter.
23. I believe that partners are less likely to ask for sexual consent the longer they are in a relationship.

Factor 4: (Pro) Assuming Consent

24. I think it is okay to assume consent and proceed sexually until the partner indicates "no."
25. If a sexual request is made and the partner indicates "no," I feel that it is okay to continue negotiating the request.
26. I think nonverbal behaviors are as effective as verbal communication to indicate sexual consent.
27. Not asking for sexual consent is not really a big deal.
28. In making a sexual advance, I believe that it is okay to assume consent unless you hear a "no."
29. I believe it is enough to ask for consent at the beginning of a sexual encounter.
30. I believe that sexual intercourse is the only sexual activity that requires explicit verbal consent.

Factor 5: Indirect Behavioral Approach

31. Typically I communicate sexual consent to my partner using nonverbal signals and body language.
32. Typically I ask for consent by making a sexual advance and waiting for a reaction, so I know whether or not to continue.
33. It is easy to accurately read my current (or most recent) partner's non-verbal signals as indicating consent or non-consent to sexual activity.
34. I always verbally ask for consent before I initiate a sexual encounter [R].
35. I don't have to ask or give my partner sexual consent because my partner knows me well enough.
36. I don't have to ask or give my partner sexual consent because I have a lot of trust in my partner to "do the right thing."

Factor 6: Awareness of Consent

37. I have discussed sexual consent issues with a friend.
38. I have heard sexual consent issues being discussed by other students on campus.
39. I have discussed sexual consent issues with my current (or most recent) partner at times other than during sexual encounters.
40. I have not given much thought to the topic of sexual consent [R].

Note. The scale follows each of the statements.

Reasons for Consenting to Unwanted Sex Scale

Terry P. Humphreys & Deborah J. Kennett,[1] *Trent University*

The purpose of the Reasons for Consenting to Unwanted Sex Scale (RCUSS; Humphreys & Kennett, 2008; Kennett, Humphreys, & Patchell, 2009) is to assess the amount of endorsement women give to a variety of reasons for why they have voluntarily consented to engage in sexual activity they did not desire. This scale was normed on heterosexual undergraduate females.

Description

The RCUSS was developed on the basis of past research that suggested women voluntarily give in to sexual activity, even though they may have little or no sexual desire

or would rather not engage in sexual activity (Meston & Buss, 2007; O'Sullivan & Allgeier, 1998). For example, Zimmerman, Sprecher, Langer, and Holloway (1995) found that, when asked how sure they were that they could say "no" if a boyfriend was trying to talk them into having sex, only 61% of females reported that they could definitely say no to unwanted sex. In a diary study, O'Sullivan and Allgeier (1998) found that 50% of the undergraduate women sampled wrote that they had consented to unwanted sexual activity, ranging from kissing to sexual intercourse, during a 2-week period.

The items of the RCUSS were chosen on the basis of past literature, suggesting that women consent to unwanted

[1]Address correspondence to either Terry P. Humphreys or Deborah J. Kennett, Psychology Department, Trent University, 1600 West Bank Drive, Peterborough, Ontario, Canada, K9J 7B8; e-mail: terryhumphreys@trentu.ca or dkennett@trentu.ca

sexual activity for a variety of reasons, including to satisfy their partner's needs, promote intimacy, avoid tension, prevent a partner from losing interest in the relationship and/or fulfill perceived relationship obligations (Impett & Peplau, 2002; O'Sullivan & Allgeier, 1998; Shotland & Hunter, 1995). Items of the RCUSS reflect how characteristic it is for a woman to voluntarily consent to unwanted sexual activity for these reasons.

The RCUSS is an 18-item, self-report questionnaire. Factor analysis with varimax rotation revealed a unidimensional scale that included all 18 items (no factor loadings below .30) accounting for 59.2% of the variance.

Response Mode and Timing

Two alternative modes are possible. When it is a pencil-and-paper survey, respondents circle a number from 0 to 8 corresponding to the degree to which they feel the statement is characteristic of themselves. When it is an online survey (using an internal or external service), respondents click on the bullet response from 0 to 8 corresponding to the degree to which they feel the statement is characteristic of themselves. The scale takes approximately 10 minutes to complete.

Scoring

Items are scored 0 for *Not at all Characteristic of Me* to 8 for *Very Characteristic of Me*. There are not any reverse-scored items. Scores are summed. Total scores can range from 0 to 144. The mean scores on this inventory for our two samples were $M = 41.2$, $SD = 33.5$ (Kennett et al., 2009) and $M = 35.9$, $SD = 32.5$ (Humphreys & Kennett, 2008), respectively.

Reliability

Based on two female undergraduate datasets, the reliability for the whole RCUSS was .96 ($N = 150$), with an average inter-item correlation of .75 (ranging from .46 to .85; Kennett et al., 2009) and .96 ($N = 152$), with an average inter-item correlation of .55 (ranging from .18 to .85; Humphreys & Kennett, 2008), respectively.

Over a 6-week period, test-retest reliability in a female student sample ($N = 63$) was .85 (Humphreys & Kennett, 2008).

Validity

Construct validity was examined by comparing the RCUSS to a number of relationship variables: a previously established scale, the Sexual Experiences Survey (SES; Koss & Oros, 1982); and two newly designed scales, Sexual Self-Efficacy and Sexual Giving-in Experiences (Kennett et al., 2009).

The RCUSS is positively correlated with both number of dating partners, $r(152) = .23$, $p = .004$, and number of

steady partners, $r(152) = .19$, $p = .017$. The greater the number of relationship partners, the more likely a woman will be endorsing a greater number of reasons for consenting to unwanted sex. This makes intuitive sense given that more relationship experience will inevitably lead to discrepancies in sexual desires that need to be negotiated. Some are resolved through relationship maintenance behaviors, such as pleasing the partner. The RCUSS is also correlated positively with two individual questions asking about the *extent* to which women have experienced unwanted sexual advances from men, $r(152) = .25$, $p = .002$, and the *percentage* of relationships in which women have experienced unwanted sexual advances, $r(152) = .26$, $p = .001$. Therefore, the greater the amount of reported unwanted sexual advances from men, the greater the endorsement of various reasons for consenting to these behaviors was observed.

As predicted, the RCUSS scale was also positively correlated with forced sex play (Koss & Oros, 1982, Items 1–3), $r(152) = .541$, $p < .001$, and attempted or completed forced intercourse (Koss & Oros, 1982, Items 4–10), $r(152) = .502$, $p < .001$, in the SES. We found that the greater the experience with nonconsensual sexual behavior, at any level, the greater the endorsement of reasons for consenting to unwanted sexual activity. This could be due to the fact that women with higher levels of nonconsensual sex are involved in more ambiguously consensual situations in total or that many nonconsensual sexual situations are later justified as consensual but not desired.

The Sexual Self-Efficacy (Kennett et al., 2009) scale assesses women's belief that they have what it takes to deal with or prevent unwanted sexual advances. As expected, this 5-item scale was negatively correlated with RCUSS, $r(152) = -.49$, $p < .001$. Clearly, believing that you have the ability to deal with unwanted sexual advances should lead to less need to endorse reasons for consenting to unwanted sexual activities. The results described in this section were reported from Humphreys and Kennett (2008); however, they were replicated in Kennett et al. (2009).

Other Information

Permission to use the RCUSS may be obtained from either T. Humphreys or D. Kennett.

References

Humphreys, T. P., & Kennett, D. J. (2008) [The reliability and validity of the Sexual Resourcefulness and Reasons for Consenting to Unwanted Sex Scales]. Unpublished raw data.

Impett, E. A. & Peplau, L. A. (2002). Why some women consent to unwanted sex with a dating partner: Insights from attachment theory. *Psychology of Women Quarterly, 26,* 360–370.

Kennett, D. J., Humphreys, T. P., & Patchell, M. (2009). The role of learned resourcefulness in helping female undergraduates deal with unwanted sexual activity. *Sex Education, 9,* 341–353.

Koss, M. P., & Oros, C. J. (1982). Sexual experiences survey: A research instrument investigating sexual aggression and victimization. *Journal of Consulting and Clinical Psychology, 50,* 455–457.

Meston, C. M., & Buss, D. M. (2007). Why humans have sex. *Archives of Sexual Behavior, 36,* 477–507.

O'Sullivan, L. F., & Allgeier, E. R. (1998). Feigning sexual desire: Consenting to unwanted sexual activity in heterosexual dating relationships. *The Journal of Sex Research, 35,* 234–243.

Shotland, R. L., & Hunter, B. A. (1995). Women's "token resistant" and compliant sexual behaviors are related to uncertain sexual intentions and rape. *Personality and Social Psychology Bulletin, 21,* 226–236.

Zimmerman, R. S., Sprecher, S., Langer, L. M., & Holloway, C. D. (1995). Adolescents' perceived ability to say "no" to unwanted sex. *Journal of Adolescent Research, 10,* 383–399.

Exhibit

Reasons for Consenting to Unwanted Sex Scale

Instructions: When answering these questions, please think of all the times in which you have consented to unwanted sexual activity. Rate each statement as to how characteristic it is of you as your reason for consenting to unwanted sexual activity using the scale provided.[a]

0	1	2	3	4	5	6	7	8
Not at all Characteristic of Me				Somewhat Characteristic of Me				Very Characteristic of Me

1. I felt that I would be jeopardizing our relationship if I did not engage in the unwanted sexual activity
2. As his girlfriend, I am obligated to engage in the unwanted sexual activity
3. He verbally pressured me to participate in the unwanted sexual behavior
4. He begged me to engage in the unwanted sexual activity until I could not argue anymore
5. I had been drinking or had consumed other types of drugs
6. I felt guilty for not participating in the unwanted sexual activity
7. I feared that I would lose my boyfriend if I did not consent to the unwanted sexual activity
8. I wanted to avoid tension in our relationship
9. I wanted to prevent my partner from losing interest in our relationship
10. I consented to the unwanted sexual activity to promote intimacy
11. I felt it was necessary to satisfy my partner's needs
12. I felt that I needed to because I consented to the sexual activity before
13. I didn't want to hurt my partner's feelings
14. He physically would not let me leave
15. I didn't want him to feel rejected
16. I felt that, if I consented to the unwanted sexual activity, he would like/love me
17. I wanted to feel accepted by my partner
18. He sweet talked me into it

[a]This scale follows each of the scale statements.

Contraceptive Attitude Scale

KELLY J. BLACK,[1] *University of Washington*

The Contraceptive Attitude Scale (CAS) is a measure of attitudes toward the use of contraceptives in general as opposed to attitudes toward a specific type of contraceptive (Brown, 1984), or toward the premarital use of contraceptives (Parcel, 1975). Potentially the scale could help distinguish between an attitude toward using a particular method of contraception (e.g., the condom) versus an attitude toward using any contraceptive.

Description

The CAS consists of 17 positively and 15 negatively worded items to which respondents indicate their agreement or disagreement. The final set of statements was selected based on the responses of 75 male and 60 female college students to a larger set of 80 statements.

Response Mode and Timing

Participants respond to each item by indicating their level of agreement with each statement. Possible responses range from 1 (*strongly disagree*) to 5 (*strongly agree*). The scale requires about 10 minutes to complete.

Scoring

All statements are scored using a 5-point scale. For positively worded statements, *strongly disagree* receives a score of 1 and *strongly agree* receives a score of 5. Negatively worded statements are reverse scored so that *strongly dis-agree* receives a score of 5 and *strongly agree* receives a score of 1. The total score is the sum of the responses to each item. Lower scores indicate more negative attitudes toward contraception.

Reliability

Test-retest reliability of the 32-item scale is very good, $r(166) = .88$, $p < .001$. Internal reliability, as measured by corrected item-total correlations is also good (rs range from .26 to .68; Black & Pollack, 1987).

Validity

Scores from the CAS correlated significantly with scores from the Premarital Contraceptive Attitude Evaluation Instrument (Parcel, 1975), $r = .72$. It also correlated with reported frequency of contraceptive use among nonvirgin male and female college students, $r = .60$.

References

Black, K. J., & Pollack, R. H. (1987, April). *The development of a contraceptive attitude scale.* Paper presented at the Annual Meeting of the Southern Society for Philosophy and Psychology, Atlanta.

Brown, I. S. (1984). Development of a scale to measure attitudes toward the condom as a method of birth control. *The Journal of Sex Research, 20,* 255–263.

Parcel, G. S. (1975). Development of an instrument to measure attitudes toward the personal use of premarital contraception. *Journal of School Health, 45,* 157–160.

Exhibit

Contraceptive Attitude Scale

Below are several statements about the use of contraceptives (birth control). We are interested in knowing your opinion about each statement. Using the scale below, please indicate your level of agreement or disagreement with each statement. Keep in mind that there are no right or wrong answers. Also remember that we are interested in your personal opinion. Therefore, we want to know how you feel about these statements and not how you think your family or friends might feel about these statements.

SA = *Strongly agree;* A = *Agree;* U = *Undecided;* D = *Disagree;* SD = *Strongly disagree*

_____ 1. I believe that it is wrong to use contraceptives.

_____ 2. Contraceptives reduce the sex drive.

_____ 3. Using contraceptives is much more desirable than having an abortion.

_____ 4. Males who use contraceptives seem less masculine than males who do not.

_____ 5. I encourage my friends to use contraceptives.

_____ 6. I would not become sexually involved with a person who did not accept contraceptive responsibility.

_____ 7. Teenagers should not need permission from their parents to get contraceptives.

_____ 8. Contraceptives are not really necessary unless a couple has engaged in intercourse more than once.

[1]Address correspondence to Kelly Black, University of Washington, WaNPRC, Box 357330, Seattle, WA 98109; e-mail: kellyblack@wanprc.org

_____ 9. Contraceptives make sex seem less romantic.

_____ 10. Females who use contraceptives are promiscuous.

_____ 11. I would not have intercourse if no contraceptive method was available.

_____ 12. I do not believe that contraceptives actually prevent pregnancy.

_____ 13. Using contraceptives is a way of showing that you care about your partner.

_____ 14. I do not talk about contraception with my friends.

_____ 15. I would feel embarrassed discussing contraception with my friends.

_____ 16. One should use contraceptives regardless of how long one has known his/her sexual partner.

_____ 17. Contraceptives are difficult to obtain.

_____ 18. Contraceptives can actually make intercourse seem more pleasurable.

_____ 19. I feel that contraception is solely my partner's responsibility.

_____ 20. I feel more relaxed during intercourse if a contraceptive method is used.

_____ 21. I prefer to use contraceptives during intercourse.

_____ 22. In the future, I plan to use contraceptives any time I have intercourse.

_____ 23. I would practice contraception even if my partner did not want me to.

_____ 24. It is no trouble to use contraceptives.

_____ 25. Using contraceptives makes a relationship seem too permanent.

_____ 26. Sex is not fun if a contraceptive is used.

_____ 27. Contraceptives are worth using, even if the monetary cost is high.

_____ 28. Contraceptives encourage promiscuity.

_____ 29. Couples should talk about contraception before having intercourse.

_____ 30. If I or my partner experienced negative side effects from a contraceptive method, we would use a different method.

_____ 31. Contraceptives make intercourse seem too planned.

_____ 32. I feel better about myself when I use contraceptives.

Contraceptive Utilities, Intention, and Knowledge Scale

LARRY CONDELLI,[1] *University of California, Santa Cruz*

The Contraceptive Utilities, Intention, and Knowledge Scale (CUIKS) was developed to test a social psychological model of contraceptive behavior developed by Condelli (1984). This model combined elements of the health belief model (Rosenstock, 1974), Luker's (1975) model of contraceptive risk taking, and Fishbein and Ajzen's (1975) behavioral intention model. Consequently, it is appropriate for use when examining any of these models or the unified model. It can also be used to study women's knowledge and perceptions about contraceptive methods, their attitudes about pregnancy, and to measure intention to use contraception.

Description

The scale is designed to be used with women and is divided into three parts. Part one has nine items (Questions 1–6 in the Exhibit) and measures perceived likelihood of becoming pregnant, both when the respondent is using her chosen method of contraception and with unprotected intercourse.

It also asks the likelihood she will use her method at each act of intercourse over the next year. This item is designed to measure intention to use contraception. One item measures attitude about becoming pregnant at the present time. This part of the scale also has the respondent rate the degree of subjective social support she expects from "people who are most important" to her for using each of four methods of contraception (diaphragm, IUD, the pill, and condoms). Part one also includes an item asking the respondent to state her current method of contraception.

Part two of the scale (Questions 7 and 8 in the Exhibit) has 16 items and measures respondent attitudes about four methods of contraception. The respondent indicates her perceptions of the effectiveness of each method. Her concerns about effects from using each method are also measured.

The third part of the scale is a multiple-choice knowledge test. This test is divided into two parts. The first part is an 8 item test of general knowledge of conception and contraception. The second part is a 4 item test that measures

[1]Address correspondence to Larry Condelli, American Institutes for Research, 1000 Thomas Jefferson Street, NW, Washington, DC 20007; e-mail: LCondelli@air.org

the respondent's knowledge of the primary birth control method she is currently using. Although the test contains four items for each of the four methods of contraception,[2] the respondent answers only the four questions dealing with her method.

The CUIKS was developed to be used in a family planning clinic. It was tested at the clinic on over 600 women of highly diverse age and educational backgrounds. Consequently, it can be used on any population of women.

Response Mode and Timing

The scale is designed to be self administered either individually or in a group setting. Respondents indicate their answers by circling the number that best represents their feelings. For the knowledge scale portion, respondents circle the letter that indicates what they believe to be the correct answer. The scale requires an average of 15 minutes to complete.

Scoring

For parts one and two of the scale, the number circled on the scale is used as the respondent's score on the item. Items 1 and 4 represent the respondent's perceived susceptibility to becoming pregnant, with higher scores indicating a greater likelihood. Item 3 measures intention to use the chosen contraceptive method; Item 6 measures the degree of subjective normative support expected by the respondent for using each method. Both items are positively scaled. Item 5 measures the perceived severity of pregnancy for the respondent and is scored by assigning a value of 7 to the first, most negative statement (It would be the worst thing that could happen) and a value of 1 to the last, most positive statement (It would be the best thing that could happen). The intermediate statements decrease in value consecutively according to their order listed in the item (e.g., the third statement down, It would be sort of bad but not terrible, is assigned a value of 5, the following statement a 4, etc.).

For part two of the scale, the value circled by the respondent is the score for that item. The scores for Item 7 on effectiveness and convenience of the methods are reverse scored.

For the knowledge portion of the scale, items are scored as correct or incorrect. Two scores are then derived by summing the number of correct answers. Items 1 through 8 comprise the general knowledge subscale; the four items relating to the respondent's chosen contraceptive method make up the specific knowledge subscale. A total score is computed by adding general and subscale scores. The correct answers are indicated by an asterisk in the Exhibit. No response on an item is scored as incorrect.

Reliability and Validity

The reliability of the knowledge scale was computed using responses from 632 women visiting a suburban family planning clinic. For the total knowledge scale, Condelli (1986) reported the Kuder Richardson 20 was .62. The reli-

ability is somewhat low due to the varied nature of the topics covered in the scale.

The validity of the scale has been demonstrated through its ability to predict contraceptive behavior and contraceptive choice. Condelli (1984) obtained four measures of contraceptive behavior from women who had completed the scale an average of 6 months previously. Using multiple regression, a significant proportion of variance of each behavioral measure was accounted for using Items 1, 5, 6, 7, and 8 as predictor variables. For Items 7 and 8, only the respondent's rating of the effectiveness, convenience, concern about minor side effects, and concern about major side effects of her own chosen contraceptive method were used in the analysis.

The behavioral measures examined included whether the respondent had unprotected intercourse at any time since completing the scale (coded 0 or 1; $R = .21$); frequency of use of her chosen contraceptive method on a 4 point scale (1 = every time, 4 = less than half the time; $R = .36$); period of time in weeks the respondent had been sexually active without using contraception ($R = .42$); and ranked actual use of effectiveness of the chosen contraceptive method ($R = .38$). All multiple Rs were significant at the .05 level or less.

Condelli (1986) also used the scale to predict choice of contraceptive. Women who chose to use the pill were compared with diaphragm users in a discriminant function analysis, with the scale items and total knowledge test score as predictors. The scale significantly distinguished pill users from diaphragm users on their reported belief the diaphragm was more inconvenient to use and the pill more convenient, expressing less concern about the pill's side effects, believing they were more protected from pregnancy when using the pill and more susceptible when not using it, and having less knowledge about contraception. More than 60% of the variance between the groups was explained by the discriminant function.

Additional Information

The CUIKS may be copied and used, with appropriate citation, without cost.

References

Condelli, L. (1984). A unified social psychological model of contraceptive behavior. Unpublished doctoral dissertation, University of California, Santa Cruz.

Condelli, L. (1986). Social and attitudinal determinants of contraceptive choice: Using the health belief model. The Journal of Sex Research, 22, 478–491.

Fishbein, M., & Ajzen, I. (1975). Belief attitude intention and behavior: An introduction to theory and research. Reading, MA: Addison Wesley.

Kirby, D. (1979). An analysis of U.S. sex education programs and evaluation methods. Washington, DC: U.S. Department of Health, Education, and Welfare.

Luker, K. (1975). Taking chances: Abortion and the decision not to contracept. Berkeley, CA: University of California Press.

Rosenstock, I. (1974). The health belief model and preventive health behavior. Health Education Monographs, 2, 354–386.

[2]In the original instrument, there were four items for the IUD. Because of the infrequent use of the IUD by women in the U.S. today, these items have been removed from this edition of the Exhibit, to save space.

Exhibit

The Contraceptive Utilities, Intention, and Knowledge Scale

Attitude Survey

1. If you were *not* to use birth control, how likely do you think it is that you would become pregnant during the next year? (Circle one category)

1	2	3	4	5
Very unlikely	Somewhat unlikely	Neutral neither likely or unlikely	Somewhat likely	Very likely

2. What form of birth control have you chosen to use? _____

3. How likely do you think it is that you will use the above method every time you have intercourse over the next year?

1	2	3	4	5
Very unlikely	Somewhat unlikely	Neutral neither likely or unlikely	Somewhat likely	Very likely

4. If you were to continue using this form of birth control, how likely do you think it is that you would become pregnant during the next year? (Circle one category)

1	2	3	4	5
Very unlikely	Somewhat unlikely	Neutral neither likely or unlikely	Somewhat likely	Very likely

5. Below are a number of statements about how you might feel about becoming pregnant within the next year. Please place a check in front of the one that best represents how you feel. (*Check one only*)

If I were to get pregnant within the next year:

____ It would be the worst thing that could happen to me.

____ It would be very bad.

____ It would be sort of bad but not terrible.

____ It would be O.K.

____ It would be sort of good but not terrific.

____ It would be very good.

____ It would be the best thing that could happen to me.

6. People who are important to you may have feelings about the type of birth control you might use. For each birth control method below, please indicate how the people who are most important to you would feel about your using that form of contraception. (Circle the number from 1–5 that best represents *their* feelings.)

They would be:

   1 = Very much opposed (would discourage use)

   2 = Somewhat opposed

   3 = Neither opposed nor in favor (neutral)

   4 = Somewhat in favor

   5 = Very much in favor (would encourage use)

Foam/condoms	1	2	3	4	5
Diaphragm	1	2	3	4	5
IUD	1	2	3	4	5
Birth control pills	1	2	3	4	5

7. Different birth control methods vary in how *effective* or *ineffective* they are in preventing pregnancy. They also vary in how *convenient* they are to use. For each birth control method listed below, please rate how *effective* you think they would be in *preventing you* from becoming pregnant, and how *convenient* or *inconvenient* they would be for you to use. (Circle the number from 1–5 that best represents your feelings).

I = Very effective
   (definitely prevents pregnancy)

I = Very convenient
   (no trouble at all)

2 = Pretty effective

2 = pretty convenient

3 = Unsure

3 = Unsure

4 = Pretty ineffective

4 = Pretty inconvenient

5 = Ineffective
   (would not prevent pregnancy)

5 = Very inconvenient
   (too much trouble to use)

	Effectiveness					Convenience				
Foams/condoms	I	2	3	4	5	I	2	3	4	5
Diaphragm	I	2	3	4	5	I	2	3	4	5
IUD	I	2	3	4	5	I	2	3	4	5
Birth control pills	I	2	3	4	5	I	2	3	4	5

8. Different forms of birth control vary in terms of how likely they are to have side effects. Some side effects may be *minor*, such as irritation of or skin problems, while others may be *major*, such as increasing risk of serious illness. For each method of birth control below, please rate how concerned you would be about the occurrence of both *minor* and *major* side effects. (Circle the number from 1–5 that best represents your feelings.)

       I = Not at all concerned

       2 = Slightly unconcerned

       3 = Unsure

       4 = Pretty concerned

       5 = Very concerned

	Minor side effects					Major side effects				
Foams/condoms	I	2	3	4	5	I	2	3	4	5
Diaphragm	I	2	3	4	5	I	2	3	4	5
IUD	I	2	3	4	5	I	2	3	4	5
Birth control pills	I	2	3	4	5	I	2	3	4	5

Knowledge Survey

Circle the correct response.

1. The pill:
   * *a. prevents ovulation
   * b. keeps cervical mucus very thin
   * c. changes the lining of the uterus to make implantation unlikely
   * d. both a & c
   * e. all of the above

2. According to the most accepted current thought, the IUD's effectiveness is due to:
   * a. changing levels of hormones
   * b. changed functioning of the fallopian tubes
   * *c. preventing implantation of the fertilized egg
   * d. preventing ovulation
   * e. all of the above

3. A diaphragm should be used:
   * a. without any cream or jelly
   * b. with any type of lubricant
   * *c. with spermicidal jelly or cream inside it
   * d. either with or without spermicidal jelly

4. Contraceptive foam is most effect in preventing pregnancy when inserted inside the vagina:
   * *a. right before intercourse
   * b. 2–4 hours before intercourse
   * c. right after intercourse
   * d. all of the above

5. The use of a condom when having sexual intercourse is recommended because:
   * a. if used right, it usually prevents getting or giving gonorrhea
   * b. it can be bought in a drug store by both men and women

    c. it does not have dangerous side effects

 *d. all of the above

6. A woman can get pregnant:

    a. a few minutes after sexual intercourse

    b. a few hours after sexual intercourse

    c. a few days after sexual intercourse

 *d. all of the above

    e. a and b

7. Over a one year period, what is the likelihood that a sexually active woman who uses no birth control will become pregnant?

    a. I in 10

    b. 5 in 10

    c. 7 in 10

 *d. 9 in 10

8. A woman is most likely to become pregnant (no matter how long or short her menstrual cycle) if she has sexual intercourse about:

    a. I week before menstruation begins

    b. 2 weeks after menstruation begins

 *c. 2 weeks before menstruation begins

    d. I week after menstruation begins

Answer these questions *only* if you decided on the *pill* as your primary method of birth control.

1. Some warning signs that may signal the onset of pill related problems are:

    a. chest pain

    b. yellowing of the skin

    c. pain in the calf of the leg

 *d. all of the above

    e. none of the above

2. Medical conditions that make it dangerous for a woman to use the pill are:

    a. high blood pressure

    b. heavy smoking

    c. diabetes

    d. both a & b

 *e. all of the above

3. Present evidence indicates that the most serious side effect of the pill is:

    a. cancer

 *b. blood clotting problems

    c. chloasma

    d. nausea

    e. creating permanent sterility

4. Which of the following group of women has the highest risk of side effects if they use the pill?

    a. women who have never had children

 *b. women over 40 who smoke

    c. women who have severe menstrual cramps and are 10–20 lbs. overweight

    d. women who have been on the pill for more than 5 years.

This completes the survey. Thank You!

Answer these questions *only* if you have decided on the *diaphragm* as your primary method of birth control.

1. After intercourse, a diaphragm:

    a. should be removed immediately to prevent infection

    b. can be taken out after 2 hours

 *c. must be left in place for at least 8 hours

    d. must be left in place for at least 12 hours

2. A problem that may result from using a diaphragm is:

    a. increased pelvic infection

    b. increased cervical infection

*c. increased urinary tract infection
d. all of the above
e. none of the above
3. When a diaphragm is properly in place:
*a. the woman *will not* be able to feel it
b. the woman *will* be able to feel it
c. both partners will be able to feel it
d. both b & c
4. A diaphragm must be fitted by a health professional because:
a. the risk of complication is high
*b. it must fit properly over the cervix
c. it is a difficult and risky medical procedure
d. all of the above
e. both a and b

This completes the survey. Thank You!

Answer these questions *only* if you have decided on the *foam* and/or *condoms* as your primary method of birth control.

1. The actual user effectiveness rate of foam and condoms is equal to or better than the actual user rates of:
a. an IUD
b. a diaphragm
c. the pill
*d. all of the above
e. none of the above
2. To use a condom correctly, a person must:
a. leave some space at the tip for the sperm
b. use one every time sexual intercourse occurs
c. hold it on the penis while withdrawing from the vagina
*d. all of the above
3. When having sexual intercourse, the use of both contraceptive foam and condoms is recommended because:
a. the man and the woman are sharing the responsibility for avoiding pregnancy
b. the woman is less likely to become pregnant than if only one of these is used
c. they can both be purchased at the drug store without prescriptions
*d. all of the above
e. a and c
4. Contraceptive (birth control) foam is most effective for the repeated acts of sexual intercourse:
a. if a single application is used
*b. if an additional application is used before each act of sexual intercourse
c. if a woman douches after each act of intercourse
d. all of the above
e. b and c

This completes the survey. Thank You!

Contraceptive Self-Efficacy Scale

RUTH ANDREA LEVINSON,[1] *Skidmore College*

The Contraceptive Self-Efficacy (CSE) scale assesses motivational barriers to contraceptive use among sexually active teenage women. The self-efficacy construct has been used by Bandura and his associates to understand motivations for apparently dysfunctional or avoidance behavior (Bandura, 1990; Bandura, Adams, Hardy, & Howells, 1980; Kazdin, 1974; McAlister, Perry, & Maccoby, 1979; Rosenthal & Bandura, 1978; Strecher, DeVellis, Becker, & Rosenstock, 1986). The nonuse of contraceptives by sexually active teenage women who say that they do not desire a pregnancy is similar to other types of phobic behaviors. Thus, teenage women's contraceptive behavior is treated as a special behavioral domain for application of the construct.

According to the self-efficacy construct, a person's expectations about whether she should and can execute a component behavior will determine initiation and persistence in achieving a desired goal (Bandura, 1977; Fishbein & Ajzen, 1975). The CSE scale measures the strength of a sexually active teenage woman's conviction that she should and can control sexual and contraceptive situations in order to make contraceptive protection a priority. Stressors are embedded within items to ascertain individual differences among young women who may have different issues that inhibit feelings of self-efficacy. The scale was designed to be used both diagnostically, by educators and clinicians as a tool for designing and assessing interventions, and as a research instrument.

Description

CSE statements evaluate the respondent's perceptions of her ability to take responsibility for sexual and contraceptive behaviors across a variety of situations. CSE is assessed using 18 items, which respondents rate on a 5-point Likert-type scale ranging from (1) *Not at all True of Me* to (5) *Completely True of Me*. The scale has been significantly and independently correlated with contraceptive use among diverse samples of young girls and women ranging in age from 13 to 45 years old, and including inner-city African American youth, predominantly White French Canadian youth, Brazilian youth, Hong Kong Chinese women, and suburban European American and Latina American youth. Research settings have included family planning clinics, high school and college classrooms, hospitals, and institutionalized youth. The results, spanning a 25-year period, indicate that a variety of methods for assessing CSE (e.g., either the sum or the average of the 18-item CSE scale, a four-factor solution, or a LISREL solution) have been predictive of contraceptive behavior among all groups of women (Bilodeau,

Forget, & Tétreault, 1994; Heinrich, 1993; Hovsepian, Blais, Manseau, Otis, & Girard, in press; Levinson, 1986, 1995; Levinson, Beamer, & Wan, 1998; Louise, 2005; Nordeen, Mann, & Sullivan, 2005; Wright, 1992).

To determine the best measure of the CSE scale, we explored the scale's relationship to contraceptive behavior with four diverse samples (for a description of the samples, see Levinson et al., 1998). A series of correlational analyses were conducted with each sample to examine scale properties. A pattern of low correlations among CSE items emerged (averaging near .15 with a small standard deviation), indicating that use of the total item set separately as the basis for CSE was warranted. Zero-order and partial correlations revealed which CSE items were correlated with contraceptive behavior, as well as which items explained unique variance in contraceptive behavior for each sample. This analytic strategy was used owing to the fact that the dependent measure assessing contraceptive behavior was on a different metric in each sample.

These results suggest that diverse groups of women and girls have different issues that inhibit their ability to use contraceptives effectively or to postpone unprotected sexual activity. It is recommended that the CSE scale be used prior to interventions in order to appropriately align interventions to the particular needs of the participants as assessed by the individual items and by the four factors. Another finding of the 1998 study was that Item 8 was consistently predictive of contraceptive behavior across three of the four samples. The predictive power of this one item suggests that the "discourse of desire" (Fine, 1988) is a very important aspect to be explored in sexuality education for the development of healthy sexual behaviors and skills (Levinson et al., 1998). Other items that were uniquely related to contraceptive behavior were those items assessing confidence in the ability to confront oneself or significant others (e.g., parents, partner, pharmacist) about issues related to sexual needs (e.g., Items 2, 3, 6, 10, 11, 12, 13c, 14). These findings dovetail with earlier research outcomes and have been largely confirmed by subsequent researchers (Nordeen et al., 2005; Hovsepian et al., in press; Louise, 2005), highlighting persistent issues that impact young women's contraceptive behavior. Educational implications for different samples have been discussed in the research cited above.

Response Mode and Timing

Respondents circle the number indicating how true or not true that statement is for them. The CSE scale requires approximately 10 minutes to complete.

[1]Address correspondence to Ruth Andrea Levinson, 1511 Peaceable Street, Ballston Spa, NY 12020; e-mail: rlevinso@skidmore.edu

Scoring

The scale is scored such that higher scores represent higher CSE. The scoring direction requires that Items 2, 5, 6, 8, 9, 11, 12, 14, and 15 be reverse scored.

Reliability

Reliability estimated across research investigations has yielded a Cronbach's alpha of .73 or higher.

Validity

In the initial phases of instrument construction, CSE items were scrutinized for face and content validity. The validity of the instrument was inspected according to two major criteria: (a) Did the items simulate the events that were both common and critical to teenage women's successful use of contraceptives, and (b) were the content and response formats of each item conducive to collecting information on expected behavior in a manner that corresponds to self-efficacy assessments of that behavior? The appearance and content of the original CSE instrument were changed several times based on information derived from pretesting the instrument within different populations and from personal communication with Bandura and associates, experts in self-efficacy assessment (Bandura, 1977; Bandura et al., 1980). Additional methods of testing validity have been used when translating the scale into languages other than English (Bilodeau et al., 1994; Louise, 2005).

In current research with the CSE scale, items pertaining to obsolete or infrequently used methods of birth control are deleted from the content of the scale items as presented here (e.g., the sponge, Encare Ovals). We are exploring adding to the scale items content that pertains to more accessible methods of birth control (e.g., the condom, Norplant, Depo-Provera, the hormonal patch, and emergency contraception). The impact of drug use on CSE and contraceptive behavior is under investigation. In addition, a gender-neutral CSE scale and a male version of the CSE scale have been used to explore contraceptive and sexual behavior in young men. Basically, the gender-neutral scale replaces the word "boyfriend" with "partner" and the male pronoun "him" is replaced with "him/her."

Other Information

The instrument is copyrighted by the author and is reproduced here with permission. It can be used for research, clinical, or educational purposes by obtaining permission from the author.

References

Bandura, A. (1977). Self-efficacy: Toward a unifying theory of behavioral change. *Psychological Review, 84,* 191–215.

Bandura, A. (1990). Perceived self-efficacy in the exercise of control over AIDS infection. *Evaluation and Program Planning, 13,* 9–17.

Bandura, A., Adams, N. E., Hardy, A. B., & Howells, G. N. (1980). Tests of the generality of self-efficacy theory. *Cognitive Therapy and Research, 4,* 39–66.

Bilodeau, A., Forget, G., & Tétreault, J. (1994). L'auto-efficacité relative à la contraception chez les adolescentes et les adolescents: La validation de la version française de l'échelle de mesure de Levinson. *Canadian Journal of Public Health, 85,* 115–120.

Fine, M. (1988). Sexuality, schooling, and adolescent females: The missing discourse of desire. *Harvard Educational Review, 58*(1), 29–53.

Fishbein, M., & Ajzen, I. (1975). *Belief, attitude, intention, and behavior.* Reading, MA: Addison-Wesley.

Heinrich, L. B. (1993). Contraceptive self-efficacy in college women. *Journal of Adolescent Health, 14,* 269–276.

Hovsepian, S. L., Blais, M., Manseau, H., Otis, J., & Girard, M.-E. (in press). Prior victimization and sexual and contraceptive self-efficacy among adolescent females under child protective services care. *Health Education and Behavior.*

Kazdin, A. E. (1974). Effects of covert modeling and reinforcement on assertive behavior. *Journal of Abnormal Psychology, 83,* 240–252.

Levinson, R. A. (1986). Contraceptive self-efficacy: A perspective on teenage girls' contraceptive behavior. *The Journal of Sex Research, 22,* 247–369.

Levinson. R. A. (1995). Reproductive and contraceptive knowledge, contraceptive self-efficacy, and contraceptive behavior among teenage women. *Adolescence, 30,* 65–85.

Levinson, R. A., Beamer, L. A., & Wan, C. K. (1998). The contraceptive self-efficacy scale: Analysis in four samples. *Journal of Youth and Adolescence, 27,* 773–793.

Louise, L. Y. S. (2005). *Knowledge, attitudes, and self-efficacy of contraception among Chinese women with unplanned pregnancies in Hong Kong.* Unpublished master's thesis, The Nethersole School of Nursing, The Chinese University of Hong Kong.

McAlister, A., Perry, C. L., & Maccoby, N. (1979). Adolescent smoking: Onset and prevention. *Pediatrics, 67,* 650–688.

Nordeen, J. L., Mann, R. J., & Sullivan, J. M. (2005). *Analysis of contraceptive self-efficacy in clients requesting emergency contraception.* Unpublished manuscript.

Rosenthal, T. L., & Bandura, A. (1978). Psychological modeling: Theory and practice. In S. L. Garfield & A. E. Bergin (Eds.), *Handbook of psychotherapy and behavior change: An empirical analysis* (pp. 621–658). New York: Wiley.

Strecher, V. J., DeVellis, B. M., Becker, M. H., & Rosenstock, I. M. (1986). The role of self-efficacy in achieving health behavior change. *Health Education Quarterly, 13*(1), 73–91.

Wright, C. (1992). *Factors associated with contraceptive behavior among Black college students.* Unpublished doctoral dissertation, University of Oregon.

Exhibit

Contraceptive Self-Efficacy Scale

The items on the following page are a list of statements. Please rate each item on a 1 to 5 scale according to how true the statement is of you. Using the scale, circle one number for each question:

1 = Not at all True of Me
2 = Slightly True of Me
3 = Somewhat True of Me
4 = Mostly True of Me
5 = Completely True of Me

1. 1 2 3 4 5   When I am with a boyfriend, I feel that I can always be responsible for what happens sexually with him.

2. 1 2 3 4 5   Even if a boyfriend can talk about sex, I can't tell a man how I really feel about sexual things.

3. 1 2 3 4 5   When I have sex, I can enjoy it as something that I really wanted to do.

4. 1 2 3 4 5   If my boyfriend and I are getting "turned on" sexually and I don't really want to have sexual intercourse (go all the way, get down), I can easily tell him "no" and mean it.

5. 1 2 3 4 5   If my boyfriend didn't talk about the sex that was happening between us, I couldn't either.

6. 1 2 3 4 5   When I think about what having sex means, I can't have sex so easily.

7. 1 2 3 4 5   If my boyfriend and I are getting "turned on" sexually and I don't really want to have sexual intercourse (go all the way, get down), I can easily stop things so that we don't have intercourse.

8. 1 2 3 4 5   There are times when I'd be so involved sexually or emotionally that I could have sexual intercourse even if I weren't protected (using a form of birth control).

9. 1 2 3 4 5   Sometimes I just go along with what my date wants to do sexually because I don't think I can take the hassle of trying to say what I want.

10. 1 2 3 4 5   If there were a man (boyfriend) to whom I was very attracted physically and emotionally, I could feel comfortable telling him that I wanted to have sex with him.

11. 1 2 3 4 5   I couldn't continue to use a birth control method if I thought my parents might find out.

12. 1 2 3 4 5   It would be hard for me to go to the drugstore and ask for foam (Encare Ovals, a diaphragm, a pill prescription, etc.) without feeling embarrassed.

13.   If my boyfriend and I were getting really heavily into sex and moving towards intercourse and I wasn't protected . . .

    a. 1 2 3 4 5   I could easily ask him if he had protection (or tell him that I didn't).
    b. 1 2 3 4 5   I could excuse myself to put in a diaphragm or foam (if I used them for birth control).
    c. 1 2 3 4 5   I could tell him that I was on the pill or had an IUD (if I used them for birth control).
    d. 1 2 3 4 5   I could stop things before intercourse, if I couldn't bring up the subject of protection.

14. 1 2 3 4 5   There are times when I should talk to my boyfriend about using contraceptives, but I can't seem to do it in the situation.

15. 1 2 3 4 5   Sometimes I end up having sex with a boyfriend because I can't find a way to stop it.

(Thank you very much for your time and thought. The answers you gave will help us prepare better services for others.)

Decreased Sexual Desire Screener

ANITA H. CLAYTON,[1] *University of Virginia*

EVAN R. GOLDFISCHER, *Hudson Valley Urology, Poughkeepsie, NY*

IRWIN GOLDSTEIN, *Alvarado Hospital, San Diego*

LEONARD R. DEROGATIS, *Center for Sexual Medicine at Sheppard Pratt, Baltimore*

DIANE J. LEWIS-D'AGOSTINO AND ROBERT PYKE, *Boehringer Ingelheim Pharmaceuticals, Inc., Ridgefield, CT*

The Decreased Sexual Desire Screener (DSDS) is a brief diagnostic instrument to assist in making the diagnosis of generalized acquired Hypoactive Sexual Desire Disorder (HSDD) in pre-, peri- and postmenopausal women. The DSDS has been validated for use by clinicians who are neither trained nor specialized in the diagnosis of Female Sexual Dysfunction (FSD).

Description

The DSDS consists of four Yes or No questions ("In the past, was your level of sexual desire or interest good and satisfying to you?" "Has there been a decrease in your level of sexual desire or interest?" "Are you bothered by your decreased level of sexual desire or interest?" "Would you like your level of sexual desire or interest to increase?") and a fifth, seven-part question covering factors relevant to the differential diagnosis of HSDD.

The DSDS was developed specifically to assist clinicians in identifying generalized acquired HSDD and not to diagnose or exclude other female sexual disorders (e.g., Female Sexual Arousal Disorder [FSAD] or Female Orgasmic Disorder [FOD]), although these may be concurrent with HSDD.

The validity of the DSDS was demonstrated in a nontreatment study (Clayton et al., 2009) and during the screening period of two Phase III trials of flibanserin (a 5-HT_{1A} agonist/5-HT_{2A} antagonist currently in development as a potential treatment for generalized acquired HSDD; Goldfischer, Clayton, Goldstein, Lewis-D'Agostino, & Pyke, 2008; Nappi, Dean, Hebert, & Pyke, 2008). The understandability of the DSDS to women and the adequacy of the items for diagnosis by clinicians who were neither trained nor specialized in the diagnosis of FSD were also evaluated in the nontreatment study (Clayton et al., 2009).

Response Mode and Timing

Patients are to answer the first four Yes or No questions relating to whether their sexual desire has decreased and whether this bothers them, and then check all the factors in Question 5 that they feel may be contributing to the decrease in sexual desire or interest that they are currently experiencing. Subsequently, their responses are reviewed with them, and adjusted if needed, by a clinician, who decides whether a diagnosis of generalized acquired HSDD according to the *DSM-IV-TR* criteria (American Psychiatric Association, 2000) is warranted.

Scoring

If the patient answers No to any of the questions 1 through 4, then she does not qualify for a diagnosis of generalized acquired HSDD. If a patient answers Yes to all of the questions 1 through 4 and No to all of the factors in Question 5 after clinician review, she would meet the criteria for a diagnosis of generalized acquired HSDD. If the patient answers Yes to all of the questions 1 through 4 and Yes to any of the factors in Question 5, then the clinician would decide whether a primary diagnosis other than generalized acquired HSDD is more appropriate. Comorbid conditions such as FSAD or FOD do not rule out a concurrent diagnosis of HSDD.

Validity

The validity of the DSDS was established in a nontreatment validation study (Clayton et al., 2009) and during the screening period of a Phase III randomized withdrawal trial of flibanserin known as the Researching Outcomes on Sustained Efficacy (ROSE) study (Goldfischer et al., 2008).

The nontreatment study included 263 pre-, peri- and postmenopausal women aged 18 to 50 years with and without FSD (141 subjects had a primary diagnosis of HSDD, 47 subjects had a primary diagnosis of another FSD [i.e., not HSDD], 75 subjects had no FSD). A total of 921 premenopausal women aged ≥18 years with decreased sexual desire were screened for enrollment into the ROSE study. Both studies were conducted in North America. Participants in both studies were required to be in a stable, communicative, monogamous heterosexual relationship with a sexually functional partner for at least 1 year. Participants were

[1]Address correspondence to Anita Clayton, University of Virginia Health System, Department of Psychiatric Medicine, 2955 Ivy Road, Northridge Suite 210, Charlottesville, VA 22903; e-mail: ahc8v@virginia.edu

excluded if they had any clinically significant condition or had used any medication that was likely to affect their sexual function within the previous 4 weeks.

Participants completed the DSDS at screening and their responses were reviewed with a clinician who was neither trained nor specialized in FSD (nonexpert clinician), who decided whether a diagnosis of generalized acquired HSDD was warranted. A clinician who was an expert in FSD then independently conducted an extensive diagnostic interview to diagnose sexual disorders. The diagnoses obtained using the two methods (generalized acquired HSDD or not) were compared. In the nontreatment study, the sensitivity and specificity of the DSDS were .836 and .878, respectively. In the ROSE study, the sensitivity of the DSDS was .946; specificity was not calculated, as this was a clinical population of women with complaints of low sexual desire.

Feedback on the use of the DSDS from a debriefing exercise involving a subset of 89 women in the nontreatment study showed that 85.4% of participants were able to understand all five questions. Further, nonexpert clinicians who were debriefed on how useful the DSDS was after 253 of the 263 interviews indicated that they could use the tool to reliably rule in or out HSDD in 93% of cases.

The validity of the DSDS was established in a sample of 513 premenopausal European women aged ≥18 years with decreased sexual desire who were screened for enrollment into the eurOpean ResearCH In Decreased sexual desire (ORCHID) trial, a Phase III trial of flibanserin in premenopausal women with HSDD (Nappi et al., 2008). Using the same methodology as described above (with patients completing the DSDS in their own language), the sensitivity of the DSDS in this sample was .956.

Other Information

Copyright © Boehringer Ingelheim International GmbH 2005. All rights reserved. Any use or reproduction of this questionnaire by a commercial organization without written authorization is prohibited.

References

American Psychiatric Association. (2000). *Diagnostic and statistical manual of mental disorders* (4th ed., text rev.). Washington, DC: Author.

Clayton, A. H., Goldfischer, E. R., Goldstein, I., Derogatis, L., Lewis-D'Agostino, D. J., & Pyke, R. (2009) Validation of the Decreased Sexual Desire Screener (DSDS): A brief diagnostic instrument for generalized acquired female Hypoactive Sexual Desire Disorder (HSDD). *Journal of Sexual Medicine, 6,* 730–738.

Goldfischer, E. R., Clayton, A. H., Goldstein, I., Lewis-D'Agostino, D. J., & Pyke, R. (2008). Decreased Sexual Desire Screener© (DSDS©) for diagnosis of Hypoactive Sexual Desire Disorder in women. *Obstetrics and Gynecology, 111,* 109S.

Nappi, R., Dean, J., Hebert, A., & Pyke, R. (2008, December). *Decreased Sexual Desire Screener (DSDS) for diagnosis of Hypoactive Sexual Desire Disorder (HSDD) in European women.* Poster presented at the Joint Congress of the European and International Societies for Sexual Medicine, Brussels, Belgium.

Exhibit

Decreased Sexual Desire Screener ©

Please answer the following questions:

Name: Age: Date: /   /

		NO	YES
1.	In the past, was your level of sexual desire or interest good and satisfying to you?	☐	☐
2.	Has there been a decrease in your level of sexual desire or interest?	☐	☐
3.	Are you bothered by your decreased level of sexual desire or interest?	☐	☐
4.	Would you like your level of sexual desire or interest to increase?	☐	☐

5. Please check all the factors that you feel may be contributing to your current decrease in sexual desire or interest:

		NO	YES
A.	An operation, depression, injuries, or other medical condition	☐	☐
B.	Medications, drugs or alcohol you are currently taking	☐	☐
C.	Pregnancy, recent childbirth, menopausal symptoms	☐	☐
D.	Other sexual issues you may be having (pain, decreased arousal or orgasm)	☐	☐
E.	Your partner's sexual problems	☐	☐
F.	Dissatisfaction with your relationship or partner	☐	☐
G.	Stress or fatigue	☐	☐

Goldfischer ER, Clayton AH, Goldstein I, Lewis-D'Agostino DJ, Pyke R. Decreased Sexual Desire Screener© (DSDS©) for diagnosis of Hypoactive Sexual Desire Disorder in women. Poster presented at the ACOG annual meeting, 3–7 May 2008, New Orleans, USA.

Brief Diagnostic Assessment for Generalized Acquired Hypoactive Sexual Desire Disorder (HSDD)

Clinician:

Verify with the patient each of the answers she has given.

The Diagnostic and Statistical Manual of Mental Disorders, 4th Edition, Text Revision® characterizes Hypoactive Sexual Desire Disorder (HSDD) as a deficiency or absence of sexual fantasies and desire for sexual activity, which causes marked distress or interpersonal difficulty, and which is not better accounted for by a medical, substance-related, psychiatric, or other sexual condition. HSDD can be either generalized (not limited to certain types of stimulation, situations, or partners) or situational, and can be either acquired (develops only after a period of normal functioning) or lifelong. To determine if symptoms are acquired, ask if there was a period of normal functioning at any time in the past.

If the patient answers "NO" to any of the questions 1 through 4, then she does not qualify for the diagnosis of generalized, acquired HSDD.

If the patient answers "YES" to all of the questions 1 through 4, and your review confirms "NO" answers to all of the factors in question 5, then she does qualify for the diagnosis of generalized, acquired HSDD.

If the patient answers "YES" to all of the questions 1 through 4 and "YES" to any of the factors in question 5, then decide if the answers to question 5 indicate a primary diagnosis other than generalized, acquired HSDD. Co-morbid conditions such as arousal or orgasmic disorder do not rule out a concurrent diagnosis of HSDD.

Based on the above, does the patient have generalized acquired Hypoactive Sexual Desire Disorder? YES ☐ NO ☐

Thank you.

Goldfischer ER, Clayton AH, Goldstein I, Lewis-D'Agostino DJ, Pyke R. Decreased Sexual Desire Screener© (DSDS©) for diagnosis of Hypoactive Sexual Desire Disorder in women. Poster presented at the ACOG annual meeting, 3–7 May 2008, New Orleans, USA.

Hurlbert Index of Sexual Desire

DAVID F. HURLBERT,[1] *U.S. Department of Health and Human Services*

The Hurlbert Index of Sexual Desire (HISD) is described by Apt and Hurlbert (1992).

Reference

Apt, C. & Hurlbert, D. F. (1992). Motherhood and female sexuality beyond one year postpartum: A study of military wives. *Journal of Sex Education and Therapy, 18,* 104–114.

[1]Address correspondence to David F. Hurlbert, 140 Farnworth Lane, Roswell, Georgia 30075; e-mail: david.hurlbert@acf.hhs.gov

Exhibit

Hurlbert Index of Sexual Desire

1. Just thinking about having sex with my partner excites me. (R)
2. I try to avoid situations that will encourage my partner to want sex.
3. I daydream about sex. (R)
4. It is difficult for me to get in a sexual mood.
5. I desire more sex than my partner does. (R)
6. It is hard for me to fantasize about sexual things.
7. I look forward to having sex with my partner. (R)
8. I have a huge appetite for sex. (R)
9. I enjoy using sexual fantasy during sex with my partner. (R)
10. It is easy for me to get in the mood for sex. (R)
11. My desire for sex should be stronger.
12. I enjoy thinking about sex. (R)
13. I desire sex. (R)
14. It is easy for me to go weeks without having sex with my partner.
15. My motivation to engage in sex with my partner is low.
16. I feel I want sex less than most people.
17. It is easy for me to create sexual fantasies in my mind. (R)
18. I have a strong sex drive. (R)
19. I enjoy thinking about having sex with my partner. (R)
20. My desire for sex with my partner is strong. (R)
21. I feel that sex is not an important aspect of the relationship I share with my partner.
22. I think my energy level for sex with my partner is too low.
23. It is hard for me to get in the mood for sex.
24. I lack the desire necessary to pursue sex with my partner.
25. I try to avoid having sex with my partner.

Note. (R) = reverse scored items. Scoring system responses: 0 points = *all of the time*, +1 point = *most of the time*, +2 points = *some of the time*, +3 points = *rarely*, +4 points = *never*.

Sexual Desire Inventory

ILANA P. SPECTOR,[1] *SMBD Jewish General Hospital*
MICHAEL P. CAREY, *Syracuse University*
LYNNE STEINBERG, *Oklahoma State University*

The Sexual Desire Inventory (SDI) is a self-administered questionnaire developed to measure sexual desire. To date, sexologists have had difficulty measuring this construct. Previous measurement of sexual desire involved either indirect measurement through examining frequency of sexual behavior, or by broad self-report of cognitions such as "rate your level of sexual desire." Both these methods are less accurate measures of sexual desire because first, sexual desire is theoretically a multidimensional construct, and second, no empirical data are available to suggest that sexual desire and behavior are perfectly correlated. For the purposes of this questionnaire, sexual desire was defined as interest in sexual activity, and it was measured as primarily a cognitive variable through amount and strength of thought directed toward approaching or being receptive to sexual stimuli.

[1]Address correspondence to Ilana P. Spector, Behavioral Psychotherapy and Research Unit, Department of Psychiatry, SMBD Jewish General Hospital, 4333 Cote St. Catherine Road, Montreal, Quebec, Canada, H3T 1E4; e-mail: ilana.spector@mcgill.ca

Description

The items of the SDI were selected by considering theoretical models of desire and clinical experience in assessing sexual desire disorders. They were presented initially to sexologists and then to a small pilot sample ($N = 20$ students) who rated the clarity and content validity of the items. Next, a sample of 300 students completed the SDI. Based on factor analytic data, items were eliminated or reworded to measure two dimensions of sexual desire: dyadic sexual desire (interest in behaving sexually with a partner) and solitary sexual desire (interest in behaving sexually by oneself).

To date, the 11-item SDI has been administered to three samples for the purpose of collecting psychometric data. These samples include 380 students (Spector, Carey, & Steinberg, 1996), 40 subjects living in geriatric long-term care facilities (Spector & Fremeth, 1996), and 40 couples (Spector & Davies, 1995). The SDI can be used to measure sexual desire in both the general population or in clinical samples. It has been used to measure sexual desire with both younger (M age $= 20.8$) and older (M age $= 82.5$) samples, and individuals and couples.

Response Mode and Timing

For each item, respondents are asked to circle the number that best reflects their thoughts and feelings about their interest in or wish for sexual activity. They are asked to use the last month as a referent. For the three frequency items (Items 1, 2, 10), respondents circle one of seven options. For the remaining eight strength items, respondents rate their level of sexual desire on an 8-point Likert-type scale. Most respondents complete the scale within 5 minutes.

Scoring

Items 1–8 are summed to obtain a Dyadic Sexual Desire score. Items 9–11 are summed to obtain a Solitary Sexual Desire score. Within a couple, female dyadic scores can be subtracted from male dyadic scores to obtain a desire discrepancy score.

Reliability

Internal consistency estimates (using Cronbach's alpha coefficients) were calculated for the Dyadic scale ($r = .86$) and the Solitary scale ($r = .96$), indicating strong evidence of reliability (Spector et al., 1996). Test-retest reliability was calculated at $r = .76$ over a 1-month period (Carey, 1995).

Validity

Evidence for factor validity has been examined. Factor analyses revealed that Items 1–8 loaded high (i.e., $> .45$) on the dyadic factor, whereas Items 9–11 loaded high on the solitary factor. Both factors had eigenvalues > 1 (Spector et al., 1996).

Concurrent validity evidence, collected from 380 students, revealed that solitary sexual desire is correlated with the frequency of solitary sexual behavior ($r = .80$, $p < .0001$), and with erotophilia ($r = -.28$, $p < .0001$; Spector, 1992). Dyadic desire is correlated with the frequency of dyadic sexual behavior ($r = .34$, $p < .0001$). Note that neither dyadic nor solitary desire is perfectly correlated with sexual behavior, indicating that measuring desire indirectly through behavior would be inaccurate. Discriminant validity evidence reveals that neither subscale of the SDI is correlated with social desirability (Spector, 1992).

A second study conducted on 40 couples revealed that, for females, dyadic desire is positively correlated with relationship adjustment as measured by the Dyadic Adjustment Scale (Spanier, 1976; $r = .54$, $p < .001$), with sexual satisfaction as measured by the Index of Sexual Satisfaction (Hudson, Harrison, & Crosscup, 1981; $r = .63$, $p < .001$), with sexual daydreams as measured by the Sexual Daydreams Scale (Giambra, 1980; $r = .53$, $p < .001$), and with sexual arousal as measured by the Sexual Arousal Inventory (Hoon, Hoon, & Wincze, 1976; $r = .71$, $p < .001$). With males, dyadic sexual desire is only correlated with sexual satisfaction ($r = .36$, $p < .01$; Spector & Davies, 1995).

Gender differences have been noted on the SDI. Males have significantly higher levels of dyadic, $F(1, 374) = 5.79$, $p < .05$, and solitary, $F(1, 376) = 55.15$, $p < .0001$, desire than do females. This difference is also found in geriatric samples (Spector & Fremeth, 1996).

References

Carey, M. P. (1995). [Test-retest reliability of the Sexual Desire Inventory.] Unpublished raw data.

Giambra, L. M. (1980). A factor analysis of the items of the Imaginal Processes Inventory. *Journal of Clinical Psychology, 36*, 383–409.

Hoon, E. F., Hoon, P. W., & Wincze, J. P. (1976). The SAI: An inventory for the measurement of female sexual arousability. *Archives of Sexual Behavior, 5*, 291–300.

Hudson, W. W., Harrison, D. F., & Crosscup, P. C. (1981). A short-form scale to measure sexual discord in dyadic relationships. *The Journal of Sex Research, 17*, 157–174.

Spanier, G. B. (1976). Measuring dyadic adjustment: New scales for assessing the quality of marriage and similar dyads. *Journal of Marriage and the Family, 38*, 15–28.

Spector, I. P. (1992). *Development and psychometric evaluation of a measure of sexual desire.* Unpublished doctoral dissertation, Syracuse University, New York.

Spector, I. P., Carey, M. P., & Steinberg, L. (1996). The Sexual Desire Inventory: Development, factor structure, and evidence of reliability. *Journal of Sex & Marital Therapy, 22, 175–190.*

Spector, I. P., & Davies, S. (1995). *The experience of sexual desire in couples.* Unpublished manuscript.

Spector, I. P., & Fremeth, S. M. (1996). Sexual behaviours and attitudes of geriatric residents in long-term care facilities. *Journal of Sex & Marital Therapy, 22,* 235–246.

Exhibit

Sexual Desire Inventory

This questionnaire asks about your level of sexual desire. By desire, we mean *interest in* or *wish for sexual activity*. For each item, please circle the number that best shows your thoughts and feelings. Your answers will be private and anonymous.

1. During the last month, *how often* would you *have liked* to engage in sexual activity with a partner (for example, touching each other's genitals, giving or receiving oral stimulation, intercourse, etc.)?

    0) Not at all
    1) Once a month
    2) Once every two weeks
    3) Once a week

    4) Twice a week
    5) 3 to 4 times a week
    6) Once a day
    7) More than once a day

2. During the last month, *how often* have you had sexual thoughts involving a partner?

    0) Not at all
    1) Once or twice a month
    2) Once a week
    3) Twice a week

    4) 3 to 4 times a week
    5) Once a day
    6) A couple of times a day
    7) Many times a day

3. When you have sexual thoughts, *how strong* is your desire to engage in sexual behavior with a partner?

0	1	2	3	4	5	6	7	8

    No desire   Strong desire

4. When you first see an attractive person, *how strong* is your sexual desire?

0	1	2	3	4	5	6	7	8

    No desire   Strong desire

5. When you spend time with an attractive person (for example, at work or school), *how strong* is your sexual desire?

0	1	2	3	4	5	6	7	8

    No desire   Strong desire

6. When you are in romantic situations (such as a candle-lit dinner, a walk on the beach, etc.), *how strong* is your sexual desire?

0	1	2	3	4	5	6	7	8

    No desire   Strong desire

7. *How strong* is your desire to engage in sexual activity with a partner?

0	1	2	3	4	5	6	7	8

    No desire   Strong desire

8. *How important* is it for you to fulfill your sexual desire through activity with a partner?

0	1	2	3	4	5	6	7	8

    Not at all   Extremely
    important   important

9. Compared to other people of your age and sex, how would you rate your desire to behave sexually with a partner?

0	1	2	3	4	5	6	7	8

    Much less   Much more
    desire   desire

10. During the last month, *how often* would you *have liked* to behave sexually by yourself (for example, masturbating, touching your genitals etc.)?

    0) Not at all
    1) Once a month
    2) Once every two weeks
    3) Once a week

    4) Twice a week
    5) 3 to 4 times a week
    6) Once a day
    7) More than once a day

11. *How strong* is your desire to engage in sexual behavior by yourself?

0	1	2	3	4	5	6	7	8
No desire								Strong desire

12. *How important* is it for you to fulfill your desires to behave sexually by yourself?

0	1	2	3	4	5	6	7	8
Not at all important								Extremely important

13. Compared to other people of your age and sex, how would you rate your desire to behave sexually by yourself?

0	1	2	3	4	5	6	7	8
Much less desire								Much more desire

14. *How long* could you go comfortably without having sexual activity of some kind?

0) Forever
1) A year or two
2) Several months
3) A month
4) A few weeks

5) A week
6) A few days
7) One day
8) Less than one day

Double Standard Scale

SANDRA L. CARON,[1] *University of Maine*
CLIVE M. DAVIS, *Syracuse University*
WILLIAM A. HALTEMAN AND MARLA STICKLE, *University of Maine*

The purpose of the Double Standard Scale is to measure acceptance of the traditional sexual double standard.

Description

The Double Standard Scale consists of 10 items arranged in a 5-point Likert format with response options labeled from (1) *Strongly Agree* to (5) *Strongly Disagree*.

Response Mode and Timing

Respondents circle the number from 1 to 5 corresponding to their answer. The scale requires an average of 5 minutes for completion.

Scoring

A total score for the instrument is obtained by summing each of the item scores, including reversing the negative item (Item 8). Scores can range from 10 to 50 points. A lower score indicates a greater adherence to the traditional double standard.

Reliability

In a sample of 330 college men and women (Caron, Davis, Halteman, & Stickle, 1993), the Cronbach alpha for the summed scores from the 10 items was 72.

Validity

In addition to the face validity of the questions, Caron et al. (1993) obtained results consistent with expectations about how those men and women who held a double standard would behave regarding some aspects of condom use.

Reference

Caron, S. L., Davis, C. M., Halteman, W. A., & Stickle, M. (1993). Predictors of condom related behaviors among first-year college students. *The Journal of Sex Research, 30,* 252–259.

[1]Address correspondence to Sandra L. Caron, Human Development, University of Maine, 5749 Merrill Hall, Orono, ME 04469; e-mail: sandy.caron@umit.maine

Exhibit

Double Standard Scale

Instructions: Please circle your response to the following questions regarding your attitudes about the sex roles of men and women. Please keep in mind that there are no right or wrong answers. Please answer honestly.

1 = Strongly Agree
2 = Agree
3 = Undecided
4 = Disagree
5 = Strongly Disagree

1 2 3 4 5   1.   It is expected that a woman be less sexually experienced than her partner.
1 2 3 4 5   2.   A woman who is sexually active is less likely to be considered a desirable partner.
1 2 3 4 5   3.   A woman should never appear to be prepared for a sexual encounter.
1 2 3 4 5   4.   It is important that the men be sexually experienced so as to teach the women.
1 2 3 4 5   5.   A "good" woman would never have a one-night stand, but it is expected of a man.
1 2 3 4 5   6.   It is important for a man to have multiple sexual experiences in order to gain experience.
1 2 3 4 5   7.   In sex the man should take the dominant role and the woman should assume the passive role.
1 2 3 4 5   8.   It is acceptable for a woman to carry condoms.
1 2 3 4 5   9.   It is worse for a woman to sleep around than it is for a man.
1 2 3 4 5   10.   It is up to the man to initiate sex.

Indicators of a Double Standard and Generational Difference in Sexual Attitudes

Ilsa L. Lottes,[1] *University of Maryland, Baltimore County*
Martin S. Weinberg, *Indiana University*

Description

The Indicators of a Double Standard and Generational Difference in Sexual Attitudes were developed by Weinberg as part of a 1992 comparative study of sexual attitudes and behaviors of university students in the United States and Sweden. Compared to the United States, Sweden is considered a much more homogeneous society and the double standard of sexuality is also thought to be less evident in Sweden (see Reiss, 1980; Weinberg, Lottes, & Shaver, 1995). Thus, the Indicators were used to test these expectations. In general, the Indicators can be used to assess the perceived heterogeneity of sexual attitudes of a population by generation and gender or to compare two or more populations with respect to such generational and gender differences.

The Indicators of sexual attitudes consist of six 5-point Likert-type items. For each item, respondents compare their sexual attitudes to those of their mother, father, close female friends, close male friends, female students their own age, and male students their own age. The response options for each item are that the specified individual(s) is (are) *much more liberal* (1), *slightly more liberal* (2), *the same* (3), *slightly more conservative* (4), or *much more conservative* (5). Because the evaluation of parent and peer sexual attitudes is provided by respondents, not respondents' parents and peers, this instrument should be regarded as providing indirect measures of a lack of homogeneity—a perception of a double standard and/or a generational difference in sexual attitudes. When evaluating a double standard of sexual behavior, researchers often ask the same respondents identical questions about

[1]Address correspondence to Ilsa L. Lottes, Department of Sociology and Anthropology, University of Maryland, Baltimore County, 5401 Wilkens Avenue, Baltimore, MD 21228; e-mail: lottes@umbc.edu

acceptable sexual behavior for women and men. These types of questions make it obvious to respondents that female/male comparisons may be made, and respondents influenced by "social desirability" and "political correctness" pressures may be careful to put the same response to corresponding pairs of female/male questions. We believe that the wording of items of the Indicators make such a social desirability bias less likely because it is less obvious that comparisons to assess a double standard will be made. The Indicators of sexual attitudes would be appropriate to administer to high school or university students.

Response Mode and Timing

Respondents circle the number from (1) to (5) corresponding to their rating of the similarity of their sexual attitudes to those of their parent or peer group. This takes less than 5 minutes to complete.

Scoring

In a society characterized by the traditional double standard of sexual behavior, men are subjected to more permissive or liberal sexual norms than women. In such a society we would expect the sexual attitudes of men to be more liberal than the sexual attitudes of women. In operationalizing the double standard, we assume that if sexual attitudes of women and men are judged to be similar with respect to a liberal/conservative dimension, then this will indicate lack of support for a double standard. If the sexual attitudes of men are judged to be more liberal than women, then this will indicate a male-permissive double standard; similarly, if the attitudes of women are judged to be more liberal than men, then this will indicate a female-permissive double standard.

For ease of interpretation and also to identify the extent of more substantial or "real" generational and gender differences in sexual attitudes, responses to the six items were recoded as follows: 1 to –1, 2 to 0, 3 to 0, 4 to 0, and 5 to 1. With this coding, a minus one indicates that a respondent rated a parent or peer group to have sexual attitudes *much more liberal* than his/her own attitudes and a plus one indicates that a respondent rated a parent or peer group to have sexual attitudes *much more conservative* than his/her own attitudes. A zero indicates that a respondent rated a parent or peer group to have sexual attitudes similar to his/her own where "similar" includes the two *slightly more liberal* or *slightly more conservative* responses and *the same* response.

To assess the extent of a double standard of sexual behavior for women and men, three new variables—Dparent, Dfriend, and Dstudent—are created by taking the difference of corresponding female and male items. Using the aforementioned variable names, Dparent equals Mother–Father, Dfriend equals Ffriend–Mfriend, and Dstudent equals Fstudent–Mstudent. Shown in Table 1 are the possible numerical values of these three double standard difference variables. A value of 0 for a double

TABLE 1
Variable Values and Difference Variable Interpretation

Female variable Mother Ffriend Fstudent Values	Male variable Father Mfriend Mstudent Values	Difference variable[a] Dparent Dfriend Dstudent Values	Interpretation of difference variables
–1	1	–2	Female more liberal, female-permissive double standard
–1	0	–1	Female more liberal, female-permissive double standard
0	1	–1	Female more liberal, female-permissive double standard
–1	–1	0	Egalitarian, no double standard
0	0	0	Egalitarian, no double standard
1	1	0	Egalitarian, no double standard
0	–1	1	Male more liberal, male-permissive double standard
1	0	1	Male more liberal, male-permissive double standard
1	–1	2	Male more liberal, male-permissive double standard

[a]The difference variable equals the female variable minus the male variable.

standard difference variable indicates a similar rating of sexual attitudes for a pair of female/male variables and is interpreted as an indicator of egalitarian sexual attitudes and no double standard. A negative difference (of –1 or –2) indicates that women's sexual attitudes were rated more liberal than those of men—a female-permissive double standard. A positive difference (of 1 or 2) indicates that men's sexual attitudes were rated more liberal than those of women—an indicator of a male-permissive double standard.

Reliability

Principal components factor analyses were performed on the six items using all five of the original responses with samples of male and female university students in the United States and Sweden. Factor analyses for each of the four country/gender groups revealed two factors—a parental factor composed of the mother and father items and a peer factor composed of the four friend and student items. For samples of male university students in the United States and Sweden, Cronbach alphas for the parental factor were .60 and .80, respectively; for these samples, Cronbach alphas for the peer factor were .85 and .84, respectively. For samples of female university students in the United States and Sweden, Cronbach alphas for the parental factor were .64 and .77, respectively; for these samples, Cronbach alphas for the peer factor were both .78.

Validity

Construct validity of the Indicators of a Double Standard and Generational Difference in Sexual Attitudes was supported by significant differences in the predicted direction for groups of Swedish and American university students. Greater proportions of Swedish than American students responded in the similar category. Between 77% and 89% of Swedish students rated their parents' sexual attitudes as similar to their own compared to between 54% and 65% for American students. Thus, these findings support the view that with respect to sexual attitudes, Sweden is a more homogeneous society, characterized by less of a generational difference in such attitudes than the United States. With respect to parents' sexual attitudes, the proportion rated *much more conservative* was higher than the proportion rated *much more liberal* (especially for Americans).

Between 80% and 94% of Swedish students rated their male peers as having sexual attitudes similar to their own compared to between 55% and 79% for American students. For comparison with male peers, there were higher homogeneity ratings for Sweden than for the United States, as expected. For ratings of male peer sexual attitudes, nonsimilar responses for each country and gender tended to occur in the *much more liberal* rather than *much more conservative* category. For comparisons with female peer sexual attitudes, similar responses were high for all four country/gender groups. Thus, with respect to comparisons with female peers, the expectation regarding greater homogeneity in Sweden was only partially supported. A greater proportion of Swedish women (88%) compared to American women (78%) rated female students their own age as having sexual attitudes similar to their own. But no greater homogeneity was found in ratings of close female friends. Over 90% of all country/gender groups rated the sexual attitudes of their close female friends as similar to their own.

For the mother-father comparison, a higher proportion of American males rated their mother as having *much more conservative* sexual attitudes than their father than rated their mother as having *much more liberal* attitudes than their father (27% vs. 10%). For the double standard variables involving gender differences for friends and students, all four country/gender groups reported a higher proportion of *much more conservative* female peers than *much more liberal* female peers. However, the ratings of *much more conservative* female peers and the difference between the *much more conservative* and *much more liberal* ratings were larger for the American students than for the Swedish students. These findings support the expectation that a male-permissive double standard of sexual behavior is more prevalent in the United States. Nevertheless, about three fourths of American students and over 90% of Swedish students gave similar evaluations of the sexual attitudes of male and female peers. Thus, only a minority of respondents in both countries (less than 10% in Sweden and about 25% in the United States) indicated perception of a male-permissive double standard of sexual attitudes.

References

Reiss, I. R. (1980). Sexual customs and gender roles in Sweden and America: An analysis and interpretation. In H. Lopata, (Ed.), *Research on the interweave of social roles: Women and men* (pp. 191–220). Greenwich, CT: JAI.

Weinberg, M. S., Lottes, I. L., & Shaver, F. M. (1995). Swedish or American heterosexual college youth: Who is more permissive? *Archives of Sexual Behavior, 24,* 409–437.

Exhibit

Indicators of a Double Standard and Generational Difference in Sexual Attitudes

Directions: Circle the number that corresponds to your answer. Do you think the sexual attitudes of the following people are more liberal or conservative than your own?

Theirs are:	Much more liberal	Slightly more liberal	The same	Slightly more conservative	Much more conservative
1. Mother	1	2	3	4	5
2. Father	1	2	3	4	5
3. Close female friends	1	2	3	4	5
4. Close male friends	1	2	3	4	5
5. Female students your own age	1	2	3	4	5
6. Male students your own age	1	2	3	4	5

Sexual Double Standard Scale

CHARLENE L. MUEHLENHARD,[1] *University of Kansas*
DEBRA M. QUACKENBUSH, *The Menninger Clinic/Baylor College of Medicine*

We developed the Sexual Double Standard Scale (SDSS; Muehlenhard & Quackenbush, 1996) to measure the extent to which respondents adhere to the traditional sexual double standard (SDS). The SDS allows men more sexual freedom than women regarding premarital sex, multiple partners, and sex at a young age or in a new or uncommitted relationship (Crawford & Popp, 2003; Komarovsky, 1976; Reiss, 1960).

Description

The SDSS consists of 26 items, using a 4-point scale from *Disagree Strongly* (0) to *Agree Strongly* (3). Six individual items compare women's and men's sexual behavior in the same item (e.g., "A man should be more sexually experienced than his wife," keyed positively, or "A woman's having casual sex is just as acceptable to me as a man's having casual sex," keyed negatively). Twenty items occur in pairs, with parallel items about women's and men's sexual behavior (e.g., "A girl who has sex on the first date is 'easy,'" and "A guy who has sex on the first date is 'easy'").

Response Mode and Timing

Researchers can select a response mode to meet their needs (e.g., written questionnaire, computerized administration). Completing the scale requires about 5 minutes.

Scoring

For individual items, reverse score for negatively keyed items. For pairs of items critical of sexually active individuals, subtract male-focused items from female-focused items; for pairs of items approving of sexually active individuals, subtract female-focused items from male-focused items; these difference scores reflect discrepancies in respondents' standards for women and men. Then add the 6 individual scores and the 10 difference scores (see Exhibit). Scores can range from 48 (reflecting acceptance of greater sexual freedom for men than for women—the traditional double standard) to 0 (reflecting identical standards for men and women, whether restrictive or permissive) to −30 (reflecting acceptance of greater sexual freedom for women than for men).

Reliability

In a sample of undergraduates (Muehlenhard & Quackenbush, 1996), coefficient alpha was .73 for women

($n = 463$) and .76 for men ($n = 255$). Alphas were calculated using 16 scores for each respondent: the 6 individual item scores (after reversing negatively keyed items) and the 10 difference scores from paired items.

In a sample of 154 male and female undergraduates, Boone and Lefkowitz (2004) reported an alpha of .68. In a sample of 342 female undergraduates, Bay-Cheng and Zucker (2007) reported alphas of .78 for the 10 items about women's sexuality, .80 for the 10 items about men's sexuality, and .57 for the 6 individual items—all calculated after appropriate reverse coding.

Validity

We developed the SDSS to investigate the sexual double standard and condom use (Muehlenhard & Quackenbush, 1996). We hypothesized that, if a woman believes that her partner accepts the SDS, she might be reluctant to provide or suggest using a condom, lest she appear too eager or experienced; men, however, would not face this dilemma. We asked each respondent about condom use during her first sexual encounter with her most recent sexual partner. We also asked each respondent to complete the SDSS twice, first as she—and then as her partner—would have completed it at the time. As expected, women who had engaged in intercourse without suggesting, providing, or using a condom believed that their partners were more accepting of the SDS (i.e., that their partners had higher SDSS scores) than did women who had provided or suggested using condoms. Also as expected, this relationship did not hold for men.

Muehlenhard and McCoy (1991) investigated (a) *token refusal (TR) situations*—situations in which women engaged in "token refusals" or "token resistance" to sex, expressing unwillingness to engage in sex but actually being willing, and (b) *open acknowledgement (OA) situations*—situations in which women openly acknowledged their interest in sex. Muehlenhard and McCoy hypothesized that (a) *token refusal* would be most likely when a woman thought her partner accepted the double standard (by offering a token refusal, she could avoid her partner's negative evaluation), and (b) *open acknowledgment* would be most likely when a woman thought her partner had egalitarian sexual attitudes (allowing her to express sexual interest without fearing negative evaluation). In a sample of 403 women, anyone who had been in TR and/or OA situations completed the SDSS twice for each situation, first as she—

[1]Address correspondence to Charlene Muehlenhard, Department of Psychology, 426 Fraser Hall, University of Kansas, 1415 Jayhawk Blvd., Lawrence, KS 66045–7556; e-mail: charlene@ku.edu

and then as her partner—would have completed it at the time. As predicted, women rated their partners as having higher SDSS scores in TR situations than in OA situations. Women's own SDSS scores did not differ significantly between the two situations.

Bay-Cheng and Zucker (2007) found that self-identified feminists had significantly lower SDSS scores than those who rejected the feminist label. Gillen, Lefkowitz, and Shearer (2006) found positive correlations between SDSS scores and orientation toward physical appearance (a component of body image) among both men and women.

In a sample of intercourse-experienced undergraduates, Boone and Lefkowitz (2004) found that high SDSS scores were related to more frequent condom use. Boone and Lefkowitz speculated that higher-SDSS men would have had more sexual partners, and higher-SDSS women would expect this, so the couple would use condoms to protect the woman. This result might seem contradictory to Muehlenhard and Quackenbush's (1996) findings; however, the significant predictor in Muehlenhard and Quackenbush's study was women's perceptions of how their *partners* would have completed the SDSS, whereas Boone and Lefkowitz used *participants' own* SDSS scores. Furthermore, Muehlenhard and Quackenbush found different patterns for women and men, but Boone and Lefkowitz's analysis combined women's and men's data.

The validity of the SDSS is also supported by its correlations with other scales. Higher SDSS scores were associated with more traditional gender role attitudes (Muehlenhard & McCoy, 1991) and with more conservative sexual attitudes (Boone & Lefkowitz, 2004).

It is important not to include the scale's title on the questionnaire. Many people claim to reject the sexual double standard—even those who endorse it when asked specific questions (Komarovsky, 1976). Including the scale's title might bias respondents' answers and lower its validity.

References

Bay-Cheng, L. Y., & Zucker, A. (2007). Feminism between the sheets: Sexual attitudes among feminists, nonfeminists, and egalitarians. *Psychology of Women Quarterly, 31,* 157–163.

Boone, T. L., & Lefkowitz, E. S. (2004). Safer sex and the health belief model: Considering the contributions of peer norms and socialization factors. *Journal of Psychology and Human Sexuality, 16,* 51–68.

Crawford, M., & Popp, D. (2003). Sexual double standards: A review and methodological critique of two decades of research. *The Journal of Sex Research, 40,* 13–26.

Gillen, M. M., Lefkowitz, E. S., & Shearer, C. L. (2006). Does body image play a role in risky sexual behavior and attitudes? *Journal of Youth and Adolescence, 35,* 243–255.

Komarovsky, M. (1976). *Dilemmas of masculinity: A study of college youth.* New York: Norton.

Muehlenhard, C. L., & McCoy, M. L. (1991). Double standard/double bind: The sexual double standard and women's communication about sex. *Psychology of Women Quarterly, 15,* 447–461.

Muehlenhard, C. L., & Quackenbush, D. M. (1996). *The social meaning of women's condom use: The sexual double standard and women's beliefs about the meaning ascribed to condom use.* Unpublished manuscript.

Reiss, I. L. (1960). *Premarital sexual standards in America.* New York: Free Press.

Exhibit

Sexual Double Standard Scale[a]

Disagree Strongly	Disagree Mildly	Agree Mildly	Agree Strongly
0	1	2	3

1. It's worse for a woman to sleep around than it is for a man.
2. It's best for a guy to lose his virginity before he's out of his teens.
3. It's okay for a woman to have more than one sexual relationship at the same time.
4. It is just as important for a man to be a virgin when he marries as it is for a woman.
5. I approve of a 16-year-old girl's having sex just as much as a 16-year-old boy's having sex.
6. I kind of admire a girl who has had sex with a lot of guys.
7. I kind of feel sorry for a 21-year-old woman who is still a virgin.
8. A woman's having casual sex is just as acceptable to me as a man's having casual sex.
9. It's okay for a man to have sex with a woman he is not in love with.[b]
10. I kind of admire a guy who has had sex with a lot of girls.
11. A woman who initiates sex is too aggressive.
12. It's okay for a man to have more than one sexual relationship at the same time.
13. I question the character of a woman who has had a lot of sexual partners.
14. I admire a man who is a virgin when he gets married.
15. A man should be more sexually experienced than his wife.
16. A girl who has sex on the first date is "easy."
17. I kind of feel sorry for a 21-year-old man who is still a virgin.
18. I question the character of a man who has had a lot of sexual partners.[b]

19. Women are naturally more monogamous (inclined to stick with one partner) than are men.
20. A man should be sexually experienced when he gets married.
21. A guy who has sex on the first date is "easy."
22. It's okay for a woman to have sex with a man she is not in love with.
23. A woman should be sexually experienced when she gets married.
24. It's best for a girl to lose her virginity before she's out of her teens.
25. I admire a woman who is a virgin when she gets married.
26. A man who initiates sex is too aggressive.

Note. Scoring: Total = Item 1 + Item 15 + Item 19 + (3 − Item 4) + (3 − Item 5) + (3 − Item 8) + (Item 2 − Item 24) + (Item 12 − Item 3) + (Item 10 − Item 6) + (Item 17 − Item 7) + (Item 9 − Item 22) + (Item 11 − Item 26) + (Item 13 − Item 18) + (Item 25 − Item 14) + (Item 16 − Item 21) + (Item 20 − Item 23).

[a]Do not use the scale's title on the form completed by respondents; this might bias their responses.

[b]The wording of this item was changed slightly from the 1998 version to make it parallel to its paired item.

Sexual Interest and Desire Inventory—Female

Anita H. Clayton,[1] *University of Virginia*
David Goldmeier, *St Mary's Hospital, London*
Rossella E. Nappi, *University of Pavia, Italy*
Glen Wunderlich, *Boehringer Ingelheim (Canada), Ltd., Burlington, Ontario*
Diane J. Lewis-D'Agostino and Robert Pyke, *Boehringer Ingelheim Pharmaceuticals, Inc., Ridgefield, CT*

The Sexual Interest and Desire Inventory—Female (SIDI-F) is a clinician-administered instrument to quantitatively assess Hypoactive Sexual Desire Disorder (HSDD) severity in women. It is a 17-page instrument available in its entirety at the companion website for this handbook: www.routledge.com/textbooks/9780415801751.

Description

The SIDI-F is a clinician-rated instrument consisting of 13 items (relationship—sexual, receptivity, initiation, desire—frequency, affection, desire—satisfaction, desire—distress, thoughts—positive, erotica, arousal—frequency, arousal ease, arousal continuation, and orgasm), as well as a 5-item diagnostic module. The items in the diagnostic module are for information purposes on common interfering conditions (e.g., fatigue, depression, and pain) and do not contribute to the total score.

The SIDI-F was developed in a collaborative effort by a group of academic sexual dysfunction researchers, pharmaceutical industry professionals, and clinicians. It originally consisted of 17 items but was modified following preliminary testing and item response analysis (Sills et al., 2005).

The resulting "near-final" version, consisting of a 13-item clinician-rated instrument with 30-day recall, was tested for reliability and validity in a two-center North American pilot validation study conducted on 90 women with HSDD, Female Orgasmic Disorder (FOD), or no Female Sexual Dysfunction (FSD; Clayton et al., 2006). The reliability and validity of the final version of the SIDI-F were subsequently established in two multicenter, nontreatment studies, conducted in North America ($n = 223$) and Europe ($n = 254$), in women with HSDD (both studies), Female Sexual Arousal Disorder (FSAD; North American study only), or no FSD (both studies; Lewis-D'Agostino et al., 2007; Nappi et al., 2008).

The SIDI-F is designed to assess HSDD severity in adult women, regardless of age, menopausal status, or country. It was validated for use by clinicians trained in FSD, so its use by untrained clinicians to evaluate patients against a normative sample can only be advisory. However, its ease of use and the low level of interpretation required by the clinician are highly compatible with use by all clinicians to monitor changes in symptoms over time with treatment, especially by clinicians experienced in treating FSD.

---

[1]Address correspondence to Anita Clayton, University of Virginia Health System, Department of Psychiatric Medicine, 2955 Ivy Road, Northridge Suite 210, Charlottesville, VA 22903; e-mail: ahc8v@virginia.edu

Response Mode and Timing

Following a brief introduction, the administering clinician progresses through the 13 items of the instrument with the respondent. Each item (written in bold) consists of one or two questions, which are read verbatim by the clinician. Supplementary information (written in plain typeface) is provided to guide more specific probes. Additional questions are asked until the respondent gives a clear answer to which the clinician can assign a specific severity score. The SIDI-F takes approximately 15 minutes to administer.

Scoring

The SIDI-F uses two kinds of ratings: 8 items are rated in terms of symptom intensity only, whereas 5 items are rated in terms of both symptom intensity and frequency. The 5 dual-rated items are arranged in a grid: symptom intensity increases from left to right and symptom frequency increases from top to bottom. The intersection of these points gives the overall severity rating.

Items are rated from 0 to 3, 4, or 5, depending on the item. The total score ranges from 0 to 51, with higher scores indicating greater levels of sexual interest. A total score of 33 or less indicates the presence of HSDD.

Reliability

For all subjects, the Cronbach's alpha for the SIDI-F was .90 on both day 0 and day 28 in the North American study ($N = 223$). In the European study ($N = 254$), the corresponding values were .93 and .92 on day 0 and day 28, respectively.

Test-retest reliability was assessed using the Pearson correlation and intraclass correlation coefficient (ICC). For all subjects, the Pearson correlation and ICC coefficients for the SIDI-F score between day 0 and day 28 were .86 and .85, respectively, in the North American study, and .91 and .90, respectively, in the European study (Lewis-D'Agostino et al., 2007; Nappi et al., 2008).

Validity

For discriminant validity, a two-way analysis of covariance, with age categories and country as fixed effects, was used. In the North American study, the SIDI-F score was significantly lower for women diagnosed with HSDD than those diagnosed with FSAD, or with no FSD, at day 0 ($p < .001$, for both; Lewis-D'Agostino et al., 2007). In the European study, the SIDI-F score was significantly lower for women diagnosed with HSDD than those with no FSD at day 0 ($p < .001$; Nappi et al., 2008). Similar findings were seen for women aged 50 years or under and aged over 50 years in both studies. Further, the SIDI-F score showed discriminant validity regardless of menopausal status (both studies), or country (European study only).

Convergent validity was assessed by comparing responses on the SIDI-F to those on the Female Sexual Function Index (FSFI; Meston, 2003; Rosen et al., 2000) and the Changes in Sexual Functioning Questionnaire—Female (CSFQ-F; Clayton, McGarvey, & Clavet, 1997) using Pearson's correlation. In both studies, the SIDI-F score was highly correlated (all correlations > .60) with FSFI and CSFQ-F total scores in women with HSDD at day 0 (irrespective of age group), demonstrating convergent validity (Lewis-D'Agostino et al., 2007; Nappi et al., 2008).

Divergent validity was assessed by comparing responses on the SIDI-F with those on the Locke-Wallace Marital Adjustment Scale (MAS; Locke & Wallace, 1959) using Pearson's correlation. In both studies, the SIDI-F score was not highly correlated (.02 and .23 for the two studies) with the MAS score in women with HSDD at day 0 (irrespective of age group), demonstrating divergent validity (Lewis-D'Agostino et al., 2007; Nappi et al., 2008).

Sensitivity to change was assessed retrospectively in the North American and European studies. At study end, the percentage change from baseline in SIDI-F score was significantly correlated with percentage change in FSFI total and desire domain scores in both studies ($p < .0001$, for all). Sensitivity to therapeutically induced change was demonstrated in two proof-of-concept trials of an agent to treat HSDD; SIDI-F score was significantly correlated with the Clinical Global Impression of Improvement score (which assesses overall improvement in sexual functioning with study medication throughout the 12-week treatment period in both studies ($p < .0001$, for all; data on file, Boehringer Ingelheim).

Other Information

The SIDI-F was copyrighted in 2004 by Drs. Anita Clayton, Sandra Leiblum, Kenneth R. Evans, Terrence Sills, Robert Pyke, Rosemary Basson, and R. Taylor Segraves. Use of this instrument by the scientific community is encouraged and free of charge as long as the abovementioned copyright notice is reproduced and as long as the instrument is not altered or modified without the express written consent of the copyright holders. Inquiries for such consents may be addressed to Dr. Robert Pyke at Boehringer Ingelheim Pharmaceuticals, Inc., 900 Ridgebury Rd, Ridgefield, CT 06877; rpyke@rdg.boehringer-ingelheim.com

References

Clayton, A. H., McGarvey, E. L., & Clavet, G. J. (1997). The Changes in Sexual Functioning Questionnaire (CSFQ): Development, reliability, and validity. *Psychopharmacology Bulletin, 33,* 731–745.

Clayton, A. H., Segraves, R. T., Leiblum, S., Basson, R., Pyke, R., Cotton, D., et al. (2006). Reliability and validity of the Sexual Interest and Desire Inventory—Female (SIDI-F), a scale designed to measure severity of female Hypoactive Sexual Desire Disorder. *Journal of Sex and Marital Therapy, 32,* 115–135.

Lewis-D'Agostino, D., Clayton, A. H., Wunderlich, G., Kimura, T., Derogatis, L., & Goldstein, A. (2007). Validating the Sexual Interest and Desire Inventory—Female (SIDI-F) in North American women. *Obstetrics and Gynecology, 109,* 23S.

Locke, H. J., & Wallace, K. M. (1959). Short marital-adjustment and prediction tests: Their reliability and validity. *Marriage and Family Living, 21,* 251–255.

Meston, C. M. (2003). Validation of the Female Sexual Function Index (FSFI) in women with Female Orgasmic Disorder and in women with Hypoactive Sexual Desire Disorder. *Journal of Sex and Marital Therapy, 29,* 39–46.

Nappi, R., van Lunsen, R., Tignol, J., Goldmeier, D., Pyke, R., & Staehle, H. (2008). Validation of the Sexual Interest and Desire

Inventory—Female© (SIDI-F©) in European women. *Sexologies, 17* (Suppl. 1).

Rosen, R., Brown, C., Heiman, J., Leiblum, S., Meston, C., Shabsigh, R., et al. (2000). The Female Sexual Function Index (FSFI): A multidimensional self-report instrument for the assessment of female sexual function. *Journal of Sex and Marital Therapy, 26,* 191–208.

Sills, T., Wunderlich, G., Pyke, R., Segraves, R. T., Leiblum, S., Clayton, A., et al. (2005). The Sexual Interest and Desire Inventory—Female (SIDI-F): Item response analyses of data from women diagnosed with Hypoactive Sexual Desire Disorder. *Journal of Sexual Medicine, 2,* 801–818.

Exhibit

Sexual Interest and Desire Inventory—Female

This measure may be viewed in its entirety at the companion website for this book: http://www.routledge.com/textbooks/9780415801751

Female Sexual Distress Scale—Revised

Leonard R. Derogatis,[1] *Center for Sexual Medicine at Sheppard Pratt, Baltimore, MD*
Robert Pyke, *Boehringer Ingelheim Pharmaceuticals, Inc., Ridgefield, CT*
Julie McCormack, Adria Hunter, and Gale Harding, *United BioSource Corporation, Bethesda, MD*

The Female Sexual Distress Scale—Revised (FSDS-R) is a self-administered questionnaire designed to assess distress related to sexual dysfunction in women with Hypoactive Sexual Desire Disorder (HSDD), and other sexual dysfunctions.

Description

The FSDS-R is a self-administered questionnaire consisting of 13 items that relate to different aspects of sex-related personal distress in women. Responses are based on the frequency with which each problem has bothered the subject or caused them distress within different recall periods (past 7 or 30 days).

The FSDS-R is an extended version of the 12-item Female Sexual Distress Scale (FSDS; Derogatis, Rosen, Leiblum, Burnett, & Heiman, 2002). The FSDS was developed by a national group of experts in human sexuality under the auspices of the American Foundation for Urologic Disease (AFUD). The FSDS-R includes an additional question (Item 13) that specifically assesses distress related to low sexual desire. The FSDS-R is for use in both pre- and postmenopausal women.

Response Mode

Respondents read a list of feelings and problems that women sometimes have concerning their sexuality and circle the number that best describes how often that problem has bothered them or caused them distress during the past 30 days. They are provided with an example before completing the questionnaire and are free to ask any questions they may have.

Scoring

All items are rated in terms of the frequency with which that problem has bothered the individual or caused her distress in the past 30 days. Respondents rate every item from 0 to 4: (*Never* [(0)], *Rarely* [(1)], *Occasionally* [(2)], *Frequently* [(3)], or *Always* [(4)]). The total score ranges from 0 to 52, with higher scores indicating more distress. A total score of ≥ 11 or more indicates a clinical level of sexual distress.

Reliability

The FSDS was tested for reliability and validity in three studies involving over 500 women with and without

[1]Address correspondence to Leonard Derogatis, Johns Hopkins Department of Psychiatry and Behavioral Sciences—Center for Sexual Medicine at Sheppard Pratt, Baltimore, MD 21285; e-mail: Lderogatis@sheppardpratt.org

sexual dysfunction (Derogatis et al., 2002). The reliability and the validity of the FSDS-R were established in a multicenter, 4-week, nontreatment study, conducted in adult North American women with generalized acquired HSDD ($n = 136$), other Female Sexual Dysfunction (FSD; Female Sexual Arousal Disorder [FSAD] or Female Orgasmic Disorder [FOD], $n = 48$); or no FSD ($n = 75$; Derogatis, Clayton, Lewis-D'Agostino, Wunderlich, & Fu, 2008).

Cronbach's coefficient alpha was used to measure the internal consistency of the FSDS-R. Cronbach's alpha was > .88 for subjects with HSDD, other FSD, and no FSD on days 0, 7, and 28 (Derogatis, Clayton, et al., 2008).

Intraclass correlation coefficient (ICC) was used to estimate test-retest reliability. For all subjects, the ICC for the FSDS-R total and Item 13 scores between days 0 and 28 wasere .88 and .83, respectively (Derogatis, Clayton, et al., 2008). A version that was identical except for using 7-day recall gave equivalent results to the standard 30-day recall version in reliability.

Validity

In the validation study, mean FSDS, FSDS-R, and FSDS-R Item 13 scores were significantly higher in women with HSDD or other FSD than in women with no FSD ($p < .001$ at all time points), demonstrating that all these tests had discriminant validity (Derogatis, Clayton, et al., 2008). Receiver operating characteristic analyses of FSDS and FSDS-R total scores confirmed these findings (Derogatis, Clayton, et al., 2008). A version that was identical except for using 7-day recall gave equivalent results to the standard 30-day recall version in discriminant validity.

The content validity (relevance, clarity, and comprehensiveness) of the FSDS-R (7-day recall version) and the potential of Item 13 (bothered by low sexual desire) as a stand-alone measure of distress associated with decreased sexual desire were assessed through saturation interviewing in women with generalized acquired HSDD in a multicenter,

single-visit study conducted in the U.S. (Derogatis, Pyke, McCormack, Hunter, & Harding, 2008). Saturation was reached (i.e., no new information obtained) with 25 subjects. Subjects completed the FSDS-R prior to undergoing cognitive debriefing to capture information on their perceptions of the instrument. Subjects rated the relevancy of every item in the FSDS-R from 0 (*Not at all Relevant*) to 4 (*Extremely Relevant*). Item 13 (bothered by low sexual desire) was rated as the most relevant item, with a mean rating of 3.33. The majority of participants found every item clear and easy to understand; the percentage of respondents answering "Yes" to the question "Was this item clear and easy to understand?" was 76% for Item 9 (regrets about your sexuality), 80% for Item 8 (sexually inadequate) and 88%–100% for the remaining items. Item 13 alone demonstrated good content validity and 56% of respondents felt that it covered all of their feelings about their decreased sexual desire.

Other Information

Copyright © 2002 by American Foundation of Urological Disease, Inc. This scale may not be used without permission.

References

Derogatis, L. R., Clayton, A., Lewis-D'Agostino, D., Wunderlich, G., & Fu, Y. (2008). Validation of the Female Sexual Distress Scale—Revised for assessing distress in women with Hypoactive Sexual Desire Disorder. *Journal of Sexual Medicine, 5,* 357–364.

Derogatis, L. R., Pyke, R., McCormack, J., Hunter, A., & Harding, G. (2008, December). *Content validity of the Female Sexual Distress Scale—Revised (FSDS-R) in women with Hypoactive Sexual Desire Disorder (HSDD).* Poster presented at the Joint Congress of the European and International Societies for Sexual Medicine, Brussels, Belgium.

Derogatis, L. R., Rosen, R., Leiblum, S., Burnett, A., & Heiman, J. (2002). The Female Sexual Distress Scale (FSDS): Initial validation of a standardized scale for assessment of sexually related personal distress in women. *Journal of Sex and & Marital Therapy, 28,* 317–330.

Exhibit

Female Sexual Distress Scale—Revised

Instructions: Below is a list of feelings and problems that women sometimes have concerning their sexuality. Please read each item carefully, and circle the number that best describes HOW OFTEN THAT PROBLEM HAS BOTHERED YOU OR CAUSED YOU DISTRESS DURING THE PAST 30 DAYS INCLUDING TODAY. Circle only one number for each item, and take care not to skip any items. If you change your mind, erase your first circle carefully. Read the example before beginning, and if you have any questions please ask about them.

Example: How often did you feel: **Personal responsibility for your sexual problems.**

Never	Rarely	Occasionally	Frequently	Always
0	1	2	3	4

HOW OFTEN DID YOU FEEL:

	Never	Rarely	Occasionally	Frequently	Always
1. Distressed about your sex life	0	1	2	3	4
2. Unhappy about your sexual relationship	0	1	2	3	4
3. Guilty about sexual difficulties	0	1	2	3	4
4. Frustrated by your sexual problems	0	1	2	3	4

5. Stressed about sex	0	1	2	3	4
6. Inferior because of sexual problems	0	1	2	3	4
7. Worried about sex	0	1	2	3	4
8. Sexually inadequate	0	1	2	3	4
9. Regrets about your sexuality	0	1	2	3	4
10. Embarrassed about sexual problems	0	1	2	3	4
11. Dissatisfied with your sex life	0	1	2	3	4
12. Angry about your sex life	0	1	2	3	4
13. Bothered by low sexual desire	0	1	2	3	4

Attitudes Related to Sexual Concerns Scale

PATRICIA BARTHALOW KOCH,[1] *The Pennsylvania State University*
CRAIG R. COWDEN, *Tacoma Community College*

The Attitudes Related to Sexual Concerns Scale (ASCS) was developed to measure those attitudes that have been conceptually, empirically, or clinically associated with specific sexual concerns/dysfunctions of men and women. Although a number of scales have previously been developed to measure overall sexual attitudes or some particular attitudes, none targeted those attitudes that were specifically associated with sexual concerns/dysfunctions. The ASCS can be used as a research tool in examining the attitudes of various subsamples of differing gender, sexual orientation, age, relationship status, ethnicity, and so forth (Cowden & Koch, 1995). It could also serve as a clinical tool for counselors and therapists in assessing the attitudes related to the sexual concerns/dysfunctions their clients are experiencing.

Description

The ASCS consists of 30 items with responses on a 5-point Likert format ranging from 1 (*Strongly Agree*) to 5 (*Strongly Disagree*). Each statement is written in a personalized manner to measure the most proximal attitude, rather than a generalized one, because proximal attitudes are more closely related to one's own personal behavior (Ajzen & Fishbein, 1980). Through pilot testing with approximately 400 college students, principal components factor analysis with promax rotation extracted eight factors that were identified as attitudes toward (a) sexual self-understanding (14% explained variance), (b) body image (8%), (c) gender roles (4%), (d) commitment (6%), (e) communication with a sexual partner (10%), (f) masturbation (42%), (g) sexual

guilt (11%), and (h) sexual performance (5%; Cowden & Koch, 1995; Koch, 1983).

Response Mode and Timing

The respondent is instructed to indicate the choice (*Strongly Agree* =1, *Agree* = 2, *Uncertain* = 3, *Disagree* = 4, *Strongly Disagree* = 5) that best represents his or her attitudes toward each statement. The statements represent attitudes that might be expressed in a variety of situations. The respondents are instructed that, if they have never personally been in such a situation, they are to imagine themselves in it and think of how they might react. The term *partner* refers to whomever the respondent might share his or her sexuality with. The scale takes approximately 15 minutes to complete.

Scoring

Scores on the ASCS range from 30, indicating the least negative attitudes, to 150, indicating the most negative attitudes. Thus, the higher a person's score, the more she or he exhibits attitudes associated with experiencing high levels of various relationship and sexual functioning concerns. The subscales consist of the following items (those with an asterisk must be reversed scored): Body Image (1, 9, *17); Sexual Self-Understanding (*2, 10, *18, 25), Gender Roles (*3, *11, 19), Communication (*4, 12, *20, *26), Guilt (*5, *13, 21, 27), Commitment (6, *14, *22, *28), Masturbation (7, 15, *23), and Sexual Performance (*8, *16, *24, *29 [for females only]/*30 [for males only]). In administering the scale to homosexually- oriented respondents, the

[1]Address correspondence to Patricia Barthalow Koch, Professor of Biobehavioral Health, The Pennsylvania State University, 304B Health and Human Development Building East, University Park, PA 16802; e-mail p3k@psu.edu

Gender Roles subscale is deleted because some items refer to other-gender pairings.

Reliability

Internal reliability has been examined with two very different samples: one from a major, predominately White northeastern university (Cowden & Koch, 1995) and another from a racially/ethnically diverse sample from smaller colleges in Washington, D.C. and North Carolina (Cowden & Bradshaw, 2007). Cronbach alpha reliability coefficients for the entire scale, as well as the subscales, were as follows for these two different samples, respectively: Overall Scale, .70, .80; Body Image, .74, .80; Sexual Self-Understanding, .84, .67; Gender Roles, .64, .63; Communications, .73, .66; Guilt, .75, .67; Commitment, .80, .66; Masturbation, .91, .90; and Sexual Performance, .66, .60.

Validity

Content validity was ensured by performing a content analysis of over 40 major sexuality education, counseling, and therapy textbooks and over 250 scientific articles written about sexual concerns/dysfunctions. Repeated pilot testing was used to determine the most reliable and valid subscales and items. Construct validity was established through factor analysis (described above). Concurrent validity for the ASCS was determined through its significant positive correlations with other established questionnaires measuring various sexual attitudes, including the Mosher Sex Guilt Inventory (Mosher, 1966), the Derogatis Sexual Attitudes Scale (Derogatis & Melisaratos, 1979), and the Sex Anxiety Inventory (Janda & O'Grady, 1980). The ASCS

has also been shown to discriminate persons experiencing high levels of relationship concerns from those with low levels of such concerns, $t(402.87) = 6.58$, $p < .001$, and persons experiencing high levels of sexual functioning concerns/dysfunctions from those with little concern with their sexual functioning, $t(400.98) = 3.50$, $p < .001$ (Koch, 1988; Koch & Cowden, 1990). It also has discriminated those who are religiously affiliated from those who are not (Cowden & Bradshaw, 2007).

References

Ajzen, I., & Fishbein, M. (1980). *Understanding attitudes and predicting social behaviors*. Englewood Cliffs, NJ: Prentice Hall.

Cowden, C. R., & Bradshaw, S. D. (2007). Religiosity and sexual concerns. *International Journal of Sexual Health, 19*(1), 15–24.

Cowden, C. R., & Koch, P. B. (1995). Attitudes related to sexual concerns: Gender and orientation comparisons. *Journal of Sex Education and Therapy, 21*(2), 78–87.

Derogatis, L. R., & Melisaratos, N. (1979). The DSFI: A multidimensional measure of sexual functioning. *Journal of Sex &and Marital Therapy, 5*, 244–281.

Janda, L. H., & O'Grady, K. E. (1980). Development of a Sex Anxiety Inventory. *Journal of Consulting and Clinical Psychology, 48*, 169–175.

Koch, P. B. (1983). The relationship between sex-related attitudes and beliefs and the sexual concerns experienced by college students. *Dissertation Abstracts International, 44*. (UMI No. DA83-20895).

Koch, P. B. (1988). The relationship of first intercourse to later sexual functioning concerns of adolescents. *Journal of Adolescent Research, 3*, 345–362.

Koch, P. B., & Cowden, C. R. (1990). *Development of a measurement of attitudes related to sexual concerns*. Unpublished manuscript.

Mosher, D. L. (1966). The development and multitrait-multimethod matrix analysis of three measures of three aspects of guilt. *Journal of Consulting Psychology, 30*, 25–29.

Exhibit

Attitudes Related to Sexual Concerns Scale

Respond to the following statements by circling the choice which best represents your attitudes. These statements represent feelings that might be experienced in a variety of situations. If you have not been in such a situation, imagine yourself in it and think of how you might feel. The term "partner" refers to whomever you might choose to share your sexuality with.

1 = Strongly Agree
2 = Agree
3 = Uncertain
4 = Disagree
5 = Strongly Disagree

1. Overall, I feel that my body is sexually attractive.[a]
2. It is difficult for me to explain my sexual thoughts, attitudes, and feelings to someone else because I really don't understand them myself.
3. When a male and female are having a sexual relationship, I feel it is the female's responsibility to set the sexual limits since the male will try to get as much as possible.
4. I would feel very uncomfortable expressing my negative feelings about our sexual relations to a partner.
5. I would feel guilty if I did *not* follow religious pronouncements about sexual behavior.
6. I would *not* be afraid of becoming involved in a committed relationship at this point in time.
7. I would *not* feel ashamed to use masturbation as a sexual release.

8. I would worry that my partner would leave me if I did not do what she or he wanted me to do in bed.
9. I feel a partner would be sexually attracted to my nude body.
10. I am *not* confused about my sexual feelings.
11. It is more acceptable to me for a male to have a one-night stand than for a female to have a one-night stand.
12. It would *not* be difficult for me to make suggestions to a partner on ways to improve his or her sexual techniques.
13. I would feel guilty if I did *not* follow my family's teachings about sexual behavior.
14. I would feel trapped if I was in a committed relationship at this time.
15. I would feel good about exploring and learning about my own body through masturbation.
16. If my partner did not reach orgasm, I would feel like a failure.
17. Because of the way my body looks, I would feel uncomfortable in the nude with a sexual partner.
18. It bothers me that I really do not understand why I behave sexually as I do.
19. I do *not* believe that males usually use love to get sex and females usually use sex to get love.
20. I would feel hurt if a sexual partner told me that something I do during lovemaking turns her or him off.
21. I would *not* feel guilty if I had genital sexual relations (such as intercourse) with a partner.
22. I am afraid to trust anyone in a sexual relationship at this time in my life.
23. I would feel guilty about masturbating.
24. I would worry that if I did not perform well sexually my partner would look for someone else.
25. It is *not* difficult for me to sort out my sexual feelings, values, and behaviors.
26. There probably would be some aspects of our sexual relationship that I just could *not* talk about with my partner.
27. I would not feel guilty fantasizing about sexual experiences.
28. I would feel like a failure if I found out that my sexual partner also engaged in solitary masturbation.

Females Only

29. I would feel inadequate if I could not reach orgasm during vaginal penetration (such as vaginal intercourse) and needed other kinds of stimulation in order to reach an orgasm.

Males Only

30. I would feel humiliated if I was unable to get an erection during a sexual encounter.

ªA scale from 1 to 5 follows each item.

Sexual Problems Self-Assessment Questionnaire

ELIZABETH RAE LARSON,[1] *Seattle Institute for Sex Therapy, Education and Research*
MALCOLM H. MCKAY, *Private Practitioner*

The Sexual Problems Self-Assessment Questionnaire (SPSAQ) was designed to assess sexual and relationship satisfaction levels in couples presenting for sex therapy; it is a clinical evaluation tool that offers a brief, comprehensive assessment of adult clients' levels of satisfaction in their sexual relationships.

Scoring forms provide client profiles. When used with a couple, a couple's form lists each partner's scores so that they can be compared. The instrument was not designed as a research tool and has not been tested for validity or reliability beyond the clinical applications it was designed to assess. Clients presenting with sexual difficulties often focus so narrowly on presenting issues that other, relevant and germane issues are not discovered until later in therapy. Even without numerical scores, a paper-and-pencil-marked questionnaire is useful in quickly providing a comprehensive assessment of problem domains.

Description

The SPSAQ was developed from the classification system presented in *A New View of Women's Sexual Problems* (Kaschak & Tiefer, 2001). In developing the item content, we sought advice from a variety of colleagues. Leonore Tiefer

[1]Address correspondence to Elizabeth Rae Larson, Seattle Institute for Sex Therapy, Education and Research, 100 NE 56th Street, Seattle WA 98105; e-mail: therapy@sextx.com

and the New View listserve have helped in the wording, design, and use of the instrument, as have other therapists and health practitioners. Prior to designing a computer-administered version, we hand scored questionnaires.

The entire form contains 73 items. The New View nosology (Kaschak & Tiefer, 2001) provides a more multidomain description of client experience than do the categories of the *Diagnostic and Statistical Manual of Mental Disorders* (American Psychiatric Association, 1994; *DSM-IV*, pp. 493–502). Items are organized into four domains. The domains as identified in the New View nosology are (a) Socio-Cultural, Political, or Economic, (b) Relationships, (c) Psychological Factors, and (d) Medical and Physiologic Factors.[2] In the SPSAQ, we shortened "Medical and Physiologic Factors" to "Physical Factors." Items in the SPSAQ have also been expanded to include male sexual concerns (Klein & Morin, 2005; Larson, 2005) and an additional domain, Overall Satisfaction, which contains two items: Sex Life and Emotional Intimacy (Larson, 2005).

The SPSAQ is administered by computer, with individual respondents completing the assessment by keyboard and mouse. Upon completion, a paper printout of the results is immediately available. In our clinical setting, neither the individual's responses nor identifying data is are electronically stored. The clinician is provided with a printed answer sheet with ample space for interview notes. For couples, an additional form provides space to list each partner's scores and facilitates comparison.

The instrument measures the subjective perceptions of each individual at the time of administration. The responses should not be confused with an objective measure of a symptom. The SPSAQ provides practitioners with quick, comprehensive feedback regarding clients' subjective state of relational and sexual satisfaction.

Response Mode and Timing

Using a hidden 100-point Likert-type scale, individuals respond to statements by marking a continuum usually ranging from *Yes* to *No*. The left—right direction of the high score is varied by the wording of the statements affirmatively or negatively throughout the instrument. Items ask for a level of agreement or disagreement. An example is the mock item used in the instructions: "I feel I have adequate access to chocolate" (see Exhibit).

Respondents can choose to mark any items as "Skip" and can change their responses to any items up until they click "Finished."

Timing is not rigid and respondents typically take 12 to 25 minutes to complete the computerized version, which provides an immediate printout of the results.

Scoring

The computer program translates the mark along the Likert-type continuum to a numerical score from 0 to 100.

Higher scores represent problem areas. Typically, glancing at a printout of the respondent's scores helps focus clinical interviews on areas of distress. The instrument is ordinarily introduced in the early stage of therapy; however, using the SPSAQ later in the course of therapy can sometimes indicate areas of improvement or areas that are being overlooked.

Reliability

No systematic assessment of reliability has been undertaken.

Validity

During development of the instrument, long-term therapy clients, usually couples, were invited to complete the instrument. Most of these clients found the questionnaire user-friendly and brief. The senior author was pleased to see "no surprises" in client responses. Then the instrument was administered to new clients. Following that, clinical interviews revealed that some clients had inaccurately marked some items. Items that proved too vaguely worded or confusing were reworded or dropped.

Except for the clinical validation in the initial population of long-term clients, no validating data have been gathered on the SPSAQ.

Other Information

We have presented this work in its development stages at meetings of the Society for the Scientific Study of Sexuality (Larson, 2005; Larson & McKay, 2006). The SPSAQ is a work in progress; future revisions of the questions and data forms are contemplated.

We typically give clients an opportunity to complete the questionnaire (in print or electronically) on the second or third visit. We often devote half, or more, of a one-on-one session to pursuing details from the questionnaire responses.

The SPSAQ lends itself to several applications beyond the satisfaction with relationships for individuals and for couples. The instrument can be used during the course of therapy as a within-subject change measure. See the companion website at www.routledge.com/textbooks/9780415801751 for a sample, fictitious printout as well as the test-retest scoring summary sheet.

No work has been done with a large population of subjects, and no standardizing procedures have been attempted.

References

American Psychiatric Association. (1994). *Diagnostic and statistical manual of mental disorders* (4th ed.). Washington, DC: Author.

---

[2]Marty Klein and Jack Morin (2005), in applying the "New View" nosology to a unified classification of women's and men's sexual problems, expanded the original Medical category to a more inclusive Physical Factors which we found more descriptive of respondents' subjective reports.

Kaschak, E., & Tiefer, L. (2001). *A new view of women's sexual problems.* Binghamton, NY: The Haworth Press.

Klein, M., & Morin, J. (2005, July). *The new view: Men are from earth, women are from earth.* Paper presented at the New View Conference, Montreal, Canada.

Larson, E. R. (2005, May). *Using the* New View of Women's Sexuality *in clinical practice.* Paper presented at the meeting of the Western

Region of the Society for the Scientific Study of Sexuality, San Francisco, CA.

Larson, E. R., & McKay, M. H. (2006, November). *Use of the New View diagnostic system in couple sex therapy.* Paper presented at the Annual Meeting of the Society for the Scientific Study of Sexuality, Las Vegas, NV.

Exhibit

Sexual Problems Self-Assessment Questionnaire

1. This questionnaire is part of a research and development project; it is unfinished and there are no scoring norms. It is being explored as a tool to aid in making a comprehensive assessment of sexual issues in women and men.

2. This information is intended for two uses:
    a. Feedback to your educator or clinician; and
    b. Data to a research project to measure the effectiveness of this questionnaire.
    Your answers might be shared anonymously with scientific, educational, or clinical professionals.

3. If you are a client or patient, know that you have the right to decline to answer all or part of the questionnaire and it will not negatively affect standard practice of treatment.

GENERAL QUESTIONS

A. FEEDBACK
1. Are you taking this survey to provide feedback to your service provider?
    ___ Yes   ___ No
2. Enter service provider's name:
    _____

3. Please create your code number with the first letter of your mother's maiden name and the last four digits of your Social Security Number. Or you may, instead, create another 5-character code that you will remember.
    ___ ___ ___ ___ ___
4. To assist us in long-term research, do you agree to have a second report sent to Seattle Institute?
    ___ Yes   ___ No

B. DEMOGRAPHICS

1. Sex: _____ Female   _____ Male   _____ Other
2. Age _____
3. Are you in a relationship? _____
4. If so, how long? _____

C. INSTRUCTIONS AND SAMPLE QUESTION
Answer each question by placing an "X" on the dotted line at the place that best describes how you feel.
Example: 1. I feel I have adequate access to chocolate.
           Yes..X..No

D. OVERALL SATISFACTION

1. In general, I am satisfied with my sex life.
    Very...Not at all
2. In general, I am satisfied with the emotional intimacy in my life.
    Very...Not at all

I. SOCIO-CULTURAL, POLITICAL, OR ECONOMIC FACTORS

A. I feel uninformed about sexuality due to inadequate sex education.
    Yes...No

B. I think my vocabulary is adequate to describe subjective or physical sexual experience.[a]
C. I have adequate information about human sexual biology and women's changes with age.
D. I have adequate information about human sexual biology and men's changes with age.
E. I think I lack information about how gender roles influence men's and women's sexuality.
F. I have adequate access to information and services for birth control.
G. I have adequate access to information and services for prevention and treatment of sexually transmitted infections.
H. I have adequate access to information and services for rape or sexual trauma.
I. I have adequate access to information and services for domestic violence.
J. I avoid having sex or experience distress during sex because I feel I don't live up to the ideals of my culture regarding sexuality or desirability.
K. I feel anxiety or shame about my body, sexual attractiveness, or sexual responses.
L. I feel confusion or shame about my sexual orientation or identity.
M. I feel confusion or shame about my sexual fantasies, desires, and preferences.
N. I feel that there are conflicts between my sexual values and those of my partner.
O. I feel that there are conflicts between my sexual values and those of my peer group.
P. I feel that there are conflicts between my sexual values and those of the mainstream culture.
Q. I feel a lack of interest, fatigue, or lack of time for sex due to family, work, or other obligations.
R. I feel inhibited about communicating preferences or initiating, pacing, or shaping sexual activities.

II. RELATIONSHIPS

A. I currently experience sexual inhibition, avoidance, or distress because of betrayal by or dislike of my partner.
   Yes..No
B. I currently experience sexual inhibition, avoidance, or distress because I fear my partner.[a]
C. I currently experience sexual inhibition, avoidance, or distress because of abuse by my partner.
D. I currently experience inhibition, avoidance, or distress arising from unequal power between myself and my partner.
E. I currently experience sexual inhibition, avoidance, or distress because of my partner's negative communication patterns.
F. I have experienced sexual inhibition, avoidance, or distress arising from betrayal, dislike, fear, or abuse in a previous relationship.
G. There are discrepancies between myself and my partner in frequency of desire for sexual activity.
H. There are discrepancies between myself and my partner in preferences for various sexual activities.
I. I trust my partner to be sensitive to my wants.
J. I have lost sexual interest as a result of conflicts with my partner over commonplace issues such as money, schedules, or relatives.
K. I have experienced loss of sexual interest due to traumatic experiences, such as infertility or the death of a child.
L. My partner's health and/or sexual problems interfere with my sexual arousal, enjoyment, or spontaneity.
M. I experience sexual aversion, mistrust, or inhibition of sexual pleasure due to my partner's personality, such as problems with rejection, cooperation, closeness, or criticalness.
N. I experience sexual aversion, mistrust, or inhibition of sexual pleasure due to my partner's depression or anxiety.

III. PSYCHOLOGICAL FACTORS

A. I experience inhibition of sexual pleasure or response that I believe is due to a history of physical, sexual, or emotional trauma.
   Yes..No
B. I avoid sexual activity or fail to experience sexual pleasure because of fears of rejection or intimacy.[a]
C. I avoid sexual activity or fail to experience sexual pleasure because of anger toward my partner.
D. I experience sexual aversion, mistrust, or inhibition of sexual pleasure due to depression or anxiety.
E. I experience sexual inhibition due to fear of sexual acts or their possible consequences, for example pain during intercourse, pregnancy, sexually transmitted infections, etc.
F. I limit my sexual feelings due to my fear of losing my partner.
G. I engage in sexual behavior that feels inappropriate and out of control.

IV. PHYSICAL FACTORS

A. I experience pain or lack of physical response during sexual activity due to medical condition(s) affecting my body.
   Yes..No
B. I believe my sexual experience and pleasure are limited by the following medical conditions (check all that apply):

1. _____ Diabetes   5. _____ Headaches
2. _____ Multiple Sclerosis   6. _____ Epilepsy
3. _____ Parkinson's Disease   7. _____ Arthritis
4. _____ Lupus   8. _____ Other

C. (men) I have been treated for prostate cancer.   ___ Yes   ___ No
D. (women) I have had a hysterectomy or had my ovary(ies) removed.   ___ Yes   ___ No
E. I have taken female hormones (estrogen, progesterone, etc.) at some time in my life.   ___ Yes   ___ No
F. I have taken male hormones (testosterone, DHEA, etc.) at some time in my life.   ___ Yes   ___ No
G. I experience pain or lack of physical response during sexual activity due to the following medical conditions:

   1. Pregnancy
   Yes...No
   2. Childbirth[a]
   3. Menopause
   4. Sexually Transmitted Disease
   5. Physical Injury
   6. Side effects of drugs, medications, or treatment for a medical condition.
   7. (women) Involuntary contractions of the vagina (vaginismus).

H. I am satisfied with my ability to control my ejaculation/orgasm.
I. I experience pain during arousal (erection, lubrication).
J. I experience pain during orgasm.
K. I experience pain during intercourse or other sexual contact for undiagnosed reasons.
L. I take medication/substance(s) (prescribed, herbal, or illegal) to enhance my sexual experience.
M. I lead a physically healthy lifestyle.
N. I smoke.
O. I drink more than 1 alcoholic beverage per day (women) or more than 2 drinks per day (men).
P. Regarding my weight, I am:
   Too Thin...Too Fat
Q. I am exposed to solvents or volatile substances, e.g., exhaust, chemical odors, etc.
   Daily...Rarely
R. I regularly engage in vigorous physical exercise.
   Daily...Rarely

Note. This questionnaire has been derived from the diagnostic classification system created by The Working Group on a New View of Women's Sexual Problems and developed by Seattle Institute for Sex Therapy, Education and Research (Elizabeth Rae Larson, Malcolm McKay, Laura Tsang, Ann Manly [Editor] and Ian Hagemann [Web Page Design]), with gratefully acknowledged critical feedback and generous assistance from Joy Davidson, Leonore Tiefer, Gerald Weeks, Marilyn McIntyre, Jack Morin, and Marty Klein. The New View of Women's Sexual Problems (2000) Working Group members were Linda Alperstein, Carol Ellison, Jennifer R. Fishman, Marny Hall, Lisa Handwerker, Heather Hartley, Ellyn Kaschak, Peggy J. Kleinplatz, Meika Loe, Laura Mamo, Carol Tavris, and Leonore Tiefer.
[a]The response option is repeated for each item.

Sexual Dysfunction Scale

Marita P. McCabe,[1] _Deakin University_

The Sexual Dysfunction Scale (SDS) is designed to evaluate the factors associated with each of the sexual dysfunctions among males and females. Respondents are asked a general question about which sexual dysfunctions they are experiencing, and then they complete a set of more specific questions on their particular sexual dysfunction(s).

[1]Address correspondence to Marita P. McCabe, School of Psychology, Deakin University, 221 Burwood Highway, Burwood, Victoria, Australia 3125; e-mail: marita.mccabe@deakin.edu.au

Description

The SDS consists of the following eight sections (see Table 1 for additional detail): (a) nature of the problem, (b) premature ejaculation, (c) erectile problems, (d) retarded ejaculation, (e) orgasmic dysfunction, (f) female unresponsiveness, (g) vaginismus, and (h) lack of sexual interest.

For each dysfunction, respondents answer questions about medical and lifestyle factors, quality of the respondent's relationship (if the person is in a relationship), length of time the dysfunction has been in place, the frequency and severity of the dysfunction, attitudes to sexual activities and responses to these activities, response to the dysfunction, and impact of the dysfunction on the respondent's relationship (if relevant).

The SDS was developed during a 10-year process in the late 1980s and 1990s. The items were initially drawn from the factors that were claimed in the literature to be associated with each particular sexual dysfunction. This resulted in the construction of a guided interview measure that elicited responses to open-ended questions. Subjects were also asked about whether the questions were relevant to their particular sexual dysfunction. This instrument was tested on 55 people with sexual dysfunction (with at least 6 subjects within any particular dysfunctional category). The measure was then converted into a forced-choice format and administered to a sexually dysfunctional population (both clinical and nonclinical subjects; McCabe, 1994a, 1994b). The scale was further modified as a result of these studies and administered to an additional 120 clinically dysfunctional subjects. This third draft of the scale is the one included in this compendium.

Response Mode and Timing

The scale is completed as a questionnaire measure and, depending upon the number of sexual dysfunctions experienced by the respondent, takes from 10 minutes to 50 minutes to complete. All items are objectively scored and consist of either yes/no responses or 5-point Likert-scale responses.

Scoring

Responses on items may be summed to provide an index of severity (nature of problem x length of time problem has been in place x frequency of problem). There are also separate questions on the medical, lifestyle, and relation-

TABLE 1
Areas Included in the Sexual Dysfunction Scale and the Reliability of These Scales

	No. of respondents in reliability study	Coefficient alpha
1. Nature of the sexual problem (30 items)	120	.63
2. Premature ejaculation (33 items)	26	.71
3. Erectile problems (33 items)	38	.72
4. Retarded ejaculation (31 items)	11	.69
5. Orgasmic dysfunction (48 items)	26	.63
6. Female unresponsiveness (51 items)	18	.73
7. Vaginismus (31 items)	14	.72
8. Lack of sexual interest (91 items)	24	.61

ship factors surrounding the problem and questions on the impact of the problem on the relationship.

Reliability and Validity

Coefficient alpha for each of the subscales was calculated for 120 subjects who presented to the sexual behaviour clinic for treatment of their sexual problem (see Table 1). The number of subjects with each dysfunction is listed in this table. As some subjects experienced more than one sexual dysfunction, the number of dysfunctions is greater than 120. Subjects with a partner ($n = 89$) were asked to report on the nature of their partner's problem. The concordance rate between their report and their partner's report was 82%, thus demonstrating the validity of the scale. Further validity is ensured by the process of the scale construction.

Other Information

The scale, along with the scoring code, may be obtained from the author for use with clinical or research subjects.

References

McCabe, M. P. (1994a). Childhood, adolescent and current psychological factors associated with sexual dysfunction. *Sexual and Marital Therapy, 9,* 267–276.

McCabe, M. P. (1994b). The influence of the quality of relationship on sexual dysfunction. *Australian Journal of Marriage and the Family, 15,* 2–8.

Family Life Sex Education Goal Questionnaire II

STEVEN GODIN[1] AND KIMBERLY RAZZANO, *East Stroudsburg University*

The initial Family Life Sex Education Goal Questionnaire (FLSE-GQ) was developed in the early 1980s as a needs assessment instrument designed to assess the attitudes of school personnel and community members toward the various goals of family life and sex education in the public schools. The FLSE-GQ-II is an updated version that includes additional items relevant for assessing family life sexuality education needs in today's public school systems. Outcome research has demonstrated that comprehensive sexuality education programs have a positive impact on delaying initiation of sexual behavior, reducing the number of new sexual partners, and reducing the incidence of unprotected sexual intercourse, to name a few (Alford, 2003, 2008; Kirby, 2001; Kirby, Laris, & Rolleri, 2005). Despite past federal governmental efforts to fund abstinence-based sex education, the Government Accountability Office Report (2006) and the Waxman Report (2004) suggest little evidence to date has been documented demonstrating program efficacy of this approach. Most experts, professional organizations, and even parents support comprehensive sexuality education (McKeon, 2006). For decades, school administrators and school boards have hesitated to include more controversial goals in their sex education programs for fear of negative community reactions or resistance from teachers or other school personnel; however, there is evidence that negative attitudes are found mostly among a small but vocal minority (Scales, 1983). The FLSE-GQ-II provides an empirical basis for determining local needs and the extent of school and community support for the various content areas of sex education and offers a means of clarifying diverse attitudes and priorities.

Description, Response Mode, and Timing

The instrument has a long and a short form. The long form consists of 60 goal items, and the short form consists of 20 goal items. Items on both forms have a 5-point Likert-type response format with response options labeled from *Very Unimportant* to *Very Important*. Respondents circle the number indicating the relative importance of each goal item for a family life sex education program. The long form takes 30 to 40 minutes for the parents to complete, and somewhat less time for the teachers. Owing to the length of the long form, the short form may be more appropriate for some parent groups. Researchers should consider the degree of literacy, interest, and so forth in the population to be sampled in determining which version to use.

The FLSE-GQ-II (or its earlier version) has been used with four major samples: 337 elementary and high school teachers, 248 parents of elementary and high school children in the Midwest, and 175 high school teachers and 157 parents of high school children in the Northeast. Separate factor analyses were carried out on the goal items from the teacher and parent samples. These analyses identified five goal dimensions or themes common to both samples: (a) facilitating sexual decision-making and life skills, (b) teaching about male and female physical development, (c) encouraging respect for diversity, (d) providing secondary prevention (e.g., to help pregnant girls to stay in school), and (e) teaching about the family and integrating sexuality in personal growth. Within the Midwest sample, Sexual Decision-Making and Life Skills was the largest factor (31% of the variance) with parent participants, whereas Family Life and Personal Growth were the largest factors (30% of the variance) in the teacher sample. Within the Northeast sample, Sexual Decision-Making and Life Skills was the sole large factor (32% of the variance). The remaining goal dimensions were minor goal dimensions in both samples (4% to 9% of the variance). The five scales of the short form correspond to each of the common goal dimensions and include items that had loadings of .5 or greater on corresponding factors in both the parent and the teacher samples.

Scoring

Investigators working with large samples will probably want to score the long form of the FLSE-GQ-II by subjecting the importance ratings for all 60 items to a principal components factor analysis. This procedure avoids any a priori assumptions about the salient goal dimensions within a particular population. The investigators can then derive scores for each goal dimension either by using computer-generated factor scores or by adding the importance ratings for the items with highest loadings on each factor. Investigators working with smaller samples and/or preferring the short form of the FLSE-GQ-II can derive scores for the Sexual Decision-Making and Life Skills (Items 8, 10, 17, 18, 21, 43), Physical Development (Items 32, 33, 44), Respect for Diversity (Items 47, 48, 49), Secondary Prevention (Items 39, 45, 57), and Family Life and Personal Growth (Items 16, 20, 22, 23, 54) scales by adding responses for each scale item and dividing by the total number of scale items.

[1]Address correspondence to Steven Godin, Department of Health Studies, East Stroudsburg University, East Stroudsburg, PA 18301; e-mail: sgodin@po-box.esu.edu

Reliability and Validity

Cronbach alphas for the five goal dimensions from the long form range from .60 to .79 for the sample of teachers, and from .65 to .85 for the sample of parents. Cronbach alphas for the five scales from the short form range from .73 to .83 for the sample of teachers, and from .79 to .87 for the sample of parents. Although the Cronbach alphas are slightly higher for the short form, researchers may want to use the longer form to assess whether new goal dimensions exist for their specific population. The questionnaire has been used to identify school personnel and community member goals for a Family Life Sex Education program in a large, midwestern urban center and the rural Northeast. Frank, Godin, Jacobson, and Sugrue (1982) and Godin, Frank, and Jacobson (1984) assessed relationships between goal dimensions derived from the long form of the FLSE-GQ-II and the teachers' and parents' demographic characteristics (i.e., age, sex, race, and religiosity). Among the teachers, religiosity was the best predictor of differing attitudes toward the goals of family life sex education in the public schools, whereas among the parents both religiosity and race contributed significantly to attitude differences. Both parents and teachers rated sexual decision-making goals as significantly less important than the other goal dimensions, contributing to the greater controversy surrounding this topic area in family life sex education. Within the Northeast sample, parents and teachers were in agreement regarding the high importance of sexual decision-making and life skills, whereas there were significant differences in importance ratings related to the minor factors (Razzano & Godin, 2006).

Other Information

The Family Life Sex Education Goal Questionnaires were copyrighted in 1985, 1994, and 2006. Electronic copies of the questionnaire, including an optional demographic questionnaire, are available by contacting the senior author.

References

Alford, S. (2003). *Science and success: Sex education and other programs that work to prevent teen pregnancy, HIV & sexually transmitted infections.* Washington, DC: Advocates for Youth.

Alford, S. (2008). *Science and success. Second edition: Programs that work to prevent teen pregnancy, HIV & sexually transmitted infections.* Washington, DC: Advocates for Youth.

Frank, S., Godin, S., Jacobson, S., & Sugrue, J. (1982, August). *Respect for diversity: Teachers' goals for a family life sex education program.* Paper presented at the meeting of the American Psychological Association, Washington, DC.

Godin, S., Frank, S., & Jacobson, S. (1984, March). *Respect for diversity: Parents' goals for a family life sex education program.* Paper presented at the Midwestern Conference of the National Council on Family Relations, Des Moines, IA.

Government Accountability Office Report. (2006). *Abstinence education: Efforts to assess the accuracy and effectiveness of federally funded programs* (Report GAO-07-8). Washington, DC: Author.

Kirby, D. (2001). *Emerging answers: Research findings on programs to reduce teen pregnancy.* Washington, DC: National Campaign to Prevent Teen Pregnancy.

Kirby, D., Laris, B. A., & Rolleri, L. (2005). *Impact of sex and HIV education programs on sexual behaviors of youth in developing and developed countries.* (Youth Research Working Paper, No. 2). Research Triangle Park, NC: Family Health International.

McKeon, B. (2006). *Effective sex education.* Washington, DC: Advocates for Youth.

Razzano, K., & Godin, S. (2006). A new paradigm in sexuality education in Pennsylvania: A descriptive analysis. *Pennsylvania Journal of Health, Physical Education, Recreation and Dance, 76*(3), 17–29.

Scales, P. (1983). The new opposition to sex education: A powerful threat to a democratic society. *Journal of School Health, 5,* 300–304.

Waxman Report. (2004). *The content of federally funded abstinence-only education programs.* Washington, DC: United States House of Representatives, Committee on Government Reform, Minority Staff, Special Investigations Division.

Exhibit

Family Life Sex Education Goal Questionnaire II

This questionnaire lists goals which some people have described as important for a family life sex education program. Some goals may be of lesser importance than others. For each of the goals listed, we would like you to indicate (on the 5-point scale provided) whether or not you view the goal as important for a family life sex education program in the _____ (specify program, school, grade level, etc.).

Instructions: In the column to the right of the goals listed on the pages which follow, indicate the importance of each goal by using the following scale:

1	2	3	4	5
Very Unimportant	Somewhat Unimportant	Neutral Importance	Somewhat Important	Very Important

Here is an example of how to use the scale:

Example Items

A. To teach children about how to stay physically healthy as they grow.　　1　2　3　4　5

B. To teach children how to play a musical instrument.　　1　2　3　4　5

If, in your opinion, the first goal ("To teach children about how to stay physically healthy as they grow") is *somewhat important* (number "4" on the scale) for a family life sex education program, you would circle "4" next to the goal statement in the column on the right. If, in your opinion, the second goal ("To teach children how to play a musical instrument") is *very unimportant* for a family life sex education program, you would circle the number "1" in the column to the right.

Remember, you may see some goals as more important than others. Please circle your opinion by circling the number that best represents your views beside each goal statement.

1. To help adolescents feel good about their physical appearance.[a]
2. To help adolescents to appreciate their special qualities and personality as well as that of other boys and girls.
3. To reduce guilt and fear about sexuality.
4. To provide information about abnormal sexual development and behavior.
5. To help adolescents understand how sexual development affects other aspects of personal growth and development.
6. To provide complete information about male and female genitalia (sex organs) and other physical differences between men and women.
7. To involve parents in selecting instruction materials and planning the curriculum of the family life sex education program.
8. To provide information about abortion and its effects on the body.
9. To provide information about the biology of human reproduction and birth.
10. To discuss ways of coping with an unexpected pregnancy.
11. To help adolescents develop skills in getting along with members of the opposite sex.
12. To provide information about how to be good parents.
13. To help adolescents learn to understand and communicate with each other better.
14. To make youth aware of community services related to health and prenatal care.
15. To emphasize the importance of the family as the keystone of American life.
16. To help adolescents understand their responsibilities to self, family, and friends as they grow up.
17. To inform youth of community services related to birth control and sexual decision-making.
18. To counsel adolescents to make their own decisions about how far to go in their sexual activities.
19. To encourage adolescents to talk more openly with their parents about sexuality.
20. To discuss the role of the family in personal growth and development.
21. To encourage adolescents to use contraceptives if they decide to have sexual intercourse.
22. To discuss ways in which families work out conflicts and solve problems.
23. To help adolescents understand people's feelings and points of view.
24. To educate adolescents about peer pressure and how to deal with it.
25. To provide information about sexually transmitted infections including HIV and AIDS.
26. To teach about abstention as a form of contraception.
27. To encourage discussion of personal family experiences in the classroom.
28. To provide special courses about family life and sexuality for disabled students.
29. To encourage adolescents to think about alternatives to abortion.
30. To bring in outside speakers to talk to youth about sexuality.
31. To counsel boys who are expectant fathers.
32. To correct myths and misinformation about the body.
33. To help adolescents to view the growth changes in their bodies as normal and healthy.
34. To discuss how the attitudes toward growth and development may be different for different ethnic groups and cultures in our society.
35. To provide information about alternative sexual behaviors and lifestyles, such as homosexuality.
36. To discuss abortion as a form of contraception.
37. To provide workshops to assist parents in talking more openly with their adolescent children about sexuality.
38. To encourage grooming and thoughtfulness about personal appearance.
39. To counsel girls who are pregnant.
40. To demonstrate how to put on a condom using a plastic teaching model or banana.
41. To refer students with special needs to social service agencies.
42. To make adolescents aware of the negative effects of sex role stereotypes.
43. To provide information about good prenatal care.
44. To provide information about contraceptives and how they work, and describe their effects on the body.
45. To teach about biological changes during puberty.
46. To provide individual counseling to students with low self-esteem or those who feel embarrassed about their bodies.
47. To meet with parents about a child who is having difficulties with sexual issues and stresses.

48. To teach about the different types of sexually transmitted infections or diseases.
49. To teach about how families may differ in how they make rules and decisions.
50. To teach students about the ways in which HIV is transmitted.
51. To provide information about how different ethnic and cultural groups differ in sexual beliefs and behaviors.
52. To work with outside community agencies to provide rap groups about sexuality and sexual decision-making.
53. To help adolescents to see that most young people are going through many of the same things as they grow toward maturity.
54. To help adolescents plan for and start working toward future goals.
55. To provide information about the roles and challenges that go along with reaching different ages in life.
56. To teach students about ways to have safer sex to reduce the risk of HIV infection.
57. To discuss ways to help families talk more openly and improve family communication.
58. To listen and respond to the opinions of the outside community and local interest groups in making family life sex education goals.
59. To encourage personal hygiene.
60. To encourage pregnant girls to stay in school and to provide special classes for them in prenatal care.

aThe 5-point scale is provided after each item.

Global Measure of Equity and Multi-Trait Measure of Equity: Measuring Equity in Close Relationships

DANIELLE M. YOUNG AND ELAINE HATFIELD,[1] *University of Hawaii*

According to equity theory, people perceive a relationship as equitable when they and their partners are getting what they both "deserve" from their romantic and marital relationships. In theory, couples are assumed to feel most comfortable when their romantic and sexual relationships are maximally profitable and (considering what they and their partners contribute to their relationship) they are reaping all the rewards they deserve—no more and certainly no less (see Hatfield, Walster, & Berscheid, 1978). Equity has been found to relate to many aspects of relationships and appears to be important throughout a couple's lifetime (Pillemer, Hatfield, & Sprecher, 2008). More recently, evolutionary theorists contend that concerns about equity have an enormous impact in the dating marketplace (Baumeister & Vohs, 2004). The Global Measure of Equity and the Multi-Trait Measure of Equity were designed to assess men's and women's perceptions of how fair and equitable their love and sexual relationships are (Traupmann, Peterson, Utne, & Hatfield, 1981; Walster, 1975.).

Description

On the Global Measure of Equity, men and women are asked to assess how fair and equitable they perceive their dating and marital relationships to be. Respondents indicate their judgments on a 7-point Likert-type scale, with answers ranging from +3 = *I am getting a much better deal* than my partner to −3 = *My partner is getting a much better deal than I am*.

On the Multi-Trait Measure of Equity, the experimenter begins by explaining the concept of equity (see Exhibit). The experimenter then hands the respondent a list of 25 items, which consist of Personal Concerns, Emotional Concerns, Day-to-Day Concerns, and Opportunities Gained and Lost (i.e., things one gains or loses simply by dating or being married). Each item can also be rated as to importance. Once again, men and women are asked to assess how fair and equitable their dating and marital relationships are and to indicate their judgments on a 7-point Likert scale, ranging from +3 = *I am getting a much better deal than my partner*, to −3 = *My partner is getting a much better deal than I am*.

Response Mode and Timing

The equity measures can be administered either individually or in groups. Respondents are asked to circle the number (ranging from +3 to −3) indicating how true each statement is for them. The Global Measure of Equity generally takes 1 minute to administer. The Multi-Trait Measure of Equity takes approximately 15 minutes to administer. If each item on the Multi-Trait Measure is weighted by importance, the scale generally takes 30 minutes to complete.

[1]Address correspondence to Elaine Hatfield, 2430 Campus Road, Honolulu, HI 96822; e-mail: elaineh1@aol.com

Scoring

On the Multi-Trait Measure of Equity, the experimenter begins by calculating a *Total Index*, by summing the respondents' estimates of how overbenefited, equitably treated, or underbenefited they consider themselves to be on each of the 25 scale items. On both the Global and the Multi-Trait Measure of Equity, participants who rate their relationships positively are generally categorized as overbenefited, those who rate them negatively are categorized as underbenefited, and those who rate them as 0 are categorized as participating in equitable relationships. Some researchers, of course, have treated the scores as a continuous variable.

Reliability

Despite its brevity, the Global Measure of Equity possesses reasonable reliability and has been used to study a variety of relationship types (see Canary & Stafford, 1992; Sprecher, 1986, 1988; Traupmann, 1978; Traupmann et al., 1981). During development of the Multi-Trait Measure of Equity, Traupmann and her colleagues (1981) demonstrated the larger scale's reliability (Cronbach's α for total inputs = .87; for total outputs scales = .90).

Validity

If the equity scales are valid, they should be related to other variables in ways expected by past theoretical and empirical work. There is some evidence for such construct validity. The Global Measure of Equity correlates with other measures of fairness and equity in intimate relationships. Sprecher (1986, 1988), for example, found that the Global Measure is positively and significantly correlated with the Sprecher Global Equity Measure (correlations range from $r = .45$ to $r = .52$, $p < .001$), which was created to measure day-to-day equity. Sprecher (2001) also correlated a multifaceted measure of equity to the Global Measure of Equity (with r's ranging from .43 to .73).

Other validity findings include the following: (a) Profitable and equitable dating relationships are associated with satisfying and comfortable relationships; inequity is associated with distress, guilt, anger, and anxiety. (b) Profitable and equitable dating relationships appear to be more stable (and more likely to lead to more serious relationships) than are inequitable relationships. (c) Those in equitable relationships are less likely to risk extramarital affairs than are their peers. (d) In close, intimate relationships, couples in equitable relationships have been found to feel more intensely about one another, share more of their lives, have more exciting sex lives, and have longer-lived relationships than do couples in fleeting affairs. (See Hatfield, Rapson, & Aumer-Ryan [2007] for a summary of this evidence.)

References

Baumeister, R. F., & Vohs, K. D. (2004). Sexual economics: Sex as female resource for social exchange in heterosexual interactions. *Personality and Social Psychology Review, 8*, 339–363.

Canary, D., & Stafford, L. (1992). Relational maintenance strategies and equity in marriage. *Communication Monographs, 59*, 243–267.

Hatfield, E., Rapson, R. L., & Aumer-Ryan, K. (2007). Equity theory: Social justice in love relationships. Recent developments. *Social Justice Research*. New York: Springer.

Hatfield, E., Walster, G. W., & Berscheid, E. (1978). *Equity: Theory and research*. Boston: Allyn & Bacon.

Pillemer, J., Hatfield, E., & Sprecher, S. (2008). The importance of fairness and equity for the marital satisfaction of older women. *Journal of Women and Aging, 20*, 215–230.

Sprecher, S. (1986). The relation between inequity and emotions in close relationships. *Social Psychology Quarterly, 49*, 309–321.

Sprecher, S. (1988). Investment model, equity, and social support determinants of relationship commitment. *Social Psychology Quarterly, 51*, 318–328.

Sprecher, S. (2001). Equity and social exchange in dating couples: Associations with satisfaction, commitment, and stability. *Journal of Marriage and Family, 63*, 599–613.

Traupmann, J. (1978). *Equity in intimate relations: An interview of marriage*. Unpublished doctoral dissertation. University of Wisconsin-Madison.

Traupmann, J., Peterson, R., Utne, M., & Hatfield, E. (1981). Measuring equity in intimate relations. *Applied Psychological Measurement, 5*, 467–480.

Walster, G. W. (1975). The Walster et al. (1973) equity formula: A correction. *Representative Research in Social Psychology, 6*, 65–67.

Exhibit

Global Measure of Equity and Multi-Trait Measure of Equity

Calculating Equity

Technically, equity is defined by a complex formula (Traupmann et al., 1981; Walster, 1975). Respondents' perceptions of the equitableness of their dating relationships or marriages are computed by entering their estimates of Inputs and Outcomes of Persons A and B (I_A, I_B, O_A, and O_B) into the equity formula:[a]

$$\frac{(O_A - I_A)}{(|I_A|)^{KA}} = \frac{(O_B - I_B)}{(|I_B|)^{KB}}$$

Respondents are classified as "overbenefited" if their relative gains exceed those of their partners. They are classified as "equitably treated" if their relative gains equal those of their partners, and as "underbenefited" if their relative gains fall short of those of their partners.

In practice, however, the equity of love relationships can reliably and validly be assessed with the use of two simple measures: the Global Measure of Equity and the Multi-Trait Measure of Equity.

Global Measure of Equity

Women were asked: "Considering what you put into your dating relationship or marriage, compared to what you get out of it . . . and what your partner puts in, compared to what (s)he gets out of it . . . how does your dating relationship or marriage 'stack up'?"

Possible responses are:

+3 = I am getting a much better deal than my partner.
+2 = I am getting a somewhat better deal.
+1 = I am getting a slightly better deal.
 0 = We are both getting an equally good, or bad, deal.
−1 = My partner is getting a slightly better deal.
−2 = My partner is getting a somewhat better deal.
−3 = My partner is getting a much better deal than I am.

On the basis of their answers, persons can be classified as overbenefited (receiving more than they deserve), equitably treated, or underbenefited (receiving less than they deserve).

Multi-Trait Measure of Equity

Introduction: Explanation of Concepts

"We're interested in the give-and-take that goes on in a dating relationship or marriage. We'd like to ask you a few questions about the things you put into your relationship . . . and the kinds of things you get out of it. We know that most people don't ordinarily keep careful track of exactly what they're giving and getting from their dating relationships or marriages. They certainly don't pull their relationship apart and think about the various aspects of their relationship, one by one. But in order for us to get some idea of what goes on in dating and marital relationships, we have to ask you and the other people we're interviewing to *spell out* some of the give-and-take that naturally occurs.

"Let us look at some of the critical areas in any dating relationship or marriage. Look over this list. [Hand respondent list.] We'd like to ask about you and your partner's Personal Concerns, your Emotional Concerns, your Day-to-Day Concerns, and a little about the things the two of you feel you gain or lose—simply by dating or being married. We'd like you to read each item.

"[Each item is read through, aloud if interviewer is used. After reading each item, respondent is asked]: Considering what you put into your dating relationship or marriage (in this area), compared to what you get out of it . . . and what your partner puts in compared to what he or she gets out of it, how does your dating relationship/marriage 'stack up'?"

+3 = I am getting a much better deal than my partner.
+2 = I am getting a somewhat better deal.
+1 = I am getting a slightly better deal.
 0 = We are both getting an equally good or bad deal.
−1 = My partner is getting a slightly better deal.
−2 = My partner is getting a somewhat better deal.
−3 = My partner is getting a much better deal than I am.

Areas Involved in Dating/Marital Give-and-Take

Personal Concerns
Social Grace
1. Social Grace: Some people are sociable, friendly, relaxed in social settings. Others are not.

Intellect
2. Intelligence: Some people are intelligent and informed.

Appearance
3. Physical Attractiveness: Some people are physically attractive.
4. Concern for Physical Appearance and Health: Some people take care of their physical appearance and conditioning, through attention to such things as their clothing, cleanliness, exercise, and good eating habits.

Emotional Concerns
Liking and Loving
5. Liking: Some people like their partners and show it. Others do not.
6. Love: Some people feel and express love for their partners.

Understanding and Concern

7. Understanding and Concern: Some people know their partner's personal concerns and emotional needs and respond to them.

Acceptance

8. Accepting and Encouraging Role Flexibility: Some people let their partners try out different roles occasionally, for example letting their partner be a "baby" sometimes, a "mother," a colleague or a friend, an aggressive as well as a passive lover, and so on.

Appreciation

9. Expressions of Appreciation: Some people openly show appreciation for their partner's contributions to the relationship—they don't take their partner for granted.

Physical Affection

10. Showing Affection: Some people are openly affectionate—touching, hugging, kissing.

Sex

11. Sexual Pleasure: Some people participate in the sexual aspect of a relationship, working to make it mutually satisfying and fulfilling.
12. Sexual Fidelity: Some people live up to (are "faithful" to) their agreements about extramarital relations.

Security/Freedom

13. Commitment: Some people commit themselves to their partners and to the future of their relationship together.
14. Respecting Partner's Need to be a Free and Independent Person: Some people allow their partners to develop as an individual in the way that they choose: for example, they allow their partners freedom to go to school or not; to work at the kind of job or career they like; to pursue outside interests; to do things by themselves or with friends; to simply be alone sometimes.

Plans and Goals for the Future

15. Plans and Goals for the Future: Some people plan for and dream about their future together.

Day-to-Day Concerns
Day-to-Day Maintenance

16. Day-to-Day Maintenance: Some people contribute time and effort to household responsibilities such as grocery shopping, making dinner, cleaning, and car maintenance. Others do not.

Finances

17. Finances: Some people contribute income to the couple's "joint account."

Sociability

18. Easy to Live With: Some people are easy to live with on a day-to-day basis; that is, they have a sense of humor, aren't too moody, don't get drunk too often, and so on.
19. Companionship: Some people are good companions, who suggest interesting activities for both of them to do together, as well as going along with their partner's ideas about what they might do for fun.
20. Conversation: Some people tell partners about their day's events and what's on their mind . . . and are also interested in hearing about their partner's concerns and daily activities.
21. Fitting in: Some people are compatible with their partner's friends and relatives; they like the friends and relatives, and the friends and relatives like them.

Decision-Making

22. Decision-Making: Some people take their fair share of the responsibility for making and carrying out decisions that affect both partners.

Remembering Special Occasions

23. Remembering Special Occasions: Some people are thoughtful about sentimental things, such as remembering birthdays, your anniversary, and other special occasions.

Opportunities Gained and Lost
Opportunities Gained

24. Chance to be Dating or Married: Dating and marriage give many people the opportunity to partake of the many life experiences that depend upon dating or being married, for example the chance to become a parent and even a grandparent, the chance to be included in "married couple" social events, and, finally, having someone to count on in old age.

Opportunities Forgone

25. Opportunities Forgone: Dating and marriage necessarily require people to give up certain opportunities . . . in order to be in this relationship. The opportunities could have been other possible mates, a career, travel, etc.

On the basis of their answers, persons can be classified as overbenefited (receiving more than they deserve), equitably treated, or underbenefited (receiving less than they deserve).

To calculate a *Total Index*, the experimenter sums the respondents' estimates of how Overbenefited, Equitably treated, or Underbenefited they are in each of the 25 areas and divides by 25.

If experimenters wish to weight the items by importance, they can simply go through the 25 items, one by one, and ask: "How important is this area to you?"

8 = Extremely Important
7 = Very Important
6 = Fairly Important
5 = Slightly Important
4 = Slightly Unimportant
3 = Fairly Unimportant
2 = Very Unimportant
1 = Extremely Unimportant

Then weight the item by importance.

---

[a]The equity formulas used by previous researchers, from Aristotle to Stacy Adams, only yield meaningful results if A and B's Inputs and Outcomes are entirely positive or entirely negative. In mixed cases the formulas yield extremely peculiar results. Thus, we proposed an equity model designed to transcend these limitations. See Walster (1975) for a discussion of the problems and the mathematical solutions. The superscript k simply "scales" equity problems (by multiplying all inputs and outcomes by a positive constant) such that the minimum of $|I_A|$ and $|I_B|$ is greater than or equal to 1.

Female Sexual Response Patterns: Grafenberg Spot/Area and Ejaculation

CAROL ANDERSON DARLING, *Florida State University*
J. KENNETH DAVIDSON, SR.,[1] *University of Wisconsin-Eau Claire*

Investigations of the physiological aspects of the Grafenberg Spot/Area have often been conducted in clinical settings; however, many social science researchers are also interested in this topic and may prefer to use a survey research design. Thus, women can be asked questions about their knowledge, attitudes, and feelings regarding their sexuality and experience with the Grafenberg Spot/Area and ejaculation. This survey instrument on Female Sexual Response Patterns was designed to obtain information about female sexuality with a special focus on experiences related to stimulation of the Grafenberg Spot/Area and female ejaculation. Various sections of the instrument contain questions concerning the Grafenberg Spot/Area and other related topics, such as experiencing orgasm and ejaculation through stimulation of the Grafenberg Spot/Area along with related urinary and bladder conditions.

Description

The entire instrument consists of 192 open-ended and closed-form items. Several variables were included concerning demographics, parent-child attachment, childhood/adolescence, socialization, partner relationships, sexual attitudes, sexual behaviors, and knowledge and/or experience with the Grafenberg Spot/Area and female ejaculation. It was important to us to obtain accurate descriptions of the location of the Grafenberg Spot/Area and source of ejaculation. Thus, these questions were open-ended and contained labeled diagrams of the female anatomy.

[1]Address correspondence to J. Kenneth Davidson, Sr., 2634 Collingwood Drive, Round Rock, TX 78665; e-mail: davidsj@uwec.edu

Although these diagrams were used each time a question related to "location" was asked, the diagrams are included only once in this description.

We chose not to use the name "Grafenberg Spot," which had been familiarized in the popular press, because its use could possibly result in preformed notions, bias, or confusion for the respondents. Thus, the terminology used throughout the questionnaire refers to an "especially sensitive area in your vagina." There were four sections of questions pertinent to the "sensitive area," including sensitive area, sensitive area orgasm, sensitive area ejaculation, and sensitive area urination/pubococcygeus musculature. These sections are not identified in the actual questionnaire, although subtitles have been included to provide clarity in this condensed version of the instrument. Because the questions pertaining to the sensitive area were distributed throughout the instrument, they are not numbered within this description. Furthermore, if the question did not apply, the respondent was directed to another question by "if and go" statements.

The instrument was first pretested with female students enrolled in an upper-division human sexuality course. A revised questionnaire was pretested utilizing acquaintances of professional colleagues in various academic settings. Finally the questionnaire was reviewed by six female professionals involved in either teaching and/or research about human sexuality and/or sex education as part of the process of developing the final draft of the questionnaire. The actual investigation involved an anonymous survey of 2,350 professional women in health-related fields in the U.S. that yielded 1,289 completed questionnaires. A purposeful sample of women employed in the fields of nursing, sex education, sex therapy, and counseling was used. Given the nature of their academic training, it was assumed that these individuals would have a degree of familiarity with the anatomical structures and physiological processes associated with sexual responsiveness. Although the respondents were well-educated, their expertise was deemed important in order to reply in more precise language to a number of open-form items contained in the survey instrument.

This survey instrument is best suited for utilization with populations that contain women with 2 or more years of college education and who are at least 25 years of age. The level of language sophistication found in the instrument would appear to preclude its application to populations that have no college education. Furthermore, given the nature of the instrument, a woman would need to be sexually experienced in order to be able to respond in a meaningful way to a substantial number of the items. It is assumed that a greater opportunity for having considerable sexual experience will exist for women ages 25 years or older.

Response Mode and Timing

Respondents are either to check the appropriate answer category or answer the open-ended items in their own words within the space provided. Given the detailed personal information being sought regarding sexuality, the survey instrument should be completed in total privacy and anonymity. Thus, this instrument is ideally suited for distribution as a mail questionnaire using a business reply envelope.

Based on the pretest results and feedback from actual respondents, an average of 45 minutes is required to complete all segments of the survey instrument, whereas only 8 to 10 minutes are needed to complete the "sensitive area" portions of the survey.

Scoring

Although some Likert-type scale items were incorporated pertaining to the Grafenberg Spot/Area and ejaculation, it was not intended that such questions would constitute a scale that could stand alone. Moreover, the open-ended questions need to be coded and categorized accordingly.

Reliability

Reliability of the instrument has not been determined.

Validity

Content validity has been established through a review of the instrument by colleagues in the field.

References

Darling, C. A., Davidson, J. K., Sr., & Conway-Welch, C. (1990). Female ejaculation: Perceived origins, role of the Grafenberg spot/area, and sexual responsiveness. *Archives of Sexual Behavior, 19*, 29–47.

Darling, C. A., Davidson, J. K., Sr., & Conway-Welch, C. (1992). Shaping women's sexuality: The role of parental attachments. *Journal of Feminist Family Therapy, 4*, 61–90.

Davidson, J. K., Sr., & Darling, C. A. (1989). The role of the Grafenberg spot and female ejaculation in the female orgasmic response: An empirical analysis. *Journal of Sex & Marital Therapy, 15*, 102–120.

Exhibit

Grafenberg Spot/Area and Ejaculation Questionnaire

Sensitive Area

Is there any especially sensitive area in your vagina which, if stimulated, produces pleasurable feelings? (Circle number)

1. Yes, always produces pleasurable feelings

2. Yes, most of the time produces pleasurable feelings
3. Yes, sometimes produces pleasurable feelings
4. No

At what age did you *first* conclude that this sensitive area exists inside your vagina?
        _____ years old
If no sensitive area exists in vagina, go to Question _____:

Under what bladder circumstances are the pleasurable sensations associated with this sensitive area in your vagina most easily detectable? (Circle number)
1. Bladder full
2. Bladder partially full
3. Bladder empty
4. Not associated with condition of bladder
5. Not aware of bladder condition when pleasurable sensations occur
6. Other

When during your menstrual cycle are the pleasurable sensations associated with this sensitive area in your vagina most easily detectable? (Circle number)
1. Just before menstrual period
2. During menstrual period
3. Just after menstrual period
4. Midway between menstrual periods
5. No difference during menstrual cycle
6. No difference, had hysterectomy with removal of uterus only
7. No difference, had hysterectomy with removal of ovaries and uterus
8. Not aware of difference in menstrual cycle when pleasurable sensations occur

When speculum is inserted and opened in your vagina during a pelvic examination, does it ever stimulate this sensitive area in your vagina so that it produces pleasurable sensations? (Circle number)
1. Never
2. Rarely
3. Occasionally
4. Frequently
5. Very frequently
6. Always

Sensitive Area—Orgasm

In your opinion, does such a sensitive area exist inside the vagina which, if stimulated, can produce an orgasm without any clitoral contact and/or stimulation? (Circle number)
1. No
2. Yes, for all females
3. Yes, for some females
If never had an orgasm go to Question _____:

Does stimulating this sensitive area in your vagina during sexual arousal produce an orgasm?
(Circle number)
1. Yes, always
2. Yes, most of the time
3. Yes, sometimes
4. No
If stimulated, sensitive area in vagina does not produce orgasm go to Question ___:

Is it possible for you and/or your sex partner to stimulate this sensitive area to produce an orgasm without causing clitoral contact to be made? (Circle number)
1. Yes

2. No
3. Never tried to stimulate sensitive area
4. Other_____ (Please specify)

If yes: Please describe how it is possible to stimulate this sensitive area to produce an orgasm independent of any clitoral stimulation.

(Note: A larger space is necessary for open-ended response.)

What is the location of this sensitive area inside your vagina which, if stimulated, will produce an orgasm?

Describe its specific, perceived location in relationship to the other genital and pelvic structures using the terminology from the diagram. Please do not just circle the terminology on the diagram and do not draw arrows.

(Note: A larger space is necessary for the open-ended response.)

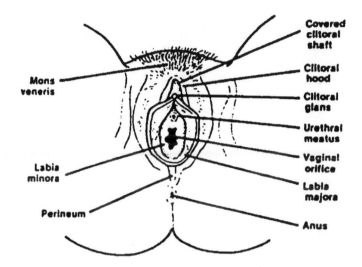

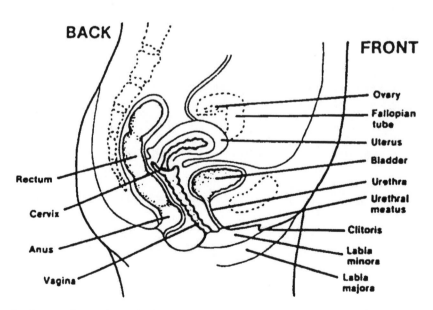

Which of the following factors play a role in whether this sensitive area in the vagina can be stimulated to produce an orgasm during sexual activity including masturbation, petting (mutual masturbation and/or oral-genital sex), or sexual intercourse. (Circle numbers for all applicable categories)

1. Not using diaphragm as a contraceptive technique
2. Long penis for vaginal penetration
3. Long internal vibrator or dildo for vaginal penetration

4. Large diameter penis for vaginal penetration
5. Large diameter internal vibrator or dildo for vaginal penetration
6. Degree of emotional involvement with sex partner
7. Angle of entry of erect penis, dildo, or vibrator during vaginal penetration
8. Use of your fingers to provide extra stimulation inside vagina
9. Use of your partner's fingers to provide extra stimulation inside vagina
10. Ability of partner to rotate pelvis during sexual activity
11. Ability to rotate your pelvis during sexual activity
12. Use of waterbed for sexual intercourse
13. Position used for sexual intercourse
14. Other _____ (Please specify)

Which position for sexual intercourse, if any, is most likely to result in stimulation of the sensitive area to produce orgasm? (Circle number)

1. Face-to-face/Male above
2. Face-to-face/Male above with legs of female over shoulders of male
3. Face-to-face/Female above
4. Face-to-face/Side
5. Prone (female lying face down)/Rear entry with vaginal penetration
6. Prone (female lying face down)/Rear entry with anal penetration
7. Kneeling/Rear entry with vaginal penetration
8. Kneeling/Rear entry with anal penetration
9. Sitting/Face-to-face
10. Sitting/Rear entry with vaginal penetration
11. Sitting/Rear entry with anal penetration
12. Standing/Face-to-face
13. Side/Rear entry with vaginal penetration
14. Supine (lying on back)/Male kneeling
15. Supine (lying on back)/Male standing
16. Side/Rear entry with anal penetration
17. Rear entry with vaginal penetration/Male on back/Female above
18. Male on side/Female on back, with knees bent
19. Other _____ (Please specify)

Sensitive Area—Ejaculation

In your opinion, does the process of ejaculation (sudden spurt of fluid at the moment of orgasm) exist in some females? (Circle number)
1. No   2. Yes

If yes: At what approximate age did you first conclude that ejaculation at the time of orgasm exists for some females?
_____ years old

At the time that you experience orgasm, do you suddenly experience a spurt of fluid (i.e., ejaculation) in the genital area? (Circle number)
1. Never
2. Rarely
3. Sometimes
4. Almost Always
5. Always
If never experience spurt of fluid during orgasm go to Question _____:

How does this spurt of fluid seem to be released at the time of your orgasm? (Please describe in your own words.)

(Note: A larger space is necessary for the open-ended response.)

What do you believe to be the source of this spurt of fluid at the time of your orgasm? (Please describe.)

(Note: A larger space is necessary for the open-ended response.)

In your own words, describe the difference, if any, between vaginal lubrication during your sexual arousal and the spurt of fluid at the moment of your orgasm.

(Note: A larger space is necessary for the open-ended response.)

During masturbation and/or sexual intercourse, are you able to consciously contract the muscles surrounding the vagina to grasp a phallic substitute (if utilized) or the penile shaft of your sex partner? (circle number)
1. Yes   2. No

Sensitive Area—Urination/Pubococcygeus Musculature

Do you ever prolong the act of urination by starting and stopping the flow of urine because of pleasurable sensations associated with contracting of the muscles involved in bladder control? (Circle number)
1. Yes   2. No

Have you ever held back from experiencing an orgasm due to the fear of urinating? (Circle number)
1. Yes   2. No
If never experienced orgasm go to Question _____:

Have you ever thought that you have urinated during your orgasm? (Circle number)
1. Yes   2. No

If yes: How often do you think you have urinated during orgasm? (Circle number)

1. Very frequently
2. Frequently
3. Occasionally
4. Seldom

Are you aware of the existence of the pubococcygeus muscle located at the vaginal entrance? (Circle number)
1. Yes   2. No

Can you consciously identify your pubococcygeus muscle through voluntary contractions? (Circle number)
1. Yes   2. No

If yes: Do you periodically exercise your pubococcygeus muscle through Kegel exercises or by another related method, such as starting and stopping the flow of urine? (Circle number)
1. Yes   2. No

Emotional Promiscuity Scale

Daniel Nelson Jones,[1] *University of British Columbia*

Research on promiscuity has focused on the sexual side with virtually no attention paid to the emotional side. I define *emotional promiscuity* as the tendency to develop romantic feelings quickly, often, and less discriminately. This tendency may be at least as important as sexual promiscuity with respect to the origins, development, and sustenance of relationships. Insofar as past behavior is predictive of future behavior in romantic relationships, emotional promiscuity in the past should influence current relationships in a variety of ways.

Researchers are beginning to confirm the longstanding notion that (at least some) people have little trouble disentangling sex and love (see Diamond, 2004). The same distinction applies to promiscuity. In one study, for example, Harms, Williams, and Paulhus (2001) found that those who are "love-prone" do not share the same individual difference correlates as those who are "lust-prone." Moreover, those seeking a mate take into consideration the emotional promiscuity of potential partners. For example, women and long-term-oriented men are averse to dating emotionally promiscuous partners and quickly end relationships with them (Jones, 2009).

Emotional promiscuity research looms large in importance when one considers the potential health consequences. Researchers have indicated that those who report being in love feel less at risk for sexually transmitted diseases (STDs; Manuel, 2005) and are less likely to use condoms (Rosenthal, Gifford, & Moore, 1998). It follows that emotionally promiscuous individuals are at higher risk for STD infection.

In sum, there appear to be health as well as relationship consequences of emotional promiscuity. Further advancement of research on this variable requires a standard instrument. This report provides an overview of my development of a reliable and valid measure of emotional promiscuity.

Description

My literature search revealed several elements of emotional promiscuity (EP): the tendency to fall in love quickly, frequently, and indiscriminately. Also associated is an exaggerated fascination with the experience of falling in love. The construct of emotional promiscuity must be distinguished from sexual promiscuity, that is, indiscriminate sexual activity (e.g., Simpson & Gangestad, 1991). It must also be distinguished from romanticism, the tendency to endorse idealistic notions of love (e.g., Sprecher & Metts, 1989).

Accordingly, a useful measure of EP would be able to assess the construct independently of sexual promiscu-ity or romanticism. This is not to say that the measures of the three constructs cannot be correlated—just not inherently confounded. To this end, I developed and validated a reliable measure of individual differences in emotional promiscuity. To permit fair comparisons with the effects of sexual promiscuity, I used the Sociosexual Orientation Inventory (SOI; Simpson & Gangestad, 1991) as a template. For robust coverage, the items span from behaviors to attitudes to identity. I used several questionnaire formats to cover both attitudes and reported behaviors.

The final set of 10 emotional promiscuity (EP) items were selected by refining a large wide-ranging item set. A series of factor analyses along with part-whole correlations were used to narrow the item set. The items were retained if they fell on the first unrotated factor in a total of four datasets.

Response Mode and Timing

The EP scale has been used successfully in paper-and-pencil as well as online survey formats. For best results, it should be administered privately and confidentially. It is appropriate for adults of any age and takes less than a minute to complete.

Scoring and Reliability

The items were evaluated separately for male and female participants in two types of samples: (a) a college student dataset ($N = 142$), and (b) two web-based surveys ($N = 775$).

College data. The data were from students attending a large northwestern university. Only individuals of European extraction were included. The item mean for males (2.99) was higher than the mean for females (2.81), marginally close to, but not reaching, statistical significance, $t(141) = 1.88, p = .07$. The alpha reliability was .69 for both male and female participants.

Web data. Two web-based surveys were aimed at a much broader community sample and included participants with a wide range of ages (16 to 71) and education. The item mean for males (3.45) was not significantly higher than the mean for females (3.36), $t(695) = 1.38, p = .17$. Alpha was .73 for male participants and .73 for female participants.

Convergent and Discriminant Validity

Correlations of EP with age were quite small—only .10 in the college sample and −.03 in the web sample. In short, individual differences in EP are evident across the adult life-span.

[1]Address correspondence to Daniel N. Jones, 2136 West Mall, Department of Psychology, UBC, Vancouver, BC, Canada, V6T 1Z4; e-mail: jonesdn@gmail.com

Student sample. For males, the correlation of the EP with sexual promiscuity (SOI) was −.01, but for females the corresponding correlation was .27. For males, a correlation of EP with the Romantic Beliefs scale was .24. For females, the correlation was .34. This pattern indicates that EP is not inherently confounded with related measures but is correlated in some cases.

Correlations with the Big Five Inventory (John & Srivastava, 1999) indicated a positive correlation with Openness to Experience (men only), which was the only significant correlation, $r = .38$, $p < .01$, two-tailed.

In Jones and Paulhus (2009), EP in women was positively and slightly associated with long-term mating orientation, but unrelated in men. EP was also positively correlated with anxious attachment style and negatively associated with avoidant attachment style. It was negatively related with IQ for both men and women.

Web sample. In the web sample, the correlation between EP and SOI was .09 for females and .13 for males. As in the student sample, the web sample revealed a moderate positive correlation with anxious attachment style and a small to moderate correlation with avoidant attachment style for both men and women. Infidelity data were available in the web sample, and EP was significantly correlated with general infidelity in men, and slightly correlated in women. Once again, EP was positively and slightly positively associated with long-term mating orientation for women, but was unrelated in men.

Criterion Validity

Of critical importance is the association that the EP scale has with relationship development, sustenance, and outcomes. In a behavioral study, Jones and Paulhus (2009) tracked participants longitudinally by coding their online logs of romantic interests and infidelities. Participants were asked to record the initials of the person they were involved with every week, along with the person or persons that they were most romantically and sexually attracted to that week.

Emotional infidelity was operationalized by the week-by-week discrepancies between the initials of participants' declared partners and the initials of their romantic interests. EP scores significantly predicted total number of romantic interests and were the lone predictor of emotional infidelity. In sum, the EP scale appears to be a valid and distinct predictor of relationship-relevant outcomes.

References

Diamond, L. M. (2004). Emerging perspectives on distinctions between romantic love and sexual desire. *Current Directions in Psychological Science, 13,* 116–119.

Harms, P. D., Williams, K. M., & Paulhus, D. L. (2001). *Predictors of love-proneness vs. lust-proneness.* Poster presented at the 109th annual convention of the American Psychological Association, San Francisco.

John, O. P., & Srivastava, S. (1999). The Big Five trait taxonomy: History, measurement, and theoretical perspectives. In L. A. Pervin & O. P. John (Eds.), *Handbook of personality: Theory and research* (pp. 102–138). New York: Guilford Press.

Jones, D. N. (2009). *The potential consequences of past sexual and emotional promiscuity: Preliminary findings.* Manuscript submitted for publication.

Jones, D. N., & Paulhus, D. L. (2009). *Emotional promiscuity and its consequences for romantic relationships and infidelity.* Manuscript in preparation.

Manuel, S. (2005). Obstacles to condom use among secondary school students in Maputo City, Mozambique. *Culture, Health and Sexuality, 7,* 293–302.

Rosenthal, D., Gifford, S., & Moore, S. (1998). Safe sex or safe love: Competing discourses? *AIDS Care, 10,* 35–45.

Simpson, J. A., & Gangestad, S. W. (1991). Individual differences in sociosexuality: Evidence for convergent and discriminant validity. *Journal of Personality and Social Psychology, 60,* 870–883.

Sprecher, S., & Metts, S. (1989). Development of the 'Romantic Beliefs Scale' and examination of the effects of gender and gender-role orientation. *Journal of Social and Personal Relationships, 6,* 387–411.

Exhibit

Emotional Promiscuity Scale

1	2	3	4	5
Strongly Disagree	Disagree	Neither Agree nor Disagree	Agree	Strongly Agree

Rate your agreement using the above guidelines

1. I fall in love easily.
2. For me, romantic feelings take a long time to develop.
3. I feel romantic connections right away.
4. I love the feeling of falling in love.
5. I am not the type of person who falls in love.
6. I often feel romantic connections to more than one person at a time.
7. I have been in love with more than one person at the same time.
8. I fall in love frequently.
9. I tend to jump into relationships.
10. During your entire life, how many people have you fallen in love with?
    A = None   B = 1   C = 2   D = 3   E = 4 or More

Sexual Anxiety Scale

ERIN E. FALLIS,[1] CHRISTINA GORDON, AND CHRISTINE PURDON, *University of Waterloo*

The Sexual Anxiety Scale (SAS) was developed to assess individuals' affective response to sexual cues, or erotophobia/philia. The term *erotophobia/philia* (EE) refers to the tendency to respond to sexual stimuli with either negative or positive affect (Fisher, Byrne, White, & Kelley, 1988), and the primary measure of EE to date has been the Sexual Opinion Survey (SOS; Fisher et al., 1988). Although exhibiting good psychometric properties, the SOS focuses primarily on responses to homosexuality, media with sexual content, and a small range of sexual behaviours. The SAS was developed to assess affective response to a broader range of sexual cues in both the public and the private domain.

Description

Respondents rate their degree of discomfort with a list of sexually relevant situations or stimuli on 11-point Likert-type scales ranging from *Extremely Pleasurable* to *Extremely Discomforting*. Items reflecting categories of sexual cues were written by members of our laboratory team and reviewed by two experts on sexuality who were not members of the team. The 56-item version of the scale was thus produced. The SAS was administered to a sample of undergraduate students at a midsized university in Ontario, Canada as part of a large test battery ($N = 701$). Reliability and validity were examined using a subset of the undergraduate students ($n = 376$) and a community sample of adults ($n = 188$). The demographic characteristics of the validation samples are shown in Table 1.

A factor analysis on responses from the undergraduate and community samples ($N = 889$) was conducted. This yielded a three-factor solution accounting for 49.5% of the variance. The first factor, Solitary and Impersonal Sexual Expression, accounted for 35.8% of the variance in the SAS and consists of 23 items pertaining to pornographic and erotic material, masturbation, and impersonal sexual experiences. The second factor, Exposure to Information, accounted for 8.1% of the variance in the SAS and consists of 14 items about giving or receiving information of a sexual nature. The third factor, Sexual Communication, accounted for 5.6% of the variance and includes 16 items reflecting openness to consensual sexual activity and communicating sexual likes and dislikes. Subscales based on these factors were then calculated and labeled accordingly.[2]

TABLE 1
Demographic Features of the Validation Samples

| | Sample | | | |
	Undergrad		Community	
Mean Age	19.2		38.9	
Gender Split	Male	Female	Male	Female
	181 (49%)	191 (51.3%)	66 (35%)	121 (64%)
Relationship Status	In Relationship 163 (44%)	Single 209 (56%)	In Relationship 140 (75%)	Single 47 (25%)
Religion Status	–		Not Practicing 99 (53%)	Practicing 67 (36%)
Modal Income	–		$40000–$59000	
Sexual Orientation	–		Heterosexual 115 (61%)	Homosexual 60 (32%)

Note. The – symbol indicates that data were not collected.

TABLE 2
Zero-Order Correlations Between Factors

| | | Sample | |
		Undergrad	Community
Factor 1	Factor 2	.34**	.32**
Factor 1	Factor 3	.68**	.64**
Factor 2	Factor 3	.40**	.35**

**$p < .01$

Correlation coefficients between the three factors were calculated for both samples, and these relationships may be seen in Table 2. Means and standard deviations for each factor for men and women in both samples are shown in Table 3.

Response Mode and Timing

The SAS is a self-report measure that takes between 5 and 15 minutes to complete.

Scoring

The SAS total score is calculated by summing the responses to each item. Higher scores indicate greater erotophobia. Individual scale scores can be calculated by summing the items in the relevant scale (see the Exhibit for the scale item key).

[1]Address correspondence to Erin Fallis, Department of Psychology, University of Waterloo, 200 University Avenue West, Waterloo, Ontario N2L 3G1, Canada; e-mail: efallis@uwaterloo.ca

[2]In these studies, respondents also rated the extent to which the sexual cue was likely to be avoided or approached so that behavior/attitude discrepancies could be explored. However, the scores on the two sets of ratings were redundant, with correlations > .92 in all samples. As such, it was decided that the approach/avoidance ratings were not a useful addition to the measure and have been dropped from the final version.

TABLE 3
Means and Standard Deviations of Total SAS Scores

	Males		Females		Combined	
	M	**SD**	**M**	**SD**	**M**	**SD**
Undergraduates						
Total	2339.4	765.9	2775.3	858.4	2563.3	842.4
Factor 1	909.6	336.4	1318.2	447.6	1119.4	457.8
Factor 2	793.3	204.2	761.4	197.5	776.9	201.1
Factor 3	476.2	274.5	518.4	338.9	497.9	309.5
Community						
Total	1736.2	565.9	2058.3	704.6	1946.5	674.0
Factor 1	596.1	291.4	937.2	412.6	815.6	406.9
Factor 2	731.7	152.3	676.4	177.1	679.1	170.8
Factor 3	278.5	161.2	301.8	208.1	295.1	193.3

Reliability

The SAS showed strong internal consistency, with Cronbach's alphas of .96 in the undergraduate sample and .95 in the community sample. The scale scores were equally strong, with alphas ranging from .87 to .95. Test-retest reliability was examined in a subset of the undergraduate sample ($n = 42$), and suggested good stability of scores over time ($r = .87, p < .01$).

Validity

In order to establish discriminant validity, measures of mood (Depression, Anxiety, Stress Scale; Lovibond & Lovibond, 1995) and personality (International Personality Item Pool; Goldberg, 1999) were administered to both samples. SAS total scores were not simply a reflection of mood, showing only a very small correlation with anxiety, and were not a reflection of neuroticism or other personality traits. See Table 4 for additional details.

In order to establish construct validity, the SAS was administered along with measures of various aspects of sexuality, with overlapping and different measures within each sample. In the community sample, the SAS had a high correlation with the SOS. As well, lower SAS scores (i.e., greater erotophilia) were significantly

TABLE 4
Zero-Order Correlations Between the SAS and Measures of Mood and Personality

	Pearson Correlations With SAS	
	Undergrad Sample	**Community Sample**
Mood		
Depression	.06	.06
Anxiety	.16**	.11
Stress	.06	.03
Personality		
Extraversion	−.21**	−.34**
Agreeableness	.03	−.07
Conscientiousness	.07	−.04
Emotional Stability	−.06	−.08
Intelligence	−.06	−.26**

**$p < .01$

correlated with greater sexual satisfaction (Global Measure of Sexual Satisfaction; Lawrance & Byers, 1995), less antigay prejudice (Heterosexual Attitudes Toward Homosexuality Scale; Larsen, 1998), better sexual functioning (Sexual Functioning Questionnaire; Lawrance & Byers, 1992), and more positive attitudes towards sex education of both male and female children (measure developed by the authors). Regression analyses indicated that the SAS was a better predictor of sexual functioning than was the SOS, particularly the Sexual Communication scale; otherwise, the two measures were equivalent in their prediction of sexual behaviour and attitudes (Purdon & Gordon, 2005).

In the undergraduate sample, lower SAS scores were significantly correlated with greater sexual satisfaction (Global Measure of Sexual Satisfaction; Lawrance & Byers, 1995), better sexual functioning (Golombok-Rust Inventory of Sexual Satisfaction; Rust & Golombok, 1998), higher scores on a measure of knowledge about sexual issues (e.g., anatomy, contraception, pregnancy, sexually transmitted infections [STIs], reproduction; developed by the authors), and more frequent use of birth control and STI protection (measure developed by the authors). The correlation between the SAS and antigay prejudice (Heterosexual Attitudes Toward Homosexuality Scale; Larsen, 1998) was not significant. However, the distribution of this measure was heavily skewed with the vast majority of the sample reporting little or no antigay prejudice, so there was little variance. See Table 5 for additional details.

Some group differences emerged. In both samples, males had lower SAS scores than females, $t(370) = -5.16$, $p < .01$ and $t(185) = -3.19$, $p < .01$ for the undergraduate and community samples respectively. Participants not currently practicing a religion had significantly lower SAS

TABLE 5
Zero-Order Correlations With Measures of Sexuality

	Pearson Correlation With SAS
Community Sample	
Sexual Opinion Survey	−.78**
Attitudes About Sex Education	
Educating Males	−.31**
Educating Females	−.32**
Sexual Functioning	.22**
Undergraduate Sample	
Effective Use of Birth Control	−.34**
Effective Use of STI Protection	−.24**
Sexual Functioning	
Males	.54**
Females	.25**
Both Samples	
Sexual Satisfaction	
Undergrad	−.27**
Community	−.20**
Antigay Prejudice	
Undergrad	−.04
Community	.22**

**$p < .01$

scores than those currently practicing a religion, $t(164) = 2.23, p < .05$. However, SAS scores did not differ according to sexual orientation.

References

Fisher, W. A., Byrne, D., White, L. A., & Kelley, K. (1988). Erotophobia-erotophilia as a dimension of personality. *The Journal of Sex Research, 25,* 123–151.

Goldberg, L. R. (1999). A broad-bandwidth, public domain, personality inventory measuring the lower-level facets of several five-factor models. In I. Mervielde, I. Deary, F. De Fruyt, & F. Ostendorf (Eds.), *Personality psychology in Europe, 7* (pp. 7–28). Tilburg, The Netherlands: Tilburg University Press.

Larsen, K. S. (1998). Heterosexual attitudes toward homosexuality scale. In C. M. Davis, W. L. Yarber, R. Bauserman, G. Schreer, & S. L. Davis (Eds.), *Handbook of sexuality-related measures* (pp. 394–395). Thousand Oaks, CA: Sage.

Lawrance, K., & Byers, E. S. (1992). *Sexual satisfaction: A social exchange perspective.* Paper presented at the Annual Meeting of the Canadian Psychological Association, Quebec.

Lawrance, K., & Byers, E. S. (1995). Sexual satisfaction in long-term heterosexual relationships: The Interpersonal Exchange Model of Sexual Satisfaction. *Personal Relationships, 2,* 267–285.

Lovibond, P. F., & Lovibond, S. H. (1995). The structure of negative emotional states: Comparison of the Depression Anxiety Stress Scales (DASS) with the Beck Depression and Anxiety Inventories. *Behaviour, Research and Therapy, 33,* 335–343.

Purdon, C., & Gordon, C. (2005, November). *Development of the Sexual Anxiety Scale.* Poster presented at the Association for the Advancement of Behavior and Cognitive Therapies Annual Meeting, Washington, DC.

Rust, J., & Golombok, S. (1998). The GRISS: A psychometric scale and profile of sexual dysfunction. In C. M. Davis, W. L. Yarber, R. Bauserman, G. Schreer, & S. L. Davis (Eds.), *Handbook of sexuality-related measures* (pp. 192–194). Thousand Oaks, CA: Sage.

Exhibit

Sexual Anxiety Scale

For each item presented below, you are asked to rate how much discomfort you would experience using the following scale:

How much discomfort would you feel in each situation? (Place this rating under column "D")

0	10	20	30	40	50	60	70	80	90	100
Extremely Pleasurable					Neutral					Extremely Discomforting

D

1. Wearing clothes that show off my sexually attractive features[c] ——
2. Seeing two people kissing or fondling each other[a] ——
3. Watching a movie scene from a major box office movie in which people were naked[a] ——
4. Talking with my friends about my sex life ——
5. Masturbating[a] ——
6. Looking at hardcore or pornographic photos in a magazine (explicit scenes of the genitals and penetration)[a] ——
7. Using sex toys, such as a vibrator, during sex with my partner[a] ——
8. Exploring the erogenous, or sexually exciting, parts of my partner's body[c] ——
9. Hearing about someone engaging in a consensual sexual act that I personally would never want to engage in[a] ——
10. Discussing my sexual fantasies with my partner[c] ——
11. Having arousing sexual thoughts that are unrelated to my current sexual partner[a] ——
12. Hearing about a woman who enjoyed sex and was sexually adventurous[a] ——
13. Watching a "hardcore" or "pornographic" film[a] ——
14. Being exposed to information about sexually transmitted infections[b] ——
15. Kissing or fondling my partner in a public place ——
16. Vocalizing my pleasure during sex with my partner[c] ——
17. Watching a movie scene from a major box office movie in which people were kissing or fondling each other[c] ——
18. Hearing about someone who has a biological sexual abnormality, such as undescended testicles, or a fertility problem[b] ——
19. Reading books with sexually explicit passages[c] ——
20. Agreeing to try sexual activities or positions that I find unusual but my partner suggests[c] ——
21. Using sex toys, such as a vibrator, when I am alone[a] ——
22. Engaging in foreplay with my partner[c] ——
23. Finding myself becoming sexually aroused in response to something I never would have expected myself to be aroused by[c] ——
24. Visiting Internet sites that feature erotic or softcore photos or video clips[a] ——
25. Having arousing sexual thoughts that are related to my current sexual partner[c] ——
26. Talking with my partner about his/her sexual fantasies[c] ——
27. Talking with my friends about general matters of a sexual nature, such as menstruation, pregnancy, childbirth[b] ——

28. Changing my clothes in a public change room that does not have privacy cubicles[b] ___
29. Being exposed to information about contraceptive devices that require intimate genital contact (e.g., diaphragm, sponge, foam)[b] ___
30. Overhearing other people (not parents) having sex[a] ___
31. Watching a scene from a major box office movie in which people were engaging in sex[a] ___
32. Exploring erogenous, or sexually exciting, parts of my body when I am alone[a] ___
33. Someone knowing that I look at/watch erotic photos/films[a] ___
34. Suggesting new sexual activities or positions to my partner[c] ___
35. Visiting Internet sites that features hardcore or pornographic photos or video clips[a] ___
36. Engaging in a casual sexual encounter (e.g., a one-night stand)[a] ___
37. Being invited by an acquaintance/friend/partner to engage in an unusual sexual act[a] ___
38. Hearing about sexual issues or matters from the newspaper or TV[b] ___
39. Fantasizing about arousing sexual acts during sex with my partner in order to enhance my sexual excitement[c] ___
40. Disclosing to my friends that I have a sexual problem[b] ___
41. Answering questions about sexual matters such as conception[b] ___
42. Someone overhearing me and my partner having sex[a] ___
43. Being around others who are changing their clothes ___
44. Being exposed to information about diseases of the sex organs, such as cervical cancer, testicular cancer, prostate cancer, breast cancer[b] ___
45. Watching an "erotic" or "softporn" film (no explicit scenes of the genitals or penetration)[a] ___
46. Allowing my partner to explore my erogenous, or sexually exciting, parts of my body[c] ___
47. Someone knowing that I look at/watch pornographic photos/films[a] ___
48. Changing activities or positions during sex with a partner to help ensure that I have an orgasm[c] ___
49. Looking at erotic or softcore photos in a magazine[a] ___
50. Telling my partner what pleases me and does not please me sexually[c] ___
51. Hearing about people I don't consider to be sexual engaging in sex, such as the elderly, my parents, disabled people[b] ___
52. Having a conversation with my friends about their sex lives[b] ___
53. Fantasizing about arousing sexual thoughts during masturbation in order to enhance my sexual excitement[a] ___
54. Watching coverage of the Gay Pride Day parade[b] ___
55. Being exposed to information about contraceptives and contraceptive use[b] ___
56. Completing questionnaires about my sexuality[b] ___

[a]Solitary and Impersonal Sexual Expression (Factor 1)
[b]Exposure to Information (Factor 2)
[c]Sexual Communication (Factor 3)

Sexual Opinion Survey

B. J. Rye,[1] *St. Jerome's University at the University of Waterloo*
Glenn J. Meaney, *Wilfrid Laurier University*
William A. Fisher, *University of Western Ontario*

The personality dimension of erotophobia-erotophilia is conceptualized as a learned disposition to respond to sexual stimuli with negative-to-positive affect and evaluation and is believed to determine avoidance or approach responses to sexual stimuli. The Sexual Opinion Survey (SOS) is a measure of this trait (Fisher, Byrne, White, & Kelley, 1988).

Description

The SOS (see Exhibit 1) consists of 21 items intended to assess affective and evaluative responses to sexual stimuli (autosexual, homosexual, heterosexual behavior; sexual fantasy; visual sexual stimuli). Each item depicts a sexual situation and an affective response to it; individuals are asked to

[1]Address correspondence to B. J. Rye, Department of Psychology, St. Jerome's University, 290 Westmount Road North, Waterloo, Ontario, Canada N2L 3G3; e-mail: bjrye@uwaterloo.ca

indicate degree of agreement or disagreement with the statement (scale development is described in Fisher, 1998, and Fisher et al., 1988). Terminology in some items was updated by Fisher (1998) because some of the original wording was no longer in use or had changed meaning. Translations of the SOS into Hebrew, French, Finnish, German, Portuguese, and Japanese are available; recently, it has also been translated into Spanish (Sierra, Ortega, & Zubeidat, 2006) and Dutch (Dodge, Sandfort, Yarber, & de Wit, 2005).

A short form of the SOS was developed by Semph (1979; see Exhibit 2) using five items established as strong predictors of full scale scores (e.g., Table 2, Sample 1: $r = .84$). A scale conceptually based on the SOS was designed for use with very young adolescent girls (Rye et al., 2008; see Exhibit 3) and highly correlated with the SOS in a sample of first-year university students ($r = .74$, $n = 55$).

Extensive construct validity for the SOS was reported by Fisher et al. (1988) and Fisher (1998); therefore, we will focus on literature published since 1998. The SOS has been used extensively with North American university students and has been used to assess erotophobia-erotophilia in university students in Australia (Beatson & Halloran, 2007), Israel (Birnbaum & Gillath, 2006), and the Netherlands (Dodge et al., 2005), as well as nonstudent populations including adult women (Graham, Sanders, & Milhausen,

2006), high-school men (Sierra et al., 2006), incarcerated men (Garland, Morgan, & Beer, 2005), women who have had an abortion and nonpregnant women at health clinics (Bradshaw & Slade, 2005), and users and nonusers of erotica (Lawyer, 2008). Normative data from these studies, when available, are summarized in Table 1; the current authors' normative data are summarized in Table 2.

Response Mode and Timing

Completion of the SOS usually takes 10 minutes or less. General instructions are provided (see Exhibit 1); additional instructions may be added for participants unfamiliar with Likert-type responding.

Scoring

Fisher (1998) specified the following scoring scheme: First, score responses from 1 (*Strongly Disagree*) to 7 (*Strongly Agree*); second, add scores from Items 2, 5, 6, 12, 13, 14, 15, 16, 19, and 20; third, subtract the sum of Items 1, 3, 4, 7, 8, 9, 10, 11, 17, 18, and 21; fourth, add 67. This scheme results in a number between 0 (erotophobic) and 126 (erotophilic); missing data can be handled for positively and negatively worded items by substituting the mean score for the other

TABLE 1
Normative Data From Published Research

Study	Subsamples	N	M	SD	Group Differences[a]	Scoring[a]	High Score	Notes
Barak et al. (1999)	n/a	31	73.36	17.21	n/a	Fisher	Erotophilia	Undergraduate men
Bogaert & Sadava (2002)	n/a	792	83.97	22.16	n/a	22 to 137	Erotophilia	Adults
Bradshaw & Slade (2005)	Abortion	98	76	19	Significant difference	Fisher	Erotophilia	Women from health clinics
	No abortion	51	69	21				
Dodge et al. (2005)	United States	133	3.07	1.03	Significant difference	Average	Erotophobia	Undergraduate men
	Netherlands	109	2.61	1.00				
Forbes et al. (2003)	n/a	211	2.68	.70	No gender difference	1 to 6 Average	Erotophilia	University students; short version
Garcia (1999)	Men	77	5.7 ± 19.1	n/a	No significant difference	Fisher −67	Erotophilia	Introductory psychology students
	Women	84	−6.7 ± 19.3	n/a		−67 to +59		
Geer & Robertson (2005)	Men	115	66.72	23.89	Significant difference	Not described	Erotophilia	Psychology undergraduates
	Women	137	59.56	19.32				
Hogben et al. (2001)	Men	177	59.88	11.86	Significant difference	Items: 1 to 6	Erotophilia	Introductory psychology students
	Women	176	71.15	15.96				
Lawyer (2008)	Erotica users	34	93.3	22.7	No significant difference	Not described	Erotophilia	Men and women
	Erotica non-users	37	84.9	22.1				
Sanders et al. (2006)	Condom appliers	102	3.9	1.2	Significant difference	Average	Erotophobia	Sexually active women
	Condom non-appliers	220	4.2	1.1				
Shim et al. (2007)	n/a	151	76	19	n/a	Fisher	Erotophilia	Introductory communications students

[a]Scoring information based on published literature or personal communication with authors. "Fisher" indicates that scores were calculated as specified by Fisher (1998) and in the *Scoring* section. "Average" indicates that negatively worded items were reverse coded and then all items were averaged. All items were scored on a 7-point Likert-type scale except where noted.

TABLE 2
Normative Data From the Authors' Research

Sample	Subsamples	N	M	SD	Group Differences	Notes
1	Men	854	3.83	.50	Significant difference	Introductory human sexuality students; 23 classes enrolled between 1999 and 2007
	Women	2007	3.60	.57		
	Heterosexual[a]	2657	3.63	.55	Significant difference	
	Queer[a]	207	4.07	.52		
2	Men	27	4.37	.83	No significant difference	Introductory psychology students agreed to participate in sex study
	Women	39	4.05	.91		
3	n/a	135	4.14	1.15	n/a	Introductory psychology students department mass-testing
4	Men	43	4.92	1.18	Significant difference	Homophobia awareness workshop (Rye & Meaney, 2009); short version without Item 21
	Women	70	4.31	1.11		
5	Heterosexual	49	4.39	.67	Lesbians more erotophilic than heterosexuals	Adult women
	AIS[b]	44	4.59	.76		
	Lesbian	45	4.85	.63		

Note. Except where noted, all samples completed the full, 21-item SOS. Scoring: Individual items were rated on a 1 to 7 scale, except for Sample 1 (1 to 5). Negatively worded items were reverse scored. Then, all items were averaged. Higher scores indicate erotophilia. Missing data were ignored provided completion of half the items.

[a]5-point self-identification scale: 1–2 = heterosexual, 3–5 = queer (bisexual or homosexual)
[b]AIS = Androgen Insensitivity Syndrome

positively or negatively worded items, respectively (stipulating completion of half the relevant items).

In practice, some researchers simply add the items after reverse coding negatively worded items (resulting in a score from 21 to 147), or average across all items (with negatively worded items reverse coded, resulting in a score from 1 to 7). There are advantages to each scoring scheme. Averaging the items, for example, results in a score on the same scale as the individual items (i.e., 1 to 7) and minimizes the impact of missing data (i.e., a few missing items can be omitted). However, researchers conducting cross-study comparisons should be aware that scores from different studies may not be directly comparable. Scoring schemes should not affect relationships between the SOS and other variables.

Reliability

Since Fisher (1998) reported on the reliability of the SOS, high internal consistency has been found among various samples of university students (Cronbach's α = .76 to .89; see References) and using a Hebrew version of the SOS (α = .85; Birnbaum & Gillath, 2006); internal consistency is about equal for men and women (e.g., Smith & Nave, 2007). Lower internal consistency (α = .63) was found for the short version (Beatson & Halloran, 2007). A scale conceptually based on the SOS designed for very young adolescent girls had similar internal consistency (α = .63; Rye et al., 2008). Substantial test-retest reliability of the full scale was found with a sample of university students over an interval of several weeks (Table 2, Sample 2: r = .61, n = 35).

Although the SOS is highly internally consistent, some researchers have attempted to identify subscales. Sierra et al. (2006), using a Spanish sample, reported four factors (erotophilia, erotophobia, homophobia, and unconventional sex); a similar factor structure was reported using a Norwegian sample (Rise, Traeen, & Kraft, 1993). Based on our analysis (Table 2, Sample 1), we recommend a two-factor solution when investigation of factors is desired: (a) open sexual display and sexual variety, and (b) homoeroticism—a refinement of the three-factor solution suggested by Gilbert & Gamache, 1984). Further investigation is required to demonstrate the generality and stability of sets of factors and the utility of factor-based subscales.

Validity

Since publication in the previous edition of the *Handbook of Sexuality-Related Measures* (Fisher, 1998), the construct validity of the SOS continues to be well established through research with theoretically relevant variables. In particular, SOS scores are predictive of prior sexual media exposure (Bogaert, 2001), subjective sexual arousal (Nobre et al., 2004), sexual arousal and anxiety (and, indirectly, sexual self-schema; Cyranowski & Andersen, 1998), self-reported sexual behavior (i.e., masturbation, multiple partners, unprotected sex; Durant, Carey, & Schroder, 2002), implicit sexual attitudes (Geer & Robertson, 2005), perceptions of consumer items as a means of attracting sexual partners or enhancing sex (Gould, 1995), sexual excitation and inhibition (Graham et al., 2006; Janssen, Vorst, Finn, & Bancroft, 2002a, 2002b; Wilson, Holm, Bishop, & Borowiak, 2002), homonegativity (Mahaffey, Bryan, & Hutchison, 2005), condom application (i.e., women who applied condoms on their male partners were more erotophilic than those who did not; Sanders et al., 2006), "short-term, unrestricted mating orientation" (Schmitt, Shackelford, Duntley, Tooke, & Buss, 2001), willingness to be exposed to unsolicited Internet pornography (Shim, Lee, & Paul, 2007), and sexual fantasy (Sierra et al., 2006). Garcia (1999) found that participants higher in erotophilia were more likely to rate themselves as sexually experienced, sexually deviant, holding liberal or permissive sexual attitudes, and being sexually responsive.

In our research (Table 2, Sample 1), SOS scores were weakly to moderately correlated with a variety of sexual attitudes (e.g., approval of premarital sexual intercourse, accessibility of birth control), sexual behaviors with others (e.g., number of sexual partners, having orally stimulated a partner's genitals), and autosexual behavior (e.g., use of mechanical aids, frequency of masturbation, also reported by Zamboni & Crawford, 2002). The SOS did not predict self-reported sexual dysfunction. Erotophilia correlated moderately with being gay or lesbian, attitudes toward homosexuality, and having gay friends or acquaintances.

Although previous research has found erotophobia-erotophilia to be a consistent predictor of sexual health behaviors (see Fisher, 1998), little current research has investigated this connection. Our data (Table 2, Sample 1) suggest that the SOS was generally unrelated to sexual health behaviors, with a few exceptions—for example, erotophilia predicted self-reported likelihood of pap exams and breast self-examination (but not testicular self-examination). Wilkinson, Holahan, and Drane-Edmundson (2002) found that erotophilia predicted safer-sex behaviors for people with cooperative partners, but not for people with uncooperative partners.

Erotophobia-erotophilia has been found to correlate with authoritarianism (Bogaert, 2001; Hogben, Byrne, Hamburger, & Osland, 2001), sensation-seeking (Bogaert, 2001), and anxious (Bogaert & Sadava, 2002) and dismissive (Schmitt et al., 2001) attachment styles. Hogben et al. (2001) found that SOS scores were related to aggression (although Bogaert did not) and gender-typing for men (again, not found by Bogaert). Our data (Table 2, Sample 4) indicate that SOS scores moderately predict authoritarianism, religiosity, and knowledge of sexual anatomy.

Discriminant validity is provided by evidence that the SOS does not correlate with social desirability, aggression, dominance, intelligence, or psychoticism (Bogaert, 2001). Our own data (Table 2, Sample 4) suggest that erotophobia-erotophilia is uncorrelated with social desirability.

Other Information

Although intended to measure an affective disposition, the SOS is generally used as an indicator of general attitudes toward sexuality. Erotophobia-erotophilia tends to be used as one of several potential predictors of an outcome measure of interest, and is occasionally used as an outcome measure in itself.

References

Barak, A., Fisher, W. A., Belfry, S., & LaShambe, D. R. (1999). Sex, guys, and cyberspace: Effects of Internet pornography and individual differences on men's attitudes toward women. *Journal of Psychology and Human Sexuality, 11*(1), 63–91.

Beatson, R. M., & Halloran, M. J. (2007). Humans rule! The effects of creatureliness reminders, mortality salience and self-esteem on attitudes towards animals. *British Journal of Social Psychology, 46*, 619–632.

Birnbaum, G. E., & Gillath, O. (2006). Measuring subgoals of the sexual behavioral system: What is sex good for? *Journal of Social and Personal Relationships, 23*, 675–701.

Bogaert, A. F. (2001). Personality, individual differences, and preferences for the sexual media. *Archives of Sexual Behavior, 30*, 29–53.

Bogaert, A. F., & Sadava, S. (2002). Adult attachment and sexual behavior. *Personal Relationships, 9*, 191–204.

Bradshaw, Z., & Slade, P. (2005). The relationships between induced abortion, attitudes towards sexuality and sexual problems. *Sexual and Relationship Therapy, 20*, 391–406.

Cyranowski, J. M., & Andersen, B. L. (1998). Schemas, sexuality, and romantic attachment. *Journal of Personality and Social Psychology, 74*, 1364–1379.

Dodge, B., Sandfort, T. G. M., Yarber, W. L., & de Wit, J. (2005). Sexual health among male college students in the United States and the Netherlands. *American Journal of Health Behavior, 29*, 172–182.

Durant, L. E., Carey, M. P., & Schroder, K. E. E. (2002). Effects of anonymity, gender, and erotophilia on the quality of data obtained from self-reports of socially sensitive behaviors. *Journal of Behavioral Medicine, 25*, 439–467.

Fisher, W. A. (1998). The Sexual Opinion Survey. In C. M. Davis, W. L. Yarber, R. Bauserman, G. Schreer, & S. L. Davis (Eds.), *Handbook of sexuality-related measures* (pp. 218–221). Thousand Oaks, CA: Sage.

Fisher, W. A., Byrne, D., White, L. A., & Kelley, K. (1988). Erotophobia-erotophilia as a dimension of personality. *The Journal of Sex Research, 25*, 123–151.

Forbes, G. B., Adams-Curtis, L. E., Hamm, N. R., & White, K. B. (2003). Perceptions of the woman who breastfeeds: The role of erotophobia, sexism, and attitudinal variables. *Sex Roles, 49*, 379–388.

Garcia, L. T. (1999). The certainty of the sexual self-concept. *Canadian Journal of Human Sexuality, 8*, 263–270.

Garland, J. T., Morgan, R. D., & Beer, A. M. (2005). Impact of time in prison and security level on inmates' sexual attitude, behavior, and identity. *Psychological Services, 2*, 151–162.

Geer, J. H., & Robertson, G. G. (2005). Implicit attitudes in sexuality: Gender differences. *Archives of Sexual Behavior, 34*, 671–677.

Gilbert, F. S., & Gamache, M. P. (1984). The Sexual Opinion Survey: Structure and use. *The Journal of Sex Research, 20*, 293–309.

Gould, S. J. (1995). Sexualized aspects of consumer behavior: An empirical investigation of consumer lovemaps. *Psychology and Marketing, 12*, 395–413.

Graham, C. A., Sanders, S. A., & Milhausen, R. R. (2006). The Sexual Excitation/Sexual Inhibition Inventory for Women: Psychometric properties. *Archives of Sexual Behavior, 35*, 397–409.

Hogben, M., Byrne, D., Hamburger, M. E., & Osland, J. (2001). Legitimized aggression and sexual coercion: Individual differences in cultural spillover. *Aggressive Behavior, 27*, 26–43.

Janssen, E., Vorst, H., Finn, P., & Bancroft, J. (2002a). The Sexual Inhibition (SIS) and Sexual Excitation (SES) Scales: I. Measuring sexual inhibition and excitation proneness in men. *Journal of Sex Research, 39*, 114–126.

Janssen, E., Vorst, H., Finn, P., & Bancroft, J. (2002b). The Sexual Inhibition (SIS) and Sexual Excitation (SES) Scales: II. Predicting psychophysiological response patterns. *The Journal of Sex Research, 39*, 127–132.

Lawyer, S. R. (2008). Probability and delay discounting of erotic stimuli. *Behavioural Processes, 79*, 36–42.

Mahaffey, A. L., Bryan, A., & Hutchison, K. E. (2005). Using startle eye blink to measure the affective component of antigay bias. *Basic and Applied Social Psychology, 27,* 37–45.

Nobre, P. J., Wiegel, M., Bach, A. K., Weisberg, R. B., Brown, T. A., Wincze, J. P., et al. (2004). Determinants of sexual arousal and the accuracy of its self-estimation in sexually functional males. *The Journal of Sex Research, 41,* 363–371.

Rise, J., Traeen, B., & Kraft, P. (1993). The Sexual Opinion Survey Scale: A study on dimensionality in Norwegian adolescents. *Health Education Research, 8,* 485–492.

Rye, B. J. & Meaney, G. J. (2009). Impact of a homonegativity awareness workshop on attitudes toward homosexuality. *Journal of Homosexuality, 56*(1), 31–55.

Rye, B. J., Yessis, J., Brunk, T., McKay, A., Morris, S., & Meaney, G. J. (2008). Outcome evaluation of *Girl Time: Grade 7/8 Healthy Sexuality Program. Canadian Journal of Human Sexuality, 17,* 15–36.

Sanders, S. A., Graham, C. A., Yarber, W. L., Crosby, R. A., Dodge, B., & Milhausen, R. R. (2006). Women who put condoms on male partners: Correlates of condom application. *American Journal of Health Behavior, 30,* 460–466.

Schmitt, D. P., Shackelford, T. K., Duntley, J., Tooke, W., & Buss, D. M. (2001). The desire for sexual variety as a key to understanding basic human mating strategies. *Personal Relationships. Special Issue: Evolutionary Approaches to Relationships, 8,* 425–455.

Semph, M. E. (1979). *Emotional orientation towards sexuality: Its relation to expecting and perceiving contraceptive side effects.* Unpublished honors thesis. University of Western Ontario, Department of Psychology, London, Ontario, Canada.

Shim, J. W., Lee, S., & Paul, B. (2007). Who responds to unsolicited sexually explicit materials on the Internet? The role of individual differences. *CyberPsychology and Behavior, 10,* 71–79.

Sierra, J. C., Ortega, V., & Zubeidat, I. (2006). Confirmatory factor analysis of a Spanish version of the sex fantasy questionnaire: Assessing gender differences. *Journal of Sex and Marital Therapy, 32,* 137–159.

Smith, G. E., & Nave, C. S. (2007). Illness transmission mode and perceiver personality: Factors affecting stigmatized perceptions of patients and sexual illness. *Social Behavior and Personality, 35,* 853–860.

Wilkinson, A. V., Holahan, C. J., & Drane-Edmundson, E. W. (2002). Predicting safer sex practices: The interactive role of partner cooperation and cognitive factors. *Psychology and Health, 17,* 697–709.

Wilson, B. A., Holm, J. E., Bishop, K. L., & Borowiak, D. M. (2002). Predicting responses to sexually aggressive stories: The role of consent, interest in sexual aggression, and overall sexual interest. *The Journal of Sex Research, 39,* 275–283.

Zamboni, B. D., & Crawford, I. (2002). Using masturbation in sex therapy: Relationships between masturbation, sexual desire, and sexual fantasy. *Journal of Psychology and Human Sexuality, 14*(2/3), 123–141.

Exhibit I

Sexual Opinion Survey

Please respond to each item as honestly as you can. There are no right and wrong answers, and your answers will be completely anonymous.

1. I think it would be very entertaining to look at hard-core erotica.
   I strongly agree   *I strongly disagree*[a]
2. Erotica is obviously filthy and people should not try to describe it as anything else.
3. Swimming in the nude with a member of the opposite sex would be an exciting experience.
4. Masturbation can be an exciting experience.
5. If I found that a close friend of mine was a homosexual, it would annoy me.
6. If people thought I was interested in oral sex, I would be embarrassed.
7. Engaging in group sex is an entertaining idea.
8. I personally find that thinking about engaging in sexual intercourse is arousing.
9. Seeing an erotic movie would be sexually arousing to me.
10. Thoughts that I may have homosexual tendencies would not worry me at all.
11. The idea of my being physically attracted to members of the same sex is not depressing.
12. Almost all sexually explicit material is nauseating.
13. It would be emotionally upsetting to me to see someone exposing themselves publicly.
14. Watching an exotic dancer of the opposite sex would not be very exciting.
15. I would not enjoy seeing an erotic movie.
16. When I think about seeing pictures showing someone of the same sex as myself masturbating, it nauseates me.
17. The thought of engaging in unusual sex practices is highly arousing.
18. Manipulating my genitals would probably be an arousing experience.
19. I do not enjoy daydreaming about sexual matters.
20. I am not curious about explicit erotica.
21. The thought of having long-term sexual relations with more than one sex partner is not disgusting to me.

Note. Score the survey as follows: First, score responses from 1 = *I strongly agree* to 7 = *I strongly disagree*. Second, add scores from Items 2, 5, 6, 12, 13, 14, 15, 16, 19, and 20. Third, subtract from this total the sum of Items 1, 3, 4, 7, 8, 9, 10, 11, 17, 18, and 21. Fourth, add 67 to this quantity. Scores range from 0 (most erotophobic) to 126 (most erotophilic). For the short form, administer Items 12, 4, 13, 17, and 21 (in this order, renumbered 1–5). Score responses from 1 = *I strongly agree* to 7 = *I strongly disagree*.

To reflect current usage, the terms *pornography* and *pornographic* from the original scale have been replaced with *erotic* or *sexually explicit material* and *stripper* has been replaced with *exotic dancer.*

[a]The scale is repeated after each item.

Exhibit 2

Sexual Opinion Survey—Short Form

1. Almost all sexually explicit material is nauseating.
        I strongly agree   *I strongly disagree*[a]
2. Masturbation can be an exciting experience.
3. It would be emotionally upsetting to me to see someone exposing themselves publicly.
4. The thought of engaging in unusual sex practices is highly arousing.
5. The thought of having long-term sexual relations with more than one sex partner is not disgusting to me.

Note. Score as follows: Score responses from 1 = *I strongly agree* to 7 = *I strongly disagree*; then reverse code items 1 and 3; then add all responses. Scores can range from 5 (most erotophilic) to 35 (most erotophobic). To reflect current usage, the terms *pornography* and *pornographic* from the original scale have been replaced with *erotic* or *sexually explicit material.*
[a]The scale is repeated after each item.

Exhibit 3

Comfort With Sexuality Matters for Very Young Adolescent Girls

Please respond to each item as honestly as you can. There are no right and wrong answers, and your answers will be completely anonymous.

1. It is *not* OK for a person to have more than one sex partner during their lifetime.
        I strongly disagree   *I strongly agree*[a]
2. It is OK for a person to masturbate if it makes him/her feel good.
3. It is OK for two men to have sex with each other or two women to have sex with each other.
4. It is *not* OK for people to have sexual intercourse unless they are in a committed relationship.
5. It is OK to enjoy being sexually aroused (turned on) by a sexy story, picture, or movie.
6. Oral sex[b] is disgusting to me.

Note. Score as follows: First, score responses from 1 (*I strongly disagree*) to 7 (*I strongly agree*); second, reverse code Items 1, 4, and 6; third, average all 6 items. Scores range from 1 (least comfortable) to 7 (most comfortable). Missing data can be ignored provided participants complete at least half of the items.
[a]The scale is repeated after each item.
[b]Our initial sample of Grade 7 girls generally did not know what "oral sex" was. The term was defined briefly by the project manager.

Sexual Inhibition/Sexual Excitation Scales—Short Form

Deanna L. Carpenter,[1] *Christopher Newport University*
Erick Janssen, *The Kinsey Institute for Research in Sex, Gender, and Reproduction*
Cynthia A. Graham, *Warneford Hospital, Oxford*
Harrie Vorst and Jelte Wicherts, *University of Amsterdam*

The central assumption of the dual control model (Bancroft & Janssen, 2000) is that sexual arousal and response result from a balance between inhibitory and excitatory mechanisms of the central nervous system. The Sexual Inhibition/Sexual Excitation Scales (SIS/SES; Janssen, Vorst, Finn, & Bancroft, 2002) consist of 45 items and feature one sexual excitation factor (SES) and two inhibition-related factors: one relevant to the threat of performance failure (SIS1) and one relevant to the threat of performance consequences (SIS2). The SIS/SES has been found to be relevant to the

[1]Address correspondence to Deanna L. Carpenter, Christopher Newport University, Department of Psychology, 1 University Place, Newport News, VA 23606; e-mail: deanna.carpenter@cnu.edu

prediction of various aspects of sexual response and behavior (for a review, see Bancroft, Graham, Janssen, & Sanders, 2009). Several studies have reported gender differences in SIS/SES scores. Women tend to score higher on sexual inhibition and lower on sexual excitation compared with men, and not all SIS/SES items may be equally relevant to men's and women's arousal (Carpenter, Janssen, Graham, Vorst, & Wicherts, 2008). The SIS/SES—Short Form (SIS/SES-SF) was designed by selecting items that represent the three-factor structure equally well for women and men.

Description

Data were provided by 2,045 Indiana University undergraduates (1,067 women and 978 men; mean age = 19.8) who completed the 45-item SIS/SES. A series of factor analyses using LISREL revealed a three-factor solution with equal factor loadings for men and women, involving 19 SIS/SES items. Several SIS/SES items showed differences in measurement characteristics between females and males, as evidenced by differences in item intercepts and residual variances. Therefore, only items that were fully "measurement invariant" for men and women were selected. This procedure yielded a 14-item solution that highlights SIS/SES themes of shared relevance to men and women. Shared SES themes included sexual arousal stemming from social interactions (vs. less relational activities like sexual fantasy or erotica). SIS1 themes for both women and men included distraction, focus on sexual performance, and past problems with arousal. SIS1 themes of greater relevance to men (excluded from the SIS/SES-SF) included concerns about pleasing partners sexually. For both men and women, SIS2 themes included risk of getting caught or contracting an STD. In contrast, concerns about pregnancy/pain were more relevant to women and are not represented on the SIS/SES-SF. Men scored higher on SES ($M = 17.1$, $SD = 2.8$), lower on SIS1 ($M = 8.2$, $SD = 1.9$), and lower on SIS2 ($M = 10.5$, $SD = 2.1$) than women ($M = 15.0$, $SD = 2.8$; $M = 8.7$, $SD = 1.8$; $M = 12.0$, $SD = 2.3$, respectively; for all, $p < .001$). Correlations between the 45-item SIS/SES and the 14-item Short Form were identical for men and women for SES ($r = .90$), SIS1 ($r = .80$) and SIS2 ($r = .80$).

Response Mode and Timing

The SIS/SES-SF consists of 14 items rated on a 4-point scale (1 = *Strongly Agree* to 4 = *Strongly Disagree*). Completion of the questionnaire takes approximately 5 minutes. General instructions are provided (see Exhibit).

Scoring

To score the SIS/SES-SF: first, recode all items so that 1 = *Strongly Disagree*, 2 = *Disagree*, 3 = *Agree*, and 4 = *Strongly Agree* (i.e., 1 = 4, 2 = 3, 3 = 2, 4 = 1). Then, add responses to Items 1, 3, 8, 10, 11, and 14 for SES; add responses to Items 4, 9, 12, and 13 for SIS1; and add responses to Items 2, 5, 6, and 7 for SIS2. This scheme will result in scores

ranging from 6 to 24 for SES, and 4 to 16 for SIS1 and SIS2. Missing data can be handled by substituting the mean score for remaining items from that subscale, but discarding incomplete data is preferable.

Reliability

A subset of our participants (50 men and 51 women) completed the SIS/SES on two occasions, at an average interim of 32 days for women and 48 days for men. After removal of three outliers, for women the test-retest reliability of the SIS/SES-SF was $r = .61$ for SES, $r = .61$ for SIS1, and $r = .63$ for SIS2. For men, test-retest reliability of the Short Form was $r = .75$ for SES, $r = .66$ for SIS1, and $r = .65$ for SIS2.

Validity

A subset of participants (141 women and 532 men) completed Neuroticism and Extraversion/Introversion Scales of the Eysenck Personality Questionnaire (Eysenck & Eysenck, 1975), the Harm Avoidance Scale of the Minnesota Personality Questionnaire (Tellegen & Waller, 1994), the Social Desirability Scale (Hays, Hayashi, & Stewart, 1989), the Behavioral Inhibition/Behavioral Activation Scales (Carver & White, 1994), the Sexual Opinion Survey (Fisher, Byrne, White, & Kelley, 1988), and the Sociosexual Orientation Inventory (Simpson & Gangestad, 1991). These data suggest that convergent and discriminant validity of the SIS/SES-SF resembles that of the 45-item measure (see Table 1).

TABLE 1
Correlations of SES, SIS1, and SIS2 With Other Measures

	SES Women	Men	SIS1 Women	Men	SIS2 Women	Men
Social Desirability Scale (SDSR-5)	−.23	.05	−.08	−.06	−.04	.10
Behavioral Inhibition/ Activation Scales						
BIS	.13	.25[a]	−.03	.20[a]	.13	.28[a]
BAS—Reward Responsiveness	.04	.35[a]	−.26	−.05	−.10	−.02
BAS—Drive	.14	.24[a]	.06	−.01	−.06	−.03
BAS—Fun Seeking	.26	.25[a]	−.23	−.14	−.27	−.16[a]
Eysenck Personality Questionnaire (EPQ)						
Neuroticism	.18	.21[a]	.19	.23[a]	.08	−.15[a]
Extraversion	.04	−.01	−.24	−.10	−.13	−.13
Harm Avoidance Subscale (MPQ)	−.10	−.04	−.04	.20[a]	.21	.27[a]
Sexual Opinion Survey (SOS)	.52[a]	.39[a]	−.20	−.13	−.31[a]	−.28[a]
Sociosexual Orientation Inventory (SOI)	.36[a]	.26[a]	−.22	.07	−.36[a]	−.29[a]

[a]$p \leq .01$; Holm's sequential Bonferroni procedure (Holm, 1979).

Other Information

In addition to the SIS/SES-SF, two measures assessing dual control model processes have been reported, including the original SIS/SES (validated in men by Janssen et al., 2002, and in women by Carpenter et al., 2008) and the SESII-W (validated in women by Graham, Sanders, & Milhausen, 2006). Although gender differences exist in factors that influence sexual excitation and inhibition, many central themes are clearly shared. The SIS/SES-SF focuses on items with similar psychometric properties in women and men. When a measure of broader scope may be preferred, the 45-item version of the SIS/SES and the 36-item SESII-W remain good alternatives.

References

Bancroft, J., Graham, C., Janssen, E., & Sanders, S. (2009). The dual control model: Current status and future directions. *The Journal of Sex Research, 46*, 121–142.

Bancroft, J., & Janssen, E. (2000). The dual control model of male sexual response: A theoretical approach to centrally mediated erectile dysfunction. *Neuroscience and Biobehavioral Reviews, 24*, 571–579.

Carpenter, D., Janssen, E., Graham, C. A., Vorst, H., & Wicherts, J. (2008). Women's scores on the Sexual Inhibition/Sexual Excitation Scales (SIS/SES): Gender similarities and differences. *The Journal of Sex Research, 45*, 36–48.

Carver, C. S., & White, T. L. (1994). Behavioral inhibition, behavioral activation, and affective responses to impending reward and punishment: The BIS/BAS Scales. *Journal of Personality and Social Psychology, 67*, 319–333.

Eysenck, H. J., & Eysenck, S. B. G. (1975). *Manual for the Eysenck Personality Questionnaire*. London: Hodder & Stoughton.

Fisher, W. A., Byrne, D., White, L. A., & Kelley, K. (1988). Erotophobia-erotophilia as a dimension of personality. *The Journal of Sex Research, 25*, 123–151.

Graham, C. A., Sanders, S., & Milhausen, R. R. (2006). The Sexual Excitation/Sexual Inhibition Inventory for Women: Psychometric properties. *Archives of Sexual Behavior, 35*, 397–409.

Hays, R. D., Hayashi, T., & Stewart, A. L. (1989). A five-item measure of socially desirable response set. *Educational and Psychological Measurement, 49*, 629–636.

Holm, S. (1979). A simple sequentially rejective multiple test procedure. *Scandinavian Journal of Statistics, 6*, 65–70.

Janssen, E., Vorst, H., Finn, P., & Bancroft, J. (2002). The Sexual Inhibition (SIS) and Sexual Excitation (SES) Scales: I. Measuring sexual inhibition and excitation proneness in men. *The Journal of Sex Research, 39*, 114–126.

Simpson, J., & Gangestad, S. (1991). Individual differences in sociosexuality: Evidence for convergent and discriminant validity. *Personality and Individual Differences, 6*, 870–883.

Tellegen, A., & Waller, N. G. (1994). Exploring personality through test construction: Development of a multidimensional personality questionnaire. In S. R. Briggs & J. M. Cheek (Eds.), *Personality measures: Development and evaluation* (Vol. 1, pp. 133–161). Greenwich, CT: Jai Press.

Exhibit

SIS/SES Questionnaire—Short Form

Instructions: In this questionnaire you will find statements about how you might react to various sexual situations, activities, or behaviors. Obviously, how you react will often depend on the circumstances, but we are interested in what would be the most likely reaction for you. Please read each statement carefully and decide how you would be most likely to react. Then circle the number that corresponds with your answer. Please try to respond to every statement. Sometimes you may feel that none of the responses seems completely accurate. Sometimes you may read a statement that you feel is "not applicable." In these cases, please circle the response you would choose if it were applicable to you. In many statements you will find words describing reactions such as "sexually aroused," or sometimes just "aroused." With these words we mean to describe "feelings of sexual excitement," feeling "sexually stimulated," "horny," "hot," or "turned on." Don't think too long before answering. Please give your first reaction. Try to not skip any questions. Try to be as honest as possible.

	Strongly Agree	Agree	Disagree	Strongly Disagree
1. When a sexually attractive stranger accidentally touches me, I easily become aroused.	A	B	C	D
2. If I am having sex in a secluded, outdoor place and I think that someone is nearby, I am not likely to get very aroused.	A	B	C	D
3. When I talk to someone on the telephone who has a sexy voice, I become sexually aroused.	A	B	C	D
4. I cannot get aroused unless I focus exclusively on sexual stimulation.	A	B	C	D
5. If I am masturbating on my own and I realize that someone is likely to come into the room at any moment, I will lose my erection/my sexual arousal.	A	B	C	D
6. If I realize there is a risk of catching a sexually transmitted disease, I am unlikely to stay sexually aroused.	A	B	C	D
7. If I can be seen by others while having sex, I am unlikely to stay sexually aroused.	A	B	C	D
8. When I think of a very attractive person, I easily become sexually aroused.	A	B	C	D
9. Once I have an erection, I want to start intercourse right away before I lose my erection/Once I am sexually aroused, I want to start intercourse right away before I lose my arousal.	A	B	C	D

10. When I start fantasizing about sex, I quickly become sexually aroused.	A	B	C	D
11. When I see others engaged in sexual activities, I feel like having sex myself.	A	B	C	D
12. When I have a distracting thought, I easily lose my erection/my arousal.	A	B	C	D
13. If I am distracted by hearing music, television, or a conversation, I am unlikely to stay aroused.	A	B	C	D
14. When an attractive person flirts with me, I easily become sexually aroused.	A	B	C	D

Note. When different item versions are used for men and women, both versions are given (male/female).

Sexual Excitation/Sexual Inhibition Inventory for Women

CYNTHIA A. GRAHAM,[1] *Warneford Hospital, Oxford, England*
STEPHANIE A. SANDERS, *The Kinsey Institute for Research in Sex, Gender, and Reproduction*
ROBIN R. MILHAUSEN, *University of Guelph*

The Sexual Excitation/Sexual Inhibition Inventory for Women (SESII-W) is designed to assess the propensity for sexual excitation (SE) and sexual inhibition (SI) in women.

Description

The theoretical model underlying the SESII-W is the dual control model (Bancroft, 1999; Bancroft, Graham, Janssen, & Sanders, 2009; Bancroft & Janssen, 2000). This model proposes that there are separate, relatively independent excitatory and inhibitory systems and that the occurrence of sexual arousal depends on the relative activation of SE and SI. A basic assumption of the model is that individuals vary in their propensity for both SE and SI.

Although a questionnaire had been developed to assess the propensity for SE and SI in men (the Sexual Inhibition/Sexual Excitation Scales (SIS/SES; Janssen, Vorst, Finn, & Bancroft, 2002), we questioned whether it was equally suited for women (Graham, Sanders, Milhausen, & McBride, 2004). For this reason, we obtained qualitative data from nine focus groups involving women of varying ages, racial/ethnic background, and sexual orientation to explore the concepts of SE and SE, and of the factors that influence sexual arousal (Graham et al., 2004). These qualitative data informed the item development of this measure, the SESII-W.

The original SESII-W contained 115 items. Initial validation involved a sample of 655 women (Graham, Sanders, & Milhausen, 2006) recruited using two methods: postal recruitment of a random sample of students and staff working at a large midwestern university (*n* = 226) and

e-mail and listserve postings about the study (*n* = 429). Factor analysis identified eight factors comprising a total of 36 items, and two higher-order factors, one related to SE and one to SI. The three lower-order factors related to inhibition were Relationship Importance (reflecting the need for sex to occur within a specific relationship context); Arousal Contingency (the potential for arousal to be easily inhibited or disrupted by situational factors); and Concerns About Sexual Function (the tendency for worries about sexual functioning to negatively affect arousal). The factors related to excitation were Sexual Arousability (the tendency to become sexually aroused in a variety of situations); Partner Characteristics (the tendency for a partner's personality or behavior to enhance arousal); Sexual Power Dynamics (the tendency to become sexually aroused by force or domination in a trusting sexual situation); Smell (the tendency for olfactory cues to enhance arousal); and Setting—Unusual or Unconcealed (the tendency for arousal to be increased by the possibility of being seen or heard having sex or having sex in a novel situation).

Close to normal distributions have been found for women's scores on the higher-order SE and SI factors (Graham et al., 2006), lending support to the idea that variation in excitation and inhibition proneness is normal, and that the mid-part of the range represents adaptive levels of inhibition.

The questionnaire was designed to be appropriate for use with women of different sexual orientation and varying degrees of sexual experience, and can be completed by women who are not in a current sexual relationship.

[1]Address correspondence to Cynthia Graham, Oxford Doctoral Course in Clinical Psychology, Isis Education Centre, Warneford Hospital, Headington, Oxford OX3 7JX, England; e-mail: cynthia.graham@hmc.ox.ac.uk

Response Mode and Timing

The 36 items on the questionnaire refer to stimulus situations that could affect SE and SI or to general statements about arousability and inhibition. The response format is a 4-point Likert-type rating scale, from *Strongly Disagree* to *Strongly Agree*. The instructions ask women to report what would be the most typical reaction now or how they think they would respond if the item does not apply to them (for full instructions, see the Exhibit). The questionnaire typically takes between 10 and 15 minutes to complete.

Scoring

For items with positive loadings (no minus sign before the item number in the Exhibit), responses should be coded as follows: 1= *Strongly Disagree*; 2 = *Disagree*; 3 = *Agree*; 4 = *Strongly Agree*. For items with negative loadings (minus sign before the item number), responses should be coded as: 4 = *Strongly Disagree*; 3 = *Disagree*; 2 = *Agree*; 1 = *Strongly Agree*. Using the items coded as indicated above, a mean score is then generated for each of the lower-order factors. To obtain higher-order factor scores for propensities for SE and SI, a mean of the mean scores for the relevant lower-order factors is calculated. That is: SE = (sum of scores for Arousability, Partner Characteristics, Sexual Power Dynamics, Smell, & Setting) divided by 5. SI = (sum of scores for Concerns about Sexual Function, Arousal Contingency, and Relationship Importance) divided by 3.

Reliability

The lower-order factor scales had Cronbach's alphas between .63 and .80, with an average of .72.

Satisfactory test-retest reliability was established (Graham et al., 2006). For the higher-order and lower-order factors, all correlations between first and second completions were significant at p < .005. The correlations for SE and SI were .81 and .82, respectively.

Validity

Good evidence of convergent and discriminant validity has been demonstrated (Graham et al., 2006). As expected, only modest correlations between scores on the Behavioral Inhibition/Behavioral Activation Scales (BIS/BAS; Carver & White, 1994) and the SESII-W were found. This suggests that the SESII-W measures distinctly sexual rather than general inhibition/activation tendencies.

Moderate positive correlations were found between SE and scores on the Sexual Opinion Survey (SOS; Fisher, 1998) and the Sexual Sensation Seeking Scale (SSSS; Kalichman & Rompa, 1995; see also Graham et al., 2006).

There were also weaker negative correlations between the SOS, and the SSSS, and both higher-order and lower-order SESII-W inhibition scores.

No correlation was found between the Social Desirability Scale (SDSR; Hays, Hayashi, & Stewart, 1989) and any of the SE or SI factor scores.

Other Information

The use of the SESII-W for research purposes is encouraged. The authors would appreciate receiving information about the results obtained with the measure.

Additional affiliation information: Cynthia A. Graham, The Kinsey Institute for Research in Sex, Gender, and Reproduction; Rural Center for AIDS/STD Prevention. Stephanie A. Sanders, Rural Center for AIDS/STD Prevention; Department of Gender Studies, Indiana University, Bloomington. Robin R. Milhausen, The Kinsey Institute for Research in Sex, Gender, and Reproduction; Rural Center for AIDS/STD Prevention, Indiana University, Bloomington.

References

Bancroft, J. (1999). Central inhibition of sexual response in the male: A theoretical perspective. *Neuroscience and Biobehavioral Reviews, 23,* 763–784.

Bancroft, J., Graham, C. A., Janssen, E., & Sanders, S. A. (2009). The dual control model: Current status and future directions. *The Journal of Sex Research, 46,* 121–142.

Bancroft, J., & Janssen, E. (2000). The dual control model of male sexual response: A theoretical approach to centrally mediated erectile dysfunction. *Neuroscience and Biobehavioral Reviews, 24,* 571–579.

Carver, C. S., & White, T. L. (1994). Behavioral inhibition, behavioral activation, and affective responses to impending reward and punishment: The BIS/BAS Scales. *Journal of Personality and Social Psychology, 67,* 319–333.

Fisher, W. A. (1998). The Sexual Opinion Survey. In C. M. Davis, W. L. Yarber, R. Bauserman, G. Schreer, & S. L. Davis (Eds.), *Handbook of sexuality-related measures* (pp. 218–223). Thousand Oaks, CA: Sage.

Graham, C. A., Sanders, S. A., & Milhausen, R. R. (2006). The Sexual Excitation and Sexual Inhibition Inventory for Women: Psychometric properties. *Archives of Sexual Behavior, 35,* 397–410.

Graham, C. A., Sanders, S. A., Milhausen, R. R, & McBride, K. R. (2004). Turning on and turning off: A focus group study of the factors that affect women's sexual arousal. *Archives of Sexual Behavior, 33,* 527–538.

Hays, R. D., Hayashi, T., & Stewart, A. L. (1989). A five-item measure of socially desirable response set. *Educational and Psychological Measurement, 49,* 629–636.

Janssen, E., Vorst, H., Finn, P., & Bancroft, J. (2002). The Sexual Inhibition (SIS) and Sexual Excitation (SES) Scales: II. Predicting psychophysiological response patterns. *The Journal of Sex Research, 39,* 127–132.

Kalichman, S. C., & Rompa, D. (1995). Sexual Sensation Seeking and Sexual Compulsivity Scales: Reliability, validity, and predicting HIV risk behavior. *Journal of Personality Assessment, 65,* 586–601.

Exhibit

Sexual Excitation/Sexual Inhibition Inventory for Women (SESII-W)

Instructions

This questionnaire asks about things that might affect your sexual arousal. Other ways that we refer to sexual arousal are feeling "turned on," "sexually excited," and "being in a sexual mood." Women describe their sexual arousal in many different ways. These can include genital changes (being "wet," tingling sensations, feelings of warmth, etc.) as well as non-genital sensations (increased heart rate, temperature changes, skin sensitivity, etc.) or feelings (anticipation, heightened sense of awareness, feeling "sexy" or "sexual," etc.).

We are interested in what would be the most *typical* reaction for you now. You may read a statement that you feel does not apply to you, or may have applied to you in the past but doesn't now. In such cases please indicate how you think you *would* respond, if you were currently in that situation. Some of the questions sound very similar but are in fact different. Please read each statement carefully and then circle the number to indicate your answer.[a]

Don't think too long before answering. Please give your first reaction to each question.

Sexual Excitation Factor (Higher-Order Factor)

Arousability

Item Number and Loading Direction	Item Content
15	Seeing an attractive partner's naked body really turns me on.
17	Just being physically close with a partner is enough to turn me on.
19	I get very turned on when someone really wants me sexually.
20	Fantasizing about sex can quickly get me sexually excited.
24	When I think about someone I find sexually attractive, I easily become sexually aroused.
25	With a new partner I am easily aroused.
26	If I see someone dressed in a sexy way, I easily become sexually aroused.
30	Certain hormonal changes definitely increase my sexual arousal.
32	Sometimes I am so attracted to someone, I cannot stop myself from becoming sexually aroused.

Partner Characteristics

Item Number and Loading Direction	Item Content
5	Someone doing something that shows he/she is intelligent turns me on.
8	If I see a partner interacting well with others, I am more easily sexually aroused.
10	Seeing a partner doing something that shows his/her talent can make me very sexually aroused.
12	Eye contact with someone I find sexually attractive really turns me on.

Sexual Power Dynamics

Item Number and Loading Direction	Item Content
2	It turns me on if my partner "talks dirty" to me during sex.
6	Feeling overpowered in a sexual situation by someone I trust increases my arousal.
−27	If a partner is forceful during sex, it reduces my arousal.
28	Dominating my partner sexually is arousing to me.

Smell

Item Number and Loading Direction	Item Content
22	Particular scents are very arousing to me.
23	Often just how someone smells can be a turn-on.

Setting (Unusual or Unconcealed)

Item Number and Loading Direction	Item Content
3	Having sex in a different setting than usual is a real turn-on for me.
−4	If it is possible someone might see or hear us having sex, it is more difficult for me to get aroused.
−7	I find it harder to get sexually aroused if other people are nearby.
13	I get really turned on if I think I may get caught while having sex.

Sexual Inhibition Factor (Higher-Order Factor)

Concerns about Sexual Function

Item Number and Loading Direction	Item Content
9	If I am concerned about being a good lover, I am less likely to become aroused.
18	If I think about whether I will have an orgasm, it is much harder for me to become aroused.
29	Sometimes I feel so "shy" or self-conscious during sex that I cannot become fully aroused.
31	If I am worried about taking too long to become aroused, this can interfere with my arousal.

Arousal Contingency

Item Number and Loading Direction	Item Content
34	It is difficult for me to stay sexually aroused.
35	When I am sexually aroused the slightest thing can turn me off.
36	Unless things are "just right" it is difficult for me to become sexually aroused.

Relationship Importance

Item Number and Loading Direction	Item Content
1	If I think that a partner might hurt me emotionally, I put the brakes on sexually.
11	It would be hard for me to become sexually aroused with someone who is involved with another person.
14	If I think that I am being used sexually it completely turns me off.
16	It is easier for me to become aroused with someone who has "relationship potential."
21	If I am uncertain about how my partner feels about me, it is harder for me to get aroused.
33	I really need to trust a partner to become fully aroused.

[a]The response choices for each question are: 1 Strongly Disagree; 2 Disagree; 3 Agree; 4 Strongly Agree.

Hurlbert Index of Sexual Excitability

DAVID F. HURLBERT,[1] U.S. Department of Health and Human Services

The Hurlbert Index of Sexual Excitability (HISE) is described by Hurlbert, Apt, and Rabehl (1993).

Reference

Hurlbert, D. F., Apt, C., & Rabehl, S. M. (1993). Key variables to understanding female sexual satisfaction: An examination of women in nondistressed marriages. *Journal of Sex & Marital Therapy, 19,* 154–165.

Exhibit

Hurlbert Index of Sexual Excitability

1. I quickly become sexually excited during foreplay. (R)
2. I find sex with my partner to be exciting. (R)
3. When it comes to having sex with my partner, I experience orgasms. (R)
4. It is difficult for me to become sexually aroused.
5. During sex, I seem to lose with initial level of sexual excitement.
6. I feel I take too long to get sexually aroused.
7. It is hard for me to become sexually excited.

[1]Address correspondence to David F. Hurlbert, 140 Farnworth Lane, Roswell, Georgia 30075; e-mail: david.hurlbert@acf.hhs.gov

8. Sex is boring.

9. I quickly become sexually excited when my partner performs oral sex on me. (R)

10. Just thinking about sex turns me on. (R)

11. I find anal sex to be exciting. (R)

12. When it comes to sex, I am easily aroused by my partner touching me. (R)

13. I find masturbation to be sexually stimulating. (R)

14. I seem to lose my sexual excitement too fast.

15. Kissing is sexually arousing for me. (R)

16. Even when I am in the mood, it is difficult for me to get excited about sex.

17. Sexual foreplay is exciting for me. (R)

18. When it comes to sex, it seems to take me a long time to get sexually aroused.

19. Pleasing my partner is sexually exciting for me. (R)

20. I have difficulty maintaining my sexual excitement.

21. I find sexual intercourse to be exciting. (R)

22. When it comes to sex, I think my level of sexual excitement is low.

23. Even when I desire sex, it seems hard for me to become excited.

24. Giving my partner oral sex is sexually exciting for me. (R)

25. In general, sex is satisfying for me. (R)

Note. (R) = Reverse-scored items. Scoring system responses: *all of the time* = 0 points; *most of the time* = +1 point; *some of the time* = +2 points; *rarely* = +3 points; *never* = +4 points.

Sexual Inhibition/Sexual Excitation Scales

ERICK JANSSEN[1] AND JOHN BANCROFT, *The Kinsey Institute for Research in Sex, Gender, and Reproduction*
CYNTHIA A. GRAHAM, *Warneford Hospital, Oxford, England*
DEANNA L. CARPENTER, *Christopher Newport University*

The Sexual Inhibition/Sexual Excitation Scales (SIS/SES) assess a person's propensity for sexual inhibition and excitation. The underlying theoretical model postulates that sexual response and associated behaviors depend on dual control mechanisms, involving excitatory and inhibitory neurophysiological systems (Bancroft & Janssen, 2000). Sexual inhibition and excitation, as measured by these scales, have been found to be predictive of sexual desire and arousal, sexual functioning, sexual risk taking, sexual compulsivity, sexual aggression, sexual infidelity, and the effects of negative mood on sexuality (see Bancroft, Graham, Janssen, & Sanders, 2009, and Janssen & Bancroft, 2007, for reviews).

Description

The SIS/SES, although initially developed for men (Janssen, Vorst, Finn, & Bancroft, 2002a, 2002b), can be used in both male and female samples. A facet design approach was used to guide scale development (e.g., Shye & Elizur, 1994). The majority of items were written in an "if-then" form. A variety of facets are covered, including the type of stimulus (e.g., social, imaginary, visual, tactile) and type of response (sexual arousal or genital response). Inhibition is conceptualized to play a specific role in the modification of sexual responses in the avoidance or reduction of threat. Threats can be intrapersonal or interpersonal in nature and can involve norms and values, physical and psychological harm, etc.

Factor analysis on the data from a sample of 408 sexually functional, heterosexual men (mean age = 23 years) identified 10 factors (Janssen et al., 2002a). A further factor analysis of the subscale scores identified a single excitation factor (SES), but differentiated sexual inhibition into two factors: Inhibition Due to Threat of Performance Failure (SIS1) and Inhibition Due to the Threat of Performance Consequences (SIS2). SES consists of 20 items and four subscales, SIS1 consists of 14 items and three subscales,

[1]Address correspondence to Erick Janssen, The Kinsey Institute for Research in Sex, Gender, and Reproduction, Indiana University, Morrison Hall 313, 1165 East Third Street, Bloomington, Indiana 47405-3700; e-mail: ejanssen@indiana.edu

and SIS2 consists of 11 items and three subscales. The factor loadings were between .6 and .9 and the three factors together accounted for 60% of the variance. Multigroup confirmatory factor analyses on the data from a second sample of 459 men (mean age = 21 years) and a third sample of 313 men (mean age = 46 years) further supported the use of the higher-level factor structure.

The three scales showed close to normal distributions in all three samples. SES and SIS1 were related to age (e.g., $r = -.24$ and .34, respectively, in the third sample). In addition, correlations between SES and the two inhibition factors were low (e.g., SES-SIS1: $r = -.07$; SES-SIS2: $r = -.11$ in the first sample), suggesting that sexual excitation and inhibition are relatively independent. A significant but modest correlation ($r = .28$, first sample) revealed limited overlap between the two inhibition scales.

A later study (Carpenter, Janssen, Graham, Vorst, & Wicherts, 2008) compared 978 men (mean age = 20 years) with 1,067 heterosexual women (mean age = 19 years), and confirmatory factor analysis suggested an acceptable fit of the three-factor structure in women.

Response Mode and Timing

Respondents are asked to indicate what their "most likely reaction" would be to a series of statements and to provide a rating on a 4-point scale (1 = *Strongly Agree* to 4 = *Strongly Disagree*) to a total of 45 questions. Completion of the questionnaire takes approximately 10 minutes.

Scoring

To compute scores, all but two (Items 17 and 45; see Exhibit) of the items first need to be reversed (1 = 4, 2 = 3, 3 = 2, 4 = 1). Missing values can be replaced with the mean of the other items making up the lower-level factor to which the missing item belongs (see Exhibit). It is recommended that no scores are computed if more than 10 out of the 45 items are missing, and that missing values are assigned to SES if more than 5 SES items are missing, to SIS1 if more than 4 SIS1 items are missing, and to SIS2 if more than 3 SIS2 items are missing. SES consists of the sum of Items 1, 3, 4, 6, 7, 11, 13, 14, 16, 25, 26, 29, 30, 32, 35, 37, 38, 39, 43, and 44. SIS1 consists of the sum of Items 5, 9, 10, 17 (not recoded) 19, 20, 21, 23, 33, 36, 40, 41, 42, and 45 (not recoded). SIS2 consists of the sum of Items 2, 8, 12, 15, 18, 22, 24, 27, 28, 31, and 34.

Reliability

Cronbach alpha scores for the three male samples were .89, .89, and .88 for SES; .81, .78, and .83 for SIS1; and .73, .69, and .75 for SIS2 (Janssen et al., 2002a). In women (Carpenter et al., 2008), the corresponding alphas were .87, .76, and .70.

A sample of 50 men (Janssen et al., 2002a) and 51 women (Carpenter et al., 2008) completed the SIS/SES questionnaire on two occasions. The average number of weeks between sessions was 7 for men and a little under 5 for women. Test-retest correlations were .76 (SES), .67 (SIS1), and .74 (SIS2) for men, and .70 (SES), .68 (SIS1), and .60 (SIS2, after removal of two outliers) for women.

Validity

In evaluating the scales' discriminant and convergent validity (see Carpenter et al., 2008; Janssen et al., 2002a), we found a small degree of overlap with measures of traits of behavioral inhibition, neuroticism, harm avoidance, and reward responsivity, suggesting that the SES scale is related to aspects of reward responsivity and the SIS scales (especially SIS2) tap aspects of behavioral inhibition (see Table 1).

However, the limited degree of overlap supports the idea that the SIS/SES questionnaire predominantly measures propensities that are specific to sexual responsivity. For more information on validity, including associations with sexual functioning and sexual risk taking, see Bancroft et al. (2009) and Janssen and Bancroft (2007).

Other Information

The SIS/SES and additional information, including an SPSS file for scoring, can be found online at http://www.indiana.edu/~sexlab. There are no fees attached to its use.

TABLE 1
Correlations of SES, SIS1, and SIS2 With Other Measures

	SES		SIS1		SIS2	
	Women	Men	Women	Men	Women	Men
Social Desirability Scale (SDSR-5)	−.23	.02	−.18	−.11	−.01	.17[a]
Behavioral Inhibition/ Activation Scales						
BIS	.16	.23[a]	−.01	.13	.16	.21[a]
BAS—Reward Responsiveness	.11	.37[a]	−.19	−.12[a]	−.08	−.01
BAS—Drive	.15	.25[a]	.06	−.01	−.09	−.07
BAS—Fun Seeking	.27[a]	.25[a]	−.19	−.18	−.31[a]	−.17[a]
Eysenck Personality Questionnaire (EPQ)						
Neuroticism	.16	.22[a]	.18	.20[a]	.07	−.09
Extraversion	.03	−.01	−.20	−.14[a]	−.12	−.10
Harm Avoidance Subscale (MPQ)	−.10	−.05	−.08	.19[a]	.23	.26[a]
Sexual Opinion Survey (SOS)	.58[a]	.42[a]	−.08	−.10	−.33[a]	−.28[a]
Sociosexual Orientation Inventory (SOI)	.38[a]	.20[a]	−.12	.08	−.47[a]	−.33[a]

Note. Women: $N = 141$ for all measures except SDSR-5: $N = 1,040$. Men: $N = 531$ for all measures except SDSR-5: $N = 971$. Table taken from Carpenter et al. (2008).
[a]$p \leq .01$; Holm's sequential Bonferroni procedure (Holm, 1979).

A short (14-item) version is also available (see this volume).

References

Bancroft, J., Graham, C, Janssen, E., & Sanders, S. (2009). The dual control model: Current status and future directions. *The Journal of Sex Research, 46,* 121–142.

Bancroft, J., & Janssen, E. (2000). The dual control model of male sexual response: A theoretical approach to centrally mediated erectile dysfunction. *Neuroscience and Biobehavioral Reviews, 24,* 571–579.

Carpenter, D. L., Janssen, E., Graham, C. A., Vorst, H., & Wicherts, J. (2008). Women's scores on the Sexual Inhibition/Sexual Excitation Scales (SIS/SES): Gender similarities and differences. *The Journal of Sex Research, 45,* 36–48.

Holm, S. (1979). A simple sequentially rejective multiple test procedure. *Scandinavian Journal of Statistics, 6,* 65–70.

Janssen, E., & Bancroft, J. (2007). The dual control model: The role of sexual inhibition and excitation in sexual arousal and behavior. In E. Janssen (Ed.), *The psychophysiology of sex* (pp. 197–222). Bloomington: Indiana University Press.

Janssen, E., Vorst, H., Finn, P., & Bancroft, J. (2002a). The Sexual Inhibition (SIS) and Sexual Excitation (SES) Scales: I. Measuring sexual inhibition and excitation proneness in men. *The Journal of Sex Research, 39,* 114–126.

Janssen, E., Vorst, H., Finn, P., & Bancroft, J. (2002b). The Sexual Inhibition (SIS) and Sexual Excitation (SES) Scales: II. Predicting psychophysiological response patterns. *The Journal of Sex Research, 39,* 127–132.

Shye, S., & Elizur, D. (1994). *Introduction to facet theory: Content design and intrinsic data analysis in behavioral research.* Thousand Oaks, California: Sage.

Exhibit

SIS/SES Scales

Instructions: In this questionnaire you will find statements about how you might react to various sexual situations, activities, or behaviors. Obviously, how you react will often depend on the circumstances, but we are interested in what would be the most likely reaction for you. Please read each statement carefully and decide how you would be most likely to react. Then circle the number that corresponds with your answer. Please try to respond to every statement. Sometimes you may feel that none of the responses seems completely accurate. Sometimes you may read a statement which you feel is "not applicable." In these cases, please circle a response which you would choose if it were applicable to you. In many statements you will find words describing reactions such as "sexually aroused," or sometimes just "aroused." With these words we mean to describe "feelings of sexual excitement," feeling "sexually stimulated," "horny," "hot," or "turned on." Don't think too long before answering; please give your first reaction. Try not to skip any questions. Try to be as honest as possible.

Item #	Item	Lower-Level Factor
1.	When I look at erotic pictures, I easily become sexually aroused.	SES_2
2.	If I feel that I am being rushed, I am unlikely to get very aroused.	SIS2_3
3.	If I am on my own watching a sexual scene in a film, I quickly become sexually aroused.	SES_2
4.	Sometimes I become sexually aroused just by lying in the sun/Sometimes just lying in the sun sexually arouses me.	SES_4
5.	Putting on a condom can cause me to lose my erection/Using condoms or other safe-sex products can cause me to lose my arousal.	SIS1_1
6.	When a sexually attractive stranger accidentally touches me, I easily become aroused.	SES_1
7.	When I have a quiet candlelight dinner with someone I find sexually attractive, I get aroused.	SES_1
8.	If there is a risk of unwanted pregnancy, I am unlikely to get sexually aroused.	SIS2_2
9.	I need my penis to be touched to maintain an erection/I need my clitoris to be stimulated to continue feeling aroused.	SIS1_1
10.	When I am having sex, I have to focus on my own sexual feelings in order to keep my erection/stay aroused.	SIS1_1
11.	When I feel sexually aroused, I usually have an erection/I usually have a genital response (e.g., vaginal lubrication, being wet).	SES_3
12.	If I am having sex in a secluded, outdoor place and I think that someone is nearby, I am not likely to get very aroused.	SIS2_1
13.	When I see someone I find attractive dressed in a sexy way, I easily become sexually aroused.	SES_1
14.	When I think someone sexually attractive wants to have sex with me, I quickly become sexually aroused.	SES_1
15.	If I discovered that someone I find sexually attractive is too young, I would have difficulty getting sexually aroused with him/her.	SIS2_3
16.	When I talk to someone on the telephone who has a sexy voice, I become sexually aroused.	SES_1

17.   When I notice that my partner is sexually aroused, my own arousal becomes stronger. *[This item should not be recoded]*   SIS1_2

18.   If my new sexual partner does not want to use a condom, I am unlikely to stay aroused/If my new sexual partner does not want to use a condom/safe-sex product, I am unlikely to stay aroused.   SIS2_2

19.   I cannot get aroused unless I focus exclusively on sexual stimulation.   SIS1_1

20.   If I feel that I'm expected to respond sexually, I have difficulty getting aroused.   SIS1_3

21.   If I am concerned about pleasing my partner sexually, I easily lose my erection/If I am concerned about pleasing my partner sexually, it interferes with my arousal.   SIS1_2

22.   If I am masturbating on my own and I realize that someone is likely to come into the room at any moment, I will lose my erection/my sexual arousal.   SIS2_1

23.   It is difficult to become sexually aroused unless I fantasize about a very arousing situation. SIS1_1

24.   If I can be heard by others while having sex, I am unlikely to stay sexually aroused.   SIS2_1

25.   Just thinking about a sexual encounter I have had is enough to turn me on sexually.   SES_3

26.   When I am taking a shower or a bath, I easily become sexually aroused.   SES_4

27.   If I realize there is a risk of catching a sexually transmitted disease, I am unlikely to stay sexually aroused.   SIS2_2

28.   If I can be seen by others while having sex, I am unlikely to stay sexually aroused.   SIS2_1

29.   If I am with a group of people watching an X-rated film, I quickly become sexually aroused.   SES_2

30.   When a sexually attractive stranger looks me straight in the eye, I become aroused/When a sexually attractive stranger makes eye-contact with me, I become aroused.   SES_1

31.   If I think that having sex will cause me pain, I will lose my erection/my arousal.   SIS2_3

32.   When I wear something I feel attractive in, I am likely to become sexually aroused.   SES_4

33.   If I think that I might not get an erection, then I am less likely to get one/If I am worried about being too dry, I am less likely to get lubricated.   SIS1_3

34.   If having sex will cause my partner pain, I am unlikely to stay sexually aroused.   SIS2_3

35.   When I think of a very attractive person, I easily become sexually aroused.   SES_1

36.   Once I have an erection, I want to start intercourse right away before I lose my erection/Once I am sexually aroused, I want to start intercourse right away before I lose my arousal.   SIS1_1

37.   When I start fantasizing about sex, I quickly become sexually aroused.   SES_3

38.   When I see others engaged in sexual activities, I feel like having sex myself.   SES_2

39.   When I see an attractive person, I start fantasizing about having sex with him/her.   SES_1

40.   When I have a distracting thought, I easily lose my erection/my arousal.   SIS1_1

41.   I often rely on fantasies to help me maintain an erection/my sexual arousal.   SIS1_1

42.   If I am distracted by hearing music, television, or a conversation, I am unlikely to stay aroused.   SIS1_3

43.   When I feel interested in sex, I usually get an erection/I usually have a genital response (e.g., vaginal lubrication, being wet).   SES_3

44.   When an attractive person flirts with me, I easily become sexually aroused.   SES_1

45.   During sex, pleasing my partner sexually makes me more aroused. *[This item should not be recoded]*   SIS1_2

Note. When different item versions are used for men and women, both versions are given (male/female). Answer categories are 1 = *Strongly Agree*, 2 = *Agree*, 3 = *Disagree*, 4 = *Strongly Disagree*.

Sexual Excitation/Sexual Inhibition Inventory for Women and Men

ROBIN R. MILHAUSEN,[1] *University of Guelph*

CYNTHIA A. GRAHAM, *Warneford Hospital, Oxford, England*

STEPHANIE A. SANDERS, *The Kinsey Institute for Research in Sex, Gender, and Reproduction*

The Sexual Excitation/Sexual Inhibition Inventory for Women and Men (SESII-W/M) was developed to assess propensity for sexual excitation (SE) and sexual inhibition (SI) in response to a broad range of stimuli and sexual situations in both women and men.

Description

The theoretical model underlying the SESII-W/M is the dual control model of sexual response (Bancroft, 1999; Bancroft, Graham, Janssen, & Sanders, 2009; Bancroft & Janssen, 2000). The model suggests that sexual arousal depends upon the relative activation of SE and SI, separate and independent systems (Bancroft, 1999; Bancroft & Janssen, 2000).

Two questionnaires assessing propensity for SE and SI were developed prior to the SESII-W/M. The Sexual Inhibition/Sexual Excitation Scales (SIS/SES; Janssen, Vorst, Finn, & Bancroft, 2002) were developed for men; however, because the SIS/SES was thought to lack factors that could be particularly important to women's sexual arousal, the Sexual Excitation/Sexual Inhibition Inventory for Women (SESII-W; Graham, Sanders, & Milhausen, 2006) was developed based on qualitative data from focus groups of women (Graham, Sanders, Milhausen, & McBride, 2004). Many of the issues raised by women in the focus groups seemed also relevant for men's arousal (e.g., self-esteem, negative mood, emotional connection to a partner, context for sexual encounter). Indeed, results from a recent focus group study of men suggest that these factors can facilitate or interfere with men's sexual arousal (Janssen, McBride, Yarber, Hill, & Butler, 2008).

Exploratory factor analysis (EFA) was conducted on the original SESII-W items, using a sample of 530 undergraduate and graduate men and women randomly selected from a list of 4,000 students attending a large, midwestern university (Milhausen, Graham, Sanders, Yarber, & Maitland, in press). EFA identified eight factors, but two factors comprised only two items and were thus removed from the confirmatory factor analysis (CFA) model. The final six-factor solution includes the following: Inhibitory Cognitions (the potential for arousal to be disrupted by worries or negative thoughts about sexual functioning and performance),

Relationship Importance (reflecting the need for sex to occur within a specific relationship context), Arousability (the tendency to become sexually aroused in a variety of situations), Partner Characteristics and Behaviors (the tendency for a partner's personality or behavior to enhance arousal), Setting (Unusual or Unconcealed; the tendency for arousal to be increased by the possibility of being seen or heard having sex or having sex in a novel situation), and Dyadic Elements of the Sexual Interaction (the tendency for negative partner dynamics during the sexual interaction to inhibit sexual arousal). Twenty of the 30 items on the SESII-W/M are also found on the SESII-W, and five of the factors (Inhibitory Cognitions, Relationship Importance, Arousability, Partner Characteristics and Behaviors, and Setting [Unusual/Unconcealed]) are highly similar to factors on the SESII-W.

The questionnaire is appropriate for use with women and men of different sexual orientations and varying degrees of sexual experience, and can be completed by persons who are not in a current sexual relationship.

Response Mode and Timing

The response format is a 4-point, Likert-type rating scale, from *Strongly Disagree* to *Strongly Agree*. For full instructions, see the Exhibit. Items should be scrambled so that items on a subscale do not appear together. The questionnaire typically takes between 10 and 15 minutes to complete.

Scoring

Items are scored in the following way: 1 = *Strongly Disagree*; 2 = *Disagree*; 3 = *Agree*; 4 = *Strongly Agree*. Items denoted with an asterisk should be reverse coded. Using the items coded as indicated above, a mean score is then generated for each of the subscales.

Reliability

Reliability and validity were assessed with a sample of men and women recruited from distance education classes at a Canadian university. The subscales had Cronbach's alphas between .66 and .76, with an average of .73. Test-retest

[1]Address correspondence to Robin R. Milhausen, Department of Family Relations and Applied Nutrition, Room 217 MINS Building, University of Guelph, Guelph, Ontario N1G 2W1, Canada; e-mail: rmilhaus@uoguelph.ca

reliability correlations ranged from $r = .66$ to $r = .82$, with a mean correlation of .76 (Milhausen et al., in press).

Validity

Convergent and discriminant validity was demonstrated and the pattern of correlations generally matched those based on the SESII-W (Graham et al., 2006). Most correlations between the SESII-W/M factors and the Behavioral Inhibition/Behavioral Activation Scales (BIS/BAS; Carver & White, 1994), the Sexual Opinion Survey (SOS; Fisher, 1998) and the Sexual Sensation Seeking Scale (SSSS; Kalichman & Rompa, 1995) were low to moderate and in the expected direction. No correlation was found between the Social Desirability Scale (SDSR; Hayes, Hayashi, & Stewart, 1989) and any of the SESII-W/M scales (Milhausen et al., in press).

Other Information

In the validation study, men's and women's scores on the subscales were significantly different at $p < .001$ (Milhausen et al., in press); effect sizes were moderate and very large (Hyde, 2005). Women scored higher on Inhibitory Cognitions, Relationship Importance, Partner Characteristics and Behaviors, and Dyadic Elements of the Sexual Interaction. Men scored higher on Arousability and Setting (Unusual or Unconcealed; Milhausen et al., in press).

The SESII-W/M will likely be a useful measure in investigations in which propensity for sexual inhibition and excitation in response to specific situations or stimuli must be measured identically for men and women. Researchers are encouraged to use the SESII-W/M for this purpose. The authors would appreciate receiving information about the results obtained with the measure.

Additional affiliation information: Robin R. Milhausen, The Kinsey Institute for Research in Sex, Gender, and Reproduction; Rural Center for AIDS/STD Prevention, Indiana University, Bloomington. Cynthia A. Graham, The Kinsey Institute for Research in Sex, Gender, and Reproduction; Rural Center for AIDS/STD Prevention.

Stephanie A. Sanders, Rural Center for AIDS/STD Prevention; Department of Gender Studies, Indiana University, Bloomington.

References

Bancroft, J. (1999). Central inhibition of sexual response in the male: A theoretical perspective. *Neuroscience and Biobehavioral Reviews, 23*, 763–784.

Bancroft, J., Graham, C. A., Janssen, E., & Sanders, S. A. (2009). The dual control model: Current status and future directions. *The Journal of Sex Research, 46*, 121–142.

Bancroft, J., & Janssen, E. (2000). The dual control model of male sexual response: A theoretical approach to centrally mediated erectile dysfunction. *Neuroscience and Biobehavioral Reviews, 24*, 571–579.

Carver, C. S., & White, T. L. (1994). Behavioral inhibition, behavioral activation, and affective responses to impending reward and punishment: The BIS/BAS Scales. *Journal of Personality and Social Psychology, 67*, 319–333.

Fisher, W. A. (1998). The Sexual Opinion Survey. In C. M. Davis, W. L. Yarber, R. Bauserman, G. Schreer, & S. L. Davis (Eds.), *Handbook of sexuality-related measures* (pp. 218–223). Thousand Oaks, CA: Sage.

Graham, C. A., Sanders, S. A., & Milhausen, R. R. (2006). The Sexual Excitation and Sexual Inhibition Inventory for Women: Psychometric properties. *Archives of Sexual Behavior, 35*, 397–410.

Graham, C. A., Sanders, S. A., Milhausen, R. R., & McBride, K. R. (2004). Turning on and turning off: A focus group study of the factors that affect women's sexual arousal. *Archives of Sexual Behavior, 33*, 527–538.

Hays, R. D., Hayashi, T., & Stewart, A. L. (1989). A five-item measure of socially desirable response set. *Educational and Psychological Measurement, 49*, 629–636.

Hyde, J. S. (2005). The gender similarities hypothesis. *American Psychologist, 60*, 581–592.

Janssen, E., McBride, K. R., Yarber, W., Hill, B. J., & Butler, S. M. (2008). Factors that influence sexual arousal in men: A focus group study. *Archives of Sexual Behavior, 37*, 252–265.

Janssen, E., Vorst, H., Finn, P., & Bancroft, J. (2002). The Sexual Inhibition (SIS) and Sexual Excitation (SES) Scales: II. Predicting psychophysiological response patterns. *The Journal of Sex Research, 39*, 127–132.

Kalichman, S. C., & Rompa, D. (1995). Sexual Sensation Seeking and Sexual Compulsivity Scales: Reliability, validity, and predicting HIV risk behavior. *Journal of Personality Assessment, 65*, 586–601.

Milhausen, R. R., Graham, C. A., Sanders, S. A., Yarber, W. L., & Maitland, S. B. (in press). Validation of the Sexual Excitation/Sexual Inhibition Inventory for Women and Men. *Archives of Sexual Behavior*.

Exhibit

Sexual Excitation/Sexual Inhibition Inventory for Women and Men

The next set of items asks about things that might affect your sexual arousal. Other ways that we refer to sexual arousal are feeling "turned on," "sexually excited," and "being in a sexual mood." Men and women describe their sexual arousal in terms of genital changes (being "hard," being "wet," tingling sensations, feelings of warmth, etc.). Men and women also mention non-genital sensations (increased heart rate, temperature changes, skin sensitivity, etc.) or feelings (anticipation, feeling "open," etc.).

We are interested in what would be the most typical reaction for you now. You might read a statement that you feel is not applicable to you, or a statement that refers to a situation that may have occurred in the past but is not likely to occur now. In such cases please indicate how you think you would respond, if you were in that situation. Some of the questions sound very similar, but are different; please read each question carefully and then mark the response which indicates your answer. Don't think too long before answering. Please give your first reaction to each question.[a]

Inhibitory Cognitions

Sometimes I have so many worries that I am unable to get aroused.

If I feel that I am expected to respond sexually, I have difficulty getting aroused.

Sometimes I feel so "shy" or self-conscious during sex that I cannot become fully aroused.

If I think about whether I will have an orgasm, it is much harder for me to become aroused.

If I am worried about taking too long to become aroused, this can interfere with my arousal.

When I am having sex, I have to focus on my own sexual feelings in order to stay aroused.

If I am concerned about being a good lover, I am less likely to become aroused.

Unless things are "just right" it is difficult for me to become sexually aroused.

Relationship Importance

It would be hard for me to become sexually aroused with someone who is involved with another person.

I really need to trust a partner to become fully aroused.

If I am very sexually attracted to someone, I don't need to be in a relationship with that person to become sexually aroused.*

If I think that I am being used sexually it completely turns me off.

If I think that a partner might hurt me emotionally, I put the brakes on sexually.

Arousability

When I think about someone I find sexually attractive, I easily become sexually aroused.

I think about sex a lot when I am bored.

Sometimes I am so attracted to someone, I cannot stop myself from becoming sexually aroused.

Just talking about sex is enough to put me in a sexual mood.

Just being physically close with a partner is enough to turn me on.

Partner Characteristics and Behaviors

Someone doing something that shows he/she is intelligent turns me on.

Seeing a partner doing something that shows his/her talent can make me very sexually aroused.

If I see a partner interacting well with others, I am more easily sexually aroused.

If a partner surprises me by doing chores, it sparks my sexual interest.

I find it arousing when a partner does something nice for me.

Setting (Unusual or Unconcealed)

If it is possible someone might see or hear us having sex, it is more difficult for me to get aroused.*

I get really turned on if I think I may get caught while having sex.

I find it harder to get sexually aroused if other people are nearby.*

Having sex in a different setting than usual is a real turn-on for me.

Dyadic Elements of the Sexual Interaction

While having sex, it really decreases my arousal if my partner is not sensitive to the signals I am giving.

If interferes with my arousal if there is not a balance of giving and receiving pleasure during sex.

If I am uncertain how my partner feels about me, it is harder for me to get aroused.

ªThe response choices for each question are: 1 Strongly Disagree; 2 Disagree; 3 Agree; 4 Strongly Agree.

*Items should be reverse coded when scoring.

Extramarital Behavioral Intentions Scale

BRAM BUUNK,[1] *University of Nijmegen, The Netherlands*

Several researchers have correlated the incidence of extramarital sex with variables such as dissatisfaction with the marital relationship, assuming that these factors could be viewed as *causes* for engaging in extramarital relationships (e.g., Bell, Turner, & Rosen, 1975). In this type of research, however, it is difficult to unravel the direction of causality (Buunk, 1980a). To make a better assessment of the factors that do indeed lead to extramarital sexual involvement, a scale assessing extramarital behavioral intentions was developed, based on Fishbein and Ajzen's (1975) theoretical perspective. From this perspective, a behavioral intention is defined as the subjective probability that someone will exhibit a certain behavior if the opportunity presents itself. As Fishbein and Ajzen have argued, and have shown in many studies, specific behavioral intentions correlate highly with actual future behavior. Another assumption behind the construction of the scale was that there is a continuum of extramarital sexual involvement, varying from flirting to a long-term sexual relationship, and that such a continuum should be included in the scale.

Description, Response Mode, and Timing

The scale consists of five items. The format for each item is the same. The respondents are asked to indicate for each of the following behaviors the probability of engaging in it, if an opportunity were to present itself: flirting, light petting, falling in love, sexual intercourse, and a long-term sexual relationship with someone other than their partner. The seven response options range from *certainly no* to *certainly yes*, with a midpoint formulated as *uncertain*. Each of the possible answers is spelled out literally. The respondents circle the number corresponding with the answer that best fits the perceived likelihood under consideration. The scale usually requires no more than 1 or 2 minutes for completion.

Scoring

The items can simply be summed. No reverse scoring is necessary. Higher scores indicate a higher intention to engage in extramarital sexual behaviors.

Reliability

Although there are slight variations across samples, the Cronbach alpha of the scale is rather high: .91 in a sample more or less representing the general Dutch population and consisting of people with diverse levels of sexual permissiveness (Buunk, 1980a); .73 in a study of people who had all been involved in extramarital relationships (Buunk, 1982); .75 in a sample of people in sexually open marriages (Buunk, 1980b), and .87 in a sample of undergraduate students. Over a 3-month period, test-retest reliability in the open marriage sample was $r(100) = .70, p < .001$. Furthermore, the scale fulfills the requirements of a Guttman scale, with a coefficient of scalability of .78 and a coefficient of reproducibility of .92. The order of the items in the Guttman scale is flirting, falling in love, light petting, sexual intercourse, and a long-term sexual relationship (Buunk, 1980a).

Validity

There is considerable evidence for the concurrent validity of the scale. In the sample from the average population, it was found that the more extensive the extramarital experience had been during the previous year, the higher the scores on the Extramarital Behavioral Intentions Scale, $r(250) = .74, p < .001$. The scale particularly differentiates between persons high and low in sexual permissiveness. Individuals from the open marriage sample scored much higher on the scale than a sample more or less representative of the average population, $t(348) = 22.46, p < .001$, and also much higher than a sample of undergraduate students, $t(478) = 15.16, p < .001$. Also, the Extramarital Behavioral Intentions Scale clearly discriminates between those whose reference group accepts extramarital sex and those who socialize with others disapproving of such behavior: The scale correlated highly with one's friends' approval of extramarital sex and the perceived opportunity for extramarital sex (Buunk, 1980a).

Construct validity of the scale has been established in several studies showing positive correlations with scales indicating permissive attitudes toward extramarital sex, and negative correlations with scales measuring the opposite. Thus, in the sample of individuals from the average population, a negative correlation was established with a scale measuring the desire for an exclusive relationship, $r(250) = -.54, p < .001$, and positive correlations were found with scales reflecting needs for intimacy outside marriage and for relational variety (see Buunk, 1980a). In the same sample, the Extramarital Behavioral Intentions Scale correlated highly and negatively with a scale measuring moral disapproval of extramarital sex, $r(250) = -.65, p < .001$ (cf. Buunk, 1981). Furthermore, in three samples strong

[1]Address correspondence to Bram Buunk, Department of Psychology University of Groningen Grote Kruisstraat 2/1, 9712 TS Groningen, The Netherlands; e-mail: apbuunk@kpnplanet.nl

negative correlations were found between the scale and a scale for anticipated sexual jealousy (Buunk, 1982). Also, in the sample of persons who had been involved in extramarital relationships, a positive correlation was found between the Extramarital Behavioral Intentions Scale and a scale for Psychosexual Stimulation developed by Frenken (1976), $r(250) = .21$, $p < .001$. This last scale measures the tendency to allow sexual perceptions and fantasizing about sexuality versus the tendency to suppress such perceptions and fantasies.

Final evidence for the validity of the Extramarital Behavioral Intentions Scale comes from the open marriage study. Here, among women, a high correlation was found between the scale and their extramarital intentions as perceived by their husbands, $r(50) = .53$, $p < .001$. The same correlation among men was somewhat lower, but also significant, $r(50) = .42$, $p < .001$.

References

Bell, R. R., Turner, S., & Rosen, L. (1975). A multivariate analysis of female extramarital coitus. *Journal of Marriage and the Family, 37*, 375-384.

Buunk, B. (1980a). Extramarital sex in the Netherlands: Motivations in social and marital context. *Alternative Lifestyles, 3*, 11-39.

Buunk, B. (1980b). Sexually open marriages. Ground rules for countering potential threats to marriage. *Alternative Lifestyles, 3*, 312-328.

Buunk, B. (1981). De samenhang van attitudes en sociale normen met de intentie tot buitenechtelijke sex [The relationships between extramarital behavioral intentions and attitudes and social norms]. *Nederlands Tijdschrift voor de Psychologie, 36*, 165-170.

Buunk, B. (1982). Anticipated sexual jealousy: Its relationships to self-esteem, dependency and reciprocity. *Personality and Social Psychology Bulletin, 8*, 310-316.

Fishbein, M., & Ajzen, I. (1975). *Belief, attitude, intention, and behavior*. Reading, MA: Addison Wesley.

Frenken, J. (1976). *Afkeer van seksualiteit* [Aversion to sexuality]. Beventer: Van Loghum Slaterus.

Exhibit

Extramarital Behavioral Intentions Scale

Would you engage in the following behavior with another man/woman if the opportunity were to present itself?

1. flirting
    a. certainly not
    b. probably not
    c. maybe not
    d. uncertain
    e. maybe yes
    f. probably yes
    g. certainly yes

2. sexual intercourse[a]
3. light petting
4. a long-term sexual relationship
5. falling in love

[a]The seven response options are repeated for each item

Intentions Towards Infidelity Scale

DANIEL NELSON JONES,[1] *University of British Columbia*
SALLY GAYLE OLDERBAK AND AURELIO JOSÉ FIGUEREDO, *University of Arizona*

Infidelity is one of the leading causes of divorce and relationship dissolution (Daly, Wilson, & Weghorst, 1982). Thus, being able to predict who will be unfaithful in the future would be critical to assessing relationship longevity and fidelity. We created the Intentions Towards Infidelity Scale (ITIS) in order

[1]Address correspondence to Daniel N. Jones, 2136 West Mall, Department of Psychology, UBC, Vancouver, BC, Canada, V6T 1Z4; e-mail: jonesdn@gmail.com

to predict who is likely to stay faithful to a romantic partner.

Description

Infidelity causes emotional pain and turmoil in addition to concerns of exposing, or actually exposing, a current partner to a sexually transmitted infection. Attitudes towards infidelity only provide some evidence for who will be unfaithful in the future, because attitudes do not always directly translate into behavior as well as behavioral intentions (Ajzen & Fishbein, 2005). Certain individual differences, such as personality, also can predict infidelity. However, such scales are long and measure global dispositions towards negative interpersonal behavior rather than specifically targeting infidelity (Hall & Fincham, 2005). As a result, we created a brief scale that measures behavioral intentions in order to assess the *likelihood* of engaging in infidelity behaviors (e.g., intentions to hide the relationship from an attractive other or be unfaithful in the future).

Response Mode and Timing

The ITIS is a self-report questionnaire with responses ranging from −3, *Not at all Likely*, to +3, *Extremely Likely*. The ITIS takes less than a minute to complete.

Scoring and Reliability

The ITIS consists of seven items. Once the third item is reverse scored, the items should then be averaged to create a single score. The ITIS has one common factor, on which all items consistently load. The Cronbach's alpha internal reliability is also consistently good across samples (Jones, 2009; Olderbak, 2008; Olderbak & Figueredo, 2009), ranging from .70 to .81. To date, there is no test-retest reliability information available on the scale.

Validity

Convergent and Discriminant Validity

The ITIS is a new scale, which demonstrates good validity in preliminary samples (Jones, 2009; Olderbak, 2008; Olderbak & Figueredo, 2009). At present, the only validity data available are on college-aged samples, although we argue that the scale is appropriate for anyone who is in a committed romantic relationship.

The ITIS shows strong overall correlations with previous and current self-reports of frequency of infidelity behavior with the average correlation of all the studies ranging from .50 to .60 (Jones, 2009). In addition, Jones (2009) also conducted several studies correlating the ITIS with a number of variables related to sexual and romantic relationships. All effect size terminology is based on Cohen's (1988) taxonomy of effect sizes. Results indicate that the ITIS correlates

moderately and positively with overall insecure attachment, as well as avoidant attachment, but does not correlate with anxious attachment. The ITIS correlates moderately and positively with unrestricted sociosexual attitudes and sexual behavior, and correlates strongly and positively with mating effort. The ITIS also correlates moderately and negatively with long-term mating orientation and relationship satisfaction.

The ITIS has small to moderate correlations with the Big Five personality traits of conscientiousness and agreeableness. The ITIS is also positively and moderately correlated with openness to experience. In addition, the ITIS has a small positive correlation with impulsive sensation seeking (ISS) and a moderate positive correlation with aggression/hostility (AH), personality traits of the "Alternative Five" personality scale (Zuckerman, Kulhman, Joireman, Teta, & Kraft, 1993). The ITIS also fully mediates the relationship between every aforementioned variable and overall number of infidelities a person has committed.

Criterion Validity: Prediction of Relationship Outcomes Over Time

In a recent longitudinal study (Olderbak, 2008), the ITIS was administered at baseline and compared to various relationship outcomes over time. The follow-up contacts were conducted 3, 6, 9, and 12 months after the initial data collection. A relationship satisfaction questionnaire was administered at intake and at every follow-up.

The ITIS correlated negatively and significantly with a validated relationship satisfaction questionnaire at baseline, 3 months after, and 6 months after baseline. However, this correlation decreased to nonsignificance 9 months and 12 months after baseline. This change is perhaps due to changes in the status of the relationship, including infidelity intentions and behavior. Thus, the ITIS was a significant predictor of relationship satisfaction up to 6 months after its administration.

Mean scores on the ITIS were also compared when disaggregated with respect to two dichotomous variables: (a) whether the participant had actually committed any acts of infidelity during the study period, and (b) whether the participant had broken up with his/her romantic partner during the study period. Mean ITIS scores were significantly higher for those who reported actually having been unfaithful and for those who reported experiencing relationship dissolution during the study period. In sum, the ITIS predicts infidelity, relationship satisfaction, and relationship dissolution longitudinally (Olderbak, 2008), as well as in one-time self-report studies (Jones, 2009).

References

Ajzen, I., & Fishbein, M. (2005). The influence of attitudes on behavior. In D. Albarracín, B. T. Johnson, & M. P. Zanna (Eds.), *Handbook of attitudes and attitude change* (pp. 173–221). Hillsdale, NJ: Erlbaum.

Cohen, J. (1988). *Statistical power analysis for the behavioral sciences* (2nd ed.). Hillsdale, NJ: Erlbaum.

Daly, M., Wilson, M., & Weghorst, S. J. (1982). Male sexual jealousy. *Ethology and Sociobiology, 3,* 11–27.

Hall, J. H., & Fincham, F. D. (2005). Relationship dissolution following infidelity. In M. Fine & J. Harvey (Eds.), *The handbook of divorce and romantic relationship dissolution* (pp. 153–168). Mahwah, NJ: Erlbaum.

Jones, D. N. (2009). *The personality of a cheater.* Manuscript in preparation.

Olderbak, S. G. (2008). *Predicting relationship satisfaction in heterosexual couples longitudinally.* Unpublished master's thesis, Department of Psychology, University of Arizona.

Olderbak, S. G., & Figueredo, A. J. (2009). Predicting romantic relationship satisfaction from life history strategy. *Personality and Individual Differences, 46,* 604–610.

Zuckerman, M., Kulhman, M. D., Joireman, J., Teta, P., & Kraft, M. (1993). A comparison of three structural models for personality: The Big Three, the Big Five, and the Alternative Five. *Journal of Personality and Social Psychology, 65,* 757–768.

Exhibit

Intentions Towards Infidelity Scale

Please indicate how likely or unlikely you would be to do the following things. Use the scale below to answer the following questions.

Not at all Likely   Extremely Likely
−3   −2   −1   0   +1   +2   +3

1. How likely are you to be unfaithful to a partner if you knew you wouldn't get caught?
2. How likely would you be to lie to a partner about being unfaithful to them?
3. How likely would you be to tell a partner if you were unfaithful to them? [R]
4. How likely do you think you would be to get away with being unfaithful to a partner?
5. How likely would you be to hide your relationship from an attractive person you just met?
6. How likely do you think you are to be unfaithful to future partners?
7. How likely do you think you are to be unfaithful to your present or future husband or wife?

Reiss Extramarital Sexual Permissiveness Scale

IRA L. REISS,[1] *University of Minnesota*

This scale was designed to measure whether people would accept extramarital coitus for themselves under any of four culturally relevant situations.

Description

The four questions combine two important aspects of an extramarital relationship: One aspect focuses on whether the extramarital relation is pleasure-centered or love-centered, and the other aspect focuses on whether one's mate accepts or rejects their partner having that sort of extramarital relationship. Together these aspects produce a way of classifying four types of extramarital relationships and measuring the degree of extramarital sexual permissiveness. One can then check responses by gender and other demographic variables.

The scale can be answered by those in a marital relationship or by those not married. The unmarried people can answer in terms of how they think they would respond if they were married. I suggest that all respondents be asked to answer the same four questions in two formats—one assuming the marriage they are in is unhappy and the other assuming that the marriage is happy. The differences in these responses would be a measure of the importance of marital happiness.

In research I carried out on four national samples, I found that three factors had a direct impact on what is accepted or rejected in extramarital attitudes: educational level, attitude toward premarital sexuality, and level of marital happiness (Reiss, 2006; Reiss, Anderson, & Sponaugle, 1980). I would suggest that any research into extramarital sexuality probe these three powerful predictors of extramarital sexual permissiveness as well as other predictors that can be tested (Buunk & Bakker, 1995; Hansen, 1987; Reiss & Miller, 1979; Weis & Jurich, 1985; Weis & Slosnerick, 1981).

[1]Address correspondence to Ira L. Reiss, 5932 Medicine Lake Road, Minneapolis, MN 55422; e-mail: irareiss@comcast.net

Response Mode and Timing

There are four response categories to each of the four questions: (a) *Definitely*, (b) *Probably*, (c) *Unlikely*, (d) *Never*. Assuming that you would ask these four questions twice—once asking the respondent to assume that he/she is in a happy marriage and once assuming that he/she is in an unhappy marriage—it would take a respondent about 5 or 6 minutes to answer all the questions.

Scoring

Respondents do seem to like having four answer categories but, for scaling purposes, I suggest dichotomizing the answers by counting "Definitely" or "Probably" as an affirmative response and counting "Unlikely" or "Never" as a rejecting response and giving one point for each question that the respondent affirms. I would, of course, do this scoring separately for the unhappy marriage condition and the happy marriage condition. So the top score in each of the two scales would be 4 and the lowest score would be 0. I would add that one could gain a rough measure of the equalitarianism of the respondents by asking them if they would have any problem if their mates gave the same answers as they did. Further, if you were studying married couples, it would be worthwhile to compare the scale scores of the two people in the marriage.

Reliability

Reliability can be established by noting that the scales have always met the general Guttman criteria concerning the coefficient of reproducibility and the coefficient of scalability.

Validity

My colleagues and I analyzed four different nationally representative samples from four different years to test for the best predictors of extramarital sexual permissiveness (Reiss et al., 1980). The national samples were carried out by the National Opinion Research Center. Our results were tested and supported by these different samples.

Construct validity was also established by finding the expected differences between men and women and between religiously devout and nondevout groups of people (Banfield & McCabe, 2001; Sponaugle, 1993). In addition, other researchers reported finding the pleasure/love and mate accepts/rejects aspects of my scale important in their work on measuring extramarital acceptance (Banfield & McCabe, 2001; Glass & Wright, 1992; Saunders & Edwards, 1984; Treas & Giesen, 2000).

Other Information

I give permission to use this scale in any research study. I would ask to be kept informed of such use and of any results of these studies. A researcher could use this same scale and just change "marriage" to a "committed relationship" and study cohabitation and other intimate dyadic arrangements. The researcher would then be measuring Extradyadic Sexual Permissiveness, and the results could be compared to those for studies of Extramarital Sexual Permissiveness.

References

Banfield, S., & McCabe, M. P. (2001). Extra relationship involvement among women: Are they different from men? *Archives of Sexual Behavior, 30,* 119–142.

Buunk, B. P., & Bakker, A. B. (1995). Extradyadic sex: The role of descriptive and injunctive norms. *The Journal of Sex Research, 32,* 313–318.

Glass, S. P., & Wright, T. L. (1992). Justifications for extramarital relationships: The association between attitudes, behaviors, and gender. *The Journal of Sex Research, 29,* 361–387.

Hansen, G. L. (1987). Extradyadic relations during courtship. *The Journal of Sex Research, 23,* 382–390.

Reiss, I. L. (2006). *An insider's view of sexual science since Kinsey.* Lanham, MD: Rowman & Littlefield.

Reiss, I. L., Anderson, R., & Sponaugle, G. C. (1980). A multivariate model of the determinants of extramarital sexual permissiveness. *Journal of Marriage and the Family, 42,* 395–411.

Reiss, I. L., & Miller, B. C. (1979). Heterosexual permissiveness: A theoretical analysis. In W. Burr, R. Hill, I. Nye and I. L. Reiss (Eds.), *Contemporary theories about the family* (Vol. 1, pp. 55–100). New York: Free Press.

Saunders, J. M., & Edwards, J. N. (1984). Extramarital sexuality: A predictive model of permissive attitudes. *Journal of Marriage and the Family, 46,* 825–835.

Sponaugle, G. C. (1993). *A study of attitudes toward extramarital relations.* Unpublished doctoral dissertation, University of Minnesota, Minneapolis.

Treas, J., & Giesen, D. (2000). Sexual infidelity among married and cohabiting Americans. *Journal of Marriage and the Family, 62,* 48–60.

Weis, D. L., & Jurich, J. (1985). Size of community of residence as a predictor of attitudes toward extramarital sexual relations. *Journal of Marriage and the Family, 47,* 173–178.

Weis, D. L., & Slosnerick, M. (1981). Attitudes toward sexual and non sexual extramarital involvements among a sample of college students. *Journal of Marriage and the Family, 43,* 349–358.

Exhibit

Reiss Extramarital Sexual Permissiveness Scale

Answer in terms of your personal values concerning what you would accept in your marriage under the conditions stated. If you are not currently married, answer in terms of a possible future marriage.

1. Would you accept extramarital sexual intercourse in which physical pleasure is your focus even though your mate would not accept your having such a relationship?

a) Definitely   b) Probably   c) Unlikely   d) Never

2. Would you accept extramarital sexual intercourse in which physical pleasure is your focus if your mate would accept your having this type of relationship?

   a) Definitely   b) Probably   c) Unlikely   d) Never

3. Would you accept extramarital sexual intercourse in which love is emphasized even though your mate would not accept your having such a relationship?

   a) Definitely   b) Probably   c) Unlikely   d) Never

4. Would you accept extramarital sexual intercourse in which love is emphasized if your mate would accept your having this type of relationship?

   a) Definitely   b) Probably   c) Unlikely   d) Never

Note. Ask the single people to assume they are in a happy marriage when answering these four questions and then give them these same four questions again and ask them to assume they are in an unhappy marriage. Also ask married people to answer these questions twice—once for being in a happy marriage and once for being in an unhappy marriage. At the end, for married people, you should ask if in their own marriage they feel they are closer to a happy marriage or closer to an unhappy marriage.

Parenting Outcome Expectancy Scale

COLLEEN DIIORIO,[1] *Emory University*

The purpose of the Parenting Outcome Expectancy Scale (POES) is to measure the parent's expectations about the outcomes associated with talking with his/her adolescent about sex-related topics.

Description

The development of the POES was based on the concept of outcome expectancy (OE), a central construct of social cognitive theory (Bandura, 1997). Bandura defines an outcome expectation as a judgment of the likely consequences that result from performance of a behavior. He proposes that people who hold more positive views about behavioral performances are more likely to perform the behavior. In the present situation, a parent who believes that talking with his/her children about sexuality issues has positive outcomes would likely initiate such discussions. Bandura further describes three types of OE—self-evaluative, social, and physical. Self-evaluative OE relates to personal reactions; social OE relates to the reactions of others; and physical OE addresses sensory effects related to a behavior. The POES includes items measuring only self-evaluative and social OE because there are no direct physical OEs that can be associated with discussions about sexuality.

For the development of the POES, outcome expectancy was defined as the parent's expectations about the outcomes associated with talking with his/her adolescent about sex-related topics. The original 15 POES items were written following a review of the literature and focus group discussions with parents of adolescents (DiIorio et al., 2001). Content and measurement specialists reviewed the wording of each item and the consistency of the idea presented in each item with the concept of OE as defined by Bandura (1997). Based on their reviews, all 15 items were retained for the final version with some minor changes in wording.

The results of the initial reliability and validity testing using the 15-item version suggested that the POES could be improved by adding one item to measure cognitive self-evaluative OE and seven items to measure social OE. The addition of these eight items increased the total number of POES items to 23.

Response Mode and Timing

Each item is rated on a 5-point Likert scale ranging from (1) *Strongly Disagree* to (5) *Strongly Agree*. Each item begins with the stem "If I talk with [my child] about sex topics." In an interview situation or when using computer-assisted

[1]Address correspondence to Colleen DiIorio, Emory University, Rollins School of Public Health, Department of Behavioral Sciences and Health Education, 1518 Clifton Road NE, Atlanta, GA 30322; e-mail: cdiiori@emory.edu

interviewing, the name of the child can be substituted by the interviewer/computer for [my child]. The POES takes about 5 to 10 minutes to complete. The items do not usually require explanation.

Scoring

Fifteen of the 23 items are positively worded, and 8 are negatively worded. The negatively worded items are reverse coded prior to summing the items. A total score is found by summing responses to the 23 individual items. Total scale scores range from 23 to 115, with higher scores indicating more positive outcome expectancies.

Reliability

The 15-item POES was assessed for reliability using scale responses from a sample of 491 mothers of 11- to 14-year-old adolescents (DiIorio et al., 2001). Cronbach's alpha for the total POES was .83, indicating an acceptable level of internal consistency among scale items. Item-to-total correlations ranged from .24 to .61, with a mean of .27. Means of individual items ranged from 3.15 to 4.50, with standard deviations ranging from .60 to 1.25. The item *"Your adolescent will do what he/she wants no matter what you say"* (the original form of Item 8) had the lowest item-to-total correlation and also demonstrated several weak (< .10) correlations with other items. The Cronbach's alphas for three subscales (cognitive self-evaluative, emotional self-evaluative, and social) resulting from a factor analysis of item responses were .82, .77, and .67, respectively, and indicated low to moderate levels of internal consistency. The 15-item POES was used in a study with mothers of 6- to 12-year-old children (Pluhar, DiIorio, & McCarty, 2008). Cronbach's alpha coefficient for responses from the 277 father participants was .85. The 23-item POES was used in a randomized controlled study of an HIV prevention intervention for fathers and their adolescent boys. Cronbach's alpha coefficient for responses from the 277 father participants was .83 (DiIorio, McCarty, & Denzmore, 2006).

Validity

The 15-item POES was assessed for validity using the same sample of 491 mothers as was used for initial reliability assessment (DiIorio et al., 2001). Construct validity was assessed by examining the association of the total POES scores with the theoretically relevant variables of sex-based communication, general communication, parenting, and self-esteem. All correlations between the POES and these scales were significant and in the predicted directions. Further analysis revealed that mothers of daughters reported higher levels of parenting OE than did mothers of sons, as was expected based on the literature.

To assess the underlying dimensions of the POES, an exploratory maximum likelihood common factor analysis with oblique rotation was conducted. The initial analysis revealed four factors with eigenvalues greater than 1.0 and explaining 59.6% of the variance. Only one item loaded on Factor 4. Thus, a second analysis was conducted requesting three factors. The resulting three factors provided a better interpretation of the data and together accounted for 52.6% of the variance. The self-evaluative items were divided across two factors with one factor representing a cognitive self-evaluative component (three items) and the second factor, an emotional self-evaluative component (six items). The third factor represented a social component (six items). The underlying theme of the strongest factor, cognitive self-evaluation, seemed to be responsibility. The second factor related to emotional self-evaluation of discussions and consisted of six items about feelings of embarrassment, discomfort, and difficulty discussing some topics. The third factor, social OE, related to discussions with adolescents. Because the cognitive self-evaluative OE factor had only three items and the social OE factor had a slightly less than adequate reliability coefficient, eight new items were written. One item was written to measure cognitive self-evaluative OE and seven items to measure social OE. In a descriptive study of correlates of sexuality communication, the POES was significantly and positively correlated with sexuality discussions, meaning that mothers who had more positive OE were more likely to talk with their children about sexuality issues (Pluhar et al., 2008).

Other Information

The format of the scale can be modified to use with computer-assisted interview (CAI) programs or face-to-face interviews. If used with CAI programs, the term [child's name] can be linked with the child's first name and appear in each item as it is presented on the screen. For paper versions, the stem of each item (If I talk with my child about sex topics) can be placed at the top of the list of items and deleted from each of the statements.

References

Bandura, A. (1997). *Self-efficacy: The exercise of control.* New York: W. H. Freeman and Company.

DiIorio, C., Dudley, W. N., Wang, D. T., Wasserman, J., Eichler, M., Belcher, L., et al. (2001). Measurement of parenting self-efficacy and outcome expectancy related to discussion about sex. *Journal of Nursing Measurement, 9,* 135–149.

DiIorio, C., McCarty, F., & Denzmore, P. (2006). An exploration of social cognitive theory mediators of father-son communication about sex. *Journal of Pediatric Psychology, 31,* 917–927.

Pluhar, E. I., DiIorio, C. K., & McCarty, F. (2008). Correlates of sexuality communication among mothers and 6–12-year-old children. *Child Care and Health Development, 34,* 283–290.

Exhibit

Parent Outcome Expectancy Scale

Read these statements about talking with your child about sex. Talking with your child about sex includes topics such as how babies are made, names of the genitals, physical changes of puberty, menstruation, wet dreams, waiting to have sex until your child is older, birth control, and HIV or AIDS. For each statement, state how much you agree or disagree.

Response Options:

1 Strongly Disagree
2 Disagree
3 Neither Disagree nor Agree
4 Agree
5 Strongly Agree

Items

1.   If I talk with [my child] about sex topics, I will feel proud.
2.   If I talk with [my child] about sex topics, I will feel like a responsible parent.
3.   If I talk with [my child] about sex topics, I will feel that I did the right thing.
4.* If I talk with [my child] about sex topics, I will be embarrassed.
5.* If I talk with [my child] about sex topics, I will find some things difficult to talk about.
6.   If I talk with [my child] about sex topics, I think [my child] will listen.
7.   If I talk with [my child] about sex topics, I will feel comfortable.
8.* If I talk with [my child] about sex topics, [my child] will do what [my child] wants no matter what I say.
9.* If I talk with [my child] about sex topics, I will feel ashamed.
10. If I talk with [my child] about sex topics, I think it will do some good.
11. If I talk with [my child] about sex topics, [my child] will be less likely to have sexual intercourse as a young teen.
12.* If I talk with [my child] about sex topics, it would be unpleasant.
13. If I talk with [my child] about sex topics, [my child] will be less likely to get pregnant or get a girl pregnant.
14. If I talk with [my child] about sex topics, I will find these issues easy to talk about.
15. If I talk with [my child] about sex topics, I will feel relieved.
16.* If I talk with [my child] about sex topics, [my child] will be embarrassed.
17.* If I talk with [my child] about sex topics, [my child] will not want to talk to me.
18. If I talk with [my child] about sex topics, I will have done what parents should do.
19. If I talk with [my child] about sex topics, [my child] will remember the discussion when [my child] is older.
20. If I talk with [my child] about sex topics, [my child] will appreciate my willingness to provide further information.
21.* If I talk with [my child] about sex topics, [my child] will be uncomfortable during the discussion.
22. If I talk with [my child] about sex topics, [my child] will be more able to resist peer pressure to have sex.
23. If I talk with [my child] about sex topics, [my child] will know where I stand on teens having sex.

*Reverse code before summing.

Parenting Self-Efficacy Scale

COLLEEN DiIORIO,[1] *Emory University*

The purpose of the Parenting Self-Efficacy Scale (PSES) is to measure parents' confidence in their ability to talk to their children about sexuality issues.

Description

The development of the PSES was based on the concept of self-efficacy (SE), a central construct of social cognitive

[1]Address correspondence to Colleen DiIorio, Emory University, Rollins School of Public Health, Department of Behavioral Sciences and Health Education, 1518 Clifton Road NE, Atlanta, GA 30322; e-mail: cdiiori@emory.edu

theory (Bandura, 1997). Bandura defined self-efficacy as the belief in personal capability to organize and execute behaviors. People who have strong beliefs in their abilities are more likely to perform behaviors and more likely to be successful. Applied to the situation of parent-child sexual communication, this means that parents who are confident that they can talk to their children about sexuality issues are more likely to do so.

Bandura (1997) noted that self-efficacy is specific to each behavior. Thus, self-efficacy scales based on his conceptualization must be behavior-specific. For the purpose of the development of the PSES, self-efficacy was defined as parents' overall belief in their capacity to talk with their children and adolescents about specific sex-related topics. Based on a literature review, three aspects of sex-based discussions were identified: (a) physiological processes (e.g., menstruation), (b) practical issues (e.g., where to get condoms), and (c) safer-sex messages (e.g., should use condoms if he/she decides to have sex). Sixteen items to measure self-efficacy related to these three aspects were developed based on a literature review of sexuality discussions and on focus groups conducted with mothers of adolescents (DiIorio et al., 2001). Content and measurement specialists reviewed the wording of each item and the consistency of the idea presented in each item with the concept of SE as defined by Bandura. Based on their reviews, all 16 items were retained for the final version with some minor changes in wording.

To assess the underlying dimensions of the PSES, an exploratory maximum likelihood common factor analysis with oblique rotation was conducted. The initial analysis revealed three factors with eigenvalues greater than 1.0 and explaining 51% of the variance. Only one item loaded on Factor 3. Thus, a second analysis was conducted requesting two factors. The resulting two factors provided a better interpretation of the data and together accounted for 44% of the variance. The first factor was composed of 10 items representing all three pre-specified aspects of sex-based discussions—physiological events, practical issues, and safer-sex messages and was labeled Basic Information. The second factor was named Relationship-Based Information, because it was composed of six items addressing relationship issues such as how to encourage a partner to wait, how to tell a partner no, and how to have fun without sex. Because the Relationship-Based Information factor had a slightly less than adequate reliability coefficient (.67), one new item was written to further define the factor; thus the current PSES has 17 items.

Response Mode and Timing

Each item is worded positively and rated on a 7-point scale anchored with the terms *Not Sure at all* (1) and *Completely Sure* (7). The midpoint of the scale is defined as *Moderately Sure*. Each item begins with the stem "I can always explain to [my child]. . . ." In an interview situation or when using computer-assisted interviewing, the name of the child can be substituted by the interviewer/computer for [my child]. The PSES takes about 5–10 minutes to complete. The items do not usually require explanation.

Scoring

All 17 items are positively worded. Total scores are found by summing responses to individual items. Total possible scores range from 17 to 119 with higher scores corresponding to a higher degree of self-efficacy to discuss sex-related issues with adolescents.

Reliability

The original 16-item PSES was assessed for reliability using scale responses from a sample of 491 mothers of 11- to 14-year-old adolescents (DiIorio et al., 2001). Cronbach's alpha for the total PSES was .85, indicating a moderately high level of internal consistency among scale items. The mean inter-item correlation was .28, with item-to-total correlations ranging from .24 to .61. Means of individual items ranged from 4.46 to 6.76 with standard deviations ranging from .78 to 2.25. The Cronbach's alphas for two subscales (Basic Information and Relationship-Based Information) were .84 and .67 and indicated low to moderate levels of internal consistency.

The 16-item POES was used in a study with mothers of 6- to 12-year-old children (Pluhar, DiIorio, & McCarty, 2008). Cronbach's alpha coefficient for responses from the 277 father participants was .94. The 17-item PSES was used in a randomized controlled study of an HIV prevention intervention for fathers and their adolescent boys. Cronbach's alpha coefficient for responses from the 277 father participants was .85 (DiIorio, McCarty, & Denzmore, 2006).

Validity

The 16-item PSES was assessed for validity using the same sample of 491 mothers as used for initial reliability assessment (DiIorio et al., 2001). Construct validity was assessed by examining the association of the total PSES scores with the theoretically relevant variables of sex-based communication, general communication, parenting, and self-esteem. All correlations between the PSES and these scales were significant and in the predicted directions. Further analysis revealed that mothers of daughters reported higher levels of parenting SE than did mothers of sons, as was expected based on the literature. In a descriptive study of correlates of sexuality communication, the PSES was significantly and positively correlated with sexuality discussions, meaning that mothers who had more positive SE were more confident in talking with their children about sexuality issues (Pluhar et al., 2008).

Other Information

The format of the scale can be modified to use with computer-assisted interview (CAI) programs or face-to-face interviews. If used with CAI programs, the term [my child] can be linked with the child's first name and appear in each item as it is presented on the screen. For paper versions, the stem of each item (I can always explain to [my child]) can be placed at the top of the list of items and deleted from each of the statements.

References

Bandura, A. (1997). *Self-efficacy: The exercise of control*. New York: W. H. Freeman and Company.

DiIorio, C., Dudley, W. N., Wang, D., Wasserman, J., Eichler, M., Belcher, L., et al. (2001). Measurement of parenting self-efficacy and outcome expectancy related to discussions about sex. *Journal of Nursing Measurement, 9,* 135–49.

DiIorio, C., McCarty, F., & Denzmore, P. (2006). An exploration of social cognitive theory mediators of father-son communication about sex. *Journal of Pediatric Psychology, 31,* 917–927.

Pluhar, E. I., DiIorio, C. K., & McCarty, F. (2008). Correlates of sexuality communication among mothers and 6–12-year-old children. *Child Care and Health Development, 34,* 283–290.

Exhibit

Parenting Self-Efficacy Scale

Read each statement about talking to your child about sexuality issues. Then chose a number on the scale from 1 (Not Sure at all) to 7 (Completely Sure) to say how sure you are about your ability to talk about each topic with [my child] as he/she grows up. Remember, 1 means Not Sure at all, 4 means Moderately Sure, and 7 means Completely Sure. You can also answer with the numbers in between. For example, a 5 or 6 would mean somewhere between Moderately Sure and Completely Sure.

Response Options:

1   Not Sure at all
2
3
4   Moderately Sure
5
6
7   Completely Sure

Items

1. I can always explain to [my child] what is happening when a girl has her period.
2. I can always explain to [my child] why a person should use a condom when he or she has sex.
3. I can always explain to [my child] ways to have fun without having sexual intercourse.
4. I can always explain to [my child] why [my child] should wait until [my child] is older to have sexual intercourse.
5. I can always explain to [my child] that [my child] should use condoms if [my child] decides to have sexual intercourse.
6. I can always explain to [my child] why wet dreams occur.
7. I can always explain to [my child] how to put on a condom.
8. I can always explain to [my child] how to use birth control pills.
9. I can always explain to [my child] how birth control pills keep girls from getting pregnant.
10. I can always explain to [my child] what I think about young teens having sex.
11. I can always explain to [my child] how to tell someone no if [my child] does not want to have sex.
12. I can always explain to [my child] how to make a partner wait until [my child] is ready to have sex.
13. I can always explain to [my child] how someone can get AIDS if they don't use a condom.
14. I can always explain to [my child] where to buy or get condoms.
15. I can always explain to [my child] where to buy or get birth control pills.
16. I can always explain to [my child] how to tell if a girl or boy really loves [my child].
17. I can always explain to [my child] how to resist peer pressure to have sex.

Sexual Daydreaming Scale of the Imaginal Processes Inventory

Leonard M. Giambra,[1] *National Institute on Aging*
Jerome L. Singer, *Yale University*

The Imaginal Processes Inventory (IPI) was developed to measure the various aspects of daydreaming and related mental processes, such as attention, distractibility, and curiosity. The IPI is intended to be taken by normally functioning persons and is meant to measure the range of normal functioning. The Sexual Daydreaming Scale (SDS) was constructed to reveal the extent to which a person has daydreams of a sexual or erotic nature.

Description

The SDS consists of 12 items selected initially by requesting a large sample of "normal" adults to record their recurrent fantasies. An additional sample of respondents reviewed these fantasies and checked off those they had experienced by indicating the degree of frequency on a Likert-type scale. Those items bearing specifically on sexuality and showing reasonable intercorrelations as well as relatively normal distributions on the 5-point scale were employed for further refinement in the procedure used for generating the 12-item scales of the IPI (Singer & Antrobus, 1963, 1972). In general, this scale has not been used to any degree independently of the other 27 scales that make up the IPI because it loads on at least two of the three second-order factors that consistently emerge from the larger questionnaire.

Response Mode and Scoring

Each of the 12 items has the same five optional responses: *Definitely Not True For Me, Usually Not True For Me, Usually True For Me, True For Me,* and *Very True For Me*. These options, in the order given, are assigned increasing larger integer values, either 0 to 4 or 1 to 5, depending upon the study cited. All items are scored directly, and a scale score consists of the sum of the values of the responses to the 12 items. Using this scoring method, the SDS can range from a minimum of zero to a maximum of 48 (or from 12 to 60). Higher scale scores indicate a greater likelihood of sexual daydreaming. An alternate method of scoring based upon a factor analysis of the IPI items is available in Giambra (1980).

Reliability

The internal consistency of the SDS as measured by Cronbach's alpha has been reported to be quite high: .87

(Singer & Antrobus, 1972), .93 (Giambra, 1977-1978), .93 (Giambra, 1979-1980). Test-retest reliability over a 1- to 3-year period based upon 45 men was .58, and no significant difference was observed between the first and second testing, $t < 1$.

Validity

In a sample of 565 men and 745 women from 17 to 92 years of age, it was found that the SDS correlated -.56 for men and -.52 for women with age; the partial correlation holding daydreaming frequency constant was -.41 for men and -.40 for women (Giambra, 1979-1980). For a life-span sample of men, Giambra and Martin (1977) determined that men who reported having a greater number of coital partners, who had a greater frequency of coitus during the first year or two of marriage, or who had a higher number of sexual events per week between ages 20 and 40 had significantly higher SDS values. For a sample of 477 women aged 40 to 60 years, the SDS was found to be significantly related to menopausal state, a menopausal symptom index, frequency of masturbation, interest in sexual relations relative to partner, and level of moodiness prior to menstrual period (Giambra, 1983a, 1983b); however, age did interact with these variables.

An extensive study of masturbatory fantasy in college students conducted by Campagna (1975) included a factor analysis of self-reports of sexual behavior as well as the scales of two factors of the IPI. One factor, reflecting a generally positive and constructive acceptance and use of daydreaming, included positive loadings for the SDS. Higher frequency and variability of sexual behavior of a relatively conventional heterosexual type was associated with higher scale scores for sexual fantasy. Those subjects who reported more elaborate "story-like" masturbation fantasies were also more likely to report more general fantasies and more sexual daydreams on the IPI.

Other Information

A revised, restandardized short form of the Imaginal Processes Inventory (SIPI) has been developed by Huba, Aneshensel, and Singer (1981). This 45-item inventory taps the three second-order factors emerging from the longer IPI. The three scales are: Poor Attentional Control

[1]Address correspondence to Leonard M. Giambra, United States Coast Guard Academy, 15 Mohegan Avenue, New London, CT 06320; e-mail: Leonard. M.Giambra@uscg.mil

(mindwandering and distractibility), Positive-Constructive Daydreaming, and Guilty-Dysphoric Daydreaming. In a study conducted by Rosenberg (1983) examining sexual fantasy and overt behavior in young male adults, there were indications that the Poor Attentional Control pattern characterized men who had more homosexual and less heterosexual fantasies or less masturbatory fantasies involving past sexual experiences. The Guilty Daydreaming Scale was more associated with masturbatory fantasies of beating or domination in masturbatory imagination ($r = .34$). The data suggested positive general daydreaming is associated with a more accepting attitude toward sexual behavior and sexual fantasies.

The longer form of the IPI is copyrighted by Singer and Antrobus and is available online at The Measurement Group (www.themeasurementgroup.com/evaluationtools/ipi.htm). Persons using the instrument should acknowledge its origin. A copy of any resulting publication would be appreciated by the authors. The SIPI is also available at that site, though at the time of the original publication, the SIPI had not been studied for clinical application.

References

Campagna, A. F. (1975). *The function of men's erotic fantasies during masturbation.* Unpublished doctoral dissertation, Yale University, New Haven, CT.

Giambra, L. M. (1977-1978). Adult male daydreaming across the lifespan: A replication, further analyses, and tentative norms based upon retrospective reports. *International Journal of Aging and Human Development, 8,* 197-228.

Giambra, L. M. (1979-1980). Sex differences in daydreaming and related mental activity from the late teens to the early nineties. *International Journal of Aging and Human Development, 10,* 1-34.

Giambra, L. M. (1980). A factor analysis of the items for the Imaginal Processes Inventory. *Journal of Clinical Psychology, 36,* 383-409.

Giambra, L. M. (1983a). Daydreaming in 40- to 60-year-old women: Menopause, health, values, and sexuality. *Journal of Clinical Psychology, 39,* 11-21.

Giambra, L. M. (1983b). Sexual daydreams in 40- to 60-year old women: The influence of menopause, sexual activity, and health. In J. E. Shorr, G. Gobel-Whittington, P. Robin, & J. Connella (Eds.), *Imagery: Theoretical and clinical applications* (Vol. 3, pp. 297-302). New York: Plenum.

Giambra, L. M., & Martin, C. E. (1977). Sexual daydreams and quantitative aspects of sexual activity: Some relations for males across adulthood. *Archives of Sexual Behavior, 6,* 497-505.

Huba, G. J., Aneshensel, C. S., & Singer, J. L. (1981). Development of scales for three second-order factors of inner experience. *Multivariate Behavioral Research, 16,* 181-206.

Rosenberg, L. G. (1983). *Sex-role identification, erotic fantasy and sexual behavior: A study of heterosexual, bisexual and homosexual males.* Unpublished predissertation research, Yale University, New Haven, CT.

Singer, J. L., & Antrobus, J. S. (1963). A factor analytic study of daydreaming and conceptually related cognitive and personality variables [Monograph]. *Perceptual and Motor Skills, 17* (Suppl. 3-V17), 187-209.

Singer, J. L., & Antrobus, J. S. (1972). Daydreaming, imaginal processes, and personality: A normative study. In P. Sheehan (Ed.), *The function and nature of imagery* (pp. 175-202). New York: Academic Press.

Exhibit

Sexual Daydreaming Scale

1. My daydreams about love are so vivid, I actually feel they are occurring.
2. I imagine myself to be physically attractive to people of the opposite sex.
3. While working intently at a job, my mind will wander to thoughts about sex.
4. Sometimes on my way to work, I imagine myself making love to an attractive person of the opposite sex.
5. My sexual daydreams are very vivid and clear in my mind.
6. While reading, I often slip into daydreams about sex or making love to someone.
7. While traveling on a train or bus [or airplane], my idle thoughts turn to love.
8. Whenever I am bored, I daydream about the opposite sex.
9. Sometimes in the middle of the day, I will daydream of having sexual relations with someone I am fond of.
10. In my fantasies, I arouse great desire in someone I admire.
11. Before going to sleep, my idle thoughts turn to love-making.
12. My daydreams tend to arouse me physically.

Note. Item 7 has been modified from the original by addition of the material in brackets.

Hurlbert Index of Sexual Fantasy

DAVID F. HURLBERT,[1] *U.S. Department of Health and Human Services*

The Hurlbert Index of Sexual Fantasy is described by Hurlbert and Apt (1993).

Reference

Hurlbert, D. F., & Apt, C. (1993). Female sexuality: A comparative study between women in homosexual and heterosexual relationships. *Journal of Sex & Marital Therapy, 19,* 315–327.

Exhibit

Hurlbert Index of Sexual Fantasy

1. I think sexual fantasies are healthy. (R)
2. I enjoy fantasizing about sex. (R)
3. I feel comfortable sharing my sexual fantasies with my partner. (R)
4. I enjoy using my sexual fantasies during masturbation. (R)
5. I am easily aroused by thoughts of sex. (R)
6. Even when I am in the mood for sex, it is difficult for me to think about sexual things.
7. I enjoy hearing my partner's sexual fantasies. (R)
8. It is hard for me to focus or concentrate on my sexual fantasies during sex.
9. I find my sexual fantasies to be boring.
10. My memories of past sexual experiences are negative.
11. It is difficult for me to think about sexual things during sex with my partner.
12. Thoughts about sex enter my mind without much effort. (R)
13. I believe sexual fantasy enhances sex. (R)
14. I feel uncomfortable discussing my sexual fantasies with my partner.
15. I don't like thinking about sex.
16. I feel uncomfortable telling my partner my sexual thoughts.
17. I feel guilty about my sexual fantasies.
18. I find my sexual fantasies to be simulating. (R)
19. When it comes to my past sexual experiences, my memories are negative.
20. It is hard for me to daydream about sex.
21. I find my partner's sexual fantasies to be exciting. (R)
22. I enjoy using my sexual fantasies during sex. (R)
23. I feel guilty when I think about sex.
24. I have negative thoughts about my past sexual experiences.
25. I experience negative feelings just thinking about sex.

Note. (R) = Reverse-scored items as indicated by the responses: *All Of The Time* = 0 points; *Most Of The Time* = +1 point; *Some Of The Time* = +2 points; *Rarely* = +3 points; *Never* = +4 points.

[1]Address correspondence to David F. Hurlbert, 140 Farnworth Lane, Roswell, Georgia 30075; e-mail: david.hurlbert@acf.hhs.gov

Women's Sexuality Questionnaire

DIANNE L. CHAMBLESS,[1] *University of Pennsylvania*
DIANE DEMARCO, *The American University*

The Women's Sexuality Questionnaire (WSQ) is a structured interview with rating scales devised to assess the frequency and subjective experience of female orgasm and activities leading to orgasm.

Description

To allow for rapport to be established, as well as to collect information on potentially confounding variables, the WSQ begins with 16 questions concerning demographics and the subject's reproductive and genital health. The second section is devoted to a brief sexual history concerning masturbation and noncoital and coital sex with a partner. Information collected includes the subject's age when beginning to engage in the activity under question, frequency, and techniques of stimulation. The third section is the heart of the questionnaire. Questions concern the frequency of orgasm during various sexual activities in addition to scales asking subjects to rate the subjective quality of the orgasmic experience and of the stimulation leading to orgasm. Information obtained in the first two sections allows the interviewer to screen for variables that would reduce the probability of orgasm, such as drugs, dyspareunia, or inadequate stimulation. Although there are a variety of question formats, the major questions in Sections II and III are on ordinal scales.

Response Mode and Timing

The WSQ is designed to be administered in a private interview of approximately 45–60 minutes duration. The interview format allows the experimenter to develop rapport and to explore answers so as to yield more careful, thoughtful answers. Experience with the interview has shown that many women are confused by sexual terms and need explanations to give valid responses. Interviewers can also provide education about sexuality in the context so that the subject truly benefits from taking part in research.

Scoring

Items are used as single-item scores with 1–5 or 1–7 ordinal scales, or as simple ages or frequencies. Items 22–25 are reverse scored.

Reliability

Test-retest reliability was established on a sample of 38 women reinterviewed by a second interviewer from 6 to 8 weeks after the first interview (median = 6 weeks). Space limitations preclude the listing of the reliability coefficient for each item, but they are available from the authors. Items concerning personal history, such as the subjects' age when first having intercourse and the frequency of sexual behaviors, were highly reliable. Pearson correlations ranged from .80 to .98, with the exception of the item concerning noncoital genital sex play with a partner, $r = .37, p < .03$.

Reliability of the remaining (ordinal) items was assessed by Kendall's tau. Taus for frequency of orgasm with clitoral stimulation by partner or self, coitus accompanied by clitoral stimulation, and coitus not accompanied by clitoral stimulation were .42, .74, and .61, respectively. Based on subjects' feedback, the item for clitoral stimulation has subsequently been rewritten to yield two items: orgasm through masturbation and orgasm through partner stimulation. Additional reliability data have yet to be collected. Although the reliability of the other two items is somewhat lower than would be desirable, we believe the subjects' responses largely reflect true variance due to the reactive nature of the interview itself rather than mostly measurement error. Interviewers provided information and reassurance on the basis of which, according to subjects' reports on retesting, the subjects made changes, often substantial ones, in their sexual behavior. Taus on items concerning the subjects' perception of the intensity and pleasurability of coitus and the orgasmic experience generally reflected good reliability, ranging from .57 to .87 (median tau = .78).

Validity

The WSQ items possess high face validity and have been examined for construct validity through a series of correlational analyses. Using a community sample of 90 heterosexual women, Chambless and Lifshitz (1984) found that, as predicted, frequency of orgasm on the WSQ was related to higher arousal on the previously validated Sexual Arousability Inventory (Hoon, Hoon, & Wincze, 1976; tau = .18, $p < .03$). In further research with these 90 women, plus 12 lesbians, we have found predictable relationships among WSQ items. For example,

[1]Address correspondence to Dianne L. Chambless, Dept. of Psychology, University of Pennsylvania, 3815 Walnut Street, Philadelphia, PA 19104-6196; e-mail: chambless@psych.upenn.edu

higher frequency of coital orgasm was related to greater emphasis on vaginal stimulation in reaching orgasm (tau = .50, p < .001) and the higher ratings on the pleasurability of vaginal sensations during the nonorgasmic phase of coitus (tau = .28, p < .01). Higher frequency of orgasm through clitoral stimulation was related to a greater emphasis on clitoral stimulation in reaching orgasm (tau = -.29, p < .005). Additional information concerning WSQ item correlations is available from the authors. Although further validation work is deemed desirable, data collected to date support the construct validity of the items.

Other Information

The WSQ, as well as accompanying information on reliability and validity, is available at no charge from Dianne Chambless.

References

Chambless, D. L., & Lifshitz, J. (1984). Self-reported sexual anxiety and arousal: The Expanded Sexual Arousability Inventory. *The Journal of Sex Research, 20*, 241–254.

Hoon, E. F., Hoon, P. W., & Wincze, J. P. (1976). An inventory for the measurement of female sexual arousability: The SAI. *Archives of Sexual Behavior, 5*, 291–300.

Exhibit

Women's Sexuality Questionnaire

Section I

1. Date of interview _____
2. Assessment no. _____
   Interviewer _____
3. S.S. Number _____   4. D.O.B. _____
5. Occupation (do not inquire about place of employment) _____
6. Highest grade completed _____
7. Affiliative status:
   Single   Married   Divorced   Separated   Cohabiting
8. Steady sexual partner: YES   NO
9. Looking over your whole life, would you say your primary sexual orientation is:
   bisexual   heterosexual   lesbian
10. What drugs do you usually take (including alcohol, caffeine, street drugs, prescribed drugs)
    In what amount and how often do you take these?

    _____

    Are any of these taken at times you plan on having sex? If so, in what way?

    _____

11. What is your present method of contraception? Do you have any problems with it?

    _____

12. Have you ever been pregnant?   YES   NO

    a. Number of full-term deliveries _____
       how long ago was each? _____
       Number of vaginal _____   Number of caesarean _____
    b. Number of premature deliveries _____
       how long ago was each? _____
       Number of vaginal _____   Number of caesarean _____
    c. Number of spontaneous or induced abortions _____
       how long ago was each? _____
       how many weeks pregnant with each? _____

13. Have you ever undergone any surgery involving the vagina, other sexual organs, or organs closely related to sexual organs (i.e., anus, urethra, kidneys, bladder)? YES   NO
    If so, please describe:

    _____

14. Do you have any physical problems with interfere with your sexual functioning or pleasure? YES   NO
    If so, please explain (including chronic illnesses, infections, vaginal tears)

    _____

    Specifically, do you get a lot of vaginal infections, and if so, how long do they usually last?

    _____

15. Have you ever done exercises for the vaginal muscle? (Show a diagram) If so, explain and describe. _____

_____

16. When not pregnant, do you ever leak urine when you cough or sneeze? _____

Section II

17. Masturbation:

a. How long ago did you begin to masturbate regularly? _____

b. On an average over the last 6 months, how often have you masturbated? _____

c. How many times would you estimate you've masturbated?

_____ under ten times

_____ 10–25

_____ 26–100

_____ 101–500

_____ over 500

d. How do you usually masturbate?

_____ by inserting object into vagina

_____ by using vibrator on external genitalia

_____ by stimulating clitoral area with fingers, etc.

_____ by manipulating the mons (define if necessary)

_____ by pressure against object or pressure from thighs

_____ by stimulating the entrance of the vagina (introitus)

_____ other (please describe unless it makes you uncomfortable)

_____

Do you need to be in one particular position to reach orgasm? YES NO

If so, please describe:

_____

18. Sex with partner excluding intercourse:

a. At what age did you begin having genital sex with another person excluding intercourse (including manual, oral stimulation, etc.)? _____

b. How often do you do so now? _____

c. Roughly how many times have you done so? _____

19. Intercourse (defined according to woman's orientation as insertion and thrusting of penis, fingers, or objects by partner):

a. At what age did you begin having intercourse? _____

b. How often do you do so now? _____

c. How many times, roughly, have you done so? _____

d. What positions do you usually use? _____

Do you generally get simultaneous clitoral stimulation while in this/these positions? If so, how? _____

_____

20. On the average, what is the duration of sex play (defined as prior to intercourse if you have intercourse)?

_____ no sex play   _____ 11–19 minutes

_____ less than 5 minutes   _____ 20 or more minutes

_____ 5–10 minutes

21. If you have intercourse, are you sufficiently lubricated at the time of insertion so that no artificial lubricant is needed for your comfort? YES NO If not, to what does this seem due? Likely factors are anxiety, insufficient stimulation, irritation from local contraceptives, menopause, infections, vaginal deodorant sprays, overwiping after diaphragm insertion, unlubricated condoms, postpartum estrogen imbalance (particularly likely if nursing), and oral contraceptive. In addition, intercourse may be uncomfortable despite lubrication during early experiences due to tightness of the vaginal entrance. _____

Section III

22. If you have intercourse, how long does it last on the average from the beginning of thrusting until thrusting stops? (Counts as one occasion if intercourse disrupted only long enough to change position or pause to prevent ejaculation)

_____

Out of all occasions of intercourse how often do you come to an orgasm, with simultaneous clitoral stimulation (include both pressure and manipulation as clitoral stimulation):

_____ almost always 90–100%   _____ sometimes 1–29%

_____ most of the time 60–89%   _____ never have 0%

_____ often 30–59%

23. Out of all occasions of intercourse how often do you come to an orgasm, *without* simultaneous clitoral stimulation (defined as pressure or manipulation)?

_____ almost always 90–100%   _____ sometimes 1–29%

_____ most of the time 60–89%   _____ never have 0%

_____ often 30–59%

24. Out of all occasions of clitoral stimulation (defined as pressure or manipulation) during masturbation, how often do you come to orgasm?

_____ almost always 90–100%   _____ sometimes 1–29%

_____ most of the time 60–89%   _____ never have 0%

_____ often 30–59%

25. If after having an orgasm you continue to receive stimulation, how often do you have sequential orgasms (a series of peaks and releases of tension)?

a. During stimulation of clitoris (exclusively)?

_____ almost always 90–100%   _____ sometimes 1–29%

_____ most of the time 60–89%   _____ never have 0%

_____ often 30–59%

b. During intervaginal stimulation (intercourse) with clitoral stimulation (defined as pressure or manipulation)?

_____ almost always 90–100%   _____ sometimes 1–29%

_____ most of the time 60–89%   _____ never have 0%

_____ often 30–59%

c. During intervaginal stimulation (intercourse) exclusively?

_____ almost always 90–100%   _____ sometimes 1–29%

_____ most of the time 60–89%   _____ never have 0%

_____ often 30–59%

26. Out of all occasions of clitoral stimulation by your partner (manual or oral, but excluding intercourse), how often do you come to orgasm?

_____ almost always 90–100%   _____ sometimes 1–29%

_____ most of the time 60–89%   _____ never have 0%

_____ often 30–59%

27. In attaining orgasm for you, what is the most accurate statement:

_____ 1. Clitoral stimulation contributes *much more* than vaginal stimulation.

_____ 2. Clitoral stimulation contributes *somewhat more* than vaginal stimulation.

_____ 3. Clitoral and vaginal stimulation are *about equal* in contribution.

_____ 4. Vaginal stimulation contributes *somewhat more* than clitoral stimulation.

_____ 5. Vaginal stimulation contributes *much more* than clitoral stimulation.

28. (If you have orgasms) which statement best describes your physical sensations during orgasm with intercourse *with clitoral stimulation* (defined as pressure or manipulation):

_____ 1. A slight pulsating feeling in the vagina

_____ 2. A distinct pulsating feeling in the vagina

_____ 3. A very strong pulsating feeling in the vagina with sensation spreading to the legs

_____ 4. An intense feeling throughout the abdomen and legs with rhythmic contractions in the vagina

_____ 5. An intense feeling traveling throughout the entire body with rhythmic contractions in the vagina

_____ 6. Other, specify: _____

29. For me, having an orgasm during intercourse (with clitoral stimulation) is:

1	2	3	4	5	6	7
blah experience						most intense experience possible

30. What kind of feeling do you typically experience in the vagina during intercourse *without* direct clitoral stimulation (defined as pressure or manipulation)?

_____ 1. Experience an unpleasant feeling the entire time

_____ 2. Experience an unpleasant feeling which eventually changes to no particular feeling at all

_____ 3. Experience an unpleasant feeling which eventually increases to a pleasant feeling

_____ 4. Experience no particular feeling the entire time

_____ 5. Experience no particular feeling which eventually increases to a pleasant feeling

_____ 6. Experience a pleasant feeling the entire time

_____ 7. Experience a pleasant feeling which eventually increases to a more pleasant feeling

_____ 8. Other, specify: _____

31. (If you have orgasms) which statement best describes your physical sensations during orgasm with intercourse *without* direct clitoral stimulation? (include pressure, manual manipulation, etc. as clitoral stimulation).

_____ 1. A slight pulsating feeling in the vagina

_____ 2. A distinct pulsating feeling in the vagina

_____ 3. A very strong pulsating feeling in the vagina with sensation spreading to the legs

_____ 4. An intense feeling throughout the abdomen and legs with rhythmic contractions in the vagina

_____ 5. An intense feeling traveling throughout the entire body with rhythmic contractions in the vagina

_____ 6. Other, specify: _____

32. For me, having an orgasm during intercourse (without clitoral stimulation, (defined as pressure or manipulation)) is:

| 1 | 2 | 3 | 4 | 5 | 6 | 7 |

blah experience   most intense experience possible

33. (If you have orgasms) when a partner stimulates your clitoris (defined as pressure or manipulation) to orgasm (no entry into the vagina) which statement best describes your feelings?

_____ 1. A slight pulsating feeling in the vagina

_____ 2. A distinct pulsating feeling in the vagina

_____ 3. A very strong pulsating feeling in the vagina with sensation spreading to the legs

_____ 4. An intense feeling throughout the abdomen and legs with rhythmic contractions in the vagina

_____ 5. An intense feeling traveling throughout the entire body with rhythmic contractions in the vagina

_____ 6. Other, specify: _____

34. For me, having an orgasm when a partner stimulates (defined as pressure or manipulation) my clitoris (no entry into vagina) is:

| 1 | 2 | 3 | 4 | 5 | 6 | 7 |

blah experience   most intense experience possible

35. If you have orgasms when you stimulate your clitoris (masturbate via pressure or manipulation) (nothing in vagina) what best describes your physical sensations?

_____ 1. A slight pulsating feeling in the vagina.

_____ 2. A distinct pulsating feeling in the vagina.

_____ 3. A very strong pulsating feeling in the vagina with sensation spreading to the legs.

_____ 4. An intense feeling throughout the abdomen and legs with rhythmic contractions in the vagina.

_____ 5. An intense feeling traveling throughout the entire body with rhythmic contractions in the vagina

_____ 6. Other, specify: _____

36. For me, having an orgasm through masturbation (nothing in vagina) is:

| 1 | 2 | 3 | 4 | 5 | 6 | 7 |

blah experience   most intense experience possible

Self-Perceptions of Female Sexuality Survey Instrument

J. Kenneth Davidson, Sr.,[1] *University of Wisconsin—Eau Claire*
Carol A. Darling, *Florida State University*

The Self-Perceptions of Female Sexuality Survey Instrument covers a wide range of beliefs, attitudes, feelings, and responses about a woman's own sexuality and, to a lesser extent, that of her partners. The instrument was developed for the primary purpose of providing further clarification of the apparently inseparable nature of clitoral and vaginal orgasms. More specifically, the instrument ascertains whether perceived differences exist with regard to experiencing orgasm via masturbation, petting, and sexual intercourse in terms of physiological and psychological sexual satisfaction.

Description

The complete instrument consists of 123 open-ended and closed-form questions concerning sexual attitudes, sexual behavior, and the female sexual response. The following categories of items appear in the instrument:

1. Demographic variables, including age, marital status, dating status, formal education, religious preference, and religiosity.
2. Physiological and psychological sexual satisfaction variables, including early knowledge about the pleasurable sensations of the clitoris, level of sexual adjustment, perceived levels of current physiological and psychological sexual satisfaction, and desired changes in sex life.
3. Peer communication and mass media variables, including sources of information about female orgasm, sources of information about any differences between orgasmic responses, discussion with peers regarding different kinds and/or types of orgasms, and ages at various stages of opinion formation regarding perceived differences in orgasmic responses.
4. Masturbatory attitude variables, including perceived acceptance of masturbation of self, acceptance of masturbation by acquaintances, and the relationship of masturbation to marital sexual adjustment.
5. Sexual history variables, including masturbatory, petting, and sexual intercourse experience; frequency of masturbation, petting, and sexual intercourse; experience with pretending orgasm; relationships with past and current sex partners; and frequency and preference for various sexual intercourse positions for achieving orgasm.
6. Orgasmic quality variables, including perceived differences, if any, in experiencing orgasm via masturbation, petting, and sexual intercourse; the relative contribution of clitoral versus vaginal stimulation in achieving orgasm during masturbation, petting, and sexual intercourse; and the degree of physiological and psychological satisfaction associated with orgasms achieved via masturbation, petting, and sexual intercourse.

The survey instrument was first pretested with students enrolled in upper-division marriage/family and human sexuality courses. After appropriate revisions, the instrument was pretested a second time utilizing the nursing staff of a large midwestern family planning organization. After making additional changes, the instrument was then critically reviewed by 10 female professionals involved either in teaching and/or research about human sexuality and/or the delivery of community-based family planning services. The recommendations received from these reviewers were incorporated into the final version of the instrument.

The survey instrument is best suited for use with populations containing women with 2 or more years of college education and who are at least 25 years of age. The level of language sophistication found in the instrument would appear to preclude its application to populations having no college education. Furthermore, given the nature of the instrument, a woman would need to have had considerable sexual experience in order to be able to respond in a meaningful way to a substantial number of the items. It is assumed that a greater opportunity for having experienced substantial sexual activity will exist for women aged 25 years or older. To date, this survey instrument has been used for data collection from professional nurses holding at least an associate degree/diploma in nursing and from professional women in academia holding at least a baccalaureate degree.

Response Mode and Timing

Respondents are either to check the appropriate answer category or to answer the open-ended items in their own words within the space provided. Given the detailed personal information being sought regarding sexuality, the

[1]Address correspondence to J. Kenneth Davidson, Sr., 2634 Collingwood Drive, Round Rock, TX 78665; e-mail: davidsj@uwec.edu

survey instrument should be completed in total privacy and anonymity. Thus, this instrument is ideally suited for distribution as a mail questionnaire using a business reply envelope.

Based on the pretest results and feedback received from actual respondents, an average of 45 minutes is required to complete all segments of the survey instrument.

Scoring

Although some attitudinal items do appear, it is not intended for this survey instrument to be employed as a scale that can stand alone. It is recommended, however, that all attitudinal items selected for use be arranged in a reverse/nonreverse response pattern to help ensure that respondents give sufficient concentration to the completion of the survey instrument.

Reliability

The test-retest reliability of the instrument has not been established.

Validity

Construct validity has been established by reviewing pretest data for the various measures, which suggest the same relationship between the variables associated with perceived differences in orgasm achieved during masturbation, petting, and sexual intercourse. The instrument has successfully delineated perceived differences in orgasmic responses between orgasms achieved via masturbation, petting, and sexual intercourse; the influence of multiple sex partners on sexual satisfaction; factors associated with pretending orgasm; and levels of sexual satisfaction and desired changes in the sexual lives of single professional women (see references).

References

Darling, C. A., & Davidson, J. K., Sr. (1985, November). *Enhancing relationships: Understanding the feminine mystique of pretending orgasm.* Paper presented at the meeting of the National Council on Family Relations, Dallas, TX.

Davidson, J. K., Sr., & Darling, C. A. (1983, October). *The stereotype of single women revisited: Sexual behavior and sexual satisfaction among professional women.* Paper presented at the annual meeting of the Mid-South Sociological Association, Birmingham, AL.

Davidson, J. K., Sr., & Darling, C. A. (1984, November). *Perceived differences in the female orgasmic response: New meanings for sexual satisfaction.* Paper presented at the annual meeting of the National Council on Family Relations, San Francisco, CA.

Davidson, J. K., Sr., & Darling, C. A. (1985, August). *The sexually experienced female: The influence of multiple sex partners.* Paper presented at the annual meeting of the Society for the Study of Social Problems, Washington, DC.

Exhibit

Self-Perceptions of Female Sexuality[a]

1. How would you rate your current level of sexual adjustment? (*Very much adjusted—Very unadjusted*; 6 point)
2. At what age did you first *become aware* of possible pleasurable sensations of the clitoris? (PLEASE SPECIFY)
3. It is necessary for a female to achieve an orgasm in a majority of the instances when she experiences masturbation, petting (mutual masturbation), and/or sexual intercourse in order to be classified as sexually adjusted. (*Strongly agree—Strongly disagree*; 4 point)
4. Do you feel that most of your female friends believe that a female must experience an orgasm in order to be sexually adjusted? (*Yes/No*)
5. What has been your *most* important source of information about the female orgasm? (15 options)
6. Have you ever consciously considered the possibility that orgasms reached through masturbation while alone and/or sexual intercourse might be different? (*Yes/No*)
7. Have you ever read any material about different kinds and/or types of orgasms? (*Yes/No*)
8. *If ever read materials about different kinds and/or types of orgasm:* From the material that you have read, what conclusions, if any, did the authors reach regarding different kinds and/or types of orgasm?
9. Have you ever discussed with a friend, relative, and/or acquaintance whether different kinds and/or types of orgasms exist for the female during sexual intercourse and/or masturbation while alone? (*Yes/No*)
10. *If ever discussed different kinds and or types of orgasm:*

    With whom have you ever discussed different kinds and/or types of orgasm? (15 categories)
11. *If ever discussed different kinds and/or types of orgasm:*

    At what age did you *first* discuss different kinds and/or types of orgasm with another person?
12. In your opinion, do different kinds and/or types of orgasm exist for the human female? (*Yes/No/Uncertain*)
13. *If yes, or uncertain that different kinds and/or types of orgasm exist:*

    Would you please describe in your own words, the different kinds and/or types of orgasm that can be achieved through masturbation while alone, petting, and/or sexual intercourse.
14. Have you ever masturbated while alone? (*Yes/No*)

15. Have you ever achieved an orgasm? *(Yes/No /Uncertain)*

16. Have you ever experienced sexual intercourse? *(Yes/No)*

17. *If ever had orgasm:*

    How did you first experience orgasm?

    _____ 1. Masturbation while alone

    _____ 2. Petting (Mutual masturbation)

    _____ 3. Sexual intercourse

    _____ 4. Other _____

18. *If ever had orgasm:*

    At what age did you experience your first orgasm?

19. *If ever had orgasm:*

    Under which of the following circumstances have you *ever* experienced an orgasm? (Check all applicable categories; 32 options)

20. *If ever had orgasm through masturbating while alone:*

    At what age did you experience your first orgasm through masturbating while alone?

21. *If ever had orgasm through petting:*

    At what age did you experience your first orgasm through petting?

22. *If ever had orgasm through sexual intercourse:*

    At what age did you experience your first orgasm through sexual intercourse?

23. *If ever masturbated while alone:*

    How old were you the first time that you masturbated while alone?

24. *If ever masturbated while alone:*

    How often do you experience an orgasm through masturbating while alone? *(Always-Never; 5 options)*

25. *If ever masturbated while alone:*

    How many orgasms do you usually experience during a single episode of masturbating alone?

26. *If masturbated while alone within the past two years:*

    During the past two years, about how many times per week, month, or year have you averaged masturbating while alone?

    (Choose only one category and do not use range of times or check the category)

    _____ 1. Times per week   _____ 2. Times per month   _____ 3. Times per year

27. *If ever had orgasm while masturbating alone:*

    In what specific area of your genital region do you most feel the sensation of orgasm occurring during *masturbating while alone?*

28. *If ever masturbated alone:*

    How would you rate your *physiological* reaction from masturbating while alone? *(Intense satisfaction-No satisfaction; 5 options)*

29. *If ever masturbated alone:*

    How would you rate your *psychological* reaction from masturbating while alone? *(No satisfaction-Intense satisfaction; 5 options)*

30. *If ever petted:*

    How often do you experience an orgasm while petting? *(Always-Never; 5 options)*

31. *If ever had orgasm during petting:*

    How many orgasms do you usually experience during a single episode of petting?

32. *If ever had orgasm during petting:*

    In what specific area of your genital region do you most feel the sensation of orgasm occurring during petting?

33. *If ever had orgasm:*

    Do you experience a *physiological* need in yourself to have an orgasm prior to any sexual arousal and/or sexual activity? *(Never-Always; 5 options)*

34. *If ever had orgasm:*

    Do you experience a *physiological* need in yourself to have more than one orgasm while engaging in masturbating while alone, petting, and/or sexual intercourse? *(Never-Always; 5 options)*

35. *If ever had orgasm:*

    Do you experience a *psychological* need in yourself to have an orgasm prior to any sexual arousal and/or sexual activity? *(Never-Always; 5 options)*

36. *If ever had orgasm:*

    Do you experience a *psychological* need in yourself to have more than one orgasm while engaging in masturbating while alone, petting, and/or sexual intercourse? *(Never-Always; 5 options)*

37. *If ever experienced more than one orgasm during a single sexual experience, including masturbation while alone:*

    Do successive orgasms during a single sexual experience become stronger or weaker? (10 options)

38. *If ever had sexual intercourse:*

    At what age did you first experience sexual intercourse?

39. *If had sexual intercourse within the past two years*:

During the past two years, about how many times per week, month, or year have you averaged having sexual intercourse? (Choose only one category and do not use a range of times or check the category)

_____ 1. Times per week _____ 2. Times per month _____ 3. Times per year

40. *If ever had sexual intercourse*:

With how many different partners have you ever had sexual intercourse?

41. *If ever had sexual intercourse*:

During sexual intercourse, at what point does your most recent male sex partner usually achieve his first orgasm? (6 options)

42. *If ever had sexual intercourse*:

Would you please indicate the most frequent position that you utilize for sexual intercourse. You are to rank the sexual intercourse positions with regard to frequency of occurrence with 1-most often, 2-second most often, and 3-third most often only. (12 options)

43. *If ever had sexual intercourse*:

How often do you experience an orgasm during sexual intercourse? (*Always-Never*; 5 options)

44. *If rarely or never have orgasm during sexual intercourse*:

Why do you believe that you experience difficulty in achieving orgasm during sexual intercourse?

45. *If ever had orgasm during sexual intercourse*:

How many orgasms do you usually experience during a single vaginal penetration while having sexual intercourse?

46. *If ever had orgasm during sexual intercourse*:

After having experienced orgasm during sexual intercourse, what is the typical extent of your *physiological* reaction? (*Intense satisfaction-No satisfaction*; 5 options)

47. *If ever had orgasm during sexual intercourse*:

After having experienced orgasm during sexual intercourse, what is the typical extent of your *psychological* reaction? (*Intense satisfaction-No satisfaction*; 5 options)

48. *If ever masturbated to orgasm while alone and had sexual intercourse*:

Do you prefer to masturbate to orgasm while alone rather than having sexual intercourse? (*Always-Never*; 5 options)

49. *If ever had orgasm*:

Would you please indicate the *most frequent* techniques that you use to achieve orgasm?

You are to rank the following techniques with regard to frequency of occurrence with 1-most often, 2-second most often, and 3-third most often only. (32 options)

50. *If ever masturbated while alone, petted, had sexual intercourse, and experienced orgasm*:

Do you experience a difference between an orgasm reached during masturbating while alone, during petting, and during sexual intercourse with vaginal penetration? (*Yes/No*)

51. *If yes, differences exist between orgasm achieved during masturbation while alone, petting, and sexual intercourse*:

In your own words, please describe the difference between orgasms achieved during masturbation while alone, petting, and sexual intercourse with vaginal penetration

52. *If ever had orgasm during sexual intercourse*:

In what specific area of your genital region do you most feel the sensation of orgasm occurring during sexual intercourse with vaginal penetration?

53. *If ever had orgasm during sexual intercourse*:

What is the relative contribution of clitoral versus vaginal stimulation in helping you to achieve orgasm *during sexual intercourse*? (7 options)

54. *If ever had orgasm during masturbation*:

What is the relative contribution of clitoral versus vaginal stimulation in helping you to achieve orgasm *during masturbating while alone*: (7 options)

55. *If ever had orgasm during petting*:

What is the relative contribution of clitoral versus vaginal stimulation in helping you to achieve orgasm *during petting*? (7 options)

56. Which of the following changes, if any, would you like to have in your current sex life? (44 options)

57. How would you rate your overall personal *physiological* level of sexual satisfaction? (*Very much satisfied-Very much dissatisfied*; 6 options)

58. How would you rate your overall personal *psychological* level of sexual satisfaction? (*Very much satisfied-Very much dissatisfied*; 6 options)

[a]In the interest of brevity, only select items specifically related to the orgasmic response have been included in this exhibit. Additional demographic, attitudinal, and behavioral items/variables that are critical to appropriate analyses and understanding of the perceived differences have been omitted due to space limitations.

Sexuality of Women Survey

CAROL RINKLEIB ELLISON,[1] *Loomis, CA*
BERNIE ZILBERGELD,[2] *Oakland, CA*

The Sexuality of Women Survey was designed to gather information for a book about how women experience and express their sexualities. The questionnaire cover letter stated that the purpose was "to learn more about the richness and variability in the sexual development, feelings, attitudes and experiences of American women of all ages, ethnic and religious groups, and sexual orientations."

Description

This 16-page questionnaire of primarily multiple-choice questions is divided into the following sections: A. Please tell us about yourself (demographics); B. Relationships; C. Family of origin; D. Early sexual experiences; E. Sexual partner(s); F. Self-stimulation; G. The experience of orgasm; H. Feelings during and immediately after self-stimulation and partner sex; I. Factors affecting sexual satisfaction within a relationship; J. Initiating sex and sexual communication; K. Sexual expression, sexual concerns, and problems; L. Body; M. Satisfaction and the frequency and quality of various kinds of touching activities; N. Sexuality and menstrual cycles; O. Pregnancy; P. Contraceptive method; Q. Sexually transmitted diseases; R. Affairs; and S. Sexual life over time.

Respondents are instructed to circle the number corresponding to the best response(s) or to fill in a blank. They also are told to "feel free to write comments on the questionnaire or on a separate page. . . . If a question doesn't accurately describe your experience, please tell us so. We want to know how **you** experience **your** sexuality."

The questionnaire was designed for and primarily surveyed (in 1993–1994) women who had attended at least some college. Thirty-two percent had some college or a 2-year degree; 21% had a 4-year degree; and 40% had done some graduate work or had a graduate degree. The 2,632 women in this sample of convenience who responded to the questionnaire were born between 1905 and 1977; 556 were age 50 or older. Even after attempts were made to have greater ethnic diversity, 83% were Caucasian. With respect to sexual orientation, 7% described themselves as lesbian, 5% as bisexual, and the remainder as heterosexual. The statistics and other research findings describe the particular group of women who were surveyed, not American women in general.

Response Mode and Timing

The questionnaire contains a number of different objective response formats and requires 30 to 45 minutes to complete.

Scoring

Many of the questions use 7-point scales; some also include a Not Applicable choice. Many of the other questions involve tabulating how many respondents choose a particular item.

For specific information, contact Carol Ellison (carol.ellison@att.net) or the statistical consultant on the project, Doug Wallace (phddoug@mi.rr.com).

Reliability and Validity

There are no available references on reliability and validity.

Other Information

This survey, and the approximately 100 in-depth interviews that preceded it, were the basis for Ellison (2000). Information from Section K was the basis for Ellison (2001, 2007). Information from Section G appeared in Ellison (2003).

I grant permission to publish the questionnaire in its entirety, but maintain the copyright in my name. The questionnaire can be viewed online at www.womenssexualities.com.

References

Ellison, C. R. (2000). *Women's sexualities: Generations of women share intimate secrets of sexual self-acceptance.* Oakland, CA: New Harbinger.

Ellison, C. R. (2001). A research inquiry into some American women's sexual concerns and problems. In E. Kaschak & L. Tiefer (Eds.), *A new view of women's sexual problems* (pp. 147–159). New York: Haworth Press.

Ellison, C. R. (2003). Facilitating orgasmic responsiveness. In S. Levine, S. Althof, & C. Risen (Eds.), *Handbook of clinical sexuality for mental health professionals* (pp. 167–185). New York: Brunner-Routledge.

Ellison, C. R. (2007). Women's sexual problems and concerns. In A. F. Owens & M. S. Tepper (Eds.), *Sexual health: Vol. 4. State-of-the-art treatments and research* (pp. 87–106). Westport, CT: Praeger.

[1]Address correspondence to Carol Rinkleib Ellison, P. O. Box 1876, Loomis, CA 95650; e-mail: carol.ellison@att.net
[2]Bernie Zilbergeld is deceased.

Exhibit

Sexuality of Women Survey

Instructions: Please answer each question by
- **CIRCLING THE NUMBER** corresponding to the best response **OR** by
- **FILLING IN THE BLANK** at the right hand margin.

Sometimes you also will be asked to **SPECIFY SOME OTHER INFORMATION** in a blank in the question itself. Some questions will ask you to circle all that apply.

If you cannot or don't want to answer a question, circle the question number and move on to the next question. Sometimes you will be directed to skip over questions that do not apply to your experience.

FEEL FREE TO WRITE COMMENTS ON THE QUESTIONNAIRE or on a separate page that you fasten securely to it. If a question doesn't accurately describe your experience, please tell us so. We want to know how **you** experience **your** sexuality.

A. PLEASE TELL US ABOUT YOURSELF.

1. **Year Born** (WRITE THE YEAR IN THE BLANK TO THE RIGHT):   19_____

2. **Ethnicity:**

   I usually describe my ethnicity as (CIRCLE ONE):

African American	1
Asian American	2
Caucasian	3
Latina	4
Native American	5
Other	
(PLEASE SPECIFY): _____	6

3. **Education:** The highest level of schooling I have completed is (CIRCLE ONE):

High school	1
Somec ollege	2
Vocational degree	3
2-year degree	4
4-year degree	5
Graduate work	6
Graduate degree	7

4. **Occupation**: My Occupation is: _____

5. **Religion/Spirituality:** The average number of times per month I attend services or other spiritual observances now, and did as a child is (PLEASE WRITE IN THE NUMBER OF TIMES):

	NOW	CHILDHOOD		NOW	CHILDHOOD
Catholic	_____	_____	Buddhist	_____	_____
Protestant	_____	_____	Atheist	_____	_____
Fundamentalist Christian	_____	_____	Agnostic	_____	_____
Jewish	_____	_____	Other spiritual		
Muslim	_____	_____	observances/meditations	_____	_____
Other (SPECIFY) _____				_____	_____

6. **Children**: The ages of the children I am raising or have raised is:

   Males   ___   ___   ___   ___   ___
   Females   ___   ___   ___   ___   ___

   (PLEASE CIRCLE THE AGES OF ANY CHILDREN NOW LIVING IN YOUR HOME.)

7. **Income:**

   a. The approximate pre-tax income I earn per year is (CIRCLE ONE):   1 2 3 4 5 6

1 **Less than $12,000**	2 **$12,001–$25,000**	3 **$25,001–$50,000**	
4 **$50,001–$75,000**	5 **$75,001–$120,000**	6 **$120,001+**	

   b. The approximate pre-tax income per year of my family unit is: 1 2 3 4 5 6

8. **Residence:**

   a. The State I now live in is _____

   b. I have lived in the United States ___ years (WRITE THE NUMBER IN THE BLANK AT THE RIGHT):   _____

9. **Orientation**: I think of myself as (CIRCLE ONE):

1 **Heterosexual**	2 **Lesbian**	3 **Bisexual**	1 2 3

B. PLEASE TELL US ABOUT YOUR RELATIONSHIP(S).

1. My current relationship and living situation is (CHOOSE ONE):

No sex partner now | 1
Seeing but not living with my sex partner(s) | 2
Living with a sex partner, <u>without</u> marriage or life commitment | 3
Living with a sex partner, <u>with</u> marriage or life commitment | 4
Other (PLEASE SPECIFY): _____ | 5

2.   The number of times I have ever (PLEASE WRITE IN THE NUMBER OR "0"):

    a. Lived with a sex partner I didn't later marry is   _____

    b. Been married is   _____

    c. Been divorced is   _____

    d. Been widowed is   _____

For many of the questions that follow you will answer by circling a number on a scale from 1 to 7:

1 = STRONGLY DISAGREE	**5 = SLIGHTLY AGREE**
2 = DISAGREE	**6 = AGREE**
3 = SLIGHTLY DISAGREE	**7 = STRONGLY AGREE**
4 = EQUALLY AGREE AND DISAGREE	**0 = NOT APPLICABLE TO MY EXPERIENCE (NA)**

C. PLEASE TELL US ABOUT YOUR FAMILY OF ORIGIN.

The questions in this section are about your growing up years.
<u>Mother</u> and <u>Father</u> refer to the "parent(s)" who raised you.
CIRCLE "0" to mean "no mother figure" or "no father figure."

While I was growing up (CIRCLE THE BEST ANSWER FOR EACH STATEMENT):

	STRONGLY DISAGREE					STRONGLY AGREE		NA
1. My mother and father openly demonstrated physical affection for each other	1	2	3	4	5	6	7	0
2. **a.** My father affectionately touched (for example, hugged) me	1	2	3	4	5	6	7	0
b. This affection was appropriately expressed	1	2	3	4	5	6	7	0
3. **a.** My mother affectionately touched me	1	2	3	4	5	6	7	0
b. This affection was appropriately expressed	1	2	3	4	5	6	7	0
4. I felt free to express my own opinions at home	1	2	3	4	5	6	7	0
5. Sexuality was often discussed in my family	1	2	3	4	5	6	7	0
6. **a.** My mother's attitude toward sex was generally positive	1	2	3	4	5	6	7	0
b. My father's attitude toward sex was generally positive	1	2	3	4	5	6	7	0

D. THESE QUESTIONS ARE ABOUT YOUR EARLY SEXUAL EXPERIENCES.

1.   As a child or adolescent, the first person with whom I engaged in an activity that
I thought of as sexual at the time was a (1 **male** OR 2 **female**) | 1   2
     0

    If you have NEVER engaged in ANY sexual activity with a male,
    CIRCLE the 0 at the right and skip to Question 4a.

2. **a.** As a child or adolescent, my first sexual activity that I thought of at the time
as sexual **with a male** occurred when I was ____ years old.   _____

	STRONGLY DISAGREE					STRONGLY AGREE		NA
b. This sexual activity was with my consent.	1	2	3	4	5	6	7	0

    c. The male involved was: (CHOOSE ONE BEST ANSWER)

           A peer (boyfriend, schoolmate, friend)   1
           A relative (PLEASE SPECIFY WHO) _____   2
           A stranger   3
           Other (PLEASE SPECIFY): _____   4
           0

    If you have NEVER had sexual intercourse, CIRCLE 0 and skip to Question 4a.

3. **a.** My first sexual intercourse was when I was ____ years old.   _____

	STRONGLY DISAGREE					STRONGLY AGREE		NA
b. My first sexual intercourse was with my consent	1	2	3	4	5	6	7	0

    c. The partner in my first intercourse was

A peer (boyfriend, schoolmate, friend)	1
A relative (PLEASE SPECIFY WHO) _____	2
A stranger	3
Other (PLEASE SPECIFY): _____	4

    d. He was (CHOOSE ONE BEST ANSWER)

Someone I wasn't then planning to marry	1
Someone I was planning to marry	2
Someone I had already married	3
None of the above	4

If you have NEVER engaged in ANY sexual activity with another female, CIRCLE "0" and skip to Question 5.   0

4. **a.** My first sexual activity that I thought of at the time as sexual **with another female** occurred when I was __ years old.

	STRONGLY DISAGREE	STRONGLY AGREE	NA
b. This sexual activity was with my consent.	1 2 3 4 5 6 7		0

    c. The female involved was (CHOOSE ONE):

A peer (girlfriend, schoolmate, friend)	1
A relative (PLEASE SPECIFY WHO) _____	2
A stranger	3
Other (PLEASE SPECIFY): _____	4

5. Compared to my female classmates, during my adolescent years:

	ABOUT AS	MORE	LESS
a. I dated (1 **about as**, 2 **more**, OR 3 **less**) often	1	2	3
b. I was (1 **about as**, 2 **more**, OR 3 **less**) sexually active	1	2	3

E. **THE QUESTIONS IN THIS SECTION ARE ABOUT YOUR SEXUAL PARTNER(S).**

A SEXUAL PARTNER is someone with whom you currently (or did in the past) engage in ANY kind of sexual activity.

1. The last time I engaged in any kind of sexual activity with a partner was (PLEASE CIRCLE **1 FOR today**, **OR WRITE IN YOUR BEST ESTIMATE OF APPROXIMATELY HOW MANY** days, months **OR** years ago):

Today	1
or Days ago	_____
or Months ago	_____
or Years ago	_____

If you have more than one current partner, interpret "current partner" to mean your "primary partner" as you fill out this questionnaire.

2. **a.** My current or most recent sexual partner is/was
       (1 **male** OR 2 **female**)
       2   1

    b. I have been (or was) with this partner ____ months OR _____ years (WRITE IN HOW MANY AT THE RIGHT):

Months	_____
or Years	_____

3. I think of myself as currently having (a) __ **male** and (b) ___ **female** sexual partners (WRITE IN HOW MANY):

a) Male	_____
b) Female	_____

4. I have had about __ sexual partners in my lifetime (WRITE IN HOW MANY):   _____

5. In my lifetime, the number of people with whom I have engaged in what is often called "casual sex" or a "one-night stand" (including instances where a relationship or friendship developed **after** the sex) is approximately __ (WRITE IN HOW MANY:)

	STRONGLY DISAGREE	STRONGLY AGREE	NA
6. My current or most recent sex partner has been (was) a good partner for me (in general, not just sexually)	1 2 3 4 5 6 7		0
7. In the past, most of my sex partners were good partners for me (in general, not just sexually)	1 2 3 4 5 6 7		0
8. In my life I have had at least one partner with whom I had what I considered to be really fantastic sex.	1 2 3 4 5 6 7		0

9. a. In the last 3 months, the number of individuals with whom I have engaged in
sexual activity of any kind is (WRITE IN HOW MANY):   _____

If your answer to 9a is "0", skip 9b.

b. The partner(s) and circumstances can be described as (CIRCLE ALL THAT APPLY):

A male partner	1
A female partner	2
My "spouse" (married or life commitment)	3
A nonspouse partner I live with	4
A partner I don't live with	5
Some one I knew at the time for more than 1 but less than 7 days	6
Some one I knew at the time for less than 24 hours	7
A partner with whom I have an on-going affair	8
A friend: we sometimes or regularly meet each other's sexual needs	9
Someone I know, in exchange for money	10
A stranger, in exchange for money	11
Other (PLEASE SPECIFY): _____	12

F. THE NEXT 4 QUESTIONS ARE ABOUT SELF-STIMULATION.

1. The first time I intentionally stimulated my genitals while alone (masturbated)
I was _____ years old (IF YOU DON'T KNOW, WRITE IN YOUR BEST GUESS)   _____

If NEVER, circle 0 and skip to Section G   0

2. In the **last month**, I have intentionally stimulated my genitals when alone approximately __ times.   _____

**If you have NOT intentionally stimulated your genitals when alone
in the LAST 3 MONTHS, circle 0 and skip to Question 4.**   0

3. In the **last 3 months**, I intentionally stimulated my genitals when alone (CIRCLE ALL THAT APPLY):

Because self-stimulation feels good	1
Because I felt a physical urge to do so	2
To comfort myself	3
To help me sleep	4
To relieve menstrual cramps	5
To relax	6
To have one or more orgasms	7
To feel more finished or relieve frustration after partner sex	8
Because a partner wasn't available right then	9
Because I was lonely	10
Because I was bored	11
Other _____	12

	STRONGLY DISAGREE					STRONGLY AGREE		NA
4. I usually fantasize when I masturbate	1	2	3	4	5	6	7	0

G. THE QUESTIONS IN THIS SECTION ARE ABOUT THE EXPERIENCE OF ORGASM:

1. Please circle the number of the best answer for you:

I have never experienced an orgasm	1
I am not sure if I have ever had an orgasm	2
My first orgasm was by myself	3
My first orgasm was during sexual activity with a partner	4
Other (PLEASE SPECIFY): _____	5

If you have NEVER experienced orgasm or are NOT SURE if you have, please skip to Question 11.

2. I think my first orgasm occurred when I was age __ years   _____
**(IF YOU DON'T KNOW FOR SURE, PLEASE WRITE IN YOUR BEST ESTIMATE OR GUESS.
IF YOU WERE YOUNG, PERHAPS YOU ONLY REALIZED LATER IT WAS AN ORGASM.)**

3. The following describe my experience (PLEASE CIRCLE ALL THAT APPLY):

My first orgasm occurred spontaneously	I
My first orgasm occurred when I was trying to have one	2
My first orgasm surprised me	3
I was frightened by the sensations of my first orgasm	4
I reach orgasm when alone but not when I'm with a partner	5
I have at some time awakened from sleep having an orgasm from dreaming	6
I have at some time had an orgasm from mental/emotional stimulation (such as a fantasy, recalling a past experience, reading) without also sexually touching myself	7
None of the above	0

If you have NEVER had an orgasm when alone, please circle 0 and skip to Question 7.   0

		STRONGLY DISAGREE					STRONGLY AGREE		NA
4.	I generally reach orgasm more easily by myself than with a partner	I	2	3	4	5	6	7	0
5.	I generally have more enjoyable orgasms by myself than I have had with a partner	I	2	3	4	5	6	7	0

6. The stimulation I use to reach orgasm when alone tends to be:

Always (or almost always) the same kind	I
Varied, I use different kinds of stimulation at different times	2

If you have NEVER experienced orgasm with a partner, please circle 0 and skip to Question 10.   0

7. The stimulation through which I reach orgasm with a partner tends to be:

Always (or almost always) the same kind	I
Varied, different kinds of stimulation at different times	2

		STRONGLY DISAGREE					STRONGLY AGREE		NA
8.	I generally have (had) more enjoyable orgasms with my most satisfying sexual partner than by myself	I	2	3	4	5	6	7	0

If you have NOT experienced orgasm with a partner in the last 3 months, please circle 0 and skip to Question 10.   0

The next question is about your orgasms with a partner IN the LAST 3 MONTHS. If you have had more than one partner, answer regarding your <u>most satisfying</u> partner.

9. In the **last 3 months** when having sex with my partner

a. I **wanted** to orgasm in approximately __ % of the sexual episodes (PLEASE WRITE IN YOUR BEST GUESS)   _____%

b. I **actually** orgasmed in approximately __ % of the sexual episodes in which I wanted to (WRITE IN YOUR BEST GUESS)   _____%

		STRONGLY DISAGREE					STRONGLY AGREE	
c.	I am satisfied with the frequency I actually orgasmed	I	2	3	4	5	6	7
d.	I am satisfied with the quality/intensity of the orgasms I had	I	2	3	4	5	6	7

10. In my life, I have (PLEASE WRITE IN YOUR <u>BEST ESTIMATE OR GUESS OF THE NUMBER</u>):

a. Cried during orgasm or had crying released by orgasm __ times   _____

b. Laughed during orgasm or had laughter released by orgasm __ times   _____

11. a. In my life, I have faked an orgasm __ times (PLEASE WRITE IN YOUR <u>BEST ESTIMATE OR GUESS</u>):   _____

b. I have faked an orgasm with __ percent of my partners   _____%

If you do not have a current partner, circle 0 and skip to Question 12.   0

c. I fake an orgasm with my current partner about __ percent of the time   _____%

If you have NEVER reached orgasm during sex with a partner, please skip to the next section, Section H.

12. In addition to getting specific physical stimulation, I often have done the following to help me reach orgasm during sex with a partner (CIRCLE ALL THAT APPLY; SOME MAY HAVE HAPPENED SPONTANEOUSLY):

Gotten myself in a sexy mood beforehand	I
Engaged in a fantasy of my own	2
Engaged in a fantasy shared with my partner	3

Thought or imagined that I might become pregnant	4
Synchronized my breathing to my partner's breathing	5
Synchronized the rhythm of my movements to my partner's	6
Felt/thought how much I love my partner	7
Tightened and released my pelvic muscles	8
Paid attention to my physical sensations	9
Focused on my partner's pleasure	10
Positioned my body to get the stimulation I needed	11
Engaged in eye contact with my partner	12
Detached from thinking about anything	13
Asked or encouraged my partner to do what I needed	14
Other (PLEASE SPECIFY): _____	15

H. THESE QUESTIONS ARE ABOUT YOUR FEELINGS DURING AND IMMEDIATELY AFTER SELF-STIMULATION AND PARTNER SEX.

If you have **NEVER** masturbated, start with Question 2; skip 1 and 3. If you have **NEVER** had sex with a partner, start with 1, skip 2 and 4.

Below is a list of feelings you may have experienced during and immediately after sexual activity, either alone or with a partner.

1. The feelings from the list that I have experienced **most typically** during and immediately after masturbation are (CIRCLE THE NUMBERS IN THE COLUMN LABELED **SELF** OF ALL THAT APPLY):

2. The feelings that I have experienced **most often** during and immediately after sex with my current or most recent partner are (CIRCLE THE NUMBERS IN THE COLUMN LABELED **PARTNER** OF ALL THAT APPLY):

	SELF	PARTNER		SELF	PARTNER		SELF	PARTNER
Anxious	1	1	Happy	20	20	Pressured	39	39
Aroused	2	2	Helpless	21	21	Resentful	40	40
Ashamed	3	3	Inadequate	22	22	Romantic	41	41
Bored	4	4	Inhibited	23	23	Sad	42	42
Coerced	5	5	Intense	24	24	Sated	43	43
Confident	6	6	Judged	25	25	Satisfied	44	44
Desirable	7	7	Lonely	26	26	Secure	45	45
Desire	8	8	Loved	27	27	Self-loving	46	46
Desired	9	9	Loving	28	28	Sensual	47	47
Disappointed	10	10	Lusty	29	29	Separate	48	48
Dissatisfied	11	11	Meditative	30	30	Sexy	49	49
Dominated	12	12	Merged	31	31	Spiritual	50	50
Dominating	13	13	"Not there"	32	32	Successful	51	51
Ecstasy	14	14	Obsessed	33	33	Tense	52	52
Embarrassed	15	15	Passionate	34	34	Tired	53	53
Erotic	16	16	Peaceful	35	35	Trusting	54	54
Excited	17	17	Playful	36	36	Victimized	55	55
Frustrated	18	18	Pleasured	37	37	Vulnerable	56	56
Guilty	19	19	Powerful	38	38	Wonderful	57	57

3. If other words better describe your masturbation experiences, please write them here:

4. If other words better describe your sexual experiences with your current or most recent partner, please write them here:

5. List the **numbers** of **up to 5 feelings** from the list above (other than "satisfied") that you associate with your most satisfying sexual experiences.

_____   _____   _____   _____   _____

If you have NEVER had satisfying sexual experiences either alone or with a partner, circle 0.   0

I. THIS SECTION IS ABOUT FACTORS AFFECTING YOUR SEXUAL SATISFACTION WITHIN A RELATIONSHIP.

If you have **NEVER** had **SATISFYING** sex with a partner within an ongoing relationship, please circle 0 and skip to the next section, Section J.

If you have **EVER** had **SATISFYING** sex with a partner within an ongoing relationship, please consider the most recent period in your life when you had satisfying sex in a relationship:

0

I   a.   In this period of my life in this relationship, the following were **USUALLY** or **ALWAYS** present in my most satisfying sexual experiences with my partner (CIRCLE THE NUMBERS OF ALL THAT APPLY):

Before Sex

Feeling close to my partner before sex	1
Arguing before having sex	2
Having an alcoholic drink before sex	3
Using marijuana or another recreational drug before (or during) sex	4

Partner and Situation

Feeling loved	5
Feeling safe in the relationship	6
Knowing we could take as much time as we wanted	7
Knowing there was no risk of getting or transmitting a disease	8
Knowing there was no risk of getting pregnant	9
Being aware that I might become pregnant	10
Knowing my partner would give me the physical stimulation I needed	11

Behaviors and Feelings During Sex

Talking with my partner during sex about what we were doing	12
Talking about or acting out a shared drama or fantasy	13
Focusing on a stimulating fantasy of my own	14
Feeling really attuned with my partner during sex	15
No pressure from my partner for me to have an orgasm	16
No pressure from myself to have an orgasm	17
My partner was accepting of my desires, preferences and responses	18
My partner got and maintained an erection	19
My partner did not ejaculate quickly	20

Stimulation

Extended stimulation of other kinds before intercourse	21
Breast stimulation	22
Manual stimulation of my genitals	23
Oral stimulation of my genitals	24
Using a vibrator	25
Using a dildo	26
Anal stimulation	27
Having intercourse	28
Steady, reliable stimulation that continued through orgasm	29

Outcomes

One or more orgasms	30
Simultaneous orgasm with my partner	31
Knowing that I gave my partner a wonderful experience	32
Emotional closeness after sexual activity	33

Other (PLEASE SPECIFY): _____   34

b.   In the period of my life I have been considering for this question I was in my

   1 Teens   2 20's   3 30's   4 40's   5 50's   6 60's   7 70's   8 80's   1   2   3   4   5   6   7   8

J.   THESE QUESTIONS ARE ABOUT INITIATING SEX AND SEXUAL COMMUNICATION.

If you have not had a sexual partner in the last year, please circle 0, skip Sections J and K, and go to Section L.

0

INITIATING SEX means letting your partner know (verbally or physically) your desire for sexual activity.

PLEASE CIRCLE THE BEST ANSWER FOR EACH STATEMENT.

		STRONGLY DISAGREE				STRONGLY AGREE		NA

1. I initiate sex whenever I want it.   1 2 3 4 5 6 7 0
2. a. I am comfortable initiating sex with my current or most recent partner.   1 2 3 4 5 6 7 0
   b. That partner is (was) comfortable with my initiating sexual activity.   1 2 3 4 5 6 7 0
3. During sex, I am comfortable telling my partner what I **don't like** or **don't want** (for example: "Ouch!" or "I don't want to do that tonight.")   1 2 3 4 5 6 7 0
4. During sex, I am comfortable telling my partner what I **want** and **like** (for example, "Would you . . ." or "A little slower . . ." or "That feels great.")   1 2 3 4 5 6 7 0
5. During sex, I communicate my desires as often as I want to.   1 2 3 4 5 6 7 0
6. One reason I don't communicate much during sex is that I usually don't know what I want.   1 2 3 4 5 6 7 0
7. My partner gives me as much feedback about his/her sexual likes and dislikes as I want.   1 2 3 4 5 6 7 0

K. THESE QUESTIONS ARE ABOUT SOME ASPECTS OF SEXUAL EXPRESSION YOU MAY HAVE EXPERIENCED IN THE PAST YEAR AND ABOUT SEXUAL CONCERNS AND PROBLEMS.

In Question 1, indicate which of the items you have experienced **IN THE PAST YEAR** by circling the number that indicates **how often** you experienced it. Skip any you have **NOT** experienced.

RAR = Rarely   **ST = Sometimes**   **OFT = Often**   **ALL = All the time**

1. a. I have experienced the following **in the last year** (CIRCLE ANY THAT APPLY):

	RAR	ST	OFT	ALL
Difficulty finding a partner I wanted to be sexual with	1	1	1	1
Lower sexual desire than I wanted to have	2	2	2	2
Being too tired to have sex	3	3	3	3
Being too busy to have sex	4	4	4	4
Not feeling sexually satisfied	5	5	5	5
My partner not as interested in sexasl was	6	6	6	6
My partner less interested incloseness after sex than I	7	7	7	7
My partner choosing inconvenient times for sex	8	8	8	8

b. **During sex in the last year** I have experienced:

	RAR	ST	OFT	ALL
Difficulty getting excited/aroused	9	9	9	9
Feeling distracted	10	10	10	10
Inability to relax	11	11	11	11
Involuntary vaginal spasm so that vaginal entry and/or intercourse was impossible or difficult	12	12	12	12
Insufficient vaginal lubrication	13	13	13	13
Pain during intercourse or other internal stimulation	14	14	14	14
Fantasizing that I am having sex with someone other than my partner	15	15	15	15
Difficulty in reaching orgasm	16	16	16	16
Inability to have an orgasm	17	17	17	17
Reaching orgasm too quickly	18	18	18	18
My partner seeming distracted	19	19	19	19
My partner wanting shorter foreplay than I wanted	20	20	20	20
My partner having difficulty getting aroused	21	21	21	21
My partner ejaculating too quickly	22	22	22	22
My partner having difficulty getting and/or maintaining an erection	23	23	23	23
Other (SPECIFY): _____	24	24	24	24
None of the above	0	0	0	0

Some of the items in Question 1 you may think of as "the way life is." Others you may think of as "problems."

2. I think or thought of these items I marked in Question 1 as <u>problems</u> (PLEASE WRITE THE NUMBER(S) OF THOSE ITEMS HERE OR CIRCLE 0 FOR NONE):

_____   _____   _____   _____   _____   _____   _____   _____   _____   0

3. In the past year I have sought the following kinds of help for sexual concerns or problems (CIRCLE ALL THAT APPLY):

None	0
Talked to my partner	I
Talked to a (nonpartner) friend	2
Talked to a relative	3
Talked to a minister or teacher	4
Read a book or article that gave advice	5
Went to a medical/health practitioner (other than a therapist)	6
Went to a therapist by myself	7
Went to a therapist with my partner	8
Enrolled in a course or program	9
Other (SPECIFY): _____	10

4. a. In the past year, my most important sexual problem or concern was (WRITE THE NUMBER FROM THE LIST IN QUESTION I OR SPECIFY) _____

   If None, circle 0 and skip 4b and 4c. 0

	STRONGLY DISAGREE	STRONGLY AGREE	NA
b. This problem or concern has been satisfactorily resolved	I 2 3 4 5 6 7		0

   If the situation is not improved, circle 0 and skip 4c. 0

   c. I attribute the improvement in this situation to (CIRCLE ALL THAT APPLY):

A solution I figured out for myself	I
Talking with my partner	2
Talking with a friend, relative, parent, or minister	3
Seeing a therapist	4
Seeing a medical/health practitioner	5
Surgery	6
Medication (starting, stopping, changing)	7
Passage of time	8
Advice in a book or article	9
Getting a new partner	10
Other (PLEASE SPECIFY): _____	11

L. THE NEXT QUESTIONS ARE ABOUT YOUR BODY.

	STRONGLY DISAGREE	STRONGLY AGREE	NA
1. Overall, I am satisfied with how my body looks	I 2 3 4 5 6 7		
2. My current or last partner is/was satisfied with how my body looks	I 2 3 4 5 6 7		0
3. My feelings about my body interfere with my sexual satisfaction	I 2 3 4 5 6 7		

4. a. My weight is ___ pounds _____ lb.
   b. My height is ___ feet ___ inches _____ ft. _____ in.

5. a. I have had the following surgery (PLEASE CIRCLE THE CORRESPONDING NUMBER(S) AND WRITE IN YOUR AGE AT THE TIME OF THE SURGERY):

	AGE AT TIME OF SURGERY	
Hysterectomy (uterus removed)	_____	I
Ovaries removed	_____	2
Mastectomy	_____	3
Other surgery (PLEASE SPECIFY): _____		4

   b. I have the following physical condition(s) (PLEASE CIRCLE THE CORRESPONDING NUMBER(S) AND INDICATE YOUR AGE WHEN THE CONDITION BEGAN):

	AGE OF ONSET	
Diabetes	_____	5
Chronic vaginal dryness (**currently**)	_____	6
Chronic bladder infections (**currently**)	_____	7
Other illness, disability, or physical condition (PLEASE SPECIFY): _____	_____	8

_____   _____   9
_____   _____   10
None   0

6. **In the past year** I have taken the following medications or hormones (PLEASE CIRCLE THE CORRESPONDING
NUMBER(S) AND WRITE IN APPROXIMATELY HOW LONG YOU HAVE TAKEN THEM):   **NO. OF YRS TAKEN**

Blood pressure medication	_____	I
Antihistamine	_____	2
Antidepressant	_____	3
Antianxiety medication	_____	4
Insulin	_____	5
Birth control pills	_____	6
Other estrogen	_____	7
Other progestin/progesterone	_____	8
Other medications or hormones (SPECIFY):		

_____   _____   9
_____   _____   10
_____   _____   11
None   0

	STRONGLY DISAGREE					STRONGLY AGREE	

7. The physical condition of my body interferes with my sexual satisfaction   1 2 3 4 5 6 7

**Answer Question 8 ONLY IF you are NOT now physically able to
become pregnant. Give ages for ALL you have experienced.**

8. I am not physically able to become pregnant because (GIVE AGES FOR ALL THAT APPLY):

I reached menopause at age ___   I _____
I had my tubes tied when I was age ___   2 _____
I had a hysterectomy when I was age ___   3 _____
I had/have had endometriosis from approximately age ___   4 _____
I had a pelvic infection when I was age ___   5 _____
Other (PLEASE SPECIFY): _____   6 _____

M. THESE QUESTIONS ARE ABOUT SATISFACTION AND THE FREQUENCY AND QUALITY OF VARIOUS KINDS OF TOUCHING ACTIVITIES:

	STRONGLY DISAGREE						STRONGLY AGREE	NA

I. I have been satisfied with my sex life (**including self-sexual activity**)
in the last 3 months   1 2 3 4 5 6 7   0

**If you have NOT engaged in sexual activity (of any kind) with a partner
in the last 3 months, please circle 0 and skip to Question 6 of this section.**   0

2. I have been satisfied with my sex life **with a partner** in the last 3 months   1 2 3 4 5 6 7   0

3. **a.** In the last 3 months, I have been satisfied with the **quality** of genital
stimulation and/or intercourse I've had with a partner   1 2 3 4 5 6 7   0

    b. With respect to the **frequency** of this kind of activity, I would like
(I **more**, 2 **less**, OR 3 **about the same**) amount

	MORE	LESS	SAME
	I	2	3

4. **a.** In the last 3 months, I have been satisfied with the **quality** of sexual/erotic
contact I've had with a partner that **did not** include or lead to sustained genital
stimulation or intercourse (For example, a passionate kiss or erotic caress).   1 2 3 4 5 6 7   0

    b. With respect to the **frequency** of this kind of activity, I would like
(I **more**, 2 **less**, OR 3 **about the same**) amount

	MORE	LESS	SAME
	I	2	3

5. **a.** In the last 3 months, I have been satisfied with the **quality** of the affectionate
nonsexual, nongenital touching I've had with a partner.   1 2 3 4 5 6 7   0

    b. With respect to the **frequency** of this kind of activity, I would like
(I **more**, 2 **less**, OR 3 **about the same**) amount

	MORE	LESS	SAME
	I	2	3

6. **a.** Regarding total amount of sexual activity (anything and everything sexual),
in my current or most recent relationship:

I want(ed) more than my partner		I
My partner wants (wanted) more		2
My partner and I want(ed) about the same amount		3

If you want(ed) about the same amount, skip 6b.

b. We (have) reached a mutually satisfying compromise   I 2 3 4 5 6 7   0

N.   THE NEXT QUESTIONS ARE ABOUT SEXUALITY AND YOUR MENSTRUAL CYCLES

	STRONGLY DISAGREE	STRONGLY AGREE	NA
I. It seems to me that my sexual **desire** has (had) predictable variations due to my menstrual cycle	I 2 3 4 5	6 7	0
2. It seems to me that my sexual **satisfaction** has (had) predictable variations due to my menstrual cycle	I 2 3 4 5	6 7	0
3. I enjoy(ed) sexual activity during my menstrual flow	I 2 3 4 5	6 7	0

4. I engage(d) in sexual intercourse during my menstrual flow
    I **Never**   2 **Rarely**   3 **Sometimes**   4 **Often**   I 2 3 4

O.   THE QUESTIONS IN THIS SECTION ARE ABOUT PREGNANCY:

If you have NEVER been pregnant AND never wanted to be pregnant,
please circle 0 and skip to the next section, Section P.   0

I. Please indicate if you have ever been pregnant and fill in any other blanks that apply:

a.	I have been pregnant ___ times.	_____ a
b.	___ of my pregnancies were planned.	_____ b
c.	___ of my pregnancies were unplanned.	_____ c
d.	___ of my pregnancies resulted in live births.	_____ d
e.	___ of my pregnancies ended in spontaneous abortion or miscarriage	_____ e
f.	___ of my pregnancies ended in an arranged abortion	_____ f
g.	___ of my babies were given up for adoption	_____ g

	STRONGLY DISAGREE	STRONGLY AGREE	NA
2. At some time in my life, trying to become pregnant **enhanced** my sexual pleasure and/or satisfaction	I 2 3 4 5	6 7	0
3. At some time in my life, I had difficulty becoming pregnant when I wanted to	I 2 3 4 5	6 7	0
4. At some time in my life, trying to become pregnant **diminished** my sexual pleasure and/or satisfaction	I 2 3 4 5	6 7	0

5. At some time in my life, I have undergone medical testing and/or
    interventions for fertility   I **Yes**   2 **No**   I   2
    If you have NEVER been pregnant, please skip to Question 8.

6. In my life, becoming pregnant has resulted in the following (CIRCLE ALL THAT APPLY):

I got married sooner than I had planned	I
I married someone I had not previously planned to marry	2
I married someone I never would have chosen to marry otherwise	3
I married someone at the time who was not the biological father	4
I had a baby in marriage before I felt ready	5
The biological father knew about the pregnancy but did not remain with me through it	6
The biological father never knew about the pregnancy	7
Other _____	8
None of the above	0

7. **a.** I am pregnant now   I **Yes**   2 **No**   3 **Not sure**   I 2 3
     b. I have a baby I currently breastfeed   I 2
     c. I have sometime had a baby delivered by Cesarean section   I 2

8. During, or as a result of, partner sex during the last 3 months I have felt (CIRCLE ALL THAT APPLY):

Desirous of becoming pregnant	I
Concerned or fearful that I might **not** become pregnant	2
Concerned or fearful that I **was** pregnant	3
Concerned or fearful that I **might become** pregnant	4
None of the above	0

P. THIS SECTION IS ABOUT YOUR CONTRACEPTIVE METHOD:

If you do NOT use a contraceptive method, circle 0 and skip to Section Q.   0

I. a. The method of contraception I use most frequently is
(PLEASE WRITE IN): _____

	STRONGLY DISAGREE					STRONGLY AGREE		NA
b. This method increases my sexual satisfaction	I	2	3	4	5	6	7	0

Q. THESE 4 QUESTIONS ARE ABOUT SEXUALLY TRANSMITTED DISEASES:

I. I have at some time in my life contracted a sexually transmitted disease (STD)
    I Yes 2 No   I   2
(IF YES, PLEASE SPECIFY WHAT IT WAS): _____

If you DO NOT use a method of disease protection, circle 0
and skip to Question 3. Note the instructions above Question 3.   0

2. a. The method of protection against sexually transmitted diseases I use most frequently is
(PLEASE WRITE IN): _____

	STRONGLY DISAGREE					STRONGLY AGREE		NA
b. This method increases my sexual satisfaction	I	2	3	4	5	6	7	0

If you have NOT had sex with a partner in the last 3 months,
please circle 0 and skip to the next section, section R.   0

3. In sex with my partner(s) during the last 3 months I have felt concerned that I might **get** an STD	I	2	3	4	5	6	7	0
4. In sex with my partner(s) during the last 3 months I have felt concerned that I might **transmit** an STD	I	2	3	4	5	6	7	0

R. THE QUESTIONS IN THIS SECTION ARE ABOUT AFFAIRS:

An AFFAIR, for the purposes of these questions, refers to YOU having sex outside of your relationship in a way that violates rules of the relationship against it. If you and your partner have agreed that outside sex is OK, then it's not an affair. If you are single and having sex with someone who is married, that is NOT an affair for you.

I. **The number of affairs I have had in my life is** ____
If you have NEVER had an affair, circle 0 and skip to Question 3.   0

2. **The most important reason(s) for my FIRST affair were (CIRCLE UP TO THREE REASONS):**

Not enough sex in my primary relationship	I
Not enough closeness in my primary relationship	2
Curiosity	3
Strong attraction to the other person	4
Desire for something different	5
To make my partner jealous	6
To get back at my partner for something done to me	7
Trying to get pregnant (I couldn't get pregnant with my partner)	8
It provided a way out of an unsatisfactory relationship	9
My partner is/was unable to engage in sex (e.g. due to a medical problem)	10
Other (PLEASE SPECIFY): _____	11

3. With respect to my **current partner** (CIRCLE THE BEST ANSWER):

I have no current partner	0
I am quite certain that while in relationship with me he/she has **not** had an affair with someone else	1
I sometimes wonder if he/she has had or is having an affair; I am not sure	2
I am quite certain that he/she has had or is having an affair	3

4. **While I was growing up**, my father and mother, or the "parents" who raised me (CIRCLE ONE ANSWER IN EACH COLUMN):

	FATHER	MOTHER
Never had an affair that I suspected or knew about	1	1
Had 1 or more affairs that I knew about	2	2
May have had an affair, I was not sure	3	3
Not applicable	0	0

Answer Questions 5 & 6 IF you have NEVER had an affair as defined above OR if you have NEVER had an affair while with your current partner.

5. The most important reason(s) I have **NEVER** had an affair or **NOT** had an affair in my **current relationship** are (up to **THREE** reasons):

I have had no desire to do so	1
I have not had an opportunity to do so	2
Having an affair is against my values	3
I am/was afraid of getting caught by my partner	4
I don't/didn't believe I could deal with the guilt	5
It would destroy my relationship	6
I am/was afraid of catching a sexually transmitted disease	7
Other (PLEASE SPECIFY): _____	8

	STRONGLY DISAGREE					STRONGLY AGREE		NA

6. I would be open to having an affair in the future (if currently in a relationship, answer in terms of still being in that relationship)   1 2 3 4 5 6 7   0

S. **THESE FINAL QUESTIONS LOOK AT YOUR SEXUAL LIFE OVER TIME:**

1. In my life, my sexual satisfaction has been/was at its peak between ages ___ and ___ years: _____ and _____

2. Looking back, I have at some time had a problem in my sexual life due to the following (CIRCLE ALL THAT APPLY):

Inadequate sex education	1
Inadequate knowledge of my body and sexual feelings	2
Inadequate information about the how-to of sex	3
Inadequate knowledge of the **physical** consequences of sex	4
Inadequate knowledge of the **emotional** consequences of sex	5
Inadequate information about birth control	6
Inadequate availability of birth control	7
None of the above	0

3. Looking back over my entire life, I **regret** the following about my sexual life (CIRCLE ALL THAT APPLY):

I got into sex when I was too young.	1
I had sex with partners I should have turned down.	2
I **did not** have sex with someone with whom I wish I had	3
I had sex without protection against pregnancy	4
I had sex without protection against disease	5
I was too often **not** assertive enough about my needs	6
I was too inhibited	7
I was celibate for too long	8
I did **not** take more time to be celibate	9
I married the wrong person because of sex	10
I stayed too long in relationship with the wrong partner	11
Other (PLEASE SPECIFY): _____	12
None of the above	0

4. Looking back, the most significant sources for me of sex information in each of the two following categories have been (CIRCLE **ONE or TWO** ANSWERS IN EACH COLUMN):

	Helpful or Useful	Misleading or Harmful
Same age friend(s)	1	1
Older friend(s)	2	2
Sexual partner(s)	3	3
Parent(s)	4	4
Sex education book(s)	5	5
Fiction books (novels, romances, etc.)	6	6
Media (TV, movies, magazines, etc.)	7	7
Erotic or pornographic material(s)	8	8
Course(s) in school or college	9	9
Religious teachings	10	10
Relative(s)	11	11
Health practitioner(s)/therapist(s)	12	12
Other (PLEASE SPECIFY): _____	13	13

	STRONGLY DISAGREE					STRONGLY AGREE		NA

5. Looking back, I believe the information I got from the parent(s) or parent figure(s) who raised me prepared me to have a healthy and fulfilling sex life

    1 2 3 4 5 6 7   0

6. Compared to how I was during the year after I became sexually active for the first time ever with a partner (in a genital way, whether or not intercourse was included), I have changed in sex in the following ways (CIRCLE THE NUMBER ON EACH LINE THAT BEST INDICATES HOW YOU HAVE CHANGED). If your first-ever genital contact with a partner occurred less than a year ago, circle 0 and skip to question 7.

0

I now:

		MORE	SAME	LESS
a.	Desire sex	1	2	3
b.	Get aroused easily	1	2	3
c.	Express my sexual needs	1	2	3
d.	Am inhibited	1	2	3
e.	Have erotic thoughts	1	2	3
f.	Orgasm easily	1	2	3
g.	Initiate	1	2	3
h.	Am sexually satisfied	1	2	3
i.	Have fun	1	2	3
j.	Engage in casual sex	1	2	3
k.	Am comfortable with sex	1	2	3
l.	Focus on my partner's satisfaction	1	2	3
m.	Focus on my own satisfaction	1	2	3

	STRONGLY AGREE					STRONGLY DISAGREE	

7. On the whole, I have been satisfied with my sexual life

    1 2 3 4 5 6 7

Thank You!

Sexual Self-Schema Scale—Women's Version

ANNA O. LEVIN AND BARBARA L. ANDERSEN,[1] *The Ohio State University*

Andersen and Cyranowski (1994) view sexual self-schema as a sexually relevant, cognitive, individual difference variable. Schemas are cognitive representations of the self. They are derived from past experience and manifest in current experiences. The sexual self-view functions to interpret and organize sexually relevant actions and experiences, provides standards for sexual behaviors, and guides decisions and inferences about future sexual circumstances. The Sexual Self-Schema Scale (SSS) is a cognitive measure of a woman's sexual self-view.

Individuals with a positive sexual self-schema tend to view themselves as emotionally romantic or passionate and behaviorally open, while reporting low levels of embarrassment or conservatism in sexual contexts. Women with negative self-descriptions report low levels of romantic or passionate emotions and low behavioral engagement in sexual and romantic relationships.

Development and Description

A construct validity method was employed in test construction, beginning with a classic approach of using trait adjectives as markers of important personality dispositions to identify a semantic representation of a "sexual" woman. Psychometric studies of internal consistency, discriminant and convergent validity, group differences, internal structure, and others were conducted. The final scale is uncorrelated with both negative affect and social desirability. Filler items were added to yield a measure for which respondents are unaware that a sexuality construct is being assessed.

The scale (entitled "Describe Yourself") has 50 items, with 26 scored and 24 fillers. Multiple factor analytic studies reveal two factors with a positive valence, Passionate/Romantic (Factor 1) and Directness/Openness (Factor 2), and one with a negative valence, Embarrassment or Conservatism (Factor 3). Use of the total score is recommended. High scores are interpreted as positively schematic and low scores negatively schematic.

Response Mode and Timing

Subjects rate items on a 7-point Likert-type scale, ranging from 0 = *Not at all Descriptive of Me* to 6 = *Very Much Descriptive of Me*. The scale takes 5–10 minutes to complete.

Scoring

The 26 items are summed within their factors, resulting in factor scores: Scale/Factor 1 items are 5, 11, 20, 35, 37, 39, 44, 45, 48, and 50; Scale/Factor 2 items are 2, 5, 9, 13, 16, 18, 24, 25, and 32; Scale/Factor 3 items are 3, 8, 22, 28, 31, 38, and 41. Item 45 is reverse scored. A total score is used and is calculated as follows: (scale 1 + scale 2) − scale 3. Total scores can range from −42 to 114. A normal distribution is typically found, with a slight positive skew. Means and standard deviations of total and scale scores were provided from college-aged women ($N = 387$) as follows: Total score: 60.47 (14.15); Scale 1: 47.44 (6.45); Scale 2: 36.26 (7.15); and Scale 3: 23.22 (5.91; Andersen & Cyranowski, 1994).

Scale scores can also be used to represent a two-dimensional model. The bivariate scoring procedure uses median-split cutoffs of the positive (sum of Factors 1 and 2) and negative (Factor 3) dimensions to delineate four types of schematic representations: positive (high on positive/low on negative schema dimensions), negative (low positive/high negative), aschematic (low on both positive and negative dimensions) and co-schematic (high on both positive and negative dimensions; Andersen & Cyranowski, 1994).

Reliability

The authors reported Cronbach's alpha values in college women ($N = 387$) as follows: Total scale, .82; Scale 1, .81; Scale 2, .77; and Scale 3, .66 (Andersen & Cyranowski, 1994). Since publication, total scale internal-consistency estimates from various other samples, including older women, cancer patients/survivors, and women with sexual dysfunctions, have been in the same range (Ns 17 to 190, $\alpha = .61$ to .86). Retest reliabilities provided from college samples at 2-week and 9-week intervals were .89 ($N = 20$) and .88 ($N = 172$; Andersen & Cyranowski, 1994).

Validity

Convergent validity data from multiple samples from Andersen, Cyranowski and colleagues (Andersen & Cyranowski, 1994; Andersen, Woods, & Copeland, 1997; Cyranowski & Andersen, 1998, 2000) showed the SSS to predict a range of sexual cognitions, behaviors, and responses. Studies with college women ($N = 220$)

[1]Address correspondence to Barbara L. Andersen, Department of Psychology, The Ohio State University, 1835 Neil Avenue, Columbus, OH 43210-1222; e-mail: andersen.1@osu.edu

indicate significant correlations of total scores with measures of sexual affects, behaviors, and arousal, as well as romantic relationships ($rs = .14$ to $.36$). Data from older women ($N = 21$) provide total score correlations with self-report measures of the sexual response cycle phases ($rs = .47$ to $.59$). Multiple regression studies showed schema scores to account for significant increments of variance beyond any contributions of other individual difference factors such as extroversion or self-esteem.

Consistent data come from other investigators. Reissing, Laliberté, and Davis (2005; $N = 84$) found the total score to predict sexual aversion and sexual self-efficacy ($\beta = .22$ and $.13$). Meston, Rellini, and Heiman (2006) found the Romantic/Passionate scale to predict negative sexual affect. Donaghue (2009; $N = 91$) reported significant correlations between schema scores and various measures of subjective well-being ($\beta = -.18$ to $.27$). Kuffel and Heiman's (2006) analog study investigated the role of schemas on responses to sexually explicit visual material. Analyses demonstrated significantly greater vaginal response, positive affect, and subjective sexual arousal when participants were told to adopt a positive schema in comparison to their responses following the negative schema induction.

Importantly, sexual self-schema appears relevant to sexual dysfunction and/or sexual distress. Studies of female cancer patients also find the SSS to predict a wide range of responses (e.g., Andersen et al., 1997; Donovan et al., 2007; Yurek, Farrar, & Andersen, 2000). Reissing, Binik, Khalife, Cohen, and Amsel (2003; $N= 87$) found that women with sexual pain disorders report a less positive score than women with no pain. Women with a sexual abuse history were found to have significantly lower Romantic/Passionate subscale scores than did nonabused women (Meston et al., 2006).

References

Andersen, B. L., & Cyranowski, J. M. (1994). Women's sexual self-schema. *Journal of Personality and Social Psychology, 67,* 1079–1100.

Andersen, B. L., Woods, X. A., & Copeland, L. J. (1997). Sexual self-schema and sexual morbidity among gynecologic cancer survivors. *Journal of Consulting and Clinical Psychology, 65,* 221–229.

Cyranowski, J. M., & Andersen, B. L. (1998). Schemas, sexuality, and romantic attachment. *Journal of Personality and Social Psychology, 74,* 1364–1379.

Cyranowski, J. M., & Andersen, B. L. (2000). Evidence of self-schematic cognitive processing in women with differing sexual self-views. *Journal of Social and Clinical Psychology, 19,* 519–543.

Donaghue, N. (2009). Body satisfaction, sexual self-schemas and subjective well-being in women. *Body Image, 6,* 37–42.

Donovan, K. A., Taliaferro, L. A., Alvarez, E. M., Jacobsen, P. B., Roetzheim, R. G., & Wenham, R. M. (2007). Sexual health in women treated for cervical cancer: Characteristics and correlates. *Gynecologic Oncology, 104,* 428–434.

Kuffel, S. W., & Heiman, J. R. (2006). Effects of depressive symptoms and experimentally adopted schemas on sexual arousal and affect in sexually healthy women. *Archives of Sexual Behavior, 35,* 163–177.

Meston, C. A., Rellini, A. H., & Heiman, R. (2006). Women's history of sexual abuse, their sexuality, and sexual self-schemas. *Journal of Consulting and Clinical Psychology, 74,* 229–236.

Reissing, E. D., Binik, Y. M., Khalife, S., Cohen, D., & Amsel, R. (2003). Etiological correlates of vaginismus: Sexual and physical abuse, sexual knowledge, sexual self-schema, and relationship adjustment. *Journal of Sex and Marital Therapy, 29,* 47–59.

Reissing, E. D., Laliberté, G. M., & Davis, H. J. (2005). Young women's sexual adjustment: The role of sexual self-schema, sexual self-efficacy, sexual aversion and body attitudes. *Canadian Journal of Human Sexuality, 14*(3/4), 77.

Yurek, D., Farrar, W., & Andersen, B. L. (2000). Breast cancer surgery: Comparing surgical groups and determining individual differences in postoperative sexuality and body change stress. *Journal of Consulting and Clinical Psychology, 68,* 697–709.

Exhibit

Sexual Self-Schema Scale

Describe Yourself

Directions: Below is a listing of 50 trait adjectives. For each word, consider whether or not the term describes you. Each adjective is to be rated on a 7-point scale, ranging from 0 = *not at all descriptive of me* to 6 = *very much descriptive of me*. For each item, fill in the appropriate circle on your computer answer sheet. Please be thoughtful and honest.

Question: To what extent does the term_____describe me?

Rating Scale:

Not at all Descriptive of Me	0	1	2	3	4	5	6	Very Much Descriptive of Me

(1) generous
(2) uninhibited
(3) cautious
(4) helpful

(26) disagreeable
(27) serious
(28) prudent
(29) humorous

(5)	loving	(30)	sensible
(6)	open-minded	(31)	embarrassed
(7)	shallow	(32)	outspoken
(8)	timid	(33)	level-headed
(9)	frank	(34)	responsible
(10)	clean-cut	(35)	romantic
(11)	stimulating	(36)	polite
(12)	unpleasant	(37)	sympathetic
(13)	experienced	(38)	conservative
(14)	short-tempered	(39)	passionate
(15)	irresponsible	(40)	wise
(16)	direct	(41)	inexperienced
(17)	logical	(42)	stingy
(18)	broad-minded	(43)	superficial
(19)	kind	(44)	warm
(20)	arousable	(45)	unromantic
(21)	practical	(46)	good-natured
(22)	self-conscious	(47)	rude
(23)	dull	(48)	revealing
(24)	straightforward	(49)	bossy
(25)	causal	(50)	feeling

Brief Index of Sexual Functioning for Women

RAYMOND C. ROSEN,[1] JENNIFER F. TAYLOR, AND SANDRA R. LEIBLUM, *University of Medicine and Dentistry of New Jersey, Robert Wood Johnson Medical School*

The Brief Index of Sexual Functioning for Women (BISF-W) was developed in response to the lack of a brief, standardized self-report measure of overall sexual function in women. Previous self-report measures have been either overly restrictive or inappropriate for use in large-scale clinical trials. None of the self-report measures to date provide a comprehensive, reliable assessment of key dimensions of sexual function in women, including sexual desire, orgasm, and satisfaction. Reynolds et al. (1988) have described the Brief Sexual Function Questionnaire (BSFQ) for men, a 21-item self-report inventory of sexual interest, activity, satisfaction, and preference. The BSFQ has been found to be highly reliable, and to discriminate between depressed, sexually dysfunctional, and healthy males (Howell et al., 1987; Reynolds et al., 1988). Surprisingly, no corresponding measures to the BSFQ for self-report assessment of female sexual function were available. The present questionnaire was developed to provide a comparable, brief self-report measure of sexual function for women.

Description

The BISF-W consists of 22 items, assessing the major dimensions of sexual desire, arousal, orgasm, and satisfaction. Several items were adapted from the BSFQ, particularly those assessing frequency of sexual behavior, fantasy, masturbation, and sexual preference. Additional items were included to address specific issues believed to affect women's sexual functioning and satisfaction, such as body image, partner satisfaction, and sexual anxiety. Several items were designed to evaluate sexual performance difficulties in women, such as diminished arousal or lubrication, pain or tightness during intercourse, and difficulties in reaching orgasm. Items assessing the impact of health problems on sexual functioning are also included. Most items are arranged in Likert-type format to rate the frequency of occurrence of sexual desire, arousal or satisfaction associated with common sexual behaviors. Based upon a principal components analysis, three major factors were identified, which were

[1]Address correspondence to Raymond C. Rosen, New England Research Institutes, Inc., 9 Galen Street, Watertown, MA 02472; e-mail: RRosen@neriscience.com

labelled Sexual Desire, Sexual Activity, and Sexual Satisfaction.

Response Mode and Timing

Respondents are required to circle the single best answer to each question. The inventory takes approximately 10–15 minutes to complete.

Scoring

Individual items are scored and the aggregate scores for each of the three major factors are computed. Items for the Sexual Desire factor are 3, 6, 8, 14, and 20. Items for the Sexual Activity factor are 3, 4, 5, 7, 9, 10, 11, 17, and 20. Items for the Sexual Satisfaction factor are 6, 9, 10, 15, 18, and 19. Item 16 is used independently as a measure of body image. Items 1, 2, 21, and 22 assess the presence of a sexual partner, sexual activity during the past month, and the respondent's sexual orientation, in terms of both experience and desire. These items are individually scored.

Reliability

In a sample of 269 women, aged 20–73, test-retest reliability was assessed by means of repeated administration of the questionnaire over a 1-month interval. Reliability was determined by means of a Pearson correlation coefficient between factor scores at the baseline and 1-month retest interval. Internal consistency was evaluated by means of Cronbach alpha coefficients for each of the factor scales. The test-retest reliability of factor scores ranged from .68 to .78. The internal consistency of the instrument ranged between .39 for Factor 1 to .83 for Factor 2. The relatively low consistency for Factor 1 was attributed to the split loading of several items with other factors.

Validity

No significant correlations were observed between the BISF-W factor scores and the Marlowe-Crowne (1964) Social Desirability Scale. This indicates that responses to the BISF-W were not biased by the effects of social desirability. Concurrent validity was assessed by means of comparison of specific factor scores with the corresponding scales of the Derogatis Sexual Function Inventory (DSFI; 1975), a comprehensive, 261-item measure of sexual information, attitudes, experience, drive, body image, sex roles, and sexual satisfaction. Correlations between BISF-W factors and subscales of the DSFI were all in a positive direction, ranging from .59 to .69. Item 16, which assesses body image, was significantly correlated with the DSFI Body Image Scale ($r = .62, p < .001$). The scale has been used for assessment of sexual functioning in a community-based sample of 329 adult women (Rosen, Taylor, Leiblum, & Bachmann, 1993).

Other Information

The DSFI may be obtained through the MAPI Institute (http://www.mapi-institute.com/).

References

Crowne, D. P., & Marlowe, D. (1964). *The approval motive: Studies in evaluative dependence.* New York: Wiley.

Derogatis, L. R. (1975). *Derogatis Sexual Functioning Inventory (DSFI): Preliminary scoring manual. Baltimor, MD: Clinical Psychometric Research Inc.*

Howell, J. R., Reynolds, C. F., Thase, M. E., Frank, E., Jennings, J. R., Houck, P. R., Berman, S., Jacobs, E., & Kupfer, D. J. (1987). Assessment of sexual function, interest, and activity in depressed men. *Journal of Affective Disorders, 13,* 61–66.

Reynolds, C. F., Frank, E., Thase, M. E., Houck, P. R., Jennings, J. R., Howell, J. R., Lilienfeld, S. O., & Kupfer, D. J. (1988). Assessment of sexual function in depressed, impotent, and healthy men: Factor analysis of a Brief Sexual Function Questionnaire for men. *Psychiatric Research, 24,* 231–250.

Rosen, R. C., Taylor, J. F., Leiblum, S. R., & Bachmann, G. A. (1993). Prevalence of sexual dysfunction in women: Results of a survey study of 329 women in an outpatient gynecological clinic. *Journal of Sex and Marital Therapy, 19,* 171–188.

Changes in Sexual Functioning Questionnaire

ANITA H. CLAYTON[1] AND ELIZABETH L. MCGARVEY, *University of Virginia School of Medicine*

Assessment of sexual functioning is an important component in many clinical encounters, and in research settings it is increasingly of interest with regard to side effects of new medications. Adequate sexual functioning for most people is an important factor for good quality of life. There is a need for brief, easy-to-use assessment instruments that provide

[1]Address correspondence to Anita H. Clayton, Department of Psychiatry and Neurobehavioral Science, University of Virginia, 2955 Ivy Road, Suite 210, Charlottesville, VA 22903; e-mail: ahc8v@virginia.edu

valid and reliable indicators of the sexual health of the individual. The Changes in Sexual Functioning Questionnaire (CSFQ) was developed with specific versions for females and males to assess sexual functioning in all the domains of the sexual response cycle. It was developed to be used in both clinical and research settings (Clayton, McGarvey, Clavet, & Piazza, 1997).

Description

The CSFQ was initially developed from patient complaints of sexual dysfunction and published sexual side effects of psychotropic medications. The clinical interview (CSFQ-I) was intended for use in the diagnosis and management of sexual dysfunction in patients who were in treatment at an outpatient psychiatric clinic. The CSFQ-I included 35 items for females and 36 items for males, and also included a section for medical disorders and medication use. At the time of its development, most research on sexual dysfunction focused on problems among males, such as erectile dysfunction, and the available research instruments did not adequately capture specific female symptoms of sexual problems relating to reduced quality of life, such as lack of desire. The CSFQ-I was used clinically and included a section to identify the sexual pattern of the individual, which permitted a documentation of how much sexual change the person experienced over time. In addition, information on medication use was collected. The documentation of change could be tied to the five domains of sexual functioning so that the clinician could better focus on strategically targeted treatment for the cause of the problem, which could be related to medication, illness, relationship problems, or a combination of difficulties. In addition, the CSFQ-I addressed the need for an assessment instrument that could differentiate current sexual dysfunction from previous "normal" sexual function and/or lifelong sexual dysfunction.

The original CSFQ items were field tested and revised on the basis of conceptual content to ensure that five aspects of sexual functioning (i.e., sexual desire, sexual frequency, sexual satisfaction, sexual arousal, and sexual completion) were captured. To establish face validity, other physicians, clinicians, and researchers reviewed the items for accuracy and clarity. Reliability and validity were established for the clinical interview version, with 14 scored items. Male- and female-specific self-report shorter versions were developed that included only the 14 scored items from the validation of the interview version: the CSFQ-14-F for females and the CSFQ-14-M for males (Clayton, McGarvey, & Clavet, 1997; Keller, McGarvey, & Clayton, 2006).

The CSFQ has been used in studies of clinical and nonclinical samples (Bobes et al., 2000; Clayton, McGarvey, Clavet, & Piazza, 1997), in a study of women survivors of gynecological cancer (Lagana, McGarvey, Classen, & Koopman, 2001), in studies on sexual dysfunction associated with medications for depression (Clayton et al., 2002), and in a study on sexual functioning in menopause

(Warnock, Swanson, Boren, Zipfel, & Brennan, 2005), among many others.

Response Mode and Timing

The CSFQ-I has items stated as questions that are rated by the clinician during a clinical interview, or for CSFQ-14-F self-scored by females and CSFQ-14-M self-scored by males in either a clinical or a research setting. Each item is scored on a 5-point scale that is linked to specific self-reported information. A "1" on the scale typically indicates *Never* or *No Enjoyment or Pleasure*, depending upon whether the response item is to determine frequency of occurrence or perception of satisfaction in a stated area, whereas a "5" indicates *Every Day* or *Always* in like manner. The response time for the CSFQ-I is between 30 and 45 minutes for the interview. The response time for the CSFQ-14-F and CSFQ-14-M is between 4 and 5 minutes.

Scoring

The CSFQ-I scoring booklet may be obtained from the first author. A CSFQ-14 total score for both female and male versions is obtained by summing the value of Items 1 to 14. Scores ≤ 41 for females and ≤ 47 for males indicate sexual dysfunction. In addition, five subscale scores with established thresholds are also provided for pleasure/overall satisfaction (Item 1 ≤ 4), desire/measured as frequency (Item 2 + Item 3 ≤ 6 for women and ≤ 8 for men), desire/measured as interest (Item 4 + Item 5 + Item 6 ≤ 9 for women and ≤ 11 for men), arousal/excitement (Item 7 + Item 8 + Item 9 ≤ 12 for females and ≤ 13 for males) and orgasm/completion (Item 11 + Item 12 + Item 13 ≤ 11 for females and ≤ 13 for males). Items 10 and 14 are included in the total score, but do not map to a subscale dimension. See the Exhibit for additional scoring information.

Reliability and Validity

For the CSFQ-I, alpha coefficients and item total correlations range from 0.45 to 0.60 with concurrent validation demonstrated using the Derogatis Interview for Sexual Functioning (Derogatis, 1997) and high test-retest reported (Clayton, McGarvey, Clavet, & Piazza, 1997). For the CSFQ-14-F and CSFQ-14-M versions, Cronbach's alpha coefficient of internal reliability for the total score and the original five subscales was established in addition to other analyses for each version of the measure. The alpha coefficient for the CSFQ-14-F was .90 and for the CSFQ-14-M was .89 (Keller at al., 2006).

Other Information

There are 51 linguistically validated translations of the CSFQ with validation of the Spanish version reported with norms established (Bobes et al., 2000). The CSFQ has been utilized in over 75 studies, including studies in psychiatric populations with diagnoses of major depressive disorder, schizophrenia, bipolar illness, OCD, ADHD, primary sexual disorders, alcohol dependence, and cognitive disorders. Other medical illnesses in which the CSFQ has been administered include cancer, obesity, diabetes mellitus/metabolic syndrome, rheumatologic illness, spinal cord injury, BPH, and vulvar pain, as well as with the administration of androgens. Use of the measures for clinical purposes is typically provided upon request to Dr. Clayton. Use of the measures for research may be approved with or without charge, depending upon the type of project being undertaken. Citation of use is always required.

All versions of the CSFQ are under copyright to Anita H. Clayton, MD, David C. Wilson Professor, Department of Psychiatry and Neurobehavioral Science, University of Virginia, 2955 Ivy Road, Suite 210, Charlottesville, VA 22903; Tel: 434-243-4646; e-mail: ahc8v@virginia.edu

References

Bobes, J., Gonzalez, M. P., Rico-Villademoros, R., Bascaran, M. T., Sarasa, P., & Clayton, A. (2000). Validation of the Spanish version of the Changes in Sexual Functioning Questionnaire-CSFQ. *Journal of Sex and Marital Therapy, 26,* 119–131.

Clayton, A. H., McGarvey, E. L., & Clavet, G. J. (1997). The Changes in Sexual Functioning Questionnaire (CSFQ): Development, reliability, and validity. *Psychopharmacology Bulletin, 33,* 731–745.

Clayton, A. H., McGarvey, E. L., Clavet, G. J., & Piazza, L. (1997). Comparison of sexual functioning in clinical and non-clinical populations using the Changes in Sexual Functioning Questionnaire (CSFQ). *Psychopharmacology Bulletin, 33,* 747–753.

Clayton, A. H., Pradko, J. F., Croft, H. A., Montano, C. B., Leadbetter, R. A., Bolden-Watson, C., et al. (2002). Prevalence of sexual dysfunction among newer antidepressants. *Journal of Clinical Psychiatry, 63,* 357–366.

Derogatis, L. R. (1997). The Derogatis Interview for Sexual Functioning (DISF/DISF-SR): An introductory report. *Journal of Sex and Marital Therapy, 23,* 291–304.

Keller, A., McGarvey, E. L., & Clayton, A. H. (2006). Reliability and construct validity of the Changes in Sexual Functioning Questionnaire Short-Form (CSFQ-14). *Journal of Sex and Marital Therapy, 32,* 43–52.

Lagana, L., McGarvey, E. L., Classen, C., & Koopman, C. (2001). Psychosexual dysfunction among gynecological cancer survivors. *Journal of Clinical Psychology in Medical Settings, 8,* 73–84.

Warnock, J. K., Swanson, S. G., Boren, R. W., Zipfel, L. M., & Brennan, J. J. (2005). Combined esterified estrogen and methyltestosterone versus esterified estrogens alone in the treatment of loss of sexual interest in surgically-menopausal women. *Menopause, 12,* 374–84.

Exhibit

Changes in Sexual Functioning Questionnaire

Changes in Sexual Functioning Questionnaire for Females (CSFQ-F-C)

Note: This is a questionnaire about sexual activity and sexual function. By sexual activity, we mean sexual intercourse, masturbation, sexual fantasies, and other activity.

1. Compared with the most enjoyable it has ever been, how enjoyable or pleasurable is your sexual life right now?
   - ☐ 1 No Enjoyment or Pleasure
   - ☐ 2 Little Enjoyment or Pleasure
   - ☐ 3 Some Enjoyment or Pleasure
   - ☐ 4 Much Enjoyment or Pleasure
   - ☐ 5 Great Enjoyment or Pleasure

2. How frequently do you engage in sexual activity (sexual intercourse, masturbation, etc.) now?
   - ☐ 1 Never
   - ☐ 2 Rarely (once a month or less)
   - ☐ 3 Sometimes (more than once a month, up to twice a week)
   - ☐ 4 Often (more than twice a week)
   - ☐ 5 Every Day

3. How often do you desire to engage in sexual activity?
   - ☐ 1 Never
   - ☐ 2 Rarely (once a month or less)
   - ☐ 3 Sometimes (more than once a month, up to twice a week)
   - ☐ 4 Often (more than twice a week)
   - ☐ 5 Every Day

4. How frequently do you engage in sexual thoughts (thinking about sex, sexual fantasies) now?
   - ☐ 1 Never
   - ☐ 2 Rarely (once a month or less)

☐ 3 Sometimes (more than once a month, up to twice a week)
☐ 4 Often (more than twice a week)
☐ 5 Every Day

5. Do you enjoy books, movies, music, or artwork with sexual content?
☐ 1 Never
☐ 2 Rarely (once a month or less)
☐ 3 Sometimes (more than once a month, up to twice a week)
☐ 4 Often (more than twice a week)
☐ 5 Every Day

6. How much pleasure or enjoyment do you get from thinking about and fantasizing about sex?
☐ 1 No Enjoyment or Pleasure
☐ 2 Little Enjoyment or Pleasure
☐ 3 Some Enjoyment or Pleasure
☐ 4 Much Enjoyment or Pleasure
☐ 5 Great Enjoyment or Pleasure

7. How often do you become sexually aroused?
☐ 1 Never
☐ 2 Rarely (once a month or less)
☐ 3 Sometimes (more than once a month, up to twice a week)
☐ 4 Often (more than twice a week)
☐ 5 Every Day

8. Are you easily aroused?
☐ 1 Never
☐ 2 Rarely (much less than half the time)
☐ 3 Sometimes (about half the time)
☐ 4 Often (much more than half the time)
☐ 5 Always

9. Do you have adequate vaginal lubrication during sexual activity?
☐ 1 Never
☐ 2 Rarely (much less than half the time)
☐ 3 Sometimes (about half the time)
☐ 4 Often (much more than half the time)
☐ 5 Always

10. How often do you become aroused and then lose interest?
☐ 5 Never
☐ 4 Rarely (much less than half the time)
☐ 3 Sometimes (about half the time)
☐ 2 Often (much more than half the time)
☐ 1 Always

11. How often do you experience an orgasm?
☐ 1 Never
☐ 2 Rarely (much less than half the time)
☐ 3 Sometimes (about half the time)
☐ 4 Often (much more than half the time)
☐ 5 Always

12. Are you able to have an orgasm when you want to?
☐ 1 Never
☐ 2 Rarely (much less than half the time)
☐ 3 Sometimes (about half the time)

☐ 4 Often (much more than half the time)
☐ 5 Always

13. How much pleasure or enjoyment do you get from your orgasms?
☐ 1 No Enjoyment or Pleasure
☐ 2 Little Enjoyment or Pleasure
☐ 3 Some Enjoyment or Pleasure
☐ 4 Much Enjoyment or Pleasure
☐ 5 Great Enjoyment or Pleasure

14. How often do you have painful orgasm?
☐ 5 Never
☐ 4 Rarely (once a month or less)
☐ 3 Sometimes (more than once a month, up to twice a week)
☐ 2 Often (more than twice a week)
☐ 1 Every Day

_____ = Pleasure (Item 1)
_____ = Desire/Frequency (Item 2 + Item 3)
_____ = Desire/Interest (Item 4 + Item 5 + Item 6)
_____ = Arousal/Excitement (Item 7 + Item 8 + Item 9)
_____ = Orgasm/Completion (Item 11 + Item 12 + Item 13)
_____ = Total CSFQ Score (Items 1 to 14)

Copyright © 1998/99 A. Clayton, Dept. of Psychiatric Medicine, University of Virginia Health Sciences Center

Changes in Sexual Functioning Questionnaire for Males (CSFQ-M-C)—sample items only

Note: This is a questionnaire about sexual activity and sexual function. By sexual activity, we mean sexual intercourse, masturbation, sexual fantasies, and other activity.

7.   How often do you have an erection related or unrelated to sexual activity?
☐ 1 Never
☐ 2 Rarely (once a month or less)
☐ 3 Sometimes (more than once a month, up to twice a week)
☐ 4 Often (more than twice a week)
☐ 5 Every Day

8.   Do you get an erection easily?
☐ 1 Never
☐ 2 Rarely (much less than half the time)
☐ 3 Sometimes (about half the time)
☐ 4 Often (much more than half the time)
☐ 5 Always

Instructions for completing and scoring the CSFQ

Ask the patient to complete all 14 items on the clinical version of the CSFQ. The patient should place a check (✓) in the box corresponding to the response for that particular item. The patient should choose only one response per item.

To score items on the CSFQ, take the numerical value or weight indicated for a particular response. For example, in Item 1, a response of "some enjoyment or pleasure" has a numerical value of 3, whereas a response of "much enjoyment or pleasure" has a numerical value of 4. Some items have responses that are reverse scored: for example, on Item 14 in the CSFQ-F-C version, a response of "never" has a numerical value of 5, whereas a response of "every day" has a value of 1.

To calculate the total CSFQ score, add up the values of the responses for all 14 items. To calculate subscale scores, add up the values for only the items that correspond to a particular subscale (see shaded box after item 14). To determine if sexual dysfunction is present, refer to the gender-specific scoring protocols below.

Scoring for CSFQ-F-C: (Female Clinical Version)

If the *female* patient obtains a score *at or below* the following cutoff points* on any of these scales, it is indicative of sexual dysfunction:

Total CSFQ score:	41.0 (range: 14 to 70)
Sexual Desire/Frequency score:	6.0 (range: 2 to 10)
Sexual Desire/Interest:	9.0 (range: 3 to 15)
Sexual Pleasure:	4.0 (range: 1 to 5)
Sexual Arousal/Excitement:	12.0 (range: 3 to 15)
Sexual Orgasm/Completion:	11.0 (range: 3 to 15)

Scoring for CSFQ-M-C: (Male Clinical Version)

If the *male* patient obtains a score *at or below* the following cutoff points* on any of these scales, it is indicative of sexual dysfunction:

Total CSFQ score:	47.0 (range: 14 to 70)
Sexual Desire/Frequency score:	8.0 (range: 2 to 10)
Sexual Desire/Interest:	11.0 (range: 3 to 15)
Sexual Pleasure:	4.0 (range: 1 to 5)
Sexual Arousal/Excitement:	13.0 (range: 3 to 15)
Sexual Orgasm/Completion:	13.0 (range: 3 to 15)

*Based on comparisons of nondepressed participants and clinically depressed patients.

Global Sexual Functioning: A Single Summary Score for Nowinski and LoPiccolo's Sexual History Form (SHF)

LAURA CRETI[1] AND CATHERINE S. FICHTEN, *SMBD-Jewish General Hospital*
RHONDA AMSEL, *McGill University*
WILLIAM BRENDER, *SMBD-Jewish General Hospital*
LESLIE R. SCHOVER, *The Cleveland Clinic Foundation*
DENNIS KALOGEROPOULOS, *Royal Victoria Hospital*
EVA LIBMAN, *SMBD-Jewish General Hospital*

The Sexual History Form (SHF: Nowinski & LoPiccolo, 1979; Schover & Jensen, 1988) is a questionnaire that evaluates sexual functioning including desire, arousal, orgasm, pain, frequency of sexual activities, and overall sexual satisfaction for men and women. Originally, it was developed for clinical use and to provide standardized data for diagnosis and research (Schover, Friedman, Weiler, Heiman, & LoPiccolo, 1982), and was limited to item-by-item analysis.

We developed a new scoring system that generates a single summary score: Global Sexual Functioning (Creti, Fichten, Libman, Amsel, & Brender, 1988; Creti, Fichten, Libman, Kalogeropoulos, & Brender, 1987), which is concise and accurate, and reflects overall level of sexual functioning. The questionnaire has been used to describe sexual functioning in different populations, in studies of various medical conditions and procedures, in sex therapy outcome, and in longitudinal assessments of the impact of chronic illness on sexuality (Creti et al., 1998; Desrosiers et al., 2008; Petersen, Ung, Holland, & Quinlivana, 2005; Weber, Walters, Schover, Church, & Piedmonte, 1999).

[1]Address correspondence to Laura Creti, ICFP, Jewish General Hospital, 4333 Chemin de la Cote Ste Catherine, Montreal, Quebec, Canada, H3T 1E4; e-mail: lcreti@mail.mcgill.ca

Description

The SHF is a self-report measure consisting of 46 multiple-choice items that have variable numbers of response options and different response scales (e.g., Item 1 has 9 options; Item 18 has 6 options). Response options are numbered and have a verbal descriptor corresponding to each number. Normative data are available for individual items (see Creti et al., 1998). Norms have yet to be established for the Global Sexual Functioning score.

Response Mode and Timing

Respondents are asked to circle the number that corresponds to the single most appropriate response for each question. The measure requires approximately 15 minutes to complete.

Scoring

The Global Sexual Functioning score is based on 12 items. Because certain items are relevant only for males, whereas others are relevant only for females, the items used to calculate the male and female scores are somewhat different. These items were selected as representative of various domains of sexual functioning: frequency of sexual activities, sexual desire, arousal, orgasmic, and erectile abilities.

To arrive at the single summary score, SHF items are grouped into a 12-item scale; this reflects either male or female global sexual functioning. The single summary score is derived by (a) converting the scores on each of the 12 items to a proportion of the maximum possible value (e.g., if on Item 1, where response options are numbered 1 to 9, the respondent answers "(4) twice a week," this is converted to $4/9 = .44$), (b) summing the 12 proportions, and (c) calculating the mean by dividing the total by the number of items that the respondent is deemed to have answered (usually 12). The resulting mean value, which is the Global Sexual Functioning score, will be greater than 0 and less than 1.

Specified in Table 1 are the items included in the calculation of the Global Sexual Functioning score. For items with an asterisk, responses equaling 6 are considered missing because this response option is *have never tried*; in this case, the summed proportions are divided not by 12 but by the number of items that are deemed to have been answered (i.e., not missing). The scoring system is summarized in Table 1. Lower scores indicate better functioning.

Reliability

Temporal stability for the GSF ranged from .92 (Creti et al., 1988) to .98 (Libman et al., 1989). Internal consistency ranged from .50 to .70 (Creti et al., 1988).

Validity

Male global sexual functioning. Data reported to date indicate the following: (a) The GSF score can differentiate

TABLE 1
Calculating the Global Sexual Functioning Score

Male Item no.	Divide by	Female Item no.	Divide by
1	9	1	9
2	9	2	9
6	9	6	9
7	9	7	9
10	6	16	5
16	5	23*	5
18	6	24*	5
19	6	25*	5
22	6	26*	5
23*	5	27*	5
24*	5	29	6
25*	5	37*	5

Note. Score as follows: (a) convert scores to proportions, (b) sum proportions, and (c) divide by number of items. Although all items included in the global sexual functioning score are present in the original 28-item version, items have been renumbered in the current 46-item version.

*Responses equaling 6 are considered missing.

sexually well-functioning from poorly functioning men, and it is responsive to changes with therapy (Creti et al., 1987; Kalogeropoulos, 1991); (b) the GSF score was found to be logically and significantly related to scores on measures of sexual satisfaction, sexual repertoire, sexual self-efficacy, sexual drive, sexual knowledge, and liberal attitudes (Creti et al. 1987; Creti & Libman, 1989; Meana & Nunnink, 2006); and (c) the GSF score is sensitive to age differences in sexual functioning (Brown et al., 2005; Creti et al., 1987, Creti & Libman, 1989; Libman et al., 1989, Libman et al., 1991).

Female global sexual functioning. Data reported by Creti et al. (1988) indicate that (a) women with diagnosed sexual dysfunction had worse scores ($M = .68$, $SD = .17$) than women who were functioning well ($M = .49$, $SD = .14$), (b) that younger women (age 21–46) had better scores ($M = .46$, $SD = .03$) than older women (age greater than 64; $M = .62$, $SD = .16$), and (c) that female GSF scores were logically and significantly correlated with sexual harmony, sexual drive, diversity of sexual repertoire, and sexual satisfaction. Meana and Nunnink (2006) also found significant correlations with sexual satisfaction, fantasies, experiences, and liberal attitudes. The GSF score was also found to be related to the female's sexual efficacy expectations for her male partner (Creti & Libman, 1989).

Reissing, Binik, Khalif, Cohen, and Amsel (2003) found worse global sexual functioning scores in women with vaginismus and women with vulvar vestibulitis syndrome than in women with no pain ($M = 38.00$).

Bergeron et al. (2001) found that scores significantly improved from posttreatment to 6-month follow-up in a sample of females who underwent cognitive-behavioral therapy, electromyographic biofeedback, or vestibulectomy in the treatment of dyspareunia resulting from vulvar vestibulitis.

The GSF score has also been used to validate the Pelvic Organ Prolapse—Urinary Incontinence Sexual

Questionnaire (PISQ; Rogers, Kammerer-Doak, Villarreal, Coates, & Qualls, 2001) and its modified short form (Rogers, Coates, Kammerer-Doak, Khalsa, & Qualls, 2003), an instrument in urogynecology that is specifically designed to measure sexual function in women with pelvic organ prolapse or incontinence.

Psychometric properties for the male and female Global Sexual Functioning scores suggest that these provide a good index of the underlying construct. Even in the absence of norms, the score is useful in research and practice. It allows investigators to classify respondents in terms of level of overall sexual functioning by using a mean or median split.

Other Information

The 28-item version of the SHF has been translated into French (Formulaire d'Histoire Sexuelle) and Spanish (Ávila Escribano, Perez Madruga, Olazabal Ulacia, & Lopez Fidalgo, 2004).

Additional affiliations: Catherine S. Fichten, Dawson College, McGill University; William Brender, Concordia University; Eva Libman, McGill University.

References

Ávila Escribano, J. J., Perez Madruga, A., Olazabal Ulacia, J. C., & Lopez Fidalgo, J. (2004). Disfunciones sexuales en el alcoholismo. *Adicciones, 16*(4), 1–6.

Bergeron, S., Binik, Y. B., Khalifé, S., Pagidas, A., Glazer, H. I., Meana M., et al. (2001). A randomized comparison of group cognitive-behavioral therapy, surface electromyographic biofeedback, and vestibulectomy in the treatment of dyspareunia resulting from vulvar vestibulitis. *Pain, 91,* 297–306.

Brown, R., Balousek, S., Mundt, M., & Fleming, M. (2005). Methadone maintenance and male sexual dysfunction. *Journal of Addictive Diseases, 24*(2), 91–106.

Creti, L., Fichten, C. S., Amsel, R., Brender, W., Schover, L. R., Kalogeropoulos, D., et al. (1998). Global sexual functioning: A single summary score for Nowinski and LoPiccolo's Sexual History Form (SHF). In C. M. Davis, W. L. Yarber, R. Bauserman, G. Schreer, & S. L. Davis (Eds.), *Handbook of sexuality-related measures* (pp. 261–267). Thousand Oaks, CA: Sage.

Creti, L., Fichten, C. S., Libman, E., Amsel, R., & Brender, W. (1988, June). *Female sexual functioning: A global score for Nowinski and LoPiccolo's Sexual History Form.* Paper presented at the annual convention of the Canadian Psychological Association, Montreal. (Abstracted in *Canadian Psychology, 29*[2a], Abstract 164)

Creti, L., Fichten, C. S., Libman, E., Kalogeropoulos, D., & Brender, W. (1987, November). *A global score for the "Sexual History Form" and its effectiveness.* Paper presented at the 21st annual convention of the Association for Advancement of Behavior Therapy, Boston.

Creti, L., & Libman, E. (1989). Cognitions and sexual expression in the aging. *Journal of Sex and Marital Therapy, 15,* 83–101.

Desrosiers, M., Bergeron, S., Meana, M., Leclerc, B., Binik, Y. B., & Khalifé, S. (2008). Psychosexual characteristics of vestibulodynia couples: Partner solicitousness and hostility are associated with pain. *Journal of Sexual Medicine, 5,* 418–427.

Kalogeropoulos, D. (1991). *Vasoactive intracavernous pharmacotherapy for erectile dysfunction: Its effects on sexual, interpersonal, and psychological functioning.* Unpublished doctoral dissertation, Concordia University, Montreal.

Libman, E., Fichten, C. S., Creti, L., Weinstein, N., Amsel, R., & Brender, W. (1989). Transurethral prostatectomy: Differential effects of age category and presurgery sexual functioning on postprostatectomy sexual adjustment. *Journal of Behavioral Medicine, 12,* 469–485.

Libman, E., Fichten, C. S., Rothenberg, P., Creti, L., Weinstein, N., Amsel, R., et al. (1991). Prostatectomy and inguinal hernia repair: A comparison of the sexual consequences. *Journal of Sex and Marital Therapy, 17,* 27–34.

Meana, M., & Nunnink, S. E. (2006). Gender differences in the content of cognitive distraction during sex. *The Journal of Sex Research, 43,* 59–67.

Nowinski, J. K., & LoPiccolo, J. (1979). Assessing sexual behaviors in couples. *Journal of Sex and Marital Therapy, 5,* 225–243.

Petersen, R. W., Ung, K., Holland, C., & Quinlivana, J. A. (2005). The impact of molar pregnancy on psychological symptomatology, sexual function, and quality of life. *Gynecologic Oncology, 97,* 535–542.

Reissing, E. D., Binik, Y. M., Khalif, S., Cohen, D., & Amsel, R. (2003). Etiological correlates of vaginismus: Sexual and physical abuse, sexual knowledge, sexual self-schema, and relationship adjustment. *Journal of Sex and Marital Therapy, 29,* 47–59.

Rogers, R. G., Coates, K. W., Kammerer-Doak, D., Khalsa, E. S., & Qualls, E. C. (2003). A short form of the Pelvic Organ Prolapse/Urinary Incontinence Sexual Questionnaire (PISQ-12). *International Urogynecology Journal and Pelvic Floor Dysfunction, 14,* 164–168.

Rogers, R. G., Kammerer-Doak, D., Villarreal, A., Coates, K. W., & Qualls, E. C. (2001). A new instrument to measure sexual function in women with urinary incontinence or pelvic organ prolapse. *American Journal of Obstetrics and Gynecology, 184,* 552–558.

Schover, L. R., Friedman, J. M., Weiler, J., Heiman, J. R., & LoPiccolo, J. (1982). Multiaxial problem-oriented system for sexual dysfunctions: An alternative to *DSM-III. Archives of General Psychiatry, 39,* 614–619.

Schover, L. R., & Jensen, S. B. (1988). *Sexuality and chronic illness: A comprehensive approach.* New York: Guilford.

Weber, A. M., Walters, M. D., Schover, L. R., Church, J. M., & Piedmonte, M. R. (1999). Functional outcomes and satisfaction after abdominal hysterectomy. *American Journal of Obstetrics and Gynecology, 181,* 530–535.

Exhibit

Sexual History Form

Please circle the most appropriate response to each question.

1. How frequently do you and your mate have sexual intercourse or activity?
   1) more than once a day
   2) once a day
   3) 3 or 4 times a week
   4) twice a week
   5) once a week
   6) once every two weeks
   7) once a month
   8) less than once a month
   9) not at all

2. How frequently would you like to have sexual intercourse or activity?

   1) more than once a day
   2) once a day
   3) 3 or 4 times a week
   4) twice a week
   5) once a week

   6) once every two weeks
   7) once a month
   8) less than once a month
   9) not at all

3. Who usually initiates sexual intercourse or activity?

   1) I always do
   2) I usually do
   3) my mate and I initiate about equally often

   4) my mate usually does
   5) my mate always does

4. Who would you ideally like to initiate sexual intercourse or activity?

   1) myself, always
   2) myself, usually
   3) my mate and I equally often

   4) my mate, usually
   5) my mate, always

5. When your mate makes sexual advances, how do you usually respond?

   1) I usually accept with pleasure
   2) accept reluctantly

   3) often refuse
   4) usually refuse

6. How often do you experience sexual *desire* (this may include wanting to have sex, planning to have sex, feeling frustrated due to lack of sex, etc.)?

   1) more than once a day
   2) once a day
   3) 3 or 4 times a week
   4) twice a week
   5) once a week

   6) once every two weeks
   7) once a month
   8) less than once a month
   9) not at all

7. How often do you masturbate (bring yourself to orgasm in private)?

   1) more than once a day
   2) once a day
   3) 3 or 4 times a week
   4) twice a week
   5) once a week

   6) once every two weeks
   7) once a month
   8) less than once a month
   9) not at all

8. For how long do you and your mate usually engage in sexual foreplay (kissing, petting, etc.) before having intercourse?

   1) less than 1 minute
   2) 1 to 3 minutes
   3) 4 to 6 minutes
   4) 7 to 10 minutes

   5) 11 to 15 minutes
   6) 16 to 30 minutes
   7) 30 minutes to one hour

9. How long does intercourse usually last, from entry of the penis to the male's orgasm/climax?

   1) less than 1 minute
   2) 1 to 2 minutes
   3) 2 to 4 minutes
   4) 4 to 7 minutes
   5) 7 to 10 minutes

   6) 11 to 15 minutes
   7) 15 to 20 minutes
   8) 20 to 30 minutes
   9) more than 30 minutes

10. Does the male ever reach orgasm while he is trying to enter the vagina with his penis?

    1) never
    2) rarely (less than 10% of the time)
    3) seldom (less than 25% of the time)

    4) sometimes (50% of the time)
    5) usually (75% of the time)
    6) nearly always (over 90% of the time)

11. Do you feel that premature ejaculation (rapid climax) is a problem in your sexual relationship?

    1) yes

    2) no

12. How satisfied are you with the *variety of sexual activities* in your current sex life? (This includes the different types of kissing and caressing with a partner, different positions for intercourse, etc.)

1) extremely satisfied
2) moderately satisfied
3) slightly satisfied

4) slightly *unsatisfied*
5) moderately *unsatisfied*
6) extremely *unsatisfied*

13. Would you like your lovemaking to include *more*:

Breast caressing
Hand caressing of your genital area
Oral caressing (kissing) of your genital area
Different positions for intercourse

1) yes 2) no
1) yes 2) no
1) yes 2) no
1) yes 2) no

14. If you would like a certain kind of sexual caress or activity, which way do you *typically* let your partner know?

1) I wait to see if my partner will do what I like without my asking
2) I show my partner what I would like by moving their hand or changing my own position
3) I tell my partner exactly what I would like

15. How have you *typically* learned about your partner's sexual likes and dislikes?

1) From my partner telling me exactly what they want
2) From my partner moving my hand or changing their position to signal what they would like me to do
3) From watching my partner's reactions during sex
4) From intuition

16. When you have sex with your mate do you feel sexually aroused (e.g., feeling "turned on," pleasure, excitement)?

1) nearly always (over 90% of the time)
2) usually (about 75% of the time)
3) sometimes (about 50% of the time)

4) seldom (about 25% of the time)
5) never

17. When you have sex with your mate, do you have negative emotional reactions (e.g., fear, disgust, shame or guilt)?

1) never
2) rarely (less than 10% of the time)
3) seldom (less than 25% of the time

4) sometimes (50% of the time)
5) usually (75% of the time)
6) nearly always (over 90% of the time)

18. Does the male have any trouble getting an erection before intercourse begins?

1) never
2) rarely (less than 10% of the time)
3) seldom (less than 25% of the time)

4) sometimes (50% of the time)
5) usually (75% of the time)
6) nearly always (over 90% of the time)

19. Does the male have any trouble keeping an erection once intercourse has begun?

1) never
2) rarely (less than 10% of the time)
3) seldom (less than 25% of the time)

4) sometimes (50% of the time)
5) usually (75% of the time)
6) nearly always (over 90% of the time)

20. If the male loses an erection, when does that usually happen?

1) before penetrating to start intercourse
2) while trying to penetrate
3) after penetration, during the thrusting of intercourse
4) not applicable, losing erections is not a problem

21. What is the male's *typical* degree of erection during sexual activity?

1) 0 to 20% of a full erection
2) 20% to 40% of a full erection
3) 40% to 60% of a full erection

4) 60% to 80% of a full erection
5) 80% to 100% of a full erection

22. Does the male ejaculate (climax) without having a full, hard erection?

1) never
2) rarely (less than 10% of the time)
3) seldom (less than 25% of the time)

4) sometimes (50% of the time)
5) usually (75% of the time)
6) nearly always (over 90% of the time)

23. If you try, is it possible to reach orgasm (sensation of climax) through masturbation?
   1) nearly always (over 90% of the time)   4) seldom (about 25% of the time)
   2) usually (about 75% of the time)   5) never
   3) sometimes (about 50% of the time)   6) have never tried to

24. If you try, is it possible for you to reach orgasm (sensation of climax) through having your genitals caressed by your mate?
   1) nearly always (over 90% of the time)   4) seldom (about 25% of the time)
   2) usually (about 75% of the time)   5) never
   3) sometimes (about 50% of the time)   6) have never tried to

25. If you try, is it possible for you to reach orgasm (sensation of climax) through sexual intercourse?
   1) nearly always (over 90% of the time)   4) seldom (about 25% of the time)
   2) usually (about 75% of the time)   5) never
   3) sometimes (about 50% of the time)   6) have never tried to

26. Can you reach orgasm (sensation of climax) through stimulation of your genitals by an electric vibrator or any other means (i.e., running water, rubbing with some object, etc.)?
   1) nearly always (over 90% of the time)   4) seldom (about 25% of the time)
   2) usually (about 75% of the time)   5) never
   3) sometimes (about 50% of the time)   6) have never tried to

27. (*Women only*) Can you reach orgasm during sexual intercourse if, at the same time, your genitals are being caressed (by yourself or your mate with a vibrator, etc.)?
   1) nearly always (over 90% of the time)   4) seldom (about 25% of the time)
   2) usually (about 75% of the time)   5) never
   3) sometimes (about 50% of the time)   6) have never tried to

28. Have you noticed a change in the intensity and pleasure of your orgasm?
   1) much more intense and pleasurable than in the past   4) somewhat less intense and pleasurable than in the past
   2) somewhat more intense and pleasurable than in the past   5) much less intense and pleasurable than in the past
   3) the same as in the past

29. Is the female's vagina so "dry" or "tight" that intercourse cannot occur?
   1) never   4) sometimes (50% of the time)
   2) rarely (less than 10% of the time)   5) usually (75% of the time)
   3) seldom (less than 25% of the time   6) nearly always (over 90% of the time)

30. Do you feel pain in your genitals (sexual parts) during intercourse?
   1) never   4) sometimes (50% of the time)
   2) rarely (less than 10% of the time)   5) usually (75% of the time)
   3) seldom (less than 25% of the time)   6) nearly always (over 90% of the time)

31. How often does pain (genital or nongenital) interfere with your ability to feel sexual pleasure?
   1) never   4) sometimes (50% of the time)
   2) rarely (less than 10% of the time)   5) usually (75% of the time)
   3) seldom (less than 25% of the time)   6) nearly always (over 90% of the time)

32. Have you noticed a change in the sensitivity to touch of your genitals?
   1) much more sensitive than in the past   4) somewhat less sensitive than in the past
   2) somewhat more sensitive than in the past   5) much less sensitive than in the past
   3) about as sensitive as in the past

33. *Overall*, how satisfactory to you is your sexual relationship with your mate?
   1) extremely *un*satisfactory   4) slightly satisfactory
   2) moderately *un*satisfactory   5) moderately satisfactory
   3) slightly *un*satisfactory   6) extremely satisfactory

34. *Overall*, how satisfactory do you think your sexual relationship is to your mate?
   1) extremely *un*satisfactory
   2) moderately *un*satisfactory
   3) slightly *un*satisfactory
   4) slightly satisfactory
   5) moderately satisfactory
   6) extremely satisfactory

35. Do you feel that your partner plays a part in causing a problem in your sex life?
   1) yes
   2) no

36. If your lovemaking does not go well, how does your partner usually react?
   1) accepting and understanding
   2) frustrated or annoyed
   3) anxious and blaming self
   4) neutral or uncaring

37. (*Women only, men go on to Question 38*) When you have sex with your mate (including foreplay and intercourse) do you notice some of these things happening: your breathing and pulse speed up, wetness in your vagina, pleasurable sensations in your breasts and genitals?
   1) nearly always (over 90% of the time)
   2) usually (about 75% of the time)
   3) sometimes (about 50% of the time)
   4) seldom (about 25% of the time)
   5) never
   6) have never tried to

38. (*Men only*) How often do you wake from sleep with a firm erection (including times when you wake up needing to urinate)?
   1) daily
   2) 3–4 times a week
   3) 1–2 times a week
   4) once every 2 weeks
   5) once a month
   6) less than once a month
   7) never

39. (*Men only*) How often do you wake from sleep with a partial (semisoft) erection?
   1) daily
   2) 3–4 times a week
   3) 1–2 times a week
   4) once every 2 weeks
   5) once a month
   6) less than once a month
   7) never

40. (*Men only*) How often are you able to get and keep a firm erection in your own masturbation (self-touch in private)?
   1) nearly always, over 90% of the time
   2) usually, 75% of the time
   3) sometimes, 50% of the time
   4) seldom, less than 25% of the time
   5) rarely, less than 10% of the time
   6) never
   7) have not tried masturbation in the past 6 months

41. (*Men only*) What is your *typical* degree of erection during masturbation (self-touch in private?
   1) 0% to 20% of a full erection
   2) 20% to 40% of a full erection
   3) 40% to 60% of a full erection
   4) 60% to 80% of a full erection
   5) 80% to 100% of a full erection

42. (*Men only*) Do you feel your erect penis has an abnormal curve to it, or have you noticed a lump or "knot" on your penis?
   1) yes
   2) no

43. (*Men only*) Do you believe your penis is abnormally small?
   1) yes
   2) no

44. (*Men only*) How does the amount of ejaculate (liquid or semen) now compare to the amount you ejaculated in the past?
   1) much greater than in the past
   2) somewhat greater than in the past
   3) about the same as in the past
   4) somewhat less than in the past
   5) much less than in the past
   6) I do not know

45. (*Men only*) Do you ever have the sensation of orgasm (climax) without any ejaculation of fluid?
   1) never
   2) rarely, less than 10% of the time
   3) seldom, less than 25% of the time
   4) sometimes, about 50% of the time
   5) usually, about 75% of the time
   6) nearly always, over 90% of the time

46. *(Men only)* Do you ever have pain and/or burning during or after ejaculation?

1) never
2) rarely, less than 10% of the time
3) seldom, less than 25% of the time
4) sometimes, about 50% of the time

5) usually, about 75% of the time
6) nearly always, over 90% of the time
7) I do not ejaculate

Note. Items 1, 2, 6, 7, 10, 16, 18, 19, 22, 23, 24, 25, 26, 27, 29, and 37 are used to compute the global sexual functioning score.

Derogatis Interview for Sexual Functioning

LEONARD R. DEROGATIS,[1] *Clinical Psychometric Research, Inc.*

The Derogatis Interview for Sexual Functioning (DISF) is a brief semistructured interview designed to provide an estimate of the quality of an individual's current sexual functioning in quantitative terms. The DISF represents quality of current sexual functioning in a multidomain format, which to some degree parallels the phases of the sexual response cycle (Masters & Johnson, 1966). The 26 interview items of the DISF are arranged into five domains of sexual functioning: I. Sexual Cognition/Fantasy, II. Sexual Arousal, III. Sexual Behavior/Experience, IV. Orgasm, and V. Sexual Drive/Relationship. In addition, the DISF total score is computed, summarizing quality of sexual functioning across the five primary DISF domains. There are distinct gender-keyed versions for men and women.

In addition to the DISF interview, there is a distinct self-report version of the test known as the DISF-SR. The DISF-SR is also composed of 26 items and was designed to be as comparable to the DISF interview as possible. With slight modifications in format, the DISF-SR may also be utilized to gain evaluations of the patient's sexual performance by the patient's spouse.

The DISF and DISF-SR were developed to address the unmet need for a set of brief, gender-keyed, multi-dimensional outcome measures that would represent the status of an individual's current sexual functioning, and do so at multiple levels of interpretation. The DISF/DISF-SR are designed to be interpreted at three distinct levels: the *discrete item* level (e.g., "A full erection upon awakening," "Your ability to have an orgasm,") the *functional domain* level (e.g., sexual arousal score), and the *global summary* level (e.g., DISF/DISF-SR total score). Because the DISF interview and the DISF-SR self-report inventory are matched on an almost item-for-item basis, clinician and patient assessments of the patient's quality of sexual functioning may be obtained in both raw and standardized score formats. Both instruments may be used repeatedly throughout efficacy or effectiveness trials, or may be implemented solely at pre- and post-intervention without significant "practice" effects or loss of validity.

Norms have been developed for both the DISF and the DISF/SR, based in each case on several hundred nonpatient community respondents. The norms are gender-keyed (i.e., separate norms for men and women) and are represented as standardized scores in terms of area *t*-scores. The area standardized score possesses distinct advantages over the simple linear transformation in that the former provides accurate percentile equivalents (i.e., *t*-score of 30 = 2nd centile; *t*-score of 40 = 16th centile; *t*-score of 50 = 50th centile; *t*-score of 60 = 84th centile; *t*-score of 70 = 98th centile, etc.). This important characteristic is not true of linear *t*-scores except when the underlying raw score distribution is perfectly normal. In addition to enabling accurate comparisons across respondents, area *t*-scores also facilitate meaningful comparisons of strengths and weaknesses within a respondent's profile of sexual functioning. A patient may reveal a relatively unremarkable profile with the exception of a profound decrement in a single functional domain, or may show a low-grade degradation of performance across multiple areas of functioning. Because DISF/DISF-SR domain scores are available in an equivalent standardized metric, such evaluations can help pinpoint the nature and extent of sexual dysfunctions.

Response Mode and Timing

The DISF and the DISF-SR are each comprised of 26 items. In the case of the former, items are cast in the format of a semistructured interview, structured via 4-point Likert-type

[1]Address correspondence to Leonard R. Derogatis, Johns Hopkins Department of Psychiatry and Behavioral Sciences—Center for Sexual Medicine at Sheppard Pratt, Baltimore, MD 21285; e-mail: LDerogatis@sheppardpratt.org

scales. The items of the DISF-SR are also represented as 4-point Likert-type scales.

The DISF interview requires between 15 to 20 minutes to complete. Time requirements for the DISF-SR are similar to the DISF; however, in most contexts the self-report version typically requires a few minutes less than the interview. Time requirements drop noticeably for both versions on successive administrations, such as in clinical efficacy or effectiveness trials, in which the test is administered sequentially.

Reliability and Validity

The DISF and DISF-SR have both demonstrated favorable profiles of psychometric characteristics. Internal consistency coefficients for the subscales range from .74 to .80. Test-retest correlations over a 1-week interval are all above .80, and interrater correlations range from .84 to .92.

An important validity demonstration for multi-dimensional or multidomain psychological outcome measures concerns the subtest intercorrelation matrix, and domain score-total score correlation vector. The pattern of these correlations represents a central psychometric characteristic of the test that relates to almost all discernable aspects of construct validity (Messick, 1995). If correlations between dimension scores are high, concerns may be raised that operational definitions of the domain constructs are redundant. If domain scores do not correlate at least moderately with the total score, then the possibility exists that the domain constructs (e.g., Sexual Arousal, Orgasm), as operationally defined by the test items, are not valid components of the higher-order, more general construct (e.g., Quality of Sexual Functioning). A theoretical optimum would find correlations between domains near zero, with each domain score showing a moderately high correlation with the total score. In such an ideal design, each domain would contribute independent true variance to the total score, with minimum redundancy or overlap.

Subtest intercorrelation matrices of the DISF/DISF-SR have been constructed based on two "normal" and one sexually dysfunctional sample. In all cases the mean interdomain correlation coefficients are relatively low (i.e., .23 to .39), whereas the average domain-total correlations for the three samples range from .60 to .71. This pattern of subtest correlations begins to approach the optimal and strongly confirms that DISF domains are contributing relatively independent variance to the DISF total score.

Much of the clinical research done with the DISF/DISF-SR has involved corporate-sponsored clinical drug trials. Although preliminary data from these studies indicated that the tests were highly sensitive to sexual dysfunction, and to a broad range of therapeutic agents, most of the data were proprietary and have not been made generally available. In two studies that have been published (Zinreich et al., 1990a, 1990b), the DISF was utilized with males suffering from prostate cancer about to undergo a course of radiation therapy. At the time of initial cancer diagnosis, the DISF was utilized in a logistic regression model as a screen for impotence, with detailed clinical evaluation as the ultimate criterion. In this study, sensitivity was found to be 86%, specificity was 80%, and the predictive value of a positive was 86%. Subsequent to treatment, patients were assigned to three functional categories on the basis of clinical evaluation: (a) totally functional, (b) marginally functional, and (c) impotent. Scores on the five domains of the DSFI were significantly different across the three groups, with mean DISF total scores being 48.2, 21.5, and 14.0, respectively. In this study, with a complex sample of patients, the DISF did a superior job of identifying those individuals who were dysfunctional prior to treatment, and it validly reflected differences in quality of sexual functioning subsequent to therapeutic intervention.

Other studies utilizing the DISF/DISF-SR have been conducted, and several new norms (e.g., geriatric, gay men) were in the process of being developed, however this information has not been updated.

Other Information

The instruments are available in English, French, Italian, Spanish, Dutch, Danish, and Norwegian. The DISF and DISF-SR are distributed exclusively by Clinical Psychometric Research, Inc. (www.derogatis-tests.com).

References

Derogatis, L. R. (1996). *Derogatis Interview For Sexual Functioning (DISF/DISF-SR): Preliminary scoring, procedures & administration manual.* Baltimore, MD: Clinical Psychometric Research Inc.

Masters, W. H., & Johnson, V. E. (1966). *Human sexual response.* Boston: Little, Brown.

Messick, S. (1995). Validity of psychological assessment: Validation of inferences from person's responses and performances as scientific inquiry into score meaning. *American Psychologist, 50,* 741–749.

Zinreich, E. Derogatis, L. R., Herpst, J., Auvil, G., Piantodosi, S., & Order, S. E. (1990a). Pre- and posttreatment evaluation of sexual function in patients with adenocarcinoma of the prostate. *International Journal of Radiation Oncology & Biological Physics, 19,* 729–732.

Zinreich, E. Derogatis, L. R., Herpst, J., Auvil, G., Piantodosi, S., & Order, S. E. (1990b). Pretreatment evaluation of sexual function in patients with adenocarcinoma of the prostate. *International Journal of Radiation Oncology & Biological Physics, 19,* 1001–1004.

Derogatis Sexual Functioning Inventory

LEONARD R. DEROGATIS,[1] *Clinical Psychometric Research, Inc.*

The Derogatis Sexual Functioning Inventory (DSFI) measures constructs believed to be fundamental to successful sexual functioning (e.g., drive, body image, sexual satisfaction) and, in addition, measures several basic indicators of general well-being (e.g., affects balance and psychological distress).

Description

The DSFI is an "omnibus" self-report inventory designed to measure the quality of the *current sexual functioning* of an individual. The DSFI is multidimensional in nature because the comprehensive study of sexual functioning has revealed it to be a highly multidetermined behavior. Although apparently straightforward, successful human sexual functioning rests on a complex interplay of endocrine, emotional, cognitive, and experiential factors that preclude the simple enumeration of sexual episodes, or orgasms, as meaningful forms of measuring the quality of sexual functioning.

The individual respondent is the basis for evaluation by the DSFI in part because it represents the most parsimonious and straightforward unit to work with, and also because, regardless of context, quality of sexual functioning is ultimately appreciated by the individual. *Current sexual functioning* is the conceptual continuum for the DSFI because it comes closest to the central evaluative question in the clinical assessment of sexual disorder: "What is the current level and nature of the patient's sexual functioning?" By quantifying the principal dimensions of the patient's sexual experience in profile form, an insight is gained into both the nature and magnitude of the individual's sexual dysfunction.

The DSFI is comprised of 10 substantive dimensions that are judged to reflect the principal components of sexual behavior. The conceptual basis for the DSFI was outlined by Derogatis in 1976, and several subsequent monographs have been published on the instrument (Derogatis, 1980; Derogatis & Melisaratos, 1979). Of the 10 subtests constituting the DSFI, two of them, Psychological Symptoms and Affects are themselves complete, multidimensional tests. The Brief Symptom Inventory (BSI; Derogatis, 1993) and the Derogatis Affects Balance Scale (ABS; Derogatis, 1975; Derogatis & Rutigliano, 1996) provide measurement of psychological distress and mood and affects, respectively.

Since its introduction in the mid-1970s, the DSFI has been utilized as an outcome measure in multiple empirical studies of sexual functioning (see references). In most instances, dimension or global score measures from the instrument have proven sufficiently sensitive to discriminate differences in the groups under study. Discriminations have ranged from relatively large effect sizes (e.g., comparisons of gender-dysphoric patients with normal heterosexuals) to much more demanding discriminations (e.g., sexual functioning in diabetic vs. normal women, inflatable vs. noninflatable prostheses in penile implant surgery).

Response Mode

The DSFI is composed of 254 items, arranged into 10 subtests. Formats vary from simple endorsements of *yes* or *no* to multiple-point Likert-type scales.

DSFI Dimensions and Global Score Descriptions

Information. The Information subtest consists of a 26-item subtest in true-false format that measures the level of accurate information possessed by the respondent concerning the physiology, anatomy, and other aspects of sexual functioning. A single information score is determined as the sum of the number of correct responses.

Experiences. The Experiences subtest consists of a list of 24 sexual behaviors ranging from very fundamental behaviors to various forms of sexual intercourse and oral-genital activities. The respondent indicates which behaviors he/she has experienced lifetime, and which experiences have occurred during the past 60 days. The Experiences score is the sum of lifetime experiences.

Drive. The Drive subtest is a composite summary measure of libidinal erotic interests expressed in the five behavioral domains of sexual intercourse, masturbation, kissing and petting, sexual fantasy, and ideal frequency of intercourse. The respondent indicates the frequencies of these behaviors during the current period. A single Drive score is developed by summing across domains.

Attitudes. Based upon work showing liberal and conservative sexual attitudes to be predictive of quality of sexual functioning, the Attitudes subtest is comprised of 30 items (15 liberal items and 15 conservative items) represented on 5-point Likert-type scales. The respondent indicates the degree to which he/she is in agreement with each item. Liberal, conservative, and total attitude scores are generated.

[1]Address correspondence to Leonard R. Derogatis, Johns Hopkins Department of Psychiatry and Behavioral Sciences—Center for Sexual Medicine at Sheppard Pratt, Baltimore, MD 21285; e-mail: LDerogatis@sheppardpratt.org

Psychological Symptoms. Psychological distress is measured by the 53 items of the Brief Symptom Inventory (BSI). Each symptom of the BSI is represented on a 5-point scale from *not at all* (0) *to extremely* (4). Scores are summed across items to achieve a single Symptoms score. The BSI may optionally be scored for the nine dimensions (e.g., Depression, Anxiety) and global scores that underlie the items of the BSI.

Affects. The Affects subtest is also a complete multi-dimensional test termed the Derogatis Affects Balance Scale (DABS). The DABS measures affect and mood through 40 adjective items endorsed by the respondent. Twenty items represent positive affects, and 20 items reflect negative affects. Scores include a Positive Affects total, a Negative Affects total and the overall Affects Balance Index. The latter is used as the affects measure for the DSFI.

Gender Role Definition. Consistent with the concept that masculinity and femininity are components of all individuals' gender role definitions, the two primary components of gender role are each measured in terms of 15 adjective items that the respondent endorses in varying degrees. A Masculinity score, a Femininity score, and a Gender Role Definition score are determined.

Fantasy. This subtest consists of 20 major sexual themes that have been culled from research on normal sexual fantasies as well as fantasies arising from clinical variations on routine sexual behaviors. The Fantasy score consists of a simple summation of the items endorsed.

Body Image. Body image has been demonstrated to be an integral aspect of self-concept and, as such, is an important determinant of successful sexual functioning. It is measured in the DSFI in terms of 15 items, 10 common and 5 gender-keyed, that reflect the individual's level of appreciation of his/her body. A single Body Image score is developed.

Sexual Satisfaction. The Sexual Satisfaction subtest is itself multidimensional in nature, being comprised of a number of distinct components (e.g., frequency of intercourse, quality of communication, quality of orgasm). Ten true-false items comprise the Satisfaction subtest, each reflecting whether the respondent is satisfied with that specific aspect of his/her sexual functioning. A single Satisfaction score is calculated as a sum of endorsements indicating satisfaction with a particular component.

SFI: The DSFI total score. The Sexual Functioning Index (SFI) is the total or global summary score of the DSFI. It is calculated as a direct unweighted linear combination of the 10 subtest or principal dimension scores. Because subtest scores are calculated along very different score continua, and some are gender-keyed (i.e., distinct for men and women), subtest scores are first transformed to area *t*-scores ($\mu = 50$; $SD = 10$) before being summed to achieve

the SFI. Because the transformation is a normalizing, area (under the curve) type, the actuarial characteristics of the resulting standardized distribution are retained.

The Global Sexual Satisfaction Index (GSSI). The GSSI is the second global measure of the DSFI, and it is quite different in nature from the SFI or DSFI total score. Whereas the DSFI total score reveals the respondent's quality of sexual functioning in psychometric terms, the GSSI reflects the individual's *subjective* perception of his/her sexual behavior. The GSSI represents quality of sexual functioning on a 9-point scale anchored at the lower extreme by 0, *could not be worse* to 8, *could not be better* at the upper limit. Each scale point is characterized by a descriptive phrase, and the respondent is provided an opportunity to globally summarize his/her perception of the quality of sexual behavior in straightforward terms.

Normative Population. Norms for the DSFI were developed based on a sample of 230 individuals in attendance at university continuing education classes. The majority of the sample were White (80%) and middle-aged, ($M = 32$) with some college education. Approximately 60% of the sample were married at the time of assessment, with the majority (75%) coming from middle-class and upper-middle-class backgrounds.

Reliability and Validity

Published studies by both the author of the scale and numerous other investigators suggest the DSFI is highly reliable and is a valid measure of the construct of sexual functioning. Derogatis and Melisaratos (1979) reported internal consistency reliability coefficients based on an *N* of 325 between .60 and .97, and test-retest coefficients across a 14-day interval ranging predominantly from the high .70s to the low .90s. Howell et al. (1987) also reported test-retest coefficients over a 14-day period, and all coefficients were $\geq .70$. Over four dozen published studies currently exist using the DSFI as a measure of functional discrimination and outcomes in a broad variety of medical treatment populations (see references). The majority show the DSFI to be highly sensitive to naturally occurring and disease-induced interference with sexual functioning, as well as positive treatment effects.

Other Information

The DSFI is available in Arabic, Chinese, English, French, French Canadian, Indian, Korean, Norwegian, Spanish, and Turkish. The DSFI is distributed exclusively by Clinical Psychometric Research, Inc. (www.derogatis-tests.com).

References

Conte, H. R. (1989). Development and use of self-report techniques for assessing sexual function: A review and critique. *Archives of Sexual Behavior, 12*, 555–576.

Derogatis, L. R. (1975). *Derogatis Sexual Functioning Inventory (DSFI): Preliminary scoring manual*. Baltimore, MD: Clinical Psychometric Research Inc.

Derogatis, L. R., Meyer, J. K., & Dupkin, C. N. (1976). Discrimination of organic versus psychogenic impotence with the DSFI (Derogatis Sexual Functioning Inventory). *Journal of Sex & Marital Therapy*, 2, 229–240.

Derogatis, L. R. (1980). Psychological assessment of psychosexual functioning. In J. K. Meyer (Ed.), *The Psychiatric Clinics of North America Symposium on Sexuality* (pp. 113–131). Philadelphia: Saunders.

Derogatis, L. R. (1993). *Brief Symptom Inventory: Administration, scoring, and procedures manual* (3rd ed.). Minneapolis, MN: National Computer Systems.

Derogatis, L. R., & Rutigliano, P. J. (1996). Derogatis Affects Balance Scale. In B. Spiker (Ed.), *Quality of life and pharmacoeconomics*

in clinical trials (2nd ed., pp. 160–177). Philadelphia: Lippincott-Raven.

Derogatis, L. R., Lopez, M. C., & Zinzeletta, E. M. (1988). Clinical applications of the DSFI in the assessment of sexual dysfunctions. In R. Brown & E. Roberts (Eds.), *Advances in the understanding and treatment of sexual disorders*. New York: PNA Publishing.

Derogatis, L. R., & Melisaratos, N. (1979). The DSFI: A multidimensional measure of sexual functioning. *Journal of Sex and Marital Therapy*, 5, 244–281.

Derogatis, L. R., Schmidt, C. W., Fagan, P. J., & Wise, T. N. (1989). Subtypes of anorgasmia via mathematical taxonomy. *Psychosomatics*, 30, 166–173.

Howell, J. R., Reynolds, C. F., Thase, M. E., Frank, E., Jennings, J. R., Houck, P. R., et al. (1987). Assessment of sexual function, interest, and activity in depressed men. *Journal of Affective Disorders*, 13, 61–66.

Garos Sexual Behavior Inventory

SHEILA GAROS,[1] *Texas Tech University*

The Garos Sexual Behavior Inventory (GSBI; Garos, 2009; Garos & Stock, 1998a, 1998b) is designed to assist forensic specialists and mental health professionals in making assessments and treatment decisions about individuals with problems related to sexuality and sexual behavior. The GSBI's subscale scores can be used to evaluate the cognitive, affective, and behavioral dimensions of an individual's overall sexual adjustment. The GSBI has been used effectively with clinical populations known to have difficulty with sexuality and sexual behavior, such as victims of sexual abuse, individuals with substance abuse problems, those with compulsive sexual behaviors, individuals with paraphilic interests (Garos & Stock, 1998b), and forensic populations (Garos, Bleckley, Beggan, & Frizzell, 2004). Yet the GSBI is sufficiently versatile that it can also be used for couples counseling to uncover differences in sexual values, feelings, and comfort levels.

Description

The first objective in development of the GSBI was to develop a conceptual model that would act as the basis for the investigation of constructs underlying disorders of sexual frequency and control. With consultation from experts in the field, a series of rationally derived item elimination procedures was instituted to identify items that best described dimensions of the constructs of interest. To evaluate the adequacy of the conceptually derived model, initial items on the GSBI were subjected to a principle components factor analysis using the varimax procedure.

In a second study, the 70-item GSBI was subjected to a maximum likelihood factor analysis with oblique rotation of the factor structure to confirm the conceptual dimensions believed to underlie the GSBI. The GSBI consists of four main scales, and three masking scales designed to reduce the potential for defensive responding, as well as an Inconsistent Responding index.

Main scales

- Discordance: Overall sexual adjustment; shame, fear, internal conflict about sexual behavior and interests
- Sexual Obsession: Preoccupation with sex and sexual stimuli
- Permissiveness: Attitudes and values about sex—conservative or unconventional
- Sexual Stimulation: Level of comfort with sexual arousal

Masking Scales

- Sexual Control Difficulties
- Sexual Excitability
- Sexual Insecurity

Response Mode and Timing

The GSBI can be completed in just 20 to 30 minutes. Items are written at a sixth-grade reading level and are easy to understand and answer. Respondents indicate the extent of

---

[1]Address correspondence to Sheila Garos, Psychology Department, Texas Tech University, Lubbock, TX 79409-2051; e-mail: sheila.garos@ttu.edu

their agreement on a 5-point Likert scale ranging from 1 (*Strongly Disagree*) to 5 (*Strongly Agree*). An AutoScore Form is designed to protect the privacy of respondents. Test items do *not* appear on the AutoScore Form. Instead, they are printed on a separate reusable Administration Card, thereby ensuring that sensitive information remains confidential.

Scoring

The GSBI generates normalized *T*-scores for the main and masking scales, making it easy to compare scores across scales and across tests. Normative data are based on a nonclinical group, spanning ages 17 to 104, with roughly equal numbers of males and females. In addition, the test manual provides average scores for males, females, and clinical and correctional subgroups (sex offenders, substance abusers, and sexual addicts). It has not been found useful to obtain a total score on the GSBI, given that the subscales are relatively independent, representing different constructs of interest.

Reliability

In Study 1 ($N = 500$; Garos & Stock, 1998b), internal reliability coefficients for the GSBI subscales for females were .75 for Sexual Obsession, .73 for Permissiveness, .74 for Sexual Stimulation, and .80 for Discordance. For males the coefficients were .72 for Sexual Obsession, .66 for Permissiveness, .67 for Sexual Stimulation, and .85 for Discordance. In Study 2 ($N = 1,000$; Garos & Stock, 1998a), internal reliability coefficients for the total sample were .80 Sexual Obsession, .70 Permissiveness, .72 Sexual Stimulation, and .82 Discordance.

The three masking scales have reported alpha reliabilities of Control (8 items, alpha = .85), Excitement (7 items, alpha = .82), and Insecurity (6 items, alpha = .74; Garos, 2009).

In Study 2 ($N = 1,000$; Garos & Stock, 1998b) the following test-retest reliability coefficients for a subset of participants were reported: .62 on the Permissiveness subscale ($n = 53$), .84 on the Sexual Obsession subscale ($n = 53$), .72 for the Discordance subscale ($n = 54$) and .79 on the Sexual Stimulation ($n = 52$) subscale. All results were significant at the $p < .001$ level. The time between administrations was 19 days.

Validity

Factorial validity for the GSBI was established through equivalence of factor structures and item retention in Studies 1 and 2 (Garos & Stock, 1998a, 1998b). The final factor structure obtained in Study 1 was replicated for males and females, and for the total sample in Study 2. To evaluate the discriminant and convergent validity of the GSBI, correlations were computed to determine the independence of GSBI subscales with related but concep-

tually distinct subscales of other behavioral and psychological measures (Garos & Stock, 1998a). These measures included the Sexual Addiction Screening Test (Carnes, 1992), the Sexuality Scale (Snell & Papini, 1989), the Zuckerman-Kuhlman Personality Questionnaire (Zuckerman, Kuhlman, Joireman, Teta, & Kraft, 1993), the Sexual Opinion Survey (Fisher, Byrne, White, & Kelley, 1988), the Beck Depression Inventory (Beck, Ward, Mendelson, Mock, & Erbaugh, 1961), and the Rosenberg Self-Esteem Scale (Rosenberg, 1962). All scales correlated as predicted ranging from .05 to .52.

A validity study was conducted with prisoners to determine how well the associated affective and cognitive characteristics of intrapsychic conflict could distinguish between incarcerated sex offenders and incarcerated nonsex offenders (Garos et al., 2004). The Discordance subscale emerged as the most significant predictor variable between sex offenders and nonoffenders (Wilks' $\lambda = .553$) $F(1,184) = 148.63, p < .001$. A discriminant function analysis was conducted to establish the GSBI's ability to correctly predict classification of group membership. For sex offenders, 80.6% were correctly classified, as were 88.3% of nonsex offenders. Overall, 84.2% of cases were correctly classified. In the cross-validation sample, results for placement in group membership for sex offenders remained the same (80.6%), whereas 87.2% of nonsex offenders were correctly classified. For this sample, an overall 83.7% of cases were correctly classified. These results indicated significant improvement over base rates, with the Discordance subscale emerging as the strongest of the four predictors. In the same study, a logistic regression was conducted as a second index of the GSBI's ability to predict group membership. A positive predictive value of 82.8% was obtained, which was a significant improvement relative to the base rate of cases in the sex offender category (53%), again with Discordance emerging as the most significant predictor. To test whether the Permissiveness, Sexual Stimulation, and Sexual Obsession subscales contributed significantly to the predictive ability of the GSBI, a logistic regression was performed with the omission of the Discordance subscale. Although the percentage of correctly classified cases decreased with the omission of Discordance relative to the base rate of cases in the sex offender category (52%), a positive predictive value of 68.4% represented a 17.6% improvement over chance.

In a study of inpatients receiving experiential therapy for sexual addiction (Klontz, Garos & Klontz, 2005), two subscales of the GSBI were sensitive to a main effect of time. Male and female patients reported less sexual preoccupation and less discordance from pretreatment to posttreatment. Changes were stable at 6-month follow-up.

Other Information

Copyright: Western Psychological Services. Testing materials are available from Western Psychological Services,

12031 Wilshire Blvd., Los Angeles, CA 90025-1251;
Telephone: (800) 648–8857; www.wpspublish.com

References

Beck, A. T., Ward, A. T., Mendelson, C. H., Mock, M., & Erbaugh, J. (1961). An inventory for measuring depression. *Archives of General Psychiatry, 4,* 53–63.

Carnes, P. (1992). *Out of the shadows: Understanding sexual addiction* (2nd ed.). Center City, MN: Hazelden.

Fisher, W. A., Byrne, D., White, L. A., & Kelley, K. (1988). Erotophobia-erotophilia as a dimension of personality. *The Journal of Sex Research, 25,* 123–151.

Garos, S. (2009). *Garos Sexual Behavior Inventory* test manual. Los Angeles: Western Psychological Services.

Garos, S., Bleckley, K. M., Beggan, J. K., & Frizzell, J. (2004). The relationship between intrapsychic conflict and deviant sexual behavior in sex offenders. *Journal of Offender Rehabilitation, 40,* 23–38.

Garos, S., & Stock, W. A. (1998a). Investigating the discriminant validity and differentiating capability of the Garos Sexual Behavior Index. *Sexual Addiction and Compulsivity: The Journal of Treatment and Prevention, 5,* 251–267.

Garos, S., & Stock, W. A. (1998b). Measuring disorders of sexual frequency and control: The Garos Sexual Behavior Index. *Sexual Addiction and Compulsivity: The Journal of Treatment and Prevention, 5,* 159–177.

Klontz, B., Garos, S., & Klontz, P. (2005). The effectiveness of multimodal experiential therapy in the treatment of sexual addiction. *Sexual Addiction and Compulsivity: The Journal of Treatment and Prevention, 12,* 275–294.

Rosenberg, M. (1962). *The Rosenberg Self-Esteem Scale.* Department of Sociology, University of Maryland, College Park.

Snell, W., & Papini, D. (1989). The sexuality scale: An instrument to measure sexual esteem, sexual depression and sexual preoccupation. *The Journal of Sex Research, 26,* 756–763.

Zuckerman, M., Kuhlman, M., Joireman, J., Teta, P., & Kraft, M. (1993). A comparison of three structural models for personality: The Big Three, the Big Five, and the Alternative Five. *Journal of Personality and Social Psychology, 65,* 757–768.

Exhibit

Garos Sexual Behavior Inventory (Sample Items)[a]

Main Scales

Discordance Subscale

I feel uncomfortable about my sexual practices.
I am afraid I am not sexually attractive enough.

Sexual Obsession

It feels impossible to stop masturbating.
Once I am aroused it is difficult not to masturbate or have sex.

Permissiveness

Birth control should be readily available to young people.
Women's sexual advances should be subtle.

Sexual Stimulation

I like not wearing underwear.
I enjoy being aroused by my sexual thoughts and feelings.

Masking Scales

Control

When I wake up from sexual dreams, I like to masturbate.
Sexual thoughts overpower my better judgment.

Excitement

As a child, I was more interested in sex than my friends were.
The smell of men's cologne/ladies' perfume makes me think of sex.

Insecurity

It is easier to have sex if my partner is the aggressor.
I feel like a failure if I cannot keep someone sexually excited.

Jewish General Hospital Sexual Self-Monitoring Form: Diary Evaluation of Sexual Behavior and Satisfaction

Eva Libman,[1] *SMBD-Jewish General Hospital and McGill University*
Ilana Spector, *SMBD-Jewish General Hospital and McGill University*
Yitzchak Binik, *McGill University and Royal Victoria Hospital*
William Brender, *SMBD-Jewish General Hospital*
Catherine S. Fichten, *SMBD-Jewish General Hospital, Dawson College, and McGill University*

Sexual diaries have been shown to have excellent temporal stability (e.g., White, Case, McWhirter, & Mattison, 1990), but there are few widely accepted structured forms to systematically self-monitor frequency, variability, or satisfaction with sexual activity. The Jewish General Hospital (JGH) Sexual Self-Monitoring Form provides information about the frequency and quality of a range of individual and couple sexual behaviors on a daily basis. Initially a clinical instrument, the JGH Sexual Self-Monitoring Form was modified to evaluate outcome in sex therapy research. The measure can also be used in process studies of sex therapy to assess the impact of various therapeutic interventions and to monitor compliance with the treatment program. It is ideally suited to assess the sexual dysfunctions consequent to antidepressant use (Serretti & Chiesa, 2009) and equally can be used to obtain descriptive and normative information in populations of single individuals or couples.

Description

This measure consists of eight questions asking respondents to indicate, on a daily basis, whether they engaged in each of 18 individual or interpersonal sexual activities, whether they experienced orgasm (and during which activities), how they felt about their partner and their sexual experience, and how satisfied they were with the amount of affection received.

Response Mode and Timing

The form takes less than 5 minutes to complete. Partners are told to complete the forms individually.

Scoring

Daily responses should each be examined and scored individually. For clinical purposes, scoring is optional; a qualitative evaluation of responses may be more appropriate for monitoring therapeutic progress and tailoring therapy to specific clients. For research purposes, the JGH Sexual Self-Monitoring Form can be scored as follows: For Question 1, item scores can be summed for 7-day periods to provide weekly measures of frequency for each sexual activity; other sexual activities may be added to this list. Enjoyment ratings (Question 2) can also be summed for each sexual activity and divided by the number of times that the activity occurred during the week. This yields a mean enjoyment score for each sexual activity. Responses to Questions 3, 6, and 7 are also summed and divided by 7 to provide a weekly estimate of feelings about one's sexual experience, satisfaction with affection received, and feelings towards one's partner.

Questions 4 and 5 examine the experience of orgasm. The weekly frequency of orgasms during each sexual activity can be counted to determine the percentage of times that the sexual activity in question resulted in orgasm (success/experience ratio: cf. Auerbach & Kilmann, 1977). If the focus of interest is not orgasmic experience but erection quality, speed of ejaculation, and so forth, Questions 4 and 5 may be replaced as needed.

To simplify scoring, activities may be clustered. Our method involves the following groupings: *Individual Sexual Activities* (dreams, fantasies, masturbation, and reading and viewing erotica), *Affectional Display* (hugging, kissing, and receiving and giving nongenital manual or oral caresses), *Couple Sexual Noncoital Activities* (receiving and giving genital manual or oral stimulation, and anal activities), and *Intercourse*. Using these clusters, we calculate frequency of type of activity cluster per week, orgasm ratio (%), and enjoyment ratings (cf. Fichten, Libman, & Brender, 1983). Averaging these data over a month is recommended to eliminate the effects of weekly variability in sexual encounters.

[1]Address correspondence to Eva Libman, Behavioral Psychotherapy and Research Unit, Institute of Community and Family Psychiatry, SMBD-Jewish General Hospital, 4333 Cote St. Catherine Rd., Montreal, Quebec, Canada H3T 1E4; e-mail: eva.libman@mcgill.ca

Reliability and Validity

Because this measure was originally developed as a clinical instrument (Burstein et al., 1985) rather than as a research tool, reliability and validity information has not been systematically obtained. However, the JGH Sexual Self-Monitoring Form has been used in several studies that address the following questions: (a) whether sexual self-monitoring adds useful information to traditional retrospective methods of measurement (Fichten, Libman, & Brender, 1986), which concluded that self-monitoring is not redundant with questionnaire methods; (b) whether completing self-monitoring forms is reactive (Fichten, Libman, Takefman, & Brender, 1988; Takefman & Brender, 1984). These findings provide preliminary evidence for the nonreactivity of sexual self-monitoring with this instrument. Findings using other sexual self-monitoring measures, however, do suggest the existence of reactivity (Ochs, Meana, Mah, & Binik, 1993). Therefore, the possible reactivity of sexual self-monitoring should be assessed in future studies; (c) whether the JGH Sexual Self-Monitoring Form can be used in treatment-outcome studies to verify compliance and to examine changes in sexual behavior frequency and satisfaction (Fichten et al., 1983, 1986; Libman, Fichten, & Brender, 1984; Takefman & Brender, 1984). Findings indicating high degrees of concordance between partners on behavioral frequency ratings provide preliminary evidence for interrater reliability. Results also show that (a) the JGH Sexual Self-Monitoring Form is effective in determining differences in treatment compliance that predict successful therapy outcome, (b) pretreatment scores on several self-monitoring variables predict posttreatment findings, and (c) the Sexual Self-Monitoring Form can highlight differences between treatments and show pre- to posttherapy changes.

Other Information

The JGH Sexual Self-Monitoring Form has been included in a recent review of questionnaires evaluating sexual quality of life (Arrington, Cofrancesco, & Wu, 2004). It is also available in French (Hôpital Général Juif [HGJ] Formulaire d'Enregistrement Quotidien des Activités Sexuelles).

References

Arrington, R., Cofrancesco, J., & Wu, A. W. (2004). Questionnaires to measure sexual quality of life. *Quality of Life Research, 13,* 1643–1658.

Auerbach, R., & Kilmann, P. R. (1977). The effects of group systematic desensitization on secondary erectile failure. *Behavior Therapy, 8,* 330–339.

Burstein, R., Libman, E., Binik, Y., Fichten, C. S., Cohen, J., & Brender, W. (1985). A short-term treatment program for secondary orgasmic dysfunction. *Psychological Documents, 15,* 9. (Ms. No. 2688)

Fichten, C. S., Libman, E., & Brender, W. (1983). Methodological issues in the study of sex therapy: Effective components in the treatment of secondary orgasmic dysfunction. *Journal of Sex & Marital Therapy, 9,* 191–202.

Fichten, C. S., Libman, E., & Brender, W. (1986). Measurement of therapy outcome and maintenance of gains in the behavioral treatment of secondary orgasmic dysfunction. *Journal of Sex & Marital Therapy, 12,* 22–33.

Fichten, C. S., Libman, E., Takefman, J., & Brender, W. (1988). Self-monitoring and self-focus in erectile dysfunction. *Journal of Sex & Marital Therapy, 14,* 120–128.

Libman, E., Fichten, C. S., & Brender, W. (1984). Prognostic factors and classification issues in the treatment of secondary orgasmic dysfunction. *Personality and Individual Differences, 5,* 1–10.

Ochs, E. P., Meana, M., Mah, K., & Binik, Y. M. (1993). The effects of exposure to different sources of sexual information on sexual behavior: Comparing a "sex-expert system" to other educational material. *Behavior Research Methods, Instruments and Computers, 25,* 189–194.

Serretti, A., & Chiesa, A. (2009). Treatment-emergent sexual dysfunction related to antidepressants: A meta-analysis. *Journal of Clinical Psychopharmacology, 29,* 259–266.

Takefman, J., & Brender, W. (1984). An analysis of the effectiveness of two components in the treatment of erectile dysfunction. *Archives of Sexual Behavior, 13,* 321–340.

White, J. R., Case, D. A., McWhirter, D., & Mattison, A. M. (1990). Enhanced sexual behavior in exercising men. *Archives of Sexual Behavior, 19,* 193–209.

Exhibit

Jewish General Hospital Sexual Self-Monitoring Form

(please fill out alone)

NAME: _____ DATE: _____

(1) Sexual Activities (please *check* in *column 1* if the activity occurred)

	1	2		1	2
	Check if Activity Occurred	Rate According to Scale A (1–10)		Check if Activity Occurred	Rate According to Scale A (1–10)
Individual activities					
a) fantasies (daydreams)			j) breast caressing		
b) dreams			k) genital touching (giving)		
c) masturbation			l) genital touching (receiving)		
d) reading erotica			m) oral stimulation (giving)		
e) seeing erotica			n) oral stimulation (receiving)		
f) other (specify below)			o) anal stimulation (giving)		
Interpersonal activities			p) anal stimulation (receiving)		
g) kissing			q) mutual masturbation		
h) caressing—nongenital (giving)			r) intercourse		
i) caressing—nongenital (receiving)			s) other (specify below)		

(2) Please look at Scale A below and then rate each activity checked above. Write the *rating in column 2* above.

Scale A

Very Unenjoyable	1	2	3	4	5	6	7	8	9	10	Very Enjoyable

(3) How did you feel about your sexual experience today? (Put X in box)

Very Negative	1	2	3	4	5	Very Positive

(4) Did you experience any orgasms? _____

(5) If yes, during which activity? _____

(6) How satisfied are you with the amount of affection you received today?

Very Dissatisfied	1	2	3	4	5	Very Satisfied

(7) In general, how did you feel about your partner today?

Very Negative	1	2	3	4	5	Very Positive

(8) Please add, in your own words, any important information or feelings concerning yourself, your marriage, your sex life, or any other issues you'd like to bring up in your session with your therapist.

Sexual Function Scale

MARITA P. MCCABE,[1] *Deakin University*

The Sexual Function Scale (SFS) is designed to evaluate the contribution of attitudes and experiences from the family of origin, the period of adolescence, and current individual and relationship factors to a person's sexual functioning. It may be completed by people who are sexually functional or sexually dysfunctional. For people who are sexually dysfunctional, it can be used as a clinical measure to evaluate the factors that need to be addressed in therapy.

Description

The SFS consists of three major sections: Childhood; Puberty and Adolescence; and Current Attitudes and Behavior. There are subsections within these three sections. These are summarized in Table 1.

TABLE 1
Subscales of the Sexual Function Scale

	Coefficient Alpha	Test–Retest
Childhood		
A. Attitudes Toward Sex in the Home (10 items)	Distinct items	
B. Emerging Sexuality (6 items)	Distinct items	
Puberty and Adolescence		
A. Sexual Education (6 items)	Distinct items	
B. Dating Behavior (2 items)	Distinct items	
C. Petting Behavior (7 items)	Distinct items	
D. Coital Experiences During Adolescence (2 items)	Distinct items	
E. (a) Homosexual Experiences (3 items)	Distinct items	
(b) Unpleasant Experiences (3 items)	.36	.71
F. Depth of Relationship (3 items)	.43	.76
Current Attitudes and Behavior		
A. Current Attitudes Towards Sex (32 items)	.85	.89
B. Sexual Identity (3 items)	Distinct items	
C. Lifestyle (6 items)	Distinct items	
D. Types of Sexual Activity		
(a) Range of Sexual Activity (16 items)	.72	.88
(b) Response to Sexual Activity and Nature of Extra Stimulation (22 items)	.78	.92
E. Sexual Communication (9 items)	.80	.90
F. Sexual Satisfaction (3 items)	.63	.98
G. Other Relationships (9 items)	.60	.88
H. Communication (10 items)	.68	.91
I. Quality of Relationship (12 items)	.80	.98
J. Performance Anxiety (10 items)	.85	.97

The SFS was originally developed as a measure to evaluate the factors that are associated with sexual dysfunction in males and females. The original questions were drawn from the literature that assessed the aetiology of sexual dysfunction.

This material was used to generate a guided interview measure, with open-ended responses. This measure was used to assess the sexuality of 55 respondents with sexual dysfunction and 58 respondents who were sexually functional. The responses of these subjects allowed scales to be created for each question. Some items were removed from the scale as analyses indicated that they had no impact on their sexual functioning. The modified scales were administered to a further sample of clinical sexually dysfunctional, nonclinical sexually dysfunctional, and sexually functional respondents (McCabe, 1994a, 1994b). The results of this study allowed the scale to be reorganized and modified to produce the present measure.

Response Mode and Timing

Respondents complete the scale as a questionnaire. Some items in the scale are categorical (e.g., What type of contraception do you use?), some are *yes/no* responses (e.g., Did you have any unpleasant sexual experiences during adolescence?), and some are on a 5-point Likert-type scale (e.g., How often do you feel highly aroused before you have intercourse?). The questionnaire takes about 1 hour to complete.

Scoring

Items are scored in the same direction, so that a total score is obtained for each subsection. Some items are categorical and so do not contribute to a total score for the subsection. Because there are different numbers of items in each subsection, the highest possible score varies from one section to another.

Reliability and Validity

Coefficient alpha have been calculated for a number of the subscales. These alphas are reported in Table 1. Some of the items in the scales tap very separate aspects of a particular construct or result in categorical responses, and so it is not appropriate to add responses or expect that respondents will answer in any consistent manner. The alphas have been calculated on a sample size of 171 cases. Of these, 82 subjects (50 females, 32 males) were sexually functional, 51

[1]Address correspondence to Marita P. McCabe, School of Psychology, Deakin University, 221 Burwood Highway, Burwood, Victoria, Australia 3125; e-mail: marita.mccabe@deakin.edu.au

subjects (27 females, 24 males) were sexually dysfunctional and not seeking treatment, and 38 subjects (20 females, 18 males) were clinical dysfunctional. The scale was also completed by 30 sexually functional and 30 sexually dysfunctional subjects on two occasions 6 weeks apart. The test-retest reliability coefficients for each subscale are reported in Table 1. The method of scale construction has ensured some level of construct validity. The scale needs to be administered along with other psychometrically sound measures of the subscales to further demonstrate the level of construct validity of the scale.

Other Information

The scale, along with the scoring code, may be obtained from the author for use with clinical or research subjects.

References

McCabe, M. P. (1994a). Childhood, adolescent and current psychological factors associated with sexual dysfunction. *Sexual and Marital Therapy, 9*, 267–276.

McCabe, M. P. (1994b). The influence of the quality of relationship on sexual dysfunction. *Australian Journal of Marriage and the Family, 15*, 2–8.

Personal Sentence Completion Inventory

L. C. MICCIO-FONSECA,[1] *Clinic for the Sexualities*

Professionals in research, educational, or clinical settings requiring information regarding a person's erotic development have limited resources, although their needs are various and extensive. The Personal Sentence Completion Inventory (PSCI; Miccio-Fonseca, 1997) is a versatile tool to be used in assessment, evaluation, and treatment of a variety of sexually related issues, particularly male and female sexually abusive individuals of all ages (including those who have been arrested and/or convicted of sex offenses). The PSCI can be used in group sessions (10–12 week segments) on such topics as erotic development, sexual health, sexual fantasies, and sexual behaviors (for all ages and both genders).

Description

The PSCI was based on a subject sample ($N = 656$) of males and females of all ages (7–75 years), who were (a) victims of sexual abuse, (b) sex offenders (who were not victims), (c) sex offenders who were also victims, and (d) individuals who were neither victims nor offenders. The subject sample was composed primarily of individuals who had received psychological evaluations and had undergone individual or group therapy or both (Miccio-Fonseca, 1996, 2000, 2001). A pilot study was completed on 185 people, ages 12–57; items were rewritten for clarification and a revised 50-item sentence-stem version of the PSCI was formulated and readministered to another 155 individuals (males and females; ages 7–61 years).

The PSCI is a paper-and-pencil inventory covering variables known to be directly related to risk and/or recidivism of sexually abusive adults and adolescents. The PSCI covers love relationships and intimacy deficits, uncovers deviant sexual fantasies, explores erotic pleasures, and gives information on unconventional sexual history and other data related to sex disorder (i.e., paraphilias). The PSCI assesses variables related to family lovemaps (Miccio-Fonseca, 2006, 2007), including the quality of family relationships and early separation from natal parents prior to the age of 16, and can also provide information on inklings of dissociative features and/or paraphilic fugue states.

The PSCI is an instructive, informative supplement to other tools, assisting the clinician in completing a comprehensive assessment of the individual's sexual background, sexual development, and sexual proclivities. The User's Manual for the PSCI has examples of actual responses given by others and comments to the item responses, along with research related to the particular area explored and a glossary of terms.

The PSCI is empirically supported and used extensively in court-ordered psychological evaluations of sex offenders. Seasoned clinicians, aware of the literature in the field of sex offenders, will find the PSCI a valuable asset eliciting empirically based information related to risk and/or recidivism from the PSCI. By considering empirically supported variables distinctive to the individual, the PSCI contrasts sharply with popular actuarial tools that compare the individual's score on a variable to groups of offenders within a particular score.

Response Mode and Timing

Respondents to the PSCI fill out the 50 sentence stems of the paper-and-pencil inventory. Depending on the individual, the entire form takes about 15 minutes to complete. The assessment's sentence completion, open-ended format is transparent to respondents and provides a valuable means of eliciting content experience from an individual in the area being explored. The PSCI capitalizes on the benefits of the sentence completion format by making responses free-form and model-focused. However, the inventory does require sensitivity on the part of the person administering it, as some respondents ask for assistance in formulating their completions, and some need to be encouraged to respond at all.

The PSCI provides qualitative rather than quantitative data. The administration of the PSCI relies on the professional skills and sophistication of the examiner, particularly during the qualitative interview phase, when the examiner's task is to draw out the subject and develop a rounded, in-depth picture of his or her sexual history. During the interview, the examiner has the opportunity to observe the subject's social skills and style of communication in action. Clinical observations help determine the best ways to approach and uncover those areas of self-disclosure that the subject did not write down in the PSCI. There is no scoring scheme for the PSCI.

Other Information

The PSCI has been used extensively in assessing male and female adolescent and adult sex offenders. It can be used by mental health professionals providing treatment in individual, couples, and/or family therapy. The PSCI can also be used as a tool to structure discussions around sexuality in group therapy with all ages. In addition, teachers of human sexuality who need a unique tool to facilitate delicate group discussions could use the PSCI.

References

Miccio-Fonseca, L. C. (1996). Research report: On sex offenders, victims and their families. *Journal of Offender Rehabilitation, 23*(3/4), 71–83.

Miccio-Fonseca, L. C. (1997). *Personal Sentence Completion Inventory: User's guide.* Brandon, VT: Safer Society Press.

Miccio-Fonseca, L. C. (2000). Adult and adolescent female sex offenders: Experiences compared to other females and male sex offenders. *Journal of Psychology and Human Sexuality, 11,* 75–88.

Miccio-Fonseca, L. C. (2001). Somatic and mental symptoms of male sex offenders: A comparison among offenders, victims, and their families. *Journal of Psychology and Human Sexuality, 13,* 103–114.

Miccio-Fonseca, L. C. (2006, Winter). Family lovemaps: Challenging the myths related to multiple paraphilias, denial, and paraphilic fugue states. ATSA Forum. Retrieved December 14, 2005, from: http://newsmanager.commpartners.com/atsa/issues/2005-12-15/1.html

Miccio-Fonseca, L. C. (2007). Challenging the myths about sex disorders: Understanding the role of bio-physio process, family lovemaps, and paraphilic fugue states. In D. S. Prescott (Ed.), *Knowledge and practice: Challenges in the treatment and supervision of sexual abusers* (pp. 91–107). Oklahoma City, OK: Wood 'N' Barnes.

Exhibit

Personal Sentence Completion Inventory (Sample Items)

Sexual Dreams

19.   My sex dreams are usually about

Erotic Pleasures

32.   What turns me on sexually is

Sexual Discomforts

40.   The thing I tried sexually once but wouldn't do again is

Sexual Interaction System Scale

JANE D. WOODY[1] AND HENRY J. D'SOUZA, *University of Nebraska at Omaha*

The Sexual Interaction System Scale (SISS) is a self-report instrument designed to measure the quality of a heterosexual couple's sexual interaction, including specific sexual dysfunctions. It provides a measure of each partner's perception (i.e., individual's scores), which may then be added for a total couple score. The SISS measures five factors believed to interact during a given sexual encounter.

1. Sexual Functioning encompasses the *Diagnostic and Statistical Manual of Mental Disorders* (American Psychiatric Association, 1987) classification of sexual dysfunctions; the subfactors are Desire, Arousal, Orgasm, (and a fourth subfactor for females, Pain Dysfunctions). In systemic terms, sexual responses at each phase of the sexual response cycle, including physiological responses, constitute communication to which the partners are constantly reacting, in part, with their own physiological responses.

2. Attitudinal Set refers to each individual's attitudes about the purpose and focus of sexual intimacy and the level of maturity that these attitudes reflect—whether self-focused, role focused, or individual connected.

3. Nonsexual Interaction refers to the presence of interactions around territoriality, ranking, attachment, and exploratory/sensory patterns that may either promote or interfere with desired sexual arousal and satisfaction. This factor taps patterns that a couple has established for dealing with these issues in their overall relationship and which may emerge and be communicated during the sexual encounter.

4. Interaction Coordination refers to the partners' action language that serves to coordinate all aspects of the sexual encounter so as to lead to the desired outcome—arousal and satisfaction. It encompasses verbal and nonverbal behaviors that serve as communication exchanges that may move the couple's sexual interaction in the desired direction.

5. Postsexual Interaction refers to the emotional tenor of the relationship following sex. It consists of each partner's evaluation of the sexual encounter relative to feelings and behaviors of distance versus closeness toward the partner as a result of the sex. These feelings, and behaviors too, constitute communication that is assumed to carry over and impact on the couple's next sexual encounter.

Description

The SISS is distinct from prior sexual functioning inventories in that it focuses on the interaction taking place during the couple's actual sexual encounters. In spite of the fact that the couple is typically the preferred unit of treatment for sexual dysfunctions, a systemic understanding of a couple's sexual relationship is a fairly recent development (Schnarch, 1991; Woody, 1992). The five factors were derived in part from Verhulst and Heiman's (1979) systemic explanation of sexual functioning as an interactional communication process. The SISS consists of 48 statements with responses to be made on a 6-point scale (0 = *none, never, does not occur in our relationship* to 5 = *high, always, always occurs in our relationship*). Of these statements, 10 items deal with Sexual Functioning, 7 with Attitudinal Set, 12 with Nonsexual Interaction, 6 with Interaction Coordination, and 10 with Postsexual Interaction. The SISS is appropriate for use with heterosexual couples in clinical practice involving sexual distress, sexual dysfunction, or general relationship problems, and for use in couple premarital and enrichment programs.

Response Mode and Timing

Partners are to complete the SISS independently, preferably on the same day, so that they have a common frame of reference (i.e., their most recent two or three sexual encounters with each other). Completion time is approximately 10 minutes. Responses, for hand scoring, are placed on the line in front of each item.

Scoring

Directions appear on the Male and Female Scoring/Profile Sheets. These directions indicate the items for which the response must be reversed in value before totaling the items within each factor to obtain the subfactor, factor, and individual scores. Reversed values are placed on the inventory, and these can be totaled on the inventory itself and then transferred to the Scoring/Profile Sheets. The couple score is the sum of both partners' total individual scores. Individual scores can range from 0 to 225, with higher scores indicating more positive sexual interaction. Maximum scores possible for the factors are Sexual Functioning (50), Attitudinal Set (35), Nonsexual Interaction (60), Interaction Coordination (30), and Postsexual

[1]Address correspondence to Jane D. Woody, School of Social Work, University of Nebraska at Omaha, Omaha, NE 68182-0293; e-mail: jwoody@unomaha.edu.

Interaction (50). Plotting scores on the profile allows comparison of the individual's scores to a Nonclinical sample ($N = 58$) and to a Sexual Dysfunction sample (Males, $N = 20$; Females, $N = 24$). The profiles show mean scores for the Nonclinical sample placed at T-score $= 50$ and the mean scores of the Sexual Dysfunction sample circled; the latter suggests a cut-off score that may be seen as clinically significant.

Reliability

In a sample of 143 couples, internal consistency, analyzed by the five SISS factors, resulted in Cronbach's alpha $= .90$ (Woody & D'Souza, 1994). This coefficient was chosen because, theoretically, a systemic explanation of the sexual encounter holds that the five factors would be correlated.

Validity

Validity was supported by several methods. Face validity was supported by the ratings of six experts on the content of the items of the scale. In addition, in a sample of 143 couples, significant differences were found on the t test between known groups: the Sexual Dysfunction group and the Nonclinical group ($t = 7.14$, $p < .001$); and the Sexual Dysfunction group and Other Problems group ($t = 2.05$,

$p < .05$). Criterion validity was supported by a Pearson's correlation coefficient ($r = .80$; $p < .001$) between the SISS couple score and the couple score on a criterion question dealing with sexual satisfaction. Finally, as expected, a moderate correlation was found between the SISS couple score and the overall couple relationship as measured by the Dyadic Adjustment Scale ($r = .61$, $p < .001$; Woody & D'Souza, 1994).

Other Information

Copyright is held by Jane D. Woody and Henry J. D'Souza. For permission to use or a copy of the complete scale, please address correspondence to the first author.

References

American Psychiatric Association. (1987). *Diagnostic and statistical manual of mental disorders* (3rd ed. rev.). Washington, DC: American Psychiatric Association.

Schnarch, D. M. (1991). *Constructing the sexual crucible*. New York: Norton.

Verhulst, J., & Heiman, J. (1979). An interactional approach to sexual dysfunction. *American Journal of Family Therapy, 7*(4), 19–36.

Woody, J. D. (1992). *Treatment for sexual distress: Integrative systems therapy*. Newbury Park, CA: Sage.

Woody, J. D., & D'Souza, H. J. (1994). The Sexual Interaction System Scale: A new inventory for assessing sexual dysfunction and sexual distress. *Journal of Sex & Marital Therapy, 20*, 210–228.

Exhibit

Sexual Interaction System Scale (sample items)

Directions. The items in this scale deal with your current sexual relationship with your spouse or regular partner. In answering each item, think of the last few times you engaged in sex with your partner.

For each of the statements, you are to answer for yourself, that is, give a response choice that reflects your own experience, your own opinion, or your own impression. You will answer each item according to a response scale of 0 to 5, which is explained below. Put your answers on the line in front of each item. Please answer all items. See the sample answers, explanations and directions below.

Response choices

For rating your experience or your opinion, select a rating from 0 to 5. The meanings of the ratings are as follows:

0	1	2	3	4	5
None or never on the characteristic described. Does not occur in our relationship.					Extremely high or always on the characteristic described. Always occurs in our relationship.

Sample Answers and Explanations

__0__ I express complaints or negative feelings during sex. This answer means that you gave a rating of 0 because you believe that you never express complaints or negative feelings during sex.

___1___   I worry about the success of my sexual performance.

This answer means that you gave a rating of 1 because only rarely do you worry about the success of your performance.

___2___   Female has consistent or recurring genital pain with intercourse. If you are a female, this answer means that you gave a rating of 2 because you occasionally have pain during intercourse. If you are a male, your answer in the response column will be NA, not applicable to you.

If an item describes a behavior that you *never engage* in or a reaction that you *never have* in your relationship, remember to look at the scale, as a rating of 0 means *none or never*, or *does not* occur in the relationship. The scale makes it possible for you to answer all questions.

Before starting to answer, take a minute to imagine yourself and your partner *during the most recent few times you engaged in sex*. This should be your frame of reference for answering the questions.

SISS Factors	Sample Items
Sexual Functioning	I am interested in sex—willing to get involved, either initiating or responding to partner's initiating.
Attitudinal Set	I worry about the success of my sexual performance.
Nonsexual Interaction	I feel my partner is too possessive of my body during sex.
Interaction Coordination	With actions and/or words, I do what it takes to make sex pleasurable for both of us.
Postsexual Interaction	I feel withdrawn and distant from my partner as a result of sex.

Masculine Gender Identity Scale for Females

RAY BLANCHARD,[1] *Centre for Addiction and Mental Health*

The Masculine Gender Identity Scale for Females (MGIS; Blanchard & Freund, 1983) was developed to measure "masculinity" occurring in homosexual females. Masculine gender identity in females was conceived as a continuous variable, inferable from the extent of an individual's departure from the usual female pattern of behavior toward the pattern typical of female-to-male transsexuals.

The MGIS was developed as a companion instrument to the Feminine Gender Identity Scale for Males (FGIS; Freund, Langevin, Satterberg, & Steiner, 1977; Freund, Nagler, Langevin, Zajac, & Steiner, 1974). The FGIS is presented elsewhere in this volume in the article by Freund and Blanchard; differences between the gender identity scales and conventional masculinity-femininity scales are also discussed there.

Description

The MGIS is a self-administered, multiple-choice questionnaire measure. It includes two subscales. The 20 items of Part A mainly concern the examinee's childhood preference for female versus male playmates, games, and toys; the predilection for stereotypically masculine household chores; childhood fantasies of adult pursuits commonly associated with the male or female sex; and the frequency of frank cross-gender wishes at various ages. Part A may be administered to any female over the age of 17. Part B consists mostly of items concerning cross-dressing and erotic preferences presupposing homosexuality. This subscale, which includes nine items, is only appropriate for homosexual females.

Scale development for both parts was conducted using all-female samples. The initial item pool for Part A was administered to 236 heterosexuals, 44 homosexuals who did not desire sex-change surgery (simple homosexuals), and 50 homosexuals who did (female-to-male transsexuals). From an initial pool of 25 items, those 20 were retained whose part-remainder correlations were greater than or equal to .30. The item pool for Part B was administered only to the 94 homosexual subjects. Because none of the nine items in the pool had a part-remainder correlation less than .30, all were retained.

[1]Address correspondence to Ray Blanchard, Centre for Addiction and Mental Health, 250 College Street, Toronto, Ontario M5T 1R8, Canada; e-mail: Ray_Blanchard@camh.net

Response Mode and Timing

Examinees may check or circle the response option of their choice. They are instructed to endorse one and only one response option per item. Part A of the scale should take no longer than 10 minutes to complete, and Part B should take no longer than 5.

Scoring

The scoring weight for each response option is shown in parentheses in the accompanying exhibit. The total score for each subscale is simply the sum of scores of its individual items; the full scale score is the sum of the two subscale scores. Higher scores indicate more masculine gender identity.

Reliability

Blanchard and Freund (1983) found an alpha reliability coefficient for Part A of .89. The alpha reliability of Part B was .92.

Validity

Blanchard and Freund (1983) found that factor analysis of Part A revealed three weak factors (each accounting for less than 6% of the total variance), and one strong factor, accounting for 31% of the total variance and 70% of the common variance. Factor loadings of the 20 items of Part A may be found in their Table 2 (p. 208). Factor analysis of

Part B revealed only one factor, accounting to 57% of the total variance.

The construct validity of Part A was supported by its reliable discrimination among three groups of females expected to show different degrees of masculine gender identity: heterosexuals, homosexuals, and female-to-male transsexuals (in ascending order). The homosexuals obtained higher scores than the heterosexuals, and the transsexuals obtained higher scores than the homosexuals. Part B, which is administered only to homosexual females (simple or transsexual), discriminated reliably between the homosexuals and the female-to-male transsexuals.

Age was not significantly correlated with Part A scores for heterosexuals, homosexuals, or transsexuals. Correlations between education and Part A scores ranged from .12 to .15, indicating that education accounts for only about 2% of the variance in Part A scores. Part B did not correlate with age or education for the homosexual or the transsexual group.

References

Blanchard, R., & Freund, K. (1983). Measuring masculine gender identity in females. *Journal of Consulting and Clinical Psychology, 51,* 205–214.

Freund, K., Langevin, R., Satterberg, J., & Steiner, B. W. (1977). Extension of the Gender Identity Scale for Males. *Archives of Sexual Behavior, 6,* 507–519.

Freund, K., Nagler, E., Langevin, R., Zajac, A., & Steiner, B. W. (1974). Measuring feminine gender identity in homosexual males. *Archives of Sexual Behavior, 3,* 249–260.

Exhibit

Masculine Gender Identity Scale for Females

Instructions: The following questions ask what sex role you have preferred at different times of your life, what were your childhood fantasies and activities, and how you felt about being born a female. Try to answer questions pertaining to childhood in terms of the way you felt then and not the way you see things now.

Please circle one and only one answer to each question. If you are not sure of the meaning of a question, you may ask the person giving the questionnaire to explain it to you. There is no time limit for answering these questions.

Part A: *Items Administered to All Females*

1. Between the ages of 6 and 12, did you prefer:
   a. to play with boys (2)
   b. to play with girls (0)
   c. didn't make any difference (1)
   d. not to play with other children (1)
   e. don't remember (1)
2. Between the ages of 6 and 12, did you:
   a. prefer boys' games and toys (soldiers, football, etc.) (2)
   b. prefer girls' games and toys (dolls, cooking, sewing, etc.) (0)
   c. like or dislike both about equally (1)
   d. had no opportunity to play games or with toys (1)

3. In childhood, were you very interested in the work of a garage mechanic? Was this:
   a. prior to age 6 (1)
   b. between ages 6 and 12 (1)
   c. probably in both periods (1)
   d. do not remember that I was very interested in the work of a garage mechanic (0)

4. Between ages 6 and 14, which did you like more: romantic stories or adventure stories?
   a. liked romantic stories more (0)
   b. liked adventure stories more (2)
   c. it did not make any difference (1)

5. Between the ages of 6 and 12, did you like to do jobs or chores which are usually done by men?
   a. yes (2)
   b. no (0)
   c. don't remember (1)

6. Between the ages of 13 and 16, did you like to do jobs or chores which are usually done by men?
   a. yes (2)
   b. no (0)
   c. don't remember (1)

7. Between the ages of 6 and 12, when you read a story did you imagine that you were:
   a. the male in the story (cowboy; detective, soldier, explorer, etc.) (2)
   b. the female in the story (the girl being saved, etc.) (0)
   c. the male sometimes and the female other times (1)
   d. neither the male nor the female (1)
   e. did not read stories (1)

8. In childhood or at puberty, did you like mechanics magazines? Was this:
   a. between ages 6 and 12 (1)
   b. between ages 12 and 14 (1)
   c. probably in both periods (1)
   d. do not remember that I liked mechanics magazines (0)

9. Between the ages of 6 and 12, did you sometimes imagine yourself as being the courageous leader of others?
   a. yes (2)
   b. no (0)
   c. unsure (1)

10. Between the ages of 6 and 12, did you wish you had been born a boy instead of a girl?
    a. often (2)
    b. occasionally (1)
    c. never (0)

11. Between the ages of 13 and 16, did you wish you had been born a boy instead of a girl?
    a. often (2)
    b. occasionally (1)
    c. never (0)

12. Since the age of 17, have you wished you had been born a boy instead of a girl?
    a. often (2)
    b. occasionally (1)
    c. never (0)

13. Do you think your appearance is:
    a. very feminine (0)
    b. feminine (0)
    c. a little masculine (1)
    d. quite masculine (2)

14. In childhood did you sometimes imagine, in your fantasies, yourself physically defending someone against a monster, a dangerous animal, or "evil" people?
    a. prior to age 6 (1)
    b. between ages 6 and 12 (1)
    c. probably in both periods (1)
    d. do not remember such fantasies (0)

15. In childhood fantasies, did you sometimes wish you could go hunting big game? Was this:
    a. prior to age 6 (1)

b. between ages 6 and 12 (1)

c. probably in both periods (1)

d. do not remember such fantasies (0)

16. In childhood, did you wish you would become very strong physically? Was this:

a. prior to age 6 (1)

b. between ages 6 and 12 (1)

c. probably in both periods (1)

d. do not remember the desire to become very strong physically (0)

17. In childhood, was there ever a period in which you wished you would, when adult, become a dressmaker or dress designer? Was this:

a. prior to age 6 (0)

b. between ages 6 and 12 (0)

c. probably in both periods (0)

d. do not remember having this desire (1)

18. In childhood fantasies, did you sometimes imagine yourself driving a racing car? Was this:

a. prior to age 6 (1)

b. between ages 6 and 12 (1)

c. probably in both periods (1)

d. do not remember having this fantasy (0)

19. In childhood, did you ever wish to become a dancer? Was this:

a. prior to age 6 (0)

b. between ages 6 and 12 (0)

c. probably in both periods (0)

d. do not remember having this desire (1)

20. In childhood, did you ever wish to become a pilot, or did you fantasize yourself being a pilot? Was this:

a. prior to age 6 (1)

b. between ages 6 and 12 (1)

c. probably in both periods (1)

d. do not remember having such a desire (0)

Part B: *Items Administered Only to Homosexual Females (Transsexual or Nontranssexual)*

21. Between the ages of 6 and 12, did you put on men's underwear or clothing?

a. once a month or more, for about a year or more (2)

b. (less often, but) several times a year for about 3 years or more (1)

c. very seldom did this during this period (0)

d. never did this during this period (0)

e. don't remember (0)

22. Between the ages of 13 and 16, did you put on men's underwear or clothing?

a. once a month or more, for a least a year (2)

b. (less often, but) several times a year for at least 2 years (1)

c. very seldom did this during this period (0)

d. never did this during this period (0)

23. Since the age of 17, have you put on men's underwear or clothing?

a. once a month or more, for at least a year (2)

b. (less often, but) several times a year for at least 2 years (1)

c. very seldom did this during this period (0)

d. never did this during this period (0)

24. If you have ever wished to have a male body rather than a female one, was this:

a. mainly to please females but also for your own satisfaction (2)

b. mainly for your own satisfaction but also to please females (2)

c. entirely for your own satisfaction (2)

d. entirely to please females (1)

e. about equally to please females and for your own satisfaction (2)

f. have never wanted to have a male body (0)

25. Have you ever felt like a man?

a. only if you were wearing a least one piece of male underwear or clothing (1)

b. while wearing at least one piece of male underwear or clothing and only occasionally at other times also (1)

c. at all times and for at least one year (2)

d. never felt like a man (2)

26. When completely dressed in female clothing (underwear, etc.), would you:

a. have a feeling of anxiety because of this (2)

b. have no feeling of anxiety but have another kind of unpleasant feeling because of this (2)

c. have no unpleasant feelings to do with above (0)

27. What kind of sexual contact with a female would you have preferred on the whole, even though you may not have done it?

a. touching your partner's privates with your hands (1)

b. touching your partner's privates with your mouth (1)

c. you would have preferred one of those two modes but you cannot decide which one (1)

d. your partner touching your privates with her hands (0)

e. your partner touching your privates with her mouth (0)

f. you would have preferred one of those two latter modes but you cannot decide which one (0)

g. you would have liked all four modes equally well (0)

h. you would have preferred some other mode of sexual contact (1)

28. What qualities did you like in females to whom you were sexually attracted?

a. slightly masculine behavior (0)

b. slightly feminine behavior (1)

c. very feminine behavior (2)

29. Would you have preferred a partner:

a. who was willing to have you lead her (2)

b. who was willing to lead you (0)

c. you didn't care (1)

Revised Mosher Guilt Inventory

DONALD L. MOSHER,[1] *University of Connecticut*

The Mosher Guilt Inventories measure three aspects of the personality disposition of guilt: Sex-Guilt, Hostility-Guilt, and Morality-Conscience. Multitrait-multimethod matrices have provided evidence for the discriminant validity of the three guilt subscales (Mosher, 1966, 1968). Sex guilt is psychologically magnified (Tomkins, 1979) in scenes involving awareness of sexual arousal, the discrete affects of interest-excitement and enjoyment-joy, and the discrete affect of shame, which appears in consciousness as guilt due to its associations with moral cognitions about sexual conduct. Hostility guilt is psychologically magnified in scenes involving the discrete affects of anger-rage and guilty affect and cognition about the immorality of aggressive behavior or cognitions. Conscience is psychologically magnified in scenes involving moral temptations and/or guilty affect about the self. The inventory is measuring three aspects of guilt conceived as a *script,* which is defined by Tomkins as a set of rules for the interpretation, prediction, production, control, and evaluation of a co-assembled set of scenes that has been further amplified by affect. The Mosher Guilt Inventories, as measures of these guilty scripts, have a considerable body of evidence supporting their construct validity.

Description

The Mosher Guilt Inventories (1961, 1966, 1968) were developed from responses given to sentence completion stems in 1960. The weights used in scoring the sentence completion were assigned to items from the scoring manual to construct true-false and forced-choice inventories for men and women, because the scoring manual had been developed to score each sex separately. O'Grady and Janda (1979) demonstrated there was no need to use weights because a 1 or 0 scoring procedure for guilty and nonguilty responses was correlated .99 with the weighted system. To compare the sexes, it was necessary either to transform the raw scores to standard scores, or to give the same

[1]Address correspondence to Donald L. Mosher, 648 Ternberry Forest Drive, The Villages, FL 32162; e-mail: dlmosher@aol.com

inventory to both sexes, which seemed to create no problems. During the past 30+ years, the range of guilt scores has been truncated as the means have dropped, particularly for sex guilt (Mosher & O'Grady, 1979). The 39 items in the female form of the forced-choice sex guilt inventory, in comparison to 28 for men, have continued to be a successful predictor of a broad range of sexually related behavior, cognitions, and affects in spite of containing items drawing 100% nonguilty choices.

Given the unusually strong evidence of construct validity for the inventories, I was reluctant to generate a new set of items that might be conceptually better but would limit generalization from past research. Instead, I submitted the nonoverlapping items contained in both male and female versions of the true-false (233 items) and the forced-choice (151 items) inventory to a sample of 187 male and 221 female University of Connecticut undergraduates for an updated item analysis. As suspected, many guilty-true items and guilty-forced-choice alternatives were uniformly rejected in that sample. The resulting Revised Mosher Guilt Inventory continues to measure Sex-Guilt, Hostility-Guilt, and Morality-Conscience, but it is now in a limited-comparison format that was selected to increase the range of response and to eliminate complaints about the forced-choice format.

The Revised Mosher Guilt Inventory consists of 114 items, arranged in pairs of responses to the same sentence completion stem, in 7-point Likert-type format to measure (a) Sex-Guilt—50 items, (b) Hostility-Guilt—42 items, and (c) Guilty-Conscience—22 items. Items were selected from an item analysis of the 151 forced-choice items in the original inventories. For the selected items, the correlations of the items with the subscale totals ranged from .32 to .62 with a median of .46. In addition, to ensure discriminant validity between the subscales, 90% of the items had a correlation with its own subscale that was significantly different from the correlation of the item with the other subscale totals. Several Morality-Conscience items were too highly correlated with Sex-Guilt, and thus were eliminated. This subscale was renamed Guilty-Conscience to reflect more adequately the retained items. The inventory is suited for adult populations.

Response Mode and Timing

Subjects respond to items by rating their response on a 7-point subscale in which 0 means *not at all true of (for) me*, and 6 means *extremely true of (for) me*. Items are arranged in sets of two different completions to a single stem—the limited-comparison format—to permit subjects to compare the intensity of *trueness* for them because people generally find one alternative is more or less *true* for them. The inventory can be completed in approximately 20 minutes. Subscales can be omitted or given separately. Answers are usually recorded on machine-scoreable answer sheets.

Scoring

Scores are summed for each subscale by reversing the nonguilty alternatives (nonitalicized item numbers in the following keys). The items for Sex-Guilt are 5, *6*, *7*, 8, 11, *12*, *13*, 14, 15, *16*, 17, *18*, *25*, 26, *31*, 32, 35, *36*, 41, *42*, *51*, 52, 53, *54*, *61*, 62, 63, *64*, 67, 78, *71*, 72, 75, 76, *81*, 82, *83*, 84, 87, *88*, *93*, 94, 101, *102*, *103*, 104, 107, *108*, 111, and *112*.

The items for Hostility-Guilt are 3, *4*, *19*, 20, 21, 22, *23*, 24, 29, *30*, *33*, 34, 37, *38*, *39*, 40, 43, *44*, *45*, 46, *55*, 56, 69, *70*, *77*, 78, *79*, 80, *85*, 86, *91*, 92, 95, 96, 97, *98*, 99, *100*, *109*, 110, *113*, and 114.

The items for Guilty-Conscience are 1, *2*, 9, *10*, 27, *28*, 47, *48*, 49, 50, *57*, 58, *59*, 60, *65*, 66, *73*, 74, *89*, 90, *105*, and 106. Higher scores indicate more scripted guilt.

Reliability

Because the Revised Mosher Guilt Inventory was constructed for inclusion in an earlier volume of the Handbook reliabilities in the new format had not yet been assessed. In past research, split-half or alpha coefficients have averaged around .90 (Mosher, 1966, 1968; Mosher & Vonderheide, 1985).

Validity

Mosher (1979) reviewed approximately 100 studies appearing by 1977 that consistently supported the construct validity of the Mosher Guilt Inventories. Subsequent research continued to add the construct validity of the inventory as a valid measure of guilt as a personality disposition (Green & Mosher, 1985; Kelley, 1985; Mosher & Vonderheide, 1985).

References

Green, S. E., & Mosher, D. L. (1985). A causal model of sexual arousal to erotic fantasies. *The Journal of Sex Research, 21*, 1–23.

Kelley, K. (1985). Sex, sex guilt, and authoritarianism: Differences in responses to explicit heterosexual and masturbatory slides. *The Journal of Sex Research, 21*, 68–85.

Mosher, D. L. (1961). *The development and validation of a sentence completion measure of guilt*. Unpublished doctoral dissertation, The Ohio State University, Columbus.

Mosher, D. L. (1966). The development and multitrait-multimethod matrix analysis of three measures of three aspects of guilt. *Journal of Consulting Psychology, 30*, 35–39.

Mosher, D. L. (1968). Measurement of guilt in females by self-report inventories. *Journal of Consulting and Clinical Psychology, 32*, 690–695.

Mosher, D. L. (1979). The meaning and measurement of guilt. In C. E. Izard (Ed.), *Emotions in personality and psychopathology*. New York: Plenum.

Mosher, D. L., & O'Grady, K. E. (1979). Sex guilt, trait anxiety, and females' subjective sexual arousal to erotica. *Motivation and Emotion, 3*, 235–249.

Mosher, D. L., & Vonderheide, S. G. (1985). Contributions of sex guilt and masturbation guilt to women's contraceptive attitudes and use. *The Journal of Sex Research, 21*, 24–39.

O'Grady, K. E., & Janda, L. H. (1979). Factor analysis of the Mosher Forced-Choice Guilt Inventory. *Journal of Consulting and Clinical Psychology, 47*, 1131–1133.

Tomkins, S. S. (1979). Script theory: Differential magnification of affects. In H. E. Howe, Jr., & R. A. Dienstbier (Eds.), *Nebraska Symposium on Motivation* (Vol. 26, pp. 201–236). Lincoln: University of Nebraska Press.

Exhibit

Revised Mosher Guilt Inventory

Instructions: This inventory consists of 114 items arranged in pairs of responses written by college students in response to sentence completion stems such as "When I have sexual dreams. . . ." You are to respond to each item as honestly as you can by rating your response on a 7-point scale from 0, which means *not at all true of (for) me* to 6, which means *extremely true of (for) me*. Ratings of 1 to 5 represent ratings of agreement-disagreement that are intermediate between the extreme anchors of *not at all true* and *extremely true* for you. The items are arranged in pairs of two to permit you to compare the intensity of a *trueness* for you. This limited comparison is often useful since people frequently agree with only one item in a pair. In some instances, it may be the case that both items or neither item is true for you, but you will usually be able to distinguish between items in a pair by using different ratings from the 7-point range for each item.

Rate each of the 114 items from 0 to 6 as you keep in mind the value of comparing items within pairs. Record your answer on the machine scoreable answer sheet by filling in the blank opposite the item number with your rating from 0 to 6. Please do not omit any items; 0s must be filled in to be read by the computer.

I punish myself . . .
1. very infrequently.
2. when I do wrong and don't get caught.

When anger builds inside me . . .
3. I let people know how I feel.
4. I'm angry myself.

"Dirty" jokes in mixed company . . .
5. do not bother me.
6. re something that make me very uncomfortable.

Masturbation . . .
7. is wrong and will ruin you.
8. helps one feel eased and relaxed.

I detest myself for . . .
9. nothing, I love life.
10. for my sins and failures.

Sex relations before marriage . . .
11. should be permitted.
12. are wrong and immoral.

Sex relations before marriage . . .
13. ruin many a happy couple
14. are good in my opinion.

Unusual sexual practices . . .
15. might be interesting.
16. don't interest me.

When I have sexual dreams . . .
17. I sometimes wake up feeling excited.
18. I try to forget them.

After an outburst of anger . . .
19. I am sorry and say so.
20. I usually feel quite a bit better.

When I was younger, fighting . . .
21. didn't bother me.
22. never appealed to me.

Arguments leave me feeling . . .
23. depressed and disgusted.
24. elated at winning.

"Dirty" jokes in mixed company . . .
25. are in bad taste.
26. can be funny depending on the company.

I detest myself for . . .

27. nothing at present.
28. being so self-centered.

When someone swears at me . . .
29. I swear back.
30. it usually bothers me even if I don't show it.

Petting . . .
31. I am sorry to say is becoming an accepted practice.
32. is an expression of affection which is satisfying.

When I was younger, fighting . . .
33. disgusted me.
34. was always a thrill.

Unusual sex practices . . .
35. are not so unusual.
36. don't interest me.

After a childhood fight, I felt . . .
37. good if I won, bad otherwise.
38. hurt and alarmed.

After an argument . . .
39. I am sorry for my actions.
40. I feel mean.

Sex . . .
41. is good and enjoyable.
42. should be saved for wedlock. and childbearing.

After an outburst of anger . . .
43. I usually feel quite a bit better.
44. I feel ridiculous and sorry that I showed my emotions.

After an argument . . .
45. I wish that I hadn't argued.
46. I feel proud in victory, understanding in defeat.

I detest myself for . . .
47. nothing, I love life.
48. not being more nearly perfect.

A guilty conscience . . .
49. is worse than a sickness to me.
50. does not bother me too much.

"Dirty jokes" in mixed company . . .
51. are coarse to say the least.
52. are lots of fun.

When I have sexual desires . . .
53. I enjoy it like all healthy human beings.

54. I fight them for I must have complete control of my body.

After an argument . . .

55. I am disgusted that I allowed myself to become involved.
56. I usually feel better.

Obscene literature . . .

57. helps people become sexual partners.
58. should be freely published.

One should not . . .

59. lose his temper.
60. say "one should not."

Unusual sexual practices . . .

61. are unwise and lead to trouble.
62. are all in how you look at it.

Unusual sexual practices . . .

63. are OK as long as they're hetersexual
64. Usually aren't pleasurable because you have preconceived feelings about their being wrong.

I regret . . .

65. all of my sins.
66. getting caught, but nothing else.

Sex relations before marriage . . .

67. in my opinion, should not be practiced.
68. are practiced too much to be wrong.

After an outburst of anger . . .

69. my tensions are relieved.
70. I am jittery and all keyed up.

As a child, sex play . . .

71. is immature and ridiculous.
72. was indulged in.

I punish myself . . .

73. by denying myself a privilege.
74. for very few things.

Unusual sex practices . . .

75. are dangerous to one's health and mental condition.
76. are the business of those who carry them out and no one else's.

Arguments leave me feeling . . .

77. depressed and disgusted.
78. proud, they certainly are worthwhile.

After an argument . . .

79. I am disgusted that I let myself become involved.
80. I feel happy if I won and still stick to my own views if I lose.

When I have sexual desires . . .

81. I attempt to repress them.
82. they are quite strong.

Petting . . .

83. is not a good practice until after marriage.

84. is justified with love.

After a childhood fight I felt . . .

85. as if I had done wrong.
86. like I was a hero.

Sex relations before marriage . . .

87. help people adjust.
88. should not be recommended.

If I robbed a bank . . .

89. I should get caught.
90. I would live like a king.

After an argument . . .

91. I am sorry and see no reason to stay mad.
92. I feel proud in victory and under-standing in defeat.

Masturbation . . .

93. is wrong and a sin.
94. is a normal outlet for sexual desire.

After an argument . . .

95. I am sorry for my actions.
96. if I have won, I feel great.

When anger builds inside me . . .

97. I always express it.
98. I usually take it out on myself.

After a fight, I felt . . .

99. relieved.
100. it should have been avoided for nothing was accomplished.

Masturbation . . .

101. is all right.
102. is a form of self destruction.

Unusual sex practices . . .

103. are awful and unthinkable.
104. are all right if both partners agree.

I detest myself for . . .

105. thoughts I sometimes have.
106. nothing, and only rarely dislike myself.

If I had sexual relations, I would feel . . .

107. all right, I think.
108. I was being used not loved.

Arguments leave me feeling . . .

109. exhausted.
110. satisfied usually.

Masturbation . . .

111. is all right.
112. should not be practiced.

After an argument . . .

113. it is best to apologize to clear the air.
114. I usually feel good if I won.

Index of Sexual Harassment

ADRIENNE L. DECKER
WALTER W. HUDSON,[1,2] *WALMYR Publishing Co.*

The Index of Sexual Harassment (ISH) is a short-form scale designed to measure sexual harassment.

Description

This ISH contains 19 category partition (Likert-type) items, each of which represents behavior that is illegal. Each item is scored on a relative frequency scale as shown in the scoring key of the instrument. Obtained scores range from 0 to 100, where higher scores indicate greater degrees of sexual harassment. The ISH can be used with all English-speaking populations aged 12 or older.

Response Mode and Timing

The ISH is a self-report scale that is normally completed in 5–7 minutes.

Scoring

The total score for the ISH scale is computed as $S = (\Sigma X_i - N)(100)/[(K-1)N]$ where X is an item response, i is item, K is the number of response categories, and N is the number of properly completed items. Total scores remain valid in the face of missing values (omitted items) provided the respondent completes at least 80% of the items. The effect of the scoring formula is to replace missing values with the mean item response value so that scores range from 0 to 100 regardless of the value of N.

Reliability

Cronbach's alpha = .90 and *SEM* = 2.97. Test-retest reliability is not available.

Validity

Known groups validity is not available for the ISH scale. Detailed information about content, factorial, and construct validity are reported in Hudson and Decker (1994) which is available from the publisher.

Other Information

The proper use of the WALMYR assessment scales is easily mastered, and the scales can be readily understood by qualified professional practitioners. These measurement tools are not intended for use by untrained individuals. The scales are simple, powerful devices that, when used by trained professionals, are capable of revealing both minor and serious problems that individuals might have in many areas of personal and social functioning. They are not intended for use by persons who are not trained to deal with such problems and should be used only by competent professionals, researchers, scholars and those who are engaged in supervised study and training.

The ISH is a copyrighted commercial assessment scale and may not be copied, reproduced, altered, or translated into other languages. The scale may not be administered online nor placed on a website for others to use. It may be purchased in tear-off pads of 50 copies each for $22.50 at www.walmyr.com.

Reference

Hudson, W. W., & Decker, A. L. (1994). The Index of Sexual Harassment: A partial validation. *The WALMYR Monograph Series*. Tempe, AZ: WALMYR Publishing Co.

Exhibit

Index of Sexual Harassment

Name: _____ Today's Date: _____

This questionnaire is designed to measure the level of sexual harassment in the workplace. It is not a test, so there are no right or wrong answers. Answer each item as carefully and as accurately as you can by placing a number beside each one as follows.

    1 = None of the time
    2 = Very rarely

[1]Walter W. Hudson, 1934–1999.
[1]Address correspondence to WALMYR Publishing Co., P.O. Box 12217, Tallahassee, FL 32317-2217; e-mail: walmyr@walmyr.com

3 = A little of the time
4 = Some of the time
5 = A good part of the time
6 = Most of the time
7 = All of the time

---

1. _____ My peer or supervisor tells sexually explicit jokes at work.
2. _____ My peer or supervisor describes me or a coworker using sexually explicit terminology.
3. _____ My peer or supervisor creates offensive rumors concerning the appearance or sexual behavior of me or a coworker.
4. _____ My peer or supervisor uses subtle questioning to determine my or my coworker's sexual behavior or availability.
5. _____ My peer or supervisor repeatedly asks me or a coworker for a date.
6. _____ My peer or supervisor asks me or a coworker for sexual favors.
7. _____ My peer or supervisor places obscene phone calls to me or a coworker.
8. _____ My peer or supervisor offers me or a coworker compensation or work benefits in exchange for sexual favors.
9. _____ My peer or supervisor demands sexual favors from me or a coworker to maintain job security.
10. _____ My peer or supervisor displays sexually explicit photographs and pictures at work.
11. _____ My peer or supervisor produces sexually explicit graffiti for display at work.
12. _____ My peer or supervisor shows pornographic videotapes at work.
13. _____ My peer or supervisor sends sexually explicit letters, cards or other written material to me or a coworker.
14. _____ My peer or supervisor uses gestures or starting considered sexually offensive by me or a coworker.
15. _____ My peer or supervisor stalks me or a coworker to pressure a personal relationship.
16. _____ My peer or supervisor blocks my or a coworker's pathway to force physical contact.
17. _____ My peer or supervisor touches self sexually in the presence of me or a coworker.
18. _____ My peer or supervisor touches me or a coworker in a sexually offensive manner.
19. _____ My peer or supervisor initiates unwelcome sexual activity with me or a coworker.

Peer Sexual Harassment Victimization Scale

JENNIFER PETERSEN[1] AND JANET SHIBLEY HYDE, *University of Wisconsin-Madison*

The purpose of this scale is to assess incidents of peer sexual harassment victimization among youth and to distinguish between same-gender and cross-gender harassment. Additionally, this scale identifies victims' reactions to peer sexual harassment victimization.

Description

The Peer Sexual Harassment Victimization Scale consists of 15 different sexual behaviors that could be considered sexually harassing. Fourteen of these behaviors were taken from the American Association of University Women (AAUW) study on peer sexual harassment (1993, 2001). The fifteenth behavior, "called you a slut or a whore," was added based on pilot interviews designed to discover sexually harassing behaviors that could be perpetrated by girls toward female victims. This scale does not ask victims to report their perceptions of sexual harassment. Instead, it asks whether specific behaviors have occurred and how upset participants were by the behaviors. Participants are asked to report the frequency of being victims of each behavior perpetrated by their peers during the past school year. For each behavior that is endorsed, participants are asked a series of follow-up questions, including how upset they were by the harassment, the gender of the perpetrator, and their reactions to the harassment. This scale was administered to a sample of 9th graders, but would be appropriate for other high school students and undergraduates as well.

[1]Address correspondence to Jennifer Petersen, University of Wisconsin-Madison, Psychology Dept., 1202 W. Johnson St., Madison, WI 53706; e-mail: Petersen1@wisc.edu

Response Mode and Timing

Although this scale may be administered as a paper-and-pencil questionnaire, we recommend the use of computer-assisted interviewing. This response mode may provide follow-up questions only when sexually harassing behaviors are endorsed, to avoid the confusion of skipping questions that are not applicable. Computer-assisted interviews also increase respondents' feelings of anonymity, thereby increasing accurate reporting. This scale is completed in approximately 15 minutes.

Scoring

Frequency of harassment is scored on a 0 (*Never*) to 3 (*Several Times*) scale. Frequency of all behaviors may be summed to obtain a frequency of harassment scale. Upset ratings for each behavior are scored from 0 (*Not Upset*) to 2 (*Very Upset*). Upset ratings for all behaviors may be summed to create a total upset score. Frequency of harassing behaviors may be multiplied by total upset score to obtain a weighted score of harassing events that caused distress.

Gender of the perpetrator may be compared to gender of the victim to assess same-gender and cross-gender sexual harassment. The responses "a girl" and "a group of girls" should be combined, and the responses "a boy" and "a group of boys" should be combined. Participants who responded "a group of boys and girls" may be analyzed separately or set to missing, if these responses are infrequent. Once these responses are combined, researchers may compare responses to victim's gender to assess same-gender and cross-gender harassment. Harassment perpetrated by girl(s) is scored as 0 and harassment perpetrated by boy(s) is scored as 1 for each behavior. These variables should be multiplied by frequencies of each corresponding behavior to create frequency of cross-gender harassment for girl victims and frequency of same-gender harassment for boy victims. Gender of the perpetrator should then be rescored as 0 for harassment perpetrated by boy(s) and 1 for harassment perpetrated by girl(s) for each behavior. These variables should again be multiplied by frequency of each corresponding behavior to create frequency of same-gender harassment for girl victims and frequency of cross-gender harassment for boy victims. Frequencies of same-gender and cross-gender harassment for each behavior may be summed for both boys and girls to create the measure's total frequency of same-gender and cross-gender harassment. Each reaction to harassment is coded as 0 (*Not Experienced*) and 1 (*Experienced*) for each behavior.

Reliability

Cronbach's alpha for harassing behaviors = .87. Test-retest reliability for the behaviors was assessed by the AAUW (1993, 2001) with a correlation of .95.

Validity

Detailed information about construct validity and scale formation is reported by the AAUW (1993, 2001).

References

American Association of University Women Educational Foundation (AAUW). (1993). *Hostile hallways: Bullying, teasing, and sexual harassment in school.* New York: Harris/Scholastic Research.

American Association of University Women Educational Foundation (AAUW). (2001). *Hostile hallways: Bullying, teasing, and sexual harassment in school.* New York: Harris/Scholastic Research.

Exhibit

Peer Sexual Harassment Victimization Scale

Participant ID _____

Gender: M   F

Below are some things that sometimes happen to kids at school. In the PAST SCHOOL YEAR how often did kids do these things to you? Circle your response.

1. Made sexual comments, jokes, gestures, or looks.[a]

Never   Once   A Few Times   Several Times

1a. If more than "Never," how upset were you by this?

Not at all Upset   Somewhat Upset   Very Upset

1b. The main time this happened, who did it to you?

A Girl   A Boy   Group of Girls   Group of Boys   Group of Boys and Girls

1c.   How did this make you feel? (check all that apply)

☐   Self-conscious
☐   Embarrassed
☐   Afraid/scared
☐   Less sure of yourself/less confident
☐   Confused about who you are
☐   Doubt whether you have what it takes to graduate
☐   Doubt whether you have what it takes to continue after graduation
☐   Doubt whether you can have a happy relationship
☐   Angry
☐   Powerless
☐   Flattered
☐   Normal
☐   Guilty/ashamed
☐   Dirty

2. Showed, gave, or left you sexual pictures, photographs, illustrations, messages, or notes.
3. Spread sexual rumors about you.
4. Said you were gay or lesbian.
5. Flashed or "mooned" you.
6. Touched, grabbed, or pinched you in a sexual way.
7. Intentionally brushed up against you in a sexual way.
8. Pulled off or down your clothing.
9. Forced you to kiss him or her.
10. Forced you to do something sexual other than kissing.
11. Called you a slut or whore.
12. Stared at a sexual part of your body.
13. Said something bad would happen to you if you did not engage in sexual relations.
14. Pulled at your clothing in a sexual way.
15. Blocked your way or cornered you in a sexual way.

[a]The response options following this statement section are repeated for each of the remaining items.

Likelihood to Sexually Harass Scale

John B. Pryor,[1] *Illinois State University*
Eric D. Wesselmann, *Purdue University*

The Likelihood to Sexually Harass (LSH) scale was developed to measure men's proclivities to sexually harass women (Pryor, 1987). The LSH measures a readiness for a specific type of sexually harassing behavior, *sexual exploitation* (Pryor & Whalen, 1997) or the tendency to use social power for sexual access or gain. Researchers have found that men's tendency to behave in a sexually exploitive manner toward women may be predicted by the LSH in combination with certain social normative factors that permit or condone such behavior (Pryor, Giedd, & Williams, 1995; Pryor, LaVite, & Stoller, 1993).

Description

The original LSH scale consists of 10 brief scenarios describing social situations in which a male protagonist has the power to sexually exploit a female with impunity. Male respondents are asked to imagine themselves in the role of the protagonist in each scenario. Following each scenario, respondents are asked to rate the likelihood that they would perform an act of quid pro quo sexual harassment. Since its initial publication in 1987, several studies have reported shorter versions of the LSH that have used a subsample

[1]Please address correspondence to John B. Pryor, Department of Psychology, Illinois State University, Normal, IL 61790-4620; e-mail: pryor@ilstu.edu

of the original scenarios. Two-scenario (Isbell, Swedish, & Gazan, 2005; Pryor & Meyers, 2001), four-scenario (in German: Siebler, Sabelus, & Bohner, 2008), and five-scenario versions have been developed (in Italian: Dall'Ara & Maass, 1999; and in Chinese: Lam & Chan, 2007).

Response Mode and Timing

Respondents typically complete the LSH scale anonymously. Ratings of the likelihood of performing sexually harassing behaviors are made on a 5-point Likert-type scale with the anchors *Not at all Likely* (1) and *Very Likely* (5). The original LSH scale takes about 15 minutes to complete.

Scoring

In the original 10-scenario version, the likelihood ratings from the key items (see *b* items in Exhibit) are summed to form a LSH score. Scores range from 10 to 50. In the Italian and German versions, blatant quid pro quo items are not used. Instead, after each scenario participants are asked to rate the likelihood of their performing several more subtle behaviors that could be seen as sexually harassing. Likelihood ratings are averaged across these more subtle items on these versions.

Reliability

Across several studies of college men reviewed by Pryor et al. (1995), the Cronbach alpha for the original LSH scale always exceeded .90. The two-scenario version produced alphas ranging from .74 to .78. The four- and five-scenario versions produced alphas ranging from .74 to .83. Initial principal components analyses of the 10-scenario version produced a single-factor solution (e.g., Pryor, 1987). Although two-factor solutions have been reported sometimes (Perry, Schmidtke, & Kulik, 1998), scales based upon these factors are highly correlated. For this reason, it is recommended that the summed score of the 10 items be viewed as a homogeneous measure of men's proclivity for sexual exploitation.

Validity

Most validity studies have examined all-male samples. Across numerous studies, the LSH has been found to be correlated with self-report scales related to sexual violence, gender roles, and sexuality (Pryor et al., 1995). Some example correlations include the following (all *p*s < .05). With regard to sexual violence, the LSH scale has been found to correlate with Attraction to Sexual Aggression (*r* = .38; Pryor & Stoller, 1994) and the Rape Myth Acceptance (*r* = .37; Begamy & Milburn, 2002). With regard to gender roles, the LSH scale has correlated significantly with Hostile Sexism (*r* = .27; Siebler et al., 2008). With regard

to sexuality, the LSH has correlated significantly with endorsing a dominance function of sex (*r* = .45; Pryor & Stoller, 1994) and the acceptability of premarital sex (*r* = .29; Lam & Chan, 2007). Pryor (1987) also examined the discriminant validity of the LSH scale. For example, he found a relatively low correlation between the LSH and the Crowne and Marlowe (1964) Social Desirability Scale (*r* = −.13). Several research teams have examined the connection between the LSH and social cognitive processes. The LSH has been found to correlate with a tendency to cognitively link concepts of sexuality with concepts of social dominance (Bargh, Raymond, Pryor, & Strack, 1995; Pryor & Stoller, 1994). With regard to behavioral validity, several studies have found that high LSH men behave in a sexually harassing manner toward women in laboratory settings when the men are exposed to social norms accepting or condoning sexual harassment (Pryor et al., 1995; Pryor et al., 1993). Investigators, using a procedure called the *computer harassment paradigm*, have found that high LSH men are more likely than low LSH men to send unsolicited pornography (Dall'Ara & Maass, 1999) and sexist jokes to women (Siebler et al., 2008) over the Internet. High LSH men are also more likely to report that they have actually engaged in sexually harassing behavior in the past and that they have viewed pornography over the Internet (Lam & Chan, 2007; Pryor & Whalen, 1997).

References

Bargh, J. A., Raymond, P., Pryor, J. B., & Strack, F. (1995). The attractiveness of the underling: An automatic power sex association and its consequences for sexual harassment. *Journal of Personality and Social Psychology, 68,* 868–781.

Begamy, J. J., & Milburn, M. A. (2002). Psychological predictors of sexual harassment: Authoritarianism, hostile sexism, and rape myths. *Psychology of Men and Masculinity, 3,* 119–126.

Crowne, D., & Marlowe, D. (1964). *The approval motive.* New York: Wiley.

Dall'Ara, E., & Maass, A. (1999). Studying sexual harassment in the laboratory: Are egalitarian women at higher risk? *Sex Roles, 38,* 557–588.

Isbell, L. M., Swedish, K., & Gazan, D. B. (2005). Who says it's sexual harassment? The effects of gender and likelihood to sexually harass on legal judgments of sexual harassment. *Journal of Applied Social Psychology, 35,* 745–772.

Lam, C. B., & Chan, D. K. S. (2007). The use of cyberpornography by young men in Hong Kong: Some psychosocial correlates. *Archives of Sexual Behavior, 36,* 588–598.

Perry, E. L., Schmidtke, J. M., & Kulik, C. T. (1998). Propensity to sexually harass: An exploration of gender differences. *Sex Roles, 38,* 443–460.

Pryor, J. B. (1987). Sexual harassment proclivities in men. *Sex Roles, 17,* 269–290.

Pryor, J. B., Giedd, J. L., & Williams, K. B. (1995). A social psychological model for predicting sexual harassment. *Journal of Social Issues, 51,* 69–84.

Pryor, J. B., LaVite, C., & Stoller, L. (1993). A social psychological analysis of sexual harassment: The person/situation interaction. *Journal of Vocational Behavior, 42,* 68–83.

Pryor, J. B., & Meyers, A. (2001). Men who sexually harass women. In L. B. Schlesinger (Ed.), *Serial offenders: Current thought, recent findings* (pp. 207–225). Boca Raton, FL: CRC Press.

Pryor, J. B., & Stoller, L. (1994). Sexual cognition processes in men who are high in the likelihood to sexually harass. *Personality and Social Psychology Bulletin, 20,* 163–169.

Pryor, J. B., & Whalen, N. J. (1997). A typology of sexual harassment: Characteristics of harassers and the social circumstances under which sexual harassment occurs. In W. O'Donohue (Ed.), *Sexual harassment: Theory, research, and treatment* (pp. 129–151). Needham Heights, MA: Allyn & Bacon.

Siebler, F., Sabelus, S., & Bohner, G. (2008). A refined computer harassment paradigm: Validation, and test of hypotheses about target characteristics. *Psychology of Women Quarterly, 32,* 22–35.

Exhibit

Likelihood to Sexually Harass Scale

Instructions: On the sheets that follow you will find 10 brief scenarios that describe 10 different interactions between males and females. In each case you will be asked to imagine that you are the main male character in the scenario. Then you will be asked to rate how likely it is that you would perform each of several different behaviors in the described social context. Assume in each scenario that, no matter what you choose to do, nothing bad would be likely to happen to you as result of your action. Try to answer each question as honestly as you can. Your answers will be completely anonymous. No one will ever try to discover your identity, no matter what you say on the questionnaire.

Scenario 1

Imagine that you are an executive in a large corporation. You are 42 years old. Your income is above average for people at your job level. You have had numerous job offers from other companies. You feel very secure in your job. One day your personal secretary decides to quit her job and you have the task of replacing her. The personnel department sends several applicants over for you to interview. All seem to be equally qualified for the job. One of the applicants, Michelle S., explains during her interview that she desperately needs the job. She is 23 years old, single and has been job-hunting for about a month. You find yourself very attracted to her. She looks at you in a way that possibly conveys she is also attracted to you. How likely are you to do the following things in this situation?

a. Would you give her the job over the other applicants? (Circle a number to indicate your response.)[a]

1...2...3...4...5
Not at all Likely   Very Likely

b. Assuming that you are secure enough in your job that no possible reprisals could happen to you, would you offer her the job in exchange for sexual favors?

c. Assuming that you fear no reprisals on your job, would you ask her to meet you later for dinner to discuss her possible employment?

Scenario 2

Imagine that you are the owner and manager of an expensive restaurant. One day, while going over the receipts, you discover that one of the waitresses has made some errors in her checks. She has undercharged several customers. The mistake costs you $100. In talking to some of the other employees, you find that the particular customers involved were friends of the waitress. You call her into your office and ask her to explain her behavior. The waitress confesses to having intentionally undercharged her friends. She promises that she will never repeat this dishonest act and tells you that she will do anything to keep her job. The waitress is someone you have always found particularly attractive. She is a divorcee and about 25 years old. How likely are you to do the following things in this situation?

a. Would you let her keep her job?

b. Would you let her keep her job in exchange for sexual favors?

c. Would you ask her to meet you for dinner after work to discuss the problem?

Scenario 3

Imagine that you are the manager of a shipping company. One day your supervisor asks you to study the possibility of buying several computers for the office. You call up several competing companies that sell computers. Each company sends a sales representative over to your office who describes the company's products. A salesperson from company "A" calls you and asks to come to your office. You agree and the next day a very attractive woman shows up. She can offer no real reason for buying her company's products over those of the other companies. However, she seems very sexy. How likely are you to do the following things in this situation?

a. Would you recommend her line of computers?

b. Assuming that you are secure enough in your job that no possible reprisals could happen to you, would you agree to recommend her line of computers in exchange for sexual favors?

c. Given the same assumptions as in the last question above, would you ask her to meet you later for dinner to discuss the choice of computers?

Scenario 4

Imagine that you are a Hollywood film director. You are casting for a minor role in a film you are planning. The role calls for a particularly stunning actress, one with a lot of sex appeal. How likely are you to do the following things in this situation?

a. Would you give the role to the actress whom you personally found sexiest?

b. Would give the role to an actress who agreed to have sex with you?

c. Would you ask the actress to whom you were most personally attracted to talk with you about the role over dinner?

Scenario 5

Imagine that you are the owner of a modeling agency. Your agency specializes in sexy female models used in television commercials. One of your models, Amy T., is a particularly ravishing brunette. You stop her after work one day and ask her to have dinner with you. She coldly declines your offer and tells you that she would like to keep your relationship with her "strictly business." A few months later you find that business is slack and you have to lay off some of your employees. You can choose to lay off Amy or one of four other women. All are good models, but someone has to go. How likely are you to do the following things in this situation?

a. Would you fire Amy?

b. Assuming that you are unafraid of possible reprisals, would you offer to let Amy keep her job in return for sexual favors?

c. Would you ask Amy to dinner so that you could talk over her future employment?

Scenario 6

Imagine that you are a college professor. You are 38 years old. You teach in a large midwestern university. You are a full professor with tenure. You are renowned in your field (Abnormal Psychology) and have numerous offers for other jobs. One day following the return of an examination to a class, a female student stops in your office. She tells you that her score is one point away from an "A" and asks you if she can do some extra credit project to raise her score. She tells you that she may not have a sufficient grade to get into graduate school without the "A." Several other students have asked you to do extra credit assignments and you have declined to let them. This particular woman is a stunning blonde. She sits in the front row of the class every day and always wears short skirts. You find her extremely sexy. How likely are you to do the following things in this situation?

a. Would you let her carry out a project for extra credit (e.g. write a paper)?

b. Assuming that you are very secure in your job and the university has always tolerated professors who make passes at students, would you offer the student a chance to earn extra credit in return for sexual favors?

c. Given the same assumptions as in the question above, would you ask her to join you for dinner to discuss the possible extra credit assignments?

Scenario 7

Imagine that you are a college student at a large midwestern university. You are a junior who just transferred from another school on the East coast. One night at a bar you meet an attractive female student named Rhonda. Rhonda laments to you that she is failing a course in English Poetry. She tells you that she has a paper due next week on the poet Shelley, and fears that she will fail since she has not begun to write it. You remark that you wrote a paper last year on Shelley at your former school. Your paper was given an A+. She asks you if you will let her use your paper in her course. She wants to just retype it and put her name on it. How likely are you to do the following things in this situation?

a. Would you let Rhonda use your paper?

b. Would you let Rhonda use your paper in exchange for sexual favors?

c. Would you ask Rhonda to come to your apartment to discuss the matter?

Scenario 8

Imagine that you are the editor for a major publishing company. It is your job to read new manuscripts of novels and decide whether they are worthy of publication. You receive literally hundreds of manuscripts per week from aspiring novelists. Most of them are screened by your subordinates and thrown in the trash. You end up accepting about one in a thousand for publication. One night you go to a party. There you meet a very attractive woman named Betsy. Betsy tells you that she has written a novel and would like to check into getting it published. This is her first novel. She is a dental assistant. She asks you to read her novel. How likely are you to do the following things in this situation?

a. Would you agree to read Betsy's novel?
b. Would you agree to read Betsy's novel in exchange for sexual favors?
c. Would you ask Betsy to have dinner with you the next night to discuss your reading her novel?

Scenario 9

Imagine that you are a physician. You go over to the hospital one day to make your rounds visiting your patients. In looking over the records of one of your patients, you discover that one of the attending nurses on the previous night shift made an error in administering drugs to your patient. She gave the wrong dosage of a drug. You examine the patient and discover that no harm was actually done. He seems fine. However, you realize that the ramifications of the error could have been catastrophic under other circumstances. You pull the files and find out who made the error. It turns out that a new young nurse named Wendy H. was responsible. You have noticed Wendy in some of your visits to the hospital and have thought of asking her out to dinner. You realize that she could lose her job if you report this incident. How likely are you to do each of the following things?

a. Would you report Wendy to the hospital administration?
b. Assuming that you fear no reprisals, would you tell Wendy in private that you will not report her if she will have sex with you?
c. Assuming that you fear no reprisals, would you ask Wendy to join you for dinner to discuss the incident?

Scenario 10

Imagine that you are the news director for a local television station. Due to some personnel changes you have to replace the anchor woman for the evening news. Your policy has always been to promote reporters from within your organization when an anchor woman vacancy occurs. There are several female reporters from which to choose. All are young, attractive, and apparently qualified for the job. One reporter, Loretta W., is someone whom you personally find very sexy. You initially hired her, giving her a first break in the TV news business. How likely are you to do the following things in this situation?

a. Would you give Loretta the job?
b. Assuming that you fear no reprisals in your job, would you offer Loretta the job in exchange for sexual favors?
c. Assuming that you fear no reprisals in your job, would you ask her to meet you after work for dinner to discuss the job?

Note. Scoring the LSH: The key items are respondents' answers to the *b* item for each scenario. Ratings for these items are simply summed to produce an overall LSH score.

[a] The following scale is reproduced after each response option.

Sexual Harassment Attitudes Questionnaire

JAYNE E. STAKE[1] AND NATALIE J. MALOVICH, *University of Missouri-St. Louis*

Description

The incidence of sexual harassment in educational settings is well documented, yet the psychological dynamics that underlie the perpetuation of sexual harassment are still only partially understood. The Sexual Harassment Attitudes Questionnaire was developed as a research tool to explore psychological factors associated with sexual harassment in educational settings. The questionnaire measures respondents' attitudes regarding (a) responsibility for harassment behaviors, (b) appropriate responses to sexual harassment, and (c) effects of sexual harassment on victims. Respondents first read two scenarios that depict clear-cut incidents of sexual harassment in a college setting. After each scenario, they indicate to whom they attribute responsibility for the incident. Two questions pertain to victim blame, two to perpetrator blame, and two to no blame. A second set of six questions taps respondents' attitudes about appropriate responses to sexual harassment. Two questions refer to confronting the harassing behavior, two to complying with the harasser, and two to ignoring the harassment. Finally, a set of eight questions measures expectations of the effects of the harassment. Two questions refer to educational effects and six to emotional effects. All questions have 6-point Likert-type scales except for the questions regarding emotional effects, which have 7-point Likert-type scales.

Validity

Based on responses of 113 female and 111 male college undergraduates, the questionnaire shows evidence of construct validity (Malovich & Stake, 1990). Perpetrator blame scores in this sample were negatively related to victim blame (−.36) and no blame (−.57) scores. Victim blame was positively related to recommendations for compliance (+.47) and expectations for positive educational effects (+.32), and negatively related to recommendations for confrontive action (−.30), expectations for negative emotional effects (−.44), and liberal sex role attitudes (Attitudes Toward Women scores and victim blame: −.22). In contrast, perpetrator blame was positively related to recommendations for confrontive action (+.45), expectations for negative emotional effects (+.54), and liberal sex role attitudes (+.22), and negatively related to recommendations for compliance (−.45) and expectations for positive educational effects (−.37).

Reference

Malovich, N. J., & Stake, J. E. (1990). Sexual harassment on campus: Individual differences in attitudes and beliefs. *Psychology of Women Quarterly, 14*, 63–81.

Exhibit

Sexual Harassment Attitudes Questionnaire

The purpose of this questionnaire is to examine relationships between instructors and students. You will read two scenarios involving instructors and students. Each will be followed by a set of questions consisting of statements about the scenario you have read. You will be asked to imagine that you or a close woman friend of yours is the student in the situation presented. There are no right or wrong answers, only opinions. If you are unsure about an answer, just indicate the response that best fits your own opinion.

Scenario 1

Suppose that you or a close woman friend of yours is attending classes on this campus. After class one day, a professor asks that you come to his office to discuss your grade with him. When you get there he notes that you barely passed the last exam and are in danger of receiving a D for the course. He then tells you at length how much he enjoys having you in the class, leading up to a dinner invitation. He states that if you "get to know each other better" he might be able to work things out so that you can get a better grade.

The following are a number of statements about the situation that might help to explain why the above incident occurred. Rate your agreement with each of the following comments. Mark the number on your answer sheet that best describes your feeling. Use the following key:

[1]Address correspondence to Jayne Stake, Department of Psychology, University of Missouri-St. Louis, St. Louis, MO 63121; e-mail: jayne_stake@umsl.edu

0 = Strongly disagree
1 = Moderately disagree
2 = Somewhat disagree
3 = Somewhat agree
4 = Moderately agree
5 = Strongly agree

1. The student is probably hoping that getting to know the professor personally will help her get a better grade in the course.
2. The professor probably meant no harm so it should not be taken too seriously.
3. The professor is using his status unfairly to pressure the student into dating him.
4. The professor is responding to normal sexual attraction and cannot really be blamed for his actions in the situation.
5. The professor's actions were unethical and could be harmful to his students.
6. The student is most likely a flirtatious type who enjoys getting special attention from her professors.

The following are a number of statements describing possible ways that you could deal with the situation. Rate your agreement with each of the following statements. Mark the number on your answer sheet that best describes your feelings. Use the following key:

0 = Strongly disagree
1 = Moderately disagree
2 = Somewhat disagree
3 = Somewhat agree
4 = Moderately agree
5 = Strongly agree

7. Change the subject and try to forget about the conversation.
8. Go to dinner with the professor and talk over the problems you are having in the class.
9. Continue to work hard in the class and avoid any individual conversations with the professor.
10. Tell the professor that you are not interested in a personal relationship, and that this should have nothing to do with your grade in the course.
11. See the professor on a social basis if he is interested as it may help your grade.
12. Go to the department head and tell him/her about the professor's actions.

Below is a set of word pairs that describe how you or a close woman friend might feel about this experience. The two feelings in each pair are separated by a 7-point scale, with one word on each side on the scale. For each word pair, mark the number on your answer sheet that is closest to how you think you or your friend might feel.

13. Insulted	0	1	2	3	4	5	6	Flattered
14. Pleased	0	1	2	3	4	5	6	Angry
15. Comfortable	0	1	2	3	4	5	6	Uncomfortable
16. Relaxed	0	1	2	3	4	5	6	Nervous
17. Intimidated	0	1	2	3	4	5	6	Powerful
18. Embarrassed	0	1	2	3	4	5	6	Proud

Scenario 2

Suppose that you or a close woman friend of yours is attending this campus. Through the course of the semester you notice that a professor in one of your classes frequently seems to be staring at you. When talking with him after class one day about an upcoming essay exam, he puts his arm around you (or the woman friend) and touches your hair. He then suggests that you come to his office at the end of the day so that the exam can be discussed further. He adds that if you fail to do so, you will probably not do as well on the exam as expected.[a]

[a]Questions 19–36 are identical to questions 1–18.

Sexual Health Services Questionnaire

SCOTT M. BUTLER,[1] *Georgia College & State University*

DAVID R. BLACK, GEORGE H. AVERY, AND JANICE KELLY, *Purdue University*

DANIEL C. COSTER, *Utah State University*

The Sexual Health Services Questionnaire (SHSQ) is a theory-based instrument designed to assess the availability of sexuality-related services among college health centers, as well as the relationship between these services and two constructs of the diffusion of innovations theory (DIT; Rogers, 2003). The SHSQ also can be used to assess services at sexual health clinics located in other settings.

Description

The 100-item questionnaire is divided into 13 sections, including employees who deal with sexuality-related problems through treatment and prevention methods (24 items), duties of human sexuality peer helpers (9 items), safer-sex products (8 items), condom distribution procedures (6 items), hormonal and barrier contraceptives (13 items), sexually transmitted infection testing methods (11 items), Human papillomavirus and Hepatitis vaccinations (2 items), gynecological services (4 items), post-sexual assault examination (1 item), testicular examination (1 item), sexuality-related counseling (6 items), Clinical Laboratory Improvement Amendment (CLIA) certificate (1 item), and participant/institutional demographics (14 items).

The first two sections of the SHSQ are grounded in the DIT and represent the complexity construct (Rogers, 2003). Rogers (2003) defines complexity as "the degree to which an organization's members possess a relatively high level of knowledge and expertise, usually measured by the member's range of occupational specialties and their degree of professionalism (expressed by formal training)" (p. 412). The DIT suggests a positive relationship with complexity and overall organizational innovativeness (Rogers, 2003). In addition, the DIT theory suggests a positive relationship between institutional size and organizational innovativeness (Rogers, 2003).

Response Mode and Timing

Directors of health centers (or appropriate representatives) are provided instructions for completing each section of items. The majority of the items require participants to place an "X" next to all services that their health center currently offers. Three items allow the participants to write in their own responses through the use of an "other" cat-

egory. One item is a ratio-based item in which directors are instructed to report the number of condoms their health center distributes per year. If they do not distribute condoms, they are instructed to report "0," and if the number distributed is unknown they are instructed to report "999." Completion of the SHSQ takes approximately 15 minutes. In order to maintain the overall validity and homogeneity of responses, it is recommended that the director of the health center (or appropriate representative) complete the SHSQ.

Scoring

The majority of the items on the SHSQ are dichotomous. Items in which the participant reports with an X are scored as 1, and items left blank are scored as 0. Responses can be summed for individual sections or multiple sections that are scored dichotomously. Responses for individual items as well as summed responses can be used for statistical analyses.

In order to assess whether the complexity items of the SHSQ can adequately predict organizational innovativeness, it is suggested all dichotomous scores from the first section be summed. An additional score of 0 or 1 is then added to this value to represent the utilization of peer helpers from the second section of the questionnaire, whereas 0 equals no utilization of peers in any form and 1 equals one or more methods. (It is not recommended that an additional value be added to the overall complexity scale for each method of peer helper utilization as this may result in over-representation of peers in the final computation.) A second value representing organization innovativeness is then created by summing the dichotomous scores on Sections 3–11. Statistical analyses can be conducted to assess the relationship between the overall score on the complexity scale and the organizational innovativeness score. Currently, there are no normative data available for services scored on the SHSQ.

The DIT theory also suggests a positive relationship between organizational innovativeness and the construct organizational size (Rogers, 2003). This assessment can be accomplished by evaluating the relationship between the organizational innovativeness scale previously described and the items addressing the number of employees within the health center and/or the item that addresses the total population of the college/university.

[1]Address correspondence to Scott M. Butler, Department of Kinesiology, Georgia College & State University, Campus Box 065, Milledgeville, GA 31061; e-mail: kanezwei@hotmail.com

Reliability

Initially, 1,200 questionnaires were mailed to a geographically representative sample of colleges/universities that house a health center in the United States. Of these, 358 (29.83% response rate) were returned. We used data from these participants to assess internal consistency and categorized items by their respective sections for assessment. We then merged Sections 6 and 7 as well as 8–10 because of similarity of service assessment. We did not include Section 12 (CLIA certificate) in the analyses. Cronbach alpha scores ranged from .62 to .93 for individual sections and .94 for the entire questionnaire.

Of the initial 358 participants, 50 were mailed a second copy of the SHSQ to establish test-retest reliability; 28 participants (56% response rate) recompleted the questionnaire. Assessment of the demographics of the test-retest participants indicated that each of the key demographic variables of the overall population was represented in the subsample on one or more occasions. Results indicated an overall rate of 87.37% consistency on service-related items.

Validity

To evaluate validity, we developed and implemented a comprehensive strategy. First, we conducted a review of the extant literature regarding sexuality-related services among college health centers. In addition, we reviewed the relevant literature regarding contemporary contraceptive, sexually transmitted infection, and other sexuality-related services. To establish face and content validity, we chose six expert panelists to review the instrument. We made initial contacts with three of the panelists through electronic mail, along with a letter of invitation and instructions to provide feedback. These individuals included a doctoral-level health promotion specialist who had served as the director of multiple college health centers, a doctoral-level psychologist with extensive leadership in peer helping, and a health behavior doctoral student with experience in coordinating collegiate sexual-health, peer-education programs and research experience in collegiate peer helping and condom use among college students. Next, we conducted three one-on-one meetings with experts in the field, one of whom was a doctoral-level psychologist who serves as the director of a comprehensive health center located within a large public university. We conducted a second interview with a doctoral-level health promotion specialist who had extensive experience in teaching collegiate-level health courses and experience as the director of a college health promotion program. The final interview occurred with a master's-level health promotion specialist who currently serves as the center's human sexuality education coordinator. The final version of the SHSQ included recommendations made by the expert panelists.

Participants who recompleted the SHSQ for test-retest reliability purposes also answered additional questions assessing response bias. We evaluated response bias by asking evaluators if the items on the questionnaire were written in a clear manner and were adequate in terms of comprehensiveness, and if they felt participants would respond honestly (Gunning, 1952). In response, 91% indicated that items were asked in a clear manner, 64% felt the sections on the questionnaire were adequate, and 98% believed that participants would respond honestly.

Other Information

This questionnaire is copyrighted © 2008 by Scott M. Butler, David R. Black, George H. Avery, Janice Kelly, and Daniel C. Coster.

References

Gunning, R. (1952). *The technique of clear writing*. New York: McGraw-Hill.

Rogers, E. M. (2003). *Diffusion of innovations* (5th ed.). New York: Free Press.

Exhibit

Sexual Health Services Questionnaire

The following questionnaire inquires about the sexual health services your student health center currently offers. If you have any questions please do not hesitate to contact the investigators.

Directions: The items below inquire about your current employment of staff involved with sexual health programs and types of sexual health services offered by your campus health center. *Please mark an "X" next to all that apply.*

Employees who deal with student sexual health concerns and/or problems *as their **primary job responsibility** at your health center* include:

Sexuality Program Coordinator ——
Sexuality Educator ——
Physician ——
Physician Assistant ——
Nurse ——

Nurse Practitioner ____
Sexual Assault Nurse Examiner (SANE) ____
Health Educator ____
Psychologist ____
Psychiatrist ____
Social Worker ____
Mental Health Counselor ____
Other (please identify): _____

Employees that deal with student sexual health concerns and/or problems *on a regular basis but* **do not consider sexual health their primary job responsibility** *include:*

Physician ____
Physician Assistant ____
Nurse ____
Nurse Practitioner ____
Sexual Assault Nurse Examiner (SANE) ____
Health Educator ____
Psychologist ____
Psychiatrist ____
Social Worker ____
Mental Health Counselor ____
Other (please identify): _____

Some health centers house volunteer or paid student peer educators/health advocates. *Please mark an "X" next to all* of the following that apply to your college health center.

Do you use student peers . . .
To organize sexuality-related events on campus
(e.g., presentations at residence halls/Greek housing) ____
To conduct counseling on relationship issues ____
To conduct sexual health outreach ____
To conduct contraceptive counseling ____
To conduct STD testing counseling ____
To conduct counseling on sexual orientation issues ____
To conduct counseling on other sexuality issues ____
To give away condoms at campus bars/restaurants ____

Other (please identify): _____

Please mark an "X" next to any of the following safer-sex products your health center distributes to students.

Male latex condoms ____
Flavored condoms ____
Non-latex male condoms ____
Specialty condoms ____
(e.g., those above or below average size) ____
Female condoms ____
Sexual lubricants ____
Latex dams (i.e., dental dams) ____

On average how many **condoms does your institution *distribute to students* per year? (If you do NOT distribute condoms please write in 0. If you are unsure about how many condoms you distribute please write in 999 for coding purposes) _____#

Please mark an "X" next to any methods in which your health center distributes condoms (includes both selling and giving away condoms for free).

At the pharmacy ____
During after-hours ____

Through appointment with health care provider   _____

Through educational outreach   _____

At campus events   _____

At bars and restaurants near campus   _____

Please mark an "X" next to any of the following contraceptive methods that are available through your health center.

Oral contraceptive pill   _____

Oral contraceptive pill (progestin only)   _____

Hormonal transdermal skin patch   _____

Hormonal vaginal ring   _____

Intrauterine device (IUD) hormonal   _____

Intrauterine device (IUD) copper   _____

Progestin-only injection   _____

Instruction for fertility awareness method (FAM)   _____

Emergency contraception pills (ECP) by prescription   _____

Emergency contraception pills (ECP) over the counter   _____

Diaphragm   _____

Cervical cap   _____

Hormonal implant   _____

Please mark an "X" next to any of the sexually transmitted infections (STIs) that your health center currently offers testing for.

HIV   _____

HIV "quick" blood test   _____

HIV oral swab test   _____

Chlamydia   _____

Gonorrhea   _____

Hepatitis B   _____

Hepatitis A   _____

Herpes simplex virus (HSV)   _____

Syphilis   _____

HPV DNA test for women   _____

Trichomonas   _____

Please mark an "X" next to *any of the following* infections that your health center currently provides a vaccine for.

HPV vaccine   _____

Hepatitis B vaccine   _____

Please mark an "X" next to *any of the following* services that your health center currently provides.

Pap test   _____

Bimanual uterine/ovarian exam   _____

Colposcopy   _____

Please mark an "X" if your health center provides the service *listed below.*

Clinical breast exam   _____

Please mark an "X" if your health center provides the service *listed below.*

Testicular exam   _____

Please mark an "X" if your health center provides the service *listed below.*

Post-sexual assault exam   _____

Please mark an "X" next to *any of the following counseling services* that your health center currently provides.

Individual counseling on general sexual health issues   _____

Group counseling on general sexual health issues _____
Relationship issues _____
Sexual orientation issues _____
Contraceptive methods _____
Service for survivors of sexual assault _____

Does your health center have a Clinical Laboratory Improvement Amendment (CLIA) certificate? *Please mark an "X" next to your response.*

Yes _____
No _____
Unsure _____

Directions: The items below ask about your personal demographics and how long you have been a college health center director. Please *respond by writing in your response or by placing an "X" in the space provided.*

Your age: _____

Your race/ethnicity:

Asian _____
Black/African American _____
Caucasian White _____
Hispanic _____
American Indian _____
Other _____

Your gender:

Male _____
Female _____

How many total years have you been the director of a college health center? If you have been the director of more than one health center, please combine your total years of experience. _____ years

Your education:
Please *mark an "X" next to all of the degrees you have earned*

Bachelor's _____
Master's _____
PhD _____
MD _____
Other _____

Total number of employees at your health center: _____

Total student population at your college/university: _____

What state is your college/university located in? _____

Directions: The items below are based upon your college/university's demographics; please *respond by placing an "X" in the space provided.*

Type of Academic Institution
Public _____
Private _____

Setting of Your Institution:
Urban _____
Small Town _____
Suburban _____
Rural _____

Student Population:

Primarily Residential	_____
Primarily Commuter	_____
Equal Numbers Residential and Commuter	_____

Degrees Awarded at Your Institution (check all that apply)

Associate	_____
Baccalaureate	_____
Master's	_____
Doctorate	_____
Professional (e.g., MD, JD)	_____
Other Degrees	_____

Does your institution have a medical school?

Yes	_____
No	_____

Additional Demographic Characteristics (Please check all that apply)

Historically Black College or University	_____
Faith-Based Institution	_____
All-Male Institution	_____
All-Female Institution	_____

Thank You for Participating in Our Study!

Address correspondence to [insert return information]:

_____

Sexual Health Survey

HEATHER EASTMAN-MUELLER,[1] DEBORAH CARR, AND STEVE OSTERLIND,
University of Missouri, Columbia

The purpose of the Sexual Health Survey (SHS) is to assess the Sexual Health Knowledge (SHK), Sexual Health Attitudes (SHA), and Sexual Health Behaviors (SHB) of students enrolled in institutes of higher education. The SHS was designed to assess a comprehensive range of five sexual health topics, including (a) contraception, (b) pregnancy prevention, (c) sexual health communication, (d) sexual behavior, and (e) sexually transmitted infections (STI) and barriers to obtaining STI testing.

Description

Items generated for this survey were based on an extensive literature review and focus group construct explication performed on priority areas. Content validity was assessed for quality, clarity, and sensitivity to culture and gender by a panel review of five experts from a variety of backgrounds, including a counseling psychologist, a registered nurse, a statistician, an expert on human sexuality, and an expert on sexual violence and lesbian, gay, bisexual, transgender, and queer (LGBTQ) issues.

A pilot test study was administered online to 600 randomly sampled university students to further refine the survey instrument. Item analysis reduced the initial number of items from 200 to 127. Items eliminated were based on failure to meet appropriate item discrimination, item difficulty/endorsement, and reliability measures.

[1]Address correspondence to Heather Eastman-Mueller, Student Health Center, 1101 Hospital Drive, Health Promotion Department, University of Missouri, Columbia, MO 65212; e-mail: eastmanmuellerh@health.missouri.edu

Response Mode and Timing

Sexual Health Knowledge (SHK) is assessed using a 6-point Likert-type scale (0 = *Strongly Disagree/Very Effective*, 5 = *Strongly Agree/Very Ineffective*) for 24 items that assess basic knowledge of sexually transmitted infection (STI) and pregnancy prevention, effects of alcohol on sexuality, and the impact of STIs among this population.

Sexual Health Attitudes (SHA) were assessed using a 6-point Likert-type scale (0 = *Very Uncomfortable/Very Unconcerned/Strongly Agree*, 5 = *Very Comfortable/Very Concerned/Strongly Disagree*) across 48 items measuring comfort level in communication with a partner about past sexual history or contraceptive methods. Other questions examine level of concern seeking STI testing, perceptions of peer's sexual activity, belief in rape myths, and communication associated with condom/dental dam procurement.

Sexual Health Behavior (SHB) was assessed using 17 multiple-choice and 16 dichotomous items requesting age at sexual debut, and sexual activity in last 30 days and across the lifespan. Other items concerned contraceptive and alcohol use, number of sexual partners, frequency of

barrier protection use, unintentional pregnancy, and sexual assault.

Demographic information included age, year in school, sexual orientation, relationship status, ethnicity, residential arrangements, and membership within a Greek (fraternity/sorority) community. The survey takes approximately 20 minutes to complete.

Scoring

The scale can be scored by construct and/or by factor. To obtain a knowledge score, add all knowledge items, 1–24, for a possible maximum score of 120. To obtain an attitude score, sum Items 1 through 10, 17 through 19, 21, 25, and 27 for a maximum score of 80.

When scoring factors independently, larger scores represent a more favorable attitude toward safer-sex practices and/or abstinence, increased comfort level with sexual health communication and barrier methods, and belief in rape myths. For Factor 4, the smaller the score, the less knowledge about latex barrier effectiveness.

TABLE 1
Items, Factor Loadings, Communality Estimates, Means, and Standard Deviations for the Four-Factor Solution for Sexual Health Survey (Rotated)

Item	Factor Loading	h^2	M	SD
Factor 1: Perceived Sexual Readiness (5 items)				
Sex should be reserved for a long-term relationship.	.68	.43	1.38	1.52
People should wait until they are married to have sex.	.73	.56	2.84	1.73
Sexual intercourse is acceptable in a relationship no matter how long the couple has been dating.	.80	.63	2.06	1.67
Engaging in sexual activity immediately after beginning a relationship is ok.	.83	.70	1.77	1.62
More students on this campus should practice being sexually abstinent.	.69	.53	2.39	1.62
Factor 2: Comfort Sexual Communication (3 items)				
Comfort level of asking a partner about their past sexual history.	.71	.52	3.56	1.46
Comfort level asking a partner if she/he has had an HIV test.	.94	.86	3.12	1.66
Comfort level asking a partner if he/she has been tested for an STD (excluding HIV).	.92	.85	3.17	1.62
Factor 3: Comfort with Barrier Methods (3 items)				
Comfort level buying a condom or a dental dam.	.60	.42	3.48	1.58
Comfort level providing a condom/dental dam if a partner did not have one available.	.96	.58	4.15	1.32
Comfort level of using/asking partner to use a condom or dental dam.	.60	.46	4.30	1.18
Factor 4: Latex Barrier Effectiveness (3 items)				
Effectiveness in preventing STDS . . .				
. . . wearing (or having a partner wear) a condom.	.83	.49	3.92	1.08
. . . wearing a condom containing spermicidal cream.	.77	.46	3.76	1.27
. . . using a dental dam during oral sex.	.62	.34	3.80	1.14
Factor 5: Belief in Rape Myths (3 items)				
A person is more likely to be raped if he/she . . .				
. . . feels that he/she owes the person something.	.68	.47	1.88	1.43
. . . has sex with multiple partners.	.65	.46	2.33	1.57
. . . is in a passive role in a relationship.	.71	.52	1.94	1.39

Reliability

To test the internal consistency, a reliability analysis was performed on each subscale and the factor model as a whole. For Factor 1, the subscale named "perceived sexual readiness," the Cronbach's alpha was .88 ($k = 5$), with all positive corrected item-total correlations of .63 and above. For Factor 2, the subscale named "comfort sexual communication," the Cronbach's alpha was .91 ($k = 3$), with all positive corrected item-total correlations .71 and above. For Factor 3, the subscale named "comfort with barrier methods" had a Cronbach's alpha of .79 ($k = 3$); all positive corrected item-total correlations were .58 and above. For Factor 4, the subscale named "latex barrier effectiveness" ($k = 3$), the Cronbach's alpha was .79; all positive corrected item-total correlations were .56 and above. For Factor 5, the subscale named "belief in rape myths" ($k = 3$), the Cronbach's alpha was .74; all positive corrected item-total correlations were .55 and above. Finally, for all subscales combined ($k = 17$), the Cronbach's alpha was .79, with corrected item-total correlations ranging from .23 to .54.

Validity

Principal axis factoring was performed to detect structure and determine dimensionality of the set of variables. The factorability indices were .784 for the Kaiser-Meyer-Olkin (KMO) measure of sampling adequacy and the Bartlett's test of sphericity ($p < .001$), indicating good factorability. A varimax rotation was performed because the majority of the variables were uncorrelated (i.e., below .32; Tabachnick & Fidell, 2001, p. 622). Following the varimax rotation, the analysis yielded a five-factor solution with eigenvalues greater than 1.0, cumulatively accounting for 71.46% of the variance. According to Heck (2000, p.188), when used alone the rule of retaining eigenvalues greater than 1.0 may over- or underestimate the number of factors; a scree plot should be used as secondary criterion for factor verification. The scree plot confirmed the five-factor solution. All of the items had loadings of .30 or greater, falling within acceptable parameters (Table 1).

Other Information

This instrument has been copyrighted in February 2006. Permission must be granted from the primary author prior to use.

References

Heck, R. H. (2000). *Factor analysis: Exploratory and confirmatory approaches.* Mahwah, NJ: Lawrence Erlbaum.

Tabachnick, B. G., & Fidell, L. S. (2001). *Using multivariate statistics* (4th ed.). Needham Heights, MA: Allyn & Bacon.

Exhibit

Sexual Health Survey (Sample Items)

Knowledge Section

The following questions are intended to access your sexual health knowledge. Please answer each question to the best of your ability by indicating to what extent you agree or disagree with the following statements. If you feel uncomfortable answering any of the questions you may skip them.

K10)   Women can become pregnant the first time they engage in vaginal-penile intercourse.

        Strongly Disagree[a]
        Moderately Disagree
        Mildly Disagree
        Mildly Agree
        Moderately Agree
        Strongly Agree

For each of the following questions, please indicate the level of effectiveness that each behavior provides in preventing sexually transmitted diseases. Select the option that best corresponds with your answer.

K13)   Giving and receiving oral sex without any form of barrier protection (condom or dental dam).

        Very Effective[b]
        Moderately Effective
        Slightly Effective
        Slightly Ineffective
        Moderately Ineffective
        Strongly Ineffective

K15)   Wearing (or having a partner wear) a condom that contains spermicidal cream.

K16)   Using (or having a partner use) a dental dam or any latex barrier used to help prevent the exchange of fluids, during oral sex.

Attitude Section

The following questions are intended to access your attitudes towards sexual health topics. Please answer each question to the best of your ability by selecting one of the following options. If you feel uncomfortable answering any of the questions you may skip them.

To what extent do you feel comfortable or uncomfortable when engaging in the following behaviors? Please indicate your answer for each behavior by selecting the corresponding option.

A6)   Speaking with a partner about using birth control (any method).
             Very Comfortable[c]
             Moderately Comfortable
             Slightly Comfortable
             Slightly Uncomfortable
             Moderately Uncomfortable
             Strongly Uncomfortable

A7)   Asking a partner about their past sexual history.

A10)   Engaging in unprotected (no condom or dental dam) sexual activity with a partner.

For the following statements, please indicate your level of concern if you were trying to decide whether or not to get tested for a sexually transmitted disease, including HIV (the virus that causes AIDS).

A19)   Having unprotected sex (sex without a condom or dental dam) is not worth the risk of contracting a sexually transmitted disease.

Behavior Section

In this survey, the definition of sexual activity refers to oral, anal, and vaginal sex. This does not include massage, touching, or mutual masturbation.

B1)   Have you ever had consensual sex (oral, anal, or vaginal)?
             Yes
             No

B8)   In the last **30 DAYS**, what type of sex did you have? Check all that apply.
             Oral
             Anal
             Vaginal
             Other

B10)   If you did NOT use a form of barrier protection such as a condom/dental dam (a latex covering used to prevent the exchange of bodily fluids) in the last **30 DAYS** you had sex please indicate the reason. Check all that apply.
             I just knew my partner was safe.
             It was a spontaneous, unplanned event.
             I was under the influence of alcohol or drugs.
             I did not feel comfortable discussing the matter with my partner.
             I did not feel I needed to because I was involved in a long-term relationship at the time.
             I was using another form of birth control.
             There was not any form of protection method available.
             The sex was nonconsensual (sex against my will).
             Other _____ (Must fill in the blank)

B15)   Which of the following barrier and/or birth control methods do you use **most often?** Check all that apply.

Condom/dental dams (latex covering used to prevent the exchange of bodily fluids)

Combination hormonal methods (such as birth control pills, Ortho Evra—the Patch, NUVA—intravaginal ring—the Ring).

Depo-Provera (the Shot)

Calendar method (rhythm or having sex only during the "safe" times of the month)

Withdrawal or "pulling out"

Diaphragm

Nothing

Other _____ (Must fill in the blank)

Demographics

D2) Which of the following do you consider yourself?

    Male
    Female
    Transgender

D5) What is your current relationship status?

    Single (not in a relationship)
    Committed relationship (only dating one person)
    Non-committed relationship (casual)
    Cohabitating (living together)
    Married or partnered

D6) Which of the following commonly used terms best describes you?

    Heterosexual
    Gay or lesbian
    Bisexual
    Transgender
    Questioning

D7) Where do you currently live?

    Campus residence halls
    Greek housing
    Other university housing
    Off-campus housing
    Parent's or guardian's house

---

aThe responses are repeated for Questions K1 through K11.

bThe responses are repeated for Questions K12 through K24.

cThe responses are repeated for Questions A1 through A10.

Sexual Health Practices Self-Efficacy Scale

PATRICIA BARTHALOW KOCH,[1] CLINTON COLACO, AND ANDREW W. PORTER,
The Pennsylvania State University

The World Health Organization defines sexual health as the state of physical, emotional, mental, and social well-being related to sexuality, not merely the absence of disease, dysfunction, or infirmity (World Health Organization, 2009). Sexual health has been identified as an important part of each person's overall wellness and quality of life (Pan American Health Organization & World Health Organization, 2000; World Association of Sexual Health, 2008). Sexual health concerns and problems may generate and/or perpetuate other problems in the individual, family, community, and population at large. In order to be sexually healthy, individuals are encouraged to learn and demonstrate a variety of behaviors (Sexuality Information and Education Council of the United States, 2009). Thus, the Sexual Health Practices Self-Efficacy Scale (SHPSES) was developed to measure respondents' confidence (self-efficacy) as described as their knowledge, skills, and comfort to carry out 20 different sexual health practices. Bandura proposed the concept of self-efficacy as the conviction or confidence that a person can successfully execute the behavior required to produce a certain outcome (Bandura, 1977, 1982). Self-efficacy is recognized as one of the most important prerequisites for behavior change (Bandura, 1997) and has been prolifically applied to research in diverse areas including smoking cessation, dietary practices, exercise behaviors, alcohol consumption, contraceptive use, and HIV prevention (Strecher, DeVellis, Becker, & Rosenstock, 1986). It has been incorporated into the frameworks of many influential theories, including social cognitive theory, the health belief model, and the transtheoretical model (DiClemente & Peterson, 1994; Glanz, Rimer, & Viswanath, 2008).

Description

The Sexual Health Practices Self-Efficacy Scale (SHPSES) consists of 20 items representing a variety of sexual health practices. Respondents indicate their confidence in performing these practices (self-efficacy) on a scale from 1 (*Not at all Confident*) to 5 (*Extremely Confident*). Through the use of factor analysis (see Validity section), six subscales were identified, including self-efficacy in regard to Sexual Relationships (5 items), Sexual Health Care (4 items), Sexual Assault (3 items), Safer Sex (4 items), Sexual Equality/Diversity (3 items), and Abstinence (1 item). SHPSES is appropriate for adolescents to older adults of all backgrounds.

Response Mode and Timing

Respondents are instructed to indicate how confident they are, at the time they are completing the survey, in carrying out each of 20 different sexual health practices. Confidence is defined as having the knowledge, skills, and comfort necessary to effectively perform the sexual health practice. Respondents use the following scale: 1 = *Not at all Confident*, 2 = *Slightly Confident*, 3 = *Moderately Confident*, 4 = *Highly Confident*, 5 = *Extremely Confident*. The term partner refers to whomever the respondent might share his or her sexuality with. The scale takes approximately 5 minutes to complete.

Scoring

Scores on the SHPSES can range from 20, indicating the least self-efficacy, to 100, indicating the most self-efficacy in performing the variety of sexual health practices. The subscales consist of the following items: Sexual Relationships (7, 8, 12, 13, 14), Sexual Health Care (1, 2, 3, 4), Sexual Assault (15, 16, 17), Safer Sex (5, 9, 10, 11), Sexual Equality/Diversity (18, 19, 20), and Abstinence (6).

Reliability

Internal reliability was calculated from 1,200 surveys completed by a convenience sample of undergraduate students attending a major northeastern university from 2004 to 2008. The Cronbach's alpha coefficient for the entire scale was .89 (Koch, 2009). Subscale reliability coefficients were as follows: Sexual Relationships, .82; Sexual Health Care, .81; Sexual Assault, .78; Safer Sex, .71; Sexual Equality/Diversity, .73. Abstinence was a single item, so no individual alpha coefficient was calculated.

Validity

Content validity was determined through examination of the sexual health content of 10 major sexuality textbooks and the syllabi of 20 sexuality classes taught at differing colleges and universities throughout the United States. A panel of three sexuality educators/researchers reviewed the initial pool of items for relevance and redundancy. Using the 1,200 surveys collected from undergraduate students, construct validity was examined with a principal component analysis using a varimax rotation with Kaiser

[1]Address correspondence to Patricia Barthalow Koch, Professor of Biobehavioral Health, The Pennsylvania State University, 304B Health and Human Development Building East, University Park, PA 16802; e-mail: p3k@psu.edu

normalization. The rotation converged in six iterations, identifying the following six factors representing sexual health practices self-efficacy: Sexual Relationships (15.4% explained variance), Sexual Health Care (13.4%), Sexual Assault (11.2%), Safer Sex (10.1%), Sexual Equality/ Diversity (10.0%), and Abstinence (5.8%). The SHPSES has been shown to discriminate undergraduate students who have taken sexuality education classes in comparison to students enrolled in nonsexuality or nonhealth-related classes at a major northeastern university (Koch, 2009). Scores from the SHPSES have also been significantly correlated with intentions to practice safer-sex behaviors in the next month and the actual practice of safer sex in the preceding month among a sample of students at a major northeastern community college (Millstein, 2006).

References

Bandura, A. (1977). Self-efficacy: Toward a unifying theory of behavioral change. *Psychological Review, 84,* 191–215.

Bandura, A. (1982). Self-efficacy mechanism is human agency. *American Psychologist, 37,* 121–147.

Bandura, A. (1997). *Self-efficacy: The exercise of control.* New York: W. H. Freeman.

DiClemente, R. J., & Peterson, J. L. (1994). *Preventing AIDS: Theories and methods of behavioral interventions.* New York: Springer.

Glanz, K., Rimer, B. K., & Viswanath, K. (2008). *Health behavior and health education: Theory, research, and practice* (4th ed.). San Francisco, CA: Jossey-Bass.

Koch, P. B. (2009, June). *Promoting positive sexual health practices for university students: What works?* Presentation at the World Congress for Sexual Health, Gothenburg, Sweden.

Millstein, S. (2006). *The effects of a human sexuality course on students' confidence to engage in healthy sexual practices.* Unpublished doctoral dissertation, Widener University, Philadelphia.

Pan American Health Organization & World Health Organization. (2000). Promotion of sexual health: Recommendations for action. Retrieved June 22, 2009, from http://new.paho.org/hq/index.php?option=com_content&task=view&id=847&Itemid=1047

Sexuality Information and Education Council of the United States. (2009). Position statements. Retrieved June 22, 2009, from http://www.siecus.org/index.cfm?pageId=494

Strecher, V. J., DeVellis, B. M., Becker, M. H., & Rosenstock, I. M. (1986). The role of self-efficacy in achieving health behavior change. *Health Education Quarterly, 13*(1), 73–92.

World Association of Sexual Health. (2008). Sexual health for the millennium. Retrieved June 22, 2009, from http://www.worldsexology.org

World Health Organization. (2009). Working definition of sexual health. Retrieved June 22, 2009, from http://www.who.int/reproductive-health/gender/sexual_health.html

Exhibit

Sexual Health Practices Self-Efficacy Scale

Please indicate how *confident* you are, at this point in time, in carrying out the following sexual health practices if you needed to. Think of confidence as having the *knowledge, skills, and comfort* necessary to effectively do these things. The term "partner" refers to whomever you might choose to share your sexuality with. Use the following scale for your answers:

1 = Not at all Confident
2 = Slightly Confident
3 = Moderately Confident
4 = Highly Confident
5 = Extremely Confident

How confident are you with:

1. Performing breast or testicular self-exams

   1   2   3   4   5

2. Getting tested for a sexually transmitted infection (STI)

   1   2   3   4   5

3. Getting an HIV test

   1   2   3   4   5

4. Talking with a health care worker about a sexual health issue like an STI

   1   2   3   4   5

5. Making thoughtful, good decisions about your sexual behaviors

   1   2   3   4   5

6. Practicing sexual abstinence

      1   2   3   4   5

7. Establishing a fulfilling sexual relationship

      1   2   3   4   5

8. Talking with a (prospective) sexual partner about your sexual histories

      1   2   3   4   5

9. Using a condom

      1   2   3   4   5

10. Using another form of birth control other than a condom

      1   2   3   4   5

11. Negotiating with a sexual partner to practice safer sex

      1   2   3   4   5

12. Talking with a sexual partner about a sexual health issue, like an STI

      1   2   3   4   5

13. Talking with a sexual partner about a relationship issue

      1   2   3   4   5

14. Dealing with a sexual functioning difficulty (like difficulty achieving orgasm or ejaculating too quickly

      1   2   3   4   5

15. Preventing a sexual assault situation from occurring

      1   2   3   4   5

16. Dealing with a sexual assault if it occurs to you

      1   2   3   4   5

17. Helping a friend who has been sexually assaulted

      1   2   3   4   5

18. Eliminating sexual double standards (based on gender) in your life

      1   2   3   4   5

19. Eliminating gender stereotyping from your life

      1   2   3   4   5

20. Accepting diversity in sexual orientation (heterosexuality, homosexuality, bisexuality)

      1   2   3   4   5

Pediatric Penile Perception Score

VERENA SCHÖNBUCHER,[1] MARKUS A. LANDOLT, RITA GOBET, AND DANIEL M. WEBER,
University Children's Hospital Zurich, Switzerland

The Pediatric Penile Perception Score (PPPS) is designed to assess both the penile self-perception of children and adolescents with hypospadias and the surgical outcome of hypospadias repair. The PPPS allows a direct comparison between children's and pediatric urologists' appraisal of penile appearance.

Description

The PPPS was developed and evaluated in a cross-sectional study on the psychosexual development and health-related quality of life of children and adolescents with hypospadias (Schönbucher, Landolt, Gobet, & Weber, 2008a, 2008b; Weber, Schönbucher, Landolt, & Gobet, 2008) because no instrument was available to objectively assess the surgical outcome and self-perception after hypospadias repair. Psychological interviews were conducted with 65 children and adolescents between the ages of 6 and 17 years who underwent surgery for hypospadias at the University Children's Hospital Zurich (Switzerland). They were asked to express their satisfaction with the following aspects of surgical outcome and penile appearance on a 4-point Likert-type scale that ranges from *Very Dissatisfied* to *Very Satisfied*: position and shape of meatus, shape of the glans, shape of penile skin, and general penile appearance. In addition, patients with hypospadias were offered a physical examination by a pediatric urologist, during which standardized photographs of the penis in four standardized views were taken, namely oblique, lateral, anteroposterior with the penis held against the abdominal wall, and anteroposterior with the penis held up straight (see Weber et al., 2008). Examinations were consented to by 56 boys.

The photographs were sent to six pediatric urologists for blind analysis, four of whom were not affiliated with the University Children's Hospital Zurich. They were asked to evaluate the standardized photographs according to the same criteria and scale as the children. To assess the stability of the instrument, in the set of 56 charts, 10 were included twice. Reliability was high (interclass correlation coefficient (ICC): .75–.88). Thus, the scores of the six pediatric urologists could be averaged to obtain an objective assessment of the quality of surgical outcome. For a more detailed description of the development of the instrument, see Weber et al. (2008).

Response Mode and Timing

Younger children's penile perception should be assessed in an interview. Alternatively, adolescents can fill in a questionnaire. (See the Exhibit for interview and questionnaire instructions.) Urologists can objectively rate the surgical outcome either from photographs or in vivo. Appraisal of the results with photographs allows evaluation by non-involved urologists and avoids the bias that occurs when judging one's own results. The use of the questionnaire by urologists is easy and self-explanatory.

The application of the PPPS takes between 5 and 10 minutes for children and 2 minutes for urologists.

Scoring

Each item of the PPPS is scored as follows: *Very Satisfied* = 3, *Satisfied* = 2, *Dissatisfied* = 1, *Very Dissatisfied* = 0. The four items are then added to a total score, ranging from 0 to 12.

Reliability

The PPPS showed an excellent internal consistency for the children's penile self-perception (α = .81), as well as for the pediatric urologists' assessment of the surgical outcome (α = .84). Interrater reliability (ICC: .75–.88) and stability of the pediatric urologists' assessment (rs between the 1st and 2nd assessment: .59–.83) were high both for the four single items and for the PPPS total score.

Validity

Validity was not examined.

Other Information

We recommend that the surgical outcome be assessed by an independent pediatric urologist who was not involved in the surgical treatment of the child, because it is assumed that pediatric urologists' assessment of their own surgical results may be distorted in the direction of a more positive judgment (Weber et al., 2008). We further suppose that the PPPS might also be a reliable

[1]Address correspondence to Verena Schönbucher, Child and Woman Abuse Studies Unit, Department of Applied Social Sciences, London Metropolitan University, Ladbroke House, 62–66 Highbury Grove, London N5 2AD, United Kingdom; e-mail: verena.schoenbucher@kispi.unizh.ch or v.schonbucher@londonmet.ac.uk

measurement for the social perception of a boy's penis after hypospadias repair, such as by the boy's parents. Assessment and possible modification of the penile perception score for the adult population as well as the social perception of the adult penis after hypospadias repair are currently being reviewed.

This research was supported by a grant of the Foundation Mercator. Verena Schönbucher is also affiliated with the Child and Woman Abuse Studies Unit, Department of Applied Social Sciences, London Metropolitan University.

References

Schönbucher, V. B., Landolt, M. A., Gobet, R., & Weber, M. A. (2008a). Health-related quality of life and psychological adjustment of children and adolescents with hypospadias. *Journal of Pediatrics, 152,* 865–872.

Schönbucher, V. B., Landolt, M. A., Gobet, R., & Weber, M. A. (2008b). Psychosexual development of children and adolescents with hypospadias. *Journal of Sexual Medicine, 5,* 1365–1373.

Weber, D. M., Schönbucher, V. B., Landolt, M. A., & Gobet, R. (2008). The Pediatric Penile Perception Score: An instrument for patient self-assessment and surgeon evaluation after hypospadias repair. *Journal of Urology, 180,* 1080–1084.

Exhibit

Pediatric Penile Perception Score

Instructions

Children

Interview version. We will talk about several aspects of your penis. Please tell me how satisfied you are with these. There are four possible answers: very satisfied, satisfied, dissatisfied, very dissatisfied. Please tell me which one is the most appropriate for you.

Questionnaire. The chart below shows various aspects of your penis. There are four possible answers: very satisfied, satisfied, dissatisfied, very dissatisfied. Please mark with a cross the box that is most appropriate for you.

Pediatric Urologists

The use of the PPPS for urologists is self-explanatory.

	Very Satisfied	Satisfied	Dissatisfied	Very Dissatisfied
Meatal position and shape	☐	☐	☐	☐
Shape of the glans	☐	☐	☐	☐
Shape of penile skin	☐	☐	☐	☐
General cosmetic appearance	☐	☐	☐	☐

Herpes Attitude Scale

Katherine Bruce,[1] *University of North Carolina at Wilmington*
Judith McLaughlin, *University of Georgia*

The Herpes Attitude Scale (HAS) assesses beliefs and feelings about genital herpes. Subject areas include feelings about self, feelings about others who have herpes, communication about herpes, intimate relationships, friendship relationships, perceived coping abilities, and myths. People who have positive attitudes about herpes can be discriminated from those who have negative attitudes.

Description

This scale is a 40-item Likert scale (5 points) with response options labeled *Strongly Agree, Agree, Neither Agree nor Disagree, Disagree,* and *Strongly Disagree.* The items on the scale were selected from an initial pool of 65 opinion statements about herpes. They were judged for readability by five undergraduate students and for acceptability for inclusion in the scale by a panel of five expert judges. The judges agreed on 45 of the original items for inclusion in the scale. The scale was administered to 250 undergraduate students in introductory psychology courses, and an item analysis was conducted to identify the statements that could best discriminate high and low scorers. Forty items had statistically significant item-total correlations ($p <$ .001). These items were arranged in random order, and the scale was tested for reliability. This scale was designed to measure college students' attitudes about herpes but could be used for other populations.

Response Mode and Timing

Respondents circle or blacken one response option for each item on a separate labeled answer sheet. Most respondents complete the scale within 15 minutes.

Scoring

The 20 positive items (2, 3, 4, 6, 9, 11, 12, 15, 17, 18, 19, 20, 21, 24, 25, 26, 27, 28, 38, and 40) are scored such that

Strongly Agree has a value of 5, *Agree* a value of 4, and so forth. For the negative items (1, 5, 7, 8, 10, 13, 14, 16, 22, 23, 29, 30, 31, 32, 33, 34, 35, 36, 37, and 39), reverse scoring is used. The total attitude score is obtained by the following formula: HAS score = $(X - N)(100)/(N)(4)$, where X is the total of the scored responses and N is the number of items properly completed. This formula standardizes scores such that they may range from 0 to 100; higher scores indicate a more positive attitude about genital herpes and coping with genital herpes.

Reliability

To measure internal consistency (split-half reliability), 148 undergraduate students in psychology and health education classes completed the scale. Reliability was high (Cronbach's alpha = .91; Bruce & McLaughlin, 1986; Bruce & Bullins, 1989).

Validity

Content and face validity were evaluated by a panel of five expert judges: a physician, a registered nurse, two health educators, and a graduate student with herpes. The judges assessed the relevance and importance of each item as well as the comprehensiveness of the entire scale (Bruce & McLaughlin, 1986).

References

Bruce, K., & McLaughlin, J. (1986). The development of scales to assess knowledge and attitudes about genital herpes. *The Journal of Sex Research, 22,* 73–84.

Bruce, K. E. M., & Bullins, C. G. (1989). Students' attitudes and knowledge about genital herpes. *Journal of Sex Education and Therapy, 15,* 257–270.

[1]Address correspondence to Katherine Bruce, Department of Psychology, UNC Wilmington, Wilmington, NC 28403; e-mail: bruce@uncw.edu

Exhibit

Herpes Attitude Scale

Instructions: For each of the following 40 statements, please note on the answer sheet whether you agree or disagree with the statements. Use the following scale:

SA: Strongly Agree With the Statement
A: Agree With the Statement
N: Neither Agree nor Disagree With the Statement
D: Disagree With the Statement
SD: Strongly Disagree With the Statement

Each statement is numbered. Be sure to match the statement's number with the number on the answer sheet. Please respond to all items on the questionnaire. There are NO right or wrong answers.

1. The thought of genital herpes is disgusting.
2. I would not feel dirty if I got genital herpes.
3. Genital herpes is not as scary as most people believe.
4. There are a lot of diseases that are worse than genital herpes.
5. People give genital herpes to others for revenge.
6. I could cope with having genital herpes.
7. If I had a roommate with genital herpes, I would move out.
8. Only bad people catch genital herpes.
9. I feel comfortable around friends who have genital herpes.
10. You can tell that someone has genital herpes just by looking at them.
11. I am pretty sure that I could handle having genital herpes if I caught it.
12. Having genital herpes is really no worse than having cold sores.
13. People who have genital herpes are looked down on.
14. I do not like to use public restrooms because I might catch genital herpes there.
15. I could remain calm if I found out that I had gotten genital herpes.
16. A person who has genital herpes got what s/he deserves.
17. If I had genital herpes, I would tell a potential sex partner.
18. There is more to a person who has genital herpes than the fact that s/he has genital herpes.
19. I would not avoid a friend if I found out that s/he had genital herpes.
20. I would consider marrying someone who has genital herpes.
21. People who have genital herpes should be treated the same as anyone else.
22. I would feel self-conscious if I got genital herpes.
23. If I found out that my sexual partner had genital herpes, I would never speak to him/her again.
24. The "new sexual leprosy" is an inappropriate term for genital herpes.
25. Catching genital herpes would not be the worst thing that could happen to me.
26. I would not be ashamed if I got genital herpes.
27. People who have genital herpes are worth getting to know.
28. Genital herpes is a manageable disease.
29. I think that people who have genital herpes are too sexually active.
30. If I caught genital herpes, I would consider suicide.
31. People who have genital herpes should never have sex again.
32. I would be embarrassed to tell anyone if I had genital herpes.
33. Only unclean people catch genital herpes.
34. If I got genital herpes, no one would want to marry me.
35. If I got genital herpes, I would not want to have children.
36. Everyone would know if I got genital herpes.
37. People who have genital herpes are promiscuous.
38. I could discuss genital herpes with my parents.
39. If I asked a friend a question about genital herpes, s/he would think that I had genital herpes.
40. I would date a person known to have genital herpes.

Herpes Knowledge Scale

KATHERINE BRUCE,[1] *University of North Carolina at Wilmington*
JUDITH MCLAUGHLIN, *University of Georgia*

The Herpes Knowledge Scale (HKS) assesses general knowledge about genital herpes. Subject areas include cause, symptoms, treatment, contagion, recurrences, prevalence, complications, myths, and the relationship between oral and genital herpes. People who have high knowledge about these areas can be discriminated from those who have low knowledge.

Description

This scale is a 54-item true-false test with response options labeled *True, False,* and *Don't Know*. The items were selected from an initial pool of 64 rationally field-derived statements about herpes. They were judged for readability by five undergraduate students and for their relevance and importance for inclusion in the scale by a panel of five expert judges. The judges agreed on 57 of the original items for inclusion. The scale was administered to 150 undergraduate students in introductory psychology courses, and an item analysis was conducted to identify the statements that could best discriminate high and low scorers. Fifty-four items had statistically significant item-total correlations ($p < .0007$). These items were arranged in random order, and the scale was tested for reliability. This scale was designed to measure college students' knowledge about herpes, but it could be used for other populations.

Response Mode and Timing

Respondents circle or blacken one response option for each item on a separately labeled answer sheet. Most respondents complete the scale within 15 minutes.

Scoring

The response to each item is scored as correct or incorrect. *Don't know* is scored as an incorrect response. Items 1, 2, 4, 7, 9, 10, 14, 15, 19, 20, 24, 25, 26, 27, 28, 29, 31, 32, 33, 34, 35, 36, 40, 41, 46, 48, and 49 are true. Items 3, 5, 6, 8, 11, 12, 13, 16, 17, 18, 21, 22, 23, 30, 37, 38, 39, 42, 43, 44, 45, 47, 50, 51, 52, 53, and 54 are false. The total score is obtained by summing the number of correct responses, dividing this by 54, and multiplying this fraction by 100 so that scores are expressed as percentage correct (0–100%).

Reliability

To measure internal consistency (split-half reliability), 148 undergraduate students in psychology and health education classes completed the scale. Reliability was high (Cronbach's alpha = .88; Bruce & McLaughlin, 1986; Bruce & Bullins, 1989).

Validity

Content and face validity were evaluated by a panel of five expert judges: a physician, a registered nurse, two health educators, and a graduate student with herpes. The judges assessed the relevance and importance of each item, as well as the comprehensiveness of the entire scale (Bruce & McLaughlin, 1986).

References

Bruce, K., & McLaughlin, J. (1986). The development of scales to assess knowledge and attitudes about genital herpes. *The Journal of Sex Research, 22,* 73–84.
Bruce, K. E. M., & Bullins, C. G. (1989). Students' attitudes and knowledge about genital herpes. *Journal of Sex Education and Therapy, 15,* 257–270.

Exhibit

Herpes Knowledge Scale

Instructions: For each of the following 54 statements, please note on the answer sheet whether you think the statement is true or false. If you do not have any idea whether or not the statement is true or false, please note that you don't know. Use the following code for your responses:

> T: The statement is true
> F: The statement is false
> DK: I don't know whether the statement is true or false

Each statement is numbered. Be sure to match the statement's number with the number on the answer sheet. Please respond to all statements on the questionnaire.

[1]Address correspondence to Katherine Bruce, Department of Psychology, UNC Wilmington, Wilmington, NC 28403; e-mail: bruce@uncw.edu

1. The length and severity of genital herpes outbreaks vary from person to person.
2. Genital herpes is caused by a virus.
3. Genital herpes was discovered five years ago.
4. Genital herpes recurrences can be triggered by menstruation (in females) or sexual intercourse.
5. Every person who has a primary (first) outbreak of genital herpes will have recurrence within the next year.
6. Genital herpes makes males infertile (sterile).
7. Between recurrences, the genital herpes virus lies dormant (inactive) in the nerve cells.
8. Herpes Type 1 cannot occur on the genitals.
9. A person having recurrences of genital herpes often experiences prodromal (early warning) sensations.
10. Years may pass between genital herpes recurrences.
11. Every sore on the genitals is herpes.
12. Once a genital herpes sore has healed, the person will never develop another herpes sore.
13. A person who gets cold sores on the mouth is immune to genital herpes.
14. Genital herpes usually looks like blisters on the genitals.
15. Prodromal (early warning) sensations of genital herpes recurrences include tingling or itching in the area where the genital herpes sores usually appear.
16. If a person has sexual intercourse with someone who has genital herpes, s/he will definitely get genital herpes too.
17. Several hundred people are expected to catch genital herpes from toilet seats this year.
18. A woman who has genital herpes will become sterile because of the herpes infection.
19. People who wear contact lenses and have oral (mouth) herpes should avoid putting the lenses in their mouths because the herpes infection could spread to their eyes.
20. A person with genital herpes is instructed to keep the sore area clean and dry.
21. Genital herpes leads to death.
22. There is a cure for genital herpes at present.
23. Genital herpes recurrences do not typically become less frequent over time.
24. A person who has genital herpes often has more psychological complications than physical complications.
25. When a person has an active outbreak of genital herpes, it is advisable not to have sexual intercourse.
26. People who have genital herpes can sometimes predict when they will have a recurrence.
27. A woman who has genital herpes should have a Pap smear at least once a year.
28. Genital herpes can be contagious even if the herpes sore has a scab on it.
29. First episodes of genital herpes infection are usually more severe than the recurrences.
30. A person who has genital herpes is immune to oral (mouth) herpes.
31. Between recurrences, the genital herpes virus lies dormant (inactive) near the spinal cord.
32. Stress can often trigger a genital herpes recurrence.
33. Herpes can be fatal to a newborn if s/he contracts the infection.
34. Genital herpes can often be detected by the use of a Pap smear.
35. After a person is exposed to genital herpes, s/he will often show symptoms in 2–20 days.
36. Anxiety can trigger a genital herpes recurrence.
37. Condoms offer 100% protection from catching genital herpes.
38. A genital herpes infection usually leads to syphilis.
39. A woman who had genital herpes must have a Caesarean section if she has a baby.
40. Most people have been exposed to oral herpes at one time or another.
41. A woman with genital herpes can deliver a baby through her vagina if she doesn't have an active herpes infection at the time of delivery.
42. If both parents have genital herpes, their children will be born with herpes.
43. A woman who has genital herpes can never have a baby.
44. Genital herpes is not contagious.
45. L-lysine is a cure for genital herpes.
46. Genital herpes may be associated with cancer of the cervix.
47. Contraceptive foam has been proven to kill genital herpes in humans.
48. In a primary (first) case of genital herpes, the person may feel like s/he has the flu.
49. Oral herpes is contagious.
50. The best way to treat genital herpes sores is to keep them moist.
51. Acyclovir (also called Zovirax or Valtrex), an anti-viral drug, can cure genital herpes.
52. A person with genital herpes is not contagious during the prodromal (early warning) stage.
53. Genital herpes is not prevalent (common) on college campuses.
54. Oral herpes cannot be transferred to the genitals during oral-genital sex.

Genital Herpes Perceived Severity Scales

JERROLD MIROTZNIK,[1] *Brooklyn College, City University of New York*

The Genital Herpes Perceived Severity Scales (GHPSS; Mirotznik, 1991) measure attitudes about contracting this sexually transmitted disease. The scales were developed to test the speculations, frequently reported as facts in the media, that (a) single, sexually active, and consequently at-risk young adults had become highly anxious about infection with the herpes virus; and (b) as a result of this heightened concern, those at risk had dramatically altered their dating behaviors. Although several researchers had addressed these issues (Aral, Cates, & Jenkins, 1985; Simkins & Eberhage, 1984; Simkins & Kushner, 1986), they used measures that suffered from important limitations, including vague conceptualizations and operationalizations in terms of a single questionnaire item. Single-item measures tend to be less reliable and, as such, have the untoward effect of attenuating associations with other measures. Another limitation concerned the use of dichotomous response options. Dichotomous response options fail to capture the variability of reactions to genital herpes. Finally, little evidence was presented regarding these measures' psychometric properties. (See Mirotznik, 1991, for a detailed discussion of these limitations.)

The primary theoretical orientation guiding the conceptualization of the GHPSS was the Health Belief Model (HBM; Janz & Becker, 1984). In the HBM it is hypothesized that people are likely to take steps to avoid a particular disease if they perceive that disease as personally threatening. A major component of perceived threat is the degree to which a disease is thought to be severe. Perceived severity, in turn, has been defined not just in terms of a disease's medical/clinical consequences but also its social and psychological effects. Accordingly, the GHPSS were constructed to measure the degree to which people believe that contracting genital herpes would lead to the latter type of consequences.

Description

Three scales were developed de novo. Each scale was hypothesized to measure a particular social or psychological consequence of infection. To enhance content and face validity, all items were constructed with the help of two clinicians, a sex therapist and a psychologist, both with expertise in treating people with genital herpes.

The Fear Scale measures whether subjects are frightened about contracting this disease by determining the degree to which they endorse seven items that characterize herpes and those who contract it in highly negative, stigmatizing terms. Each item has a 6-point Likert-type response format ranging from (1) *strongly disagree* to (6) *strongly agree.*

The Family Impediment Scale measures the degree to which respondents believe that contracting genital herpes would be a hinderance in establishing a family. It consists of one overall question asking respondents to rate how difficult it would be for a single person with genital herpes to experience each of five family life-course events. Each item has a 6-point Likert-type response format ranging from (1) *not difficult at all* to (6) *very difficult.*

The Emotional Response Scale assesses possible emotional reactions to infection with genital herpes. The scale lists seven emotions. For each emotion, respondents indicate on a 4-point Likert-type format whether they would (1) *not react* with the emotion or (4) *strongly experience* the emotion.

Response Mode and Timing

For the items for each scale, respondents can circle on the questionnaire the number of the response option that best corresponds to their attitude, or they can mark the number on separate machine-scoreable answer sheets. The three scales take approximately 5 minutes to complete.

Scoring

Items within each scale and between scales are keyed in the same direction with higher scores indicating that respondents perceive herpes to be more severe. For each scale, a total score is calculated by first summing the response number for all answered items and then dividing by the number of answered items. The resulting mean score has the beneficial properties of having the same range as the individual items and also of adjusting for any missing items.

Reliability

To assess the psychometric properties of the GHPSS and the consistency of those properties across varied populations, the scales were initially administered to two convenience samples: 998 college and graduate students, and 178 residents of a therapeutic community for alcohol and drug rehabilitation (Mirotznik, 1991). Subsequently, the questionnaire was administered to an additional sample of 439 college students. Each sample was subdivided into those who were single, sexually active and thereby at risk of infection and those not at risk. For each of the resulting six

[1]Address correspondence to Jerrold Mirotznik, Office of the Associate Provost, Brooklyn College, 2900 Bedford Avenue, Brooklyn, NY 11210; e-mail: jmirotznik@brooklyn.cuny.edu

subsamples, internal consistency reliability was then calculated using Cronbach's alpha. For the Fear Scale the mean alpha across the six subsamples was .80 with a range of .73 to .83. The mean alpha for the Family Impediment Scale was .77 with a range of .73 to .81, and for the Emotional Response Scale, it was .77 with a range of .75 to .82. Generally, the scales exhibited somewhat better reliability for the student subsamples than for the therapeutic community subsamples.

Validity

Two tests were conducted to assess validity (Mirotznik, 1991). Given that these three scales were hypothesized to measure the same overarching construct, perceived severity of genital herpes, they should be more highly correlated with each other than with measures of other constructs. As Nunnally (1978) pointed out, an indication that variables cluster as theoretically predicted is important evidence of construct validity. A principal-components factor analysis with varimax rotation conducted on the initial subsample of at-risk students indicated that the GHPSS generally factored as expected. Specifically, all three scales loaded highly on one factor (i.e., Fear Scale, .76; Family Impediment Scale, .75; Emotional Reaction Scale, .68), whereas measures of knowledge about genital herpes and preventive behaviors loaded on other factors. When the factor analysis was rerun on the remaining five subsamples, generally the same factor structure appeared.

A second important test of construct validity involves determining if a measure of a construct fits predictions from a well accepted theory (Nunnally, 1978). According to the HBM, the greater people's perceived severity of disease, the more likely they are to engage in preventive health behaviors. To assess this, a measure of preventive behavior (i.e., change in dating behaviors in light of knowledge about genital herpes) was correlated with the three perceived severity scales separately for the at-risk respondents from each of the three convenience samples. Each scale was significantly associated in the theoretically predicted direction, albeit modestly so, with the measure of preventive behavior in the two subsamples of at-risk students. The mean correlations for these two subsamples were .25 for the Fear Scale, .17 for the Family Impediment Scale, and .18 for the Emotional Response Scale. It is conceivable that the magnitude of these correlations may have been attenuated by the single-item used to operationalize preventive behavior.

References

Aral, S. O., Cates, W., & Jenkins, W. C. (1985). Genital herpes: Does knowledge lead to action? *American Journal of Public Health, 75,* 69–71.

Janz, N. K., & Becker, M. H. (1984). The health belief model: A decade later. *Health Education Quarterly, 11,* 1–47.

Mirotznik, J. (1991). Genital herpes: A survey of the attitudes, knowledge, and reported behaviors of college students at-risk for infection. *Journal of Psychology and Human Sexuality, 4,* 73–99.

Nunnally, J. C. (1978). *Psychometric theory.* New York: McGraw-Hill.

Simkins, L., & Eberhage, M.G. (1984). Attitudes toward AIDS, herpes II, and toxic shock syndrome. *Psychological Reports, 55,* 779–786.

Simkins, L., & Kushner, A. (1986). Attitudes toward AIDS, herpes II, and toxic shock syndrome: Two years later. *Psychological Reports, 59,* 883–891.

Exhibit

Genital Herpes Perceived Severity Scales

Instructions: The following items measure your beliefs about genital herpes. Some of the questions concern your views about others who have contracted the virus and the general consequences of infection. Other questions concern how you would personally react if you contracted the virus. For each item, please circle the response option that best corresponds to your feelings.

Fear Scale

For the following statements please select a number from 1 to 6, 1 meaning that you strongly disagree and 6 that you strongly agree.

1. Genital herpes will ruin your sex life.
2. Having genital herpes is as bad as having cancer.
3. No one will want me if I had genital herpes.
4. Genital herpes is a dirty disease.
5. I would not trust anybody who has genital herpes.
6. My opinion of a person would change if I found out he/she had genital herpes.
7. Even though I would be very understanding of people I knew had genital herpes, I would be tempted to stay away from them.

Family Impediment Scale

How difficult to deal with would each of the following things be for a single person who has genital herpes? Choose a number from 1 to 6, 1 indicating *not difficult at all* and 6 *very difficult.*

1. Meeting a boyfriend/girlfriend.
2. Telling a boyfriend or girlfriend that you have genital herpes.
3. Having sex.
4. Getting married.
5. Having children.

Emotional Reaction Scale

People may have different reactions to contracting genital herpes. How would you react? For each emotion listed below indicate if you would: 1. not react with the emotion, 2. mildly feel the emotion, 3. moderately feel the emotion or 4. strongly experience the emotion.

1. Angry.
2. Punished.
3. Fearful.
4. Numbed.
5. Damaged.
6. That it was expected.
7. Guilty.

Inventory of Dyadic Heterosexual Preferences and Inventory of Dyadic Heterosexual Preferences—Other

DANIEL M. PURNINE, MICHAEL P. CAREY,[1] AND RANDALL S. JORGENSEN, *Syracuse University*

The Inventory of Dyadic Heterosexual Preferences (IDHP) was developed to measure men's and women's affinity for a broad range of fairly conventional sexual behavior preferences within the context of a dyadic heterosexual relationship. Six scales, reflecting different domains of behavioral preference, are derived. The IDHP allows researchers to explore relationships between specific preferences or profiles of preference and various behavioral, personality, or dyadic correlates. Sex therapists may be interested in comparing the profile of one's sexual preferences with that of one's partner. An other-focused version of the inventory (IDHP-O) asks the respondent to indicate how he or she believes the partner would respond to the IDHP.

Description

A complete description of the IDHP and its development may be found elsewhere (Purnine, Carey, & Jorgensen, 1996). The IDHP is a 27-item self-report inventory that measures the following six areas of sexual preference: Erotophilia, Use of Contraception, Conventionality, Use of Erotica, Use of Drugs/Alcohol, and Romantic Foreplay.

Seventy-four statements, applicable to both men and women, were generated to elicit responses to specific behaviors or elements of a sexual scene. Each item was followed by a 6-point Likert-type scale, ranging from *strongly agree* to *strongly disagree*. Items regarding fantasy, opinion, or motivation were generally excluded. The perfect tense ("I would enjoy") rather than the present tense ("I enjoy") was employed in order that items outside one's habitual range of experience may be applicable. This use of the hypothetical allows the IDHP to be applicable to those not currently involved in a sexually intimate relationship.

The 74 items were administered to 258 undergraduate and graduate university students (Sample 1), aged 18 to 59 years of age ($M = 23$). After eliminating items that failed to elicit a broad range of responses or that were unreliable over a 1- to 2-week period, 46 items remained. Factor analyses suggested a six-factor, 27-item solution. This solution was based on a covariance matrix in which the variance attributable to gender had been removed. A gender-neutral factor structure was considered necessary in order to allow meaningful comparisons between the profiles of male and female partners.

[1]Address correspondence to Michael P. Carey, Department of Psychology, 430 Huntington Hall, Syracuse University, Syracuse, NY 13244–2340; e-mail: mpcarey@psych.syr.edu

These results were cross-validated using new data (Sample 2) from 228 students, aged 17 to 53, ($M = 21$). Six items were reworded to improve their clarity. Three new items were introduced to enlarge certain factors. A six-factor maximum likelihood solution, with promax rotation, incorporated the new items and suggested the elimination of three others. The final 27-item factor structure accounted for 51% of the variance among the 27 items.

Response Mode and Timing

Using a paper/pencil format, respondents circle the number indicating their personal level of agreement/disagreement with each statement of preference. It takes approximately 5 minutes to complete the IDHP and, if administered, an additional 5 minutes to complete the IDHP-O.

Scoring

IDHP scale scores (individual preferences). Higher scores on each of the six IDHP scales indicate stronger preference for the behaviors in that scale. First, Items 3, 24, and 26 must be reverse scored by subtracting the number circled from 7. Each scale is then derived by adding across the items as follows—Erotophilia: 1, 7, 8, 11, 16, 17, 18; Use of Contraception: 3, 6, 13, 26; Conventionality: 5, 10, 22, 23; Use of Erotica: 4, 9, 24, 27; Use of Drugs/Alcohol: 12, 14, 15, 20; and Romantic Foreplay: 2, 19, 21, 25. To standardize the scales, each ranging from 1 to 6, sums may be divided by the number of items added.

Exploratory scores. Several dyadic variables are currently under investigation. Agreement, or similarity between two partners' preferences may be observed by comparing the IDHP of each partner. Female Understanding (of the male) is reflected by comparing the male's IDHP with the IDHP-O of the female; Male Understanding (of the female) is reflected by comparing the female's IDHP with the male's IDHP-O. An individual variable, Perceived Agreement, is reflected in the difference between one's own IDHP and IDHP-O. These variables may be generated through correlational procedures or as difference-scores (by adding the absolute value of point differences across the 27 items). Because these variables are exploratory, the following sections pertain only to the IDHP scale scores.

Reliability

Listed in Table 1 are alpha coefficients, test-retest reliability correlations, means and standard deviations across the six IDHP scales, based on data from Sample 2. The scales are internally consistent (mean alpha coefficient = .72) and stable over time (mean test-retest $r = .84$). Item analysis from Sample 1 required a test-retest reliability of .70 for each item.

Validity

In a subgroup of 45 women and 20 men from Sample 2, seven additional scales were administered for purposes of establishing concurrent and discriminant validity with the six IDHP scales. Of 42 predictions in this 6 x 7 matrix of correlations, 36 were supported. Absence of any relationship between each IDHP scale and the Marlowe-Crowne Social Desirability Scale (Crowne & Marlowe, 1960) provides discriminant evidence that the IDHP is not confounded by a bias toward presenting oneself in a socially desirable light. The Sexual Opinion Survey (SOS; Fisher, White, Byrne, & Kelley, 1988), a 21-item measure of erotophilia, correlated with the IDHP scale, Erotophilia ($r = .54$). However, discriminant validity for this scale is currently lacking, because the SOS also was related to Use of Erotica, Use of Drugs/Alcohol, and Conventionality. It should be noted, however, that similar relationships exist among the IDHP factors themselves. This is an allowance of oblique factor rotation. In fact, it would be surprising if erotophilia were *not* related to other, possibly more specific, domains of preference.

Both concurrent and discriminant validity were evidenced for the following IDHP scales: Use of Contraception, Conventionality, and Use of Drugs/Alcohol. The Use of Contraception scale positively correlated only with a measure entitled Affective Response Toward Contraceptive Topics and Behavior (Kelley, 1979). Conventionality was related to the Sexual Irrationality Questionnaire (Jordan & McCormick, 1988), a measure with factors such as "conformity," and "cautious control." Both the global and sexual subscales of the Alcohol Expectancy Questionnaire (Brown, Christiansen, & Goldman, 1987) were positively related to the IDHP Use of Drugs/Alcohol only. Validity of Romantic Foreplay and Use of Erotica remain without support, as the former was uncorrelated with its criterion measure and no relevant measure was available to test the latter.

TABLE 1

Psychometric Properties of the Inventory of Dyadic Heterosexual Preferences (IDHP)

Scale	Alpha Coefficients	Test-Retest Correlations[a]	Means (SD)			
			Male		Female	
1. Erotophilia	.73	.84	4.77	(.56)	4.27	(.73)
2. Use of Contraception	.65	.80	4.36	(.93)	4.59	(.84)
3. Conventionality	.59	.83	2.89	(.83)	3.20	(.91)
4. Use of Erotica	.83	.92	4.04	(.97)	3.22	(1.12)
5. Use of Drugs/Alcohol	.87	.91	3.15	(1.34)	2.43	(1.18)
6. Romantic Foreplay	.62	.73	4.43	(.71)	4.91	(.71)

[a]Test-retest interval was 2 weeks, including 45 women and 20 men ($N = 65$).

Other Information

Further research regarding reliability, validity, and factor structure across diverse populations is encouraged for clinicians and researchers using the IDHP and IDHPO.

References

Brown, S. A., Christiansen, B. A., & Goldman, M. S. (1987). The Alcohol Expectancy Questionnaire: An instrument for the assessment of adolescent and adult alcohol expectancies. *Journal of Studies on Alcohol, 48*, 483–491.

Crowne, D. P., & Marlowe, D. (1960). A new scale of social desirability independent of psychopathology. *Journal of Consulting Psychology,* 24, 349–354.

Fisher, W. A., White, L. A., Byrne, D., & Kelley, K. (1988). Erotophilia-erotophobia as a dimension of personality. *The Journal of Sex Research, 25*, 123–151.

Jordan, T. J., & McCormick, N. B. (1988). Sexual Irrationality Questionnaire. In C. M. Davis, W. L. Yarber, & S. L. Davis (Eds.), *Sexually-related measures: A compendium* (pp. 46–49). Lake Mills, IA: Graphic Publishing Company.

Kelley, K. (1979). Socialization factors in contraceptive attitudes: Roles of affective responses, parental attitudes, and sexual experience. *The Journal of Sex Research, 15*, 6–20.

Purnine, D. M., Carey, M. P., & Jorgensen, R. S. (1996). The Inventory of Dyadic Heterosexual Preferences: Development and psychometric evaluation. *Behaviour Research and Therapy, 34*, 375–387.

Exhibit

Inventory of Dyadic Heterosexual Preferences

Instructions.[a] Please read the following statements carefully and indicate how much you agree or disagree that the statement is true for you. Respond to each item as you would actually like things to be in relations with your partner. Feel free to ask the investigator about any statement that is not clear to you. Please respond to all items.

There are no right or wrong answers; respond as truthfully as possible.

1. I would like to initiate sex.

Strongly agree	Agree	Somewhat agree	Somewhat disagree	Disagree	Strongly[b] disagree
6	5	4	3	2	1

2. An intimate, romantic dinner together would be a real turn on to me.
3. Using spermicide would spoil sex for me.
4. I would like to use a vibrator or other sexual toy (or aid) during sex.
5. I would prefer to have sex under the bedcovers and with the lights off.
6. Having myself or my partner use a condom would not spoil sex for me.
7. Having sex in rooms other than the bedroom would turn me on.
8. I would prefer to have sex everyday.
9. Looking at sexually explicit books and movies would turn me on.
10. I would not enjoy looking at my partner's genitals.
11. I would like to have sex after a day at the beach.
12. I would like to mix alcohol and sex.
13. Using a contraceptive would not affect my sexual satisfaction or pleasure.
14. I would enjoy having sex after smoking marijuana.
15. I would prefer to have sex while using drugs that make me feel aroused.
16. I would enjoy having sex outdoors.
17. My preferred time for having sex is in the morning.
18. Swimming in the nude with my partner would be a turn-on.
19. I would enjoy dressing in sexy/revealing clothes to arouse my partner.
20. I would like to mix drugs and sex.
21. I would get turned on if my partner touched my chest and nipples.
22. I would prefer to avoid having sex during my (partner's) period.
23. I would not enjoy having my partner look at my genitals.
24. Sexually explicit books and movies are disgusting to me.
25. I would find deep kissing with the tongue quite arousing to me.
26. Using a vaginal lubricant (KY jelly) would spoil sex for me.
27. Watching erotic movies with my partner would turn me on.

[a]Instructions for the IDHP-O: Please read the following statements carefully and indicate how much you believe that *your partner* would agree or disagree that the statement is true for him/her. That is, respond to each item *as you think your partner would respond*—how he or she would actually like things to be in relations with you.

[b]This scale is repeated after each item.

The Meharry Questionnaire: The Measurement of Attitudes Toward AIDS-Related Issues

FREDERICK A. ERNST,[1] RUPERT A. FRANCIS, JOYCE PERKINS, *Centre for Addiction and Mental Health*

QUINTESSA BRITTON-WILLIAMS, AND AJAIPAL S. KANG, *Meharry Medical College*

The Meharry Questionnaire was developed to measure the attitudes and behaviors of workers in health care facilities concerning AIDS-related issues. We were particularly concerned about attitudes which would be expected to compromise quality of care. Furthermore, we wished to identify differences in attitudes related to specific differences in demographics, specifically race, gender, education, and religious preference. In 1989, we used a convenience sample of 2,006 employees in the mental health and retardation residential facilities throughout the state of Tennessee. A follow-up questionnaire was administered in 1994 for the same population, using Items 4, 5, 6, and 8 from the original survey. The 1994 sample consisted of 857 respondents. Each administration of the survey achieved a fairly representative cross-section of socioeconomic strata by including respondents from all occupational categories at each of the facilities.

The combined 1989 and 1994 populations had a racial composition of 38% Blacks and 55% Whites; 68% of the sample were females. The highest levels of education completed by the respondents were as follows: 45% with high school or less, 33% with Bachelor's degree or some college and 8% with Master's or Doctorate degrees. The respondents who chose not to answer any of the demographics were not included in the statistics above.

Previous analyses from this data set revealed that Blacks were significantly more likely than Whites to affirm personal habit changes to prevent HIV infection and significantly more likely to reject the notion that AIDS is not a threat to rural areas of the United States (Ernst, Francis, Nevels, Collipp, & Lewis, 1991). Findings from the same questionnaire demonstrated that condemnation of homosexuality is stronger in the Black community deriving primarily from relatively less tolerant attitudes of Black females (Ernst, Francis, Nevels, & Lemeh, 1991).

Description

The Meharry Questionnaire consists of 13 statements to which subjects respond on a 6-point Likert scale of 0 (*strongly disagree*) to 5 (*strongly agree*). It was originally designed to assess attitudes of physicians and was later modified for general public comprehension.

Response Mode and Timing

The questionnaire requires approximately 5 to 10 minutes to complete, including the time in which respondents are providing cursory demographic information.

Scoring

Each of the 13 items was analyzed independently to compare differences in responses which might have been related to specific demographic characteristics. In unpublished work, a moral conservatism score was derived from responses to Items 2, 4, 6 (scored as a negative number), 9, 10, 11, and 13. The mean score on this measure of moral conservatism was 6.11, $SD = .18$ (range: –5 to 30).

Reliability

Reliability analyses yielded a Cronbach alpha of .70 with an average inter-item correlation of .16. Split-half reliability was .74. Test-retest correlation coefficients ranged from .24 to .72 for the 13 items.

Validity

Although no validity studies have been published to date, we have data supporting the validity of the questionnaire. For example, we have found that moral conservatism is strongly and inversely related to educational level ($p < .000001$). Religious preference is also predictable from scores on moral conservatism but this relationship is more complex because the more conservative religions (e.g., Church of God) tend to be over-represented by subjects with less formal education.

References

Ernst, F. A., Francis, R. A., Nevels, H., Collipp, D., & Lewis, A. (1991). Racial differences in affirmation of personal habit change to prevent HIV infection. *Preventive Medicine, 20*, 529–533.

Ernst, F. A., Francis, R. A., Nevels, H., & Lemeh, C. A. (1991). Condemnation of homosexuality in the Black community: A gender-specific phenomenon? *Archives of Sexual Behavior, 20*, 579–585.

[1]Address correspondence to Frederick A. Ernst, Department of Psychology and Anthropology, University of Texas–Pan American, 1201 West University Drive, Edinburg, TX 78541-2999; e-mail: fernst@utpa.edu

Exhibit

The Meharry Questionnaire: The Measurement of Attitudes Toward AIDS-Related Issues

Please *circle the number* which reflects the amount of your agreement or disagreement with each statement.

1. AIDS will never be a threat to the rural areas of the U.S.A.

0	1	2	3	4	5[a]
Strongly Disagree					Strongly Agree

2. AIDS is the result of God's punishment ("Divine Retribution").
3. Most of the AIDS patients in the 1990s will have to be treated by family doctors.
4. AIDS will help the society by decreasing the number of homosexuals (gay people).
5. I have made changes in my personal habits to prevent being infected by the AIDS virus.
6. Sterilized needles should be made available to needle-using drug abusers to prevent the spread of AIDS.
7. All pregnant women should be required to have their blood tested for the AIDS virus.
8. It is easier to catch the AIDS virus than the experts are leading us to believe.
9. The AIDS epidemic is a fulfillment of biblical prophecy.
10. AIDS will help the society by decreasing the number of drug abusers.
11. People with AIDS have gotten what they deserve.
12. In the 1990s, a large increase in health care manpower will be required because of AIDS.
13. Needle-using drug abusers who get AIDS are not worthy of extensive medical attention.

[a]This scale follows each of the statements.

HIV/AIDS Knowledge and Attitudes Scales for Teachers

PATRICIA BARTHALOW KOCH[1] AND MAUREEN D. SINGER, *The Pennsylvania State University*

HIV is increasing among children and adolescents in the United States, with an estimate that at least one-half of all new infections occur in people younger than 25 years of age (Centers for Disease Control and Prevention, 2007). It is predicted that, in the near future, all school professionals will have contact with at least one student who is infected or affected by the disease (Landau, Pryor, & Haefli, 1995). Education about prevention and how best to live with HIV-infected family members, friends, and co-workers, as well as how to deal with the disease if one is personally infected, is the key to disarming the devastating health effects of this disease and the stigma attached to it. Education at each school level (elementary, intermediate, and high school) has been recommended so that children can grow up knowing how to protect themselves. Yet researchers have indicated that children and adolescents continue to have many fears and questions about HIV/AIDS arising from a lack of

education and from misunderstanding (Kistner et al., 1997; Steitz & Munn, 1993). Although the majority of states mandate HIV/AIDS education, and teachers indicate their support for it (Brucker & Hall, 1996), the implementation of HIV/AIDS education in the classroom is questionable (di Mauro, 1989–1990). Researchers have shown that teachers at various levels and from various backgrounds may lack basic factual knowledge of the cause, transmission, and prevalence of HIV/AIDS or lack sufficient comfort to teach about this topic (Boscarino & DiClemente, 1996; Dawson, Chunis, Smith, & Carboni, 2001).

Thus, the HIV/AIDS Knowledge and Attitudes Scales for Teachers were developed to serve as measurement instruments in determining teachers' level of knowledge and attitudes toward HIV disease, in general, and specific educational issues. These scales can be and have been used with preservice education students, teachers in the field, and

[1]Address correspondence to Patricia Barthalow Koch, Department of Biobehavioral Health, The Pennsylvania State University, 304B Health and Human Development Building East, University Park, PA 16802; e-mail: p3k@psu.edu

related professionals including school counselors (Costin, Page, Pietrzak, Kerr, & Symons, 2002; Singer, 1991). The data can be useful in designing college programs and in-service workshops to prepare more effective AIDS educators.

Description

The HIV/AIDS Knowledge Scale for Teachers consists of two parts. The first part, General Knowledge, includes 14 true-false items regarding the HIV disease process (e.g., cause, symptoms, diagnosis, effects, treatment) and 4 true-false items specific to classroom issues. The second part, Likelihood of Transmission, contains 17 possible modes of HIV transmission. Thus, the entire knowledge scale contains 35 items.

The HIV/AIDS Attitudes Scale for Teachers contains 25 items regarding HIV/AIDS, persons with HIV/AIDS, and educational issues. The respondent indicates her or his attitudes using a 5-point Likert-type scale.

Response Mode and Timing

For the General Knowledge part of the HIV/AIDS Knowledge Scale for Teachers, respondents identify the statements as (1) *True*, (2) *False*, or (3) *Not Sure*. For the Likelihood of Transmission part of the knowledge scale, respondents are given 17 possible modes of HIV transmission and asked if transmission through each mode is (1) *Very Likely*, (2) *Somewhat Likely*, (3) *Somewhat Unlikely*, (4) *Very Unlikely*, (5) *Definitely Not Possible*, or (6) *Don't Know*. The entire scale takes approximately 20 minutes to complete.

For the HIV/AIDS Attitudes Scale for Teachers, respondents indicate, using a Likert-type scale, if they (1) *Strongly Agree*, (2) *Agree*, (3) are *Uncertain*, (4) *Disagree*, or (5) *Strongly Disagree* with each of the 25 statements. This scale takes approximately 10 to 15 minutes to complete.

Scoring

The highest possible score on the HIV/AIDS Knowledge Scale for Teachers is 35. One point is given for every correct answer on the General Knowledge part of the knowledge scale, with the highest possible score being 18. Correct answers are as follows: *Definitely True* (1) for Items 3, 4, 6, 7, 9, 11, 14, 15, 17, and 18; *Definitely False* (2) for Items 1, 2, 5, 8, 10, 12, 13, and 16. All *Unsure* responses are considered incorrect.

The highest possible score for the Likelihood of Transmission part of the knowledge scale is 17, with one point given for each correct answer. The correct answers are as follows: *Very Likely* (1) for Items 27, 30, and 32; *Very Likely* or *Somewhat Likely* (1 or 2) for Items 20, 29, and 34; *Very Unlikely* for Items 21, 23, 31, 33, and 35; *Definitely Not Possible* for Items 19, 22, 24, 25, 26, and 28.

Scores on the HIV/AIDS Attitudes Scale for Teachers can range from 25 (most unsupportive attitudes) to 125 (most supportive attitudes). A mean score can be calculated, with a mean of 1.00 representing the most unsupportive attitudes and 5.00 indicating the most supportive attitudes toward dealing with HIV disease inside and outside of the classroom. The following items on the scale are reverse scored: 1, 5, 7, 9, 10, 13, 15, 17, 20, 21, 22, 25.

Research using these instruments involving 128 elementary education students completing their student teaching experiences indicated that they had very poor knowledge about HIV disease ($M = 18.9$), representing a 54% correct response level (Singer, 1991). These student teachers possessed uncertain to slightly positive attitudes toward dealing with HIV disease, with an average score of 87.6 ($M = 3.46$). The knowledge levels of preservice and in-service school counselors were very similar, with mean scores of 18.9 and 18.5, respectively. The preservice and in-service school counselors reported more positive attitudes, with scores of 97.39 and 97.64 ($M = 3.89$ and 3.90), respectively.

Reliability

Reliability for the knowledge and attitudes scales was established using two different methods (Singer, 1991). First, a test-retest of the instruments was conducted with 59 elementary education majors. Pearson product-moment correlations were established for the knowledge scale at .87 and for the attitudes scale at .89. Internal reliability for the knowledge scale, using Kuder-Richardson's statistic, was established using a sample of 128 elementary education student teachers. The reliability for the General Knowledge section was .78 and for the Likelihood of Transmission section was .88, yielding an overall reliability for the entire scale of .89. Cronbach's alpha coefficient was used to establish reliability for the attitude scale at .89. It is recommended that reliability be further tested with groups of education majors, student teachers, and teachers of differing content areas and levels of school (elementary, intermediate, and high school).

Validity

The HIV/AIDS Knowledge and Attitude Scales for Teachers were constructed adapting items and/or format from the National Health Interview Survey (Hardy, 1989), the Nurses' Attitudes About AIDS Scale (Preston, Young, Koch, & Forti, 1995), and an instrument previously used in a study of preservice elementary education teachers (Ballard, White, & Glascoff, 1990). A panel of three experts in the area of HIV/AIDS disease and education reviewed the items and answers for relevancy and accuracy when the instruments were developed and at 5-year intervals to ensure their continued accuracy and relevancy. A pilot test for content validity was conducted with 10 elementary education majors. It is recommended that construct validity be further tested with groups of education majors, student teachers, and teachers of differing content areas and levels of school.

References

Ballard, D., White, D., & Glascoff, M. (1990). HIV/AIDS education for preservice elementary teachers. *Journal of School Health, 60,* 262–269.

Boscarino, J. A., & DiClemente, R. J. (1996). AIDS knowledge, teaching comfort, and support for AIDS education among school teachers: A statewide study. *AIDS Education and Prevention, 8,* 267–277.

Brucker, B. W., & Hall, W. H. (1996). Teachers' attitudes toward HIV/AIDS: An American national assessment. *Early Child Development and Care, 115,* 85–98.

Centers for Disease Control and Prevention. (2007). Cases of HIV infection and AIDS in the United States and dependent areas. *HIV/AIDS Surveillance Report, 19,* 1–63.

Costin, A. C., Page, B. J., Pietrzak, D. R., Kerr, D. L., & Symons, C. W. (2002). HIV/AIDS knowledge and beliefs among pre-service and in-service school counselors. *Professional School Counseling, 6*(1), 79–86.

Dawson, L. J., Chunis, M. L., Smith, D. M., & Carboni, A. A. (2001). The role of academic discipline and gender in high school teachers' AIDS-related knowledge and attitudes. *Journal of School Health, 71*(1), 3–8.

di Mauro, D. (1989–1990, December/January). Sexuality education 1990: A review of state sexuality and AIDS education curricula. *SIECUS Report, 18*(2), 1–9.

Hardy, A. M. (1989). *AIDS knowledge and attitudes for April-June 1989.* Provisional data from the National Health Interview Survey. (Advance Data from Vital and Health Statistics, No. 179.) (DHHS Publication No. PHS 90-1250.) Hyattsville, MD: National Center for Health Statistics.

Kistner, J., Eberstein, I. W., Guadagno, D., Sly, D., Sittig, L., Foster, K., et al. (1997). Children's AIDS-related knowledge and attitudes: Variations by grade, race, gender, socioeconomic status, and size of community. *AIDS Education and Prevention, 9,* 285–298.

Landau, S., Pryor, J. B., & Haefli, K. (1995). Pediatric HIV: School-based sequelae and curricular interventions for prevention and social acceptance. *School Psychology Review, 24,* 213–229.

Preston, D. B., Young, E. W., Koch, P. B., & Forti, E. M. (1995). The Nurses' Attitudes About AIDS Scale (NAAS): Development and psychometric analysis. *AIDS Education and Prevention, 7,* 443–454.

Singer, M. D. (1991). *Elementary student teachers' knowledge and attitudes of HIV/AIDS and HIV/AIDS education.* Unpublished thesis, Pennsylvania State University, University Park, PA.

Steitz, J. A., & Munn, J. A. (1993). Adolescents and AIDS: Knowledge and attitude. *Adolescence, 28*(111), 609–619.

Exhibit

HIV/AIDS Knowledge and Attitudes Scales for Teachers

HIV/AIDS Knowledge Scale for Teachers

Please indicate, to the best of your knowledge, if the following statements are true (1) or false (2) by circling a number from the scale for your answer. If you are not sure of the correct answer, circle 3.

1 = True	2 = False	3 = Not Sure

1. AIDS is an infectious disease caused by a bacteria.[a]
2. AIDS breaks down the body's immunity by destroying the B cells in the endocrine system.
3. AIDS can damage the brain.
4. It may be more than 5 years before an HIV-infected person develops AIDS.
5. HIV lives and functions in warm, moist environments for days outside of the body.
6. Early symptoms of HIV infection include fatigue, fever, weight loss, and swelling of the lymph nodes.
7. A person who has tested negatively on one HIV antibody blood test could still transmit HIV to a sexual partner.
8. The number of HIV-infected persons will be decreasing during the next two years.
9. Two common disorders found in persons with AIDS are pneumocystis carinii pneumonia and Kaposi's sarcoma.
10. Latex condoms are not as effective as "lambskin" or natural membrane condoms in preventing the spread of HIV.
11. Drugs can be used to slow down the rate of reproduction of HIV and lengthen the life of an infected person.
12. It is possible to detect HIV antibodies in the bloodstream immediately after becoming infected.
13. There is a vaccine available in Europe that can protect a person from getting AIDS.
14. There have been no cases of AIDS spread by students to their teachers or classmates through usual daily contact.
15. In recent years, adolescents are among the groups with the largest increase of HIV infection.
16. Less than one-half of the states have mandated that AIDS education be included in their schools' curricula.
17. There is a federal law that protects children with HIV or AIDS from educational discrimination.
18. There is no cure for AIDS at the present time.

To what degree do you think the following are likely to transmit HIV? Please use the numbers from the scale for your answers.

1 = Very Likely	2 = Somewhat Likely	3 = Somewhat Unlikely
4 = Very Unlikely	5 = Definitely Not Possible	6 = Don't Know

19. Working near someone with AIDS.

20. HIV-infected mother to baby during pregnancy/birth.
21. Kissing someone who has AIDS.
22. Eating in a restaurant where the cook has AIDS.
23. Receiving a blood transfusion.
24. Sharing plates, forks, or glasses with someone who has AIDS.
25. Living with a person who has AIDS (without sexual involvement).
26. Donating blood.
27. Sharing needles for drug use with someone who has AIDS.

How likely do you think the following situations are in transmitting HIV? Please use the numbers from the scale for your answers.

| 1 = Very Likely | 2 = Somewhat Likely | 3 = Somewhat Unlikely |
| 4 = Very Unlikely | 5 = Definitely Not Possible | 6 = Don't Know |

28. Mosquito bites.
29. HIV-infected mother to baby through nursing.
30. Receiving anal intercourse from an HIV-infected person without using a condom.
31. Receiving anal intercourse from an HIV-infected person with using a condom.
32. Having sexual intercourse with an HIV-infected person without using a condom.
33. Having sexual intercourse with an HIV-infected person with using a condom.
34. Performing oral sex on an HIV-infected man without using a condom.
35. Performing oral sex on an HIV-infected woman using a dental dam.

HIV/AIDS Attitudes Scale for Teachers

The following statements reflect attitudes about HIV and AIDS. Circle the number that best describes your reactions to each statement.

| 1 = Strongly Agree | 2 = Agree | 3 = Uncertain | 4 = Disagree | 5 = Strongly Disagree |

1. I believe I have enough information about HIV/AIDS to protect myself in my social life.[a]
2. I worry about possible casual contact with a person with AIDS.
3. Activities that spread HIV, such as some forms of sexual behavior, should be illegal.
4. I feel uncomfortable when coming in contact with gay men because of the risk that they may have AIDS.
5. I believe I have enough information about HIV/AIDS to protect myself in my future work setting.
6. Persons with AIDS are responsible for getting their illness.
7. Civil rights laws should be enacted/enforced to protect people with AIDS from job and housing discrimination.
8. Male homosexuality is obscene and vulgar.
9. HIV antibody blood test results should be confidential to avoid discrimination against people with positive results.
10. I feel that more time should be spent teaching future teachers about HIV/AIDS in their college courses.
11. I feel disgusted when I consider the state of sinfulness of male homosexuality.
12. I would quit my job before I would work with someone who has AIDS.
13. People should not blame the homosexual community for the spread of AIDS in the U.S.
14. AIDS is a punishment for immoral behavior.
15. I feel secure that I have reduced all risks of personally contracting HIV.
16. I think all children should be tested for HIV before entering school.
17. I believe it is the regular elementary classroom teacher's responsibility to teach AIDS education.
18. In my opinion, parents of all students in the class should be notified if there is a student with HIV or AIDS in the class.
19. I feel that all school personnel who have direct contact with a student with HIV or AIDS should be notified.
20. I think that students with HIV or AIDS should be allowed to fully participate in the day-to-day activities of the regular classroom.
21. I would support including AIDS education in the curriculum in a school where I was teaching.
22. A teacher with HIV or AIDS should be allowed to continue teaching.
23. It scares me to think that I may have a student with HIV or AIDS in my classroom.
24. I believe that teachers should have the right to refuse to have students with HIV or AIDS in their classroom.
25. I feel that I could comfortably answer students' questions about HIV/AIDS.

[a]The appropriate scale of numbers follows each item in the scale.

HIV/AIDS Knowledge and Beliefs Scales for Adolescents

CHERYL KOOPMAN,[1] *Stanford University*
HELEN REID, *University of California, Los Angeles*
ELIZABETH MCGARVEY, *University of Virginia*
ADELAIDA CRUZ CASTILLO, *Stanford University*

Assessment is essential to the evaluation of educational and other interventions designed to increase knowledge and encourage the adoption of safer beliefs about preventing HIV/AIDS. We developed and evaluated measures for adolescents, who were at particularly high risk, owing to their sexual risk behaviors, for contracting HIV/AIDS and other sexually transmitted diseases (Whaley, 1999).

Description

Two advisory councils, composed of experts in the area, evaluated a pool of items on the basis of content, accuracy, reading level, and clarity. After revising items, knowledge and beliefs measures were developed, which were revised again based on pilot testing with adolescents.

These instruments were then administered to adolescents involved in research programs with homeless and gay-identified adolescents in New York City (Koopman, Rotheram-Borus, Henderson, Bradley, & Hunter, 1990) and with incarcerated delinquents in Virginia (Canterbury, Clavet, McGarvey, & Koopman, 1998; Chang, Bendel, Koopman, McGarvey, & Canterbury, 2003; Otto-Salaj, Gore-Felton, McGarvey, & Canterbury, 2002). In the research with homeless and gay-identified adolescents, a consecutive series of 450 youths aged 11 to 19 years ($M = 16.0$, $SD = 1.7$) were recruited at four homeless shelters and one agency providing social and recreational services to gay-identified youths in New York City. Participants included 153 homeless females, 158 homeless males, and 139 gay or bisexual males. Ethnicities were African American (49%), Hispanic/Latino (35%), White (10%), and other (6%).

Incarcerated youths were recruited from a juvenile detention facility in Virginia. Youths ranged in age from 12 to 19 years old, with a mean of 15.8. A total of 893 participants were assessed, including 754 male participants and 139 female participants. Participants' ethnic backgrounds were 55% African American, 39% Caucasian, 3% Native American, and 3% other.

Since their original development, these measures have been adapted for other purposes. To ascertain that participants had at least a minimal level of HIV/AIDS knowledge (Patel, Gutnik, Yoskowitz, O'Sullivan, & Kaufman, 2006;

Patel, Yoskowitz, & Kaufman, 2007), a modified, 12-item Knowledge scale was used as a screening instrument of heterosexual undergraduate college students (ages 18 to 24) in New York City. Items from the HIV/AIDS Knowledge and Beliefs measures have been included in research with adult Kenyan males and females (Volk & Koopman, 2001), Indian women (Ananth & Koopman, 2003), and adult women in Botswana (Greig & Koopman, 2003).

Response Mode and Timing

The HIV/AIDS Knowledge Scale uses true-false response options and also includes a separate Safer Alternatives subscale in which the respondent is asked to identify the safer action of two alternatives. The response format for the Beliefs About Preventing HIV/AIDS instrument is a 4-point Likert-type scale for each item (1 = *Agree Strongly* to 4 = *Disagree Strongly*). It takes respondents about 20 minutes to complete the HIV/AIDS Knowledge Scale and 15 minutes to complete the Beliefs About Preventing HIV/AIDS Scale.

Scoring

For the HIV/AIDS Knowledge Scale, item scores are recoded as correct = 1 or incorrect = 0 and then summed for the total score. In the computation of the Beliefs About Preventing HIV/AIDS scores, 19 items are first reverse scored, as shown in the scoring instructions. Higher Beliefs scores indicate stronger endorsement of beliefs about preventing HIV/AIDS.

Reliability and Validity

For both measures, the process used in their development contributed to the content validity of the measures (Koopman et al., 1990). Items were generated to ensure content validity across relevant domains.

Homeless and Gay-Identified Adolescents

Of the original 49 HIV/AIDS Knowledge items, 45 loaded on three factors: Medical/Scientific Knowledge (23 items,

[1]Address correspondence to Cheryl Koopman, Department of Psychiatry and Behavioral Sciences, MC 5718, Stanford University, Stanford, CA 94305-5718; e-mail: koopman@stanford.edu

alpha = .71), Myths of HIV Transmission (9 items, alpha = .72), and Knowledge of High-Risk and Prevention Behaviors (13 items, alpha =. 68). For the full 45-item true-false scale, alpha = .85 and test-retest reliability at 1 week was strong (r = .82, p < .0001). For the seven Safer Alternative subscale items, alpha = .69 and test-retest reliability was r = 40, p < .01.

Of the Beliefs items, 36 loaded on five factors that generated five corresponding subscales. Internal consistencies for these subscales were calculated: Peer Support for Safe Acts, alpha = .61; Expectation to Prevent Pregnancy, alpha = .72; Perceived Threat, alpha = .81; Self-Control, alpha = .82; and Self-Efficacy, alpha = .90. Test-retest reliability of the overall Beliefs measure was r = .49, p < .001.

Correlations among the HIV/AIDS Knowledge subscales ranged from .26 to .61 (p < .0001); among the Beliefs subscales, correlations ranged from .37 to .74 (p < .0001 for all). However, the correlations between Knowledge and Beliefs subscales ranged from .00 to .19. Subscales were significantly correlated with age (r = .12 to r = .34), with the exception of Expectation to Prevent Pregnancy.

Gay/bisexual males scored highest on every Knowledge subscale. Homeless females scored significantly lower than gay/bisexual males on the Expectation to Prevent Pregnancy subscale. No other significant differences between male homeless, female homeless, and gay/bisexual male youths were found.

Incarcerated Adolescents

In the research with incarcerated adolescents, for the overall Knowledge true-false scale, the alpha equaled .81. The Safer Alternatives subscale was not administered, so it could not be evaluated with this sample. The Beliefs measure demonstrated strong internal consistency for the overall scale when administered to incarcerated adolescents (alpha = .88). The subscales demonstrated marginal to good internal consistencies: Peer Support for Safe Acts (alpha = .56); Perceived Threat (alpha = .58); Expectation to Prevent Pregnancy (alpha = .60); Self-Control (alpha = .75); and Self-Efficacy (alpha = .79).

Other Information

This research was funded by the following grants: 1P50MH43520 from the National Institute of Mental Health and the National Institute on Drug Abuse (Mary Jane Rotheram-Borus, principal investigator); 1R01MH54930 from the National Institute of Mental Health (David Spiegel, principal investigator); and 1R01DAO7900-01A1 from the National Institute on Drug Abuse (Randy Canterbury, principal investigator).

References

Ananth, P., & Koopman, C. (2003). HIV/AIDS knowledge, beliefs, and behavior among women of childbearing age in India. *AIDS Education and Prevention, 15*, 529–546.

Canterbury, R. J., Clavet, G. J., McGarvey, E. L., & Koopman, C. (1998). HIV risk-related attitudes and behaviors of incarcerated adolescents: Implications for public school students. *High School Journal, 82*, 1–10.

Chang, V. Y., Bendel, T. L., Koopman, C., McGarvey, E. L., & Canterbury, R. J. (2003). Delinquents' safe sex attitudes: Relationships with demographics, resilience factors, and substance use. *Criminal Justice and Behavior, 30*, 210–229.

Greig, F. E., & Koopman, C. (2003). Multilevel analysis of women's empowerment and HIV prevention: Quantitative survey results from a preliminary study in Botswana. *AIDS and Behavior, 7*, 195–208.

Koopman, C., Rotheram-Borus, M. J., Henderson, R., Bradley, J. S., & Hunter, J. (1990). Assessment of knowledge of AIDS and beliefs about AIDS prevention among adolescents. *AIDS Education and Prevention, 2*, 58–70.

Otto-Salaj, L. L., Gore-Felton, C., McGarvey, E., & Canterbury, R. J. (2002). Psychiatric functioning and substance use: Factors associated with HIV risk among incarcerated adolescents. *Child Psychiatry and Human Development, 33*, 91–106.

Patel, V. L., Gutnik, L. A., Yoskowitz, N. A., O'Sullivan, L. F., & Kaufman, D. R. (2006). Patterns of reasoning and decision making about condom use by urban college students. *AIDS Care, 18*, 918–930.

Patel, V. L., Yoskowitz, N. A., & Kaufman, D. R. (2007). Comprehension of sexual situations and its relationship to risky decisions by young adults. *AIDS Care, 19*, 916–922.

Volk, J. E. & Koopman, C. (2001). Factors associated with condom use in Kenya: A test of the health belief model. *AIDS Education and Prevention, 13*, 495–508.

Whaley, A. L. (1999). Preventing the high-risk behavior of adolescents: Focus on HIV/AIDS transmission, unintended pregnancy, or both? *Journal of Adolescent Health, 24*, 376–382.

Exhibit

HIV/AIDS Knowledge Scale

Directions: Read each of the following statements and decide whether you think the statement is true or false. If you think the statement is true, mark "T." If you think the statement is false, mark "F."

1. AIDS means Acquired Immune Deficiency Syndrome.
2. Most scientists today believe that AIDS is caused by a virus, called HIV (Human Immunodeficiency Virus).
3. Most people who develop AIDS eventually recover.
4. A baby born to a mother with HIV infection can get AIDS.
5. HIV is carried in the blood.
6. Most people who have HIV infection are sick with AIDS.
7. Prostitutes in New York City have a low chance of getting HIV (which can lead to AIDS).
8. HIV (which can lead to AIDS) is carried in men's cum (semen).
9. The number of men and women infected with HIV will probably be less in the next several years than it is now.

10. AIDS weakens the body's ability to fight off disease.
11. People have been known to get HIV and develop AIDS from toilet seats.
12. A negative HIV antibody test means that a person probably has AIDS.
13. You can't get HIV (which can lead to AIDS) if you only have intercourse with one person for the rest of your life.
14. It is a good idea to ask someone about his/her past sexual activities before having sex with them, even though some partners may lie to you.
15. If the HIV test comes out negative, it means that the person has AIDS.
16. People get other diseases because of AIDS.
17. You can die from AIDS.
18. Men have a higher chance of getting AIDS from having sex with a woman than from having sex with a man.
19. Using a condom will lessen the chance of getting AIDS.
20. People who have AIDS get pneumonia more often than the average person.
21. Women are more likely to get AIDS from having sex with a straight (heterosexual) man than with a bisexual man.
22. It is safe to have intercourse without a condom with a person who shoots drugs as long as you don't shoot drugs.
23. People have been known to get HIV and develop AIDS from a swimming pool used by someone with AIDS.
24. People of any race can get HIV and develop AIDS.
25. People have been known to get HIV and develop AIDS by tongue kissing a person who is infected.
26. Lambskin condoms are better than latex condoms for preventing HIV infection.
27. People usually become very sick with AIDS a few days after being infected with HIV.
28. Getting AIDS depends on whether or not you practice safe sex, not on the group you hang out with.
29. People have been known to get HIV and develop AIDS from insect bites.
30. It is safer not to have sexual intercourse at all than to have sexual intercourse using a condom.
31. You only need one HIV test to come out positive to be sure that you are infected.
32. Pregnant women are safe from getting HIV infection.
33. A vaccine has recently been developed that prevents people from getting HIV infection (which can lead to AIDS).
34. The virus that can lead to AIDS can be passed by an infected person even though that person isn't sick.
35. If you are really healthy, then exercising daily can prevent getting HIV (which can lead to AIDS).
36. If the person you are now having sex with has been tested and does not have HIV infection, it means that you are not infected.
37. People have been known to get HIV and develop AIDS by eating at a restaurant where a worker has AIDS.
38. When using condoms, it is better to use one with a spermicide like Nonoxynol-9.
39. You can get HIV and eventually AIDS through an open cut or wound.
40. You are safe from AIDS if you have oral sex (with mouth to penis or mouth to vagina) without a condom.
41. If you get a "false positive" result on your HIV antibody test, it means you are infected.
42. Anal (rear end) sex without a condom is one of the safer sexual practices.
43. You can get HIV and eventually AIDS by donating blood.
44. Using drugs like marijuana, alcohol, cocaine, and crack makes it more likely that you may have unsafe sex.
45. You can get HIV (which can lead to AIDS) by getting tested for it.

Safer Alternatives

Directions: For each pair of choices below, show which you think is safer by marking your choice (either A or B) on your answer sheet. If you do not know, take a guess.

Which is safer?

1. A) Giving blood.
   B) Getting a blood transfusion.
2. A) Working in the same office with someone who has AIDS or HIV.
   B) Contact with HIV or the AIDS virus through an open cut or sore.
3. A) Heterosexual vaginal intercourse with a woman who has AIDS.
   B) Anal intercourse with a man who has AIDS.
4. A) Using a needle just used by a person with HIV.
   B) A man having unprotected vaginal intercourse with a woman who has AIDS.
5. A) Having sexual intercourse with a person who shoots drugs.
   B) Spending time in the same house or room with a person who has AIDS.
6. A) Homosexual anal intercourse with someone who has AIDS.
   B) Receiving a blood transfusion.
7. A) Unprotected sexual intercourse with a lesbian.
   B) Unprotected sexual intercourse with a bisexual man.

Note. True/False answer key: 1-T, 2-T, 3-F, 4-T, 5-T, 6-F, 7-F, 8-T, 9-F, 10-T, 11-F, 12-F,13-F, 14-T, 15-F, 16-T, 17-T, 18-F, 19-T, 20-T, 21-F, 22-F, 23-F, 24-T, 25-F, 26-F, 27-F, 28-T, 29-F, 30-T, 31-F, 32-F, 33-F, 34-T, 35-F, 36-F, 37-F, 38-F, 39-T, 40-F, 41-F, 42-F, 43-F, 44-T, 45-F. Subscales: Medical/Scientific Knowledge (1, 2, 3, 4, 5, 6, 8, 9, 10, 12, 15, 16, 17, 20, 26, 31, 33, 34, 35, 36, 38, 39, 41); Myths of HIV Transmission (11, 23, 25, 27, 29, 32, 37, 43, 45); Knowledge of High Risk/Prevention Behaviors (7, 13, 14, 18, 19, 21, 22, 24, 28, 30, 40, 42, 44). Safer Alternatives answer key: 1-A, 2-A, 3-A, 4-B, 5-B, 6-B, 7-A.

Beliefs About Preventing HIV/AIDS

Directions: Read each statement carefully. Then show your agreement or disagreement with each statement by marking 1, 2, 3, or 4.

Mark:

1 if you agree strongly
2 if you agree somewhat
3 if you disagree somewhat
4 if you disagree strongly

1. I would feel uncomfortable buying condoms.
2. I would be too embarrassed to carry a condom around with me, even if I kept it hidden.
3. It doesn't bother me if others make fun of me because I believe in having safe sex.
4. If my partner won't use (or let me use) a condom, I won't have sex.
5. My friends have changed the way they have sex because of the AIDS epidemic.
6. I will have safe sex even if people make fun of me for it.
7. AIDS is a health scare that I take very seriously.
8. There is a good chance I will get AIDS during the next five years.
9. If I ask to use condoms, it might make my partner not want to have sex with me.
10. A person who gets AIDS has a good chance of being cured.
11. I plan on being very careful about who I have sex with.
12. My friends practice safe sex.
13. I have no control over my sexual urges.
14. My friends feel that it is too much trouble to use condoms.
15. I have a high chance of getting AIDS because of my past history.
16. My partner will know I really care about him/her if I ask to use condoms.
17. I don't know how to use a condom.
18. AIDS is the scariest disease I know.
19. If I was going to have sex with someone and they made fun of me for wanting to have safe sex, I would probably give in.
20. There is still time for me to protect myself against AIDS.
21. Trying to have safe sex gets in the way of having fun.
22. I feel almost sure that I will get AIDS.
23. I know how to have safe sex.
24. Using condoms would be a sexual "turn-off" for me.
25. I am not doing anything now that is sexually unsafe.
26. In the future I will always be able to practice safe sex.
27. Before I decide to have intercourse, I will make sure we have a condom.
28. Once I get sexually excited, I lose all control over what happens.
29. Most of my friends think that practicing safe sex can lower the spread of AIDS.
30. If I ask to use a condom, it will look like I don't trust my partner.
31. Carrying condoms with me every day is a habit I can keep.
32. I am too young to take care of a baby right now.
33. Not getting pregnant (or not getting a girl pregnant) is very important to me.
34. I will not bother with birth control when I have intercourse with a member of the opposite sex.
35. In the future, whenever I have sexual intercourse with a member of the opposite sex, I plan to make sure we are using birth control.
36. If I wanted to have sex with a member of the opposite sex, and did not have protection, I would go ahead and have intercourse anyway.

Note. Reverse scored: 3, 4, 5, 6, 7, 11, 12, 16, 18, 20, 23, 25, 26, 27, 29, 31, 32, 33, 35. Subscales: Perceived Threat (7, 8, 10, 15, 18, 22); Self-Control (9, 13, 19, 21, 24, 28, 30, 36); Self-Efficacy (1, 2, 3, 4, 6, 11, 16, 17, 20, 23, 25, 26, 27, 31); Peer Support for Safe Acts (5, 12, 14, 29); Expectation to Prevent Pregnancy (32, 33, 34, 35, 36).

Attitudes About HIV/AIDS for Hispanic College Students

RAFFY R. LUQUIS,[1] *Penn State Harrisburg*
PATRICIA BARTHALOW KOCH, *The Pennsylvania State University*

The HIV/AIDS attitudes scale for Hispanics was adapted from the attitudes survey used by the Centers for Disease Control and Prevention (Dawson, 1990) and the Nurse's Attitudes about AIDS Scale (Preston, Young, Koch, & Forti, 1995).

Description

The scale includes 26 items to measure attitudes about HIV and people who may be infected, sexual behaviors and safer sexual practices, and discussion and learning about AIDS.

Response Mode and Timing

Participants respond according to how they feel about each item using a 5-point Likert scale from *Strongly Agree* (1) to *Strongly Disagree* (5).

Scoring

A mean score is calculated for the scale, with 1 representing negative attitudes to 5 representing positive attitudes. The following items are reverse scored: 1, 5, 8, 9, 10, 12, 13, 15, 16, 20, 21, 23, 25, and 26.

Reliability

Reliability analysis was conducted on the scale using a Cronbach's alpha measure of the internal consistency. As part of a study with Hispanic and non-Hispanic college students (Luquis, 1991), the reliability analysis resulted in an alpha of .85 for the entire scale.

Validity

The initial version of the scale was subject to focus groups analysis with Hispanic college students to determine culturally relevant issues to be included. The revised instrument was pilot-tested with Hispanic and non-Hispanic students for feedback regarding content, format, and vocabulary. The English version of the instrument was translated into Spanish and back-translated into English by two separate bilingual professionals to ensure the validity of the Spanish version of the scale.

References

Dawson, D. A. (1990). *AIDS knowledge and attitudes for July–September*. Provisional data from the National Health Interview Survey. (Advance Data from Vital and Health Statistics No. 183.) Hyattsville, MD: Department of Health and Human Services, Public Health Services, Centers for Disease Control, National Center for Health Statistics.

Luquis, R. (1991). *Knowledge of and attitudes about HIV/AIDS among Hispanic college students at the Pennsylvania State University*. Unpublished master's thesis, Pennsylvania State University, University Park, PA.

Preston, D. B., Young, E. W., Koch, P. B., & Forti, E. M. (1995). The Nurses' Attitudes about AIDS Scale (NAAS): Development and psychometric analysis. *AIDS Education and Prevention, 7*, 443–454.

Exhibit

Attitudes About HIV/AIDS for Hispanic College Students

Attitudes About HIV/AIDS

The following statements reflect attitudes about HIV and AIDS. Circle the number that best describes your feeling about each statement.

Scale: 1 = *Strongly Agree*, 2 = *Agree*, 3 = *Uncertain*, 4 = *Disagree*, 5 = *Strongly Disagree*

1. I believe I have enough information about HIV/AIDS to protect myself.
2. I believe women should not have sexual intercourse before marriage.
3. Activities that spread HIV/AIDS, such as some forms of sexual behaviors, should be illegal.
4. I feel uncomfortable when coming in contact with gay men because of the risk that they may have HIV/AIDS.
5. Civil rights laws should be enacted/enforced to protect people with HIV/AIDS from job and housing discrimination.

[1]Address correspondence to Raffy R. Luquis, School of Behavioral Sciences and Education, W331 Olmsted, Penn State Harrisburg, 777 West Harrisburg Pike, Middletown PA 17057; e-mail: rluquis@psu.edu

6. Male homosexuality is obscene and vulgar.

7. I believe men should not have sexual intercourse before marriage.

8. HIV test results should be confidential to avoid discrimination against people with positive results.

9. I feel that more time should be spent teaching students about HIV/AIDS in my college courses.

10. People should not blame the homosexual community for the spread of HIV/AIDS in the U.S.

11. AIDS is a punishment for immoral behavior.

12. I feel secure that I have reduced all risk of personally contracting HIV.

13. It would not bother me to attend class with a person with HIV/AIDS.

14. Anyone who has had more than one sexual partner is promiscuous.

15. I could comfortably discuss HIV/AIDS with a friend.

16. I would not avoid a friend if she/he had HIV/AIDS.

17. If I discovered that my roommate had HIV/AIDS, I would move out.

18. I do not believe in using condoms.

19. I could not discuss HIV/AIDS with my parents.

20. I would date a person with HIV/AIDS.

21. I would feel comfortable discussing HIV/AIDS in a course.

22. I would not engage in sexual intercourse before marriage.

23. I would feel comfortable asking a new partner about his/her sexual history.

24. I would use HIV/AIDS as an excuse to avoid any sexual relationships.

25. I would limit myself to one sexual partner.

26. I would use a condom every time I had sex.

Actitudes Acerca del VIH/SIDA

Las siguientes oraciones reflejan actitudes acerca del VIH/SIDA. Circule el numero qua mejor describe tu reacción a cada oración.
Escala: 1 = Muy de Acuerdo, 2 = De Acuerdo, 3 = Inseguro, 4 = En Desacuerdo, 5 = Muy en Desacuerdo

1. Creo tener suficiente información acerca del VIH/SIDA para protegerme.

2. Creo que las mujeres no deberían tener relaciones sexuales antes de casarse.

3. Actividades que trasmiten el VIH/SIDA, tal como algunos comportamientos sexuales, deberían ser ilegales.

4. Me siento incomodo cuando estoy en contacto con hombres homosexuales por miedo de que puedan tener VIH/SIDA.

5. Leyes de Derechos Civiles deben ser promulgadas e impuestas para proteger personas con HIV/SIDA de discriminación de trabajo y casa.

6. La homosexualidad masculina es vulgar y obscena.

7. Creo que los hombres no deberían tener relaciones sexuales antes de casarse.

8. Resultados de la prueba de sangre para el VIH deben ser confidenciales para prevenir discriminación en contra de personas con resultados positivos.

9. Siento que deberían dedicar más tiempo a la enseñanza sobre el VIH/SIDA en mis clases de universidad.

10. La comunidad homosexual no debe ser culpada por la transmisión del VIH/SIDA en los Estados Unidos.

11. El SIDA es un castigo por comportamiento inmoral.

12. Creo haber reducido todos los riesgos que me exponen al VIH/SIDA.

13. No me importaría ir a clases con una persona con VIH/SIDA.

14. Cualquier persona que haya tenido más de un compañero sexual es promiscuo.

15. Podría hablar abiertamente del VIH/SIDA con un amigo.

16. Yo no me alejaría de un amigo si él/ella tuviera VIH/SIDA.

17. Si yo descubriera que mi compañero de apartamento tuviera el VIH/SIDA, yo me mudaría a otro lugar.

18. Yo no estoy de acuerdo con en el uso de condones.

19. Yo no podría hablar el tema del VIH/SIDA con mis padres.

20. Yo saldría con una persona que tuviera VIH/SIDA.

21. Me sentiría cómodo hablando del tema del VIH/SIDA en clase.

22. Me abstendría de relaciones sexuales antes del matrimonio.

23. Me sentiría cómodo al preguntar a mi compañero acerca de su vida sexual pasada.

24. Usaría el VIH/SIDA como excusa para no tener relaciones sexuales.

25. Me limitaría a un solo compañero en mi relación sexual.

26. Siempre que tenga sexo usare un condón.

Nurses' Attitudes About HIV/AIDS Scale—Version 2

DEBORAH BRAY PRESTON,[1] *The Pennsylvania State University*
ELAINE WILSON YOUNG, *Massachusetts General Hospital Institute of Health Professions*
PATRICIA BARTHALOW KOCH, *The Pennsylvania State University*
ESTHER M. FORTI, *Medical University of South Carolina*

The Nurses' Attitudes About HIV/AIDS Scale (NAAS) is a paper-and-pencil test designed to assess nurses' attitudes about people living with HIV/AIDS (PLWHAs; homosexuals, intravenous drug users, and women), nursing care concerns, and societal/professional concerns. It is a 1997 revision of the original NAAS (Preston, Young, Koch, & Forti, 1995).

Suggested applications of the NAAS are: (a) as a descriptive tool to investigate HIV/AIDS-related attitudes in a variety of nursing populations, (b) as a means of describing models of nursing practice behavior related to PLWHAs, (c) as a means of predicting practice outcomes related to care of PLWHAs in varying nursing populations—specifically the use of Standard Precautions, (d) as a needs assessment for educational programming related to HIV/AIDS, and (e) as an evaluative tool to assess attitude change as the result of educational programming. In addition, adaption of the NAAS for use with other health care providers, that is, health educators, social workers, and physicians, is recommended.

Description

The scale comprises 45 items pertaining to Homosexuality (12 items), Women with HIV (4 items), IV Drug Abusers (9 items), Nursing Care Concerns (8 items), and Social/Professional Issues (12 items). The scale should be administered in its entirety and not as a series of subscales. We suggest that the items be randomly ordered to avoid response bias.

Response Mode and Timing

Respondents indicate their degree of agreement/disagreement with the statements on a scale ranging from 1 (*Strongly Disagree*) to 5 (*Strongly Agree*). The scale requires approximately 20 minutes to complete.

Scoring

For the Homosexuality items, reverse score Items 2, 7, 11, and 12. For the items on Women with HIV, reverse score Items 2 and 3. For the items pertaining to IV Drug Abusers, reverse score Items 3, 4, 5, and 7. For the Nursing Care Concerns, reverse score Items 1, 2, 6, 7, and 8. For the Social/Professional Issues, reverse score Items 1, 3, 4, 5, 6, 7, 8, 9, 10, 11, and 12. After adding all scores, possible scores range from 45 to 225, with higher scores indicating greater tolerance toward or favorable attitudes about HIV/AIDS.

Reliability

Cronbach's alpha for the Homosexuality items is .95, for the Women items, $\alpha = .64$, for the IV Drug Abusers subscale, $\alpha = .75$, for the Nursing Care Concerns, $\alpha = .80$, and for the Social/Professional Issues, $\alpha = .82$.

Reference

Preston, D. B., Young, E. W., Koch, P. B., & Forti, E. M. (1995). The Nurses' Attitudes About AIDS Scale (NAAS): Development and psychometric analysis. *AIDS Education and Prevention, 7,* 443–454.

Exhibit

Nurses' Attitudes About HIV/AIDS Scale—Version 2

The following are some statements regarding opinions about HIV/AIDS and PWAs. There may be no "right" or "wrong" response. Place the number from the scale that best represents your reaction in the space provided.

1 Strongly Agree	4 Disagree
2 Agree	5 Strongly Disagree
3 Neither Agree nor Disagree	

[1]Address correspondence to Deborah Bray Preston, Professor Emerita, The Pennsylvania State University, 3296 Shellers Bend, Unit 144, State College, PA 16801; e-mail: dqp@psu.edu

Homosexuality:

1. Homosexual men should be given social equality.

2. Male homosexuality is obscene and vulgar.

3. The homosexual civil rights movement is positive for society.

4. The love between two males is the same as heterosexual love.

5. Homosexual men are a viable part of our society.

6. I would be comfortable knowing that my clergy was a homosexual man.

7. I feel disgusted when I consider the state of sinfulness of male homosexuality.

8. I feel comfortable when I think that male homosexuality is a natural human occurrence.

9. I feel confident that homosexual men are just as emotionally healthy as heterosexual men.

10. I would feel comfortable if I learned that my son's teacher was a homosexual man.

11. Male homosexuality should be considered immoral.

12. I feel revolted when I think of two men engaged in private sexual behaviors with each other.

1. _____
2. _____
3. _____
4. _____
5. _____
6. _____
7. _____
8. _____
9. _____
10. _____
11. _____
12. _____

Women:

1. Women with HIV ought to have equal access to health care services.

2. I feel disgusted when I think of an HIV-infected woman.

3. A woman with HIV deserves what she gets.

4. I would feel comfortable giving nursing care to an HIV positive woman.

1. _____
2. _____
3. _____
4. _____

IV Drug Abusers:

1. The government should provide free syringes to IV drug abusers.

2. IV drug abusers are victims of society.

3. I feel disgusted when I consider the immorality of IV drug abuse.

4. IV drug abusers ought to be locked up.

5. People who contract HIV through IV drug abuse should not be entitled to free medical care.

6. People who shoot drugs cannot help themselves.

7. I feel upset around IV drug abusers.

8. IV drug abusers are mistreated in our society.

9. I would feel comfortable giving nursing care to an IV drug abuser.

1. _____
2. _____
3. _____
4. _____
5. _____
6. _____
7. _____
8. _____
9. _____

Nursing Care Concerns:

1. I feel worried about the possibility of acquiring AIDS from patients.

2. I am bothered that I might not be able to prevent myself from contracting AIDS.

3. It is comforting to know that there isn't much difference in caring for AIDS patients than caring for other terminally ill persons.

4. I have enough information to protect myself against AIDS in my workplace.

1. _____
2. _____
3. _____
4. _____

5. I worry about possible casual contact with a person with AIDS.   5. _____

6. I am fearful of caring for persons with AIDS because there is no cure.   6. _____

7. Nurses need to know the HIV antibody status of patients they are caring for.   7. _____

8. I am not bothered about possibly caring for an infant who was born HIV positive.   8. _____

Social/Professional Concerns:

1. Nurses who are HIV positive should be prevented from participating in direct patient care.   1. _____

2. Persons with AIDS are not dangerous to other people with whom they come in casual contact.   2. _____

3. I think the homosexual community has brought the problem of AIDS upon itself.   3. _____

4. I feel angry about possibly caring for a person with AIDS who contracted the disease through high-risk
   sexual behaviors.   4. _____

5. There is too much money spent on AIDS research.   5. _____

6. Persons with AIDS should be quarantined.   6. _____

7. Pregnant nurses should be excused from caring for persons with AIDS.   7. _____

8. Civil rights laws should be enacted to protect people with AIDS from job and housing discrimination. 8. _____

9. Activities that spread AIDS, such as some forms of sexual behaviors, should be outlawed.   9. _____

10. It distresses me to think that so many nursing procedures have to be changed or modified as a result of AIDS. 10. _____

11. Nurses should be allowed to refuse to care for a person with AIDS.   11. _____

12. Public school officials should not be required to accept an AIDS child into classes.   12. _____

AIDS Attitude Scale

JACQUE SHRUM,[1] NORMA TURNER, AND KATHERINE BRUCE,[2]
University of North Carolina at Wilmington

The purpose of the AIDS Attitude Scale (AAS) is to measure attitudes about AIDS and people who have AIDS or HIV infection. The scale can be used to discriminate people who are more empathetic or tolerant toward people who have HIV infection from those who are less tolerant or empathetic. Subject areas on the AAS include fears related to contagion and casual contact, moral issues, and topics related to legal and social welfare issues.

Description

This scale is a 54-item Likert scale (5 points) with response options labeled *Strongly Agree, Agree, Neither Agree nor Disagree, Disagree,* and *Strongly Disagree.* The items on the scale were selected from an initial pool of 94 items written by undergraduate students in health education and nursing classes, or derived from literature review and interviews with experts knowledgeable about AIDS. They were reviewed for readability by five different undergraduate and graduate students and for acceptability for inclusion on the scale by a panel of four expert judges. The judges agreed on 67 of the original items for inclusion in the scale. The scale was administered to 164 undergraduate students in health education courses, and an item analysis was conducted to identify the statements that could best discriminate high and low scorers. Fifty-four items had statistically significant item-total correlations ($p < .001$). These items were arranged in random order, and the scale was tested for reliability. This scale was designed to measure college students' attitudes about AIDS, but could be used for other populations.

Response Mode and Timing

Respondents circle or blacken one response option for each item on a separate answer sheet. Most respondents complete the scale within 15 minutes.

Scoring

The 25 tolerant items (2, 3, 5, 6, 9, 12, 14, 15, 19, 21, 22, 23, 24, 26, 28, 31, 32, 34, 36, 38, 41, 46, 51, 52, and 53) are scored such that *Strongly Agree* has a value of 5, *Agree* a value of 4, and so forth. For the intolerant items (1, 4, 7, 8, 10, 11, 13, 16, 17, 18, 20, 25, 27, 29, 30, 33, 35, 37, 39, 40, 42, 43, 44, 45, 47, 48, 49, 50, 54), reverse scoring is used. The total attitude score is obtained by the following

formula: AAS score $= (X - N)(100)/(N)(4)$, where X is the total of the scored responses and N is the number of items properly completed. This formula standardizes scores such that they may range from 0 to 100; higher scores indicate more empathy or tolerance related to AIDS and people who have AIDS.

Reliability

To measure internal consistency (split-half reliability), 135 undergraduates completed the scale. Reliability was high (Cronbach's alpha = .96; Shrum, Turner, & Bruce, 1989). Reliability was confirmed in another independent sample of students (Cronbach's alpha = .94; Bruce & Reid, 1998).

Validity

Content and face validity were evaluated by a panel of four expert judges: a social worker, a university health educator, a health education faculty member, and an experimental psychologist. Experts were chosen because of their expertise related to AIDS, either in education, counseling, or support services, or related to attitude scale development. The panel assessed the relevance of each item, as well as the content of the entire scale (Shrum et al., 1989). Evidence for construct validity through factor analysis shows three consistent factors related to contagion concerns, moral issues, and legal/social welfare issues. These account for over 40% of the variance (Bruce, Shrum, Trefethen, & Slovik, 1990; Shrum et al., 1989). Evidence for known-groups, concurrent, convergent, and discriminant validity of the AAS has been documented by Bruce and Reid (1998) and Bruce and Walker (2001). In addition, AAS scores predicted AIDS-related information seeking, as measured before and after celebrity announcements about having AIDS (Bruce, Pilgrim, & Spivey, 1994). The AAS also differentiated attitudes of college students and clients at sexually transmitted disease clinics (Bruce & Moineau, 1991). Further, females consistently score more tolerantly than males across college samples (Bruce & Walker, 2001).

Other Information

The scale is published in its entirety in Shrum et al. (1989). In the original scale, "AIDS" was used throughout. Now half of the references to AIDS have been changed to "HIV infection" as more appropriate.

[1]Jacque Shrum is deceased.
[2]Address correspondence to Katherine Bruce, Department of Psychology, UNC Wilmington, Wilmington, NC 28403; e-mail: bruce@uncw.edu

References

Bruce, K., & Moineau, S. (1991). A comparison of sexually transmitted disease clinic patients and undergraduates: Implications for AIDS prevention and education. *Health Values, 15,* 5–12.

Bruce, K., Pilgrim, C., and Spivey, R. (1994). Assessing the impact of Magic Johnson's HIV positive announcement on a university campus. *Journal of Sex Education and Therapy, 20,* 264–276.

Bruce, K., Shrum, J., Trefethen, C., & Slovik, L. (1990). Students' attitudes about AIDS, homosexuality, and condoms. *AIDS Behavior and Prevention, 2,* 220–234.

Bruce, K. E., & Reid, B. C. (1998). Assessing the construct validity of the AIDS Attitude Scale. *AIDS Education and Prevention, 10,* 75–89.

Bruce, K. E., & Walker, L. J. (2001). College students' attitudes about AIDS: 1986 to 2000. *AIDS Education and Prevention, 13,* 428–437.

Shrum, J., Turner, N., & Bruce, K. (1989). Development of an instrument to measure attitudes towards AIDS. *AIDS Education and Prevention, 1,* 222–230.

Exhibit

AIDS Attitude Scale

For each of the following statements, please note whether you agree or disagree with the statement. There are no correct answers, only your opinions. Use the following scale:

SA: Strongly Agree With the Statement
A: Agree With the Statement
N: Neither Agree nor Disagree With the Statement
D: Disagree With the Statement
SD: Strongly Disagree With the Statement

1. Limiting the spread of AIDS is more important than trying to protect the rights of people with AIDS.
2. Support groups for people with HIV (Human Immunodeficiency Virus) infection would be very helpful to them.
3. I would consider marrying someone with HIV infection.
4. I would quit my job before I would work with someone who has AIDS.
5. People should not be afraid of catching HIV from casual contact, like hugging or shaking hands.
6. I would like to feel at ease around people with AIDS.
7. People who receive positive results from the HIV blood tests should not be allowed to get married.
8. I would prefer not to be around homosexuals for fear of catching AIDS.
9. Being around someone with AIDS would not put my health in danger.
10. Only disgusting people get HIV infection.
11. I think that people with HIV infection got what they deserved.
12. People with AIDS should not avoid being around other people.
13. People should avoid going to the dentist because they might catch HIV from dental instruments.
14. The thought of being around someone with AIDS does not bother me.
15. People with HIV infection should not be prohibited from working in public places.
16. I would not want to be in the same room with someone who I knew had AIDS.
17. The "gay plague" is an appropriate way to describe AIDS.
18. People who give HIV to others should face criminal charges.
19. People should not be afraid to donate blood because of AIDS.
20. A list of people who have HIV infection should be available to anyone.
21. I would date a person with AIDS.
22. People should not blame the homosexual community for the spread of HIV infection in the United States.
23. No one deserves to have a disease like HIV infection.
24. It would not bother me to attend class with someone who has AIDS.
25. An employer should have the right to fire an employee with HIV infection regardless of the type of work s/he does.
26. I would allow my children to play with children of someone known to have AIDS.
27. People get AIDS by performing unnatural sex acts.
28. People with HIV should not be looked down upon by others.
29. I could tell by looking at someone if s/he had AIDS.
30. It is embarrassing to have so many people with HIV infection in our society.
31. Health care workers should not refuse to care for people with HIV infection regardless of their personal feelings about the disease.
32. Children who have AIDS should not be prohibited from going to schools or day care centers.
33. Children who have AIDS probably have a homosexual parent.
34. HIV blood test results should be confidential to avoid discrimination against people with positive results.

35. HIV infection is a punishment for immoral behavior.
36. I would not be afraid to take care of a family member with AIDS.
37. If I discovered that my roommate had AIDS, I would move out.
38. I would contribute money to an HIV infection research project if I were making a charitable contribution.
39. The best way to get rid of HIV infection is to get rid of homosexuality.
40. Churches should take a strong stand against drug abuse and homosexuality to prevent the spread of AIDS.
41. Insurance companies should not be allowed to cancel insurance policies for AIDS-related reasons.
42. Money being spent on HIV infection research should be spent instead on diseases that affect innocent people.
43. A person who gives HIV to someone else should be legally liable for any medical expenses.
44. The spread of AIDS in the United States is proof that homosexual behavior should be illegal.
45. A list of people who have HIV infection should be kept by the government.
46. I could comfortably discuss AIDS with others.
47. People with AIDS are not worth getting to know.
48. I have no sympathy for homosexuals who get HIV infection.
49. Parents who transmit HIV to their children should be prosecuted as child abusers.
50. People with AIDS should be sent to sanitariums to protect others from AIDS.
51. People would not be so afraid of AIDS if they knew more about the disease.
52. Hospitals and nursing homes should not refuse to admit patients with HIV infection.
53. I would not avoid a friend if s/he had AIDS.
54. The spread of HIV in our society illustrates how immoral the United States has become.

AIDS Discussion Strategy Scale

WILLIAM E. SNELL, JR.,[1] *Southeast Missouri State University*

In order to gain insight into the nature of how people discuss sexual topics, such as AIDS, with a potential sex partner, Snell and Finney (1990) developed the AIDS Discussion Strategy Scale (ADSS), an objective self-report instrument designed to measure the types of interpersonal discussion strategies that women and men use if they want to discuss AIDS with an intimate partner. The ADSS was found to have subscales involving the use of six specific types of discussion tactics: *rational strategies*, defined as straightforward, reasonable attempts to discuss AIDS in a forthright manner with an intimate partner; *manipulative strategies*, defined as deceptive and indirect efforts to persuade an intimate partner to engage in conversation about AIDS; *withdrawal strategies*, defined as attempts to actually avoid any extended interpersonal contact with an intimate partner until this individual agrees to a discussion about AIDS; *charm strategies*, defined as acting in pleasant and charming ways toward an intimate partner in order to promote a discussion about AIDS; *subtlety strategies*, defined as involving the use of hinting and subtle suggestions in order to elicit a conversation about AIDS; and *persistence strategies*, defined as persistent and continuous attempts to try to influence an intimate partner to discuss AIDS.

Description

The ADSS consists of 72 items. Subjects respond to the 72 items on the ADSS using a 5-point Likert-type scale: –2 = *definitely would not do this*, –1 = *might not do this*, 0 = *not sure whether I would do this*, 1 = *might do this*, and 2 = *would definitely do this*. To determine whether the 72 items on the ADSS would form independent clusters of items, a principal components factor analysis with varimax rotation was conducted. Six factors with eigenvalues greater than 1 were extracted. Those items that loaded on unique factors (coefficients greater than .30) were used to construct six subscales for the ADSS. The number of items on the respective subscales were as follows: Rational (26 items), Manipulation (20 items), Withdrawal (4 items), Charm (5 items), Subtlety (3 items), and Persistence (4 items).

Response Mode and Timing

Respondents indicate their response on a computer scan sheet by darkening in a response from A to E for each item. The questionnaire usually requires about 45 minutes to complete.

[1]Address all correspondence to William E. Snell, Jr., Department of Psychology, Southeast Missouri State University, One University Plaza, Cape Girardeau, Missouri 63701; e-mail: wesnell@semo.edu

Scoring

The labels and items for the ADSS subscales are Rational (Items 2, 4, 8, 9, 11, 12, 14, 16, 17, 18, 21, 23, 25, 28, 29, 31, 32, 35, 37, 43, 49, 53, 55, 61, 65, 67); Manipulation (Items 5, 6, 13, 20, 22, 24, 27, 38, 40, 42, 44, 45, 48, 52, 54, 57, 58, 69, 70, 72); Withdrawal (Items 39, 51, 56, 63); Charm (Items 9, 36, 60, 64, 66); Subtlety (Items 3, 10, 50); and Persistence (Items 7, 41, 46, 47). The ADSS items are coded so that A = −2, B = −1, C = 0, D = +1, and E = +2 (no items are reverse coded). Then, the items on each subscale are averaged so that higher scores indicate a greater likelihood of using this type of AIDS-related discussion strategy.

Reliability

Reliability analyses were conducted on each subscale using Cronbach's alpha measure of interitem consistency. In two investigations reported by Snell and Finney (1990), all six subscales were found to have more than adequate internal consistency: Rational (.96, .96), Manipulation (.93, .92), Withdrawal (.83, 85), Charm (.81, .82), Subtlety (.74, .66), and Persistence (.81, .80).

Validity

Gender comparisons on the ADSS (Snell & Finney, 1990) indicate that females reported they would be more likely than males to use rational approaches to discuss AIDS with an intimate partner; that females were less likely than males to report that they would use manipulative tactics to persuade an intimate partner to discuss the topic of AIDS; and that females reported that they would be less likely than males to use charm to persuade an intimate partner to talk about AIDS. Although no other gender effects were found, it is informative to note that both males and females reported that they would use subtlety in trying to discuss AIDS with an intimate partner. By contrast, both males and females indicated that they would be less likely to use with-drawal tactics to elicit a discussion on AIDS with a close partner.

Correlations between the ADSS and the Stereotypes About AIDS Scale (Snell & Finney, 1990) indicated that people's use of AIDS-related discussion strategies were associated with their privately held stereotypes about AIDS. Also, people's willingness to use a variety of strategies to discuss the topics of AIDS with an intimate partner was associated with their own personal sexual dispositions, sexual attitudes, and sexual behaviors. Moreover, the pattern of findings indicated both some similar as well as some unique gender-related findings. For both males and females, the use of manipulative AIDS-related discussion strategies was directly related to their sexual traits (i.e., sexual depression and sexual preoccupation), their sexual attitudes (i.e., manipulative and casual sexual attitudes), and their sexual behaviors (i.e., an exchange orientation to sexual relations). Other gender similarities showed that both men and women who held sexually manipulative attitudes endorsed the use of charm as a tactic for discussing AIDS with a potential sexual partner; and both men and women whose orientation toward their sexual relations was based on mutual caring and concern reported that they would use persistence as a strategy for discussing AIDS with a potential sex partner. Although there was considerable similarity in the way that men's and women's sexual dispositions, attitudes, and behaviors impacted their use of AIDS-related discussion strategies, other findings were more gender specific. For example, women with greater sexual esteem were more likely to report that they would use rational strategies and were less likely to use manipulation and charm as avenues for discussing AIDS. Among males, by contrast, sexual esteem was associated with less willingness to use charm to elicit a conversation about AIDS with a partner.

Reference

Snell, W. E., Jr., & Finney, P. D. (1990). Interpersonal strategies associated with the discussion of AIDS. *Annals of Sex Research, 3,* 425–451.

Exhibit

The AIDS Discussion Strategy Scale

Instructions: Suppose you wanted to talk to a potential or current sexual partner about AIDS. The following statements concern the types of things you might do if you wanted to discuss the topic of AIDS (Acquired Immune Deficiency Syndrome) with a sexual partner (either a current sexual partner or a future sexual partner). More specifically, we are interested in whether you would use each of the behaviors listed below. To provide your responses, use the following scale:

A	=	Definitely would not do this.
B	=	Might not do this.
C	=	Not sure whether I would do this.
D	=	Might do this.
E	=	Would definitely do this.

Remember: Be sure to respond to each and every statement; leave no blanks.

1. My partner and I would compromise about the aspects of the topic of AIDS we'd discuss.
2. I would try to reason with my partner to influence him/her to discuss AIDS.
3. I would drop hints about wanting to discuss the topic of AIDS.
4. I would simply tell my partner that I wanted to discuss AIDS with him/her.
5. I would put on a sweet face to induce my partner to discuss AIDS-related issues.
6. I would try to get my partner to discuss AIDS by doing some fast talking.
7. I would continually attempt to discuss the issue of AIDS.
8. I would try to discuss AIDS with my partner.
9. I would explain the reason that it's important for us to discuss AIDS.
10. I would subtly bring up the topic of AIDS.
11. I would state in a matter-of-fact way that I wanted to talk about AIDS.
12. I would try to look sincere to make the person more willing to talk about AIDS.
13. I would persuade my partner to discuss AIDS by telling some small white lies.
14. I would try to discuss the topic of AIDS, despite any obstacles from my partner.
15. I would try to negotiate what AIDS-related topics we'd be willing to discuss.
16. I would argue in a logical way that it's important for us to discuss AIDS.
17. I would make suggestions that we discuss AIDS.
18. I would simply ask to discuss AIDS with my partner.
19. I would try to put my partner in a good mood before trying to talk about AIDS.
20. I would use deception to get my partner to talk about AIDS.
21. I would talk with my partner about AIDS even if s/he didn't want to.
22. I would tell my sexual partner that I'd do something special if s/he'd discuss AIDS with me.
23. I would explain the reason why I want to discuss AIDS.
24. I would try to make my partner think that s/he wanted to talk about AIDS.
25. I would tell my partner it's in his/her best interest to discuss the issue of AIDS.
26. I would get mad if my partner didn't want to discuss the topic of AIDS.
27. I would make my partner believe that s/he would be doing me a favor by discussing AIDS.
28. I would try to persuade my partner to discuss AIDS related issues.
29. I would try to discuss the topic by convincing my partner that it's really important.
30. I would make my partner realize that I have a legitimate right to demand we talk about AIDS.
31. I would try to make my partner feel like discussing topics related to AIDS.
32. I would demand to discuss aspects of our relationship that deal with AIDS.
33. I would try to make my partner feel bad or guilty if s/he didn't discuss AIDS with me.
34. I would moralize about the topic of AIDS.
35. I would talk my partner into discussing issues dealing with AIDS.
36. I would give my partner a big hug to put her/him in a good mood to discuss AIDS.
37. I would tell my partner that it's important for us to discuss AIDS.
38. I would con my partner into discussing things about AIDS.
39. I would tell my partner that we couldn't have sex until we discussed AIDS.
40. I would try to manipulate my partner into a discussion on AIDS.
41. I would keep bugging my partner to discuss the topic of AIDS.
42. I would use flattery to persuade my partner to discuss AIDS.
43. I would tell my partner I want to talk about AIDS.
44. I would pout or threaten to cry if I didn't get my way in discussing AIDS.
45. I would promise sexual rewards if we first discussed AIDS.
46. I would repeatedly remind my partner that I want to discuss AIDS.
47. I would keep trying to discuss AIDS issues with my partner.
48. I would become especially affectionate so my partner would agree to discuss AIDS issues.
49. I would insist that my partner and I discuss AIDS.
50. I would drop subtle hints that I want to talk about AIDS.
51. I would refrain from sexual contact until we discussed AIDS.
52. I would try to use coercion or blackmail to make my partner discuss AIDS.
53. I would try my hardest to make my partner discuss AIDS.
54. I would blow up in anger if s/he would not discuss the issue of AIDS.
55. I would state my need to discuss AIDS with my partner.
56. I would withhold affection and act cold until s/he discusses the topic of AIDS with me.
57. I would tell my partner that unless we discussed AIDS, I would never talk with him/her again.

58. I would get angry and demand that s/he talk about AIDS with me.
59. I would give up if my partner refused to discuss any AIDS-related issues.
60. I would appeal to my partner's love/affection for me as a basis for our discussing AIDS.
61. I would ask my partner if s/he wanted to discuss AIDS.
62. I would argue until my partner agreed to discuss the topic of AIDS with me.
63. I would refuse to interact further with my partner unless we first discussed AIDS.
64. I would act nice so that my partner could not refuse to discuss AIDS with me.
65. I would convince my partner that we need to discuss AIDS.
66. I would be especially sweet, charming, and pleasant before bringing up the subject of AIDS.
67. I would tell my partner we are close enough to discuss AIDS.
68. I would loudly voice my desire to discuss the topic of AIDS.
69. I would pretend to be an expert about AIDS.
70. I would plead or beg my partner to talk about the disease AIDS.
71. I would get someone else to help persuade my partner to discuss AIDS.
72. I would tell my partner I have a lot of knowledge about the topic of AIDS.

Multidimensional AIDS Anxiety Questionnaire

WILLIAM E. SNELL, JR.[1] AND PHILLIP D. FINNEY, *Southeast Missouri State University*

Although considerable medical attention has been recently focused on AIDS, relatively little is known about the amount and nature of anxiety that this disease may be fostering in segments of society. To better understand the public's reaction to AIDS, a multidimensional self-report measure of anxiety experienced about AIDS was developed, the Multidimensional AIDS Anxiety Questionnaire (MAAQ; Finney & Snell, 1989; Snell & Finney, 1996). Factor analysis indicated that the MAAQ items correspond to five concepts concerned with AIDS anxiety: (a) AIDS-related anxiety manifested as physiological arousal, (b) AIDS-related anxiety manifested as fear, (c) AIDS-related anxiety manifested as cognitive worry, (d) AIDS-related anxiety manifested as sexual inhibition, and (e) AIDS-anxiety manifested as discussion inhibition.

Description

The MAAQ consists of 50 items. In responding to the MAAQ, individuals are asked to indicate how characteristic each statement is of them. A 5-point Likert-type scale is used to collect data on the subjects' responses, with each item being scored from 0 to 4: *not at all characteristic of me* (A), *slightly characteristic of me* (B), *somewhat characteristic of me* (C), *moderately characteristic of me* (D), and *very characteristic of me* (E). In order to create subscale scores, the items on each subscale are averaged. Higher

scores thus correspond to greater amounts of each respective type of AIDS-related anxiety.

Response Mode and Timing

Individuals are asked to record their responses to the MAAQ on a computer scan sheet by darkening in a response from A to E for each MAAQ item. Alternatively, one could prepare the MAAQ so that respondents write directly on the instrument itself. The questionnaire usually takes between 20 and 25 minutes to complete.

Scoring

The MAAQ consists of five subscales designed to measure several aspects of anxiety about AIDS. (The items on the sixth subscale are indicated here also, although the eigenvalue from the factor analysis for this subscale was less than 1. Although this sixth subscale appears to be psychometrically weak, we anticipate that it will gain more prominence in future research.) The labels for these subscales are (with a listing of the items on each subscale) Physiological Arousal (Items 13, 14, 23, 27, 28, 29, 31, 33, 34, 38, 39, 43, 44, 46, 47, 48); Fear of AIDS (Items 5, 6, 10, 15, 16, and 21); Sexual Inhibition (Items 18, 30, 35, 37, 40, 42); Cognitive Worry (Items 1, 3, 4, 8, and 9); Discussion Inhibition (Items 2, 7, 12, 19, and 24); and Anxiety About AIDS Exposure

[1]Address correspondence to William E. Snell, Jr., Department of Psychology, Southeast Missouri State University, One University Plaza, Cape Girardeau, MO 63701; e-mail: wesnwll@semo.edu

(Items 20, 49, 50). The MAAQ items are scored so that A = 0, B = 1, C = 2, D = 3, and E = 4. Next, they are averaged for each subscale so that higher scores correspond to greater amounts of anxiety about AIDS (score range for each subscale = 0 to 4).

Reliability

Internal consistency coefficients for the MAAQ were reported by Finney and Snell (1989). All five scales had high internal consistency, with Cronbach alphas ranging from a low of .85 to a high of .94. Test-retest reliability coefficients for the Physiological Arousal (.65), Fear of AIDS (.78), and Sexual Inhibition (.63) subscales of the MAAQ were quite high; the coefficients for the Cognitive Worry (.40) and Discussion Inhibition (.40) subscales were somewhat lower.

Validity

To determine whether the 50 MAAQ items would cluster into unique groups, a principal components factor analysis with varimax rotation was conducted. There were five factors with eigenvalues greater than 1. Factor 1 had an eigenvalue of 17.00 (accounting for 34% of the variance) and consisted of 16 items concerned with signs of general physiological arousal about AIDS. Factor 2 had an eigenvalue of 4.43 (accounting for 8.9% of the variance) and consisted of six items reflecting a stronger fear of AIDS. Factor 3 consisted of six statements concerned specifically with sexual inhibition resulting from AIDS (eigenvalue = 2.24; 4.5% percent of the variance). The five items that characterized Factor 4 concerned cognitive worry about AIDS (eigenvalue = 1.23; 2.5% of the variance). Factor 5 consisted of five items concerned with discussion inhibition about AIDS (eigenvalue = 1.16; 2.3% of the variance). As anticipated, physiological (the arousal and fear factors), cognitive (the worry factor), and behavioral (the sexual

inhibition and discussion inhibition factors) manifestations of AIDS anxiety were apparent in these data.

Researchers (Finney & Snell, 1989; Snell & Finney, 1996) have indicated that physiological arousal about AIDS and discussion inhibition about AIDS are associated with more positive personal approaches to AIDS. Additionally, in our research findings, we found that the MAAQ is related to the Stereotypes About AIDS Scale (Snell, Finney & Godwin, 1991) and the AIDS Discussion Strategy Scale (Snell & Finney, 1990). Still other results demonstrate convergent validity for the MAAQ with other measures of general anxiety and discriminant validity from social desirability and other personality characteristics. Also, AIDS anxiety was found to be broadly related to individuals' underlying general anxiety level but unrelated to other specific forms of anxiety (e.g., relationship anxiety). Furthermore, scores on the MAAQ have been shown to be related to the contraceptive behavior of university students. More specifically, the physiological arousal type of AIDS anxiety was positively correlated with reliable contraceptive behaviors among males. Males who reported AIDS anxiety, manifested as physiologically arousal, were also more likely to report a change in sexual practices due to the possibility of contracting AIDS. In addition, there was a trend for physiological arousal to be positively related to self-reported use of condoms or spermicides to protect against AIDS among males.

References

Finney, P., & Snell, W. E., Jr. (1989, April). *The AIDS Anxiety Scale: Components and correlates.* Paper presented at the annual meeting of the Southwestern Psychological Association, Houston, TX.

Snell, W. E., Jr., & Finney, P. (1990). Interpersonal strategies associated with the discussion of AIDS. *Annals of Sex Research, 3,* 435–451.

Snell, W. E., Jr., Finney, P., & Godwin, L. J. (1991). Stereotypes about AIDS. *Contemporary Social Psychology, 15,* 18–38.

Snell, W. E., Jr., & Finney, P. (1996). *The Multidimensional AIDS Anxiety Questionnaire.* Unpublished manuscript.

Exhibit

The Multidimensional AIDS Anxiety Questionnaire

Instructions: The items listed below refer to feelings and reactions that people may experience about the disease AIDS (Acquired Immune Deficiency Syndrome). As such, there are no right or wrong answers, only the individual reactions that people have. We are interested in how typical these feelings and behaviors are of you. To provide your responses, use the following scale to indicate how characteristic the following statements are for you.

A = *Not at all* characteristic of me.
B = *Slightly* characteristic of me.
C = *Somewhat* characteristic of me.
D = *Moderately* characteristic of me.
E = *Very* characteristic of me.

Note: Remember to respond to all items, even if you are not completely sure. Also, please be honest in responding to these statements.

1. Thinking about AIDS makes me feel anxious.
2. I sometimes find it hard to discuss issues dealing with AIDS.
3. I feel tense when I think about the threat of AIDS.
4. I feel quite anxious about the epidemic of AIDS.
5. I feel scared about AIDS when I think about sexual relationships.
6. I'm afraid of getting AIDS.
7. I have trouble talking about AIDS with an intimate partner.
8. I feel flustered when I realize the threat of AIDS.
9. The disease AIDS makes me feel nervous and anxious.
10. I feel scared when I think about catching AIDS from a sexual partner.
11. I'm not worried about getting AIDS.
12. I would feel shy discussing AIDS with an intimate partner.
13. My heart beats fast with anxiety when I think about AIDS.
14. I feel anxious when I talk about AIDS with people.
15. Because of AIDS, I feel nervous about initiating sexual relations.
16. All these discussions of AIDS leaves me feeling a bit alarmed.
17. I would not find it hard to discuss AIDS with an intimate partner.
18. AIDS makes me feel jittery about having sex with someone.
19. I feel uncomfortable when discussing AIDS.
20. I sometimes worry that one of my past sexual partners may have had AIDS.
21. Thinking about catching AIDS leaves me feeling concerned.
22. I would not hesitate to ask a former sex partner about AIDS-related concerns.
23. The issue of AIDS is a very stressful experience for me.
24. I feel nervous when I discuss AIDS with another person.
25. The threat of getting AIDS makes me feel uneasy about sex.
26. I worry about what I should do about AIDS.
27. Anxiety about AIDS is beginning to affect my personal relationships.
28. In general, the media attention on AIDS makes me feel restless.
29. I have feelings of worry when I think about AIDS.
30. Were I to have sexual relations, I would worry about getting AIDS.
31. All this recent media attention about AIDS leaves me feeling on edge.
32. AIDS does not influence my willingness to engage in sexual relationships.
33. When I think about AIDS, I feel tense.
34. I am more anxious than most people are about the disease AIDS.
35. If I were to have sex with someone, I would worry about AIDS.
36. I'm pretty indifferent to the idea of catching AIDS.
37. I would hesitate to involve myself in a sexual relationship because of AIDS.
38. When talking about AIDS with someone, I feel jumpy and high-strung.
39. I become really frightened when I think about the threat of AIDS.
40. The fear of AIDS makes me feel nervous about engaging in sex.
41. The increased chances of being infected with AIDS leaves me feeling troubled.
42. Because of AIDS, I feel too nervous to start a new sexual relationship.
43. The spread of AIDS is causing me to feel quite a bit of stress.
44. I worry that AIDS may directly influence my life.
45. I had a better attitude towards sex before the AIDS epidemic.
46. I get pretty upset when I think about the possibility of catching AIDS.
47. The discussion of AIDS makes me feel uncomfortable.
48. All this talk about AIDS has left me feeling strained and tense.
49. I'm concerned that I might be carrying the AIDS virus.
50. I feel nervous when I think that a past sexual partner could have given me AIDS

Stereotypes About AIDS Scale

WILLIAM E. SNELL, JR.,[1] PHILLIP D. FINNEY, AND LISA J. GODWIN, *Southeast Missouri State University*

The spread of AIDS (i.e., Acquired Immune Deficiency Syndrome) poses such a severe threat to society that a variety of stereotypes have proliferated about this disease. Snell, Finney, and Godwin (1991) conducted an investigation to examine several stereotypes about AIDS. More specifically, they developed and provided preliminary validation of the psychometric properties of the Stereotypes About AIDS Scale (SAAS), a multidimensional measure of stereotypes about AIDS. The selection of the particular stereotypes about AIDS measured by the SAAS was based on a literature review about AIDS stereotypes. Four categories of AIDS-related stereotypes (with multiple subscales in each category) are measured by the SAAS: (a) global stereotypic beliefs about AIDS, (b) personal attitudes about AIDS, (c) medical issues about AIDS, and (d) sexual issues about AIDS. The items in Section A of the SAAS (Global Stereotypes about AIDS) form four separate subscales concerned with stereotypes about the need for AIDS-related education, AIDS-related confidentiality, the transmission of AIDS, and AIDS is caused by homosexuality. The items in Section B of the SAAS (Personal Attitudes About AIDS) form five separate subscales concerned with stereotypes about the desire to avoid those afflicted with AIDS, AIDS is not perceived as self-relevant, a closed-minded approach to AIDS, the issue of AIDS is being exaggerated, and the notion that AIDS is a moral punishment. The items in Section C of the SAAS (Medical Issues about AIDS) form four separate subscales concerned with stereotypes about the belief that AIDS is a threat to medical staff, protecting the U.S. blood supply system from AIDS, a cure for AIDS, and AIDS testing should be conducted. The items in Section D of the SAAS (Sexual Issues about AIDS) form two separate subscales concerned with stereotypes about the relationship between AIDS and sexual activity and the prevention of AIDS through the use of condoms.

Description

The SAAS consists of four sections. Section A has 30 items, Section B has 35 items, Section C has 30 items, and Section D has 20 items. In responding to the SAAS, individuals are asked to indicate how much they agree versus disagree with each statement, using a 5-point Likert format: *agree* (+2), *slightly agree* (+1), *neither agree nor disagree* (0), *slightly disagree* (−1), and *disagree* (−2). In order to create subscale scores, the items on each subscale are averaged. Higher positive (negative) scores correspond to greater

agreement (disagreement) with the stereotypes measured by the SAAS.

Response Mode and Timing

People respond to the SAAS by using a computer scan sheet to darken a response (either A, B, C, D, or E) for each item. The entire questionnaire (i.e., all four sections) usually takes about 35–45 minutes to complete.

Scoring

The SAAS consists of 15 separate subscales. Several SAAS items are reversed-scored (A8, A20, A21, C2, C12, and D4) before the subscales are computed. The four subscales for Section A are the need for AIDS-related education (A4, A6, A12, A18, A20, A22, A24, A28, A30), AIDS-related confidentiality (A2, A3, A8, A9, A14, A21, A26, A27), the transmission of AIDS (A5, A11, A15, A17, A23, A29), and AIDS is caused by homosexuality (A1, A7, A13, A19, A25). The five subscales for Section B are the desire to avoid those afflicted with AIDS (B1, B22, B23, B24, B34, B35), AIDS was not perceived as self-relevant (B5, B6, B7, B8), a closed-minded approach to AIDS (B13, B16, B17), the issue of AIDS is being exaggerated (B3, B10, B25, B29), and the notion that AIDS is a moral punishment (B9, B32, B33). The four subscales for Section C are the belief that AIDS is a threat to medical staff (C3, C4, C6, C11, C12, C18), protecting the U.S. blood supply system from AIDS (C2, C5, C7, C17, C25, C27), cure for AIDS (C9, C10, C23), and AIDS testing should be conducted (C13, C14). The two subscales for Section D are the relationship between AIDS and sexual activity (D1, D2, D4 to D12, D13) and the prevention of AIDS through the use of condoms (D3, D10, D17, D18, D19).

Reliability

Snell, Finney, and Godwin (1991) found that for Section A (Stereotypic Beliefs About AIDS) of the SAAS, the reliabilities ranged from a low of .75 to a high of .85; for Section B (Personal Attitudes About AIDS) of the SAAS, the reliabilities ranged from a low of .72 to a high of .87; for Section C (Medical Issues Related to AIDS) of the SAAS, the reliabilities ranged from a low of .64 to a high of .83; and for Section D (Sexuality and AIDS) of the SAAS, the Cronbach alphas were .86 and .78, respectively.

---

[1]Address correspondence to William E. Snell, Jr., Department of Psychology, Southeast Missouri State University, One University Plaza, Cape Girardeau, MO 63701; e-mail: wesnwll@semo.edu

Validity

Snell et al. (1991) reported that those individuals who endorsed a wide range of "negative," inaccurate stereotypes about AIDS, as measured by their responses to SAAS, reported greater AIDS-related anxiety. In particular, people who believed that AIDS was not relevant to them, who were closed-minded about AIDS, and who believed that the media was exaggerating the issue of AIDS indicated that they felt sufficient AIDS anxiety to inhibit their sexual activity. Additionally, it was found that those who believed in the importance of AIDS education reported that they would be more likely to use direct, rational strategies to start a conversation about AIDS with a potential sexual partner. One other set of findings reported by Snell et al. dealt with the issue of men's and women's stereotypic reactions to AIDS. It was found that both males and females were supportive of greater educational efforts about AIDS, although, interestingly enough, they also were somewhat supportive of widespread mandatory testing for AIDS.

In addition, other evidence indicated a consistent pattern of gender differences in men's and women's stereotypic beliefs about AIDS, with the findings generally suggesting that women expressed more positive and less prejudicial AIDS-related attitudes than did males. Snell et al. also found that females' endorsement of several socially undesirable stereotypes about women was predictive of their agreement (and disagreement) with a number of prejudicial (and nonprejudicial) stereotypes about AIDS and AIDS-afflicted individuals, as measured by the SAAS. Females who held a set of disparaging beliefs about women (e.g., that women are more passive, vulnerable, and moral than men; that women are sexually passive and sexual teases) reported adhering to a variety of stigmatizing beliefs and attitudes about AIDS, as measured by the SAAS.

Reference

Snell, W. E., Jr., Finney, P. D., & Godwin, L. J. (1991). Stereotypes about AIDS. *Contemporary Social Psychology, 15*, 18–38.

Exhibit

The Stereotypes about AIDS Scale

AIDS – Section A

Instructions: The items listed below refer to people's beliefs about the topic of AIDS (Acquired Immune Deficiency Syndrome). We are interested in whether you agree or disagree with these statements. As such, there are no right or wrong answers, only your own individual opinions. To indicate your reactions to these statements, use the following scale:

A   =   Agree
B   =   Slightly agree
C   =   Neither agree nor disagree
D   =   Slightly disagree
E   =   Disagree

Remember: There are no right or wrong responses; only your opinions. Be sure to respond to each and every statement; leave no blanks.

1. Homosexuality is the cause of AIDS.
2. People with AIDS don't really have a right to confidentiality about their disease.
3. People ought to notify their employees if they contract AIDS.
4. Not enough money is being spent on AIDS-related research.
5. AIDS can be transmitted by being in the same room with an AIDS patient.
6. People need education to learn how to avoid getting the virus AIDS.
7. If it weren't for homosexuals, we wouldn't have the disease AIDS.
8. AIDS victims have a right to privacy about their lives and lifestyles.
9. Businesses should have the right to fire people if they have AIDS.
10. The cost of medical care for AIDS patients should be paid by the government.
11. AIDS can be transmitted by shaking hands with an AIDS patient.
12. AIDS education is an appropriate task for schools to perform.
13. The sexual promiscuity of homosexuals is the reason why AIDS exists.
14. The government should be able to test anyone for AIDS.
15. A person can get AIDS from fellow workers at a job.
16. The government is not doing enough to fight AIDS.
17. AIDS can be transmitted by sharing eating utensils with an AIDS patient.
18. Sexual education about AIDS is necessary at school.
19. AIDS is really a punishment sent from God for the sinful acts of homosexuality.

20. AIDS infected children should be kept out of public school.
21. Having a co-worker with AIDS would not bother me.
22. AIDS is a serious national problem that deserves government attention.
23. AIDS can be transmitted by kissing an individual with AIDS.
24. It is important that students learn about AIDS in their classes.
25. AIDS is God's way of getting rid of homosexuals.
26. Identifying those people with AIDS should be a high priority.
27. Employees have a right to know if any of their co-workers have AIDS.
28. The Federal government ought to fund education on AIDS.
29. People can catch AIDS by giving CPR to an individual with AIDS.
30. Children need instruction about AIDS in their school curriculum.

AIDS – Section B

Instructions: The items listed below refer to people's beliefs about the topic of AIDS (Acquired Immune Deficiency Syndrome). We are interested in whether you agree or disagree with these statements. As such, there are no right or wrong answers, only your own individual opinions. To indicate your reactions to these statements, use the following scale:

A = Agree
B = Slightly agree
C = Neither agree nor disagree
D = Slightly disagree
E = Disagree

Remember: There are no right or wrong responses; only your opinions. Be sure to respond to each and every statement; leave no blanks.

1. I don't want to talk or interact with anyone with AIDS.
2. We have a social obligation to help those with AIDS.
3. People who describe AIDS as an epidemic are exaggerating its true nature.
4. As always, science will eventually find a cure for AIDS.
5. AIDS is really not my problem; it's somebody else's.
6. AIDS is not my problem.
7. AIDS is not a threat to me.
8. The AIDS crisis is really removed from me.
9. People who die from AIDS are being punished for their past wrongs.
10. People are blowing the issue of AIDS way out of proportion.
11. People should test themselves for AIDS.
12. People who get AIDS can blame only themselves.
13. Only people from California have been affected by AIDS.
14. Part of the problem with AIDS is that people don't talk about it.
15. The AIDS epidemic will soon be a financial burden on the U.S. economy.
16. You can't teach young children about AIDS.
17. Men and women don't really need to discuss AIDS with each other.
18. AIDS has become a significant problem in prison populations.
19. A cure for AIDS is inevitable.
20. AIDS is easy to get.
21. AIDS may eventually bankrupt the U.S. health care system.
22. People with AIDS should not be allowed to work in public schools.
23. People with AIDS should not be allowed to handle food in restaurants.
24. People with AIDS should not be allowed to work with patients in hospitals.
25. AIDS is not as big a problem as the media suggests.
26. I am not the kind of person who is likely to get AIDS.
27. I am less likely than most people to get AIDS.
28. I'd rather get any other disease than AIDS.
29. I've heard enough about AIDS, and I don't want to hear any more about it.
30. Living in San Francisco would increase anyone's chances of getting AIDS.
31. If a free blood test was available to see if you have the AIDS virus, I would take it.

32. AIDS is God's punishment for immorality.
33. AIDS patients offend me morally.
34. If I knew someone with AIDS, it would be hard for me to continue that relationship.
35. Children with AIDS should not be allowed to attend public schools.

AIDS – Section C

Instructions: The items listed below refer to people's beliefs about the topic of AIDS (Acquired Immune Deficiency Syndrome). We are interested in whether you agree or disagree with these statements. As such, there are no right or wrong answers, only your own individual opinions. To indicate your reactions to these statements, use the following scale:

A   =   Agree
B   =   Slightly agree
C   =   Neither agree nor disagree
D   =   Slightly disagree
E   =   Disagree

Remember: There are no right or wrong responses; only your opinions. Be sure to respond to each and every statement; leave no blanks.

1. The family of AIDS victims ought to have the right to participate in medical decisions.
2. People with AIDS should not be admitted to medical hospitals.
3. Doctors can catch AIDS if they treat patients with this disease.
4. AIDS patients will contaminate medical staff and other hospital patients.
5. It's important to maintain a safe blood banking system, because of AIDS.
6. Health care workers can catch AIDS in medical situations.
7. Medicine has a test to identify whether a person has AIDS.
8. The medical test for AIDS will not always identify a recently-infected person.
9. There's a vaccine that prevents the spread of AIDS.
10. There are effective medical treatments for those with AIDS.
11. Doctors and nurses are at risk for catching AIDS from infected patients.
12. No medical assistance person has ever caught AIDS from a patient.
13. AIDS blood tests should be administered to everyone in hospitals.
14. Hospitals should have the right to test all patients for AIDS.
15. A doctor with AIDS should not be allowed to treat patients.
16. A hospital worker should not be required to work with AIDS patients.
17. AIDS patients have as much right to quality medical care as anyone else.
18. AIDS makes a medical job a high-risk occupation.
19. Dealing with AIDS patients is different from dealing with other types of patients.
20. The high cost of treating AIDS patients is unfair to other people in need of care.
21. Working with AIDS patients can be a rewarding experience for medical personnel.
22. Hospital personnel should go out of their way to be helpful to a patient with AIDS.
23. People with AIDS can be cured if they seek medical attention.
24. To get AIDS, a person must have intimate sexual or blood contact with an AIDS carrier.
25. The disease AIDS can be transmitted by the exchange of blood (or blood products).
26. AIDS has been identified in hemophiliacs (people who bleed easily).
27. AIDS has been linked to blood transfusion.
28. AIDS is probably in most of the nation's blood supply.
29. A blood test can identify testing for AIDS.
30. People get AIDS from blood transfusion.

AIDS – Section D

Instructions: The items listed below refer to people's beliefs about the topic of AIDS (Acquired Immune Deficiency Syndrome). We are interested in whether you agree or disagree with these statements. As such, there are no right or wrong answers, only your own individual opinions. To indicate your reactions to these statements, use the following scale:

A = Agree
B = Slightly agree
C = Neither agree nor disagree
D = Slightly disagree
E = Disagree

Remember: There are no right or wrong responses; only your opinions. Be sure to respond to each and every statement; leave no blanks.

1. AIDS is a serious challenge to the notion of recreational sex.
2. Because of AIDS, everyone has a responsibility to practice healthful sexual behaviors.
3. Condoms offer protection against the spread of AIDS.
4. AIDS cannot be transmitted by heterosexual (male-female) sexual activity.
5. People catch AIDS from their sexual partners.
6. The more sexual partners people have, the greater their chance of acquiring AIDS.
7. AIDS is associated with multiple anonymous sexual contacts.
8. AIDS is transmitted by intimate sexual contact.
9. People can contract AIDS even though they have had sex with only one person.
10. Condoms are a safe shield against AIDS.
11. AIDS is essentially a sexually transmitted disease.
12. People can contract AIDS from sexual contact with a single infected person.
13. Any sexually active people can get AIDS.
14. People get AIDS from sex.
15. People don't engage in sex very much nowadays because of AIDS.
16. AIDS is transmitted primarily through sexual relations.
17. Proper use of condoms can reduce the risk of catching AIDS.
18. The use of condoms can prevent the spread of AIDS.
19. Heterosexuals who use condoms can lessen their risk for getting AIDS.
20. People who have "one-night stands" will probably catch AIDS.

Alternate Forms of HIV Prevention Attitude Scales for Teenagers

Mohammad R. Torabi and William L. Yarber,[1] *Indiana University*

The lack of valid devices for measuring attitudes toward HIV prevention for adolescents has remained an obstacle to HIV/AIDS education evaluation. Many national authority groups, such as the National Research Council (Coyle, Boruch, & Turner, 1989), have recognized the importance of construction of reliable survey questionnaires in evaluating HIV prevention programs. In addition to knowledge and behavioral outcomes, it is imperative to determine attitude status and how it changes in health education settings.

Research indicates that attitudes are best described as multidimensional, having the three components of cognitive (belief), affective (feeling), and conative (intention to act; Ajzen & Fishbein, 1980; Kothandapani, 1971; Ostrom, 1969). This model has been successfully applied in measurement of attitudes toward alcohol among teenagers (Torabi & Veenker, 1986), prevention of cancer for college students (Torabi & Seffrin, 1986), and sexually transmitted diseases (Yarber, Torabi, & Veenker, 1989).

In testing situations, especially for test-retest design, there is a need for parallel, equivalent, or alternate forms of tests. Tests are considered to be parallel whenever their information functions are identical (Timminga, 1990).

[1]Address correspondence to William L. Yarber, Department of Applied Health Science, Indiana University, HPER Building, Bloomington, IN 47405; e-mail: yarber@indiana.edu

For most of educational evaluation using pretest/posttest design, the use of alternate forms is preferred over single forms. Our purpose was to develop alternate, attitude-scale forms, using the three-component model, to measure adolescents' attitudes toward HIV and prevention of HIV infection.

Description

A large pool of Likert-type items was generated, guided by a table of specifications using a three-component attitude theory and conceptual areas related to HIV and HIV prevention. A preliminary scale with 50 items was prepared and reviewed by a jury of experts. The jurors provided feedback regarding clarity and content validity. Following revision, the preliminary scale was administered to 210 Midwestern high school students. After extensive item analyses, two comparable forms with 15 maximally discriminatory items were identified. These alternate forms were simultaneously administered to a representative sample of 600 teenagers in a Midwestern high school. Data were subjected to various techniques of item analysis, factor analysis, and reliability estimation.

The item analysis results provided strong evidence of internal consistency and comparability. The item correlation coefficients were positive and statistically significant for both forms. Additionally, the normative data regarding means, the standard deviations of item scores, and the total scale scores for the two forms were comparable.

Response Mode and Timing

Respondents indicate whether they *strongly agree, agree, undecided, disagree,* or *strongly disagree* to each statement. It takes about 10 minutes to complete the scale.

Scoring

The minimum and maximum possible points for each form are 15 and 75 points, with higher scores indicating more positive attitudes toward HIV and HIV prevention.

Scoring for Form A. For Items 7, 8, 11, 13, 15, *strongly agree* = 5 points, *agree* = 4, *undecided* = 3; *disagree* = 2, *strongly disagree* = 1. For the remaining items, *strongly agree* = 1, *agree* = 2, *undecided* = 3, *disagree* = 4, *strongly disagree* = 5.

Scoring for Form B. For Items 1, 3, 8, 9, 10, 11, 12, 13, 14, 15, *strongly agree* = 5, *agree* = 4, *undecided* = 3, *disagree* = 2, *strongly disagree* = 1. For the remaining items, *strongly agree* = 1, *agree* = 2, *undecided* = 3, *disagree* = 4, *strongly disagree* = 5.

Reliability

Alternate reliability across the form was .82. The alpha reliability for Forms A and B was .78 and .77, and split-half method was .76 and .69 (Torabi, & Yarber, 1992).

Validity

Evidence of content validity was provided by using a jury of experts, table of specifications, and factor analysis procedures. The factor analyses of both forms identified reasonably comparable factor structures for each form, indicating further evidence of content validity and comparability. It would have been ideal to provide evidence of criterion-related validity by surveying actual behaviors or practices. However, due to serious resistance to assessing minors' sexual and injecting drug behaviors, no such data were obtained.

Because the evidence of validity and reliability of the alternate forms were obtained from a sample of predominantly White, in-school student, the forms may not be very appropriate for minority or out-of-school youth.

Other Information

The scales may be utilized for needs assessment and evaluation of HIV/AIDS education measuring teenagers' attitudes toward prevention of HIV infection. The alternate forms are probably more suitable to pretest/posttest HIV education evaluation design.

References

Ajzen, I., & Fishbein, M. (1980). *Understanding attitudes and predicting social behavior.* Englewood Cliffs, NJ: Prentice Hall.

Coyle, S., Boruch, R. F., & Turner, C. F. (1989). *Evaluating AIDS prevention programs.* Washington, DC: National Academy Press.

Kothandapani, V., (1971). *A psychological approach to the prediction of contraceptive behavior.* Chapel Hill Carolina Population Center, University of North Carolina.

Ostrom, T. M. (1969). The relationship between the affective, behavioral, and cognitive components of attitude. *Journal of Experimental Psychology, 5,* 12–30.

Timminga, E. B. (1990). The construction of parallel tests from IRT-based item banks. *Journal of Educational Statistics, 15*(2), 129–145.

Torabi, M. R., & Seffrin, J. R. (1986). A three component cancer attitude scale. *Journal of School Health, 56,* 170–174.

Torabi, M. R., & Veenker, C. H. (1986). An alcohol attitude scale for teenagers. *Journal of School Health, 56,* 96–100.

Torabi, M. R., & Yarber, W. L. (1992). Alternate forms of the HIV prevention attitude scales for teenagers. *AIDS Education and Prevention, 4,* 172–182.

Yarber, W. L., Torabi, M. R., & Veenker, C. H. (1989). Development of a three component sexually transmitted diseases attitude scale for young adults. *Journal of Sex Education and Therapy, 15,* 36–49.

Exhibit

Alternate Forms of HIV Prevention Attitude Scales for Teenagers

Form A

Directions: Please read each statement carefully. *Record your immediate reaction to the statement by blackening the proper oval on the answer sheet.* There is no right or wrong answer for each statement, so mark your own response. Use the below key:

KEY: A = Strongly agree
      B = Agree
      C = Undecided
      D = Disagree
      E = Strongly disagree

Example: Doing something to prevent getting HIV is the responsibility of each person.

                                            A   B   C   D   E

1. I would feel very uncomfortable being around someone with HIV.
2. I feel that HIV is a punishment for immoral behavior.
3. If I were having sex, it would be insulting if my partner insisted we use a condom.
4. I dislike the idea of limiting sex to just one partner to avoid HIV infection.
5. I would dislike asking a possible sex partner to get the HIV antibody test.
6. It would be dangerous to permit a student with HIV to attend school.
7. It is easy to use the prevention methods that reduce one's chance of getting HIV.
8. It is important to talk to a sex partner about HIV prevention before having sex.
9. I believe that sharing IV drug needles has nothing to do with HIV.
10. HIV education in schools is a waste of time.
11. I would be supportive of a person with HIV.
12. Even if a sex partner insisted, I would not use a condom.
13. I intend to talk about HIV prevention with a partner if we were to have sex.
14. I intend not to use drugs so I can avoid HIV.
15. I will use condoms when having sex if I'm not sure if my partner has HIV.

Form B

Directions: Please read each statement carefully. *Record your immediate reaction to the statement by blackening the proper oval on the answer sheet.* There is no right or wrong answer for each statement, so mark your own response. Use the below key:

KEY: A = Strongly agree
      B = Agree
      C = Undecided
      D = Disagree
      E = Strongly disagree

Example: Doing something to prevent getting HIV is the responsibility of each person.

                                            A   B   C   D   E

1. I am certain that I could be supportive of a friend with HIV.
2. I feel that people with HIV got what they deserve.
3. I am comfortable with the idea of using condoms for sex.
4. I would dislike the idea of limiting sex to just one partner to avoid HIV infection.
5. It would be embarrassing to get the HIV antibody test.
6. It is meant for some people to get HIV.
7. Using condoms to avoid HIV is too much trouble.
8. I believe that AIDS is a preventable disease.
9. The chance of getting HIV makes using IV drugs stupid.
10. People can influence their friends to practice safe behavior.
11. I would shake hands with a person having HIV.
12. I will avoid sex if there is a slight chance that the partner might have HIV.
13. If I were to have sex I would insist that a condom be used.
14. If I used IV drugs, I would not share the needles.
15. I intend to share HIV facts with my friends.

Sexual Health Knowledge Questionnaire for HIV+ MSM

PETER A. VANABLE,[1] JENNIFER L. BROWN, MICHAEL P. CAREY, AND REBECCA A. BOSTWICK,
Syracuse University

Most conceptual models of sexual risk behavior identify knowledge about HIV and STDs as an important determinant of risk behavior (e.g., Fisher & Fisher, 1992). Moreover, effective interventions to reduce risks for contracting HIV include modules that focus on improving HIV-related knowledge as part of broader strategy to motivate behavior change (e.g., Johnson, Carey, Marsh, Levin, & Scott-Sheldon, 2003). Although a few validated measures of HIV- and STD-related knowledge exist for use in primary prevention contexts (e.g., Carey & Schroder, 2002), there are no published measures to assess knowledge of specific relevance to sexual risk reduction for persons living with HIV. In this report, we describe reliability and validity data for the Sexual Health Knowledge Questionnaire (SHKQ) for HIV+ men who have sex with men (MSM), a measure developed to assess prevention-related knowledge pertinent to risk reduction among HIV+ MSM. Interventions to promote knowledge of health risks associated with sexual behavior among HIV+ MSM are an important public health priority (Vanable & Carey, 2006).

The SHKQ was developed as part of a program of research to evaluate a sexual risk reduction intervention for HIV+ MSM (Vanable et al., 2009). Knowledge domains assessed by the SHKQ correspond to core knowledge modules that were included in our sexual risk reduction curriculum. Reliability and validity information for the SHKQ are derived from baseline and 3-month follow-up data collected among HIV+ MSM who participated in our pilot intervention trial (Vanable, Carey, Brown, Bostwick, & Blair, 2008).

Description

The SHKQ consists of 18 true-false questions that assess prevention-related knowledge relevant to risk reduction among HIV+ MSM. The SHKQ focuses on health risks associated with sexual behavior rather than knowledge about medical aspects of HIV. In particular, items assess knowledge regarding the impact of STD co-infections on HIV infectivity and disease progression, health risks related to unprotected sex involving two HIV+ partners, the relationship of HIV viral load to infectivity, differences in HIV transmission risks associated with being the receptive or insertive partner for anal sex, and STD and HIV transmission risk associated with oral sex. The measure also includes items that assess knowledge of specific STDs that can affect the health of HIV+ MSM.

Response Mode and Timing

For each item, respondents are asked to indicate whether the statement is *True* or *False*. If they are unsure whether the statement is true or false, respondents are instructed to select *Don't Know*, rather than guessing. The scale takes approximately 5 minutes to complete.

Scoring

For each item, responses are coded to indicate whether the respondent provided a correct or incorrect answer. Correct responses are assigned a value of one, whereas selection of an incorrect response or *Don't Know* is assigned a value of zero. For the following items, true is the correct response: 1, 2, 3, 4, 6, 9, 11, 13, 15, 17, 18. False is the correct response for these items: 5, 7, 8, 10, 12, 14, 16. A total score is calculated by summing the number of correct responses across the 18 items. Higher scores indicate greater sexual health knowledge.

Reliability and Validity

African American (26%) and White (63%) HIV+ MSM were recruited from an infectious disease clinic in upstate New York to participate in the sexual risk reduction program ($N = 80$). Participants' ages ranged between 22 and 62 (M age = 40.6, $SD = 8.0$). Participants had been infected with HIV for 9.0 years, on average ($SD = 5.6$). Participants were randomly assigned to an immediate intervention condition ($n = 40$) or a time-delayed intervention control condition ($n = 40$).

Test-Retest Reliability

Test-retest reliability data for the SHKQ were obtained using baseline and 3-month follow-up data among participants in the delayed intervention control condition. A total of 35 respondents in the delayed intervention condition completed the SHKQ both at baseline and at a 3-month follow-up. Test-retest reliability for SHKQ for this subsample was .78, $p < .001$. Based on established benchmarks

[1]Address correspondence to Peter A. Vanable, Department of Psychology & Center for Health and Behavior, Syracuse University, 430 Huntington Hall, Syracuse, NY 13244; e-mail: pvanable@syr.edu

(Cicchetti, 1994), our findings provide evidence of moderate to excellent test-retest agreement.

Validity

To provide evidence of convergent validity, the correlation between participants' SHKQ scores and responses to five items assessing medical knowledge related to HIV (e.g., "A low CD4 count indicates that an HIV+ person has minimal damage to the immune system") and five items assessing attitudes toward condom use (Sacco, Levine, Reed, & Thompson, 1991) was calculated. SHKQ scores were positively correlated with higher levels of medical knowledge related to HIV ($r = .34$, $p < .005$) and positively associated with having more favorable attitudes toward condom use ($r = .24$, $p < .05$). SHKQ scores also correlated positively with participants' education level ($r = .23$, $p < .05$).

We conducted analyses to determine whether the SHKQ was sensitive to changes in knowledge following participation in a two-session group intervention to promote sexual risk reduction among HIV+ MSM. Our results demonstrated that knowledge scores improved from baseline ($M = 9.3$, $SD = 3.3$) to follow-up ($M = 10.7$, $SD = 2.4$) among participants in the immediate intervention condition who attended at least one intervention workshop, whereas knowledge showed no improvement from baseline to 3-month follow-up among participants in the delayed intervention condition, $F(1, 63) = 9.0$, $p < .005$. To examine whether there was a similar pattern of results for the delayed-intervention participants after receiving the intervention, we conducted paired t-tests evaluating change from the pre-intervention assessment to the 3-month follow-up. Delayed-intervention participants reported greater HIV transmission knowledge at the 3-month assessment ($M = 12.0$, $SD = 2.1$) than before receiving the intervention ($M = 10.1$, $SD = 2.4$), $t(23) = -4.8$, $p < .001$. Using these data, we suggest that our scale is sensitive to change in sexual health knowledge following participation in a two-session intervention program designed to address the unique health risks posed to HIV+ MSM.

Other Information

Support for this research was provided by NIMH Grants R21-MH65865 and F31MH081751.

References

Carey, M. P., & Schroder, K. E. (2002). Development and psychometric evaluation of the brief HIV Knowledge Questionnaire. *AIDS Education and Prevention, 14,* 172–182.

Cicchetti, D. V. (1994). Guidelines, criteria, and rules of thumb for evaluating normed and standardized assessment instruments in psychology. *Psychological Assessment, 6,* 284–90.

Fisher, J. D., & Fisher, W. A. (1992). Changing AIDS-risk behavior. *Psychological Bulletin, 111,* 455–474.

Johnson, B. T., Carey, M. P., Marsh, K. L., Levin, K. D., & Scott-Sheldon, L. A. (2003). Interventions to reduce sexual risk for the human immunodeficiency virus in adolescents, 1985–2000: A research synthesis. *Archives of Pediatric and Adolescent Medicine, 157,* 381–388.

Sacco, W. P., Levine, B., Reed, D. L., & Thompson, K. (1991). Attitudes about condom use as an AIDS-relevant behavior: Their factor structure and relation to condom use. *Psychological Assessment: A Journal of Consulting and Clinical Psychology, 3,* 265–272.

Vanable, P. A., & Carey, M. P. (2006). Behavioral medicine interventions in HIV/AIDS: Challenges and opportunities for promoting health and adaptation. In A. R. Kuczmierczyk & A. Nikcevic (Eds.), *A clinician's guide to behavioral medicine: A case formulation approach.* New York: Brunner-Routledge.

Vanable, P. A., Carey, M. P., Brown, J. L., Bostwick, R., & Blair, D. (2008, March). *A pilot intervention trial to promote sexual health and stress management among HIV+ MSM.* Poster presented at the Annual Meeting of the Society of Behavioral Medicine, San Diego, CA.

Vanable, P. A., Carey, M. P., Brown, J., Littlewood, R., Bostwick, R. A., and Blair, D. (2009). *What HIV+ men who have sex with men say is needed to promote sexual risk reduction.* Manuscript submitted for publication.

Exhibit

Sexual Health Knowledge Scale

Directions: For each statement, please tell us whether the statement is "True" or "False." If you do not know the answer, please do not guess; please say "Don't Know."

1. Having an undetectable viral load reduces the risk of transmitting HIV.	True	False	Don't Know
2. Having another STD makes it easier for an HIV+ person to give HIV to an HIV-negative partner.	True	False	Don't Know
3. Infection with another STD can speed up HIV disease progression for a person who is HIV+.	True	False	Don't Know
4. Human Papillomavirus (HPV) sometimes leads to rectal cancer in gay men.	True	False	Don't Know
5. Having an undetectable viral load eliminates the chance that a person with HIV will infect a sexual partner.	True	False	Don't Know
6. Among gay men, Hepatitis A is transmitted through rimming (oral-anal contact).	True	False	Don't Know
7. Doctors have now proven that reinfection with another strain of HIV worsens the health of an HIV+ person.	True	False	Don't Know
8. Unlike HIV, most other viral STDs can be cured.	True	False	Don't Know

9. A person can get an STD through oral sex.	True	False	Don't Know
10. An HIV+ person is less likely to transmit HIV to a sexual partner if he is the insertive partner (top) than if he is the receptive partner (bottom).	True	False	Don't Know
11. Transmission of drug- resistant HIV to HIV-negative sexual partners is more common than transmission of drug- resistant HIV to HIV+ partners.	True	False	Don't Know
12. If you"re HIV positive, infections like gonorrhea and chlamydia in your penis can decrease the amount of HIV in your semen.	True	False	Don't Know
13. Syphilis is a bacterial STD.	True	False	Don't Know
14. It is a good idea to use Vaseline or baby oil with latex condoms.	True	False	Don't Know
15. Gonorrhea can be found in the throat.	True	False	Don't Know
16. For two HIV+ partners, STDs are less of a concern than contracting drug- resistant HIV.	True	False	Don't Know
17. HIV can be transmitted through oral sex, but the risks are much lower than for anal or vaginal sex.	True	False	Don't Know
18. An HIV+ person who has sex with another HIV+ person should still use a condom to avoid new health problems.	True	False	Don't Know

Adolescent AIDS Knowledge Scale

GREGORY D. ZIMET,[1] *Indiana University School of Medicine*

The Adolescent AIDS Knowledge Scale (AAKS) was developed as part of a comprehensive questionnaire to evaluate adolescents' knowledge, beliefs, and attitudes about acquired immunodeficiency syndrome (AIDS; Zimet et al., 1989). The knowledge scale was developed with two principal issues in mind. First, we wanted to ensure that the scale covered relevant material. To accomplish this goal, item content was derived from a 1988 informational brochure distributed to every household by the U.S. Government (Centers for Disease Control, 1988). As a result, the scale addresses multiple AIDS-related domains, including modes of transmission, high-risk behaviors, mortality, the existence of a cure, prevention of transmission, and the appearance of persons with AIDS (PWAs).

A second issue considered during scale development was that most existing AIDS knowledge scales confounded knowledge (i.e., awareness of scientific facts about AIDS) with beliefs. It seemed likely that a person might "know" the facts according to experts, but not believe them. In considering the design of AIDS education interventions, it appeared particularly important to assess AIDS awareness/knowledge separately from AIDS beliefs. To address this issue, each item on the AAKS was constructed to begin with the phrase "Do most experts say . . .?" A separate but parallel AIDS Beliefs scale was developed to evaluate the extent to which adolescents believed what experts were saying.

Description

The AAKS has 22 items. Each item takes the form of a question (e.g., "Do most experts say you can get AIDS by giving blood?"). Transmission-related items cover true modes of transmission (e.g., sharing needles), low- or no-risk behaviors (e.g., sharing a glass of water), behaviors that increase risk of transmission (e.g., prostitution), and transmission of human immunodeficiency virus (HIV) without clinical AIDS. Two protection items address effective (i.e., condom use) and ineffective (i.e., eating healthy foods) protective behaviors. Finally, single items cover such topics as the mortality associated with AIDS, whether there is a cure for AIDS, and whether it is possible to determine if someone has AIDS by looking at him or her.

Response Mode and Timing

To each question, respondents are asked to circle *yes*, *no*, or *don't know*. Response times vary, but typically the scale requires less than 5 minutes to complete.

Scoring

A correct response receives a score of 1. An incorrect answer or a *don't know* response each receives a score of 0. For the following items, *no* is the correct response: 1, 3,

[1]Address correspondence to Gregory D. Zimet, Indiana University School of Medicine, Section of Adolescent Medicine, 410 West 10th Street, HS 1001, Indianapolis, IN 46202; e-mail: gzimet@iupui.edu

4, 5, 9, 11, 13, 15, 17, and 19. For the following items, *yes* is the correct response: 2, 6, 7, 8, 10, 12, 14, 16, 18, 20, 21, and 22. The total score for the scale, which is calculated by summing across items, can range from 0 to 22.

Reliability

An AIDS-knowledge scale such as this one represents multiple content areas, not a single construct. Therefore, standard measures of internal reliability that assess overall internal consistency (e.g., Cronbach's coefficient alpha or Kuder-Richardson formula 20) are inappropriate (Anastasi, 1982; Zimet, 1992b). A more useful approach involves a specialized form of Spearman-Brown split-half reliability in which items from one half are matched for content with items from the other half (Zimet, 1992b). Given that the AAKS was not designed with this approach to reliability in mind, it is not possible to match all items perfectly (e.g., only one item addresses mortality associated with AIDS). Nonetheless, in a sample of 721 junior and senior high school students, the Spearman-Brown matched-item split-half method resulted in a coefficient of .82, indicating good internal reliability (Zimet, 1992b).

Validity

The content validity of the scale was established through the use of the U.S. government brochure on AIDS to guide item selection (Centers for Disease Control, 1988). Furthermore, in addressing major AIDS-related domains (i.e., HIV transmission, protection, mortality, appearance, etc.), the scale demonstrates good face validity.

Support for the construct validity of the AAKS is demonstrated by expected relationships with other variables. For example, it may be expected that older students have more accurate knowledge about AIDS than younger students. For the AAKS, analysis of variance indicated a linear increase in scores across grade level among 617 7th to 12th graders, $F(5, 611) = 8.8, p < .0001$ (Zimet, DiClemente, et al., 1993).

Another expectation is that greater AIDS knowledge is likely to be negatively correlated to inaccurate beliefs about AIDS. Among 438 junior and senior high school students, increases in scores on the AAKS, in fact, were associated significantly with decreases in inaccurate beliefs about AIDS, $r = -.65, p < .001$ (Zimet et al., 1991).

Finally, it is reasonable to expect that more accurate knowledge about AIDS will be negatively related to fears about interacting with PWAs. Among the same 438 students, AAKS scores correlated significantly and negatively with anxiety about interacting with PWAs, $r = -.28, p < .001$ (Zimet et al., 1991).

References

Anastasi, A. (1982). *Psychological testing* (5th ed.). New York: Macmillan.

Centers for Disease Control. (1988). Understanding AIDS [An information brochure being mailed to all U.S. households]. *Morbidity and Mortality Weekly Report, 37*, 261–269.

Zimet, G. D. (1992a). Attitudes of teenagers who know someone with AIDS. *Psychological Reports, 70*, 1169–1170.

Zimet, G. D. (1992b). Reliability of AIDS knowledge scales: Conceptual issues. *AIDS Education and Prevention, 4*, 338–344.

Zimet, G. D., Anglin, T. M., Lazebnik, R., Bunch, D., Williams, P., & Krowchuk, D. P. (1989). Adolescents' knowledge and beliefs about AIDS: Did the government brochure help? *American Journal of Diseases of Children, 143*, 518–519.

Zimet, G. D., Bunch, D. L., Anglin, T. M., Lazebnik, R., Williams, P., & Krowchuk, D. P. (1992). Relationship of AIDS-related attitudes to sexual behavior changes in adolescents. *Journal of Adolescent Health, 13*, 493–498.

Zimet, G. D., DiClemente, R. J., Lazebnik, R., Anglin, T. M., Ellick, E. M., & Williams, P. (1993). Changes in adolescents' knowledge and attitudes about AIDS over the course of the AIDS epidemic. *Journal of Adolescent Health, 14*, 85–90.

Zimet, G. D., Hillier, S. A., Anglin, T. M., Ellick, E. M., Krowchuk, D. P., & Williams, P. (1991). Knowing someone with AIDS: The impact on adolescents. *Journal of Pediatric Psychology, 16*, 287–294.

Zimet, G. D., Lazebnik, R., DiClemente, R. J., Anglin, T. M., Williams, P., & Ellick, E. M. (1993). The relationship of Magic Johnson's announcement of HIV infection to the AIDS attitudes of junior high school students. *The Journal of Sex Research, 30*, 129–134.

Exhibit

Adolescent AIDS Knowledge Scale

Instructions: Experts on AIDS have talked about the spread and prevention of AIDS. Please circle your answer for each question.

1. Do most experts say there's a high chance of getting AIDS by kissing someone on the mouth who has AIDS?	Yes	No	Don't Know
2. Do most experts say AIDS can be spread by sharing a needle with a drug user who has AIDS?	Yes	No	Don't Know
3. Do most experts say you can get AIDS by giving blood?	Yes	No	Don't Know
4. Do most experts say there's a high chance that AIDS can be spread by sharing a glass of water with someone who has AIDS?	Yes	No	Don't Know
5. Do most experts say there's a high chance you can get AIDS from a toilet seat?	Yes	No	Don't Know
6. Do most experts say AIDS can be spread if a man has sex with a woman who has AIDS?	Yes	No	Don't Know
7. Do most experts say AIDS can be spread if a man has sex with another man who has AIDS?	Yes	No	Don't Know
8. Do most experts say a pregnant woman with AIDS can give AIDS to her unborn baby?	Yes	No	Don't Know

9. Do most experts say you can get AIDS by shaking hands with someone who has AIDS?	Yes	No	Don't Know
10. Do most experts say a woman can get AIDS by having sex with a man who has AIDS?	Yes	No	Don't Know
11. Do most experts say you can get AIDS when you masturbate by yourself?	Yes	No	Don't Know
12. Do most experts say using a condom (rubber) can lower your chance of getting AIDS?	Yes	No	Don't Know
13. Do most experts say that there's a high chance of getting AIDS if you get a blood transfusion?	Yes	No	Don't Know
14. Do most experts say that prostitutes have a higher chance of getting AIDS?	Yes	No	Don't Know
15. Do most experts say that eating healthy foods can keep you from getting AIDS?	Yes	No	Don't Know
16. Do most experts say that having sex with more than one partner can raise your chance of getting AIDS?	Yes	No	Don't Know
17. Do most experts say that you can always tell if someone has AIDS by looking at them?	Yes	No	Don't Know
18. Do most experts say that people with AIDS will die from it?	Yes	No	Don't Know
19. Do most experts say there is a cure for AIDS?	Yes	No	Don't Know
20. Do most experts say that you can have the AIDS virus without being sick from AIDS?	Yes	No	Don't Know
21. Do most experts say that you can have the AIDS virus and spread it without being sick from AIDS?	Yes	No	Don't Know
22. Do most experts say that if a man or woman has sex with someone who shoots up drugs, they raise their chance of getting AIDS?	Yes	No	Don't Know

Modern Homonegativity Scale

MELANIE A. MORRISON[1] AND TODD G. MORRISON, *University of Saskatchewan*

The Modern Homonegativity Scale (MHS; M. A. Morrison & Morrison, 2002) is a brief measure designed to assess contemporary negative attitudes toward gay men and lesbian women. Unlike many measures of homonegativity, items on the MHS do not assess traditional, moral, or religious objections to lesbian women and gay men, but rather objections to members of these social groups based on the following beliefs: (a) gay men and lesbian women are making unnecessary or illegitimate demands for changes to the status quo (e.g., the right to legally wed and to parent an adopted child), (b) discrimination against homosexual men and women is a thing of the past, and (c) gay men and lesbian women exaggerate the importance of their sexual orientation and, in so doing, prevent themselves from assimilating into mainstream culture (i.e., they are responsible for their own marginalization given their participation in events such as "Gay Pride" parades).

Description

The MHS is suitable for use both with students (M. A. Morrison & Morrison, 2002; M. A. Morrison, Morrison, & Franklin, 2009; T. G. Morrison, Kenny, & Harrington, 2005) and with nonstudents (M. A. Morrison & Morrison, 2009). The items were originally developed via input from members of organizations serving sexual minority men and women, members of academic faculty, and gay, lesbian, and heterosexual graduate students. The 50-item version of the MHS was then distributed to both university and college students. Using specific scale item reduction criteria, principal components analysis, and reliability assessments, the number of items was ultimately reduced to a 12-item version (M. A. Morrison & Morrison, 2002). Factor analyses were conducted on the 12-item MHS, with results indicating that the scale was both unidimensional and conceptually distinct from measures of "old-fashioned" homonegativity (e.g., the Homonegativity Scale; T. G. Morrison, Parriag, & Morrison, 1999). There are two parallel forms of the MHS: one focusing on gay men (MHS-G) and the other focusing on lesbian women (MHS-L). Results from M. A. Morrison and Morrison (2002) indicate that both 12-item forms are reliable (alphas exceeded .90), unidimensional, and construct valid (total scale scores correlated in anticipated directions with constructs that are theoretically linked such as modern racism and modern sexism).

[1]Address correspondence to Melanie A. Morrison, Department of Psychology, University of Saskatchewan, 9 Campus Drive, 184 Arts Bldg., Saskatoon, SK, Canada S7N 5A5; e-mail: melanie.morrison@usask.ca

Response Mode and Timing

Study participants report the extent to which they agree or disagree with the written MHS items. Specifically, participants are given instructions that read "After the statement, please circle the number which best represents your opinion." A 5-point Likert response format is often used in which 1 represents *Strongly Disagree*, 2 represents *Disagree*, 3 represents *Don't Know*, 4 represents *Agree*, and 5 represents *Strongly Agree*. The MHS also has used a 7-point Likert-type scale, with no noticeable differences observed in terms of psychometric properties. Participants take less than 5 minutes to complete the MHS.

Scoring

Total scale scores are calculated by summing participants' responses across all MHS items. If researchers are using a 5-point Likert response format, for example, the possible range of scores is 12 (a low-scoring participant) to 60 (a high-scoring participant). It should be noted that three scale items require reverse scoring, and calculation of subscale or factor scores are not applicable to the MHS.

Reliability

Using student and nonstudent samples, alpha coefficients for the MHS have been consistently high. Specifically, they have ranged from .81 to .95 (MHS-G) and .84 to .91 (MHS-L; M. A. Morrison & Morrison, 2002; M. A. Morrison et al., 2009).

Validity

Construct validation of the MHS when used with Canadian and American university students has been obtained via confirmation of hypothesized relationships between modern homonegativity and political conservatism, religious behavior, religious self-schema, modern and neosexism, humanitarian-egalitarianism, motivation to control prejudiced reactions, interpersonal contact, anti-fat attitudes, and prejudice toward Aboriginal men and women (M. A. Morrison & Morrison, 2002; M. A. Morrison et al., 2009; M. A. Morrison, Morrison, Harriman, & Jewell, 2008). Further, responses to the MHS do not appear to be contaminated by social desirability bias (M. A. Morrison & Morrison, 2002). Tests of construct validation also were conducted using a sample of Irish university students. Specifically, T. G. Morrison et al. (2005) found participants'

level of modern homonegativity correlated positively with their levels of old-fashioned and modern racism, patriotism, nationalism, religious fundamentalism, social dominance, and perceived political conservatism. The authors also found inverse correlations between scores on the MHS and support for the human rights of gay men and lesbian women. A series of confirmatory factor analyses also provided evidence of divergent validity, with MHS items loading on a different factor than items taken from a popular measure of old-fashioned homonegativity (M. A. Morrison et al., 2009). Fit statistics for this two-factor model were superior to those obtained for a unidimensional model. Finally, behavioral studies (M. A. Morrison & Morrison, 2002, 2009) offered additional construct validation, with significant differences emerging between high- and low-scoring participants on the MHS in terms of the degree to which they socially distanced themselves from a lesbian or gay individual and supported the candidacy of a gay male running for political office.

Other Information

The MHS is available for use by any individual conducting research in accordance with the American Psychological Association's *Ethical Principles for Psychologists*. Individuals wishing to use the MHS can do so without obtaining permission from the authors.

References

Morrison, M. A., & Morrison, T. G. (2002). Development and validation of a scale measuring modern prejudice toward gay men and lesbian women. *Journal of Homosexuality, 43,* 15–37.

Morrison, M. A., & Morrison, T. G. (2009). *Sexual orientation bias toward gay men and lesbian women: Modern homonegative attitudes and their association with discriminatory behavioural intentions.* Manuscript submitted for publication.

Morrison, M. A., Morrison, T. G., & Franklin, R. (2009). Modern and old-fashioned homonegativity among samples of Canadian and American university students. *Journal of Cross-Cultural Psychology, 40,* 523–542.

Morrison, M. A., Morrison, T. G., Harriman, R. L., & Jewell, L. M. (2008). Old-fashioned and modern prejudice toward Aboriginals in Canada. In M. A. Morrison & T. G. Morrison (Eds.), *The Psychology of Modern Prejudice* (pp. 277–306). New York: Nova Science.

Morrison, T. G., Kenny, P., & Harrington, A. (2005). Modern prejudice toward gay men and lesbian women: Assessing the viability of a measure of modern homonegative attitudes with an Irish context. *Genetic, Social, and General Psychology Monographs, 131,* 219–250.

Morrison, T. G., Parriag, A. V., & Morrison, M. A. (1999). The psychometric properties of the Homonegativity Scale. *Journal of Homosexuality, 37,* 111–126.

Exhibit

Modern Homonegativity Scale

Scale Items

MHS-G

1. Gay men have all the rights they need.*
2. Gay men have become far too confrontational in their demand for equal rights.*
3. Gay men should stop shoving their lifestyle down other people's throats.*
4. Gay men seem to focus on the ways in which they differ from heterosexuals, and ignore the ways in which they are similar.*
5. Gay men who are "out of the closet" should be admired for their courage.* [R]
6. Many gay men use their sexual orientation so that they can obtain special rights and privileges.*
7. Gay men no longer need to protest for equal rights.*
8. In today's tough economic times, Canadians' tax dollars shouldn't be used to support gay men's organizations.*
9. The notion of universities providing degrees in gay and lesbian studies is ridiculous.
10. Gay men should stop complaining about the way they are treated in society, and simply get on with their lives.
11. Celebrations such as "Gay Pride Day" are ridiculous because they assume that an individual's sexual orientation should constitute a source of pride.
12. If gay men want to be treated like everyone else, then they need to stop making such a fuss about their sexuality/culture.

MHS-L

1. The notion of universities providing degrees in gay and lesbian studies is ridiculous.*
2. Celebrations such as "Gay Pride Day" are ridiculous because they assume that an individual's sexual orientation should constitute a source of pride.*
3. Lesbian women should stop shoving their lifestyle down other people's throats.*
4. Lesbian women seem to focus on the ways in which they differ from heterosexuals, and ignore the ways in which they are the same.*
5. Many lesbian women use their sexual orientation so that they can obtain special rights and privileges.*
6. Lesbian women have become far too confrontational in their demand for equal rights.*
7. Lesbian women who are "out of the closet" should be admired for their courage.* [R]
8. In today's tough economic times, Canadians' tax dollars shouldn't be used to support lesbian organizations.*
9. If lesbians want to be treated like everyone else, then they need to stop making such a fuss about their sexuality/culture.*
10. Lesbian women should stop complaining about the way they are treated in society, and simply get on with their lives.*
11. Lesbian women no longer need to protest for equal rights.
12. Lesbian women have all the rights they need.

Note. [R] = Item requires reverse scoring. If using the invariant items only, standardized scores are recommended (total MHS-L score divided by 10 and total MHS-G score divided by 8).

*Items identified as invariant between Canadian and American samples of university students (M. A. Morrison et al., 2009).

Index of Homophobia (Index of Attitudes Toward Homosexuals)

WENDELL A. RICKETTS AND WALTER W. HUDSON,[1,2] *WALMYR Publishing Co.*

The Index of Homophobia (IHP) is a short-form scale designed to measure homophobic versus nonhomophobic attitudes (the fear of being in close quarters with homosexuals).

Description

The IHP contains 25 category-partition (Likert-type) items, some of which are worded negatively to partially offset the potential for response-set bias. Each item is scored on a relative frequency scale as shown in the scoring key of the instrument. Obtained scores range from 0 to 100 where higher scores indicate greater degrees of homophobia. The IHP has a cutting score of 50, such that scores above that value indicate the presence of an increasingly homophobic attitude toward human sexual expression, whereas scores below that value indicate the presence of an increasing nonhomophobic orientation. A score of 0 represents the most nonhomophobic position, and a score of 100 represents the most homophobic position. The IHP can be used with all English-speaking populations aged 12 or older.

The readability statistics for the IHP are Flesch Reading Ease: 68, Gunning's Fog Index: 10, Flesch-Kincaid Grade Level: 7.

Response Mode and Timing

The IHP is normally completed in 5–7 minutes.

Scoring

Items 3, 4, 6, 9, 10, 12, 13, 14, 15, 17, 19, 21, and 24 must first be reverse-scored by subtracting the item response from $K+1$ where K is the number of response categories in the scoring key. After making all appropriate item reversals, compute the total score as $S = (\Sigma X_i - N)(100) / [(K-1)N]$ where X is an item response, i is item, K is the number of response categories, and N is the number of properly completed items. Total scores remain valid in the face of missing values (omitted items) provided the respondent completes at least 80% of the items. The effect of the scoring formula is to replace missing values with the mean item response

value so that scores range from 0 to 100 regardless of the value of N.

Reliability

Cronbach's alpha = .90, and the *SEM* = 4.43. Test-retest reliability is not available.

Validity

Known groups validity is not available for the IHP scale. Detailed information about content, factorial, and construct validity is reported in the *WALMYR Assessment Scale Scoring Manual* which is available from the publisher.

Other Information

The proper use of the Walmyr assessment scales is easily mastered, and the scales can be readily understood by qualified professional practitioners. These measurement tools are not intended for use by untrained individuals. The scales are simple, powerful devices that, when used by trained professionals, are capable of revealing both minor and serious problems that individuals might have in many areas of personal and social functioning. They are not intended for use by persons who are not trained to deal with such problems and should be used only by competent professionals, researchers, scholars and those who are engaged in supervised study and training.

The IHP is a copyrighted commercial assessment scale and may not be copied, reproduced, altered, or translated into other languages. The scale may not be administered online nor placed on a website for others to use. It may be purchased in tear-off pads of 50 copies each for $22.50 at www.walmyr.com.

References

Hudson, W. W., & Ricketts, W. A. (1980). A strategy for the measurement of homophobia. *Journal of Homosexuality, 5*, 357–372.

Nurius, P. S., & Hudson, W. W. (1993), *Human services practice, evaluation & computers.* Pacific Grove, CA: Brooks/Cole.

[1]Walter W. Hudson, 1934–1999.

[2]Address correspondence to WALMYR Publishing Co., P.O. Box 12217, Tallahassee, FL 32317-2217; e-mail: walmyr@walmyr.com

Exhibit

Index of Attitudes Toward Homosexuals (IAH)

Name: _____ Today's Date: _____

This questionnaire is designed to measure the way you feel about working or associating with homosexuals. It is not a test, so there are no right or wrong answers. Answer each item as carefully and as accurately as you can by placing a number beside each one as follows.

1 = Strongly agree
2 = Agree
3 = Neither agree nor disagree
4 = Disagree
5 = Strongly disagree

1. _____ I would feel comfortable working closely with a male homosexual.
2. _____ I would enjoy attending social functions at which homosexuals were present.
3. _____ I would feel uncomfortable if I learned that my neighbor was homosexual.
4. _____ If a member of my sex made a sexual advance toward me I would feel angry.
5. _____ I would feel comfortable knowing that I was attractive to members of my sex.
6. _____ I would feel uncomfortable being seen in a gay bar.
7. _____ I would feel comfortable if a member of my sex made an advance toward me.
8. _____ I would be comfortable if I found myself attracted to a member of my sex.
9. _____ I would feel disappointed if I learned that my child was homosexual.
10. _____ I would feel nervous being in a group of homosexuals.
11. _____ I would feel comfortable knowing that my clergyman was homosexual.
12. _____ I would be upset if I learned that my brother or sister was homosexual.
13. _____ I would feel that I had failed as a parent if I learned that my child was gay.
14. _____ If I saw two men holding hands in public I would feel disgusted.
15. _____ If a member of my sex made an advance toward me I would be offended.
16. _____ I would feel comfortable if I learned that my daughter's teacher was a lesbian.
17. _____ I would feel uncomfortable if I learned that my spouse or partner was attracted to members of his or her sex.
18. _____ I would feel at ease talking with a homosexual person at a party.
19. _____ I would feel uncomfortable if I learned that my boss was homosexual.
20. _____ It would not bother me to walk through a predominantly gay section of town.
21. _____ It would disturb me to find out that my doctor was homosexual.
22. _____ I would feel comfortable if I learned that my best friend of my sex was homosexual.
23. _____ If a member of my sex made an advance toward me I would feel flattered.
24. _____ I would feel uncomfortable knowing that my son's male teacher was homosexual.
25. _____ I would feel comfortable working closely with a female homosexual.

Note. 3, 4, 6, 9, 10, 12, 13, 14, 15, 17, 19, 21 and 24 are reverse scored.

Homophobic Behavior of Students Scale

PAUL VAN DE VEN,[1] LAUREL BORNHOLT, AND MICHAEL BAILEY, *University of Sydney*

The Homophobic Behavior of Students Scale (HBSS; Van de Ven, Bornholt, & Bailey, 1993, 1996) was developed to measure students' behavioral intentions toward gay males and lesbians, in the context of teaching about homosexuality. The HBSS complements existing cognitive and affective measures of homophobia, thereby giving researchers of antigay and antilesbian prejudice an efficient strategy to measure the much neglected, though highly important, behavioral dimension of homophobic responses (Van de Ven, 1994a). Previous assessments of homophobic behavior have relied on highly contrived experimental manipulations which are unsuitable for everyday classroom use and, with their reliance on naive participants, cannot be used in the repeated measures designs of behavior change studies. The HBSS has the advantages of being practical and plausible, and of being a measure of personal commitment to action which can be assessed on multiple occasions. The HBSS can be treated as an individual-differences measure of homophobic behavioral intentions or as a dependent variable when evaluating the impact on behavioral intentions of homophobia reduction strategies (see Van de Ven, 1994b, 1995a, 1995b).

Description

The HBSS consists of 10 items arranged in a 5-point Likert-type format to rate strength of intention from 1 (*definitely false*) to 5 (*definitely true*). The first six items are designed to measure, across classroom and social situations, the extent to which students associated willingly or avoided contact with gay males and lesbians. These items were construed as a measure of social distance aspects of behavior. The remaining items were selected to measure additional and related aspects of behavior expressed as willingness to act in support of gay and lesbian rights. Separate analyses of the responses of 97 undergraduate students (26 males; 71 females) and 40 high school students (24 males; 16 females) suggested that the items contributed to a single factor of behavioral intentions. The HBSS is appropriate to use with both high school and college populations. A posttest version of the HBSS is created by changing the instructions minimally as specified in the Exhibit.

Response Mode and Timing

Students circle the number from 1 to 5 that corresponds with their willingness to participate in each activity. The HBSS takes approximately 3 minutes to complete.

Scoring

A combination of positive and negative items is used to control for potential response set bias. The positively phrased items (i.e., Items 1, 2, 4, 6, 7, 9, & 10) have their scoring reversed in the analysis so that higher scores, following convention, indicate more negative behavioral intentions toward homosexuals. Computed HBSS scores, which can range from 0 (least homophobic) to 100 (most homophobic), are determined by using the equation: HBSS computed score = (HBSS summed raw score −10) × 2.5.

Reliability

For the sample of 97 undergraduate students, Cronbach's alpha was .81, $M = 37.65$; $SD = 19.94$. For the sample of 40 high school students, Cronbach's alpha was .86, $M = 65.25$; $SD = 24.29$ (Van de Ven et al., 1993, 1996).

Validity

As expected, Van de Ven et al. (1993, 1996) found that the computed score of the HBSS was significantly correlated with Homophobic Cognition, $r = .78$, as measured by the Modified Attitudes Toward Homosexuality Scale (Price, 1982). Also in line with expectations, homophobic behavioral intentions were significantly correlated with both Homophobic Anger, $r = .66$, and Homophobic Guilt, $r = .38$, and significantly negatively correlated with Warmth Toward Homosexuals, $r = −.56$, as measured by the Affective Reactions to Homosexuality Scale (Van de Ven, 1994a; Van de Ven et al., 1993, 1996; after Ernulf & Innala, 1987).

To assess the predictive validity of the HBSS, the 40 high school students were given the opportunity to participate in each of the 10 activities of the HBSS (Van de Ven et al., 1993, 1996). As expected, the group of participants for each activity had a lower HBSS mean than the corresponding

[1]Address correspondence to Paul Van de Ven, 11 John St, Ashfield NSW 2131, Australia; e-mail: p.vandeven@bigpond

group that abstained from participation. Group means were significantly different at the .005 alpha level (for a family-wise error rate of .05) for six of the HBSS activities.

Other Information

If the HBSS is used by researchers, notification to the first author of the use and the results obtained would be appreciated.

This scale was developed while the authors were at the School of Educational Psychology, Measurement and Technology, University of Sydney. Laurel Bornholt is now at Charles Darwin University.

References

Ernulf, K. E., & Innala, S. M. (1987). The relationship between affective and cognition components of homophobic reaction. *Archives of Sexual Behavior, 16,* 501–509.

Price, J. H. (1982). High school students' attitudes toward homosexuality. *Journal of School Health, 52,* 469–474.

Van de Ven, P. (1994a). *Challenging homophobia in schools.* Unpublished doctoral thesis, University of Sydney.

Van de Ven, P. (1994b). Comparisons among homophobic reactions of undergraduates, high school students, and young offenders. *The Journal of Sex Research, 31,* 117–124.

Van de Ven, P. (1995a). Effects on high school students of a teaching module for reducing homophobia. *Basic and Applied Social Psychology, 17,* 153–172.

Van de Ven, P. (1995b). Effects on young offenders of two teaching modules for reducing homophobia. *Journal of Applied Social Psychology, 25,* 632–649.

Van de Ven, P., Bornholt, L., & Bailey, M. (1993, November). *Homophobic attitudes and behaviours: Telling which teaching strategies make a difference.* Paper presented at the Annual Conference of the Australian Association for Research in Education, Freemantle, Western Australia.

Van de Ven, P., Bornholt, L., & Bailey, M. (1996). Measuring cognitive, affective, and behavioral components of homophobic reaction. *Archives of Sexual Behavior, 25,* 155–179.

Exhibit

Homophobic Behavior of Students Scale

Instructions: As part of the unit of work (Posttest version: As part of the follow-up to the unit of work) on lesbian and gay issues, it may be possible to organize some additional activities and guest speakers. So that these can be planned, please indicate in which of the following activities, if any, you would participate. Circle the number that comes closest to representing your willingness to participate. Please do not leave any statements unanswered.

1. I would speak in a small class group with a gay person or lesbian about homosexual issues.

Definitely false 1 2 3 4 5 Definitely true[a]

2. I would speak individually, in class, with a gay person or lesbian about homosexual issues.
3. I would NOT like to have a gay person or lesbian address the class about homosexual issues.
4. I would take the opportunity to talk in an informal lunch-time meeting with a group of four lesbians or gay males.
5. I would NOT attend a lunch-time barbecue at which four gay males or lesbians were present.
6. I would watch a video in class in which a lesbian or gay person is featured.
7. I would sign my name to a petition asking the government to do more to stop violence against gay men and lesbians.
8. I would NOT sign my name to a petition asking the government to make sure gays and lesbians have equal rights with everybody else.
9. I would sign my name to a petition asking the government to allow lesbian and gay couples to officially register their marriage or partnership.
10. I would sign my name to a petition asking the government to allow lesbian and gay couples to adopt children.

[a]The scale is repeated after each item.

Internalized Homophobia Scale

GLENN J. WAGNER,[1] *New York State Psychiatric Institute*

The Internalized Homophobia Scale was developed for use with gay men and is intended to measure the extent to which negative attitudes and beliefs about homosexuality are internalized and integrated into one's self-image and identity as gay. The significance of measuring internalized homophobia is its negative impact on the mental health of gay and lesbian individuals as it is often associated with guilt, shame, depression, and feelings of worthlessness. Several clinical reports documenting the effects and dynamics of internalized homophobia have been published, but research studies in which internalized homophobia has been systematically measured have been confined (by and large) to studies of gay men with Human Immunodeficiency Virus (HIV). In research conducted by our group, and others, we have found that internalized homophobia is associated with demoralization, depression, and general psychological distress, as well as low self-esteem and avoidant coping.

Description

The Internalized Homophobia Scale consists of 20 items, 9 of which are from the Nungesser Homosexual Attitudes Inventory (Nungesser, 1983), with the other 11 items developed by the HIV Center for Clinical and Behavioral Studies at the New York State Psychiatric Institute. A principal components factor analysis with a varimax rotation was performed on a sample of 142 gay men who completed the IHS and a 22-item scale of demoralization (Dohrenwend, Shrout, Egri, & Mendelsohn, 1987), and the 7-item depression subscale of the Brief Symptom Inventory (Derogatis & Melisaratos, 1983). Using all items a two-factor solution resulted, with all but one (Item 4) of the IHS items loading on Factor 1. All of the items from the depression scale loaded on Factor 2, as did 17 of the items from the demoralization scale. None of the items from the three factors loaded on discrepant factors (Wagner, Brondolo, & Rabkin, 1996).

Response Mode and Timing

Each item is scored on a 5-point Liker-type scale with 1 = *strongly disagree* and 5 = *strongly agree*, and each response represents the degree to which the respondent endorses the statement or item. The scale requires approximately 5 minutes to complete.

Scoring

There are 10 items that are positively keyed and 10 that are negatively keyed. The range for the total score is 20 to 100, with higher scores representing greater internalized homophobia.

Reliability

The scale was tested for internal consistency reliability in a sample of 142 gay men, yielding a Cronbach alpha of .92 for the total score (Wagner, Serafini, Rabkin, Remien, & Williams, 1994). Based on this statistic and the previously described factor analysis, it is recommended that the total summed score of the 20 items be regarded as a homogeneous measure of internalized homophobia.

Validity

Research using the Internalized Homophobia Scale has revealed the construct to be positively correlated with mental health measures including demoralization ($r = .49$), global psychological distress ($r = .37$), and depression ($r = .36$; Wagner et al., 1994, 1996). Other correlates include age at which one first accepted being gay ($r = .46$), and degree of integration into the gay community ($r = -.54$; Wagner et al., 1994). In a study of HIV+ gay men in which the scale was completed twice, with a 2-year interval, results indicated that greater internalized homophobia, specifically among those who had not yet experienced any HIV-related physical symptoms, predicted higher levels of distress over time; within this subgroup, internalized homophobia at the first assessment was correlated .61 with distress 2 years later.

These research findings indicate that internalized homophobia may have a negative impact on mood, self-esteem, and quality of life. Mental health professionals working with gay men, regardless of HIV status, may be more effective in targeting resources and interventions aimed at improving mental health and overall quality of life if they address issues related to internalized homophobia.

References

Derogatis, L. R., & Melisaratos, N. (1983) The Brief Symptom Inventory: An introductory report. *Psychological Medicine, 13*, 595–605.

Dohrenwend, B. P., Shrout, P. E., Egri, G., & Mendelsohn, F. S. (1987). Nonspecific psychological distress and other dimensions of psychopathology. *Archives in General Psychiatry, 9*, 114–122.

Nungesser, L. G. (1983). *Homosexual acts, actors and identities.* New York, NY: Praeger.

Wagner, G., Brondolo, E., & Rabkin, J.G. (1996). Internalized homophobia in a sample of HIV+ gay men, and its relationship to psychological distress, coping, and illness progression. *Journal of Homosexuality, 32*(2), 91–106.

Wagner, G., Serafini, J., Rabkin, J., Remien, R., & Williams, J. (1994). Integration of one's religion and homosexuality: A weapon against internalized homophobia? *Journal of Homosexuality, 26*(4), 91–109.

[1]Address correspondence to Glenn J. Wagner, RAND Corporation, 1776 Main St., Santa Monica, CA 90407; e-mail: gwagner@rand.org

Exhibit

Internalized Homophobia Scale

Instructions: The following are some statements that individuals can make about being gay. Please read each one carefully and decide the extent to which you agree with the statement, then circle the number that best reflects how much you agree or disagree with the statement.

Response format: 1 Strongly Disagree
2 Disagree
3 Neutral
4 Agree
5 Strongly Agree

1. Male homosexuality is a natural expression of sexuality in human males.
2. I wish I were heterosexual.
3. When I am sexually attracted to another gay man, I do not mind if someone else knows how I feel.
4. Most problems that homosexuals have come from their status as an oppressed minority, not from their homosexuality per se.
5. Life as a homosexual is not as fulfilling as life as a heterosexual.
6. I am glad to be gay.
7. Whenever I think a lot about being gay, I feel critical about myself.
8. I am confident that my homosexuality does not make me inferior.
9. Whenever I think a lot about being gay, I feel depressed.
10. If it were possible, I would accept the opportunity to be completely heterosexual.
11. I wish I could become more sexually attracted to women.
12. If there were a pill that could change my sexual orientation, I would take it.
13. I would not give up being gay even if I could.
14. Homosexuality is deviant.
15. It would not bother me if I had children who were gay.
16. Being gay is a satisfactory and acceptable way of life for me.
17. If I were heterosexual, I would probably be happier.
18. Most gay people end up lonely and isolated.
19. For the most part, I do not care who knows I am gay.
20. I have no regrets about being gay.

Self-Identified Lesbian Internalized Homophobia Scale

STACY WEIBLEY[1] AND MICHELLE HINDIN, *Johns Hopkins University*

The Self-Identified Lesbian Internalized Homophobia Scale (SLIHS) was developed to gain a greater understanding of internalized homophobia in the lives of women who identify as lesbian and to address significant gaps in the literature regarding this topic. It has been hypothesized that internalized homophobia is linked to the elevated rates of mental health and substance abuse issues experienced by gay, lesbian, bisexual, and transgender (GLBT) individuals, including the disproportionately high rates of suicide among GLBT youth. However, although previous research suggests internalized homophobia is a statistically significant and distinct factor in the lives of gay men (Meyer, 1995), there is a dearth of research regarding this issue among other GLBT groups, including lesbians.

Of the few existing empirical studies regarding internalized homophobia among lesbians, many rely on

[1]Address correspondence to Stacy Weibley; e-mail: sweibley@msn.com

questions developed to measure this construct among gay men rather than those that appropriately address lesbian culture (Radonsky & Borders, 1995). Other studies are limited owing to a lack of theoretical support, small sample size, or additional methodological issues (DiPlacido, 1998; Peterson & Gerrity, 2006). Although there are several published scales that assess internalized homophobia among men, only one scale addresses women (Szymanski & Chung, 2001). However, this scale was validated using a sample that included a significant number (approximately 30%) of participants who did not identify as lesbian and was biased in terms of education level, and it includes questions that confound internalized homophobia with other psychological issues or personality traits.

Description

The SLIHS is a self-administered survey that is completed by women who self-identify as lesbian. The instrument includes four subscales, Visibility, Connectedness, Self-Acceptance, and Judgment, and a total of 30 closed-ended questions.

Response Mode and Timing

This two-page self-administered survey takes approximately 3 minutes to complete. The response has been very high: Over 95% completed the survey.

Scoring

Overall and subscale scores can be calculated. Possible overall scores range from 30 to 120 (with higher numbers representing greater internalized homophobia), whereas subscale scores range from 7 to 28 for Visibility (Items 1–7) and Connectedness (Items 8–14), 5 to 20 for Self-Acceptance (Items 15–19), and 11 to 44 for Judgment (Items 20–30). The Likert-type scale response categories and associated points for about half of the items are the following: *Strongly Agree* = 1, *Agree* = 2, *Disagree* = 3, and *Strongly Disagree* = 4. The remaining items are reversed (R), with point structures as follows: *Strongly Agree* = 4, *Agree* = 3, *Disagree* = 2, and *Strongly Disagree* = 1.

Reliability and Validity

The SLIHS was validated with a sample of 786 women, ranging in age from 18 to 82, from 39 states across the United States (Weibley, 2009). The sample was 81.7% White, 4.7% Hispanic, 4.6% Asian, 4.4% African American, 3.8% Biracial, and 0.8% other. Confirmatory factor analysis confirmed the internal reliability of the four subscales, with Cronbach coefficient alpha values ranging from .74 to .85. The original scale items were developed by lesbian focus group participants using the concept mapping technique (Trochim, 1989), and the construct validity was assessed and affirmed by a total of 14 face and content validity reviewers.

Other Information

The scale was copyrighted by Stacy Weibley in 2009.

References

DiPlacido, J. (1998). Minority stress among lesbians, gay men, and bisexuals: A consequence of heterosexism, homophobia, and stigmatization. In G. Herek (Ed.), *Stigma and sexual orientation: Understanding prejudice against lesbians, gay men, and bisexuals* (pp. 138–159). Thousand Oaks, CA: Sage.

Meyer, I. H. (1995). Minority stress and mental health in gay men. *Journal of Health and Social Behavior, 36,* 38–56.

Peterson, T. L., & Gerrity, D. A. (2006). Internalized homophobia, lesbian identity development, and self-esteem in undergraduate women. *Journal of Homosexuality, 50*(4), 49–75.

Radonsky, V. E., & Borders, L. D. (1995). Factors influencing lesbians' direct disclosure of their sexual orientation. *Journal of Gay and Lesbian Psychotherapy, 2*(3), 17–37.

Szymanski, D. M., & Chung, Y. B. (2001). The lesbian internalized homophobia scale: A rational/theoretical approach. *Journal of Homosexuality, 41*(2), 37–52.

Trochim, W. (1989). An introduction to concept mapping for planning and evaluation. *Evaluation and Program Planning, 12,* 1–16.

Weibley, S. (2009). *Creating a scale to measure internalized homophobia among self-identified lesbians.* Unpublished doctoral dissertation, Johns Hopkins University, Baltimore, MD.

Exhibit

Self-Identified Lesbian Internalized Homophobia Scale

	Strongly Agree	Agree	Disagree	Strongly Disagree
I am comfortable being "out."				
I am "out" to my boss/employer.				
I am "out" to my co-workers.				
I am "out" to my parents.				
I feel comfortable discussing homosexuality in a public setting.				
When discussing your partner, it is all right to use gender neutral pronouns to make heterosexual people more comfortable. [R]				

When/if I am in a relationship, I feel comfortable talking about my lesbian partner.					
I feel comfortable about the idea of another woman making an advance toward me.					
I feel comfortable at lesbian-centered events or places.					
I feel comfortable in social situations with other lesbians.					
I have stopped myself from coming out because no heterosexuals are truly accepting. [R]					
I have very little in common with other lesbians. [R]					
It is important for me to be part of the lesbian community.					
It is important to have people in my life who know I am a lesbian.					
I am comfortable being a lesbian.					
I feel comfortable thinking about my homosexuality.					
I sometimes feel disappointed in myself for being a lesbian. [R]					
I sometimes feel embarrassed to be a lesbian. [R]					
I would prefer to be heterosexual. [R]					
Being a lesbian is all right when you are young, but I worry how people will perceive me as an older lesbian. [R]					
Children should be taught that being gay or lesbian is normal.					
I find myself making negative comments about other lesbians. [R]					
I sometimes think heterosexual people's judgments of lesbians are, at least in part, justified. [R]					
I think of lesbians as sexually predatory. [R]					
I wish other lesbians would not flaunt their lesbianism. [R]					
It is understandable that people judge lesbians who do not dress or act "straight." [R]					
It is understandable that some people believe that lesbians are not worthy of the same treatment as other women. [R]					
Lesbians should try to look as non-offensive as possible. [R]					
Lesbians who have a very masculine appearance make me uncomfortable. [R]					
Most lesbians grow out of their lifestyles. [R]					

Note. [R] = reverse-scored items.

Homophobia Scale

LESTER W. WRIGHT, JR.,[1] HENRY E. ADAMS,[2] AND JEFFREY BERNAT, *University of Georgia*

The Homophobia Scale (HS) was developed to assess the cognitive, affective, and behavioral components of homophobia.

Description

The HS consists of 25 statements to which respondents answer on a 5-point Likert scale of 1 (*Strongly Agree*) to 5 (*Strongly Disagree*). The majority of the homophobia scales currently in use measure attitudes toward gay and lesbian individuals and what has been referred to as homonegativity, but do not capture the entire construct of homophobia. The inclusion of items that assess social avoidance and aggressive acting, in addition to the attitudinal items found on many homophobia measures, differentiates the HS from other scales.

The participants for the development and validation studies (N = 321 for the initial field trial and N = 122 for test-retest reliability) were students from a large midwestern university. Their average age was 22.38 (SD = 4.12).

[1]Address correspondence to Lester W. Wright, Jr., Department of Psychology, Western Michigan University, Kalamazoo, MI 49008; e-mail: lester.wright@wmich.edu
[2]Henry E. Adams died October 16, 2000.

The mean total score for the scale based on 145 participants was 32.04 (SD = 19.76). The mean score for the male participants (n = 47) was 41.38 (SD = 19.32). The mean score for the female participants (n = 98) was 27.56 (SD = 18.44). It is recommended that users of the scale conduct statistics on their samples to determine cut scores for high and low responding.

The scale contains three factors that accounted for 68.69% of the scale's variance. The first factor, Behavioral/ Negative Affect, accounted for 40.88% of the scale's variance and contained 10 items that assess primarily negative affect and avoidance behaviors. The mean score for Factor 1 = 10.79 (SD = 8.22). The second factor, Affect/Behavioral Aggressive, accounted for 23.05% of the scale's variance and contained 10 items that assess primarily aggressive behavior and negative affect. The mean score for Factor 2 = 14.28 (SD = 12.51). The third factor, Cognitive Negativism, accounted for 4.77% of the scale's variance and contained five items that assess negative attitudes and cognitions. The mean score for Factor 3 = 7.10 (SD = 4.84).

Response Mode and Timing

Respondents can indicate their level of agreement or disagreement with the statements by circling the number on the Likert scale that most closely matches their thoughts, feelings, or behavior. The scale can be completed in approximately 5 to 7 minutes.

Scoring

A total score and three subscale scores can be calculated for the scale.

1. Reverse score the following items: 1, 2, 4, 5, 6, 9, 12, 13, 14, 15, 17, 19, 21, 23, 24, 25 (to reverse score the items 1 = 5, 2 = 4, 3 = 3, 4 = 2, 5 = 1). Use these reverse scores to calculate total score and factor subscale scores.
2. To calculate the total scale score: Add the responses to items 1–25; then subtract 25 from the total scale score. The range of scores will be between 0 and 100, with a score of 0 being the least homophobic and 100 being the most homophobic.

3. To calculate the subscale (factor) scores:
   Factor 1 (Behavior/Negative Affect): Add items 1, 2, 4, 5, 6, 7, 9, 10, 11, and 22; then subtract 10. Scores should range between 0 and 40.
   Factor 2 (Affect/Behavioral Aggression): Add items 12, 13, 14, 15, 17, 19, 21, 23, 24, and 25; then subtract 10. Scores should range between 0 and 40.
   Factor 3 (Cognitive Negativism): Add items 3, 8, 16, 18, and 20; then subtract 5. Scores should range between 0 and 20.

Reliability

The scale yielded an overall α reliability coefficient of $r = .94$, $p < .01$ and a 1-week test-retest reliability coefficient of $r = .96$, $p < .01$.

Validity

Concurrent validity was established using the Index of Homophobia (IHP; Hudson & Ricketts, 1980). A Pearson correlation coefficient was computed using overall scores for the IHP and the HS. The results yielded a significant correlation, $r = .66$, $p < .01$, indicating the two scales are measuring a similar construct. The moderately strong correlation suggests the HS measures something different than the IHP.

Other Information

A copy of the scale can be obtained at no cost from the corresponding author. Appropriate citation of the scale (Wright, Adams, & Bernat, 1999) is requested.

References

Hudson, W. W., & Ricketts, W. A. (1980). A strategy for the measurement of homophobia. *Journal of Homosexuality, 5,* 357–372.

Wright, L. W., Jr., Adams, H. E., & Bernat, J. (1999). Development and validation of the Homophobia Scale. *Journal of Psychopathology and Behavioral Assessment, 21,* 337–347.

Exhibit

Homophobia Scale

This questionnaire is designed to measure your thoughts, feelings, and behaviors with regard to homosexuality. It is not a test, so there are no right or wrong answers. Answer each item by circling the number after each question as follows:

1 Strongly Agree
2 Agree
3 Neither Agree nor Disagree
4 Disagree
5 Strongly Disagree

1. Gay people make me nervous.
   1   2   3   4   5

2. Gay people deserve what they get.
   1   2   3   4   5

3. Homosexuality is acceptable to me.
   1   2   3   4   5

4. If I discovered a friend was gay I would end the friendship.
   1   2   3   4   5

5. I think homosexual people should not work with children.
   1   2   3   4   5

6. I make derogatory remarks about gay people.
   1   2   3   4   5

7. I enjoy the company of gay people.
   1   2   3   4   5

8. Marriage between homosexual individuals is acceptable.
   1   2   3   4   5

9. I make derogatory remarks like "faggot" or "queer" to people I suspect are gay.
   1   2   3   4   5

10. It does not matter to me whether my friends are gay or straight.
    1   2   3   4   5

11. It would not upset me if I learned that a close friend was homosexual.
    1   2   3   4   5

12. Homosexuality is immoral.
    1   2   3   4   5

13. I tease and make jokes about gay people.
    1   2   3   4   5

14. I feel that you cannot trust a person who is homosexual.
    1   2   3   4   5

15. I fear homosexual persons will make sexual advances towards me.
    1   2   3   4   5

16. Organizations which promote gay rights are necessary.
    1   2   3   4   5

17. I have damaged property of gay persons, such as "keying" their cars.
    1   2   3   4   5

18. I would feel comfortable having a gay roommate.
    1   2   3   4   5

19. I would hit a homosexual for coming on to me.
    1   2   3   4   5

20. Homosexual behavior should not be against the law.
    1   2   3   4   5

21. I avoid gay individuals.
    1   2   3   4   5

22. It does not bother me to see two homosexual people together in public.
    1   2   3   4   5

23. When I see a gay person I think, "What a waste."
    1   2   3   4   5

24. When I meet someone I try to find out if he/she is gay.
    1   2   3   4   5

25. I have rocky relationships with people that I suspect are gay.
    1   2   3   4   5

Gay Identity Questionnaire

STEPHEN BRADY,[1] *Boston University School of Medicine*

The Gay Identity Questionnaire (GIQ) can be used by clinicians and researchers to identify gay men in the developmental stages of "coming out" proposed by Cass (1979) in the Homosexual Identity Formation (HIF) Model. These stages include Confusion, Comparison, Tolerance, Acceptance, Pride, and Synthesis. Test construction procedures included the selection of questionnaire items based upon the constructs of the HIF model, and the establishment of reliability and validity for the GIQ through two pilot tests and one final administration of the instrument (Brady, 1983; Brady & Busse, 1994).

Description

The GIQ is comprised of 45 true-false items and can easily be scored for the purpose of identifying the respondent's stage of HIF. Findings suggest that the GIQ is a reliable and valid measure that can be used by clinicians and researchers to examine the coming-out process. Two hundred twenty-five male respondents were administered the final version of the GIQ and a psychosocial/background questionnaire. Efforts were made to recruit a developmentally heterogeneous sample of men with same-sex thoughts, feelings, and/or behavior. The majority of the respondents (179) were young (*M* age = 28.8 years), non-Hispanic White men residing in Southern California in 1983. All respondents indicated they had homosexual thoughts, feelings, or engaged in homosexual behavior. In addition to the author's use, the instrument has been used in a number of doctoral dissertations and Master's theses.

Response Mode and Timing

The GIQ consists of 45 randomly ordered, true-false statements to which respondents respond by circling either the letter T or F depending upon whether they agree or disagree with the statement. The instrument takes approximately 15–20 minutes to complete.

Scoring

The scoring of the GIQ includes the following. Three items (Items 4, 22, & 40) are used as validity checks and identify that an individual has thoughts, feelings, or engages in behavior that can be labeled as homosexual. Respondents must mark at least one of these three items as True for the instrument to be considered appropriate for use in classifying the stage of homosexual identity formation.

The other 42 items are used to determine respondents' stage designation. Each of the six stages of HIF is represented by seven items that are characteristic of individuals at that stage. For each item a respondent marks as true, he accrues one point in the HIF stage represented by that item. For every item a respondent marks false, he receives a zero point subscore. The subset of items in which a respondent accrues the most points is his given stage designation. If a respondent accrues the same number of points in two or more stages, he is given a dual stage designation.

Reliability

Interitem consistency scores for the GIQ were obtained using the Kuder-Richardson formula (Hays, 1973). Too few respondents were identified in the first two stages of HIF for data analytic procedures to be utilized. The reliabilities for the other four stages were: Stage 3 (Identity Tolerance), $r = .76$; Stage 4 (Identity Acceptance), $r = .71$; Stage 5 (Identity Pride), $r = .44$; Stage 6 (Identity Synthesis), $r = .78$.

Validity

No statistically significant relationships were found between respondent age, education, income, religiosity, political values, and HIF stages. Findings that most demographic variables did not confound the HIF process supports the validity of the HIF model for predicting stages of coming out independent of those variables.

Findings also support a central construct of the HIF model which describes the importance of psychological factors in the evolution of a homosexual identity. Statistical tests revealed a significant positive relationship between respondent stage of HIF and a composite measure of nine self-report items assessing psychological well-being, $F(3, 189) = 8.67$, $p < .01$. Subsequent post-hoc analysis of ANOVA results using Tukey's HSD test (Hays, 1973) revealed that respondents in Stage 3, Identity Tolerance, reported having less psychological well-being compared to their counterparts in Stages 4, 5, and 6.

Significant relationships were also found between respondent's stage of HIF and five indices assessing homosexual adjustment. More specifically, respondents in Stage 3, Identity Tolerance, compared to respondents in the later stages of HIF, reported homosexuality as being a less viable identity, $F(3, 190) = 9.86$, $p < .01$; they were less exclusively homosexual, $F(3, 188) = 14.34$, $p < .01$; they were less likely to have "come out" to significant others, $F(3,

[1]Address correspondence to Stephen Brady, Division of Psychiatry, Boston University School of Medicine, 715 Albany Street, Robinson 2 B-2903, Boston, MA 02118; e-mail: sbrady@bu.edu

190) = 25.04, $p < .01$; they were less sexually active, $F(3, 191) = 4.52$, $p < .01$); and they had fewer involvements in intimate homosexual relationships, $\chi^2 (3, N = 194), = 9.68$, $p < .01$.

Respondents in the latter three stages of HIF did not differ appreciably from one another on measures of psychological well-being or homosexual adjustment. These latter findings suggest that homosexual identity formation may be a two-stage process rather than the six stages proposed by Cass (1979) in the HIF model. In the first stage (Identity Confusion/Comparison/Tolerance) respondents remain unclear about or do not like their homosexual identity, whereas in the second stage (Identity Acceptance/Pride/Synthesis) respondents know and approve of their identity while maintaining different public identities.

Findings support the use of the GIQ as a brief measure for identifying young middle-class White men at one of the stages of homosexual identity formation proposed by Cass (1979). In order to increase the generalizability of the instrument, future researchers should recruit a sample that includes women and people of color. In addition, a refinement of the instrument so that homosexual identity is treated as a continuous variable with a summed scale score, rather than a categorical variable with a stage designation, would be an improvement in the measurement of homosexual identity formation.

References

Brady, S. M. (1983). The relationship between differences in stages of homosexual identity formation and background characteristics, psychological well-being and homosexual adjustment. *Dissertation Abstracts International, 45*, 3328(10B).

Brady, S. M., & Busse, W. J. (1994). The Gay Identity Questionnaire: A brief measure of homosexual identity formation. *Journal of Homosexuality, 26*(4), 1–22.

Cass, V. C. (1979). Homosexual identity formation: A theoretical model. *Journal of Homosexuality, 4*, 219–235.

Cass, V. C. (1984). Testing a theoretical model. *The Journal of Sex Research, 20*, 143–167.

Hays, W. L. (1973). *Statistics for the social sciences.* New York: Holt, Rinehart and Winston.

Exhibit

Gay Identity Questionnaire

Directions: Please read each of the following statements carefully and then circle whether you feel the statements are true (T) or false (F) for you at this point in time. A statement is circled as true if the entire statement is true, otherwise it is circled as false.

	True	False
1. I probably am sexually attracted equally to men and women. (Stage 2)	T	F
2. I live a homosexual lifestyle at home, while at work/school I do not want others to know about my lifestyle. (Stage 4)	T	F
3. My homosexuality is a valid private identity, that I do not want made public. (Stage 4)	T	F
4. I have feelings I would label as homosexual. (validity check item)	T	F
5. I have little desire to be around most heterosexuals. (Stage 5)	T	F
6. I doubt that I am homosexual, but still am confused about who I am sexually. (Stage 1)	T	F
7. I do not want most heterosexuals to know that I am definitely homosexual. (Stage 4)	T	F
8. I am very proud to be gay and make it known to everyone around me. (Stage 5)	T	F
9. I don't have much contact with heterosexuals and can't say that I miss it. (Stage 5)	T	F
10. I generally feel comfortable being the only gay person in a group of heterosexuals. (Stage 6)	T	F
11. I'm probably homosexual, even though I maintain a heterosexual image in both my personal and public life. (Stage 3)	T	F
12. I have disclosed to 1 or 2 people (very few) that I have homosexual feelings, although I'm not sure I'm homosexual. (Stage 2)	T	F
13. I am not as angry about treatment of gays because even though I've told everyone about my gayness, they have responded well. (Stage 6)	T	F
14. I am definitely homosexual but I do not share that knowledge with most people. (Stage 4)	T	F
15. I don't mind if homosexuals know that I have homosexual thoughts and feelings, but I don't want others to know. (Stage 3)	T	F
16. More than likely I'm homosexual, although I'm not positive about it yet. (Stage 3)	T	F
17. I don't act like most homosexuals do, so I doubt that I'm homosexual. (Stage 1)	T	F
18. I'm probably homosexual, but I'm not sure yet. (Stage 3)	T	F
19. I am openly gay and fully integrated into heterosexual society. (Stage 6)	T	F
20. I don't think that I'm homosexual. (Stage 1)	T	F
21. I don't feel as if I am heterosexual or homosexual. (Stage 2)	T	F
22. I have thoughts I would label as homosexual. (validity check item)	T	F
23. I don't want people to know that I may be homosexual, although I'm not sure if I am homosexual or not. (Stage 2)	T	F

24. I may be homosexual and I am upset at the thought of it. (Stage 2)	T	F
25. The topic of homosexuality does not relate to me personally. (Stage 1)	T	F
26. I frequently confront people about their irrational, homophobic (fear of homosexuality) feelings. (Stage 5)	T	F
27. Getting in touch with homosexuals is something I feel I need to do, even though I'm not sure I want to. (Stage 3)	T	F
28. I have homosexual thoughts and feelings but I doubt that I'm homosexual. (Stage 1)	T	F
29. I dread having to deal with the fact that I may be homosexual. (Stage 2)	T	F
30. I am proud and open with everyone about being gay, but it isn't the major focus of my life. (Stage 6)	T	F
31. I probably am heterosexual or non-sexual. (Stage 1)	T	F
32. I am experimenting with my same sex, because I don't know what my sexual preference is. (Stage 2)	T	F
33. I feel accepted by homosexual friends and acquaintances, even though I'm not sure I'm homosexual. (Stage 3)	T	F
34. I frequently express to others, anger over heterosexuals' oppression of me and other gays. (Stage 5)	T	F
35. I have not told most of the people at work that I am definitely homosexual. (Stage 4)	T	F
36. I accept but would not say I am proud of the fact that I am definitely homosexual. (Stage 4)	T	F
37. I cannot imagine sharing my homosexual feelings with anyone. (Stage 1)	T	F
38. Most heterosexuals are not credible sources of help for me. (Stage 5)	T	F
39. I am openly gay around heterosexuals. (Stage 6)	T	F
40. I engage in sexual behavior I would label as homosexual. (validity check item)	T	F
41. I am not about to stay hidden as gay for anyone. (Stage 5)	T	F
42. I tolerate rather than accept my homosexual thoughts and feelings. (Stage 3)	T	F
43. My heterosexual friends, family, and associates think of me as a person who happens to be gay, rather than as a gay person. (Stage 6)	T	F
44. Even though I am definitely homosexual, I have not told my family. (Stage 4)	T	F
45. I am openly gay with everyone, but it doesn't make me feel all that different from heterosexuals. (Stage 6)	T	F

Lesbian, Gay, and Bisexual Knowledge and Attitudes Scale

FRANK R. DILLON, *Florida International University*
ROGER L. WORTHINGTON,[1] *University of Missouri*

Recent scholars have conceptualized attitudes toward lesbian, gay, and bisexual (LGB) individuals as multidimensional and wide-ranging (Worthington, Savoy, Dillon, & Vernaglia, 2002). There are two concurrent yet divergent trends in the United States with respect to attitudes toward LGB individuals. Although Yang (2000) has reported data that suggest a gradual trend over the past 25 years toward more positive attitudes among the general population, there also has been a corresponding increase in highly publicized violence (Cloud, 2008) and a mixture of outcomes in a variety of judicial and legislative legal battles over LGB civil rights issues. Furthermore, as LGB individuals become more visible in the mainstream of United States culture, knowledge of LGB history, symbols, and community is likely to evidence corresponding increases. Therefore, as attitudes toward LGB individuals reflect widening complexities in society, it is critical that scientific measurement provides increasing precision of range and dimensionality.

The Lesbian, Gay, and Bisexual Knowledge and Attitudes Scale (LGB-KAS) measures respondents' attitudes and knowledge levels regarding LGB individuals. The multidimensional and wide-ranging factors assessed by the LGB-KAS include (a) Internalized Affirmativeness: a willingness to engage in proactive social activism for LGB issues and internalized sense of comfort with same-sex attractions, (b) Civil Rights Attitudes: beliefs about the civil rights of LGB individuals with respect to marriage, child rearing, health care, and insurance benefits, (c) Knowledge: basic knowledge about the history, symbols, and organizations related to the LGB community, (d) Religious Conflict: conflictual beliefs and ambivalent homonegativity with respect to LGB individuals, often of a religious nature, and (e) Hate: attitudes about avoidance, self-consciousness, hatred, and violence toward LGB individuals.

[1]Address correspondence to Roger L. Worthington, 217 Jesse Hall, University of Missouri, Columbia, MO 65211; e-mail: WorthingtonR@missouri.edu

Description

The LGB-KAS consists of 28 items. Each item represents an attitude or fact concerning LGB individuals or issues. Higher factor scores are indicative of a stronger endorsement of beliefs (or a higher level of knowledge) concerning each of the five factors (Internalized Affirmativeness, Civil Rights Attitudes, Knowledge, Religious Conflict, and Hate). The scale is intended for self-identifying heterosexual respondents.

The development and validation of the LGB-KAS included four studies (Worthington, Dillon, & Becker-Schutte, 2005). In Study 1, item development procedures and an exploratory factor analysis of an initial item pool were conducted. Discriminant validity estimates also were examined (described in *Validity* section). A review of (a) measures of homophobia, racism, and sexism, (b) literature examining attitudes toward LGB individuals, and (c) the Worthington et al. (2002) model of sexual identity yielded 211 initial items. Pilot studies decreased the item pool to 32 items. The remaining items reflected the following dimensions: *violent homonegativity* (e.g., "I sometimes feel violent toward gay men/lesbian women/bisexual individuals"); *homophobic intolerance* (e.g., "Same-sex marriage just does not make sense to me"); *negatively ambivalent attitudes* (e.g., "I do not care what LGB individuals do as long as they do not draw attention to themselves"); *indifference* (e.g., "I have never given much thought to my beliefs about lesbian, gay, or bisexual people"); *positively ambivalent attitudes* (e.g., "I'm not sure what to say or do when someone makes an anti-LGB joke or statement"); *affirmative or supportive attitudes* (e.g., "It is important to teach children positive attitudes about LGB people"); and *specific attitudes toward lesbians or gay men or bisexual persons* (e.g., "Lesbian women [Gay men] should be allowed to adopt children"; "Gay men [Lesbian women] deserve the hatred they receive"). In addition, 28 items were developed to expand the range of items included in the measure. These new items reflected more contemporary issues related to civil rights (e.g., "Hospitals should acknowledge same-sex partners equally to any other next of kin"), items intended to reflect differential negativity toward lesbians versus gay men versus bisexual individuals (e.g., ["Lesbian/Gay/Bisexual] individuals should not be allowed to work with children"), and issues of religiosity (e.g., "I keep my religious views to myself in order to accept LGB people"). These items also were intended to reflect the present literature on attitudes and offer the foundation for multiple forms of the LGB-KAS to independently examine attitudes and knowledge regarding gay men or lesbians or bisexual men and women. An exploratory factor analysis (EFA) using principal axis factor extraction was performed on the remaining 60 items of the LGB-KAS. A five-factor solution using an oblique rotation yielded the most interpretable solution.

In Study 2, the factor stability of the initial EFA solution was established via confirmatory factor analyses, and construct validity estimates were obtained (described in the *Validity* section). Study 3 provided the test-retest reliability estimates of the instrument (described in the *Reliability* section) and evidence of convergent validity (described in the *Validity* section). In Study 4, another indication of construct validity of the LGB-KAS was investigated, that is, the sensitivity of the LGB-KAS to change across sexual orientation identities (described in the *Validity* section).

Response Mode and Timing

Participants respond to each item using a 6-point Likert-type scale ranging from 1 (*Very Uncharacteristic of Me or My Views*) to 6 (*Very Characteristic of Me or My Views*). It typically takes a participant approximately 10 minutes to complete the LGB-KAS.

Scoring

LGB-KAS subscale scores are obtained by summing all items within each of the five subscales and dividing by the number of items on the subscales receiving responses (i.e., items with missing data are not scored or included in the averaging). There are no reverse-scored items.

Reliability

The LGB-KAS subscales have evidenced adequate internal consistency (Cronbach's $\alpha > .70$) in past studies (Worthington et al., 2005). Test-retest reliability estimates indicated LGB-KAS subscale scores as highly stable over a 2-week time period (Worthington et al., 2005).

Validity

Discriminant validity was evidenced by an absence of relations between the total scale and subscales and a measure of impression management (Worthington et al., 2005). Construct validity was supported through (a) exploratory and confirmatory factor analyses, (b) correlations between LGB-KAS subscales and social dominance orientation and sexual identity exploration, and (c) findings indicating differences between heterosexual and LGB individuals on all five subscales (Worthington et al., 2005). Convergent validity for subscales was supported by correlations with measures of attitudes toward bisexuality, as well as lesbian women and gay men (Worthington et al., 2005). More recently, Worthington & Reynolds (2009) have demonstrated that the LGB-KAS can be administered to LGB individuals to obtain information about internalized homonegativity.

Other Information

Ann M. Becker-Schutte was one of the original authors of the scale.

References

Cloud, J. (2008, February 18). Prosecuting the gay teen murder. *Time, 172*. Retrieved September 26, 2008, from http://www.time.com/time/nation/article/0,8599,1714214,00.html

Worthington, R. L., Dillon, F. R., & Becker-Schutte, A. M. (2005). Development, reliability, and validity of the LGB Knowledge and Attitudes Scale for Heterosexuals (LGB-KASH). *Journal of Counseling Psychology, 52*, 104–118.

Worthington, R. L., & Reynolds, A. L. (2009). Within group differences in sexual orientation and identity. *Journal of Counseling Psychology, 56*, 44–55.

Worthington, R. L., Savoy, H. B., Dillon, F. R., & Vernaglia, E. R. (2002). Heterosexual identity development: A multidimensional model of individual and social identity. *The Counseling Psychologist, 30*, 496–531.

Yang, A. (2000). *From wrong to rights: Public opinions on gay and lesbian Americans' move toward equality*. Washington, DC: National Gay and Lesbian Task Force Institute.

Exhibit

Lesbian, Gay, and Bisexual Knowledge and Attitudes Scale

Instructions: Please use the scale below to respond to the following items. Circle the number that indicates the extent to which each statement is characteristic or uncharacteristic of you or your views. Please try to respond to every item.

1	2	3	4	5	6
Very Uncharacteristic of Me or My Views					Very Characteristic of Me or My Views

Note: LGB = Lesbian, Gay, or Bisexual.

Please consider the ENTIRE statement when making your rating, as some statements contain two parts.

1. I feel qualified to educate others about how to be affirmative regarding LGB issues.[a]

1	2	3	4	5	6

2. I have conflicting attitudes or beliefs about LGB people.
3. I can accept LGB people even though I condemn their behavior.
4. It is important to me to avoid LGB individuals.
5. I could educate others about the history and symbolism behind the "pink triangle."
6. I have close friends who are LGB.
7. I have difficulty reconciling my religious views with my interest in being accepting of LGB people.
8. I would be unsure what to do or say if I met someone who is openly lesbian, gay, or bisexual.
9. Hearing about a hate crime against an LGB person would not bother me.
10. I am knowledgeable about the significance of the Stonewall Riot to the Gay Liberation Movement.
11. I think marriage should be legal for same-sex couples.
12. I keep my religious views to myself in order to accept LGB people.
13. I conceal my negative views toward LGB people when I am with someone who doesn't share my views.
14. I sometimes think about being violent toward LGB people.
15. Feeling attracted to another person of the same sex would not make me uncomfortable.
16. I am familiar with the work of the National Gay and Lesbian Task Force.
17. I would display a symbol of gay pride (pink triangle, rainbow, etc.) to show my support of the LBG community.
18. I would feel self-conscious greeting a known LGB person in a public place.
19. I have had sexual fantasies about members of my same sex.
20. I am knowledgeable about the history and mission of the PFLAG organization.
21. I would attend a demonstration to promote LGB civil rights.
22. I try not to let my negative beliefs about LGB people harm my relationships with the lesbian, gay, or bisexual individuals I know.
23. Hospitals should acknowledge same-sex partners equally to any other next of kin.
24. LGB people deserve the hatred they receive.
25. It is important to teach children positive attitudes toward LGB people.
26. I conceal my positive attitudes toward LGB people when I am with someone who is homophobic.
27. Health benefits should be available equally to same-sex partners as to any other couple.
28. It is wrong for courts to make child custody decisions based on a parent's sexual orientation.

Scoring:

Hate = 4, 24, 8, 14, 9, 18
Knowledge = 20, 10, 16, 5, 1
Civil Rights = 27, 23, 11, 28, 25
Religious Conflict = 26, 12, 22, 7, 3, 13, 2
Internalized Affirmativeness = 19, 15, 17, 6, 21

There are no reverse-scored items. Subscale scores are obtained by averaging ratings on items receiving a response for each participant. Thus, if Item 19 is not rated by a specific respondent, only the remaining four items on the Internalized Affirmativeness subscale are used to obtain the average, and so on. This method ensures comparable scores when there are missing data.

[a]The 6-point rating scale follows each of the items.

Sexual Correlates of Female Homosexual Experience

ERICH GOODE,[1] *State University of New York at Stony Brook*

Goode and Haber (1977) investigated whether and to what extent college women who have engaged in homosexual behavior have had different sexual experiences than those who have not engaged in such behavior. Hence, setting aside the direction of causality, whether the respondent *engaged in* versus *did not engage in* homosexual or lesbian experiences was taken as the "independent" variable. We used a questionnaire that consisted of 66 questions about a wide variety and range of sexual behaviors and experiences. These included age of first heterosexual intercourse, total number of sexual partners, sex partners with whom the respondent was not in love, experiences with fellatio and heterosexual cunnilingus, types of sexual experiences with a woman, age of the respondent when she first engaged in homosexual experience, whether she engaged in masturbation and how often, and so on. We took the answers to these 66 questions as the "dependent" variables.

Description

We distributed the questionnaire/instrument during the spring of 1975 to all the female residents of several dormitories at the State University of New York at Stony Brook; the questionnaires were delivered on a door-to-door basis. When completed, residents sealed them in an envelope; we picked them up a week later. The response rate for the initial wave was just under 50%; the total response rate following the third and final wave was 64%, which is considered good for this type of survey. The sample *N* was 160. We consider the findings from this survey explor-

atory rather than definitive. Because the respondents were college students, their average age was between 19 and 20; no respondent was older than 23.

Among our respondents, 86% had engaged in heterosexual intercourse at least once in their lives; only 16 respondents (10%) had engaged in at least one form of homosexual experience we asked about at least once, and 9 out of the 16 had never achieved an orgasm in this fashion. We found that the homosexually experienced women had engaged in a wider range of *heterosexual* experiences, and with a substantially larger number of partners, than was true of the homosexually naive women. For instance, the modal number of men the women *with* homosexual experience had engaged in intercourse with was 2, the median was 5, and the mean was 7.4; for those *without* homosexual experience, these figures were 1, 2, and 3.6, respectively. The median age at first heterosexual intercourse for the homosexually experienced was 16.7, with a mode of 15 and a median of 16; for the homosexually inexperienced, the figures were 18.3, 17, and 17, respectively. Women *with* homosexual experience were more likely to have experienced or engaged in fellatio, heterosexual cunnilingus, loveless sex, regular self-masturbation, and fantasy during heterosexual intercourse. Women *without* homosexual experience were more likely to enjoy fellatio and rank heterosexual intercourse as the source of their most pleasurable orgasm. Attainment of orgasm in heterosexual sex (at all) was slightly more likely among homosexually experienced women, but *always or almost always* attaining orgasm during heterosexual intercourse was slightly less likely.

[1]Address correspondence to Erich Goode, 3 Washington Square Village, Apartment 3B, New York, NY 10012; e-mail: egoode2001@aol.com

In short, homosexually experienced women appeared to be more *heterosexually* experienced as well, at least at this stage of their lives. We speculated that this category includes a "mixed bag": young women who are sexual "adventurers," experimenting with a variety of sexual experiences, most of whom will go on to become exclusively heterosexual; those who will decide to have a bisexual lifestyle; and those who will come to regard themselves as lesbians. Members of the last of these categories will, in all likelihood, abandon heterosexuality activity later in their lives. Possible indicators of the last of these categories include the following: nonenjoyment of fellatio; the predominance of loveless heterosexual sex; mention of homosexual sex as the source of their most pleasurable sexual activity; and mention of women in sexual fantasies.

Response Mode and Timing

The questions were framed in the form of a forced-choice checklist or a question requesting that the respondent write out a specific answer, often a number. Most respondents needed between 30 and 60 minutes to complete the questionnaire.

Scoring

No scoring is required (see below).

Reliability and Validity

Because the study for which the instrument was developed (Goode & Haber, 1977) was descriptive and exploratory and not explanatory and definitive, we did not conduct tests of reliability, validity, and significance. We used simple percentage differences—as determined by magnitude—to determine the differences between our two categories of respondents.

Reference

Goode, E., & Haber, L. (1977). Sexual correlates of homosexual experience: An exploratory study of college women. *The Journal of Sex Research, 13,* 12–21.

Exhibit

Sexual Correlates of Female Homosexual Experience: Sexual Experience Questionnaire/Instrument

Instructions: The intent of this study is to find out what and how women feel about their own sexuality. These questions are designed as a means of understanding what women experience in their sexual relationships and activities.

It is my belief that we, as women, have been letting one another down by allowing men to define out sexuality for us. The time has come for us to speak candidly and frankly about our sexual lives. Only in this way can we know the nature of our collective experiences.

It will not be easy to shed the beliefs we were taught and expected to accept pertaining to our sexuality, but it is something we must do for ourselves and for each other.

Several hundred questionnaires will be distributed to a sample of women on the Stony Brook campus. *All returned questions will remain confidential.* There is no need to write your name on this questionnaire.

Please answer all questions honestly, completely, and seriously. Your cooperation is very much appreciated. Thank you![a]

1. Have you ever engaged in sexual intercourse with a man or a boy? (Please check one) Yes _____ No _____
   (If *no,* skip to Question 2; if *yes,* proceed to Question 1a)

   1a. Please write the age when you first engaged in sexual intercourse with a man or boy _____
   1b. Please write in the total number of men or boys with whom you have engaged in sexual intercourse _____
   1c. Have you ever engaged in sexual intercourse with a man or boy you were not in love with? Yes _____ No _____
   1d. If *yes* to Question 1c, how did you usually feel right after engaging in sexual intercourse when you were not in love? (Please check the alternative that comes closest to your feeling)
      Negative (sad, depressed, guilty, etc.) _____
      Positive (It was what I wanted to do at the time) _____
      Neutral (it didn't bother me) _____
      It depended on the man; I felt different with different men _____
      It depended on my mood at the time_____
      Other (please explain) _____
   1e. About what proportion of the time do you generally achieve orgasm during intercourse with a man? (Please check the appropriate category)
      Never _____
      Rarely (less than 10% of the time) _____

Occasionally (less than a quarter of the time but more than 10% of the time) _____

About half the time, more or less _____

Usually _____

Always or almost always _____

1f. Please estimate the total number of *times* that you have had intercourse with any boy or man. (Please write in the number)
_____

2. Have you ever engaged in fellatio with a boy or man (oral stimulation of a man's penis) *whether or not it led to his orgasm*?

Yes _____ No _____

2a. Could you estimate the number of times that you have engaged in fellatio, with any boy or man _____

2b. About what proportion of this number did your oral stimulation of a boy or a man's penis lead to his orgasm? Please estimate about what percentage of the time this happened) _____

2c. With how many boys or men have you engaged in fellatio when it did not lead to his orgasm? _____

2d. With how many men have you engaged in fellatio when it did lead to his orgasm? _____

2e. How old were you when you first engaged in fellatio with a boy or man? _____

2f. How old were you when you first engaged in fellatio when it led to his orgasm? _____

2g. Do you usually enjoy fellating a man? Yes _____ No _____

2h. Do you usually fellate a man spontaneously, or does the man usually request you to do it?

Usually spontaneously _____

At first, I was asked; later, it's usually been spontaneous _____

It depends on how much I like the man _____

I usually have to be asked to do it _____

There's no particular pattern to it _____

It's some other way (please explain) _____

3. Has a man ever engaged in cunnilingus (oral stimulation of the woman's genitals) with you? Yes _____ No _____

If *no*, have you ever wanted a man to engage in cunnilingus with you? Yes _____ No _____; if *yes*, how often has this happened and with how many men? _____; If yes, a man has engaged in cunnilingus with you, could you please estimate the total number of times that this has taken place? _____

(If *no*, a man has not engaged in cunnilingus with you, please skip to Question 4; if at least one has, please continue with Question 3a)

3a. About what proportion of the time would you say you have achieved orgasm during cunnilingus with a man? (Please check the appropriate category):

Never _____

Rarely (less than 10 % of the time) _____

Occasionally (less than a quarter of the time but more than 10% of the time) _____

About half the time, more or less _____

Usually _____

Always or almost always _____

3b. If you achieved orgasm during cunnilingus with a man less than half the time, why do you think this is so?
(Please explain) _____

3c. If a man engages in cunnilingus with you, do you usually ask him to do it or does he usually do it without you having to ask him?

I always have to ask _____

I usually have to ask _____

It depends on the man _____

It happens both ways about half the time _____

The man usually does it without my asking _____

The man always does it without my asking _____

3d. How many men have performed cunnilingus with you? _____

3e. How old were you when a man first performed cunnilingus with you? _____

3f. How old were you when a man first performed cunnilingus with you when it led to your orgasm? _____

3g. Have you ever been afraid to ask a man to perform cunnilingus with you because you thought he wouldn't like it?

Yes _____ No _____

3h. If yes, about how many times has that taken place? (Please estimate the number of times) _____

3i. If yes, with how many men have you been afraid to ask? (Please estimate the number of men) _____

4. Have you ever engaged in any of the following sexual experiences with another woman?

Nude hugging and kissing and caressing without genital contact? Yes _____ No _____

Cunnilingus? Yes _____ No_____

Mutual pubic rubbing? Yes _____ No _____

Manual genital contact? Yes _____ No _____

(If you have not engaged in any of these activities, please skip to Question 5; if you have, please proceed with Question 4a)

If you have engaged in any other sexual experiences with another woman, what were they?

(Please explain) _____

4a. Could you estimate the total number of times that you have had sexual experiences with another woman asked about in Question 4—caressing, cunnilingus, pubic rubbing, and manual genital contact? (Please write in the total number) _____

4b. About what proportion of the time have you engaged in the following activities when you have engaged in sexual experiences with another woman? (Please write in the percentage)

Nude hugging, kissing, and caressing, without genital contact _____%

Cunnilingus _____%

Mutual pubic rubbing _____%

Manual genital contact _____%

4c. How old were you when you had any of these sexual experiences with another woman? _____

4d. With how many women have you engaged in any of these experiences? _____

4e. Have you ever engaged in any of these sexual experiences with a woman, with a man present? Yes _____ No _____

4f. If so, how often has this happened? _____

4g. About what proportion of the time that you had a sexual experience with another woman did you achieve orgasm?

Never _____ Rarely_____ Occasionally _____ About half the time _____

Usually _____ Always or almost always _____

5. Have you ever masturbated yourself? Yes _____ No _____

(If no, skip to Question 6; if yes, proceed with Question 5a)

5a. How old were you when you first masturbated yourself? _____

5b. How old were you when you first masturbated yourself to orgasm? _____

5c. How frequently would you say you have masturbated yourself per month in the past year? _____

5d. About what proportion of the time would you say that you achieved orgasm when you masturbated yourself?

Never _____ Rarely _____ Occasionally _____

5e. Do you feel that masturbation is a substitute for having orgasms during sex with another person, or do you think that it is an enjoyable activity in itself? A substitute _____ Enjoyable in itself _____ Something else (Please explain) _____

6. Are some of your orgasms significantly more enjoyable than others, or are they equally enjoyable?

Some are far more enjoyable than others _____

They are about equally enjoyable _____

I have never had an orgasm _____

Something else (Please explain) _____

6a. If some of your orgasms are far more pleasurable than others, what do you think makes them this way?

(Please explain) _____

6b. Which of the following activities gives you the most pleasurable orgasm? Which one the least? Please rank all of the following activities in terms of how pleasurable your orgasms have been when you engaged in each one:

Intercourse with a man _____

Cunnilingus with a man _____

Masturbating yourself _____

A man masturbating me _____

Sexual experience with another woman _____

My orgasms are about equally enjoyable _____

I have orgasms only one way _____

I have never had an orgasm _____

Something else (Please explain) _____

7. If you fail to achieve an orgasm with a man during intercourse, are you usually:

Extremely disappointed and frustrated _____

Somewhat disappointed and frustrated _____

Indifferent; if it happens, it happens, if it doesn't, it doesn't _____

I usually feel some other way (Please explain) _____

8. How do you know you are having an orgasm? What are the signs? What happens to your body or mind that tells you that you are having an orgasm? (Please explain) _____

9. Are there any sexual activities that you have not participated in but you would like to try? Yes _____ No _____

   If yes, what are they? (Write it/them out) _____

10. When you've been in bed with another person, have there been times when you would have liked to engage in a certain activity but didn't because you were afraid to ask your partner? Yes _____ No _____

    If yes, what were they? (Please explain) _____

11. When you have been in bed with someone for the first time, have you ever felt reluctant to take off your clothes, or to have your partner take off your clothes, because you were afraid the other person might not like your body? Yes _____ No _____

12. About how many orgasms per week do you feel is ideal for yourself? _____

13. In the best of all possible worlds, how often would you engage in sexual activity each week? _____

14. Do you fantasize during sex, any form of sex? Yes _____ No _____

15. When you have sex, any form of sex, and have an orgasm, do you feel that one orgasm is satisfying for the next few hours, or do you feel that you would like to have more than one?

    One is usually satisfying _____

    I usually would like to have more than one _____

    It depends _____ (If it depends, what does it depend on? _____)

    Something else (Please explain) _____

    I rarely or never have orgasms _____

16. If you could have things more or less exactly the way you wanted sexually, what would they be like? How would you change your life? What would your sex life be like? _____

17. What is your age? _____

18. What is your grandparents' religion? _____

19. How religious would you say you are?

    Very religious _____

    Somewhat religious _____

    Not very religious _____

    I'm not religious at all _____

20. Father's education: _____ Mother's education: _____

21. Race: Black _____ White _____ Asian _____ Latino _____

    Other (Please write in your race if it is Other) _____

22. How influential do you feel your parents are now in your life? (Check one)

    Very influential now _____

    Somewhat influential now _____

    Not very influential now _____

    Not at all influential now _____

23. Have you ever smoked marijuana? Yes _____ No _____

24. During the past six months or so, how often would you estimate that you have smoked marijuana?

    Not at all _____

    Less than monthly _____

    More than monthly but less than weekly _____

    About once a week _____

    Several times a week _____

    Daily or so _____

    More than once a day _____

25. Are there any questions that we should have asked in this questionnaire but didn't? _____

[a] The original introductory instructions were written by Goode's collaborator, Lynn Haber.

Attitudes Toward Lesbians and Gay Men Scale

GREGORY M. HEREK[1] AND KEVIN A. MCLEMORE, *University of California at Davis*

The Attitudes Toward Lesbians and Gay Men (ATLG) Scale is a brief measure of heterosexuals' attitudes toward gay men and lesbians. The original scale consisted of 20 different statements, 10 about gay men (ATG subscale) and 10 about lesbians (ATL subscale), to which respondents indicated their level of agreement or disagreement. Shorter versions have subsequently been developed, consisting of ATG and ATL subscales with parallel versions of 3, 4, or 5 items. These shorter versions have been found to be highly correlated with the original, longer subscales (e.g., *r*s > .95 between 5-item versions of the ATG and ATL and their 10-item counterparts), and their use is now recommended instead of the original subscales.

Response Mode and Timing

The ATLG can be self-administered (presented on paper or on a computer) or administered orally (as in a telephone survey). When presented visually, scale items are typically accompanied by a 5-, 7-, or 9-point Likert-type scale with anchor points of *Strongly Disagree* and *Strongly Agree*. When administered orally during telephone or face-to-face interviews, four response options are usually offered (*Strongly Disagree, Disagree Somewhat, Agree Somewhat, Strongly Agree*), and respondents are allowed to volunteer a middle response (e.g., "Neither Agree nor Disagree"). Completion time is roughly 30–60 seconds per item.

Scoring

Scoring is accomplished by assigning numerical values to the response options (e.g., for a 7-point response format, 1 = *Strongly Disagree*, 7 = *Strongly Agree*) and summing across items for each subscale. Some items are reverse scored as indicated below. For ease of interpretation, the sum of item values can be divided by the total number of items to yield a score that matches the response scale metric. The possible range of scores depends on the response scale used.

Scores on the original ATL and ATG subscales, which are based on responses to differently worded items, were not directly comparable. Researchers wishing to compare respondents' attitudes toward gay men with their attitudes toward lesbians were advised to use parallel forms of one subscale (usually the ATG items). The use of such parallel forms (with each item presented once in reference to gay men and once in reference to lesbians) is now recommended for all ATLG scale users, as shown in the Exhibit.

Reliability and Validity

The ATLG subscales have high levels of internal consistency. When self-administered, α > .85 with most college student samples and α > .80 with most nonstudent adult samples. For telephone surveys with oral administration to adult samples, α > .80 for 5-item versions and α > .70 for 3-item versions. Test-retest reliability (*r*s > .80) has been demonstrated with alternate forms (Herek, 1988, 1994).

Scores on the ATLG subscales are reliably correlated with other theoretically relevant constructs (e.g., Herek, 1994, 2009; Herek & Capitanio, 1996, 1999a). Higher scores are associated with high religiosity, lack of interpersonal contact with gay men and lesbians, adherence to traditional gender-role attitudes, belief in a traditional family ideology, and endorsement of policies that discriminate against sexual minorities. In addition, ATG scores are reliably correlated with AIDS-related stigma.

The ATLG's discriminant validity also has been established. Members of lesbian and gay organizations scored at the extreme positive end of the range, and nonstudent adults who publicly supported a gay rights ballot measure scored significantly lower on the ATLG than did community residents who publicly opposed the initiative (Herek, 1988, 1994).

Administration in Other Languages and Outside the United States

Although the ATLG was originally developed for administration to English-speaking heterosexual adults in the United States, it has also been used in research conducted in England (Hegarty, 2002) and Canada (Mohipp & Morry, 2004), and translated versions have been administered in the Netherlands (Meerendonk, Eisinga, & Felling, 2003), Singapore (Detenber et al., 2007), Brazil (DeSouza, Solberg, & Elder, 2007), Chile (Cardenas & Barrientos, 2008; Nierman, Thompson, Bryan, & Mahaffey, 2007), and Turkey (Gelbal & Duyan, 2006). In addition, a Spanish-language version was created for a study of California adults of Mexican descent (Herek & Gonzalez-Rivera, 2006). In these studies, scale reliability has been consistently acceptable (typically, α > .80), and the patterns of correlations between ATLG scores and theoretically related constructs have been similar to those obtained with U.S. English-speaking samples.

[1]Address correspondence to Gregory Herek, Department of Psychology, University of California, Davis, CA 95616-8686; e-mail through http://psychology.ucdavis.edu/Herek/

Other Information

Item order effects have been observed among heterosexual males in telephone surveys, which may indicate a gender-linked pattern in heterosexuals' attitudes (Herek, 2002; Herek & Capitanio, 1999b). For more information about the ATLG's development and usage, see Herek (1994, 2009). Researchers need not obtain the author's permission to use the ATLG in not-for-profit research that is consistent with the American Psychological Association's Ethical Principles of Psychologists.

References

Cardenas, M., & Barrientos, J. (2008). The Attitudes Toward Lesbians and Gay Men Scale (ATLG): Adaptation and testing the reliability and validity in Chile. *The Journal of Sex Research, 45,* 140–149.

DeSouza, E., Solberg, J., & Elder, C. (2007). A cross-cultural perspective on judgments of woman-to-woman sexual harassment: Does sexual orientation matter? *Sex Roles, 56,* 457–471.

Detenber, B., Cenite, M., Ku, M., Ong, C., Tong, H., & Yeow, M. (2007). Singaporeans' attitudes toward lesbians and gay men and their tolerance of media portrayals of homosexuality. *International Journal of Public Opinion Research, 19,* 367–379.

Gelbal, S., & Duyan, V. (2006). Attitudes of university students toward lesbians and gay men in Turkey. *Sex Roles, 55,* 573–579.

Hegarty, P. (2002). "It's not a choice, it's the way we're built": Symbolic beliefs about sexual orientation in the US and Britain. *Journal of Community and Applied Social Psychology, 12,* 153–166.

Herek, G. M. (1988). Heterosexuals' attitudes toward lesbians and gay men: Correlates and gender differences. *The Journal of Sex Research, 25,* 451–477.

Herek, G. M. (1994). Assessing heterosexuals' attitudes toward lesbians and gay men: A review of empirical research with the ATLG scale. In B. Greene & G. M. Herek (Eds.), *Lesbian and gay psychology: Theory, research, and clinical applications* (pp. 206–228). Thousand Oaks, CA: Sage.

Herek, G. M. (2002). Gender gaps in public opinion about lesbians and gay men. *Public Opinion Quarterly, 66,* 40–66.

Herek, G. M. (2009). Sexual stigma and sexual prejudice in the United States: A conceptual framework. In D. A. Hope (Ed.), *Contemporary perspectives on lesbian, gay and bisexual identities: The 54th Nebraska Symposium on Motivation* (pp. 65–111). New York: Springer.

Herek, G. M., & Capitanio, J. (1996). "Some of my best friends": Intergroup contact, concealable stigma, and heterosexuals' attitudes toward gay men and lesbians. *Personality and Social Psychology Bulletin, 22,* 412–424.

Herek, G. M., & Capitanio, J. (1999a). AIDS stigma and sexual prejudice. *American Behavioral Scientist, 42,* 1130–1147.

Herek, G. M., & Capitanio, J. (1999b). Sex differences in how heterosexuals think about lesbians and gay men: Evidence from survey context effects. *The Journal of Sex Research, 36,* 348–360.

Herek, G. M., & Gonzalez-Rivera, M. (2006). Attitudes toward homosexuality among U.S. residents of Mexican descent. *The Journal of Sex Research, 43,* 122–135.

Meerendonk, B. van de, Eisinga, R., & Felling, A. (2003). Application of Herek's Attitudes Toward Lesbians and Gay Men Scale in the Netherlands. *Psychological Reports, 93,* 265–275.

Mohipp, C., & Morry, M. (2004). The relationship of symbolic beliefs and prior contact to heterosexuals' attitudes toward gay men and lesbian women. *Canadian Journal of Behavioural Science, 36,* 36–44.

Nierman, A. J., Thompson, S., Bryan, A., & Mahaffey, A. (2007). Gender role beliefs and attitudes toward lesbians and gay men in Chile and the U.S. *Sex Roles, 57,* 61–67.

Exhibit

Attitudes Toward Lesbians and Gay Men Scale, Revised 5-Item Version

Attitudes Toward Gay Men (ATG-R-S5) Subscale

1. Sex between two men is just plain wrong.[*]
2. I think male homosexuals are disgusting.[*]
3. Male homosexuality is a natural expression of sexuality in men.[*] (Reverse scored)
4. Male homosexuality is a perversion.
5. Male homosexuality is merely a different kind of lifestyle that should not be condemned. (Reverse scored)

Attitudes Toward Lesbians (ATL-R-S5) Subscale

1. Sex between two women is just plain wrong.[*]
2. I think female homosexuals (lesbians) are disgusting.[*]
3. Female homosexuality is a natural expression of sexuality in women.[*] (Reverse scored)
4. Female homosexuality is a perversion.
5. Female homosexuality is merely a different kind of lifestyle that should not be condemned. (Reverse scored)

[*]This item is included in the 3-item version (ATLG-R) of the subscale.

Attitudes Toward Lesbians and Gay Men Scale: Spanish-Language Version

Attitudes Toward Gay Men (ATG)

1. Las relaciones sexuales entre dos hombres simplemente están mal. [Sex between two men is just plain wrong.]
2. Yo pienso que los hombres homosexuales son repugnantes. [I think that male homosexuals are disgusting.]

3. La homosexualidad masculina es una expresión natural de la sexualidad del hombre. [Male homosexuality is a natural expression of sexuality in men.]

4. La homosexualidad masculina es una perversión. [Male homosexuality is a perversion.]

Attitudes Toward Lesbians (ATL)

1. Las relaciones sexuales entre dos mujeres simplemente están mal. [Sex between two women is just plain wrong.]

2. Yo pienso que las lesbianas son repugnantes. [I think that lesbians are disgusting.]

3. La homosexualidad femenina es una expresión natural de la sexualidad de la mujer. [Female homosexuality is a natural expression of sexuality in women.]

4. La homosexualidad femenina es una perversión. [Female homosexuality is a perversion.]

Note. The Spanish-language version was adapted for use by Herek and Gonzales-Rivera (2006).

Component Measure of Attitudes Toward Homosexuality

MARY E. KITE,[1] *Ball State University*

Researchers have demonstrated that attitudes toward gay men and lesbians are multidimensional and that, to fully understand antigay prejudice, these different aspects of people's attitudes and perceptions should be considered (see Kite & Whitley, 1996; LaMar & Kite, 1998). Because attitudes toward homosexuality can serve different functions for different people (Herek, 1986), antigay prejudice can best be understood by considering these differing perspectives. One attitude component reflects the general belief that homosexuality violates traditional values, for example, whereas another component reflects the possibility that people fear contact with gays and lesbians in general or sexual advances from a same-sex other specifically. These attitudes are separate from the stereotypic beliefs people hold about gay men and women and from people's tendency to support or deny gay men and lesbians' civil rights.

Description

To construct this measure, established measures of attitudes toward homosexuality, summarized in Beere (1990), were reviewed. Initially, 174 items were selected that conceptually represented five components of attitudes toward homosexuality: Civil Rights, Condemnation/Tolerance, Contact, Morality, and Stereotypes. These items were categorized by component, and overlapping items were eliminated. For those categories not well represented by previous measures, new items were written.

A sample of 270 college students completed the measure, and their responses were analyzed using a varimax factor analysis. Results revealed five factors that accounted for 56.8% of the variance. Most parallel items for lesbians and gay men loaded on the same factor; the exception was that the gay male and lesbian contact items emerged as separate factors. Contrary to expectations, civil rights did not emerge as a separate factor. Rather, those items loaded on the Condemnation/Tolerance factor, thereby resulting in four final components.

The final measure consists of 91 items assessing attitudes toward gay men and lesbians. Of these, 42 items address attitudes toward gay men and 42 parallel items address attitudes toward lesbians. An additional seven items refer to homosexuality or same-sex interactions (and do not vary by sex of target). Number of items per subscale and Cronbach's alpha, based on LaMar and Kite (1998), are as follows: Gay Male Condemnation/Tolerance (11 items; alpha = .92); Lesbian Condemnation/Tolerance (11 items; alpha = .89); Gay Male Morality (10 items; alpha = .92); Lesbian Morality (10 items; alpha = .93); Neutral Morality (3 items; alpha = .80); Gay Male Contact (14 items; alpha = .96); Lesbian Contact (14 items; alpha = .95); Neutral Contact (4 items; alpha = .75); Gay Male Stereotypes (7 items; alpha = .78); Lesbian Stereotypes (7 items; alpha = .75). This measure was developed using a college student sample; however, it can be used with any population.

Response Mode and Timing

Participants evaluate these items using a 5-point Likert scale ranging from 1, *Strongly Agree*, to 5, *Strongly*

[1]Address correspondence to Mary E. Kite, Department of Psychological Science, Ball State University, Muncie, IN 47306; e-mail: mkite@bsu.edu

TABLE 1
Correlations Among Subscales of Component Measure of Attitudes Toward Homosexuality

	Gay Condemnation-Tolerance	Lesbian Condemnation-Tolerance	Gay Morality	Lesbian Morality	Gay Contact	Lesbian Contact	Neutral Contact	Gay Stereotypes	Lesbian Stereotypes
Gay Condemnation-Tolerance		.90	.83	.75	.83	.55	.46	.62	.61
Lesbian Condemnation-Tolerance			.79	.79	.78	.67	.50	.62	.63
Gay Morality				.91	.85	.64	.58	.63	.61
Lesbian Morality					.76	.75	.59	.62	.63
Gay Contact						.61	.67	.60	.56
Lesbian Contact							.63	.54	.54
Neutral Contact								.42	.42
Gay Stereotypes									.79
N	263	264	264	264	263	263	264	264	264

Note. All correlations are significant at $p < .001$. Reprinted from LaMar and Kite (1998), Table 2, with permission from Taylor & Francis.

Disagree. It is recommended that the item order be randomized and parallel items not appear contiguously on the measure. At administration, items from the four factors can be intermixed. However, each factor can be used as a standalone instrument to assess a specific component of attitudes toward homosexuality. The instrument takes approximately 15 minutes to complete.

Scoring

Subscales are created for each of the 10 factors by first reverse scoring items that are worded negatively. Items that are reverse scored are marked on the instrument (see the Exhibit). Subscale scores are then created by averaging participants' ratings on the items. LaMar and Kite (1998) reported correlations among the subscales. Correlations between the gay male and lesbian versions of the subscales are high for Condemnation/Tolerance ($r = .90$) and Morality ($r = .91$) and smaller for Contact and Stereotype (see Table 1).

Reliability

Information concerning the internal consistency of the subscales is presented in the description of the development of the scale (see above). Additional information is provided in Table 1. Test-retest reliability of the measure has not been established.

Validity

To establish validity of the factors, LaMar and Kite (1998) compared mean subscale scores for each target sex for male and female respondents. Results showed that men evaluated gay men more negatively than they evaluated lesbians on both the Condemnation/Tolerance and the Morality subscales. On these two subscales, women respondents evaluated gay men and lesbians similarly. For the Contact subscale, men rated contact with gay men more negatively than contact with lesbians, and women rated contact with lesbians more negatively than contact with gay men. There were no sex of respondent differences on the Stereotype subscale, but gay men were evaluated more negatively than lesbians on that subscale. These results provide support for the idea that attitudes toward homosexuality are multidimensional.

Whitley (1999) found that, averaged across two samples, the Stereotype subscale (for gay men and lesbians combined) was correlated with Right-Wing Authoritarianism (Altemeyer, 1988; $r = .44$) and Social Dominance Orientation (Pratto, Sidanius, Stallworth, & Malle, 1994; $r = .37$) but was unrelated to affective responses to gays and lesbians ($r = -.14$). Wilkinson (2006) reported correlations between subscales assessing attitudes toward lesbians and attitudes toward gender roles. Specifically, he found the Attitude Toward Women Scale (AWS; Spence & Hahn, 1997) was correlated with the Contact subscale ($r = .41$), the Morality subscale ($r = .47$), and the Stereotype subscale ($r = .43$). He also reported that Hostile Sexism (HS), as assessed by the Ambivalent Sexism Inventory (ASI; Glick & Fiske, 1996), was correlated with the Contact ($r = .26$), Morality ($r = .30$), and Stereotype ($r = .44$) subscales. Benevolent Sexism (BS), as assessed by the ASI, was correlated with the Contact ($r = .35$), Morality ($r = .37$), and Stereotype ($r = .43$) subscales. Finally, he reported that the Benevolence Toward Men (BM) subscale of the Ambivalence Toward Men Inventory (Glick & Fiske, 1999) correlated with the Contact ($r = .47$), Morality ($r = .47$), and Stereotype ($r = .54$) subscales. Similar relationships between HS and BM are reported in Wilkinson (2008).

References

Altemeyer, B. (1988). *Enemies of freedom: Understanding right-wing authoritarianism.* San Francisco: Jossey-Bass.

Beere, C. A. (1990). *Sex and gender issues: A handbook of tests and measures.* New York: Greenwood Press.

Glick, P., & Fiske, S. T. (1996). The Ambivalent Sexism Inventory: Differentiating hostile and benevolent sexism. *Journal of Personality and Social Psychology, 127,* 199–208.

Glick, P., & Fiske, S. T. (1999). The Ambivalence Toward Men Inventory:

Differentiating hostile and benevolent sexism toward men. *Psychology of Women Quarterly, 23,* 519–536.

Herek, G. M. (1986). The instrumentality of attitudes: Toward a neofunctional theory. *Journal of Social Issues, 42*(2), 99–114.

Kite, M. E., & Whitley, B. E., Jr. (1996). Sex differences in attitudes toward homosexual persons, behavior, and civil rights. *Personality and Social Psychology Bulletin, 22,* 336–353.

LaMar, L., & Kite, M. E. (1998). Sex differences in attitudes toward gay men and lesbians: A multi-dimensional perspective. *The Journal of Sex Research, 35,* 189–196.

Pratto, F., Sidanius, J., Stallworth, L. M., & Malle, B. F. (1994). Social dominance orientation: A personality variable predicting social and political attitudes. *Journal of Personality and Social Psychology, 67,* 741–763.

Spence, J. T., & Hahn, E. D. (1997). The Attitudes Toward Women Scale and attitude change in college students. *Psychology of Women Quarterly, 21,* 17–34.

Whitley, B. E., Jr. (1999). Right-wing authoritarianism, social dominance orientation, and prejudice. *Journal of Personality and Social Psychology, 77,* 126–134.

Wilkinson, W. W. (2006). Exploring heterosexual women's anti-lesbian attitudes. *Journal of Homosexuality, 51*(2), 139–155.

Wilkinson, W. W. (2008). Threatening the patriarchy: Testing an explanatory paradigm of anti-lesbian attitudes. *Sex Roles, 59,* 512–520.

Exhibit

Component Measure of Attitudes Toward Homosexuality

Record your responses to each item using the following scale:

1	2	3	4	5
Strongly Agree				Strongly Disagree

Condemnation/Tolerance

1. Apartment complexes should not accept lesbians (gay men) as renters.
2. Lesbians (gay men) should be required to register with the police department where they live.
3. Lesbians (gay men) should not be allowed to hold responsible positions.
4. Job discrimination against lesbians (gay men) is wrong.*
5. Lesbians (gay men) are a danger to young people.
6. Lesbians (gay men) are more likely to commit deviant acts such as child molestation, rape, voyeurism (peeping Toms) than are heterosexuals.
7. Lesbians (gay men) dislike members of the opposite sex.
8. Finding out an artist was a gay man (lesbian) would have no effect on my appreciation of his (her) work.*
9. Lesbians (gay men) should be allowed to serve in the military.*
10. Lesbians (gay men) should not be discriminated against because of their sexual preference.*
11. Lesbians (gay men) should not be allowed to work with children.

Gay Male/Lesbian Social Norms/Morality

1. The increasing acceptance of gay men (lesbians) in our society is aiding in the deterioration of morals.
2. Gay men (lesbians) endanger the institution of the family.
3. Many gay men (lesbians) are very moral and ethical people.*
4. Gay male (lesbian) couples should be able to adopt children the same as heterosexual couples.*
5. The idea of marriages between gay men (lesbians) seems ridiculous to me.
6. State laws regulating private, consenting behavior between gay men (lesbians) should be loosened.*
7. Gay men (lesbians) just can't fit into our society.
8. Gay men (lesbians) do need psychological treatment.
9. Gay men (lesbians) are a viable part of our society.*
10. Homosexual behavior between two men (women) is just plain wrong.

Neutral Morality

1. Homosexuality, as far as I am concerned, is not sinful.*
2. Homosexuality is a perversion.
3. I find the thought of homosexual acts disgusting.

Gay Male/Lesbian Contact

1. I enjoy the company of gay men (lesbians).*
2. It would be upsetting to me to find out I was alone with a gay man (lesbian).

3. I avoid gay men (lesbians) whenever possible.
4. I would feel nervous being in a group of gay men (lesbians).
5. I think gay men (lesbians) are disgusting.
6. I would enjoy attending social functions at which gay men (lesbians) were present.*
7. Bars that cater solely to gay men (lesbians) should be placed in a specific and known part of town.
8. I would feel comfortable working closely with a gay man (lesbian).*
9. If a gay man (lesbian) approached me in a public restroom, I would be disgusted.
10. I would not want a gay man (lesbian) to live in the house next to mine.
11. Two gay men (lesbians) holding hands or displaying affection in public is revolting.
12. I would be nervous if a gay man (lesbian) sat next to me on a bus.
13. I would decline membership in an organization if I found out it had gay male (lesbian) members.
14. If I knew someone was a gay male (lesbian), I would go ahead and form a friendship with that individual.*

Neutral Contact

1. If a member of my sex made advances toward me, I would feel angry.
2. I would feel comfortable knowing I was attractive to members of my sex.*
3. I would be comfortable if I found myself attracted to a member of my sex.*
4. I would feel uncomfortable if a member of my sex made an advance toward me.

Gay Male/Lesbian Stereotypes

1. Lesbians (gay men) prefer to take roles (passive or aggressive) in their sexual behavior.
2. The love between two lesbians (gay men) is quite different from the love between two persons of the opposite sex.
3. Lesbians (gay men) have weaker sex drives than heterosexuals.
4. A lesbian's (gay man's) mother is probably very domineering.
5. Most lesbians (gay men) have a life of one-night stands.
6. Most lesbians (gay men) like to dress in opposite-sex clothing.
7. Most lesbians (gay men) have identifiable masculine (feminine) characteristics.

*Items reverse scored.

Gay Peer Crowds Questionnaire

BETTY S. LAI,[1] *University of Miami*
BRIAN L. B. WILLOUGHBY, *Massachusetts General Hospital and Harvard Medical School*
NATHAN D. DOTY, *Children's Hospital of Philadelphia*
NEENA M. MALIK, *University of Miami Miller School of Medicine*

The Gay Peer Crowds Questionnaire (GPCQ) assesses self-identified gay men's affiliations with distinct subgroups that may exist within the larger gay community. Peer crowds of interest include Activist, Artsy, Bear, Circuit Partier, Drag Queen, Goth, Granola, Leather Men, Muscle Boy, Professional, Suburban, and Twink. Men are asked to give their opinions on whether these crowds exist, rate their identification with each crowd, and indicate their primary affiliation. Additional information, such as the reputation and attractiveness of each crowd, is also assessed.

Description

The GPCQ is a 23-item self-report measure. The format of the GPCQ is based upon the Peer Crowds Questionnaire, a measure of adolescents' peer crowd affiliations (La Greca, Prinstein, & Fetter, 2001; Mackey & La Greca, 2006). To examine the existence of gay peer crowds, respondents are provided with descriptions of 12 key peer crowds and asked whether they believe that each group exists. For example, men are asked, "Is there a group of gay men who are boyish-looking, with a slim or athletic figure and little

[1]Address correspondence to Betty Lai, Department of Psychology, University of Miami, P. O. Box 249229, Coral Gables, FL 33124; e-mail: bettylai10@gmail.com

body hair ('Bois/Twinks')?" Response options include *Yes*, *No*, and *Unsure*. Respondents are also asked to provide other common names for each crowd and asked to list other adult gay peer crowds in an open-ended format (i.e., "What *other* adult gay peer crowds may exist?").

To examine the degree of identification with gay peer crowds, respondents are then asked to rate the degree to which they identify with 12 peer crowds on a 5-point Likert-type scale (1 = *Not at all*, 5 = *Very Much*). In addition, participants are asked, "Which *one* of these groups, if any, do you identify with?" Participants are also asked how other groups view the individual's peer crowd on a 5-point Likert scale (1 = *Very Disliked*, 5 = *Very Liked*), whether others who are not in the group are able to identify the group (*Yes* or *No*), and whether there are symbols, behaviors, or values associated with the group (*Yes* or *No*). Affiliation with gay peer crowds is measured through five questions related to perception of peer crowds, and close social network ties to peer crowds (e.g., "Which group does your *closest gay male friend* (not including your partner) belong to?" "Which group are you *most attracted* to?" "Which group does your *relationship partner* belong to?").

Several steps were involved in developing the GPCQ. First, a preliminary list of gay subcommunities was generated from the limited empirical data available in this area (i.e., Clausell & Fiske, 2005; Peacock, Eyre, Quinn, & Kegeles, 2001). Next, this list was given to an informal focus group of gay men and to researchers who are experts in the area of psychological research and sexuality. Each person commented on the list by providing written descriptions of the peer crowds, listing other crowds that may exist, and providing general feedback. Descriptions from the focus group and researchers were combined with definitions provided by Peacock et al. (2001) to create the final list of gay peer crowds with their descriptions.

Response Mode and Timing

Respondents are provided with a copy of the GPCQ and asked to read instructions carefully. For each question, respondents should check the box corresponding with their answer. The GPCQ was developed specifically for self-identified gay men. A full administration of the GPCQ takes approximately 10 minutes.

Scoring

Items on the GPCQ should be examined individually; that is, no summary scores need to be calculated. Some of the items are categorical in nature, whereas others (i.e., Items 14 and 16) are continuous, ranging from 1 (*Not at all*; *Very Disliked*) to 5 (*Very Much*; *Very Liked*).

Validity

The GPCQ has been implemented and examined in a large empirical investigation (Willoughby, Lai, Doty, Mackey, & Malik, 2008). In this initial study, 340 self-identified adult gay men were recruited for a web-based study. Participants ranged in age from 18 to 72 (*M* = 35.11, *SD* = 11.32). Participants were 80% Anglo-European, 7% Hispanic/Latino, 5% Asian or Pacific Islander, 2% African or Caribbean American/Canadian, 5% Mixed Ethnicity, and 1% Other. Participants were diverse with regard to highest level of education obtained (4% High School, 16% Some College, 37% Bachelor's Degree, 29% Master's Degree, 14% MD, PhD, JD or advanced degree). For all 12 peer crowds, the majority of men believe they exist. Men in the study were most certain about the existence of the following peer crowds: Drag Queens (97% yes), Bears (96% yes), Circuit Partiers (96% yes), Activists (94% yes), Twinks (93% yes), and Professionals (92% yes). Participants were less likely to endorse the existence of Granolas (22% unsure) and Goths (20% unsure).

There is initial evidence supporting the criterion validity of the GPCQ (Willoughby et al., 2008). For instance, identification with peer crowds was associated with health risk behaviors over and above the effects of age, income, and education. Greater identification with Circuit Partiers, Bears, Muscle Boys, Granolas, Goths, and Artsys was significantly associated with greater risk for at least one adverse health behavior (e.g., high-risk sexual behavior, binge drinking). For example, increased identification with the Circuit Partier peer crowd was associated with higher levels of binge drinking, club drug use, and unprotected anal sex in the past 30 days. Greater identification with Suburbans, Professionals, and Twinks, on the other hand, was associated with significantly less risk-taking behavior.

Content validity was established during the development of the GPCQ. Experts in psychological and sexuality-related research and a small sample of gay men were asked to examine the GPCQ and provide feedback about the content of the GPCQ and its representativeness in assessing gay peer crowds. Additionally, men who identified a primary peer crowd affiliation also endorsed that their friends would place them in that same crowd and noted being attracted to men from the same group. For instance, 63% of men who identified primarily as a Bear also endorsed being primarily attracted to Bears. Further, 59% of men identifying as Professionals indicated they were primarily attracted to other Professionals.

References

Clausell, E., & Fiske, S. T. (2005). When do the parts add up to the whole? Ambivalent stereotype content for gay male subgroups. *Social Cognition, 23,* 157–176.

La Greca, A. M., Prinstein, M. J., & Fetter, M. D. (2001). Adolescent peer crowd affiliation: Linkages with health-risk behaviors and close friendships. *Journal of Pediatric Psychology, 26,* 131–143.

Mackey, E. R., & La Greca, A. M. (2006). Adolescents' eating, exercise, and weight control behaviors: Does peer crowd affiliation play a role? *Journal of Pediatric Psychology, 32,* 13–23.

Peacock, B., Eyre, S. L., Quinn, S. C., & Kegeles, S. (2001). Delineating differences: Sub-communities in the San Francisco gay community. *Culture, Health, and Sexuality, 3,* 183–201.

Willoughby, L. B., Lai, B. S., Doty, N. D., Mackey, E., & Malik, N. M. (2008). Peer crowd affiliations of adult gay men: Linkages with health risk behaviors. *Psychology of Men and Masculinity, 9,* 235–247.

Exhibit

Gay Peer Crowds Questionnaire

Certain groups or "peer crowds" of gay men may exist in the United States or Canada. We'd like to ask you about whether or not *you* believe these different groups exist.

Section I. Existence of Peer Crowds

Please check the box indicating your answer.

	Yes	No	Unsure
1. Is there a group of gay men who are interested in political and social issues and promote/protest certain views and policies ("Activists")? What might be *other* names for gay men who are "Activists"? _____	☐	☐	☐
2. Is there a group of gay men who are hairy (e.g., beards) and have husky builds ("Bears")? What might be *other* names for gay men who are "Bears"? _____	☐	☐	☐
3. Is there a group of gay men who are very interested in arts, such as writing, poetry, galleries, and/or theatre performances ("Artsy")? What might be *other* names for gay men who are "Artsy"? _____	☐	☐	☐
4. Is there a group of gay men who rebel against the norm (in clothing or ideas, for example), or attempt not to conform to social ideals ("Goths/Alternatives")? What might be *other* names for gay men who are "Goths/Alternatives"? _____	☐	☐	☐
5. Is there a group of gay men who follow the club scene and go to circuit parties ("Circuit Partiers")? What might be *other* names for gay men who are "Circuit Partiers"? _____	☐	☐	☐
6. Is there a group of gay men who live in suburban areas, enjoy the comfort of home, and shy away from the gay social scene ("Suburbans")? What might be *other* names for gay men who are "Suburbans"? _____	☐	☐	☐
7. Is there a group of gay men who spend a lot of time working out and like to maintain a muscular physique ("Muscle Boys")? What might be *other* names for gay men who are "Muscle Boys"? _____	☐	☐	☐
8. Is there a group of gay men who are well educated, have white-collar jobs, and/or lead wealthy lifestyles ("Professionals")? What might be *other* names for gay men who are "Professionals"? _____	☐	☐	☐
9. Is there a group of gay men who wear leather or uniforms for social activities ("Leather Men")? What might be *other* names for gay men who are "Leather Men"? _____	☐	☐	☐
10. Is there a group of gay men who dress up and/or perform as women ("Drag Queens")? What might be *other* names for gay men who are "Drag Queens"? _____	☐	☐	☐
11. Is there a group of gay men who are concerned about the environment and nature, liberal in political beliefs, and/or vegetarian, vegan, or have other dietary restrictions ("Granola")? What might be *other* names for gay men who are "Granola"? _____	☐	☐	☐
12. Is there a group of gay men who are boyish-looking, with a slim or athletic figure and little body hair ("Bois/Twinks")? What might be *other* names for gay men who are "Bois/Twinks"? _____	☐	☐	☐

13. What *other* adult gay peer crowds may exist? (please list) _____

Section II. Self-Identification

Please check the box indicating your answer.

14. How much *do you identify* with the:

	Not at All 1	 2	Somewhat 3	 4	Very Much 5
Activists	☐	☐	☐	☐	☐
Bears	☐	☐	☐	☐	☐
Artsy	☐	☐	☐	☐	☐
Goths/Alternatives	☐	☐	☐	☐	☐
Circuit Partiers	☐	☐	☐	☐	☐
Suburbans	☐	☐	☐	☐	☐
Muscle Boys	☐	☐	☐	☐	☐
Professionals	☐	☐	☐	☐	☐

	Very Disliked	Moderately Disliked	Neutral	Moderately Liked	Very Liked
Leather Men	☐	☐	☐	☐	☐
Drag Queens	☐	☐	☐	☐	☐
Granolas	☐	☐	☐	☐	☐
Bois/Twinks	☐	☐	☐	☐	☐

15. Which *one* of these groups, if any, do you identify with? (Select one that fits you best)

Activists	☐
Bears	☐
Artsy	☐
Goths/Alternatives	☐
Circuit Partiers	☐
Suburbans	☐
Muscle Boys	☐
Professionals	☐
Leather Men	☐
Drag Queens	☐
Granolas	☐
Twinks	☐
None/Average	☐

	Very Disliked	Moderately Disliked	Neutral	Moderately Liked	Very Liked
16. How is *your group* treated by most other gay men? (Select one)	☐	☐	☐	☐	☐

17. Can *your group* be identified by other gay men who are not part of your group? Yes ☐ No ☐

18. Does *your group* have symbols (e.g., certain clothes), behaviors (e.g., hanging out at similar places), or values (e.g., believe in same things)? Yes ☐ No ☐

Section III. Group Affiliation

Please select one group for each column.

	19. Which one of these groups, if any, would you *most like to be a part of?*	20. Which one of these groups would *your friends say you are most similar to?*	21. Which group does your *closest gay male friend* (not including your partner) belong to?	22. Which group are you *most attracted to?*	23. Which group does your *relationship partner* belong to?
Activists	☐	☐	☐	☐	☐
Bears	☐	☐	☐	☐	☐
Artsy	☐	☐	☐	☐	☐
Goths/Alternatives	☐	☐	☐	☐	☐
Circuit Partiers	☐	☐	☐	☐	☐
Suburbans	☐	☐	☐	☐	☐
Muscle Boys	☐	☐	☐	☐	☐
Professionals	☐	☐	☐	☐	☐
Leather Men	☐	☐	☐	☐	☐
Drag Queens	☐	☐	☐	☐	☐
Granolas	☐	☐	☐	☐	☐
Twinks	☐	☐	☐	☐	☐
None/Average	☐	☐	☐	☐	☐

Power Sharing in Lesbian Partnerships

Jean M. Lynch,[1] *Miami University*
Mary Ellen Reilly, *University of Rhode Island*

The instrument was developed to determine egalitarianism in lesbian partnerships as a function of similarity in social status variables. Specifically, it investigates whether couples who are similar in age, income, occupation, education, and financial assets tend to characterize their relationships as equal in a variety of areas. Previous researchers have typically investigated one partner's perception of power in the relationship (e.g., Blood & Wolfe, 1960; Peplau et al., 1982). Our instrument is designed to assess similarities and differences in each partner's assets so that it can be determined whether differences in these demographic variables are related to social status. Additionally, our instrument allows a determination of whether type of couple (i.e., equal, unequal but in agreement about who has more power, and couples with differing perceptions about power sharing) is related to social status variables.

Description

The power sharing instrument consists of demographic items, such as respondent's age as of the last birthday, income, educational attainment, occupation and occupational classification, and several items which assess the respondent's assets. A number of items also investigate financial sharing by partners, such as whether the couple are cosignatories on saving and checking accounts, and whether the partner is a sole or partial beneficiary. Respondents also indicate how financial contributions in the household are divided, such as whether the respondent or her partner pays, or whether equal or proportional payments are made for a variety of household needs.

The remainder of the questionnaire measures egalitarianism in a variety of areas. Specifically, these items refer to responsibility for household chores and financial decision making. Three items query respondents regarding sexual equality in terms of initiation, decisions about the frequency of sex, and sexual satisfaction. As above, responses to the items indicate whether respondents are equal or whether the partner or respondent has more control in the relationship.

Finally, single items ask respondents about a number of issues related to equality, for example, self-disclosure, degree of commitment, and yielding in disagreements. Potential responses indicate whether the respondent or her partner or both tend to dominate in these areas. Two items, ideal and actual power (i.e., who has more say and who should have more say) are included from Peplau, Cochran, Rook, and Padesky's (1978) instrument.

Reliability and Validity

No reliablity data are available. The instrument evidences face and content validity, covering the areas most significant to power in relationships. Results from studies using the instrument (e.g., Lynch & Reilly, 1986; Peplau et al., 1978; Peplan et al., 1982; Reilly & Lynch, 1990) indicate considerable consistency across diverse samples (college and adult populations in relationships of at least 1 year's duration). For both populations, respondents professed a belief in the importance of power sharing, and there was evidence of a great deal of egalitarianism in lesbian relationships. When inequity was found, power sharing arrangements did not seem to be explained by social status differences.

References

Blood, R. O., & Wolfe, D. M. (1960). *Husbands and wives*. Glencoe, IL: Free Press.

Lynch, J., & Reilly, M. E. (1985–1986). Role relationships: Lesbian perspectives. *Journal of Homosexuality, 12*(2), 53–69.

Peplau, L., Cochran, S., Rook, K., & Padesky, C. (1978). Loving women: Attachment and autonomy in lesbian relationships. *Journal of Social Issues, 34*(3), 7–27.

Peplau, L., Padesky, C., & Hamilton, M. (1982). Satisfaction in lesbian relationships. *Journal of Social Homosexuality, 8*(2), 23–35.

Reilly, M. E., & Lynch, J.M. (1990). Power-sharing in lesbian partnerships. *Journal of Homosexuality, 19*(3), 1–30.

[1]Address correspondence to Jean M. Lynch, Department of Sociology and Anthropology, Miami University, Oxford, OH 45056; e-mail: lynchjm@muohio.edu.

Exhibit

Power Sharing in Lesbian Relationships

This questionnaire is the main source of data for a study of lesbian relationships. It should only take a few minutes to complete.

Your replies will be completely anonymous since there are no identifying marks on the questionnaire. *Please do not sign the questionnaire.* It is important that each partner fills out her questionnaire separately and places it in one of the blank envelopes. Both should be returned to me together in the stamped, addressed envelope provided. Since I am studying couples, this is essential. Thank you very much for your time and cooperation.

1. What is your age as of your last birthday? _____years.
2. What is *your* income (as reported on all W-2 forms)? _____
3. Which of the following best describes your highest level of educational attainment?
   ( ) Completed grammar school
   ( ) Completed high school
   ( ) Some college or technical school
   ( ) Completed college
   ( ) Master's degree
   ( ) Ph.D., M.D., Ed.D., J.D.L.
   ( ) Other, please describe _____
4. What is your occupation? _____
5. Which of the following would you use to describe your occupation?
   ( ) Homemaker
   ( ) Professional
   ( ) Manager or Administrator
   ( ) Sales worker
   ( ) Clerical
   ( ) Craftsworker
   ( ) Farm worker
   ( ) Machinist or Transportation Worker
   ( ) Laborer
   ( ) Service worker
   ( ) Private household worker
   ( ) Other
6. What is the current worth of your *personal* financial assets? (stocks, bonds, property, cars, savings and checking accounts). Please estimate:
   ( ) $0
   ( ) $1,001–$9,999
   ( ) $10,000–$19,999
   ( ) $20,000–$34,999
   ( ) $35,000–$49,999
   ( ) $50,000–$74,999
   ( ) $75,000–$100,000 or more
7. Which of the following are currently held by you? Check all that apply.
   A ( ) Savings accounts in my name only
   B. ( ) Checking accounts in my name only
   C. ( ) Investments in my name only
   D. ( ) Joint savings accounts
   E. ( ) Joint checking accounts
   F. ( ) Investments in my name and someone else's
8. If you checked A, B, or C in Question 7 above, are the account(s) or investment(s) arranged so that your partner could manage your personal finances in the event that you were unable to do so?
   ( ) Yes
   ( ) No

9. If you checked C, E, or F in Question 7 above, is the other name on the account(s) or investment(s):

	Partner	Relative	Some other person, not related
Checking	( )	( )	( )
Savings	( )	( )	( )
Investments	( )	( )	( )

10. If you have a will, is your partner named as:
   ( ) A beneficiary of all of your estate
   ( ) A beneficiary of part of your estate
   ( ) Not mentioned in your will
   ( ) I do not have a will

11. If you have life insurance, who is your beneficiary?
   ( ) Partner
   ( ) Relative
   ( ) Some other person, not related
   ( ) Both partner and relative
   ( ) I do not have any insurance

12. If you are currently renting, and have a lease, whose name is it in?
   ( ) My name
   ( ) My partner's name
   ( ) Both of our names
   ( ) Someone else's name
   ( ) No lease

13. If you own your own home, whose name is on the mortgage title or title to the house?
   ( ) My name
   ( ) My partner's name
   ( ) My partner and I are tenants in common
   ( ) My partner and I are joint tenants

14. If you currently own a car, who paid (or is paying) for it?
   ( ) I
   ( ) My partner
   ( ) Both own it equally
   ( ) Each has her own car which she owns
   ( ) Other, please explain _____

15. In our current residence, household furnishings are:
   ( ) Predominantly mine
   ( ) Predominantly hers
   ( ) Each person owns approximately half of the furnishings
   ( ) Ours jointly

16. In your household, how are contributions to the following arranged:

	I pay	My partner pays	We split bills based on our ability to pay	We split bills equally	Included in the rent	Does not apply
A. Mortgage payments	( )	( )	( )	( )	( )	( )
B. Property taxes	( )	( )	( )	( )	( )	( )
C. Rent payments	( )	( )	( )	( )	( )	( )
D. Insurance (house or apartment)	( )	( )	( )	( )	( )	( )
E. Heating bills	( )	( )	( )	( )	( )	( )
F. Electric bills	( )	( )	( )	( )	( )	( )
G. Telephone bills	( )	( )	( )	( )	( )	( )
H. Groceries	( )	( )	( )	( )	( )	( )
I. Household repairs	( )	( )	( )	( )	( )	( )

17. Reviewing the items in Question 16 above, how would you describe your overall contributions to these household expenses?
   ( ) I contribute more
   ( ) My partner contributes more
   ( ) We contribute according to our ability to pay
   ( ) We contribute equally

18. How long have you and your partner been living together? _____ years
19. When you and your partner first began living together, whose residence did you use?
　　( ) Mine
　　( ) Partner's
　　( ) A new residence chosen by us
20. Our current residence is:
　　( ) Mine, where I lived before meeting my partner
　　( ) Hers, where she lived before meeting me
　　( ) Ours, since we met
21. Do you have children?
　　( ) Yes
　　( ) No (Please skip to Question 25)
22. How many children do you have?
　　_____ Girls
　　_____ Boys
23. Where are the children presently living? Please describe _____
24. Who is financially responsible for the support of the children?
　　( ) I am primarily responsible for their support
　　( ) Father is primarily responsible for their support
　　( ) Father and I support them equally
　　( ) Father, partner and I support them
　　( ) Partner and I support them equally
　　( ) Partner is primarily responsible for their support
　　( ) Other. Please describe _____
25. For the following items, please indicate who has the major responsibility for the following chores:

	Always I	Usually I	Partner and I exactly equal	Usually partner	Always partner	Does not apply or done by hired person
A. Cooking	( )	( )	( )	( )	( )	( )
B. Laundry	( )	( )	( )	( )	( )	( )
C. Dishwashing and cleaning up	( )	( )	( )	( )	( )	( )
D. Household repairs	( )	( )	( )	( )	( )	( )
E. Dusting and vacuuming	( )	( )	( )	( )	( )	( )
F. Housecleaning (windows, floors, cleaning drapes)	( )	( )	( )	( )	( )	( )
G. Child care	( )	( )	( )	( )	( )	( )
H. Payment of bills	( )	( )	( )	( )	( )	( )
I. Bathroom cleaning	( )	( )	( )	( )	( )	( )
J. Outdoor maintenance (e.g., washing windows, cleaning gutters, painting)	( )	( )	( )	( )	( )	( )
K. Lawn care	( )	( )	( )	( )	( )	( )
L. Gardening (flowers and vegetables)	( )	( )	( )	( )	( )	( )
M. Car repairs	( )	( )	( )	( )	( )	( )
N. Decorating	( )	( )	( )	( )	( )	( )

26. Who do you think is more involved in your relationship—your partner or you?
　　_____ Partner is much more involved
　　_____ Partner is somewhat more involved
　　_____ We are involved to exactly the same degree
　　_____ I am somewhat more involved
　　_____ I am much more involved
27. Who do you think has revealed more about herself to the other—your partner or you?
　　_____ Partner has revealed much more
　　_____ Partner has revealed somewhat more
　　_____ We have revealed exactly the same amount
　　_____ I have revealed somewhat more
　　_____ I have revealed much more
28. Who do you think has more of a say about what you and your partner do together—your partner or you?

_____ Partner has much more say
_____ Partner has somewhat more say
_____ We have exactly the same amount of say
_____ I have somewhat more say
_____ I have much more say

29. Who do you think is more satisfied in the relationship—your partner or you?
_____ Partner is much more satisfied
_____ Partner is somewhat more satisfied
_____ We are exactly equally satisfied
_____ I am somewhat more satisfied
_____ I am much more satisfied

30. Who do you think is more committed to the relationship—your partner or you?
_____ Partner is much more committed
_____ Partner is somewhat more committed
_____ We are committed to exactly the same degree
_____ I am somewhat more committed
_____ I am much more committed

31. Who do you think <u>should</u> have more of a say about what you and your partner do together—your partner or you?
_____ Partner should have much more say
_____ Partner should have somewhat more say
_____ We should have exactly equal say
_____ I should have somewhat more say
_____ I should have much more say

32. If my partner and I disagreed on political issues or candidates,
_____ Partner would definitely change her opinion
_____ Partner would probably change her opinion
_____ Neither of us would change our opinion
_____ I would probably change my opinion
_____ I would definitely change my opinion

33. When my partner and I argue,
_____ Partner always gives in first
_____ Partner usually gives in first
_____ Sometimes she gives in first, sometimes I give in first
_____ I usually give in first
_____ I always give in first

34. If my partner expressed dislike for a friend of mine,
_____ I would definitely reevaluate my opinion of the friend
_____ I would probably reevaluate my opinion of my friend
_____ Neither of us would change our opinion
_____ I would probably not reevaluate my opinion of the friend
_____ I would definitely not reevaluate my opinion of the friend

35. If your partner were offered an attractive job opportunity in another city, how likely is it that you would move with your partner?
_____ I would definitely move with my partner
_____ I would probably move with my partner
_____ Uncertain if I would move or not
_____ I would probably not move with my partner
_____ I would definitely not move with my partner

36. If you were offered an attractive job opportunity in another city, how likely is it that your partner would move with you?
_____ My partner would definitely move with me
_____ My partner would probably move with me
_____ Uncertain if my partner would move with me
_____ My partner would probably not move with me
_____ My partner would definitely not move with me

37. Who do you think takes more of the initiative in your sexual relationship?
_____ My partner takes much more of the initiative
_____ My partner takes somewhat more of the initiative
_____ We both initiate sex to exactly the same degree

_____ I take somewhat more of the initiative

_____ I take much more of the initiative

38. Who do you think makes more of the decisions about the frequency of sex?

_____ My partner makes much more of the decisions

_____ My partner makes somewhat more of the decisions

_____ We make mutual decisions

_____ I make somewhat more of the decisions

_____ I make much more of the decisions

39. Who do you think is more sexually satisfied in your relationship?

_____ My partner is much more satisfied

_____ My partner is somewhat more satisfied

_____ We are both satisfied to exactly the same degree

_____ I am somewhat more satisfied

_____ I am much more satisfied

40. For the following, please check the appropriate responses:

Who usually makes the final decision about:	Partner always	Partner more than I	Partner and I exactly equal	Usually I	Always I	Does not apply; has never been an issue
A. What car to get	( )	( )	( )	( )	( )	( )
B. Whether or not to buy life insurance	( )	( )	( )	( )	( )	( )
C. How much money to spend per week on food	( )	( )	( )	( )	( )	( )
D. Where to go on vacation	( )	( )	( )	( )	( )	( )
E. What restaurants to frequent	( )	( )	( )	( )	( )	( )
F. How to spend leisure time	( )	( )	( )	( )	( )	( )
G. Which friends to spend time with	( )	( )	( )	( )	( )	( )
H. Where to go on holidays	( )	( )	( )	( )	( )	( )
I. What house or apartment to take	( )	( )	( )	( )	( )	( )

41. Do any of the following know that you are a lesbian?

Your mother _____ Your father _____ Brothers _____ Sisters _____ Other relatives _____

Neighbors _____ Friends _____ Colleagues at work _____

42. How many friends are aware of your relationship?

All _____ Most _____ Half _____ A few _____ None _____

43. Do you and your partner participate in any lesbian organizations?

_____ Yes

_____ No

44. How often do you see your family?

Weekly _____ Monthly _____ Several times a year _____ Never _____

Identification and Involvement With the Gay Community Scale

PETER A. VANABLE,[1] DAVID J. MCKIRNAN, AND JOSEPH P. STOKES,
University of Illinois at Chicago

The Identification and Involvement with the Gay Community Scale (IGCS) is designed to measure involvement with and perceived closeness to the gay community among men who have sex with men. Although bisexually and homosexually active men are often considered to be part of the same homogeneous group, there are substantial individual differences in the extent to which these men perceive themselves to be part of a larger gay community and in the degree to which they self-identify as gay (Stokes, McKirnan, & Burzette, 1993; Vanable, McKirnan, Stokes, Taywaditep, & Burzette, 1993). The IGCS was developed to characterize these individual differences. The scale was initially developed as part of a larger research program designed to identify both individual and community level variables associated with HIV risk behavior among a heterogenous group of bisexually active men (see McKirnan, Stokes, Doll, & Burzette, 1995, for a description). Thus, although the construct tapped by this scale may be equally relevant to women who have sex with women, reliability and validity data have been gathered only for men.

Description

The scale consists of a eight self-report items. Four items require respondents to rate how much their degree of agreement with attitude statements regarding the importance of self-identifying as gay and associating with a gay community. Response options range from *completely disagree* (1) to *completely agree* (5). In previous testing of this instrument, these four questions were embedded within a larger set of questions assessing attitudes toward sexuality and AIDS. Three items tap the frequency with which respondents read a gay or lesbian newspaper, attend gay or lesbian organizational activities, and frequent gay bars. The final item assesses the overall number of gay friends in the respondent's social network.

An earlier version of this scale, focussing only on behavioral indices of involvement in the gay community, was described by Stokes et al. (1993). The present version, which includes subjective ratings of identification with the gay community, was initially tested using a face-to-face interview format in which responses were elicited by trained interviewers. In a more recent study (McKirnan & Vanable, 1995), the scale was administered using a self-report format, yielding similar psychometric properties.

Response Mode and Timing

Respondents are instructed to circle the response that most accurately describes their personal attitudes and experiences. The scale requires 2 to 3 minutes to complete.

Scoring

Prior to computing scale scores, responses to questions 5 through 8 should be converted to numeric values (A = 1, B = 2, C = 3, D = 4, E = 5). Final scale scores are obtained by computing a mean across the eight items. Item 4 must be reverse coded. Higher scores indicate more identification and involvement with the gay community.

Reliability

Reliability and validity data come from a large, diverse sample of bisexual and gay men living in the metropolitan Chicago area ($N = 750$). African-American (51%) and White (49%) respondents between the ages of 18 and 30 were recruited on the basis of specific sexual behavior criteria. During the first phase of the research, interviews were conducted with men reporting that they had both male and female partners within the past 3 years ($n = 536$). The remaining 214 men were recruited on the basis of having only male sexual partners in past 3 years. For the complete sample, 43% of respondents self-identified as bisexual, 48% self-identified as gay, and 7% self-identified as being straight (2% refused to provide a label).

The Cronbach alpha for the complete sample was .78. A subgroup of respondents ($n = 218$) completed a 1-year follow-up interview. Test-retest reliability for this subsample was .74.

Validity

In the sample described above, scores on the IGCS were positively correlated with 7-point Kinsey ratings of sexual orientation ($r = .58$, $p < .0001$) such that people with stronger involvement and identification with the gay community tended to rate themselves as more homosexual in orientation. Similarly, scores on the IGCS reliably differentiated between men who variously described their sexual orientation as either gay, bisexual, or straight ($Ms = 3.09$, 2.38, & 1.51); $F(2, 733) = 159.0$, $p < .0001$. In addition, men showing greater identification with the gay community were more "out" to others about their same-sex activity, were

[1]Address correspondence to Peter A. Vanable, Department of Psychology & Center for Health and Behavior, Syracuse University, 430 Huntington Hall, Syracuse, NY 13244; e-mail: pvanable@syr.edu

less self-homophobic, reported that their friends were more accepting of their sexual preferences, and were more oriented toward using gay bars as a social resource, $rs = .53, -.35, .56, .47, ps < .0001$. Similar construct validity data are reported by Stokes et al. (1993), using an earlier version of this scale.

Of greater theoretical interest are data linking scores on the IGCS to differences in sexual behavior with men and women, and specific practices that place homosexually active men at increased risk for HIV infection. In our sample, we found that rates of sexual behavior with men and women were directly related to differences in identification and involvement with the gay community, with high scorers on the IGCS reporting more overall sexual behavior with men and low scorers reporting more sexual behavior with women in the past 6 months (McKirnan, Vanable, & Stokes, 1995). In comparison to men who were less identified with the gay community, high scorers on the IGCS were more likely to report having had unprotected anal contact with another man. However, when the sample was restricted to only those men who had any anal sex with men in the past 6 months, these differences were eliminated. These data suggest that men showing greater identification and involvement with the gay community are at increased risk for HIV as a direct function of their being more likely to have anal sex with men at all (for a discussion of related findings, see McKirnan, Stokes, Vanable, Burzette, & Doll., 1993; Vanable et al., 1993). A reversal in this pattern occurs for behaviors with women, with lower scores on the IGCS being associated with an increased likelihood of having unprotected vaginal or anal sex with a woman in the past 6 months. Again, these differences were eliminated when the sample was limited to only those men who had some sex with women in the past 6 months.

Other Information

Support for this research was provided through Cooperative Agreement Number U64/CCU506809-02 with the Centers for Disease Control and Prevention.

References

McKirnan, D. J., Stokes, J. P., Doll, L. S., & Burzette, R. G. (1995). Bisexually active men: Social characteristics and sexual behavior. *The Journal of Sex Research, 32*, 64–75.

McKirnan, D. J., Stokes, J. P., Vanable, P. A., Burzette, R. G., & Doll, L. S. (1993, June). *Predictors of unsafe sex among bisexual men: The role of gay identification.* Poster presentation to the IX International Conference on AIDS, Berlin, Germany.

McKirnan, D. J., & Vanable, P. A. (1995). [Centers for Disease Control Collaborative HIV Sero-Incidence Study]. Unpublished raw data.

McKirnan, D. J., Vanable, P. A., & Stokes, J. P. (1995). *HIV-risk sexual behavior among bisexually active men: The role of gay identification and social norms.* Unpublished manuscript.

Stokes, J. P., McKirnan, D. J., & Burzette R. G. (1993). Sexual behavior, condom use, disclosure of sexuality, and stability of sexual orientation in bisexual men. *The Journal of Sex Research, 30*, 202–213.

Vanable, P. A., McKirnan, D. J., Stokes, J. P., Taywaditep, K. J., & Burzette, R. G. (1993, November). *Subjective sexual identification among bisexually active men: Effects on sexual behavior and sexual risk.* Paper presented at the Annual Meeting of the Society for the Scientific Study of Sex, Chicago, IL.

Exhibit

Identification and Involvement With the Gay Community Scale

Directions: This questionnaire concerns some of your general attitudes and experiences. For each question, circle the response that is most accurate for you personally. Answer the questions quickly, giving your first "gut reactions."

	Do not agree at all				Strongly agree
(1) It is very important to me that at least some of my friends are bisexual or gay.	1	2	3	4	5
(2) Being gay makes me feel part of a community.	1	2	3	4	5
(3) Being attracted to men is important to my sense of who I am.	1	2	3	4	5
(4) I feel very distant from the gay community.	1	2	3	4	5

For questions 5–7, please think in terms of the last six months or so.

(5) How often do you read a gay or lesbian oriented paper or magazine, such as the *Advocate* or other local gay/bisexual papers?

A = Never   C = Several times a month   E = Several times a week or daily
B = Once a month or less   D = About once a week

(6) How often do you attend any gay or lesbian organizational activities, such as meetings, fund-raisers, political activities, etc.?

A = Never   C = Several times a month   E = Several times a week or daily
B = Once a month or less   D = About once a week

(7) How often do you go to a gay bar?

A = Never   C = Several times a month   E = Several times a week or daily
B = Once a month or less   D = About once a week

(8) About how many gay men would you call personal friends (as opposed to casual acquaintances)?

A = None   C = 2 gay friends   E = 5 or more gay friends
B = 1 gay friend   D = 3 or 4 gay friends

Perceived Parental Reactions Scale

Brian L. B. Willoughby,[1] *Department of Psychiatry, Massachusetts General Hospital and Harvard Medical School*
Nathan D. Doty, *Department of Psychology, Children's Hospital of Philadelphia*
Ellen B. Braaten, *Department of Psychiatry, Massachusetts General Hospital and Harvard Medical School*
Neena M. Malik, *Department of Pediatrics, University of Miami Miller School of Medicine*

The Perceived Parental Reactions Scale (PPRS) assesses gay, lesbian, and bisexual (LGB) individuals' perceptions of their parents' initial reactions to their coming out. It evaluates eight theoretical dimensions of perceived parental reactions, including negative shock, denial, anger, bargaining, depression, acceptance, general homophobia, and parent-focused concerns.

Description

The PPRS is a 32-item scale wherein self-identified LGB individuals are asked to rate their mother's or father's initial reactions to their coming out. Maternal and paternal reactions are rated on separate versions of the scale, which are identical except for references to parent gender. Individuals are required to think back to the week their mother or father found out about their sexual orientation and indicate agreement or disagreement with several possible reactions (e.g., cried tears of sadness) using a 5-point Likert scale. The PPRS was developed on the basis of Weinberg's (1972) love versus conventionality theory and Savin-Williams' (2001) initial reactions model.

The scale was initially developed to assess nine theoretical dimensions of parents' initial reactions to coming out, including negative shock, denial, anger, bargaining, depression, acceptance, general homophobia, parent-focused concerns, and child-focused concerns. Four items assess each dimension. Items assessing the child-focused dimension were later removed based on the results of the initial scale development study. Child-focused items were written to address parental responses of concern for their child (e.g., "My mother was worried about my chances of finding a relationship partner"), which were initially conceptualized as positive reactions from parents. However, these items did not correlate with the PPRS total as expected and lowered overall reliability estimates (i.e., alpha) in both the mother and the father versions of the scale. The result, therefore, was a 32-item scale assessing eight theoretical dimensions of perceived parental reactions.

Response Mode and Timing

During administration, individuals are provided with copies of the mother and father versions of the PPRS, asked to read the instructions carefully, and asked to respond to each item by circling a number on a Likert scale. Respondents should complete the PPRS only if (a) they have directly disclosed their sexual orientation to a parent *or* (b) they have had direct discussion with a parent about their sexuality following the parent's discovery of their sexual orientation through other means (e.g., parent discovered gay material on the Internet, read a diary, or was told by someone else). It takes approximately 15 minutes to complete both the mother and the father versions of the PPRS.

Scoring

Before calculating the scale total, Items 1, 5, 8, and 10 are reverse scored. The PPRS total score is obtained by summing all items, with possible scores ranging from 32 to 160. Higher scores represent more negative perceived reactions from parents. Items assessing the various theoretical domains are as follows: negative shock (Items 13, 18, 23, 28), denial (Items 14, 19, 24, 29), anger (Items 15, 20, 25, 30), bargaining (Items 16, 21, 25, 31), depression (Items 17, 22, 26, 32), acceptance (Items 1, 5, 8, 10), general homophobia (Items 3, 6, 9, 11), and parent-focused concerns (Items 2, 4, 7, 12). Despite these various theoretical domains, the scale should be used as a whole, because factor analyses have not yet supported the use of individual domain scores as discrete subscales.

Reliability

The reliability of the PPRS has been examined in two independent empirical investigations. In the initial development study (Willoughby, Malik, & Lindahl, 2006), the PPRS was administered to 72 gay men (ages 18 to 26) recruited from LGB community- and university-based organizations. Participants were ethnically diverse (39% Hispanic, 39% White-Anglo European, 10% Caribbean/African American, 12% Mixed/Other). The majority of participants had completed some college or a bachelor's degree (83%), whereas others reported high school (15%) or elementary school (1%) as their highest level of education. Of the 72 respondents, 70 were out to their mothers and 45 were out to their fathers. Means and standard deviations for the PPRS total score were as follows: mother version $M = 90.16$, $SD = 35.21$; father version $M = 86.87$, $SD = 31.73$. In this study, all items on both the mother and the father versions of the PPRS showed item-total correlations of .40 or above and demonstrated good internal consistencies (mother version [$n = 70$], $\alpha = .97$; father version [$n = 45$], $\alpha = .97$). Using a subset of participants, both versions of the PPRS showed good test-retest reliability after a 14-day interval (mother version [$n = 19$], $r = .97$; father version [$n = 12$], $r = .95$).

The mother version of the PPRS was administered as part of a larger protocol examining the family and peer relationships of LGB young people. Participants included 81 young men (69%) and women (31%), who identified as gay, lesbian, bisexual, or queer. Ages ranged from 14 to 25 ($M = 19.70$, $SD = 1.76$), and the sample included young people from diverse ethnic backgrounds (54% White-Anglo European, 20% Hispanic/Latino, 14% African/Caribbean American, 6% Asian, and 6% Mixed/Other). Participants were recruited from LGB social and college groups, as well as via study advertisements and friend referrals. Of the 81 young people, 65 were out to their mother. In this sample, the mean of the PPRS total score was 89.64 ($SD = 34.37$). Similar to the development study, all items showed item-total correlations of .39 and above. Internal consistency was also adequate ($n = 65$), $\alpha = .97$.

Validity

Initial evidence supports the construct validity of the PPRS. First, as reported by Willoughby et al. (2006), gay men reporting to have grown up in families with low cohesion (i.e., family togetherness) and low adaptability (i.e., family flexibility) reported greater negativity from parents at coming out. Further, gay men who reported coming from families with authoritarian parents endorsed greater negativity from parents at coming out, compared with men who reported having authoritative or indulgent parents. Regarding convergent validity, the PPRS is related to hypothetically similar constructs. For instance, the mother version of the PPRS was highly correlated ($r = .55$, $p < .001$) with the Family Reactions subscale of the Measure of Gay Related Stressors (Lewis, Derlega, Berndt, Morris, & Rose, 2001), a measure of LGB individuals' current perceptions of family rejection due to sexual orientation. Lastly, higher scores on the mother version of the PPRS were also found to relate to higher levels of youth internalizing symptoms, school problems, and depressive symptoms, as measured by the Behavior Assessment System for Children (Reynolds & Kamphaus, 2004).

References

Lewis, R., Derlega, V., Berndt, A., Morris, L., & Rose, S. (2001). An empirical analysis of stressors for gay men and lesbians. *Journal of Homosexuality, 42,* 63–88.

Reynolds, C. R., & Kamphaus, R. W. (2004). *Behavior Assessment Scale for Children* (2nd ed.). Circle Pines, MN: AGS Publishing.

Savin-Williams, R. (2001). *Mom. Dad. I'm gay.* Washington, DC: American Psychological Association.

Weinberg, G. (1972). *Society and the healthy homosexual.* New York: Doubleday.

Willoughby, B. L. B., Malik, N. M., & Lindahl, K. L. (2006). Parental reactions to their sons' sexual orientation disclosures: The roles of family cohesion, adaptability, and parenting style. *Psychology of Men and Masculinity, 7,* 14–26.

Exhibit

Perceived Parental Reactions Scale—Mother Version

Instructions: Think only about *your mother* when filling out this questionnaire.

Think back *to the week* when your mother first became aware of your sexual orientation. Read the following statements and indicate how much you agree or disagree with each statement by circling a number. Remember, there are no correct or incorrect answers. These are your opinions.

Strongly Disagree	Disagree	Neutral	Agree	Strongly Agree[a]
1	2	3	4	5

The week when I *told* my mother I was gay/lesbian/bisexual (or when she *found out* I was gay/lesbian/bisexual) she:

1. supported me
2. was worried about what her friends and other parents would think of her
3. had the attitude that homosexual people should not work with children
4. was concerned about what the family might think of her
5. was proud of me
6. believed that marriage between homosexual individuals was unacceptable
7. was concerned about the potential that she wouldn't get grandchildren from me
8. realized I was still "me," even though I was gay/lesbian/bisexual

9. believed that homosexuality was immoral
10. thought it was great
11. would have had a problem seeing two homosexual people together in public
12. was concerned about having to answer other people's questions about my sexuality
13. kicked me out of the house
14. didn't believe me
15. yelled and/or screamed
16. prayed to God, asking him to turn me straight
17. blamed herself
18. called me derogatory names, like "faggot" or "queer"
19. pretended that I wasn't gay/lesbian/bisexual
20. was angry at the fact I was gay/lesbian/bisexual
21. wanted me not to tell anyone else
22. cried tears of sadness
23. said I was no longer her child
24. told me it was just a phase
25. was mad at someone she thought had "turned me gay/lesbian/bisexual"
26. wanted me to see a psychologist who could "make me straight"
27. was afraid of being judged by relatives and friends
28. severed financial support
29. brought up evidence to show that I must not be gay/lesbian/bisexual, such as "You had a girlfriend/boyfriend; you can't be gay/lesbian/bisexual."
30. was mad at me for doing this to her
31. wanted me not to be gay/lesbian/bisexual
32. was ashamed of my homosexuality

[a]The 5-point scale is repeated following each item.

Measure of Sexual Identity Exploration and Commitment

RACHEL L. NAVARRO, *New Mexico State University*
HOLLY BIELSTEIN SAVOY, *Charlotte, North Carolina*
ROGER L. WORTHINGTON,[1] *University of Missouri*

Identity encompasses a coherent sense of one's values, beliefs, and roles, including but not limited to gender, race, ethnicity, social class, spirituality, and sexuality. Identity development is an active process of exploring and assessing one's identity and establishing a commitment to an integrated identity. Marcia (1966) generated a four-status model for understanding ego identity development based on the processes of exploration and commitment to identity: (a) *foreclosure* (commitment without prior exploration), (b) *moratorium* (withholding commitment during the process of exploration), (c) *achievement* (commitment following exploration), and (d) *diffusion* (a lack of commitment and exploration).

Fassinger and colleagues described two models of gay and lesbian identity development that define sexual identity development as including four phases (awareness, exploration, deepening/commitment, and internalization/synthesis) conceptualized along the dimensions of individual and group membership identity (Fassinger & Miller, 1996; McCarn & Fassinger, 1996). Building upon the work of Fassinger and colleagues, Worthington, Savoy, Dillon, and Vernaglia (2002) conceptualized a developmental model of sexual identity that more broadly establishes sexual orientation identity as just one of six components of individual sexual identity (i.e., perceived sexual needs, preferred sexual activities, preferred characteristics of sexual partners,

[1]Address correspondence to Roger L. Worthington, 217 Jesse Hall, University of Missouri, Columbia, MO 65211; e-mail: WorthingtonR@missouri.edu

sexual values, recognition and identification of sexual orientation, and preferred modes of sexual expression).

The Measure of Sexual Identity Exploration and Commitment (MoSIEC) is a theoretically based multi-dimensional measure of the processes of sexual identity development. The purposes of this measure are to (a) quantitatively assess the processes associated with Marcia's (1966) model of identity development as applied to the construct of sexual identity and (b) assess the processes of sexual identity development among individuals of any sexual orientation identity. The MoSIEC is comprised of four interrelated, but independent, dimensions underlying the construct of sexual identity, namely (a) *commitment*, (b) *exploration*, (c) *sexual orientation identity uncertainty*, and (d) *synthesis/integration*.

Description

The MoSIEC consists of 22 items within four subscales: (a) Commitment (6 items), (b) Exploration (8 items), (c) Sexual Orientation Identity Uncertainty (3 items), and (d) Synthesis/Integration (5 items). The Commitment subscale assesses the degree of commitment to a sexual identity. The Exploration subscale measures "a general orientation toward or away from sexual exploration" (Worthington, Navarro, Savoy, & Hampton, 2008, p. 31). The Sexual Orientation Identity Uncertainty subscale assesses commitment or a lack of commitment to a sexual orientation identity. The Synthesis/Integration subscale measures the degree of commitment to a unified, cohesive sexual identity. On the Commitment subscale, 3 items are reverse scored; on the Sexual Orientation Identity Uncertainty subscale, 1 item is reverse scored. Thus, higher scores on each of the subscales are indicative of higher levels of the construct being measured.

The MoSIEC is intended for persons of any sexual orientation identity. Thus the instrument is not constrained for use in samples in which all participants are from LGB or heterosexual orientations, as is the case for earlier measures. In fact, the sexual orientation identities of participants need not be known at the time of administration in order to use the MoSIEC in psychological research, a feature unique to this instrument at the time of its development.

The MoSIEC was developed and validated across four studies. In Study 1, scale development procedures and exploratory factor analysis were conducted. Additionally, initial reliability and validity estimates were examined (described in *Reliability* and *Validity*). Using Marcia's (1966) model of identity formation, Klein's (1993) extension of Kinsey and colleagues' (1948, 1953) model of sexual identity, and Worthington et al.'s (2002) model of heterosexual identity development, an initial pool of 48 MoSIEC items were generated. These items reflected exploration (i.e., past, current, and future) and commitment (i.e., not committed, committed, or synthesis/integration) across six dimensions of sexual identity: "(a) sexual needs, (b) sexual values, (c) characteristics of sexual partners, (d) preferred sexual activities, (e) sexual orientation identity, and (f) models of sexual expression" (Worthington et al., 2008, p. 24). A principal-axis factor analysis with oblique rotation was conducted with the initial 48 MoSIEC items. A four-factor solution with 22 items was retained.

In Study 2, confirmatory factor analyses were used to establish the factor reliability and construct validity of the MoSIEC retained in Study 1 across two samples. In Study 3, convergent validity and additional reliability data was examined (described in *Reliability* and *Validity*). In Study 4, the authors assessed test-retest reliability (described in *Reliability*).

Response Mode and Timing

Participants respond to each item using a 6-point Likert-type scale ranging from 1 (*very uncharacteristic of me*) to 6 (*very characteristic of me*). It typically takes a participant 10 minutes to complete the MoSIEC.

Scoring

After reverse scoring the necessary items, MoSIEC subscale scores are obtained by averaging the ratings within each of the four subscales: (a) Commitment, (b) Exploration, (c) Sexual Orientation Identity Uncertainty, and (d) Synthesis/Integration (see the Exhibit).

Reliability

In past studies (Dillon, Worthington, Soth-McNett, & Schwartz, 2008; Worthington et al., 2008), findings have demonstrated the high internal consistency (Cronbach's $\alpha > 0.70$) of the MoSIEC subscales. Furthermore, test-retest reliability estimates are indicative of the MoSIEC subscales' stability across a 2-week interval (Worthington et al., 2008).

Validity

Exploratory and confirmatory factor analyses (Worthington et al., 2008) support the construct validity of the MoSIEC. Convergent validity was supported by "correlations indicating that the MoSIEC subscales were related to age, religiosity, sexual conservatism, and multiple aspects of sexual self-awareness in expected and logically consistent ways" (Worthington et al., 2008, p. 31). Criterion-related validity was established by demonstrated MoSIEC subscale differences across sexual orientation groups in expected and logically consistent ways. Dillon and colleagues (2008) provided further validity evidence for the Exploration and Commitment subscales in that these scores correlated or did not correlate with age, income, professional experience, sexual orientation, gender self-definition, gender self-acceptance, and lesbian, gay, bisexual (LGB) affirmative counseling self-efficacy as logically expected. Worthington and Reynolds (2009) found that all four of the subscales of the MoSIEC were useful for independently differentiating between research participants with different sexual orientation identities. Worthington, Dillon, and Becker-Schutte (2005) also found that heterosexual attitudes regarding LGB individuals were related to all four subscales of the MoSIEC, with the strongest correlations between sexual identity exploration and attitudes regarding LGB civil rights and "internalized affirmativeness" regarding homosexuality.

Other Information

Dustin Hampton contributed to the original research on the scale.

References

Dillon, F. R., Worthington, R. L., Soth-McNett, A. M., & Schwartz, S. J. (2008). Gender and sexual identity based predictors of lesbian, gay, and bisexual affirmative counseling self-efficacy. *Professional Psychology: Research and Practice, 39,* 353–360.

Fassinger, R. E., & Miller, B. A. (1996). Validation of an inclusive model of sexual minority identity formation on a sample of gay men. *Journal of Homosexuality, 32,* 53–78.

Kinsey, A. C., Pomeroy, W. B., & Martin, C. E. (1953). *Sexual behavior in the human female.* Philadelphia: W. B. Saunders.

Kinsey, A. C., Pomeroy, W. B., Martin, C. E., & Gebhard, P. (1948). *Sexual behavior in the human male.* Philadelphia: W. B. Saunders.

Klein, F. (1993). The bisexual option (2nd ed.). New York: Haworth Press.

Marcia, J. E. (1966). Development and validation of ego identity status. *Journal of Personality and Social Psychology, 5,* 551–558.

McCarn, S. R., & Fassinger, R. E. (1996). Revisioning sexual minority identity formation: A new model of lesbian identity and its implications for counseling and research. *The Counseling Psychologist, 24,* 508–534.

Worthington, R. L., Dillon, F. R., & Becker-Schutte, A. M. (2005). Development, reliability and validity of the LGB Knowledge and Attitudes Scale for Heterosexuals (LGB-KASH). *Journal of Counseling Psychology, 52,* 104–118.

Worthington, R. L., Navarro, R. L., Savoy, H. B., & Hampton, D. (2008). Development, reliability and validity of the measure of sexual identity exploration and commitment (MoSIEC). *Developmental Psychology, 44,* 22–33.

Worthington, R. L., & Reynolds, A. L. (2009). Within group differences in sexual orientation and identity. *Journal of Counseling Psychology, 56,* 44–55.

Worthington, R. L., Savoy, H., Dillon, F. R., & Vernaglia, E. R. (2002). Heterosexual identity development: A multidimensional model of individual and group identity [Monograph]. *The Counseling Psychologist, 30,* 496–531.

Exhibit

Measure of Sexual Identity Exploration and Commitment

Please read the following definitions before completing the survey items:

Sexual needs are defined as an internal, subjective experience of instinct, desire, appetite, biological necessity, impulses, interest, and/or libido with respect to sex.

Sexual values are defined as moral evaluations, judgments and/or standards about what is appropriate, acceptable, desirable, and innate sexual behavior.

Sexual activities are defined as any behavior that a person might engage in relating to or based on sexual attraction, sexual arousal, sexual gratification, or reproduction (e.g., fantasy to holding hands to kissing to sexual intercourse).

Modes of sexual expression are defined as any form of communication (verbal or nonverbal) or direct and indirect signals that a person might use to convey her or his sexuality (e.g., flirting, eye contact, touching, vocal quality, compliments, suggestive body movements or postures).

Sexual orientation is defined as an enduring emotional, romantic, sexual, or affectional attraction to other persons that ranges from exclusive heterosexuality to exclusive homosexuality and includes various forms of bisexuality.

Please use the following scale to respond to Items 1–22.

1	2	3	4	5	6
Very Uncharacteristic of Me					Very Characteristic of Me

1. My sexual orientation is clear to me.[a]

1	2	3	4	5	6

2. I went through a period in my life when I was trying to determine my sexual needs.

3. I am actively trying to learn more about my own sexual needs.

4. My sexual values are consistent with all of the other aspects of my sexuality.

5. I am open to experiment with new types of sexual activities in the future.

6. I am actively trying new ways to express myself sexually.

7. My understanding of my sexual needs coincides with my overall sense of sexual self.
8. I went through a period in my life when I was trying different forms of sexual expression.
9. My sexual values will always be open to exploration.
10. I know what my preferences are for expressing myself sexually.
11. I have a clear sense of the types of sexual activities I prefer.
12. I am actively experimenting with sexual activities that are new to me.
13. The ways I express myself sexually are consistent with all of the other aspects of my sexuality.
14. I sometimes feel uncertain about my sexual orientation.
15. I do not know how to express myself sexually.
16. I have never clearly identified what my sexual values are.
17. The sexual activities I prefer are compatible with all of the other aspects of my sexuality.
18. I have never clearly identified what my sexual needs are.
19. I can see myself trying new ways of expressing myself sexually in the future.
20. I have a firm sense of what my sexual needs are.
21. My sexual orientation is not clear to me.
22. My sexual orientation is compatible all of the other aspects of my sexuality.

Scoring:

Exploration = 2, 3, 5, 6, 8, 9, 12, 19
Commitment = 10, 11, **15**, **16**, **18**, 20
Synthesis = 4, 7, 13, 17, 22
Sexual Orientation Identity Moratorium = 1, 15, 21

Reverse-scored items are listed in bold typeface. Subscale scores are obtained by averaging ratings on items receiving a response for each participant. Thus, if Item 17 is not rated by a specific respondent, only the remaining four items on the Synthesis subscale are used to obtain the average, and so on. This method ensures comparable scores when there are missing data.

[a]The 6-point rating scale follows each of the items.

Sexual Ideology Instrument

ILSA L. LOTTES,[1] *University of Maryland, Baltimore County*

The original purpose of the Sexual Ideology Instrument (SII) was to test Reiss's (1981, 1983, 1986) hypotheses about the sexual ideologies of Americans. Reiss proposed three sexual ideologies: Traditional Romantic, Modern Naturalistic, and Abstinence. A *sexual ideology* is a coherent set of beliefs regarding what is appropriate, acceptable, desirable, and innate sexual behavior. A *tenet* is a specific belief of an ideology. The SII contains scales and specific items designed to measure attitudes toward the tenets of the three ideologies and toward the four controversial topics mentioned below.

The five tenet types in the Reiss ideologies are concerned with g*ender role equality*, the value of *body-centered sexuality*, the *power of sexual emotions*, the importance of

coital focus in sexual relations, and the necessity of love for satisfactory sex or the *love need in sex*. These are described more specifically in Table 1, in conjunction with the three ideologies. Reiss also claimed that adherents of each ideology would have predictable attitudes on the following four areas of public controversy: abortion, gender genetic differences, pornography, and homosexuality. The expected views, as linked to each ideology, are also indicated in Table 1. Although the SII was originally constructed to test hypotheses about sexual ideologies, its use would also be appropriate in studies requiring assessment of a wide range of sexual attitudes. In addition, because the SII contains several small scales, the use of all or some of its scales would be appropriate in studies assessing many variables

[1]Address correspondence to Ilsa L. Lottes, Department of Sociology and Anthropology, University of Maryland, Baltimore County, 5401 Wilkens Avenue, Baltimore, MD 21228; e-mail: lottes@umbc.edu

TABLE 1
Tenets and Attitudes of Sexual Ideologies

Tenet Type 1. Gender Role Equality
Traditional Romantic: Gender roles should be distinct and interdependent,with the male gender role as dominant.
Modern Naturalistic: Gender roles should be similar for males and females and should promote egalitarian participation in the society.

Tenet Type 2. Body-Centered Sexuality
Traditional Romantic: Body-centered sexuality is to be avoided by females.
Modern Naturalistic: Body-centered sexuality is of less worth than person-centered sexuality, but it still has a positive value for both genders.
Abstinence: Body-centered sexuality is to be avoided by males and females.

Tenet Type 3. Power of Sexual Emotions
Traditional Romantic: Sexuality is a very powerful emotion and one that should be particularly feared by females.
Modern Naturalistic: One's sexual emotions are strong but manageable, by both males and females, in the same way as are other basic emotions.
Abstinence: Sexuality is a very powerful emotion and one that should be feared by males and females.

Tenet Type 4. Coital Focus
Traditional Romantic: The major goal of sexuality is heterosexual coitus and that is where the man's focus should be placed.
Modern Naturalistic: The major goals of sexuality are physical pleasure and psychological intimacy in a variety of sexual acts and this is so for
                         both genders.

Tenet Type 5. Love Need in Sex
Traditional Romantic: Love redeems sexuality from its guilt, particularly for females.
Modern Naturalistic: A wide range of sexuality should be accepted without guilt by both genders providing it does not involve force or fraud.
Abstinence: Love redeems sexuality from guilt for males and females.

Abortion
Traditional Romantic
and Abstinence: Laws should prohibit abortion.
Modern Naturalistic: Women should be allowed to make their own decisions about abortion.

Genetic Differences
Traditional Romantic
and Abstinence: Differences between men and women are due more to genetics than to social conditioning.
Modern Naturalistic: Differences between men and women are due more to social conditioning than to genetics.

Pornography
Traditional Romantic
and Abstinence: Pornography produces harmful effects for society.
Modern Naturalistic: Most pornography does not produce harmful effects for society.

Homosexuality
Traditional Romantic
and Abstinence: Homosexuality is not acceptable.
Modern Naturalistic: Homosexuality is acceptable

and where the length of the questionnaire is an important consideration.

Description

The SII is a 72-item questionnaire containing 15 scales. The response options to each item are *strongly agree* (1), *agree* (2), *undecided* (3), *disagree* (4), or *strongly disagree* (5). The items are ordered so that items in any one scale are not grouped together. Tenet Types 2, 3, and 5 each require a comparison of beliefs about males and females. Therefore, 15 pairs of equivalent male and female items are included. To reduce the tendency of respondents to give the same answer for pairs of equivalent items, they are placed on different pages. For the test sample, correlations between equivalent items ranged from .24 to .72, with the average equal to .56. Thus, for that sample, respondents in general did not answer these pairs of items identically.

Lottes (1983b) analyzed the psychometric properties of a preliminary version of the SII. The weakest items were

eliminated. It was tested on a sample of 395 adults in the northeastern United States. This sample was composed of 259 students and 136 nonstudents, and contained 60% females and 40% males. For the students, the mean ages of both the males and females were 22. For the nonstudents, the mean ages of the males and females were 31 and 40, respectively. The SII is appropriate to administer to adults.

Response Mode and Timing

The SII is distributed with an answer sheet, preferably for computer scoring. Respondents indicate the number reflecting their agreement/disagreement with each item. The SII requires an average of 30 minutes for completion.

Scoring

To determine the score for each scale, add the responses (coded 1–5) to the individual items of the scale. The reverse-scored items are indicated by an asterisk in Table 2.

TABLE 2
Reliability and Item Numbers of the Scales of the SII

Scale	Cronbach's Alpha	Item numbers in Scale[a]
Gender Role Equality[b]	.75	*1, 6, *11, 16, 24, *43, 51, *64
Body-Centered Sexuality		
Scale 1	.80	*35, *40, *50
Scale 2	.75	*7, *15, *30
Scale 3	.56	12, 13, 17
Scale 4	.64	2, 65
Power of Sexual Emotions		
Scale 1	.46	28, 34
Scale 2	.51	53, 60
Scale 3	.57	*3, *18, *23, *39, *52, *72
Coital Focus	.72	4, 19, *22, 44, *48, 56, *57, 63, *66
Love Need in Sex[c]		
Scale 1	.80	*5, 9, 20, 21, 33, 41, 55, *62, *68
Scale 2	.86	*8, 10, *25, *31, *32, *36, *37, *38, *42, *46, *49, *58, *67, *69, *71
Abortion	.65	29, *54, 70
Gender Genetic Differences	.52	27, 45, 61
Pornography	.63	26, *47, *59
Homosexuality	.81	14, *38, *67

[a]The asterisk before a number indicates a reverse-scored item.
[b]Items 6, 24, 51, and 64 of this scale are from National Opinion Research Center (1980).
[c]Items 20, 41, 42, 55, 68, and 71 are from Weis and Slosnerick (1981).

For the Gender Role Equality and Coital Focus scales, a high score indicates support for the Modern Naturalistic tenets and a low score indicates support for the Traditional Romantic tenets.

For the four Body-Centered Sexuality scales, high scores on all scales indicate support for the Modern Naturalistic tenet, and low scores on all scales indicate support for the Abstinence tenet. Low scores on Body-Centered Sexuality scales 1 and 3 and a high score on scale 2 indicate support for the Traditional Romantic tenet (i.e., the view that body-centered sexuality is acceptable for men but not women).

For the three Power of Sexual Emotions scales, high scores on all scales indicate support for the Modern Naturalistic tenet, and low scores on all scales indicate support for the Abstinence tenet. A high score for Power of Sexual Emotions scale 1 and a low score for scale 2 indicate support for the Traditional Romantic tenet (i.e., the view that men's sexual emotions are more powerful and unmanageable than women's).

For the two Love Need in Sex scales, high scores indicate support for the Modern Naturalistic tenet and low scores indicate support for the Abstinence tenet. To determine support for the Traditional Romantic tenet, the results of items 41 and 55 need to be compared. A high score for item 41 and a low score for item 55 would indicate support for the Traditional Romantic tenet (i.e., for the view that love in sexual relations is necessary for women but not men).

For the Abortion, Gender Genetic Differences, Pornography, and Homosexuality scales, high scores indicate respectively, support for belief in (a) freedom of choice for abortion, (b) environment over heredity as the primary basis of personality difference, (c) tolerant attitudes toward pornography, and (d) acceptance of homosexuality.

Reliability

The reliability of each scale was estimated by computing Cronbach's alpha. Listed in Table 2 are the 15 scales used in the SII, their items, and their reliabilities.

Validity

The construct validity of the 15 scales was generally supported by both interscale correlations and factor analysis. Exceptions were the Body-Centered Sexuality and Love Need in Sex scales. Both high interscale correlations and factor analysis suggested that these two types of scales were measuring the same construct. However, Lottes (1983a) found significant differences in response to these two types of scales for young women students.

The construct validity was supported by examining (a) correlations with background variables of age, sex, and religiosity and (b) differences between scale means for men and women students and for women students and women nonstudents. Both correlations and differences between scale means, significant at the .001 level, were consistent with predictions suggested by previous research.

Further information concerning the reliability and validity of the scales is reported by Lottes (1983b).

References

Lottes, I. L. (1983a, April). *An investigation of the tenet patterns in the Reiss sexual ideologies.* Paper presented at the Eastern Region meeting of the Society for the Scientific Study of Sex, Philadelphia, PA.

Lottes, I. L. (1983b). *Psychometric characteristics of a sexual ideology instrument.* Unpublished manuscript.

Lottes, I. L. (1985). The use of cluster analysis to determine belief patterns of sexual attitudes. *The Journal of Sex Research, 21,* 405–421.

National Opinion Research Center. (1980). *General social surveys, 1972–1980: Cumulative codebook.* Chicago: University of Chicago Press.

Reiss, I. L. (1981). Some observations on ideology and sexuality in America. *Journal of Marriage and the Family, 43,* 271–283.

Reiss, I. L. (1983). Sexuality: A research and theory perspective. In P. Houston (Ed.), *Sexuality and the family life span* (pp. 141–147). Iowa City: University of Iowa Press.

Reiss, I. L. (1986). *Journey into sexuality.* Englewood Cliffs, NJ: Prentice Hall.

Weis, D. L., & Slosnerick, M. (1981). Attitudes toward sexual and nonsexual extramarital involvements among a sample of college students. *Journal of Marriage and the Family, 43,* 349–358.

Exhibit

Sexual Ideology Instrument

Directions: Put your answers on side 1, beginning with question 1. For each of the statements, indicate whether you *strongly agree* (SA) = 1, *agree* (A) = 2, are *undecided* (U) = 3, *disagree* (D) = 4, or *strongly disagree* (SD) = 5.

SA	A	U	D	SD
1	2	3	4	5

Remember: (1) Be sure that the number of the statement you are reading corresponds to the number you are marking on the answer sheet.

(2) Mark only one response for each statement.

(3) Respond the way you really feel, which may or may not be in agreement with the majority of public opinion.

_____ 1. I am in favor of laws that promote gender equality.

_____ 2. Women who emphasize sexual pleasure in their lives overlook life's more important pursuits.

_____ 3. Sexual emotions are strong but manageable by most males.

_____ 4. A mature man and woman should get their greatest sexual pleasure from intercourse rather than from some other sexual activity.

_____ 5. Having a physical attraction to someone would be sufficient for me to enjoy sex with that person.

_____ 6. A preschool child is likely to suffer if the mother works.

_____ 7. It is acceptable for a 16–17 year old unmarried male to have sexual intercourse.

_____ 8. Masturbation is an acceptable activity for males.

_____ 9. I would feel very guilty if I had sexual relations with someone I did NOT love.

_____ 10. I would be very upset if my spouse had had many previous sexual relationships.

_____ 11. I hope that the family, social, and career roles of men and women become more alike.

_____ 12. Since many men seem to be unable to control their sex drive, it is important for women to be in control of theirs.

_____ 13. I do NOT respect women who appear in pornographic films or magazines.

_____ 14. Homosexuals should NOT be teaching school. It is too risky to allow the possibility of such a teacher taking advantage of or influencing the sexual orientation of even one student.

_____ 15. I approve of a man having premarital sex with someone he likes but is NOT in love with.

_____ 16. If a woman really loves her husband, she will want to include the vow "to obey" her husband in the marriage ceremony.

_____ 17. Women degrade themselves when they show obvious sexual interest in a man they are NOT in love with.

_____ 18. Men can have affairs that do NOT disrupt their life style.

_____ 19. The primary goal of sexual activity between men and women should be intercourse.

_____ 20. A successful and satisfying sex partnership CANNOT be established unless the sex partners are quite willing to be sexually faithful to one another.

_____ 21. It would be difficult for me to enjoy sex with someone I did NOT love.

_____ 22. Orgasm resulting from manual genital stimulation by the sex partner can be as satisfying as intercourse.

_____ 23. Women can have affairs without significant emotional involvement.

_____ 24. It is more important for a wife to help her husband's career than to have one herself.

_____ 25. I approve of a woman having extramarital sex WITH her husband's consent.

_____ 26. Pornography influences men to commit sexual crimes including rape.

_____ 27. Men are generally more interested in sex than women.

_____ 28. If women yield to their sexual feelings, these feelings will probably disrupt and dominate their lives in destructive ways.

_____ 29. The Supreme Court ruling making abortions legal should be reversed.

_____ 30. I approve of a man having premarital sex with someone he is strongly attracted to but knows only casually.

_____ 31. Group sex (sex involving more than two people) is an acceptable sexual activity for men and women.

_____ 32. John is married to Ann. John is strongly attracted to, but not in love with Mary. I approve of John and Mary having sexual relations.

_____ 33. Extramarital sex is always wrong.

_____ 34. Sexuality is a very powerful force and females should do all they can to control it in their lives.

_____ 35. It is acceptable for a 16–17 year old unmarried female to have sexual intercourse.

_____ 36. I approve of a man having extra-marital sex WITHOUT his wife's consent.

_____ 37. I would *NOT* object to my spouse having had a couple of previous sexual relationships.

_____ 38. I can accept and do *NOT* condemn homosexual activities for females.

_____ 39. Sexual emotions are strong but manageable by most females.

_____ 40. I approve of a woman having premarital sex with someone she likes but is *NOT* in love with.

_____ 41. A man *CANNOT* have a satisfactory and satisfying sex life without being in love with his sex partner.

_____ 42. Sexual intercourse with someone other than the regular sex partner can bring about an improvement in the sexual relationship of the established pair.

_____ 43. It would be best for our society if there were about an equal number of men and women in all high-level positions of government, business and education.

_____ 44. To advocate an emphasis on sexual pleasure is to forget that the major purpose of sexual relations is procreation.

_____ 45. The innate differences in men and women's strengths and weaknesses are the major source of satisfaction in male-female relationships.

_____ 46. I approve of a man having extra marital sex *WITH* his wife's consent.

_____ 47. I enjoy looking at the pictures of nude men and women that appear in "Playgirl" and "Playboy" type magazines.

_____ 48. Oral or mouth-genital sex is a good substitute for intercourse.

_____ 49. Masturbation is an acceptable activity for females.

_____ 50. I approve of a woman having premarital sex with someone she is strongly attracted to but knows only casually.

_____ 51. It is much better for everyone involved if the man is the achiever outside the home and the woman takes care of the home and family.

_____ 52. Men can have affairs without significant emotional involvement.

_____ 53. If men yield to their sexual feelings, these feelings will probably disrupt and dominate their lives in destructive ways.

_____ 54. The decision about an abortion should be left up to a woman and her doctor.

_____ 55. A woman cannot have a satisfactory and satisfying sex life without being in love with her sex partner.

_____ 56. Having intercourse is the best way to end sex.

_____ 57. Anal intercourse is a good substitute for vaginal intercourse.

_____ 58. Ann is married to John. Ann is strongly attracted to, but not in love with Jim. I approve of Ann and Jim having sexual relations.

_____ 59. Non-violent pornography is harmless to our society.

_____ 60. Sexuality is a very powerful force and males should do all they can to control it in their lives.

_____ 61. Men and women have different sexual needs that are based on differences in male and female anatomy and hormones.

_____ 62. Basically, I simply love sex and would enjoy making love to many different people.

_____ 63. It is a mistake to allow oral sex to become as important as intercourse in one's sex life.

_____ 64. A working mother can establish just as warm and secure a relationship with her children as a mother who is *NOT* employed.

_____ 65. Men who emphasize sexual pleasure in their lives overlook life's more important pursuits.

_____ 66. Sexual intercourse does *NOT* have to be the major focus of positive and pleasurable sexual activity for men and women.

_____ 67. I can accept and do *NOT* condemn homosexual activities for males.

_____ 68. Sexual intercourse is often best when enjoyed for its own sake, rather than for the purpose of expressing love.

_____ 69. I approve of a woman having extramarital sex *WITHOUT* her husband's consent.

_____ 70. Where abortions are legal, the father should have the right to veto the abortion.

_____ 71. Casual sexual intercourse with a variety of sex partners can be as satisfying and satisfactory as intercourse that is limited to an established sex partnership.

_____ 72. Women can have affairs that do *NOT* disrupt their lifestyle.

Sexual Rights Instrument

ILSA L. LOTTES,[1] *University of Maryland, Baltimore County*

The purpose of the Sexual Rights Instrument is to assess the 11 sexual rights formulated and adopted by the World Association of Sexology (WAS; WAS, 1999) and listed in Table 1. The Sexual Rights Instrument can be used to assess all 11 sexual rights of WAS or a subset. The construction and psychometric properties of this instrument were originally discussed by Lottes and Adkins (2003).

Description

The Sexual Rights Instrument contains 94 Likert items where the response options to each item are one of five choices: (a) *Strongly Agree*, (b) *Agree*, (c) *Neither Agree nor Disagree*, (d) *Disagree*, and (e) *Strongly Disagree*. The 94 items are ordered in the questionnaire so that items assessing one sexual right are not all listed consecutively but rather placed throughout with measures of other rights. Each of the 11 sexual rights of WAS is assessed by a single scale except for the right to sexual equity, and for that right there are separate scales corresponding to groups of the population that are known for their lack of sexual equity. Thus, for the right to sexual equity there are five scales: one for each of the following groups: Poor People, Gays and

Lesbians, Handicapped People, Adolescents, and Elderly People.

One of the fundamental principles of human rights, in general, and sexual rights, in particular, is their interconnectivity. Violation of one right often implies violation of another. Thus, it is not possible to assess multiple sexual rights using mutually exclusive items in all scales. From both theoretical and content perspectives, items could apply to more than one scale. For example, although the sexual health professionals who formulated the right to comprehensive sex education intended for this right to mean that sexuality information should be provided to people throughout their lifetime, these same professionals acknowledge that adolescence is a critical period when youth need to acquire sexual knowledge. Thus, items of the scale assessing the right to sexual equity for adolescents overlap with the items of the scale assessing the right to comprehensive sex education.

The Sexual Rights Instrument was administered to two samples of college students in the northeastern United States. Sample 1 included students from a human sexuality class and students who were not taking the human sexuality class but who were recruited by students in that class.

TABLE 1
Sexual Rights Formulated by the World Association of Sexology

The right to sexual freedom—Sexual freedom encompasses the possibility for individuals to express their full sexual potential. However, this excludes all forms of sexual coercion, exploitation and abuse at any time and situations in life.

The right to sexual autonomy, sexual integrity, and safety of the sexual body—This right involves the ability to make autonomous decisions about one's sexual life within a context of one's own personal and social ethics. It also encompasses control and enjoyment of our own bodies free from torture, mutilation, and violence of any sort.

The right to sexual privacy—This involves the right for individual decisions and behaviors about intimacy as long as they do not intrude on the sexual rights of others.

The right to sexual equity—This refers to freedom from all forms of discrimination regardless of sex, gender, sexual orientation, age, race, social class, religion, or physical and emotional disability.

The right to sexual pleasure—Sexual pleasure, including autoeroticism, is a source of physical, psychological, intellectual, and spiritual well-being.

The right to emotional sexual expression—Sexual expression is more than erotic pleasure or sexual acts. Individuals have a right to express their sexuality through communications, touch, emotional expression, and love.

The right to sexually associate freely—This means the possibility to marry or not, to divorce, and to establish other types of responsible sexual associations.

The right to make free and responsible reproductive choices—This encompasses the right to decide whether or not to have children, the number and spacing of children, and the right to full access to the means of fertility regulation.

The right to sexual information based upon scientific inquiry—This right implies that sexual information should be generated through the process of unencumbered and yet scientifically ethical inquiry, and disseminated in appropriate ways at all societal levels.

The right to comprehensive sexuality education—This is a lifelong process from birth throughout the lifecycle and should involve all social institutions.

The right to sexual health care—Sexual health care should be available for prevention and treatment of all sexual concerns, problems, and disorders.

[1]Address correspondence to Ilsa L. Lottes, University of Maryland, Baltimore County, Department of Sociology and Anthropology, 1000 Hilltop Circle, Baltimore, MD 21250; e-mail: lottes@umbc.edu

TABLE 2
Reliability and Item Numbers of the Scales of the Sexual Rights Instrument for Sample 1 (Sample 2)

Right	Number of Items	Cronbach's Alpha	Item Numbers in Scale
Sexual freedom	4	.72 (.65)	1*, 16*, 42, 60*
Sexual autonomy and safety	13	.84 (.79)	10*, 15, 21, 24*, 28*, 29*, 34*, 35*, 36*, 43*, 61*, 72*, 84*
Sexual privacy	9	.71 (.57)	1*, 2, 11, 16*, 22, 53, 60*, 62, 78
Sexual equity			
Poor people	5	.77 (.81)	26*, 27*, 41*, 73*, 94
Gays and lesbians	13	.93 (.92)	3, 5*, 8*, 11, 15, 23*, 47*, 61*, 63, 68, 75, 83, 92
Handicapped people	5	.75 (.75)	9, 67, 70*, 81*, 93*
Adolescents	15	.87 (.83)	10*, 19*, 22, 28*, 35*, 36*, 40*, 51*, 52*, 57*, 62, 72*, 76*, 84*, 89*
Elderly people	6	.74 (.72)	37, 45*, 54, 74*, 78, 86*
Sexual pleasure	9	.83 (.82)	4*, 14*, 56, 64, 65*, 69, 79*, 87, 88*
Emotional sexual expression	7	.64 (.67)	13*, 23*, 45, 46, 50*, 55*, 91*
Sexually associate freely	11	.83 (.72)	1*, 5*, 8*, 12, 16*, 25*, 30*, 31, 39, 47, 60
Responsible reproductive choices	18	.90 (.85)	6, 17*, 19*, 26*, 32*, 40*, 51*, 52*, 62, 71, 76*, 80, 82*, 85*, 86*, 90*, 92, 94
Information based on scientific inquiry	10	.82 (.79)	6, 17*, 19*, 33*, 38, 44*, 57*, 58*, 66, 77*
Comprehensive sexuality education	27	.91 (.90)	6, 7*, 8*, 10*, 17*, 18, 19*, 24*, 28*, 33*, 35*, 36, 38, 40*, 44*, 48, 52*, 57*, 58*, 66, 70*, 72*, 74*, 76*, 81*, 83, 89*
Sexual health care	11	.86 (.86)	20*, 26*, 27*, 43*, 47*, 49, 58*, 59, 72*, 77*, 94

Note. Rights are from the World Association of Sexology (1999). Item codes range from 1 to 5, with a higher score indicating greater support for the sexual right. Items 1, 16, 38, 48, 67, and 68 are from the Sexuality Attitudes Scale in either their original or slightly revised forms (Hudson, Murphy, & Nurius, 1983). Item 61 is a slightly revised item from the Homophobic Behavior of Students Scale (Van de Ven, Bornholt, & Bailey, 1998). Item 72 is a slightly revised item from the Sexuality Education Feature/Program Outcome Inventory (Klein, 1998). Item 62 is a slightly revised item from the Attitudes Toward Sexuality Scale (Fisher & Hall, 1998). Items 33, 76, 84, and 89 are taken from the Family Life Sex Education Goal Questionnaire in either their original or slightly revised forms (Godin, Frank, & Jacobson, 1998). Items 45, 50, and 78 are all slightly revised items from the Aging Sexual Knowledge and Attitudes Scale (White, 1998). Items 71, 80, and 90 are all from the Abortion Attitude Scale in either their original or slightly revised forms (Berne, 1998).
*Indicates item is reverse scored.

Students responded to the survey on their own time. This was part of a project that was enthusiastically supported by students in the human sexuality class. The final number of usable questionnaires was 388. This sample was 41% male and 59% female with a mean age of 26.5. The data collection method for Sample 2 was similar except that the class recruiting other students was a research methods class. Members of this class were later involved in analyzing the responses to the Sexual Rights Instrument. This sample included 175 students of whom 38% were male and 62% female. The mean age of this sample was 28.6. In general, the Sexual Rights Instrument would be appropriate to administer to adult samples.

Most of the Sexual Rights Instrument's items were constructed by Lottes and Adkins (2003), with 19 items taken from previously published scales. The final list of items was sent to a sexuality researcher with expertise in sexual rights. Two items were revised according to this researcher's suggestions. A list of the item numbers corresponding to each scale can be found in Table 2, which identifies the items that were reverse scored and the reference for the items used from previously constructed scales.

Response Mode and Timing

Two response modes are possible. If machine-scored sheets that can be scanned and then transferred to a dataset readable by a statistical data analysis program are used, respondents shade in the circle of the number indicating their agreement/disagreement with each item. If machine-scored sheets are not used, then the numbers 1 through 5 need to be included next to each item, and respondents should be instructed to circle the number indicating their agreement/disagreement with each item. The Sexual Rights Instrument requires an average of 40 minutes to complete.

Scoring

To determine the score for each scale, add the responses (coded 1 through 5) to the individual items of each scale. The reverse-scored items are indicated in Table 2, and these items need to be recoded before summing the responses to each item in a scale. For all scales, the higher the score, the more a respondent supports sexual rights.

Reliability

The reliability of each scale was estimated by computing Cronbach's alpha. Table 2 lists the 15 sexual rights scales with their reliabilities.

Validity

The construct validity of the 15 scales was supported by examining (a) correlations of the scales with measures of conservative political views, religiosity, support for feminist causes, and personal value of sex and (b) differences between scale means for those who had only heterosexual sex partners and those who had at least one same-sex partner. Nearly all the correlations and mean differences were highly significant, supporting predictions that more support for sexual rights is given by less conservative and less religious people, people with more rather than less feminist views, people who place a high value on sex in their personal lives, and people who have had at least one same-sex partner.

References

Berne, L. (1998) Abortion Attitude Scale. In C. M. Davis, W. L. Yarber, R. Bauserman, G. Schreer, & S. L. Davis (Eds.), *Handbook of sexuality-related measures* (pp. 1–2). Thousand Oaks, CA: Sage.

Fisher, T., & Hall, R. (1998). Attitudes Toward Sexuality Scale. In C. M. Davis, W. L. Yarber, R. Bauserman, G. Schreer, & S. L. Davis (Eds.), *Handbook of sexuality-related measures* (pp. 32–33). Thousand Oaks, CA: Sage.

Godin, S., Frank, S., & Jacobson, S. (1998). Family Life Sex Education Goal Questionnaire. In C. M. Davis, W. L. Yarber, R. Bauserman, G. Schreer, & S. L. Davis (Eds.), *Handbook of sexuality-related measures* (pp. 203–205). Thousand Oaks, CA: Sage.

Hudson, W., Murphy, G., & Nurius, P. (1983). A short-form scale to measure liberal vs. conservative orientations toward human sexual expression. *The Journal of Sex Research, 19,* 258–272.

Klein, D. (1998). The Sexuality Education Program Feature/Program Outcome Inventory. In C. M. Davis, W. L. Yarber, R. Bauserman, G. Schreer, & S. L. Davis (Eds.), *Handbook of sexuality-related measures* (pp. 206–208). Thousand Oaks, CA: Sage.

Lottes, I., & Adkins, C. (2003). The construction and psychometric properties of an instrument to assess support for sexual rights. *The Journal of Sex Research, 40,* 286–295.

Van de Ven, P., Bornholt, L., & Bailey, M. (1998). Homophobic Behavior of Students Scale. In C. M. Davis, W. L. Yarber, R. Bauserman, G. Schreer, & S. L. Davis (Eds.), *Handbook of sexuality-related measures* (pp. 369–370). Thousand Oaks, CA: Sage.

White, C. (1998). Aging Sexual Knowledge and Attitudes Scale. In C. M. Davis, W. L. Yarber, R. Bauserman, G. Schreer, & S. L. Davis (Eds.), *Handbook of sexuality-related measures* (pp. 66–69). Thousand Oaks, CA: Sage.

World Association of Sexology. (1999). *Declaration of sexual rights.* Retrieved May 5, 2001, from http://www.worldsexology.org/about_sexualrights.html

Exhibit

Sexual Rights Instrument

Directions: Circle the response that best corresponds to your view about each statement using the following choices:

Strongly Agree	Agree	Neither Agree nor Disagree	Disagree	Strongly Disagree
SA	A	N	D	SD

1. There should be no laws prohibiting sexual acts between consenting adults. — SA A N D SD
2. Candidates for public office should be willing to disclose their sexual histories to the public. — SA A N D SD
3. The federal government has done enough already to eliminate discrimination against gay men. — SA A N D SD
4. A pleasurable sex life is very important to the vast majority of men's overall sense of well-being. — SA A N D SD
5. Homosexual couples should have the same legal rights as married couples. — SA A N D SD
6. Women do NOT need to be educated about the most up to date means of fertility regulation/contraception. — SA A N D SD
7. It is a responsibility of the media, including TV and the Internet, to inform people about scientific research relating to contraception/birth control. — SA A N D SD
8. Sex education courses in public high schools should discuss issues related to sexual orientation. — SA A N D SD
9. It is unreasonable to try to provide ways for physically handicapped people to enjoy their sexuality. — SA A N D SD
10. High school students should be taught negotiating skills enabling them to avoid unwanted sexual activities. — SA A N D SD
11. It is still important to investigate the sexual orientation (that is, finding out if they are gay, lesbian, or bisexual) of those people working in any branch of the armed forces. — SA A N D SD
12. Laws should make it financially difficult for married couples with children to get divorced. — SA A N D SD
13. It is perfectly normal to have sexual fantasies. — SA A N D SD
14. A pleasurable sex life is very important to the vast majority of women's overall sense of well-being. — SA A N D SD
15. National policy has successfully protected lesbians from discrimination. — SA A N D SD
16. What two consenting adults do together sexually is their business. — SA A N D SD
17. Men should be educated about the most up-to-date means of fertility regulation/contraception. — SA A N D SD
18. It is NOT the obligation of the media to inform the public about the harmful effects and treatment of sexually transmitted diseases. — SA A N D SD
19. Teenagers should be given up-to-date information on how to avoid becoming a parent before they are ready. — SA A N D SD

20. Health insurance companies should routinely cover the majority of costs to treat the most common and curable sexually transmitted diseases.   SA   A   N   D   SD

21. It is acceptable to put pressure on someone to participate in a sexual activity that was initially refused.   SA   A   N   D   SD

22. Health care professionals should have to get parental consent before treating an adolescent (<18) for a sexually transmitted disease.   SA   A   N   D   SD

23. It should be acceptable for gay men to hold hands in public.   SA   A   N   D   SD

24. The media, including TV and the Internet, should take a major role in educating people about the harmful effects of sexual abuse on its victims.   SA   A   N   D   SD

25. It should be socially acceptable for two people to live together without being married.   SA   A   N   D   SD

26. Low-income women should be given financial assistance for the purchase of contraception.   SA   A   N   D   SD

27. There should be a place where uninsured people with low incomes can get immediate treatment for curable sexually transmitted diseases.   SA   A   N   D   SD

28. Young children (<12) need to be taught ways to help them minimize their risk of being sexually abused.   SA   A   N   D   SD

29. It is wrong to psychologically pressure someone to engage in sexual activity.   SA   A   N   D   SD

30. Laws giving cohabiting couples the same legal opportunities as married couples, with respect to health insurance, need to be enacted.   SA   A   N   D   SD

31. If a non-married couple conceives a child, they should get married.   SA   A   N   D   SD

32. Safe and legal abortions should be available to all women, before the 4th month of pregnancy.   SA   A   N   D   SD

33. Sex education courses in high school should help adolescents understand how different ethnic and cultural groups vary in sexual beliefs and behaviors.   SA   A   N   D   SD

34. Affordable health services should be available to help victims recovering from sexual abuse.   SA   A   N   D   SD

35. Public high schools should provide programs to try to eliminate forms of non-consensual sexual activity.   SA   A   N   D   SD

36. The media should provide examples demonstrating to young people how to say 'No' to unwanted sexual activity.   SA   A   N   D   SD

37. Sexual activity for senior citizens should be discouraged.   SA   A   N   D   SD

38. Sex education should be restricted to the home.   SA   A   N   D   SD

39. It is much too easy to get a divorce in the United States.   SA   A   N   D   SD

40. Teenage girls should be educated in high school about how sexually transmitted diseases influence their ability to get pregnant.   SA   A   N   D   SD

41. Policies in the United States should enable health providers to offer all people affordable diagnosis and treatment of sexually transmitted diseases.   SA   A   N   D   SD

42. I approve of state laws which make anal sex illegal.   SA   A   N   D   SD

43. A person should be able to stop a sexual interaction at any point, no matter how far that sexual interaction has gone.   SA   A   N   D   SD

44. Sexuality instructors should have training in the health, social, cultural, and biological aspects of sexuality.   SA   A   N   D   SD

45. Sexual activity is often psychologically beneficial for older (>65) people.   SA   A   N   D   SD

46. For most people, emotional expression is of little value to their long-term sexual relationships.   SA   A   N   D   SD

47. The union of homosexual couples deserves some form of public recognition.   SA   A   N   D   SD

48. Sex education should only be given to people ready for marriage.   SA   A   N   D   SD

49. The government already contributes enough for the health care of its citizens.   SA   A   N   D   SD

50. Sexual activity is typically a lifelong need.   SA   A   N   D   SD

51. It should be easy for teenagers to get contraceptives.   SA   A   N   D   SD

52. Teenage girls should be educated in high school about the harmful effects of a mother's sexually transmitted disease or her drug use on her baby.   SA   A   N   D   SD

53. The media should be able to report on the sexuality of any person.   SA   A   N   D   SD

54. Nursing homes should restrict the sexual activities of their residents.   SA   A   N   D   SD

55. Sexual intimacy provides a way for many people to express their love for their partner.   SA   A   N   D   SD

56. Self-masturbation as an adult is juvenile and immature.   SA   A   N   D   SD

57. Teenagers should be taught ways to reduce their risk for getting a sexually transmitted disease.   SA   A   N   D   SD

58. Physicians should be educated on how illnesses and their treatments affect a patient's sexual response.   SA   A   N   D   SD

59. The government should NOT help small businesses provide health insurance for their employees.   SA   A   N   D   SD

60. It is wrong to investigate the sexual activities of two consenting adults.   SA   A   N   D   SD

61. I would sign my name to a petition asking the government to protect gay men from physical violence.   SA   A   N   D   SD

62. Parents should be informed if their children (<18) have been to a health professional to obtain a contraceptive device.   SA   A   N   D   SD

63. Heterosexual men have more positive characteristics than gay men.   SA   A   N   D   SD

64. Women who emphasize sexual pleasure in their lives overlook life's more important pursuits.   SA   A   N   D   SD
65. Self-masturbation in childhood can help a person develop a natural and healthy attitude toward sex.   SA   A   N   D   SD
66. It is the duty of parents and NOT the schools to provide sex education for their children.   SA   A   N   D   SD
67. Physically handicapped people should NOT have sex.   SA   A   N   D   SD
68. Too much social approval has been given to gay men.   SA   A   N   D   SD
69. Self-masturbation by a person who is married is NOT healthy.   SA   A   N   D   SD
70. Sexuality courses should be provided for those who are disabled.   SA   A   N   D   SD
71. Abortion is wrong, no matter what the circumstances are.   SA   A   N   D   SD
72. Sex education courses in high school should help adolescents express their desire NOT to be involved
    sexually if they do NOT wish to be.   SA   A   N   D   SD
73. The government should provide more financial assistance to hospitals and doctors to help cover the
    cost of the health care of poor people.   SA   A   N   D   SD
74. Care takers of the aged should be educated about the sexual needs of their patients.   SA   A   N   D   SD
75. Homosexual men are treated justly in our society.   SA   A   N   D   SD
76. Sex education courses in high school should help adolescents use protection (condom/birth control) if
    they plan to have intercourse.   SA   A   N   D   SD
77. Physicians should communicate to patients how illnesses and their treatments affect sexual response.   SA   A   N   D   SD
78. Nursing homes have no obligation to provide privacy for residents who wish to express their sexuality,
    either alone or with their partner.   SA   A   N   D   SD
79. Self-masturbation in private should be considered a normal and healthy activity for adolescents.   SA   A   N   D   SD
80. The Supreme Court should make abortion illegal in the United States.   SA   A   N   D   SD
81. Care takers of the disabled should be educated about the sexual needs of their patients.   SA   A   N   D   SD
82. I believe contraceptive use is a responsibility for both men and women.   SA   A   N   D   SD
83. Heterosexual women have more positive characteristics than lesbians.   SA   A   N   D   SD
84. Sex education courses in high school should help adolescents deal with the negative aspects of peer
    pressure.   SA   A   N   D   SD
85. Artificial insemination should be available to lesbians.   SA   A   N   D   SD
86. Nursing homes should provide condoms for their residents.   SA   A   N   D   SD
87. Men who emphasize sexual pleasure in their lives overlook life's more important pursuits.   SA   A   N   D   SD
88. Adults who self-masturbate in private should be considered normal and healthy.   SA   A   N   D   SD
89. Adolescents in high school should be taught skills to reduce guilt and fear about sexual issues.   SA   A   N   D   SD
90. The final decision to have an abortion should be up to the pregnant woman.   SA   A   N   D   SD
91. Sexual relationships provide an important and fulfilling part of life for most people.   SA   A   N   D   SD
92. Gay men should NOT be able to adopt children.   SA   A   N   D   SD
93. Institutions for the physically disabled should provide privacy to allow residents to engage in sexual
    activities.   SA   A   N   D   SD
94. The government does NOT need to provide family planning services to low-income women.   SA   A   N   D   SD

Sexual Polarity Scale

DONALD L. MOSHER[1] AND JAMES SULLIVAN, *University of Connecticut*

Sexual polarity is defined as a sexual ideology (a) consisting of a more or less organized set of ideas about sexuality that orders information about the ideals and aspirations in a sexual world view; (b) polarizing into a left-wing (*naturalist*) and a right-wing (*jehovanist*) set of ideas; and (c) serving as a script, often shared by a community of believers, to interpret, to predict, to explain, to evaluate, or to control past, present, and future sexual scenes. The concepts of *jehovanist* and *naturalist*, introduced by Davis (1983), suggested the content of the items. Jehovanists believe that sex is dirty and aside from moderate intensity— marital coitus—threatens the dissolution of the individual's self

[1]Address correspondence Donald L. Mosher, 648 Ternberry Forest Drive, The Villages, FL 32162; e-mail: dlmosher@aol.com

and the destruction of the social order. Naturalists are modernists who place sex into a nonsacred, biological context of natural behavior that occurs commonly in humans across cultures and in other species of animals.

The Sexual Polarity Scale (SPS), in addition, contains selected items from Tomkins' (1965) Polarity Scale (TPS). Tomkins (1965) defined ideology as "any organized set of ideas about which humans are most passionate and for which there is no evidence and about which they are least certain" (p. 78). The left-wing of the polarity, called *humanist*, is rooted in the view, introduced by Protagoras, of man as the measure of all things. The right-wing of the polarity, called *normative*, is anchored to the Platonic conception of Ideas and Essences as the realm of reality and value. Humanists, who view people as basically good, view science as promoting human realization, government as promoting social welfare, and socialization as requiring unconditional love, sympathy, and play. Normatives, who view people as basically bad, view science as establishing truth, government as preserving law and order, and socialization as requiring conditional love to promote respect for rules and authority.

Description

The SPS consists of 30 forced-choice items measuring the sexual polarity of jehovanist or the naturalist ideology and 30 selected forced-choice items from the TPS measuring the polarity in world-views of the normative or humanist ideology. The 60 items are randomly mixed. Thus, the scale measures a relative preference for a left-wing world-view (humanist ideology) and a left-wing sexual ideology (naturalist) or a right-wing world-view (normative ideology) and a right-wing sexual ideology (jehovanist).

Response Mode and Timing

Respondents can circle the letter of the preferred alternative in each pair or respond on a machine-scoreable answer sheet. Approximately 13 minutes is required for completion.

Scoring

Alternatives assigned to the jehovanist ideology are scored 1, and naturalist alternatives are scored 0. The jehovanist item numbers and letters for that choice are: 1a, 4b, 8a, 9b, 10b, 11a, 14a, 15b, 16b, 17b, 19b, 20a, 22b, 23b, 25b, 27b, 28b, 29a, 30b, 35a, 36a, 37b, 39b, 40a, 41b, 43b, 44a, 46b, 51b, and 52a.

Alternatives assigned to the normative ideology are scored 1, and humanist alternatives are scored 0. The normative item numbers and letters for that choice are: 2b,

3b, 5a, 6b, 7b, 12a, 13a, 18a, 21b, 24a, 26b, 31a, 52b, 33a, 34a, 38b, 42b, 45b, 47b, 48b, 49a, 50b, 53a, 55b, 56b, 57a, 58a, 59b, and 60a. Scores for normative and jehovanist ideologies can range from 0, if only humanist and naturalist alternatives are selected, to 30, if only normative and jehovanist alternatives are selected.

Reliability

Internal consistency item analyses, from a sample of 140 male University of Connecticut undergraduates, were used to select 30 items from 40 items sampling the content of the sexual polarity and 30 items from the 59 items of the TPS. In the pool of 40 items measuring the sexual polarity, 37 items had discriminated the jehovanist/naturalist polarity at the .95 level of significance; for the TPS, 45 of 59 items significantly discriminated the normative/humanist polarity. The Cronbach alpha coefficient for the sexual jehovanist/humanist polarity was .86. The Cronbach alpha coefficient for Tomkins's normative/humanist polarity was .79.

Validity

Evidence of construct validity is limited to a study of 140 male undergraduates (Mosher & Sullivan, 1986). A pattern of significant Pearson correlations with other measures revealed a pattern that confirmed expectations. More jehovanist men, in comparison to more naturalist men, attended church more frequently, $r(138) = .23$; reported more involvement in church activities, $r(138) = .33$; scored higher on sex-guilt, $r(138) = .56$; had a normative rather than a humanist world-view, $r(138) = .36$; were more intolerant of ambiguity, $r(138) = .32$, and accepted more rape myths, $r(138) = .16$.

Tomkins (1965) summarized evidence from diverse experimental methods that supported the construct validity of the normative/humanist ideology. In addition to being more jehovanist, more normative men, in comparison to more humanist men, were more macho, $r(138) = .22$; intolerant of ambiguity, $r(138) = .20$; and had a higher proclivity to rape, $r(138) = .19$.

References

Davis, M. S. (1983). *Smut: Erotic reality/obscene ideology.* Chicago: University of Chicago Press.

Mosher, D. L., & Sullivan, J. (1986). *The development of a measure of sexual ideology: The polarity of jehovanist or naturalist.* Unpublished manuscript. University of Connecticut, Storrs.

Tomkins, S. S. (1965). Affect and the psychology of knowledge. In S. S. Tomkins & C. E. Izard (Eds.), *Affect, cognition, and personality* (pp. 72–97). New York: Springer.

Exhibit

Sexual Polarity Scale

Instructions: An ideology is an organized set of ideas that offers a world view. An ideology can be concerned with theories of value, education, science, sex, or socialization. These are just a few examples. A sexual ideology is an organized set of ideas about sex reflecting the ideas and aspirations of the individual, society, and culture. In the 60 items that follow, polar or contrasting ideas are presented. Your task is to select the item in each pair which is closest to your personal point of view. If you prefer alternative (a) circle letter (a); if you prefer alternative (b) circle letter (b). Although your cooperation is appreciated, you are, of course, free not to answer any item.

1. a) Pornography is disgusting.
    b) So-called pornography can be enjoyable.
2. a) The most important aspect of science is that it enables man to realize himself by gaining understanding and control of the world around him.
    b) The most important aspect of science is that it enables man to separate the true from the false, the right from the wrong, reality from fantasy.
3. a) To assume that most people are well-meaning brings out the best in others.
    b) To assume that most people are well-meaning is asking for trouble.
4. a) Abandoning yourself to pleasure helps to produce orgasmic response.
    b) Sexual abandonment endangers the person's ability to control his or her own body.
5. a) No government should sanction legalized gambling. Ultimately this will undermine the very foundations of authority.
    b) Legalized gambling is at worst innocuous. At best it lends spice and zest to life.
6. a) What children demand should be of little consequence to their parents.
    b) What children demand, parents should take seriously and try to satisfy.
7. a) The most important thing in the world is to know yourself and be yourself.
    b) The most important thing in the world is to try to live up to the highest standards.
8. a) The sin of fornication can be a worse crime than murder.
    b) It is better to make love than to fight.
9. a) Homosexual teachers have no necessary affect on children's personality sexual orientation.
    b) Homosexual teachers can corrupt a young mind.
10. a) Sexual fantasy is a way for a person to increase their erotic pleasure through the use of imagination.
    b) Too much thinking about sex is a sign of an impure mind that will be easy prey to sexual temptation.
11. a) Sex undermines the distinction between humans and animals, making people more bestial.
    b) Sex affirms the essential similarity of all of nature's creatures.
12. a) Juvenile delinquency is simply a reflection of the basic evil in human beings. It has always existed in the past and it always will.
    b) Juvenile delinquency is due to factors we do not understand. When we do understand these we will be able to prevent it in the future.
13. a) When man faces death he learns how basically insignificant he is.
    b) When man faces death he learns who he really is and how much he loved life.
14. a) Pornography pollutes the senses, the self, and the society.
    b) Erotica arouses the senses, frees the self, and purges false prudery from society.
15. a) The child molester deserves society's help, treatment, and rehabilitation.
    b) The child molester should receive their just deserts-punishment.
16. a) Scientific knowledge provides the best guide to leading a satisfying sex life.
    b) The Bible and religious leaders provide the best guide to leading a moral sex life.
17. a) Pornography is protected by the freedom of speech clause in the First Amendment.
    b) Pornography should not be protected by the First Amendment because it creates a clear and present danger to society.
18. a) The important thing in science is to be right and make as few errors as possible.
    b) The important thing in science is to strike out into the unknown-right or wrong.
19. a) Sexually explicit materials can be used in the classroom to educate young people about the facts of human sexuality.
    b) The danger of sex education in the classroom is that it will corrupt the minds of young people who are open to immoral influences.
20. a) Nudity at public beaches endangers the well-being of the young.
    b) Nudity at public beaches can lead to an appreciation of the human body as part of nature.

21. a) Great achievements require first of all great imagination.
    b) Great achievements require first of all severe self-discipline.
22. a) Engaging in a single homosexual act does not necessarily mean the person has, or will adopt, an identity as a homosexual.
    b) Engaging in a single homosexual act identifies a person as homosexual.
23. a) Although child pornography is distasteful, its influence is overrated.
    b) If child pornography is permitted in any form, civilization, as we know it, is doomed.
24. a) If human beings were really honest with each other, there would be a lot more antipathy and enmity in the world.
    b) If human beings were really honest with each other, there would be a lot more sympathy and friendship in the world.
25. a) Leaders in the public eye have no special moral obligations-they are fallible like all humans.
    b) Sexual morality is necessary in our clergy, government officials, and teachers to uphold the standards of society.
26. a) The beauty of theorizing is that it has made it possible to invent things which otherwise never would have existed.
    b) The trouble with theorizing is that it leads people away from the facts and substitutes opinion for truth.
27. a) Sometimes abortion is the best choice available to a young, unmarried woman.
    b) Abortion is immoral because it takes a human life.
28. a) Sex education in the schools, including teaching about contraception, is the most effective way to reduce teenage pregnancies.
    b) Sex education in the schools threatens to undermine the authority of the family and the morality of the community.
29. a) People should wash their hands and genitals after engaging in sexual relations.
    b) Washing after sex destroys the relaxed mood that is created since it implies that sex is dirty.
30. a) The loss of control during sexual intercourse heightens orgasmic and interpersonal fulfillment.
    b) Sexual intercourse and orgasm resemble having an epileptic fit, lacking the gracefulness and beauty of more refined social interaction.
31. a) Imagination leads people into self-deception and delusions.
    b) Imagination frees people from the dull routines of life.
32. a) Thinking is responsible for all discovery and invention.
    b) Thinking keeps people on the straight and narrow.
33. a) Observing the world accurately enables human beings to separate reality from imagination.
    b) Observing the world accurately provides a human being with constant excitement and novelty.
34. a) Some people can only be changed by humiliating them.
    b) No one has the right to humiliate another person.
35. a) Sex is so powerful that it alters your moral character, making you more like your partner.
    b) Sex has no more power to alter personality or character than any other form of social interaction.
36. a) The wages of sexual sin is death.
    b) The wages of sexual guilt is sexual inhibition.
37. a) Marital sex can remain exciting if the couple is imaginative and uninhibited.
    b) Marriage is a good remedy for sexual temptation.
38. a) Those who err should be forgiven.
    b) Those who err should be corrected.
39. a) Consenting sex is a worthwhile moral end.
    b) Too often, sex leads people to relate to one another as means rather than as ends.
40. a) Oral and anal sex are more depraved than sexual intercourse.
    b) Oral and anal sex are as morally acceptable as intercourse as long as the couple agrees.
41. a) Any position a couple wants to use during intercourse is normal because preferences for positions vary from culture to culture.
    b) There are natural and unnatural positions for men and women to use during sexual intercourse.
42. a) Whenever a person has difficulty in deciding which of two things to do he should do that which will give him the greatest satisfaction. In the long run that will be the right choice.
    b) Whenever a person has difficulty in deciding which of two things to do he should do what he ought to do, whether it gives him satisfaction or not.
43. a) All of sex is natural, without necessarily having any cosmic or religious significance.
    b) Marital sex, and only marital sex, is sacred-to be regarded with wonder.
44. a) Human sex was set apart forever from animal sex by the divine act that created the human soul.
    b) Human sex is similar, biologically and behaviorally, to sex in primates like the apes.
45. a) Anger should be directed against the oppressors of mankind.
    b) Anger should be directed against those revolutionaries who undermine law and order.
46. a) Masturbation is a normal sexual behavior that has produced needless worries.
    b) At best, masturbation must be controlled; at worst, it is a sinful waste of human seed.

47. a) Familiarity, like absence, makes the heart grow fonder.
    b) Familiarity breeds contempt.
48. a) Reason is the chief means by which human beings make great discoveries.
    b) Reason has to be continually disciplined and corrected by reality and hard facts.
49. a) The changeableness of human feelings is a weakness in human beings.
    b) The changeableness of human feelings makes life more interesting.
50. a) There are a great many things in the world which are good for human beings and which satisfy them in different ways. This makes the world an exciting place and enriches the lives of human beings.
    b) There are a great many things which attract human beings. Some of them are proper, but many are bad for human beings, and some are degrading.
51. a) Psychology studies sexual behavior with the same scientific methods used to study other forms of experience and behavior.
    b) Psychology can only study the surface of sex, not its essence.
52. a) The Kinsey Reports are an example of poor science.
    b) The Kinsey Reports reduced irrational guilt by describing how common many sexual behaviors were.
53. a) Children should be seen and not heard.
    b) Children are entirely delightful.
54. a) For a human being to live a good life he must act like a good man, i.e., observe the rules of morality.
    b) For a human being to live a good life he must satisfy both himself and others.
55. a) Mystical experiences may be sources of insight into the nature of reality.
    b) So-called mystical experiences have most often been a source of delusion.
56. a) Man must always leave himself open to his own feelings—alien as they may sometimes seem.
    b) If sanity is to be preserved, man must guard himself against the intrusion of feelings which are alien to his nature.
57. a) There is no surer road to insanity than surrender to the feelings, particularly those which are alien to the self.
    b) There is a unique avenue to reality through the feelings, even when they seem alien.
58. a) Life sometimes smells bad.
    b) Life sometimes leaves a bad taste in the mouth.
59. a) The mind is like a lamp which illuminates whatever it shines on.
    b) The mind is like a mirror which reflects whatever strikes it.
60. a) Things are beautiful or ugly independent of what human beings think.
    b) Beauty and ugliness are in the eye of the beholder.

Sexually Assertive Behavior Scale

PETER B. ANDERSON,[1] *Walden University*
MARIA NEWTON, *University of Utah*

The purpose of the Sexually Assertive Behavior Scale (SABS) is to assess women's behaviors and motives relative to initiating sexual contact with men.

Description

The SABS is a 19-item scale composed of six factors—Sexual Arousal, Hidden Motives, Verbal Pressure, Retaliation or Gain, Physical Force, and Exploitation. Factor 1 (Sexual Arousal) relates to mutually consenting sexual contact and attempts to arouse a partner. Factor 2 (Hidden Motives) items relate to a woman initiating a sexual relationship with a man other than her partner to make her partner jealous, to hurt him, or to terminate their relationship. Factor 3 (Verbal Pressure) items relate to verbally persuasive tactics. Factor 4 (Retaliation or Gain)

[1] Address correspondence to Peter B. Anderson, School of Counseling and Social Services, Walden University, 155 Fifth Ave. South, Suite 100, Minneapolis, MN 55401; e-mail: Peter.Anderson@Waldenu.edu

items relate to initiating sexual contact with a partner out of anger, to retaliate, or to gain favor. Factor 5 (Physical Force) items specify the threat and use of physical force. Factor 6 (Exploitation) items relate to initiating sexual contact while the partner is vulnerable.

The SABS was developed to assess a wide range of behaviors and motives relative to women initiating sexual contact. Thirteen of the items in the SABS were adapted from the Sexual Experiences Survey (SES) developed by Koss and Oros (1982). The SES is a self-report instrument using dichotomous (yes-no) responses to 13 questions that reflect various degrees of male sexual aggression and female victimization. For example, women responding to the SES were asked, "Have you had sexual intercourse when you didn't want to because a man used his position of authority (boss, teacher, camp counselor, supervisor) to make you?" This work was chosen for adaptation because it was previously tested and shown to have good internal consistency reliability (Cronbach's alpha = .74 for women, .89 for men), test-retest reliability of .93, and external validity established through face-to-face interview (Pearson r = .61, p < .001) (Koss & Gidycz, 1985).

In addition to the 13 items adapted from the SES for inclusion in the SABS, 6 more items were generated from a review of the literature on male sexual aggression and item suggestions by a panel of experts in sexual aggression, for example "How many times have you attempted to have sexual contact with a man by taking advantage of a compromising position he was in (being where he did not belong or breaking some rule)?" or "How many times have you attempted to have sexual contact with a man to get even with or hurt another man?" All items were worded to conform to the interviewing style used by Kinsey, Pomeroy, and Martin (1948), who assumed all respondents had engaged in each behavior mentioned and allowed for specific numerical responses (i.e., "How many times have you . . .?" rather than "Have you ever . . .?"). Also, we attempted to arrange the order of items in the SABS to ask what we judged to be the more comfortable questions first.

Response Mode and Timing

The SABS contains written instructions directing the respondents to write in the number of times they have initiated sexual contact as described in each question. Completion of the 19-item questionnaire typically takes approximately 5 minutes.

Scoring

Actual frequency counts are elicited for each question. To date, we have compiled and transformed the responses into dichotomous scores of 0 for those who reported no experience and 1 for those who reported engaging in the behavior

or motive one or more times. One may also choose to create a response distribution per item and then subdivide the distribution into quartiles. Items contained in each subscale are Sexual Arousal (Items 1–5), Hidden Motives (Items 9–11), Verbal Pressure (Items 6–8), Retaliation or Gain (Items 12–14), Physical Force (Items 18–19), and Exploitation (Items 15–17).

Reliability

Anderson and Newton (1997) found that the Hidden Motives subscale demonstrated satisfactory reliability (alpha coefficient .75). Internal consistency for the Sexual Arousal, Retaliation or Gain, and Verbal Pressure subscales was marginally acceptable (alphas = .64, .56, and .61, respectively). The Exploitation subscale (alpha = .43) yielded low reliability and should be interpreted with caution. The Physical Force subscale contained only two items (alpha = .58).

Validity

This instrument was reviewed for face and content validity, pretested, pilot tested, and reviewed twice by a panel of experts to establish consensual validation (Anderson, 1990). Construct validity, in relation to factor structure, was supported by factor analyses (Anderson & Newton, 1997).

Updates

The SABS has been modified for use by the principal authors and others since it was first introduced (see Anderson, Kontos, & Struckman-Johnson, 2008; Anderson, Kontos, Tanigoshi, & Struckman-Johnson, 2005). Subsequent versions have expanded the number of questions asked and shown similar reliability and validity scores. The original SABS remains the most parsimonious scale designed to assess women's sexual aggression toward men.

References

Anderson, P. B. (1990, November). *Aggressive sexual behavior by females: Incidence, correlates, and implications.* Paper presented at the Annual Meeting of the Mid-South Educational Research Association, New Orleans, LA.

Anderson, P. B., Kontos, A. P., & Struckman-Johnson, C. (2008). Relationships between college women's responses to the multidimensional sexuality questionnaire and the heterosexual contact scale. *Electronic Journal of Human Sexuality, 11.* http://www.ejhs.org/volume11/anderson.htm

Anderson, P. B., Kontos, A. P., Tanigoshi, H., & Struckman-Johnson, C. (2005). A comparison of sexual strategies used by urban southern and rural midwestern university women. *The Journal of Sex Research, 42,* 335–341.

Anderson, P., & Newton, M. (1997). The Initiating Heterosexual Contact Scale: A factor analysis. *Sexual Abuse: A Journal of Research and Treatment, 9,* 179–186.

Kinsey, A., Pomeroy W., & Martin, C. (1948). *Sexual behavior in the human male.* Philadelphia: Saunders.

Koss, M., & Gidycz, C. (1985). Sexual Experiences Survey: Reliability and validity. *Journal of Consulting and Clinical Psychology, 53,* 422–423.

Koss, M., & Oros, C. (1982). Sexual Experiences Survey: A research instrument investigating sexual aggression and victimization. *Journal of Consulting and Clinical Psychology, 50,* 455–457.

Exhibit

Sexually Assertive Behavior Scale

This portion of the questionnaire is an attempt to discover some of the behavior that you employ in your sexual activities. Sexual contact is defined as fondling, kissing, petting, or intercourse. There are no right or wrong answers to the questions. Please answer as honestly as you can.

1. How many times have you had sexual contact (fondling, kissing, petting, or intercourse) with a man when you both wanted to?
2. How many times have you initiated sexual contact (fondling, kissing, petting, or intercourse) with a man?
3. In initiating sexual contact with a man, how many times have you overestimated the level of sexual activity he desired to have with you?
4. How many times have you attempted to have sexual contact with a man because you were so sexually aroused you did not want to stop?
5. How many times have you attempted to have sexual contact with a man by getting him sexually aroused?
6. How many times have you attempted to have sexual contact (fondling, kissing, petting, or intercourse) with a man by threatening to end your relationship?
7. How many times have you attempted to have sexual contact with a man by saying things that you didn't mean?
8. How many times have you attempted to have sexual contact with a man by pressuring him with verbal arguments?
9. How many times have you attempted to have sexual contact with a man in order to make another man jealous?
10. How many times have you attempted to have sexual contact with a man in order to get even with or hurt another man?
11. How many times have you attempted to have sexual contact with a man in order to end a relationship with another man?
12. How many times have you attempted to have sexual contact with a man in a position of power or authority over you (boss, teacher, or supervisor) in order to better your situation or gain something?
13. How many times have you attempted to have sexual contact with a man because you were angry at him?
14. How many times have you attempted to have sexual contact with a man to retaliate for something he did to you?
15. How many times have you attempted to have sexual contact (fondling, kissing, petting, or intercourse) with a man to gain power or control over him?
16. How many times have you attempted to have sexual contact with a man while his judgment was impaired by drugs or alcohol?
17. How many times have you attempted to have sexual contact with a man by taking advantage of a compromising position he was in (being where he did not belong or breaking some rule)?
18. How many times have you attempted to have sexual contact with a man by threatening to use some degree of physical force (holding him down, hitting him, etc.)?
19. How many times have you attempted to have sexual contact with a man by using some degree of physical force?

Depth of Sexual Involvement Scale

MARITA P. McCABE[1] AND JOHN K. COLLINS, *Macquarie University*

The purpose of this instrument is to measure the depth or intimacy of desired and experienced sexual behaviors during various stages of heterosexual dating.

Description

A Guttman-type scale of 16 behaviors (Guttman, 1944) was constructed by extending the scale used by Collins (1974) with items from Luckey and Nass (1969). This scale was administered to 259 high school and university students who were asked to indicate which of 16 behaviors they would like to experience in a heterosexual dating relationship. The scale was reduced to 12 items by combining adjacent scale items which showed similar responses by males and females over a number of stages of dating. Examples of items that were combined were "hand holding" and "light embrace," redefined as "hand holding: holding hands or locking arms, generally while walking." Three other items which were combined were "necking," "deep kissing," and "general body contact." These were redefined as "necking: close body contact, with hugging and prolonged kissing." The final scale is a Guttman-type scale of 12 behaviors which could measure either the heterosexual desires or experiences of adolescents and young adults during dating.

The three stages of dating for which the instrument has been used are the first date (defined as "the first time you go out with a new dating partner to whom you are attracted"), several dates (defined as "when going out with a partner consistently, but both partners feeling free to go out with others"), and going steady (defined as "when both partners come to a mutual and implicit understanding that dating will exclude others"). The scale could also be used for other relationship stages.

Response Mode and Timing

Respondents circle *yes* if they have experienced (or want to experience) a particular behavior, and *no* if they have not experienced (or do not want to experience) a particular behavior at the stage of dating being studied. The length of time taken to complete the scale will depend upon the number of aspects of the dating relationships under consideration; that is, the number of times the scale is administered. Any single administration of the scale requires an average of 3 minutes.

Scoring

As the scale is of a Guttman-type, a score may be obtained by determining the last item which received an affirma-

tive response. Alternatively, the number of affirmative responses for each use of the scale may be totalled. Higher scores indicate a greater desire for, or experience of, sexual intimacy at the stage of dating being studied.

Reliability

McCabe and Collins (1984) reported test-retest reliability over an 8-week period with 61 student volunteers for behavior on a first date as .83; after several dates, .73; and when going steady, .96. For desires, over the same time period, the coefficient for the first date was .85; after several dates, .80; and when going steady, .78. McCabe and Collins also administered the scale to 2,001 volunteers ranging in age from 16 to 25 years to evaluate the scalability of the component items of each of the six uses of the scale. The coefficient of reproducibility exceeded .90 and the corresponding coefficient of scalability was greater than .70. These same data show the scale to be internally consistent and predominantly unidimensional with coefficient alpha exceeding .87 for each use of the scale.

Validity

Construct validity has been established by McCabe and Collins (1984). The scale was administered to 156 subjects ranging in age from 18 to 48 years. Results showed that as dating became more involved, the level of sexual activity both desired and experienced by males and females also increased. A further study of 259 subjects demonstrated that the desire for sexual experience was higher for males than for females until a committed relationship was established, and that females desire greater sexual involvement with increasing age.

Criterion validity was demonstrated by McCabe and Collins (1984). Twenty-nine couples who were going steady at the time of testing were asked to indicate their desired level of sexual experience for this stage of dating. Results showed that 62% of couples indicated the same number of *yes* responses, with a total of 77% scoring within one *yes* response of their partners.

References

Collins, J. K. (1974). Adolescent data intimacy: Norms and peer expectations. *Journal of Youth and Adolescence, 3,* 317–328.

Collins, J. K., & McCabe, M. P. (1980). The influence of sex roles on psychobiological and psychoaffectional orientations to dating. In C. A. Rigg & L. B. Sherin (Eds.), *Adolescent medicine: Present*

[1]Address correspondence to Marita P. McCabe, School of Psychology, Deakin University, 221 Burwood Highway, Burwood, Victoria, Australia 3125; e-mail: marita.mccabe@deakin.edu.au

and future concepts (pp. 181–195). Chicago: Year Book Medical Publishers.

Guttman, L. (1944). A basis for scaling qualitative ideas. *American Sociological Review, 9,* 139–150.

Luckey, E., & Nass, G. A. (1969). A comparison of sexual attitudes and behavior in an international sample. *Journal of Marriage and the Family, 31,* 364–379.

McCabe, M. P. (1982). The influence of sex and sex role on the dating attitudes and behavior of Australian youth. *Journal of Adolescent Health Care, 3,* 54–62.

McCabe, M. P., & Collins, J. K. (1981). Dating desires and experiences: A new approach to an old question. *Australian Journal of Sex, Marriage and the Family, 2,* 165–173.

McCabe, M. P., & Collins, J. K. (1983). The sexual and affectional attitudes and experiences of Australian adolescents during dating: The effects of age, church attendance, type of school and socioeconomic class. *Archives of Sexual Behavior, 12,* 525–539.

McCabe, M. P., & Collins, J. K. (1984). Measurement of depth of desired and experienced sexual involvement at different stages of dating. *The Journal of Sex Research, 20,* 377–390.

Exhibit

Depth of Sexual Involvement Scale

The following instructions accompany the scale, depending upon the purpose for which it is used.

Desire on First Date

This task is to determine what you *would like* at different stages in the dating relationship.

Indicate which of the following you *would like* on the FIRST DATE (i.e., the first time you go out with a new dating partner to whom you are attracted).

Circle the response which is applicable.

Behavior on First Date

Instructions as above, but "*would like*" is replaced by "*have never experienced.*"

Desires After Several Dates

Instructions as for Desires on First Date but "FIRST DATE" is replaced by "SEVERAL DATES" with the definition of this stage of dating given earlier in this paper.

Behavior After Several Dates

Instructions as for Behavior on First Date but "FIRST DATE" is replaced by "SEVERAL DATES" with the definition of this stage of dating given earlier in this paper.

Desires When Going Steady

Instructions as for Desires on First Date but "FIRST DATE" is replaced by "when GOING STEADY" with the definition of this stage of dating given earlier in this paper.

Behavior When Going Steady

Instructions as for Behavior on First Date but "FIRST DATE" is replaced by "when GOING STEADY" with the definition of this stage of dating given earlier in this paper.

Scale of Sexual Activities

1. Hand holding: holding hands or locking arms, generally while walking.
2. Light kissing: casual goodnight kiss on the lips.
3. Necking: close body contact, with hugging and prolonged kissing.
4. Light breast petting: caress of the girl's breasts outside the clothing.
5. Heavy breast petting: fondling or kissing of the girl's breasts under the clothing.
6. Light genital petting of the female: touching genital area of the girl, outside the clothing.
7. Heavy genital petting of female: touching genital area of the girl, under the clothing.
8. Manual stimulation of male genitals.
9. Oral stimulation of female genitals.
10. Oral stimulation of male genitals.
11. Petting of each other's genitals resulting in orgasm for one or both partners.
12. Intercourse.

Sexual Path Preferences Inventory

Donald L. Mosher,[1] *University of Connecticut*

In Mosher's (1980) sexual involvement theory, orgasmic response is potentiated by effective sexual stimulation that is subjectively experienced as pleasurable: (a) sensory signals, (b) the discrete affects of interest-excitement and enjoyment-joy, and (c) the cognitive interpretation and evaluation of sensory and affective pleasure as ordered by rules contained in facilitating sexual scripts. Effective sexual stimulation is a joint function of the optimal density of physical sexual stimulation and depth of involvement in the sexual episode. The *optimal density* of physical stimulation is a function of scripted rules for ordering information about the intensity times duration of sexual touching. *Involvement* is defined as a latent or theoretical construct consisting of a complex of interacting psychological processes that motivate and define the state of absorption in the sexual episode. The involvement complex consists of (a) the affects of interest-excitement and enjoyment-joy, (b) affect-cognition blends of anticipatory excitement and sexual pleasure with the sexual goal, image, and plan (i.e., the sexual motive) for the episode, and (c) the facilitating sexual scripts of involvement potential and path preference.

The Sexual Path Preferences Inventory measures involvement potential and path preferences. In addition, it measures, for couples, the compatibility of path preferences and potential involvement. Involvement is manifested as a state of absorption in the inherently acceptable affective scene of the sexual episode. To be involved or absorbed means the person is fully attending to or totally engrossed in the possibilities of the sexual image and plan and the unfolding actualities or expressive action, subject experience, and interpersonal engagement emergent in the present moment of the sexual episode. Depth of involvement in the sexual episode is a function of a deepening involvement within three (so far identified) general paths, or families of plans, that are distinguished conceptually as (a) the path of involvement in sexual role enactment, (b) the path of involvement in sexual trance, and (c) the path of involvement with the sex partner.

A *path* is defined as a general sexual script containing (a) the ordered set of rules for generating, predicting, interpreting, controlling, and evaluating a related family of sexual scenes and (b) its associated affect. The potentiality for deep involvement in a particular sexual scene is a function of (a) involvement potential; (b) multiple, highly valued path preferences; and (c) flexibility in responding to feedback from auxiliary information about the goodness-of-fit of the unfolding incidents and events to the sexual image and plan. *Involvement potential* is defined as a latent

capacity, realized in an actual sexual scene, for absorption in the sexual episode as a function of the total set of facilitating sexual scripts. *Path preference* is defined as a relative preference for a specific set of plans sharing a family resemblance, the three paths to involvement identified above. *Compatible involving path or paths* is defined as the sharing by a couple of one of more paths which are involving for them as individuals and on which they overlap, preferring the same specific features within the path. This inventory is appropriate for use in research on sexual involvement theory and for clinical use with clients experiencing sexual dysfunction.

Description

This inventory consists of 90 7-point Likert items, arranged into 30 item triplets by categories, with response options labeled 0, *not at all true of (for) me* to 6, *extremely true of (for) me*. Each item triplet consists of an item from the sexual role enactment, sexual trance, and sex partner paths in categories that define path preference (e.g., sexual metaphors, mood, settings, sexual techniques, etc.). This novel item arrangement in sets of three is named a *limited comparison format* because respondents are encouraged to compare their responses within the set to delineate gradations in preference. The inventory is appropriate for use with sexually experienced adults who have had an opportunity to develop preferences.

Response Mode and Timing

Respondents rate each item on a 0 to 6 scale by circling a number on the test booklet or filling in a blank on a machine-scoreable answer sheet. Approximately 20 minutes are required for completion.

Scoring

The sum of the scores for all 90 items measures involvement potential. The summed scores of the following 30 items measure Preference for the Path of Sexual Role Enactment: 1, 5, 9, 11, 13, 18, 19, 23, 26, 28, 33, 35, 38, 42, 44, 46, 49, 52, 55, 59, 62, 66, 68, 70, 74, 78, 80, 83, 86, and 90. The summed scores of the following 30 items measure Preference for the Path of Sexual Trance: 3, 4, 8, 12, 14, 16, 20, 24, 27, 29, 31, 36, 39, 40, 43, 47, 50, 54, 56, 60, 61, 65, 69, 72, 75, 77, 81, 84, 85, and 89. The summed scores of the following 30 items measure Preference for the Path of Partner Engagement: 2, 6, 7, 10, 15, 17, 21, 22,

[1]Address correspondence to Donald L. Mosher, 648 Ternberry Forest Drive, The Villages, FL 32162; e-mail: dlmosher@aol.com

25, 30, 32, 34, 37, 41, 45, 48, 51, 53, 57, 58, 63, 64, 67, 71, 73, 76, 79, 82, 87, and 88. An individual might have one, two, three, or no highly valued paths as defined by scores above 120 for a particular path. If each partner of a couple has completed the inventory independently, then indices of compatibility of involving path preference can be scored. A score for Compatible Role Path is a count of the 30 items keyed above on which both members of the couple rated the same item as 5, 6, or 7 (i.e., it was true of them both). A score for Compatible Trance Path is a similar count of the 30 items keyed in that path which both members of the couple endorsed as true for them; likewise, a count is made for Compatible Partner Path. A sum of these three scores yields an index of Potential for Compatible Involvement.

Reliability

Cronbach alpha coefficients were computed on a sample of 100 sexually experienced adult men and women for Involvement Potential, alpha = .93; Preference for Role Path, alpha = .92; Preference for Trance Path, alpha = .86; and Preference for Partner Path, alpha = .91.

Validity

Sirkin (1985) found that 76 college men scored significantly higher on the Path of Role Enactment, $M = 100.01$, than 62 college women, $M = 87.52$, $t(136) = 2.72$, $p < .01$. For the women in the sample, Involvement Potential, Trance Path Preference, and Role Path Preference were significantly correlated (Mdn $r(60) = .43$) with self-reports of sexual behavior, sexual pleasure, and sexual fantasy. Partner Path Preference was correlated, also for women, with reported

sexual pleasure. For the men, there were only three significant correlations. Two were for Partner Path Preference and reports of sexual behavior, $r(74) = -.28$, and masturbation, $r(73) = .32$ (i.e., men who scored higher on the Partner Path reported less sexual behavior with partners and more masturbation). Men scoring higher on the Role Path reported more sexual fantasy, $r(72) = .25$.

Moreover, Sirkin (1985), using a method of guided sexual imagery, experimentally varied conditions of hypnotic trance induction with a relaxation control and a no-treatment control to test for a theoretically predicted interaction between the Path of Sexual Trance and hypnotic induction. Using ratings of sexual arousal as the dependent variable, men and women who scored above the median on the Path of Sexual Trance and who received the hypnotic trance induction reported significantly higher sexual arousal than all of the other subjects in various conditions, $t(136) = 2.83$, $p < .01$. Preference for the Trance Path was also associated, alone or in interaction with the other two path preferences, with reports of experiencing the positive affects of enjoyment-joy and interest-excitement during the guided sexual imagery. Furthermore, Involvement Potential, after partialing out the treatment effects, was predictive of greater depth of involvement in the guided imagery, more subjective sexual arousal across three measures, and more affective enjoyment and interest.

References

Mosher, D. L. (1980). Three dimensions of depth of involvement in human sexual response. *The Journal of Sex Research, 16*, 1–42.

Sirkin, M. I. (1985). *Sexual involvement theory, sexual trance, and hypnotizability: The experimental use of guided imagery.* Unpublished doctoral dissertation, The University of Connecticut, Storrs.

Exhibit

Sexual Path Preferences Inventory

Instructions: This Inventory of Sexual Preferences provides you with an opportunity to clarify what your sexual preferences are. It consists of 90 items arranged into 30 triplets. Each set of three items is related to some aspect of a sexual episode between two partners. You are to respond to each of the 90 items as honestly as you can by rating your response on a 7-point scale where 0 means *not at all true of (for) me*, and 6 means *extremely true of (for) me*. Ratings of 1 through 5 represent ratings of disagreement/agreement that are intermediate between *not at all true* and *extremely true*. The items are arranged in sets of three to permit you to compare the intensity of agreement/disagreement among the set since they all relate to the same feature of the sexual situation. This limited comparison is often useful since people frequently most or least prefer one item in each set. In some instances it is possible that all items in a set may be *not at all true* or *extremely true* for you. Most often, there will be a gradation in preference. You may prefer or believe some items to be more characteristically true of you than others, and you may not prefer some items which are much less true for you than others. Rate each of the 90 items from 0 to 6 as you keep in mind the value of comparing items within the triplets.

Sexual metaphors

1. Sex is artful and dramatic play.
2. Sex is union.
3. Sex is trance.

Mood

4. My favorite mood for enjoying sex is like a tranquil meditative state or the relaxation that you might get from a massage or marijuana.
5. When I'm feeling that "All the world's a stage, and all the people are sex players," then I know I want to get it on.
6. When my heart is bursting with love, I know our sex will be bursting with loving pleasure.

Settings

7. I like to have sex in a romantic context in which my partner and I are feeling loving toward one another.
8. I could enjoy having sex in a setting close to nature (e.g., on a mountain top or by the ocean), if I knew that we were totally alone and sure of privacy.
9. I would enjoy having sex in a dramatic setting, like in an oriental harem or an elegant New Orleans brothel.

Sexual techniques

10. Regardless of contemporary views on sexual variety, for me nothing will replace my favorite position for coitus of being face to face with the one I love.
11. I enjoy having sexual intercourse in a wide variety of positions.
12. I prefer slow and rhythmic movement that permits me to really sense the shades and nuances of pleasure that can exist during sexual intercourse.

Sexual metaphors

13. Sex is a drama that begins with attraction, develops a plot filled with intrigue, mystery, and sex play, and ends in tumultuous climax worthy of an audience's applause.
14. Sex is a trip into your own sensory nerves and erotic images.
15. I consider sex to be the organ of love.

Mood

16. The most important aspect of my mood when I get into sex is that I be physically relaxed and mentally receptive.
17. To really want sex my mood must be one of really loving my partner.
18. I love serious sex play when I'm in a playful mood.

Settings

19. I believe that I would feel very excited by having secret sex in a semi-public place.
20. I like a setting for having sex that ensures total privacy.
21. I enjoy having sex in a place that has special meanings for me and my partner.

Sexual techniques

22. Ideally, all sexual techniques begin and build from kissing the face and lips.
23. I pride myself in being quite accomplished in the techniques of oral sex.
24. The most important thing about sexual technique is pacing and repetition that permits you and your partner to become absorbed into the sex.

Sexual style

25. My sexual style is affectionate and loving.
26. My sexual style is as varied as my mood suggests and my fantasies can create.
27. I concentrate on my inward sensations and experience during sex.

Ideal partner

28. Sexual skill and a flair for experimenting make an ideal sex partner.
29. An ideal sex partner flows with your mood and the situation rather than trying to dictate just how sex is to be done.
30. My ideal sex partner is my ideal love object.

Sex talk

31. If I talk during sex it's liable to be to say something like "oh, that feels so good, oh more, mmmh good, etc."
32. Most of all during sex I like to hear and say "I love you."
33. I really get off when my partner is urging, begging, or directing me by saying, for example, "fuck me, fuck me, fuck me!"

Sex fantasies

34. Sometimes I imagine that my partner through his/her sexual participation is pledging his/her love to me for life.
35. I can enjoy a wide range of sexual fantasies that create novelty in partners, activities, and settings.
36. I like to use my imagination to increase my absorption into the sensory experience of sex.

Sexual techniques

37. My sexual style concentrates on mutual pleasuring to bond us closer together.
38. Sexual variety is the spice of a love life.
39. When I have truly good sex I care less about what and how we are doing it sexually than I do about what I am sensing, feeling, and experiencing as a consequence.

Sexual style

40. For me the sexual experience is truly entrancing, and you would never know how intensely I am experiencing the sex by just looking at me.
41. In my sexual style I try to blend the romantic with the erotic to offer a full rich gift of sexual love.
42. I like to play different sexual roles and scripts that act out fantasies while having sex.

Ideal partner

43. I expect my sexual partner to help create and sustain an ambiance of sensual pleasure.
44. I like a partner who moans and writhes and is carried away by his/her passion.
45. I expect my sex partner to be truly sexually considerate and loving.

Sex talk

46. I can enjoy lusty sex talk that uses erotic language for erotic acts.
47. During sex I like little talk and more sensual friction.
48. Sex talk should be love talk.

Sex fantasies

49. I have several fantastic sex fantasies with dramatic and exciting plots that help turn me on during ordinary sex.
50. I may imagine how I look or how my own and my partner's sex organs look, etc. during sex to enhance my erotic pleasure.
51. Sometimes I imagine my partner is telling me how much he/she loves me during our lovemaking in ways that exceed the limits of mere words.

Ideal sex

52. Truly good sex for me usually entails a wide variety of sex practices and coital positions.
53. Good sex is the physical expression through sexual union of an interpersonal loving union.
54. Good sex for me is characterized by an intense involvement into the sensual and sexual sensation of the moment.

Music

55. Music to have sex by should have dramatic changes in rhythm, tempo, and volume while building to a lively crescendo.
56. Music to have sex by should be soft, low, and repetitive to form a rhythmic background that facilitates the flow without setting a pace to be followed.
57. Music to have sex by should be lyrical, romantic, and poetic in tone to match the partner's loving mood.

Orgasms

58. I most enjoy orgasms in which I seem to flow into my partner and lose myself in our union.

59. I love it when sex moves me to uninhibited self-expression that leaves me with no sense of control of my sounds, movements, and orgasm.
60. I most enjoy orgasms in which I experience sensations that are so intense that I actually lose consciousness or at least waking consciousness fades in the face of the culminative sensations and experience.

Ideal partner

61. An ideal sex partner knows exactly what I like and want now.
62. I enjoy a partner who is open to playing different roles so that we can create a novel and dramatic sexual script.
63. If a person cannot look me in the eye before, during and after sex, I suspect the attraction is to my body and not to me.

Sex fantasies

64. Most of my fantasies during sex are really memories of past shared moments in which we felt especially close and loving.
65. Sometimes I experience visual and auditory images that accompany the sensual sensory experience during sex.
66. Sometimes I imagine that I could enjoy sex on a stage surrounded by an admiring audience.

Ideal sex

67. The best sex for me is loving sex.
68. The best sex occurs when sexual expression becomes so ecstatic that it becomes nonvolitional and I lose all sense of conscious control.
69. When I'm having the best sex, my sex organs become alive and their sensations demand and direct the action.

Orgasms

70. I love it when my orgasms are nearly convulsive and I involuntarily scream in pleasure, and grab, and/or bite, or scratch.
71. To orgasm, I must be secure in my love for and from my partner.
72. During orgasms my awareness is flooded with intense sensations.

Emotions

73. Love is the predominant emotion in my sexual experience.
74. Excitement is the predominant emotion in my sexual experience.
75. Enjoyment is the predominant emotion in my sexual experience.

Meanings of sex

76. Sex is the merger of two into a unity of physical and spiritual love.
77. The meaning of sex is that it permits me to set aside my daily existence and to be transported into an underworld of sensations.
78. Sex when most meaningful is a cathartic drama that requires mastery and artful performance of one's sexual identity.

Sex fantasies

79. I sometimes imagine that my partner and I have been selected to symbolize the essence of love in a religious-like, sexual-spiritual ritual.
80. I can enjoy imagining that I am an amazingly successful porno film star and sex symbol in our culture.
81. I rarely have a sex fantasy with a plot; usually I only have a series of nonconnected, visual, sexual images of, for example, sex organs.

Ideal sex

82. The best sex occurs when I enter into a loving warm union with my partner, when we become two in one.
83. Sexual ecstasy is my criterion of good sex.
84. Good sex is total absorption into the sexual experience.

Orgasms

85. The moment of orgasm is a moment of total surrender to intense sensations.
86. The best orgasm is like an involuntary dramatic shock that overwhelms yet releases my sexual tension.
87. Orgasms are a unique moment of fusion in which my soul cries out its love through my body, and my longing for my partner is fulfilled.

Meanings of sex

88. Sharing sex with my partner can become a ritual that celebrates the profound meaning of life.
89. During sex I feel transported into another level of consciousness or plane of existence that gives me a new understanding of my life and the universe.
90. When I have a super sexual experience I feel as if I embody all men/women in a universal and timeless sexual ritual.

Anticipated Sexual Jealousy Scale

BRAM BUUNK,[1] *University of Nijmegen, The Netherlands*

Sexual jealousy can be defined as an aversive emotional reaction that occurs as the result of the partner's sexual attraction to a rival that is real, imagined, or considered likely to occur (Bringle & Buunk, 1985). In line with this definition, the Anticipated Sexual Jealousy Scale (ASJS) measures the degree to which the idea of sexual attraction felt by one's partner for another person evokes a negative emotional response. Because sexual attraction can be manifested in divergent ways, a range of sexually laden behaviors that could be exhibited by the partner are described, and the respondent's reaction to these hypothetical events is assessed. Another consideration behind the construction of the scale was that the negative emotional reactions to such events are not necessarily labeled as jealousy. As the word *jealous* has a negative connotation in Western culture, individuals may resist labeling their feelings as such. Therefore, the word jealous is avoided in the scale: people are simply asked how bothered they would be. Furthermore, it was assumed that extradyadic sexual behaviors exhibited by the partner can evoke negative, neutral, and positive emotional reactions (see Buunk, 1981a) and that this should be reflected in the response code.

Description, Response Mode, and Timing

The scale consists of five items. The format for each item is the same: the respondents are asked how they would feel if their partner were to engage in flirting, light petting, falling in love, sexual intercourse, and a long-term sexual relationship with another person of the opposite sex. The nine response options range from *extremely bothered* to *extremely pleased*. The midpoint is described as *neutral*. Each of the possible answers is spelled out literally. The respondents circle the number corresponding with the answer that best fits their anticipated feelings. The scale usually requires no more than 1 or 2 minutes for completion.

Scoring

The items can simply be summed. No reverse scoring is necessary. Higher scores indicate a higher degree of jealousy.

Reliability

The Cronbach alpha of the scale was .94 in a sample more or less representative of the general Dutch population and consisting of people with diverse levels of sexual permissiveness (Buunk, 1978); .90 in a study of people who had all been involved in extramarital relationships (Buunk, 1982); .91 in a sample of people in sexually open marriages (Buunk, 1981a); and .91 in a sample of undergraduate students (Buunk, 1981b). Over a 3-month period, test-retest reliability in the open marriage sample was $r(100) = .76$, $p < .001$.

Validity

There is considerable evidence for the concurrent validity of the ASJS. Individuals who said they were presently less jealous than before scored significantly lower on the scale than people who indicated they were as jealous now as they had been in the past (Buunk, 1981a). The scale particularly discriminates between persons high and low in sexual permissiveness. The sample described above, consisting of people who had been involved in extramarital relationships, scored much lower on the scale than a sample of undergraduate students, $t(596) = 19.78$, $p < .001$, and also much lower than the sample more or less representative of the average population, $t(466) = 11.27$, $p < .001$.

Further evidence for the concurrent validity of the ASJS is provided by the strong negative correlations that were found between this scale and a scale for extramarital behavioral intentions in three samples (Buunk, 1982). Finally, in

[1]Address correspondence to Bram Buunk, University of Nijmegen, Postbus 9104, 6500 HE Nijmegen, The Netherlands; e-mail: apbuunk@kpnplanet.nl

the aforementioned sample of individuals from the average population, the scale showed a high correlation with a scale measuring moral disapproval of extramarital sex, $r(250) = .77, p < .001$.

Construct validity of the ASJS has been established in several studies showing positive and rather high correlations with other scales measuring jealousy or related constructs. A correlation of $r(218) = .56, p < .001$, was found with a scale measuring jealousy as a consequence of a spouse's real extramarital relationship that had occurred in the recent past (see Buunk, 1984). Additionally, in the sample of persons from the average population, a positive correlation was established with a scale measuring the desire for an exclusive relationship, $r(250) = .63, p < .01$. In the undergraduate student sample mentioned previously, the ASJS correlated rather strongly, $r(380) = .59, p < .001$, with a scale based on the factor Threat to Exclusive Relationship, the first and main factor that was found in a factor analysis of jealousy related items by Hupka et al. (1985).

In the same study, Rubin's (1970) love scale correlated significantly with the scale described here, and his liking scale did not (Buunk, 1981a). These last findings support the construct validity of the ASJS because the love scale—as opposed to the liking scale as conceptualized by Rubin (1970)—refers to the emotional bond in a relationship, and jealousy is supposed to stem from a threat to such a bond.

Final evidence for the validity of the ASJS comes from the open marriage study. Here, among women, a high correlation was found between the scale and their jealousy as perceived by their husbands, $r(50) = .61, p < .001$. The same correlation among men was lower, but also significant, $r(50) = .39, p < .01$.

References

Bringle, R. G., & Buunk, B. (1985). Jealousy and social behavior: A review of person, relationship and situational determinants. In P. Shaver (Ed.), *Review of personality and social psychology* (Vol. 6). Beverly Hills, CA: Sage.

Buunk, B. (1978). Jaloezie 2. Ervaringen van 250 Nederlanders [Jealousy: Experiences of 250 Dutch people]. *Intermediair, 14*(11), 43–51.

Buunk, B. (1981a). Jealousy in sexually open marriages. *Alternative Lifestyles, 4*, 357–372.

Buunk, B. (1981b). Liefde, sympathie en jaloezie. [Loving, liking and jealousy]. *Gedrag, Tijdschrift voor Psychologie, 9*, 189–202.

Buunk, B. (1982). Anticipated sexual jealousy: Its relationship to self-esteem, dependency, and reciprocity. *Personality and Social Psychology, 8*, 310–316.

Buunk, B. (1984). Jealousy as related to attributions for the partner's behavior. *Social Psychology Quarterly, 47*, 107–112.

Hupka, R. B., Buunk, B., Falus, G., Fulgosi, A., Ortega, E., Swain, R., & Tarabrina, N. V. (1985). Romantic jealousy and romantic envy. A seven nation study. *Journal of Cross-Cultural Psychology, 16*, 423–446.

Rubin, Z. (1970). Measurement of romantic love. *Journal of Personality and Social Psychology, 16*, 265–273.

Exhibit

Anticipated Sexual Jealousy Scale

How would you feel if your partner were to engage in the following behavior with another man/woman?

1. Flirting
   a. extremely pleased
   b. very pleased
   c. fairly pleased
   d. somewhat pleased
   e. neutral
   f. somewhat bothered
   g. fairly bothered
   h. very bothered
   i. extremely bothered

2. Sexual intercourse[a]
3. Light petting
4. A long-term sexual relationship
5. Falling in love

[a]The nine response options are repeated for each item.

Sexual Knowledge, Experience, Feelings, and Needs Scale

MARITA P. McCABE,[1] *Deakin University*

The Sexual Knowledge, Experience, Feelings and Needs Scale (SexKen) is designed to evaluate the knowledge, experience, feelings, and needs of respondents in a range of sexual areas. There are four parallel versions of the scale: for people from the general population (SexKen), for people with mild intellectual disability (SexKen-ID), for people with physical disability (SexKen-PD), and for caregivers of people with disabilities (SexKen-C). The development of these parallel forms allows the similarities and differences in the sexuality of different groups of respondents to be evaluated and also the report of people with disabilities to be contrasted with the report of their caregivers. The measures may be completed as either a questionnaire or interview.

Description

Each of the versions of SexKen consists of 13 subscales. Within each subscale there are questions on the knowledge, experience, feelings, and needs of respondents as they relate to that area of sexuality. The number of items within each of these areas is different for each subscale, as the need for questions in each of these areas is different for the various aspects of sexuality. The subscales, with the number of questions in each area, are summarized in Table 1.

The first version of the scale to be developed was SexKen-ID. The reason for its development was the lack of an instrument which adequately evaluated the sexuality of people with mild intellectual disability across a broad range of areas. The scale was designed to focus on sexual knowledge, experience, feelings and needs. SexKen-ID was generally intended to be administered as an interview. The areas covered by the scale and the original questions included in the scale came from a review of the sexuality literature and other sexuality scales, mainly those developed for the general population. The original scale was tested with five people with mild intellectual disability, and feedback was obtained from professionals working in the sexuality area, carestaff working with people with intellectual disability, and academics who specialised in psychometrics.

The revised scale and the parallel SexKen and SexKen-C versions of the scale, which were designed for the general population and caregiver assessment of the sexuality of people with intellectual disability, were administered to 25 people with mild intellectual disability, 39 volunteer students, and 10 carestaff working with people with

intellectual disability (Szollos & McCabe, 1995). SexKen and SexKen-C were completed as questionnaire measures and SexKen-ID was administered as an interview. From this study, it was clear that some items in the scale were not readily understood by people with mild intellectual disability. Items in the scale were altered or removed to address the problems of relevance and comprehension that were evident from this study.

Modified versions of SexKen-ID and SexKen were used to evaluate the sexuality of people with mild intellectual disability and a student population in two further studies (McCabe & Cummins, 1996; McCabe, Cummins, & Reid, 1994). Analysis of responses and discussions with respondents led to further modification of the scales. SexKen-ID was restructured so that it comprised three separate interviews. The subscales were organised so that they ranged from the least intrusive to the most intrusive subscales in successive interviews. Interview 1 comprised the subscales of Friendship, Dating and Intimacy, Marriage, and Body Part Identification; Interview 2 comprised Sex and Sex Education, Menstruation, Sexual Interaction, Contraception, and Pregnancy, Abortion and Childbirth; and Interview 3 comprised Sexually Transmitted Diseases, Masturbation, and Homosexuality. There were knowledge questions at the end of each interview to determine whether respondents had sufficient knowledge to proceed to the next interview. SexKen and SexKen-C were also reorganised, but remained as questionnaire measures, with the subscales in the same order as for SexKen-ID. A further parallel questionnaire measure was developed for people with physical disability (SexKen-PD).

SexKen, SexKen-ID, and SexKen-PD have been used to gather data among people from the general population ($n = 100$), people with mild intellectual disability ($n = 60$), and people with physical disability ($n = 60$). Test-retest data have been collected on 30 people in each group. These data are available from the author.

Response Mode and Timing

Each of the SexKen measures may be completed as either an interview or questionnaire measure. However, SexKen-ID is designed to be completed as an interview, and SexKen, SexKen-C, and SexKen-PD are designed as questionnaire measures. If completed as a questionnaire, the measure takes about 1 hour to complete. SexKen-ID is divided into

[1]Address correspondence to Marita P. McCabe, School of Psychology, Deakin University, 221 Burwood Highway, Burwood, Victoria, Australia 3125; e-mail: marita.mccabe@deakin.edu.au

three interviews, with each interview taking about 1 hour to complete.

TABLE 1
A Description of the Subscales, Areas, and Range of Scores for the Sexual Knowledge, Experience, Feelings, and Needs Scale (SexKen, SexKen-ID, SexKen-PD, SexKen-C)

Subscale	Area	Number of Items	Range of Scores
Friendship (23 items)	Knowledge:	1	0–2
	Experience:	13	5–22
	Feelings:	4	4–20
	Needs:	5	5–25
Dating and Intimacy (16 items)	Knowledge:	2	0–4
	Experience:	4	3–9
	Feelings:	6	4–11
	Needs:	4	4–20
Marriage (16 items)	Knowledge:	2	0–4
	Experience:	0	—
	Feelings:	13	6–10
	Needs:	1	1–5
Body Part Identification (21 items)	Knowledge:	21	0–42
	Experience:	0	—
	Feelings:	0	—
	Needs:	0	—
Sex and Sex Education (16 items)	Knowledge:	1	0–2
	Experience:	7	6–27
	Feelings:	5	5–25
	Needs:	3	3–15
Menstruation (16 items)	Knowledge:	11	0–22
	Experience:	2	2–4
	Feelings:	2	2–10
	Needs:	1	1–5
Sexual Interaction (52 items)	Knowledge:	21	0–42
	Experience:	15	8–31
	Feelings:	14	8–31
	Needs:	2	2–10
Contraception (19 items)	Knowledge:	9	0–18
	Experience:	8	4–11
	Feelings:	1	1–5
	Needs:	1	1–5
Pregnancy, Abortion and Childbirth (24 items)	Knowledge:	15	0–30
	Experience:	3	—
	Feelings:	4	4–20
	Needs:	2	2–10
Sexually Transmitted Diseases (19 items)	Knowledge:	11	0–22
	Experience:	2	1–2
	Feelings:	4	4–20
	Needs:	2	2–10
Masturbation (16 items)	Knowledge:	3	0–6
	Experience:	6	4–20
	Feelings:	6	5–25
	Needs:	1	1–5
Homosexuality (10 items)	Knowledge:	1	0–2
	Experience:	1	1–5
	Feelings:	6	4–20
	Needs:	2	2–10

Scoring

Whether completed as an interview or questionnaire, the experience, feelings and needs items are either *yes/no* (scored as 1 or 2) responses or are scored on a 5-point Likert scale (ranging from 1 to 5). The knowledge questions are open-ended, with responses scored 0, 1, or 2 depending upon the accuracy of the responses. The nature of the acceptable responses for each question was determined through pilot work. Some items are categorical (e.g., What do you do with your friends?) and do not contribute to the total score. All other items are scored in the same direction. A total score is obtained for each area within each subscale. The range of scores for each subarea and each subscale is listed in Table 1.

Reliability and Validity

Data have been gathered on people with mild intellectual disability, physical disability, and the general population, which will allow the internal consistency of each of the scales and the test-retest reliability of the scales to be evaluated.

The validity of the scale has been ensured through the initial development of the scale with close attention being paid to the wording of items (Sigelman, Budd, Winer, Schoenrock, & Martin, 1982). Subsequent modification of the scale has been based on feedback from professionals working with people with intellectual disability, psychometricians, and subjects from each group who completed the various versions of the scale. There have been three revisions of the scale. It was not possible to assess the validity of the scale using another measure of sexuality because at the time of the original publication, no other psychometrically sound measure of sexuality had been developed for people with disabilities or carestaff working with these people.

Other Information

The scale, along with the scoring code, may be obtained from the author for use with clinical or research subjects.

References

McCabe, M. P., & Cummins, R. A. (1996). The sexual knowledge, experience, feelings and needs of people with mild intellectual disability. *Education and Training in Mental Retardation and Development Disabilities, 31,* 13–22.

McCabe, M. P., Cummins, R. A., & Reid, S. B. (1994). An empirical study of the sexual abuse of people with intellectual disability. *Journal of Sexuality and Disability, 12,* 297–306.

Sigelman, C., Budd, E. C., Winer, J. L., Schoenrock, C. J., & Martin, P. W. (1982). Evaluating alternative techniques of questioning mentally retarded persons. *American Journal of Mental Deficiency, 86,* 511–518.

Szollos, A., & McCabe, M. P. (1995). The sexuality of people with mild intellectual disabilities: Perceptions of clients and caregivers. *Australia and New Zealand Journal of Developmental Disabilities, 20,* 205–222.

Dyadic Sexual Regulation Scale

JOSEPH A. CATANIA,[1] *University of California, San Francisco*

The Dyadic Sexual Regulation Scale (DSR) measures the extent to which an individual perceives sexual activity to be regulated from an internal versus an external locus of control. In developing a locus of control scale specific to the dyadic sexual situation, we sought to develop a scale that assesses perceptions of the ability to emit behaviors that (a) influence the acquisition and termination of sexual rewards, (b) effect events between these latter two points, and (c) prevent or avoid aversive sexual encounters. Moreover, the scale would reflect control flexibility, which is generally defined as an individual's ability either to relinquish or to accept control, dependent on the variant nature of social/sexual interactions.

Description

The DSR is an 11-item, subject- or interviewer-administered, Likert-type scale with seven points (1 = *strongly disagree*, 7 = *strongly agree*). The scale items were derived from open-ended interviews about sexual attitudes with heterosexual and homosexual couples. Five items are reversed (Items 2, 5, 6, 8, 10) for counter-balancing purposes. A shortened five-item interviewer-administered form of the DSR is also available.

Response Mode and Timing

All forms of the scale are available in English and Spanish. The expanded form is self-administered; the briefer revised form is interviewer administered. Both forms take 1–2 minutes to complete.

Scoring

After reversing the reverse-worded items, total scores are computed so that higher scores indicate a greater degree of internal control. Sum across scores to obtain total score. Scale scores range from 11 (external) to 77 (internal).

Reliability and Validity

The DSR has been administered to varied populations, including college students, national urban probability samples constructed to adequately represent White, Black, and Hispanic ethnic groups, and high HIV-risk-factor groups (Catania, Coates, Kegeles, et al., 1992; Catania, Coates, Stall, et al., 1992). The DSR scale has also been administered to respondents from introductory psychology classes at a university recruited to participate in a sexual survey study that assessed locus of control in sexual contexts (Catania, McDermott, & Wood, 1984). The college-age analyses (Catania et al., 1984) examined only heterosexuals who had a current, regular sexual partner. Sample 1 consisted of 151 White students (59 males and 92 females) with a mean age of 27. Sample 2 consisted of 27 males and 43 females with similar demographic features as Sample 1. Reliability was good (Cronbach's alpha = .74 in Sample 1, and .83 in Sample 2). A principal component analysis with varimax rotation was conducted on the DSR items for Sample 1. There were no item loadings greater than .30 beyond the first factor, and the first factor accounted for 95% of the variance. Test-retest reliability was .77, with a 2-week interval. The DSR revealed convergent validity with the Nowicki-Strickland Adult Internal-External Control Scale (NSLC; Nowicki & Duke, 1974), $r = .19$, $p < .05$, $df = 149$ (Catania et al., 1984). The DSR was found to be related with each dyadic measure of sexual activity. The scale was not found to be related to monadic activities (i.e., masturbation), further supporting the concurrent validity of the DSR with locus of control. Internality with regard to sexual activity is associated with higher frequencies of intercourse, oral sex from partner, orgasms with partner, sexual relations, affectionate behaviors, and sexual satisfaction, and with lesser anxiety in sexual situations. DSR was not found to be related to gender. In contrast the NSLC was more weakly associated with each criterion.

The five-item, shortened version of the DSR was administered to respondents recruited to participate in the 1990–1991 National AIDS Behavior Survey[2] (NABS) longitudinal cohort study, which was composed of three interlaced samples designed to oversample African Americans and Hispanics for adequate representation (Catania, Coates, Kegeles, et al., 1992). The interlaced samples included a national sample, an urban sample of 23 cities with high prevalences of AIDS cases, and a special Hispanic urban sample. The revised version of the DSR was administered to 4,620 respondents between the ages of 18–49. Reliability was good (Cronbach's alpha = .62 total sample). Means, standard deviations, range, median, and reliabilities are given for White, Black, and Hispanic groups, males and

[1]Address correspondence to Joseph A. Catania, College of Health and Human Sciences, Oregon State University, 320 B Waldo Hall, Corvallis, OR 97331; e-mail: Joseph.Catania@oregonstate.edu
[2]For further details on sample construction and weighting of the NABS study, see Catania Coates, Stall, et al. (1992).

TABLE 1
Normative Data for Dyadic Sexual Regulation Scale

| | NABS[a] Study (Wave 2) | | | | | |
	N	Mean	SD	Range	Mdn	Alpha
National Sample	1,022	15.62	2.83	15.0	16.0	.59
High Risk Cities	3,598	15.37	2.86	15.0	15.0	.57
Ethnicity						
White						
National Sample	747	15.75	2.75	15.0	16.0	.61
High Risk Cities	1,565	15.62	2.68	15.0	16.0	.61
Black						
National Sample	162	15.23	2.99	14.0	15.0	.47
High Risk Cities	1,181	15.18	3.06	15.0	15.0	.52
Hispanic						
National Sample	90	15.45	3.03	14.0	15.6	.61
High Risk Cities	764	14.98	3.20	15.0	15.0	.60
Gender						
Male						
National Sample	410	15.37	2.65	14.0	15.0	.86
High Risk Cities	1,553	15.24	2.77	15.0	15.0	.56
Female						
National Sample	612	15.85	2.98	15.0	16.0	.61
High Risk Cities	2,043	15.53	2.94	15.0	16.0	.58
Education						
< 12 years						
National Sample	82	14.74	2.89	12.0	15.0	.38
High Risk Cities	483	14.76	3.12	15.0	15.0	.53
= 12 years						
National Sample	273	15.75	2.93	13.0	16.0	.59
High Risk Cities	807	15.41	2.96	15.0	16.0	.54
> 12 years						
National Sample	668	15.71	2.76	15.0	16.0	.59
High Risk Cities	2,308	15.54	2.72	15.0	16.0	.58
	AMEN[b] Study					
Total	954	15.08	3.01	15.0	15.0	.58
Ethnicity						
White	418	15.14	2.88	13.0	15.0	.63
Black	238	15.0	13.24	15.0	15.0	.53
Hispanic	229	14.98	3.08	15.0	15.0	.55
Gender						
Male	410	15.22	2.74	15.0	15.0	.52
Female	544	14.98	3.20	15.0	15.0	.61
Education						
< 12 years	109	15.44	3.30	13.0	16.0	.57
= 12 year	213	14.64	3.21	15.0	15.0	.54
> 12 years	626	15.26	2.86	14.0	15.0	.59

Note. Because weights for probability of selection are used, all frequencies may not
sum to equal total frequencies.
[a]National AIDS Behavior Study.
[b]AIDS in Multi-Ethnic Neighborhoods.

females, and levels of education for both national and urban-high risk city samples (Table 1). The shortened five-item version was also administered to 954 respondents who participated in the third wave of the AIDS in Multi-ethnic Neighborhoods (AMEN)[3] study (Catania, Coates, Stall, et al., 1992). The AMEN study is a longitudinal study (three waves) in which the distribution of HIV, sexually transmitted diseases, related risk behaviors, and their correlates across social strata were examined. Respondents ranged from 20–44 years of age and included White ($n = 418$) African-American ($n = 124$) and Hispanic ($n = 229$) ethnic groups. Reliability was moderate (Cronbach's alpha = .59). The mean, standard deviation, median, range, and reliabilities of ethnic groups, gender, and levels of education are provided in Table 1.

References

Catania, J. A., Coates, T., Kegeles, S., Thompson-Fullilove, M., Peterson, J., Marin, B., et al. (1992). Condom use in multi-ethnic neighborhoods of San Francisco: The population-based AMEN (AIDS in Multi-Ethnic Neighborhoods) study. *American Journal of Public Health, 82*, 284–287. (See also Erratum, June 1992, *82*, 998)

Catania, J. A., Coates, T., Peterson, J., Dolcini, M., Kegeles, S., Siegel, D., et al. (1993). Changes in condom use among Black, Hispanic, and White heterosexuals in San Francisco: The AMEN cohort survey. *The Journal of Sex Research, 30*, 121–128.

Catania, J. A., Coates, T. J., Stall, R., Turner, H., Peterson. J., Hearst, N., et al. (1992). Prevalence of AIDS-related risk factors and condom use in the United States. *Science, 258*, 1101–1106.

Catania, J. A., McDermott, L. J., & Wood, J. A. (1984). The assessment of locus of control: Situational specificity in the sexual context. *The Journal of Sex Research, 20*, 310–324.

Nowicki, S., & Duke, M. (1974). A Locus of Control Scale for noncollege as well as college adults. *Journal of Personality Assessment, 38*, 136–137.

[3]For further details on sample construction and weighting of the AMEN cohort study, see Catania Coates, Stall, et al. (1992).

Exhibit

Dyadic Sexual Regulation Scale

Instructions: The following statements describe different things people do and feel about sex. Please tell me how much you agree or disagree with these statements.

1	2	3	4	5	6	7
Strongly agree						Strongly disagree

1. I often take the initiative in beginning sexual activity.
2. If my sexual relations are not satisfying there is little I can do to improve the situation.
3. I have sexual relations with my partner as often as I would like.
4. My planning for sexual encounters leads to good sexual experiences with my partner.
5. I feel that it is difficult to get my partner to do what makes me feel good during sex.
6. I feel that my sexual encounters with my partner usually end before I want them to.
7. When I am not interested in sexual activity I feel free to reject sexual advances by my partner.
8. I want my partner to be responsible for directing our sexual encounters.
9. I find it pleasurable at times to be the active member during sexual relations while my partner takes a passive role.
10. I would feel uncomfortable bringing myself to orgasm if the stimulation my partner was providing was inadequate.
11. During some sexual encounters I find it pleasurable to be passive while my partner is the active person.

Note. Items 2, 3, 4, 5, and 6 make up the brief revised form. Items 3 and 8 are reworded in the short form, as follows: 3. You have sexual relationships as often as you like. Do you agree or disagree? 8. Your sexual partner makes most of the decisions about when the two of you will have sex. Do you agree or disagree?

Juvenile Love Scale: A Child's Version of the Passionate Love Scale

ELAINE HATFIELD[1] AND DANIELLE YOUNG, *University of Hawaii*

Hatfield and Walster (1978) defined passionate love as "a state of intense longing for union with another." Reciprocation is "associated with fulfillment and ecstasy," whereas unrequited love is "associated with emptiness, anxiety, or despair (p. 9)." Though the Passionate Love Scale (PLS) for adults has been used for several decades (Hatfield, Rapson, & Martel, 2007), it was not until 1983 that we developed a companion scale to measure passionate love in young children and adolescents. Because passionate love has been described as "puppy love," "lovesickness," and "infatuation" (labels all ideologically associated with young love), it seems to be specifically relevant to measure this concept in younger age groups. The Juvenile Love Scale (JLS) is an exact equivalent of the PLS. (A detailed description of the PLS is provided elsewhere in this volume.) The JLS taps cognitive, emotional, and behavioral indicants of "desire for union."

Description

The JLS is designed to measure passionate love in children from 3 to 18 years of age. The JLS, like the PLS, comes in a short form (15 items) and a long form (30 items). Researchers have used two techniques in administering the JLS, depending on the age of the participants.

If children are 3 to 7. The first step in administering the JLS is to make sure the children understand the concepts of *boyfriend* and *girlfriend* (almost all do), the 15 or 30 test items (almost all do), and how to use the response scale.

The response scale is explained first. Essentially, one wants to teach children that, when the experimenter makes a statement, they can indicate how much they agree via a 9-point scale. This is done in the following way: Children are shown a large "ruler" with dimensions of 4 × 20 inches.

[1]Address correspondence to Elaine Hatfield, 2430 Campus Road, Honolulu, HI 96822; e-mail: elaineh1@aol.com

It is divided into nine blocks. The first block is labeled (1) *Agree Very Little*. The last block is labeled (9) *Agree Very Much*. The experimenter then conducts several tests to teach children how to respond via the scale. (For a more detailed example, see Hatfield, Schmitz, Cornelius, & Rapson, 1988.)

After it has been confirmed that children understand and can use the scale, the experimenter then proceeds to administer the JLS. Researchers, such as Greenwell (1983), have found that even children as young as 3 or 4 years of age have no trouble understanding this scale. (For more information on these procedures, see Greenwell, 1983.)

If children are older. Once children are 7 or 8 years old, one can simply follow the same procedure used in administering the PLS to older adolescents and adults.

Response Mode and Timing

Respondents either put a block in the appropriate square (if they are young) or circle the number indicating how true each statement is for them (if they are older). The JLS is generally given individually. Once children are 7 or 8, it can be given in groups. How long it takes to explain the scale depends on the children. Usually, the short (15 items) version of the JLS takes appropriately 25 minutes and the long version (30 items) takes 40 minutes to complete.

Scoring

The individual items are simply summed to produce a total score. Some researchers, such as Hatfield and Sprecher (1986), have interpreted the scores (in adolescents and adults) this way:

- 106–135 points = Wildly, recklessly, in love
- 86–105 points = Passionate but less intense
- 66–85 points = Occasional bursts of passion
- 45–65 points = Tepid, infrequent passion
- 15–44 points = The thrill is gone

Generally, however, the scale has been used to investigate gender and group differences.

Reliability

Greenwell (1983) provides statistical evidence that the JLS is internally consistent and reliable. In various samples, coefficient alphas were found to range from .94 to .98. When older children and adolescents were asked to complete *both* the PLS and the JLS, they received identical scores on the two scales. This is not surprising, since the scales are designed to be identical, differing only in the difficulty of the language. In various populations, the JLS and PLS have been found to correlate .88 for children and .87 for adults. Thus, it is clear that the PLS and the JLS are measuring the same construct.

Greenwell (1983) also provided information on item-by-item correspondences. She found items to be highly intercorrelated. She also correlated each item with its own scale total, the other scale total, and the combined total of all 60 items (i.e., she used the long versions of both the JLS and the PLS). All items correlated highly with all totals, with 67 items in the .25 to .50 range, 221 in the .51 to .75 range, and 59 in the .76 to 1.00 range.

Validity

If the JLS is valid, it should be related to other variables in ways expected by past theoretical and empirical work. There is some evidence for such construct validity. Greenwell (1983) provided evidence that the JLS and the PLS are virtually equivalent measures of passionate love, and that both scales reflect the real-world experience of "being in love." For example, she asked children and adolescents to describe their feelings for a person whom they currently love or had loved in the past, or (if they had never been in love) with whom it was as close as they had come to being in love. She found that individuals who had experienced passion did score higher on both the JLS and the PLS than did those who had never been in love. (For more information on the JLS, see Hatfield et al., 1988, who provided information on the JLS scores typically secured by boys and girls, from 4 to 18 years of age.) Furthermore, Hatfield, Brinton, and Cornelius (1989) found that children and adolescents prone to anxiety tended to score higher on the PLS than did their less anxious peers.

Other Information

The JLS is copyrighted by Elaine Hatfield and Marilyn Easton. Permission is automatically given to all clinicians and researchers who wish to use the scale in their research (free of charge).

References

Greenwell, M. E. (1983). *Development of the Juvenile Love Scale.* Unpublished master's thesis, University of Hawaii at Manoa, Honolulu.

Hatfield, E., Brinton, C., & Cornelius, J. (1989). Passionate love and anxiety in young adolescents. *Motivation and Emotion, 13,* 271–289.

Hatfield, E., Rapson, R. L., & Martel, L. D. (2007). Passionate love and sexual desire. In S. Kitayama & D. Cohen. (Eds.), *Handbook of cultural psychology* (pp. 760–779). New York: Guilford Press.

Hatfield, E., Schmitz, E., Cornelius, J., & Rapson, R. (1988). Passionate love: How early does it begin? *Journal of Psychology and Human Sexuality, 1,* 35–52.

Hatfield, E., & Sprecher, S. (1986). Measuring passionate love in intimate relations. *Journal of Adolescence, 9,* 383–410.

Hatfield, E., & Walster, G. W. (1978). *A new look at love.* Lanham, MD: University Press of America.

Exhibit

Juvenile Love Scale (Forms A and B)

Instructions for both scale forms: We are trying to find out how children feel when they love somebody in a very special way. Some children think about a special person a lot, get very excited about him or her, and want to get very, very close. Sometimes we call this a "crush." Please list on the lines that follow the name of the eight people you have loved or liked most in your life:

Name   Male or female

1. _____   _____
2. _____   _____
3. _____   _____
4. _____   _____
5. _____   _____
6. _____   _____
7. _____   _____
8. _____   _____

Now draw a circle around the name of the person you'd feel most excited about seeing right now or used to get excited about seeing if that person isn't around anymore. Do not choose mother, father, or brother or sister. If you aren't excited about him/her right now, try to remember how you felt when you did feel the most excited. If you don't think you have ever felt *very* excited, try to answer anyway, remembering how you *did* feel.

Each question is followed by a 9-point rating scale. If you circle the 9, it means you agree very much with what the item says. If you circle the 1, it means you agree very little with what the item says. Try to circle the number that most closely explains how you *do* feel.

Juvenile Love Scale (Form A)

1. I feel like things would always be sad and gloomy if I had to live without _____ forever.
2. Did you ever keep thinking about ____ when you wanted to stop and couldn't?
3. I feel happy when I am doing something to make _____ happy.
4. I would rather be with _____ than anybody else.
5. I'd feel bad if I thought _____ liked somebody else better than me.
6. I want to know all I can about _____.
7. I'd like _____ to belong to me in every way.
8. I'd like it a lot if _____ played with me all the time.
9. If I could, when I grow up I'd like to marry (live with) _____.
10. When _____ hugs me my body feels warm all over.
11. I am always thinking about _____.
12. I want _____ to know me, what I am thinking, what scares me, what I am wishing for.
13. I look at _____ a lot to see if he/she likes me.
14. When _____ is around I really want to touch him/her and be touched.
15. When I think _____ might be mad at me, I feel really sad.

Possible answers range from

1	2	3	4	5	6	7	8	9
Agree Very Little								Agree Very Much

Juvenile Love Scale (Form B)

1. When _____ is around I laugh and cry more often.
2. I feel like things would always be sad and gloomy if I had to live without _____ forever.
3. Sometimes I feel shaky all over when I see _____.
4. Sometimes I think it is fun just to watch _____ move around.
5. Did you ever keep thinking about ____ when you wanted to stop and couldn't?
6. I feel happy when I am doing something to make _____ happy.

7. I would rather be with _____ than anybody else.

8. I'd feel bad if I thought _____ liked somebody else better than me.

9. No one else could like _____ as much as I do.

10. I want to know all I can about _____.

11. I'd like _____ to belong to me in every way.

12. I will always like _____.

13. I feel all happy inside when _____ looks at me and I look at _____.

14. I'd like it a lot if _____ played with me all the time.

15. If I could, when I grow up I'd like to marry (live with) _____.

16. _____ is the person who can make me feel the happiest.

17. When _____ hugs me my body feels warm all over.

18. I feel all soft and happy inside about _____.

19. I am always thinking about _____.

20. If I were away from _____ for a long time I would be very lonely.

21. Sometimes I can't do my school work because I am thinking about _____.

22. I want _____ to know me, what I am thinking, what scares me, what I am wishing for.

23. Knowing that _____ cares about me makes me feel more like I am OK.

24. I look at _____ a lot to see if he/she likes me.

25. If _____ needed help from me, I'd stop what I was doing, even if it was lots of fun and go help him (her).

26. _____ can make me feel bubbly, like coke.

27. When _____ is around I really want to touch him/her and be touched.

28. Living without _____ would be very, very sad.

29. I want to hug _____ very, very tight.

30. When I think _____ might be mad at me, I feel really sad.

Possible answers range from

1	2	3	4	5	6	7	8	9
Agree Very Little								Agree Very Much

Passionate Love Scale

ELAINE HATFIELD,[1] *University of Hawaii*
SUSAN SPRECHER, *Illinois State University*

Many classifications and typologies of love exist in the literature, but the most common distinction is between passionate love and companionate love. Hatfield and Walster (1978) described passionate love as "a state of intense longing for union with another. Reciprocated love (union with the other) is associated with fulfillment and ecstasy; unrequited love (separation) is associated with emptiness, anxiety, or despair" (p. 9).

In 1986, Hatfield and Sprecher published the Passionate Love Scale (PLS) for the purpose of promoting more research on this intense type of love. Although a companion scale to measure companionate love was not also developed by this team of researchers, other measures exist in

the literature designed to assess this type of love (see, e.g., Grote & Frieze's [1994] Friendship-Based Love Scale).

Description

The PLS scale was specifically designed to assess the cognitive, emotional, and behavioral components of passionate love. The *cognitive components* consist of Intrusive thinking; Preoccupation with the partner; Idealization of the other or of the relationship; and Desire to know the other and be known by him/her. *Emotional components* consist of Attraction to the partner, especially sexual attraction; Positive feelings when things go well; Negative feelings

[1]Address correspondence to Elaine Hatfield, 2430 Campus Road, Honolulu, HI 96822; e-mail: elaineh1@aol.com

when things go awry; Longing for reciprocity—passionate lovers not only love but want to be loved in return; Desire for complete and permanent union; and Physiological (sexual) arousal. Finally, *behavioral components* consist of Actions aimed at determining the other's feelings; Studying the other person; Service to the other; and Maintaining physical closeness.

The most common form of the PLS is a 15-item scale (Form A), but an alternative 15-item version (Form B) is also available. The two scales can be combined to form a 30-item scale. Although the scale was originally designed using North American young adults in pilot studies, the scale has subsequently been revised to be administered to children and has been translated into many languages and administered to samples in other countries.

Response Mode and Timing

Participants are presented with statements such as "I would feel deep despair if ____ left me" and are asked to indicate how true the statement is of them. Possible responses range from 1 = *Not at all True* to 9 = *Definitely True*. (The ____ in each statement refers to the partner.) The scale takes only a few minutes to complete, although often it is embedded in a larger questionnaire with other measures.

Scoring

The total score of the scale can be represented either by the mean of the scores for the items or by the sum of the ratings. Higher scores indicate greater passionate love. An average score for young adults across the items is approximately 7. Recently, for a popular press article, Hatfield and Sprecher (2004) provided for readers the following rubric to interpret their summed scores across 15 items:

- 106–135 points = Wildly, recklessly, in love
- 86–105 points = Passionate but less intense
- 66–85 points = Occasional bursts of passion
- 45–65 points = Tepid, infrequent passion
- 15–44 points = The thrill is gone

Reliability

Hatfield and Sprecher (1986) reported a coefficient alpha of .91 for the 15-item version and .94 for the 30-item version. Others have also reported high levels of reliability for the scale (e.g., Sprecher & Regan, 1998). The PLS appears to be primarily unidimensional, with one primary factor emerging from a principal components factoring.

Validity

The scale is uncontaminated by a social desirability bias, as indicated by a nonsignificant correlation between the PLS and their scores on the 1964 Crowne and Marlowe Social Desirability Scale (Hatfield & Sprecher, 1986). There is

some evidence for the construct validity of the PLS. For example, it has been found to be associated positively with conceptually similar scales and measures (Aron & Henkemeyer, 1995; Hatfield & Sprecher, 1986; Hendrick & Hendrick, 1989; Sprecher & Regan, 1998).

Other Information

Researchers have used the PLS in exploring many different topics, including cross-cultural differences in passionate love (Hatfield, Rapson, & Martel, 2007; Landis & O'Shea, 2000), prototype approaches to love (Fehr, 2005), neural bases of passionate love (Aron et al., 2005; Bartels & Zeki, 2004), changes in passionate love over the family life cycle (Tucker & Aron, 1993), correlates of sexual desire (Beck, Bozman, & Qualtrough, 1991), the effects of an emotionally focused couples therapy (James, 2007), degree of bonding with an abusive partner (Graham et al., 1995), and the effects of having married couples engage in novel activities (Aron, Norman, Aron, McKenna, & Heyman, 2000). The PLS is copyrighted by Hatfield and Sprecher (1986). Permission is given to all clinicians and researchers who wish to use the scale in their research (free of charge).

References

Aron, A., Fisher, H., Mashek, D. J., Strong, G., Li, H., & Brown, L. L. (2005). Reward, motivation, and emotion systems associated with early-stage intense romantic love. *Journal of Neurophysiology, 94,* 327–337.

Aron, A., & Henkemeyer, L. (1995). Marital satisfaction and passionate love. *Journal of Social and Personal Relationships, 12,* 139–146.

Aron, A., Norman, C. C., Aron, E. N., McKenna, C., & Heyman, R. (2000). Couples' shared participation in novel and arousing activities and experienced relationship quality. *Journal of Personality and Social Psychology, 78,* 273–284.

Bartels, A., & Zeki, S. (2004). The neural correlates of maternal and romantic love. *Neuroimage, 21,* 1155–1166.

Beck, J. G., Bozman, A. W., & Qualtrough, T. (1991). The experience of sexual desire: Psychological correlates in a college sample. *The Journal of Sex Research, 28,* 443–456.

Crowne, D. P., & Marlowe, D. (1964). *The approval motive: Studies in evaluative dependence.* New York: Wiley.

Fehr, B. (2005). Prototype-based assessment of laypeople's views of love. *Personal Relationships, 1,* 309–331.

Graham, D. L., Rawlings, E. I., Ihms, K., Latimer, D., Foliano, J., Thompson, A., et al. (1995). A scale for identifying "Stockholm syndrome" reactions in young dating women: Factor structure, reliability, and validity. *Violence and Victims, 10,* 3–22.

Grote, N. K., & Frieze, I. H. (1994). The measurement of friendship-based love in intimate relationships. *Personal Relationships, 1,* 275–300.

Hatfield, E., Rapson, R. L., & Martel, L. D. (2007). Passionate love and sexual desire. In S. Kitayama & D. Cohen (Eds.), *Handbook of cultural psychology* (pp. 760–779). New York: Guilford Press.

Hatfield, E., & Sprecher, S. (1986). Measuring passionate love in intimate relations. *Journal of Adolescence, 9,* 383–410.

Hatfield, E., & Sprecher, S. (January 19, 2004). In Jeffrey Kluger, "Why we love," *Time Magazine,* p. 60. http://www.time.com/time/2004/sex/scale

Hatfield, E., & Walster, G. W. (1978). *A new look at love.* Lanham, MD: University Press of America.

Hendrick, C., & Hendrick, S. S. (1989). Research on love: Does it measure up? *Journal of Personality and Social Psychology, 56,* 784–794.

James, P. (2007). Effects of a communication training component added to an emotionally focused couples therapy. *Journal of Marital and Family Therapy, 17,* 263–275.

Landis, D., & O'Shea, W. A., III. (2000). Cross-cultural aspects of passionate love: An individual difference analysis. *Journal of Cross-Cultural Psychology, 31,* 754–779.

Sprecher, S., & Regan, P. C. (1998). Passionate and companionate love in courting and young married couples. *Sociological Inquiry, 68,* 163–185.

Tucker, P., & Aron, A. (1993). Passionate love and marital satisfaction at key transition points in the family life cycle. *Journal of Social and Clinical Psychology, 12,* 135–147.

Exhibit

Passionate Love Scale

Passionate Love Scale (Form A)

We would like to know how you feel (or once felt) about the person you love, or have loved, most *passionately*. Some common terms for passionate love are romantic love, infatuation, love sickness, or obsessive love.

Please think of the person whom you love most passionately *right now*. If you are not in love, please think of the last person you loved. If you have never been in love, think of the person you came closest to caring for in that way.

Try to describe the way you felt when your feelings were most intense. Answers range from (1) *Not at all True* to (9) *Definitely True.*

Whom are you thinking of?

- Someone I love *right now.*
- Someone I *once* loved.
- I have never been in love.

1. I would feel deep despair if _____ left me.

1	2	3	4	5	6	7	8	9[a]
Not at all True								Definitely True

2. Sometimes I feel I can't control my thoughts; they are obsessively on _____.
3. I feel happy when I am doing something to make _____ happy.
4. I would rather be with _____ than anyone else.
5. I'd get jealous if I thought _____ were falling in love with someone else.
6. I yearn to know all about _____.
7. I want _____ physically, emotionally, mentally.
8. I have an endless appetite for affection from _____.
9. For me, _____ is the perfect romantic partner.
10. I sense my body responding when _____ touches me.
11. _____ always seems to be on my mind.
12. I want _____ to know me—my thoughts, my fears, and my hopes.
13. I eagerly look for signs indicating _____'s desire for me.
14. I possess a powerful attraction for _____.
15. I get extremely depressed when things don't go right in my relationship with _____.

Total: _____

Results:

- 106–135 points = Wildly, even recklessly, in love
- 86–105 points = Passionate, but less intense
- 66–85 points = Occasional bursts of passion
- 45–65 points = Tepid, infrequent passion
- 15–44 points = The thrill is gone

Passionate Love Scale (Form B)

We would like to know how you feel (or once felt) about the person you love, or have loved, most passionately. Some common terms for passionate love are romantic love, infatuation, love sickness, or obsessive love.

Please think of the person whom you love most passionately *right now*. If you are not in love, please think of the last person you loved. If you have never been in love, think of the person you came closest to caring for in that way.

Try to describe the way you felt when your feelings were most intense. Answers range from (1) *Not at all True* to (9) *Definitely True*.

Whom are you thinking of?

- Someone I love *right now*.
- Someone I *once* loved.
- I have never been in love.

1. Since I've been involved with _____, my emotions have been on a roller coaster.

   1   2   3   4   5   6   7   8   9[a]
   Not at all True   Definitely True

2. Sometimes my body trembles with excitement at the sight of _____.
3. I take delight in studying the movements and angles of _____'s body.
4. No one else could love _____ like I do.
5. I will love _____ forever.
6. I melt when looking deeply into _____'s eyes.
7. _____ is the person who can make me feel happiest.
8. I feel tender toward _____.
9. If I were separated from _____ for a long time, I would feel intensely lonely.
10. I sometimes find it difficult to concentrate on work because thoughts of _____ occupy my mind.
11. Knowing that _____ cares about me makes me feel complete.
12. If _____ were going through a difficult time, I would put away my own concerns to help him/her out.
13. _____ can make me feel effervescent and bubbly.
14. In the presence of _____, I yearn to touch and be touched.
15. An existence without _____ would be dark and dismal.

        Total: _____

Results:

- 106–135 points = Wildly, even recklessly, in love
- 86–105 points = Passionate, but less intense
- 66–85 points = Occasional bursts of passion
- 45–65 points = Tepid, infrequent passion
- 15–44 points = The thrill is gone

[a]This response scale follows each item.

Gender Identity and Erotic Preference in Males

KURT FREUND[1] AND RAY BLANCHARD,[2] *Centre for Addiction and Mental Health*

This test package includes seven scales. Six of these are concerned with the assessment of erotic preference and erotic anomalies; one is concerned with the assessment of gender identity. This last instrument, in its present form and in earlier versions, has a longer history in the published literature than the other six. All seven instruments are intended for use with adult males.

The Feminine Gender Identity Scale (FGIS, see Exhibit 1) was developed to measure that "femininity" occurring in homosexual males (Freund, Langevin, Satterberg, & Steiner, 1977; Freund, Nagler, Langevin, Zajac, & Steiner, 1974). There were two reasons to develop a special instrument to measure this attribute rather than rely upon conventional masculinity-femininity tests. First, conventional masculinity-femininity tests are usually assembled from items that are differentially endorsed by males and females. Such differential endorsement may reflect other differences between the sexes besides gender identity (e.g., body build and upbringing). Moreover, femininity in homosexual males need not be identical with what psychologically differentiates males from females. Therefore, rather than using biological females as a reference group, Freund identified the "feminine" behavioral patterns and self-reports of homosexual male-to-female transsexuals as the extreme of that femininity observable in homosexual males. Accordingly, feminine gender identity in males was conceived as a continuous variable, inferable from the extent of an individual's departure from the usual male pattern of behavior toward the pattern typical of male-to-female transsexuals.

The second reason for developing a new instrument was that conventional masculinity-femininity scales did not include those items pointed out by the classical sexologists (e.g., Hirschfeld and Krafft-Ebing) as indicative of femininity in homosexual males (e.g., whether, as a child, the subject had preferred to be in the company of males or females; whether he had preferred girls' or boys' games and toys). In Freund's clinical experience, such developmental items seemed to be of particular importance.

The item content of the six erotic interest scales was derived from Freund's clinical experience. The Androphilia and Gynephilia Scales (Exhibits 2 and 3) were originally assembled to measure the extent of bisexuality reported by androphilic males and to measure the erotic interest in other persons reported by patients with cross-gender identity problems. The term *androphilia* refers to erotic attraction to physically mature males, and *gynephilia*, to erotic attraction to physically mature females. The Heterosexual Experience Scale (Exhibit 4) was intended to assess sexual experience with women, as opposed to sexual interest in them. The Fetishism, Masochism, and Sadism Scales (Exhibits 5–7) were constructed from face-valid items as self-report measures of these anomalous erotic preferences.

The interested reader should note the availability of certain closely related instruments. We have developed a companion instrument for the FGIS, the Masculine Gender Identity Scale for Females (Blanchard & Freund, 1983), presented elsewhere in this volume. Modifications of the Androphilia and Gynephilia Scales specifically intended for male patients with gender identity disorders have been developed by Blanchard (1985a, 1985b). Blanchard (1985a) includes a scale for measuring *cross-gender* fetishism (roughly *transvestism*), also reprinted in this volume.

Description

All seven scales are presented in full (see Exhibits 1–7). Most of the scales are a mixture of dichotomous and multiple-choice items. The number of items in each scale is summarized in Table 1, along with the types and numbers of subjects used in item analysis, the alpha reliability of each scale, and the proportion of total variance accounted for by the largest single factor found with principal components analysis.

With the exception of the FGIS, all scales are appropriate for any adult male with sufficient reading comprehension. Part A of the FGIS, which was constructed by selecting items differentially endorsed by adult gynephiles and (nontranssexual) androphiles may also be administered to any adult male.

Parts B and C of the FGIS were constructed from items differentially endorsed by transsexual and nontranssexual homosexuals. Part B consists of three items, which also appear on the Androphilia Scale, and which presuppose homosexuality. Part B is only appropriate for homosexual subjects; hence the full scale (Parts A, B, and C) may only be administered to homosexual subjects: androphilic transsexuals, androphiles, homosexual hebephiles (men who erotically prefer pubescent males), or homosexual pedophiles (men who erotically prefer male children). Part C consists of items aimed at transsexualism and is appropriate for males presenting with any cross-gender syndrome, including transvestism.

[1]Kurt Freund is deceased.

[2]Address correspondence to Ray Blanchard, Centre for Addiction and Mental Health, 250 College Street, Toronto, Ontario M5T 1R8, Canada; e-mail: Ray_Blanchard@camh.net

TABLE 1
Psychometric Information

Scale[a]	N of items	Subjects used in item analysis[b]	N of subjects	Alpha[c]	% Variance[d]
FGI(A)	19	CGI patients; andro patients; courtship disorder; sadists	743	.93	43.8
FGI(BC)	10	CGI patients; andro patients	332	.89	51.4
Andro	13	CGI patients; andro controls; andro patients; homo pedohebe	437	.93	59.8
Gyne	9	CGI patients; hetero controls; andro controls; andro patients; homo pedohebe; hetero pedohebe	605	.85	40.4
Het Exp	6	As above	606	.82	47.8
Fetish	8	CGI patients; hetero controls; andro controls; homo pedohebe; hetero pedohebe; courtship disorder; sadists; hyperdominants; masochists	444	.91	59.6
Maso	11	As above	491	.83	33.7
Sadism	20	As above	491	.87	28.0

Note. The FGI Scale data were prepared for this table by Blanchard. The data for the other six scales are from Freund, Steiner, and Chan, 1982.
[a]FGI(A), Feminine Gender Identity Scales for Males—Part A; FGI(BC), Feminine Gender Identity Scale for Males—Parts B and C combined; Andro, Androphilia Scale; Gyne, Gynephilia Scale; Het Exp, Heterosexual Experience Scale; Fetish, Fetishism Scale; Maso, Masochism Scale; Sadism, Sadism Scale.
[b]CGI, patients with cross-gender identity; courtship disorder, patients with voyeurism, exhibitionism, toucherism, frotteurism, obscene telephone calling, or the preferential rape pattern; pedohebe, pedophiles or hebephiles; hyperdominants, borderline sadists.
[c]Alpha reliability coefficient.
[d]Percentage of total variance accounted for by the strongest principal component.

Response Mode and Timing

Subjects check one and only one response option for each item. The shortest scale takes only a few minutes to complete; the longest (the full FGIS) takes about 15 minutes. Subjects are permitted to ask for clarification on any item whose meaning they do not understand.

Scoring

Scoring weights for each response option of each item follow that option in parentheses in the Exhibits. The total scores for each scale (and for the three subscales of the FGIS) are obtained by totaling the subject's scores for each item in that scale (or subscale). For all scales, high scores indicate that the relevant attribute (e.g., sadism, feminine gender identity) is strongly present, and low scores indicate that it is absent.

Reliability

The alpha reliability coefficient of each scale is presented in Table 1. Test-retest reliabilities have never been computed.

Validity

The main line of evidence for the construct validity of the FGIS is the demonstration of reliable group differences among heterosexual, nontranssexual homosexual, and transsexual homosexual males. Two studies have cross-validated Part A of the most recent version of the FGIS (Freund et al., 1977) and have also shown the relative insensitivity of the scale to socioeconomic variables. Freund, Scher, Chan, and Ben-Aron (1982) found no difference in the FGIS scores of gynephilic prisoners (whose modal education was less than high school graduation) and gynephilic university students; both groups produced lower FGIS scores than a sample of androphilic volunteers, who, in turn, scored lower than androphilic male-to-female transsexuals.

Part A scores on the FGIS have also been shown to enter into orderly relationships with a variety of other sexological variables and questionnaire measures. Freund, Scher et al. (1982) found a positive correlation between the degree of homosexuals' femininity and the age group to which they are most attracted sexually. The androphilic subjects in this study produced higher FGIS scores than the homosexual hebephiles or pedophiles. The homosexual pedophiles did not differ in feminine gender identity from gynephiles. Freund and Blanchard (1983) found that those androphiles who produced the highest (most feminine) FGIS scores also tended to report the worst childhood relationships with their fathers. Blanchard, McConkey, Roper, and Steiner (1983) found a high negative correlation (−.71) between Part A of the FGIS and retrospectively reported boyhood aggressiveness, defined as a generalized disposition to engage in physically combative or competitive interactions with male peers.

Freund (1977) reported a moderate correlation (.46) between Part A of the FGIS and the MMPI Masculinity-Femininity (Mf) Scale, and Hooberman (1979) reported a similar correlation (.52) between Part A of the 1974 version of the FGIS and the femininity scale of the Bem Sex-Role Inventory (BSRI; Bem, 1981). Hooberman did not report the correlation between the FGIS and the BSRI masculinity scale; presumably it was lower and not statistically significant. Guloien (1983) found a statistically significant negative correlation (−.20) between Part A of the FGIS and Jackson's (1974) social desirability scale in a mixed sample of heterosexual and homosexual male university students; Blanchard, Clemmensen, and Steiner (1985) found a significant positive correlation (.37) between Part A and the Crowne-Marlowe (1964) Social Desirability Scale among male patients at a gender identity clinic, most of whom were seeking sex reassignment surgery.

Freund, Scher et al. (1982) found that the Gynephilia and Heterosexual Experience Scales differentiated between two groups of androphiles, one claiming considerable, the other only minimal, bisexuality. The two scales discriminated between groups about equally well. Freund, Steiner, and Chan (1982) reported good agreement between clinicians' assessment of erotic partner preference (heterosexual vs. homosexual) and assessment by means of the Androphilia and Gynephilia Scales. They also found, among the various syndromes of cross-gender identity that they investigated, group differences in all seven measures presented here. Of particular interest was the confirmation they obtained with the Sadism, Masochism, and Fetishism Scales of their clinical impression that these anomalies tend to be differentially associated with heterosexual-type cross-gender identity.

References

Bem, S. L. (1981). *Bem Sex-Role Inventory professional manual*. Palo Alto, CA: Consulting Psychological Press.

Blanchard, R. (1985a). Research methods for the typological study of gender disorders in males. In B. W. Steiner (Ed.), *Gender dysphoria: Development, research, management* (pp. 227–257). New York: Plenum.

Blanchard, R. (1985b). Typology of male-to-female transsexualism. *Archives of Sexual Behavior, 14*, 247–261.

Blanchard R., Clemmensen, L. H., & Steiner, B. W. 1985). Social desirability response set and systematic distortion in the self-report of adult male gender patients. *Archives of Sexual Behavior, 14*, 505–516.

Blanchard, R., & Freund, K. (1983). Measuring masculine gender identity in females. *Journal of Consulting and Clinical Psychology, 51*, 205–214.

Blanchard, R., McConkey, J. G., Roper, V., & Steiner, B. W. (1983). Measuring physical aggressiveness in heterosexual, homosexual, and transsexual males. *Archives of Sexual Behavior, 12*, 511–524.

Crowne, D. P., & Marlowe, D. (1964). *The approval motive: Studies in evaluative dependence*. New York: Wiley.

Freund, K., & Blanchard, R. (1983). Is the distant relationship of fathers and homosexual sons related to the sons' erotic preference for male partners, or to the sons' atypical gender identity, or to both? *Journal of Homosexuality, 9*, 7–25.

Freund, K., Langevin, R., Satterberg, J., & Steiner, B. W. (1977). Extension of the Gender Identity Scale for Males. *Archives of Sexual Behavior, 6*, 507–519.

Freund, K., Nagler, E., Langevin, R., Zajac, A., & Steiner, B. W. (1974). Measuring feminine gender identity in homosexual males. *Archives of Sexual Behavior, 3*, 249–260.

Freund, K., Steiner, B. W., & Chan, S. (1982). Two types of cross-gender identity. *Archives of Sexual Behavior, 11*, 49–63.

Freund, K., Scher, H., Chan, S., & Ben-Aron, M. (1982). Experimental analysis of pedophilia. *Behavior Research & Therapy, 20*, 105–112.

Guloien, E. H. (1983). *Childhood gender identity and adult erotic orientation in males*. Unpublished master's thesis, University of Guelph, Guelph, Ontario.

Hooberman, R. E. (1979). Psychological androgyny, feminine gender identity, and self-esteem in homosexual and heterosexual males. *The Journal of Sex Research, 15*, 306–315.

Jackson, D. (1974). *Personality research form manual*. Goshen, NY: Research Psychologist's Press.

Exhibit I

Feminine Gender Identity Scale for Males

Part A

1. Between the ages of 6 and 12, did you prefer
   a. to play with boys (0)
   b. to play with girls (2)
   c. didn't make any difference (0)
   d. not to play with other children (1)
   e. don't remember (1)

2. Between the ages of 6 and 12, did you
   a. prefer boys' games and toys (soldiers, football, etc.) (0)
   b. prefer girls' games and toys (dolls, cooking, sewing, etc.) (2)
   c. like or dislike both about equally (1)
   d. had no opportunity to play games or with toys (1)

3. In childhood, were you very interested in the work of a garage mechanic? Was this
   a. prior to age 6 (0)
   b. between ages 6 and 12 (0)
   c. probably in both periods (0)
   d. do not remember that I was very interested in the work of a garage mechanic (1)

4. Between the ages of 6 and 14, which did you like more, romantic stories or adventure stories?
   a. liked romantic stories more (2)
   b. liked adventure stories more (0)
   c. it did not make any difference (1)

5. Between the ages of 6 and 12, did you like to do jobs or chores which are usually done by women?
   a. yes (2)
   b. no (0)
   c. don't remember (1)
6. Between the ages of 13 and 16, did you like to do jobs or chores which are usually done by women?
   a. yes (2)
   b. no (0)
   c. don't remember (1)
7. Between the ages of 6 and 12, were you a leader in boys' games or other activities?
   a. more often than other boys (0)
   b. less often than other boys (1)
   c. about the same, or don't know (0)
   d. did not partake in children's games and/or other activities (1)
8. Between the ages of 6 and 12, when you read a story did you imagine that you were
   a. the male in the story (cowboy, detective, soldier, explorer, etc.) (0)
   b. the female in the story (the girl being saved, etc.) (2)
   c. the male sometimes and the female other times (1)
   d. neither the male nor the female (1)
   e. did not read stories (1)
9. In childhood or at puberty, did you like mechanics magazines? Was this
   a. between ages 6 and 12 (0)
   b. between ages 12 and 14 (0)
   c. probably in both periods (0)
   d. do not remember that I liked mechanics magazines (1)
10. Between the ages of 6 and 12, did you wish you had been born a girl instead of a boy
    a. often (2)
    b. occasionally (1)
    c. never (0)
11. Between the ages of 13 and 16, did you wish you had been born a girl instead of a boy
    a. often (2)
    b. occasionally (1)
    c. never (0)
12. Since the age of 17, have you wished you had been born a girl instead of a boy
    a. often (2)
    b. occasionally (1)
    c. never (0)
13. Do you think your appearance is
    a. very masculine (0)
    b. masculine (0)
    c. a little feminine (1)
    d. quite feminine (2)
14. In childhood, did you sometimes imagine yourself a well-known sports figure, or did you wish you would become one? Was this
    a. prior to age 6 (0)
    b. between ages 6 and 12 (0)
    c. probably in both periods (0)
    d. do not remember such fantasies (1)
15. In childhood fantasies did you sometimes wish you could go hunting big game? Was this
    a. prior to age 6 (0)
    b. between ages 6 and 12 (0)
    c. probably in both periods (0)
    d. do not remember such fantasies (1)
16. In childhood fantasies did you sometimes imagine yourself as being a policeman or soldier? Was this
    a. prior to age 6 (0)
    b. between ages 6 and 12 (0)
    c. probably in both periods (0)
    d. do not remember that I had such a fantasy (1)

17. In childhood was there ever a period in which you wished you would, when adult, become a dressmaker or dress designer?
    a. prior to age 6 (1)
    b. between ages 6 and 12 (1)
    c. probably in both periods (1)
    d. do not remember having this desire (0)
18. In childhood fantasies did you sometimes imagine yourself driving a racing car? Was this
    a. prior to age 6 (0)
    b. between ages 6 and 12 (0)
    c. probably in both periods (0)
    d. do not remember having this fantasy (1)
19. In childhood did you ever wish to become a dancer? Was this
    a. prior to age 6 (1)
    b. between ages 6 and 12 (1)
    c. probably in both periods (1)
    d. do not remember having this desire (0)

Part B

20. What kind of sexual contact with a male would you have preferred on the whole, even though you may not have done it?
    a. inserting your privates between your partner's upper legs (thighs) (0)
    b. putting your privates into your partner's rear end (0)
    c. you would have preferred one of those two modes but you cannot decide which one (0)
    d. your partner putting his privates between your upper legs (thighs) (1)
    e. your partner putting his privates into your rear end (2)
    f. you would have preferred one of these two latter modes but you cannot decide which one (1)
    g. you would have liked all four modes equally well (1)
    h. you would have preferred some other mode of sexual contact (1)
    i. had no desire for physical contact with males (*exclude subject*)
21. What qualities did you like in males to whom you were sexually attracted?
    a. strong masculine behavior (2)
    b. slightly masculine behavior (1)
    c. rather feminine behavior (0)
    d. did not feel sexually attracted to males (*exclude subject*)
22. Would you have preferred a partner
    a. who was willing to have you lead him (0)
    b. who was willing to lead you (2)
    c. you didn't care (1)
    d. did not feel sexually attracted to males (*exclude subject*)

Part C

23. Between the ages of 6 and 12, did you put on women's underwear or clothing
    a. once a month or more, for about a year or more (2)
    b. (less often, but) several times a year for about 3 years or more (1)
    c. very seldom did this during this period (0)
    d. never did this during this period (0)
    e. don't remember (0)
24. Between the ages of 13 and 16, did you put on women's underwear or clothing
    a. once a month or more, for about a year or more (2)
    b. (less often, but) several time a year for about 2 years or more (1)
    c. very seldom did this during this period (0)
    d. never did this during this period (0)
25. Since the age of 17, did you put on women's underwear or clothing
    a. once a month or more, for at least a year (2)
    b. (less often, but) several times a year for at least 2 years (1)
    c. very seldom did this during this period (0)
    d. never did this during this period (0)

26. Have you ever wanted to have an operation to change you physically into a women?
    a. yes (2)
    b. no (0)
    c. unsure (1)
27. If you have ever wished to have a female body rather than a male one, was this
    a. mainly to please men but also for your own satisfaction (2)
    b. mainly for your own satisfaction but also to please men (2)
    c. entirely for your own satisfaction (2)
    d. entirely to please men (1)
    e. about equally to please men and for your own satisfaction (2)
    f. have never wanted to have a female body (0)
28. Have you ever felt like a woman
    a. only if you were wearing at least one piece of female underwear or clothing (1)
    b. while wearing at least one piece of female underwear or clothing and only occasionally at other times also (1)
    c. at all times and for at least 1 year (female clothing or not) (2)
    d. never felt like a woman (0)
29. When completely dressed in male clothing (underwear, etc.) would you
    a. have a feeling of anxiety because of this (2)
    b. have no feeling of anxiety but have another kind of unpleasant feeling because of this (2)
    c. have no unpleasant feelings to do with above (0)

Exhibit 2

Androphilia Scale

1. About how old were you when you first made quite strong efforts to see males who were undressed or scantily dressed?
    a. younger than 12 (1)
    b. between 12 and 16 (1)
    c. older than 16 (1)
    d. never (0)
2. About how old were you when you first felt sexually attracted to males?
    a. younger than 6 (1)
    b. between 6 and 11 (1)
    c. between 12 and 16 (1)
    d. older than 16 (1)
    e. never (0)
3. Since what age have you been sexually attracted to males only?
    a. younger than 6 (1)
    b. between 6 and 11 (1)
    c. between 12 and 16 (1)
    d. older than 16 (1)
    e. never (0)
4. Since the age of 16, have you ever fallen in love with a person of the male sex?
    a. yes (1)
    b. no (0)
5. How old were you when you first kissed a male because you felt sexually attracted to him?
    a. younger than 12 (1)
    b. between 12 and 16 (1)
    c. older than 16 (1)
    d. never (0)
6. Since age 12, how old were you when you first touched the privates of a male to whom you felt sexually attracted?
    a. between 12 and 16 (1)
    b. older than 16 (1)
    c. never (0)

7. What kind of sexual contact with a male would you have preferred on the whole, even though you may not have done it?
   a. inserting your privates between your partner's upper legs (thighs) (1)
   b. putting your privates into your partner's rear end (1)
   c. you would have preferred one of those two modes but you cannot decide which one (1)
   d. your partner putting his privates between your upper legs (thighs) (1)
   e. your partner putting his privates into your rear end (1)
   f. you would have preferred one of those two latter modes but you cannot decide which one (1)
   g. you would have liked all four modes equally well (1)
   h. you would have preferred some other mode of sexual contact (1)
   i. had no desire for physical contact with males (0)
8. What qualities did you like in males to whom you were sexually attracted?
   a. strong masculine behavior (1)
   b. slightly masculine behavior (1)
   c. rather feminine behavior (1)
   d. did not feel sexually attracted to males (0)
9. Would you have preferred
   a. male homosexual partners (1)
   b. male partners who were not homosexual (1)
   c. had no preference (1)
   d. did not feel sexually attracted to males (0)
10. Since age 18, how old was the oldest male to whom you could have felt sexually attracted?
    a. younger than 6 (1)
    b. between 6 and 11 (1)
    c. between 12 and 16 (1)
    d. between 17 and 19 (1)
    e. between 20 and 30 (1)
    f. between 31 and 40 (1)
    g. between 41 and 50 (1)
    h. older than 50 (1)
    i. did not feel sexually attracted to males (0)
11. Would you have preferred a partner
    a. who was willing to have you lead him (1)
    b. who was willing to lead you (1)
    c. you didn't care (1)
    d. did not feel sexually attracted to males (0)
12. Since age 16 and up to age 25 (or younger if you are less than 25) how did the preferred age of male partners change as you got older?
    a. became gradually younger (1)
    b. became gradually older (1)
    c. remained about the same (1)
    d. never felt attracted to males (0)
13. Since age 16, have you even been equally, or more, attracted sexually by a male age 17 and over than by females at 17–40?
    a. yes (1)
    b. no (0)

Exhibit 3

Gynephilia Scale

1. Since the age of 17 when you went dancing, was this to
   a. mainly meet girls at the dance (1)
   b. mainly meet male friends at the dance (0)
   c. mainly because you liked dancing itself (0)
   d. never went dancing since age 17 (0)

2. How old were you when you first tried (on your own) to see females 13 or older naked or dressing or undressing (including strip-tease, movies or pictures)?
   a. younger than 12 (1)
   b. between 12 and 16 (1)
   c. older than 16 (1)
   d. never (0)
3. Since age 13, have you ever fallen in love with or had a crush on a female who was between the ages of 13–40?
   a. yes (1)
   b. no (0)
4. Have you ever desired sexual intercourse with a female age 17–40?
   a. yes (1)
   b. no (0)
5. How do you prefer females age 17–40 to react when you try to come into sexual contact (not necessarily intercourse) with them?
   a. cooperation on the part of the female (1)
   b. indifference (1)
   c. a little resistance (1)
   d. considerable resistance (1)
   e. you don't care (0)
   f. do not try to come into sexual contact with females age 17–40 (0)
6. Do you prefer females of age 17–40
   a. who have no sexual experience (1)
   b. who have had a little experience (1)
   c. who have had considerable experience (1)
   d. you don't care how much experience (1)
   e. not enough interest in females age 17–40 to know (0)
7. Between 13 and 16, when you first saw females 13 or over in the nude (or dressing or undressing) including strip-tease, movies or picture, did you feel sexually aroused?
   a. very much (1)
   b. mildly (1)
   c. not at all (0)
   d. never saw females 13 or over in the nude, dressing or undressing (including striptease, movies or pictures) (0)
8. When you have a wet dream (reach climax while dreaming), do you always, or almost always, dream of a female age 17–40?
   a. yes (1)
   b. no (0)
   c. don't remember any wet dreams (0)
9. In your sexual fantasies, are females age 17–40 always, or almost always involved?
   a. yes (1)
   b. no (0)
   c. haven't had such fantasies (0)

Exhibit 4

Heterosexual Experience Scale

1. Since age 13, how old were you when you first kissed a female age 13–40 who seemed to be interested in you sexually?
   a. between the ages 13–16 (1)
   b. between the ages 17–25 (1)
   c. 26 or older (1)
   d. never after age 12 (0)
2. Since age 13, how old were you when you first petted (beyond kissing) with a female age 13–40 who seemed to be interested in you sexually?
   a. between the ages 13–16 (1)
   b. between the ages 17–25 (1)

    c. 26 or older (1)

    d. never after age 12 (0)

3. Have you ever attempted sexual intercourse with a female age 17–40?

    a. yes (1)

    b. no, and you are older than 25 (0)

    c. no, and you are 25 or younger (0)

4. When did you first have sexual intercourse with a female age 17–40?

    a. before age 16 (1)

    b. between 16 and 25 (1)

    c. 26 or older (1)

    d. never, and you are older than 25 (0)

    e. never, and you are 25 or younger (0)

5. When did you first get married or begin living common-law?

    a. before 30 (1)

    b. between 30–40 (1)

    c. age 41 or older (1)

    d. never married or had common-law relations, and you are older than 30 (0)

    e. never, and you are 30 or younger (0)

6. Was there any period of 14 days or less when you had sexual intercourse with a female age 17–40 more than 5 times?

    a. yes (1)

    b. no, and you are older than 25 (0)

    c. no, and you are 25 or younger (0)

Exhibit 5

Fetishism Scale

1. Do you think that certain inanimate objects (velvet, silk, leather, rubber, shoes, female underwear, etc.) have a stronger sexual attraction for you than for most other people?

    a. yes (1)

    b. no (0)

2. Has the sexual attractiveness of an inanimate (not alive) thing ever increased if it had been worn by, or had been otherwise in contact with

    a. a female (1)

    b. a male (1)

    c. preferably a female but also when in contact or having been in contact with a male (1)

    d. preferably a male but also when in contact or having been in contact with a female (1)

    e. a female or male person equally (1)

    f. contact between a person and a thing never increased its sexual attractiveness (1)

    g. do not feel sexually attracted to any inanimate thing (0)

3. Did the sexual attractiveness to you of such a thing ever increase if you wore it or were otherwise in contact with it yourself?

    a. yes (1)

    b. no (0)

    c. have never been sexually attracted to inanimate things (0)

4. Were you ever more strongly sexually attracted by inanimate things than by females or males?

    a. yes (1)

    b. no (0)

5. What was the age of persons who most increased the sexual attractiveness for you of a certain inanimate object by their contact with it?

    a. 3 years or younger (1)

    b. between 4 and 6 years (1)

    c. between 6 and 11 years (1)

    d. between 12 and 13 years (1)

    e. between 14 and 16 years (1)

    f. between 17 and 40 years (1)

g. over 60 years (1)

h. contact between a person and a thing never increased its sexual attractiveness (1)

i. have never been sexually attracted to inanimate things (0)

6. Is there more than one kind of inanimate thing which arouses you sexually?

   a. yes (1)

   b. no (1)

   c. have never been sexually attracted to inanimate things (0)

7. Through which of these senses did the thing act most strongly?

   a. through the sense of smell (1)

   b. through the sense of taste (1)

   c. through the sense of sight (1)

   d. through the sense of touch (1)

   e. through the sense of hearing (1)

   f. have never been sexually attracted to inanimate objects (0)

8. At about what age do you remember first having a special interest in an inanimate thing which later aroused you sexually?

   a. younger than 2 (1)

   b. between 2 and 4 (1)

   c. between 5 and 7 (1)

   d. between 8 and 10 (1)

   e. between 11 and 13 (1)

   f. older than 13 (1)

   g. have never been sexually attracted to inanimate objects (0)

Exhibit 6

Masochism Scale

1. If you were insulted or humiliated by a person to whom you felt sexually attracted, did this ever increase their attractiveness?

   a. yes (1)

   b. no (0)

   c. unsure (0)

2. Has imagining that you were being humiliated or poorly treated by someone ever excited you sexually?

   a. yes (1)

   b. no (0)

3. Has imagining that you had been injured by someone to the point of bleeding ever excited you sexually?

   a. yes (1)

   b. no (0)

4. Has imagining that someone was causing you pain ever aroused you sexually?

   a. yes (1)

   b. no (0)

5. Has imagining that someone was choking you ever excited you sexually?

   a. yes (1)

   b. no (0)

6. Has imagining that you have become dirty or soiled ever excited you sexually?

   a. yes (1)

   b. no (0)

7. Has imagining that your life was being threatened ever excited you sexually?

   a. yes (1)

   b. no (0)

8. Has imagining that someone was imposing on you heavy physical labor or strain ever excited you sexually?

   a. yes (1)

   b. no (0)

9. Has imagining a situation in which you were having trouble breathing ever excited you sexually?

   a. yes (1)

   b. no (0)

10. Has imagining that you were being threatened with a knife or other sharp instrument ever excited you sexually?
    a. yes (1)
    b. no (0)
11. Has imagining that you are being tied up by somebody ever excited you sexually?
    a. yes (1)
    b. no (0)

Exhibit 7

Sadism Scale

1. Did you ever like to read stories about or descriptions of torture?
    a. yes (1)
    b. no (0)
2. Did you usually re-read a description of torture several times?
    a. yes (1)
    b. no (0)
    c. don't remember (0)
3. Were you
    a. very interested in descriptions of torture (1)
    b. a little interested (0)
    c. not at all interested (0)
    d. never read such descriptions (0)
4. Between the ages of 13 and 16, did you find the sight of blood
    a. exciting (1)
    b. only pleasant (1)
    c. unpleasant (0)
    d. did not affect you in any way (0)
5. Has beating somebody or imagining that you are doing so ever excited you sexually?
    a. yes (1)
    b. no (0)
6. Have you ever tried to tie the hands or legs of a person who attracted you sexually?
    a. yes (1)
    b. no (0)
7. Has cutting or imagining to cut someone's hair ever excited you sexually?
    a. yes (1)
    b. no (0)
8. Has imagining that you saw someone bleeding ever excited you sexually?
    a. yes (1)
    b. no (0)
9. Has imagining someone being choked by yourself or somebody else ever excited you sexually?
    a. yes (1)
    b. no (0)
10. Has imagining yourself or someone else imposing heavy physical labor or strain on somebody ever excited you sexually?
    a. yes (1)
    b. no (0)
11. Has imagining that someone was being ill-treated in some way by yourself or somebody else ever excited you sexually?
    a. yes (1)
    b. no (0)
12. Has imagining that you or someone else were causing pain to somebody ever excited you sexually?
    a. yes (1)
    b. no (0)
13. Has imagining that you or somebody else were threatening someone's life ever excited you sexually?
    a. yes (1)
    b. no (0)

14. Has imagining that someone other than yourself was crying painfully ever excited you sexually?
   a. yes (1)
   b. no (0)
15. Has imagining that someone other than yourself was dying ever excited you sexually?
   a. yes (1)
   b. no (0)
16. Has imagining that you or someone else were making it difficult for somebody to breathe ever excited you sexually?
   a. yes (1)
   b. no (0)
17. Has imagining that you or someone else were tying up somebody ever excited you sexually?
   a. yes (1)
   b. no (0)
18. Has imagining that you or somebody else were threatening someone with a knife or other sharp instrument ever excited you sexually?
   a. yes (1)
   b. no (0)
19. Has imagining that someone was unconscious or unable to move ever excited you sexually?
   a. yes (1)
   b. no (0)
20. Has imagining that someone had a very pale and still face ever excited you sexually?
   a. yes (1)
   b. no (0)

Stereotypes About Male Sexuality Scale

WILLIAM E. SNELL, JR.,[1] *Southeast Missouri State University*

Cognitive approaches to human sexuality have recently received considerable attention. However, there has been a paucity of instruments designed to deal with the types of cognitive beliefs that might influence sexual feelings and behaviors. Snell and his colleagues attempted to address this concern through the development and validation of the Stereotypes About Male Sexuality Scale (SAMSS; Snell, Belk, & Hawkins, 1986, 1990; Snell, Hawkins, & Belk, 1988). The SAMSS is an objective self-report questionnaire that is designed to measure 10 distinctive stereotypic beliefs about males and their sexuality (cf. Zilbergeld, 1978; Chap. 4): (a) Inexpressiveness, (b) Sex Equals Performance, (c) Males Orchestrate Sex, (d) Always Ready for Sex, (e) Touching Leads to Sex, (f) Sex Equals Intercourse, (g) Sex Requires Erection, (h) Sex Requires Orgasm, (i) Spontaneous Sex, and (j) Sexually Aware Men. The 10 subscales on the SAMSS can be used in research as individual-tendency measures of stereotypes about males and their sexuality.

Description

The SAMSS consists of 60 items. Individuals respond to the 60 items on the SAMSS using a 5-point Likert-type scale: *agree* (+2); *slightly agree* (+1); *neither agree nor disagree* (0); *slightly disagree* (–1); and *disagree* (–2).

Response Mode and Timing

Individuals typically indicate their responses on a computer scan sheet by darkening in a response ranging from A (*agree*) to E (*disagree*). The questionnaire usually takes about 20–25 minutes to complete.

Scoring

Individuals respond to the 60 statements on the SAMSS using a 5-point Likert-type scale. The items are recoded so that A = +2, B = +1, C = 0, D = –1, and E = –2, so that the anchors range from *agree* (+2) to *disagree* (–2). The items

[1]Address all correspondence to William E. Snell, Jr., Department of Psychology, Southeast Missouri State University, One University Plaza, Cape Girardeau, MO 63701; e-mail: wesnell@semo.edu

assigned to each subscale are (a) Inexpressiveness (1, 11, 21, 31, 41, 51); (b) Sex Equals Performance (2, 12, 22, 32, 42, 52); (c) Males Orchestrate Sex (3, 13, 23, 33, 43, 53); (d) Always Ready for Sex (4, 14, 24, 34, 44, 54); (e) Touching Leads to Sex (5, 15, 25, 35, 45, 55); (f) Sex Equals Intercourse (6, 16, 26, 36, 46, 56); (g) Sex Requires Erection (7, 17, 27, 37, 47, 57); (h) Sex Requires Orgasm (8, 18, 28, 38, 48, 58); (i) Spontaneous Sex (9, 19, 29, 39, 49, 59); and (j) Sexually Aware Men (10, 20, 30, 40, 50, 60). Higher subscale scores thus correspond to greater agreement with the 10 cognitive beliefs measured by the SAMSS.

Reliability

The alpha values for these 10 subscales range from a low of .63 to a high of .93 with an average of .80 (Snell et al., 1986).

Validity

Snell et al. (1990) reported the results of two investigations involving the SAMSS. In the first study, the relationship between the SAMSS and two gender-role measures were examined. The results were that the restrictive emotionality aspect of the masculine role was strongly associated with stereotypic beliefs about male sexuality (Doyle, 1989; Gould, 1982; Gross, 1978; Herek, 1987; Mosher & Anderson, 1986; Mosher & Sirkin, 1984). Other gender-role preferences and behaviors were also found to be positively associated with conventional "performance" approaches to male sexuality. In the second investigation, counseling trainees were asked to describe how mentally healthy adult men and women would respond to the SAMSS. The responses of both male and female in-training counselors indicated that they expected mentally healthy males (a) to reject inhibited, control, and constant readiness approaches to the expression of male sexuality and (b) to express greater disagreement toward defining male sexuality only in terms of sexual intercourse and toward viewing males as inherently knowledge-able about sex. These results thus provide evidence for the importance of the SAMSS and a cognitive approach to the study of male sexuality. Finally, the SAMSS has been found to correlate significantly and negatively with the use of bilateral social influence strategies (Snell et al., 1988), thus providing evidence for the validity of the SAMSS in that conventional beliefs about sex, as measured by the SAMSS, were expected to be associated with the use of selfish (vs. bilateral) influence strategy use with an intimate partner.

References

Doyle, J. A. (1989). *The male experience* (2nd ed.). Dubuque, IA: Brown.

Gould, R. (1982). Sexual functioning in relation to the changing roles of men. In K. Solomon & N. Levy (Eds.), *Men in transition: Theory and therapy* (pp. 165–173). New York: Plenum.

Gross, A. E. (1978). The male role and heterosexual behavior. *Journal of Social Issues, 34*(1), 87–107.

Herek, G. M. (1987). On heterosexual masculinity: Some psychical consequences of the social construction of gender and sexuality. In M. S. Kimmel (Ed.), *Changing men: New directions in research on men and masculinity* (pp. 68–82). Newbury Park, CA: Sage.

Mosher, D. L., & Anderson, R. D. (1986). Macho personality, sexual aggression, and reactions to guided imagery of realistic rape. *Journal of Research in Personality, 20*, 77–94.

Mosher, D. L., & Sirkin, M. (1984). Measuring a macho personality constellation. *Journal of Research in Personality, 18*, 150–163.

Snell, W. E., Jr., Belk, S. S., & Hawkins, R. C., II. (1986). The Stereotypes About Male Sexuality Scale (SAMSS): Components, correlates, antecedents, consequences, and counselor bias. *Social and Behavioral Sciences Documents, 16*, 10. (Ms. No. 2747)

Snell, W. E., Jr., Belk, S. S., & Hawkins, R. C., II (1990). Cognitive beliefs about male sexuality: The impact of gender roles and counselor perspectives. *Journal of Rational-Emotive Therapy, 8*, 249–265.

Snell, W. E., Jr., Hawkins, R. C., II, & Belk, S. S. (1988). Stereotypes about male sexuality and the use of social influence strategies in intimate relationships. *Journal of Social and Clinical Psychology, 7*, 42–48.

Tiefer, L. (1987). In pursuit of the perfect penis: The medicalization of male sexuality. In M. Kimmel (Ed.), *Changing men: New directions in research on men and masculinity* (pp. 165–184). Newbury Park, CA: Sage.

Zilbergeld, B. (1978). *Male sexuality*. Boston: Little, Brown.

Exhibit

Stereotypes About Male Sexuality Scale

Instructions: We would like to know something about people's beliefs about male sexuality. For this reason we are asking you to respond to a number of items that deal with male sexuality, indicating the extent to which you disagree/agree with the statements. For each of the items on this page, you will be indicating your answer on the computer-scoreable answer sheet by darkening in the number (or letter) that corresponds to your response. Your response should be based on the sorts of things that you believe about male sexuality. Use the following scale to indicate your degree of agreement/disagreement with each item:

A	B	C	D	E
Agree	Slightly Agree	Neither Agree nor Disagree	Slightly Disagree	Disagree

There are no right or wrong answers. Your choices should be a description of your own personal beliefs.

1. Men should not be held.
2. Most men believe that sex is a performance.
3. Men generally want to be the guiding participant in sexual behavior.

4. Most men are ready for sex at any time.
5. Most men desire physical contact only as a prelude to sex.
6. The ultimate sexual goal in men's mind is intercourse.
7. Lack of an erection will always spoil sex for a man.
8. From a man's perspective, good sex usually has an "earthshaking" aspect to it.
9. Men don't really like to plan their sexual experiences.
10. Most men are sexually well-adjusted.
11. Only a narrow range of emotions should be permitted to men.
12. Men are almost always concerned with their sexual performance.
13. Most men don't want to assume a passive role in sex.
14. Men usually want sex, regardless of where they are.
15. Among men, touching is simply the first step towards sex.
16. Men are not sexually satisfied with any behavior other than intercourse.
17. Without an erection a man is sexually lost.
18. Quiet, lazy sex is usually not all that satisfying for a man.
19. Men usually like good sex to "just happen."
20. Most men have healthy attitudes toward sex.
21. A man who is vulnerable is a sissy.
22. In sex, it's a man's performance that counts.
23. Sexual activity is easier if the man assumes a leadership role.
24. Men are always ready for sex.
25. A man never really wants "only" a hug or caress.
26. Men want their sexual experiences to end with intercourse.
27. A sexual situation cannot be gratifying for a man unless he "can get it up."
28. Sexual climax is a necessary part of men's sexual behavior.
29. Most men yearn for spontaneous sex that requires little conscious effort.
30. In these days of increased openness about sex, most men have become free of past inhibiting ideas about their sexual behavior.
31. A man should be careful to hide his feelings.
32. Men's sexuality is often goal-orientated in its nature.
33. Sex is a man's responsibility.
34. Most men come to a sexual situation in a state of constant desire.
35. Men use physical contact as a request for sex.
36. Men believe that every sexual act should include intercourse.
37. Any kind of sexual activity for a man requires an erection.
38. Satisfying sexual activity for a man always includes increasing excitement and passion.
39. A satisfying sexual experience for a man does not really require all that much forethought.
40. Most men have progressive ideas about sex.
41. It is unacceptable for men to reveal their deepest concerns.
42. Men usually think of sex as work.
43. A man is supposed to initiate sexual contact.
44. Men are perpetually ready for sex.
45. Many men are dissatisfied with any bodily contact which is not followed by sexual activity.
46. Many men are only interested in sexual intercourse as a form of sexual stimulation.
47. An erection is considered by almost all men as vital for sex.
48. Men's sexual desire is often "imperative and driven" in nature.
49. Men consider sex artificial if it is preplanned.
50. In these days of wider availability of accurate information, most men are realistic about their sexual activities.
51. Intense emotional expressiveness should not be discussed by men.
52. Sex is a pressure-filled activity for most men.
53. Men are responsible for choosing sexual positions.
54. Men usually never get enough sex.
55. For men, kissing and touching are merely the preliminaries to sexual activity.
56. During sex, men are always thinking about getting to intercourse.
57. Without an erection, sexual activity for a man will end in misery.
58. Sexual activity must end with an orgasm for a man to feel satisfied.
59. For men, natural sex means "just doing it instinctively."
60. Most men have realistic insight into their sexual preferences and desires.

Negative Attitudes Toward Masturbation

DONALD L. MOSHER,[1] *University of Connecticut*

Abramson and Mosher (1975) developed an inventory, Attitudes Toward Masturbation, as a measure of *negative* attitudes toward masturbation, to measure the construct of masturbation-guilt (Mosher, 1979b; Mosher & Vonderheide, 1985). Although the inventory is regarded as a homogeneous measure, a factor analysis conducted for descriptive purposes found three factors: (a) positive attitudes toward masturbation, (b) false beliefs about the harmful nature of masturbation, and (c) personally experienced negative affects associated with masturbation (Abramson & Mosher, 1975). Masturbation-guilt is regarded as a script—a set of rules for ordering a co-assembled family of scenes—learned scenes in which the negative affects of guilt, disgust, shame, and fear have reciprocally interacted with cognitions about masturbation (including general fantasies and sex myths). Masturbation-guilt, as a script, predicts, interprets, regulates, and evaluates conduct in scenes entailing masturbation or in scenes associatively linked through family resemblance of affect, objects, or scene features to past imagined masturbatory scenes.

Description

This inventory is a 30-item (10 of which have reversed scoring), 5-point Likert-type scale anchored by *not at all true for me* to *extremely true for me*. Because items were taken from college subjects' responses to open-ended questions about the consequences of masturbation (Abramson, 1973), the items are useful with educated populations of men and women.

Response Mode and Timing

Respondents can circle the number indicating the relative truth of the statement for them, but the more common scoring has had the subjects indicate response choices on machine-scoreable answer sheets. The scale requires approximately 7 minutes to complete.

Scoring

The 10 items with reversed scoring are 3, 5, 8, 11, 13, 14, 17, 22, 27, and 29. To obtain an index of masturbation-guilt, scores are summed to yield a score from 30 to 150.

Reliability

A corrected split-half reliability of .75 was reported for the original sample of 198 male and female college students (Abramson & Mosher, 1975). A Cronbach alpha of .94 was found for a sample of 186 college women (Mosher & Vonderheide, 1985).

Validity

The scale has successfully predicted decreased frequency and lower percentage of orgasm to masturbatory behavior (Abramson & Mosher, 1975; Mosher & O'Grady, 1979); less subjective sexual arousal and more negative affective responses to explicit films of male and female masturbation (Mosher & Abramson, 1977); less positive projective stories to films of masturbation (Abramson & Mosher, 1979); less subjective sexual arousal and more negative affects to films of male homosexuality and male masturbation (Mosher & O'Grady, 1979); less pelvic vasocongestion, as measured by thermography, in women reading an erotic story (Abramson, Perry, Rothblatt, Seeley, & Seeley, 1981); more negative affect when recalling a memory of past masturbation (Green & Mosher, 1985); and more negative attitudes toward contraceptives and avoidance of selecting the diaphragm as a method of birth control (Mosher & Vonderheide, 1985). Although masturbation-guilt and sex-guilt (Mosher, 1966, 1968, 1979a) can be viewed as measuring a latent construct of *guilt over sexuality*, there is also evidence of discriminant validity from sex-guilt (which is a more general sexual script) in a number of the studies cited above.

References

Abramson, P. R. (1973). The relationship of the frequency of masturbation to several aspects of behavior. *The Journal of Sex Research, 9,* 132–142.

Abramson, P. R., & Mosher, D. L. (1975). The development of a measure of negative attitudes toward masturbation. *Journal of Consulting and Clinical Psychology, 43,* 485–490.

Abramson, P. R., & Mosher, D. L. (1979). Am empirical investigation of experimentally induced masturbatory fantasies. *Archives of Sexual Behavior, 8,* 24–39.

Abramson, P. R., Perry, L. B., Rothblatt, A., Seeley, T. T., & Seeley, D. M. (1981). Negative attitudes toward masturbation and pelvic vasocongestion: A thermographic analysis. *Journal of Research in Personality, 15,* 497–509.

Green, S. E., & Mosher, D. L. (1985). A causal model of arousal to erotic fantasies. *The Journal of Sex Research, 21,* 1–23.

Mosher, D. L. (1966). The development and multitrait-multimethod matrix analysis of three measures of three aspects of guilt. *Journal of Consulting Psychology, 30,* 35–39.

Mosher, D. L. (1968). Measurement of guilt in females by self-report inventories. *Journal of Consulting and Clinical Psychology, 32,* 690–695.

[1]Address correspondence to Donald L. Mosher, 648 Ternberry Forest Drive, The Villages, FL 32162; e-mail: dlmosher@aol.com

Mosher, D. L. (1979a). The meaning and measurement of guilt. In C. E. Izard (Ed.), *Emotions in personality and psychopathology* (pp. 105–129). New York: Plenum.

Mosher, D. L. (1979b). Negative attitudes toward masturbation in sex therapy. *Journal of Sex & Marital Therapy, 5*, 315–333.

Mosher, D. L., & Abramson, P. R. (1977). Subjective sexual arousal to films of masturbation. *Journal of Consulting and Clinical Psychology, 45*, 796–807.

Mosher, D. L., & O'Grady, K. E. (1979). Homosexual threat, negative attitudes toward masturbation, sex guilt, and male's sexual and affective reactions to explicit sexual films. *Journal of Consulting and Clinical Psychology, 47*, 860–873.

Mosher, D. L., & Vonderheide, S. G. (1985). Contributions of sex guilt and masturbation guilt to women's contraceptive attitudes and use. *The Journal of Sex Research, 21*, 24–39.

Exhibit

Negative Attitudes Toward Masturbation

The following 30 items sample diverse opinions and attitudes about masturbation. Masturbation means stimulating your own genitals to enjoy the pleasurable sensations or experience orgasm. Answers are to be marked on the separate answer sheet. Marking 1 means the item is *not at all true for you*; marking 2 means it is *somewhat untrue*; marking 3 means you are *undecided*; marking 4 means it is *somewhat true*; marking 5 means it is *strongly true for you.*

1. People masturbate to escape feelings of tension and anxiety.
2. People who masturbate will not enjoy sexual intercourse as much as those who refrain from masturbation.
3. Masturbation is a private matter which neither harms nor concerns anyone else.
4. Masturbation is a sin against yourself.
5. Masturbation in childhood can help a person develop a natural, healthy attitude toward sex.
6. Masturbation in an adult is juvenile and immature.
7. Masturbation can lead to homosexuality.
8. Excessive masturbation is a needless worry, as it is physically impossible.
9. If you enjoy masturbating too much, you may never learn to relate to the opposite sex.
10. After masturbating, a person feels degraded.
11. Experience with masturbation can potentially help a woman become orgasic in sexual intercourse.
12. I feel guilty about masturbating.
13. Masturbation can be a "friend in need" when there is no "friend in deed."
14. Masturbation can provide an outlet for sex fantasies without harming anyone else or endangering oneself.
15. Excessive masturbation can lead to problems of impotence in men and frigidity in women.
16. Masturbation is an escape mechanism which prevents a person from developing a mature sexual outlook.
17. Masturbation can provide harmless relief from sexual tension.
18. Playing with your own genitals is disgusting.
19. Excessive masturbation is associated with neurosis, depression, and behavioral problems.
20. Any masturbation is too much.
21. Masturbation is a compulsive, addictive habit which once begun is almost impossible to stop.
22. Masturbation is fun.
23. When I masturbate, I am disgusted with myself.
24. A pattern of frequent masturbation is associated with introversion and withdrawal from social contacts.
25. I would be ashamed to admit publicly that I have masturbated.
26. Excessive masturbation leads to mental dullness and fatigue.
27. Masturbation is a normal sexual outlet.
28. Masturbation is caused by an excessive preoccupation with thoughts about sex.
29. Masturbation can teach you to enjoy the sensuousness of your own body.
30. After I masturbate, I am disgusted with myself for losing control of my body.

Attitudes Toward Masturbation Scale

CHANTAL D. YOUNG AND CHARLENE L. MUEHLENHARD,[1] *University of Kansas*

The Attitudes Toward Masturbation Scale (ATMS) was developed to measure individuals' complex and often conflicting thoughts and feelings about masturbating (Young & Muehlenhard, 2009). We found two existing scales for measuring attitudes about masturbation: Abramson and Mosher's (1975) Negative Attitudes Toward Masturbation Inventory and Miller and Lief's (1976) Masturbation Attitude Scale. Both are more than 30 years old, both yield only one global score, and both assess respondents' attitudes about masturbation in general rather than about *their own* masturbation. The purpose of the ATMS is to measure respondents' (a) reasons for wanting (or being tempted) to masturbate, (b) reasons for avoiding (or trying to avoid) masturbating, and (c) positive and negative feelings related to masturbating.

Description

The ATMS was developed using a multistep process. First, in a pilot study, 236 undergraduate women and men wrote answers to open-ended questions about their attitudes and feelings about masturbation. Second, we compiled their responses and used them to create scale items. We also created scale items reflecting themes identified in prior studies of attitudes toward masturbation (e.g., Clifford, 1978; Elliott & Brantley, 1997). Our preliminary scale included 223 items divided into three sections reflecting reasons for wanting—or being tempted—to masturbate, reasons for avoiding—or trying to avoid—masturbation, and feelings about masturbating. Third, a new sample of 518 undergraduate women and men rated these items on a 7-point scale. We used their responses to divide the items into subscales, based on factor loadings derived from principal components analysis, Cronbach's alphas, and conceptual considerations (Young & Muehlenhard, 2009).

The ATMS consists of 179 items, divided into 28 subscales in three categories. (a) The 13 reasons-for-wanting-to-masturbate subscales assess themes such as pleasure, self-exploration and improvement, and mood improvement. Items are rated on a 7-point scale, from 0 (*Not a Reason*) to 6 (*A Very Important Reason*). (b) The 10 reasons-for-avoiding-masturbation subscales assess themes such as immorality, lack of desire or interest, and preference for partner sex. The same 7-point scale is used. (c) The 5 feelings-related-to-masturbation subscales assess satisfaction, guilt, anger, anxiety, and indifference.

Respondents rate the strength of each feeling, using a 7-point scale ranging from 0 (*Not at all*) to 6 (*Very Strongly*).

The scale was developed and tested using samples of college students, but it could be used with other populations. It is designed so that anyone can complete it, regardless of whether they masturbate.

Response Mode and Timing

The ATMS is a paper-and-pencil questionnaire. It can be completed in about 15 to 30 minutes.

Scoring

Subscale scores are calculated by averaging the respondent's ratings for the items on the subscale. Subscale scores can range from 0 to 6. For the reasons-for-wanting-to-masturbate subscales and the reasons-for-avoiding-masturbation subscales, higher scores reflect a greater importance of the reason tapped by that subscale. For the feelings-related-to-masturbation subscales, higher scores reflect greater intensity of feeling.

Each subscale score can be used individually to assess the specific content of each subscale. In addition, four composite scores can be calculated: the Wanting Composite (the mean of the 13 reasons-for-wanting-to-masturbate subscales), the Avoiding Composite (the mean of the 10 reasons-for-avoiding-masturbation subscales), the Negative-Feelings Composite (the mean of the Guilt, Anger, Anxiety, and Indifference subscales), and the Positive-Feelings Composite (the Satisfaction subscale score). These composites can be used to assess the respondent's overall positive and negative attitudes toward masturbation.

The subscales and items on each are as follows:

Reasons-for-Wanting-to-Masturbate Subscales
Pleasure: 1, 2, 35, 41, 42, 44, 50, 51, 52
Self-Exploration and Improvement: 11, 13, 17, 23, 39, 54, 55, 56, 63, 68
Mood Improvement: 47, 60, 62, 67
Relaxation and Stress Relief: 6, 7, 16, 40, 46, 58, 61, 64
Avoidance of Partner Sex: 26, 28, 29, 30, 34, 65
Arousal Decrease: 18, 21, 33, 49, 59, 69
Compulsion: 8, 25, 27, 32, 43
Pleasure of Partner: 15, 66, 70
Adherence to Social Norms: 12, 14, 19, 20, 38, 57

[1]Address correspondence to Charlene Muehlenhard, Department of Psychology, 426 Fraser Hall, University of Kansas, 1415 Jayhawk Blvd, Lawrence, KS 66045–7556; e-mail: charlene@ku.edu

Substitution for Partner Sex: 4, 9, 10, 22, 24, 31
Importance of Fantasy: 36, 37, 48, 72
Feeling Unattractive: 45, 53, 71
Boredom: 3, 5

Reasons-for-Avoiding-Masturbation Subscales

Immorality: 73, 74, 75, 79, 81, 83, 105, 122, 123, 124, 125, 126, 127, 131, 132, 134
No Desire or Interest: 76, 77, 86, 87, 88, 100, 101, 114, 118, 119, 120
Preference for Partner Sex: 90, 103, 104, 107, 110, 128, 129, 133
Fear of Negative Social Evaluation: 84, 91, 93, 95, 102, 121
Sex Negativity: 78, 82, 85, 94, 96, 97
Negative Mood State: 92, 106, 109, 117
Detraction from Partner Sex: 111, 112
In Committed Relationship: 80, 98, 108, 115
Bothered by Thoughts: 116, 130
Self-Control: 89, 99, 113

Feelings-Related-to-Masturbation Subscales

Guilt: 136, 138, 142, 143, 153, 154, 155, 167, 168, 169, 171, 179
Satisfaction: 135, 139, 146, 147, 149, 150, 151, 152, 156, 157, 158, 163, 166, 170, 173, 174, 176, 177, 178
Anger: 159, 160, 161, 165
Anxiety: 144, 145, 148, 162
Indifference: 137, 140, 141, 164, 172, 175

Reliability

Based on a sample of 518 undergraduate women and men (Young & Muehlenhard, 2009), Cronbach's alphas for the subscales ranged from .71 to .97, providing evidence that the subscales have good internal consistency.

Validity

Based on data from 518 undergraduate women and men, Young and Muehlenhard (2009) found numerous significant differences between participants who masturbated and those who did not, even after controlling for gender. Compared with nonmasturbators, masturbators scored significantly higher on 9 of the 13 reasons-for-wanting-to-masturbate subscales and the Satisfaction subscale and significantly lower on 5 of the 10 reasons-for-avoiding-masturbation subscales and the Guilt, Anger, Anxiety, and Indifference subscales.

Consistent with meta-analytic findings that more men than women masturbate (Oliver & Hyde, 1993; Petersen & Hyde, 2007), there were significant gender differences on 18 of the 28 subscales. Men generally reported stronger reasons for wanting to masturbate, weaker reasons for avoiding masturbation, and stronger positive and weaker negative feelings related to masturbation. When controlling for masturbation status, there were fewer gender differences, but some remained: For the reasons-for-wanting-to-masturbate subscales, women scored higher on Self-Exploration and Improvement, Avoidance of Partner Sex, and Pleasure of Partner; men scored higher on Boredom. For reasons-for-avoiding-masturbation subscales, women scored higher on No Desire or Interest, Fear of Negative Social Evaluation, and Sex Negativity. For feelings-related-to-masturbation subscales, women scored higher on Anxiety.

Young and Muehlenhard (2009) performed a cluster analysis on participants' subscale scores. They identified four clusters: The *enthusiastic cluster* had *high* Wanting subscale scores and *low* Avoiding subscales scores. The *lukewarm cluster* had *low* Wanting subscale scores and *even lower* Avoiding subscales scores. The *high-guilt cluster* had *low* Wanting subscale scores and *high* Avoiding subscales scores. The *ambivalent cluster* had the *highest* Wanting subscale scores and the *highest* Avoiding subscales scores. These clusters showed numerous differences in the percentages of women and men in the cluster, the percentages who reported masturbating, and their qualitative comments about masturbation.

In another study (Stroupe, 2008), 210 undergraduate women completed the ATMS. Compared with women who had never masturbated, those who masturbated had significantly higher Wanting Composite and Positive-Feelings Composite scores and significantly lower Avoiding Composite and Negative-Feelings Composite scores; scores for women who masturbated infrequently were intermediate. Analyses of subscale scores provided additional information.

Other Information

With appropriate citation, the ATMS may be copied and used for educational, research, and clinical purposes, without permission. The authors would appreciate receiving a summary of any research using this scale.

References

Abramson, P., & Mosher, D. (1975). Development of a measure of negative attitudes toward masturbation. *Journal of Counseling and Clinical Psychology, 43*, 485–490.

Clifford, R. (1978). Development of masturbation in college women. *Archives of Sexual Behavior, 7*, 559–573.

Elliott, L., & Brantley, C. (1997). *Sex on campus: The naked truth about the real sex lives of college students.* New York: Random House.

Miller, W. R., & Lief, H. I. (1976). Masturbatory attitudes, knowledge, and experience: Data from the sex knowledge and attitude test (SKAT). *Archives of Sexual Behavior, 5*, 447–467.

Oliver, M. B., & Hyde, J. S. (1993). Gender differences in sexuality: A meta-analysis. *Psychological Bulletin, 114*, 29–51.

Petersen, J., & Hyde, J. S. (2007, November). *A meta-analytic review of gender differences in sexuality: 1990–2007.* Paper presented at the 50th Anniversary Meeting of the Society for the Scientific Study of Sexuality, Indianapolis, IN.

Stroupe, N. (2008). *How difficult is too difficult? The relationships among women's sexual experience and attitudes, difficulty with orgasm, and perception of themselves as orgasmic or anorgasmic.* Unpublished master's thesis, University of Kansas, Lawrence.

Young, C. D., & Muehlenhard, C. L. (2009). *The meanings of masturbation.* Manuscript in preparation.

Exhibit

Attitudes Toward Masturbation Scale

Reasons for **Wanting** to Masturbate

Whether they masturbate or not, people may **want** to masturbate (or be **tempted** to masturbate) for many different reasons. Below is a list of possible reasons. Please rate how strong each of the reasons is for your **wanting** to masturbate or being tempted to masturbate, *regardless of whether or not you actually masturbate.*

0	1	2	3	4	5	6
Not a Reason			A Moderately Important Reason			A Very Important Reason

For you, how strong are the following reasons for **wanting** to (or being **tempted** to) masturbate?

1. If I'm feeling horny
2. I find it pleasurable
3. If there is nothing else to do
4. If I'm not getting as much sex as I want
5. If I'm bored
6. To relieve stress
7. If I'm anxious
8. Because—even though I try—I just can't stop myself
9. Because it's a substitute for sex with a partner
10. Out of sexual frustration
11. I hope that masturbating will help me reach orgasm with a partner
12. Someone else thinks I should (e.g., a friend or a dating partner)
13. To explore my own sexuality
14. So I could say that I've done it (it's something to talk about)
15. My partner wants to watch me do it
16. It's a good way to take a break (e.g., a break from studying, etc.)
17. I'm curious about it
18. If I want to avoid unwanted arousal later
19. My friends have masturbated, and I want to be able to talk with them about it
20. "Everyone" does it, and I want to feel "sexually normal"
21. If I'm so sexually aroused that it's interfering with other things I want or need to do
22. If I don't have a partner to have sex with
23. To make myself a better sexual partner (e.g., to figure out how to achieve orgasm or to become more comfortable having orgasms with my partner)
24. Masturbating helps me keep my mind off sex with a partner
25. It's a compulsive sexual behavior
26. Masturbating helps me remain a virgin
27. I just do it without really thinking about it
28. Masturbating makes it easier to avoid sex with a partner, and I don't want to have sex with a partner for moral reasons (e.g., I don't want to have sex before marriage)
29. Masturbating makes it easier to avoid sex with a partner, and I don't want to have sex with a partner for health reasons (e.g., I don't want to risk sexually transmitted diseases or pregnancy)
30. Masturbating makes it easier to avoid sex with a partner, and I don't want to have sex with a partner for self-esteem reasons (e.g., I don't feel comfortable being sexual with someone else)
31. If I have a partner, but my partner refuses to have sex
32. I feel an uncontrollable urge to do it
33. If I want to decrease my sexual arousal so I can focus on something else
34. It's more moral to masturbate than to have sex with a partner
35. If I want to have an orgasm
36. I get aroused by sexual activities that are not socially acceptable, so I fantasize about them during masturbation

37. I get aroused by sexual activities that are not possible in real life, so I fantasize about them during masturbation (e.g., sex with a movie star, sex on a beach, etc.)
38. Because I hear about it from TV, movies, magazines, etc.
39. Masturbating improves my sexual health
40. To help me fall asleep
41. Because it's fun
42. Because I know exactly how to stimulate myself and maximize my pleasure
43. It's a habit
44. If I am already sexually aroused (e.g., from watching a movie, reading a magazine)
45. Because I feel like no one is attracted to me
46. If I want to relax
47. If I'm angry
48. If I want to exercise my imagination
49. So that I can focus my concentration on a task after masturbating
50. Because I deserve to experience pleasure
51. If I see someone or something that is arousing
52. If I have an urge to do something sexual
53. Because I'm not comfortable enough with my body to be sexual with someone else
54. To learn how to give myself pleasure
55. To gain more sexual confidence
56. Because it's good exercise
57. Because my friends masturbate
58. To calm myself down
59. So that I can stop thinking about masturbating
60. If I feel frustrated about something else
61. It makes me feel peaceful
62. It distracts me when I'm feeling down
63. To try a new method (e.g., sex toys, pornography)
64. It's an escape
65. To avoid using another person for sex
66. Because it arouses my partner when he/she knows that I masturbated
67. If I'm in a bad mood
68. To learn how to have better orgasms
69. If I'm already sexually aroused, and I want to decrease my level of sexual arousal
70. Because it arouses my partner when I masturbate in front of him/her
71. If I'm feeling unattractive
72. I enjoy my fantasies during masturbation

Reasons for *Avoiding* (or for Trying to Avoid) Masturbating

Whether they masturbate or not, people might **avoid** (or try to avoid) masturbating for many different reasons. Below is a list of possible reasons. Please rate how strong each of the reasons is for you **avoiding** (or trying to avoid) masturbating, *regardless of whether or not you actually masturbate.*

0	1	2	3	4	5	6
Not a Reason			A Moderately Important Reason			A Very Important Reason

For you, how strong are the following reasons for **avoiding** (or trying to avoid) masturbating?

73. It's against my religion
74. It's against my morals or values
75. It's against my parents' morals or values
76. I'm just not interested
77. It just doesn't appeal to me
78. I am uncomfortable with any sexual behavior

79. It would make me feel cheap
80. If I am committed to someone
81. I would feel guilty about it
82. I am anxious about sexual behavior
83. I know I'd regret it
84. I fear it will damage my reputation
85. I feel uncomfortable or embarrassed about my body
86. I think it would be physically uncomfortable
87. It seems weird to me
88. I feel strange doing it
89. I think I should have more self-control
90. If I'm currently sexually satisfied
91. Society says it's wrong
92. If I'm stressed
93. I'm afraid of someone knowing I masturbate
94. It makes me feel lonely
95. If I'm afraid of being caught
96. It makes me feel sexually inadequate
97. It's bad for my health
98. If I'm in a committed relationship
99. I like to feel in control of my urges
100. I'm not sure how to masturbate
101. I don't like how it feels
102. It's embarrassing to me
103. Because I like intercourse better
104. Because I like any sexual contact with a partner better
105. I feel bad about myself afterwards
106. If I'm depressed
107. Orgasms are better with a partner
108. My partner doesn't want me to do it
109. If I'm worried about something else
110. If I've recently had sex
111. It makes me less able to orgasm during sex
112. It makes me less horny during sex
113. I want to improve my self-discipline
114. It's boring
115. I feel like I'm cheating on my partner
116. My fantasies during masturbation bother me
117. If I've had a bad day
118. It's a waste of time
119. It seems pointless
120. I don't find it sexually arousing
121. Other people might find me gross
122. My family is against it
123. My friends are against it
124. It makes me feel empty inside
125. I was raised to believe it's wrong
126. It makes me feel ashamed
127. It's disrespectful to myself
128. If I'm satisfied with the quantity of the sex I'm having
129. If I'm satisfied with the quality of the sex I'm having
130. My sexual thoughts during masturbation bother me
131. Masturbation in an adult is immature
132. It makes me feel like I'm sinning against myself
133. It's not as good as sex
134. It does not fit with my religious views

Feelings About Masturbation

Check which set of directions applies to you:

_____ **If you masturbate:** People feel many different things when they masturbate. Below is a list of possible feelings. *How strongly, if at all, do you usually experience these feelings when you masturbate?*

_____ **If you don't masturbate:** People feel many different things when they masturbate. Below is a list of possible feelings. *How strongly, if at all, do you think you **would** usually experience these feelings if you **did** masturbate?*

0	I	2	3	4	5	6
Not at all			Somewhat			Very Strongly

How strongly do you experience this feeling when you masturbate?

OR

How strongly would you experience this feeling if you did masturbate?

135. happy
136. guilty
137. empty
138. pathetic
139. healthy
140. indifferent
141. nothing
142. strange
143. embarrassed
144. anxious
145. tense
146. horny
147. focused
148. awkward
149. good
150. calm
151. relieved
152. in control
153. ashamed
154. regretful
155. degraded
156. pleased
157. connected to myself

158. refreshed
159. frustrated
160. aggressive
161. angry
162. nervous
163. content
164. unemotional
165. stressed
166. attractive
167. immoral
168. remorseful
169. disgusted
170. thrilled
171. disappointed
172. detached
173. aroused
174. relaxed
175. passive
176. comfortable
177. satisfied
178. invigorated
179. sinful

Hurlbert Index of Sexual Narcissism

DAVID F. HURLBERT,[1] *U.S. Department of Health and Human Services*

The Hurlbert Index of Sexual Narcissism (HISN) is described by Hurlbert, Apt, Gasar, Wilson, and Murphy (1994).

Reference

Hurlbert, D. F., Apt, C., Wilson, N. E., & Murphy, Y. (1994). Sexual narcissism: A validation study. *Journal of Sex & Marital Therapy, 20,* 24–34.

Exhibit

Hurlbert Index of Sexual Narcissism

1. In sex, I like to be the one in charge.
2. My partner has difficulty understanding my sexual needs.
3. In general, most people take sex too seriously.
4. When it comes to sex, I consider myself a knowledgeable person.
5. In a close relationship, sex is an entitlement.
6. I believe I have a special style of making love.
7. I think people have the right to do anything they please in sex.
8. My partner tends to place too many emotional demands on me.
9. Pleasing yourself in sex is most important because it is hard to please someone sexually if you do not know how to please yourself first.
10. A relationship can keep one from engaging in a lot of fulfilling sexual activities.
11. Not enough people have sex for fun anymore.
12. I have no sexual inhibitions.
13. Too much relationship closeness can interfere with sexual pleasure.
14. In certain situations, sexually cheating on a partner is justifiable.
15. I think I am better at sex than most people my age.
16. In a close relationship, I would expect my partner to fulfill my sexual wishes.
17. My partner seldom gives me the sexual praise I deserve.
18. In a relationship where I commit myself, sex is a right.
19. In order to have a good sexual relationship, at least one partner needs to take charge.
20. Relationships that are too close are often too demanding.
21. When it comes to sex, not enough people live for the moment.
22. I know some pretty unique sexual techniques.
23. Emotional closeness can easily get in the way of sexual pleasure.
24. Couples should leave a relationship when they find sex to no longer be enjoyable.
25. In a close relationship, if a sexual act feels good, it is right.

Note. Respondents are asked to write in their choices. Scoring is based on the following choices: SA = *I strongly agree* (+4); A = *I agree* (+3); U = *I am undecided* (+2); D = *I disagree* (+1); SD = *I strongly disagree* (+0). Scores range from 0 to 100, with higher scores corresponding to greater sexual narcissism.

[1]Address correspondence to David F. Hurlbert, 140 Farnworth Lane, Roswell, Georgia 30075; e-mail: david.hurlbert@acf.hhs.gov

Sexual Narcissism Scale

LAURA WIDMAN[1] AND JAMES K. MCNULTY, *University of Tennessee, Knoxville*

Narcissism—a personality style characterized by tendencies toward exploiting others, a general lack of empathy for others, a pervasive pattern of grandiosity, and an excessive need for admiration (American Psychiatric Association, 2000)—has numerous implications for sexual behavior (e.g., Baumeister, Catanese, & Wallace, 2002; Buss & Shackelford, 1997). Yet, owing to the situation-specific nature of personality (see Mischel & Shoda, 1995), global assessments of narcissism, such as the frequently used Narcissistic Personality Inventory (NPI; Raskin & Terry, 1988), may be imprecise tools for assessing the extent to which the components of narcissism are active in the sexual domain and predict sexual behavior. In an effort to allow researchers to demonstrate more consistent links between narcissism and sexual behavior, Widman and McNulty (in press) developed the Sexual Narcissism Scale (SNS).

Description

The 20-item SNS assesses the extent to which self-centered, narcissistic personality traits are manifested in sexual situations. The SNS comprises four 5-item subscales: (a) Sexual Exploitation, (b) Sexual Entitlement, (c) Low Sexual Empathy, and (d) Sexual Skill. The Sexual Exploitation subscale assesses the ability and willingness to manipulate a person to gain sexual access. The Sexual Entitlement subscale assesses a sense of sexual entitlement and belief that the fulfillment of one's sexual desires is a personal right. The Low Sexual Empathy subscale assesses a general lack of empathy and devaluation of sexual partners. The Sexual Skill subscale assesses a tendency to hold a grandiose sense of sexual skill or an exaggerated sense of sexual success. Items are rated on a 5-point Likert scale ranging from 1 (*Strongly Disagree*) to 5 (*Strongly Agree*). Two reverse-scored items are included to help control response sets.

Response Mode and Timing

The SNS can be administered in either paper-and-pencil or computerized response formats. Respondents should be instructed to choose the Likert rating that best describes their current attitudes or beliefs and assured that there are no "right or wrong" sexual attitudes. The SNS generally takes less than 5 minutes to complete.

Scoring

Items are coded such that higher scores indicate greater sexual narcissism. A total SNS score is computed by reverse scoring two items from the Low Sexual Empathy subscale (see Exhibit) and then summing all scores (possible range = 20–100). Individual subscale scores are computed by summing the 5 items from each subscale (possible range = 5–25).

Reliability

Widman and McNulty (in press) recently reported evidence supportive of the factor structure of the SNS using confirmatory factor analyses in a sample of 299 male and female virgin and nonvirgin college students. Adequate fit of the four-factor model was observed for the entire sample ($N = 299$, $MFF \chi^2[164] = 433.47$, $p < .01$, χ^2/df ratio = 2.64, $CFI = .95$, $RMSEA = .077$), and individually for men ($N = 152$, $MFF \chi^2[164] = 282.29$, $p < .01$, χ^2/df ratio = 1.76, $CFI = .94$, $RMSEA = .07$), women ($N = 147$, $MFF \chi^2[164] = 323.39$, $p < .01$, χ^2/df ratio = 1.97, $CFI = .93$, $RMSEA = .08$), nonvirgins ($N = 206$, $MFF \chi^2[164] = 377.90$, $p < .01$, χ^2/df ratio = 2.30, $CFI = .93$, $RMSEA = .082$), and virgins ($N = 93$, $MFF \chi^2[164] = 310.63$, $p < .01$, χ^2/df ratio = 1.89, $CFI = .90$, $RMSEA = .095$). Likewise, Widman and McNulty (in press) reported adequate internal consistency of the SNS in two independent samples of male and female virgin and nonvirgin college students for the full scale ($\alpha = .81–.86$) and each subscale (Sexual Exploitation $\alpha = .72–.78$; Sexual Entitlement $\alpha = .76–.84$; Low Sexual Empathy $\alpha = .70–.79$; Sexual Skill $\alpha = .80–.89$).

Validity

The SNS has also demonstrated convergent, divergent, and predictive validity. Regarding convergent validity, the SNS demonstrated strong positive correlations with another published scale of sexual narcissism, the Index of Sexual Narcissism (ISN; Hurlbert, Apt, Gasar, Wilson, & Murphy, 1994), $r = .72$, $p < .001$, and with the NPI, $r = .41$, $p < .001$, in a sample of 163 college men (Widman & McNulty, 2009). These results suggest the SNS is related to but unique from existing measures of narcissism. Regarding divergent validity, the SNS demonstrated null or weak relationships with each of the Big Five personality traits using the same sample of 163 college men (Widman & McNulty, 2009) (Extraversion $r = -.04$, Agreeableness $r = -.24$, Conscientiousness $r = -.09$, Neuroticism $r = .21$, Openness $r = .03$), suggesting that sexual narcissism can emerge independent of these traits. Finally, the SNS has demonstrated predictive validity in several samples. In a sample of 211 college men, those higher in sexual narcis-

[1]Address correspondence to Laura Widman, Department of Psychology, University of Tennessee, Knoxville, TN 37996; e-mail: lwidman@utk.edu

sism reported an earlier age of first intercourse, a higher number of sex partners, more acceptance of rape myths, more hostility toward women, and more adversarial sexual beliefs (Widman & McNulty, 2008). Likewise, in a recent study of 378 college men, those higher in sexual narcissism reported more frequent past sexual aggression (including unwanted sexual contact, sexual coercion, and attempted/ completed rape) and a greater likelihood of future sexual aggression (Widman & McNulty, in press). Importantly, consistent with the proposed need for a sexual-specific measure of narcissism, associations between the SNS and sexual aggression were more robust than associations between sexual aggression and a global measure of narcissism (Widman & McNulty, in press) and between sexual aggression and the existing ISN (Widman & McNulty, 2009).

Other Information

Future researchers may benefit by examining the extent to which the SNS accounts for variance in additional sexual behaviors and outcomes, such as sexual satisfaction, sexual frequency, sexual exploration, contraceptive use, and infidelity (for discussion of future research possibilities, see Widman & McNulty, in press).

References

American Psychiatric Association. (2000). *Diagnostic and statistical manual of mental disorders* (4th ed., text revision). Washington, DC: Author.

Baumeister, R. F., Catanese, K. R., & Wallace, H. M. (2002). Conquest by force: A narcissistic reactance theory of rape and sexual coercion. *Review of General Psychology, 6*, 92–135.

Buss, D. M., & Shackelford, T. K. (1997). Susceptibility to infidelity in the first year of marriage. *Journal of Research in Personality, 31*, 193–221.

Hurlbert, D. F., Apt, C., Gasar, S., Wilson, N. E., & Murphy, Y. (1994). Sexual narcissism: A validation study. *Journal of Sex and Marital Therapy, 20*, 24–34.

Mischel, W., & Shoda, Y. (1995). A cognitive-affective system theory of personality: Reconceptualizing situations, dispositions, dynamics, and invariance in personality structure. *Psychological Review, 102*, 246–268.

Raskin, R. & Terry, H. (1988). A principal-components analysis of the Narcissistic Personality Inventory and further evidence of its construct validity. *Journal of Personality and Social Psychology, 54*, 890–902.

Widman, L., & McNulty, J. K. (2008, August). *Sexual narcissism and the confluence model of sexual aggression*. Presentation at the meeting of the American Psychological Association, Boston, MA.

Widman, L., & McNulty, J. K. (2009). *"If I ruled the world . . . I would have sex with anyone I choose." Sexual narcissism and sexual aggression*. Unpublished manuscript.

Widman, L., & McNulty, J. K. (in press). Sexual narcissism and the perpetration of sexual aggression. *Archives of Sexual Behavior*.

Exhibit

Sexual Narcissism Scale

Item Wording	Subscale
If I ruled the world for one day, I would have sex with anyone I choose.	Exp
One way to get a person in bed with me is to tell them what they want to hear.	Exp
When I want to have sex, I will do whatever it takes.	Exp
I could easily convince an unwilling person to have sex with me.	Exp
I would be willing to trick a person to get them to have sex with me.	Exp
I feel I deserve sexual activity when I am in the mood for it.	Ent
I am entitled to sex on a regular basis.	Ent
I should be permitted to have sex whenever I want it.	Ent
I would be irritated if a dating partner said no to sex.	Ent
I expect sexual activity if I go out with someone on an expensive date.	Ent
When I sleep with someone, I rarely know what they are thinking or feeling.	Emp
It is important for me to know what my sexual partner is feeling when we make love.[a]	Emp
I enjoy sex more when I feel I really know a person.[a]	Emp
The feelings of my sexual partners don't usually concern me.	Emp
I do not usually care how my sexual partner feels after sex.	Emp
I am an exceptional sexual partner.	Skill
My sexual partners think I am fantastic in bed.	Skill
I really know how to please a partner sexually.	Skill
I have been very successful in my sexual relationships.	Skill
Others have told me I am very sexually skilled.	Skill

Note. Items were randomized for survey administration. Exp = Sexual Exploitation, Ent = Sexual Entitlement, Emp = Low Sexual Empathy, Skill = Sexual Skill.

[a]Reverse-scored item.

Causal Attribution for Coital Orgasm Scale

Joseph W. Critelli,[1] *North Texas State University*
Charles F. Bridges, *Terrell State Hospital, Terrell, Texas*
Victor E. Loos, *Galveston Family Institute*

The Causal Attribution for Coital Orgasm Scale is designed to evaluate causal attributions for orgasm and nonorgasm during sexual intercourse.

Description

This scale was developed to evaluate attributions of coital outcomes, along the two major attributional dimensions identified by Weiner (1979; Weiner & Kukla, 1970): internal versus external, and stable versus unstable. The scale uses a paired-comparison forced-choice format as suggested by McMahan (1973), Weiner, Nierenberg, and Goldstein (1976), and Girodo, Dotzenroth, and Stein (1981). The labels in the questionnaire were judged to translate most adequately Weiner's notions of ability (internal-stable), effort (internal-unstable), task difficulty (external-stable), and luck (external-unstable). For both orgasmic and non-orgasmic coital outcomes, subjects are presented with every possible pairing of causal attributions. With four attributional categories (internal-stable, internal-unstable, external-stable, external-unstable), this yields two sets of six forced-choice options. Whether respondents refer to simultaneous clitoral stimulation does not seem to affect causal attributions (Loos, Bridges, & Critelli, 1987). The scale is designed for use with women who have had at least 15 coital contacts and have experienced coital orgasm at least one time.

Response Mode and Timing

Respondents place a check mark in front of the one choice in each pair of choices which they believe is more accurate for them. The questionnaire requires no more than 10 minutes to complete.

Scoring

One point is credited for each check mark; no points are given for unchecked items. For both Question I (orgasm) and Question II (nonorgasm), items are summed to form an attributional score (ranging from 0 to 3) for each of the four causal categories, as follows: internal-stable (1a + 4b + 5b); internal-unstable (1b + 2a + 6a); external-stable (2b + 3a + 5a); external unstable (3b + 4a + 6b). The two underlying causal dimensions are formed by summing across quad-

rants, as follows: locus of control (internal-stable + internal-unstable); stability (internal-stable + external-stable).

Reliability

The paired-comparison forced-choice format has been used reliably in a number of other studies investigating Weiner's four categories of causal attribution (Girodo et al., 1981; McMahan, 1973; Weiner & Kukla, 1970; Weiner et al., 1976), and is a standard method of assessing attributions in achievement-motivation situations (Crandall, Katkovsky, & Crandall, 1965). Girodo et al. reported a test-retest reliability ranging from .65 to .78 ($p < .001$) for success and failure ascriptions, and a high internal consistency of causal preferences across the four causal categories, with Kendall's tau ranging from .22 ($p < .05$) to .70 ($p < .001$).

Validity

Construct validity for Weiner's four attributional categories has been established in numerous studies in which respondents were asked to explain spontaneously the causes of certain imagined and real outcomes (Frieze, 1976; Weiner, 1979; Weiner, Russell, & Lerman, 1978; Wong & Weiner, 1981). The Causal Attribution for Coital Orgasm Scale has been used successfully to differentiate between attributional styles of women with high and low orgasm frequency (Bridges, 1981; Loos et al., 1987).

References

Bridges, C. F. (1981). *Orgasm consistency, causal attribution, and inhibitory control.* Unpublished master's thesis, North Texas State University, Denton, TX.

Crandall, V. C., Katkovsky, W., & Crandall, V. J. (1965). Children's beliefs in their own control of reinforcements in intellectual-academic achievement situations. *Child Development, 46,* 91–109.

Frieze, I. H. (1976). Causal attributions and information seeking to explain success and failure. *Journal of Research in Personality, 10,* 293–305.

Girodo, M., Dotzenroth, S. E., & Stein, S. J. (1981). Causal attribution bias in shy males: Implications for self-esteem and self-confidence. *Cognitive Therapy and Research, 5,* 325–338.

Loos, V. E., Bridges, C. F., & Critelli, J. W. (1987). Weiner's attribution theory and female orgasmic consistency. *The Journal of Sex Research, 23,* 348–361.

McMahan, I. D. (1973). Relationships between causal attributions and expectancy of success. *Journal of Personality and Social Psychology, 28,* 108–114.

[1]Address correspondence to Joseph W. Critelli, Department of Psychology, North Texas State University, P.O. Box 13587, Denton, TX 76203–3587; e-mail: critelli@unt.edu

Weiner, B. (1979). A theory of motivation for some classroom experiences. *Journal of Educational Psychology, 71*, 3–25.

Weiner, B., & Kukla, A. (1970). An attributional analysis of achievement motivation. *Journal of Personality and Social Psychology, 15*, 1–20.

Weiner, B., Nierenberg, R., & Goldstein, M. (1976). Social learning (locus of control) versus attributional (causal stability) interpretations of expectancy of success. *Journal of Personality, 44*, 52–68.

Weiner, B., Russell, D., & Lerman, D. (1978). Affective consequences of causal ascriptions. In J. H. Harvey, W. J. Ickes, & R. F. Kidd (Eds.), *New directions in attribution research* (Vol. 1, pp. 59–90). Hillsdale, NJ: Lawrence Erlbaum.

Wong, T. P., & Weiner, B. (1981). Why people ask "why" questions, and the heuristics of attributional search. *Journal of Personality and Social Psychology, 40*, 650–663.

Exhibit

Causal Attributions for Coital Outcome Scale

I. Complete the following sentence by placing a check mark in front of the ONE CHOICE IN EACH PAIR of choices which you believe is MORE ACCURATE FOR YOU. Please respond to *all six choices*.

When I have an orgasm *during coitus*, it is typically because: (Select one answer from each pair.)

1. a) _____ I am typically sexually responsive.

   OR

   b) _____ I particularly wanted to have an orgasm.

2. a) _____ I particularly wanted to have an orgasm.

   OR

   b) _____ My partner is a good lover.

3. a) _____ My partner is a good lover.

   OR

   b) _____ It was a matter of luck.

4. a) _____ It was a matter of luck.

   OR

   b) _____ I am typically sexually responsive.

5. a) _____ My partner is a good lover

   OR

   b) _____ I am typically sexually responsive.

6. a) _____ I particularly wanted to have an orgasm.

   OR

   b) _____ It was a matter of luck.

II. Complete the following sentence by placing a check mark in front of the ONE CHOICE IN EACH PAIR of choices which you believe is MORE ACCURATE FOR YOU. Please respond to *all six choices*.

When I *do not* have an orgasm *during coitus*, it is typically because: (Select one answer from each pair.)

1. a) _____ I am typically sexually unresponsive.

   OR

   b) _____ I did not particularly want to have an orgasm.

2. a) _____ I did not particularly want to have an orgasm.

   OR

   b) _____ My partner is not a good lover.

3. a) _____ My partner is not a good lover.

   OR

   b) _____ It was a matter of luck.

4. a) _____ It was a matter of luck.

   OR

   b) _____ I am typically sexually unresponsive.

5. a) _____ My partner is not a good lover.

   OR

   b) _____ I am typically sexually unresponsive.

6. a) _____ I did not particularly want to have an orgasm.

   OR

   b) _____ It was a matter of luck.

Orgasm Rating Scale

KENNETH MAH,[1] *Toronto General Hospital*
YITZCHAK M. BINIK, *McGill University Health Centre*

The Orgasm Rating Scale (ORS) employs a multidimensional approach to assess and quantify the psychological experience of orgasm in both men and women. It was developed to address the lack of a comprehensive, theoretically based self-report measure of orgasm.

Description

The ORS is a 40-item, self-report adjective-rating scale. Two subscales assess sensory and cognitive-affective dimensions, reflecting a two-dimensional model of the psychological experience of orgasm that has been previously theorized and/or investigated by others (e.g., Davidson, 1980; Mah & Binik, 2001; Warner, 1981). The sensory dimension represents the perception of physiological events (e.g., contractile sensations), whereas the cognitive-affective dimension represents the subjective evaluations (e.g., intensity, satisfaction) and emotions (e.g., elation, intimacy) associated with orgasm. Each of these dimensions further encompasses multiple components. The ORS contains 40 adjectives, 28 of which are employed in subscale scoring. Individuals are asked to rate each adjective on a 0–5 rating scale according to how well it describes their most recent orgasm experience. The ORS was developed to describe orgasm experiences attained under two sexual-context conditions: solitary masturbation and sex with a partner.

To create the scale (see Mah & Binik, 2002), an initial pool of 141 adjectives was compiled from the available self-report literature in which individuals had been asked to describe their subjective experience of orgasm. Pilot ratings of items reduced the pool to a final set of 60 adjectives. These adjectives were formatted into a preliminary version of the ORS, which was then employed in two cross-sectional studies of the two-dimensional model of the experience of orgasm. Undergraduate and graduate student participants rated the set of adjectives, using the 0–5 rating scale, to describe orgasm experiences attained through solitary masturbation and through sex with a partner. When rating orgasm experienced with a partner, individuals were also asked to indicate from a list of options the particular sexual behavior by which they attained the orgasm (e.g., through intercourse, oral stimulation, manual stimulation, etc.). Exploratory factor analysis of the ratings data resulted in the current reduced pool of 28 adjectives; the remaining 12 adjectives included in the current 40-item version

reflect aspects hypothesized to be relevant to the orgasm experience (e.g., intensity, altered state of consciousness) but were not specifically evaluated.

Response Mode and Timing

The ORS is a self-administered measure and may be used to assess orgasm experiences attained during solitary masturbation or sex with a partner. In both cases, individuals are asked to recall their most recent orgasm experience attained under the specific contextual condition and to rate each adjective, using the 0–5 scale (0 = *Does Not Describe It At All*, 5 = *Describes It Perfectly*), according to how well each describes that orgasm experience. The ORS requires approximately 5 to 10 minutes to rate the 40 adjectives.

Scoring

Only 28 of a total of 40 adjectives are employed in scoring the ORS. The ORS contains two primary subscales reflecting the sensory and cognitive-affective dimensions of orgasm experience. The sensory dimension further encompasses six components that are represented by particular adjectives (listed in brackets after each component): building sensations (building, swelling), flooding sensations (flooding, flowing), flushing sensations (flushing, spreading), shooting sensations (shooting, spurting), throbbing sensations (throbbing, pulsating), and general spasms (shuddering, trembling, quivering). The cognitive-affective dimension includes four components represented by particular adjectives: emotional intimacy (close, loving, passionate, tender, unifying), ecstasy (ecstatic, elated, euphoric, rapturous), pleasurable satisfaction (pleasurable, satisfying, fulfilling), and relaxation (relaxing, peaceful, soothing).

Total scores for each of the 10 components are obtained by summing the ratings of a component's respective adjectives (e.g., the total score for the building-sensations component is the sum of the ratings for its adjectives, "building" and "swelling"). Total scores for each of the two-dimensional subscales are obtained by summing the total scores of the components for that dimension (e.g., the total score for the cognitive-affective dimension would be the sum of the total scores for the "emotional-intimacy," "ecstasy," "pleasurable-satisfaction," and "relaxation" components; see Exhibit).

[1]Address correspondence to Kenneth Mah, Behavioural Sciences and Health Research Division, Toronto General Hospital, Eaton North, 9EN 220, 200 Elizabeth Street, Toronto, Ontario, Canada M5G 2C4; e-mail: kmah@uhnres.utoronto.ca

Reliability

Internal consistency of the ORS was examined in the initial and cross-validation studies (Mah & Binik, 2002). Results in both studies indicated high internal consistency for both men and women across sexual contexts (Cronbach's alphas ranging from .88 to .92).

Validity

The two-dimensional model of the orgasm experience, comprising the sensory and cognitive-affective dimensions and their respective components, was evaluated in initial and cross-validation studies, using the ORS as the corresponding measure of the model (Mah & Binik, 2002). Fit of the model was assessed using confirmatory factor analysis in both studies. In addition, gender and sexual-context (i.e., comparison of orgasm attained through solitary masturbation versus sex with a partner) effects on the components were investigated.

Results indicated that the two-dimensional model provided an adequate representation of the orgasm experience in both men and women across both sexual contexts. The model was superior to an alternative one-dimensional model, in which all components were loaded onto a single global dimension of orgasm experience. It was also comparable to an alternative three-dimensional model that retained the sensory dimension but separated the cognitive-affective into distinct cognitive and affective dimensions. Significant gender differences were observed in both studies for primarily sensory-type components, with women reporting higher subscale scores than men, but these differences were generally small. The only consistently large gender difference across both studies involved the shooting-sensations component, with men reporting higher scores than women. This was interpreted to reflect the male capacity for ejaculation. Similarly, significant sexual-context differences were observed with several components, but only the difference involving the emotional-intimacy component appeared consistent and substantial, with higher scores in the sex-with-partner context. This finding may reflect the impact of the sex-with-partner context's inherent psychosexual and emotional qualities on the orgasm experience.

We also examined potential determinants of orgasmic pleasure and satisfaction as a critical aspect of the subjective orgasm experience (Mah & Binik, 2005). This was accomplished by employing one of the cognitive-affective components, the pleasurable-satisfaction component, as an index of orgasmic pleasure and satisfaction and regressing it on all of the other cognitive-affective and sensory components. Within both the solitary-masturbation and sex-with-partner contexts, more of the other cognitive-affective components than the sensory components significantly predicted scores on the pleasurable-satisfaction component. The pleasurable-satisfaction component scores were also significantly associated with ratings of overall psychological intensity and physical intensity of orgasm within both sexual contexts, as well as relationship satisfaction within the sex-with-partner context. Although reported anatomical location of the orgasm experience did predict pleasurable-satisfaction component scores, this relation disappeared when overall psychological or physical intensity was taken into account. The results were taken generally to support the hypothesized importance of psychological and psychosocial factors, in addition to physiological mechanisms, in the subjective orgasm experience.

These findings offer preliminary evidence for the utility of the ORS as a measure of the psychological experience of orgasm. However, the ORS has been evaluated only in university student populations to date. Further psychometric-evaluation studies involving healthy and clinical nonstudent samples spanning a range of age and sexual/relationship experiences are recommended. Researchers might also investigate the potential of the ORS in assessing orgasm difficulties or in evaluating the efficacy of medical or psychotherapeutic interventions targeting such difficulties.

References

Davidson, J. M. (1980). The psychobiology of sexual experience. In J. M. Davidson & R. J. Davidson (Eds.), *The psychobiology of consciousness* (pp. 271–332). New York: Plenum.

Mah, K., & Binik, Y. M. (2001). The nature of human orgasm: A critical review of major trends. *Clinical Psychology Review, 21*, 823–856.

Mah, K., & Binik, Y. M. (2002). Do all orgasms feel alike? Evaluating a two-dimensional model of the orgasm experience across gender and sexual context. *The Journal of Sex Research, 39*, 104–113.

Mah, K., & Binik, Y. M. (2005). Are orgasms in the mind or the body? Psychosocial versus physiological correlates of orgasmic pleasure and satisfaction. *Journal of Sex and Marital Therapy, 31*, 187–200.

Warner, J. E. (1981). *A factor analytic study of the physical and affective dimensions of peak of female sexual response in partner-related sexual activity.* Unpublished doctoral dissertation. Teachers College, Columbia University, New York.

Exhibit

Orgasm Rating Scale

[*Instructions for solitary-masturbation context*]
Recall to the best of your ability the most recent orgasm you experienced during solitary masturbation. This would include any sexual activity in which you engaged while alone.

[*Instructions for sex-with-partner context*]
Recall to the best of your ability the most recent orgasm you experienced during sex with a partner. This would include any sexual activity with your partner in which you had orgasm while your partner was present.

1. To the best of your memory, how did you have this orgasm with your partner? (circle letter)
    a. through intercourse (vaginal/anal/other)
    b. through oral stimulation from partner
    c. through manual stimulation from partner
    d. through manual stimulation from myself
    e. other (describe briefly on line below, e.g., clitoral stimulation/vaginal intercourse at same time)

_____

Below is a list of words that might be used to describe the experience of orgasm. Different people may use different words to describe their personal experience, and so there is no "right" answer. After each word, write the number that best indicates how well that word describes your most recent orgasm experienced through [*indicate sexual context, either* **solitary masturbation** *or* **sex with a partner**].

   If you have never had an orgasm in this way, please place an X on this line _____ and rate the words according to how you think orgasm experienced through [*indicate sexual context, either* **solitary masturbation** *or* **sex with a partner**] would feel.

To rate each of the words below, use the following scale.

0	1	2	3	4	5
Does Not Describe It At All					Describes It Perfectly

Please rate all of the words; do not skip any

absorbed _____	blissful _____	building _____	close _____	ecstatic _____
elated _____	engulfing _____	euphoric _____	exciting _____	exploding _____
flooding _____	flowing _____	flushing _____	fulfilling _____	hot _____
immersing _____	loving _____	passionate _____	peaceful _____	pleasurable _____
pulsating _____	quivering _____	rapturous _____	relaxing _____	rising _____
satisfying _____	shooting _____	shuddering _____	soothing _____	spreading _____
spurting _____	swelling _____	tender _____	throbbing _____	trembling _____
uncontrolled _____	unifying _____	unreal _____	warm _____	wild _____

Scoring the Orgasm Rating Scale

To obtain total scores for each component: Sum the adjective ratings for that component to obtain a total score (e.g., for total score for the Building-Sensations component, add up the ratings for the adjectives listed for that component, "building" and "swelling").

To obtain total scores for each dimension: Sum the total scores for each component within that dimension to obtain a total score (e.g., for a total score for the Cognitive-Affective dimension, add up the total scores for the Emotional-Intimacy, Ecstasy, Pleasurable-Satisfaction, and Relaxation components).

Dimension	*Component*	*Adjectives*
Sensory	Building Sensations	building + swelling
	Flooding Sensations	flooding + flowing
	Flushing Sensations	flushing + spreading
	Shooting Sensations	shooting + spurting
	Throbbing Sensations	throbbing + pulsating
	General Spasms	shuddering + trembling + quivering
Cognitive-Affective	Emotional Intimacy	close + loving + passionate + tender + unifying
	Ecstasy	ecstatic + elated + euphoric + rapturous
	Pleasurable Satisfaction	pleasurable + satisfying + fulfilling
	Relaxation	relaxing + peaceful + soothing

Female Orgasm Scale

ALEXANDRA MCINTYRE-SMITH AND WILLIAM A. FISHER,[1] *University of Western Ontario*

This scale assesses the consistency of female orgasm during partnered sexual activities (e.g., intercourse, oral stimulation, self-stimulation with partner present) and overall satisfaction with orgasm frequency and quality.

Description

The scale comprises seven items. Five items inquire about the frequency of orgasm during different sexual activities: (a) intercourse, (b) intercourse with additional direct clitoral stimulation, (c) hand/manual stimulation of the clitoris and/or genitals by a partner, (d) self-stimulation of the clitoris and/or genitals in the presence of a partner, and (e) oral stimulation. Respondents indicate the percentage of time they experience orgasm on an 11-point scale in 10% increments ranging from 0% to 100%. Respondents are also provided with the option, "Does not apply to me (I do not have sexual interactions involving . . .)" to allow the 0% response option to identify respondents who engage in the type of stimulation described in the item but do not experience orgasm from it. Two other items assess perceived satisfaction with the number and quality of orgasms experienced during sexual activity with a partner. They are rated on a 7-point scale ranging from *Very Satisfied* to *Very Unsatisfied*.

Scale development followed an iterative process, whereby items were developed and refined over a series of three studies. An initial pool of 17 items was developed and administered to 198 female undergraduate students. Items were subject to individual item analyses and exploratory factor analyses. Nine items were deleted owing to poor empirical performance or poor conceptual overlap with the construct, and five new items were written. The 13 items were then administered to a second sample of 242 female undergraduate participants, and items were subjected to item analyses and exploratory factor analyses. Six items were deleted and two additional items were written. The nine items were administered to 211 female undergraduate participants, and responses were subjected to item analyses and test-retest reliability analyses. Seven items were retained for the final scale.

Decision-making regarding item deletion was based on the following scale-development guidelines (see Netemeyer, Bearden, & Sharma, 2003; Streiner & Norman, 2008): (a) range restriction problems (i.e., more than 50% of the sample endorsed a single response option, low standard deviations), (b) poor inter-item correlations with two or more scale items ($r < .30$), (c) poor corrected item-total correlations ($r < .30$), (d) high cross-loadings on nontarget factors ($> .35$ or more), (e) low percentage of variance accounted for within items (i.e., poor communalities; $< .30$), (f) poor item-wording as judged by scale developers, (g) redundancy with other items, (h) poor conceptual overlap (i.e., item was judged to be too dissimilar from other items and/or to poorly reflect the construct).

Sampling was conducted with three groups of female undergraduate students, aged 17–49 ($M = 18.83$–19.24, $SD = 2.67$–3.38), who were heterosexually active (i.e., they reported having sexual intercourse with a male partner at least twice per month). As this scale was developed based on responses from undergraduate female participants, it is most appropriate for use with this population. Future studies examining the use of this measure with additional populations are needed.

Response Mode and Timing

Respondents are provided with the scale and instructions, and are asked to complete the survey on their own, and with as much privacy as possible. Sampling for the purposes of scale development was conducted using the Internet. Paper-and-pencil administration of the scale requires 2 to 5 minutes.

No particular time frame was assigned to the scale (i.e., it provides a global overview of a woman's orgasm experience rather than being limited to the past 4 weeks, current partner, etc.). This approach was chosen to allow the scale to be applicable to a broad range of temporal and relationship contexts. If one were interested in limiting the use of the scale to a specific time frame or sexual relationship (e.g., current partner), the scale could be prefaced with additional instructions specifying this constraint. The Female Orgasm Scale was strongly correlated with the Orgasm subscale of the Female Sexual Function Index (Rosen et al., 2000), $r = .71$, which measures orgasmic function over the past 4 weeks. This provides preliminary support for the consistency of female orgasmic experience as measured by the Female Orgasm Scale, and for tailoring the scale to a specific time frame.

Scoring

1. Examine the number of responses marked "Does not apply to me." These responses can be coded either as missing data or as 0, depending on the rationale of the researcher and use of the scale.

[1]Address correspondence to Alexandra McIntyre-Smith or William Fisher, Department of Psychology, The University of Western Ontario, London, Ontario, Canada N6A 5C2; e-mail: amcsmith@gmail.com or fisher@uwo.ca

2. Score Items 1–5 as follows: 0% = 0, 10% = 1, 20% = 2, ... 100% = 10.
3. Score Items 6–7 as follows: *Very Unsatisfied* = 1 ... *Very Satisfied* = 7.
4. Because Items 1–5 are essentially keyed on a 10-point scale (i.e., there is no conceptual equivalent to the 0% response option on the 7-point scale for Items 6–7), and the rest of the items are coded on a 7-point scale, items should be weighted in the following manner:

   a. Multiply Items 1–5 by 7.
   b. Multiply Items 6–7 by 10.

5. Calculate the average score or the total score for all items. Higher scores indicate greater orgasm consistency and satisfaction.
6. Calculate subscale scores if desired:

   a. Orgasm from Clitoral Stimulation—Items 2–5
   b. Satisfaction with Orgasm—Items 6–7

When calculating subscale scores, items do not need to be weighted within a given subscale, because the response options are the same for all items (e.g., Items 2–5 are answered on a 7-point scale).

Reliability

Internal consistency of the Female Orgasm Scale was good in all three studies (α = .84–.86), and for both subscales: Orgasm from Clitoral Stimulation (α = .81–.82) and Satisfaction with Orgasm (α = .72–.90). Corrected item-total correlations ranged from r = .41 to .77 for the total scale, and from r = .56 to .81 for the subscales. Inter-item correlations ranged from r =.19 to .61 for the total scale, and from r = .43 to .68 for both subscales. Four-week test-retest reliability was excellent for the total scale (r = .82) and both subscales (r = .62–.78).

Validity

As expected, the Female Orgasm Experiences Scale was highly correlated (r = .71) with the Orgasm subscale of the Female Sexual Function Index (FSFI; Rosen et al., 2000), providing evidence of convergent validity. The current scale was also correlated with the total FSFI score and the other subscales scores (r = .20–.55), except for the Desire subscale. The Satisfaction with Orgasm subscale was correlated with the Satisfaction subscale of the FSFI (r = .31), providing some evidence of convergent validity. The Female Orgasm Scale, subscales, and individual items were not correlated with the Marlowe-Crowne Social Desirability Scale (MCSD; Crowne & Marlowe, 1964) or with measures of depression and anxiety (Henry & Crawford, 2005), providing evidence of discriminant validity and freedom from response bias.

References

Crowne, D. P., & Marlowe, D. (1964). *The approval motive: Studies in evaluative dependence*. New York: Wiley.

Henry, J. D., & Crawford, J. R. (2005). The short-form version of the Depression Anxiety Stress Scales (DASS-21): Construct validity and normative data in a large non-clinical sample. *British Journal of Clinical Psychology, 44*, 227–239.

Netemeyer, R. G., Bearden, W. O., & Sharma, S. (2003). *Scaling procedures: Issues and applications*. Thousand Oaks, CA: Sage.

Rosen, R., Brown, C., Heiman, J., Leiblum, S., Meston, C., Shabsigh, R., et al. (2000). The Female Sexual Function Index (FSFI): A multidimensional self-report instrument for the assessment of female sexual function. *Journal of Sex and Marital Therapy, 26*, 191–208.

Streiner, D. L., & Norman, G. R. (2008). *Health measurement scales: A practical guide to their development and use* (4th ed.). New York: Oxford University Press.

Exhibit

Female Orgasm Scale

Instructions: The following questions ask about your sexual experiences (such as sexual activities with a partner). You are asked to rate each item on the scale provided. Please check off one box per item to indicate your response.

1. How often do you have an orgasm from *vaginal penetration only* (no direct clitoral stimulation) during *intercourse* with a partner? Please indicate what percentage of the time:

☐	☐	☐	☐	☐	☐	☐	☐	☐	☐	☐
0%	10%	20%	30%	40%	50%	60%	70%	80%	90%	100%

OR ☐ Does not apply to me
(i.e., I do not have sexual interactions involving vaginal penetration only during intercourse with a partner)

2. How often do you have an orgasm from *intercourse* with a partner that includes *both vaginal penetration and direct clitoral stimulation*? Please indicate what percentage of the time:

☐   ☐   ☐   ☐   ☐   ☐   ☐   ☐   ☐   ☐   ☐

0%   10%   20%   30%   40%   50%   60%   70%   80%   90%   100%

OR ☐ Does not apply to me
(i.e., I do not have sexual interactions involving vaginal penetration and simultaneous clitoral stimulation)

3. How often do you have an orgasm from *HAND/MANUAL stimulation* of your genitals/clitoris by a partner?
Please indicate what percentage of the time:

☐   ☐   ☐   ☐   ☐   ☐   ☐   ☐   ☐   ☐   ☐

0%   10%   20%   30%   40%   50%   60%   70%   80%   90%   100%

OR ☐ Does not apply to me
(i.e., I do not have sexual interactions involving manual stimulation of the genitals/clitoris with a partner)

4. How often do you have an orgasm when you *yourself manipulate or rub your own genitals/clitoris* when you are with a partner?
Please indicate what percentage of the time:

☐   ☐   ☐   ☐   ☐   ☐   ☐   ☐   ☐   ☐   ☐

0%   10%   20%   30%   40%   50%   60%   70%   80%   90%   100%

OR ☐ Does not apply to me
(i.e., I do not have sexual interactions where I self-manipulate my own genitals/clitoris when I am with a partner)

5. How often do you have an orgasm from *ORAL stimulation* of your genital/clitoris by a partner?
Please indicate what percentage of the time:

☐   ☐   ☐   ☐   ☐   ☐   ☐   ☐   ☐   ☐   ☐

0%   10%   20%   30%   40%   50%   60%   70%   80%   90%   100%

OR ☐ Does not apply to me
(i.e., I do not have sexual interactions involving oral stimulation of the genitals/clitoris with a partner)

6. In general, how satisfied . . . unsatisfied are you with the *number* of orgasms that you have during sexual activity with a partner?

☐   ☐   ☐   ☐   ☐   ☐   ☐

Very **Satisfied**   Moderately **Satisfied**   Slightly **Satisfied**   Neither **Satisfied** nor **Unsatisfied**   Slightly **Unsatisfied**   Moderately **Unsatisfied**   Very **Unsatisfied**

7. In general, how satisfied . . . unsatisfied are you with the *quality or experience* of orgasm that you have during sexual activity with a partner?

☐   ☐   ☐   ☐   ☐   ☐   ☐

Very **Satisfied**   Moderately **Satisfied**   Slightly **Satisfied**   Neither **Satisfied** nor **Unsatisfied**   Slightly **Unsatisfied**   Moderately **Unsatisfied**   Very **Unsatisfied**

Paraphilia Scales From Kurt Freund's Erotic Preferences Examination Scheme

RAY BLANCHARD,[1] *Centre for Addiction and Mental Health*

Kurt Freund, MD, DSc (1914–1996), was one of the most influential researchers in the areas of sexual orientation, gender identity, and paraphilias in the latter half of the 20th century. Freund was born into a German-speaking Jewish family in Czechoslovakia, and he conducted his pioneering research on penile plethysmography (phallometry) while living and working in Prague. He fled from Czechoslovakia to Canada in 1968, in the wake of the "Prague Spring," and accepted a position at the Clarke Institute of Psychiatry (now the Centre for Addiction and Mental Health; CAMH) in Toronto. Shortly after arriving at the Clarke Institute, he began developing the first English-language version of his self-report questionnaire for erotic preferences and gender identity in men.

Freund's questionnaire sections for pedophilia and hebephilia, voyeurism and exhibitionism, sadism and masochism, fetishism, and transvestism and transsexualism all have date stamps indicating that they were revised for the first time on October 15, 1971. This suggests that his questionnaire development must have been well under way prior to the autumn of 1971.

The last major revision, according to the date stamps, was completed during April 3–9, 1974. This version was referred to in Freund's laboratory as Questionnaire III (Q-III). This is the only version of the questionnaire for which computerized data still exist; in other words, the laboratory's electronic database at the CAMH currently includes Freund questionnaire data for subjects going back to 1974.

Major changes to Q-III after 1974 consisted primarily of additions. Freund added a new section on courtship disorders (voyeurism, exhibitionism, toucheurism, frotteurism, telephone scatologia, and preferential rape) on July 17, 1980—the same week that I began work at the Clarke Institute—and with his encouragement I added a questionnaire section on transvestism and autogynephilia in the next month. In later years, Freund occasionally inserted extra items into various sections, when he became dissatisfied with an existing item or perceived the need for an additional one.

Freund eventually needed a better name than Q-III for the purpose of describing the instrument in publications. I suggested *Erotic Preferences Examination Scheme* (EPES), which he readily adopted. The EPES has never been published in its entirety, and there would be little purpose in doing so at this point. Many of its multi-item scales have been published in scholarly journals or book chapters, often in appendices or tables. These include scales intended to assess parent-child relations, childhood gender identity, gynephilia (the erotic preference for physically mature females), androphilia (the erotic preference for physically mature males), and degree of heterosexual experience.

It is not my purpose to collect and review all of the EPES scales here. My purpose in this document is to bring together, in one place, all of the scales corresponding to the specific paraphilias listed in the American Psychiatric Association's *Diagnostic and Statistical Manual of Mental Disorders* (*DSM*). I am doing this partly for historical purposes and partly because the scales' contents illustrate many of the points an experienced clinician might cover in interviewing a potentially paraphilic patient. These scales have not been copyrighted for commercial purposes, and any clinician or researcher who wishes to use them as they are, or to quote them, or to modify them for his or her own purposes is free to do so.

The first thing to point out is that the EPES is designed for men. Freund never attempted, at least after moving to Canada, to produce a parallel version for women. That is because the majority of Freund's patients were sex offenders, and the overwhelming majority of sex offenders are men.

Freund made no attempt, in writing these items, to mislead or distract the patient from the meaning of the item or its implications. The items were designed on the sole principle of face validity. Of course Freund understood as well as anyone that patients, especially those accused of criminal sexual behavior, are not candid about their erotic interests. Patients' scores on these scales are influenced both by whether they have a paraphilia and by whether they are willing to admit a paraphilia if they have one. Freund chose to stress the latter source of variance when he called his measures of pedophilia and hebephilia the *Pedo Admitter Scale* and the *Hebe Admitter Scale* rather than the *Pedo Scale* and the *Hebe Scale*.

Freund was also well aware of the repetitiousness of the items in some of the scales; he commented wryly about that on one occasion I remember. That repetitiousness results, in part, from the fact that paraphilias are essentially monosymptomatic conditions. He did vary item content when he could. He included, for example, items about love as well as items about lust in his pedophilia and hebephilia measures.

[1]Address correspondence to Ray Blanchard, Centre for Addiction and Mental Health, 250 College Street, Toronto, Ontario M5T 1R8, Canada; e-mail: Ray_Blanchard@camh.net

Freund often went over patients' questionnaire responses with them and helped them complete the questionnaire if they had difficulty answering the items on their own. He naturally used their responses to key items (along with their sexual offense histories and their phallometric results) in making clinical diagnoses. He did not, to the best of my knowledge, habitually use the computed scale totals for diagnostic purposes. He therefore did not conduct much, if any, research to identify cutting scores for the various scales, so cutting scores for classifying a patient as paraphilic or nonparaphilic are not available. The computed scale totals were primarily for the purposes of research rather than individual diagnosis.

It is necessary to know one aspect of Freund's standard operating procedure in order to understand what psychometric data are and are not available. I have already explained that the EPES was physically divided into sections. Freund did not give every patient every section. In general, he gave patients only those sections that were relevant to their clinical presentations. Thus, a patient who presented with exhibitionism would not get the section on fetishism (unless he also acknowledged fetishism). A patient who presented with fetishism, on the other hand, might also be given the section on sadism and masochism without his having mentioned those interests spontaneously, because fetishism is commonly found in association with sadism and masochism. Freund did this for a variety of practical reasons, one being that patients who had no interest in a particular paraphilia (e.g., transvestism or pedophilia) were sometimes upset and offended to be asked about cross-dressing or sexual feelings toward children. The upshot of this is that it was never feasible to conduct a grand, omnibus factor analysis of all paraphilia measures on all patients. Thus, the available psychometric data are alpha reliability coefficients.

These scales, whatever their psychometric flaws, did yeoman's service in a large number of studies, which I have not attempted to list comprehensively in this document. They still offer, at the very least, a starting point for the further development of self-report scales that canvass patients' sexual desires as well as their sexual actions.

A more complete description of these scales as well as the individual scales (with scoring weights in parentheses after each response option), references, and some psychometric data about the scales may be found online at http://www.routledge.com/textbooks/9780415801751.

Sexual Socialization Instrument

ILSA L. LOTTES,[1] *University of Maryland, Baltimore County*
PETER J. KURILOFF, *University of Pennsylvania*

The purpose of the Sexual Socialization Instrument (SSI) is to measure permissive sexual influences of parents and peers on adolescents and young adults. The term *permissive* here means acceptance of nonmarital sexual interactions. A permissive influence is one that would encourage sexual involvement in a wide variety of relationships—from casual to long term. A nonpermissive influence is one that discourages casual sexual encounters and promotes either abstinence or sex for individuals only in loving, long-term relationships.

Description

The SSI was developed for use in a longitudinal study investigating the relationships among background variables, residential and social affiliations, and the attitudes, values, and sexual experiences of university students. The items of this instrument were included in a questionnaire completed by 557 first-year students (48% female) in 1987 and 303 of these same students (55% female) in 1991 when they were seniors.

The SSI consists of two scales, the Parental Sexual Socialization Scale and the Peer Sexual Socialization Scale. When the SSI was given to first-year students, short forms of the parental and peer scales, containing 4 items (numbered 1, 3, 19 and 20) and 6 items (numbered 2, 4, 5, 8, 15, and 18), respectively, were used. To improve the internal consistency reliability of both scales for the second administration of the questionnaire to seniors, the number of items in the parental and peer scales was increased to 8 (numbered 1, 3, 6, 9, 12, 16, 19, and 20) and 12 (numbered 2, 4, 5, 7, 8, 10, 11, 13, 14, 15, 17, and 18), respectively. These versions of the scales are referred to as long forms. The response options to each item are one of the 5-point Likert-type choices: *strongly agree* (1), *agree* (2), *undecided* (3), *disagree* (4), and *strongly disagree* (5).

If one is interested in an overall measure of sexual socialization from parents and peers, the items of the parental and

[1]Address correspondence to Ilsa L. Lottes, Department of Sociology and Anthropology, University of Maryland, Baltimore County, 5401 Wilkens Avenue, Baltimore, MD 21228; e-mail: lottes@umbc2.umbc.edu

peer scales can be combined to form such a measure as was done by Bell et al. (1992), Bell, Lottes, and Kuriloff (1995), and Kuriloff, Lottes, and Bell (1995).

Response Mode and Timing

Respondents can circle the number from 1 to 5 corresponding to their degree of agreement/disagreement with each item or if computer scoring is available, machine-scoreable answer sheets can be provided for responses. The instrument requires about 5 minutes for completion.

Scoring

Eleven of the 20 items are scored in the reverse direction: Items 1, 4, 6, 8, 11, 13, 14, 15, 16, 18, and 19. For reverse direction items, recoding for scoring needs to transform all 5s to 1s and 4s to 2s and vice versa before responses to the items are summed to give a scale score. For the long form of the Parental Sexual Socialization Scale, scores can range from 8 to 40, and for the short form of this scale scores can range from 4 to 20. For the long form of the Peer Sexual Socialization Scale, scores can range from 12 to 60, and for the short form of this scale scores can range from 6 to 30. The higher the score, the more permissive the parental or peer influence for respondents.

Reliability

In a sample of 557 first-year college students (Lottes & Kuriloff, 1994), Cronbach alphas for the short forms of the Parental and Peer Sexual Socialization Scales were both .60. Test-retest reliabilities comparing first-year students with seniors for a sample of 303 college students were .55 and .47, respectively. In this sample of 303 seniors, Cronbach alphas

for the short forms of the parental and peer scales were .73 and .70, respectively, and alphas for the long forms of these scales were .78 and .85, respectively (Lottes & Kuriloff, 1994).

Validity

The construct validity of the Parental and Peer Sexual Socialization Scales was supported by statistically significant results for predicted correlations and group differences. As expected, Lottes and Kuriloff (1994) found that men reported significantly higher scores on both the short and long forms of the parental and peer scales. Also, as expected, future fraternity members as first-year students reported significantly higher scores on the short form of the Peer Socialization Scale than did first-year male students who remained independent. Similarly, compared to nonfraternity senior men, senior fraternity men reported significantly higher scores on the long form of the Peer Sexual Socialization Scale (Lottes & Kuriloff, 1994). In addition, the short forms of the Parental and Peer Sexualization Scales were found to be positively significantly correlated with number of sex partners and negatively significantly correlated with age of first intercourse.

References

Bell, S. T., Kuriloff, P. J., Lottes I. L., Nathanson, J., Judge, T., & Fogelson-Turet, K. (1992). Rape and callousness in college freshmen: An empirical investigation of a sociocultural model of aggression towards women. *Journal of College Student Development, 33*, 454–461.

Bell, S. T., Lottes, I. L., & Kuriloff, P. J. (1995). *Understanding rape callousness in college students: Results of a panel study.* Unpublished manuscript.

Kuriloff, P. J., Lottes, I. L., & Bell, S. T. (1995). *The socialization of sexual misconduct in college students.* Unpublished manuscript.

Lottes, I. L., & Kuriloff, P. J. (1994). Sexual socialization differences by gender, Greek membership, ethnicity, and religious background. *Psychology of Women Quarterly, 18*, 203–219.

Exhibit

Sexual Socialization Instrument

Directions: Below you will see five numbers corresponding to five choices. Choose the response that best describes your degree of agreement/disagreement with each statement. Write or shade in only one response for each statement. Because all responses will remain anonymous you can respond truthfully with no concerns about anyone connecting responses with individuals.

Strongly Agree (1)   Agree (2)   Undecided (3)   Disagree (4)   Strongly Disagree (5)

____ 1. My mother would have felt okay about my having sex with many different people.

____ 2. I am uncomfortable around people who spend much of their time talking about their sexual experiences.

____ 3. My father would have felt upset if he'd thought I was having sex with many different people.

____ 4. Among my friends, men who have the most sexual experience are the most highly regarded.

____ 5. My friends disapprove of being involved with someone who was known to be sexually easy.

____ 6. According to my parents, having sexual intercourse is an important part of my becoming an adult.

____ 7. Most of my friends don't approve of having multiple sexual partners.

____ 8. My friends and I enjoy telling each other about our sexual experiences.

____ 9. My parents stress that sex and intimacy should always be linked.

____ 10. Most of my friends believe that you should only have sex in a serious relationship.

____ 11. Among my friends alcohol is used to get someone to sleep with you.

____ 12. My parents would disapprove of my being sexually active.

—   13. My friends approve of being involved with someone just for sex.
—   14. My friends brag about their sexual exploits.
—   15. My friends suggest dates to each other who are known to be sexually easy.
—   16. My parents encourage me to have sex with many people before I get married.
—   17. Among my friends, people seldom discuss their sexuality.
—   18. Among my friends, women who have the most sexual experience are the most highly regarded.
—   19. My father would have felt okay about my having casual sexual encounters.
—   20. My mother would only have approved of me having sex in a serious relationship.

Reiss Premarital Sexual Permissiveness Scale (Short Form)

IRA L. REISS,[1] *University of Minnesota*

This scale measures the level of premarital sexual permissiveness that an individual accepts. The scale allows one to precisely place a respondent on the cumulative, low to high, scale of permissiveness. This newer short form focuses on only the measures of coital permissiveness and consists of just four questions (Reiss, 1989; Schwartz & Reiss, 1995).

Description

The short-form scale and the original form are Guttman scales (i.e., they produce a ladder from low to high permissiveness; Reiss, 1967, 1989; Schwartz & Reiss, 1995). The original form consisted of a 12-question scale asking about the person's acceptance of kissing, petting, and intercourse in relationships involving no affection, strong affection, love, or engagement (Hampe & Ruppel, 1974; Reiss, 1964). That scale met all Guttman scaling criteria in both a nationally representative sample and several regional samples. It has been tested in a number of other countries (Huang & Uba, 1992; Sprecher & Hatfield, 1996; Stillerman & Shapiro, 1979). It led to the development of the "Autonomy Theory," explaining changes in premarital sexuality (Crawford & Popp, 2003; Reiss, 1965, 1967; Weis, 1998; Weis, Rabinowitz, & Ruckstuhl, 1992; Weis & Slosnerick, 1981). I would add here that my use of the term *premarital* does not involve any assumption that everyone will marry, but rather it indicates that the scale focuses on attitudes toward sexual behavior of young unmarried people.

In 1989, I composed a revision consisting of a simple four-item scale that used three of the original coital questions and added a fourth question (Reiss, 1989). The fourth question was added because the old scale lacked a "moderate" affection category. The focus on only coital relationships in this newer short-form scale derived from the fact that our culture had changed from a minority of young people accepting premarital intercourse to a majority of young people accepting and having premarital intercourse (Reiss, 2006). This short version has been tested both in the United States and in Sweden and found to meet all Guttman scaling requirements (Schwartz & Reiss, 1995). Although this scale focuses on heterosexual penile/vaginal intercourse, a similar scale measuring the role of affection in same-gender sexual relations could be devised. Doing that could produce some very interesting comparisons.

Response Mode and Timing

The short form of the Premarital Sexual Permissiveness Scale (PSPS) offers three degrees of agreement and three degrees of disagreement with each question (see Exhibit). Respondents circle the degree of agreement or disagreement they have with each item. The four questions take only a couple of minutes for almost everyone to answer.

Scoring

Because Guttman scaling has been proven to work on both the old form and this newer short form of the scale, respondents could simply be scored by dichotomizing their answers into agree or disagree and assigning one point for each question to which they agreed. Dichotomizing each question's answers would yield a total permissiveness scale score for each respondent ranging from a low of 0 to a high of 4. But keep the six choices in each question because it does make respondents feel that they can more accurately express their feelings on the questions, and some researchers may want to use all six categories.

[1]Address correspondence to Ira L. Reiss, 5932 Medicine Lake Road, Minneapolis, MN 55422; e-mail: irareiss@comcast.net

Reliability

Reliability is indicated in that both the original and the short form of the scale always met Guttman Scale criteria, such as the coefficient of reproducibility and the coefficient of scalability. This held up in the U.S. and other industrialized countries (Reiss & Miller, 1979; Schwartz & Reiss, 1995; Walsh, Zey-Ferrell, & Tolone, 1976; Whitbeck, Simons, & Kao, 1994).

Validity

Construct validity was established by finding the expected differences between parents and college students, Whites and Blacks, and males and females (Crawford & Popp, 2003; Liao & Tu, 2006; Reiss, 1967; Schwartz & Reiss, 1995). In the short form the results fit precisely with what was expected when comparing Swedish and American college students (e.g., Swedish students were much more acceptant of Question 4 than were U.S. students).

Other Information

In the last five decades, the PSPS, in one form or the other, has been widely used. For research today, I would recommend using the newer short form of the scale. It incorporates the theoretical structure of the original scale, and three of its four questions are from the coital part of that scale. It can be compared to earlier results with confidence that it is measuring the same thing as the original. I give my permission to use this scale in any research project, but I would ask that you let me know your results.

References

Crawford, M., & Popp, D. (2003). Sexual double standards: A review and methodological critique of two decades of research. *The Journal of Sex Research, 40*, 13–26.

Hampe, G., & Ruppel, H. (1974). The measurement of premarital sexual permissiveness: A comparison of two Guttman scales. *Journal of Marriage and the Family, 36*, 451–464.

Huang, K., & Uba, L. (1992). Premarital sexual behavior among Chinese college students in the U.S. *Archives of Sexual Behavior, 21*, 227–240.

Liao, P. S., & Tu, S. H. (2006). Examining the scalability of intimacy permissiveness in Taiwan. *Social Indicators Research, 76*, 207–232.

Reiss, I. L. (1964). The scaling of premarital sexual permissiveness. *Journal of Marriage and the Family, 26*, 188–198.

Reiss, I. L. (1965). Social class and premarital sexual permissiveness: A re-examination. *American Sociological Review, 29*, 747–756.

Reiss, I. L. (1967). *The social context of premarital sexual permissiveness.* New York: Holt, Rinehart & Winston.

Reiss, I. L. (1989). Is this my scale? *Journal of Marriage and the Family, 51*, 1079–1080.

Reiss, I. L. (2006). *An insider's view of sexual science since Kinsey.* Lanham, MD: Rowman & Littlefield.

Reiss, I. L., & Miller, B. C. (1979). Heterosexual permissiveness: A theoretical analysis. In W. Burr, R. Hill, I. Nye, & I. L. Reiss (Eds.), *Contemporary theories about the family* (Vol. 1, pp. 57–100). New York: Free Press.

Schwartz, I., & Reiss, I. L. (1995). The scaling of premarital sexual permissiveness revisited. Test results of Reiss's new short-form version. *Journal of Sex and Marital Therapy, 21*, 78–86.

Sprecher, S., & Hatfield, E. (1996). Premarital sexual standards among U.S. college students: Comparison with Russian and Japanese students. *Archives of Sexual Behavior, 25*, 261–288.

Stillerman, E. D., & Shapiro, C. M. (1979). Scaling sex attitudes and behavior in South Africa. *Archives of Sexual Behavior, 8*, 1–14.

Walsh, R. H., Zey-Ferrell, M., & Tolone, W. L. (1976). Selection of reference group, perceived reference group permissiveness, and personal permissiveness attitudes and behavior: A study of two consecutive panels (1967–71; 1970–74). *Journal of Marriage and the Family, 38*, 495–507.

Weis, D. L. (1998). The use of theory in sexuality research. *The Journal of Sex Research, 35*, 1–9.

Weis, D. L., Rabinowitz, B., & Ruckstuhl, M. F. (1992). Individual changes in sexual attitudes and behavior within college level human sexuality courses. *The Journal of Sex Research, 29*, 43–59.

Weis, D. L., & Slosnerick, M. (1981). Attitudes toward sexual and non-sexual extramarital involvements among a sample of college students. *Journal of Marriage and the Family, 43*, 349–358.

Whitbeck, L. B., Simons, R. L., & Kao, M. (1994). The effects of divorced mothers' dating behaviors and sexual attitudes on the sexual attitudes and behaviors of their adolescent children. *Journal of Marriage and the Family, 56*, 615–621.

Exhibit

Reiss Premarital Sexual Permissiveness Scale (Short Form)

The following four questions concern your personal attitude regarding premarital sexual intercourse. First decide whether you agree or disagree with the view expressed; then indicate the level of your agreement or disagreement by circling the answer that best expresses your view. The six choices below follow each question.

Agree:	Strongly	Moderately	Slightly
Disagree:	Strongly	Moderately	Slightly

1. I believe that premarital sexual intercourse is acceptable if one is in a love relationship.
2. I believe that premarital sexual intercourse is acceptable if one is in a relationship involving strong affection.
3. I believe that premarital sexual intercourse is acceptable if one is in a relationship involving moderate affection.
4. I believe that premarital sexual intercourse is acceptable even if one is in a relationship without much affection.

Note. The wording presented above asks what is acceptable for "one" and that term includes both the respondent and others. If you wished to know only what the respondent believes is acceptable for her- or himself, then you could change the wording of each question to a more personalized form. For example change Question 1 to read: ". . . acceptable if I am in a love relationship." It would be interesting to compare the two different wordings of this scale to see what differences, if any, would be found. My own testing of this with students found very little difference.

Premarital Sexual Permissiveness Scale

SUSAN SPRECHER,[1] *Illinois State University*

The Premarital Sexual Permissiveness Scale (PSPS) was developed to assess people's attitudes about the acceptability of premarital sex at different levels of relational development (Sprecher, McKinney, Walsh, & Anderson, 1988). It was modeled after the Reiss (1964, 1967) Premarital Sexual Permissiveness Scale, but with sexual behaviors and relationship stages that my colleagues and I believed would more adequately measure variation in sexual permissiveness. Multiple-item scales, such as the PSPS, are more discriminating measures of sexual standards than the single items often found in national studies, such as the one used in the General Social Survey: "If a man and a woman have sex relations before marriage, do you think it is always wrong, almost always wrong, wrong only sometimes, not wrong at all or don't know." That is, people may be accepting of premarital sex under some relational conditions (e.g., a serious, committed relationship) but not others (e.g., casual dating), and the PSPS can assess this interesting variation.

In addition, multiple versions of the scale can be administered, either with the same participants or with different participants, with each version focusing on a different target in the scale items. This allows the investigator not only to examine a sample's general sexual permissiveness but also to examine how sexual permissiveness may vary for different targets. The most common comparisons that have been made are standards for self versus standards for others and standards for males versus females (i.e., a double standard).

Description

The original version (Sprecher et al., 1988) of the PSPS was created containing 15 items that asked about acceptance of three sexual behaviors (heavy petting [touching of genitals], sexual intercourse, and oral-genital sex) for each of five relationship stages (first date, casually dating, seriously dating, pre-engaged, and engaged). Not surprisingly, people were found to be least accepting of premarital sex at the first date stage, and most accepting at the engaged stage. With each increasing relationship stage, more acceptance was expressed. Variation in acceptability was also found among the sexual activities. People were most accepting of heavy petting; and sexual intercourse was viewed as slightly more acceptable than oral-genital sex.

In some of my research (Sprecher, 1989) I found that the "pre-engaged stage" (defined further as "seriously discussed the possibility of getting married") was dropped. In

addition, in recent research, I have reduced the scale to only the sexual intercourse items.

Response Mode and Timing

In our research, the scale items of the PSPS are followed by a 6-point response scale. The response options are *Agree Strongly, Agree Moderately, Agree Slightly, Disagree Slightly, Disagree Moderately, Disagree Strongly.* Interpretation of results is facilitated by reverse coding the responses so that the higher number indicates greater acceptance.

The scale, even if it is administered multiple times, does not take long to complete. The version that includes five items takes 1 to 2 minutes to complete.

Scoring

To create a total score presenting degree of sexual permissiveness, a mean of the items is recommended (although a sum is also all right). If multiple versions are included (i.e., a version for self, a version for a male target, a version for a female target), it is recommended that a total score be computed separately for each version. Also, as noted above, it is recommended, for ease of interpretation, that the response options first be reverse scored so that the higher number indicates greater agreement.

Reliability

The scale has high internal consistency. With unpublished data collected from over 6,000 undergraduate students at a Midwest university, Cronbach's alpha for the 5-item subscale measuring acceptability of sexual intercourse for the self was .82.

Validity

Construct validity is evidenced by findings of expected differences between male and female participants (e.g., Sprecher, 1989; Sprecher et al., 1988). That is, men are found to be more permissive than women, especially at the stages of first date and casually dating. In addition, in unpublished data, the subscale of acceptability of sexual intercourse for the self was found to be significantly and positively correlated with the sexual attitude items from the Sociosexuality Orientation Inventory (Simpson & Gangestad, 1991).

[1]Address correspondence to Susan Sprecher, Dept. of Sociology and Anthropology, Illinois State University, Normal, IL 61790; e-mail: Sprecher@ilstu.edu

Other Information

If the researcher has the space for only a few items of the scale, my suggestion is that the three items asking about acceptability of sexual intercourse for first date, casual dating, and serious dating be selected. The greatest variation is found for the items asking about first date and casual dating.

Although the scale has been used primarily to examine young adults' attitudes about their own and peers' sexual activity prior to marriage, it could also be used in other ways, including to assess parents' attitudes about their adult children's sexual behavior (e.g., "I believe that sexual intercourse is acceptable for my son when he is casually dating").

Researchers interested in assessing premarital sexual attitudes may continue to adapt and modify the scale, to explore other interesting nuances of sexual attitudes.

References

Reiss, I. L. (1964). The scaling of premarital sexual permissiveness. *Journal of Marriage and the Family, 26,* 188–198.

Reiss, I. L. (1967). *The social context of premarital sexual permissiveness.* New York: Holt, Rinehart and Winston.

Simpson, J. A., & Gangestad, S. W. (1991). Individual differences in sociosexuality: Evidence for convergent and discriminant validity. *Journal of Personality and Social Psychology, 60,* 870–883.

Sprecher, S. (1989). Premarital sexual standards for different categories of individuals. *The Journal of Sex Research, 26,* 232–248.

Sprecher, S., McKinney, K., Walsh, R., & Anderson, C. (1988). A revision of the Reiss Premarital Sexual Permissiveness Scale. *Journal of Marriage and the Family, 50,* 821–828.

Exhibit

Premarital Sexual Permissiveness Scale

Following are the items for *sexual intercourse* in reference to the *self*.

Directions. For each of the following statements, indicate to what extent you agree or disagree with it. These statements concern what you think is appropriate behavior *for you*.

Response option: The following response options follow each item.

1 Agree Strongly
2 Agree Moderately
3 Agree Slightly
4 Disagree Slightly
5 Disagree Moderately
6 Disagree Strongly

The items:[a]

1. I believe that sexual intercourse is acceptable for me on a first date.
2. I believe that sexual intercourse is acceptable for me when I'm casually dating my partner (dating less than one month).
3. I believe that sexual intercourse is acceptable for me when I'm seriously dating my partner (dating almost a year).
4. I believe that sexual intercourse is acceptable for me when I am pre-engaged to my partner (we have seriously discussed the possibility of getting married).
5. I believe that sexual intercourse is acceptable for me when I'm engaged to my partner.

[a]The researcher may also ask about the acceptability of other sexual behaviors. For example, the researcher may include similar items that ask about acceptability of heavy petting (e.g., touching of genitals) and oral-genital sex for the five different relationship stages, as was done in Sprecher et al. (1988). Furthermore, the researcher may ask about acceptability of sexual behaviors for different targets—for example, for a male and a female (see Sprecher, 1989; Sprecher et al., 1988). An example item to measure standards for a female would be "I believe that sexual intercourse is acceptable for a female who is seriously dating her partner." An example item from the male version is "I believe that sexual intercourse is acceptable for a male who is engaged to his partner."

Need for Sexual Intimacy Scale

WILLIAM D. MARELICH[1] AND ERIN SHELTON, *California State University, Fullerton*

The Need for Sexual Intimacy Scale (NSIS) was developed to look specifically at motivations for sexual intimacy, including the needs for sex, affiliation, and dominance. It is intended to complement existing sexuality measures that focus on sexual desires and drives for sexual intercourse, in that it addresses additional aspects of sexual motivations often overlooked (e.g., affiliation and dominance). In application, the NSIS may be used as part of a larger battery of assessment scales addressing sexual health, as individuals with strong sexual intimacy motivations are more likely to engage in risky sexual behaviors that may lead to increased exposure to sexually transmitted diseases (such individuals could then be targeted for primary prevention efforts). The scale may also be used with general or college populations for research on issues surrounding intimate and close relationships.

Description

The scale consists of 22 items that are divided into three subscales: need for sex, need for affiliation, and need for dominance. These needs come from Murray (1938) and were chosen based on their relationship with issues surrounding sexual intimacy. According to Murray, the need for sex addresses the formation and progression of sexual relationships and sexual intercourse. The need for affiliation concerns one's need for affection and to be close to others, whereas the need for dominance focuses on controlling and influencing one's environment (and those in the environment) through persuasion and seduction. Of the 22 items in the NSIS, 8 address the need for sex, 9 address the need for affiliation, and 5 refer to the need for dominance. The items are rated on a 5-point scale, with responses ranging from 1 (*Disagree Definitely*) to 5 (*Agree Definitely*). The compilation of the 22 items and 3 subscales was determined through exploratory factor analyses utilizing principal axis factoring, and confirmed through confirmatory factor analysis.

Response Mode and Timing

Respondents are to fill in the blank next to each item with a number that corresponds to the 5-point scale. The measure requires 5 minutes to complete.

Scoring

A separate score is generated for each of the three subscales. Although a second-order factor analysis suggests

the possibility of a viable total score measure (see Marelich & Lundquist, 2008), no psychometrics for a total score are available at this time. Scores for items corresponding to a given subscale are summed and divided by the total number of items in that subscale to produce a mean score. As illustrated in the Exhibit, Items 1–8 correspond to the need for sex, Items 9–17 correspond to the need for affiliation, and Items 18–22 correspond to the need for dominance. Item 14 should be reverse coded, and is marked with an "R" in the Exhibit. For each subscale, higher mean scores indicate higher needs. When originally assessed, items were randomly arranged across subscales, and this remains the current recommendation when using the scale.

Reliability

Principal axis factoring was performed on the final 22 items, utilizing an oblique rotation to allow the resulting factors to correlate. The number of factors was determined through a parallel analysis, scree plot inspection, and the interpretability of the factor solution. All items had sufficient pattern matrix loadings on at least one of the three factors, and two of the factors (sex and dominance) correlated at .39. The three factors reflect the three needs subscales.

Internal consistency reliabilities were .88 for need for sex, .82 for need for affiliation, and .74 for need for dominance. Test-retest reliabilities are not available.

Validity

Confirmatory factor analysis was performed on the 22-item solution obtained from the principal axis factor analysis. The factor structure was confirmed with good fit. In addition, a second-order factor analysis was found to fit the data well, suggesting that the three resulting subscales reflect a broader need for sexual intimacy construct. Construct and criterion validity were assessed by looking at the significant associations of each subscale with a series of 21 items addressing sexual communication and behaviors, attitudes toward relationships, and demographics.

Need for Sex

Individuals with a higher need for sex had higher numbers of sexual partners, had higher numbers of one-night stands, were more likely to dominate their partners sexually, reported using condoms less often, and used intoxicants during sexual encounters more often. They also had a harder time talking with their partners about safe sex,

[1]Address correspondence to William D. Marelich, Dept. of Psychology, CSU Fullerton, 800 N. State College Blvd., Fullerton, CA 92834; e-mail: wmarelich@fullerton.edu

were more likely to lie about HIV testing, and reported that the most important aspect of a relationship was sex. Men tended to report higher needs for sex compared to women.

Need for Affiliation

Individuals higher in need for affiliation report being consumed with thoughts of their partners more frequently, were less likely to misinform their partners about being HIV tested, were more truthful when revealing information about the number of sexual partners they have had, and report that being in a relationship was something they need. Women tended to report higher need for affiliation than men.

Need for Dominance

Individuals higher in need for dominance showed a preference for dominating partners in a sexual manner. In addition, they report using condoms less often, and in circumstances where condoms were not available were less likely to be turned away by a sexual partner for sex. Individuals higher on this measure were more likely to ask partners about their past sexual experiences, report that being in a relationship is something they needed, and that sex was an important aspect of relationships. No gender differences were noted.

Other Information

It is important when administering this measure that items are presented in a random order and mixed between sub-scales in order to avoid response bias.

References

Marelich, W. D., & Lundquist, J. (2008). Motivations for sexual intimacy: Development of a needs-based sexual intimacy scale. *International Journal of Sexual Health, 20,* 177–186.

Murray, H. (1938). *Explorations in personality.* New York: Oxford University Press.

Exhibit

Need for Sexual Intimacy Scale

Directions: The next few items address things we may "need" in life. Some say we "need" many things in order to survive (e.g., food, shelter, etc.). Below we have presented a series of items and would like you to rate each item as to how much you agree or disagree with them as things you may "need." The term "partner" below refers to a sexual partner (e.g. dating partner, boyfriend/girlfriend, long-term partner/spouse). Please read each statement carefully, and then fill in the blank (_____) with a number that corresponds to the scale description.

Disagree Definitely				Agree Definitely
1	2	3	4	5

I need . . .

_____ 1. To have more sex.
_____ 2. Sex every day.
_____ 3. To have an orgasm every day.
_____ 4. To let myself go sexually with someone.
_____ 5. Sex every couple of days.
_____ 6. Someone who is "great in bed."
_____ 7. Sex with a lot of partners.
_____ 8. To take control of my partner when we are intimate.
_____ 9. A partner who loves me.
_____ 10. Somebody to love.
_____ 11. Companionship.
_____ 12. A companion in life.
_____ 13. Complete trust in the people I am intimate with.
_____ 14. Nobody special in my life. [R]
_____ 15. Somebody to hold my hand.
_____ 16. A few really good friends.
_____ 17. Someone to sleep next to me.
_____ 18. My partner to tell me where they are at all times.
_____ 19. Control over my partner.
_____ 20. My partner to give me what I want (such as financial support, clothes, a car).
_____ 21. A partner I can manipulate.
_____ 22. The ability to order my partner to have sex with me if I want to.

Rape Supportive Attitude Scale

ILSA L. LOTTES,[1] *University of Maryland, Baltimore County*

The purpose of the Rape Supportive Attitude Scale is to measure attitudes that are hostile to rape victims, including false beliefs about rape and rapists. Seven beliefs measured by this scale are (a) women enjoy sexual violence, (b) women are responsible for rape prevention, (c) sex rather than power is the primary motivation for rape, (d) rape happens only to certain kinds of women, (e) a woman is less desirable after she has been raped, (f) women falsely report many rape claims, and (g) rape is justified in some situations. Researchers (Burt, 1980; Marolla & Scully, 1982; Russell, 1975; Williams & Holmes, 1981) have found support for the views that these beliefs not only promote rape but also hinder and prolong the recuperative process for survivors of a rape.

Description

The Rape Supportive Attitude Scale was developed from a pool of 40 items from the rape attitude measures of Barnett and Feild (1977), Burt (1980), Koss (1981), and Wheeler and Utigard (1984). The 20 items selected for the scale meet two criteria: (a) the items have content validity (i.e., they assess one of the seven victim-callous beliefs listed above), and (b) the items have high item-total scale correlations and high factor loadings on the same factor. The response options for each item are one of the five Likert scale choices: *strongly disagree* (1), *disagree* (2), *undecided* (3), *agree* (4), or *strongly agree* (5).

The Rape Supportive Attitude Scale was administered to two college student samples in the northeastern United States (Lottes, 1991). Students completed the scale in their regularly scheduled classes. For both samples, the 20 scale items were randomly distributed in a questionnaire containing 70 other items requiring similar Likert-type responses. The first sample consisted of 98 males and 148 females from education, health, and sociology classes at two universities. The second sample consisted of 195 males and 195 females from business, engineering, English, education, history, mathematics, physics, political science, and sociology classes at three universities. The majority of the students in both samples were single and in the 19 to 22 age range. The Rape Supportive Attitude Scale is appropriate to administer to adults.

Response Mode and Timing

Two response modes are possible. If a machine-scoreable sheet is used, respondents should shade in the circle of the number indicating their agreement/disagreement with each item. If a machine-scoreable sheet is not used, then the numbers 1 through 5 need to be included next to each item

and the respondents should circle the number indicating their agreement/disagreement with each item. The 20-item scale takes about 10 minutes to complete.

Scoring

All of the items are scored in the same direction. To break up any response set, the 20 items of this scale can be randomly placed among Likert-type items assessing other characteristics. To determine each respondent's score for the scale, add the responses (coded 1 through 5) to the 20 items. The higher the score, the more rape supportive or victim-callous attitudes are supported by a respondent.

Reliability

For the first sample of 246 college students, the Cronbach alpha was .91. For the second sample of 390 students, the Cronbach alpha also was .91.

Validity

For both college student samples (n = 246 and n = 390, respectively), scores for the Rape Supportive Attitude Scale were significantly correlated ($p < .001$) in the predicted direction with (a) nonegalitarian gender role beliefs (r = .58, r = .64), (b) traditional attitudes toward female sexuality (r = .50, r = .42), (c) adversarial sexual beliefs (r = .65, r = .70), (d) arousal to sexual violence (r = .32, r = .37), and (e) nonacceptance of homosexuality (r = .25, r = .34). For males in both samples, the Rape Supportive Attitude Scale was significantly correlated ($p < .001$) in the predicted direction with the Hypermasculinity Inventory of Mosher and Sirkin (1984; r = .44, r = .52). Finally, for both samples, the correlations of sex with the scale (r = .36, r = 35) were significant ($p < .001$) and in the predicted direction. Males indicated more victim-callous attitudes than females.

A principal components analysis of the data from both samples revealed that a single, dominant factor emerged, accounting for 37% of the variance in each case. In both analyses, all items loaded on this factor at .39 or greater.

Other Information

Bell et al. (1992) found that a 12-item subset (containing items numbered 2, 3, 4, 5, 6, 7, 11, 12, 13, 15, 17, and 19) of the Rape Supportive Attitude Scale produced an alpha of .77 for a sample of 521 first-year university students. As seniors, 300 of the original first-year student sample completed a questionnaire containing the 12-item subset.

[1]Address correspondence to Ilsa L. Lottes, Department of Sociology and Anthropology, University of Maryland, Baltimore County, 5401 Wilkens Avenue, Baltimore, MD 21228; e-mail: lottes@umbc.edu.

Test-retest reliability was .53 and the Cronbach alpha for the senior sample was .76 (Bell, Lottes, & Kuriloff, 1995).

Construct validity of this shortened Rape Supportive Attitude Scale was supported by significant correlations in the predicted directions between this scale and measures of feminist attitudes, male dominant attitudes, liberalism, and social conscience for both the first-year student and senior samples (Bell et al., 1992, 1995). For both samples, men reported significantly higher ($p < .001$) scores on the Rape Supportive Attitude Scale than did women (Bell et al., 1992, 1995).

References

Barnett, N. J., & Feild, H. S. (1977). Sex differences in university students' attitudes toward rape. *Journal of College Student Personnel, 18*, 93–96.

Bell, S., Kuriloff, P., Lottes, I., Nathanson, J., Judge, T., & Fogelson-Turet, K. (1992). Rape callousness in college freshmen: An empirical investigation of a sociocultural model of aggression towards women. *Journal of College Student Development, 33*, 454–461.

Bell, S., Lottes, I., & Kuriloff, P. (1995). *Understanding rape callousness in college students: Results of a panel study*. Unpublished manuscript.

Burt, M. R. (1980). Cultural myths and supports for rape. *Journal of Personality and Social Psychology, 38*, 217–230.

Koss, M. P. (1981). *Hidden rape on a university campus* (Grant No. R01MH31618). Rockville, MD: National Institute of Health.

Lottes, I. L. (1991). Belief systems: Sexuality and rape. *Journal of Psychology and Human Sexuality, 4*, 37–59.

Marolla, J., & Scully, D. (1982). *Attitudes toward women, violence, and rape: A comparison of convicted rapists and other felons* (Grant No. R01MH33013–01A1). Rockville, MD: National Institute of Health.

Mosher, D. L., & Sirkin, M. (1984). Measuring a macho personality constellation. *Journal of Research in Personality, 18*, 150–163.

Russell, D. (1975). *The politics of rape*. New York: Stein and Day.

Wheeler, J. R., & Utigard, C. N. (1984, June). *Gender, stereotyping, rape attitudes, and acceptance of interpersonal violence*. Paper presented at the combined annual meeting of the Society for the Scientific Study of Sex and the American Association of Sex Educators, Counselors, and Therapists, Boston, MA.

Williams, J. E., & Holmes, K. A. (1981). *The second assault: Rape and public attitudes*. Westport, CT: Greenwood Press.

Exhibit

Rape Supportive Attitude Scale

Directions: Write all your responses on the computer answer sheet. Use a No. 2 lead pencil. To indicate your opinion about each statement, shade in the number corresponding to one of the five circles. Indicate whether you *strongly disagree* (1), *disagree* (2), are *undecided* or *have no opinion* (3), *agree* (4), or *strongly agree* (5).

Strongly Disagree (1)   Agree (2)   Undecided (3)   Disagree (4)   Strongly Agree (5)

Remember: Be sure that the statement you are reading corresponds to the statement number you are marking on the answer sheet. Mark only one response for each statement.

1. Being roughed up is sexually stimulating to many women.
2. A man has some justification in forcing a female to have sex with him when she led him to believe she would go to bed with him.
3. The degree of a woman's resistance should be the major factor in determining if a rape has occurred.
4. The reason most rapists commit rape is for sex.
5. If a girl engages in necking or petting and she lets things get out of hand, it is her fault if her partner forces sex on her.
6. Many women falsely report that they have been raped because they are pregnant and want to protect their reputation.
7. A man has some justification in forcing a woman to have sex with him if she allowed herself to be picked up.
8. Sometimes the only way a man can get a cold woman turned on is to use force.
9. A charge of rape two days after the act has occurred is probably not rape.
10. A raped woman is a less desirable woman.
11. A man is somewhat justified in forcing a woman to have sex with him if he has had sex with her in the past.
12. In order to protect the male, it should be difficult to prove that a rape has occurred.
13. Many times a woman will pretend she doesn't want to have intercourse because she doesn't want to seem loose, but she's really hoping the man will force her.
14. A woman who is stuck-up and thinks she is too good to talk to guys deserves to be taught a lesson.
15. One reason that women falsely report rape is that they frequently have a need to call attention to themselves.
16. In a majority of rapes the victim is promiscuous or had a bad reputation.
17. Many women have an unconscious wish to be raped, and may then unconsciously set up a situation in which they are likely to be attacked.
18. Rape is the expression of an uncontrollable desire for sex.
19. A man is somewhat justified in forcing a woman to have sex with him if they have dated for a long time.
20. Rape of a woman by a man she knows can be defined as a "woman who changed her mind afterwards."

Sexual Assault Treating/Reporting Attitudes Survey

VETTA L. SANDERS THOMPSON[1] AND SHARON WEST SMITH, *Washington University in St. Louis*

The Sexual Assault Treatment/Reporting Attitudes Survey is a 46-item survey designed to assess community attitudes on a variety of issues related to sexual assault. The survey consists of three sections: demographic data, sexual assault treatment and reporting attitudes, and vignette responses.

The first section of the survey elicits demographic data. Participants are asked to report age, sex, income, education, and marital status. The second section of the survey examines attitudes related to decisions to report or seek treatment in cases of sexual assault. The survey addresses knowledge of both short- and long-term effects of rape and child sexual abuse, attitudes toward the need for treatment, preferences for who provides treatment, as well as expectations and fears related to entering the treatment process. In addition, concerns regarding the involvement of the judicial system and various social service agencies are addressed.

The third section of the instrument is based on a prior survey (Howard, 1988). It consists of 10 vignettes, depicting either child molestation or rape. Three vignettes depict the sexual molestation of a female child; three, the sexual molestation of a male child; three, the rape of a female; and one vignette depicts the rape of a male by a stranger. Participants read each vignette and indicate whether a sexual assault has occurred, the need for treatment, type of treatment, and treatment source preferred. They also indicate the extent to which there is victim responsibility for the incident described using a 5-point rating scale.

Other Information

A copy of this instrument may be obtained from the Health and Psychosocial Instruments database, Behavioral Measurement Database Services, P.O. Box 110287, Pittsburgh, PA 15232–0787.

Reference

Howard, J. (1988). A structural approach to sexual attitudes. *Sociological Perspectives, 31,* 88–121.

Exhibit

Sexual Assault Treating/Reporting Attitudes Survey (sample items)

Do you believe there are detrimental or bad effects for a child who has been sexually abused or molested?

If your child were sexually abused or molested, would you seek treatment or counseling (beyond medical treatment)?

Which of the following do you think/feel might be long-term effects of child sexual abuse or molestation:

If a family member or friend were raped or sexually assaulted, would you recommend that they seek treatment or counseling (beyond medical treatment)?

Would you be more likely to seek treatment if you knew that there would be no police or judicial involvement?

Can males be sexually molested or raped?

Where would you go for help or treatment?

[1]Address correspondence to Vetta L. Sanders Thompson, Washington University in St. Louis, George Warren Brown School of Social Work, Campus Box 1009, 700 Rosedale Avenue, St. Louis, MO 63112–1408; e-mail: vthompson@gwbmail.wustl.edu

Multidimensional Sexual Approach Questionnaire

WILLIAM E. SNELL, JR.,[1] *Southeast Missouri State University*

The Multidimensional Sexual Approach Questionnaire (MSAQ; Snell, 1992) is a self-report questionnaire designed to assess several different ways in which people can approach their sexual relationships (e.g., from a caring vs. an exchange perspective). More specifically, the MSAQ was developed to measure eight separate approaches to sexual relations (cf. Hughes & Snell, 1990): (a) a passionate, romantic approach to sexual relations; (b) a game-playing approach to sexual relations; (c) a companionate, friendship approach to sexual relations; (d) a practical, logical, and shopping-list approach to a sexual partner and a sexual relationship; (e) a dependent, possessive approach to sexual relations; (f) an altruistic, selfless, and all-giving approach to sexual partners and sexual relations; (g) a communal approach to sex (i.e., a sensitive approach to sexual relations that emphasizes caring and concern for a partner's sexual needs and preferences); and (h) an exchange approach to sex (i.e., a quid pro quo approach to sex, in which a sexual partner keeps "tabs" on the sexual activities and favors that she or he does for a partner, expecting to be repaid in an exchange fashion at some time in the future of the relationship). Snell (1992) found significant relationships between the ways that people approach their sexual relations, as measured by the MSAQ, and both their sexual and love attitudes. Other findings reported by Snell (1992) revealed that several demographic/psychosocial variables (e.g., dating status) were also associated with the sexual styles measured by the MSAQ.

Description

The MSAQ consists of 56 items. In responding to the MSAQ, subjects are asked to indicate how much they agree-disagree with each statement. A 5-point Likert-type scale is used to collect data on the subjects' responses, with each item being scored from +2 to –2: *agree* (+2), *slightly agree* (+1), *neither agree nor disagree* (0), *slightly disagree* (–1), *disagree* (–2). In order to create subscale scores, the items on each subscale are summed. Higher positive (vs. negative) scores thus correspond to the tendency to approach one's sexual relations in the manner described by each respective MSAQ subscale. A varimax factor analysis with an orthogonal rotation extracted eight factors that corresponded to the eight approaches measured by the MSAQ.

Response Mode and Timing

Respondents indicate their responses on a computer scan sheet by darkening in a response from A to E. The questionnaire usually takes 15–20 minutes to complete.

Scoring

For purposes of analyses, the statements are keyed so that A=2, B = 1, C = 0, D = –1, and E = –2 (no items are reverse scored). This procedure results in six subscale scores, based on the sum of the items assigned to a particular subscale (i.e., add up the seven item scores). An overall scale score for the MSAQ is not particularly useful. The MSAQ subscales are coded so that a higher score indicates greater agreement with the respective MSAQ statements. Subscale scores can range from –14 to 14. The items assigned to each subscale are (a) a passionate, romantic approach to sexual relations (Items 1–7); (b) a game-playing approach to sexual relations (Items 8–14); (c) a companionate, friendship approach to sexual relations (Items 15–21); (d) a practical, logical, and shopping-list approach to a sexual partner and a sexual relationship (Items 22–28); (e) a dependent, possessive approach to sexual relations (Items 29 to 35); (f) an altruistic, selfless, and all-giving approach to sexual partners and sexual relations (Items 36 to 42); (g) sexual communion and a sensitive approach to sexual relations that emphasizes caring and concern for a partner's sexual needs and preferences (Items 43 to 48); and (h) sexual exchange (Items 49 to 56).

Reliability

To examine the internal reliability of the subscales on the MSAQ, Cronbach alpha coefficients were computed for males and females, separately and in combination (Snell, 1992). The results clearly indicated that the subscales on the MSAQ have high internal reliability among both males and females. Specifically, the Cronbach alphas ranged from a low of .72 for males (.73 for females) to a high of .92 for males (.85 for females), average for males = .80 (average for females = .78).

Validity

As expected, Snell (1992) found that males who took a friendly, companionate approach to their sexual relations were characterized by sexual possessiveness, selflessness, and sensitivity. Not surprisingly, it was also found that, among males, a game-playing sexual style was directly related to a logical, rational way of approaching their sexual relations. In contrast, females who approached sex as a game were less likely to engage in friendly, companionate sexual relations. Other results reported by Snell indicated that males reported higher scores than females on the

---

[1] Address all correspondence to William E. Snell, Jr., Department of Psychology, Southeast Missouri State University, One University Plaza, Cape Girardeau, MO 63701; e-mail: wesnell@semo.edu

measure of the altruistic sexual style (a selfless, all-giving approach to sexual relations). In contrast, females, relative to males, were more rejecting of an exchange approach to sex. Men's and women's scores on the remaining MSAQ subscales were quite similar; they endorsed a romantic, companionate, and communal approach to their sexual relations, while disavowing a game-playing sexual style. A final set of results reported by Snell examined the impact of sexual attitudes on the way that people approach their sexual relations (i.e., their sexual styles). As expected, sexually permissive attitudes were found to be positively associated with a game-playing approach to sex; people with sexually responsible attitudes toward contraceptives approached their sexual relations with a sensitive, caring sexual style; and a sexual attitude favoring idealized communal sex, as measured by the Sexual Attitudes Scale (Hendrick & Hendrick, 1987), was positively and strongly associated with all of the following MSAQ sexual styles: passionate, companionate, possessive, selfless, and caring approaches to sex.

References

Hendrick, S. S., & Hendrick, C. (1987). Multidimensionality of sexual attitudes. *The Journal of Sex Research, 23,* 502–526.

Hughes, T. G., & Snell, W. E., Jr. (1990). Communal and exchange approaches to sexual relations. *Annals of Sex Research, 3,* 149–164.

Snell, W. E., Jr. (1992, April). *Sexual styles: A multidimensional approach to sexual relations.* Presented at the annual meeting of the Southwestern Psychological Association, Austin, TX.

Exhibit

Multidimensional Sexual Approach Questionnaire

Instructions: Listed below are several statements that reflect different attitudes about sex. For each statement fill in the response on the answer sheet that indicates how much you agree or disagree with that statement. Some of the items refer to a specific sexual relationship, while others refer to general attitudes and beliefs about sex. Whenever possible, answer the questions with your current partner in mind. If you are not currently dating anyone, answer the questions with your most recent partner in mind. If you have never had a sexual relationship, answer in terms of what you think your responses would most likely be in a future sexual relationship. For each statement:

A = Strongly *agree* with the statement.
B = Moderately *agree* with the statement.
C = Neutral—*Neither* agree nor disagree.
D = Moderately *disagree* with the statement.
E = Strongly *disagree* with the statement.

1. I was sexually attracted to my partner immediately after we first met.
2. I feel a strong sexual "chemistry" toward my partner.
3. I have a very intense and satisfying sexual relationship with my partner.
4. I was sexually meant for my partner.
5. I became sexually involved rather quickly with my partner.
6. I have a strong sexual understanding of my partner.
7. My partner fits my notion of the ideal sexual partner.
8. I try to keep my partner a little uncertain about my sexual commitment to him/her.
9. I believe that what my partner doesn't know about my sexual activity won't hurt him/her.
10. I have not always told my partner about my previous sexual experiences.
11. I could end my sexual relationship with my partner rather easily and quickly.
12. My partner wouldn't like hearing about some of the sexual experiences I've had with others.
13. When my partner becomes too sexually involved with me, I want to back off a little.
14. I like playing around with a number of people, including my partner and others.
15. The sexual relationship between myself and my partner started off rather slowly.
16. I had to "care" for my partner before I could make love to him/her.
17. I expect to always be a friend of my sexual partner.
18. The sex I have with my partner is better because it was preceded by a long friendship.
19. I was a friend of my sexual partner before we became lovers.
20. The sex my partner and I have is based on a deep friendship, not something mystical and mysterious.
21. Sex with my partner is highly satisfying because it developed out of a good friendship.
22. Before I made love with my partner, I spent some time evaluating her/his career potential.
23. I planned my life in a careful manner before I chose my sexual partner.

24. One of the reasons I chose my sexual partner is because of our similar backgrounds.
25. Before I made love with my sexual partner, I considered how s/he would reflect on my family.
26. It was important to me that my sexual partner be a good parent.
27. I thought about the implications for my career before I made love with my sexual partner.
28. I didn't have sex with my partner until after I had considered our hereditary backgrounds.
29. When sex with my partner isn't going right, I become upset.
30. If my sexual relationship with my partner ended, I would become extremely despondent and depressed.
31. Sometimes I am so sexually attracted to my partner that I simply can't sleep.
32. When my partner sexually ignores me, I feel really sick.
33. Since my partner and I started having sex, I have not been able to concentrate on anything else.
34. If my partner became sexually involved with someone else, I wouldn't be able to take it.
35. If my partner doesn't have sex with me for a while, I sometimes do stupid things to get her/his sexual attention.
36. If my partner were having a sexual difficulty, I would definitely try to help as much as I could.
37. I would rather have a sexual problem myself than let my partner suffer though one.
38. I could never be sexually satisfied unless first my partner was sexually satisfied.
39. I am usually willing to forsake my own sexual needs in order to let my partner achieve her/his own sexual needs.
40. My partner can use me the way s/he chooses in order for him/her to be sexually satisfied.
41. When my partner is sexually dissatisfied with me, I still accept him/her without reservations.
42. I would do practically any sexual activity that my partner wanted.
43. It would bother me if my sexual partner neglected my needs.
44. If I were to make love with a sexual partner, I'd take that person's needs and feelings into account.
45. If a sexual partner were to do something sensual for me, I'd try to do the same for him/her.
46. I expect a sexual partner to be responsive to my sexual needs and feelings.
47. I would be willing to go out of my way to satisfy my sexual partner.
48. If I were feeling sexually needy, I'd ask my sexual partner for help.
49. If a sexual partner were to ignore my sexual needs, I'd feel hurt.
50. I think people should feel obligated to repay an intimate partner for sexual favors.
51. I would feel somewhat exploited if an intimate partner failed to repay me for a sexual favor.
52. I would probably keep track of the times a sexual partner asked me for a sensual pleasure.
53. When a person receives sexual pleasures from another, s/he ought to repay that person right away.
54. It's best to make sure things are always kept "even" between two people in a sexual relationship.
55. I would do a special sexual favor for an intimate partner, only if that person did some special sexual favor for me.
56. If my sexual partner performed a sexual request for me, I would probably feel that I'd have to repay him/her later on.
57. I responded to the following items based on:
    (A)   A current sexual relationship.
    (B)   A past sexual relationship.
    (C)   An imagined sexual relationship.

Sexual Relationship Scale

WILLIAM E. SNELL, JR.,[1] *Southeast Missouri State University*

Clark and Mills (1979) proposed a theory of relationship orientation based on the rules governing the giving and receiving of benefits. An exchange-relationship orientation was defined as one in which benefits are given on the assumption that a similar benefit would be reciprocated. The recipient of a benefit in such a relationship presumably incurs a debt to make a suitable, comparable return. By contrast, a communal-relationship orientation was defined by Clark and Mills as one in which benefits are given on the assumption that they are in response to some need. In

[1]Address all correspondence to William E. Snell, Jr., Department of Psychology, Southeast Missouri State University, One University Plaza, Cape Girardeau, MO 63701; e-mail: wesnell@semo.edu

communal relationships, concern for a partner's welfare mediates interpersonal giving rather than anticipation of a reciprocated benefit. Sexual relationships may also be viewed from a communal perspective, which emphasizes caring and concern for a partner's sexual needs and preferences, or else from an exchange perspective, which emphasizes a quid pro quo approach to sexual relations.

The Sexual Relationship Scale (SRS; Hughes & Snell, 1990) is an objective self-report instrument that was designed to measure communal and exchange approaches to sexual relationships. More specifically, the SRS was developed to assess chronic dispositional differences in the type of orientation that people take toward their sexual relations. Some individuals take a communal approach to their sexual relations in which they feel responsible for and involved in their partner's sexual satisfaction and welfare. They want to respond to their partner's sexual needs and desires. In this sense, they contribute to their partner's sexual satisfaction and welfare in order to please the partner and to demonstrate a desire to respond to that person's sexual welfare. Moreover, people who take a communal approach to sexual relations also expect their partner to be responsive and sensitive to their own sexual welfare and needs. In contrast, those who approach sexual relations from an exchange orientation do not feel any special responsibility for their partner's sexual satisfaction and welfare. Nor do they feel any inherent need or desire to be attuned to or responsive to their partner's sexual pleasure. Rather, they give sexual pleasure only in response to sexual benefits they have received in the past or have been promised in the future. An exchange approach to sexual relations often involves sexual debts and obligations. The individuals involved in this type of sexual relationship are usually concerned with how many sexual favors they have given and received, and the comparability of these sexual exchanges. To examine these ideas, the SRS was developed to measure exchange and communal approaches to sexually intimate relations. The SRS was based on the Communal Orientation scale developed by Clark, Ouellette, Powell, and Milberg (1987) and the Exchange Orientation scale developed by Clark, Taraban, Ho, and Wesner (1989) and was intended to represent an extension of their ideas.

Description

The SRS consists of 24 items arranged in a 5-point Likert-type format, in which respondents rate how characteristic the SRS items are of them from (A) *not at all characteristic of me* to (E) *very characteristic of me*.

Response Mode and Timing

Typically, individuals respond to the items on the SRS by indicating their responses on a computer scan sheet, using a response range from A to E. The questionnaire usually takes about 10–15 minutes to complete.

Scoring

People are asked to respond to the SRS items by indicating how much each statement describes them, using a 5-point Likert-type scale: (0) *not at all characteristic of me*, (1) *slightly characteristics of me*, (2) *somewhat characteristic of me*, (3) *moderately characteristic of me*, and (4) *very characteristic of me*. The SRS items are coded so that A = 0, B = 1, C = 2, D = 3, and E = 4. Items 6, 8, 10, and 18 are reverse coded so that 0 = 4, 1 = 3, 2 = 2, 3 = 1, and 4 = 0. The SRS consists of two subscales, each containing eight separate items. The labels and items for these two subscales are (a) The Exchange Approach to Sexual Relations (Items 2, 6, 8, 10, 12, 14, 16, and 18) and (b) The Communal Approach to Sexual Relations (Items 1, 3, 4, 9, 13, 15, 21, and 24). Finally, the eight items on each subscale are summed so that higher scores indicate a stronger communal and exchange approach, respectively, to sexual relations.

Reliability

The internal consistency of the two SRS subscales was determined by computing Cronbach alpha coefficients for both females and males, as well as for the combined group of subjects (Hughes & Snell, 1990). For the sexual communion subscale, the coefficients were .77 for males, .79 for females, and .78 for both together. The coefficients for the sexual exchange subscale were .59 for males, .67 for females, and .67 for both. These findings indicate that the two subscales had sufficient internal consistency to justify their use in research. Other analyses have revealed that among females the two SRS subscales are essentially orthogonal to one another (Hughes & Snell, 1990).

Validity

Factor analysis (a principal components factor analysis with oblique rotation) was performed on the SRS items to determine whether the statements on the SRS would form two separate clusters. Because several items were unrelated to the initial factor solutions, they were first deleted, and the same factor analysis procedure was reconducted. The pattern matrix loadings for the females clearly provided support for the expected two factor structure, with conceptually similar items loading together (the results for the males were less clear, given the small sample size). Factor I consisted of sexual communion items (eigenvalue = 4.81, percent of variance = 20%), and Factor II contained sexual exchange items (eigenvalue = 2.98, percent of variance = 12%).

Hughes and Snell (1990) also found that males reported significantly higher scores than females on the sexual exchange subscale, but no difference was found for the sexual communion subscale. Further evidence for the validity of the SRS was obtained by correlating the SRS subscales with Clark's Communal and Exchange Orientation scales. The sexual communion subscale was significantly and positively correlated with the Communal Orientation scale for females and for the subjects as a whole. Significant and positive correlations were also found between the sexual exchange orientation subscale and scores on the Exchange Orientation scale for males, females, and both together. In addition, the SRS was found to be related to relationship satisfaction. Among males, a significant negative relationship was found between an exchange approach to sexual relations and their relationship satisfaction. The analysis for the females, in contrast, revealed a statistically significant positive correlation between relationship satisfaction and a communal approach to sexual relations.

These patterns of correlations thus provide preliminary evidence for the construct validity of the SRS, in that (a) those individuals characterized by a stronger communal approach to their sexual relations were expected to report greater satisfaction with their intimate relationships and to approach their partners with a more caring and companionate perspective and (b) those individuals characterized by an exchange approach to their sexual relations were expected to have a similar exchange approach to their adult romantic relationships and to report less satisfaction with their romantic relationships.

References

Clark, M. S., & Mills, J. (1979). Interpersonal attraction in exchange and communal relationships. *Journal of Personality and Social Psychology, 37*, 12–24.

Clark, M. S., Ouellette, R., Powell, M. C., & Milberg, S. (1987). Recipient's mood, relationship type, and helping. *Journal of Personality and Social Psychology, 53*, 94–103.

Clark, M. S., Taraban, C., Ho, J., & Wesner, K. (1989). *A measure of exchange orientation.* Unpublished manuscript, Carnegie Mellon University, Pittsburgh, PA.

Hughes, T., & Snell, W. E., Jr. (1990). Communal and exchange approaches to sexual relations. *Annals of Sex Research, 3*, 149–163.

Exhibit

Sexual Relationship Scale

Instructions: Listed below are several statements that concern the topic of sexual relationships. Please read each of the following statements carefully and decide to what extent it is characteristic of you. Some of the items refer to a specific relationship. Whenever possible, answer the questions with your current partner in mind. If you are not currently dating anyone, answer the questions with your most recent partner in mind. If you have never had a relationship, answer in terms of what you think your responses would most likely be. Then, for each statement fill in the response on the answer sheet that indicates how much it applies to you by using the following scale:

A = *Not at all* characteristic of me.
B = *Slightly* characteristic of me.
C = *Somewhat* characteristic of me.
D = *Moderately* characteristic of me.
E = *Very* characteristic of me.

Note: Remember to respond to all items, even if you are not completely sure. Your answers will be kept in the strictest confidence. Also, please be honest in responding to these statements.

1. It would bother me if my sexual partner neglected my needs.
2. When I make love with someone, I generally expect something in return.
3. If I were to make love with a sexual partner, I'd take that person's needs and feelings into account.
4. If a sexual partner were to do something sensual for me, I'd try to do the same for him/her.
5. I'm not especially sensitive to the feelings of a sexual partner.
6. I don't think people should feel obligated to repay an intimate partner for sexual favors. (R)
7. I don't consider myself to be a particularly helpful sexual partner.
8. I wouldn't feel all that exploited if an intimate partner failed to repay me for a sexual favor. (R)
9. I believe sexual lovers should go out of their way to be sexually responsive to their partner.
10. I wouldn't bother to keep track of the times a sexual partner asked for a sensual pleasure. (R)
11. I wouldn't especially enjoy helping a partner achieve their own sexual satisfaction.
12. When a person receives sexual pleasures from another, s/he ought to repay that person right away.
13. I expect a sexual partner to be responsive to my sexual needs and feelings.
14. It's best to make sure things are always kept "even" between two people in a sexual relationship.
15. I would be willing to go out of my way to satisfy my sexual partner.
16. I would do a special sexual favor for an intimate partner, only if that person did some special sexual favor for me.
17. I don't think it's wise to get involved taking care of a partner's sexual needs.

18. If my sexual partner performed a sexual request for me, I wouldn't feel that I'd have to repay him/her later on. (R)
19. I'm not the sort of person who would help a partner with a sexual problem.
20. If my sexual partner wanted something special from me, s/he would have to do something sexual for me.
21. If I were feeling sexually needy, I'd ask my sexual partner for help.
22. If my sexual partner became emotionally upset, I would try to avoid him/her.
23. People should keep their sexual problems to themselves.
24. If a sexual partner were to ignore my sexual needs, I'd feel hurt.

Note. R = reverse-coded item.

Index of Sexual Satisfaction

WALTER W. HUDSON,[1,2] *WALMYR Publishing Co.*

The Index of Sexual Satisfaction (ISS) is short-form scale designed to measure the degree of dissatisfaction in the sexual component of a dyadic relationship.

Description

The ISS contains 25 category-partition (Likert-type) items, some of which are worded negatively to partially offset the potential for response set bias. Each item is scored on a relative frequency scale as shown in the scoring key of the instrument. Obtained scores range from 0 to 100, with higher scores indicating greater degrees of sexual discord. The ISS has a clinical cutting score of 30 such that scores above that value indicate the presence of a clinically significant degree of sexual discord in the relationship. The ISS can be used with all English speaking populations aged 12 or older.

The readability statistics for the ISS are Flesch Reading Ease: 79; Gunning's Fog Index: 8; and Flesch-Kincaid Grade Level: 5.

Response Mode and Timing

The ISS is a self-report scale that is normally completed in 5–7 minutes.

Scoring

Items 1, 2, 3, 9, 10, 12, 16, 17, 19, 21, 22, and 23 must first be reverse scored by subtracting the item response from $K+1$, where K is the number of response categories in the scoring key. After making all appropriate item reversals, compute the total score as $S = (\Sigma X_i - N)(100) / [(K-1)N]$, where X is an item response, i is item, K is the number of response categories, and N is the number of properly completed items. Total scores remain valid in the face of missing values (omit-

ted items) provided the respondent completes at least 80% of the items. The effect of the scoring formula is to replace missing values with the mean item response value so that scores range from 0 to 100 regardless of the value of N.

Reliability

Cronbach's alpha is .92 and the *SEM* is 4.24. Test-retest reliability is not available.

Validity

The known groups validity coefficient is .76 as determined by the point biserial correlation between group status (troubled vs. untroubled criterion groups) and the ISS scores. Detailed information about content, factorial, and construct validity are reported in the *WALMYR Assessment Scale Scoring Manual*, which is available from the publisher.

Other Information

The proper use of the WALMYR assessment scales is easily mastered, and the scales can be readily understood by qualified professional practitioners. These measurement tools are not intended for use by untrained individuals. The scales are simple, powerful devices that, when used by trained professionals, are capable of revealing both minor and serious problems that individuals might have in many areas of personal and social functioning. They are not intended for use by persons who are not trained to deal with such problems and should be used only by competent professionals, researchers, scholars and those who are engaged in supervised study and training.

The ISS is a copyrighted commercial assessment scale and may not be copied, reproduced, altered, or translated into other languages. The scale may not be administered

[1] Walter W. Hudson, 1934–1999.

[2] Address correspondence to WALMYR Publishing Co., P.O. Box 12217, Tallahassee, FL 32317-2217; e-mail: walmyr@walmyr.com

online nor placed on a website for others to use. It may be purchased in tear-off pads of 50 copies each for $22.50 at www.walmyr.com.

References

Hudson, W. W., Harrison, D. F., & Crosscup, P. C. (1981). A short-form scale to measure sexual discord in dyadic relationships. *The Journal of Sex Research, 17*, 157–174.

Murphy, G. J. (1978). *The family in later life: A cross-ethnic study in marital and sexual satisfaction.* Unpublished doctoral dissertation, Tulane University, New Orleans.

Murphy, G. J., Hudson, W. W., & Cheung, P. P. L. (1980). Marital and sexual discord among older couples. *Social Work Research & Abstracts, 161*, 11–16.

Nurius, P. S., & Hudson, W. W. (1993), *Human services practice, evaluation & computers.* Pacific Grove, CA: Brooks/Cole Publishing.

Exhibit

Index of Sexual Satisfaction (ISS)

Name: _____   Today's Date: _____

This questionnaire is designed to measure the degree of satisfaction you have in the sexual relationship with your partner. It is not a test, so there are no right or wrong answers. Answer each item as carefully and as accurately as you can by placing a number beside each one as follows.

1 = None of the time
2 = Very rarely
3 = A little of the time
4 = Some of the time
5 = A good part of the time
6 = Most of the time
7 = All of the time

1. _____ I feel that my partner enjoys our sex life.
2. _____ Our sex life is very exciting.
3. _____ Sex is fun for my partner and me.
4. _____ Sex with my partner has become a chore for me.
5. _____ I feel that our sex is dirty and disgusting.
6. _____ Our sex life is monotonous.
7. _____ When we have sex it is too rushed and hurriedly completed.
8. _____ I feel that my sex life is lacking in quality.
9. _____ My partner is sexually very exciting.
10. _____ I enjoy the sex techniques that my partner likes or uses.
11. _____ I feel that my partner wants too much sex from me.
12. _____ I think that our sex is wonderful.
13. _____ My partner dwells on sex too much.
14. _____ I try to avoid sexual contact with my partner.
15. _____ My partner is too rough or brutal when we have sex.
16. _____ My partner is wonderful sex mate.
17. _____ I feel that sex is a normal function of our relationship.
18. _____ My partner does not want sex when I do.
19. _____ I feel that our sex life really adds a lot to our relationship.
20. _____ My partner seems to avoid sexual contact with me.
21. _____ It is easy for me to get sexually excited by my partner.
22. _____ I feel that my partner is sexually pleased with me.
23. _____ My partner is very sensitive to my sexual needs and desires.
24. _____ My partner does not satisfy me sexually.
25. _____ I feel that my sex life is boring.

Note. 1, 2, 3, 9, 10, 12, 16, 17, 19, 21, 22, and 23 are reverse scored.

Interpersonal Exchange Model of Sexual Satisfaction Questionnaire

KELLI-AN LAWRANCE, *Brock University*
E. SANDRA BYERS,[1] *University of New Brunswick*
JACQUELINE N. COHEN, *Correctional Service of Canada*

The Interpersonal Exchange Model of Sexual Satisfaction (IEMSS) Questionnaire assesses the components of the IEMSS, a conceptual framework for understanding sexual satisfaction within relationships. It addresses a number of methodological limitations associated with previous research on sexual satisfaction, namely use of single-item measures with unknown reliability and validity, inclusion in multi-item scales of items that are used as predictors of sexual satisfaction (e.g., sexual frequency), and failure to validate measures for sexual-minority individuals.

The IEMSS proposes that sexual satisfaction is influenced by (a) the balance of sexual rewards and sexual costs in the relationship, (b) how these rewards and costs compare to the expected levels of rewards and costs, (c) the perceived equality of rewards and costs between partners, and (d) the nonsexual aspects of the relationship (Lawrance & Byers, 1995). Sexual rewards are exchanges that people experience as pleasurable and gratifying; sexual costs are exchanges that demand effort or cause pain, anxiety, or other negative affect. Because sexual satisfaction is a function of the history of sexual exchanges, repeated assessments of these components provides a better indication of sexual satisfaction than does a single assessment (Byers & MacNeil, 2006; Lawrance & Byers 1995).

Description and Scoring

The IEMSS Questionnaire comprises three self-report measures that assess the components of the model as well as a checklist of sexual rewards and costs. The Global Measure of Sexual Satisfaction (GMSEX) assesses overall sexual satisfaction. Respondents rate their sex life on five 7-point dimensions: *Good-Bad, Pleasant-Unpleasant, Positive-Negative, Satisfying-Unsatisfying, Valuable-Worthless*. Ratings are summed such that possible scores range from 5 to 35, with higher scores indicating greater sexual satisfaction. The Global Measure of Relationship Satisfaction (GMREL) is identical to the GMSEX except that respondents rate their overall relationship satisfaction. Higher summed scores indicate greater relationship satisfaction. The Exchanges Questionnaire assesses respondents' levels of sexual rewards and costs. Using 9-point scales, respondents indicate (a) their level of rewards, from *Not at all Rewarding* to *Extremely Rewarding*, (b) how their level

of rewards compares to the level of rewards they expected to receive, from *Much Less Rewarding in Comparison* to *Much More Rewarding in Comparison*, and (c) how their level of rewards compares with the level of rewards their partner receives, from *My Rewards Are Much Higher* to *My Partner's Rewards Are Much Higher*. Parallel items are used to assess respondents' level of sexual costs, relative level of sexual costs, and perceived equality of sexual costs. The perceived equality items are coded such that the midpoint, which represents perfect equality, is assigned a score of 4 and the endpoints are assigned scores of 0. Thus higher scores represent greater equality between partners. Scores on the two equality scales (EQ_{REW} and EQ_{CST}) consitute one of the components of the IEMSS. The two other components ($REW - CST$ and $CL_{REW} - CL_{CST}$) are calculated by subtracting the cost score from the reward score so that the possible range of scores is -8 to 8.

The 58-item Rewards/Costs Checklist (RCC) was developed based on open-ended questions about the sexual rewards and costs experienced by university students in mixed-sex relationships (Lawrance & Byers, 1992) and revised to include the sexual rewards and costs identified by lesbians and gay men (Cohen, Byers, & Walsh, 2008). Respondents are presented with the checklist twice (in counterbalanced order). They indicate whether each item is a reward in their sexual relationship and whether each item is a cost in their sexual relationship. The total number of sexual rewards and costs are determined by summing the number of rewards and costs endorsed. Responses to individual items indicate the types of rewards and costs experienced.

Response Mode and Timing

For each item, respondents mark a response on a Likert-type scale or checklist. Together, the GMSEX, GMREL, and Exchanges Questionnaire take 10 minutes to complete. The RCC takes another 10 minutes to complete.

Reliability

Studies using married or cohabiting individuals in mixed-sex relationships, married individuals in China, and sexual-minority women indicate that the GMSEX and GMREL

[1]Address correspondence to E. Sandra Byers, Department of Psychology, University of New Brunswick, Bag Service #45444, Fredericton, New Brunswick, Canada E3B 6E4; e-mail: byers@unb.ca

have high internal consistency, ranging from .90 to .96 for the GMSEX and from .91 to .96 for GMREL (Cohen, 2008; Lawrance & Byers, 1992, 1995; Peck, Shaffer, & Williamson, 2004; Renaud, Byers, & Pan, 1997). Test-retest reliabilities also are high: .84 at 2 weeks, .78 at 3 months, and .73 at 18 months for GMSEX, and .81 at 2 weeks, .70 at 3 months, and .61 at 18 months for GMREL (Byers & MacNeil, 2006; Lawrance & Byers, 1995). As anticipated, for individuals in long-term relationships, test-retest reliabilities are moderate for REW, CST, CL_{REW}, CL_{CST}, REW − CST, and CL_{REW} − CL_{CST}, ranging from .43 to .67 at 3 months and from .25 to .56 at 18 months (Byers & MacNeil, 2006; Lawrance & Byers, 1995).

Validity

Evidence for the validity of the IEMSS Questionnaire is based on a sample of university students (Lawrance & Byers, 1992). Construct validity for GMSEX was supported by a significant correlation of −.65 ($p < .001$) with scores on the Index of Sexual Satisfaction (ISS; Hudson, Harrison, & Crosscup, 1981). For GMREL, construct validity was supported by a significant correlation with the Dyadic Adjustment Scale (Spanier, 1976; $r = .69, p < .001$). Further, a higher level of rewards was negatively correlated with the ISS ($r = −.66, p < .001$) as well as a single-item measure of sexual satisfaction ($r = .64, p < .001$). The level of costs was significantly correlated with the ISS ($r = .30, p < .01$) and a single-item measure of sexual satisfaction ($r = .70, p < .001$); however, it was not significantly correlated with a single-item measure of sexual satisfaction ($r = −.15$) Recent researchers have found that higher scores on the GMSEX and/or GMREL are associated with each other as well as with multiple indicators of sexual and relationship functioning, including sexual communication, sexual esteem, sexual cognitions, sexual desire, sexual frequency, and communality (Cohen, 2008; MacNeil & Byers, 2009; Peck et al., 2004; Renaud & Byers, 2001). Finally, the items on the Exchanges Questionnaire and the components of the model are all significantly and uniquely correlated with GMSEX, and multiple assessments enhance the prediction of sexual satisfaction, providing strong support for the validity of the IEMSS (Byers & MacNeil, 2006; Lawrance & Byers, 1995). The IEMSS is tested by entering GMREL in the first step of a hierarchical regression analysis and the four exchange components in the second step.

References

Byers, E. S., & MacNeil, S. (2006). Further validation of the Interpersonal Exchange Model of Sexual Satisfaction. *Journal of Sex and Marital Therapy, 32,* 53–69.

Cohen, J. N. (2008). *Minority stress, resilience, and sexual functioning in sexual-minority women.* Unpublished doctoral dissertation, University of New Brunswick.

Cohen, J. N., Byers, E. S., & Walsh, L. P. (2008). Factors influencing the sexual relationships of lesbians and gay men. *International Journal of Sexual Health, 20,* 162–246.

Hudson, W., Harrison, D., & Crosscup, P. (1981). A short-form scale to measure sexual discord in dyadic relationships. *The Journal of Sex Research, 17,* 157–174.

Lawrance, K., & Byers, E. S. (1992). Development of the Interpersonal Exchange Model of Sexual Satisfaction in long-term relationships. *Canadian Journal of Human Sexuality, 1,* 123–128.

Lawrance, K., & Byers, E. S. (1995). Sexual satisfaction in long-term heterosexual relationships: The Interpersonal Exchange Model of Sexual Satisfaction. *Personal Relationships, 2,* 267–285.

MacNeil, S., & Byers, E. S. (2009). Role of sexual self-disclosure in the sexual satisfaction of long-term heterosexual couples. *The Journal of Sex Research, 46,* 1–12.

Peck, S. R., Shaffer, D. R., & Williamson, G. M. (2004). Sexual satisfaction and relationship satisfaction in dating couples: The contributions of relationship communality and favorability of sexual exchanges. *Journal of Psychology and Human Sexuality, 16,* 17–37.

Renaud, C., Byers, E. S., & Pan, S. (1997). Sexual and relationship satisfaction in mainland China. *The Journal of Sex Research, 34,* 339–410.

Renaud, C. A., & Byers, E. S. (2001). Positive and negative sexual cognitions: Subjective experience and relationships to sexual adjustment. *The Journal of Sex Research, 38,* 252–262.

Spanier, G. (1976). Measuring dyadic adjustment: New scales for assessing the quality of marriage and similar dyads. *Journal of Marriage and the Family, 38,* 15–28.

Exhibit

Interpersonal Exchange Model of Sexual Satisfaction Questionnaire

GMSEX

Overall, how would you describe your sexual relationship with your partner?

1.

   Very Bad   ☐   ☐   ☐   ☐   ☐   ☐ Very Good
        ☐

2.

   Very Unpleasant   ☐   ☐   ☐   ☐   ☐ Very Pleasant
        ☐   ☐

3.

Very Negative ☐ ☐ ☐ ☐ ☐ ☐ Very Positive
☐ ☐

4.

Very Unsatisfying ☐ ☐ ☐ ☐ ☐ ☐ Very Satisfying
☐ ☐

5.

Worthless ☐ ☐ ☐ ☐ ☐ ☐ Very Valuable
☐ ☐

GMREL

In general, how would you describe your *overall* relationship with your partner?

1.

Very Bad ☐ ☐ ☐ ☐ ☐ ☐ Very Good
☐ ☐

2.

Very Unpleasant ☐ ☐ ☐ ☐ ☐ ☐ Very Pleasant
☐ ☐

3.

Very Negative ☐ ☐ ☐ ☐ ☐ ☐ Very Positive
☐ ☐

4.

Very Unsatisfying ☐ ☐ ☐ ☐ ☐ ☐ Very Satisfying
☐ ☐

5.

Worthless ☐ ☐ ☐ ☐ ☐ ☐ Very Valuable
☐ ☐

Exchanges Questionnaire

When people think about their sexual relationship with their partner, most can think of both rewards and costs about their sexual relationship. Rewards are things that are positive or pleasing: things they like about their sexual relationship. Costs are things that are negative or displeasing: things they don't like about their sexual relationship.

1. Think about the *rewards* that you have received in *your sexual relationship with your partner* within the past three months. How rewarding is your sexual relationship with your partner?

☐ ☐ ☐ ☐ ☐ ☐ ☐
Not at all Rewarding   Extremely Rewarding

2. Most people have a general *expectation* about *how rewarding* their sexual relationship "should be." Compared to this general expectation, they may feel that their sexual relationship is more rewarding, less rewarding, or as rewarding as it "should be."
Based on your own expectation about how rewarding your sexual relationship with your partner "should be," how does your level of rewards compare to that expectation?

☐ ☐ ☐ ☐ ☐ ☐ ☐

Much Less
Rewarding in
Comparison

Much More
Rewarding in
Comparison

3. How does the level of *rewards* that you get from your sexual relationship with your partner compare to the level of rewards that your partner gets from the relationship?

☐ ☐ ☐ ☐ ☐ ☐ ☐

My Rewards
Are Much
Higher

Partner's
Rewards Are
Much Higher

4. Think about the costs that you have incurred in *your sexual relationship with your partner* within the past three months. How costly is your sexual relationship with your partner?

☐ ☐ ☐ ☐ ☐ ☐ ☐

Not at all
Costly

Extremely
Costly

5. Most people have a general *expectation* about *how costly* their sexual relationship "should be." Compared to this general expectation, they may feel that their sexual relationship is more costly, less costly, or as costly as it "should be." Based on your own expectation about how costly your sexual relationship with your partner "should be," how does your level of costs compare to that expectation?

☐ ☐ ☐ ☐ ☐ ☐ ☐

Much Less
Costly in
Comparison

Much More
Costly in
Comparison

6. How does the level of *costs* that you incur in your sexual relationship with your partner compare to the level of costs that your partner gets from the relationship?

☐ ☐ ☐ ☐ ☐ ☐ ☐

My Costs
Are Much
Higher

Partner's
Costs Are
Much Higher

Rewards/Costs Checklist (RCC)

Note to researcher: The presentation order of the Rewards Checklist and the Costs Checklist is counterbalanced across participants. The items are identical in both Checklists. The response options for the Rewards Checklist are **Reward** and **Not a Reward**. The response options for the Costs Checklist are **Cost** and **Not a Cost**.

Instructions. We will be asking you some more questions about your sexual relationship with your partner. Before answering them, it is important that you carefully read the following information.

When people think about their sexual relationship with their partner, most can give concrete examples of positive/pleasing things they like about their sexual relationship. These are **rewards**. Most people can also give concrete examples of negative/displeasing things they don't like about their sexual relationship. These are **costs**.

For example, take *oral sex*.

Oral sex would be a **reward** if you feel that you engage in this sexual activity "just the right amount" and you enjoy it.

Oral sex would be a **cost** if you would like to engage in oral sex more often or less often than you do, or you do not enjoy it.

You will be asked to complete the same list twice. One time you will be asked to indicate whether each item in this list is generally a **reward** in your sexual relationship with your partner or **not a reward**. The other time you will be asked to indicate whether each item is a **cost** in your sexual relationship with your partner or **not a cost**.

Note that things can be both rewards and costs. For example, *oral sex* would be both a reward and a cost if you enjoy oral sex but want it more or less frequently. Further, some items may be neither rewards nor costs in your sexual relationship.

Rewards Checklist

This is a list of possible rewards and costs in your sexual relationship. Please indicate whether each item in this list is generally a ***reward*** in your sexual relationship with your partner or ***not a reward***.

In brief, things that are positive, pleasing, or "just right" are rewards.

1. Level of affection you and your partner express during sexual activities
2. Degree of emotional intimacy (feeling close, sharing feelings)
3. Extent to which you and your partner communicate about sex
4. Variety in sexual activities, locations, times
5. Extent to which you and your partner use sex toys
6. Sexual activities you and your partner engage in to arouse each other
7. How often you experience orgasm (climax)
8. How often your partner experiences orgasm (climax)
9. Extent to which you and your partner engage in intimate activities (e.g., talking, cuddling) after sex
10. Frequency of sexual activities
11. How much privacy you and your partner have for sex
12. Oral sex: extent to which your partner stimulates you
13. Oral sex: extent to which you stimulate your partner
14. Physical sensations from touching, caressing, hugging
15. Feelings of physical discomfort or pain during/after sex
16. How much fun you and your partner experience during sexual interactions
17. Who initiates sexual activities
18. Extent to which you feel stressed/relaxed during sexual activities
19. Extent to which you and your partner express enjoyment about your sexual interactions
20. Extent to which you and your partner communicate your sexual likes and dislikes to each other
21. Ability/inability to conceive a child
22. Extent to which you and your partner engage in role-playing or act out fantasies
23. How you feel about yourself during/after engaging in sexual activities with your partner
24. Extent to which your partner shows consideration for your wants/needs/feelings
25. How your partner treats you (verbally and physically) when you have sex
26. Having sex when you're not in the mood
27. Having sex when your partner is not in the mood
28. Extent to which you let your guard down with your partner
29. Extent to which your partner lets their guard down with you
30. Method of protection (from sexually transmitted infections and/or pregnancy) used by you and your partner
31. Extent to which you and your partner discuss and use protection (from sexually transmitted diseases and/or pregnancy)
32. How comfortable you and your partner are with each other
33. Extent to which/way in which your partner influences you to engage in sexual activity
34. Extent to which you and your partner argue after engaging in sexual activity
35. Extent to which you and your partner are/are not sexually exclusive (i.e., have sex only with each other)
36. How much time you and your partner spend engaging in sexual activities
37. How easy it is for you to have an orgasm (climax)
38. How easy it is for your partner to have an orgasm (climax)
39. Extent to which your sexual relationship with your partner reflects or breaks down stereotypical gender roles (the way women and men are expected to behave sexually)
40. How your partner responds to your initiation of sexual activity
41. Being naked in front of your partner
42. Your partner being naked in front of you
43. Extent to which your partner talks to other people about your sex life
44. Extent to which you and your partner read/watch sexually explicit material (e.g., erotic stories, pornographic videos)
45. Pleasing/trying to please your partner sexually
46. Extent to which sexual interactions with your partner make you feel secure in the relationship
47. Extent to which you get sexually aroused

48. Amount of spontaneity in your sex life
49. Extent of control you feel during/after sexual activity
50. Extent to which you engage in sexual activities that you dislike but your partner enjoys
51. Extent to which you engage in sexual activities that you enjoy but your partner dislikes
52. Worry that you or your partner will get a sexually transmitted infection from each other
53. How confident you feel in terms of your ability to please your partner sexually
54. Extent to which you and your partner engage in anal sex/anal play
55. Your partner's ability to please you sexually
56. Extent to which you think your partner is physically attracted to/sexually desires you
57. Extent to which you are physically attracted to/sexually desire your partner
58. Extent to which you and your partner are sexually compatible (i.e., well matched in terms of your sexual likes/dislikes)

Costs Checklist

This is a list of possible rewards and costs in your sexual relationship. Please indicate whether each item in this list is a **cost** in your sexual relationship with your partner or **not a cost**.

In brief, things that are negative, displeasing, or "too little or too much" are costs.

Note to researcher: The same 58 checklist items are repeated here.

The New Sexual Satisfaction Scale and Its Short Form

ALEKSANDAR ŠTULHOFER[1] **AND VESNA BUŠKO,** *University of Zagreb*
PAMELA BROUILLARD, *Texas A&M University-Corpus Christi*

The New Sexual Satisfaction Scale (NSSS; $k = 20$) was developed as a universal tool for assessing sexual satisfaction and tested in two cultures (Croatia and the United States; Štulhofer, Buško, & Brouillard, in press). Unlike the majority of similar measures, the NSSS is not gender, sexual orientation, or relationship status specific. Its conceptual framework is derived from the sex counseling and psychotherapy literature and includes the following five dimensions: (a) sexual sensations, (b) sexual presence/awareness, (c) sexual exchange, (d) emotional connection/closeness, and (e) sexual activity. In order to facilitate the use of the NSSS in clinical and nonclinical studies, a short version of the scale (NSSS-S; $k = 12$) was developed. The NSSS-S demonstrates reliability and validity comparable to the full-scale instrument.

Description

The NSSS was created within a research project more broadly focused on the impact of pornography on young people's sexual socialization (Štulhofer, Buško, & Landripet, 2010; Štulhofer et al., 2007). Scale construction and validation were carried out using seven independent samples with over 2,000 participants, aged 18–55 years, in Croatia and the U.S. Of the seven, three were college student samples, two were community samples, one was a clinical sample (sex therapy clients), and the final one was a sample of nonheterosexual Croatian men and women. In all but two samples, online surveying tools were used to collect data.

Principal component analysis was carried out on an initial pool of 35 Likert items generated by the proposed five-dimensional conceptual framework. It extracted six components with eigenvalues > 1, which were than rotated to oblique position using the oblimin method. Closer inspection of this structure suggested that a forced two-factor solution would be the best strategy to pursue. The obtained two-factor solution proved stable in both student and adult Croatian and the U.S. samples, among female and male participants, as well as in the nonheterosexual Croatian sample. The first factor was primarily focused on personal experiences and sensations, whereas the second

[1]Address correspondence to Aleksandar Štulhofer, Sexology Unit, Department of Sociology, Faculty of Humanities and Social Sciences, I. Lučića 3, 10000 Zagreb, Croatia; e-mail: astulhof@ffzg.hr

factor reflected the participant's perception of the partner's reactions and sexual activity in general. Taking into account the strong association between the two domains (factor correlations ranged from .52 to .61), our findings pointed to a relatively high homogeneity of the sexual satisfaction construct.

The selection of items per component was performed according to standard criteria of simple structure, factor loadings, and content overlap (redundancy). Respecting both statistical and content-related characteristics, 20 items (10 per component) were retained from the initial set. The two following subscales were created: the Ego-Centered subscale, which measures sexual satisfaction generated by personal experiences/sensations, and the Partner/Sexual Activity-Centered subscale, which measures sexual satisfaction derived from an individual's perception of the partner's sexual behaviors and reactions, and the diversity and/or frequency of sexual activities. The two subscales represent the New Sexual Satisfaction Scale (NSSS).

The Short Version of the NSSS (NSSS-S) was created following a somewhat different procedure. The 20 NSSS items were first divided into five clusters representing the initial conceptual dimensions, and then two to three items per cluster were selected (depending on cluster size) according to their item-total correlation in the NSSS subscales. Additional principal component analysis of the 12 NSSS-S items showed that all items loaded highly ($> .59$ in student, and $> .58$ in community samples) on a single factor with eigenvalue > 1.

In all samples, the NSSS scores ranged between 20 and 100, and the NSSS-S scores between 12 and 50, covering the full range. The NSSS, its subscales, and the NSSS-S scores displayed a characteristic asymmetric distribution with the mean scores leaning toward more satisfaction. No differences in sexual satisfaction scores between students and adults were found. However, Croatian participants consistently displayed higher sexual satisfaction than the U.S. participants.

Response Mode and Timing

For each item, respondents are asked to circle the number that best reflects their satisfaction with a particular aspect of their sex life in the preceding six months ("Thinking about your sex life during the last six months, please rate your satisfaction with the following aspects"). Respondents rate their level of satisfaction using the following 5-point Likert-type scale: 1 = *Not at all Satisfied*, 2 = *A Little Satisfied*, 3 = *Moderately Satisfied*, 4 = *Very Satisfied*, 5 = *Extremely Satisfied*. Most respondents complete the full scale within 5 minutes.

Scoring

The Ego-Centered subscale (Items 1–10), Partner and Activity-Centered subscale (Items 11–20), NSSS (Items 1–20), and NSSS-S (Items 2–3, 5–6, 8, 10–12,

14, 17, 19–20) are computed by summing the related items.

Reliability

Internal consistency in two student samples ($N_{CRO} = 544$, M age = 21.3; $N_{US} = 356$, M age = 20.4), two community samples ($N_{CRO} = 729$, M age = 34.1; $N_{US} = 212$, M age = 40.7), and a sample of Croatian nonheterosexual men and women ($N = 360$, M age = 26.1) was satisfactory for the full scale ($\alpha = .94–.96$), both subscales ($\alpha = .91–.93$ and .90–.94, respectively), and the short version ($\alpha = .90–.93$). No substantial differences related to either gender or sexual orientation were observed. Additional analysis performed on the Croatian student sample dataset showed that the NSSS and NSSS-S internal consistency coefficients were similar in the group of participants currently in a relationship and those who were single ($\alpha = .87–.96$). This remained the case even after separate analyses were done for men and women.

Test-retest reliability of the NSSS and NSSS-S was shown to be satisfactory in a sample of Croatian students ($N = 219$) over a 1-month period. Stability coefficients ranged from .72 to .84, with somewhat stronger associations reported among women.

Validity

Both the NSSS and the NSSS-S were shown to be significantly associated with a global measure of life satisfaction, in the expected direction. Negative correlations with the shortened Sexual Boredom Scale (Watt & Ewing, 1996) scores and positive correlations with relationship intimacy, partner communication about sex, and relationship status were also found to be significant among men and women in both the Croatian and the U.S. student samples. In support of convergent validity, associations between a global (single-item) measure of sexual satisfaction and the NSSS/NSSS-S scores were significant and strong in both samples ($r = .44–.67$). Correlation coefficients were systematically lower in the U.S. sample.

There were significant differences in the average NSSS and NSSS-S scores between participants in the clinical sample (sex therapy clients; $N = 54$; M age = 34.6) and nonclinical community sample ($N = 729$; M age = 34.1), $t_{NSSS} = -8.64$, $df = 709$, $p < .001$; $t_{NSSS-S} = -8.74$, $df = 735$, $p < .001$. Participants with sexual difficulties systematically reported lower sexual satisfaction. Cohen's d values (ranging from -1.07 to -1.39) suggested that the observed differences are large in size. For example, the overlap between the full NSSS scores in the clinical and nonclinical sample was 32%.

Discriminant analysis was carried out to predict membership in the clinical vs. nonclinical community sample. The inclusion criterion in the first group was the persistent or recurrent distressful presence of one or more sexual disorders related to sexual desire, sexual arousal, orgasm, or sexual pain according to the *Diagnostic and Statistical*

Manual of Mental Disorders (*DSM–IV-TR*) criteria (American Psychiatric Association, 2000). With the probability of group membership set to equal, the analysis correctly classified a total of 80.3% of cases. In the clinical group, the procedure correctly classified 64.8% of cases. Using the NSSS-S as independent variable resulted in only slightly lower percentages of correct classifications (79.6% and 63%, respectively).

References

American Psychiatric Association. (2000). *Diagnostic and statistical manual of mental disorders* (text rev.). Washington, DC: Author.

Štulhofer, A., Buško, V., & Brouillard, P. (in press). Development and bicultural validation of the New Sexual Satisfaction Scale. *The Journal of Sex Research.*

Štulhofer, A., Buško, V., & Landripet, I. (2010). Pornography, sexual socialization, and satisfaction among young men. *Archives of Sexual Behavior, 39,* 168–178.

Štulhofer, A., Landripet, I., Momčilović, A., Matko, V., Kladarić, P. G., & Buško, V. (2007). Pornography and sexual satisfaction in young women and men. In S. V. Knudsen, L. Lofgren-Martenson, & S. A. Mansson (Eds.), *Generation P? Youth, gender and pornography* (pp. 66–84). Copenhagen: Danish University Press.

Watt, J. D., & Ewing, J. E. (1996). Toward the development and validation of a measure of sexual boredom. *The Journal of Sex Research, 33,* 57–66.

Exhibit

The New Sexual Satisfaction Scale (NSSS)

	Subscale A (Ego-Focused)	Subscale B (Partner and Activity-Focused)	Short Version (NSSS-S)
Thinking about your sex life during the last six months, please rate your satisfaction with the following aspects:[a]			
1. The intensity of my sexual arousal	X		
2. The quality of my orgasms	X		X
3. My "letting go" and surrender to sexual pleasure during sex	X		X
4. My focus/concentration during sexual activity	X		
5. The way I sexually react to my partner	X		X
6. My body's sexual functioning	X		X
7. My emotional opening up in sex	X		
8. My mood after sexual activity	X		X
9. The frequency of my orgasms	X		
10. The pleasure I provide to my partner	X		X
11. The balance between what I give and receive in sex		X	X
12. My partner's emotional opening up during sex		X	X
13. My partner's initiation of sexual activity		X	
14. My partner's ability to orgasm		X	X
15. My partner's surrender to sexual pleasure ("letting go")		X	
16. The way my partner takes care of my sexual needs		X	
17. My partner's sexual creativity		X	X
18. My partner's sexual availability		X	
19. The variety of my sexual activities		X	X
20. The frequency of my sexual activity		X	X

[a]Responses are anchored on the following scale: 1 = *Not at all Satisfied*, 2 = *A Little Satisfied*, 3 = *Moderately Satisfied*, 4 = *Very Satisfied*, 5 = *Extremely Satisfied.*

The Meaning of My Sexual Self

ANNIE LAURA COTTEN,[1] *Central Connecticut State University*

Whereas measures have been developed for assessing sexual self-schemas as cognitive representations of one's self view (Andersen & Cyranowski, 1994; Andersen, Cyranowski, & Espindle, 1999) and for associations between sexual self-concept and self-efficacy (Rostosky, Dekhtyar, Cupp, & Anderman, 2008), a measure for the meaning of the sexual self has been lacking. Using the technique of Osgood, Suci, and Tannenbaum (1957) for the measurement of meaning, bipolar adjectives were determined for measuring "my sexual self."

Description

The scale's development was a continuation from previous dissertation research that included 125 college students who responded to 18 bipolar choices, nine of which determined the three dimensions of meanings: evaluation, potency, and activity. Students were also given the Bem Sex-Role Inventory (BSRI; Bem, 1974) for comparison. The hypothesis for that research was significantly confirmed; the more androgynous, the more positive were the responses on the meaning of "my sexual self" (Cotten-Huston, 1981). Participants rated the bipolar adjectives on a scale from 1 (*Most Positive*) to 7 (*Least Positive*).

Bipolar adjectives were derived from eight business and psychology class responses to the question of what bipolar adjective pairs respondents would use to evaluate each of the three dimensions. For sexual evaluation meanings, most frequent responses were good-bad, valuable-worthless, and honest-dishonest. Most frequent adjective pairs for sexual activity meanings were assertive-nonassertive, involved-uninvolved, and flexible-rigid. For most frequent meanings of sexual-self potency, the most frequent adjective pairs were together-alone, loved-unloved, and strong-weak. Within each dimension, other suggested adjective pairs were included for a total of 18 bipolar choices that were rotated from left to right, so that on every other adjective pair the order of numbers was reversed to avoid rater bias. The design included demographic variables for age, gender, lifestyle, religiosity, and sexual experience, which were included on a separate page.

Research was conducted with a larger sample to examine in particular the construct of the semantic measure and,

again, any associations with masculinity and femininity trait responses from the BSRI (Bem, 1974). Androgyny and undifferentiated scores were not computed; however, the masculinity and femininity traits were included along with demographic variables. There were 294 participants, ages 17–87, divided into three age groups: 17–25; 26–55; 56–87. Participants in the age group 17–55 were undergraduates and graduate students at Central Connecticut State University. Those over age 55 were Elderhostelers enrolled in programs at the University from diverse geographical regions of the country. The measure was suitable for all adult-age groups.

Response Mode and Timing

Participants included those who wished to assist in research about the meaning of "my sexual self." Instructions included a one-sentence request to circle the number that came closest to how they felt about their sexual selves. Most participants completed the measure in 30 minutes.

Other Information

Statistical collaboration was provided by the Biostatistics Laboratory, University of North Carolina, Chapel Hill.

References

Andersen, B. L., & Cyranowski, J. M. (1994). Women's sexual self-schema. *Journal of Personality and Social Psychology, 67,* 1079–1100.

Andersen, B. L., Cyranowski, J. M., & Espindle, D. (1999). Men's sexual self-schema. *Journal of Personality and Social Psychology, 76,* 645–661.

Bem, S. (1974). The measurement of psychological androgyny. *Journal of Consulting and Clinical Psychology, 42,* 155–162.

Cotten-Huston, A. L. (1981). *Androgyny and the sexual self.* Unpublished doctoral dissertation, The Union Institute and University, Cincinnati, OH.

Osgood, C. E., Suci, G. J., & Tannenbaum, P. H. (1957). *The measurement of meaning.* Chicago: University of Illinois Press.

Rostosky, S. S., Dekhtyar, O., Cupp, P. K., & Anderman, E. M. (2008). Sexual self-concept and sexual self-efficacy in adolescents: A possible clue to promoting sexual health? *The Journal of Sex Research, 45,* 277–286.

[1]Address correspondence to Annie Laura Cotten, 5 Melstone Turn, Durham, NC 27707; e-mail: anniecotten@nc.rr.com

Exhibit

The Meaning of My Sexual Self

Please circle the number which comes closest to the way you feel about your sexual self.

Good	1	2	3	4	5	6	7	Bad
Sad	7	6	5	4	3	2	1	Happy
Beautiful	1	2	3	4	5	6	7	Ugly
Dirty	7	6	5	4	3	2	1	Clean
Honest	1	2	3	4	5	6	7	Dishonest
Worthless	7	6	5	4	3	2	1	Valuable
Pleasant	1	2	3	4	5	6	7	Unpleasant
Unfair	7	6	5	4	3	2	1	Fair
Healthy	1	2	3	4	5	6	7	Sick
Rigid	7	6	5	4	3	2	1	Flexible
Assertive	1	2	3	4	5	6	7	Submissive
Tense	7	6	5	4	3	2	1	Relaxed
Together	1	2	3	4	5	6	7	Fragmented
Unloved	7	6	5	4	3	2	1	Loved
Involved	1	2	3	4	5	6	7	Uninvolved
Inactive	7	6	5	4	3	2	1	Active
Strong	1	2	3	4	5	6	7	Weak
Subjective	7	6	5	4	3	2	1	Objective

Comments you wish to make about your sexual self:

Sexual Self-Concept Inventory

LUCIA F. O'SULLIVAN,[1] *University of New Brunswick*
HEINO F. L. MEYER-BAHLBURG, *New York State Psychiatric Institute*
IAN MCKEAGUE, *Columbia University*

This measure was designed to assess the gender-specific sexual self-concepts of early adolescent girls based on extensive formative work with ethnically diverse samples. Respondents complete 34 items assessing three dimensions of sexual self-concepts. Details regarding this measure can be found in O'Sullivan, Meyer-Bahlburg, & McKeague (2006).

Description

The Sexual Self-Concept Inventory (SSCI) is a 34-item instrument comprising three scales that are shown to be distinct and reliable dimensions of early adolescent girls' sexual self-concepts. These scales assess Sexual Arousability, Sexual Agency, and Negative Sexual Affect. Sexual Arousability reflects sexual responsiveness, whereas Sexual Agency incorporates items relating to sexual curiosity. Negative Sexual Affect addresses sexual anxiety as well as some concerns relating to sexual monitoring. The measure was developed following extensive formative work using both qualitative and quantitative methods with samples of ethnically diverse, urban, early adolescent girls (12–14 years of age). The formative data were used to generate an item pool using the exact wording from transcripts of girls' interviews and focus groups to help ensure item comprehension and authenticity amongst the target population. Principal components analytic procedures were used to ascertain the instrument's factor structures,

[1]Address correspondence to Lucia F. O'Sullivan, Department of Psychology, 38 Dineen Drive, Keirstead Hall, Rm. 216, University of New Brunswick, Fredericton, New Brunswick, Canada E3B 5A3; e-mail: osulliv@unb.ca

from which the three scales emerged.

Response Mode and Timing

Respondents indicate their degree of agreement with 34 items on a Likert-type scale ranging from 1 (*Strongly Disagree*) to 6 (*Strongly Agree*). The questionnaire takes approximately 4 minutes to complete.

Scoring

Scores for each of the three SSCI scales are computed by summing the respective items: Sexual Arousability (17 items), Sexual Agency (10 items), and Negative Sexual Affect (7 items). There are no filler or reverse-scored items.

Reliability

Coefficient alphas for the three scales were .91 (Sexual Arousability), .76 (Sexual Agency), and .67 (Negative Sexual Affect). These coefficients are considered to be good to very good (DeVellis, 1991). Fifty participants were retested 3 weeks after the first administration of the instrument. The test-retest reliability coefficients for the three scales were also substantial: $r = .68$, $p < .001$ (Sexual Arousability); $r = .69$, $p < .001$ (Sexual Agency); and $r = .67$, $p < .001$ (Negative Sexual Affect). In addition, 162 girls were administered the SSCI on two occasions, 1 year apart, to examine how girls' scores changed over the 1-year period. Test-retest coefficients were $r = .59$, $p < .001$ (Sexual Arousability); $r = .84$, $p < .001$ (Sexual Agency); and $r = .69$, $p < .001$ (Negative Sexual Affect), indicating stability in scores.

Validity

The construct validity of the SSCI was assessed using correlations between the scale scores and sexual self-esteem (Rosenthal, Moore, & Flynn, 1991) and abstinence attitudes (Miller, Norton, Fan, & Christopherson, 1998) using a sample of 180 girls. As expected, Sexual Arousability and Sexual Agency correlated positively with sexual self-esteem ($rs = .37$ and .43, $ps < .001$), whereas Negative Sexual Affect correlated negatively with this scale ($r = -.18$, $p < .05$). Negative Sexual Affect was positively correlated with abstinence attitudes ($r = .43$, $p < .001$), whereas Sexual Arousability and Sexual Agency were negatively correlated with these attitudes ($rs = -.44$ and $-.22$, $p < .001$). As a test of discriminant validity, we assessed correlations of SSCI scale scores with parenting attitudes (Unger, Molina, & Teran, 2000), as girls frequently dissociate sexual experiences from reproduction (O'Sullivan & Meyer-Bahlburg, 2003). That is, scores on measures regarding the value that they place on parenting were expected to be unrelated to girls' views of themselves as sexual people. As predicted, none of the three scales was significantly correlated with parenting attitudes ($ps > .05$). Sexual Arousability, but not Sexual Agency, was positively correlated with scores on a measure of perceived maternal approval of sexual activity ($r = .23$, $p < .01$) (Treboux &

Busch-Rossnagel, 1990), and Negative Sexual Affect was negatively correlated with these ratings ($r = -.20$, $p < .01$). Girls with high Sexual Arousability and Sexual Agency had scores reflecting less disapproval/more approval ($rs = .32$ and .31, $ps < .01$) on a measure of perceived peer approval for sexual intercourse experience (Treboux & Busch-Rossnagel, 1990); Negative Sexual Affect was unrelated. Girls with higher Sexual Arousability and Sexual Agency perceived a greater proportion of their friends to have sexual intercourse experience ($r = .24$, $p < .01$ and $r = .33$, $p < .001$); Negative Sexual Affect was unrelated. Girls' Sexual Arousability and Sexual Agency were positively correlated with future orientation ($rs = .45$ and .21, $p < .01$), whereas Negative Sexual Affect was negatively correlated with this variable ($r = -.26$, $p < .001$).

We also examined correlations between SSCI scores and sexual experience. Given that relatively few girls in this age range report sexual intercourse experience (Paikoff, 1995), we examined associations with intentions to engage in intercourse in the near future, as well as lifetime reports of having had a crush, having had a boyfriend, having been in love, having engaged in kissing, having engaged in breast fondling with a partner, having engaged in genital touching with a partner, having engaged in oral sex, and having engaged in vaginal intercourse. Girls with higher levels of sexual experience tended to have more positive sexual self-concepts (i.e., higher Sexual Arousability and Sexual Agency and lower Negative Sexual Affect). Participation in romantic activities and the range of lower-level sexual activities was positively correlated with Sexual Arousability scores (O'Sullivan et al., 2006). This was also true of Sexual Agency, although the associations were notably less strong, and only significant for participation in kissing and breast fondling. This pattern suggests that Sexual Arousability and Sexual Agency tap overlapping, but somewhat different, constructs. Girls who reported sexual intercourse experience (at least once in the past) tended to report higher Sexual Arousability scores. Girls' reports of breast fondling, touching a penis, oral sex, and/or intercourse tended to be negatively and moderately correlated with scores for Negative Sexual Affect. (Note: Higher levels of sexual experiences were relatively uncommon among girls at these ages).

References

DeVellis, R. F. (1991). *Scale development: Theory and applications.* Newbury Park, CA: Sage.

Miller, B. C., Norton, M. C., Fan, X., & Christopherson, C. R. (1998). Pubertal development, parental communication, and sexual values in relation to adolescent sexual behaviors. *Journal of Early Adolescence, 18,* 27–52.

O'Sullivan, L. F., & Meyer-Bahlburg, H. F. L. (2003). African-American and Latina inner-city girls' reports of romantic and sexual development. *Journal of Social and Personal Relationships, 20,* 221–238.

O'Sullivan, L. F., Meyer-Bahlburg, H. F. L., & McKeague, I. W. (2006). The development of the Sexual Self-Concept Inventory for early adolescent girls. *Psychology of Women Quarterly, 30,* 139–149.

Paikoff, R. L. (1995). Early heterosexual debut: Situations of sexual possibility during the transition to adolescence. *American Journal of Orthopsychiatry, 65,* 389–401.

Rosenthal, D., Moore, S., & Flynn, I. (1991). Adolescent self-efficacy, self-esteem and sexual risk-taking. *Journal of Community and Applied Social Psychology, 1,* 77–88.

Treboux, D., & Busch-Rossnagel, N. A. (1990). Social network influences on adolescent sexual attitudes and behavior. *Journal of Adolescent Research, 5,* 175–189.

Unger, J. B., Molina, G. B., & Teran, L. (2000). Perceived consequences of teenage childbearing among adolescent girls in an urban sample. *Journal of Adolescent Health, 26,* 205–212.

Exhibit

Sexual Self-Concept Inventory

The questions below are about your views about yourself and other people your age. Please read each statement carefully and then rate each statement according to how much you agree with it using a number from 1 (*Strongly Disagree*) to 6 (*Strongly Agree*). An answer is correct to the extent it truly reflects how much you agree with it.

1	2	3	4	5	6
Strongly Disagree					Strongly Agree

(SEXUAL AROUSABILITY)

____ 1. I sometimes think I'd like to try doing the sexual things my friends are doing with their boyfriends.

____ 2. When I kiss a guy, I get hot.

____ 3. I would really want to touch a boyfriend if we were left alone together.

____ 4. I sometimes want to know how different types of sex feel.

____ 5. If I'm going to see a guy I like, I like to dress sexy.

____ 6. If a guy kisses me, I also want him to touch my body.

____ 7. When I flirt with a guy, I like to feel him up.

____ 8. Sometimes I dress sexy to get attention from guys.

____ 9. If I were to kiss a guy, I'd get really turned on.

____ 10. There are things about sex I want to try.

____ 11. If a boy kisses me, my body feels good.

____ 12. I enjoy talking about sex or talking sexy with boys I know really well.

____ 13. If I were kissing and touching a guy, I would get hyped, real excited.

____ 14. I enjoy talking about sex with my girl friends.

____ 15. It's okay to feel up on a guy.

____ 16. I like it when a guy tells me I look good.

____ 17. I think I'm ready to have sex.

(SEXUAL AGENCY)

____ 1. Girls always wonder what sex is going to be like the first time.

____ 2. I sometimes think about who I would want to have sex with.

____ 3. When I decide to have sex with a guy, it will be because I wanted to have sex and not because he really wanted me to have sex with him.

____ 4. Girls sometimes have sex because they're curious and want to see what it's like.

____ 5. Sex is best with a guy you love.

____ 6. I like to let a guy know when I like him.

____ 7. If I have sex, my friends will want to know all about it.

____ 8. If I had sex with a guy, I would be running the risk of being played (taken advantage of).

____ 9. Flirting is fun and I am good at it.

____ 10. If I have sex with a guy, I would worry that I could get my feelings really hurt.

(NEGATIVE SEXUAL AFFECT)

____ 1. If I kiss a guy I don't really know, I'm afraid of what people will think about me.

____ 2. Sex is nasty.

____ 3. Sex isn't fun for girls my age.

____ 4. I would be scared to be really alone with a boyfriend.

____ 5. Some girls have sex just to be accepted or popular.

____ 6. I think I am too young to have sex.

____ 7. If I have sex, my friends will want to know all about it.

Multidimensional Sexual Self-Concept Questionnaire

WILLIAM E. SNELL, JR.,[1] *Southeast Missouri State University*

The Multidimensional Sexual Self-Concept Questionnaire (MSSCQ; Snell, 1995) is an objective self-report instrument designed to measure the following 20 psychological aspects of human sexuality: (1) *sexual anxiety*, defined as the tendency to feel tension, discomfort, and anxiety about the sexual aspects of one's life; (2) *sexual self-efficacy*, defined as the belief that one has the ability to deal effectively with the sexual aspects of oneself; (3) *sexual consciousness*, defined as the tendency to think and reflect about the nature of one's own sexuality; (4) *motivation to avoid risky sex*, defined as the motivation and desire to avoid unhealthy patterns of risky sexual behaviors (e.g., unprotected sexual behavior); (5) *chance/luck sexual control*, defined as the belief that the sexual aspects of one's life are determined by chance and luck considerations; (6) *sexual preoccupation*, defined as the tendency to think about sex to an excessive degree; (7) *sexual assertiveness*, defined as the tendency to be assertive about the sexual aspects of one's life; (8) *sexual optimism*, defined as the expectation that the sexual aspects of one's life will be positive and rewarding in the future; (9) *sexual problem self-blame*, defined as the tendency to blame oneself when the sexual aspects of one's life are unhealthy, negative, or undesirable in nature; (10) *sexual monitoring*, defined as the tendency to be aware of the public impression which one's sexuality makes on others; (11) *sexual motivation*, defined as the motivation and desire to be involved in a sexual relationship; (12) *sexual problem management*, defined as the tendency to believe that one has the capacity/skills to effectively manage and handle any sexual problems that one might develop or encounter; (13) *sexual esteem*, defined as a generalized tendency to positively evaluate one's own capacity to engage in healthy sexual behaviors and to experience one's sexuality in a satisfying and enjoyable way; (14) *sexual satisfaction*, defined as the tendency to be highly satisfied with the sexual aspects of one's life; (15) *power-other sexual control*, defined as the belief that the sexual aspects of one's life are controlled by others who are more powerful and influential than oneself; (16) *sexual self-schemata*, defined as a cognitive framework that organizes and guides the processing of information about the sexual-related aspects of oneself; (17) *fear of sex*, defined as a fear of engaging in sexual relations with another individual; (18) *sexual problem prevention*, defined as the belief that one has the ability to prevent oneself from developing any sexual problems or disorders; (19) *sexual depression*, defined as the experience of feelings of sadness, unhappiness, and depression regarding one's sex life; and (20) *internal sexual control*, defined as the belief that the sexual aspects of one's life are determined by one's own personal control.

The MSSCQ (Snell, 1995) was based on previous work by Snell and Papini (1989), Snell, Fisher, and Schuh (1992), Snell, Fisher, and Miller (1991), and Snell, Fisher, and Walters (1993). Scores on the MSSCQ can be treated as individual difference measures of the 20 sexuality-related constructs measured by this instrument or as dependent variables when examining predictive correlates of these concepts.

Description

The MSSCQ consists of 100 items arranged in a format in which respondents indicate how characteristic of them each statement is. A 5-point Likert-type scale is used to collect data on peoples' responses, with each item scored from 0 to 4: *not at all characteristic of me* (0), *slightly characteristic of me* (1), *somewhat characteristic of me* (2), *moderately characteristic of me* (3), and *very characteristic of me* (4). In order to create subscale scores (discussed below), the items on each subscale are averaged. Higher scores thus correspond to greater amounts of the relevant MSSCQ tendency.

Response Mode and Timing

People respond to the 100 items on the MSSCQ by marking their answers on separate machine-scoreable answer sheets. In most instances, the scale usually requires about 45–60 minutes to complete.

Scoring

After several items are reverse coded (Items 27, 47, 68, 77, 88, and 97, designated with an R), the relevant items on each subscale are then coded so that A = 0; B = 1; C = 2; D = 3; and E = 4. Next, the items on each subscale are averaged, so that higher scores correspond to greater amounts of each tendency. Scores on the 20 subscales can thus range from 0 to 4. The items on the MSSCQ subscales alternate in ascending numerical order for each subscale (e.g., Subscale 1 consists of Items 1, 21, 41, 61, and 81; Subscale 2 consists of Items 2, 22, 42, 62, and 82).

Reliability

The internal consistency of the 20 subscales on the MSSCQ was determined by calculating Cronbach alpha coefficients, using 473 participants (302 females; 170

[1]Address correspondence to William E. Snell, Jr., Department of Psychology, One University Plaza, Southeast Missouri State University, Cape Girardeau, MO 63701; e-mail: wesnell@semo.edu

males; 1 gender unspecified) drawn from lower division psychology courses at a small midwestern university (Snell, 1995). Most of the sample (85%) was between 16 and 25 years of age. Based on five items per subscale, the alphas for all subjects on the 20 subscales were: .84, .85, .78, .72, .88, .94, .84, .78, .84, .84, .89, .84, .88, .91, .85, .87, .85, .85, .85, and .76 (respectively). In brief, the 20 MSSC subscales have more than adequate internal consistency.

Validity

Evidence for the validity of the MSSCQ comes from a research investigation in which Snell (1995) found that among university students, the MSSCQ subscales were related in predictable ways to men's and women's contraceptive use. Among males, a history of reliable, effective contraception was negatively associated with (1) sexual anxiety, (5) chance/luck sexual control, (17) sexual fear, and (19) sexual depression; and positively associated with (2) sexual self-efficacy, (8) sexual optimism, (11) sexual motivation, (13) sexual esteem, (14) sexual satisfaction, and (16) sexual self-schemata. By contrast, among females, long-term effective contraception use was negatively associated with (17) sexual fear, (19) sexual depression, and (20) internal sexual control; and positively associated with (2) sexual self-efficacy, (7) sexual assertiveness, (11) sexual motivation, (14) sexual satisfaction, and (16) sexual self-schemata.

Additional findings indicated that males reported higher levels of (5) chance/luck sexual control, (6) sexual preoccupation, (9) sexual problems self-blame, and (11) motivation to be sexually active than did females. By contrast, females reported greater (4) motivation to avoid risky sexual behavior and (17) fear of sexual relations than did males.

References

Fisher, T. D., & Snell, W. E., Jr. (1995). *Validation of the Multidimensional Sexuality Questionnaire.* Unpublished manuscript, The Ohio University at Mansfield.

Snell, W. E., Jr. (1995, April). *The Extended Multidimensional Sexuality Questionnaire: Measuring psychological tendencies associated with human sexuality.* Paper presented at the annual meeting of the Southwestern Psychological Association, Houston, TX.

Snell, W. E., Jr., Fisher, T. D., & Miller, R. S. (1991). Development of the Sexual Awareness Questionnaire: Components, reliability, and validity. *Annals of Sex Research, 4,* 65–92.

Snell, W. E., Jr., Fisher, T. D., & Schuh, T. (1992). Reliability and validity of the Sexuality Scale: A measure of sexual-esteem, sexual-depression, and sexual-preoccupation. *The Journal of Sex Research, 29,* 261–273.

Snell, W. E., Jr., Fisher, T. D., & Walters, A. S. (1993). The Multidimensional Sexuality Questionnaire: An objective self-report measure of psychological tendencies associated with human sexuality. *Annals of Sex Research, 6,* 27–55.

Snell, W. E., Jr., & Papini, D. R. (1989). The Sexuality Scale: An instrument to measure sexual-esteem, sexual-depression, and sexual-preoccupation. *The Journal of Sex Research, 26,* 256–263.

Exhibit

Multidimensional Sexual Self-Concept Questionnaire

Instructions: The items in this questionnaire refer to people's sexuality. Please read each item carefully and decide to what extent it is characteristic of you. Give each item a rating of how much it applies to you by using the following scale:

    A = *Not at all* characteristic of me.
    B = *Slightly* characteristic of me.
    C = *Somewhat* characteristic of me.
    D = *Moderately* characteristic of me.
    E = *Very* characteristic of me.

Note: Remember to respond to all items, even if you are not completely sure. Your answers will be kept in the strictest confidence. Also, please be honest in responding to these statements.

1. I feel anxious when I think about the sexual aspects of my life.
2. I have the ability to take care of any sexual needs and desires that I may have.
3. I am very aware of my sexual feelings and needs.
4. I am motivated to avoid engaging in "risky" (i.e., unprotected) sexual behavior.
5. The sexual aspects of my life are determined mostly by chance happenings.
6. I think about sex "all the time."
7. I'm very assertive about the sexual aspects of my life.
8. I expect that the sexual aspects of my life will be positive and rewarding in the future.
9. I would be to blame if the sexual aspects of my life were not going very well.
10. I notice how others perceive and react to the sexual aspects of my life.
11. I'm motivated to be sexually active.
12. If I were to experience a sexual problem, I myself would be in control of whether this improved.

13. I derive a sense of self-pride from the way I handle my own sexual needs and desires.
14. I am satisfied with the way my sexual needs are currently being met.
15. My sexual behaviors are determined largely by other more powerful and influential people.
16. Not only would I be a good sexual partner, but it's quite important to me that I be a good sexual partner.
17. I am afraid of becoming sexually involved with another person.
18. If I am careful, then I will be able to prevent myself from having any sexual problems.
19. I am depressed about the sexual aspects of my life.
20. My sexuality is something that I am largely responsible for.
21. I worry about the sexual aspects of my life.
22. I am competent enough to make sure that my sexual needs are fulfilled.
23. I am very aware of my sexual motivations and desires.
24. I am motivated to keep myself from having any "risky" sexual behavior (e.g., exposure to sexual diseases).
25. Most things that affect the sexual aspects of my life happen to me by accident.
26. I think about sex more than anything else.
27. I'm not very direct about voicing my sexual needs and preferences. (R)
28. I believe that in the future the sexual aspects of my life will be healthy and positive.
29. If the sexual aspects of my life were to go wrong, I would be the person to blame.
30. I'm concerned with how others evaluate my own sexual beliefs and behaviors.
31. I'm motivated to devote time and effort to sex.
32. If I were to experience a sexual problem, my own behavior would determine whether I improved.
33. I am proud of the way I deal with and handle my own sexual desires and needs.
34. I am satisfied with the status of my own sexual fulfillment.
35. My sexual behaviors are largely controlled by people other than myself (e.g., my partner, friends, family).
36. Not only would I be a skilled sexual partner, but it's very important to me that I be a skilled sexual partner.
37. I have a fear of sexual relationships.
38. I can pretty much prevent myself from developing sexual problems by taking good care of myself.
39. I am disappointed about the quality of my sex life.
40. The sexual aspects of my life are determined in large part by my own behavior.
41. Thinking about the sexual aspects of my life often leaves me with an uneasy feeling.
42. I have the skills and ability to ensure rewarding sexual behaviors for myself.
43. I tend to think about my own sexual beliefs and attitudes.
44. I want to avoid engaging in sex where I might be exposed to sexual diseases.
45. Luck plays a big part in influencing the sexual aspects of my life.
46. I tend to be preoccupied with sex.
47. I am somewhat passive about expressing my own sexual desires. (R)
48. I do not expect to suffer any sexual problems or frustrations in the future.
49. If I were to develop a sexual disorder, then I would be to blame for not taking good care of myself.
50. I am quick to notice other people's reactions to the sexual aspects of my own life.
51. I have a desire to be sexually active.
52. If I were to become sexually maladjusted, I myself would be responsible for making myself better.
53. I am pleased with how I handle my own sexual tendencies and behaviors.
54. The sexual aspects of my life are personally gratifying to me.
55. My sexual behavior is determined by the actions of powerful others (e.g., my partner, friends, family).
56. Not only could I relate well to a sexual partner, but it's important to me that I be able to do so.
57. I am fearful of engaging in sexual activity.
58. If just I look out for myself, then I will be able to avoid any sexual problems in the future.
59. I feel discouraged about my sex life.
60. I am in control of and am responsible for the sexual aspects of my life.
61. I worry about the sexual aspects of my life.
62. I am able to cope with and to handle my own sexual needs and wants.
63. I'm very alert to changes in my sexual thoughts, feelings, and desires.
64. I really want to prevent myself from being exposed to sexual diseases.
65. The sexual aspects of my life are largely a matter of (good or bad) fortune.
66. I'm constantly thinking about having sex.
67. I do not hesitate to ask for what I want in a sexual relationship.
68. I will probably experience some sexual problems in the future. (R)
69. If I were to develop a sexual problem, then it would be my own fault for letting it happen.

70. I'm concerned about how the sexual aspects of my life appear to others.
71. It's important to me that I involve myself in sexual activity.
72. If I developed any sexual problems, my recovery would depend in large part on what I myself would do.
73. I have positive feelings about the way I approach my own sexual needs and desires.
74. The sexual aspects of my life are satisfactory, compared to most people's.
75. In order to be sexually active, I have to conform to other more powerful individuals.
76. I am able to "connect" well with a sexual partner, and it's important to me that I am able to do so.
77. I don't have much fear about engaging in sex. (R)
78. I will be able to avoid any sexual problems, if I just take good care of myself.
79. I feel unhappy about my sexual experiences.
80. The main thing which affects the sexual aspects of my life is what I myself do.
81. I feel nervous when I think abut the sexual aspects of my life.
82. I have the capability to take care of my own sexual needs and desires.
83. I am very aware of the sexual aspects of myself (e.g. habits, thoughts, beliefs).
84. I am really motivated to avoid any sexual activity that might expose me to sexual diseases.
85. The sexual aspects of my life are a matter of fate (destiny).
86. I think about sex the majority of the time.
87. When it comes to sex, I usually ask for what I want.
88. I anticipate that in the future the sexual aspects of my life will be frustrating. (R)
89. If something went wrong with my own sexuality, then it would be my own fault.
90. I'm aware of the public impression created by my own sexual behaviors and attitudes.
91. I strive to keep myself sexually active.
92. If I developed a sexual disorder, my recovery would depend on how I myself dealt with the problem.
93. I feel good about the way I express my own sexual needs and desires.
94. I am satisfied with the sexual aspects of my life.
95. My sexual behavior is mostly determined by people who have influence and control over me.
96. Not only am I capable of relating to a sexual partner, but it's important to me that I relate very well.
97. I'm not afraid of becoming sexually active. (R)
98. If I just pay careful attention, I'll be able to prevent myself from having any sexual problems.
99. I feel sad when I think about my sexual experiences.
100. My sexuality is something that I myself am in charge of.
101. I responded to the above items based on:
    (A) A current relationship.
    (B) A past close relationship.
    (C) An imagined close relationship.

Note. R = reverse-scored item.

Sexual Self-Disclosure Scale

JOSEPH A. CATANIA,[1] *University of California, San Francisco*

The Sexual Self-Disclosure Scale (SSDS) is a 19-item, Likert-type scale measuring the degree of threat associated with sexuality questions. The scale items assess respondent's self-reported ease or difficulty with disclosing information in different contexts and interpersonal situations.

Description

The self-administered scale requires respondents to imagine themselves in the different situations described by each item and then rate how easy or difficult it would be to reveal sexual information under each circumstance. A short, 7-

[1]Address correspondence to Joseph A. Catania, College of Health and Human Sciences, Oregon State University, 320B Waldo Hall, Corvallis, OR 97331; e-mail: Joseph.Catania@oregonstate.edu

item form is also shown in the Exhibit. An interviewer-administered version of the scale and English and Spanish versions are also available.

Response Mode and Timing

Ratings made on 6-point Likert-type scales, in which 1 = *extremely easy*, to 6 = *extremely difficult*. All forms take approximately 3–5 minutes to complete.

Scoring

Scores are produced by summing across items. Lower scores indicate less threat.

Reliability and Validity

The SSDS has been administered to college students and a national probability sample. The scale was administered to participants recruited from introductory social science classes at a large western university (N = 66 males, 127 females) who were asked to participate in a study assessing response bias in self-administered questionnaires and sample bias in face-to-face interviews (Catania, McDermott, & Pollack, 1986). Respondents' mean age was 24.6 years; education, 12–19 years; 100% Caucasian heterosexuals; 89% with prior coital experience; 65 respondents having had coitus with their current partner. Internal consistency reliability (Cronbach's alpha) was .93; Test-retest r was .92.

In terms of construct validity, the scale was also found to correlate significantly with Chelune's (1976) General Self-Disclosure Scale, $r(72)$= –.51, p <.0001. Note that lower SSDS scores indicate less threat, whereas higher scores on Chelune's scale indicate less threat. One item from the Chelune Scale concerning sexuality was removed to eliminate redundancy between scales.

The discriminant validity of the SSDS was assessed in a separate analysis in which introductory psychology students (n = 90) were compared with students in a human sexuality course (n = 84). We hypothesized that the human sexuality students, on the basis of self-selection for a course of that nature, would be more sexually self-disclosing than the average introductory psychology student. This hypothesis was supported: Intro Psych M = 60.7, SD = 16.2; Sex Course M = 54.6, SD = 17.1; $t(172)$ = 1.66, p < .05. Note that groups did not differ in age, $t(172)$ = 1.14, p > .10; number of sex books read, $t(172)$ = .30, p > .10; number of lifetime sexual partners, $t(172)$ = .09, p >.10; virginity status, $\chi^2(1, N = 174)$ = .01, p > .10; and sex composition, $\chi^2(1, N = 174)$ = .01, p > .10. Both the number of sexuality books read and total sex partners had small but significant negative

correlations with threat, $r(86)$ = –.24, p <.03; $r(86)$= .23, p <.05, respectively. There was no difference in number of partial responders; 24% of participants who circled one or more items were detected when comparing respondents who did versus did not receive the SSDS at baseline, $\chi^2(1, N = 193)$ = .06, p > .10. This finding indicates that the SSDS did not sensitize respondents to making fewer nonresponses. Volunteers, relative to nonvolunteers, were significantly less threatened about disclosing sexual information, $t(191)$ = 7.22, p < .0001. Furthermore, the order of presentation of SSDS or general self-disclosure scales had no significant effects on sexual behavior and pathology summary scores. Summary scores included variety (the total number of different sexual behaviors performed), frequency (total frequency of sexual behaviors performed, and pathology (average percentage of sexual episodes negatively influenced by sexual problems). All t values were less than 1.49, and all two-tailed p values were greater than .14.

The shortened version was administered by phone to 2,018 respondents who were randomly selected, through probability sampling using random-digit dialing of the contiguous United States, to participate in the recently completed (1995) National Survey Methods study (unpublished data, information is available from the author); reliability (Cronbach's alpha) = .80. Normative data are provided for gender and levels of education; ethnic groups were excluded because there was an insufficient number of non-White ethnic groups to pursue differences (see Table 1).

TABLE 1
Normative Data for Sexual Self-Disclosure Scale/National Methods Survey Study

	N	M	SD	Range	Mdn	Alpha
National sample	2,018	21.68	.09	21.0	22.00	.80
Male national sample	953	21.82	4.24	21.0	22.00	.82
Female national sample	1,065	21.54	4.17	20.0	22.00	.81
Education						
< 12–National sample	144	21.35	4.62	21.0	21.65	.83
= 12–High risk cities	642	21.65	4.34	21.0	22.00	.81
> 12–National sample	1,215	21.80	3.96	20.0	22.00	.80

References

Catania, J. A., McDermott, L. J., & Pollack, L. M. (1986). Questionnaire response bias and face-to-face interview sample bias in sexuality research. *The Journal of Sex Research, 22,* 52–72.

Chelune, G. (1976). Self-disclosure situations survey: A new approach to measuring self-disclosure. *Journal Supplement Abstract Service: Catalog of Selected Documents in Psychology, 6,* 11–112. (Ms. No. 1367)

Exhibit

Sexual Self-Disclosure Scale

Instructions: The following describe different situations in which people may or may not wish to discuss sexual matters. Imagine yourself in each of the situations listed below and circle that number which best shows how easy or difficult it would be for you to reveal sexual information in that situation. Use the key below as a guide for making your answer.

Key   1   Extremely easy   4   Somewhat difficult
         2   Moderately easy   5   Moderately difficult
         3   Somewhat easy   6   Extremely difficult

1. If you were asked to complete an anonymous questionnaire containing personal questions on sexuality, the answers to which you had been told would never be publicly associated with you personally, how easy or difficult would this be in the following situation:
   a. In the privacy of your own home, with no one else present.[a]
   b. During a large (25 or more people) group meeting, where most others are also filling-out the questionnaire.
2. If you were asked personal sexual questions in a private face-to-face situation (for instance, only you and an interviewer), the answers to which you had been told would never be revealed, how much difficulty or ease would you have in doing this in the following situations:
   a. With a young (20–30 years) female interviewer
   b. With a young (20–30 years) male interviewer
   c. With an older (50 years and older) female interviewer
   d. With an older (50 years and older) male interviewer
   e. With a young (25–35 years) female medical doctor
   f. With a young (25–35 years) male medical doctor
   g. With an older (50+ years) female medical doctor
   h. With an older (50+ years) male medical doctor
3. How difficult or easy would it be for you to discuss a personal sexual problem or difficulty in the following situation (assume you are in private circumstances)?
   a. With a close female friend
   b. With a close male friend
   c. With a spouse or sexual partner
   d. With a personal physician
   e. With a specialist in sexual problems
4. How easy or difficult would it be for you to openly discuss your sex life and history in a group of three to five people who are:
   a. Both female and male (mixed company) that you have known only briefly
   b. All members of your own sex that you have known only briefly
5. How easy or difficult would it be for you to discuss a personal sexual problem or difficulty with your parents, or if your parents are deceased how easy or difficult would it have been to discuss such with them? (answer for both parents separately below):
   a. With your mother
   b. With your father

Sexual Self-Disclosure Scale—Short Form

1. Do you think that talking about sex in an AIDS survey is . . .
   Very easy
   Kind of easy
   Kind of hard or
   Very hard
   Declined to answer
   Don't know[b]
2. How easy or hard would it be to fill out an anonymous questionnaire that asked questions about your sexual behavior in the privacy of your own home with no one else present? Would it be . . .
3. How easy or hard would it be for you to fill out an anonymous questionnaire that asked questions about your sexual behavior in the waiting room of a medical clinic with other patients present, who could not see what you were writing? Would it be . . .

4. How easy or hard would it be for you to answer questions about your sexual behavior if they were asked by a medical doctor in the privacy of his/her own office? Would it be . . .

5. How easy or hard would it be to answer questions about your sexual behavior if they were asked by a marriage counselor in the privacy of his/her office? Would it be . . .

6. How easy would it be for you to discuss a sexual problem (read each)
   With a good friend? Would it be . . .

7. With a spouse or sexual partner? Would it be . . .

---

[a]The 1–6 scale is repeated after each item.

[b]These response options follow each item.

Sexual Self-Disclosure Scale

EDWARD S. HEROLD[1] AND LESLIE WAY, *University of Guelph*

Although there has been considerable research about self-disclosure, there has been little research regarding disclosure of sexual topics. In particular, researchers have not differentiated disclosure about specific sexual topics. This differentiation is important because sexuality covers a wide range of attitudinal and behavioral areas.

Our first objective was to construct a scale consisting of sexual topics and to determine the extent of disclosure for each. The question of whether subjects vary in their disclosure to different target persons has been examined extensively. When disclosing information on sexual topics, adolescents and young adults prefer to disclose to friends and dating partner than to parents (Herold, 1984).

Our second objective was to analyze sexual self-disclosure separately for each of the target groups of mother, father, close friend of the same sex, and dating partner.

Description and Response Mode

The Sexual Self-Disclosure Scale (SSDS) was based on Jourard's Self-Disclosure Questionnaire (Jourard, 1971). The SSDS differs from Jourard's in three respects. The SSDS measures only sexual topics. The SSDS measures disclosure to the target groups of mother, father, close friend of the same sex, and dating partner. Unlike Jourard, we did not measure self-disclosure to a close friend of the opposite sex as we believed some people might have difficulty in distinguishing between close friend of the opposite sex and dating partner.

Timing and Scoring

The scale requires about 5 minutes for completion. Self-disclosure scores are obtained separately for each of the target groups. Item scores for each target group are summed and mean scores are obtained.

Reliability and Validity

Data were obtained from 203 unmarried university females aged 18–22 (Herold & Way, 1988). The respective scale means and Cronbach alpha coefficients were: disclosure to mother ($M = 13.2$; alpha = .84); disclosure to father ($M = 10.1$; alpha = .71); disclosure to friend ($M = 19.7$; alpha = .89) and disclosure to dating partner ($M = 21.9$; alpha = .94). Validity for the scale is indicated by the fact that the mean scores are consistent with previous research which has found greater disclosure to friends and dating partner than to parents and the least amount of disclosure to father (Herold, 1984).

Other Information

There is no charge for use of the scale and no restriction in its use.

References

Herold, E. S. (1984). *The sexual behavior of Canadian young people.* Markham, Ontario: Fitzhenry & Whiteside.

Herold, E. S., & Way, L. (1988). Sexual self-disclosure among university women. *The Journal of Sex Research, 24,* 1–14.

Jourard, S. (1971). *Self-disclosure: An experimental analysis of the transparent self.* New York: Wiley.

---

[1]Address correspondence to Edward S. Herold, Department of Family Studies, University of Guelph, Guelph, Ontario N1G 2W1, Canada; e-mail: eherold@uoguelph.ca

Exhibit

Sexual Self-Disclosure Scale

You are to read each item in the next section of the questionnaire and then indicate the extent that you have talked about that item to each person (i.e., the extent to which you have made your attitudes and/or behaviours known to that person). Use the rating scale below to describe the extent that you have talked about each item.

The rating scale is:

(1) Have told the person *nothing* about this aspect of me.
(2) Have talked only in *general terms* about this item.
(3) Have talked in *some detail* about this item but have not fully discussed my own attitudes or behaviors.
(4) Have talked in *complete detail* about this item to the other person. He or she knows me fully in this respect.

Choose one number in the row which corresponds to the amount of your disclosure. For example, if you have talked in general terms to your mother about your attitudes and/or behaviors regarding masturbation, you would place a 2 in column 6 of the computer card.

Items: Disclosure to mother	No Disclosure	Only General Terms	Some Detail	Complete Detail
1. My personal views on sexual morality.	1	2	3	4
2. Premarital sexual intercourse.	1	2	3	4
3. Oral sex.	1	2	3	4
4. Masturbation.	1	2	3	4
5. My sexual thoughts or fantasies.	1	2	3	4
6. Sexual techniques I find or would find pleasurable.	1	2	3	4
7. Use of contraception.	1	2	3	4
8. Sexual problems or difficulties I might have.	1	2	3	4

Sexual Deception Scale

WILLIAM D. MARELICH[1] AND RHONA I. SLAUGHTER, *California State University, Fullerton*

The Sexual Deception Scale is designed to measure the use of sexual deception in intimate relationships by specifically focusing on the lies and deceptive practices individuals use in order to engage in sexual activity with a current or prospective partner. The scale is designed for use with general or college populations for research on intimate and close relationships.

Description

In accordance with social exchange theory (Thibaut & Kelley, 1959), the scale addresses the use of sexually deceptive practices in order to gain and/or maintain specific resources. In some cases, the rewards are sexual in nature (e.g., when one partner deliberately lies in order to have sexual intercourse with another partner). Likewise, the use of deception may occur when an individual uses sexual intimacy as a cost in order to maintain an existing resource (e.g., providing sexual services in order to maintain the relationship).

The instrument consists of a 15-item questionnaire in a forced-choice, dichotomous format. Participants indicate *Yes* or *No* to having ever engaged in a particular act or

[1]Address correspondence to William D. Marelich, Dept. of Psychology, CSU Fullerton, 800 N. State College Blvd., Fullerton, CA 92834; e-mail: wmarelich@fullerton.edu

behavior. The measure consists of three subscales that reflect the different types of lies or deceptions used by individuals: blatant lies, self-serving lies, and lies told to avoid confrontation. Items that address blatant lying tactics involve the individual's use of deception to gain access to sexual activity. The use of deception for self-serving purposes employs the practice of engaging in sexual behavior in order to gain specific resources such as material items or companionship. Finally, items that address the use of deception to avoid confrontation signify the individual's willingness to engage in sexual behaviors to avoid conflict.

Response Mode and Timing

Respondents answer *Yes* or *No* to each item based on whether they have ever participated in the act/behavior. The instrument can be administered by traditional paper-and-pencil method or by utilizing online data collection techniques. The measure takes 5 minutes to complete.

Scoring

The Sexual Deception Scale comprises three subscales (Blatant Lying, Self-Serving, Avoiding Confrontation). No total score is available, although a second-order factor analysis (see Marelich, Lundquist, Painter, & Mechanic, 2008) suggests that a total score measure may be viable. The Blatant Lying subscale consists of Items 1, 2, 9, 11, 12, 13, and 15. The Self-Serving subscale consists of Items 4, 7, and 8. The Avoiding Confrontation subscale consists of Items 3, 5, 6, 10, and 14. According to Marelich et al. (2008), each item is assigned the value of 1 for a *Yes* response and 2 for a *No* response. To obtain a score for each individual subscale:

1. Reverse code all scale items (0 = *No*, 1 = *Yes*).
2. Sum the items of the particular subscale.
3. Divide by the number of items in that particular subscale.

Scores yielded for each subscale indicate the amount of deception used; higher scores signify the greater use of sexually deceptive practices.

Reliability

Principal components analysis was utilized, and an oblique rotation was utilized to allow the resulting components to correlate. Items showed good pattern matrix loadings on at least one of the subscales. After a confirmatory factor analysis was performed (see *Validity* below), internal consistency reliabilities were performed, and ranged from .71 to .75 for the three subscales.

Validity

A confirmatory factor analysis was performed to validate the principal components analysis. Based on these results, the final set of 15 items and their respective subscales was derived. This final model showed good fit, and a second-order factor analysis showed that the three resulting subscales reflect a broader sexual deception construct.

Construct and criterion validity of the instrument was assessed by correlating the three subscales with additional items designed to address attitude and behavioral issues toward sexual intimacy and sexual needs. Across all three subscales, those noting more sexual deceptions reported a greater number of lifetime sexual partners, engaging in one-night stands, and misrepresenting the total number of lifetime sexual partners to the current/prospective partners. These correlations were the strongest for those using blatant lies. Individuals showing greater self-serving deceptions were significantly associated with greater perceived sexual need, and greater need to manipulate their partners. Items assessing intimacy-related attitudes, such as the desire to be in a relationship and/or maintain the current relationship, were found to positively correlate with the use of deceptions to avoid confrontation.

In addition to the significant associations found between subscales and various acts and behaviors, each component was found to fall in accordance with the cost/benefit structure of social exchange theory. For example, items that constitute the Blatant Lying subscale address the use of deception to gain sexual favors (i.e., sex as a benefit), whereas items associated with the Self-Serving or Avoiding Confrontation subscales construe the use of sexual favors as a means to gain or maintain resources (i.e., sex as a cost to maintain the relationship).

References

Marelich, W. D., Lundquist, J., Painter, K., & Mechanic, M. B. (2008). Sexual deception as a social-exchange process: Development of a behavior-based sexual deception scale. *The Journal of Sex Research, 45*, 27–35.

Thibaut, J., & Kelley, H. (1959). *The social psychology of groups.* New York: Wiley.

Exhibit

Sexual Deception Scale

Directions: Below are a number of items addressing things you may or may not have done sometime in your life. Please answer each item Yes or No. "Sex" below can refer to intercourse or other forms of sexual intimacy (e.g., oral sex, manual stimulation).

Have you ever . . .

1. Told someone "I love you" but really didn't just to have sex with them?
Yes _____ No_____

2. Told someone "I care for you" just to have sex with them?
Yes _____ No_____

3. Had sex with someone so they would leave you alone?
Yes _____ No_____

4. Had sex with someone so you would have someone to sleep next to?
Yes _____ No_____

5. Had sex with someone even though you didn't want to?
Yes _____ No_____

6. Had sex with someone in order to maintain your relationship with them?
Yes _____ No_____

7. Had sex with someone in order to maintain resources you get from them (e.g., money, clothes, companionship)?
Yes _____ No_____

8. Had sex with someone in order to get resources from them (e.g., money, clothes, companionship)?
Yes _____ No_____

9. Had sex with someone just so you could tell your friends about it?
Yes _____ No_____

10. Had sex with someone so they wouldn't break up with you?
Yes _____ No_____

11. Gotten a partner really drunk or stoned in order to have sex with them?
Yes _____ No_____

12. Told someone they'd be your boyfriend/girlfriend just so they would have sex with you?
Yes _____ No_____

13. Had sex with someone, then never returned their calls after that?
Yes _____ No_____

14. Had sex with someone because you wanted to please them?
Yes _____ No_____

15. Faked "who you are" in order to have sex with somebody?
Yes _____ No_____

Sexual Self-Disclosure Scale

WILLIAM E. SNELL, JR.,[1] *Southeast Missouri State University*

The literature on human sexuality emphasizes the need for people to discuss the sexual aspects of themselves with others. Snell, Belk, Papini, and Clark (1989) examined women's and men's willingness to discuss a variety of sexual topics with parents and friends by developing an objective self-report instrument, the Sexual Self-Disclosure Scale (SSDS). The first version of the SSDS consists of 12 subscales that measure the following sexual topics (Snell & Belk, 1987): sexual behavior, sexual sensations, sexual fantasies, sexual attitudes, the meaning of sex, negative sexual affect, positive sexual affect, sexual concerns, birth control, sexual responsibility, sexual dishonesty, and rape. In another study reported by Snell et al. (1989), women's and men's willingness to discuss a variety of sexual topics with an intimate partner was examined by extending the SSDS to include a greater variety of sexual topics. The Revised Sexual Self-Disclosure Scale (SSDS-R) consists of 24 three-item subscales measuring people's willingness to discuss the following sexual topics with an intimate partner (reported in Study 3 by Snell et al., 1989): sexual behaviors, sexual sensations, sexual fantasies, sexual preferences, meaning of sex, sexual accountability, distressing sex, sexual dishonesty, sexual delay preferences, abortion and pregnancy, homosexuality, rape, AIDS, sexual morality, sexual satisfaction, sexual guilt, sexual calmness, sexual depression, sexual jealousy, sexual apathy, sexual anxiety, sexual happiness, sexual anger, and sexual fear.

Description

The initial version of the SSDS consists of 120 items that form 12 separate five-item subscales for each of two disclosure targets (male and female therapists). To respond to this version of the SSDS, individuals are asked to indicate how willing they would be to discuss the SSDS sexual topics with the disclosure targets. A 5-point Likert-type scale (scored 0 to 4) is used to measure the responses: (0) *I am not at all willing to discuss this topic with this person*, (1) *I am slightly willing to discuss this topic with this person*, (2) *I am moderately willing to discuss this topic with this person*, (3) *I am almost totally willing to discuss this topic with this person*, and (4) *I am totally willing to discuss this topic with this person*. Subscale scores are created for each disclosure target person by summing the 5 items on each subscale. Higher scores thus indicate greater willingness to disclose a particular SSDS sexual topic with a particular person.

The SSDS-R used by Snell et al. (1989) consists of 72 items that form 24 three-item subscales for the disclosure target (i.e., an intimate partner). In responding to the SSDS-R, individuals are asked to indicate how much they are willing to discuss the SSDS-R topics with an intimate partner. A 5-point Likert-type scale is used to collected data on the subjects' responses, with each item being scored from 0 to 4: (0) *I would not be willing to discuss this topic with an intimate partner*, (1) *I would be slightly willing to discuss this topic with an intimate partner*, (2) *I would be moderately willing to discuss this topic with an intimate partner*, (3) *I would be mostly willing to discuss this topic with an intimate partner*, and (4) *I would be completely willing to discuss this topic with an intimate partner*. In order to create SSDS-R subscale scores, the three items on each subscale are summed (no items are reverse scored). Higher scores thus correspond to greater willingness to discuss the SSDS-R sexual topics with an intimate partner.

The sample version of the SSDS-R in the exhibit is an example of how the SSDS-R may be modified for use with different target persons (e.g., mother, father, best female friend, best male friend).

Response Mode and Timing

Respondents indicate their responses typically on a computer scan sheet by darkening in a response from A to E. Alternatively, responses to the SSDS can be written directly on the questionnaire itself. Usually, 20–30 minutes are needed to complete the SSDS.

Scoring

The SSDS consists of 12 subscales, each containing five separate items. The labels and items for each of these subscales are: (a) Sexual Behavior (Items 1, 13, 25, 37, 49); (b) Sexual Sensations (Items 2, 14, 26, 38, 50); (c) Sexual Fantasies (Items 3, 15, 27, 39, 51); (d) Sexual Attitudes (Items 4, 16, 28, 40, 52); (e) Meaning of Sex (Items 5, 17, 29, 41, 53); (f) Negative Sexual Affect (Items 6, 18, 30, 42, 54); (g) Positive Sexual Affect (Items 7, 19, 31, 43, 55); (h) Sexual Concerns (Items 8, 20, 32, 44, 56); (i) Birth Control (Items 9, 21, 33, 45, 57); (j) Sexual Responsibility (Items 10, 22, 34, 46, 58); (k) Sexual Dishonesty (Items 11, 23, 35, 47, 59); and (l) Rape (Items 12, 24, 36, 48, 60). The items are coded so that A = 0; B = 1; C = 2; D = 3; and E = 4. The five items on each subscale are then summed, so that higher scores correspond to greater sexual self-disclosure.

The SSDS-R consists of 24 subscales, each containing three separate items: (a) Sexual Behaviors (Items 1, 5, 9);

[1]Address all correspondence to William E. Snell, Jr., Department of Psychology, Southeast Missouri State University, One University Plaza, Cape Girardeau, MO 63701; e-mail: wesnell@semo.edu

(b) Sexual Sensations (Items 2, 6, 10); (c) Sexual Fantasies (Items 3, 7, 11); (d) Sexual Preferences (Items 4, 8, 12); (e) Meaning of Sex (Items 13, 18, 23); (f) Sexual Accountability (Items 14, 19, 24); (g) Distressing Sex (Items 15, 20, 25); (h) Sexual Dishonesty (Items 16, 21, 26); (i) Sexual Delay Preferences (Items 17, 22, 27); (j) Abortion and Pregnancy (Items 28, 33, 38); (k) Homosexuality (Items 29, 34, 39); (l) Rape (Items 30, 35, 40); (m) AIDS (Items 31, 36, 41); (n) Sexual Morality (Items 32, 37, 42); (o) Sexual Satisfaction (Items 43, 53, 63); (p) Sexual Guilt (Items 44, 54, 64); (q) Sexual Calmness (Items 45, 55, 65); (r) Sexual Depression (Items 46, 56, 66); (s) Sexual Jealousy (Items 47, 57, 67); (t) Sexual Apathy (Items 48, 58, 68); (u) Sexual Anxiety (Items 49, 59, 69); (v) Sexual Happiness (Items 50, 60, 70); (w) Sexual Anger (Items 51, 61, 71); and (x) Sexual Fear (Items 52, 62, 72).

Reliability

The internal consistency of the 12 subscales on the original SSDS was determined by calculating Cronbach alpha coefficients. These alphas ranged from a low of .83 to a high of .93 (average = .90) for the female therapist, and from a low of .84 to a high of .94 (average = .92) for the male therapist.

The reliability coefficients for the SSDS-R ranged from a low of .59 to a high of .91 (average = .81). These reliability coefficients were all sufficiently high to justify using either version of the scale in research investigations.

Validity

Snell et al. (1989) reported that women's and men's responses to the SSDS varied as a function of the disclosure recipient and the content of the sexual disclosure. Women indicated that they were more willing to discuss the topics on the SSDS with a female than a male therapist. Also, it was found that people's responses to the SSDS-R varied as a function of respondent gender and sexual topic.

References

Snell, W. E., Jr., & Belk, S. S. (1987, April). *Development of the Sexual Self-Disclosure Scale (SSDS): Sexual disclosure to female and male therapists.* Paper presented at the 33rd annual meeting of the Southwestern Psychological Association, New Orleans, LA.

Snell, W. E., Jr., Belk, S. S., Papini, D. R., & Clark, S. (1989). Development and validation of the Sexual Self-Disclosure Scale. *Annals of Sex Research, 2,* 307–334.

Exhibit

Sexual Self-Disclosure Scale

Instructions: This survey is concerned with the extent to which you have discussed the following 60 topics about sexuality with several different people. Listed below you will notice four columns[a] which represent the following individuals: (A) your mother, (B) your father, (C) your best male friend, and (D) your best female friend. For each of these people, indicate how much you have discussed these topics with them. Use the following scale for your responses:

Have not discussed this topic:	Have slightly discussed this topic:	Have moderately discussed this topic:	Have mostly discussed this topic:	Have fully discussed this topic:

(A) with your mother.
(B) with your father.
(C) with your best male friend.
(D) with your best female friend.

1. My past sexual experiences
2. The things that sexually arouse me
3. My imaginary sexual encounters
4. The sexual behaviors which I think people ought to exhibit
5. What sex means to me
6. How guilty I feel about sex
7. How satisfied I feel about the sexual aspects of my life
8. Times when sex was distressing for me
9. What I think about birth control
10. My private notion of sexual responsibility
11. The times I have faked orgasm
12. My private views about rape

13. The types of sexual behaviors I've engaged in
14. The sexual activities that "feel good" to me
15. My private sexual fantasies
16. What I consider "proper" sexual behaviors
17. What it means to me to make love together with someone
18. How anxious I feel about my sex life
19. How content I feel about the sexual aspects of my life
20. Times when I had undesired sex
21. How I feel about abortions
22. The responsibility one ought to assume for one's sexuality
23. The times I have pretended to enjoy sex
24. The "truths and falsehoods" about rape
25. The number of times I have had sex
26. The behaviors that are sexually exciting to me
27. My sexually exciting imaginary thoughts
28. The sexual conduct that people ought to exhibit
29. What I think and feel about having sex with someone
30. How depressed I feel about my own sexuality
31. How happy I feel about my sexuality
32. Times when I was pressured to have sex
33. How I feel about pregnancy
34. My own ideas about sexual accountability
35. The times I have lied about sexual matters
36. What women and men really feel about rape
37. The sexual positions I've tried
38. The sensations that are sexually arousing to me
39. My "juicy" sexual thoughts
40. My attitudes about sexual behaviors
41. The meaning that sexual intercourse has for me
42. How frustrated I feel about my sex life
43. How much joy that sex gives me
44. The aspects of sex that bother me
45. My private beliefs about pregnancy prevention
46. The idea of having to answer for one's sexual conduct
47. What I think about sexual disloyalty
48. Women's and men's reactions to rape
49. The places and times-of-day when I've had sex
50. The types of sexual foreplay that feel arousing to me
51. The sexual episodes that I daydream about
52. My personal beliefs about sexual morality
53. The importance that I attach to making love with someone
54. How angry I feel about the sexual aspect of my life
55. How enjoyable I feel about my sexuality
56. Times when I wanted to leave a sexual encounter
57. The pregnancy precautions that people ought to take
58. The notion one is answerable for one's sexual behaviors
59. How I feel about sexual honesty
60. Women's and men's reactions to rape

Revised Sexual Self-Disclosure Scale (illustrated for the "intimate partner" target only)

Instructions: This survey is concerned with the extent to which you have discussed the following topics about sexuality with an intimate partner. To respond, indicate how much you have discussed these topics with an intimate partner. Use the following scale for your responses:[b]

1. My past sexual experiences
2. The kinds of touching that sexually arouse me

 3. My private sexual fantasies
 4. The sexual preferences that I have
 5. The types of sexual behaviors I have engaged in
 6. The sensations that are sexually exciting to me
 7. My "juicy" sexual thoughts
 8. What I would desire in a sexual encounter
 9. The sexual positions I have tried
10. The types of sexual foreplay that feel arousing to me
11. The sexual episodes that I daydream about
12. The things I enjoy most about sex
13. What sex in an intimate relationship means to me
14. My private beliefs about sexual responsibility
15. Times when sex was distressing for me
16. The times I have pretended to enjoy sex
17. Times when I prefer to refrain from sexual activity
18. What it means to me to have sex with my partner
19. My own ideas about sexual accountability
20. Times when I was pressured to have sex
21. The times I have lied about sexual matters
22. The times when I might not want to have sex
23. What I think and feel about having sex with my partner
24. The notion that one is accountable for one's sexual behaviors
25. The aspects of sex that bother me
26. How I would feel about sexual dishonesty
27. My ideas about not having sex unless I want to
28. How I feel about abortions
29. My personal views about homosexuals
30. My own ideas about why rapes occur
31. My personal views about people with AIDS
32. What I consider "proper" sexual behavior
33. My beliefs about pregnancy prevention
34. Opinions I have about homosexual relationships
35. What I really feel about rape
36. Concerns that I have about the disease AIDS
37. The sexual behaviors that I consider appropriate
38. How I feel about pregnancy at this time
39. My reactions to working with a homosexual
40. My reactions to rape
41. My feelings about working with someone who has AIDS
42. My personal beliefs about sexual morality
43. How satisfied I feel about the sexual aspects of my life
44. How guilty I feel about the sexual aspects of my life
45. How calm I feel about the sexual aspects of my life
46. How depressed I feel about the sexual aspects of my life
47. How jealous I feel about the sexual aspects of my life
48. How apathetic I feel about the sexual aspects of my life
49. How anxious I feel about the sexual aspects of my life
50. How happy I feel about the sexual aspects of my life
51. How angry I feel about the sexual aspects of my life
52. How afraid I feel about the sexual aspects of my life
53. How pleased I feel about the sexual aspects of my life
54. How shameful I feel about the sexual aspects of my life
55. How serene I feel about the sexual aspects of my life
56. How sad I feel about the sexual aspects of my life
57. How possessive I feel about the sexual aspects of my life
58. How indifferent I feel about the sexual aspects of my life
59. How troubled I feel about the sexual aspects of my life

60. How cheerful I feel about the sexual aspects of my life
61. How mad I feel about the sexual aspects of my life
62. How fearful I feel about the sexual aspects of my life
63. How delighted I feel about the sexual aspects of my life
64. How embarrassed I feel about the sexual aspects of my life
65. How relaxed I feel about the sexual aspects of my life
66. How unhappy I feel about the sexual aspects of my life
67. How suspicious I feel about the sexual aspects of my life
68. How detached I feel about the sexual aspects of my life
69. How worried I feel about the sexual aspects of my life
70. How joyful I feel about the sexual aspects of my life
71. How irritated I feel about the sexual aspects of my life
72. How frightened I feel about the sexual aspects of my life

---

[a]The columns are not shown here to conserve space.
[b]The scale is the same as that for the SSDS except that "with an intimate partner" follows each descriptor.

Sexual Self-Efficacy Scale for Female Functioning

SALLY BAILES,[1] LAURA CRETI, CATHERINE S. FICHTEN, EVA LIBMAN, AND WILLIAM
BRENDER, *SMBD-Jewish General Hospital*
RHONDA AMSEL, *McGill University*

The evaluation and alteration of self-efficacy expectations is important in the cognitive-behavioral treatment of psychosexual problems. The Sexual Self-Efficacy Scale for females (SSES-F) is a measure of perceived competence in the behavioral, cognitive, and affective dimensions of female sexual response. Recently, researchers studying women's perceived sexual self-efficacy, using the SSES-F, have focused on sexual adjustment (Reissing, Laliberté, & Davis, 2005), marital satisfaction (Oluwole, 2008), and the treatment of genital pain (Sutton, Pukall, & Chamberlain, 2009).

Description

The SSES-F was developed as a multidimensional counterpart to the SSES-E (erectile function in men), and has been used for clinical screening and assessment, as well as for research (Fichten et al., 2010; Libman, Rothenberg, Fichten, & Amsel, 1985).

The SSES-F has 37 items, sampling capabilities in four phases of sexual response: interest, desire, arousal, and orgasm. In addition, the measure samples diverse aspects of female individual and interpersonal sexual expression (e.g., communication, body comfort and acceptance, and enjoyment of various sexual activities). The instrument includes the following subscales determined by factor

analysis (items in parentheses): Interpersonal Orgasm (4, 28, 29, 30, 32, 33, 34, 36, 37), Interpersonal Interest/Desire (1, 5, 6, 7, 9, 22), Sensuality (17, 18, 19, 20, 21, 27), Individual Arousal (24, 25, 26, 31), Affection (8, 15, 16), Communication (12, 13, 14, 23, 35), Body Acceptance (2, 3), and Refusal (10, 11).

The SSES-F may be used by single or partnered women of all ages. Female respondents indicate those activities they can do and, for each of these, rate their confidence level. In addition, their partners can rate how they perceive the respondents' capabilities and confidence levels.

Response Mode and Timing

For each item, respondents check whether the female can do the described activity and rate her confidence in being able to engage in the activity. Confidence ratings range from 10 (*Quite Uncertain*) to 100 (*Quite Certain*). If an item is unchecked, the corresponding confidence rating is assumed to be zero. The measure takes about 10 to 15 minutes to complete.

Scoring

The SSES-F yields an overall self-efficacy strength score as well as eight subscale scores. The total strength score is

[1]Address correspondence to Sally Bailes, Department of Psychiatry, SMBD-Jewish General Hospital, 4333 Cote Ste. Catherine, Montreal, Quebec, H3T 1E4, Canada; e-mail: sally.bailes@mail.mcgill.ca

given by the average of the confidence ratings; items not checked in the "Can Do" column are scored as zero. The strength scores for the separate subscales are given by the average of the confidence ratings for that subscale.

Reliability

The SSES-F was administered to a nonclinical sample of 131 women (age range = 25 to 68 years). The sample included 51 married or cohabiting women and 80 single women. Thirty-six of the women completed the SSES-F a second time, after an interval of 4 weeks. The male partners of the 51 married or cohabiting women also completed the SSES-F.

Evaluation of the women's confidence ratings *(N = 131)* included a factor analysis to identify subscales and analyses to assess test-retest reliability and internal consistency. Item analysis demonstrated a high degree of internal consistency (Cronbach's alpha = .93) for the overall test. A factor analysis, using a varimax rotation, yielded eight significant factors, accounting for 68% of the total variance. Internal consistency coefficients for the separate subscales ranged from α = .70 to α = .87. Subscale-total and intersubscale correlations, carried out on the mean confidence score for each subscale, indicated reasonably high subscale-total correlations (range = .31 to .85) and moderate intersubscale correlations (range = .08 to .63).

Test-retest correlations for the total scores *(r = .83, p < .001)* and for the subscales (range = .50 to .93) indicate good stability over time. For the married or cohabiting couples, the correlation between the partners' total SSES-F scores was *r = .46, p < .001.*

Validity

Creti et al. (1989) reported on a preliminary validity analysis for the SSES-F. Both nonclinical and clinical samples were administered the SSES-F along with a test battery including measures of psychological, marital, and sexual adjustment and functioning. The overall strength score of the SSES-F was found to correlate significantly with other measures of sexual functioning, such as the Sexual History Form (Nowinski & LoPiccolo, 1979), the Golombok Rust Inventory of Sexual Satisfaction (Rust & Golombok, 1985), and the Sexual Interaction Inventory (LoPiccolo & Steger, 1974), and with marital satisfaction (Locke Wallace Marital Adjustment Scale; Kimmel & Van der Veen, 1974). In addition, the overall strength scores of the SSES-F were significantly lower for sexually dysfunctional women who

presented for sex therapy at our clinic than for those of a sample of women from the community who reported no sexual dysfunction. Sexually dysfunctional women also showed significantly lower scores than the community sample on the Interpersonal Orgasm, Interpersonal Interest/Desire, Sensuality, and Communication subscales. Creti et al. (1989) found that older women (age > 50) had significantly lower total strength scores than younger women (age < 50). Recently, Sutton et al. (2009) reported that women with provoked vestibulodynia had lower scores on the total SSES-F score as well as on the sensuality, affection, and communication subscales compared to controls. Reissing et al. (2005) found that sexual self-efficacy, as measured by the SSES-F, was a mediating variable between sexual self-schema and sexual adjustment.

Other Information

The SSES-F is available in the French language.

References

Creti, L., Bailes, S., Fichten, C., Libman, E., Amsel, R., Liederman, G., et al. (1989, August). *Validation of the Sexual Self-Efficacy Scale for Females.* Poster presented at the annual convention of the American Psychological Association, New Orleans, LA.

Fichten, C. S., Budd, J., Spector, I., Amsel, R., Creti, L., Brender, W., et al. (2010). Sexual Self-Efficacy Scale—Erectile Functioning. In T. D. Fisher, C. M. Davis, W. L. Yarber, & S. L. Davis (Eds.), *Handbook of sexuality-related measures.* New York: Routledge.

Kimmel, D., & Van der Veen, F. (1974). Factors of marital adjustment. *Journal of Marriage and the Family, 36,* 57.

Libman, E., Rothenberg, I., Fichten, C. S., & Amsel, R. (1985). The SSES-E: A measure of sexual self-efficacy in erectile functioning. *Journal of Sex and Marital Therapy, 11,* 233–244.

LoPiccolo, J., & Steger, J. C. (1974). The Sexual Interaction Inventory: A new instrument for assessment of sexual dysfunction. *Archives of Sexual Behavior, 1,* 585–595.

Nowinski, J. K., & LoPiccolo, J. (1979). Assessing sexual behavior in couples. *Journal of Sex and Marital Therapy, 5,* 225–243.

Oluwole, D. A. (2008). Marital satisfaction: Connections of self-disclosure, sexual self-efficacy and spirituality among Nigerian women. *Pakistan Journal of Social Sciences, 5,* 464–469.

Reissing, E. D., Laliberté, G. M., & Davis, H. J. (2005). Young women's sexual adjustment: The role of sexual self-schema, sexual self-efficacy, sexual aversion and body attitudes. *The Canadian Journal of Human Sexuality, 14*(3), 77–85.

Rust, J., & Golombok, S. (1985). The Golombok Rust Inventory of Sexual Satisfaction (GRISS). *British Journal of Clinical Psychology, 24,* 63–64.

Sutton, K. S., Pukall, C. F., & Chamberlain, S. (2009). Pain ratings, sensory thresholds, and psychosocial functioning in women with provoked vestibulodynia. *Journal of Sex and Marital Therapy, 35,* 262–281.

Exhibit

Sexual Self-Efficacy Scale for Female Functioning

The attached form lists sexual activities that women engage in.

For women respondents only:

Under **column I** (Can Do), check (✓) the activities **you think you could do** if you were asked to do them today. For **only** those activities you checked in column I, rate your **degree of confidence** that you could do them by selecting a number from 10 to 100 using the scale given below. Write this number in **column II** (Confidence).

For partners only:

Under **column I** (Can Do), check (✓) the activities you think **your female partner could do** if she were asked to do them today. For only those activities you checked in column I, rate your **degree of confidence** that your female partner could do them by selecting a number from 10 to 100 using the scale given below. Write this number in **column II** (Confidence).

10	20	30	40	50	60	70	80	90	100
Quite Uncertain				Moderately Certain					Quite Certain

If you think your partner is **not** able to do a particular activity, leave columns I **and** II **blank** for that activity.

10 Quite Uncertain 20 30 40 50 Moderately Certain 60 70 80 90	100 Quite Certain	**I** Check if Female **Can Do**	**II** Rate **Confidence** 10–100
1. Anticipate (think about) having intercourse without fear or anxiety.			
2. Feel comfortable being nude with the partner.			
3. Feel comfortable with your body.			
4. In general, feel good about your ability to respond sexually.			
5. Be interested in sex.			
6. Feel sexual desire for the partner.			
7. Feel sexually desirable to the partner.			
8. Initiate an exchange of affection without feeling obliged to have sexual relations.			
9. Initiate sexual activities.			
10. Refuse a sexual advance by the partner.			
11. Cope with the partner's refusal of your sexual advance.			
12. Ask the partner to provide the type and amount of sexual stimulation needed.			
13. Provide the partner with the type and amount of sexual stimulation requested.			
14. Deal with discrepancies in sexual preference between you and your partner.			
15. Enjoy an exchange of affection without having sexual relations.			
16. Enjoy a sexual encounter with a partner without having intercourse.			
17. Enjoy having your body caressed by the partner (excluding genitals and breasts).			
18. Enjoy having your genitals caressed by the partner.			
19. Enjoy having your breasts caressed by the partner.			
20. Enjoy caressing the partner's body (excluding genitals).			
21. Enjoy caressing the partner's genitals.			
22. Enjoy intercourse.			
23. Enjoy a lovemaking encounter in which you do not reach orgasm.			
24. Feel sexually aroused in response to erotica (pictures, books, films, etc.).			
25. Become sexually aroused by masturbating when alone.			
26. Become sexually aroused during foreplay when both partners are clothed.			

27. Become sexually aroused during foreplay when both partners are nude.			
28. Maintain sexual arousal throughout a sexual encounter.			
29. Become sufficiently lubricated to engage in intercourse.			
30. Engage in intercourse without pain or discomfort.			
31. Have an orgasm while masturbating when alone.			
32. Have an orgasm while the partner stimulates you by means other than intercourse.			
33. Have an orgasm during intercourse with concurrent stimulation of the clitoris.			
34. Have an orgasm during intercourse without concurrent stimulation of the clitoris.			
35. Stimulate a partner to orgasm by means other than intercourse.			
36. Stimulate a partner to orgasm by means of intercourse.			
37. Reach orgasm within a reasonable period of time.			

Lesbian, Gay, and Bisexual Affirmative Counseling Self-Efficacy Inventory

FRANK R. DILLON, *Florida International University*
ROGER L. WORTHINGTON,[1] *University of Missouri*

LGB-affirmative psychotherapy is defined as "therapy that celebrates and advocates the authenticity and integrity of lesbian, gay and bisexual persons and their relationships" (Bieschke, McClanahan, Tozer, Grzegorek, & Park, 2000, p. 328). Theoretical tenets of social cognitive theory (Bandura, 1986) were applied to LGB-affirmative psychotherapist training to better delineate ways to train psychotherapists in LGB-affirmative practices (Bieschke, Eberz, Bard, & Croteau, 1998). Exposure of psychotherapists and trainees to four sources of self-efficacy (performance accomplishments, vicarious learning, verbal reinforcement, and physiological states/reactions) is posited to foster increases in LGB-affirmative counselor self-efficacy. An optimal level of LGB-affirmative counseling self-efficacy may serve as a mechanism for implementing LGB-affirmative counseling behaviors and positive therapeutic outcomes, as well as for promoting psychotherapists' interest in LGB-affirmative psychotherapy.

The Lesbian, Gay, and Bisexual Affirmative Counseling Self-Efficacy Inventory (LGB-CSI) measures participants' self-efficacy to perform LGB-affirmative counseling behaviors. LGB-affirmative counseling behaviors include (a) *advocacy skills*: identifying and utilizing community resources that are supportive of LGB clients' concerns; (b) *application of knowledge*: counseling LGB clients through unique issues using knowledge of LGB issues in psychology; (c) *awareness*: maintaining awareness of attitudes toward one's own and others' sexual identity development; (d) *assessment*: assessing relevant issues and problems

of LGB clients; and (e) *relationship*: building a working alliance with LGB clients. An optimal level of self-efficacy is one that slightly exceeds one's ability. Successful performance requires both high efficacy beliefs and acquisition of knowledge and skills (Bandura, 1986).

Description

The LGB-CSI consists of 32 items. Each item represents an LGB-affirmative counseling behavior. Higher scores are indicative of higher levels of self-efficacy to counsel gay, lesbian, and/or bisexual clients.

The scale is intended for mental health professionals (e.g., psychologists, social workers, counselors) ranging in professional background and level of experience.

The development and validation of the LGB-CSI included five studies. In Study 1, item development procedures and an exploratory factor analysis of an initial item pool were conducted. Item development involved investigating LGB-affirmative counseling competencies. First, literature was reviewed to determine the competencies. Five categories were hypothesized to represent the current conceptualization of LGB-affirmative counseling: (a) application of knowledge of LGB issues and the counseling behaviors reliant on a priori understanding of LGB issues, including: the impacts of race, ethnicity, gender, religion, locale, and other cultural variables on sexual identity development; internalized homophobia/heterosexism and biphobia; anti-LGB violence; causality

[1]Address correspondence to Roger L. Worthington, 217 Jesse Hall, University of Missouri, Columbia, MO 65211; e-mail: WorthingtonR@missouri.edu

questions; career issues; interpersonal isolation/marginality; relationship issues; LGB family issues; impact of aging; HIV/AIDS; substance abuse; domestic violence; sexual abuse; sexual identity theory; exploration of sexual identity and management; (b) advocacy skills; (c) awareness of one's own and others' sexual identity development; (d) development of a working relationship with an LGB client; (e) assessment of the relevant issues and problems of an LGB client. Items were generated for each issue after a thorough review of the literature. A pool of 101 items was developed on the basis of the preliminary framework. The item pool included counseling behaviors that go beyond simple microskills to reflect the complexity of behaviors needed for effective LGB-affirmative counseling. Three counseling psychologists and two doctoral-level graduate students (one self-identified gay male, one self-identified bisexual male, two self-identified lesbian women, and one self-identified heterosexual woman), each of whom had extensive experience in the practice of LGB-affirmative and/or multicultural counseling and research, assessed the content validity of the 101 items. The experts were asked to examine the items to (a) determine whether they were reflective of the critical issues that were gleaned from the literature, (b) ensure coverage of the content domains, (c) eliminate unnecessary items, (d) revise any confusing items, and (e) provide general feedback that would assist in developing items representative of LGB-affirmative counseling. The experts rated each item on content appropriateness and clarity by using a 5-point scale that ranged from 1 (*Not at all Appropriate or Clear*) to 5 (*Very Appropriate or Clear*). Items receiving a mean rating between 1 and 3 were reworded or deleted. Revisions to the LGB-CSI were made on the basis of feedback from experts. A principal axis factor extraction analysis (EFA) was performed on the remaining items of the LGB-CSI. A five-factor solution using a promax rotation yielded the most interpretable solution.

In Study 2, the factor stability of the initial EFA solution was established via confirmatory factor analyses. Study 3 provided evidence of convergent and discriminant validity of the instrument, as well as internal consistency (described in *Reliability* section). In Study 4 we assessed the test–retest reliability of the instrument (described in *Reliability* section), and in Study 5 we investigated the sensitivity of the LGB-CSI to change across professionals and counselor trainees (described in *Validity* section).

Response Mode and Timing

Participants respond to each item using a 6-point Likert-type scale ranging from 1 (*Not at all Confident*) to 6 (*Extremely Confident*). It typically takes a participant 15 minutes to complete the LGB-CSI.

Scoring

LGB-CSI subscale scores are obtained by summing all items within each of the five subscales: application of knowledge, advocacy skills, awareness, assessment, and relationship. LGB-CSI total scores are obtained by summing all items across the subscales.

Reliability

The LGB-CSI total scale and subscales have evidenced high internal consistency (Cronbach's $\alpha > .70$) in past studies (Dillon & Worthington, 2003; Dillon, Worthington, Soth-McNett, & Schwartz, 2008). However, test-retest reliability estimates indicated LGB-CSI total and subscale scores as relatively unstable over a 2-week time period.

Validity

Content validity of the LGB-CSI items was determined through expert panel review (Dillon & Worthington, 2003). Construct validity was supported through exploratory and confirmatory factor analyses (Dillon & Worthington, 2003). Convergent validity for total scale and subscales was supported by correlations with measures of general counseling self-efficacy and attitudes toward LGB individuals (Dillon & Worthington, 2003). Discriminant validity was evidenced by an absence of relations between the total scale and subscales and measures of social desirability, self-deceptive positivity, and impression management (Dillon & Worthington, 2003). Construct validity was supported by findings indicating varying levels of self-efficacy commensurate with status in the field (Dillon & Worthington, 2003).

References

Bandura, A. (1986). *Social foundations of thought and action: A social cognitive theory.* Englewood Cliffs, NJ: Prentice Hall.

Bieschke, K. J., Eberz, A. B., Bard, C. C., & Croteau, J. M. (1998). Using social cognitive career theory to create affirmative lesbian, gay, and bisexual research training environments. *The Counseling Psychologist, 26,* 735–753.

Bieschke, K. J., McClanahan, M., Tozer, E., Grzegorek, J. L., & Park, J. (2000). Programmatic research on the treatment of lesbian, gay, and bisexual clients: The past, the present, and the course for the future. In R. M. Perez, K. A. DeBord, & K. J. Bieschke (Eds.), *Handbook of counseling and psychotherapy with lesbian, gay, and bisexual clients* (pp. 309–336). Washington, DC: American Psychological Association.

Dillon, F. R., & Worthington, R. L. (2003). The Lesbian, Gay, and Bisexual Affirmative Counseling Self-Efficacy Inventory (LGB-CSI): Development, validation, and training implications. *Journal of Counseling Psychology, 50,* 235–251.

Dillon, F. R., Worthington, R. L., Soth-McNett, A. M., & Schwartz, S. J. (2008). Gender and sexual identity based predictors of lesbian, gay, and bisexual affirmative counseling self-efficacy. *Professional Psychology: Research and Practice, 39,* 353–360.

Exhibit

Lesbian, Gay, and Bisexual Affirmative Counseling Self-Efficacy Inventory

Instructions: Below is a list of activities regarding counseling/psychotherapy. Indicate your confidence in your current ability to perform each activity by marking the appropriate answer below each question ranging from **Not at all Confident** to **Extremely Confident**. Please answer each item based on how you feel now, not on your anticipated (or previous) ability. I am interested in your actual judgments, so please be **honest** in your responses.

How confident am I in my ability to . . .?

1. Directly apply sexual orientation/identity development theory in my clinical interventions with lesbian, gay, and bisexual (LGB) clients.[a]

   Not at all Confident ◯   ◯   ◯   ◯   ◯   ◯ Extremely Confident

2. Directly apply my knowledge of the coming out process with LGB clients.
3. Identify specific mental health issues associated with the coming out process.
4. Understand the socially constructed nature of categories and identities such as lesbian, bisexual, gay, and heterosexual.
5. Explain the impact of gender role socialization on a client's sexual orientation/identity development.
6. Apply existing American Psychological Association guidelines regarding LGB-affirmative counseling practices.
7. Use current research findings about LGB clients' critical issues in the counseling process.
8. Assist LGB clients to develop effective strategies to deal with heterosexism and homophobia.
9. Evaluate counseling theories for appropriateness in working with an LGB client's presenting concerns.
10. Help a client identify sources of internalized homophobia and/or biphobia.
11. Select affirmative counseling techniques and interventions when working with LGB clients.
12. Assist in the development of coping strategies to help same-sex couples who experience different stages in their individual coming out processes.
13. Facilitate an LGB-affirmative counseling/support group.
14. Recognize when my own potential heterosexist biases may suggest the need to refer an LGB client to an LGB-affirmative counselor.
15. Examine my own sexual orientation/identity development process.
16. Identify the specific areas in which I may need continuing education and supervision regarding LGB issues.
17. Identify my own feelings about my own sexual orientation and how it may influence a client.
18. Recognize my real feelings versus idealized feelings in an effort to be more genuine and empathic with LGB clients.
19. Provide a list of LGB-affirmative community resources, support groups, and social networks to a client.
20. Refer an LGB client to affirmative social services in cases of estrangement from their families of origin.
21. Refer LGB clients to LGB-affirmative legal and social supports.
22. Provide a client with city, state, federal, and institutional ordinances and laws concerning civil rights of LGB individuals.
23. Help a same-sex couple access local LGB-affirmative resources and support.
24. Refer an LGB elderly client to LGB-affirmative living accommodations and other social services.
25. Refer an LGB client with religious concerns to an LGB-affirmative clergy member.
26. Integrate clinical data (e.g., mental status exam, intake assessments, presenting concern) of an LGB client.
27. Complete an assessment for a potentially abusive same-sex relationship in an LGB-affirmative manner.
28. Assess for post-traumatic stress felt by LGB victims of hate crimes based on their sexual orientations/identities.
29. Assess the role of alcohol and drugs on LGB clients' social, interpersonal, and intrapersonal functioning.
30. Establish an atmosphere of mutual trust and affirmation when working with LGB clients.
31. Normalize an LGB client's feelings during different points of the coming out process.
32. Establish a safe space for LGB couples to explore parenting.

---

[a]The 6-point scale is repeated after each item.

Sexual Self-Efficacy Scale—Erectile Functioning

CATHERINE S. FICHTEN,[1] *SMBD-Jewish General Hospital*
JILLIAN BUDD, *Adaptech Research Network*
ILANA SPECTOR, *SMBD-Jewish General Hospital*
RHONDA AMSEL, *McGill University*
LAURA CRETI, WILLIAM BRENDER, SALLY BAILES, AND EVA LIBMAN,
SMBD-Jewish General Hospital

The Sexual Self-Efficacy Scale—Erectile Functioning (SSES-E) is a brief self-report measure of the cognitive dimension of erectile functioning and adjustment in men. It evaluates a man's beliefs about his sexual and erectile competence in a variety of situations. The scale may be completed by a man to obtain self-ratings or by his partner to obtain corroboration. Self-efficacy refers to confidence in the belief that one can perform a certain task or behave adequately in a given situation (Bandura, 1982). Sexual self-efficacy is of great concern to most men and a topic of increasing interest with an aging population.

Description

The SSES-E is a 25-item self-report measure that follows Bandura, Adams, and Beyer's (1977) format. Item content is based on questionnaires by Lobitz and Baker (1979) and Reynolds (1978). Respondents indicate which sexual activities they expect they can complete. For each, they rate their confidence level on a scale ranging from 10 to 100. To obtain both partners' views about the male's self-efficacy beliefs, the SSES-E can be completed by both the male subject and his partner.

Response Mode and Timing

The respondent places a check mark in the "Can Do" column next to each sexual activity that he expects he could do if he tried it today. For each activity checked, he also selects a number from 10 to 100 indicating confidence in his ability to perform the activity. The reference scale labels a confidence rating of 10 as *Quite Uncertain*, a rating of 50–60 as *Moderately Certain*, and a rating of 100 as *Quite Certain*. Partners rate sexual functioning according to the same format. This takes 10 minutes.

Scoring

The SSES-E yields a self-efficacy strength score obtained by summing the values in the Confidence column and dividing by 25 (the number of activities rated). Any activity not checked in the Can Do column is presumed to have a 0 confidence (i.e., strength) rating. Some are reluctant to use the 10-point interval, so any continuous number recorded may be used in the Confidence column. Higher scores indicate greater confidence in the man's erectile competence. In case of missing scores, prorating is possible. There must, however, be at least one response in either the Can Do or the Confidence column on items 14 to 25. To deal with missing data, if Can Do is checked and Confidence is left empty, mean score substitution can be used when this occurs fewer than three times. If it occurs more often, the test is invalid.

Reliability

To collect evidence for the reliability of the SSES-E, dysfunctional and control samples were examined. The dysfunctional sample consisted of 17 men presenting with sexual difficulties (13 with Erectile Disorder, 2 with Hypoactive Sexual Desire, 2 with Rapid Ejaculation) at the sex therapy service of a large metropolitan hospital (Libman, Rothenberg, Fichten, & Amsel, 1985). Nine men presented with their female sexual partners. The control group consisted of 15 married couples with nonproblematic sexual functioning, who were matched to the dysfunctional group on demographic variables: the entire sample was composed of middle-class Caucasians with a mean age of 34.

To determine internal consistency, standardized alpha coefficients were calculated for the dysfunctional and control males and females separately. The following estimates were obtained: .92 for dysfunctional males and .94 for their female partners' ratings of their male partners, .92 for control males and .86 for their female partners.

Test-retest reliability, using the control group, was calculated over a 1-month period. Results showed a reliability coefficient of .98 for males and .97 for females.

Validity

Concurrent validity estimates were reported in the original (Libman et al., 1985) study. Recently, Latini et al. (2002)

[1]Address correspondence to Catherine S. Fichten, Behavioural Psychotherapy and Research Unit, Institute of Community and Family Psychiatry, SMBD-Jewish General Hospital, 4333 Cote St. Catherine Rd., Montreal, Quebec, Canada H3T 1E4; e-mail: catherine.fichten@mcgill.ca

correlated men's SSES-E and Psychological Impact of Erectile Dysfunction Scale (PIED) scores. The SSES-E was significantly correlated (−.57 and −.51) with both PIED scales, suggesting that lower sexual self-efficacy about erectile functioning is associated with greater negative impact of erectile dysfunction.

Convergent validity was also established by Swindle, Cameron, Lockhart, and Rosen (2004), who found a correlation of .67 between SSES-E and Psychological and Interpersonal Relationship Scales scores.

Predictive validity was shown by Kalogeropoulos (1991), who found that scores significantly improved in a sample of 53 males who had undergone vasoactive intracavernous pharmacotherapy for erectile dysfunction. Similarly, Latini, Penson, Wallace, Lubeck, and Lue's (2006b) longitudinal study of therapy for erectile dysfunction showed that treatment had an important and significant effect on SSES-E scores. Godschalk et al. (2003) used low-dose human chorionic gonadotropin and placebo in the treatment of benign prostatic hyperplasia. In addition to significant improvement in urine flow in the active treatment sample, the authors also showed improved sexual self-efficacy after treatment relative to placebo subjects ($p < .036$).

The SSES-E has also demonstrated good criterion validity. For example, Latini, Penson, Wallace, Lubeck, and Lue (2006a) found that the SSES-E score was the best predictor of erectile dysfunction severity out of a large number of clinical and psychosocial predictors. Evidence for known-groups criterion validity has also been collected. In our initial sample of 17 dysfunctional men and 15 controls (Libman et al., 1985), dysfunctional men ($M = 53.6$, $SD = 21.1$) and their partners ($M = 47.2$, $SD = 26.7$) scored significantly ($p < .001$) lower on the SSES-E than did functional men ($M = 88.0$, $SD = 10.0$) and their partners ($M = 89.5$, $SD = 10.4$). Moreover, a stepwise discriminant analysis indicated that SSES-E scores were able to classify dysfunctional and nondysfunctional men with 88% accuracy. In addition, data indicate that older married men (age = 65+) had significantly lower self-efficacy scores ($M = 54.10$) than their middle-aged (age = 50–64) counterparts ($M = 70.03$; Libman et al., 1989). Also, men who underwent a transurethral prostatectomy were found to rate their postsurgery sexual self-efficacy lower ($M = 59.3$, $SD = 20.3$) than presurgery ($M = 64.3$, $SD = 18.8$) (Libman et al., 1989, 1991). A study by Latini et al. (2006a) found that men with mild ($M = 74.7$, $SD = 9.31$), moderate ($M = 56.3$, $SD = 10.69$), and severe erectile dysfunction ($M = 34.3$, $SD = 18.38$) differed significantly, $p < .0001$. The findings above were replicated in studies of men with erectile dysfunction who had illness known to affect erectile functioning. For example, Penson et al. found that men with erectile dysfunction as well as prostate cancer (2003a) and diabetes (2003b) reported worse sexual self-efficacy than men with erectile dysfunction but no known underlying medical illness (prostate cancer $M = 37.7$, no prostate cancer $M = 50.6$, $p < .001$; diabetes $M = 38.2$, $SD = 17.75$, no diabetes $M = 47.5$, $SD = 20.30$, $p = .063$).

These results indicate that the SSES-E has excellent psychometric properties. The measure has good internal consistency and test-retest reliability as well as good concurrent, convergent, criterion, and predictive validity. Moreover, the measure has been successfully used in studies of psychological and medical interventions for men with erectile difficulties caused by known disease processes as well as erectile dysfunction of unknown etiology.

Other Information

GlaxoSmithKline (2009) had the measure, which was originally developed in English and French, translated into several languages (cf. Eremenco, 2003) and has been using it in its worldwide Levitra evaluation program. A companion measure, the Sexual Self-Efficacy Scale for Female Functioning (SSES-F), is available in this volume (Bailes et al., 2010).

References

Bailes, S., Creti, L., Fichten, C. S., Libman, E., Brender, W., & Amsel, R. (2010). Sexual Self-Efficacy Scale for Female Functioning. In T. D. Fisher, C. M. Davis, W. L. Yarber, & S. L. Davis (Eds.). *Handbook of sexuality-related measures*. New York: Routledge.

Bandura, A. (1982). Self-efficacy mechanism in human agency. *American Psychologist, 37,* 122–147.

Bandura, A., Adams, N. E., & Beyer, J. (1977). Cognitive processes mediating behavioral change. *Journal of Personality and Social Psychology, 35,* 125–139.

Eremenco, S. (2003). FACIT Multilingual Translations Project, Center on Outcomes, Research, and Education (CORE), Evanston Northwestern Healthcare, Evanston, IL. Available tel: 847-570-7313, s-eremenco@ northwestern.edu

GlaxoSmithKline. (2009). *BAY38-9456, 5/10/20mg, vs. placebo in erectile dysfunction—clinical trial.* Retrieved June 1, 2009, from http:// clinicaltrials.gov/ct2/show/NCT00665054

Godschalk, M. F., Unice, K. A., Bergner, D., Katz, G., Mulligan, T., & McMichael, J. (2003). A trial study: The effect of low dose human chorionic gonadotropin on the symptoms of benign prostatic hyperplasia. *Journal of Urology, 170,* 1264–1269.

Kalogeropoulos, D. (1991). *Vasoactive intracavernous pharmacotherapy for erectile dysfunction: Its effects on sexual, interpersonal, and psychological functioning.* Unpublished doctoral dissertation, Concordia University, Montreal, Canada.

Latini, D. M., Penson, D. F., Colwell, H. H., Lubeck, D. P., Mehta, S. S., Henning, J. M., et al. (2002). Psychological impact of erectile dysfunction: Validation of a new health related quality of life measure for patients with erectile dysfunction. *Journal of Urology, 168,* 2086–2091.

Latini, D. M., Penson, D. F., Wallace, K. L., Lubeck, D. P., & Lue, T. F. (2006a). Clinical and psychosocial characteristics of men with erectile dysfunction: Baseline data from ExCEED. *Journal of Sexual Medicine, 3,* 1059–1067.

Latini, D. M, Penson, D. F., Wallace, K. L., Lubeck, D. P., & Lue, T. F. (2006b). Longitudinal differences in psychological outcomes for men with erectile dysfunction: Results from ExCEED. *Journal of Sexual Medicine, 3,* 1068–1076.

Libman, E., Fichten, C. S., Creti, L., Weinstein, N., Amsel, R., & Brender, W. (1989). Transurethral prostatectomy: Differential effects of age category and presurgery sexual functioning on post prostatectomy sexual adjustment. *Journal of Behavioral Medicine, 12,* 469–485.

Libman, E., Fichten, C. S., Rothenberg, P., Creti, L., Weinstein, N., Amsel, R., et al. (1991). Prostatectomy and inguinal hernia repair: A comparison of the sexual consequences. *Journal of Sex and Marital Therapy, 17,* 27–34.

Libman, E., Rothenberg, I., Fichten, C. S., & Amsel, R. (1985). The SSES-E: A measure of sexual self-efficacy in erectile functioning. *Journal of Sex and Marital Therapy, 11,* 233–244.

Lobitz, W. C., & Baker, E. C. (1979). Group treatment of single males with erectile dysfunction. *Archives of Sexual Behavior, 8,* 127–138.

Penson, D. F., Latini, D. M., Lubeck, D. P., Wallace, K. L., Henning, J. M., & Lue, T. F. (2003a). Do impotent men with diabetes have more severe erectile dysfunction and worse quality of life than the general population of impotent patients? Results from the Exploratory Comprehensive Evaluation of Erectile Dysfunction (ExCEED) database. *Diabetes Care, 26,* 1093–1099.

Penson, D. F., Latini, D. M., Lubeck, D. P., Wallace, K. L., Henning, J. M., & Lue, T. F. (2003b). Is quality of life different for men with erectile dysfunction and prostate cancer compared to men with erectile dysfunction due to other causes? Results from ExCEED data base. *Journal of Urology, 169,* 1458–1461.

Reynolds, B. S., (1978). *Erectile Difficulty Questionnaire.* Unpublished manuscript, Human Sexuality Program, University of California, Los Angeles.

Swindle, R. W., Cameron, A. E., Lockhart, D. C., & Rosen, R. C. (2004). The Psychological and Interpersonal Relationship Scales: Assessing psychological and relationship outcomes associated with erectile dysfunction and its treatment. *Archives of Sexual Behavior, 33,* 19–30.

Exhibit

Sexual Self-Efficacy Scale for Erectile Functioning

NAME:

DATE:

The following form lists sexual activities that men engage in.

For male respondents only:

Under column I (*Can Do*), check (✓) the activities *you expect you could do* if you were asked to do them today.

For *only* those activities you checked in column I, rate your *degree of confidence* in being able to perform them by selecting a number from 10 to 100 using the scale given below. Each activity is independent of the others. Write this number in column II (*Confidence*).

Remember, check (✓) what you *can do.* Then, rate your *confidence* in being able to do each activity if you tried to do it today. Each activity is independent of the others.

For (female) partners only:

Under column I (*Can Do*), check (✓) the activities you think *your male partner could do* if he were asked to do them today.

For only those activities you checked in column I, rate your *degree of confidence* that your male partner could do them by selecting a number from 10 to 100 using the scale given below. Write this number in column II (*Confidence*).

Remember, check (✓) what you expect your male partner *can do.* Then rate your *confidence* in your partner's ability to do each activity if he tried to do it today. Each activity is independent of the others.

10 Quite Uncertain 20 30 40 50 Moderately Certain 60 70 80 90 100 Quite Certain	I Check if Female **Can Do**	II Rate **Confidence** 10–100
1. Anticipate (think about) having intercourse without fear or anxiety.		
2. Get an erection by masturbating when alone.		
3. Get an erection during foreplay when both partners are clothed.		
4. Get an erection during foreplay while both partners are nude.		
5. Regain an erection if it is lost during foreplay.		
6. Get an erection sufficient to begin intercourse.		
7. Keep an erection during intercourse until orgasm is reached.		
8. Regain an erection if it is lost during intercourse.		
9. Get an erection sufficient for intercourse within a reasonable period of time.		
10. Engage in intercourse for as long as desired without ejaculating.		
11. Stimulate the partner to orgasm by means other than intercourse.		
12. Feel sexually desirable to the partner.		
13. Feel comfortable about one's sexuality.		

14. Enjoy a sexual encounter with the partner without having intercourse.		
15. Anticipate a sexual encounter without feeling obliged to have intercourse.		
16. Be interested in sex.		
17. Initiate sexual activities.		
18. Refuse a sexual advance by the partner.		
19. Ask the partner to provide the type and amount of sexual stimulation needed.		
20. Get at least a partial erection when with the partner.		
21. Get a firm erection when with the partner.		
22. Have an orgasm while the partner is stimulating the penis with hand or mouth.		
23. Have an orgasm while penetrating (whether there is a firm erection or not).		
24. Have an orgasm by masturbation when alone (whether there is a firm erection or not).		
25. Get a morning erection.		

NOM:

DATE:

Échelle d'efficacité sexuelle (Forme E)

Le questionnaire suivant donne la liste d'activités sexuelles dans lesquelles les hommes s'engagent.

Pour les hommes:

Cochez dans la colonne *Peut le Faire*, les activités que vous pensez être capable de faire si l'on vous demandait de les faire aujourd'hui.

Seulement pour les activités où vous avez coché *Peut le Faire*, évaluez votre degré de confiance dans le fait que vous pouvez les faire, en choisissant un nombre de 10 à 100, en utilisant l'échelle en bas de la page.

Écrivez les nombres dans la colonne *Confiance*. Rappelez-vous de cocher ce que pensez que vous *pouvez faire*. Évaluez ensuite votre *Confiance* dans le fait d'être capable de faire chaque activité si vous essayiez de le faire aujourd'hui. Chaque activité est indépendante des autres.

Pour les femmes:

Cochez dans la colonne *Peut le Faire*, les activités que vous pensez que votre partenaire pourrait faire, si on lui demandait de les faire aujourd'hui.

Seulement pour les activités où vous avez coché *Peut le Faire*, évaluez votre degré de confiance dans le fait que votre partenaire puisse les faire, en choisissant un nombre de 10 à 100, en utilisant l'échelle en bas de la page.

Écrivez les nombres dans la colonne *Confiance*. Rappelez-vous: Cochez ce que vous pensez que votre partenaire peut faire. Évaluez alors votre *Confiance* dans la capacité de votre partenaire de faire chaque activité, s'il essayait de les faire aujourd'hui. Chaque activité est indépendante des autres.

10 20 30 40 50 60 70 80 90 100	I Cochez (T) si l'Homme **Peut le Faire**	II Évaluez votre Degré de **Confiance** 10–100
Tout à fait Incertain *Modérément Certain* *Certain*		
1. Anticiper (penser à) la pénétration sans peur ni anxiété.		
2. Obtenir une érection en se masturbant seul.		
3. Obtenir une érection pendant les caresses préliminaires quand les deux partenaires sont habillés.		
4. Obtenir une érection pendant les caresses préliminaires quand les deux partenaires sont nus.		
5. Regagner une érection si elle a été perdue pendant les caresses préliminaires.		
6. Obtenir une érection suffisante pour tenter la pénétration.		
7. Conserver une érection pendant la pénétration jusqu'à ce que l'orgasme soit atteint par l'homme.		
8. Regagner une érection si elle est perdue durant la pénétration.		
9. Obtenir une érection suffisante pour la pénétration dans un délai de temps raisonnable.		

10. S'engager dans la pénétration pour aussi longtemps que désiré sans éjaculer.		
11. Stimuler la partenaire jusqu'à l'orgasme de façon autre que par la pénétration.		
12. Se sentir sexuellement désirable pour la partenaire.		
13. Se sentir à l'aise au niveau sexuel.		
14. Avoir du plaisir au cours d'une activité sexuelle avec la partenaire sans qu'il n'y ait de pénétration.		
15. Anticiper une activité sexuelle sans se sentir obligé de faire la pénétration.		
16. Être intéressé au sexe.		
17. Initier les activités sexuelles.		
18. Refuser les avances sexuelles de la partenaire.		
19. Demander à la partenaire de procurer le type et la quantité de stimulation sexuelle désirée.		
20. Obtenir au moins une érection partielle en présence de la partenaire durant les activités sexuelles.		
21. Obtenir une érection ferme en présence de la partenaire durant les activités sexuelles.		
22. Obtenir un orgasme avec la partenaire pendant qu'elle stimule le pénis avec ses mains ou sa bouche.		
23. Obtenir un orgasme pendant la pénétration (que l'érection soit ferme ou non).		
24. Obtenir un orgasme en se masturbant seul (que l'érection soit ferme ou non).		
25. Obtenir une érection le matin au réveil.		

Clitoral Self-Stimulation Scale

ALEXANDRA MCINTYRE-SMITH AND WILLIAM A. FISHER,[1] *University of Western Ontario*

This scale assesses the frequency of women's self-stimulation of the clitoris and genitals in the presence of a partner, as well as their attitudes and affective reactions to such self-stimulation.

Description

The scale is composed of five items measuring attitudinal and affective states in relation to self-stimulation of the clitoris and genitals in the context of sexual interaction with a partner, and one item assessing the frequency of self-stimulation in such situations. Response options vary, reflecting the content of the item.

Scale development followed an iterative process, whereby items were developed and refined over a series of three studies. An initial pool of 18 items was developed and administered to 198 female undergraduate students. Items were subject to individual item analyses and exploratory factor analyses. Ten items were deleted owing to poor empirical performance or poor conceptual overlap with the construct. The eight remaining items and four new items were provided to 16 graduate students, who rated the items for clarity and provided feedback and suggestions for wording changes (see Hinkin, 1998; Streiner & Norman, 2008, for evidence for the use of students as item judges). Recommendations to improve item wording were considered if two or more people suggested them; word-

ing changes were made to three items. The 12 items were then administered to a second sample of 242 female undergraduate participants, and items were subjected to item analyses and exploratory factor analyses. Five items were deleted and two additional items were written. The seven items were administered to 211 female undergraduate participants, and responses were subjected to item analyses and test-retest reliability analyses. Six items were retained for the final scale.

Decision-making regarding item deletion was based on the following scale-development guidelines (see Netemeyer, Bearden, & Sharma, 2003; Streiner & Norman, 2008): (a) range restriction problems (i.e., more than 50% of the sample endorsed a single response option, low standard deviations), (b) poor inter-item correlations with two or more scale items ($r < .30$), (c) poor corrected item-total correlations ($r < .30$), (d) high cross-loadings on nontarget factors ($> .35$ or more), (e) low percentage of variance accounted for within items (i.e., poor communalities, $< .30$), (f) low clarity ratings by expert raters ($M < 5.5$ on a 7-point scale), (g) poor item wording as judged by expert raters, (h) redundancy with other items, (i) poor conceptual overlap (i.e., item was judged to be too dissimilar from other items and/or to poorly reflect the construct).

Sampling was conducted with three groups of female undergraduate students, aged 17–49 years ($M = 18.83$–19.24, $SD = 2.67$–3.38), who were heterosexually active

[1]Address correspondence to Alexandra McIntyre-Smith or William Fisher, Department of Psychology, The University of Western Ontario, London, Ontario, Canada N6A 5C2; e-mail: amcsmith@gmail.com or fisher@uwo.ca

(i.e., they reported having sexual intercourse with a male partner at least twice per month). As this scale was developed based on responses from undergraduate female participants, it is most appropriate for use with this population. Future studies examining the use of this measure with additional populations are needed.

Response Mode and Timing

Respondents are provided with the scale and instructions, and are asked to complete the survey on their own and with as much privacy as possible. The scale was administered using the Internet for the purpose of scale development research. Paper-and-pencil administration of the scale requires 2 to 5 minutes.

This scale was designed to measure individual differences in attitudinal, affective, and behavioral components of the tendency to engage in self-stimulation of the clitoris and genitals in the context of sexual interaction with a partner. No particular time frame or relationship context was assigned to the scale. This approach was chosen so that the scale assesses individual difference dispositions more broadly, rather than being limited to a particular relationship or temporal context. If one were interested in limiting the use of the scale to a specific time frame or sexual relationship (e.g., current partner), the scale could be prefaced with additional instructions specifying this constraint. It should be noted, however, that the scale was not designed or validated with this purpose in mind.

Scoring

1. Score Items 2, 3, and 5 as follows: *Very Unimportant, Strongly Disagree, Very Difficult* = 1. *Moderately Unimportant/Disagree/Difficult* = 2. *Slightly Unimportant/ Disagree/Difficult* = 3. *Neither . . .* = 4. *Slightly Important/ Agree/Easy* = 5. *Moderately Important/Agree/Easy* = 6. *Very Important, Strongly Agree, Very Easy* = 7.
2. Score Items 1 and 4 as follows: *Very Bad, Strongly Agree* = 1. *Moderately Bad/Agree* = 2. *Slightly Bad/Agree* = 3. *Neither . . .* = 4. *Slightly Good/Disagree* = 5. *Moderately Good/Disagree* = 6. *Very Good, Strongly Disagree* = 7.
3. Score Item 6 as follows: 0% = 0, 1–25% = 1, 26–50% = 2, 51–75% = 3, 76–99% = 4, 100% = 5.
4. Because Item 6 is essentially keyed on a 5-point scale (i.e., there is no conceptual equivalent to the 0% response option on the 7-point scales for Items 1–5), and the rest of the items are coded on a 7-point scale, items should be weighted in the following manner:

   a. Multiply Items 1–5 by 5.
   b. Multiply Item 6 by 7.

5. Calculate the average score or the total score for all items. Higher scores indicate a greater proclivity for engaging in self-stimulation of the clitoris or genitals during sexual interaction with a partner.
6. Calculate subscale scores if desired as follows:

a. Attitudes Towards Clitoral Self-Stimulation—Items 1, 2, 5
b. Affective Reactions to Clitoral Self-Stimulation— Items 3–4

When calculating subscale scores, items do not need to be weighted within a given subscale, because the response options are the same for all items (e.g., they are all answered on a 7-point scale).

Reliability

Internal consistency of the total scale was good in all three studies (α = .82–.86). Four-week test-retest reliability was good for the total scale (r = .84) and both subscales (r = .74–.77). The internal consistency of the Attitudes Towards Clitoral Self-Stimulation subscale was excellent in two of the three studies (α = .81–.86) and was adequate in the third study (α = .72), providing good evidence of internal consistency, particularly for a three-item measure. The internal consistency of the Affective Reactions to Clitoral Self-Stimulation Subscale was adequate for two of the three studies (α = .70–.71) but was less desirable in the third study (α = .59), though still acceptable for a two-item subscale.

Validity

Clitoral self-stimulation is a sexual behavior that may not usually be part of the typical sexual script (Gagnon, 1977) and may require a certain degree of openness to sexual experience. Evidence for the convergent validity of the Clitoral Self-Stimulation Scale was explored using measures of openness to a broad range of sexual experiences. The Clitoral Self-Stimulation Scale and subscale scores were correlated with the Sexual Opinion Survey measure of erotophobia-erotophilia (SOS; Fisher, Byrne, White, & Kelley, 1988), r = .39–.48, which is the tendency to respond to sexual stimuli with negative-to-positive affect, and avoidant-to-approach behavior. SOS scores were calculated without two of the 21 items that inquire about self-stimulation ("Manipulating my genitals would probably be an arousing experience" and "Masturbation can be an exciting experience") to reduce inflated estimates of the correlation between the Clitoral Self-Stimulation Scale and erotophobia-erotophilia.

Other evidence of convergent validity includes the correlation of the total score and subscale scores with the Sociosexual Inventory (Simpson & Gangestad, 1991), r = .15–.22, a measure of respondents' willingness to engage in casual, uncommitted sexual relationships; and with frequency of intercourse with a dating partner (r = .20–.27) and a casual sexual partner (r = .53–.66), as well as frequency of masturbation (r = .33–.49). The total scale and subscales were not correlated with the Marlowe-Crowne Social Desirability Scale (Crowne & Marlowe, 1964) or with measures of depression and anxiety (Henry & Crawford,

2005), providing evidence of discriminant validity and freedom from response bias.

References

Crowne, D. P., & Marlowe, D. (1964). *The approval motive: Studies in evaluative dependence.* New York: Wiley.

Fisher, W. A., Byrne, D., White, L. A., & Kelley, K. (1988). Erotophobia-erotophilia as a dimension of personality. *The Journal of Sex Research, 25,* 123–151.

Gagnon, J. H. (1977). *Human sexualities.* Dallas, TX: Scott, Foresman.

Henry, J. D., & Crawford, J. R. (2005). The short-form version of the Depression Anxiety Stress Scales (DASS-21): Construct validity and normative data in a large non-clinical sample. *British Journal of Clinical Psychology, 44,* 227–239.

Hinkin, T. R. (1998). A brief tutorial on the development of measures for use in survey questionnaires. *Organizational Research Methods, 1,* 104–121.

Netemeyer, R. G., Bearden, W. O., & Sharma, S. (2003). *Scaling procedures: Issues and applications.* Thousand Oaks, CA: Sage.

Simpson, J. A., & Gangestad, S. W. (1991). Individual differences in sociosexuality: Evidence for convergent and discriminant validity. *Journal of Personality and Social Psychology, 60,* 870–883.

Streiner, D. L. & Norman, G. R. (2008). *Health measurement scales: A practical guide to their development and use* (4th ed.). New York: Oxford University Press.

Exhibit

Clitoral Self-Stimulation Scale

Instructions: The following questions ask about your thoughts and feelings concerning your sexual experiences and sexual activities with a partner. You are asked to rate each item on the scale provided. Please check off one box per item to indicate your response.

Stimulating myself (i.e., massaging my genitals/clitoris) to help me have an orgasm during intercourse with a partner would be:

1. Good

☐	☐	☐	☐	☐	☐	☐
Very **Good** Good	Moderately Good	Slightly nor Bad	Neither Good Bad	Slightly Bad	Moderately	Very **Bad**

2. Important

☐	☐	☐	☐	☐	☐	☐
Very **Unimportant**	Moderately Unimportant	Very Unimportant	Neither Important nor Unimportant	Slightly Important	Moderately Important	Very **Important**

3. Exciting

☐	☐	☐	☐	☐	☐	☐
Strongly **Disagree**	Moderately Disagree	Slightly Disagree	Neither Agree nor Disagree	Slightly Agree	Moderately Agree	Strongly **Agree**

4. Embarrassing

☐	☐	☐	☐	☐	☐	☐
Strongly **Disagree**	Moderately Disagree	Slightly Disagree	Neither Agree nor Disagree	Slightly Agree	Moderately Agree	Strongly **Agree**

5. Easy

☐	☐	☐	☐	☐	☐	☐
Very **Difficult**	Moderately Difficult	Slightly Difficult	Neither Easy nor Difficult	Slightly Easy	Moderately Easy	Very **Easy**

6. When having sex with a partner, how *often* do you stimulate your clitoris to orgasm?

☐ 0% of the time
☐ 1–25% of the time
☐ 26–50% of the time
☐ 51–75% of the time
☐ 76–99% of the time
☐ 100% of the time

Sexual Sensation Seeking Scale

SETH C. KALICHMAN,[1] *University of Connecticut*

The Sexual Sensation Seeking Scale assesses the dispositional need for varied, novel, and complex sexual experiences and the willingness to take personal physical and social risks for the sake of enhancing sexual sensations. Sexual sensation seeking is therefore a behaviorally specified derivative of the personality disposition sensation seeking, which in turn is derived from the trait known as extraversion (Zuckerman, 1994). Sexual sensation seeking is behaviorally defined as a dimension of sensation seeking and should not be considered an alternative or replacement for the sensation-seeking construct. The item content of the Sexual Sensation Seeking Scale is sex-specific and does not confound substance use or other conceptual factors with sexual risk taking. The Sexual Sensation Seeking Scale was designed as a psychometric assessment of sexual adventurism or sexual risk taking in adolescents and adults. The scale has been used primarily in research with adults on their risks for sexually transmitted infections, including HIV/AIDS.

Description

The Sexual Sensation Seeking Scale was originally derived from the Sensation Seeking Scale (Zuckerman, 1994), with items redefined for sexual relevance. A three-step process was used to develop the original scale. The first step involved carefully examining the item content of Zuckerman's Sensation Seeking Scale and selecting items that demonstrated the highest loadings on the factors from Zuckerman's original factor analysis (e.g., thrill and adventure seeking, disinhibition, boredom susceptibility). The second step involved conducting focus groups with adults on the appropriateness of the item content and framing of items for sexual content. For example, we revised the item "I like wild and uninhibited parties" to "I like wild and uninhibited sexual encounters." The final step involved clarifying content and refining wording of the original scale items with additional focus groups of gay, bisexual, and heterosexual men and women. Items were refined following community feedback and were placed on 4-point scales, 1 = *Not at all Like Me*, 2 = *Slightly Like Me*, 3 = *Mainly Like Me*, 4 = *Very Much Like Me*. Following initial scale development research (Kalichman et al., 1994), the items were further refined with original items that tapped sexually coercive behavior replaced with items reflecting sexual adventurism. The final scale consists of 10 items

developed for use with men and women and has shown utility with adolescents and adults of all ages.

Response Mode, Timing, and Scoring

The 10-item Sexual Sensation Seeking Scale requires less than 5 minutes to self-administer or interview administer. The scale does not have formally developed subscales. Scoring involves summing the items or taking the mean response (sum of items/10). There are no reverse-scored items.

Reliability

The Sexual Sensation Seeking Scale has demonstrated excellent internal consistency across several relevant diverse populations, including male (α = .83) and female (α = .81) college students (Gaither & Sellbom, 2003), community samples of men and women (α's = .79–.83; Hendershot, Stoner, George, & Norris, 2007; Maisto et al., 2004), sexually transmitted disease clinic patients in South Africa (α = .71; Kalichman, Simbayi, Jooste, Vermaak, & Cain, 2008), gay and bisexual men (α's range from .75 to .79; Kalichman et al., 1994; Kalichman & Rompa, 1995), and HIV-positive men (α = .83; O'Leary, Fisher, Purcell, Spikes, & Gomez, 2007). Item-to-total correlations range from .25 to .79, with no single item substantially reducing or improving the internal consistency when deleted from the total scale. The scale has also demonstrated acceptable time stability over 2 weeks (r = .69; Kalichman & Rompa, 1995) and 3 months (r = .78; Kalichman et al., 1994).

Validity

The Sexual Sensation Seeking Scale has demonstrated evidence for its construct validity. Kalichman et al. (1994) found that among gay and bisexual men the scale correlated with rates of unprotected intercourse (r = .32), numbers of sexual partners (r = .38), and alcohol use in sexual contexts (r = .23). Kalichman and Rompa (1995) found the scale correlated with numbers of sex partners in men (r = .22) and women (r = .39). Gaither and Sellbom (2003) reported that the scale correlated with number of one-night-stand sexual encounters for men (r = .31) and women (r = .40), an association also reported by Hendershot et al. (2007). Sexual Sensation Seeking Scale scores also correlate significantly

[1]Address correspondence to Seth C. Kalichman, Department of Psychology, 406 Babbidge Road, University of Connecticut, Storrs, CT 06269; e-mail: seth.k@uconn.edu

with the perceived pleasure of an array of sexual activities, whereas the scale is inversely associated with sexual risk reduction practices, including condom use (Kalichman & Rompa, 1995). A similar pattern of associations between sexual sensation seeking and a variety of sexual practices was found in a sample of adolescents in Spain (Gutiérrez-Martínez, Bermúdez, Teva, & Buela-Casal, 2007). Hart et al. (2003) found that gay and bisexual men who practice anal sex as both the receptive and the insertive partner score higher on the scale than men who practice either receptive or insertive anal sex. Evidence for the scale's discriminant validity was demonstrated by Berg (2008), who found that the Sexual Sensation Seeking Scale was the single best discriminating factor between gay and bisexual men who practice unprotected sex with limited concern about becoming HIV infected and men who do not.

Other Information

The Sexual Sensation Seeking Scale is in the public domain and available for open use. National Institute of Mental Health (NIMH) grant R01-MH71164 supported preparation of this chapter.

References

Berg, R. C. (2008). Barebacking among MSM Internet users. *AIDS and Behavior, 12,* 822–833.

Gaither, G. A., & Sellbom, M. (2003). The sexual sensation seeking scale: Reliability and validity within a heterosexual college student sample. *Journal of Personality Assessment, 81,* 157–167.

Gutiérrez-Martínez, O., Bermúdez, M. P., Teva, I., & Buela-Casal, G. (2007). Sexual sensation-seeking and worry about sexually transmitted diseases (STD) and human immunodeficiency virus (HIV) infection among Spanish adolescents. *Psicothema, 19,* 661–666.

Hart, T. A., Wolitski, R. J., Purcell, D. W., Gómez, C., Halkitis, P., & the Seropositive Urban Men's Study Team. (2003). Sexual behavior among HIV-positive men who have sex with men: What's in a label? *The Journal of Sex Research, 40,* 179–188.

Hendershot, C. S., Stoner, S. A., George, W. H., & Norris, J. (2007). Alcohol use, expectancies, and sexual sensation seeking as correlates of HIV risk behavior in heterosexual young adults. *Psychology of Addictive Behaviors, 21,* 365–372.

Kalichman, S. C., Adair, V., Rompa, D., Multhauf, K., Johnson, J., & Kelly, J. (1994). Sexual sensation-seeking: Scale development and predicting AIDS-risk behavior among homosexually active men. *Journal of Personality Assessment, 62,* 385–397.

Kalichman, S. C., & Rompa, D. (1995). Sexual sensation seeking and sexual compulsivity scales: Reliability, validity, and predicting HIV risk behaviors. *Journal of Personality Assessment, 65,* 586–602.

Kalichman, S. C., Simbayi, L., Jooste, S., Vermaak R., & Cain, D. (2008). Sensation seeking and alcohol use predict HIV transmission risks: Prospective study of sexually transmitted infection clinic patients, Cape Town, South Africa. *Addictive Behaviors, 33,* 1630–1633.

Maisto, S. A., Carey, M. P., Carey, K. B., Gordon, C. M., Schum, J. L., & Lynch, K. G. (2004). The relationship between alcohol and individual differences variables on attitudes and behavioral skills relevant to sexual health among heterosexual young adult men. *Archives of Sexual Behavior, 33,* 571–584.

O'Leary, A., Fisher, H. H., Purcell, D. W., Spikes, P. S., & Gomez, C. A. (2007). Correlates of risk patterns and race/ethnicity among HIV-positive men who have sex with men. *AIDS and Behavior, 11,* 706–715.

Zuckerman, M. (1994). *Biological expression and biological bases of sensation seeking.* New York: Cambridge University Press

Exhibit

Sexual Sensation Seeking Scale

A number of statements that some people have used to describe themselves are given below. Read each statement and then circle the number to show how well you believe the statement describes you.

	Not at all Like Me	Slightly Like Me	Mainly Like Me	Very Much Like Me
1. I like wild "uninhibited" sexual encounters.	1	2	3	4
2. The physical sensations are the most important thing about having sex.	1	2	3	4
3. My sexual partners probably think I am a "risk taker."	1	2	3	4
4. When it comes to sex, physical attraction is more important to me than how well I know the person.	1	2	3	4
5. I enjoy the company of sensual people.	1	2	3	4
6. I enjoy watching "X-rated" videos.	1	2	3	4
7. I am interested in trying out new sexual experiences.	1	2	3	4
8. I feel like exploring my sexuality.	1	2	3	4
9. I like to have new and exciting sexual experiences and sensations.	1	2	3	4
10. I enjoy the sensations of intercourse without a condom.	1	2	3	4

Sexual Self-Consciousness Scale

J. J. D. M. van Lankveld,[1] *Maastricht University, The Netherlands*
H. Sykora, *Manë Center, Maasmechelen, Belgium*
W. E. H. Geijen, *Maastricht University, The Netherlands*

The Sexual Self-Consciousness Scale (SSCS) aims to measure individual variability with regard to the propensity to become self-conscious in sexual situations. Self-focused attention was found to have impeding effects on genital sexual responsiveness, presumably because it also reduces processing capacity (Meston, 2006). Next to this effect of a state of self-focused attention, experimentally induced self-focus was found to interact with the personality trait of sexual self-consciousness in its effect on genital arousal (Meston, 2006; van Lankveld & Bergh, 2008; van Lankveld, van den Hout, & Schouten, 2004). Subjective experience of sexual excitement was not affected in these studies. Sexual self-consciousness may thus constitute a vulnerability factor for the development of sexual dysfunction.

Description

Based on the sexological literature and on the opinion of a local panel of sexological experts, Hendriks (1997) selected 15 items to construct the SSCS. The items represented private and public aspects of self-consciousness proneness in sexual situations and of sexual anxiety and discomfort, analogous to the subscales of the Self-Consciousness Scale (Fenigstein, Scheier, & Buss, 1975). In a psychometric study (van Lankveld, Geijen, & Sykora, 2008), 282 participants between the ages of 16 and 75 years completed questionnaires. A total of 253 participants provided both demographic and SSCS data. Eighty percent of the 171 female participants (*M* age, 25.6 years; *SD* = 7.7; range, 16–58) had a steady male partner; 20% were single. Of 82 men (*M* age, 34.1 years; *SD* = 11.8; range, 16–70) 89% had a steady female partner; 11% were single. In a principal components analysis (PCA) on the initial 15-item questionnaire, the best-fitting solution contained two components (Sexual Embarrassment, Sexual Self-Focus) with eigenvalues > 1. Based on this PCA, multitrait scaling analysis (Hays & Hayashi, 1990), and subscale internal consistency, 12 items were retained. The final subscales both consisted of six items. The oblimin-rotated PCA on the final 12-item version again revealed two factors together explaining 53.7% of the variance (see Table 1). Normative scores of the SSCS have not yet been published.

TABLE 1
Principal Components Analysis of the 12-Item Sexual Self-Consciousness Scale: Oblimin-Rotated Pattern Matrix

Item	Component 1	Component 2
Sexual Embarrassment Subscale		
It takes quite some time for me to overcome my shyness in sexual situations.	.84	
I quickly feel embarrassed in sexual situations.	.80	
I feel uncomfortable in sexual situations.	.79	
I find it difficult to sexually let myself go in front of the other person.	.76	
When I see myself during sex, I am irritatingly aware of myself.	.60	
I continuously feel being observed by the other person during sex.	.57	
Sexual Self-Consciousness Subscale		
I am aware during sex of the impression I make on the other person.		.73
I pay much attention to my sexual thoughts and feelings.		.73
I often wonder during sex what the other person thinks of me.		.68
I am preoccupied by the way I behave sexually.		.68
During sex, I pay much attention to what happens inside my body.		.62
I often imagine how I behave during sex.		.55
Eigenvalue	4.58	1.87
Percentage of explained variance	38.10	15.60

Note: Loadings < .40 have been suppressed; together, both components explained 53.7% of the total variance.

Response Mode and Timing

Items are presented as brief descriptive statements. Participants rate their level of endorsement on a 5-point Likert-type scale. Scale interval anchors are: *Strongly Disagree* = 0, *Disagree a Little* = 1, *Neither Agree nor Disagree* = 2, *Agree a Little* = 3, and *Strongly Agree* = 4. Completion requires less than 5 minutes.

[1]Address correspondence to J. J. D. M. van Lankveld, Department of Clinical Psychological Science, Maastricht University, P. O. Box 616, Maastricht 6200 MD, The Netherlands; e-mail: J.vanLankveld@DEP.Unimaas.nl

Scoring

Subscales representing the Sexual Embarrassment and Sexual Self-Focus components are calculated as sum scores (see Exhibit).

Reliability

The internal consistency of the current version is good for the Sexual Embarrassment subscale (Cronbach's α =.84), satisfactory for the Sexual Self-Focus subscale (Cronbach's α = .79), and good for the full 12-item scale (Cronbach's α =.85). Correlations between the subscales in our full sample were $r = .44$ ($p < .001$), which is less than their respective reliability coefficients, and is considered as solid evidence that the subscales measure distinct concepts. Test-retest reliability after a 4-week interval was satisfactory for the subscales (for Sexual Embarrassment, $r = .84$; for Sexual Self-Focus, $r = .79$), and for the total score ($r = .79$; all $ps < .001$; van Lankveld, Geijen, & Sykora, 2008).

Validity

In the psychometric study (van Lankveld, Geijen, & Sykora, 2008), 61 sexually dysfunctional participants were identified (42 women, 19 men). Sexually dysfunctional participants were older (M_{dysf} = 34.1 year; M_{func} = 26.6 year, $p < .001$), more often had a steady partner (M_{dysf} = 93.2%; M_{func} = 79.7%, $p < .05$), and had longer relationships (M_{dysf} = 10.5 year; M_{func} = 6.0 year, $p < .01$).

Sexual Embarrassment and Sexual Self-Focus scores were significantly related to age, $F(2, 234) = 9.60$, $p < .001$. Independent main effects were found of Sex, $F(2, 234) = 8.48$, $p < .001$; Group, $F(2, 234) = 7.02$, $p = .001$; and Partner Status, $F(2, 234) = 4.11$, $p < .05$. Post hoc tests revealed that, compared with sexually functional participants, sexually dysfunctional participants scored higher on Sexual Embarrassment, $F(1, 235) = 10.98$, $p = .001$, and on Sexual Self-Focus, $F(1, 235) = 8.97$, $p < .005$.

Compared to men, women scored higher on Sexual Embarrassment, $F(1, 235) = 12.07$, $p = .001$, whereas women's and men's Sexual Self-Focus scores did not differ. Participants without a partner scored higher on Sexual Embarrassment, $F(1, 235) = 8.26$, $p < .005$, whereas participants with and without partners did not differ significantly on Sexual Self-Focus. In repeated MANCOVA in the subsample of participants with a partner ($N = 189$), with duration of the relationship added as a covariate, the main effects of Group and Sex were retained. Convergent and divergent construct validity were investigated by inspecting the Pearson product-moment correlation matrix of the SSCS subscales and the putative similar construct of general self-consciousness, on the one hand, and the putative dissimilar construct of psychological distress on the other hand.

For the purpose of interpretation, following Cohen (1988), we considered $r < |.15|$ as small, $|.15| < r < |.35|$ as medium, and $r > |.35|$ as large. As expected, the SSCS Sexual Embarrassment and Sexual Self-Focus subscales were both found to show medium- to large-size correlations with the subscales of the general Self-Consciousness Scale (Fenigstein et al., 1975). As expected, nonsignificant or medium-size correlation coefficients ($.20 > r > .24$, $p < .05$) were found on the SSCS Sexual Self-Focus and the Psychological Distress subscales of the SCL-90. However, large-size correlations were found between SSCS Sexual Embarrassment and the psychological distress subscales of the SCL-90, varying between $r = .36$ (SCL-90 Somatic Complaints) and $r = .49$ (SCL-90 Depression).

References

Cohen, J. (1988). *Statistical power analysis for the behavioral sciences* (2nd ed.). Hillsdale, NJ: Lawrence Erlbaum.

Fenigstein, A., Scheier, M. F., & Buss, A. H. (1975). Public and private self-consciousness: Assessment and theory. *Journal of Consulting and Clinical Psychology, 43,* 522–527.

Hays, R., & Hayashi, T. (1990). Beyond internal consistency reliability: Rationale and user's guide for Multitrait Analysis Program on the microcomputer. *Behavior Research Methods, Instruments, and Computers, 22,* 167–175.

Hendriks, T. (1997). *Een hypothetisch cognitief verklaringsmodel voor seksuele dysfuncties* [A hypothetical cognitive explanatory model of sexual dysfunction]. Unpublished master's thesis, Maastricht University, Maastricht, The Netherlands.

Meston, C. M. (2006). The effects of state and trait self-focused attention on sexual arousal in sexually functional and dysfunctional women. *Behaviour Research and Therapy, 44,* 515–532.

van Lankveld, J. J. D. M., & Bergh, S. (2008). The interaction of state and trait aspects of self-focused attention affects genital, but not subjective, sexual arousal in sexually functional women. *Behaviour Research and Therapy, 46,* 514–528.

van Lankveld, J. J. D. M., Geijen, W., & Sykora, H. (2008). Reliability and validity of the Sexual Self-Consciousness Scale: Psychometric properties. *Archives of Sexual Behavior, 37,* 925–933.

van Lankveld, J. J. D. M., van den Hout, M. A., & Schouten, E. G. (2004). The effects of self-focused attention, performance demand, and dispositional sexual self-consciousness on sexual arousal of sexually functional and dysfunctional men. *Behaviour Research and Therapy, 42,* 915–935.

Exhibit

Sexual Self-Consciousness Scale

Instructions: Every question has 5 possible answers: *Strongly Disagree* (0), *Disagree a Little* (1), *Neither Agree nor Disagree* (2), *Agree a Little* (3), and *Strongly Agree* (4). Please encircle the number that you feel best represents your opinion.

You don't need to take much time to consider each item. However, it is important that you give the answer that best represents your opinion, not what you think your opinion should be.

  Please respond to each item.

1. I feel uncomfortable in sexual situations.	0	1	2	3	4
2. I often imagine how I behave during sex.	0	1	2	3	4
3. I pay much attention to my sexual thoughts and feelings.	0	1	2	3	4
4. I quickly feel embarrassed in sexual situations.	0	1	2	3	4
5. I often wonder during sex what the other person thinks of me.	0	1	2	3	4
6. I am preoccupied by the way I behave sexually.	0	1	2	3	4
7. I am aware during sex of the impression I make on the other person.	0	1	2	3	4
8. During sex, I pay much attention to what happens inside my body.	0	1	2	3	4
9. I find it difficult to sexually let myself go in front of the other person.	0	1	2	3	4
10. When I see myself during sex, I am irritatingly aware of myself.	0	1	2	3	4
11. It takes quite some time for me to overcome my shyness in sexual situations.	0	1	2	3	4
12. I continuously feel being observed by the other person during sex.	0	1	2	3	4

Sexual History Questionnaire

CAROLINE CUPITT,[1] *Oxleas NHS Foundation Trust, London*

The Sexual History Questionnaire (SHQ) was devised to assess the degree to which an individual's sexual behavior is putting him or her at risk of infection by HIV, the virus that leads to AIDS. Respondents are asked to self-report such behavior and, in addition, are questioned regarding their beliefs about their risk of contracting HIV.

Description

The SHQ was originally designed for use with college students and has since been used to study the sexual behavior of this population across several cultures, including the UK (Cupitt & de Silva, 1994), Turkey (Askun & Ataca, 2007), South Africa (Aitken, 2005), and North America (Ehrhardt, Krumboltz, & Koopman, 2006; Lam & Barnhart, 2006; Peterson, 2006).

    The questionnaire first asks for information concerning basic demographic characteristics and is then divided into four sections. Section A begins by asking whether respondents have sex with men or women (see Exhibit instructions for the definitions used for "have sex"). This makes the important distinction between sexual identity and sexual behavior, which may be very different (Bancroft, 1989). Two questions follow, asking whether the respondent has ever had protected or unprotected penetrative sex.

    Section B asks for details of all sexual encounters over the past month. Because retrospective self-report of sexual behavior has been criticized for its unreliability, Section C then asks about the last occasion the respondent had sex. This allows for more detailed questioning about interpersonal and situational variables involved in the last sexual encounter.

    Finally, Section D includes a brief set of questions relating to contact with HIV counseling, sufferers, and risk

[1]Address correspondence to Caroline Cupitt, Consultant Clinical Psychologist, Oxleas NHS Foundation Trust, Assertive Outreach Team, Erith Centre, Park Crescent, Bexley, Kent, UK, DA8 3EE; e-mail: caroline.cupitt@oxleas.nhs.uk

assessment. There is substantial evidence that sexual-behavior change is affected by knowing someone who has died of HIV (e.g., Becker & Joseph, 1988) and some evidence that it may be affected by HIV antibody test counseling. Respondents are asked to make a general assessment of their perceived risk for HIV/AIDS using a standard scale.

Response Mode and Timing

A combination of multiple-choice, yes/no, 5-point scale, and numerical questions are used. The questionnaire takes between 5 and 10 minutes to complete, depending on the complexity of the respondent's sexual history.

Scoring

The questionnaire was not originally designed to be scored. However, the information in Section B gives an indication of the respondent's current risk of HIV infection. If a respondent has had unprotected penetrative sex in the past month, he or she can be said to be at high risk. This assumes that the risk from oral sex is not significant.

Peterson (2006) describes calculating a sexual risk composite score using the responses to four items, which are then assigned values as follows: age of first penetrative sex (question 2: values range from 6 to 1), number of sexual partners (question 4: values range from 1 to 6), history of unprotected penetrative sex (question 3: 3 or 0), and unprotected penetrative sex in the last encounter (question 9: 3 or 0). By assigning values within the ranges given, weight is given to items that have been demonstrated to be associated with increased risk of contracting sexually transmitted infections and/or unplanned pregnancies (DiClemente, 1992; Roosa, Tein, Reinholtz, & Angelini, 1997).

Reliability

By its nature, the behavior this questionnaire seeks to measure is ever changing. In an endeavor to increase the reliability of the information gained, there is a focus on the last occasion the respondent had sex. In the original research (Cupitt, 1992), the final section, D, was submitted to a test-retest reliability measurement. The questions in Section D were repeated over a 2-week interval with a group of 18 postgraduate students, and all were found to have an intraclass correlation of above .80 ($p < .001$), indicating a high level of reliability.

Validity

Most of the questions are considered to have high face validity. To ensure that the respondent shared the same understanding of the different sexual practices mentioned, a summary of definitions was included at the beginning of the questionnaire. Critically, these definitions distinguish penetrative from nonpenetrative forms of sexual contact. The concept of *penetrative partner* has been advocated by Project SIGMA (Socio-Sexual Investigations of Gay Men and AIDS; Hunt, Davies, Weatherburn, Coxon, & McManus, 1991). They argue that the notion of sexual partner per se is not valid to estimate risk behavior for HIV and that the concept of a penetrative sexual partner is considerably more accurate.

References

Aitken, L. (2005). *The influence of HIV knowledge, beliefs, and religiosity on sexual risk behaviours of private school adolescents.* Minithesis, University of the Western Cape, Bellville, South Africa. Retrieved from http://etd.uwc.ac.za/usrfiles/modules/etd/docs/etd_init_3582_1174044987.pdf

Askun, D., & Ataca, B. (2007). Sexuality related attitudes and behaviors of Turkish university students. *Archives of Sexual Behavior, 36,* 741–752.

Bancroft, J. (1989). *Human sexuality and its problems* (2nd ed.). Edinburgh, UK: Churchill Livingstone.

Becker, M. H., & Joseph, J. G. (1988). AIDS and behavioral change to reduce risk: A review. *American Journal of Public Health, 78,* 394–410.

Cupitt, C. (1992). *Cognitive factors in the decision to adopt safer sex practices.* Unpublished master's thesis, University of London, UK.

Cupitt, C., & de Silva, P. (1994). Zilbergeld's myths and sexual activity in the age of AIDS: An empirical study. *Sexual and Marital Therapy, 9,* 17–31.

DiClemente, R. J. (1992). Psychosocial determinants of condom use among adolescents. In R. J. DiClemente (Ed.), *Adolescents and AIDS: A generation in jeopardy* (pp. 34–51). Newbury Park, CA: Sage.

Ehrhardt, B. L., Krumboltz, J. D., & Koopman, C. (2006). Training peer sexual health educators: Changes in knowledge, counseling self-efficacy and sexual risk behavior. *American Journal of Sexuality Education, 2,* 39–55.

Hunt, A. J., Davies, P. M., Weatherburn, P., Coxon, A. P., & McManus, T. J. (1991). Sexual partners, penetrative sexual partners and HIV risk. *AIDS, 5,* 723–728.

Lam, A. G., & Barnhart, J. E. (2006). It takes two: The role of partner ethnicity and age characteristics on condom negotiations of heterosexual Chinese and Filipina American college women. *AIDS Education and Prevention, 18,* 68–80.

Peterson, S. H. (2006). The importance of fathers: Contextualizing sexual risk taking in "low risk" African-American adolescent girls. *Journal of Human Behavior in the Social Environment, 13*(3), 67–83.

Roosa, M. W., Tein, J., Reinholtz, C., & Angelini, P. J. (1997). The relationship of childhood sexual abuse to teenage pregnancy. *Journal of Marriage and the Family, 59,* 119–130.

Exhibit

Sexual History Questionnaire

Instructions: This questionnaire asks questions about your recent sexual history. Your answers are entirely confidential. Some words used in this questionnaire may not be familiar to you, or you may not be sure of their exact meaning. The following definitions may be helpful: *Vaginal sex* is sex in which the penis enters the vagina. *Oral sex* is sex in which the mouth or tongue is in contact with the genitals. *Anal sex* is sex in which the penis enters the anus, or back passage. *Penetrative sex* is sex in which the penis enters the vagina or anus. *Nonpenetrative sex* includes oral sex, and also many other forms of sex such as massage, touching, and mutual masturbation. *Protected sex* refers to sex with a condom or oral sex with a latex barrier or condom. A *regular partner*, for the purposes of this study, is someone with whom you have had sex more than once.

Please indicate your gender   male/female

        your age   _____ years

        your status   undergraduate/postgraduate

        the religion which influences you most (please circle):

I Christianity   2 Judaism   3 Islam   4 Hinduism   5 Other

Section A

1. Who do you have sex with? (please circle):

    I only men   2 mostly men   3 equally men and women   4 mostly women   5 only women

2. Have you ever had penetrative sex (sex in which the penis penetrates the vagina or anus)?
   Yes/no
   If yes, at what age did you first have penetrative sex? _____

3. Have you ever had unprotected penetrative sex (penetrative sex without a condom)?
   Yes/no

Section B

The following questions relate to your sexual encounter(s) over the last month. This includes nonpenetrative sex such as oral sex and mutual masturbation. If you have not had sex in the last month please move on to Section C. If you have never had sex please move on to Section D.

4. In the last month how many sexual partners have you had? _____
5. How many of these were regular partners (people with whom you have had sex more than once)? _____

6. (a) How many times have you had sex with a regular partner in the last month? _____
   (b) On how many of these occasions did you have penetrative sex? _____
   (c) On how many of these occasions did you use a condom? _____

7. (a) How many times have you had sex with other partners in the last month? ___
   (b) On how many of these occasions did you have penetrative sex? _____
   (c) On how many of these occasions did you use a condom? _____

Section C

The following questions refer specifically to your last sexual encounter.

8. How long ago was your last sexual encounter? Please circle.
   I less than a week ago
   2 between one week and one month ago
   3 between one month and three months ago
   4 between three months and six months ago
   5 between six months and one year ago
   6 more than one year ago

9. What kind(s) of sex did you have on this occasion? Please answer yes or no to the following activities:

Unprotected vaginal sex	yes/no
Vaginal sex with a condom	yes/no
Unprotected anal sex	yes/no
Anal sex with a condom	yes/no

Oral sex   yes/no

Other forms of nonpenetrative sex (such as massage and mutual masturbation)   yes/no

10. What gender was your partner on this occasion?
    Male/female

11. On this occasion did you or your partner mention using a condom?
    1 you
    2 your partner
    3 neither

12. On this occasion did you or your partner mention practicing nonpenetrative sex?
    1 you
    2 your partner
    3 neither

13. Was s/he a regular sexual partner (a partner with whom you have had sex more than once)?
    Yes/no

    If yes, have you discussed practicing safer sex with this partner (using condoms or latex barriers, or having nonpenetrative sex)?
    Yes/no

14. If you had heterosexual vaginal sex on this occasion, did you use a form of contraception? Please circle one or more:
    1 the condom
    2 the pill
    3 the diaphragm or cap
    4 IUD (the coil)
    5 spermicidal sponge, creams, or pessaries
    6 the rhythm (calendar) method
    7 the withdrawal method
    8 other (please specify) _____
    9 none

15. With this partner, have you discussed what kind of sex you like and don't like
    Yes/no

Using the scale below, write a number beside each statement to indicate how you felt.

1	2	3	4	5
Not at all				A Great Deal

16. How much did you feel like having sex on this occasion? _____
17. How much did your partner feel like having sex on this occasion? _____
18. With this partner on this occasion, how able did you feel to express your wishes regarding sex? _____

Section D
Using the same scale, answer the following, more general question.

1	2	3	4	5
Not at all				A Great Deal

19. How much at risk do you consider yourself from HIV/AIDS? _____

20. Have you ever had an HIV antibody test?
    Yes/no

21. Did you get the result of the test?
    Yes/no/nonapplicable

22. To your knowledge, do you know or have you known anyone personally with HIV or AIDS?
    Yes/no

23. Please feel free to add anything which may give a clearer picture of your answers to this questionnaire.

Affective and Motivational Orientation Related to Erotic Arousal Questionnaire

CRAIG A. HILL,[1] *Indiana University-Purdue University Fort Wayne*

The Affective and Motivational Orientation Related to Erotic Arousal Questionnaire (AMORE) is a self-report questionnaire designed to measure individual differences in eight dispositional sexual motives proposed within a construct of intrinsic sexual motivation. A dispositional sexual motive is a relatively stable interest in obtaining gratification from a specific outcome associated with sexual behavior or sexual interaction. Intrinsic sexual motivation is the desire or interest in outcomes inherent in sexual expression, those that cannot be experienced except through sexual expression. The eight sexual motives assessed by the AMORE are the desire to (a) feel valued by one's partner, (b) express value for one's partner, (c) obtain relief from negative emotional states, (d) provide nurturance and comfort to one's partner, (e) enhance one's power, (f) experience the power of one's partner, (g) experience sensuality and physical pleasure, and (h) procreate. The eight motives are considered to be important factors influencing individuals to engage in sexual behavior (Hill & Preston, 1996).

Description

The AMORE comprises 62 statements dealing with the tendency to desire or find pleasure in specific aspects of sexual expression; these specific tendencies are called sexual motives. The focus of each statement is one of the eight sexual motives identified within the construct of intrinsic sexual motivation presented in the previous section. To begin the instrument development process, an initial pool of 101 statements was constructed in such a way as to convey the theoretical and conceptual essence of a given sexual motive, a theory-driven process.

Principal components analysis of responses to the statements by 612 college students confirmed the existence of eight motive dimensions for 62 of the items; 39 items were eliminated based on this analysis because of low factor loadings, or loading highly on more than one factor. The selected 62 items were administered to two additional groups of college students (Ns = 586 and 396), and each set of responses was separately factor analyzed. Both analyses produced solutions highly similar to the one for the initial sample of respondents, confirming the presence of eight stable factors. The instrument has been employed with noncollege-student samples, as well.

Response Mode and Timing

The AMORE is a self-report questionnaire. Each of the 62 statements is evaluated by respondents on a 5-point Likert-type scale. The response scale is labeled at the low extreme with *Not at all True*, *Moderately True* at the midpoint, and *Completely True* at the high extreme. The alphabetic letters A through E represent each of the points on the scale. In early research, respondents marked their ratings on a Scantron sheet. More recently, the questionnaire has been presented on computers employing MediaLab software, with responses recorded electronically.

Scoring

The AMORE consists of eight subscales measuring each of the theoretically derived sexual motive dimensions. Responses are converted to numeric values in the following way: A = 1, B = 2, C = 3, D = 4, and E = 5. Item 21 is coded in the reverse direction. Values for items on each subscale are added together to create a total subscale score. The items belonging to each subscale are shown in Table 1.

Reliability

Internal consistency coefficients (alphas) for the subscales have ranged from .76 (for the Procreation subscale) to .94 (for the Relief From Stress and Partner Power subscales) across a number of samples. Most coefficients are typically greater than .85 (Hill, 1997b, 2002; Hill & Preston, 1996).

TABLE 1
Items Belonging to Subscales of the AMORE

Subscale	Item Numbers
Valued by Partner	1, 9, 14, 26, 35, 36, 38
Value for Partner	17, 43, 44, 49, 55, 59, 60, 61
Relief from Stress	3, 12, 20, 27, 28, 31, 37, 39, 40, 45
Nurturance	2, 10, 33, 52, 57, 62
Expression of Power	6, 7, 11, 16, 41, 46, 48, 53, 56, 58
Experience Partner's Power	5, 13, 19, 23, 25, 29, 47, 50, 51, 54
Pleasure and Sensuality	18, 22, 24, 30, 34
Procreation	4, 8, 15, 21, 32, 42

[1]Address correspondence to Craig Hill, Department of Psychology, IPFW, Fort Wayne, IN 46805; e-mail: hillc@ipfw.edu

Validity

A number of studies have supported the validity of the eight AMORE subscales. The convergent and divergent validity of the AMORE subscales have been established through correlations with scores on measures of constructs theoretically related and unrelated, respectively, to the sexual motivation constructs (Hill & Preston, 1996). The distinctiveness of the subscales was supported in reactions to eight role-played sexual scenarios designed to be uniquely relevant to each of the eight sexual motives. Reported likelihood of engaging in sexual behavior in each situation was correlated most strongly with scores on the theoretically most relevant AMORE scale (e.g., likelihood of sexual behavior in a situation focused on expressing one's power was most highly correlated with the AMORE Power subscale (Hill 1997b, 2002).

The AMORE subscales have been shown to correlate with differences in various aspects of sexual behavior and contraception use (Hill & Preston, 1996), as well as to sexual fantasies that are theoretically most relevant to specific sexual motives (Hill, 2007a). The subscales also correlate with attraction to a potential partner in a situation in which participants believed they were involved in a dating service opportunity (Hill, 2005). Interest in engaging in sexual behavior with someone one has just met or knows only slightly is likewise associated with theoretically relevant AMORE subscales (Hill, 2007b). The Valued by Partner and Value for Partner subscales are related to greater sexual satisfaction, relationship satisfaction, and relationship commitment among couples involved in romantic relationships (Hill, 1997a), as well as to changes in satisfaction and commitment over time (Hill, 1998). Many of the AMORE subscales correlate as predicted with attachment anxiety (Davis, Shaver, & Vernon, 2004; Schachner & Shaver, 2004).

Other Information

I am grateful to Leslie K. Preston for earlier assistance in the development of this scale.

References

Davis, D., Shaver, P. R., & Vernon, M. L. (2004). Attachment style and subjective motivations for sex. *Personality and Social Psychology Bulletin, 30,* 1076–1090.

Hill, C. A. (1997a, August). *Dispositional sexual motives and relationship quality.* Paper presented at the Annual Meeting of the American Psychological Association, Chicago, IL.

Hill, C. A. (1997b). The distinctiveness of sexual motives in relation to sexual desire and desirable partner attributes. *The Journal of Sex Research, 34,* 139–153.

Hill, C. A. (1998, May). *Sexual motivation, romantic attraction, and intimate relationships.* Paper presented at the Annual Meeting of the Midwestern Psychological Association, Chicago, IL.

Hill, C. A. (2002). Gender, relationships stage, and sexual behavior: The importance of partner emotional investment within specific situations. *The Journal of Sex Research, 39,* 228–240.

Hill, C. A. (2005, August). *Romantic and sexual interest as a function of dispositional sexual motives.* Paper presented at the Annual Convention of the American Psychological Association, Washington, DC.

Hill, C. A. (2007a, May). *Sexual fantasies relate to the theoretically most relevant dispositional sexual motives.* Paper presented at the Annual Convention of the Association for Psychological Science, Washington, DC.

Hill, C. A. (2007b, November). *Sexual interest in casual and newly acquainted partners relative to sexual motivation and relationship status.* Paper presented at the Annual Meeting of the Society for the Scientific Study of Sexuality, Indianapolis, IN.

Hill, C. A., & Preston, L. K. (1996). Individual differences in the experience of sexual motivation: Theory and measurement of dispositional sexual motives. *The Journal of Sex Research, 33,* 27–45.

Schachner, D. A., & Shaver, P. R. (2004). Attachment dimensions and sexual motives. *Personal Relationships, 11,* 179–195.

Exhibit

Affective and Motivational Orientation Related to Erotic Arousal

Please be extremely honest and think about yourself very carefully when responding to each statement!
There are no right or wrong answers.

This questionnaire asks you about reasons that you typically experience sexual feelings or that you become interested in sexual issues or behaviors. When you experience these feelings or interests, you may or may not always act on those feelings. "Sex," "having sex," or "sexual activity" can include sexual behavior with another person (e.g., your spouse or lover), as well as sexual behavior by yourself (e.g., masturbation, viewing or reading erotic materials). "Partner" can refer to either your spouse or regular romantic partner or any individual with whom you have sex. If you have never had sex or are not currently involved sexually with anyone, respond to the statements below like you think you would feel if you were involved in a sexual relationship or were sexually active.

Not all reasons for being interested in sexual issues or sexual behavior may be listed below. Many of the reasons included may not describe you well at all. If this is the case, please indicate that they are not true for you when rating them.

If a particular statement describes your typical reaction or feelings well, indicate that it is "Completely True" by filling in the letter "E" on the computer sheet. If a particular statement does not describe you well or is opposite of the way you feel, indicate that it is "Not at all True" by filling in the letter "A" on the computer sheet. Of course, you may choose any letter in between A and E to indicate the degree to which the statement describes you or not.

Please use the rating scale below to indicate how true or descriptive each of following statements is for you:

A	B	C	D	E
Not at all True		Moderately True		Completely True

1. Often when I need to feel loved, I have the desire to relate to my partner sexually because sexual intimacy really makes me feel warm and cared for.
2. I enjoy having sex most intensely when I know that it will lift my partner's spirits and improve his or her outlook on life.
3. When bad or frustrating things happen to me, many times I feel like engaging in sexual fantasy or doing something sexual to try to get to feeling better.
4. Sex is important to me largely for reproductive reasons.
5. Sexual activities and fantasies are most stimulating when my partner seems extremely self-assured and demanding during sex.
6. I find that I often feel a sense of superiority and power when I am expressing myself sexually.
7. One of the most exciting aspects of sex is the sense of power I feel in controlling the sexual pleasure and stimulation my partner experiences.
8. Often while I am engaging in sex or fantasy, the idea that children might result from sexual behavior is extremely arousing.
9. Frequently, when I want to feel that I am cared for and that someone is concerned about me, relating to my partner sexually is one of the most satisfying ways to do so.
10. Often the most pleasurable sex I have is when it helps my partner forget about his or her problems and enjoy life a little more.
11. I find sexual behavior and sexual fantasy most exciting when I can feel forceful and dominant with my partner.
12. Thinking about sex or engaging in sex sometimes seems to help me keep on going when things get rough.
13. It is frequently very arousing when my partner gets very forceful and aggressive during sex.
14. I frequently want to have sex with my partner when I need him or her to notice me and appreciate me.
15. I especially enjoy sex when my partner and I are trying to have a baby.
16. Often engaging in sex with my partner makes me feel like I have established myself as a force to be reckoned with.
17. A major reason I enjoy having sex with my partner is because I can communicate how much I care for and value him or her.
18. The sensations of physical pleasure and release are major reasons that sexual activity and fantasy are so important to me.
19. Sex and sexual fantasies are most exciting when I feel like my partner has totally overpowered me and has taken complete control.
20. When I am going through difficult times, I can start feeling better simply by engaging in some type of sexual fantasy or behavior.
21. The idea of having children is not very significant in my feelings about why sexual activity is important to me.
22. In many ways, I think engaging in sex and sexual fantasy are some of the most exciting and satisfying activities I can experience.
23. Many times it is extremely thrilling when my partner takes complete charge and begins to tell me what to do during sex.
24. I really value sexual activity as a way of enjoying myself and adding an element of adventure to my life.
25. Often I have a real need to feel dominated and possessed by my partner while we are engaged in sex or sexual fantasy.
26. One of the best ways of feeling like an important part of my partner's life is by relating to him or her sexually.
27. I find that thinking about or engaging in sexual activity can frequently help me get through unpleasant times in my life.
28. I often feel like fantasizing about sex or expressing myself sexually when life isn't going very well and I want to feel better about myself.
29. Engaging in sexual activity is a very important way for me to experience and appreciate the personal strength and forcefulness that my partner is capable of.
30. I find it extremely exciting to be playful and to have fun when I am expressing myself sexually.
31. Thinking about sex or engaging in sexual behavior can frequently be a source of relief from stress and pressure for me.
32. I would prefer to have sex primarily when I am interested in having a child.
33. Often when my partner is feeling down on life or is unhappy about something, I like to try to make him or her feel better by sharing intimacy together sexually.
34. The experience of sexual tension and energy are in many ways the most thrilling and important aspects of sexual activity and fantasy.
35. I often feel like having sex with my partner when I need to feel understood and when I want to relate to him or her on a one-to-one level.
36. When I need to feel a sense of belongingness and connectedness, having sex with my partner is really an important way of relating to him or her.
37. Doing something sexual often seems to greatly improve my outlook on life when nothing seems to be going right.
38. I frequently feel like expressing my need for emotional closeness and intimacy by engaging in sexual behavior or fantasy with my sexual partner.
39. Many times when I am feeling unhappy or depressed, thinking about sex or engaging in sexual activity will make me feel better.
40. When things are not going well, thinking about sex or doing something sexual is often very uplifting for me and helps me to forget about my problems for a while.

41. Engaging in sexual activity is very important to me as a means of feeling powerful and charismatic.

42. One of the main reasons I am interested in sex is for the purpose of having children.

43. The sense of emotional bonding with my partner during sexual intercourse is an important way of feeling close to him or her.

44. One of the most satisfying aspects of engaging in sex is expressing the intensity of my feelings for my partner while we are having sex.

45. I often have a strong need to fantasize about sex or to do something sexual when I feel upset or unhappy.

46. I really enjoy having sex as a way of exerting dominance and control over my partner.

47. I often find it a real turn-on when my partner takes charge and becomes authoritative during sexual activity or fantasy.

48. I am often very excited by the sense of power that I feel I have over my partner when I am sexually attractive to him or her.

49. Being able to experience my partner's physical excitement and sexual release is incredibly thrilling and stimulating for me.

50. I find it very exciting when my partner becomes very demanding and urgent during sex and sexual fantasy, as if he or she needs to possess me completely.

51. I frequently become very aroused when I sense that my partner is excited by controlling and directing our sexual activity or fantasy.

52. I frequently want to have sex with my partner because I know how much he or she enjoys it and how good it makes my partner feel as a person.

53. Expressing myself sexually generally makes me feel personally strong and in control of things.

54. I am especially excited by the feeling of domination and being controlled by my partner during sex and sexual fantasy.

55. One of the most satisfying features of sex is when my partner really seems to need the love and tenderness it conveys.

56. Often the sense of power that I have over my sexual partner can be extremely exhilarating.

57. I find it very rewarding when I can help my partner get through rough times by showing how much I care and being sexually intimate with him or her.

58. I frequently find it quite arousing to be very directive and controlling while having sex with my partner.

59. Sexual intercourse is important in creating a great deal of emotional closeness in my relationship with my partner.

60. Sharing affection and love during sexual intercourse is one of the most intense and rewarding ways of expressing my concern for my partner.

61. The sense of emotional closeness I experience from having sex with my partner is one of the most satisfying ways I know of feeling valued.

62. To me, an extremely rewarding aspect of having sex is that it can make my partner feel good about himself or herself.

Sexual Wanting Questionnaire

Zoë D. Peterson,[1] *University of Missouri-St. Louis*
Charlene L. Muehlenhard, *University of Kansas*

Sexual activity is often classified as wanted or unwanted, reflecting a unidimensional, dichotomous model of sexual wanting. In reality, individuals' feelings about wanting or not wanting sex often are more complex (Muehlenhard & Peterson, 2005). The Sexual Wanting Questionnaire was developed to measure a new, more complex model of sexual wanting. The questionnaire measures sexual wanting taking into account the following: (a) multiple levels of wanting rather than a dichotomy, acknowledging that sex can be wanted and unwanted to varying degrees; (b) multiple dimensions of wanting, acknowledging that sex can be wanted in some ways and unwanted in other ways; (c) an act-consequences distinction, acknowledging that wanting or not wanting a sexual act differs from wanting or not wanting its consequences; and (d) a wanting-consenting distinction, acknowledging that wanting or not wanting sex differs from consenting or not consenting to sex (Peterson & Muehlenhard, 2007).

Description

The Wanting Questionnaire consists of 106 items assessing participants' reasons for wanting or not wanting a particular sexual experience (e.g., respondents' first

[1]Address correspondence to Zoë Peterson, Department of Psychology, 325 Stadler Hall, University of Missouri-St. Louis, One University Blvd, St. Louis, MO 63121; e-mail: petersonz@umsl.edu

sexual experience or most recent sexual experience). It measures reasons for wanting and not wanting the sexual act itself, the consequences of engaging in the sexual act, and the consequences of not engaging in the sexual act. Questionnaire items describe reasons for wanting or not wanting sex that relate to sexual arousal, morals and values, situational characteristics, social status, fear of pregnancy and sexually transmitted infections (STIs), and relationship concerns.

The scale was developed and tested for use with college students, although it could be adapted for use with other populations. The scale has been used to measure the "wantedness" of college men's and women's first sexual intercourse (Muehlenhard, Peterson, MacPherson, & Blair, 2002) and the wantedness of college women's experiences with consensual and nonconsensual sexual intercourse (Peterson & Muehlenhard, 2007).

Response Mode and Timing

For each item, respondents are asked to indicate whether the statement was true for them prior to the particular sexual experience in question. If the item was true, they are asked to rate the extent to which that item was a reason for wanting or not wanting the sexual activity using a 7-point scale ranging from −3 (*A Strong Reason for Not Wanting to Have Sex*), to 0 (*Not a Reason for Wanting or Not Wanting to Have Sex*), to 3 (*A Strong Reason for Wanting to Have Sex*). Participants also are asked to make three global ratings of wantedness, which provide summaries of the wantedness of the sexual act itself, the wantedness of the consequences of the sexual activity, and the overall wantedness of the sexual activity. These global wantedness items also are rated on a scale ranging from −3 (*Strongly Unwanted*) to 3 (*Strongly Wanted*). It takes approximately 15 to 20 minutes to complete the entire scale.

Scoring

In order to calculate scores on the Reasons for Wanting and the Reasons for Not Wanting subscales, the "not true" items are set equal to 0. When calculating the Reasons for Wanting subscale scores, negative ratings are replaced with zeros, and, when calculating the Reasons for Not Wanting subscale scores, positive ratings are replaced with zeros. Ratings for items on each subscale are averaged to calculate subscale scores. Scores on the Reasons for Wanting subscales can range from 0 to 3; higher scores indicate stronger feelings of wanting to have sex for that reason. Scores on the Reasons for Not Wanting subscales can range from −3 to 0; lower scores indicate stronger feelings of not wanting to have sex for that reason. The following is a breakdown of items belonging to each subscale:

Reasons for Wanting Subscales
In the Mood: 1a, 2a, 3a, 6a, 7a, 10, 11a, 12a, 13a, 14, 16a, 17, 19, 22a, 26, 78

Negative Consequences of Refusing: 49, 62, 66, 67, 68, 71, 75, 80, 82
Personal Gain: 47, 48, 54, 79a
Social Benefits: 40a, 41a, 45
Fear of Physical Harm: 69, 74
Strengthen the Relationship: 50, 51, 59, 61
Not Intoxicated: 20a, 21a
Not a Virgin: 29b, 30b

Reasons for Not Wanting Subscales
Not in the Mood: 1b, 2b, 3c, 5, 12b, 13b, 16b
Negative Consequences: 23, 31, 33, 34, 35, 36, 37, 39
Lack of Confidence: 4b, 18, 25, 28, 29a
Cheating: 63, 64
Disliked the Other Person: 6b, 7b
Negative Social Consequences: 40b, 41b

Reliability

Based on a sample of 213 college women who answered the questionnaire based on their experiences with consensual and nonconsensual sexual intercourse, Cronbach's alphas for the subscales ranged from .72 to .95, providing evidence that the subscales had adequate internal consistency.

Validity

Items for the Sexual Wanting Questionnaire were developed based on themes identified in prior studies of individuals' reasons for wanting and not wanting sex (e.g., Muehlenhard & Cook, 1988; O'Sullivan & Allgeier, 1998; O'Sullivan & Gaines, 1998) and based on discussions with a group of undergraduate college students. The subscales were developed using exploratory factor analysis and scale reliability analyses.

Because wanting and not wanting sex was conceptualized as distinct from consenting and not consenting to sex, scores on the Sexual Wanting Questionnaire were expected to be associated with—but distinct from—sexual consent. Peterson and Muehlenhard (2007) found evidence for this. A group of 87 college women who answered the questionnaire based on their most recent experience with consensual sexual intercourse (i.e., the consensual sex group) was compared with a group of 77 college women who answered based on their experience with nonconsensual sexual intercourse (i.e., the rape group). Not surprisingly, findings suggested that wanting sex and consenting to sex were closely related; on average, the rape group wanted the sexual intercourse significantly less than the consensual sex group. However, also as expected, there were large within-group variations in the wantedness of women's consensual and nonconsensual sexual experiences; the results demonstrated that individuals sometimes consent to unwanted sex and sometimes do not consent to wanted sex. These findings provide some evidence of construct validity.

Other Information

With appropriate citation, the Sexual Wanting Scale may be copied and used for educational and research purposes without permission. The authors would appreciate receiving a summary of any research utilizing this scale.

References

Muehlenhard, C. L., & Cook, S. W. (1988). Men's self-reports of unwanted sexual activity. *The Journal of Sex Research, 24,* 58–72.

Muehlenhard, C. L., & Peterson, Z. D. (2005). Wanting and not wanting sex: The missing discourse of ambivalence. *Feminism and Psychology, 15,* 15–20.

Muehlenhard, C. L., Peterson, Z. D., MacPherson, L. A., & Blair, R. L. (2002, June). *First experiences with sexual intercourse: Wanted, unwanted, or both? Application of a multidimensional model.* Paper presented at the Midcontinent and Eastern Region Joint Conference of the Society for the Scientific Study of Sexuality, Big Rapids, MI.

O'Sullivan, L. F., & Allgeier, E. R. (1998). Feigning sexual desire: Consenting to unwanted sexual activity in heterosexual dating relationships. *The Journal of Sex Research, 35,* 234–243.

O'Sullivan, L. F., & Gaines, M. E. (1998). Decision-making in college students' heterosexual dating relationships: Ambivalence about engaging in sexual activity. *Journal of Social and Personal Relationships, 15,* 347–363.

Peterson, Z. D., & Muehlenhard, C. L. (2007). Conceptualizing the "wantedness" of women's consensual and nonconsensual sexual experiences: Implications for how women label their experiences with rape. *The Journal of Sex Research, 44,* 72–88.

Exhibit

Sexual Wanting Questionnaire

Indicate whether each statement was true for you shortly before the sexual activity started.

- If this statement **was not true** for you at the time, check **Not True** and go to the next line.
- If this statement **was true** for you at the time, then check **True**.

Circle a number from −3 to 3 indicating how much, if at all, it was a reason for **not wanting** or **wanting** to engage in sexual intercourse, based on the scale below.

It was a reason for **not wanting** to engage in the sexual activity			It had no influence	It was a reason for **wanting** to engage in the sexual activity		
−3	−2	−1	0	1	2	3
a strong reason	a moderate reason	a weak reason	not a reason for wanting or not wanting to have sex	a weak reason	a moderate reason	a strong reason
	for *not wanting* to **have sex**				for *wanting* to **have sex**	

Was this statement true for you shortly before the sexual activity began?	**Not True** Check and go to the next line	**True** Check and then circle your rating	A reason for **not wanting** the sexual activity			A reason for **wanting** the sexual activity		
1a. I was sexually aroused before the sexual intercourse began.			−3	−2	−1	0	1	2	3
1b. I was not sexually aroused before the sexual intercourse began.			−3	−2	−1	0	1	2	3
2a. I expected to be aroused during the sexual intercourse.			−3	−2	−1	0	1	2	3
2b. I did not expect to be aroused during the sexual intercourse.			−3	−2	−1	0	1	2	3
3a. I felt interested in and excited about the possibility of the sexual act.			−3	−2	−1	0	1	2	3
3b. I felt indifferent about the possibility of the sexual act; I didn't care one way or another.			−3	−2	−1	0	1	2	3
3c. I felt uninterested in and bored about the possibility of the sexual act.			−3	−2	−1	0	1	2	3
4a. I felt comfortable about my body.			−3	−2	−1	0	1	2	3
4b. I felt uncomfortable about my body.			−3	−2	−1	0	1	2	3
5. I felt disgusted or revolted by the possibility of the sexual intercourse.			−3	−2	−1	0	1	2	3

6a. I found the other person physically attractive.			−3	−2	−1	0	I	2	3
6b. I found the other person physically unattractive.			−3	−2	−1	0	I	2	3
7a. I liked the other person.			−3	−2	−1	0	I	2	3
7b. I disliked the other person.			−3	−2	−1	0	I	2	3
8. I didn't know the other person well.			−3	−2	−1	0	I	2	3
9a. The sexual activity in question was socially acceptable.			−3	−2	−1	0	I	2	3
9b. The sexual activity in question was socially unacceptable.			−3	−2	−1	0	I	2	3
10. I felt curious to try sexual intercourse with this person in this situation.			−3	−2	−1	0	I	2	3
11a. There was a good location available (it was comfortable, there was privacy, etc.).			−3	−2	−1	0	I	2	3
11b. There was a problem with the location (it was uncomfortable, there was little privacy, etc.).			−3	−2	−1	0	I	2	3
12a. I was in the mood to engage in sexual intercourse.			−3	−2	−1	0	I	2	3
12b. I was not in the mood to engage in sexual intercourse.			−3	−2	−1	0	I	2	3
13a. I found the other person's behavior appealing or attractive in this situation.			−3	−2	−1	0	I	2	3
13b. The other person's behavior was unappealing or obnoxious in this situation.			−3	−2	−1	0	I	2	3
14. It seemed that the other person wanted to engage in the sexual intercourse at least to some degree.			−3	−2	−1	0	I	2	3
15. It seemed that the other person was at least somewhat reluctant to engage in the sexual intercourse.			−3	−2	−1	0	I	2	3
16a. I expected emotional closeness during this sexual activity.			−3	−2	−1	0	I	2	3
16b. I did not expect emotional closeness during this sexual activity.			−3	−2	−1	0	I	2	3
17. There would have been a great deal of physical closeness during this sexual activity.			−3	−2	−1	0	I	2	3
18. I expected the sexual intercourse to be painful or physically uncomfortable.			−3	−2	−1	0	I	2	3
19. I expected the sexual intercourse to be pleasurable.			−3	−2	−1	0	I	2	3
20a. I was not intoxicated (on alcohol or drugs).			−3	−2	−1	0	I	2	3
20b. I was mildly intoxicated (on alcohol or drugs).			−3	−2	−1	0	I	2	3
20c. I was extremely intoxicated (on alcohol or drugs).			−3	−2	−1	0	I	2	3
21a. The other person was not intoxicated (on alcohol or drugs).			−3	−2	−1	0	I	2	3
21b. The other person was mildly intoxicated (on alcohol or drugs).			−3	−2	−1	0	I	2	3
21c. The other person was extremely intoxicated (on alcohol or drugs).			−3	−2	−1	0	I	2	3
22a. The other person consented (or agreed) to engage in the sexual intercourse.			−3	−2	−1	0	I	2	3
22b. The other person did not consent (or agree) to engage in the sexual intercourse.			−3	−2	−1	0	I	2	3

23. I felt that engaging in the sexual intercourse would make me feel uncomfortable because it would be going against my morals and values.			−3	−2	−1	0	I	2	3
24. I or the other person was menstruating.			−3	−2	−1	0	I	2	3
25. I was nervous about my ability to perform sexual intercourse.			−3	−2	−1	0	I	2	3
26. I was confident about my ability to perform sexual intercourse.			−3	−2	−1	0	I	2	3
27. I felt physically unwell or sick.			−3	−2	−1	0	I	2	3
28. It would have been my first time engaging in the sexual activity in question.			−3	−2	−1	0	I	2	3
29a. I was a virgin.			−3	−2	−1	0	I	2	3
29b. I was not a virgin.			−3	−2	−1	0	I	2	3
30a. The other person was a virgin.			−3	−2	−1	0	I	2	3
30b. The other person was not a virgin.			−3	−2	−1	0	I	2	3
31. I thought that, if I had sex, I might get a sexually transmitted disease.			−3	−2	−1	0	I	2	3
32. I thought I might give the other person a sexually transmitted disease.			−3	−2	−1	0	I	2	3
33. I thought I might get pregnant or get the other person pregnant.			−3	−2	−1	0	I	2	3
34. I thought I might get into trouble (e.g., with my parents, my boss, the police).			−3	−2	−1	0	I	2	3
35. I thought I might feel bad or guilty because it was against my morals or values.			−3	−2	−1	0	I	2	3
36. I thought I might feel bad or guilty because it was against my parents' morals or values.			−3	−2	−1	0	I	2	3
37. I thought my parents might find out.			−3	−2	−1	0	I	2	3
38. I thought that having sex would improve my self-esteem or self-image at least in some ways.			−3	−2	−1	0	I	2	3
39. I thought that having sex would harm my self-esteem or self-image at least in some ways.			−3	−2	−1	0	I	2	3
40a. I thought it would improve my reputation among my female friends and acquaintances.			−3	−2	−1	0	I	2	3
40b. I thought it would harm my reputation among my female friends and acquaintances.			−3	−2	−1	0	I	2	3
41a. I thought it would improve my reputation among my male friends and acquaintances.			−3	−2	−1	0	I	2	3
41b. I thought it would harm my reputation among my male friends and acquaintances.			−3	−2	−1	0	I	2	3
42. I thought it would prevent me from doing something else I needed to do (e.g., studying, going to work).			−3	−2	−1	0	I	2	3
43. I thought it would prevent me from doing something else fun or pleasant (e.g., watching TV, going to a movie).			−3	−2	−1	0	I	2	3
44a. I thought it would make the other person happy.			−3	−2	−1	0	I	2	3
44b. I thought it would make the other person unhappy			−3	−2	−1	0	I	2	3
45. I thought it would give me something to talk about with friends and acquaintances.			−3	−2	−1	0	I	2	3
46. I thought that, if I had sex, the other person might think I was cheap or easy.			−3	−2	−1	0	I	2	3

47. I thought it might result in my getting something I really needed (e.g., food, money, transportation, shelter).			−3	−2	−1	0	I	2	3
48. I thought it might result in my getting something I really wanted (e.g., a gift, a vacation).			−3	−2	−1	0	I	2	3
49. I felt like it would fulfill my obligation to the other person.			−3	−2	−1	0	I	2	3
50. I thought that it would demonstrate my love for the other person.			−3	−2	−1	0	I	2	3
51. I thought that it would make me feel closer to the other person.			−3	−2	−1	0	I	2	3
52. I thought that it would make the other person fall in love with me.			−3	−2	−1	0	I	2	3
53. I thought that it would make me feel needed or wanted.			−3	−2	−1	0	I	2	3
54. I thought that it would result in the other person doing something I wanted.			−3	−2	−1	0	I	2	3
55. I felt like it would be fair to the other person because, in the past, he/she had engaged in sexual intercourse with me when I wanted to.			−3	−2	−1	0	I	2	3
56. I thought that it would result in my being accused of rape or sexual coercion.			−3	−2	−1	0	I	2	3
57. I thought that I might regret it later.			−3	−2	−1	0	I	2	3
58. I thought that the other person might regret it later.			−3	−2	−1	0	I	2	3
59. I thought that having sex would strengthen my relationship with the other person in some ways.			−3	−2	−1	0	I	2	3
60. I thought that having sex would damage my relationship with the other person in some ways.			−3	−2	−1	0	I	2	3
61. I thought that it might lead to a steady relationship with the other person.			−3	−2	−1	0	I	2	3
62. I thought that it would cause the other person to stop pressuring me.			−3	−2	−1	0	I	2	3
63. It would have been "cheating," and I was afraid that it would damage my relationship with my spouse or steady dating partner.			−3	−2	−1	0	I	2	3
64. It would have been "cheating," and I was afraid that it would hurt my spouse or steady dating partner.			−3	−2	−1	0	I	2	3
65a. I wanted to be more sexually experienced.			−3	−2	−1	0	I	2	3
65b. I did not want to be more sexually experienced.			−3	−2	−1	0	I	2	3
66. I wanted to avoid hurting the other person's feelings.			−3	−2	−1	0	I	2	3
67. Refusing sex would have made me feel guilty.			−3	−2	−1	0	I	2	3
68. I was afraid that, if I refused, the other person would become angry.			−3	−2	−1	0	I	2	3
69. I was afraid that, if I refused, the other person might harm me physically.			−3	−2	−1	0	I	2	3
70. There was nothing else to do.			−3	−2	−1	0	I	2	3
71. I was afraid that, if I refused, the other person might accuse me of being a tease or leading him/her on.			−3	−2	−1	0	I	2	3

			-3	-2	-1	0	1	2	3
72. I was afraid that, if I refused, the other person might think I was ungrateful because he/she had done something for me.			-3	-2	-1	0	1	2	3
73. I was afraid that refusing would make me seem selfish.			-3	-2	-1	0	1	2	3
74. I was afraid that, if I refused, the other person might try to force me to do it.			-3	-2	-1	0	1	2	3
75. I was afraid that the other person would be disappointed if we didn't have sex.			-3	-2	-1	0	1	2	3
76. I thought that this was my only chance to have sex with this person—that it was now or never.			-3	-2	-1	0	1	2	3
77. I was afraid that, if I refused, the other person might carry out some threat against me.			-3	-2	-1	0	1	2	3
78. This was an experience that I didn't want to miss out on.			-3	-2	-1	0	1	2	3
79a. I felt like having sex would have made me feel powerful.			-3	-2	-1	0	1	2	3
79b. I felt like having sex would have made me feel powerless.			-3	-2	-1	0	1	2	3
80. I thought that refusing might damage my relationship with the other person at least in some ways.			-3	-2	-1	0	1	2	3
81. I thought that refusing might strengthen my relationship with the other person at least in some ways.			-3	-2	-1	0	1	2	3
82. I was afraid that, if I refused, the other person might break up with me.			-3	-2	-1	0	1	2	3
83. I was afraid that, if I refused, the other person might have sex with someone else.			-3	-2	-1	0	1	2	3
84. It was a situation where sex was expected (e.g., it was prom night; the other person was my girlfriend/boyfriend visiting from out of town, etc.).			-3	-2	-1	0	1	2	3

Overall, how much did you want or not want to engage in the **sexual act itself** (not considering the consequences)?

-3	-2	-1	0	1	2	3
Strongly unwanted	Moderately unwanted	Slightly unwanted	No opinion	Slightly wanted	Moderately wanted	Strongly wanted

Overall, how much did you want or not want the **possible consequences** of engaging in the sexual activity?

-3	-2	-1	0	1	2	3
Strongly unwanted	Moderately unwanted	Slightly unwanted	No opinion	Slightly wanted	Moderately wanted	Strongly wanted

Overall, how much did you want or not want to engage in sexual activity in this situation (taking into account the sexual act itself, the possible consequences of engaging in the sexual act, and the possible consequences of not engaging in the sexual act)?

-3	-2	-1	0	1	2	3
Strongly unwanted	Moderately unwanted	Slightly unwanted	No opinion	Slightly wanted	Moderately wanted	Strongly wanted

Age, Gender, and Sexual Motivation Inventory

DAVID QUADAGNO,[1] *Florida State University*

The Age, Gender, and Sexual Motivation Inventory (AGSMI) was originally developed to measure the relationships between gender and age and motivations for engaging in sexual activities, favored part of a sexual experience (foreplay, intercourse, and afterplay), ideal benefit to be gained from engaging in sexual activities, and other aspects of sexual behavior and satisfaction (Sprague & Quadagno, 1989). The literature on sexual motivation consistently indicates that males are primarily motivated by physical and women by emotional factors when college-aged individuals are the subjects (e.g., see Bardwick, 1971; Carroll, Volk, & Hyde, 1985; Denney, Field, & Quadagno, 1984). When a diverse age group was sampled, the results from AGSMI indicated very clearly that inferences about sexual motivations for the whole population couldn't be drawn from studies of a very limited and relatively inexperienced segment of it. In addition, in using the AGSMI, we found only a moderate relationship between usual motive for engaging in sexual intercourse and the respondent's assessment of its most important benefit. The AGSMI can be used to examine gender differences in many aspects of sexual behaviors, satisfaction, and motivations in a similar age group, or changes in sexuality in men and women at varying ages.

Description

The AGSMI begins with a demographic section, in which the respondents record information including, but not limited to, age, gender, marital status, employment status, sexual orientation, and combined family income. The demographic section is followed by 25 questions, 23 of which are multiple choice and 2 of which call for short answers. The sample used in the development of the instrument included 95 women and 84 men ranging in age from 22 to 57 years of age; mean age for the women was 31.2 and for the men was 31.7 years.

Response Mode and Timing

Respondents can circle the letter of choice for each question on the instrument and can also write their responses to the short-answer items on the instrument. As an alternative, if it is administered to a large group at the same time, a separate answer sheet can be used to record responses. The majority of the test items have three to five response choices. The inventory requires approximately 5 to 8 minutes to complete.

Scoring

The instrument is not designed to produce any combined or total scores for groups of items. Comparisons between individuals or between groups on individual items can be made.

Reliability

A rough indication of the reliability of responses to the instrument can be gained from a comparison of the answers of male and female respondents to three items that asked average frequency of sexual intercourse per week, usual time spent in foreplay, and usual time spent in afterplay. Assuming the respondents and their sex partners are all from the same heterosexual population, there should be no aggregate gender differences on any of these items (i.e., if men in the population are averaging sexual intercourse three nights per week then females in the population should also have this average frequency). In addition, if men or women have a tendency to overstate or understate the time spent in foreplay or afterplay, this response bias would be reflected in differences between their means in the sample. No significant gender differences in responses to these questions were found, suggesting that whatever response biases may be operating in these data are not strongly associated with gender.

In addition, two differently phrased questions (Questions 16 and 23) probed the favored part of a sexual encounter and found agreement for both male and female respondents.

Validity

The results reported in the questionnaire responses of the younger age groups (22–25, 26–30, and 31–35 years of age) were in perfect agreement with previously published studies of college-aged individuals (Bardwick, 1971; Carroll et al., 1985; Denney et al., 1984). The findings from our older age groups (36–57 years of age) do not have a comparable sample because of the lack of studies of this type using older individuals.

References

Bardwick, J. (1971). *The psychology of women*. New York: Harper and Row.

Carroll, J., Volk, K., & Hyde, J. (1985). Differences between males and females in motives for engaging in sexual intercourse. *Archives of Sexual Behavior, 14*, 131–139.

Denney, N., Field, J., & Quadagno, D. (1984). Sex differences in sexual needs and desires. *Archives of Sexual Behavior, 13*, 233–245.

Sprague, J., & Quadagno, D. (1989). Gender and sexual motivation: An exploration of two assumptions. *Journal of Psychology & Human Sexuality, 2*, 57–76.

[1]Address correspondence to David Quadagno, Department of Biological Science, Florida State University, Tallahassee, FL 32306-2043; e-mail: quadagno@bio.fsu.edu

Exhibit

Age, Gender, and Sexual Motivation Inventory

1. Age _____
2. Sex _____; *For women only*: Past menopause? Yes _____; No _____
3. What is your marital status? (Check one)

_____ never married

_____ separated

_____ married

_____ divorced

_____ widowed

4. If married, how long in current marriage? _____
5. Age of current spouse _____
6. What is your employment status? (Check one)

_____ full-time homemaker

_____ employed part-time outside the home

_____ employed full-time outside the home

_____ student

7. What is your approximate yearly household income? (Check one)

_____ below $20,000

_____ $20,001–30,000

_____ $30,001–40,000

_____ $40,001–50,000

_____ $50,001–60,000

_____ $60,001–80,000

_____ over $80,000

8. Sexual orientation (Check one)

_____ heterosexual; _____ bisexual; _____ homosexual

9. How religious do you think you are? (Check one)

_____ very religious

_____ moderately religious

_____ not religious

For the remainder of the questions please circle the best answer.

10. How many individuals have you had sexual intercourse with?

a. none

b. only one

c. between two and five

d. between six and ten

e. between eleven and twenty

f. over twenty

11. How many times per week do you usually engage in sexual intercourse?

a. less than once

b. between one and two

c. between three and four

d. between five and seven

e. more than seven

12. How often do you experience orgasm during your sexual encounters (does not have to be sexual intercourse)?

a. never

b. 1–25% of the time

c. 26–50% of the time

d. 51–75% of the time

e. 76–99% of the time

f. 100% of the time

Foreplay is a word that has been used to refer to sexual activity that occurs before intercourse. *Afterplay* refers to interactions such as hugging, holding, talking, etc. that occur after intercourse. Not all sexual encounters involve sexual intercourse, but foreplay and afterplay are defined here because many of the following questions will refer to them.

13. During which of the following phases of a sexual encounter are you most likely to experience an orgasm?
    a. foreplay
    b. sexual intercourse
    c. afterplay
    d. equally in foreplay, intercourse, or afterplay
    e. I don't experience orgasms in my sexual encounters

14. *For women only*: If you experience orgasm during foreplay do you usually like to then have intercourse?
    a. yes
    b. no

15. When you engage in sexual intercourse or other intimate sexual acts, which of the following reasons best describes your motivation on most occasions?
    a. I want the physical release
    b. I want to show my love for my partner
    c. I am afraid my partner will leave me if I don't

16. Which aspect of a sexual experience do you enjoy the most?
    a. foreplay
    b. intercourse
    c. afterplay

17. Which of the following is the most important thing that you could get from a sexual experience?
    a. a feeling of being emotionally close to my partner
    b. the physical release and/or orgasm
    c. a feeling that I am in control of my partner

18. Do you usually want to spend more or less time in foreplay than your partner(s)?
    a. I want to spend more time
    b. I want to spend less time
    c. We want to spend about the same amount of time

19. Do you usually want to spend more or less time in afterplay than your partner(s)?
    a. I want to spend more time
    b. I want to spend less time
    c. We want to spend about the same amount of time

20. When you and your partner(s) disagree on the amount of time that should be spent in foreplay, who is more likely to get his/her way?
    a. I am more likely to get my way
    b. My partner is more likely to get his/her way
    c. We are each likely to get our way half of the time
    d. We don't disagree

21. When you and your partner(s) disagree on the amount of time that should be spent in afterplay, who is more likely to get his/her way?
    a. I am more likely to get my way
    b. My partner is more likely to get his/her way
    c. We are each likely to get our way half of the time
    d. We don't disagree

22. When you and your partner(s) disagree on the amount of time that should be spent in foreplay or afterplay do you discuss the problem?
    a. We do communicate our disagreements
    b. We do not communicate our disagreements
    c. We do not disagree on this

23. Which of the following rank orders best describes the importance of the various parts of a sexual encounter to you (the first listed part should be the most important and the last the least important to you)?
    a. foreplay, intercourse, afterplay
    b. intercourse, foreplay, afterplay
    c. afterplay, intercourse, foreplay
    d. foreplay, afterplay, intercourse

    e. intercourse, afterplay, foreplay

    f. afterplay, foreplay, intercourse

24. How often do you initiate your sexual encounters?

    a. never

    b. 1–25% of the time

    c. 26–50% of the time

    d. 51–75% of the time

    e. 76–99% of the time

    f. 100% of the time

25. Would you prefer your partner(s) to initiate sexual encounters?

    a. more than she/he does

    b. less than she/he does

    c. the same as she/he does

26. In most cases, do you get more sexually aroused by initiating or being pursued during a sexual encounter?

    a. initiating the encounter

    b. being pursued by my partner

27. What percentage of your sexual encounters would you say you find to be satisfying?

    a. none

    b. 1–25%

    c. 26–50%

    d. 51–75%

    e. 76–99%

    f. 100%

28. How satisfied are you with your typical sexual encounter?

    a. extremely satisfied

    b. moderately satisfied

    c. slightly satisfied

    d. not at all satisfied

29. During which of the three phases (foreplay, intercourse, afterplay) of a sexual encounter are you usually most dissatisfied with how your partner responds?

    a. foreplay

    b. intercourse

    c. afterplay

    d. I am not dissatisfied with any part

30. Have you ever communicated your dissatisfaction to your partner(s)?

    a. yes

    b. no

31. If you are dissatisfied, why are you dissatisfied?_____

32. With which of the three phases (foreplay, intercourse, afterplay) are you most satisfied with how your partner responds?

    a. foreplay

    b. intercourse

    c. afterplay

    d. I am not satisfied with any part

33. If you are satisfied, what do you find particularly satisfying?_____

34. Do you sometimes have sex to please your partner even though you don't want to have sex?

    a. yes

    b. no

Multidimensional Sexual Perfectionism Questionnaire

WILLIAM E. SNELL, JR.,[1] *Southeast Missouri State University*

Previous researchers have indicated that people some-times apply highly rigid and perfectionistic standards of personal conduct to themselves. Snell and Rigdon (1995) developed a new multidimensional self-report instrument, the Multidimensional Sexual Perfectionism Questionnaire (MSPQ), to measure five distinct psychological tendencies associated with people's standards of sexual conduct: (a) self-oriented sexual perfectionism, (b) perceived socially prescribed sexual perfectionism, (c) partner-directed sexual perfectionism, (d) partner's self-oriented sexual perfectionism, and (e) perceived self-directed sexual per-fectionism from one's partner. The MSPQ can be used in a variety of ways: as a research instrument in correlational or experimental research designs; as a pretest and posttest instrument for therapy effectiveness and recovery studies; and as a predictive correlate of sexual affect, attitudes, and behaviors.

Description

The MSPQ contains five subscales: (a) Self-oriented Sexual Perfectionism, designed to measure excessively high, rigid, and perfectionistic sexual standards that are applied to oneself; (b) Socially Prescribed Sexual Perfection, which involves the belief that society and "generalized" others are imposing perfectionistic sexual standards and expectations for oneself; (c) Partner-directed Sexual Perfectionism, which involves the application of perfectionistic sexual standards to one's partner; (d) Partner's Self-oriented Sexual Perfectionism, designed to measure people's per-ception that their partners impose rigid and perfectionistic sexual standards to themselves (i.e., to the partners them-selves); and (e) Self-directed Sexual Perfectionism from one's partner, which involves people's belief that their partners are applying excessively rigid and perfectionis-tic sexual standards to themselves (i.e., to the respondents themselves).

Response Mode and Timing

In responding to the MSPQ, individuals are asked to indi-cate how characteristic each statement is of them. A 5-point Likert-type scale is used for their responses, with each item being scored from 0 to 4: *not at all characteristic of me* (0), *slightly characteristic of me* (1), *somewhat characteristic of me* (2), *moderately characteristic of me* (3), and *very*

characteristic of me (4). Although the MSPQ can be for-matted so that respondents can circle a response between A and E (or 0 to 4), corresponding to how characteristic the statement is of them, the more common scoring technique is to mark the answers on a machine-scoreable answer sheet. The MSPQ requires approximately 15 minutes to complete.

Scoring

The MSPQ consists of 31 statements that are assigned to five subscales. To create subscale scores for the five sub-scales, several statements (16 through 30) are first recoded so that A = E, B = D, C = C, D = B, and E = A. Then the items are scored so that A = 0; B = 1; C = 2; D = 3; and E = 4. Next, they are averaged for each subscale so that higher scores correspond to greater amounts of the relevant tendency: (a) Self-oriented Sexual Perfectionism (2, 7, 12, 17R, 22R, 27R); (b) Socially Prescribed Sexual Perfectionism (3, 8, 13, 18R, 23R, 28R); (c) Partner-directed Sexual Perfectionism (4, 9, 14, 19R, 23R, 29R); (d) Partner's Self-oriented Sexual Perfectionism (5, 10, 15, 20R, 25R, 30R); and (e) Self-directed Sexual Perfectionism from one's partner (6, 11, 16, 21R). Statement 1 on the MSPQ is used for informational purposes only; it is not assigned to any MSPQ subscale. Statements 30 and 31 are response-con-sistency filler items; they too are not assigned to any MSPQ subscale.

Reliability

In order to provide preliminary evidence for the reliability (i.e., internal consistency) of the MSPQ, Cronbach alphas were computed for each of the MSPQ subscales (Snell & Rigdon, 1995). These results revealed the following alphas for each MSPQ subscale: (a) Self-oriented Sexual Perfectionism (alpha = .71); (b) Socially Prescribed Sexual Perfectionism (alpha = .37); (c) Partner-directed Sexual Perfectionism (alpha = .67); (d) Partner's Self-oriented Sexual Perfectionism (alpha = .67); and (e) Self-directed Sexual Perfectionism from one's partner (alpha = .75). Except for MSPQ subscale 2 (Socially Prescribed Sexual Perfectionism; alpha of .51 for the three non-reversed-worded items and .40 for the reverse-coded items), these reliability indexes were sufficiently high to justify their use in research analyses.

[1]Address all correspondence to William E. Snell, Jr., Department of Psychology, Southeast Missouri State University, One University Plaza, Cape Girardeau, MO 63701; e-mail: wesnell@semo.edu

Validity

Preliminary evidence (Snell & Rigdon, 1995) revealed that males reported greater self-oriented sexual perfectionism than did females, and that males, relative to their female counterparts, also expected greater self-directed sexual perfectionism from their sexual partners and applied similar perfectionistic standards of sexual conduct to their partners. Other findings reported by Snell and Rigdon showed a strong pattern of similarity between people's sexual perfectionism and their tendency to be aware of the public image of their sexuality. More specifically, it was found that both males and females who were characterized by higher levels of each of the components of sexual perfectionism—especially Self-oriented Sexual Perfectionism—reported greater sexual monitoring. That is, those with greater sexual perfectionism were more likely to be highly concerned with others' scrutiny of their sexuality. A final set of results revealed that the various types of sexual perfectionism measured by the MSPQ were related in predictable ways to the four attachment styles measured by the Relationship Scales Questionnaire (Scharfe & Bartholomew, 1994). More specifically, it was found that

those males and females who possessed a secure attachment style (i.e., those with a positive relational view of themselves and others) were less likely to apply perfectionistic sexual standards either to themselves or to their sexual partners, and in addition they were less likely to expect that their partners would apply such perfectionistic sexual standards to either partner. By contrast, an almost identical *inverse* pattern of findings was discovered for the measure of fearful attachment. In particular, it was found that a fearful attachment style was characteristic of both males and females who applied an excessively rigid and perfectionistic set of sexual standards of conduct to themselves as well as expected such standards from their partners.

References

Scharfe, E., & Bartholomew, K. (1994). Reliability and stability of adult attachment patterns. *Personal Relationships, 1*, 23–43.

Snell, W. E., Jr., & Rigdon, K. (1995, April). *The Sexual Perfectionism Questionnaire: Preliminary evidence for reliability and validity*. Paper presented at the annual meeting of the Southwestern Psychological Association, San Antonio, TX.

Exhibit

Multidimensional Sexual Perfectionism Questionnaire

Instructions: Listed below are several statements that concern the topic of sexual relationships. Please read each item carefully and decide to what extent it is characteristic of you. Some of the items refer to a specific sexual relationship. Whenever possible, answer the questions with your current partner in mind. If you are not currently dating anyone, answer the questions with your most recent partner in mind. If you have never had a sexual relationship, answer in terms of what you think your responses would most likely be. Then, for each statement fill in the response on the answer sheet that indicates how much it applies to you by using the following scale:

A = *Not at all* characteristic of me.
B = *Slightly* characteristic of me.
C = *Somewhat* characteristic of me.
D = *Moderately* characteristic of me.
E = *Very* characteristic of me.

1. I will respond to the following items based on:
   (A) A current sexual relationship.
   (B) A past sexual relationship.
   (C) An imagined sexual relationship.
2. I set very high standards for myself as a sexual partner.
3. Others would consider me a good sexual partner even if I'm not responsive every time.
4. My partner sets very high standards of excellence for her/himself as a sexual partner.
5. My partner expects me to be a perfect sexual partner.
6. I expect my partner to be a top-notch and competent sexual partner.
7. I must always be successful as a sexual partner.
8. People often expect more of me as a sexual partner than I am capable of giving.
9. My partner is perfectionistic in that this person expects to sexually satisfy me each and every time.
10. My partner demands nothing less than perfection of me as a sexual partner.
11. My partner should never let me down when it comes to my sexual needs.
12. One of my goals is to be a "perfect" sexual partner.
13. Most people expect me to always be an excellent sexual partner.
14. It makes my partner uneasy for him/her to be less than a perfect sexual partner.
15. My partner always wants me to try hard to sexually please him/her.

16. I cannot stand for my partner to be less than a satisfying sexual partner.

17. I seldom feel the need to be a "perfect" sexual partner.

18. Most people would regard me as okay, even if I did not perform well sexually.

19. My partner does not set very high goals for herself (himself) as a sexual partner.

20. My partner seldom pressures me to be a perfect sexual partner.

21. I do not expect perfectionism from my sexual partner.

22. I do not have to be the best sexual partner in the world.

23. In general, people would readily accept me even if I were not the greatest sex partner in the world.

24. My partner never aims at being perfect as a sexual partner.

25. My sexual partner does not have very high goals for me as a sexual partner.

26. In general, people would readily accept me even if I were not a great sex partner.

27. I do not have very high goals for myself as a sexual partner.

28. Most people don't expect me to be perfectionistic when it comes to sex.

29. My partner does not feel that she/he has to be the best sexual partner.

30. My partner appreciates me even if I am not a perfect sexual lover. (*response consistency filler item*)

31. Most people don't expect me to be perfectionistic when it comes to sex. (*response consistency filler item*)

Sexual Risk Behavior Beliefs and Self-Efficacy Scales

Karen Basen-Engquist,[1] *University of Texas, M.D. Anderson Cancer Center*
Louise C. Mâsse, *Center for Health Promotion Research and Development,*
University of Texas, School of Public Health
Karin Coyle and Douglas Kirby, *ETR Associates*
Guy Parcel, *Center for Health Promotion Research and Development,*
University of Texas, School of Public Health
Stephen Banspach, *Centers for Disease Control and Prevention*
Jesse Nodora, *Arizona Department of Health Services*

The Sexual Risk Behavior Beliefs and Self-Efficacy (SRBBS) scales were developed to measure important psychosocial variables affecting sexual risk-taking and protective behavior. It was originally a component of a larger questionnaire used in evaluating the effectiveness of a multicomponent, school-based program to prevent Human Immunodeficiency Virus (HIV), sexually transmitted disease (STD), and pregnancy among high school students (Coyle et al., 1996). The variables measured by the SRBBS scales are attitudes, norms, self-efficacy, and barriers to condom use. These variables were derived from the Theory of Reasoned Action (Fishbein & Ajzen, 1975), Bandura's Social Learning Theory (1986), and the Health Belief Model (Rosenstock, 1974).

Description

The instrument development process for the SRBBS scales involved four stages: (a) identifying the psychosocial constructs relevant to risk behavior for HIV, STD, and pregnancy; (b) generating questionnaire items by a team of investigators, based on the theories and models described above, empirical research, and other instruments that measured these constructs; (c) pretesting the draft instrument with focus groups of high school students; and (d) revising the instrument and testing it with additional focus groups.

The scales consist of 22 items with a 3- or 4-point Likert-type response format. Three of the scales address sexual risk-taking behavior: attitudes about sexual intercourse (ASI), norms about sexual intercourse (NSI), and self-efficacy in refusing sex (SER). Five scales address protective behavior: attitudes about condom use (ACU), norms about condom use (NCU), self-efficacy in communication about condoms (SECM), self-efficacy in using and buying condoms (SECU), and barriers to condom use (BCU). These scales have been used with students of various ethnic groups and have been translated into Spanish. In our

[1]Address correspondence to Karen Basen-Engquist, University of Texas M.D. Anderson Cancer Center, Department of Behavioral Science—Box 243, 1515 Holcombe, Houston, TX 77030; e-mail: kbasenen@mdanderson.org

research, we have used the SRBBS scales with high school students (aged 14 to 18). They have also been used with middle school students (grades 7 and 8) in another study; however, data from this research are not yet available.

Response Mode and Timing

The SRBBS scales have been used as part of a larger 110-item self-administered questionnaire that takes approximately 30–45 minutes to complete. The scales were originally printed on a form that can be optically scanned. In that form, respondents marked the circle corresponding to their response (the form did not include a numeric value for the responses). The scales can be adapted so that respondents circle or mark the appropriate response on a form that cannot be optically scanned.

Scoring

The items that belong in each scale are identified in the Exhibit, along with values for the responses. Two items (ASI2 and NSI2) should be scored in reverse. Scores on individual items in a scale are totaled and then divided by the number of items in the scale. This gives the scale scores the same range as the response values, enabling the user to compare the scale scores to the original response categories with ease. The range of the ASI, ACU, NSI, NCU, and BCU is 1 to 4, and the range of SER, SECM, and SECU is 1 to 3.

Reliability and Validity

An analysis of data from a multiethnic sample of 6,213 high school students from Texas and California provides all information on reliability and validity (Basen-Engquist et al., 1996).

Reliability. In a sample of 6,213 high school students from Texas and California (Basen-Engquist et al., 1996), the Cronbach alpha measuring internal consistency reliability for the each of the scales was as follows: attitudes about sexual intercourse, .78; norms about sexual intercourse, .78; self-efficacy for refusing sex, .70; attitudes about condom use, .87; norms about condom use, .84; self-efficacy in communicating about condoms, .66; self-efficacy in buying and using condoms, .61; and barriers to condom use, .73.

Construct validity. Confirmatory factor analysis was used to assess construct validity. Two models were evaluated, one with items relating to sexual risk-taking behavior, the other with items relating to protective behavior. The sexual risk behavior model included three scales: ASI, NSI, and SER. In the development of the model, we discovered that correlated error terms were required between norm and attitude items that were grammatically similar in order to obtain a model that fit the data. The fit indices indicated that the final data fit the model well (that is, the χ^2 was not sig-

nificant, the residuals were normally distributed, and root mean square error of approximation was < .05).

The final protective behavior model included five scales: CU, NCU, SECM, SECU, and BCU. The fit indices indicated a good fit for this model as well, once paths for correlated error terms between grammatically similar attitude and norm items were added.

Concurrent validity. Concurrent validity was assessed by examining specific relationships between the scales and sexual experience in the high school sample. The sexual risk behavior scales differentiated between sexually experienced and those who have never had sexual intercourse. The results indicated that attitudes and perceived norms of students who had never had sexual intercourse were less supportive of having sexual intercourse than were those of sexually experienced respondents (Effect size$_{ASI}$ = 1.09; Effect size$_{NSI}$ = .90 [Effect size = | Mean$_1$–Mean$_2$ |/ Pooled standard deviation]). In addition, students who were sexually experienced had lower self-efficacy for refusing sex than did students who were not (Effect size$_{SER}$ = .57). Similar findings were observed in comparisons of students who had sexual intercourse in the last 3 months with those who did not.

We also examined students' condom use and their related attitudes and norms. Protective behavior scales differentiated sexually active students who were consistent condom users from those who were not. Consistent condom users had more positive attitudes toward condom use and more favorable perceived norms about condom use than inconsistent users (Effect size$_{ACU}$ = .78; Effect size$_{NCU}$ = .56). Self-efficacy for using and buying condoms and communicating about condom use with partners also were higher for the consistent condom users (Effect size$_{SECM}$ = .47; Effect size$_{SECU}$ = .23; Effect size$_{BCU}$ = .20). In addition, the consistent users found carrying or buying condoms to be less of a barrier than did the inconsistent users.

Concurrent validity also was assessed by hypothesizing specific relationships between the scales and age and gender, and then testing these hypotheses in the high school sample. We hypothesized that girls would have higher scores on norms about sexual intercourse, attitudes about sexual intercourse, self-efficacy for refusing sexual intercourse, attitudes about condom use, norms about condom use, and self-efficacy in communicating about condoms, but lower scores on condom use self-efficacy. These hypotheses were confirmed. We also hypothesized that age would be positively related to all three self-efficacy scales and negatively related to norms and attitudes. These hypotheses were also confirmed, with one exception. Younger students reported higher self-efficacy in refusing sex than older students (Basen-Engquist et al., 1996).

Other Information

This work was conducted under Contract #200–91–0938 with the Centers for Disease Control and Prevention.

References

Bandura A. (1986). *Social foundations of thought and action*. Englewood Cliffs, NJ: Prentice Hall.

Basen-Engquist, K., Masse, L., Coyle, K., Parcel, G. S., Banspach, S., Kirby, D., et al. (1996). *Validity of scales measuring the psychosocial determinants of HIV/STD-related risk behavior in adolescents*. Unpublished manuscript.

Coyle, K., Kirby, D., Parcel, G., Basen-Engquist, K., Banspach, S., Rugg, D., et al. 1996). Safer Choices: A multi-component school-based HIV/STD and pregnancy prevention program for adolescents. *Journal of School Health, 66*, 89–94.

Fishbein, M., & Ajzen, I.(1975). *Beliefs, attitudes, intentions, and behavior: An introduction to theory and research*. Reading, MA: Addison-Wesley.

Rosenstock, I. M. (1974). Historical origins of the Health Belief Model. In: M. H. Becker (Ed.), *The Health Belief Model and personal health behavior* (Vol. 2, pp. 328–335). Thorofare, NJ: Charles B. Slack.

Exhibit

Student Health Questionnaire

Your beliefs

Please fill in the answer for each question that best describes how *you* feel.

ASI1.   *I believe* people my age should wait until they are older before they have sex.

*ASI2.   *I believe* it's OK for people my age to have sex with a steady boyfriend or girlfriend.

ACU1.   *I believe* condoms (rubbers) should always be used if a person my age has sex.

ACU2.   *I believe* condoms (rubbers) should always be used if a person my age has sex, *even if the girl uses birth control pills.*

ACU3.   *I believe* condoms (rubbers) should always be used if a person my age has sex, *even if the two people know each other very well.*

What do your friends believe?

The following questions ask you about your FRIENDS and what they think. Even if you're not sure, mark the answer that you think best describes what they think.

NSI1.   Most of *my friends* believe people my age should wait until they are older before they have sex.

*NSI2.   Most of *my friends* believe it's OK for people my age to have sex with a steady boyfriend or girlfriend.

NCU1.   Most of *my friends* believe condoms (rubbers) should always be used if a person my age has sex.

NCU2.   Most of *my friends* believe condoms (rubbers) should always be used if a person my age has sex, *even if the girl uses birth control pills.*

NCU3.   Most of *my friends* believe condoms (rubbers) should always be used if a person my age has sex, *even if the two people know each other very well.*

How sure are you?

What if the following things happened to you? Imagine that these situations were to happen to you. Then tell us how sure you are that you could do what is described.

SER1.   Imagine that you met someone at a party. He or she wants to have sex with you. Even though you are very attracted to each other, you're not ready to have sex. How sure are you that you could *keep from having sex?*

SER2.   Imagine that you and your boyfriend or girlfriend have been going together, but you have not had sex. He or she really wants to have sex. Still, you don't feel ready. How sure are you that you could *keep from having sex until you feel ready?*

SER3.   Imagine that you and your boyfriend or girlfriend decide to have sex, but he or she will not use a condom (rubber). You do not want to have sex without a condom (rubber). How sure are you that you *could keep from having sex, until your partner agrees it is OK to use a condom (rubber)?*

SECM1.   Imagine that you and your boyfriend or girlfriend have been having sex but have not used condoms (rubbers). You really want to start using condoms (rubbers). How sure are you that you could *tell your partner you want to start using condoms (rubbers)?*

SECM2.   Imagine that you are having sex with someone you just met. You feel it is important to use condoms (rubbers). How sure are you that you could *tell that person that you want to use condoms (rubbers)?*

SECM3.   Imagine that you or your partner use birth control pills to prevent pregnancy. You want to use condoms (rubbers) to keep from getting STD or HIV. How sure are you that you could *convince your partner that you also need to use condoms (rubbers)?*

SECU1.   How sure are you that you could use a condom (rubber) correctly or explain to your partner how to use a condom (rubber) correctly?

SECU2.   If you wanted to get a condom (rubber), how sure are you that you could go to the store and buy one?

SECU3.   If you decided to have sex, how sure are you that you could have a condom (rubber) with you when you needed it?

What do you think about condoms?

Please tell us how much you agree or disagree with the following statements.

BCU1.   It would be embarrassing to buy condoms (rubbers) in a store.
BCU2.   I would feel uncomfortable carrying condoms (rubbers) with me.
BCU3.   It would be wrong to carry a condom (rubber) with me because it would mean that I'm planning to have sex.

Key to identification of scale items and description of response formats:

ASI   =   Attitudes about sexual intercourse
ACU   =   Attitudes about condom use
NSI   =   Norms about sexual intercourse
NCU   =   Norms about condom use
        Response format for attitude and norm items:
                4 = Definitely Yes
                3 = Probably Yes
                2 = Probably No
                1 = Definitely No
SER   =   Self-efficacy for refusing sexual intercourse
SECM   =   Self-efficacy for communicating about condom use
SECU   =   Self-efficacy for buying and using condoms
        Response format for self-efficacy items:
                1 = Not Sure at All
                2 = Kind of Sure
                3 = Totally Sure
BCU   =   Barriers to condom use
        Response format for barrier items:
                4 = I Strongly Agree
                3 = I Kind of Agree
                2 = I Kind of Disagree
                1 = I Strongly Disagree

*Item should be scored in reverse.

Health Protective Sexual Communication Scale

JOSEPH A. CATANIA,[1] *University of California, San Francisco*

The Health Protective Sexual Communication Scale (HPSC) is a self-report scale that assesses how often respondents discuss health protective topics while interacting with a new, first-time sexual partner. Items address health protective concerns related to safer sex, sexual histories, and contraceptive use. Moreover, the scale assesses communication that has health protective consequences as distinct from sexual communication that may be related to enhancement of sexual pleasure. The expanded 10-item scale was based on an extension of two brief scales that have been used in two national survey studies to assess the ability to discuss sexual histories and condom use with prospective sexual partners. Findings indicate both the brief and expanded HPSC scales to be strongly linked to high-risk sexual behaviors that include multiple partners, condom use, and alcohol use before sex (Catania, 1995; Catania, Coates, & Kegeles, 1994; Dolcini, Coates, Catania, Kegeles, & Hauck, 1995).[2]

[1]Address correspondence to Joseph A. Catania, College of Health and Human Sciences, Oregon State University, 320B Waldo Hall, Corvallis, OR 97331; e-mail: Joseph.Catania@oregonstate.edu
[2]Portions of the NABS survey data collected from the NABS cohort study used to report indexes of reliability and validity are available on request from the author.

Description

The original self- or interviewer-administered scale is composed of three items rated on a 3-point scale (1, *happened with all partners*; 2, *happened with some partners*; 3, *didn't happen*). The revised, expanded scale is a 10-item Likert-type rating scale with two questions that need to be excluded when administering the scale to gay individuals. Each item is rated on a 4-point scale (4 = *always*, 1 = *never*).

Response Mode and Timing

The scales are available in Spanish and English. Both the short and the expanded forms are self- or interviewer-administered and take approximately 1–2 minutes to complete.

Scoring

Total scores on the brief three-item HPSC scale are produced by reverse scoring and summing across items for a total scale score. Total scores on the expanded HPSC scale are obtained by summing across items.

Reliability and Validity

The HPSC scale has been administered to varied populations, including adolescents and national urban probability samples constructed to adequately represent White, Black, and Hispanic ethnic groups, as well as high HIV-risk groups (Catania et al., 1994; Catania, Kegeles, & Coates, 1990; Dolcini et al., 1995). The original brief version of the HPSC scale was used on a population of 114 adolescent females who participated in a study (Catania et al., 1990) that examined psychosocial correlates of condom use and multiple partner sex. Respondents, recruited from a family planning clinic in California, were White (92%), Hispanic (4%), and other (4%) and ranged in age from 12 to 18 years. The majority of respondents were heterosexual, unmarried, and sexually active. Reliability was good (Cronbach's alpha = .67). A hierarchical multiple regression model, in which several predictor variables known to be related to sexual risk were examined, revealed that a greater willingness to request partners to use condoms as indicated by HPSC scores was associated with more frequent condom use and multiple partners (Catania et al., 1990).

The original three-item Health Communication Sexual Scale was also administered to respondents who participated in a study (Catania et al., 1994) examining the incidence of multiple partners and related psychosocial correlates, as part of the AIDS in Multi-Ethnic Neighborhoods (AMEN)[3] study (Catania, Coates, Kegeles, et al., 1992). The AMEN study is a longitudinal study (three waves) examining the distribution of HIV, sexually transmitted diseases (STDs), related risk behaviors, and their correlates across social

strata. The multiple partner study sample, which used data generated from Wave 2, restricted inclusion criteria to unmarried heterosexuals who revealed an HIV-related risk marker at Wave 2, and being sexually active between Wave 1 and 2. Respondents ranged from 20–44 years of age. Reliability was excellent (Cronbach's alpha = .84). The mean, standard deviation, median, range, and reliabilities of ethnic groups, gender, and levels of education are provided in Table 1.

TABLE 1
Normative Data for the Health Protective Sexual Communication Scale

	n	Mean	SD	Range	Mdn	Alpha
NABS study[a]						
National sample	155	23.82	8.21	30.0	24.0	.88
High-risk cities	810	22.93	7.32	30.0	22.0	.84
Ethnicity						
White						
National sample	101	23.06	8.19	30.0	22.3	.88
High-risk cities	342	22.53	7.02	30.0	21.9	.83
Black						
National sample	47	25.62	8.13	29.0	28.0	.87
High-risk cities	329	24.35	7.33	30.0	24.0	.83
Hispanic						
National sample	8	23.01	3.30	15.0	24.0	.60
High-risk cities	125	21.90	8.12	30.0	21.0	.87
Gender						
Male						
National sample	81	22.57	8.22	29.0	22.1	.90
High-risk cities	414	21.22	6.72	29.0	20.0	.64
Female						
National sample	68	25.88	7.85	30.0	27.2	.84
High-risk cities	379	25.30	7.46	30.0	25.0	.82
Education						
< 12 years						
National sample	14	22.24	6.01	17.0	24.0	.76
High-risk cities	97	24.78	7.89	30.0	24.0	.55
= 12 years						
National sample	49	23.67	8.50	29.0	22.9	.88
High-risk cities	196	22.36	7.53	30.0	22.0	.85
> 12 years						
National sample	91	24.53	8.48	30.0	25.0	.88
High-risk cities	517	22.74	7.02	30.0	22.0	.83
The AMEN[b] Study						
Total	320	22.82	7.81	30.0	22.0	.84
Ethnicity						
White	146	23.05	7.86	30.0	22.1	.86
Black	72	23.69	7.79	30.0	23.0	.83
Hispanic	85	21.57	7.65	30.0	20.0	.84
Gender						
Male	155	20.64	7.34	30.0	19.0	.84
Female	165	24.86	7.71	30.0	24.0	.83
Education						
< 12 years	41	20.32	7.30	24.0	21.0	.83
= 12 years	65	23.34	8.34	30.0	22.0	.87
> 12 years	212	23.11	7.72	30.0	22.0	.84

[a]National AIDS Behavior Survey
[b]AIDS in Multi-Ethnic Neighborhoods

---

[3]For further details on sampling methods for the AMEN cohort study, see Catania, Coates, Kegeles, et al. (1992).

In earlier analysis with the HPSC scale, we examined whether its relationship to condom use was continuous across all scale values (Catania, Coates, Kegeles, et al., 1992). The scale was found to have a significant relationship to condom use primarily for those respondents scoring in the upper one third of the scale, indicating that people who consistently communicate about sexual matters across sexual encounters and partners are significantly more likely to use condoms. Thus, the HPSC scale was scored by dichotomizing the measure so that high scores included the upper one third of scores and low scores were composed of the lower two thirds of scores. Findings from the AMEN study revealed that high levels of health protective sexual communication were significantly correlated with high levels of condom use.

In another AMEN cohort analysis, the original HPSC scale was examined in relationship to incidence of multiple partners (Dolcini et al., 1995). Reliability was fair (Cronbach's alpha = .50) for respondents who also reported two or more sex partners in the past year. A regression model for all respondents with a primary sexual partner revealed that those who also had a new sexual partner in the past year ($n = 201$), and low heath protective communication (odds ratio = 1.3 per unit decrease in health protective communication, 95% confidence interval = 1.05, 1.5), were associated with having multiple partners.

We conducted further analyses on the expanded Health Communication Scale Measure used in the 1990–1991 National AIDS Behavior Survey[4] (NABS) longitudinal study (Wave 2), which was composed of three interlaced samples designed to oversample African Americans and Hispanics for adequate representation. The interlaced samples included a national sample, an urban sample of 23 cities with high prevalences of AIDS cases, and a special Hispanic urban sample. In our analyses of the expanded HPSC scale, we limited our sample to respondents who reported having at least one partner in the past 12 months, were heterosexual (defined as respondents who only had opposite gender sexual partners in the past 5 years), aged 18–49, and completed the HSPC scale. Respondents who described themselves as Asians, Native Americans, and Pacific Islanders were excluded because they were not adequately represented for analysis purposes ($n = 24$). Because the intent of our analyses was to examine relationships between variables, sample segments were combined without the use of poststratification weights. The resulting increase in power allowed for the detection of even very small relationships. Internal reliability was excellent (Cronbach's alpha = .85). Means, standard deviations, range, median, and reliability are given for White, Black, and Hispanic ethnic groups; males and females; and levels of education (Table 1).

A factor analysis of the expanded HPSC scale obtained a single large eigenvalue (4.3), with an additional value falling near one (1.15), suggesting that there may be an additional factor, but it is not a strong element in the expanded scale. The second factor that may exist consists of items asking specifically about condom use. Given the small amount of variance accounted for by the second (6%) versus the first factor (37%), we opted for a single-factor scale. We recommend further work that would expand the number of condom items in the scale to examine additional factors.

We examined an array of psychosocial and experiential factors that previous models and studies have indicated are important determinants of sexual communication and negotiation. From a multiple regression in which we analyzed primary antecedents, background, and demographic variables, we found respondents with higher HPSC expanded scale scores to be more likely to have greater sexual and condom relations skills, to be sexually assertive, to have ever used a condom, to be committed to using condoms in the future, to have been tested for HIV, and to be 18 to 29 years old (Catania, 1995). Respondents with high HPSC scores were also less likely to feel susceptible to STDs and less likely to report having used alcohol before sex.

We also examined a number of hypothesized gender and race interactions. An inverse relationship between sexual guilt and HPSC among Hispanic women was revealed. In contrast, Hispanic men who scored higher on sexual guilt also scored higher in HPSC. Higher communicators were also somewhat more likely to be Black than Hispanic and were almost three times more likely to be women than men.

References

Catania, J. (1995). [NABS Survey Data]. Unpublished raw data.

Catania J., Coates, T., Golden, E., Dolicini, M., Peterson, J., Kegeles, S., Siegel, D., & Fullilove, M. (1994). Correlates of condom use among Black, Hispanic, and White heterosexuals in San Francisco: The AMEN Longitudinal Survey. *AIDS Education and Prevention, 6,* 12–26.

Catania, J., Coates, T., & Kegeles, S. (1994). A test of the AIDS risk reduction model: Psychosocial correlates of condom use in the AMEN cohort survey. *Health Psychology, 13,* 548–555.

Catania, J., Coates, T., Kegeles, S., Thompson-Fullilove, M., Peterson, J., Marin, B., et al. (1992). Condom use in multi-ethnic neighborhoods of San Francisco: The population-based AMEN (AIDS in Multi-Ethnic Neighborhoods) Study. *American Journal of Public Health, 82,* 284–287.

Catania, J., Coates, T. J., Stall, R., Turner, H., Peterson, J., Hearst, N., et al. (1992). Prevalence of AIDS-related risk factors and condom use in the United States. *Science, 258,* 1101–1106.

Catania, J., Kegeles, S., & Coates, T. (1990). Towards an understanding of risk behavior: An AIDS risk reduction model (ARRM). *Health Education Quarterly, 17,* 53–72.

Dolcini, M. M., Coates, T. J., Catania, J. A., Kegeles, S. M., & Hauck, W. W. (1995). Multiple sexual partners and their psychosocial correlates: The population-based AIDS in Multi Ethnic Neighborhoods (AMEN) Study. *Health Psychology, 14,* 1–10.

---

[4]For further details on sample construction and weighting of the NABS cohort study, see Catania, Coates, Stall, et al. (1992).

Exhibit

Health Protective Sexual Communication Scale

Instructions: Now I am going to read a list of things that people talk about before they have sex with each other for the first time. How often in the past 12 mos. have you . . . (read each). Would you say *always*, *almost always*, *sometimes*, or *never*?

1 = Never   2 = Sometimes   3 = Almost always   4 = Always   6 = Don't know   7 = Declined to answer

1. Asked a new sex partner how (he/she) felt about using condoms before you had intercourse.
2. Asked a new sex partner about the number of past sex partners (he/she) had.
3. Told a new sex partner about the number of sex partners you have had.
4. Told a new sex partner that you won't have sex unless a condom is used.
5. Discussed with a new sex partner the need for both of you to get tested for the AIDS virus before having sex.
6. Talked with a new sex partner about not having sex until you have known each other longer.
7. Asked a new sex partner if (he/she) has ever had some type of VD, like herpes, clap, syphilis, gonorrhea.
8. Asked a new sex partner if (he/she) ever shot drugs like heroin, cocaine, or speed.
9. Talked about whether you or a new sex partner ever had homosexual experiences.
10. Talked to a new sex partner about birth control before having sex for the first time.

Note. Items 1, 2, and 4 were used in the original short version. Items 9 and 10 are excluded for gay men and lesbians.

Safe Sex Behavior Questionnaire

COLLEEN DiIORIO,[1] *Emory University*

The Safe Sex Behavior Questionnaire (SSBQ) was designed to measure frequency of use of recommended practices that reduce one's risk of exposure to, and transmission of, HIV.

Description

An information pamphlet sent in May and June of 1988 to all U.S. households by the Surgeon General's office, *Understanding AIDS*, was used as a guide to select items that reflect safe-sex practices (DiIorio, Parsons, Lehr, Adame, & Carlone, 1992). All references to safe-sex practices within the pamphlet were identified and classified into one of the following categories: (a) protection during intercourse, (b) avoidance of risky behaviors, (c) avoidance of bodily fluids, and (d) interpersonal skills. Based on these statements, 27 items were written and selected for review by content experts. Experts were asked to evaluate each item for meaning, clarity, and correspondence to the definition of safe-sex behaviors, which were defined as "sexually-related practices, which avoid or reduce the risk of exposure to HIV and the transmission of HIV." Based on their reviews, all 27 items were retained for the final version, with some minor changes in wording. Following factor analysis, three items were deleted from the scale.

Response Mode and Timing

Each of the 24 SSBQ items is rated on a 4-point scale from 1 (*Never*) to 4 (*Always*). The SSBQ takes about 5 to 10 minutes to complete. The items do not usually require explanation.

Scoring

Of the 24 SSBQ items, 15 are worded positively and 9 negatively. The 15 positively worded items are 1, 3, 4, 5, 6, 8, 9, 10, 11, 12, 16, 17, 18, 19, 21. The original items 6, 7, and 16 were deleted from the scale because of the results of factor analysis.

[1]Address correspondence to Colleen DiIorio, Emory University, Rollins School of Public Health, Department of Behavioral Sciences and Health Education, 1518 Clifton Road NE, Atlanta, GA 30322; e-mail: cdiiori@emory.edu

The negatively worded items are reverse coded prior to summing the items. A total score is found by summing responses to the 24 individual items. Total scale scores range from 24 to 96, with higher scores indicating greater frequency of use of safer-sex practices.

Reliability

Initial reliability of the 27-item SSBQ based on responses from a sample of 89 sexually active college students was .82 (coefficient alpha), indicating a moderate degree of internal consistency reliability. Test-retest reliability was assessed using responses from a sample of 100 sexually active college students who completed the scale twice, 2 weeks apart. The correlation was .82, indicating moderate stability. Internal consistency reliability was assessed using a second sample of sexually active college students ($N =$ 531). The alpha coefficient for the 24 items was .82. Based on data collected from a sample ($N = 584$) of sexually active college students in 1994, the estimated reliability coefficient (Cronbach's alpha) for the SSBQ 24-item instrument was .82 (DiIorio, Dudley, Lehr, & Soet, 2000).

Validity

Construct validity of the scale was assessed using hypothesis testing and factor analysis. The SSBQ correlated in the predicted directions with the concepts of risk taking and assertiveness (DiIorio, Parsons, Lehr, Adame, & Carlone, 1993). Factor analysis revealed five factors with eigenvalues greater than 1.0: risky behaviors, assertiveness, condom use, avoidance of bodily fluids, and avoidance of anal sex. Three weak items (6, 7, and 16) were identified and dropped to form the 24-item SSBQ.

Other Information

The format of the scale can be modified to use with computer-assisted interview (CAI) programs or face-to-face interviews.

References

DiIorio, C., Dudley, W., Lehr, S., & Soet, J. (2000). Correlates of safer sex communication among college students. *Journal of Advanced Nursing, 32*, 658–665.

DiIorio, C., Parsons, M., Lehr, S., Adame, D., & Carlone, J. (1992). Measurement of safe sex behavior in adolescents and young adults. *Nursing Research, 41*, 203–208.

DiIorio, C., Parsons, M., Lehr, S., Adame, D., & Carlone, J. (1993). Factors associated with use of safer sex practices among college freshmen. *Research in Nursing and Health, 16*, 343–350.

Exhibit

Safe Sex Behavior Questionnaire

Directions: Below is a list of sexual practices. Please read each statement and respond by indicating **your degree of use of these practices**.

I = Never	2 = Sometimes	3 = Most of the Time	4 = Always

	Never	Sometimes	Most of the Time	Always
1. I insist on condom use when I have sexual intercourse.	I	2	3	4
*2. I use cocaine or other drugs prior to or during sexual intercourse.	I	2	3	4
3. I stop foreplay long enough to put on a condom (or for my partner to put on a condom).	I	2	3	4
4. I ask potential sexual partners about their sexual histories.	I	2	3	4
5. I avoid direct contact with my sexual partner's semen or vaginal secretions.	I	2	3	4
6. I ask my potential sexual partners about a history of bisexual/homosexual practices.	I	2	3	4
*7. I engage in sexual intercourse on a first date.	I	2	3	4
8. I abstain from sexual intercourse when I do not know my partner's sexual history.	I	2	3	4
9. I avoid sexual intercourse when I have sores or irritation in my genital area.	I	2	3	4
10. If I know an encounter may lead to sexual intercourse, I carry a condom with me.	I	2	3	4
11. I insist on examining my sexual partner for sores, cuts, or abrasions in the genital area.	I	2	3	4
12. If I disagree with information that my partner presents on safer sex practices, I state my point of view.	I	2	3	4
*13. I engage in oral sex without using protective barriers such as a condom or rubber dam.	I	2	3	4
*14. If swept away in the passion of the moment, I have sexual intercourse without using a condom.	I	2	3	4

*15. I engage in anal intercourse.	I	2	3	4
16. I ask my potential sexual partners about a history of IV drug use.	I	2	3	4
17. If I know an encounter may lead to sexual intercourse, I have a mental plan to practice safer sex.	I	2	3	4
18. If my partner insists on sexual intercourse without a condom, I refuse to have sexual intercourse.	I	2	3	4
19. I avoid direct contact with my sexual partner's blood.	I	2	3	4
*20. It is difficult for me to discuss sexual issues with my sexual partners.	I	2	3	4
21. I initiate the topic of safer sex with my potential sexual partner.	I	2	3	4
*22. I have sexual intercourse with someone who I know is a bisexual or gay person.	I	2	3	4
*23. I engage in anal intercourse without using a condom.	I	2	3	4
*24. I drink alcoholic beverages prior to or during sexual intercourse.	I	2	3	4

*Negatively worded items.

Risk Behavior Assessment

Dennis G. Fisher,[1] **Lucy E. Napper, and Grace L. Reynolds,** *California State University, Long Beach*
Mark E. Johnson, *University of Alaska, Anchorage*

The instrument was developed to document behaviors that put individuals at risk for infection with the Human Immunodeficiency Virus (HIV). A companion instrument, the Risk Behavior Follow-up Assessment (RBFA), is available in 3-month and 6-month versions. The RBA-RBFA system was originally designed to measure intervention effects in the National Institute on Drug Abuse (NIDA) Cooperative Agreement for HIV/AIDS Community-Based Outreach/Intervention Research program (CA).

Description

The instrument was developed by the Community Research Branch of NIDA along with principal investigators in the NIDA CA. The original RBA was revised twice with the final version consisting of the following sections: preliminary data, such as ID number, and interview date and time (Section P); demographics (A); drug use (B); C is only for those respondents who have injected drugs in the 30 days prior to interview (C); recent drug use in the last 48 hours (D); drug treatment history (E); sexual risk behavior with separate subsections for men who have sex with men, men who have sex with women, men who have sex with both men and women, women who have sex with women, women who have sex with men, and women who

have sex with both men and women (F); sex trading (G); health-related conditions (H); arrest and incarceration (I); economic questions (J); and interviewer's impressions of interviewee's understanding, honesty, and accuracy (K).

Response Mode and Timing

The RBA takes from 18 to 60 minutes to administer depending upon the interviewer's skill and the interviewee's responses. Most items are responded to as a single-, a double-, a triple-, or a quadruple-digit answer. There are a few yes/no and categorical questions, and some questions, such as other race or country of origin, require word responses. All items have the capability of being coded *Don't Know/Unsure* or *Refused*. Skip patterns are included in most sections to expedite completion of the interview.

Scoring

As all items are self-report of behavior, no scoring is required. A data entry package, NOVA-DE, is available, which produces a raw ASCII file. This file is readable by either SAS or SPSS code, includes labels and formats, and can be saved as either a permanent SAS dataset or an SPSS SAV file.

[1]Address correspondence to Dennis G. Fisher, Center for Behavioral Research and Services, 1090 Atlantic Ave., Long Beach, CA 90813; e-mail: dfisher@csulb.edu

Reliability and Validity

The original reliability study collected data on 48-hour test-retest administration and found that, with the exception of needle sharing, most questions had acceptable reliability and validity (Needle et al., 1995; Weatherby, Needle, Cesari, & Booth, 1994). The reliability and validity of a revision of the RBA, with improved needle-sharing questions, was conducted using a 48-hour test-retest interval for the basic drug and sex variables, and a comparison of recent drug use and urine test results (Dowling-Guyer, Johnson, Fisher, & Needle, 1994). Subsequent analyses have examined the reliability and validity of the questions pertaining to amphetamine use (Napper, Fisher, Johnson, & Wood, 2008); hepatitis infection (Fisher, Kuhrt-Hunstiger, Orr, & Davis, 1999; Schlicting et al., 2003); syphilis infection (Fisher, Reynolds, Creekmur, Johnson, & Deaugustine, 2007); and HIV/AIDS testing and infection (Fisher, Reynolds, Jaffe, & Johnson, 2007). Similarly, further analyses have examined the reliability of questions pertaining to homelessness (Klahn, Fisher, Wood, Reynolds, & Johnson, 2004); gonorrhea infection (Paschane, Fisher, Cagle, & Fenaughty, 1998); drug treatment (Edwards, Fisher, Johnson, Reynolds, & Redpath, 2007); economic issues (Johnson, Fisher, & Reynolds, 1999); and alcohol use (Johnson, Pratt, Neal, & Fisher, in press). Finally, the reliability and validity of the RBFA 6-month follow-up version have been reported (Johnson et al., 2000).

Relative to the RBA sexual risk items, the 48-hour test-retest reliability coefficients ranged from a low of .07 for male reporting of oral sex (cunnilingus) with barrier, to a high of .92 for the number of different sex partners in the last 30 days (Dowling-Guyer et al., 1994). Four of the sexual risk behavior items have reliability coefficients greater than .80, and four have reliability coefficients greater than .70. Two have reliability coefficients greater than .60, one each for .50 and .40, and two greater than .30 (Dowling-Guyer et al., 1994). For the RBFA, the 48-hour test-retest reliability coefficients for the sexual risk behavior questions range from a low of .57 for the number of drug-injecting sex partners, to a high of .87 for the male reporting of number of times for vaginal sex (Johnson et al., 2000).

Other Information

Annotated versions of all Cooperative Agreement instruments are in the public domain and are available as .pdf files from the Inter-University Consortium for Political and Social Research, Substance Abuse Mental Health Data Archive at the University of Michigan, http://www.icpsr. umich.edu/SAMHDA/survey-inst/CAA_1.pdf.

References

Dowling-Guyer, S., Johnson, M. E., Fisher, D. G., & Needle, R. (1994). Reliability of drug users' self-reported HIV risk behaviors and validity of self-reported recent drug use. *Assessment, 1*, 383–392.

Edwards, J. W., Fisher, D. G., Johnson, M. E., Reynolds, G. L., & Redpath, D. P. (2007). Test-retest reliability of self-reported drug treatment variables. *Journal of Substance Abuse Treatment, 33*, 7–11.

Fisher, D. G., Kuhrt-Hunstiger, T. I., Orr, S. M., & Davis, D. C. (1999). Hepatitis B validity of drug users' self-report. *Psychology of Addictive Behaviors, 13*, 33–38.

Fisher, D. G., Reynolds, G. L., Creekmur, B., Johnson, M. E., & Deaugustine, N. (2007). Reliability and criterion-related validity of self-report of syphilis. *Sexually Transmitted Diseases, 34*, 389–391.

Fisher, D. G., Reynolds, G. L., Jaffe, A., & Johnson, M. E. (2007). Reliability, sensitivity and specificity of self-report of HIV test results. *AIDS Care, 19*, 692–696.

Johnson, M. E., Fisher, D. G., Montoya, I., Booth, R., Rhodes, F., Andersen, M., et al. (2000). Reliability and validity of not-in-treatment drug users' follow-up self-reports. *AIDS and Behavior, 4*, 373–380.

Johnson, M. E., Fisher, D. G., & Reynolds, G. L. (1999). Reliability of drug users' self-report of economic variables. *Addiction Research, 7*, 227–238.

Johnson, M. E., Pratt, D. K., Neal, D. B., & Fisher, D. G. (in press). Drug users' test-retest reliability of self-reported alcohol use on the Risk Behavior Assessment. *Substance Use and Misuse*.

Klahn, J. A., Fisher, D. G., Wood, M. M., Reynolds, G. L., & Johnson, M. E. (2004). Homelessness among out-of-treatment drug users in Long Beach, CA. *Journal of Social Distress and the Homeless, 13*, 345–368.

Napper, L. E., Fisher, D. G., Johnson, M. E., & Wood, M. M. (2008, October 25–29). *Reliability and validity of drug users' self-reports of amphetamine use*. Paper presented at the 136th Annual Meeting and Exposition of the American Public Health Association, San Diego, CA.

Needle, R., Fisher, D. G., Weatherby, N., Chitwood, D., Brown, B., Cesari, H., et al. (1995). Reliability of self-reported HIV risk behaviors of drug users. *Psychology of Addictive Behaviors, 9*, 242–250.

Paschane, D. M., Fisher, D. G., Cagle, H. H., & Fenaughty, A. M. (1998). Gonorrhea among drug users: An Alaskan versus a national sample. *American Journal of Drug and Alcohol Abuse, 24*, 285–297.

Schlicting, E. G., Johnson, M. E., Brems, C., Wells, R. S., Fisher, D. G., & Reynolds, G. L. (2003). Validity of injecting drug users' self report of hepatitis A, B, and C. *Clinical Laboratory Science, 16*, 99–106.

Weatherby, N. L., Needle, R., Cesari, H., & Booth, R. E. (1994). Validity of self-reported drug use among injection drug users and crack cocaine users recruited through street outreach. *Evaluation and Program Planning, 17*, 347–355.

Exhibit

Risk Behavior Assessment (sample items)

Now, we are going to talk about your sexual practices, including each of the times you have had vaginal, oral, and anal sex. We are also talking about all types of partners: regular partners, partners for money, drugs, or whatever.

Q25.   How many days in the last 30 days have you had sex (vaginal, oral, and/or anal)?

	DK/Unsure	Refused
Days ___ ___	77	88

Q26.   During the last 30 days, *how many different people* have you had vaginal, oral, and/or anal sex with?

	DK/Unsure	Refused	Skip
___ ___ ___	777	888	999

Q27.   *How many* of your sex partners were likely to have been drug injectors or shooters?

	DK/Unsure	Refused	Skip
___ ___ ___	777	888	999

Q28.   *How many* of your sex partners were female?

	DK/Unsure	Refused	Skip
___ ___ ___	777	888	999

Q29.   *How many* of your sex partners were male?

	DK/Unsure	Refused	Skip
___ ___ ___	777	888	999

Now I want to ask you more specific questions about your vaginal, oral, and/or anal sexual practices. When I ask you these questions, I want you to think about all the partners that you have had sex with in the last 30 days, not just your main or last partner.

Q30.   How many times in the last 30 days when you had sex did you put your penis in your partner's vagina?

	DK/Unsure	Refused	Skip	NA
Times ___ ___ ___	777	888	999	666

(IF "000," GO TO Q31.)

Q30a. Of these ____ (NUMBER FROM Q30) times, how many times did you use a condom?

	DK/Unsure	Refused	Skip	NA
Times ___ ___ ___	777	888	999	666

Q31.   How many times in the last 30 days when you had sex did you put your penis in your partner's mouth?

	DK/Unsure	Refused	Skip	NA
Times ___ ___ ___	777	888	999	666

(IF "000," GO TO Q32.)

Q31a. Of these ____ (NUMBER FROM Q31) times, how many times did you use a condom?

	DK/Unsure	Refused	Skip	NA
Times ___ ___ ___	777	888	999	666

Q32.   How many times in the last 30 days when you had sex did *you put your mouth on your partner's vagina?*

	DK/Unsure	Refused	Skip	NA
Times ___ ___ ___	777	888	999	666

(IF "000," GO TO Q33.)

Q32a. How many of those _____ (NUMBER FROM Q32) times did your partner use latex or other barrier protection?

	DK/Unsure	Refused	Skip	NA
Times ___ ___ ___	777	888	999	666

Q33. How many times in the last 30 days when you had sex did you put your penis in your partner's anus?

	DK/Unsure	Refused	Skip	NA
Times ___ ___ ___	777	888	999	666

Q33a. Of these _____ (NUMBER FROM Q33) times, how many times did you use a condom?

	DK/Unsure	Refused	Skip	NA
Times ___ ___ ___	777	888	999	666

Q58. In the last 30 days, how many times have you used the following drugs immediately before or during sex?

	Times	DK/Unsure	Refused	Skip
A Alcohol	— — —	777	888	999
B Marijuana/hashish (weed, grass, reefers)?	— — —	777	888	999
C Crack?	— — —	777	888	999
D Cocaine by itself (other than crack) that you injected or snorted?	— — —	777	888	999
E Heroin (by itself)?	— — —	777	888	999
F Heroin and cocaine mixed together (e.g., speedball)?	— — —	777	888	999
G Nonprescription methadone?	— — —	777	888	999
H Other opiates (e.g., demerol, codeine, dilaudid)?	— — —	777	888	999
I Amphetamines (e.g., speed, uppers, bennies)?	— — —	777	888	999
J Some other drug? (Specify: _ _ _ _ _ _ _ _ _ _ _ _ _ _ _ _ _ _)	— — —	777	888	999

Sexual Risk Survey

JESSICA A. TURCHIK[1] AND JOHN P. GARSKE, *Ohio University*

Risky sexual behavior among college students is a significant problem that warrants scientific investigation. Other measures of sexual risk taking either are too narrowly focused to be used with college students or do not have adequate psychometric properties. The Sexual Risk Survey (SRS; Turchik & Garske, 2009) was developed to provide a broad and psychometrically sound measure of sexual risk taking to researchers interested in studying college students.

Description

The SRS was developed to assess the frequency of sexual risk behaviors in the past 6 months among college students. The SRS was developed at a midsized midwestern university with a sample of 613 male and female undergraduate students (Turchik & Garske, 2009). The survey was originally composed of 37 items taken from past surveys of sexual risk behaviors and from suggestions in the literature. Descriptive analyses and a principal components analysis with varimax rotation were used to reduce data from the original 37 SRS items. Items were eliminated based on low number of responses above 0 (< 10%), low item-total correlations (< .40), low communalities (< .40), and low factor loadings (< .40). Fourteen items were eliminated based on these criteria; the final survey comprises 23 items.

Response Mode and Timing

Participants are asked to read the 23 items, each describing a sexual risk behavior, and to indicate in a free-response format the number of times they engaged in each behavior over the past 6 months. The SRS was developed as a paper-and-pencil self-administered survey that can be given in groups. The survey typically takes participants 5 to 10 minutes to complete. The SRS has also been given in an individual-structured interview format. The responses to the survey and the interview were found to be highly correlated ($r = .90$).

Scoring

Given that sexual risk-taking scores are typically positively skewed, the data will likely need to be recoded or transformed to reduce skewness in the frequencies reported by the students. In the original study (Turchik & Garske, 2009), the responses to the 23 items were recoded into an ordinal series of categories to reduce the variability and skewness in the raw score totals. The raw numbers for each item were recoded into categories coded as 0 to 4. Codes of "0" only included frequencies of 0. Next, the remaining frequencies were examined for the sample and were treated as if they represented 100% of the frequencies. Because the data were negatively skewed, the following guideline was used to classify the frequencies greater than 0: 1 = 40% of responses, 2 = 30% of responses, 3 = 20% of responses, and 4 = 10% of responses. However, in practice, with the restricted variability of frequencies in many of the items, it was often not possible to classify the frequencies in this manner. Also, the distribution of frequencies will likely be different based on the sample, and researchers should not assume the ordinal categories used in one study would be valid in another sample. An alternative way to reduce skewness in the data is to perform some other normalizing technique, such as a logarithmic or inverse transformation, because the distribution will likely not be normally distributed. Researchers should refer to the original article for more discussion on this issue (Turchik & Garske, 2009).

Once the items are recoded with scores from 0 to 4, all 23 items are summed for the total sexual risk-taking score, with scores ranging from 0 to 92 based on the original score "blocking" technique. A principal components analysis revealed five subscales that can also be scored: Sexual Risk Taking With Uncommitted Partners (8 items), Risky Sex Acts (5 items), Impulsive Sexual Behaviors (5 items), Intent to Engage in Risky Sexual Behaviors (2 items), and Risky Anal Sex Acts (3 items).

Reliability

The SRS has demonstrated good internal consistency and test-retest reliability (Turchik & Garske, 2009). The internal consistency of the total Sexual Risk Survey with all 23 items was .88. For the five subscales, the Cronbach's alphas were .88, .80, .78, .89, and .61 for Sexual Risk Taking With Uncommitted Partners, Risky Sex Acts, Impulsive Sexual Behaviors, Intent to Engage in Risky Sexual Behaviors, and Risky Anal Sex Acts, respectively. The 2-week test-retest reliability for the total Sexual Risk Survey was .93. The 2-week test-retest reliabilities for the Sexual Risk Taking With Uncommitted Partners, Risky Sex Acts, Impulsive Sexual Behaviors, Intent to Engage in Risky Sexual Behaviors, and Risky Anal Sex Acts factors were .90, .89, .79, .70, and .58, respectively. The inclusion or exclusion of the Risky Anal Sex Act items did not affect

[1]Address correspondence to Jessica A. Turchik, Ohio University, 200 Porter Hall, Athens, OH 45701; e-mail: jt865504@ohio.edu

the internal consistency or test-retest reliability of the total scale.

Validity

The SRS has demonstrated evidence of content, concurrent, and convergent validity (Turchik & Garske, 2009). Content validity was supported by inclusion of items based on a review of the literature, an examination of previous measures of sexual risk taking, and a pilot study of college students. The SRS demonstrated evidence of convergent and concurrent validity by its relationships with a number of other measures predicted to be related to sexual risk behaviors based on past literature. The SRS evidenced discriminant validity with low correlations with measures of social desirability and sexual threat of disclosure.

Other Information

The measure was originally given with a glossary of terms that might not be familiar to some participants and with a calendar of the last 6 months. Questions to help participants remember their sexual experiences over this time period were also included to help enhance accurate recall.

Further information concerning the measure can be found in the original article (Turchik & Garske, 2009) or by contacting the first author.

Reference

Turchik, J. A., & Garske, J. P. (2009). Measurement of sexual risk taking among college students. *Archives of Sexual Behavior, 38*, 936–948.

Exhibit

Sexual Risk Survey

Instructions: Please read the following statements and record the number that is true for you over the past six months for each question on the blank. If you do not know for sure how many times a behavior took place, try to estimate the number as close as you can. Thinking about the average number of times the behavior happened per week or per month might make it easier to estimate an accurate number, especially if the behavior happened fairly regularly. If you've had multiple partners, try to think about how long you were with each partner, the number of sexual encounters you had with each, and try to get an accurate estimate of the total number of each behavior. If the question does not apply to you or you have never engaged in the behavior in the question, put a "0" on the blank. Please do not leave items blank. **Remember that in the following questions "sex" includes oral, anal, and vaginal sex and that "sexual behavior" includes passionate kissing, making out, fondling, petting, oral-to-anal stimulation, and hand-to-genital stimulation.** Refer to the Glossary[a] for any words you are not sure about. Please consider only the last six months when answering and please be honest.

In the **past six months**:

1. _____ How many partners have you engaged in sexual behavior with but not had sex with?
2. _____ How many times have you left a social event with someone you just met?
3. _____ How many times have you "hooked up" but not had sex with someone you didn't know or didn't know well?
4. _____ How many times have you gone out to bars/parties/social events with the intent of "hooking up" and engaging in sexual behavior but not having sex with someone?
5. _____ How many times have you gone out to bars/parties/social events with the intent of "hooking up" and having sex with someone?
6. _____ How many times have you had an unexpected and unanticipated sexual experience?
7. _____ How many times have you had a sexual encounter you engaged in willingly but later regretted?

For the next set of questions, follow the same direction as before. However, for questions 8–23, if you have never had sex (oral, anal, or vaginal), please put a "0" on each blank.

8. _____ How many partners have you had sex with?
9. _____ How many times have you had vaginal intercourse without a latex or polyurethane condom? Note: Include times when you have used a lambskin or membrane condom.
10. _____ How many times have you had vaginal intercourse without protection against pregnancy?
11. _____ How many times have you given or received fellatio (oral sex on a man) without a condom?
12. _____ How many times have you given or received cunnilingus (oral sex on a woman) without a dental dam or "adequate protection" (please see definition of dental dam for what is considered adequate protection)?
13. _____ How many times have you had anal sex without a condom?

14. ____ How many times have you or your partner engaged in anal penetration by a hand ("fisting") or other object without a latex glove or condom followed by unprotected anal sex?

15. ____ How many times have you given or received analingus (oral stimulation of the anal region, "rimming") without a dental dam or "adequate protection" (please see definition of dental dam for what is considered adequate protection)?

16. ____ How many people have you had sex with that you know but are not involved in any sort of relationship with (i.e., "friends with benefits," "fuck buddies")?

17. ____ How many times have you had sex with someone you don't know well or just met?

18. ____ How many times have you or your partner used alcohol or drugs before or during sex?

19. ____ How many times have you had sex with a new partner before discussing sexual history, IV drug use, disease status and other current sexual partners?

20. ____ How many times (that you know of) have you had sex with someone who has had many sexual partners?

21. ____ How many partners (that you know of) have you had sex with who had been sexually active before you were with them but had not been tested for STIs/HIV?

22. ____ How many partners have you had sex with that you didn't trust?

23. ____ How many times (that you know of) have you had sex with someone who was also engaging in sex with others during the same time period?

---

[a]The Glossary is available upon request from Jessica A. Turchik.

Attitudes Toward Erotica Questionnaire

ILSA L. LOTTES,[1] *University of Maryland, Baltimore County*
MARTIN S. WEINBERG, *Indiana Universtiy*

The Attitudes Toward Erotica Questionnaire (ATEQ) was developed by a University Task Force on Pornography. At a Midwestern university, a student was arrested for showing a sexually explicit film to raise funds for his dormitory. The arrest sparked controversy and brought the issue of pornography into sharp focus among students, faculty, and administrators. Subsequently, a task force was appointed to investigate attitudes toward sexually explicit materials by the student body.

The ATEQ includes scales measuring attitudes about harmful and positive effects of erotica, as well as attitudes toward its restriction and regulation. Because of the wide variety of sexually explicit material, the questionnaire is not designed to investigate attitudes toward erotica in general. A social scientist can adapt the questionnaire to examine attitudes about the type of erotic material most appropriate for her/his research—either a specific medium (e.g., *Playboy*) or a general form (e.g., X-rated movie).

Description

For each type of erotica, nine items (numbered 1, 4, 6, 7, 9, 10, 12, 20, and 21) assess its harmful effects and form

a Harmful scale; seven items (numbered 5, 11, 13, 15, 17, 18, and 19) assess its positive effects and form a Positive scale; and five items (numbered 2, 3, 8, 14, and 16) assess its restriction and form a Restrict scale. In the study at the university in the Midwest, 663 students (52% female) responded to items about four types of sexually explicit materials—"magazines like *Playboy*," "magazines like *Hustler*," "adult bookstore magazines," and "X-rated movies and videos like Deep Throat" (Lottes, Weinberg, & Weller, 1993). From a varimax factor analysis with an orthogonal rotation of the 84 responses (21 per erotic type) of these students, one major factor emerged. This factor accounted for 63% of the variance with all factor loadings having an absolute value greater than .71. Thus, although properties of the individual Harmful, Positive, and Restrict scales are presented here, analysis based on one large random student sample (70% response rate) suggests that attitudes toward erotica are organized along a simple binary good/bad dimension.

The response options to each item are one of the 5-point Likert-type choices: *strongly disagree* (1), *disagree* (2), *no opinion* (3), *agree* (4), and *strongly agree* (5). This questionnaire is designed for a college student or general adult

[1]Address correspondence to Ilsa L. Lottes, Department of Sociology and Anthropology, University of Maryland, Baltimore County, 5401 Wilkens Avenue, Baltimore, MD 21228; e-mail: lottes@umbc.edu

population. Obscenity law is strongly linked to "community standards" and the ATEQ is a tool to assess such standards.

Response Mode and Timing

Respondents write the number from 1 to 5 corresponding to their degree of agreement/disagreement with each item or if computer scoring is available, machine-scoreable answer sheets can be provided for responses. Each set of 21 items for a particular type of erotica takes 8 minutes for completion.

Scoring

For 11 of the items, an agree response indicates a pro-erotica attitude and for 10 items an agree response indicates an anti-erotica attitude. To decrease the probability of a response set, the 21 items of the Harmful, Positive, and Restrict scales are not grouped together but placed randomly in the questionnaire. To obtain the scale scores for the Harmful and Positive scales, the responses to the items of each respective scale are summed. For the Harmful scale, scores can range from 9 to 45 and the higher the score, the more harm has been attributed to the erotica. For the Positive scale, scores can range from 7 to 35, and the higher the score, the more positive the effect attributed to the erotica. For the Restrict scale, four of the five items (items numbered 2, 3, 8, and 16) are scored in the reverse direction. For these reverse-direction items, recoding needs to transform all 5s to 1s and 4s to 2s and vice-versa before responses to the five items are summed to give the Restrict scale score. For this scale, scores can range from 5 to 25 and the higher the score, the more restrictions on the erotica are supported.

Reliability

In a sample of 663 college students, Cronbach alphas for the Harmful scale associated with *Playboy, Hustler*, adult bookstore magazines, and X-rated movies or videos were .90, .85, .84, and .85, respectively. Cronbach alphas for these same materials for the Positive scale were .73, .76, .78, and .78, respectively, and Cronbach alphas for the Restrict scale were .85, .85, .84, and .85, respectively (Lottes, Weinberg, & Weller, 1993).

Validity

The construct validity of the Harmful, Positive, and Restrict scales was supported by statistically significant results for predicted correlations and group differences. As expected, Lottes, Weinberg, and Weller (1993) found that respondents who were more religious, less sexually active, and viewed erotica less often evaluated all four types of sexually explicit material as being more harmful and having fewer positive effects, and supported more restrictions on their availability than did respondents who were less religious, more sexually active, and viewed erotica more often. Also as expected, males and those who had seen a specific type of sexually explicit material reported higher scores on the Positive scale and lower scores on the Harmful and Restrict scales than did females and those who had not seen the erotic material.

Reference

Lottes, I. L., Weinberg, M. S., & Weller, I. (1993). Reactions to pornography on a college campus: For or against? *Sex Roles, 29*, 69–89.

Exhibit

Attitudes Toward Erotica Questionnaire

Directions: Indicate how strongly you agree or disagree with each of the following statements by writing the number corresponding to one of the five response options below in the space provided.

Strongly Disagree	Disagree	No Opinion	Agree	Strongly Agree
1	2	3	4	5

1. The material exploits women. ____
2. The material should be publicly sold (magazines) and publicly shown (movies). ____
3. The material should be available to adults. ____
4. The availability of the material leads to a breakdown in community morals. ____
5. The material can improve sex relations among adults. ____
6. I feel the material is offensive. ____
7. The material exploits men. ____
8. The material should be available to minors (under 18). ____
9. The material increases the probability of sexual violence. ____
10. In this material, the positioning and treatment of men is degrading to men. ____
11. The material may provide an outlet for bottled-up sexual pressures. ____
12. In this material, sex and violence are often shown together. ____

13. This material can enhance the pleasure of masturbation for women. ____
14. This material should be made illegal. ____
15. The material may teach people sexual techniques. ____
16. This material should be protected by the 1st Amendment (freedom of speech and the press). ____
17. People should be made aware of the positive effects of this material. ____
18. This material serves a more positive than negative function in society. ____
19. This material can enhance the pleasure of masturbation for men. ____
20. People should be made aware of the negative effects of this material. ____
21. In this material, the positioning and treatment of women is degrading to women. ____

Sexual Scripts Overlap Scale—Short Version

ALEKSANDAR ŠTULHOFER[1] AND IVAN LANDRIPET, *University of Zagreb*

Little is known about the possible impact of sexually explicit material (SEM) or pornography use on young people's sexual socialization. The efforts so far have been characteristically brief (1-item measures assessing self-rated influence of pornography on one's sex life were often used) and direct—thus vulnerable to normative expectations and socially desirable answers. According to our conceptualization, pornographic imagery competes with other socially available sexual narratives in the process of sexual scripting, particularly in the formation of personal sexual scripts (Simon & Gagnon, 2003). It should be possible, therefore, to retrospectively assess the impact of SEM on sexual socialization by measuring the overlap between a pornographic and personal depiction of sex, which is what the Sexual Scripts Overlap Scale (SSOS) does. Recently, the SSOS has been found to be a useful tool in modeling mediated effects of early SEM use on sexual satisfaction of young adults (Štulhofer, Buško, & Landripet, 2010; Štulhofer et al., 2007). To facilitate wider application of this composite measure, a brief but more robust version of the scale (SSOS-S; $k = 20$) has been developed and validated using two online surveys.

Description

The original SSOS was developed by asking a group of Croatian college students ($N = 41$) to make a list of things/activities/sensations that are important for the pornographic depiction of sex. The other group ($N = 35$) was asked to do the same for what they personally considered to be "great sex." The two inventories—the *pornographic inventory* and the *great sex inventory*—were then merged. Judged for relevance and occurrence, 42 items were selected and combined into the final inventory, which was pretested on 277 students. In 2006 and 2007, two online surveys were carried out to validate this new instrument among sexually active young adults (18–25) with at least some experience with SEM. In 2006 the questionnaire was completed by 1,914 participants and in 2007 by another 600. In the first part of the questionnaire, participants were asked to assess the importance of the listed 42 items for great sex. Near the end of the questionnaire, participants were asked to assess the inventory again, but this time they were asked about each item's importance for the pornographic presentation of sex. In both cases, answers were anchored on a 5-point Likert scale. The scores were computed on each of the 42 paired items by subtracting the pornographic item value from the great sex item value. After the SSOS scores were reverse recoded, greater overlap between the values—which implied greater influence of pornography on sexual socialization—was represented by higher SSOS scores (for the list of the SSOS items, see Štulhofer et al., 2010). The SSOS items reflected five important dimensions of sexual socialization: (a) personal and partner sexual role expectations, (b) content of "successful" sex, (c) sexiness and body image, (d) relationship between emotions, intimacy, and sexuality, and (e) power dynamics within sexual relationship.

To make the SSOS more efficient, items from both inventories were arranged according to their sample means to determine the most characteristic aspects of the great sex and pornographic script. The top 10 items from both inventories were identical in 2006 and 2007. The resulting 20-item version of the scale (SSOS-S) was normally distributed (2006: range 8–80, $M = 45.0$, $SD = 11.3$; 2007: range 17–79, $M = 44.2$, $SD = 11.1$) and highly correlated

[1]Address correspondence to Aleksandar Štulhofer, Sexology Unit, Department of Sociology, Faculty of Humanities and Social Sciences, I. Lučića 3, 10000 Zagreb, Croatia; e-mail: astulof@ffzg.hr

with the SSOS, both in total and by gender ($r = .90-.94, p < .001$). Principal component analysis indicated the presence of four dimensions (eigenvalues > 1) in the 2006 dataset, accounting for 57% of the total item variance. However, a scree test suggested a forced two-factor solution: 10 items loaded high (> .4) on the Sexual Intimacy factor and the remaining 10 on the Sexual Performance factor. Similar structure and factor loadings were found in the 2007 sample.

Response Mode and Timing

To minimize self-censorship, the great sex inventory should be placed closer to the beginning of the questionnaire and the pornographic inventory closer to its end (or vice versa). Respondents are asked to assess the importance of the 20 items for what they consider to be great sex ("How important for great sex do you personally find . . .?") and for pornographic representation of sex ("How important for pornographic depiction of sex do you find . . .?"). Responses are recorded on a 5-point scale ranging from 1 = *Not at all Important* to 5 = *Exceptionally Important*. Most participants complete both scales in less than 8 minutes.

Scoring

Twenty overlap items are calculated from the paired great sex and pornographic inventory items by subtracting the second from the first (negative signs are ignored). The SSOS-S is additive and represents a linear combination of the overlap-item scores. Absolute range of the scale is 0 (all paired items have identical values) to 80 (all paired items have opposite values). The SSOS-S scores are reverse recoded ($80-n$), so that higher scores indicate greater overlap between the scripts.

Reliability

The SSOS-S had satisfactory internal consistency in both samples (Cronbach's $\alpha_{2006} = .84$ and $\alpha_{2007} = .83$), with reliability coefficients lower for women (2006: $\alpha_{Female} = .80$ and $\alpha_{Male} = .86$; 2007: $\alpha_{Female} = .79$ and $\alpha_{Male} = .85$). In 2007, an English version of the SSOS-S was tested in a sample of 356 U.S. college students. Obtained reliability was satisfactory (Cronbach's $\alpha = .88$).

Validity

Construct validity was assessed by zero-order correlations between the SSOS-S and theoretically relevant constructs/indicators: partner intimacy, exposure to SEM at the age of 14 and 17, range of sexual experiences, the acceptance of myths about sexuality, attitudes towards SEM, and the presence of sexually compulsive sexual thoughts and behaviors (Kalichman & Rompa, 1995). All the associations were found significant and in the expected direction in both samples ($r = .21-.50, p < .001$). Convergent validity was investigated by relating the SSOS-S to the real-life desirability of SEM-portrayed sexuality ("To what extent would you like your sex life to resemble a pornographic movie?"), personal importance of SEM, and the perceived realism of pornographic depictions of sex. Again, significant and moderately strong associations were found ($r = .35-.40, p < .001$).

The SSOS-S was shown to differentiate between male and female participants, as well as between users of mainstream vs. nonmainstream SEM. Women reported lesser overlap than men ($p < .001$), whereas users of nonmainstream SEM (S&M and B&D, fetishism, bestiality, and/or sexually violent/coercive material) reported higher overlap than those who preferred mainstream SEM ($p < .05$). Effect size of the observed differences was medium to small.

References

Kalichman, S. C., & Rompa, D. (1995). Sexual sensation seeking and sexual compulsivity scales: Reliability, validity, and predicting HIV risk behaviors. *Journal of Personality Assessment, 65*, 586–602.

Simon, W., & Gagnon, J. H. (2003). Sexual scripts: Origins, influences and changes. *Qualitative Sociology, 26*, 491–497.

Štulhofer, A., Buško, V., & Landripet, I. (2010). Pornography, sexual socialization and sexual satisfaction among young men. *Archives of Sexual Behavior, 39*, 168–178.

Štulhofer, A., Landripet, I., Momčilović, A., Matko, V., Kladarić, P. G., & Buško, V. (2007). Pornography and sexual satisfaction in young women and men. In S. V. Knudsen, L. Lofgren-Martenson, & S. A. Mansson (Eds.), *Generation P? Youth, Gender and Pornography* (pp. 66–84). Copenhagen: Danish School of Education Press.

Exhibit

Sexual Scripts Overlap Scale—Short Version

The "Great Sex" Script Items	The Pornographic Script Items
How important for great sex do you personally find:[a]	How important for pornographic depiction of sex do you find:
1 = Not at all 2 = Somewhat 3 = Moderately 4 = A Great Deal 5 = Exceptionally	
1. I am always ready for sex[b]	1. Men are always ready for sex
2. My partner is always ready to have sex[c]	2. Women are always ready for sex
3. It is easy to initiate sex	3. *(same)*

4. Sex is possible in any situation	4. (same)
5. Oral sex	5. (same)
6. Anal sex	6. (same)
7. Partner's sexual pleasure	7. (same)
8. Emotions, love	8. (same)
9. Intimate communication	9. (same)
10. Penetration	10. (same)
11. Being constantly horny[b]	11. Men are constantly horny
12. Partner is constantly horny[c]	12. Women are constantly horny
13. Trust in partner	13. (same)
14. Commitment	14. (same)
15. Intense passion	15. (same)
16. Feeling safe and well cared for	16. (same)
17. Spontaneity	17. (same)
18. Imagination	18. (same)
19. Unselfishness	19. (same)
20. "Pumping" (fast and deep penetration)	20. (same)

[a]The questions regarding the "great sex" script should be placed closer to the beginning of the questionnaire, whereas the questions concerning the pornographic script should be closer to the end.

[b]If a respondent is male, the item should be paired with the corresponding item on the pornography inventory; if a respondent is female, the item should be paired with the next item on the pornography inventory.

[c]The item should be paired according to participant's sexual orientation.

STI Education Efficacy Survey

Patricia Barthalow Koch,[1] Andrew W. Porter, and Clinton Colaco,
The Pennsylvania State University

As of June 1, 2009, 35 states plus the District of Columbia mandate STI/HIV education in their public schools (Guttmacher Institute, 2009). Yet teachers often do not have the training, including the accurate knowledge, positive attitudes, and appropriate skills, needed to implement effective STI/HIV education (Cozzens, 2006; Rodriguez, Young, Renfro, Ascencio, & Haffner, 1995–1996). Thus, the STI Education Efficacy Survey (SEES) was developed to measure educators' level of STI knowledge, attitudes toward adolescent sexuality and sexuality education, STI education confidence, and readiness to implement STI education. Improving the educational efficacy of educators will then improve students' learning and improve STI prevention. (James-Traore, Finger, Ruland, & Savariaud, 2004).

Description

The STI Education Efficacy Survey (SEES) consists of four sections: Knowledge of Sexually Transmitted Infections (STIs; 25 items), Attitudes Toward Adolescent Sexuality and Sexuality Education (10 items), STI Education Confidence (8 items), and STI Education Readiness (5 items). It was designed to ascertain the areas in which educators, particularly those working with young people in schools or community educational settings, need additional training, resources, or other type of support.

Response Mode and Time

For Part One, Knowledge of Sexually Transmitted Infections, respondents are instructed to indicate if they definitely know if each of the 25 statements is *True* (1) or *False* (2). If they do not definitely know the answer, they are to respond *Don't Know* (3). For Part Two, Attitudes Toward Adolescent Sexuality and Sexuality Education Scale, respondents are asked to indicate their reactions to each of 10 statements using a 5-point Likert scale: 1= *Strongly Agree*, 2 = *Agree*, 3 = *Uncertain*, 4 = *Disagree*, 5 = *Strongly*

[1]Address correspondence to Patricia Barthalow Koch, Department of Biobehavioral Health, The Pennsylvania State University, University Park, PA 16802; e-mail: p3k@psu.edu

Disagree. For Part Three, STI Education Confidence, respondents are directed to indicate how confident they feel about each of eight aspects of teaching about STIs, using a 5-point Likert-type scale: 1 = *No Confidence at all,* 2 = *Very Little Confidence,* 3 = *Somewhat Confident,* 4 = *Very Confident,* 5 = *Extremely Confident.* If an item does not apply to them, they mark 6 for "Does Not Apply." For the final part, STI Education Readiness, respondents are asked to describe their readiness (including their willingness and ability) to perform each of five educational tasks using a 5-point Likert-type scale: 1 = *Not Ready at all,* 2 = *Hardly Ready,* 3 = *Somewhat Ready,* 4 = *Very Ready,* 5 = *Extremely Ready.* If an item does not apply to them, they mark 6 for "Does Not Apply." The SEES takes approximately 20 minutes to complete.

Scoring

Scores on the Knowledge of Sexually Transmitted Infections scale can range from 0 (none correct) to 25 (all correct). A score of 0 is given to an incorrect response or a response that the respondent marked as "Don't Know." The following items are true: 3, 4, 5, 7, 12, 13, 17, 19, 21. The following items are false: 1, 2, 6, 8, 9, 10, 11, 14, 15, 16, 18, 20, 22, 23, 24, 25. Scores on the Attitudes Toward Adolescent Sexuality and Sexuality Education scale can range from 10 (least positive attitudes) to 50 (most positive attitudes). The following items are reverse scored: 26, 29, 32, 34. Scores on the STI Education Confidence scale can range from 8 (if all the items applied to the respondent), indicating the least confidence, to 40 (if all the items applied to the respondent), indicating the most confidence. Scores on the STI Education Readiness scale can range from 5 (if all the items apply to the respondent), indicating the least readiness, to 25 (if all the items apply to the respondent), indicating the highest level of readiness.

Reliability

Reliability was calculated from a sample of 120 middle and high school teachers from around the state of Pennsylvania (Koch, 2009). Approximately two-thirds were women and 75% had been working in their position for more than 5 years. Using the Kuder-Richardson alpha statistic, the reliability of the Knowledge of Sexually Transmitted Infections scale was calculated to be .89. Using the Cronbach alpha statistical method, the reliabilities for the Attitudes Toward Adolescents and Sexuality and Sexuality Education, STI Education Confidence, and STI Education Readiness scales were determined to be .75, .92, and .89, respectively.

Validity

Content validity for the Knowledge of Sexually Transmitted Infections scale was determined from information gathered from the Centers for Disease Control and Prevention (2009)

and the Kaiser Family Foundation (2006). A panel of five sexuality educators, three of whom were experienced with providing STI/HIV education to professionals and two of whom taught STI/HIV education to youth, reviewed the initial pool of items for relevance and redundancy and reached a consensus of 25 items using the Delphi method (Adler & Ziglio, 1996). Guided by Ajzen and Fishbein's attitudinal theory (1980), this same panel generated separate items for the Attitudes Toward Adolescent Sexuality and Sexuality Education, using recommended guidelines and evaluation research provided by the Sexuality Information and Education Council of the United States (2004). Using the Delphi method to reach consensus, 10 items were agreed upon. Finally, the panel of experts independently generated lists of tasks that are relevant to providing effective sexuality education. Using the Delphi method to reach consensus, eight items were identified for the STI Education Confidence scale and five items for the STI Education Readiness scale. Once these scales were completed, five middle and high school teachers reviewed them for relevance and wording. The SEES was then used for pre- and posttest evaluation of three professional workshops attended by teachers from around the state of Pennsylvania. After attending the all-day workshops, the participants demonstrated significant improvement in STI knowledge ($p < .001$), positive attitudes toward adolescent sexuality and sexuality education ($p < .05$), and STI education confidence ($p < .001$; Koch, 2009).

References

Adler, M., & Ziglio, E. (1996). *Gazing into the oracle: The Delphi method and its application to social policy and public health.* London: Jessica Kingsley.

Ajzen, I., & Fishbein, M. (1980). *Understanding attitudes and predicting social behaviors.* Englewood Cliffs, NJ: Prentice Hall.

Centers for Disease Control and Prevention. (2009). *Sexual health.* Retrieved June 22, 2009, from http://www.cdc.gov/sexualhealth

Cozzens, J. (2006). Assessing the awareness of adolescent sexual health among teachers-in-training. *American Journal of Sexuality Education, 1*(3), 25–50.

Guttmacher Institute (2009). *Sex and STD/HIV education, state policies in brief.* Retrieved June 22, 2009, from http://www.guttmacher.org/statecenter/spibs/spib_SE.pdf

James-Traore, T. A., Finger, W., Ruland, C. D., & Savariaud, S. (2004). Teacher training: Essential for school health and HIV/AIDS education. *Youthnet Issues, Paper 3.* Arlington, VA: Family Health International.

Kaiser Family Foundation. (2006). *Sexual health statistics for teenagers and young adults in the United States.* Retrieved June 22, 2009, from http://www.kff.org/womenshealth/upload/3040-03.pdf

Koch, P. B. (2009). *STI/HIV workshops for K-16 educators: Report to the Pennsylvania Department of Education.* University Park: Pennsylvania State University, The Pennsylvania Learning Academy for Sexuality Education.

Rodriguez, M., Young, R., Renfro, S., Ascencio, M., & Haffner, D. (1995–1996). Teaching our teachers to teach: A SIECUS study on training and preparation for HIV/AIDS prevention and sexuality education. *SIECUS Report, 28*(2), 15–23.

Sexuality Information and Education Council of the United States. (2004). *Guidelines for comprehensive sexuality education.* Retrieved June 22, 2009, from http://www.siecus.org/_data/images/guidelines.pdf

Exhibit

STI Education Efficacy Survey

The following statements are to assess your understanding of STIs.

If you definitely know that a statement is *True*, answer 1
If you definitely know that a statement is *False*, answer 2
If you do *not* definitely know the answer (*Don't Know*), answer 3

1. About one-half of 12th graders have engaged in intercourse and one-half have not.
2. About one in five young people have had intercourse before their 15th birthday.
3. Oral sex is more common among many teenagers than is engaging in vaginal-penile intercourse.
4. About one in 10 sexually active youth have a sexually transmitted infection (STI).
5. Half of the people in the U.S. will acquire at least one STI by age 35.
6. Human papilloma virus (HPV) is the most common bacterial STI in the U.S.
7. The majority of females with chlamydia do not have any detectable symptoms.
8. Vaginal infections, like trichomoniasis, can *not* be transmitted to males.
9. People know when they get syphilis because a very painful sore, or chancre, appears.
10. Females are more likely to have symptoms of gonorrhea than are males.
11. All bacterial STIs can be cured with penicillin.
12. HPV accounts for about 90% of cervical cancer risk.
13. HPV can still be spread even when there are no warts present.
14. The most effective method to cure genital warts is through surgical removal.
15. Herpes is only infectious when there are open lesions present.
16. Herpes Simplex I (oral herpes/cold sores) can *not* be transmitted to the genital area.
17. Hepatitis B is more infectious than HIV.
18. HIV can *not* be transmitted through oral sex.
19. A person can be HIV-infected but still test negative.
20. Heterosexual females and males are at little risk for AIDS.
21. The most common cause of infertility among U.S. females is chlamydial infection.
22. Currently there are no vaccines to prevent becoming infected with any type of STI caused by a virus.
23. Natural membrane condoms are more effective in preventing STIs than latex condoms.
24. Oil-based products, such as Vaseline, are good to use for added lubrication with condoms so that they don't break.
25. Because of an emphasis on abstinence-only education, the U.S. has lower rates of STIs than western European countries.

Adolescents and Sexuality/Sex Education

Please indicate your reactions to the following statements on your response sheet:

1 Strongly Disagree
2 Disagree
3 Uncertain
4 Agree
5 Strongly Agree

26. Sexual expression is a natural part of development for adolescents.
27. Most high school students are not mature enough to act sexually responsible even when they know the facts.
28. Young people need to remain sexually abstinent until marriage.
29. Young people should *not* think of sexuality as taboo, shameful, or dirty.
30. Most teenagers do *not* want sexuality education from their parents or in school.
31. Having information about contraceptives, including condoms, only encourages young people to be promiscuous.
32. Young people need as much information as possible in order to make responsible decisions.
33. Abstinence-only education is more effective in preventing STIs than education that discusses safer sex as well.
34. Young people who receive more comprehensive sexuality education are *less* likely to engage in intercourse at younger ages and are *more* likely to use contraception when they do have intercourse.
35. Most parents in the U.S. do not support the teaching of sexuality education in the schools.

STI Education Efficacy

In teaching about STIs/HIV, please indicate how you feel about the following using this scale:

1 No Confidence at all
2 Very Little Confidence
3 Somewhat Confident
4 Very Confident
5 Extremely Confident

36. The currency and accuracy of my knowledge.
37. The comprehensiveness of my knowledge.
38. My comfort level in talking about these topics with young people.
39. My comfort level in talking about these topics with my colleagues and supervisors.
40. My ability to develop lessons and learning activities to effectively teach about these topics.
41. My skill in developing open communication with young people about these topics.
42. My ability to develop curriculum or programs on these topics.
43. My understanding of the experiences of today's young people that impact their sexuality and STI risk.

When it comes to STI education, how would you describe your readiness (including your willingness and ability) to:

1 Not Ready at all
2 Hardly Ready
3 Somewhat Ready
4 Very Ready
5 Extremely Ready

44. Advocate for better education and services for teens.
45. Share my knowledge and skills with my colleagues.
46. Serve as a resource person for people who need help with these topics.
47. Influence curriculum/program development in my school or agency related to these topics.
48. Influence policy either in my school, agency, or community related to these topics.

STD Attitude Scale

WILLIAM L. YARBER,[1] AND MOHAMMAD R. TORABI, *Indiana University*
C. HAROLD VEENKER, *Purdue University*

Researchers have found that attitudes are best described as multidimensional, having the three components of cognitive (belief), affective (feeling), and conative (intention to act). Beliefs express one's perceptions or concepts toward an attitudinal object; feelings are described as an expression of liking or disliking relative to an attitudinal object; and intention to act is an expression of what the individual says he/she would do in a given situation (Bagozzi, 1978; Kothandapani, 1971; Ostrom, 1969; Torabi & Veenker,

1986). Attitudes are one important component determining individual health-risk behavior. More attention is now given by health educators to improving or maintaining health-conducive attitudes. A scale designed specifically to measure the components of attitudes toward sexually transmitted diseases (STDs) can be valuable to educators and researchers in planning STD education and determining risk correlates of individuals.

[1]Address correspondence to William L. Yarber, Department of Applied Health Science, Indiana University, HPER Building, Bloomington, IN 47405; e-mail: yarber@indiana.edu.

Description

The STD Attitude Scale was developed to measure young adults' beliefs, feelings, and intentions to act regarding sexually transmitted diseases. The scale discriminates between individuals with high-risk attitudes toward STD contraction and those with low-risk attitudes. A summated rating scale utilizing the 5-point Likert-type format and having three subscales reflecting the attitude components was constructed. Items were developed according to a table of specifications containing three conceptual areas: nature of STD, STD prevention, and STD treatment. Each subscale contained items from the three conceptual areas.

An extensive pool of items was generated from the literature, expert contribution, and via item solicitation from students. To avoid the possibility of a response set, both positive and negative items were developed. Attention was given to the readability of each item. From the item pool, three preliminary forms with 45 items each (15 items per subscale) were administered to 457 college students. Following statistical analysis, one scale containing the 45 items (15 per subscale) that best met item selection criteria of internal consistency and discrimination power was given to 100 high school students.

A further refined scale of 33 items (11 items per subscale), subjected to jury review, was given to 2,980 secondary school students. Analysis of these data produced the final scale of 27 items, 9 items for each subscale. The final scale has items with highly significant levels of internal consistency (item score vs. subscales and total scale score) and discriminating power (upper group vs. lower group for each item).

Response Mode and Timing

Respondents indicate whether they *strongly agree, agree, are undecided, disagree,* or *strongly disagree* with each statement. The scale takes an average of 15 minutes to complete.

Scoring

Scoring is as follows: Total scale, Items 1–27; Belief subscale, Items 1–9; Feeling subscale, Items 10–18; and Intention to Act subscale, Items 19–27. Calculate total points for each subscale and total scale by using the following point values. For Items 1, 10–14, 16, and 25: *strongly agree* = 5, *agree* = 4, *undecided* = 3, *disagree* = 2, and *strongly disagree* = 1. For Items 2–9, 15, 17–24, 26, and 27: *strongly agree* = 1, *agree* = 2, *undecided* = 3, *disagree* = 4, and *strongly disagree* = 5.

Higher subscale or total scale scores are interpreted as reflecting an attitude that predisposes one toward high-risk STD behavior, and lower scores predispose the person toward low-risk STD behavior.

Reliability

Yarber, Torabi, and Veenker (1988) reported a test-retest reliability over a 5- to 7-day period to be the following: Total scale = .71; Belief subscale = .50; Feeling subscale = .57; Intention to Act subscale = .63. Cronbach's alpha was as follows: Total scale = .73; Belief subscale = .53; Feeling subscale = .48; Intention to Act subscale = .71.

Validity

Scale items have evidence of content and face validity as they were developed according to a table of specifications reflecting the behavioral aspects of STD and the content emphasis—preventive health behavior—of an STD education school curriculum (Yarber, 1985). Further, a panel of experts judged each item's merit. The scale was developed, in part, as one component of a project for assessing the efficacy of a Centers for Disease Control education program (Yarber, 1985). Evidence of construct validity is provided by the fact that secondary school students exposed to the STD curriculum, in contrast to students receiving no STD instruction, showed improvement in scores from pretest to posttest when assessed by the scale (Yarber, 1988).

Other Information

The scale development was supported in part by U.S. Public Health Service grant award #R30/CCR500638–01.

References

Bagozzi, R. P. (1978). The construct validity of the affective, behavioral and cognitive components of attitude by using analysis of covariance of structure. *Multivariate Behavior Research, 13,* 9–31.

Kothandapani, V. (1971). *A psychological approach to the prediction of contraceptive behavior.* Chapel Hill, NC: Carolina Population Center, University of North Carolina.

Ostrom, T. M. (1969). The relationship between the affective, behavioral and cognitive components of attitude. *Journal of Experimental Psychology, 5,* 12–30.

Torabi, M. R., & Veenker, C. H. (1986). An alcohol attitude scale for teenagers. *Journal of School Health, 56,* 96–100.

Yarber, W. L. (1985). *STD: A guide for today's young adults* [student and instructor's manual]. Waldorf, MD: American Alliance Publications.

Yarber, W. L. (1988). Evaluation of the health behavior approach to school STD education. *Journal of Sex Education and Therapy, 14,* 33–38.

Yarber, W. L., Torabi, M. R., & Veenker, C. H. (1988). Development of a three-component sexually transmitted diseases attitude scale. *Journal of Sex Education and Therapy, 15,* 36–49.

Exhibit

STD Attitude Scale

Directions: Please read each statement carefully. STD means sexually transmitted diseases, once called venereal diseases. Record your reaction by marking an "X" through the letter which best describes how much you agree or disagree with the idea.

Use this key: SA = strongly agree

A = agree

U = undecided

D = disagree

SD = strongly disagree

Example: Doing things to prevent getting an STD is the job of each person.

SA   X̸   U   D   SD

1. How one uses his/her sexuality has nothing to do with STD.
2. It is easy to use the prevention methods that reduce one's chances of getting an STD.
3. Responsible sex is one of the best ways of reducing the risk of STD.
4. Getting early medical care is the main key to preventing harmful effects of STD.
5. Choosing the right sex partner is important in reducing the risk of getting an STD.
6. A high rate of STD should be a concern for all people.
7. People with an STD have a duty to get their sex partners to medical care.
8. The best way to get a sex partner to STD treatment is to take him/her to the doctor with you.
9. Changing one's sex habits is necessary once the presence of an STD is known.
10. I would dislike having to follow the medical steps for treating an STD.
11. If I were sexually active, I would feel uneasy doing things before and after sex to prevent getting an STD.
12. If I were sexually active, it would be insulting if a sex partner suggested we use a condom to avoid STD.
13. I dislike talking about STD with my peers.
14. I would be uncertain about going to the doctor unless I was sure I really had an STD.
15. I would feel that I should take my sex partner with me to a clinic if I thought I had an STD.
16. It would be embarrassing to discuss STD with one's partner if one were sexually active.
17. If I were to have sex, the chance of getting an STD makes me uneasy about having sex with more than one person.
18. I like the idea of sexual abstinence (not having sex) as the best way of avoiding STD.
19. If I had an STD, I would cooperate with public health persons to find the sources of STD.
20. If I had an STD, I would avoid exposing others while I was being treated.
21. I would have regular STD checkups if I were having sex with more than one person.
22. I intend to look for STD signs before deciding to have sex with anyone.
23. I will limit my sex activity to just one partner because of the chances I might get an STD.
24. I will avoid sex contact anytime I think there is even a slight chance of getting an STD.
25. The chance of getting an STD would not stop me from having sex.
26. If I had a chance, I would support community efforts toward controlling STD.
27. I would be willing to work with others to make people aware of STD problems in my town.

Female Sexual Resourcefulness Scale

TERRY P. HUMPHREYS AND DEBORAH J. KENNETT,[1] *Trent University*

The Female Sexual Resourcefulness Scale (FSRS; Humphreys & Kennett, 2008; Kennett, Humphreys & Patchell, 2009) assesses the self-control strategies women use to deal with unwanted sexual encounters. Unwanted sexual encounters often involve some form of verbal and/or nonverbal persuasion on the part of the male, creating more perceived pressure on a woman to consent. Hence, being sexually resourceful empowers women with a variety of specific strategies for saying no or leaving the situation when in these circumstances.

Description

The FSRS was developed after Rosenbaum's (1990, 2000) model of self-control. The key component in this model is learned resourcefulness: the basic self-regulatory skills needed to handle everyday life challenges. Individuals possessing a large, general repertoire of learned resourcefulness skills make use of positive self-instructions, delay gratification, apply problem-solving methods, and employ other self-control strategies when dealing with negative emotions (Rosenbaum & Cohen, 1999), breaking bad habits (Kennett, Morris, & Bangs, 2006), adhering to medical regimens (Zauszniewski & Chung, 2001), carrying out boring but necessary tasks (Kennett & Nisbet, 1998), or overcoming other adversities they encounter (Chislett & Kennett, 2007). However, how readily one is able to draw on this general repertoire of well-learned skills depends on other factors. In particular, the extent to which a woman is able to be sexually resourceful when confronted with unwanted sexual advances depends on process regulating cognitions (PRCs) such as sexual self-efficacy (i.e., the belief that she is capable of stopping unwanted sexual advances/activities). These beliefs are shaped over time by the outcomes and personal explanations of past unwanted sexual experiences, and they are further affected by physiological (e.g., one's sexual arousal level) and situational (e.g., relationship status, sexual coercion, environmental setting) variables that interact among each other by either facilitating or preventing the use of specific sexual resourcefulness strategies to put a halt to the unwanted sexual advance/activity.

Response Mode and Timing

Two alternative modes are possible. As a paper-and-pencil survey, respondents circle a number from 1 to 6 corresponding to the degree to which they feel the statement is characteristic of themselves. As an online survey (using an internal or external service), respondents click on the bullet response from 1 to 6 corresponding to the degree to which they feel the statement is characteristic of themselves. The FSRS takes approximately 10 minutes to complete.

Scoring

Items are scored 1 for *Very Uncharacteristic of Me* to 6 for *Very Characteristic of Me*. Items 2, 3, 5, 6, 7, 16, 17, and 18 are reverse scored. Total scores can range from 19 to 114. The mean score on this inventory for our two samples was $M = 80.5$, $SD = 18.4$ (Kennett et al., 2009) and $M = 85.9$, $SD = 16.1$ (Humphreys & Kennett, 2008), respectively.

Reliability

Based on two female undergraduate datasets, the reliability for the whole FSRS was .91 ($N = 150$; Kennett et al., 2009) and .91 ($N = 152$; Humphreys & Kennett, 2008), respectively.

Over a 6-week period, test-retest reliability in a female student sample ($N = 63$) was .78 (Humphreys & Kennett, 2008).

Validity

Construct validity was examined by comparing the FSRS to previously established scales: the Self-Control Schedule (SCS; Rosenbaum, 1980) and the Sexual Experiences Survey (SES; Koss & Oros, 1982), as well as a number of newly designed scales: Sexual Self-Efficacy (Kennett et al., 2009), Reasons for Consenting to Unwanted Sex (Kennett et al., 2009; Humphreys & Kennett, 2008), and Sexual Giving-In Experiences (Kennett et al., 2009).

Demographically, FSRS is unrelated to age, relationship stage, or length of relationship. This is important given that Rosenbaum's conceptualization of learned resourcefulness suggests that skill level should not change dramatically once one reaches early adulthood or because of changes in relationship partners without significant intervention (Rosenbaum, 1990, 2000).

Rosenbaum's (1980) SCS measures an individual's general repertoire of learned resourcefulness skills, by assessing one's use of positive self-statements to control emotional and physiological responses and ability to

---

[1]Address correspondence to either Terry P. Humphreys or Deborah J. Kennett, Psychology Department, Trent University, 1600 West Bank Drive, Peterborough, Ontario, Canada, K9J 7B8; e-mail: terryhumphreys@trentu.ca or dkennett@trentu.ca

problem solve and delay gratification. The FSRS was designed to measure a specific type of learned resourcefulness focused on dealing with unwanted sexual situations. As predicted, the SCS and the FSRS are correlated, $r(152) = .26$, $p = .001$. Again, as predicted, FSRS is negatively correlated with forced sex play (Items 1–3), $r(152) = -.48$, $p < .001$, and attempted or completed forced intercourse (Items 4–10), $r(152) = -.41$, $p < .001$, in the SES (Koss & Oros, 1982). In addition, FSRS was negatively correlated with a single item assessing the extent to which female students have experienced unwanted sexual advances from men, $r(152) = -.21$, $p = .008$. Therefore, being sexually resourceful is related to less involvement in unwanted and forced sexual situations.

The Sexual Self-Efficacy scale (Kennett et al., 2009) assesses women's belief that they have what it takes to deal with or prevent unwanted sexual advances. This 5-item scale was positively correlated with FSRS, $r(152) = .59$, $p < .001$. Clearly, believing that you have the ability to deal with unwanted sexual advances is positively linked with actually using a variety of resourcefulness skills when engaged in these situations.

The Reasons for Consenting to Unwanted Sex Scale (RCUSS) (Kennett et al., 2009; Humphreys & Kennett, 2008) assesses the amount of endorsement women give to a variety of reasons why they have voluntarily consented to engage in sexual activity they did not desire. Reasons for consent are in accordance with previous research suggesting that women consent to unwanted sexual activity to satisfy their partner's needs, promote intimacy, avoid tension, prevent a partner from losing interest in the relationship, and/or fulfill perceived relationship obligations (O'Sullivan & Allgeier, 1998; Impett & Peplau, 2002; Shotland & Hunter, 1995). As predicted, the RCUSS negatively correlated with the FSRS, $r(152) = -.67$, $p < .001$. The FSRS was also negatively correlated with actual percentage of time women "gave in" to sexual experiences, $r(152) = -.60$, $p < .001$. The results described in this section were reported from Humphreys and Kennett (2008); however, they were replicated in Kennett et al. (2009).

Other Information

Permission to use the FSRS may be obtained from either T. Humphreys or D. Kennett.

References

Chislett, G., & Kennett, D. J. (2007). The effects of the Nobody's Perfect Program on parenting resourcefulness and competency. *Journal of Child and Family Studies, 16,* 473–482.

Humphreys, T. P., & Kennett, D. J. (2008) [The reliability and validity of the Sexual Resourcefulness and Reasons for Consenting to Unwanted Sex Scales]. Unpublished raw data.

Impett, E. A., & Peplau, L. A. (2002). Why some women consent to unwanted sex with a dating partner: Insights from attachment theory. *Psychology of Women Quarterly, 26,* 360–370.

Kennett, D. J., Humphreys, T. P., & Patchell, M. (2009). The role of learned resourcefulness in helping female undergraduates deal with unwanted sexual activity. *Sex Education, 9,* 341–353.

Kennett, D. J., Morris, E., & Bangs, A. (2006). Learned resourcefulness and smoking cessation revisited. *Patient Education and Counseling, 60,* 206–211.

Kennett, D. J., & Nisbet, C. (1998). The influence of body mass index and learned resourcefulness skills on body image and lifestyle practices. *Patient Education and Counseling, 33,* 1–12.

Koss, M. P., & Oros, C. J. (1982). Sexual experiences survey: A research instrument investigating sexual aggression and victimization. *Journal of Consulting and Clinical Psychology, 50,* 455–457.

O'Sullivan, L. F., & Allgeier, E. R. (1998). Feigning sexual desire: Consenting to unwanted sexual activity in heterosexual dating relationships. *The Journal of Sex Research, 35,* 234–243.

Rosenbaum, M. (1980). A schedule for assessing self-control behaviors: Preliminary findings. *Behavior Therapy, 11,* 109–121.

Rosenbaum, M. (1990). The role of learned resourcefulness in the self-control of health behavior. In M. Rosenbaum (Ed.), *Learned resourcefulness: On coping skills, self-control and adaptive behavior* (pp. 4–25). New York: Springer.

Rosenbaum, M. (2000). The self-regulation of experience: Openness and construction. In P. Dewe, A. M. Leiter, & T. Cox (Eds.), *Coping, health and organizations* (pp. 51–67). London: Taylor & Francis.

Rosenbaum, M., & Cohen, E. (1999). Equalitarian marriages, spousal support, resourcefulness and psychological distress among Israeli working women. *Journal of Vocational Behavior, 54,* 102–113.

Shotland, R. L., & Hunter, B. A. (1995). Women's "token resistant" and compliant sexual behaviors are related to uncertain sexual intentions and rape. *Personality and Social Psychology Bulletin, 21,* 226–236.

Zauszniewski, J. A., & Chung, C. W. (2001). Resourcefulness and health practices of diabetic women. *Research in Nursing and Health, 21,* 113–121.

Exhibit

Female Sexual Resourcefulness Scale

Instructions: This questionnaire is designed to find out how different people view their thinking and their behavior about unwanted sexual activities/advances.

Unwanted sexual advances/activities are defined as *anything from an unwanted intimate hand on the shoulder to unwanted sexual intercourse.* Other unwanted sexual advances/activity could include things such as verbal advances, touching, hugging, kissing, or dancing.

A statement may range from very uncharacteristic of you to very characteristic of you. Please answer every statement, and circle only one answer for each statement. Use the following scale to indicate whether a statement describes your thinking or behavior.

1 = Very Uncharacteristic of Me[a]
2 = Rather Uncharacteristic of Me

  3 = Somewhat Uncharacteristic of Me
  4 = Somewhat Characteristic of Me
  5 = Rather Characteristic of Me
  6 = Very Characteristic of Me

1. When I am in the middle of sexual play and am aroused, but do not want the activity to progress any further, I am often able to change my aroused feelings so that I am able to prevent the activity from progressing.
2. I often give in to unwanted sexual activity.
3. When I feel upset while engaged in unwanted sexual activity, I try not to think about it.
4. When I am faced with unwanted sexual activity/advances, I have no difficulty leaving the situation.
5. While engaged in unwanted sexual activity, I think I'm making a mistake, but I'm at a loss to do anything about it.
6. I usually consent to unwanted sexual activity when my partner is pressuring me.
7. When I am experiencing unwanted sexual activity/advances, I prefer to not think about it and go along with the activity instead.
8. If I was in the middle of sexual play which I no longer wanted to continue, I could tell him to stop.
9. When I have become aroused from sexual play, but do not want to continue any further, I am able to resist engaging in the sexual activity by thinking about the good reasons for stopping.
10. Although I feel bad about hurting my partner's feelings, I am able to let him know when I am uncomfortable with a sexual situation.
11. I feel good about myself when I resist unwanted sexual advances.
12. When experiencing unwanted sexual activity/advances, I often tell myself that I can do something about it.
13. When I am about to engage in unwanted sexual activity, I tell myself to stop and think before I do anything.
14. I consider my actions very carefully when deciding whether or not to participate in unwanted sexual activity.
15. I always have a back-up plan for when I am faced with unwanted sexual advances/activity that get out of control.
16. It takes a lot of effort on my part to bring unwanted sexual advances/activity to a halt.
17. When presented with unwanted sexual advances/activity, I base my decision on my arousal and how I feel in the moment, even if I know I will regret it later.
18. When engaging in unwanted sexual activity, I try to divert my thoughts from how uncomfortable I feel.
19. I plan in advance how far I want to go with any sexual activity, and am able to stop the activity before it goes too far.

[a]This scale follows each of the scale statements.

Questionnaire of Cognitive Schema Activation in Sexual Context

PEDRO J. NOBRE,[1] *Universidade de Trás-os-Montes e Alto Douro, Portugal*
JOSÉ PINTO-GOUVEIA, *Universidade de Coimbra, Portugal*

The Questionnaire of Cognitive Schema Activation in Sexual Context (QCSASC; Nobre & Pinto-Gouveia, 2009) assesses the activation of negative self-schemas to negative sexual events. The measure assesses the activation of these self-schemas (using a list proposed by Judith Beck, 1995), following the presentation of four negative sexual events associated with the most common sexual dysfunctions in men and women. The QCSASC is a measure that might be clinically useful in helping to assess the role of cognitive variables on sexual functioning, and eventually contribut-

ing to a better understanding of cognitive processes underlying sexual problems.

Description

The QCSASC is a 28-item instrument that assesses cognitive schemas presented by the participants when facing negative sexual situations. The first part consists of the presentation of four sexual situations related to the most common sexual dysfunctions: desire disorder, erectile

[1]Please address correspondence to Pedro Nobre, Universidade de Trás-os-Montes e Alto Douro, Apartado 1013, 5001–801 Vila Real, Portugal; e-mail: pnobre5@gmail.com

disorder, premature ejaculation, and orgasmic difficulties in the male version and desire disorder, subjective arousal difficulties, orgasmic problems, and vaginismus in the female version. These four situations are presented in the questionnaire in the form of vignettes and were developed by a panel of sex therapists based on material from clinical cases. The QCSASC also presents a list of 10 emotions (worry, sadness, disillusion, fear, guilt, shame, anger, hurt, pleasure, and satisfaction) in order to assess the emotional response to the negative sexual events previously presented. Finally, the QCSASC uses a list of 28 self-statements reproducing the core beliefs or self-schemas proposed by Beck (1995).

The list of 28 self-schemas of the QCSASC was submitted to factor analysis (Nobre & Pinto-Gouveia, 2009). A principal component analysis with varimax rotation identified five factors accounting for 62% of the total variance: (a) Undesirability/Rejection, (b) Incompetence, (c) Self-Deprecation, (d) Difference/Loneliness, and (e) Helpless (see Table 1).

TABLE 1
Items, Minimums, and Maximums of the QCSASC

Factors	Item Numbers	Minimum	Maximum
Undesirability/ Rejection	15, 17, 19, 20, 24, 26, 27	7	35
Incompetence	2, 4, 8, 9, 10, 11, 13	7	35
Self-Deprecation	16, 21, 22	3	15
Difference/ Loneliness	5, 23, 28	3	15
Helpless/Betrayed	1, 6	2	10
Total		22	110

Response Mode and Timing

Participants may respond to the QCSASC using paper and pencil or computer. The response scales are Likert-type. Respondents first indicate the negative event (if any) which is most similar to their sexual experience, and rate the frequency with which it usually happens (from 1 = *Never Happens* to 5 = *Happens Often*). They are also asked to identify the emotions aroused by the situation (checking all that apply from a list of 10 emotions: worry, sadness, disillusion, fear, guilt, shame, anger, hurt, pleasure, satisfaction). After being instructed to concentrate on the identified situation and emotions, they are asked to rate on a 5-point Likert-type scale the degree of concordance with 28 self-schemas. Respondents take an average of 10 minutes to complete the QCSASC.

Scoring

Specific indexes for the five domains and for the total scale can be calculated through the sum of the schema items (higher scores reflecting greater negative schema activation).

Reliability

Internal consistency. Internal consistency was assessed using Cronbach's alpha statistics for the full scale and the different domains of the questionnaire. High inter-item correlations were observed for the subscales and the total scale. Cronbach's alpha values ranged from .59 (Difference/Loneliness) to .91 (Undesirability/Rejection), with the full scale presenting .94. Except for the Difference/Loneliness and the Helpless domains, all other Cronbach's alpha results were higher than .71, supporting the homogeneity of the scale and the contribution from all the factors to the overall score (Nobre & Pinto-Gouveia, 2009).

Test-retest reliability. Test-retest reliability was assessed by computing correlations for the total scale in two consecutive administrations of the questionnaire with a 4-week interval. The results ranged between $r = .49$ and $r = .74$ for the specific domains, with the full scale presenting r = .66. Although some correlations were not so strong, all reliability coefficients were statistically significant ($p < .01$). These results indicated a moderate stability of the scale over time (Nobre & Pinto-Gouveia, 2009).

Validity

Convergent validity. Convergent validity was assessed by correlating the QCSASC with validated measures oriented to assess cognitive structures linked to psychopathology: the Schema Questionnaire (SQ; Young, 1990) and the Sexual Self-Schema (SSS; Andersen & Cyranowski, 1994; Andersen, Cyranowski, & Espindle, 1999). The QCSASC was significantly correlated with the SQ, indicating that the measure assesses concepts that are partially related to more general cognitive schemas. Results regarding the relationship between the QCSASC and the Sexual Self-Schema Questionnaire showed moderate to high correlations, supporting our prediction that negative views about oneself as a sexual individual (particularly conservative ideas) would be related to the activation of negative self-schemas when facing unsuccessful sexual situations (Nobre & Pinto-Gouveia, 2009).

Incremental validity. Findings from the incremental validity analysis indicate that the QCSASC presents with higher clinical utility compared to already existing related measures (e.g., SQ, SSS). Partial correlations with measures of sexual functioning in men (IIEF) and women (FSFI) were higher for the QCSASC compared to the SQ and SSS, suggesting that this new measure presents a unique contribution for the explanation of sexual functioning beyond previous existing measures (Nobre & Pinto-Gouveia, 2009).

Discriminant validity. A discriminant validity analysis was conducted, using a clinical (men and women with sexual dysfunction) and a control group (matched men and women without sexual dysfunction). We hypothesized that the higher the activation of negative cognitive schemas facing unsuccessful sexual situations, the greater the probability of developing a sexual dysfunction. Regarding women, we found statistically significant differences between clinical and control groups in three of the five domains of the QCSASC: Incompetence, Self-Deprecation, and Difference/Loneliness. Women with sexual dysfunction also scored significantly higher in the total QCSASC scale. Men with sexual dysfunction presented significantly higher scores, compared to the control group, on the Incompetence dimension, and the total scale (Nobre & Pinto-Gouveia, 2009, in press).

Other Information

For more information regarding the QCSASC and permission for its use please contact Pedro J. Nobre (pnobre5@gmail.com).

References

Andersen, B. L., & Cyranowski, J. M. (1994). Women's sexual self-schema. *Journal of Personality and Social Psychology, 67,* 1079–1100.

Andersen, B. L., Cyranowski, J. M., & Espindle, D. (1999). Men's sexual self-schema. *Journal of Personality and Social Psychology, 76,* 645–61.

Beck, J. S. (1995). *Cognitive therapy: Basics and beyond.* New York: Guilford Press.

Nobre, P. J., & Pinto-Gouveia, J. (2009). Questionnaire of cognitive schema activation in sexual context: A questionnaire to assess cognitive schemas activated in sexual failure situations. *The Journal of Sex Research, 46,* 425–437.

Nobre, P. J., & Pinto-Gouveia, J. (in press). Cognitive schemas associated with negative sexual events: A comparison of men and women with and without sexual dysfunction. *Archives of Sexual Behavior.*

Young, J. (1990). *Cognitive therapy for personality disorders.* Sarasota, FL: Professional Resource Exchange, Inc.

Exhibit

Questionnaire of Cognitive Schema Activation in Sexual Context

Female Version

Read carefully each one of the episodes presented below and indicate the extent to which they have ever happen to you by circling a number (1 *Never* to 5 *Often*).

I'm alone with my partner. He looks as if he wants to have sex, and he's going to extraordinary lengths to try to arouse me. However, I don't feel like it at all. So instead, I pretend to be tired and change the subject. Yet he persists. He looks disappointed, and says that I don't love him as much as I used to.

Never Happened 1 _____ 2 _____ 3 _____ 4 _____ 5 Happened Often

I'm having sex with my partner. He is really trying to arouse me, but I am experiencing no pleasure at all. Instead, I feel as if I am fulfilling an obligation. I ask myself, "Does it always have to be like this?"

Never Happened 1 _____ 2 _____ 3 _____ 4 _____ 5 Happened Often

My partner is touching me and I am very aroused. A few moments later he tries to penetrate me, but my vaginal muscles seem to clamp shut and my partner can't penetrate. He persists with no success, and what could have been an unforgettable moment turns into a frustrating experience.

Never Happened 1 _____ 2 _____ 3 _____ 4 _____ 5 Happened Often

My partner and I are engaged in foreplay, and he has tried different ways of stimulating me, which I'm enjoying. But in spite of it all I can't reach orgasm. My partner seems to be getting tired and I start to feel frustrated. I begin to feel anxious as I realize that the likelihood of reaching orgasm is becoming more and more remote.

Never Happened 1 _____ 2 _____ 3 _____ 4 _____ 5 Happened Often

Circle all emotions you felt when you imagined the episode which more often happens to you.

Worry   Sadness   Disillusionment   Fear   Guilt   Shame   Anger   Hurt   Pleasure   Satisfaction

Keeping in mind the episode which more often happens to you, read the statements presented below carefully and circle the degree to which they describe the way you think and feel about yourself (1 *Completely False* to 5 *Completely True*).

Schemas	Completely False	False	Sometimes True some false	True	Completely True
1. I'm helpless	1	2	3	4	5
2. I'm powerless	1	2	3	4	5
3. I'm out of control	1	2	3	4	5
4. I'm weak	1	2	3	4	5
5. I'm vulnerable	1	2	3	4	5
6. I'm needy	1	2	3	4	5
7. I'm trapped	1	2	3	4	5
8. I'm inadequate	1	2	3	4	5
9. I'm ineffective	1	2	3	4	5
10. I'm incompetent	1	2	3	4	5
11. I'm a failure	1	2	3	4	5
12. I'm disrespected	1	2	3	4	5
13. I'm defective (less than others)	1	2	3	4	5
14. I'm not good enough (achieve)	1	2	3	4	5

Schemas	Completely False	False	Sometimes True some false	True	Completely True
15. I'm unlovable	1	2	3	4	5
16. I'm unlikable	1	2	3	4	5
17. I'm undesirable	1	2	3	4	5
18. I'm unattractive	1	2	3	4	5
19. I'm unwanted	1	2	3	4	5
20. I'm uncared for	1	2	3	4	5
21. I'm bad	1	2	3	4	5
22. I'm unworthy	1	2	3	4	5
23. I'm different	1	2	3	4	5
24. I'm defective (not loved)	1	2	3	4	5
25. I'm not good enough (loved)	1	2	3	4	5
26. I'm bound to be rejected	1	2	3	4	5
27. I'm bound to be abandoned	1	2	3	4	5
28. I'm bound to be alone	1	2	3	4	5

Male Version

Read carefully each one of the episodes presented below and indicate the extent to which they usually happen to you by circling a number (1 *Never* to 5 *Often*).

I'm alone with my partner. She looks as if she wants to have sex, and she's going to extraordinary lengths to try to arouse me. However, I don't feel like it at all. So instead, I pretend to be tired and change the subject. Yet she persists. She looks disappointed, and says that I don't love her as much as I used to.

Never Happened 1 _____ 2 _____ 3 _____ 4 _____ 5 Happened Often

I'm caressing my partner, and she is enjoying it and seems to be ready for intercourse. Upon attempting penetration, I notice that my erection isn't as firm as it normally is and full penetration seems impossible. I try to no avail, and finally quit.

Never Happened 1 _____ 2 _____ 3 _____ 4 _____ 5 Happened Often

My partner is stimulating me, and I'm becoming very aroused. I'm getting very excited and I immediately try to penetrate her. I feel out of control and reach orgasm very quickly, at which point intercourse stops. She looks very disappointed, as if she expected much more from me.

Never Happened 1 _____ 2 _____ 3 _____ 4 _____ 5 Happened Often

I'm completely involved in lovemaking and I start to penetrate my partner. In the beginning everything is going fine, but time passes and I can't seem to reach orgasm. She seems to be getting tired. No matter how hard I try, orgasm seems to be farther and farther out of my reach.

Never Happened 1 _____ 2 _____ 3 _____ 4 _____ 5 Happened Often

Circle all emotions you felt when you imagined the episode which more often happens to you

Worry Sadness Disillusionment Fear Guilt Shame Anger Hurt Pleasure Satisfaction

Keeping in mind the episode which more often happens to you, read the statements presented below carefully and circle the degree to which they describe the way you think and feel about yourself (1 *Completely False* to 5 *Completely True*).

Schemas	Completely False	False	Sometimes True some false	True	Completely True
1. I'm helpless	1	2	3	4	5
2. I'm powerless	1	2	3	4	5
3. I'm out of control	1	2	3	4	5
4. I'm weak	1	2	3	4	5
5. I'm vulnerable	1	2	3	4	5
6. I'm needy	1	2	3	4	5
7. I'm trapped	1	2	3	4	5
8. I'm inadequate	1	2	3	4	5
9. I'm ineffective	1	2	3	4	5
10. I'm incompetent	1	2	3	4	5
11. I'm a failure	1	2	3	4	5
12. I'm disrespected	1	2	3	4	5
13. I'm defective (less than others)	1	2	3	4	5
14. I'm not good enough (achieve)	1	2	3	4	5

Schemas	Completely False	False	Sometimes True some false	True	Completely True
15. I'm unlovable	1	2	3	4	5
16. I'm unlikable	1	2	3	4	5
17. I'm undesirable	1	2	3	4	5
18. I'm unattractive	1	2	3	4	5
19. I'm unwanted	1	2	3	4	5
20. I'm uncared for	1	2	3	4	5
21. I'm bad	1	2	3	4	5
22. I'm unworthy	1	2	3	4	5
23. I'm different	1	2	3	4	5
24. I'm defective (not loved)	1	2	3	4	5
25. I'm not good enough (loved)	1	2	3	4	5
26. I'm bound to be rejected	1	2	3	4	5
27. I'm bound to be abandoned	1	2	3	4	5
28. I'm bound to be alone	1	2	3	4	5

Women's Nontraditional Sexuality Questionnaire

RONALD F. LEVANT,[1] *The University of Akron*
K. BRYANT SMALLEY, *Georgia Southern University*
THOMAS J. RANKIN, *The University of Akron*
ALEXANDER COLBOW, *Boston College*
KRISTIN DAVID, *Brown University*
CHRISTINE M. WILLIAMS, *The University of Akron*

The Women's Nontraditional Sexuality Questionnaire (WNSQ) was created to investigate women's nontraditional sexual behaviors and attitudes as broadly as possible by including forms of sexuality that are prohibited by the traditional norm, such as recreational sex, using sex as a means to gain an end, and participating in commercial sex by paying for, or receiving payment for, a sexual experience.

Description

The WNSQ is a 40-item self-report measure that is divided into three general sections. The first section asks six preliminary questions about the respondent's relationship status, sexual activity, sexual orientation, and current engagement in casual sex. The second section forms the bulk of the questionnaire and assesses the frequency of 26 sexual behaviors that occur for reasons other than the expression of love within a committed sexual relationship. The third section addresses attitudes about nontraditional sexuality by asking the respondent the strength of her agreement or disagreement with eight statements assessing attitudes toward sex. Six additional demographic items—age, gender, race/ethnicity, family/household income, highest educational level completed, and socioeconomic status—assisted in the validation of the instrument but are not included here in order to maintain focus on the core sexuality-related items.

[1]Address correspondence to Ronald Levant, Buchtel College of Arts and Sciences, The University of Akron, Akron, OH 44325-1901; e-mail: levant@uakron.edu

The psychometric properties of the WNSQ were assessed with a sample drawn from college-aged women at a large midwestern university. Of the 243 women who completed the instrument, 85% identified as White/European American, 7% identified as Black/African American, and 2% or less each identified as Asian/Asian American, Arab/Arab American, Bi-/Multi-Racial, or Latino(a)/Hispanic. Respondents' ages ranged from 18 to 49 years old, but 90% of participants were 26 years of age or younger, and the average age was approximately 21. Annual household income varied considerably, with about one-fifth of the sample making less than $20,000 per year, about half the sample making between $20,000 and $80,000, and slightly more than a quarter of the sample making $80,000 or more. Self-descriptions of socioeconomic status were consistent with the financial responses except that only 4% self-described lower/working class and only 2% self-described as upper class.

Of the respondents, 92% reported that they always preferred a male sexual partner. An additional 4% usually preferred a male partner, and 3% preferred a female partner exclusively or at least as often as a male partner. About 45% of the respondents were seriously dating someone, and 43% were single. Only 10% were married or partnered, and 2% were divorced. Although 89% of the sample had been sexually active at some point in their lives, only 72% were sexually active when they completed the survey, and 67% said that their sexual activity occurred in the context of a relationship. Thus, 5% of the sample engaged exclusively in nontraditional sexual activity.

Response Mode and Timing

The WNSQ has been administered solely online but was adapted to a paper-and-pencil format in the Exhibit. Online administration used a commercial survey administration website that permits responses to automatically be downloaded into Excel and then imported into SPSS for analysis. Participants simply clicked their answer choice using their computer's mouse. The measure is usually completed within 15 to 30 minutes.

Scoring

All items receive a score of 1–7, according to the numbers across the top of each page of the survey. Items 36, 38, 39, and 40 are reverse scored (designated with an *R*) such that a response of 1 is scored as a 7 and a response of 7 is scored as a 1, and so forth for each value 1–7. *Never* is scored as a 1 and *Frequently* is scored as a 7 in Items 7–32, whereas *Agree Strongly* is scored as a 7 and *Disagree Strongly* is scored as a 1 in Items 33–40. Items 1–6 are nominal or categorical variables and are scored as such.

To obtain the total scale score, reverse the scores of Items 36, 38, 39, and 40 and then average Items 7–40. To obtain the Degree of Sexual Interest subscale score, average the scores of responses to Items 7, 11, 14, 20, 21, and 27. To obtain the Casual Sex subscale score, average the scores of responses to Items 9, 10, 17, 22, 23, 28, and 29. To obtain the Involvement in Commercial Sex subscale score, average the scores of responses to Items 12, 13, 18, 19, 24, 25, 31, and 32. To obtain the Sex as a Means to an End subscale score, reverse Item 39 and then average the scores of responses to Items 8, 15, 16, 26, 30, 35, and 39R. To obtain the Nontraditional Attitudes About Sex subscale score, reverse Items 36, 38, and 40 and then average the scores of responses to Items 33, 34, 36R, 37, 38R, and 40R.

Reliability

Reliability for the total scale was excellent, with a Cronbach's alpha of .88. Subscale reliabilities were good for four subscales: alphas were .80, .84, .72, and .80 for the subscales Degree of Sexual Interest, Casual Sex, Sex as a Means to an End, and Commercial Sex, respectively. The fifth theorized subscale, Nontraditional Attitudes About Sex, displayed poor reliability ($\alpha = .22$). Exploratory and confirmatory factor analyses suggested a four-factor solution in which three of the four factors corresponded to the Degree of Sexual Interest, Casual Sex, and Sex as a Means to an End subscales. On the Commercial Sex subscale, only items relating to Self-Pleasuring survived the factor analyses, and the Nontraditional Attitudes About Sex did not emerge as a stable factor. The four factors accounted for 33.5% of the variance (Levant, Rankin, Hall, Smalley, & Williams, 2009).

Validity

Convergent construct validity for the WNSQ was supported by its moderate-to-large correlation ($r = .72, p < .01$) with the Sociosexual Orientation Index (SOI; Simpson & Gangestad, 1991), which measures men's and women's willingness to engage in sex with a partner who is not committed to them. The Casual Sex subscale had the highest correlation with the SOI ($r = .73, p < .01$), whereas the other four subscales had moderate correlations (ranging from $r = .28$ to .57, $p < .01$). This is consistent with the intention that the WNSQ was constructed to measure casual sex *plus* other nontraditional sexuality behaviors such as self-pleasuring, using sex as a means to an end, degree of sexual interest, and involvement in commercial sex. In addition, convergent construct validity was supported by a moderate negative correlation ($r = -.44, p < .01$) between the total scale score of the WNSQ and the Purity subscale of the Femininity Ideology Scale (FIS; Levant, Richmond, Cook, House, & Aupont, 2007), which measures the degree to which women endorse traditional feminine sexual norms. The Sex as a Means to an End subscale had the lowest correlation with the Purity subscale of the FIS ($r = -.17, p < .01$), whereas the other four subscales had small to moderate correlations (ranging from $r = -.24$ to $-.46, p < .01$).

Other Information

We gratefully acknowledge the assistance of Korenna Barto, The University of Akron; Katherine Frank, University of Wisconsin-Madison; Chassity Angeny, Nova Southeastern University; and Katherine Richmond, Muhlenberg College.

References

Levant, R. F., Rankin, T. J., Hall, R. J., Smalley, K. B., & Williams, C. M. (2009). *The development and assessment of a scale to measure nontraditional sexuality in women.* Manuscript submitted for publication.

Levant, R. F., Richmond, K., Cook, S., House, A., & Aupont, M. (2007). The Femininity Ideology Scale: Factor structure, reliability, validity, and social contextual variation. *Sex Roles, 57,* 373–383.

Simpson, J. A., & Gangestad, S. (1991). Individual differences in sociosexuality: Evidence for convergent and discriminant validity. *Journal of Personality and Social Psychology, 60,* 870–883.

Exhibit

Women's Nontraditional Sexuality Questionnaire

Sexual Practices and Attitudes Survey

Thank you for your help with our study! We are looking at current sexual practices and attitudes in our society. We are very interested in your honest responses to our questions. We would like this survey to remain anonymous, so please do not put your name on the survey.

Please circle the response that best describes yourself.

1. Relationship Status:

    a. Married/Partnered/Engaged
    b. Single: Casual, non-exclusive dating
    c. Single: Dating one person with the expectation of exclusivity
    d. Single: Not currently dating anyone
    e. Divorced/Separated
    f. Widowed

For the following questions, please consider the term "sex" to refer to any form of intimate physical contact involving more than kissing between you and another person (opposite or same sex).

2. Have you ever had sex (based on the above definition)?

    a. Yes
    b. No

3. Are you currently sexually active (based on the above definition)?

    a. Yes
    b. No

4. Are you currently involved in a sexual relationship in which you and your partner have agreed not to have sex (based on the above definition) with other people?

    a. Yes
    b. No

5. Are you currently or have you recently been sexually active (based on the above definition) with someone who is not your exclusive sexual partner (e.g., one-night stand; having sex with two or more people in a short time period; or casual sexual activity)?

    a. Yes
    b. No

6. Whether or not you are sexually active, would your preferred sexual partner be:

    a. Always male
    b. Usually male, but sometimes female
    c. Equally likely to be either
    d. Usually female, but sometimes male
    e. Always female

For the following questions, please provide your answer using the 7-point scale provided. Check the circle that best describes where you fall between those two extremes. Please remember that the definition of sex is any form of intimate physical contact involving more than kissing between you and another person (opposite or same sex).

	Never						Frequently
	1	2	3	4	5	6	7
7. Given the chance, how often would you choose to have sex?	O	O	O	O	O	O	O
8. How often have you had sex to end a fight?	O	O	O	O	O	O	O
9. How often do you go somewhere (e.g., bar, social event) to find someone to have sex with?	O	O	O	O	O	O	O
10. How often would you have anonymous sex with someone you are *very* attracted to if you are/were single?	O	O	O	O	O	O	O
11. How often do you masturbate?	O	O	O	O	O	O	O
12. How often do you use sex toys alone?	O	O	O	O	O	O	O
13. How often have you **been paid** for sex?	O	O	O	O	O	O	O
14. How often do you fantasize about having sex with someone **other than** your current partner?	O	O	O	O	O	O	O
15. How often have you had sex to keep your partner in the relationship?	O	O	O	O	O	O	O
16. How often have you had sex to help get a promotion or some other benefit at work or school?	O	O	O	O	O	O	O
17. How often do you cheat sexually on a partner?	O	O	O	O	O	O	O
18. How often do you purchase sex toys?	O	O	O	O	O	O	O
19. How often do **you** pay for sex?	O	O	O	O	O	O	O
20. How often do you talk to your friends about your sexual experiences?	O	O	O	O	O	O	O
21. How often do you say what you want or need during sex?	O	O	O	O	O	O	O
22. How often do you have sex outside of an exclusive relationship?	O	O	O	O	O	O	O
23. How often would you have anonymous sex with someone you were **very** attracted to if you were in a relationship and knew for sure that your partner would not find out?	O	O	O	O	O	O	O
24. How often do you buy an X-rated video?	O	O	O	O	O	O	O
25. How often do you go to a strip club?	O	O	O	O	O	O	O
26. How often do you use sex to get something you want?	O	O	O	O	O	O	O
27. How often do you fantasize about having sex with your **current** partner?	O	O	O	O	O	O	O
28. Do you ever have sex with a friend with whom you are not interested in dating (so-called "friends with benefits")?	O	O	O	O	O	O	O
29. How often do you have sex with someone you just met?	O	O	O	O	O	O	O
30. How often have you had sex to get someone to do something for you?	O	O	O	O	O	O	O
31. How often do you watch pornography alone?	O	O	O	O	O	O	O
32. How often do you have phone-sex or cyber-sex with someone you are not in a relationship with?	O	O	O	O	O	O	O

For the following questions, please indicate to what extent you agree or disagree with the following statements. Keep in mind that the definition of sex is any form of intimate physical contact involving more than kissing between you and another person (opposite or same sex).

	Strongly Disagree			Neutral			Strongly Agree
	1	2	3	4	5	6	7
33. Sex should be unplanned, rather than planned ahead of time.	○	○	○	○	○	○	○
34. One should always be ready for sex.	○	○	○	○	○	○	○
35. Sex can be a useful tool in some situations.	○	○	○	○	○	○	○
36. Hugging and kissing should not always lead to sex.	○	○	○	○	○	○	○
37. I am not sexually satisfied with any behavior other than intercourse.	○	○	○	○	○	○	○
38. Orgasm is not a necessary part of sex for me.	○	○	○	○	○	○	○
39. I would not use sex to get something I wanted.	○	○	○	○	○	○	○
40. Sex should only take place between two people who are in love.	○	○	○	○	○	○	○

Revised Sociosexual Orientation Inventory

LARS PENKE,[1] *University of Edinburgh*

The construct of sociosexuality or sociosexual orientation captures individual differences in the tendency to have casual, uncommitted sexual relationships. The term was introduced by Alfred Kinsey, who used it to describe the individual differences in sexual permissiveness and promiscuity that he found in his groundbreaking survey studies on sexual behavior (Kinsey, Pomeroy, & Martin, 1948; Kinsey, Pomeroy, Martin, & Gebhard, 1953). The amount of scientific research on sociosexuality increased markedly when Simpson and Gangestad (1991) published the Sociosexual Orientation Inventory (SOI), a 7-item self-report questionnaire that assesses sociosexual orientations along a single dimension from *restricted* (indicating a tendency to have sex exclusively in emotionally close and committed relationships) to *unrestricted* (indicating a tendency for sexual relationships with low commitment and investment, often after short periods of acquaintance and with changing partners). On average, men tend to be more unrestricted than women in their sociosexual orientations, though there are also large individual differences within both sexes (Schmitt, 2005). The SOI has been successfully applied in over 50 published studies from fields as diverse as social, personality, and evolutionary psychology, sexuality research, gender studies, biological anthropology, and cross-cultural research (Simpson, Wilson, & Winterheld, 2004).

Despite its popularity, the SOI has repeatedly been criticized (Asendorpf & Penke, 2005; Penke & Asendorpf, 2008; Townsend, Kline, & Wasserman, 1995; Voracek, 2005; Webster & Bryan, 2007). Conceptually, it has been doubted that a single unitary dimension accurately reflects individual differences in sociosexuality. Psychometrically, the SOI has received criticism for its sometimes low internal consistency, its multifactorial structure, its skewed score distribution, its open response items that invite exaggerated responses, its multiple alternative scoring methods that yield incoherent results, and the formulation of one item (number 4) that makes the SOI inappropriate for singles.

[1]Address correspondence to Lars Penke, Centre for Cognitive Ageing and Cognitive Epidemiology, Department of Psychology, University of Edinburgh, 7 George Square, Edinburgh, EH8 9JZ, UK; e-mail: lars.penke@ed.ac.uk

The Revised Sociosexual Orientation Inventory (SOI-R) is a nine-item self-report questionnaire that was developed to fix all these issues (Penke & Asendorpf, 2008). It assesses three facets of sociosexuality: past *Behavior* in terms of number of casual and changing sex partners, the explicit *Attitude* towards uncommitted sex, and sexual *Desire* for people with whom no romantic relationship exists.

Description

The SOI-R consists of nine items, three for each of the three facets. All are answered on rating scales. The first two items of the Behavior facet are taken from the original SOI. They ask for the number of sexual partners in the last 12 months and the lifetime number of "one-night stands." The third behavioral item assesses the number of partners with whom one had sex despite a lack of long-term relationship interest. Similarly, the first two Attitude items (asking for acceptance of sex without love and for comfort with casual sex) are identical with two items from the SOI, whereas a new item (asking for requiring the prospect of a long-term relationship before consenting to sex) replaces an SOI attitude item with overly long and complicated text. Finally, three new items assess the Desire facet, which was not very well represented in the original SOI (Penke & Asendorpf, 2008). They ask for the frequency with which one experiences spontaneous sexual fantasies or sexual arousal when encountering people in everyday life with whom no committed romantic relationship exists.

In a series of studies, the SOI-R items were chosen from a pool of 47 items using exploratory factor analysis and item analysis (Penke, 2006). Confirmatory factor analysis supported that they represent distinctive facets of sociosexuality with low to moderate positive intercorrelations (.17 to .55). The correlation between the Attitude and Behavior facets was significantly larger in women than in men, but otherwise the factorial structure is invariant between the sexes, showing that the SOI-R is equally appropriate for men and women (Penke & Asendorpf, 2008).

An analysis of 8,522 participants from an online study indicates that the SOI-R is appropriate for individuals of any normal-range educational level, including hetero-, bi- and homosexuals, singles and individuals of any relationship/marital status, and at least the age range of 18 to 60 years (Penke, 2006; data partly available on www.larspenke.eu/soi-r/). However, some facets do not work very well for sexually inexperienced and asexual individuals.

Response Mode and Timing

All items of the SOI-R use Likert-type rating scales with the same number of response alternatives, which makes the SOI-R appropriate for both paper-and-pencil and online studies. Two alternative response scale formats exist for the SOI-R, one with nine and the other with five response alternatives. Both show comparable psychometric properties. The 9-point response scale was developed to allow for

combining the SOI-R with the original SOI (for details, see Penke & Asendorpf, 2008). However, for the majority of applications I recommend the 5-point response scale, because most subjects (especially nonstudents) find it easier to discriminate between five than between nine response alternatives. The SOI-R takes 1 to 2 minutes to complete.

Scoring

For Items 1 to 3, values of 1 to 5 (5-point response scale) or values of 1 to 9 (9-point response scale) should be assigned to the responses. Thus, all nine items have values from 1 to 5 (5-point scale) or 1 to 9 (9-point scale). Item 6 should be reverse keyed. Items 1 to 3 are aggregated (summed or averaged) to form the Behavior facet, Items 4 to 6 form the Attitude facet, and Items 7 to 9 form the Desire facet. Finally, all nine items can be aggregated to form a full-scale score that represents the global sociosexual orientation, similar to the full score of the original SOI. Because most SOI-R scores (except Behavior) usually show marked sex differences, results should be analyzed separately for men and women, or alternatively sex should be statistically controlled in all analyses. Descriptive statistics for average facet and full-scale scores for both response formats can be found in Table 1.

Reliability

As can be seen in Table 1, the SOI-R facet and total scores show good internal consistencies for both response formats. Additionally, all scores except the Desire facet show good 1-year retest stability, at least when the 9-point scale is used. The lower retest stability of the Desire facet appears to relate to its transactions with romantic relationship status, with women in particular showing more restrictive desires when starting a new relationship and less restrictive desires when separating (see Penke & Asendorpf, 2008).

Validity

In two large studies, Penke and Asendorpf (2008) showed that the SOI-R full-scale score and the SOI showed very similar relationships to established correlates of sociosexuality, including sex differences, past and future relationship and sexual behaviors, infidelity, mate choice preferences, sex drive, personality traits like shyness and sensation seeking, and flirting behavior towards an attractive opposite-sex stranger. Thus, there is strong evidence that the SOI-R offers the same predictive validity that has been shown for the SOI (Simpson et al., 2004).

However, more detailed analyses revealed a highly distinctive pattern of relationships for the three SOI-R facets, supporting their discriminant validity. For example, sex differences were pronounced for Desire, mediocre for Attitude, and nonexistent for Behavior (Table 1). Only Desire made unique contributions to the prediction of past sexual and relationship behaviors, observer-rated

TABLE 1
Descriptive Statistics, Reliabilities, and Effect Sizes for Sex Differences for Both SOI-R Response Scale Formats

		N	Cronbach's α	r_{tt} (1 year)	M	SD	Cohen's d
5-point scale							
SOI-R	male	2728	.85	—	2.19	1.10	.00
Behavior	female	5821	.78	—	2.19	.95	
SOI-R	male	2706	.81	—	3.54	1.18	.45
Attitude	female	5794	.81	—	3.01	1.20	
SOI-R	male	2687	.82	—	3.45	1.01	.86
Desire	female	5748	.82	—	2.61	.96	
SOI-R	male	2647	.82	—	3.07	.82	.57
	female	5632	.83	—	2.60	.80	
9-point scale							
SOI-R	male	1026	.85	.83	2.76	1.83	.06
Behavior	female	1682	.84	.86	2.65	1.73	
SOI-R	male	1026	.87	.73	6.42	2.33	.43
Attitude	female	1682	.83	.79	5.41	2.37	
SOI-R	male	1026	.86	.68	5.62	1.91	.86
Desire	female	1682	.85	.39	3.96	1.94	
SOI-R	male	1026	.83	.83	4.93	1.50	.61
	female	1682	.83	.78	4.01	1.52	

Note. r_{tt} = test-retest correlation. The results for the 5-point response scale are from an unpublished online study (Penke, 2006). The results for the 9-point response scale are from Study 1 in Penke and Asendorpf (2008). More detailed results, split by subsamples, can be found on www.larspenke.eu/soi-r/.

attractiveness, self-perceived mate value, and female flirting behavior, whereas Attitude appeared responsible for the effects of sociosexuality on mate preferences, assortative mating, and a romantic partner's flirtatiousness outside the relationship, and Desire had strong independent effects on relationships with sex drive, relationship quality, and male flirting behavior. Furthermore, Behavior and Desire, but not Attitude, predicted the number of sexual partners and changes in romantic relationship status over the next 12 month. Thus, Behavior, Attitude, and Desire apparently reflect rather unique components of sociosexuality that should be studied separately in order to understand the dynamics that underlie sociosexual orientations.

Other Information

The SOI-R can freely be used for research purposes. The items of 10 different language versions (Chinese, Dutch, English, French, German, Icelandic, Italian, Malaysian, Spanish, and Swedish) can be downloaded from www. larspenke.eu/soi-r/.

References

Asendorpf, J. B., & Penke, L. (2005). A mature evolutionary psychology demands careful conclusions about sex differences. *Behavioral and Brain Sciences, 28*, 275–276.

Kinsey, A., Pomeroy, W., & Martin, C. (1948). *Sexual behavior in the human male.* Philadelphia: Saunders.

Kinsey, A., Pomeroy, W., Martin, C., & Gebhard, P. (1953). *Sexual behavior in the human female.* Philadelphia: Saunders.

Penke, L. (2006). *Development of the revised Sociosexual Orientation Inventory (SOI-R).* Unpublished manuscript, Institute of Psychology, Humboldt University of Berlin.

Penke, L., & Asendorpf, J. B. (2008). Beyond global sociosexual orientations: A more differentiated look at sociosexuality and its effects on courtship and romantic relationships. *Journal of Personality and Social Psychology, 95*, 1113–1135.

Schmitt, D. P. (2005). Sociosexuality from Argentina to Zimbabwe: A 48-nation study of sex, culture, and strategies of human mating. *Behavioral and Brain Sciences, 28*, 247–275.

Simpson, J. A., & Gangestad, S. W. (1991). Individual differences in sociosexuality: Evidence for convergent and discriminant validity. *Journal of Personality and Social Psychology, 60*, 870–883.

Simpson, J. A., Wilson, C. L., & Winterheld, H. A. (2004). Sociosexuality and romantic relationships. In J. H. Harvey, A. Wenzel, & S. Sprecher (Eds.), *Handbook of sexuality in close relationships* (pp. 87–111). Mahwah, NJ: Erlbaum.

Townsend, J. M., Kline, J., & Wasserman, T. H. (1995). Low-investment copulation: Sex differences in motivations and emotional reactions. *Ethology and Sociobiology, 16*, 25–51.

Voracek, M. (2005). Shortcomings of the Sociosexual Orientation Inventory: Can psychometrics inform evolutionary psychology? *Behavioral and Brain Sciences, 28*, 296–297.

Webster, G. D., & Bryan, A. (2007). Sociosexual attitudes and behaviors: Why two factors are better than one. *Journal of Research in Personality, 41*, 917–922.

Exhibit

Revised Sociosexual Orientation Inventory[a]

Please respond honestly to all of the following questions. Your responses will be treated confidentially and anonymously.

1. With how many different partners have you had sex within the past 12 months?[b]

☐	☐	☐	☐	☐
0	1	2 to 3	4 to 7	8 or More

☐	☐	☐	☐	☐	☐	☐	☐	☐
0	1	2	3	4	5–6	7–9	10–19	20 or More

2. With how many different partners have you had sexual intercourse on *one and only one* occasion?

3. With how many different partners have you had sexual intercourse without having an interest in a long-term committed relationship with this person?

4. Sex without love is OK.[c]

1 ☐   2 ☐   3 ☐   4 ☐   5 ☐
Totally Disagree   Totally Agree

1 ☐   2 ☐   3 ☐   4 ☐   5 ☐   6 ☐   7 ☐   8 ☐   9 ☐
Strongly Disagree   Strongly Agree

5. I can imagine myself being comfortable and enjoying "casual" sex with different partners.
6. I do *not* want to have sex with a person until I am sure that we will have a long-term, serious relationship.
7. How often do you have fantasies about having sex with someone you are *not* in a committed romantic relationship with?[d]

1 ☐	2 ☐	3 ☐	4 ☐	5 ☐
Never	Very Seldom	About Once a Month	About Once a Week	Nearly Every Day

1 ☐	2 ☐	3 ☐	4 ☐	5 ☐	6 ☐	7 ☐	8 ☐	9 ☐
Never	Very Seldom	About Once Every Two or Three Months	About Once a Month	About Once Every Two Weeks	About Once a Week	Several Times per Week	Nearly Every Day	At Least Once a Day

8. How often do you experience sexual arousal when you are in contact with someone you are *not* in a committed romantic relationship with?
9. In everyday life, how often do you have spontaneous fantasies about having sex with someone you have just met?

[a]Both the 5-response option and the 9-response option are shown in the exhibit that follows.
[b]These response options are used for the first three questions.
[c]These response options are used for the next three questions.
[d]These response options are used for the last three questions.

Sociosexual Orientation Inventory

JEFFRY A. SIMPSON,[1] *University of Minnesota*
STEVEN W. GANGESTAD, *University of New Mexico*

In the 1940s and 1950s, comprehensive surveys of the sexual practices of North American men (Kinsey, Pomeroy, & Martin, 1948) and women (Kinsey, Pomeroy, Martin, & Gebhard, 1953) documented that people differ dramatically on several "sociosexual" attitudes and behaviors. Although men, as a group, displayed greater sexual permissiveness than women on most sociosexual attitudes and behaviors (e.g., men have more permissive attitudes toward casual sex, and they are more likely to have sexual affairs), one of the most striking features of the Kinsey data is that much more variability in sociosexual attitudes and behaviors exists *within* each sex than between men and women. Some women, for example, are more sexually permissive than

most men, and some men are less permissive than most women.

The Sociosexual Orientation Inventory (SOI; Simpson & Gangestad, 1991) was developed to measure individual differences in willingness to engage in casual, uncommitted sexual relationships. The SOI assesses individuals' past sexual behavior, anticipated (future) sexual behavior, the content of their sexual fantasies, and their attitudes toward engaging in casual sex without commitment and emotional investment. Individuals who score high on the SOI have an *unrestricted* sociosexual orientation. These individuals report having a larger number of different sexual partners in the past year, anticipate having more partners in the next

[1]Address correspondence to Jeffry A. Simpson, Department of Psychology, University of Minnesota, Minneapolis, MN 55455; e-mail: simps108@umn.edu or to Steven W. Gangestad, Department of Psychology, University of New Mexico, Albuquerque, NM 87131.

5 years, have had more one-night stands ("hook-ups"), fantasize more often about having sex with people other than their current (or most recent) romantic partner, and believe that sex without emotional ties is acceptable. Individuals who score low on the SOI have a *restricted* sociosexual orientation. These individuals report fewer sexual partners in the past year, anticipate fewer partners in the next 5 years, are less likely to engage in "one-night stands," rarely fantasize about extra-pair sex, and do not believe in having sex without love and commitment.

Description

The SOI has seven items. Two items ask respondents to report on their past sexual behavior: Item 1 (the number of sexual partners in the past year) and Item 3 (the number of times they have had sex with someone on only one occasion). Item 2 assesses future sexual behavior (the number of partners anticipated in the next 5 years). Item 4, answered on a Likert-type scale, inquires about sexual fantasies (how often they fantasize about having sex with someone other than their current [or most recent] romantic partner). Items 5, 6, and 7, all answered on Likert-type scales, ask about respondents' attitudes toward engaging in casual sex. These seven items load on a higher-order factor labeled sociosexuality.

Response Mode and Timing

Items 1–3 on the SOI (those that inquire about past and future sexual behavior) require respondents to write down specific numbers of sexual partners. Items 4–7 (those that inquire about fantasies and sexual attitudes) are answered on Likert-type scales. The SOI takes 1–2 minutes to complete.

Scoring

Item 7 of the SOI must be reverse keyed. Items 5, 6, and 7 are then aggregated (summed) to create the attitudinal component of the SOI. The following weighting scheme is used when aggregating the five components: SOI = 5X (Item 1) + 1X (Item 2) + 5X (Item 3) + 4X (Item 4) + 2X (aggregate of Items 5–7). To ensure that Item 2 does not have disproportionate influence on the total SOI score, the maximum value of Item 2 is limited to 30 partners. This weighting scheme approximates the scores that individuals would receive if the five SOI components were transformed to z scores, unit-weighted, and then summed. Scores based on the current weighting scheme correlate at or above .90 with a unit-weighting system (Simpson & Gangestad, 1991).

SOI scores can range from 10 (a maximally restricted orientation) to 1,000 (a maximally unrestricted orientation). The normal range in college samples is 10–250. Because men tend to score higher on the SOI than women (Simpson & Gangestad, 1991, 1992), respondents' gender should be partialed before statistical analyses are conducted, or analyses should be performed separately on women and men.

Some respondents will occasionally report very high numbers for Items 1–3. In college samples, 30 is the maximum value for Item 2. If respondents report more than 20 partners for Items 1 or 2, these individuals may be outliers who could have undue influence on the results. Thus, outlier detection should *always* be done prior to analyzing SOI scores.

Reliability

The SOI is internally consistent (average Cronbach alpha = .75; Simpson & Gangestad, 1991, 1992). Test-retest reliability over 2 months is high (r = .94; Simpson & Gangestad, 1991; see Simpson, Wilson, & Winterheld, 2004, for additional information).

Validity

Predictions for individuals who have restricted or unrestricted sociosexual orientations can be derived from the theoretical construct of sociosexuality (see Gangestad & Simpson, 1990; Simpson et al., 2004). Predictive validity evidence for the SOI is reviewed in Simpson et al. (2004). Evidence for its convergent and discriminant validity properties also exists. With regard to convergent validity, for example, more unrestricted individuals (relative to more restricted ones): (a) engage in sex earlier in their romantic relationships, (b) are more likely to have sex with more than one partner during a given time period, and (c) tend to be involved in sexual relationships characterized by less investment, less commitment, less love, and weaker emotional ties (Simpson & Gangestad, 1991). More unrestricted individuals also score higher on other scales known to tap related constructs (e.g., sexual permissiveness, impersonal sex).

More unrestricted people also desire, choose, and acquire romantic partners who have different attributes compared to more restricted people (Simpson & Gangestad, 1992). For example, more unrestricted individuals prefer partners who are more physically attractive and have higher social status, and they place less emphasis on kindness, loyalty, and stability. More restricted persons prefer partners who are kinder and more affectionate, more faithful and loyal, and more responsible, and they place less weight on attractiveness and social status. In dating initiation studies (Simpson, Gangestad, & Biek, 1993), more unrestricted persons—especially men—display more nonverbal behaviors known to facilitate rapid relationship development (e.g., more smiling, laughing, maintaining direct eye contact, flirtatious glances; for further validity information, see Simpson et al., 2004).

In terms of discriminant validity, Simpson and Gangestad (1991) found that more restricted persons (a) do *not* have appreciably lower sex drives and (b) do *not* score higher on scales assessing sexuality-based constructs that should not correlate with the SOI (e.g., sexual satisfaction, sex guilt, sex-related anxiety).

References

Gangestad, S., & Simpson, J. A. (1990). Toward an evolutionary history of female sociosexual variation. *Journal of Personality, 58,* 69–96.

Kinsey, A., Pomeroy, W., & Martin, C. (1948). *Sexual behavior in the human male.* Philadelphia: Saunders.

Kinsey, A., Pomeroy, W., Martin, C., & Gebhard, P. (1953). *Sexual behavior in the human female.* Philadelphia: Saunders.

Simpson, J. A., & Gangestad, S. (1991). Individual differences in socio-sexuality: Evidence for convergent and discriminant validity. *Journal*

of Personality and Social Psychology, 60, 870–883.

Simpson, J. A., & Gangestad, S. (1992). Sociosexuality and romantic partner choice. *Journal of Personality, 60,* 31–51.

Simpson, J. A., Gangestad, S. W., & Biek, M. (1993). Personality and nonverbal social behavior: An ethological perspective of relationship initiation. *Journal of Experimental Social Psychology, 29,* 434–461.

Simpson, J. A., Wilson, C. L., & Winterheld, H. A. (2004). Sociosexuality and romantic relationships. In J. H. Harvey, A. Wenzel, & S. Sprecher (Eds.), *Handbook of sexuality in close relationships* (pp. 87–112). Mahwah, NJ: Erlbaum.

Exhibit

Sociosexual Orientation Inventory

Please answer all of the following questions *honestly*. Your responses will be treated as confidential and anonymous. For the questions dealing with behavior, write your answers in the blank spaces provided. For the questions dealing with thoughts and attitudes, circle the appropriate number on the scales provided. The term "sexual intercourse" refers to genital sex.

1. With how many different partners have you had sex (sexual intercourse) within the past year? _____
2. How many different partners do you foresee yourself having sex with during the next five years? (Please give a specific, *realistic* estimate.) _____
3. With how many different partners have you had sex on *one and only one* occasion? _____
4. How often do you fantasize about having sex with someone other than your current dating partner (when you are in a relationship)? (Circle one.)

    1 Never
    2 Once Every Two or Three Months
    3 Once a Month
    4 Once Every Two Weeks
    5 Once a Week
    6 A Few Times Each Week
    7 Nearly Every Day
    8 At Least Once a Day

5. Sex without love is OK.

    1   2   3   4   5   6   7   8   9

    1 Strongly Disagree   1 Strongly Agree

6. I can imagine myself being comfortable and enjoying "casual" sex with different partners.

    1   2   3   4   5   6   7   8   9

    1 Strongly Disagree   1 Strongly Agree

7. I would have to be closely attached to someone (both emotionally and psychologically) before I could feel comfortable and fully enjoy having sex with him or her.

    1   2   3   4   5   6   7   8   9

    1 Strongly Disagree   1 Strongly Agree

Source. This scale was originally published in "Individual Differences in Sociosexuality: Evidence for Convergent and Discriminant Validity" by J. A. Simpson and S. Gangestad, 1991, *Journal of Personality and Social Psychology, 60,* 870–883. Reprinted with permission.

Tactics to Obtain Sex Scale

JOSEPH A. CAMILLERI,[1] *Westfield State College, Massachusetts*

The Tactics to Obtain Sex Scale (TOSS; Camilleri, Quinsey, & Tapscott, 2009) is a 31-item self-report attitude measure with two subscales designed to evaluate a person's current propensity to engage in sexual coaxing or sexual coercion with one's sexual partner.

Previous measures of partner sexual coercion evaluated the frequency and severity of sexual coercion in relationships (e.g., Shackelford & Goetz, 2004; Straus, Hamby, Boney-McCoy, & Sugarman, 1996). Using these *temporally fixed dynamic variables* (i.e., historic events, such as history of alcohol abuse) limits assessments to determining the presence of partner sexual coercion and limits research to quasi-experimental designs. If, however, clinicians or researchers are interested in changes in risk before and after treatment or after experimental manipulation, they require measures that are sensitive to proximal change in risk, known as *temporally variable dynamic variables* (e.g., being intoxicated; see Quinsey, Jones, Book, & Barr, 2006). Examples of measures that assess sexual coercion propensity include the various rape attitude and empathy measures (e.g., Deitz, Blackwell, Daley, & Bentley, 1982; Payne, Lonsway, & Fitzgerald, 1999), but none are specific to sexual offending in relationships.

Because the behaviors people use to obtain sex vary, a comprehensive measure of tactics people use also needs to capture benign and seductive tactics, known as *sexual coaxing* (Camilleri et al., 2009). Because sexual coaxing is more prevalent than sexual coercion, and only one measure exists to evaluate past instances of sexual coaxing in relationships (Jesser, 1978), a subscale that evaluates current propensity for sexual coaxing could be useful for couples research.

Description

To evaluate current propensity, participants are asked how they would respond to a hypothetical situation—their partner refusing sexual intercourse that evening. Given that scenario, participants rate a total of 31 items on how likely they would use each tactic and how effective each tactic would be in obtaining sex on a 5-point scale that ranges from 0 (*Definitely Not*) to 4 (*Definitely*). Current propensity was therefore defined as a respondent reporting a high likelihood of using tactics that the individual considered to be effective in obtaining sex from a reluctant partner.

Thirty-six items that varied on sexual coercion and sexual coaxing, and on verbal and physical acts, were initially selected from behaviors described in the literature and from the author's clinical experience and research. Factor analytic techniques reduced the number of items and confirmed a two-factor structure: 19 tactics were sexually coercive (COERCE) and 12 tactics were sexually coaxing (COAX).

The TOSS was developed and validated among student and community participants who were sexually active in heterosexual dating, cohabiting, common-law, or marital relationships.

Response Mode and Timing

Participants should complete the TOSS in a private room using either a paper-and-pencil format (see Exhibit) or a computer program that randomizes item order. Internal consistency and factor structure are similar across modalities (Camilleri et al., 2009). It should take participants no longer than 10 minutes to complete the TOSS.

Scoring

Likelihood and effectiveness ratings are summed for each item; then sexual coercion item total scores are summed for the partner sexual coercion subscale score (COERCE), and sexual coaxing item total scores are summed for the partner sexual coaxing subscale (COAX). COERCE scores can range from 0 to 152, where higher scores indicate a greater current propensity for partner sexual coercion. COAX scores range from 0 to 96, where higher scores indicate a greater current propensity for partner sexual coaxing. A total TOSS score could also be calculated by summing COAX and COERCE total scores. Higher scores would indicate a higher propensity for using any tactic to obtain sex from a partner.

Reliability

Camilleri et al. (2009) reported internal consistency estimates that ranged from .87 to .89 (COERCE); .92 to .93 (COAX); and .90 to .91 (TOSS).

Validity

Construct validity of the TOSS was established by finding significant correlations between the COERCE subscale and other measures of antisociality, including psychopathy and attraction to sexual aggression, whereas significant correlations were found between COAX and measures of

[1]Address correspondence to Joseph A. Camilleri, Psychology Department, Westfield State College, 577 Western Ave, Westfield, MA 01086; e-mail: jcamilleri@wsc.ma.edu

general sexual interest measures and self-perceived mating success (Camilleri & Quinsey, 2009a; Camilleri et al., 2009).

Initial criterion validity of the TOSS was demonstrated from a relationship between COERCE and sexually coercive behaviors with one's partner in the last month and year, and no relationship with nonsexual violence against a partner. COAX, on the other hand, correlated with instances of signaling sexual interest with one's partner.

Temporal sensitivity of the COERCE subscale is supported by finding higher scores among men who experienced many recent cues to infidelity than men who did not experience such cues (Camilleri & Quinsey, 2009b). Temporal sensitivity of COAX was supported by finding scores varied by age and finding lower COAX scores among younger participants who were in committed relationships (common-law or marital) than dating or cohabiting relationships (Camilleri et al., 2009).

Other Information

Because of its unique properties, the TOSS has been used to test novel hypotheses about individual difference characteristics and social predictors of sexually coercive and sexually coaxing behaviors in relationships (Camilleri & Quinsey, 2009a, 2009b). Not only are further psychometric refinements to the scale possible and encouraged, but I hope this scale encourages further discourse into the causes and consequences of sexual conflict in relationships. The scale could be further validated among clinical and correctional populations and used experimentally to measure changes in coercive and coaxing interests.

Acknowledgements

The author would like to thank Vern Quinsey for his helpful comments on an earlier draft of this manuscript.

References

Camilleri, J. A., & Quinsey, V. L. (2009a). Individual differences in the propensity for partner sexual coercion. *Sexual Abuse: A Journal of Research and Treatment, 21,* 111–129.

Camilleri, J. A., & Quinsey, V. L. (2009b). Testing the cuckoldry risk hypothesis of partner sexual coercion in community and forensic samples. *Evolutionary Psychology, 7,* 164–178.

Camilleri, J. A., Quinsey, V. L., & Tapscott, J. L. (2009). Assessing the propensity for sexual coaxing and sexual coercion in relationships: Factor structure, reliability, and validity of the Tactics to Obtain Sex Scale. *Archives of Sexual Behavior, 38,* 959–973.

Deitz, S. R., Blackwell, K. T., Daley, P. C., & Bentley, B. J. (1982). Measurement of empathy toward rape victims and rapists. *Journal of Personality and Social Psychology, 43,* 372–384.

Jesser, C. J. (1978). Male response to direct verbal sexual initiatives of females. *The Journal of Sex Research, 14,* 118–128.

Payne, D. L., Lonsway, K. A., & Fitzgerald, L. F. (1999). Rape myth acceptance: Exploration of its structure and its measurement using the Illinois Rape Myth Acceptance Scale. *Journal of Research in Personality, 33,* 27–68.

Quinsey, V. L., Jones, G. B., Book, A. S., & Barr, K. N. (2006). The dynamic prediction of antisocial behavior among forensic psychiatric patients: A prospective field study. *Journal of Interpersonal Violence, 21,* 1539–1565.

Shackelford, T. K., & Goetz, A. T. (2004). Men's sexual coercion in intimate relationships: Development and initial validation of the Sexual Coercion in Intimate Relationships Scale. *Violence and Victims, 19,* 541–556.

Straus, M. A., Hamby, S. L., Boney-McCoy, S., & Sugarman, D. B. (1996). The revised Conflict Tactics Scales (CTS2). *Journal of Family Issues, 17,* 283–316.

Exhibit

Tactics to Obtain Sex Scale

Suppose you were with your partner this evening, and he/she did not want to have sex with you: Please rate **how effective** the following acts would be to persuade your partner into having sex. Remember, you may skip questions you are uncomfortable in answering.

	Effectiveness of Acts				
	Definitely Not	Unlikely	Maybe	Probably	Definitely
Massage his/her neck or back	0	1	2	3	4
Threaten to leave	0	1	2	3	4
Try to make him/her feel bad about not having sex	0	1	2	3	4
Play with his/her hair	0	1	2	3	4
Suggest you may harm him/her	0	1	2	3	4
Offer to buy him/her something	0	1	2	3	4
Lie down near him/her	0	1	2	3	4
Tie partner up	0	1	2	3	4
Block partner's retreat	0	1	2	3	4
Tickle	0	1	2	3	4
Provide him/her with drugs	0	1	2	3	4
Call him/her names	0	1	2	3	4
Threaten self-harm	0	1	2	3	4
Massage feet/thighs	0	1	2	3	4

	Definitely Not	Unlikely	Maybe	Probably	Definitely
Use humor	0	1	2	3	4
Say you might break partner's property	0	1	2	3	4
Wait until he/she is sleeping	0	1	2	3	4
Attempt to blackmail	0	1	2	3	4
Caress near/on partner's genitals	0	1	2	3	4
Rub leg with his/her legs	0	1	2	3	4
Whisper in his/her ear	0	1	2	3	4
Softly kiss his/her ears, neck, or face	0	1	2	3	4
Question partner's sexual orientation	0	1	2	3	4
Break partner's property	0	1	2	3	4
Say sweet things	0	1	2	3	4
Provide him/her with alcohol	0	1	2	3	4
Explain that your needs should be met	0	1	2	3	4
Take advantage of him/her if he/she's already drunk or stoned	0	1	2	3	4
Slap or hit	0	1	2	3	4
Caress his/her chest/breasts	0	1	2	3	4
Physically restrain	0	1	2	3	4

Suppose you were with your partner this evening, and he/she did not want to have sex with you: Please rate **how likely** you would engage in the following acts to persuade your partner into having sex. Remember, you may skip questions you are uncomfortable in answering.

	Likelihood You Would Use Acts				
	Definitely Not	*Unlikely*	*Maybe*	*Probably*	*Definitely*
Massage his/her neck or back	0	1	2	3	4
Threaten to leave	0	1	2	3	4
Try to make him/her feel bad about not having sex	0	1	2	3	4
Play with his/her hair	0	1	2	3	4
Suggest you may harm him/her	0	1	2	3	4
Offer to buy him/her something	0	1	2	3	4
Lie down near him/her	0	1	2	3	4
Tie partner up	0	1	2	3	4
Block partner's retreat	0	1	2	3	4
Tickle	0	1	2	3	4
Provide him/her with drugs	0	1	2	3	4
Call him/her names	0	1	2	3	4
Threaten self-harm	0	1	2	3	4
Massage feet/thighs	0	1	2	3	4
Use humor	0	1	2	3	4
Say you might break partner's property	0	1	2	3	4
Wait until he/she is sleeping	0	1	2	3	4
Attempt to blackmail	0	1	2	3	4
Caress near/on partner's genitals	0	1	2	3	4
Rub leg with his/her legs	0	1	2	3	4
Whisper in his/her ear	0	1	2	3	4
Softly kiss his/her ears, neck, or face	0	1	2	3	4
Question partner's sexual orientation	0	1	2	3	4
Break partner's property	0	1	2	3	4
Say sweet things	0	1	2	3	4
Provide him/her with alcohol	0	1	2	3	4
Explain that your needs should be met	0	1	2	3	4
Take advantage of him/her if he/she's already drunk or stoned	0	1	2	3	4
Slap or hit	0	1	2	3	4
Caress his/her chest/breasts	0	1	2	3	4
Physically restrain	0	1	2	3	4

Token Resistance to Sex Scale

SUZANNE L. OSMAN,[1] *Salisbury University*

The Token Resistance to Sex Scale (TRSS; Osman, 1995) was developed to measure the predispositional belief that women use token resistance to sexual advances; that is, they say "no" to sexual advances but mean "yes." The belief in token resistance has been recognized as an important determinant of perceptions, opinions, and outcomes of date rape (Muehlenhard, Friedman, & Thomas, 1985; Muehlenhard & Hollabaugh, 1988; Muehlenhard & Linton, 1987; Shotland & Goodstein, 1983). Although the concept of *token resistance* has been documented, this is the first scale to measure this predispositional belief by examining the situational factors known to be associated with belief in token resistance. Prior to the development of this scale, past researchers had measured belief in token resistance as a dependent variable by asking questions about whether sexual activity was desired. As a predispositional measure, this scale allows the belief in token resistance to be treated as an independent variable.

Description

The TRSS consists of eight items arranged on a 7-point Likert-type scale ranging from 1 (*Strongly Disagree*) to 7 (*Strongly Agree*).

Response Mode and Timing

Respondents can write the number from 1 to 7 that corresponds to their agreement with an item. The scale can be completed in less than 5 minutes.

Scoring

All eight items are keyed in the same direction, with a higher score indicating a stronger belief in token resistance and a lower score indicating a weaker belief in token resistance. Scores can range from 8 to 56.

Reliability

In a sample of 81 college men (Osman, 1995), the original Cronbach alpha reliability coefficient for the TRSS was .86. In subsequent studies, the Cronbach alpha for this scale has ranged from .83 to .87 in samples of men and women (*n*'s ranging from 131 to 541) (Osman, 2003, 2004, 2007b; Osman & Davis, 1997, 1999a, 1999b).

Validity

Across several studies, it has been found consistently that greater belief in token resistance is associated with weaker perceptions of date rape (Osman, 2003; Osman & Davis, 1997, 1999a, 1999b). With related measures, Osman and Davis (1999a) found that the TRSS significantly correlated with Burt's (1980) Sex Role Stereotyping Scale, $r = .28$, and with Mosher and Sirkin's (1984) Hypermasculinity Inventory, including Callous Sexual Attitudes, $r = .60$, Danger as Exciting, $r = .28$, and Violence as Manly, $r = .28$. Of these scales, the TRSS was the best dispositional predictor of date rape perceptions, supporting its construct validity. Furthermore, Osman and Davis (1997) found that the TRSS significantly correlated in the expected directions with all five subscales of Muehlenhard and Felts's (1998) Sexual Beliefs Scale, including Token Refusal, No Means Stop, Leading on Justifies Force, Men Should Dominate, and Women Like Force.

Predictive utility for the TRSS has been demonstrated in studies examining men's perceptions of date rape based on experimentally manipulated scenarios. For example, Osman and Davis (1997) found that men with higher scores on the TRSS attended relatively more to nonverbal cues of sexual availability (i.e., provocative clothing, going to the man's apartment, timing of protest) in their judgments of whether rape occurred, whereas men who scored lower were more sensitive to the victim's verbal refusals. Furthermore, Osman and Davis (1999a) found that men with a stronger belief in token resistance were less certain that the situation was rape when the woman verbally resisted the man's sexual advances than when she fought back physically. Men with a weaker belief did not make this distinction and were more certain than their stronger belief counterparts that rape occurred as long as the woman offered some type of resistance. Lastly, Osman (2003) presented participants with a date rape, a consensual sex, or an ambiguous scenario. Men with lower TRSS scores had stronger rape perceptions than men with higher scores, in the rape condition only. Results suggested that the woman's verbal refusal to sexual intercourse was not taken seriously by those with higher TRSS scores.

More recently, the concept of token resistance has been applied to sexual harassment (Osman, 2004, 2007a, 2007b). As with date rape, some individuals may think that women use token resistance in response to sexual attention from men: that they say "stop" to sexual attention but truly want it to continue. Consistent with this, higher scores on

[1]Address correspondence to Suzanne L. Osman, Department of Psychology, Salisbury University, Salisbury, MD 21801; e-mail: slosman@salisbury.edu

the TRSS have been associated with weaker perceptions of sexual harassment (Osman, 2004, 2007b). Furthermore, whereas those with lower TRSS scores were more certain that harassment occurred when any type of resistance was present in sexual harassment scenarios, this was not true for those scoring higher. When the woman offered verbal or physical resistance to sexual attention, those with higher TRSS scores had weaker harassment perceptions than those with lower scores (Osman, 2007b).

References

Burt, M. R. (1980). Cultural myths and supports for rape. *Journal of Personality and Social Psychology, 38,* 217–230.

Mosher, D. L., & Sirkin, M. (1984). Measuring a macho personality constellation. *Journal of Research in Personality, 18,* 150–163.

Muehlenhard, C. L., & Felts, A. S. (1998). Sexual Beliefs Scale. In C. M. Davis, W. L. Yarber, R. Bauserman, G. Shreer, & S. L. Davis (Eds.), *Handbook of sexuality-related measures* (pp. 116–118). Newbury Park, CA: Sage.

Muehlenhard, C. L., Friedman, D. E., & Thomas, C. M. (1985). Is date rape justifiable? The effects of dating activity, who initiated, who paid, and men's attitudes toward women. *Psychology of Women Quarterly, 9,* 297–309.

Muehlenhard, C. L., & Hollabaugh, L. C. (1988). Do women sometimes say no when they mean yes? The prevalence and correlates of women's token resistance to sex. *Journal of Personality and Social Psychology, 54,* 872–879.

Muehlenhard, C. L., & Linton, M. A. (1987). Date rape and sexual aggression in dating situations: Incidence and risk factors. *Journal of Counseling Psychology, 34,* 186–196.

Osman, S. L. (1995, April). *Predispositional and situational factors influencing men's perceptions of date rape.* Paper presented at the Eastern Regional Meeting of the Society for the Scientific Study of Sexuality, Atlantic City, NJ.

Osman, S. L. (2003). Predicting men's rape perceptions based on the belief that "no" really means "yes." *Journal of Applied Social Psychology, 33,* 683–692.

Osman, S. L. (2004). Victim resistance: Theory and data on understanding perceptions of sexual harassment. *Sex Roles, 50,* 267–275.

Osman, S. L. (2007a). The continuation of perpetrator behaviors that influence perceptions of sexual harassment. *Sex Roles, 56,* 63–69.

Osman, S. L. (2007b). Predicting perceptions of sexual harassment based on type of resistance and belief in token resistance. *The Journal of Sex Research, 44,* 340–346.

Osman, S. L., & Davis, C. M. (1997). Predicting men's perceptions of date rape using the heuristic-systematic model. *Journal of Sex Education and Therapy, 22,* 25–32.

Osman, S. L., & Davis, C. M. (1999a). Belief in token resistance and type of resistance as predictors of men's perceptions of date rape. *Journal of Sex Education and Therapy, 24,* 189–196.

Osman, S. L. & Davis, C. M. (1999b). Predicting perceptions of date rape based on individual beliefs and female alcohol consumption. *Journal of College Student Development, 40,* 701–709.

Shotland, R. L., & Goodstein, L. (1983). Just because she doesn't want to doesn't mean it's rape: An experimental based causal model of the perception of rape in a dating situation. *Social Psychology Quarterly, 46,* 220–232.

Exhibit

Token Resistance to Sex Scale

Respond to the following statements by indicating the degree to which you agree or disagree with the statement. Respond using the following scale for each statement.

1 = Strongly Disagree
2 = Disagree
3 = Slightly Disagree
4 = Undecided, Neither Agree nor Disagree
5 = Slightly Agree
6 = Agree
7 = Strongly Agree

____1. Women usually say "no" to sex when they really mean "yes."

____2. When a man only has to use a minimal amount of force on a woman to get her to have sex, it probably means she wanted him to force her.

____3. When a woman waits until the very last minute to object to sex in a sexual interaction, she probably really wants to have sex.

____4. A woman who initiates a date with a man probably wants to have sex.

____5. Many times a woman will pretend she doesn't want to have intercourse because she doesn't want to seem too loose, but she's really hoping the man will force her.

____6. A woman who allows a man to pick her up for a date probably hopes to have sex that night.

____7. When a woman allows a man to treat her to an expensive dinner on a date, it usually indicates that she is willing to have sex with him.

____8. Going home with a man at the end of a date is a woman's way of communicating to him that she wants to have sex.

Cross-Gender Fetishism Scale

RAY BLANCHARD,[1] *Centre for Addiction and Mental Health*

The Cross-Gender Fetishism Scale (CGFS; Blanchard, 1985) is a measure (for males) of the erotic arousal value of putting on women's clothes, perfume, and make-up, and shaving the legs. The term *cross-gender fetishism* was coined by Freund, Steiner, and Chan (1982) to designate fetishistic activity that is accompanied by fantasies of being female and carried out with objects symbolic of femininity. It is therefore roughly equivalent to the term *transvestism* as defined in the *Diagnostic and Statistical Manual of Mental Disorders* (American Psychiatric Association, 1980).

Description

The CGFS is primarily intended to discriminate fetishistic from nonfetishistic cross-dressers (e.g., gender dysphorics, transsexuals, "drag queens," self-labeled transvestites). All items, however, contain one response option appropriate for non-cross-dressing males, so that it may be administered to control samples as well.

The scale is a self-administered, multiple-choice questionnaire. It contains 11 items: 6 with three response options and 5 with two options. Scoring weights for these response options were determined with the optimal scaling procedure for multiple-choice items outlined by Nishisato (1980). This procedure directly determines the set of scoring weights that optimizes the alpha reliability of a scale for a given population. This analysis, as well as others yielding the psychometric information reported below, was carried out on 99 adult male patients of the behavioral sexology department or gender identity clinic of a psychiatric teaching hospital. All had reported that they felt like females at least when cross-dressed, if not more generally.

Response Mode and Timing

Examinees may check or circle the response option of their choice. They are instructed to endorse one and only one response option per item. Examinees are permitted to ask for clarification on the meaning of an item. The CGFS was intended to round out a larger battery of erotic preference and gender identity measures (see the paper by Freund and Blanchard elsewhere in this volume) and should not, by itself, take longer than 1 or 2 minutes to complete.

Scoring

The scoring weight for each response option is shown in parentheses in the accompanying exhibit. Because empirically derived scoring weights can vary from sample to sample, users might wish to substitute the scoring weights given here with a simple dichotomous scheme: 1 for each positive response and 0 for each negative one.

The total score is simply the (algebraic) sum of scores on the 11 individual items. Higher (i.e., more positive) scores indicate a more extensive history of cross-gender fetishism.

Reliability

Blanchard (1985), using the scoring weight presented here, found an alpha reliability coefficient of .95.

Validity

Blanchard (1985) found that two factors with eigenvalues greater than 1.0 emerged from principal components analysis, accounting for 68% and 9% of the total variance. The part-remainder correlations ranged from .56 to .89.

Blanchard (1985) demonstrated the expected strong association (within the clinical population previously described) between high scores on the CGFS and heterosexual partner preference. Blanchard, Clemmensen, and Steiner (1985), predicting that heterosexual male gender patients motivated to create a favorable impression at clinical assessment would tend to minimize their history of fetishistic arousal in their self-reports, found a high significant correlation of −.48 between the CGFS and the Crowne-Marlowe (1964) Social Desirability Scale. The correlation between these two measures among homosexual gender patients–who rarely or never have fetishistic histories–was virtually zero.

Other Information

No permission or fee is required to use the CGFS.

References

American Psychiatric Association. (1980). *Diagnostic and statistical manual of mental disorders* (3rd ed.). Washington, DC: Author.

Blanchard, R. (1985). Research methods for the typological study of gender disorders in males. In B. W. Steiner (Ed.)., *Gender dysphoria: Development, research, management* (pp. 227–257). New York: Plenum.

Blanchard, R., Clemmensen, L. H., & Steiner, B. W. (1985). Social desirability response set and systematic distortion in the self-report of adult male gender patients. *Archives of Sexual Behavior, 14*, 505–516.

Crowne, D. P., & Marlowe, D. (1964). *The approval motive: Studies in evaluative dependence*. New York: Wiley.

Freund, K., Steiner, B. W., & Chan, S. (1982). Two types of cross-gender identity. *Archives of Sexual Behavior, 11*, 49–63.

Nishisato, S. (1980). *Analysis of categorical data: Dual scaling and its applications*. Toronto: University of Toronto Press.

[1]Address correspondence to Ray Blanchard, Centre for Addiction and Mental Health, 250 College Street, Toronto, Ontario M5T 1R8, Canada; e-mail: Ray_Blanchard@camh.net

Exhibit

Cross-Gender Fetishism Scale

Instructions to Subjects

The following questions ask about your experiences in dressing or making up as the opposite sex. These questions are meant to include experiences you may have had during puberty or early adolescence as well as more recent experiences.

Please circle one and only one answer to each question. If you are not sure of the meaning of a question, you may ask the person giving the questionnaire to explain it to you. There is no time limit for answering these questions.

1. Have you ever felt sexually aroused when putting on women's underwear, stockings, or a nightgown?
   a. Yes (1.0)
   b. No (−1.1)
   c. Have never put on any of these (−1.1)

2. Have you ever felt sexually aroused when putting on women's shoes or boots?
   a. Yes (1.5)
   b. No (−.7)
   c. Have never put on either of these (−.7)

3. Have you ever felt sexually aroused when putting on women's jewelry or outer garments (blouse, skirt, dress, etc.)?
   a. Yes (1.2)
   b. No (−1.0)
   c. Have never put on any of these (−1.0)

4. Have you ever felt sexually aroused when putting on women's perfume or make-up, or when shaving your legs?
   a. Yes (1.3)
   b. No (−.8)
   c. Have never done any of these (−.8)

5. Have you ever masturbated while thinking of yourself putting on (or wearing) women's underwear, stockings, or a nightgown?
   a. Yes (1.1)
   b. No (−1.0)

6. Have you ever masturbated while thinking of yourself putting on (or wearing) women's shoes or boots?
   a. Yes (1.7)
   b. No (−.4)

7. Have you ever masturbated while thinking of yourself putting on (or wearing) women's jewelry or outer garments?
   a. Yes (1.4)
   b. No (−.8)

8. Have you ever masturbated while thinking of yourself putting on (or wearing) women's perfume or make-up, or while thinking of yourself shaving your legs (or having shaved legs)?
   a. Yes (1.5)
   b. No (−.7)

9. Has there ever been a period in your life of one year (or longer) during which you always or usually felt sexually aroused when putting on female underwear or clothing?
   a. Yes (1.1)
   b. No (−1.0)
   c. Have never put on female underwear or clothing (−1.0)

10.   Has there ever been a period in your life of one year (or longer) during which you always or usually masturbated if you put on female underwear or clothing?
      a. Yes (1.2)
      b. No (−.8)
      c. Have never put on female underwear or clothing (−.8)

11.   Have you ever put on women's clothes or make-up for the main purpose of becoming sexually excited and masturbating?
      a. Yes (1.3)
      b. No (−.4)

Attitudes About Sadomasochism Scale

MEGAN R. YOST,[1] *Dickinson College*

The Attitudes About Sadomasochism Scale (ASMS; Yost, 2010) assesses stereotypical and prejudicial attitudes about individuals involved in consensual, sexual sadomasoch- ism. Sadomasochism (SM), in this context, refers to the safe and consensual sexual activities of an adult subculture that practices bondage, discipline, domination, submission, sadism, and masochism as part of their sexual interactions (Scott, 1980; Weinberg, Williams, & Moser, 1984). Many SM activists claim that identifying as a sadomasochist is similar to identifying as a lesbian, gay man, or bisexual, in that SM is an identity that defines their sexuality and their preferred manner of sexual interaction (Taylor & Ussher, 2001). Others argue that SM is best conceptualized as a set of sexual practices or activities, with no implication for identity (Langdridge, 2006). In either case, prejudicial attitudes about such individuals have begun to be docu- mented (Wright, 2006), just as prejudice and discrimina- tion against individuals based on sexual orientation have been well documented over the past few decades (Herek & Capitanio, 1996).

Psychotherapists reporting discomfort working with clients who engage in SM (Ford & Hendrick, 2003), and reports of therapist bias from SM practitioners seeking therapy (Kolmes, Stock, & Moser, 2006), indicate a need for greater understanding about SM within the mental health professions. Furthermore, recent custody cases in which a parent's involvement in SM is used as evidence of unfit parenting (Klein & Moser, 2006), and raids in which police charge consenting adults with lewd behav- ior, nudity, and assault for engaging in SM in semiprivate settings (Ridinger, 2006), demonstrate anti-SM bias in the legal system.

The ASMS is a multidimensional measure of prejudicial attitudes about sadomasochism, which provides a reliable and valid means of assessing such prejudice. It is a useful tool to examine the prevalence of anti-SM attitudes, par- ticularly among populations that come into contact with SM practitioners in settings where discriminatory attitudes could have serious consequences. By using the ASMS to survey these attitudes, educational programs could specifi- cally address the anti-SM bias held by psychotherapists, lawyers, judges, and the police. More broadly, this mea- sure is a useful tool for sex researchers and social scientists interested in discrimination against sexual minorities.

Description

The ASMS is a 23-item measure that was developed using a sample of 213 participants and validated using a sample of 258 participants. In the first sample, 58 items were administered and explored through factor analysis. After deleting items that lacked variance or loaded highly on multiple factors, an exploratory factor analysis yielded four subscales: *Socially Wrong* (the belief that SM behav- ior is morally wrong and socially undesirable); *Violence* (linking SM activity to violence against an unwilling partner); *Lack of Tolerance* (suggesting that SM can be an acceptable form of sexuality among willing partners [reverse scored]); and *Real Life* (the belief that SM prac- titioners carry their SM interests into their daily lives). Confirmatory factor analysis using a second sample fur- ther supported the structure of the ASMS, with fit indi- ces above .90 indicating that the four-structure model adequately fit the data.

[1]Address correspondence to Megan R. Yost, Department of Psychology, Dickinson College, P. O. Box 1773, Carlisle, PA 17013; e-mail: yostm@dickinson.edu

Response Mode and Timing

Response options range on a Likert-type scale from 1 (*Disagree Strongly*) to 7 (*Agree Strongly*) with a neutral midpoint of 4 (*Neither Agree nor Disagree*). The instrument can be completed in 10 minutes.

Scoring

So that higher scores indicate negative attitudes about SM or SM practitioners, the four items phrased in a positive direction (all items in *Lack of Tolerance*) are first reverse coded. Then items within each subscale are averaged to form a subscale score.

Reliability

To measure internal consistency, reliability analyses were conducted using all 471 participants. Cronbach's alpha for each subscale ranged from .78 to .92, indicating very good internal consistency for each subscale.

Validity

Validation analyses using all 471 participants showed that the ASMS demonstrated good concurrent validity at the subscale level by correlating in expected ways with other established scales. All subscales were positively correlated with prejudicial attitudes about lesbians and gay men, and with a measure of general sexual conservatism, suggesting that prejudicial SM attitudes are an extension of more general sex-negative attitudes. The *Socially Wrong* subscale was most strongly correlated with a measure of right-wing authoritarianism, which would be expected given that the items in this subscale are closely related to moral judgments and society's role in maintaining order. Lastly, the only subscale significantly correlated with a measure of rape myths was *Violence*, showing that participants who supported inaccurate beliefs about rape (such as blaming the victim) also believed inaccurate statements associating SM with rape.

However, a multiple regression analysis showed that over half of the variance in the ASMS (58%) remained unexplained by the four established scales, indicating that the ASMS measures specific attitudes about SM and SM practitioners that cannot be accounted for by social and sexual conservatism alone. In other words, the ASMS captures a set of attitudes specific to SM that do not overlap with already-developed attitudinal scales.

Finally, the ASMS demonstrated validity through its ability to discriminate between groups of participants (based on their prior knowledge of SM, their self-identification as being involved in SM, and friendships with SM practitioners). The more participants knew about SM prior to this study, the more positive their attitudes, consistent with the idea that knowledge creates a more accurate perception of SM practices. Also, participants who identified themselves as involved in SM had more positive attitudes, consistent with social psychological research on in-group favoritism showing that group members perceive others in their group in positive terms, even if the group is stigmatized in the broader society (Frable, Platt, & Hoey, 1998). Lastly, participants who had a friend who was involved in SM also had more positive attitudes, consistent with the contact hypothesis of stigma reduction (Allport, 1954), which explains that positive attitude change occurs when intergroup contact takes place under optimal circumstances.

References

Allport, G. W. (1954). *The nature of prejudice*. Reading, MA: Addison-Wesley.

Ford, M. P., & Hendrick, S. S. (2003). Therapists' sexual values for self and clients: Implications for practice and training. *Professional Psychology: Research and Practice, 34,* 80–87.

Frable, D. E. S., Platt, L., & Hoey, S. (1998). Concealable stigmas and positive self-perceptions: Feeling better around similar others. *Journal of Personality and Social Psychology, 74,* 909–922.

Herek, G. M., & Capitanio, J. (1996). "Some of my best friends": Intergroup contact, concealable stigma, and heterosexuals' attitudes toward gay men and lesbians. *Personality and Social Psychology Bulletin, 22,* 412–424.

Klein, M., & Moser, C. (2006). SM (Sadomasochistic) interests as an issue in child custody proceedings. *Journal of Homosexuality, 50*(2/3), 233–242.

Kolmes, K., Stock, W., & Moser, C. (2006). Investigating bias in psychotherapy with BDSM clients. *Journal of Homosexuality, 50,* 301–324.

Langdridge, D. (2006). Voices from the margins: SM and sexual citizenship. *Citizenship Studies, 10,* 373–389.

Ridinger, R. B. (2006). Negotiating limits: The legal status of SM in the United States. *Journal of Homosexuality, 50,* 189–216.

Scott, G. G. (1980). *Erotic power: An exploration of dominance and submission*. Secaucus, NJ: Citadel.

Taylor, G. W., & Ussher, J. M. (2001). Making sense of S&M: A discourse analytic account. *Sexualities, 4,* 293–314.

Weinberg, M. S., Williams, C. J., & Moser, C. (1984). The social constituents of sadomasochism. *Social Problems, 31,* 379–389.

Wright, S. (2006). Discrimination of SM-identified individuals. *Journal of Homosexuality, 50,* 217–231.

Yost, M. R. (2010). Development and validation of the Attitudes About Sadomasochism Scale. *The Journal of Sex Research, 47,* 79–91.

Exhibit

Attitudes About Sadomasochism Scale

Instructions: For each of the following statements, please note whether you agree or disagree using the following scale:

1	2	3	4	5	6	7
Disagree Strongly	Disagree Moderately	Disagree Mildly Disagree	Neither Agree nor	Agree Mildly	Agree Moderately	Agree Strongly

Use the following definitions when considering your responses:

Sadomasochism: sexual practices that involve dominance and submission (the appearance that one person has control over the other), sometimes involve role-playing (such as Master-Slave or Teacher-Student), and are always consensual (all partners participate willingly and voluntarily)

Sadomasochist: someone who deliberately uses physical stimulation (possibly pain) and/or psychological stimulation and control to produce sexual arousal and to achieve sexual pleasure

Dominant: someone who always or mostly is the person in control during an SM sexual encounter

Submissive: someone who always or mostly is the person who does not have control during an SM sexual encounter

Factor 1: Socially Wrong

Sadomasochists just don't fit into our society.

Practicing sadomasochists should not be allowed to be members of churches or synagogues.

Sadomasochism is a perversion.

Sadomasochistic behavior is just plain wrong.

Sadomasochism is a threat to many of our basic social institutions.

I think sadomasochists are disgusting.

Sadomasochistic activity should be against the law.

Parents who engage in SM are more likely to physically abuse their children.

Sadomasochism is an inferior form of sexuality.

If I was alone in a room with someone I knew to be a Dominant, I would feel uncomfortable.

SM rarely exists in a psychologically healthy individual.

If I was alone in a room with someone I knew to be a Submissive, I would feel uncomfortable.

Factor 2: Violence

People who engage in SM are more likely to become involved in domestic violence.

A Dominant is more likely to rape a romantic partner than the average person.

A Dominant is more likely to rape a stranger than the average person.

A Dominant is more likely to sexually molest a child than the average person.

A variety of serious psychological disorders are associated with sadomasochism.

Factor 3: Lack of Tolerance

Sadomasochists are just like everybody else. (R)

Sadomasochism is erotic and sexy. (R)

Many sadomasochists are very moral and ethical people. (R)

Sadomasochistic activity should be legal, as long as all participants are consenting adults. (R)

Factor 4: Real Life

Submissives are passive in other aspects of their lives (besides sex).

Dominants are aggressive and domineering in other aspects of their lives (besides sex).

Virginity Beliefs Scale

JONAS ERIKSSON AND TERRY P. HUMPHREYS,[1] *Trent University*

The Virginity Beliefs Scale (VBS) assesses beliefs and motivations for engaging in sexual intercourse for the first time.

Description

The statements contained in the VBS were developed using Carpenter's (2002) qualitative study of virginity loss. Carpenter found that individuals generally perceived of their virginity loss in three different ways: as a *gift*, a *stigma*, or a *process*. Gift individuals were proud of their virginity and considered it to be a valuable gift to their first partner. Those identified as perceiving their virginity as a stigma were anxious to lose their virginity, believing it to be an embarrassment. Process individuals saw their virginity loss as a step in their natural development towards becoming an adult. Carpenter suggested that these three frameworks influence first intercourse experiences. For example, those identifying virginity as a stigma were more likely to choose their first sexual partner based on opportunity, whereas those identifying virginity as a gift chose their partner based on love and commitment. Carpenter presented support for the notion that how individuals perceive their virginity loss may shape their sexual development and behavior in the years following their first sexual intercourse experience. For instance, individuals identifying virginity as a gift take a risk when deciding to lose their virginity. If their partner does not reciprocate, it is likely that these individuals feel that their experience was a mistake.

Response Mode and Timing

The scale can be completed either in paper-and-pencil form or as an online survey. In both modes, individuals indicate their agreement with each statement on a Likert-type scale from 1 (*Strongly Disagree*) to 7 (*Strongly Agree*). The VBS can be completed in approximately 10 minutes.

Scoring

The three frames contained in the VBS are scored separately. Items are scored 1 for *Strongly Disagree* and 7 for *Strongly Agree*. Mean gift scores are calculated by summing Items 2, 3, 5, 7, 10, 12, 14, 16, 18, and 20 and dividing by 10. Mean stigma scores are calculated by summing Items 1, 6, 8, 11, 15, 17, 19, and 21 and dividing by 8. Process mean scores are calculated by summing Items 4, 9, 13, and 22 and dividing by 4. Mean scores on all three subscales can thus range between 1 and 7.

Reliability

In a sample of undergraduates ($N = 243$) from a small university in Ontario, Canada, reliability was .89 for gift, .92 for stigma, and .80 for process (Eriksson & Humphreys, 2009).

Validity

Gift individuals tend to engage in intercourse for the first time for reasons related to improving their relationship with their partner and therefore choose their first partner with care (Carpenter, 2002). The concept of virginity as a gift is compatible with mainstream religious conceptions of virginity. As such, we expected that individuals scoring high on the gift subscale would generally hold less permissive attitudes towards sexuality and be more religious. As expected, gift individuals reported having had fewer lifetime sexual partners, $r(243) = -.267, p < .001$. These individuals also reported less sexual permissiveness as measured by the permissiveness subscale of the Brief Sexual Attitudes Scale (Hendrick, Hendrick, & Reich, 2006), $r(243) = -.495, p < .001$, and greater involvement in religion (i.e., frequency of religious services/activities), $r(242) = .144, p = .025$ (Eriksson & Humphreys, 2009).

Individuals perceiving of their virginity as a stigma hold more traditional sex role beliefs as indicated by the Double Standard Scale (DSS; Caron, Davis, Halteman, & Stickle, 1993), $r(243) = -.316, p < .001$, and also hold more hypergendered beliefs as measured by the Hypergender Ideology Scale (HIS; Hamburger, Hogben, McGowan, & Dawson, 1996), $r(243) = .356, p < .001$. The concept of virginity as a stigma is closely tied to traditional masculine beliefs having to do with greater sexual readiness and activity. Along the same lines, individuals scoring high on the stigma subscale are also more sexually permissive (Hendrick et al., 2006), $r(243) = .436, p < .001$.

Individuals perceiving their virginity as a process typically fall in between gift and stigma individuals in terms of traditional gender roles. Although their agreement with such roles is not as strong as stigma individuals, significant relationships exist between process scores and the HIS, $r(243) = .190, p < .003$, and the DSS, $r(243) = -.183$, $p = .004$. They also hold more permissive beliefs than gift individuals, but less permissive beliefs than stigma individuals, $r(243) = .266, p < .001$.

[1]Address correspondence to Terry P. Humphreys, Psychology Department, Trent University, 1600 West Bank Drive, Peterborough, Ontario, Canada, K9J 7B8; e-mail: terryhumphreys@trentu.ca

Other Information

Permission to use the Virginity Beliefs Scale may be obtained from T. Humphreys.

References

Caron, S. L., Davis, C. M., Halteman, W. A., & Stickle, M. (1993). Predictors of condom-related behaviors among first-year college students. *The Journal of Sex Research, 30,* 252–259.

Carpenter, L. M. (2002). Gender and the meaning and experience of virginity loss in the contemporary United States. *Gender and Society, 16,* 345–365.

Eriksson, J., & Humphreys, T. (2009). [Reliability and validity of the Virginity Beliefs Scale]. Unpublished raw data.

Hamburger, M. E., Hogben, M., McGowan, S., & Dawson, L. J. (1996). Assessing hypergender ideologies: Development and initial validation of a gender-neutral measure of adherence to extreme gender-role beliefs. *Journal of Research in Personality, 30,* 157–178.

Hendrick, C., Hendrick, S. S., & Reich, D. A. (2006). The Brief Sexual Attitudes Scale. *The Journal of Sex Research, 43,* 76–86.

Exhibit

Virginity Beliefs Scale

Instructions: Please think back to the first time you engaged in sexual intercourse. Indicate on the following scale how much you agree with each statement in regard to your first sexual intercourse experience.

> 1 = Strongly Disagree
> 2 = Disagree
> 3 = Somewhat Disagree
> 4 = Neutral
> 5 = Somewhat Agree
> 6 = Agree
> 7 = Strongly Agree

1. I actively tried to hide my status as a virgin.
2. I chose the person I lost my virginity to with care.
3. I planned my first time carefully.
4. I saw my virginity loss as a natural step in my development.
5. It was important to me that the circumstances under which I lost my virginity were perfect.
6. I felt my virginity was a burden that I needed to get rid of as soon as possible.
7. It was important to me that my first time was romantic.
8. I felt embarrassed over being a virgin.
9. I considered virginity loss to be an inevitable part of growing up.
10. I dated the person I lost my virginity to for a long time before we engaged in intercourse.
11. I was worried about what others might think if they found out I was a virgin.
12. The reason I did not lose my virginity earlier was because I had not found the right partner.
13. I felt that losing my virginity was an important step towards becoming a man/woman.
14. I believed I would stay in a relationship with the person I lost my virginity to for a long time.
15. I lost my virginity later than I would have wanted.
16. I felt in love with the person I lost my virginity to.
17. I regarded my virginity as something negative.
18. My virginity was a gift to my first partner.
19. I was afraid my partner would find out I was a virgin.
20. I planned my virginity loss with my partner.
21. I was afraid to tell my partner that I was a virgin.
22. I felt losing my virginity was a step in the transition between adolescence and becoming an adult.

First Coital Affective Reaction Scale

Israel M. Schwartz,[1] *Hofstra University*

Research on premarital coital activity has generally focused on incidence, prevalence, and changing trends, with little attention given to the affective aspects of the experience. However, affective variables are an important component of human sexual behavior. The importance of assessing affect to facilitate a better understanding of the relationship between feelings (as predictors or consequences) and sexual behaviors, attitudes, and norms has been highlighted by the findings of several researchers (Byrne, Fisher, Lamberth, & Mitchell, 1974; Schwartz, 1993; Weis, 1983). Scales used by Byrne et al. (1974) and Weis (1983), in their assessment of affect, stimulated the development of the First Coital Affective Reaction Scale (FCARS). The scale was developed as part of a cross-cultural research project comparing first coital experiences of American and Swedish women from an affective, behavioral, and attitudinal perspective (Schwartz, 1993). This scale measures subjects' (male or female) reported affective reactions to their first coital experience.

Description

The FCARS consists of 13 bipolar items, using a 7-point Likert format for the measurement of each item. Respondents answering *Yes* to the question "Have you ever had sexual intercourse (defined as penile-vaginal penetration)?" are asked to indicate the degree to which they had experienced the following feelings in reaction to their first coitus at the time that it occurred: confused, satisfied, anxious, guilty, romantic, pleasure, sorry, relieved, exploited, happy, embarrassed, excited, and fearful. The responses range from 1 (representing *Not Experiencing the Feeling at all*) to 7 (representing *Strongly Experiencing the Feeling*), with the numbers in between representing various gradations between these extremes. (To protect anonymity, two versions of the scale are provided to respondents. The respondents who have never engaged in sexual intercourse can complete a version asking about how they think they would feel during their first sexual intercourse. Thus far, only the version for coitally experienced participants has been used for analysis.)

In a cross-cultural study, the scale, included in a self-report anonymous questionnaire focusing on coital initiation and the circumstances surrounding the event, was administered to a sample of 217 female undergraduates drawn from institutions in the northeast, southeast, mideastern, and western regions of the United States (Schwartz, 1993). As part of the same study, the scale was administered to a sample of 186 female undergraduates from institutions in the northern, middle, and southern regions of Sweden. The entire questionnaire, including the FCARS, was translated into Swedish. A complete description of the translation procedure is provided in Schwartz's article.

Response Mode and Timing

Respondents are asked to circle the number (1 to 7) in each item that most closely represents the way they felt. The scale takes approximately 2 minutes to complete, making it easy to include in questionnaires in which time and length are important considerations.

Scoring

Each scale item uses a 7-point Likert response format yielding a possible score range of 1 to 7. Items 2 (satisfied), 5 (romantic), 6 (pleasure), 8 (relieved), 10 (happy), and 12 (excited) are reversed in scoring so that on all items 1 represents a positive response and 7 represents a negative response. Thus, greater positive FCARS affect would be represented by a lower total score and greater negative affect would be represented by a higher total score. Items may be scored and looked at separately to assess the degree to which a specific affective reaction was experienced (e.g., guilt, exploitation, pleasure, confusion, etc.).

Reliability

Internal consistency of the scale was estimated using Cronbach's alpha. The alpha coefficient with a sample of 217 female undergraduate students in the U.S. was .89 (Schwartz, 1993). With a sample of 186 female undergraduate students in Sweden (using the Swedish version of the scale), the alpha coefficient was .85. An unpublished pilot test of the research instrument used by Schwartz, with a sample of 37 female undergraduate students from a university in the New York metropolitan area, yielded an alpha coefficient of .87 for the FCARS.

Validity

For face validity the scale was reviewed by a panel of three sexuality experts. In addition, 10 of the participants in the pilot test were individually interviewed to get their opinions regarding format, readability, clarity, and

[1]Address correspondence to Israel M. Schwartz, Department of Health, Physical Education and Recreation, Hofstra University, 1000 Fulton Avenue, Hempstead, New York 11550-1090; e-mail: Israel.M.Schwartz@hofstra.edu

possible bias. Recommendations were incorporated into the final version of the scale. The FCARS construct validity was supported by Schwartz's (1993) findings of expected differences between the American and Swedish samples (greater negative affect among the American group) based on Christensen's (1969) theoretical assertions. These findings were also consistent with Christensen's earlier findings comparing Danish and American cultures (Christensen & Carpenter, 1962a, 1962b; Christensen & Gregg, 1970).

Other Information

The FCARS has recently been translated to Arabic and administered in modified version to Turkish university students (Askun & Ataca, 2007).

This scale is copyrighted by the author. With appropriate citation, it may be used without permission for the purpose of research.

References

Askun, D., & Ataca, B. (2007). Sexuality related attitudes and behaviors of Turkish university students. *Archives of Sexual Behavior, 36,* 741–752.

Byrne, D., Fisher, J. D., Lamberth, J., & Mitchell, H. E. (1974). Evaluations of erotica: Facts or feelings? *Journal of Personality and Social Psychology, 29,* 111–119.

Christensen, H. T. (1969). Normative theory derived from cross-cultural family research. *Journal of Marriage and the Family, 31,* 209–222.

Christensen, H. T., & Carpenter, G. R. (1962a). Timing patterns in the development of sexual intimacy: An attitudinal report on three modern western societies. *Journal of Marriage and the Family, 24,* 30–35.

Christensen, H. T., & Carpenter, G. R. (1962b). Value-behavior discrepancies regarding premarital coitus in three western cultures. *American Sociological Review, 27,* 66–74.

Christensen, H. T., & Gregg, C. F. (1970). Changing sex norms in America and Scandinavia. *Journal of Marriage and the Family, 32,* 616–627.

Schwartz, I. M. (1993). Affective reactions of American and Swedish women to their first premarital coitus: A cross-cultural comparison. *The Journal of Sex Research, 30,* 18–26.

Weis, D. L. (1983). Affective reactions of women to their initial experience of coitus. *The Journal of Sex Research, 19,* 209–237.

Exhibit

First Coital Affective Reaction Scale

1. Have you ever had sexual intercourse (defined as penile-vaginal penetration)?
   a. ___ Yes   b. ___ No

(If your answer to this question is "Yes" then complete Question 2. If your answer to this question is "No" skip Question 2 and complete Question 3.)

2. *Directions*: The following items deal with your feelings about your first sexual intercourse. Please try to answer as accurately and honestly as possible. Please answer *all items* "a" through "m" by using a 7-point scale, in which "1" represents not experiencing the feeling at all, and "7" represents strongly experiencing the feeling, with the numbers in between representing various gradations between these extremes. *Please circle the number in each item that most closely represents the way you felt.*

What were your reactions to your first sexual intercourse at the time that it occurred? I felt:

a.	Not at all Confused	1	2	3	4	5	6	7	Very Confused
b.	Not at all Satisfied	1	2	3	4	5	6	7	Very Satisfied
c.	Not at all Anxious	1	2	3	4	5	6	7	Very Anxious
d.	Not at all Guilty	1	2	3	4	5	6	7	Very Guilty
e.	Not at all Romantic	1	2	3	4	5	6	7	Very Romantic
f.	No Pleasure at all	1	2	3	4	5	6	7	Much Pleasure
g.	Not at all Sorry	1	2	3	4	5	6	7	Very Sorry
h.	Not at all Relieved	1	2	3	4	5	6	7	Very Relieved

i.	Not at all Exploited	1	2	3	4	5	6	7	Very Exploited
j.	Not at all Happy	1	2	3	4	5	6	7	Very Happy
k.	Not at all Embarrassed	1	2	3	4	5	6	7	Very Embarrassed
l.	Not at all Excited	1	2	3	4	5	6	7	Very Excited
m.	Not at all Fearful	1	2	3	4	5	6	7	Very Fearful

3. *Directions*: The following items deal with your anticipated reactions to your first sexual intercourse. Please answer *all items* "a" through "m" by using a 7-point scale, in which "1" represents not anticipating the feeling at all, and "7" represents strongly anticipating the feeling, with the numbers in between representing various gradations between these extremes. *Please circle the number in each item that most closely represents the way you anticipate feeling.*

How do you think you will react to your first sexual intercourse at the time that it occurs?
I anticipate feeling: (The 13 responses for Question 2 are repeated.)

Credit Lines

McBride, K. R., Reece, M., & Sanders, S. A., *Cognitive and Behavioral Outcomes of Sexual Behavior Scale*. Copyright © 2010 by Kimberly R. McBride, Michael Reece, and Stephanie A. Sanders. Used by permission of the authors.

McCabe, M. P., & Collins, J. K., *Depth of Sexual Involvement Scale*. Copyright © 1988 by Marita P. McCabe and John K. Collins. Used by permission of the authors.

McDonagh, L. K., Morrison, T. G., & McGuire, B. E., *Male Body Image Self-Consciousness Scale*, initially published in McDonagh, L. K., Morrison, T. G., & McGuire, B. E. (2008). The naked truth: Development of a scale designed to measure male body image self-consciousness during physical intimacy. *Journal of Men's Studies, 16,* 253–265. Copyright © 2008 by Men's Studies Press. Used by permission of Men's Studies Press and the authors.

McIntyre-Smith, A., & Fisher, W. A., *Clitoral Self-Stimulation Scale*. Copyright © 2010 by Alexandra McIntyre-Smith and William A. Fisher. Used by permission of the authors.

McIntyre-Smith, A., & Fisher, W. A., *Female Orgasm Scale*. Copyright © 2010 by Alexandra McIntyre-Smith and William A. Fisher. Used by permission of the authors.

McIntyre-Smith, A., & Fisher, W. A., *Female Partner's Communication During Sexual Activity Scale*. Copyright © 2010 by Alexandra McIntyre-Smith and William A. Fisher. Used by permission of the authors.

Miccio-Fonseca, L. C., *Personal Sentence Completion Inventory*. Copyright © 1998 by L. C. Miccio-Fonseca. Used by permission of the author.

Milhausen, R. R., Sales, J. M., & DiClemente, R. J., *Partner Communication Scale*, initially published in Milhausen, R. R., Sales, J. M., Wingood, G. M., DiClemente, R. J., Salazar, L. F., & Crosby, R. A. (2007). Validation of a partner communication scale for use in HIV/AIDS prevention interventions. *Journal of HIV/AIDS Prevention in Children & Youth, 8,* 11–33. Copyright © 2007 by Taylor & Francis. Used by permission of Taylor & Francis and the authors.

Milhausen, R. R., Graham, C. A., & Sanders, S. A., *Sexual Excitation/Sexual Inhibition Inventory for Women and Men*. Copyright © 2010 by Robin R. Milhausen, Cynthia A. Graham, and Stephanie A. Sanders. Used by permission of the authors.

Miller, R. S., & Johnson, J. A., *Early Sexual Experiences Checklist*, initially published in Miller, R. S., Johnson, J. A., & Johnson J. K. (1991). Assessing the prevalence of unwanted childhood sexual experiences. *Journal of Psychology & Human Sexuality, 4,* 43–54. Copyright © 1991 by Taylor & Francis. Used by permission of Taylor & Francis and the authors.

Mirotznik, J., *Genital Herpes Perceived Severity Scales*, initially published in Mirotznik, J. (1991). Genital herpes: A survey of attitudes, knowledge, and reported behaviors of college students at-risk of infection. *Journal of Psychology and Human Sexuality, 4,* 73–99. Copyright © 1991 by Taylor & Francis. Used by permission of Taylor & Francis and the author.

Morrison, M. A., & Morrison, T. G., *Modern Homonegativity Scale*, initially published in Morrison, M. A., & Morrison, T. G. (2002). Development and validation of a scale measuring modern prejudice toward gay men and lesbian women. *Journal of Homosexuality, 43,* 15–37. Copyright © 2002 by Taylor & Francis. Used by permission of Taylor & Francis and the authors.

Mosher, D. L., *Aggressive Sexual Behavior Inventory*. Copyright © 1988 by Donald L. Mosher. Used by permission of the author.

Mosher, D. L., *Multiple Indicators of Subjective Sexual Arousal*. Copyright © 1988 by Donald L. Mosher. Used by permission of the author.

Mosher, D. L., *Negative Attitudes Toward Masturbation*. Copyright © 1988 by Donald L. Mosher. Used by permission of the author.

Mosher, D. L., *Revised Mosher Guilt Inventory*. Copyright © 1988 by Donald L. Mosher. Used by permission of the author.

Mosher, D. L., *Sexual Path Preferences Inventory*. Copyright © 1988 by Donald L. Mosher. Used by permission of the author.

Mosher, D. L., & Sullivan, J., *Sexual Polarity Scale*. Copyright © 1988 by Donald L. Mosher and James Sullivan. Used by permission of the authors.

Muehlenhard, C. L., & Felts, A. S., *Sexual Beliefs Scale*. Copyright © 1998 by Charlene L. Muehlenhard and Albert S. Felts. Used by permission of the authors.

Muehlenhard, C. L., & Quackenbush, D. M., *Sexual Double Standard Scale*. Copyright © 1998 by Charlene L. Muehlenhard and Debra M. Quackenbush. Used by permission of the authors.

Navarro, R. L., Savoy, H. B., & Worthington, R. L., *Measure of Sexual Identity Exploration and Commitment*. Copyright © 2010 by Rachel L. Navarro, Holly Bielstein Savoy, and Roger L. Worthington. Used by permission of the authors.

Nemerofsky, A. G., & Carran, D. T., *What-If-Situations-Test*. Copyright © 1986 by Alan G. Nemerofsky. Used by permission of the author.

Nobre, P., & Pinto-Gouveia, J., *Questionnaire of Cognitive Schema Activation in Sexual Context*, initially published in Nobre, P.J., & Pinto-Gouveia, J. (2009). Questionnaire of cognitive schema activation in sexual context: A questionnaire to assess cognitive schemas activated in sexual failure situations. *The Journal of Sex Research, 46,* 425–437. Copyright © 2009 by Taylor & Francis. Used by permission of Taylor & Francis and the authors.

Nobre, P. J., & Pinto-Gouveia, J., *Sexual Dysfunctional Beliefs Questionnaire*, initially published in Nobre, P. J. & Pinto-Gouveia, J, & Gomes, F. A. (2003). Sexual dysfunctional beliefs questionnaire: An instrument to assess sexual dysfunctional beliefs as vulnerability factors to sexual problems. *Sexual & Relationship Therapy, 18,* 171–204. Copyright © 2003 by Taylor & Francis. Used by permission of Taylor & Francis and the authors.

Nobre, P., & Pinto-Gouveia, J., *Sexual Modes Questionnaire*, initially published in Nobre, P. J., & Pinto-Gouveia, J. (2003). Sexual modes questionnaire: Measure to assess the interaction between cognitions, emotions and sexual response. *The Journal of Sex Research, 40,* 368–382. Copyright © 2003 by Taylor & Francis. Used by permission of Taylor & Francis and the authors.

Osman, S. L., *Token Resistance to Sex Scale*. Copyright © 1998 by Suzanne L. Osman. Used by permission of the author.

O'Sullivan, L. F., Meyer-Bahlburg, H. F. L., & McKeague, I., *Sexual Self-Concept Inventory*, initially published in O'Sullivan, L. F., Meyer-Bahlburg, H. F. L., & McKeague, I. W. (2006). The development of the Sexual Self-Concept Inventory for early adolescent girls. *Psychology of Women Quarterly, 30,* 139–149. Copyright © 2006 by John Wiley & Sons, Ltd. Used by permission of John Wiley & Sons, Ltd and the authors.

Patton, W., & Mannison, M., *The Revised Attitudes Toward Sexuality Inventory*, initially published in Patton, W., &

Snell, W. E., Jr., *Stereotypes About Male Sexuality Scale.* Copyright © 1998 by William E. Snell, Jr. Used by permission of the author.

Snell, W. E., Jr., & Finney, P. D., *Multidimensional AIDS Anxiety Questionnaire.* Copyright © 1998 by William E. Snell, Jr. and Phillip D. Finney. Used by permission of the authors.

Snell, W. E., Jr., Finney, P. D., & Godwin, L. J., *Stereotypes About AIDS Scale.* Copyright © 1998 by William E. Snell, Jr., Phillip D. Finney, and Lisa J. Godwin. Used by permission of the authors.

Snell, W. E. Jr., Fisher, T. D., & Miller, R. S. *Sexual Awareness Questionnaire.* Copyright © 1998 by William E. Snell, Jr., Terri D. Fisher, and Rowland S. Miller. Used by permission of the authors.

Spector, I. P., Carey, M. P., & Steinberg, L., *Sexual Desire Inventory,* initially published in Spector , I. P., Carey, M. P., & Steinberg, L. (1996). The Sexual Desire Inventory: Development, factor structure, and evidence of reliability. *Journal of Sex & Marital Therapy, 22,* 175–190. Copyright © 1996 by Taylor & Francis. Used by permission of Taylor & Francis and the authors.

Sprecher, S., *Premarital Sexual Permissiveness Scale.* Copyright © 1998 by Susan Sprecher. Used by permission of the author.

Stake, J. E., & Malovich, N. J., *Sexual Harassment Attitudes Questionnaire.* Copyright © 1998 by Jayne E. Stake and Natalie J. Malovich. Used by permission of the authors.

Stevenson, M. R., *Unwanted Childhood Sexual Experiences Questionnaire.* Copyright © 1998 by Michael R. Stevenson. Used by permission of the author.

Štulhofer, A., Buško, V., & Brouillard, P., *The New Sexual Satisfaction Scale and Its Short Form,* initially published in Štulhofer, A., Buško, V., & Brouillard, P. (in press). Development and bicultural validation of the New Sexual Satisfaction Scale. *The Journal of Sex Research.* Copyright © 2010 by Taylor & Francis. Used by permission of Taylor & Francis and the authors.

Štulhofer, A., & Landripet, I., *Sexual Scripts Overlap Scale— Short Version.* Copyright © 2010 by Aleksandar Štulhofer and Ivan Landripet. Used by permission of the authors.

Thompson, V. L. S., & Smith, S. W., *Sexual Assault Treating/ Reporting Attitudes Survey.* Copyright © 1998 by Vetta L. Sanders Thompson and Sharon West Smith. Used by permission of the authors.

Torabi, M. R., & Yarber, W. L., *Alternate Forms of HIV Prevention Attitude Scales for Teenagers,* initially published in Torabi, M. R., & Yarber, W. (1992). Alternate forms of HIV prevention attitude scales for teenagers. AIDS Education and Prevention, 4, 172–182. Copyright © 1992 by the Guilford Press. Used by permission of the Guilford Press and the authors.

Tromovitch, P., *Multidimensional Measure of Comfort with Sexuality.* Copyright © 2010 by Philip Tromovitch. Used by permission of the author.

Turchik, J. A., & Garske, J. P., *Sexual Risk Survey,* initially published in Turchik, J. A., & Garske, J. P. (2009). Measurement of sexual risk taking among college students. *Archives of Sexual Behavior, 38,* 936–948. Copyright © 2009 by Springer. Used with kind permission from Springer Science+Business Media and the authors.

Vail-Smith, K., Durham, T. W., & Howard, H. A., *Condom Embarrassment Scale,* initially published in Vail-Smith, K., Durham, T. W., & Howard, H. A. (1992). A scale to measure embarrassment associated with condom use. *Journal of Health Education, 29,* 209–214. Copyright © 1992 by the American Association for Health Education. Used by permission of the American Association for Health Education and the authors.

Van de Ven, P., Bornholt, L., & Bailey, M., *Homophobic Behavior of Students Scale.* Copyright © 1998 by Paul Van de Ven, Laurel Bornholt, and Michael Bailey. Used by permission of the authors.

Vanable, P. A., Brown, J. L., Carey, M. P., & Bostwick, R. A., *Sexual Health Knowledge Questionnaire for HIV+ MSM.* Copyright © 2010 by Peter A. Vanable, Jennifer L. Brown, Michael P. Carey, and Rebecca A. Bostwick. Used by permission of the authors.

Vanable, P. A., McKirnan, D. J., & Stokes, J. P., *Identification and Involvement with the Gay Community Scale.* Copyright © 1998 by Peter A. Vanable, David J. McKirnan, and Joseph P. Stokes. Used by permission of the authors.

Wagner, G. J., *Internalized Homophobia Scale.* Copyright © 1998 by Glenn J. Wagner. Used by permission of the author.

Warren, C., *Family Sex Communication Quotient,* initially published in Warren, C., & Neer, M. (1986). Family sex communication orientation, *Journal of Applied Communication Research, 14,* 86–107. Copyright © 1986 by Taylor & Francis. Used by permission of Taylor & Francis and the authors.

Weibley, S., & Hindin, M., *Self-Identified Lesbian Internalized Homophobia Scale.* Copyright © 2010 by Stacy Weibley and Michelle Hindin. Used by permission of the authors.

Weinstein, E., *Senior Adult Sexuality Scales.* Copyright © 1988 by Estelle Weinstein. Used by permission of the author.

Wenner, C. A., Russell, V. M, & McNulty, J. K., *Attitudes Toward Unconventional Sex Scale.* Copyright © 2010 by Carolyn A. Wenner, V. Michelle Russell, and James K. McNulty. Used by permission of the authors.

White, C. B., *Aging Sexual Knowledge and Attitudes Scale.* Copyright © 1988 by Charles B. White. Used by permission of the author.

Widman, L., & McNulty, J. K., *Sexual Narcissism Scale,* initially published in Widman, L., & McNulty, J. K. (in press). Sexual narcissism and the perpetration of sexual aggression. *Archives of Sexual Behavior.* Copyright © 2010 by Springer. With kind permission from Springer Science+Business Media and the authors.

Willoughby, B. L. B., Doty, N. D., Braaten, E. B., & Malik, N. M., *Perceived Parental Reactions Scale.* Copyright © 2010 by Brian L. B. Willoughby, Nathan D. Doty, Ellen B. Braaten, and Neena M. Malik. Used by permission of the authors.

Woody, J. D., & D'Souza, H. J., Sexual Interactions System Scale. Copyright © 1998 by Jane D. Wood and Henry J. D'Souza. Used by permission of the authors.

Wright, L. W., Jr., Adams, H. E., & Bernat, J., *Homophobia Scale,* initially published in Wright, L. W., Jr., Adams, H. E., & Bernat, J. (1999). Development and validation of the Homophobia Scale. *Journal of Psychopathology and Behavioral Assessment, 21,* 337–347. Copyright © 1999 by Springer. With kind permission from Springer Science+Business Media and the authors.

Yarber, W. L., Torabi, M. R., & Veenker, C. H., *STD Attitude Scale,* initially published in Yarber, W. L., Torabi, M. R., & Veenker, C. H. (1988). Development of a three-component sexually transmitted diseases attitude scale. *Journal of Sex Education and Therapy, 15,* 36–49. Copyright © 1988 by the American Association of Sexuality Educators, Counselors and Therapists (AASECT). Used by permission of AASECT and the authors.